Personal Finance

^{13e}

E. THOMAS GARMAN
Virginia Tech University

RAYMOND E. FORGUE
University of Kentucky

CENGAGE
Learning·

Australia • Brazil • Mexico • Singapore • United Kingdom • United States

Personal Finance, Thirteenth Edition
Garman/Forgue

Vice President, General Manager, Social Science & Qualitative Business: Erin Joyner

Senior Product Manager: Joe Sabatino

Content Developer: Conor Allen and Tara Slagle, MPS North America, LLC

Product Assistant: Denisse Zavala-Rosales

Senior Marketing Manager: Nate Anderson

Senior Marketing Coordinator: Eileen Corcoran

Art and Cover Direction, Production Management, and Composition: Lumina Datamatics, Inc.

Intellectual Property Analyst: Brittani Morgan

Project Manager: Julie Dierig

Manufacturing Planner: Kevin Kluck

Cover Image: Strejman/Shutterstock.com

Interior Images: iStockphoto.com/Faysal Ahamed, iStockphoto.com/istock-designer, iStockphoto.com/pictafolio, djdarkflower/Shutterstock.com, Pixel Embargo/Shutterstock.com, DVARG/Shutterstock.com, DeiMosz/Shutterstock.com, Pixel Embargo/Shutterstock.com, inxti/Shutterstock.com

For product information and technology assistance, contact us at
Cengage Learning Customer & Sales Support, 1-800-354-9706

For permission to use material from this text or product, submit all requests online at **www.cengage.com/permissions**
Further permissions questions can be emailed to
permissionrequest@cengage.com

Library of Congress Control Number: 2016960526

Student Edition:
ISBN:978-1-337-09975-2

Loose-leaf Edition:
ISBN: 978-1-337-28831-6

Cengage Learning
20 Channel Center Street
Boston, MA 02210
USA

Cengage Learning is a leading provider of customized learning solutions with employees residing in nearly 40 different countries and sales in more than 125 countries around the world. Find your local representative at **www.cengage.com.**

Cengage Learning products are represented in Canada by Nelson Education, Ltd.

To learn more about Cengage Learning Solutions, visit **www.cengage.com**

Purchase any of our products at your local college store or at our preferred online store **www.cengagebrain.com**

Printed in the United States of America
Print Number: 02   Print Year: 2017

Brief Contents

Contents

CHAPTER 3
Financial Statements, Tools, and Budgets 72

PART 2   MONEY MANAGEMENT   113

CHAPTER 4
Managing Income Taxes   114

CHAPTER 5
Managing Checking and Savings Accounts   150

CHAPTER 8
Vehicle and Other Major Purchases ... 228

CHAPTER 9
Obtaining Affordable Housing ... 258

PART 3   INCOME AND ASSET PROTECTION   297

CHAPTER 10
Managing Property and Liability Risk   298

CHAPTER 11

Planning for Health Care Expenses 332

CHAPTER 12

Life Insurance Planning 360

CHAPTER 17
Retirement and Estate Planning   518

Preface

TO THE INSTRUCTOR

This 13th edition of *Personal Finance* has been happily revised, and it sets a high standard in the field. When revising, we once again surprised ourselves: We improved the book a lot! We absolutely loved revising because it is fun and we know how valuable the book is for students. This edition is a winner.

More Pizzazz   We got "fired up" when revising because we know instructors want students to actually *read* the book before coming to class. A book must have some pizzazz to keep students reading, so we tried to make the style of writing a bit breezier as we updated the topical coverage. We think this edition has much more zip!

Involves the Student   The text genuinely involves the student in learning the subject, particularly through information presented in more than 180 new boxes, enhanced end-of-chapter activities, and innovative "do-it soon" prescriptions from the authors. We are the "Doctors of Personal Finance"—with over 80 combined years of teaching experience, 70 years of writing 40 college textbooks, and authors of 200 refereed research articles.

Learn How to Learn   By drawing on our years of experience, we have made the 13th edition more than just a compilation of what to know. In addition to providing the most up-to-date knowledge base in personal finance, we recognize that the role of the instructor has changed from teaching facts to teaching students how to learn. Thus, the book's many tools show students how to discover and where to find accurate facts and other essentials in personal finance that they need to know. Students need to learn how to replace the old personal finance knowledge they currently possess with the latest knowledge that is new, accurate, and reliable.

The Right Things to Do in Personal Finance   *Personal Finance* emphasizes the "right things" to do in personal finance, and why, and then how to do them. Why such an emphasis? Because today's students—despite their many abilities—need more guidance than those of yesteryear. Personal finance has become much more complicated. Plus, advertising and marketing are nothing less than relentless in their aim to persuade one to buy, buy, and buy stuff as well as to confuse people about who is telling them the "truth."

Gets Students to Think   This book's many features offer normative, value-laden suggestions on getting ahead in one's personal finances. It requires the reader to reflect on the facts and opinions presented, the advice they are given, the available choices in their communities and on the Internet, and finally to apply their personal values in their decision-making. In short, *Personal Finance* gets students to contemplate, deliberate, and think!

NOTES TO THE STUDENT

"Personal finance knowledge is obsolete." It's over. It's done for. It's history. This is great news! But, read on because this quote does not mean to skip reading this book.

Obsolete knowledge is that which we believe may have been valid at one time, if it ever was true in the first place. When we are confident about erroneous knowledge we are not motivated to look for new information. As the Jedi master Yoda told Luke Skywalker, "You must unlearn what you have learned." If you believe the world is changing and recognize that some of your knowledge is obsolete, you can begin to move past your outdated knowledge.

But how? Your response will be your true challenge in learning personal finance *and* applying it to your money matters in the many years of your life. Both are goals of this book.

Making good personal financial decisions for you and your loved ones requires making informed choices. To do this, you must learn the vocabulary of personal finance, consider reasonable prescriptions for success, and then apply your newly acquired beliefs in your everyday decision making. If you do these tasks soon—by reading this book from cover to cover—you absolutely, positively will reap big financial benefits in the future.

Ignore these suggestions at your peril, however, because a lack of financial literacy will guarantee your financial failure. No kidding. That warning is for real. It is not easy to succeed financially, but sometimes it can be challenging. We'll show you how to do it correctly.

Our goal as authors is to provide the knowledge, tools, skills, and attitudes you need to become financially savvy and successful. Along with the textbook, we have developed a full, rich MindTap student resource and a companion website that you can use to learn as much as possible about personal finance as well as develop your own financial plans.

The 13th edition of *Personal Finance* offers confidence to readers about how to succeed financially. Yes, this book provides you with facts—the most up-to-date and best available—and much of the information is evolving and as such it will need to be replaced. *In today's world you need to learn how and where to accurately find the facts you need to know.* Without understanding the basics of personal finance, how could you even know what questions to ask?

This book is very good at giving you the tools to strengthen your knowledge. First, the authors provide you with fundamental knowledge in personal finance, lots of it. You need an excellent base of know-how in personal finance to work with, otherwise you will remain ignorant about some money matters and occasionally you will make small and sometimes big mistakes. Second, we provide a number of tools to guide you through the process of searching the Internet and resources in your community to find the best answers to your personal finance questions. Thus, you need to learn how to learn, and this book aims to help you accomplish that goal.

The 13th edition of *Personal Finance* is the language of today and tomorrow! Successfully handling your money today is important. All the tools—and we mean ALL—are here for you to learn to use to your advantage so you will do well financially throughout life.

You need the best knowledge, tools, and skills to successfully manage your financial resources because so much of the responsibility of financial accomplishment today rests solely upon your shoulders.

While personal finance is not rocket science, it sometimes feels like it. In fact, personal finance actually is not very complicated. But there are a lot of topics in personal finance, so please try to stay focused!

You are lucky because you are holding in your hands the 13th edition of *Personal Finance*. This book carefully lays out your financial "marching orders" for challenging economic times. The mantra of this book is *"What to do, why do it, when to do it, and how to do it."* We give you "prescriptions" to follow that will guide you to success in your personal finances. If you pay attention, learn, and apply the knowledge contained herein you will enjoy a taste of the good life while still in college, plus you will have enough resources left over to start building an extremely successful financial future.

This 13th edition balances all the pieces of wise financial planning. In addition to updating and enhancing the quality of the content, this edition stimulates student interest in several new ways.

Each chapter of *Personal Finance* starts with a brief case with some questions that ask *"What Do You Recommend?"* And the student usually does not know much at that early point, and that is okay. At the end of the chapter, the question is repeated with *"What Do You Recommend NOW?"* Now the student should know a lot more after having read the chapter and the learning gained from class discussion. Then they can answer the questions more knowledgeably. Every chapter also contains dozens of Internet website addresses of high-quality sources of information to help replace some of your obsolete knowledge.

Throughout every chapter are prescriptions to achieve personal financial success in the form of box inserts. One such box is titled *"To-Do Soon List."* These boxes suggest five tasks to accomplish in the next few months or years. Then there is a new box called *"Your Grandparents Say"* that offers tips from those who have lived long and succeeded in their personal finances. There also is a new box titled *"There Is an App for That!"* that lists some good ones and almost all can be used on both Apple and Android devices. This is complemented by updated boxes on the best quality *"Money Websites."* Another new box series is *"Numbers on"* that highlight important numbers relevant to the subject of each chapter. Finally there are new *"Common Sense"* thoughts for readers to contemplate. Collectively, these boxes are full of prescriptions and insights to help students achieve financial success.

Every chapter also includes lots of interesting *"Did You Know?"* boxes that offer surprises in current understanding. There also is a robust list of concrete suggestions on how to *"Turn Bad Habits INTO Good Ones."* All chapters have one or more boxes revealing *"Advice From a Seasoned Pro."* The latter chapters also have boxes on *"The Tax Consequences of (name of chapter)"* to help the reader always think of the impact of income taxes when making financial decisions. The *"Bias Toward"* boxes give the reader a reality check on the behavioral economics biases that plague us into making bad financial decisions, and they also explain how to overcome them. Finally the reader may recall that we told you earlier there are a few things to not do wrong. So, we inserted new *"Never Ever!"* boxes in every chapter that headline what one should absolutely, positively not do in personal finance.

The revised end-of-chapter questions are extremely well organized and are designed to walk you to and through the most important topics in each chapter. The authors want you to learn how to find the best and most reliable sources of new information throughout your life and use it to your advantage.

The end-of-chapter activities begin with a thorough *"Summary of Learning Objectives Recapped."* Next are several *"Let's Talk About It"* questions designed to help you and your instructor create some lively class discussions. This is followed by *"Do the Math"* activities that require the student to practice the key mathematical applications in the chapter. Even more down to earth are the five or six *"Financial Planning Cases"* because they make the student think realistically about the information. The continuing case of *"Harry and Belinda"* has been updated and the couple eventually age into their mid-forties. So, too, has the *"Victor and Maria"* case, which now follows them almost into retirement. The other continuing case is that of *"Julia Price,"* whose successful financial life evolves through challenging economic times. Her cases always end with a question to challenge the student: *"Offer your opinions about her thinking."*

The end-of-chapter questions continue with *"Be Your Own Personal Financial Planner"* that focuses on personalizing the concepts and lessons to your life. The forms and questions are contained in the student workbook, *My Personal Financial Planner*, which can be found on the book's MindTap. These activities are not busy-work. They are questions and tasks that require applying the knowledge provided in each chapter at a personal level—in your life. All of the *"On the 'Net"* activities have been designed to carefully direct students to reliable online materials that are truly useful and appropriate to use in your financial life. The end-of-chapter questions close with *"Action Involvement Projects"* that get the reader into their local community or on the Internet to expert sources to help you apply chapter concepts.

This edition connects all the dots in personal finance in a comprehensive manner, shows students the relevancy of the topics, and requires students to carefully think about their own financial lives. As a result, you will achieve genuine success in your personal finances!

Changes in This Edition

The 13th edition contains lots of up-to-the minute original material, and the major changes include the following:

- **Personal financial planning spread over three chapters.** We did not jam the whole boring and esoteric "financial planning process" down the readers' throats in Chapter 1. If we put the all the steps in there, probably only a handful of students would read the details and fewer would understand it completely. Instead, the key concepts and examples in the financial planning process are explained and illustrated over the first three chapters. This is a personal finance textbook so we try to attract and keep student interest in the first chapter as well as throughout the remaining chapters of the book.

- **Exchange traded funds.** The growing popularity of ETFs as an investment is explored fully in chapter 15, now retitled as "Mutual and Exchange Traded Funds." The chapter also includes a new table of ETFs that allows one to compare which ones in which to invest.

- **Five new types of box inserts.** Every chapter has five new types of boxes: "To-Do Soon List," "Numbers on," "There is an App for That!," "Your Grandparents Say," and "Never Ever."

- **New material.** Newness prevails as we have added some 90 new headings, 180 new boxed inserts, 10 new tables and figures, 70 new terms, and 40 new boxed inserts on "Advice from a Seasoned Pro" (formerly called "Advice From a Professional"). We also retitled and expanded "Your Next Five Years" into the new "To-Do Soon List" that opens each chapter.

- **Continuing cases updated.** Both continuing cases—Harry and Belinda, and Victor and Maria—have been edited and they had all their numbers updated, thus income, ages, expenses, assets, liabilities, and everything else has been rationalized.

- **Definitions.** Hundreds of definitions that in the past were long considered quite clearly written have been tightened up for even more clarity. And we have added new terms with well-structured definitions.

- **Deletions.** Several headings and subheadings have been deleted as well as five tables and figures. To incorporate the latest thinking in personal finance and to save space, we also deleted the series of boxes on "Sean's Success Stories" and "Financial Power Point."

- **Stronger emphasis on budgeting, emergency fund saving, and investing for retirement.** From the first chapter onward, we are major cheerleaders for focusing on budgeting, emergency fund savings and investing for retirement. We encourage readers to think about the critical importance of saving, why they should save, how to do it when they believe they cannot, and then how to wisely invest for retirement. It all starts with creating a simple budget.

- **Breezier writing for more reading by students.** We know instructors want students to actually *read* the book before coming to class, so we paid careful attention to adding more pizzazz. To keep students reading, we livened up the style of writing and added more examples as we updated the topical coverage.

TOPICAL COVERAGE OF THE 13TH EDITION

We have carefully constructed the 13th edition to address instructors' concerns about getting through all the necessary material for this course. The table of contents outlines 17 chapters divided into four parts: Financial Planning, Money Management, Income and Asset Protection, and Investments. We also include a comprehensive chapter on "Career Planning" that provides students with innovative 21st century suggestions necessary to obtain and succeed in their careers.

FEATURES TO STRENGTHEN LEARNING OPPORTUNITIES

We have carefully designed pedagogical features to strengthen learning opportunities for students. Each feature is designed to communicate vital information meaningfully and to maintain student interest. The following features support student understanding and retention.

You Must Be Kidding, Right?   If you typically skip the opening case, now is the time to change your ways. This feature opens every chapter with a short narrative about a financial topic and a question with four possible answers. The often surprising (and sometimes funny) answers provide an excellent opportunity to quickly engage students in a concept that is critically important to understanding the chapter.

Learning Objectives   Concise behavioral objectives that can be measured against the content of each chapter, its activities, and then tested.

What Do You Recommend?   These concise, realistic cases are actually "pretests" at the beginning of each chapter followed by leading questions asking about the most important fundamental concepts in the chapter. The case acts as a pretest because a student who has not read the chapter will be able to offer only simplistic, experience-based opinions and suggestions to respond to the questions. This will communicate to them how much they have to learn from an instructor-led classroom discussion of the chapter. A corresponding posttest, *"What Do You Recommend NOW?"* appears as part of the end-of-chapter pedagogy. At that point, after reading and classroom discussion, student responses should be very different: informed, practical, and action oriented.

Boxed Inserts on Key Topics   Many of the authors' prescriptions for success in personal finance and other important topics are explained in boxes, and these include:

To-Do Soon List   These boxes list the most important tasks students need to take to get off to a great start financially. Every chapter includes five specific prescriptions for the student to accomplish in the next few months or years in life.

Did You Know?   These boxes have interesting, catchy titles that encourage students to actually read the information. These offer some surprises in current understanding that rejects obsolete knowledge.

Numbers On   These highlight important numbers relevant to the subject of each chapter.

Never Ever!   The reader may recall that we wrote that there are a few things to not do wrong. Accordingly, we have two new boxes that feature what one should absolutely, positively in no way ever do in personal finance.

Your Grandparents Say   These offer tips from those who have lived long and succeeded in their personal finances.

There Is an App for That!   Many good apps are listed and almost all can be used on both Apple and Android devices.

Money Websites   These are updated lists of top quality websites that can be truly useful for readers to update their knowledge.

Turn Bad Habits Into Good Ones   A robust list of concrete suggestions is offered.

Advice from a Seasoned Pro   These boxes are written by some of the nation's best personal finance experts. They offer authoritative, real-world advice on topics such as getting out of credit card debt, buying a safe car, and paying for retirement on the layaway plan.

YOU MUST BE KIDDING, RIGHT?

The world of personal finances is getting more complicated and challenging each year. Recent economic times have been tough with some negative impacts on people's personal finances. Which one of the following statements is false?

A. Half of Americans have less than one month's income saved for a rainy day.

B. Half of adults say they do not budget.

C. Sixty percent of Americans say they live paycheck-to-paycheck.

D. Forty percent of Americans say they find it difficult to meet monthly expenses

The answer is "none of the above" is false because all the statements are true. Clearly, many Americans are experiencing trouble with their personal finances. You can get smart about personal finances so these statements do not apply to you!

TO-DO SOON

Do the following to begin to achieve financial success:

1. *Get up to date on future economic conditions by going to www.conference-board.org to read their expectations for economic growth.*

2. *Do some time value of money calculations until you are comfortable using them.*

3. *Harness the power of compounding by starting early to save a consistent amount each month for a long-term goal.*

4. *When employed take advantage of tax sheltering through your employer's benefits program.*

5. *Use marginal and opportunity costs when making an important financial decision.*

The Tax Consequences of   These boxes focus on the income tax aspects in key chapters, so the reader is pushed to always think of the impact of income taxes when making important financial decisions.

Bias Toward   These give the reader a reality check on the behavioral economics biases that plague us into making bad financial decisions. They also explain how to overcome them.

Common Sense   Here we offer thoughts for readers to contemplate. These boxes are basic prescriptions to achieve financial success.

Concept Checks   At the end of each major segment of each chapter, we provide a box of concept check questions tied to the major topics in that part. They may aid classroom discussion, serve as student assignments, or simply provide students with a self-check for a fuller understanding of the material.

Run the Numbers   These boxes guide students to their best personal finance decisions that require mathematics, and they illustrate commonly confronted choices following a step-by-step process.

Do It in Class   This feature highlights with icons the topics in the chapter that are most suitable for students to "turn the class upside down" by choosing perhaps to do in-class learning activities for 20–25 minutes.

End-of-Chapter Pedagogy   The end of chapter pedagogy—much of which has been revised—carefully directs student learning of the concepts and principles that are key to success in personal finance.

What Do You Recommend NOW?   This end-of-chapter section asks the same leading questions pertaining to the case at the beginning of the chapter. At this point, however, instructors can anticipate higher-quality responses and a deeper level of understanding because students have read the chapter and likely listened to instructor-led class discussion.

Summary of Learning Objectives Recapped   Three to six sentences review the most important content cited in each of the chapter's learning objectives.

Let's Talk about It   Students are given an opportunity to discuss their personal experiences related to the chapter by addressing these questions.

Do the Math   These questions apply the relevant quantitative mathematical calculations used in personal finance decision making. The companion website includes Excel calculators for these exercises.

Financial Planning Cases   Students must apply key concepts when analyzing typical personal financial problems, dilemmas, and challenges that face individuals and couples. Because some cases are designed to be both continuous and independent of the other chapters' cases, each case can be analyzed by itself. One continuing case is that of "Julia Price," whose sometimes complicated financial life evolves through challenging economic times, and each of her cases ends with a question for the student: *"Offer your opinions about her thinking."* Two other continuing cases are "Harry and Belinda Johnson," starting out married life as a young couple, and "Victor and Maria Hernandez," a family starting in their thirties. This edition also features five or six cases in each chapter. The series of case questions requires data analysis and critical thinking, and this effort reinforces mastery of chapter concepts.

MY PERSONAL
FINANCIAL
PLANNER

Be Your Own Personal Financial Planner   This end-of-chapter section provides concrete, personalized activities that engage students in developing aspects of their own financial plans. Most are keyed to the "My Personal Financial Planner" worksheets— available in MindTap—complete with interactive spreadsheets.

On the 'Net All of these exercises have been updated to carefully focus the student to online materials that are genuinely useful and appropriate for this time in their personal financial lives. Each chapter includes several Internet-based exercises, activities, and focused questions that expand the student's learning in a guided manner, allowing the student to research and apply chapter concepts while finding the best and most accurate answers available.

Action Involvement Projects Each out-of-class project points the student toward taking specific steps in their communities or on the Internet that require communicating with experts to apply the knowledge provided in each chapter at a personal level, particularly aiming to have an impact on their thoughts about personal finance.

"Flip the Classroom" icons tell instructors and students about "Do It in Class" Exercises for Instructors to Flip the Classroom The traditional pattern of teaching and learning has been for instructors to assign students to read a textbook and have them work on problems, cases, and exercises outside of school. Then the students come to class to listen to lectures, participate in discussions, and take tests.

Flip teaching or a **flipped classroom** is a pedagogical model in which the typical lecture and homework elements of a course are reversed. It is a form of learning where students learn new content by what used to be class work (the "lecture") that is usually done online at home by students who watch video lessons and what used to be "homework" (assigned problems and cases) is now done in class with instructors who offer more personalized guidance and interaction with students.

In a flipped classroom, the instructor has decided that students will study the chapter before coming to class, often using videos, podcasts or screencasts prepared by the instructor or a third party. Sometimes these can be found online from YouTube, the Khan Academy, MIT's OpenCourseWare, Coursera, or other similar sources. As a result the students may watch, rewind, and fast-forward as needed. Then the students the come to class to apply their knowledge by working on problems, cases, and various exercises, including short discussions, for part or all of what used to be the usual class time.

In the flipped class the instructor tutors the students when they become stuck working on problems, rather than imparting the initial lesson by lecturing in person. The flipped classroom frees up class time for hands-on work. Students learn by doing and asking questions. Students can also help each other, a process that benefits both the advanced and less advanced learners.

A breakthrough approach for instructors is offered with this *Personal Finance* textbook. You do not have to, but you may try out a flipped classroom. If instructors provide students some at-home video lessons or if they simply want to take a crack at flipping the classroom, they may review the end-of-chapter "Do It in Class" icons and decide which questions might be most suitable for their students. They might plan for perhaps 20 to 25 minutes of class time for students to solve appropriate problems.

DO IT IN CLASS

To assist with this endeavor we have placed several "Do It in Class" icons within each chapter that are suitable for students to "turn the class upside down" should they choose to do the related in-class learning activities marked with icons at the end of the chapter. The in-chapter icons have no meaning upon first reading the chapter. However, their importance becomes apparent when the student sees the selected end-of-chapter questions that are marked with the same icons. Each of these questions also has page numbers that direct the student to the appropriate section of the chapter (marked with the same icon) where the content exists for them to review and learn so they may perform the tasks requested. The instructor needs only to assign some end-of-chapter "Do It in Class" activities and supervise the student learning.

Glossary A comprehensive end-of-text glossary includes precise definitions of all key terms and concepts. More than 80 terms new have been added and hundreds of others have been rewritten for more clarity.

COMPLETE INSTRUCTOR SUPPORT

- **Instructor Website.** The instructor website that accompanies *Personal Finance* provides a wealth of supplemental materials to enhance learning and aid in course management. Features of the site include PowerPoint slides, downloadable Instructor Manual and Solution Manual files, and test bank content.

- **Instructor's Manual.** Written by coauthor author, Ray Forgue, this ancillary includes a variety of useful components: suggested course syllabi to emphasize a general, insurance, or investments approach to personal finance; learning objectives; a summary overview for use as a lecture outline; and teaching suggestions including student application exercises and tips for bringing the Web into the classroom. This item is found on the instructor companion website.

- **Solutions Manual.** Answers and solutions to all end-of-chapter questions and problems are included. This item is found on the instructor companion website.

- **PowerPoint Slides.** The PowerPoint slides contain chapter outlines, figures, and tables from the main text, which were written by coauthor Ray Forgue. Lecture material is available within the PowerPoint slides.

- **Test Bank.** Each chapter boasts a Test Bank of multiple choice and true/false questions varying in difficulty level and covering the key concepts. The Test Bank for each chapter will be available through *Cognero*, an online, fully customizable version of the Test Bank, which provides instructors with all the tools they need to create, author/edit, and deliver multiple types of tests. Instructors can import questions directly from the *Test Bank,* create their own questions, or edit existing questions.

COMPLETE STUDENT SUPPORT

- **My Personal Financial Planner** is a fantastic tool for students to use in planning and organizing their personal finances. This online product contains over **60** useful worksheets, schedules, and planners for personal finance. They are not busywork for students. Some of the worksheets mimic the calculations and planning exercises covered in the book; others help students develop their own personal financial plans and details for future actions. A student's use of this tool virtually guarantees positive changes in their personal financial behaviors and quick success in money matters. "My Personal Financial Planner" is available in the MindTap student resource for *Personal Finance.*

- **Student Companion Website** is accessible *without* an access code. Among other assets, students can find a short interactive quiz for each chapter.

- **Quizlet.** We know that in a lot of courses, terminology is an important part of how you study. We also know that you may love to use Quizlet on your phone or tablet to help you create flashcards as a study tool. To make it easier for you to use Quizlet with this book, we have created flashcard templates for you. You'll find instructions and the templates on this book's companion site.

Acknowledgments

We would like to thank our reviewers and other experts, who offered helpful suggestions and criticisms to this and previous editions. This book is their book, too. We especially appreciate the assistance of the following individuals:

Tim Alzheimer, *Montana State University*

Gary Amundson, *Montana State University-Billings*

Jan D. Andersen, *California State University, Sacramento*

Dori Anderson, *Mendocino College*

Sophia Anong, *University of Georgia*

Robert E. Arnold, Jr., *Henry Ford Community College*

Bala Arshanapalli, *Indiana University Northwest*

Hal Babson, *Columbus State Community College*

Anne Bailey, *Miami University*

Rosella Bannister, *Bannister Financial Education Services*

Richard Bartlett, *Muskingum Area Technical College*

Katie Barrow, *Louisiana Tech University*

Anne Baumgartner, *Navy Family Service Center-Norfolk*

John J. Beasley, *Georgia Southern University*

Kim Belden, *Daytona Beach Community College*

Pamela J. Bennett, *University of Central Arkansas*

Daniel A. Bequette, *Harwell College*

Peggy S. Berger, *Colorado State University*

David Bible, *Louisiana State University-Shreveport*

George Biggs, *Southern Nazarene University*

Robert Blatchford, *Tulsa Junior College*

Susan Blizzard, *San Antonio College*

Karin B. Bonding, *University of Virginia*

Linda A. Bradley, *California State University-Northridge*

Dean Brassington, *Joint Expeditionary Base Little Creek-Fort Story*

Morgan Bridge, *Colorado Mesa University*

Bryan Brullon, *Polk State College*

Philip Corwin Bryant, *Ivy Tech Community College*

Anne Bunton, *Cottey College*

Bruce Brunson, *Tidewater Community College*

Paul L. Camp, *Galecki Financial Management*

Chris Canellos, *Stanford University*

Andrew Cao, *American University*

Melinda Carlson, *Eastern Michigan University*

Diana D. Carroll, *Carson-Newman College*

Gerri Chaplin, *Joliet Junior College*

Gerry Chambers, *The Villages, FL*

Steve Christian, *Jackson Community College*

Ron Christner, *Loyola University*

Charlotte Churaman, *University of Maryland*

Carol N. Cissel, *Roanoke College*

Thomas S. Coe, *Xavier University of Louisiana*

Edward R. Cook, *University of Massachusetts-Boston*

Patricia Cowley, *Omni Travel*

Kathy Crall, *Des Moines Area Community College*

Sheran Cramer, *University of Nebraska-Lincoln*

Brenda Cude, *University of Georgia*

Ellen Daniel, *Harding University*

Jamey Darnell, *College of Central Florida*

Howard Davidoff, *Brooklyn College*

Joel J. Dauten, *Arizona State University*

William Dean, *Southern University*

Lorraine R. Decker, *Decker & Associates Inc.*

Lucy Delgadillo, *Utah State University*

Carl R. Denson, *University of Delaware*

Dale R. Detlefs, *William M. Mercer, Inc.*

Nancy C. Deringer, *University of Idaho*

A. Terrence Dickens, *California State University*

Jenn J. Dorwart, *Chardron State College*

Charles E. Downing, *Massasoit Community College*

Alberto Duarte, *Access Counseling*

Dottie B. Durband, *Kansas State University*

Sidney W. Eckert, *Appalachian State University*

Marc Eiger, *Standard & Poor's*

Gregg Edwards, *Monroe Community College*

Jacolin P. Eichelberger, *Hillsborough Community College*

Gregory J. Eidleman, *Alvernia College*

Richard English, *Augustana College*

Evan Enowitz, *Grossmont College*

Don Etnier, *University of Maryland-European Division*

David A. Evans, *Purdue University*

Judy Farris, *South Dakota State University*

Patti Fisher, *Virginia Tech*

Vicki Fitzsimmons, *University of Illinois*

Jonathan Fox, *Iowa State University*

Elizabeth Fletcher, *Evangel University*

Fred Floss, *Buffalo State College*

Brian Fraser, *Colorado Mesa University*

Paula G. Freston, *Colby Community College*

H. Swint Friday, *University of South Alabama*

Carol S. Fulmer, *University of Alabama*

Wafica Ghoul, *Davenport University*

Richard Gianni, *North Greenville University*

Joel Gold, *University of South Maine*

Gerson M. Goldberg, *Northeastern University*

Elizabeth Goldsmith, *Florida State University*

Jordan E. Goodman, *MoneyAnswers.com*

Joseph D. Greene, *Augusta State University*

Paul Gregg, *University of Central Florida*

Jeri W. Griego, *Laramie County Community College*

Michael P. Griffin, *University of Massachusetts-Dartmouth*

Richard C. Grimm, *Grove City College*

David R. Guarino, *Standard & Poor's*

Mark Guild, *Southern Adventist University*

Hilda Hall, *Surry Community College*

Sherman Hanna, *The Ohio State University*

Patty Hatfield, *Bradley University*

Andrew Hawkins, *Lake Area Technical Institute*

Deborah Haynes, *Montana State University*

Janice Heckroth, *Indiana University of Pennsylvania*

Diane Henke, *University of Wisconsin-Sheboygan*

Roger P. Hill, *University of North Carolina-Wilmington*

Jeanne Hilton, *University of Nevada*

Steve Holcombe, *North Greenville University*

Laura Horvath, *University of Detroit Mercy*

David Houghton, *Northwest Nazarene College*

George Hruby, *University of Akron*

Holly Hunts, *Montana State University*

Samira Hussein, *Johnson County Community College*

Roger Ignatius, *University of Maine-Augusta*

Alena C. Johnson, *Utah State University*

Xiaohui Sophie Li, *Northern Illinois University*

James R. Isherwood, *Community College of Rhode Island*

Naheel Jeries, *Iowa State University*

Clarence W. Jones, Jr., *Lane College*

Karen Jones, *SWBC Mortgage Corporation*

Marilyn S. Jones, *Friends University*

Ellen Joyner, *Liberty National Bank-Lexington*

Virginia W. Junk, *University of Idaho*

Peggy D. Keck, *Western Kentucky University*

Dennis Keefe, *Michigan State University*

Jim Keys, *Florida International University*

Heidi Kilmer, *Northeastern University*

Haejeong Kim, *Central Michigan University*

Hyungsoo Kim, *University of Kentucky*

Jinhee Kim, *University of Maryland-College Park*

Kyoung Tae (KT) Kim, *The University of Alabama*

Richard Koza, *Chadron State College*

Joan Koonce, *University of Georgia*

Konnie G. Kustron, *Eastern Michigan University*

Karen Eilers Lahey, *University of Akron*

Eloise J. Law, *State University of New Tork-Plattsburgh*

Andrew H. Lawrence, *Delgado Community College*

Frances C. Lawrence, *Louisiana State University*

David W. Leapard, *Eastern Michigan University*

Hongbok Lee, *Western Illinois University*

Irene Leech, *Virginia Tech*

Xiaohai Sophia Li, *Northern Illinois University*

Charles J. Lipinski, *Marywood University*

Lori Lothringer, *Metropolitian Community College*

Jean Lown, *Utah State University*

Janet K. Lukens, *Mississippi State University*

Lee McClain, *Western Washington University*

Wayne Mackie, *Saginaw Valley State University*

Ashwin Madia, *Metropolitan State University*

Kenneth Marin, *Aquinas College*

Kenneth Mark, *Kansas Community College*

Julia Marlowe, *University of Georgia*

Allen Martin, *California State University Northridge*

Lisa Cole-Martin, *Texas Tech University*

Gerard J. Mellnick, *Schoolcraft College*

Linda Meltzer, *Queensborough Community College*

Billy Moore, *Delta State University*

John R. Moore, *Navy Family Services Center-Norfolk*

Byron L. Morgan, *Texas State University*

Diane R. Morrison, *University of Wisconsin-La Crosse*

Diann Moorman, *University of Georgia*

Steven J. Muck, *El Camino College*

Randolph J. Mullis, *WEATrust*

James Nelson, *East Carolina State University*

Donald Neuhart, *Central Missouri State University*

Oris L. Odom II, *University of Texas-Tyler*

William S. Phillips, *Memphis State University*

John Piccione, *Rochester Institute of Technology*

Jennifer H. Plantier, *Hardin-Simmons University*

Carl H. Pollock, *Jr., Portland State University*

Angela J. Rabatin, *Prince George's Community College*

Ann Ranczuch, *Monroe Community College*

Robert Reagan, *Western Dakota Tech*

Gwen M. Reichbach, *Dealers' Financial Services*

Mary Ellen Rider, *University of Nebraska*

Eloise Lorch Rippie, *Iowa State University*

Edmund L. Robert, *Front Range Community College*

Clarence C. Rose, *Radford University*

David E. Rubin, *Glendale Community College*

Michael Ruff, *Monroe Community College*

Michael Rupured, *University of Georgia*

Peggy Schomaker, *University of Maine*

Oscar Solis, *Virginia Tech*

Barry B. Schweig, *Creighton University*

Elaine D. Scott, *Bluefield State University*

Michelle Singletary, *The Washington Post*

James Scott, *Southwest Missouri State University*

Wilmer E. Seago, *Virginia Tech University*

Kim Simons, *Madisonville Community College*

Marilyn K. Skinner, *Macon Technical Institute*

Kelsie Smathers, *University of Idaho*

Feliccia Smith, *North Greenville University*

Rosalyn Smith, *Morningside College*

Horacio Soberon-Ferrer, *University of Florida*

Edward Stendard, *St. John Fisher College*

Mary Stephenson, *University of Maryland-College Park*

Vicky Swank, *Heritage University*

Eugene Swinnerton, *University of Detroit Mercy*

Lisa Tatlock, *The Master's College*

Angela W. Taunton, *Athens State College*

Anastasia Theisen, *Northern Illinois University*

Francis C. Thomas, *Port Republic, New Jersey*

Erica Tobe, *Michigan State University*

Stephen Trimby, *Worcester State College*

Sherry Tshibangu, *Monroe Community College*

John W. Tway, *Amber University*

Shafi Ullah, *Broward Community College*

Dick Verrone, *University of North Carolina-Wilmington*

Jerry A. Viscione, *Boston College*

Stephen E. Wagner, *Attorney at Law, Blacksburg, Virginia*

Rosemary Walker, *Michigan State University*

Robert O. Weagley, *University of Missouri-Columbia*

David Wendle, *Baker College*

Grant J. Wells, *Michigan State University*

Jon D. Wentworth, *Southern Adventist University*

Dorothy West, *Michigan State University*

Mary Ann Whitehurst, *Southeastern Crescent Technical College*

James J. Williams, *Hudson Valley Community College*

Brianne Wilson, *Huntingdon College*

David Windle, *Baker College*

Dana Wolff, *Southeast Technical Institute*

Gloria Worthy, *State Technical Institute-Memphis*

Stephanie R. Yates, *University of Alabama at Birmingham*

Rui Yau, *South Dakota State University*

Alex R. Yguado, *L.A. Mission College*

Robert P. Yuyuenyongwatana, *Cameron University*

Martha Zenns, *Jamestown Community College*

Larry Zigler, *Highland College*

Virginia S. Zuiker, *University of Minnesota*

This 13th edition also has benefited from the contributions of some of the best personal finance experts in the United States, who have shared some specialized expertise by contributing to a series of boxes titled "Advice From a Seasoned Pro":

Dennis R Ackley, *Ackley & Associates*

Katie Barrow, *Louisiana Tech University*

Linda A. Bradley, *California State University*

Morgan Bridge, *Colorado Mesa University*

Bryan Brullon, *Polk State College*

Melinda Carlson, *Eastern Michigan University*

Gerry Chambers, *The Villages, FL*

Philip Corwin Bryant, *Ivy Tech Community College*

Jamey Darnell, *College of Central Florida*

Howard Davidoff, *Brooklyn College*

William Dean, *Southern University*

Lucy Delgadillo, *Utah State University*

Nancy C. Deringer, *University of Idaho*

Jenn J. Dorwart, *Chardron State College*

Dorothy B. Durband, *Kansas State University*

David A. Evans, *Purdue University*

xxviii **ACKNOWLEDGMENTS**

Brian Fraser, *Colorado Mesa University*

Richard Gianni, *North Greenville University*

Jordan E. Goodman, *MoneyAnswers.com*

Gerson M. Goldberg, *Northeastern University*

Mark Guild, *Southern Adventist University*

Sherman Hanna, *The Ohio State University*

Deborah Haynes, *Montana State University*

Steve Holcombe, *North Greenville University*

Holly Hunts, *Montana State University*

Alena C. Johnson, *Utah State University*

Clarence W. Jones, *Jr., Lane College*

Heidi Kilmer, *Northeastern University*

Hyungsoo Kim, *University of Kentucky*

Kyoung Tae (KT) Kim, *The University of Alabama*

Richard Koza, *Chadron State College*

Konnie G. Kustron, *Eastern Michigan University*

Frances C. Lawrence, *Louisiana State University*

David W. Leapard, *Eastern Michigan University*

Irene Leech, *Virginia Tech*

Xiaohui Sophie Li, *Northern Illinois University*

Lori Lothringer, *Metropolitian Community College*

Jean Lown, *Utah State University*

Wayne Mackie, *Saginaw Valley State University*

Lisa Cole-Martin, *Texas Tech University*

Ashwin Madia, *Metropolitan State University*

Gerard J. Mellnick, *Schoolcraft College*

Linda Meltzer, *Queensborough Community College*

Diann Moorman, *University of Georgia*

Byron L. Morgan, *Texas State University*

Jennifer H. Plantier, *Hardin-Simmons University*

Ann Ranczuch, *Monroe Community College*

Michael Ruff, *Monroe Community College*

Michelle Singletary, *The Washington Post*

Kelsie Smathers, *University of Idaho*

Oscar Solis, *Virginia Tech*

Robert Reagan, *Western Dakota Tech*

Felicia Smith, *North Greenville University*

Vicky Swank, *Heritage University*

Angela W. Taunton, *Athens State College*

Anastasia Theisen, *Northern Illinois University*

Erica Tobe, *Michigan State University*

Sherry Tshibangu, *Monroe Community College*

Robert O. Weagley, *University of Missouri-Columbia*

Jon Wentworth, *Southern Adventist University*

David Windle, *Baker College*

Brianne Wilson, *Huntingdon College*

Stephanie R. Yates, *University of Alabama at Birmingham*

Dana Wolff, *Southeast Technical Institute*

We definitely wish to thank the many students who had the opportunity to read, critique, and provide input for various components of the *Personal Finance* project. Please keep sending us your e-mails.

This edition of *Personal Finance* benefited enormously from the editorial efforts of Conor Allen. In addition to being a fine manager and editor, he brought much insight, creativity, intelligence, and wisdom to the project. His staff also was kind enough to provide some excellent insights. Conor is a master of his art, and it has been a privilege to work with him on this as well as others of our books. Many thanks go to Conor's successors for their strong efforts to manage the many complex decisions as they completed the book on schedule: Tara Slagle and Julie Dierig. Finally, and this is a first in our 13 editions, sincere appreciation is given to the firm that composed the book—implementing hundreds of critical decisions as well as making the content perfectly fit the pages—Lumina Datamatics, and the team led by Joseph Malcolm, Senior Project Manager.

A project of this dimension could never have been completed without the patience, support, understanding, and sacrifices of our friends and families during the book's development, revision, and production. Tom Garman, professor emeritus and fellow at Virginia Tech University, retired to life in The Villages, Florida, and stays in contact with his children and their spouses and significant others: Scott and his husband Dave, Dana and her husband Tom with Julia, Alieu and his wife Isatou with Kumba, Alimatou, and Ousman. Thanks are owed to all. Tom also credits the mentors in his life—Ron West, Bill Boast, Bill McDivitt, and John Binnion—for guiding him along the way, particularly through their noble examples of compassion, commitment, and excellence. Most helpful of all, most encouraging and inspiring, and most deserving of my wholehearted gratitude, is my wife, Gerry. I thank her for being the love of my life. Her laughter, love, and support guarantees that the fourth quarter of my life is and will continue to be blessed with tremendous happiness.

Ray Forgue, retired from University of Kentucky, lives in Easley, South Carolina, with his wife Snooky. They take great pleasure in traveling to visit their children. Ray's son, Matthew, and his wife, Kat, live in Oregon. His daughter, Amy, her husband, Mack, and their two daughters live in Colorado. Snooky's children, Stuart and Dru, live in South Carolina. Her son, Seth, his wife, Alexandra, and their two boys live in New York. Ray wishes to thank his mother, Mary, and brothers Bob, Gary, Joe, and Dave for their patience over the years as he spent time during vacation and holiday visits working on this book. Special thanks to Snooky, whose assistance on the first edition of *Personal Finance* continues to shine through to this current edition.

Finally, we wish to say "thank you" to the hundreds of personal finance instructors around the country, who have generously shared their views, in person, via telephone, mail, fax, text, Facebook, and e-mail on what should be included in a high-quality textbook and ancillary materials. Some of you thankfully have communicated multiple times, especially Professors Sherman Hanna of The Ohio State University, Jonathan Fox of Iowa State University, and Jean Lown of Utah State University. Their views have always been astute and insightful, and they are among the nation's best college personal finance professors.

Instructors around the country demand the best for their students, and we have listened. *Personal Finance* is your book! The two of us and the quality team of professionals at Cengage have tried very hard to meet your needs in every possible way. We hope we have exceeded your expectations. Why? Because we share the belief that students need to study personal finance principles thoroughly and learn them well so that they will be genuinely financially successful throughout their lives.

E. Thomas Garman
ethomasgarman@yahoo.com

Raymond E. Forgue
perfinypm@yahoo.com

P.S. Dear students: If you are going to save any of your college textbooks, be certain to keep this one because the basic principles of personal finance are everlasting. Also, you might want to present the book as a gift to a significant other, spouse, sibling, or parent.

PART 1

Monkey Business Images/Shutterstock.com

1 Understanding Personal Finance

YOU MUST BE KIDDING, RIGHT?

Lauren Crawford, age 23, earns $50,000 a year and she invests 6 percent of her salary, $3,000 annually, through her employer-sponsored 401(k) retirement account. Because her employer also contributions 50 cents for every dollar she contributes, Lauren is saving $4,500 each year ($3,000 + $1,500). Even if she never increases her 401(k) contributions, about how much money will she have in the account after 40 years if she earns an 8 percent return?

A. Less than one-quarter of a million dollars

B. More than one-quarter million dollars but less than one-half million

C. Close to $1 million

D. Over $1 million

The answer is D; approximately $1,165,750. This is even though her total contributions will only be $180,000 ($4,500 x 40). Lauren will make the big money from "the annual compounding of money," not just on the amounts she puts into her retirement plan each month (the $180,000). Growing wealth is all about the magic of compound interest over time!

mstanley/Shutterstock.com

Learning Objectives

After reading this chapter, you should be able to:

1 Recognize the keys to achieving financial success.

2 Understand how the economy affects your personal financial success.

3 Think like an economist when making financial decisions.

4 Perform time value of money calculations in personal financial decision making.

5 Make smart decisions about your employee benefits.

6 Identify the professional certifications of providers of financial advice.

WHAT DO YOU RECOMMEND?

Jing Wáng, age 23, recently graduated with her bachelor's degree in accounting. She is about to take her first professional position as an accountant with a large firm in an expanding area in California. While in school, Jing worked part time for that firm during the summers, earning about $15,000 per year. For the past two years, she has managed to put $1,000 each year into an individual retirement account (IRA). Jing owes $35,000 in student loans on which she will soon start to make payments. Her new job will pay $80,000. Jing may begin participating in her employer's 401(k) retirement plan immediately, and she can contribute up to 8 percent of her salary to the plan. Her employer will contribute 1/2 of 1 percent for every 1 percent that Jing contributes.

qingqing/Shutterstock.com

What do you recommend to Jing on the importance of personal finance regarding:

1. **Participating in her employer's 401(k) retirement plan?**
2. **Understanding the effects of her marginal tax rate on her financial decisions?**
3. **Considering the current state of the economy in her personal financial planning?**
4. **Using time value of money considerations to project what her IRA might be worth at age 63?**
5. **Using time value of money considerations to project what her 401(k) plan might be worth when she is age 63 if she were to participate fully?**

personal finance

*The study of personal and family
resources considered important in
achieving financial success; it involves
how people spend, save, protect, and
invest their financial resources.*

financial literacy

*Knowledge of facts, concepts,
principles, and technological tools
that are fundamental to being smart
about money.*

financial well-being

*A state of being wherein a person can
fully meet current and ongoing financial obligations, can feel secure in their
financial future, and make choices that
allow them to enjoy life.*

financially responsible

*Means that you are accountable for
your future financial well-being and
that you strive to make wise personal
financial decisions.*

Learning Objective 1

Recognize the keys to achieving
financial success.

Can you successfully manage your personal finances in today's economy? Yes you can! Most people realize that the key to long-term financial stability and success is to live below your means, have an emergency fund to handle financial surprises, pay off credit cards and student loans, and save and invest for your future. But it is tough to accomplish today with all the demands on your money.

In the years ahead many opportunities will arise for you to take smart actions to help assure your future financial success. Financial success may seem like a far-off prospect when you are in your twenties. But the personal finance patterns you put into practice while enrolled in your personal finance course and immediately after graduation will help you manage, as well as accumulate, money in the years ahead.

This book is your ticket for a financially successful life! You can have it all by becoming a wealth builder. You can become financially responsible and economically independent. And you will learn to handle any financial surprises along the way.

Personal finance is the study of personal and family resources considered important in achieving financial success. It involves how people spend, save, protect, and invest their financial resources. A good understanding of personal finance topics offers you a great chance of success in facing the financial challenges, responsibilities, and opportunities of life.

At the heart of it, personal finance is totally about money. On the question of "What makes the world go around, love or money?" The answer: "Love makes it very special. But without money you are in serious trouble. And the trouble is so bad that it is like being up the proverbial creek without a paddle." So, please, continue reading and get started on how to be very smart in your personal finances.

This book provides prudent guidance for every step of the way. Careful study will enhance your **financial literacy**, which is your knowledge of facts, concepts, principles, and technological tools that are fundamental to being smart about money. Financial literacy empowers you. It improves your ability to handle day-to-day financial matters, helps you avoid the consequences of poor financial decisions that could take years to overcome, helps you make informed and confident personal money decisions, and makes you more financially responsible.

Financial well-being, says the federal government, is a state of being wherein a person can fully meet current and ongoing financial obligations, can feel secure in their financial future, and is able to make choices that allow them to enjoy life. To achieve financial well-being, one must be **financially responsible**. This means that you are accountable for your future financial well-being and that you strive to make good decisions in personal finance. The best example of not being financially responsible is to live like you are rich *before* you are. Being financially responsible means you will control your personal financial destiny and be successful.

At the beginning of each chapter, we provide a short case vignette titled "What Do You Recommend?" Each story focuses on the financial challenges that can be experienced by someone who has not learned about the material in that chapter. You will be asked to think about what advice you might give the person as you study the chapter. At the end of each chapter, you will again be asked to provide more informed advice based on what you have learned. The question at that point is "What Do You Recommend NOW?" You will be much better informed then!

1.1 ACHIEVING PERSONAL FINANCIAL SUCCESS

Today's marketplace provides a constant barrage of messages suggesting that you can spend and borrow your way to financial success, security, and wealth. Well, they are wrong because you can't. These messages are very enticing for those starting out in their financial lives. It is hard to resist the immediate gratification of spending. In truth, however, overspending and overuse of consumer credit seriously impedes financial success.

The fact is that "you" are the result of your financial decisions. If you regularly purchase things you cannot afford, that is who you are. There is a right and a wrong way, and that is the wrong way. If this sounds like you, then you must learn to make better financial decisions.

Many people think that being wealthy is a function of how much one earns or inherits. In reality, it is much more closely related to your ability to make good decisions that generate wealth for you. The most important point in this book is to realize that you must live within your means, save some of what you earn, and avoid the temptation of having to purchase every new thing your friends buy.

You must have the discipline to delay gratification and make the right decisions to succeed in your finances. You have to do only a *few* things right in personal finance during your lifetime, as long as you don't do too many things wrong. Personal finance is not rocket science. You can succeed very well in your personal finances by making appropriate plans and taking sensible actions to implement those plans.

1.1a The Five Fundamental Steps in the Financial Planning Process

There are five fundamental steps to the personal financial planning process, and these are examined in this chapter and the two that follow:

(1) Evaluate your financial condition relative to your education and career choice;
(2) Define your financial goals;
(3) Develop a plan of action to achieve your goals;
(4) Periodically develop and implement spending plans to monitor and control progress toward goals; and
(5) Review your financial progress and make changes as appropriate.

1.1b You Must Plan for Financial Success and Happiness

Financial success is the achievement of financial aspirations that are desired, planned, or attempted. Success is defined by the person who seeks it. Some define financial success as being able to actually live according to one's standard of living. Many seek **financial security**, which provides the comfortable feeling that your financial resources will be adequate to fulfill any needs you have as well as most of your wants. Others want to be **wealthy** and have an abundance of money, property, investments, and other resources.

Financial happiness encompasses a lot more than just making money. It is the experience you have when you are satisfied with your money matters. People who are happy about their finances are likely to be spending within a budget and taking steps to achieve their goals, and this happiness spills over in a positive way to feelings about their overall enjoyment of life. Financial happiness is in part a result of practicing good financial behaviors. Examples of such behaviors include paying bills on time, spending less than you earn, knowing where your money goes, and investing some money for the future. The more good financial behaviors you practice, the greater your financial happiness. In fact, simply setting financial goals contributes to financial happiness.

1.1c You Must Spend Less So You Can Save and Invest More

Financial objectives are rarely achieved without forgoing or sacrificing current **consumption** (spending on goods and services). This restraint is accomplished by putting money into **savings** (income not spent on current consumption) for use in achieving future goals. Some savings are actually **investments** (assets purchased with the goal of providing additional future income from the asset itself). By saving and investing, people are much more likely to have funds available for future consumption. If you save for tomorrow, you will be happier today *and* tomorrow.

Effective financial management often separates the *haves* from the *have-nots*. The haves are those people who learn to live on less than they earn and are the savers and investors of society. The have-nots are the spenders who live paycheck-to-paycheck, usually with high consumer debt. They fail to manage money and as a result money manages them.

financial success

The achievement of financial aspirations that are desired, planned, or attempted, as defined by the person who seeks it.

financial security

The comfortable feeling that your financial resources will be adequate to fulfill any needs you have as well as most of your wants.

financial happiness

The experience you have when you are satisfied with your money matters, which is in part a result of practicing good financial behaviors.

savings

Income not spent on current consumption.

investments

Assets purchased with the goal of providing additional future income from the asset itself.

Being frugal is not about abstinence. It is about being smart in personal finance. Saving money does not make you cheap; it makes you smarter than those who just spend and spend. Spending less is about prioritizing your choices. You should think about making good choices in life when making every day spending decisions by asking yourself "What is most important to me?" This helps you get out of the habit of simply spending money and instead making choices that will enhance your life.

Saving for future consumption represents a good illustration of the human desire to achieve a certain **standard of living**. This standard is what an individual or group earnestly desires and seeks to attain, to maintain if attained, to preserve if threatened, and to regain if lost. Our standards include our wants and needs—as well as our comforts and luxuries too. In contrast, individuals actually experience their **level of living** at any particular time. In essence, your standard of living is where you would like to be, and your level of living is where you actually are.

standard of living

Material well-being and peace of mind that individuals or groups earnestly desire and seek to attain, to maintain if attained, to preserve if threatened, and to regain if lost.

level of living

Refers to the level of wealth, comfort, material goods and necessities one is currently living.

1.1d What You Will Accomplish Studying Personal Finance

Learning about and succeeding in money matters means that by the time you finish this book you will:

1. Recognize how to manage the unexpected and unplanned financial events.
2. Pay as little as possible in income taxes to the Internal Revenue Service (IRS).
3. Understand how to effectively comparison shop for vehicles and homes.
4. Protect what you own.
5. Invest wisely.
6. Accumulate and protect wealth that you may choose to spend during your non-working years or donate it.

Figure 1-1 shows the building blocks to achieving financial success and how they fit together. Figure 1-2 shows how to get your financial house in order by age 30. Accomplish these steps and you will be well on your way to being truly financially successful.

obsolete knowledge

That which we believe may have been valid at one time, if it ever was true in the first place.

1.1e Replace Your Obsolete Knowledge

Obsolete knowledge is that which we believe may have been valid at one time, if it ever was true in the first place. When we are sure of erroneous knowledge we are not

Figure 1-1   **Building Blocks to Achieving Financial Success**

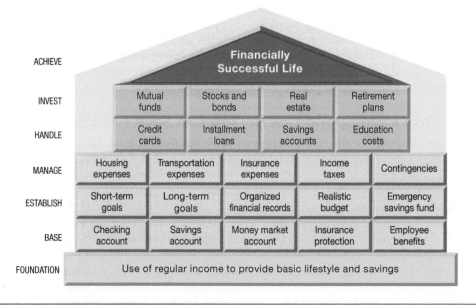

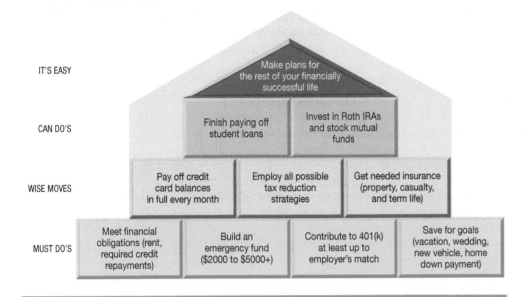

Figure 1-2 **Get Your Financial House in Order by Age 30**

IT'S EASY

Make plans for the rest of your financially successful life

CAN DO'S

Finish paying off student loans

Invest in Roth IRAs and stock mutual funds

WISE MOVES

Pay off credit card balances in full every month

Employ all possible tax reduction strategies

Get needed insurance (property, casualty, and term life)

MUST DO'S

Meet financial obligations (rent, required credit repayments)

Build an emergency fund ($2000 to $5000+)

Contribute to 401(k) at least up to employer's match

Save for goals (vacation, wedding, new vehicle, home down payment)

motivated to look for new information. As the Jedi master Yoda told Luke Skywalker, "You must unlearn what you have learned." If you believe the world is changing and recognize that some of your knowledge is obsolete, you can begin to move past your outdated knowledge.

But how? Your response will be your true challenge in learning personal finance *and* applying it to your money matters in the many years of your life. This book provides you with the most up-to-date and best facts available, and much of the information is evolving and as such it will need to be replaced. In today's world you need to learn how and where to accurately find the facts you want to know. This book will show you.

CONCEPT CHECK 1.1

1. Explain the five fundamental steps in the financial planning process.
2. Distinguish among financial success, financial security, and financial happiness.
3. Summarize what you will accomplish studying personal finance.
4. What are the building blocks to achieving financial success?

1.2 THE ECONOMY AFFECTS YOUR PERSONAL FINANCIAL SUCCESS

Your success in personal finance depends in part on how well you understand the economic environment; the current stage of the business cycle; and the future direction of the economy, inflation, and interest rates.

1.2a How to Tell Where We Are in the Business Cycle

An economy is an economic and political system of managing the productive and employment resources of a country, state, or community. The U.S. economy is **capitalism**. Here a country's trade and industry are controlled by private owners who seek profit.

Learning Objective 2

Understand how the economy affects your personal financial success.

capitalism

Here a country's economy, its trade and industry, are controlled by private owners who see profit.

economic growth

A condition of increasing production (business spending) and consumption (consumer spending) in the economy and hence increasing national income.

business cycle/economic cycle

Business cycles can be depicted as a wavelike pattern of rising and falling economic activity; the phases of the business cycle include expansion, peak, contraction (which may turn into recession), and trough.

deleveraging

A time period when credit use shrinks in an economy instead of expanding as during normal economic times.

recession

A recurring period of decline in total output, income, employment, and trade, usually lasting from six months to a year and marked by widespread contractions in many sectors of the economy.

The U.S. federal government attempts to regulate the country's overall economy to maintain stable prices (low inflation) and stable levels of employment (low unemployment). In this way, the government seeks to achieve sustained **economic growth**, which is a condition of increasing production (business activity) and consumption (consumer spending) in the economy—and hence increasing national income. Specific government policies also affect the economy. For example, tax cuts keep money in consumers' pockets, money that they are then likely to spend. Tax increases, in contrast, depress consumer demand.

1.2b   The Business Cycle

Growth in the U.S. economy varies over time. The **business cycle** (also called the **economic cycle**) is a process by which the economy grows and contracts over time. It can be depicted as a wavelike pattern of rising and falling economic activity in which the same pattern occurs again and again over time. As illustrated in Figure 1-3, the phases of the business cycle are expansion (when the economy is increasing), peak (the end of an expansion and the beginning of a contraction), contraction (when the economy is falling), and trough (the end of a contraction and beginning of an expansion).

The preferred stage of the economic cycle is the **expansion phase,** where production is at high capacity, unemployment is low, retail sales are high, and prices and interest rates are low or falling. Under these conditions, consumers find it easier to buy homes, cars, and expensive goods on credit, and businesses are encouraged to borrow to expand production to meet the increased consumer demand. The stock market also rises because investors expect higher profits in the future.

As the demand for credit increases, short-term interest rates rise because more borrowers want money. Consumers and businesses purchase more goods, exerting upward pressure on prices. Eventually, prices and interest rates climb high enough to stifle consumer and business borrowing, send stock prices down, and choke off the expansion. One effect of such economic turmoil is **deleveraging**, meaning that instead of normal economic times when credit usage grows, it shrinks because companies and individuals pay down their debts. When businesses and consumers use less debt, home and car sales decline as does employment. The result is a period of negligible economic growth or even a decline in economic activity.

In such situations, the economy often contracts and moves toward a **recession**. During recessions, consumers become pessimistic about their future buying plans. The typical U.S. recession is marked by an average economic decline of 2 percent that lasts for ten months with an average unemployment rate exceeding 6 percent.

There have been five recessions since 1980. The federal government's Business Cycle Dating Committee of the National Bureau of Economic Research officially defines a recession as "a period of falling economic activity spread across the economy, lasting

Figure 1-3   **Business Cycle Phases**

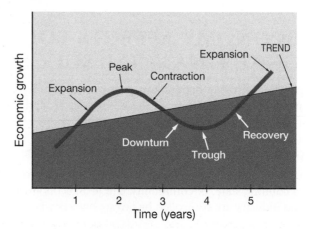

more than a few months, normally visible in real gross domestic product, real income, employment, industrial production, and wholesale-retail sales."

The Great Recession The Great Recession began in 2007 and lasted 18 months, which makes it the longest of any recession since 1929–1941. The economy contracted 5.1 percent, which was of historic proportions. Nine million people had their jobs disappear as unemployment surpassed 10 percent. Half of all American workers suffered job losses, pay cuts, or reduced hours at work, or they were forced into part-time employment. The decline was almost a genuine depression.

The Great Recession reduced the asset values and wealth of individuals. Many people of your parents' ages saw the value of their homes shrink 25 to 65 percent while at the same time half of their retirement funds evaporated. In total, it destroyed 20 percent of Americans' wealth in both home values and investments. Surveys revealed that over 60 percent of those between ages 50 and 61 had to delay their retirements; the average age at retirement rose three years. Consumer confidence dropped to an all-time low.

Some people feared a **double dip recession**. This happens when the economy has a recession and then, soon after emerging from the recession with a short period of growth, falls back into recession. Fortunately, this did not occur although rebound growth was slow.

The Economic Future Will Be Expansion Despite the severity or length of any recession, eventually the economic contraction ends, and consumers and businesses become more optimistic. The economy then moves beyond the trough toward recovery and expansion, where levels of production, employment, and retail sales begin to improve, allowing the overall economy to experience some growth from its previously weakened state. The entire business cycle typically takes about six years.

Politicians and economic advisors struggle with which path to take to create economic growth. Most of the world has followed the Keynesian economic theory since the 1930s, which is to increase demand with stimulus spending even if it creates large temporary government deficits. The logic is that when consumers and businesses spend less, the economy will be further depressed unless the government spends more. Such spending creates additional economic growth that results in increased tax revenues, thus resulting in budget surpluses that can be used to pay down the debts.* Now, however, the deficits themselves are seen as the problem by some U.S. politicians and in other countries resulting in calls to slash public outlays. Others say such an austerity approach will lead to lower demand, lower growth, lower tax revenues, stock market declines, and an even higher national debt.

1.2c How to Tell the Future Direction of the Economy

To make sound financial decisions, you need to know where we are in the business cycle, how well the economy is doing, and where the economy might be headed. You can do this by paying attention to some economic statistics that are regularly reported in the news as well as on cable TV business shows. Your knowledge can help guide your long-term financial strategy. An **economic indicator** is any economic statistic, such as the unemployment rate, GDP, or the inflation rate (terms discussed in the next few paragraphs), that suggests how well the economy is doing and how well the economy might do in the future.

Look at Procyclic Indicators, like GDP and Jobs A **procyclic** (or **procyclical**) economic indicator is one that moves in the same direction as the economy. Thus, if the economy is doing well, this number typically is increasing. If we are in a recession, this indicator is decreasing. Examples of procyclic indicators are retail sales, industrial production, new orders for durable goods (like household appliances), number of employees on nonagricultural payrolls, and the gross domestic product. Consumer spending accounts for about 70 percent of the total U.S. economy.

The best understood example of a procyclic economic indicator is the **gross domestic product (GDP)**, which is the market value of all the goods and services produced in

COMMON SENSE
Be Optimistic About Your Future

During poor economic times people face uncertain financial futures. However, this does not mean that they should stop saving and investing for their futures. Every generation has faced similar uncertainties. You should be positive about the long-term economic future. Make good decisions regarding spending, saving, investing, and donating by putting in practice what you learn in this book.

economic indicator
Any economic statistic, such as the unemployment rate, GDP, or the inflation rate, that suggests how well the economy is doing now and how well it might be doing in the future.

gross domestic product (GDP)
The nation's broadest measure of economic health; it reports how much economic activity (all goods and services) has occurred within the U.S. borders during a given period.

---

*Every year since 1970, Congress has authorized more spending than projected revenue, except for the last two years of the William Jefferson Clinton presidency (1999 and 2000), which had budget surpluses.

the country. It is the broadest measure of the economic health of the nation. The federal government reports every quarter the value of all the goods and services produced in the country (www.bea.gov/newsreleases/rels.htm).

In the United States, an annual rate of 2 percent or less is considered very low growth (usually not even enough to create jobs for new entrants to the job market, such as college graduates), and 3 percent is considered growth occurring at a safe speed that is not likely to induce excessive inflation. A sustained rate of 4 percent or higher starts to worry economists and investors as they fear future inflation. The United States needs a GDP growth rate of about 2.5 percent just to keep unemployment from rising.

Look at Countercyclic Indicators　A **countercyclic** (or **countercyclical**) economic indicator is one that moves in the opposite direction from the economy. For example, the unemployment rate is countercyclic because it gets larger as the economy gets worse.

leading economic indicators

Statistics that change before the economy changes, thus helping predict how the economy will do in the future, such as the stock market, the number of new building permits, and the consumer confidence index.

Look at Leading Indicators　**Leading economic indicators** are those that change before the economy changes, thus, they help predict how the economy will do in the future. The stock market is a leading economic indicator because it usually begins to decline shortly before the overall economy slows down. Also, the stock market advances before the economy begins to pull out of a recession. Other examples of leading economic indicators are the number of new building permits, existing home sales, home prices, jobless claims (average number of weekly first-time filings for unemployment benefits), the Standard & Poor's 500 Stock Index, and the consumer confidence index.

The **consumer confidence index** is a widely watched leading economic indicator that gauges how consumers feel about the economy and their personal finances. It gives a sense of consumers' willingness to spend (www.conference-board.org). Growing confidence suggests increased consumer spending. Consumers worried about the future postpone purchases, and the reduced spending acts as a drag on the economy.

index of leading economic indicators (LEI)

Four composite index reported monthly by the Conference Board that suggests the future direction of the U.S. economy.

The **index of leading economic indicators (LEI)** is a composite index, reported monthly by the Conference Board, that suggests the future direction of the U.S. economy (www.conference-board.org). The LEI averages ten components of growth from different segments of the economy, such as building permits, factory orders, and new private housing starts. Leading economic indicators are important to investors as they help predict what the economy will be like in the future.

inflation

The process by which the cost of goods and services tends to rise over time.

1.2d　The Future Direction of Inflation and Interest Rates

Prices and interest rates typically move in the same direction. A steady rise in the general level of prices is called **inflation**, which is the process by which the cost of goods and services tends to rise over time. Inflation often occurs when the supply

ADVICE FROM A SEASONED PRO

Seven Money Mantras for a Richer Life

1. It's not an asset if you are wearing it!
2. Is this a need or is it a want?
3. Sweat the small stuff.
4. Cash is better than credit.

5. Keep it simple.
6. Priorities lead to prosperity.
7. Enough is enough!

Michelle Singletary, Washington, DC
Nationally syndicated *Washington Post* columnist for *"The Color of Money"* and author of *"The 21 Day Financial Fast: Your Path to Financial Peace and Freedom."* Reprinted with permission of the author.

of money (or credit) rises faster than the supply of goods and services available for purchases. It also may be attributed to excessive demand or sharply increasing costs of production.

Inflation Is the Typical Economic Condition Some level of inflation is the typical condition in any economy. It can be beneficial in moderation as inflation encourages job creation and economic growth. But when there is high inflation in the United States, perhaps as high as 5 or 6 percent, workers begin to demand higher wages, thereby adding to the cost of production. In response to the increases in the costs of labor and raw materials, manufacturers will charge more for their products. Lenders, in turn, will require higher interest rates to offset the lost purchasing power of the loaned funds. Consumers will lessen their resistance to price increases because they may fear even higher prices in the future. Thus, inflation can have a snowball effect. In times of moderate to high inflation, buying power declines rapidly, and people on fixed incomes suffer the most.

A very negative complication of inflation that sometimes occurs is **stagflation**. This is the condition of stagnant economic growth and high unemployment accompanied by rising prices.

How Inflation Is Measured The U.S. Bureau of Labor Statistics measures inflation on a monthly basis using the **consumer price index (CPI)**. The CPI is a broad measure of changes in the prices of all goods and services purchased for consumption by urban households. The prices of more than 400 goods and services (a "market basket" of food, transportation, housing, health care, and entertainment) sold across the country are tracked, recorded, weighted for importance in a hypothetical budget, and totaled. In essence, the CPI is a cost of living index.

consumer price index (CPI)
A broad measure of changes in the prices of all goods and services purchased for consumption by urban households.

The index has a base time period—or starting reference point—from which to make comparisons. The 1982 to 1984 time period represents the base period of 100. For example, if the CPI were 251 on January 1, 2018, the cost of living would have risen 151 percent since the base period [(251 − 100) / 100 = 1.51 or 151%]*. Similarly, if the index rises from 251 to 257 on January 1, 2019, then the cost of living will have increased by 2.4 percent over the year [(257 − 251) / 251 = 0.024 or 2.4%].

How Inflation Affects Your Income From an income point of view, inflation has significant effects. Consider the case of Scott Wade of Sioux Falls, South Dakota, a single man who took a job in retail management three years ago at a salary of $50,000 per year. Since that time, Scott has received three annual raises of $1,000, but he still cannot make ends meet because of inflation. Although Scott received raises, his current income of $53,000 ($50,000 + $1,000 + $1,000 + $1,000) did not keep pace with the annual inflation rate of 2.4 percent ($50,000 × 1.024 = $51,200; $51,200 × 1.024 = $52,429; $52,429 × 1.024 = $53,687). If Scott's own cost of living rose at the same rate as the general price level, in the third year he would be $687 ($53,687 − $53,000) short of keeping up with inflation. He would need $687 more in the third year to maintain the same purchasing power that he enjoyed in the first year.

Personal incomes rarely keep up in times of high inflation. Your **real income** (income measured in constant prices relative to some base time period) is the more important number. It reflects the actual buying power of the **nominal income** (also called **money income**) that you have to spend as measured in current dollars. Rising nominal income during times of inflation creates the illusion that you are making more money, when in actuality that may not be true.

real income
Income measured in constant prices relative to some base time period. It reflects the actual buying power of the money you have as measured in constant dollars.

To compare your annual wage increase with the rate of inflation for the same time period, you first convert your dollar raise into a percentage, as follows:

nominal income
Also called money income; income that has not been adjusted for inflation and decreasing purchasing power.

$$\text{Percentage change} = \frac{\text{nominal annual income after raise} - \text{nominal annual income last year}}{\text{nominal annual income last year}} \times 100 \quad \textbf{(1.1)}$$

---

*This equation shows how the percentage change is calculated for any difference between two measurements. Divide the difference between measurement 1 and measurement 2 by the value of measurement 1. For example, a stock selling for $65 per share on January 1 and for $76 on December 31 of the same year would have risen 16.92 percent during the year: [($76 − $65) ÷ $65 = 0.1692 or 16.92%].

For example, imagine that Javier Gomez, a single parent and assistant manager of a convenience store in Durham, New Hampshire, received a $1,600 raise to push his $47,000 annual salary to $48,600. Using Equation (1.1), Javier calculated his percentage change in personal income as follows:

$$\frac{\$48,600 - \$47,000}{\$47,000} = 0.034 \times 100 = 3.4\%$$

After a year during which inflation was 2.4 percent, Javier did better than the inflation rate because his raise amounted to 3.4 percent. Measured in real terms, his raise was 1.0 percent (3.4 − 2.4). In dollars, Javier's real income after the raise can be calculated by dividing his new nominal income by 1.0 plus the previous year's inflation rate (expressed as a decimal):

$$\text{Real income} = \frac{\text{nominal annual income after raise}}{1.0 + \text{previous inflation rate}}$$

(1.2)

$$\frac{\$48,600}{1 + 0.024} = \$47,460$$

DO IT IN CLASS

Clearly, a large part of the $1,600 raise Javier received was eaten up by inflation. To Javier, only $460 ($47,460 − $47,000) represents real economic progress, while $1,140 ($1,600 − $460) was used to pay the inflated prices on goods and services. The $460 real raise is equivalent to 0.98 percent ($460 / $47,000, or less than 1 percent) of his previous income, reflecting the difference between Javier's percentage raise in nominal dollars and the inflation rate.

How Inflation Affects Your Consumption When prices are rising, an individual's income must rise at the same rate to maintain its **purchasing power**, which is a measure of the goods and services that one's income will buy. When prices rise, the purchasing power of the dollar declines, but not by the same percentage. Instead, it falls by the *reciprocal amount* of the price increase.

purchasing power

Measure of the goods and services that one's income will buy.

DO IT IN CLASS

Rule of 70

A formula to determine how long it will take for the value of a dollar to decline by one-half.

In the preceding illustration where prices increase between 2018 and 2019, prices rose 2.4 percent, whereas the purchasing power of the dollar declined 2.07 percent over the same period. [The previous year base of 251 divided by the index of 257 equals 0.9767; the reciprocal is 0.0233 (1 − 0.9767), or 2.33%.].

The **Rule of 70** can be used to determine how long it will take for the value of the dollar to go down by one-half. Simply divide 70 by the current inflation rate. In our example, a 2.4 percent inflation rate would reduce the value of a dollar by one-half in 29 years (70 / 2.4). As you can see, even a low inflation rate means that by the time a young worker retires, the purchasing power of their initial income will have dropped significantly.

Inflation pushes up the costs of the products and services we consume. If automobile prices rose 15 percent over the past five years, for example, then it will take $32,200 now to buy a car that once sold for $28,000 ($28,000 × 1.15). If your market basket of goods and services differs from that used to calculate the CPI, you might have a very different **personal inflation rate** (the rate of increase in prices of items purchased by a particular person). Inflation pushes up the cost of borrowing, so monthly car payments and home mortgage rates can increase when inflation rises.

Deflation Also Can Be Bad During a severe recession there is the possibility of **deflation**, which is a broad, sustained decline in prices of goods and services. Deflation last occurred in the United States in 2009 as prices declined 0.34 percent during the year, and prices continued to decline during the early months of 2010. When faced with deflation, government policymakers often embark on massive spending programs to stimulate the economy. Such spending, of course, creates high national liabilities that ideally could be repaid when the economy is stronger.

deflation

A broad, sustained decline in prices of goods and services that is hard to stop once it takes hold, causing less consumer spending, lower corporate profits, declining home values, rising unemployment, and lower incomes.

interest

The price of borrowing money.

How Inflation Affects Your Borrowing, Saving, and Investing **Interest** is the price of money. During times of high inflation, interest rates rise on new loans for cars, homes, and credit cards. Even though nominal interest rates for savers rise as well, the increases do not provide "real" gains if the inflation rate is higher than the interest rate on savings accounts.

Smart investors recognize that the degree of inflation risk is higher for long-term lending (5 to 20 years, for example) than for short-term lending (such as a year) because the likelihood of error when estimating inflation increases when lots of time is involved. Therefore, long-term interest rates are generally higher than short-term interest rates.

Similarly, stock market investors are negatively affected when inflation causes businesses to pay more when they borrow, thereby reducing their profits and depressing stock prices. When inflation is at 5 percent annually, a dollar of profit that a company will earn a year from now will be worth only 95 cents in today's prices. If instead inflation were only 2 percent, that dollar would be worth 98 cents today. Such differences add up to significant amounts over many years.

You Can Track the Federal Funds Rate to Forecast Interest Rates and Inflation One of the mandates of the Federal Reserve Board (an agency of the federal government commonly referred to as the **"Fed"**) is to "promote maximum employment and price stability." You can forecast interest rates and inflation by paying attention to changes in the **federal funds rate**, which is the short-term rate at which banks lend funds to other banks overnight so that the borrowing bank has sufficient reserves as mandated by the Fed.

The federal funds rate is set by the Fed and is a benchmark for business and consumer loans and an indication of future Fed policy. The Fed lowers the federal funds rate to boost the economy in slow economic times and raises it to slow down an overheated economy. The Fed has kept the federal funds rate at zero or very low for the past decade, and as the economy expands it will raise rates. The Fed's goals are inflation at 2 percent or a bit lower, interest rates at 3 percent or a bit lower, and unemployment at 5 percent or a bit higher.

Unfortunately, it is impossible for regular people, or anyone else, to accurately forecast inflation. This is made clear by Professor Sherman Hanna of The Ohio State University, who has long studied the topic. The Fed has hundreds of professional economists making estimates as do virtually all large corporations in the USA.

Probably no one forecasts the future correctly beyond about a year. One's views on inflation depend in part on when you were born and what inflation rates you experienced over your life so far. For you it might be best to use the past few years of inflation to formulate an estimate what inflation might be in the year or so. It is better to be close in your estimates of inflation than not making any estimates at all. Throughout your financial life, you will want to factor the impact of inflation into your financial decisions in an effort to reduce its negative effects.

In summary, to assess the economic outlook for the United States, watch these indicators: (1) GDP and jobs, including unemployment rate changes; (2) procyclic items like inflation and interest rates; (3) countercyclic items like unemployment and gold prices; (4) leading indicators like the consumer confidence index, LEI, and the stock market; (5) interest rates; and (6) the federal funds rate.

fed
The Federal Reserve Board, an agency of the federal government.

federal funds rate
The short-term rate at which banks lend funds to other banks overnight so that the borrowing bank has sufficient reserves as mandated by the Fed.

DO IT IN CLASS

The Fed meets regularly to discuss the economy and review federal interest rates.

Xinhua/Sipa USA/Newscom

DID YOU KNOW

The Peer-to-Peer Sharing Economy

The **sharing economy** refers to person-to-person (P2P) sharing of access to goods and services where owners rent out something they are not using, such as a car, house or bicycle to a stranger. This is coordinated through community-based online services.

Today we are hopping into strangers' cars (Lyft, Sidecar, Uber), welcoming them into our spare rooms (Airbnb), dropping our dogs off at their houses (DogVacay, Rover), eating food in their dining rooms (Feastly), and getting food delivered from popular restaurants (Caviar). We hire their handymen (Handy), get goods delivered in an hour (Postmates), and oursource household errands (TaskRabbit). They rent our cars (RelayRides, Getaround), boats (Boatbound), houses (HomeAway), and power tools (Zilok).

We are entrusting complete strangers with our personal experiences and sometimes our lives. This is also known as *shareconomy* or *collaborative consumption*.

CONCEPT CHECK 1.2

1. Summarize the phases of the business cycle.
2. Describe two statistics that help predict the future direction of the economy.
3. Give an example of how inflation affects income and consumption.

Learning Objective 3

Think like an economist when making financial decisions.

sharing economy

Refers to person-to-person (P2P) sharing of access to goods and services where owners rent out something they are not using, such as a car, house, or bicycle to a stranger.

opportunity cost

The opportunity cost of any decision is the value of the next best alternative that must be forgone.

trade-off

Giving up one thing for another.

1.3   THINK LIKE AN ECONOMIST WHEN MAKING FINANCIAL DECISIONS

Understanding and applying basic economic principles will affect your financial success. The most notable of these are opportunity costs, marginal utility and costs, marginal income tax rate, and the importance of tax-free and tax-sheltered income.

1.3a   Consider Opportunity Costs When Making Decisions

The **opportunity cost** of a decision is the value of the next best alternative that must be forgone. A simple example of opportunity costs in personal finance is spending money on current living expenses, which, of course, reduces the amount you can save and invest and you gain the opportunity to earn interest. Also, buying on credit results in monthly payments later, which reduces the opportunity to make desired purchases in the future. It is not just the payments and interest that is the cost of credit but other uses of those funds. If opportunity costs are underestimated, then decisions will be based on faulty information, and judgments may prove wrong. Properly valuing opportunity costs of alternatives represents a key step in rational decision making.

Using the concept of opportunity costs in your thinking allows you to address the personal consequences of choices because every decision inevitably involves trade-offs. A **trade-off** is giving up one thing for another. For example, it is wise to give up some current spending in order to enjoy a financially comfortable future. For example, suppose that instead of reading this book you could have gone to a movie or watched television, but mainly you wanted to sleep.

The lost benefit of reading—the next best alternative—is the opportunity cost when you choose to sleep. Similarly, keeping the money in a savings account has the opportunity cost of the higher return on investment that a stock market mutual fund might pay. This opportunity to earn a higher rate of return is a primary opportunity cost when making low-risk investment decisions. Other challenging opportunity cost decisions are renting versus buying housing, buying a new or used car, working or borrowing to pay for college, and starting early or late to save and invest for retirement.

1.3b Identify Marginal Utility and Costs in Decision Making

Utility is the ability of a good or service to satisfy a human want. A key task in personal finance is to determine how much utility you will gain from a particular decision. For example, if you decide to spend $150 on a ticket to a concert, you might begin by thinking about what you might gain from the expenditure. Perhaps you'll enjoy a nice evening, good music, and so on.

Marginal utility is the extra satisfaction derived from having one more incremental unit of a product or service. **Marginal cost** is the additional (marginal) cost of one more incremental unit of some item. When known, this cost can be compared with the marginal utility received. Thinking about marginal utility and marginal cost can help in decision making because it reminds us to compare only the most important variables. It requires that we examine what we will really gain if we also experience a certain extra cost.

marginal utility
The extra satisfaction derived from gaining one more incremental unit of a product or service.

marginal cost
The additional (marginal) cost of one more incremental unit of some item.

To illustrate this idea, assume that you will consider spending $250 instead of $150 (an additional $100) for a ground floor, close-to-the-front seat at the concert. What marginal utility will you gain from that decision? Perhaps it is the ability to see and hear more or the satisfaction of having one of the best seats in the house. You would then ask yourself whether those extra benefits are worth 100 extra dollars. In practice, people are inclined to seek additional utility as long as the marginal utility exceeds the marginal cost.

In another example, imagine that two new automobiles are available on a dealership lot in Fayetteville, Arkansas, where assistant plant manager Pamela Hicks, of nearby Wyman, is trying to make a purchase decision. The first, with a sticker price of $29,100, has a moderate number of options; the second, with a sticker price of $32,800, has numerous options. Marginal analysis suggests that Pamela does not need to consider all of the options when comparing the vehicles. Instead, the concept of marginal cost says to compare the benefits of the additional options with the additional costs—$3,700 in this instance ($32,800 − $29,100). Pamela needs to decide if the additional options are worth $3,700.

1.3c Factor Your Marginal Income Tax Rate When Making Financial Decisions

Financial decisions often have an impact on the income taxes one must pay. Of particular importance is your **marginal tax rate**, which is the rate at which your *last* dollar earned (not all your income) is taxed. It is the highest tax bracket that your taxable income puts you in.

marginal tax rate
The tax rate at which your last dollar earned is taxed, and it refers to the highest tax bracket that your taxable income puts you in.

As income rises, taxpayers pay progressively higher marginal income tax rates. Financially successful people often pay U.S. federal income taxes at the 25 percent, or higher, marginal tax rate on the top segment of their income. For example, if Isatou Demba, an unmarried office manager working in Rockville, Maryland, has a taxable income of $66,000 and receives a $1,000 bonus from her employer, she has to pay an extra $250 in taxes on the bonus income ($1,000 × 0.25 = $250). Isatou also has to pay state federal income taxes of 6 percent, or $60 ($1,000 × 0.06 = $60), local income taxes of 2 percent and Social Security and Medicare taxes of 7.65 percent, or $76.50 ($1,000 × 0.0765 = $76.50). Therefore, Isatou pays an effective marginal tax rate of just over 40 percent (25% + 6% + 2% + 7.65% = 40.65%), or $406.50, on the extra $1,000 of earned income.

1.3d Know that the Very Best Kind of Income Is Tax-Exempt Income

The best kind of income, as this discussion implies, is **tax-exempt income**, which generally is from an investment whose earnings are free, or exempt, from taxation. Examples are interest on municipal bonds issued by agencies of state and local governments. People who pay high marginal tax rates often seek out tax-exempt investments. For example, Serena Miller, a married chiropractor with two children from Portland, Oregon, currently earns $250 per year on $5,000 in invested in bonds and pays $62.50 in federal income tax on that income

tax-exempt income
Income from an investment whose earnings are free, or exempt, from taxation.

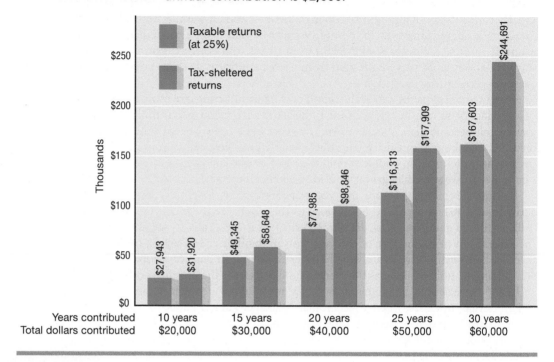

Figure 1-4   **Tax-Sheltered Returns Are Greater Than Taxable Returns**
In the illustration, the annual return is 8 percent and the annual contribution is $2,000.

	10 years	15 years	20 years	25 years	30 years
Years contributed					
Taxable returns (at 25%)	$27,943	$49,345	$77,985	$116,313	$167,603
Tax-sheltered returns	$31,920	$58,648	$98,846	$157,909	$244,691
Total dollars contributed	$20,000	$30,000	$40,000	$50,000	$60,000

tax-sheltered income

Income that is legitimately exempt from income taxes and may or may not be subject to taxation in a later tax year.

at her 25 percent marginal tax rate ($250 × 0.25). Alternatively, a tax-exempt $5,000 state bond paying 4 percent will provide Serena with a better after-tax return, $200.00 instead of $187.50 ($250 − $62.50).

1.3e   Realize that the Second Best Kind of Income Is Tax-Sheltered Income

Tax-sheltered income is income that is legitimately exempt from income taxes and may or may not be subject to taxation in a later tax year. **Tax-deferred income** occurs when the payment of tax on the earnings from the investment can be postponed for a period of time.

Figure 1-4 shows that tax-sheltered and tax-deferred returns on savings and investments provide much greater returns than returns on which income taxes have to be paid because more money remains available to be invested. In addition, tax-sheltered funds grow more rapidly because compounding (the subject of the next section in this chapter) is enhanced when larger dollar amounts continue to grow especially during the latter years of an investment.

CONCEPT CHECK 1.3

1. Define *opportunity cost* and give an example of how opportunity costs might affect your financial decision making.
2. Explain and give an example of how marginal utility and marginal cost makes some financial decisions easier.
3. Describe and give an example of how your marginal income tax rate can affect financial decision making.

1.4 PERFORM TIME VALUE OF MONEY CALCULATIONS

Learning Objective 4

Perform time value of money calculations in personal financial decision making.

A dollar in your pocket today is worth more than a dollar to be received five years from now. Why? Time is money.

The **time value of money** (TVM) is perhaps the single most important concept in personal finance. TVM is the cost of money that is borrowed or lent, and it is commonly referred to as interest. TMV adjusts for the fact that dollars to be received or paid out in the future are not equivalent to those received or paid out today. It is easy to understand that a dollar received today is worth more than a dollar received five years from now because today's dollar can be saved or invested and earn some kind of return, such as interest, so that in five years you expect it to be worth more than a dollar. The time value of money involves two components: future value and present value.

time value of money

A method by which one can compare cash flows across time, either as what a future cash flow is worth today (present value) or what an investment made today will be worth in the future (future value). Also, the cost of money that is borrowed or lent; it is commonly referred to as interest and adjusts for the fact that dollars to be received or paid out in the future are not equivalent to those received or paid out today.

1.4a There Are Only Two Common Questions About Money

To illustrate the time value of money, two questions in personal finance are commonly asked:

1. *What will an investment (or a series of investments) be worth after a period of time?* This question asks for a future value, which is referred to as compounding.

2. *How much has to be put away today (or as a series of investments) to provide some dollar amount in the future?* This question asks for a present value.

As you can see from these two questions, comparisons between time periods cannot be made without making adjustments to money values. Accordingly, time value of money calculations compare future and present values by taking into account the interest rate (or investment rate of return) and the time period involved.

Simple Interest The calculation of interest involves (1) the dollar amount, called the **principal**, (2) the rate of interest earned on the principal, and (3) the amount of time the principal is invested. One way of calculating interest is called simple interest and is illustrated by the simple interest formula

principal

The original amount invested.

$i = prt$ where

p = the *principal* set aside

r = the *rate* of interest

(1.3)

t = the *time* in years that the funds are left on deposit

If someone saved or invested $1,000 at 8 percent for four years, he would receive $320 in interest ($1,000 × 0.08 × 4) over the four years.

Compounding Is the Basis of All Time Value of Money Considerations
But something is missing in the simple interest calculation. The simple interest formula assumes that the interest is withdrawn each year and only the $1,000 stays on deposit for the entire four years, and thus interest is not added to the principal.

Most people do not invest this way. Instead, they leave the interest earned in the account so that it will earn additional interest. By compounding we mean interest that is paid on interest, which been reinvested; in other words, "interest on interest." To understand why, consider that Albert Einstein once said that, "Compound interest is the eighth wonder of the world. He who understands it, earns it ... He who doesn't, pays it."

This earning of interest on interest is referred to as **compound interest**. It arises when interest is added to the principal, so that from that moment on the interest that has been added also itself earns interest. This addition of interest to the principal is called **compounding**. The effect of compounding depends on the frequency with which interest is paid and the periodic interest rate that is applied. Compound interest is always assumed in time value of money calculations.

compound interest

Compound interest is earning of interest on interest and arises when interest is added to the principal so that, from that moment on, the interest that has been added also earns interest.

compounding

The addition of interest to principal; the effect of compounding depends on the frequency with which interest is compounded and the periodic interest rate that is applied.

Compounding is the best way to build investment values over time. Because of compounding, money grows much faster when the income from an investment is left in the account. In fact, the deposit of $1,000 in our example would grow to $4,661 after 20 years (the calculation is described below). Many of the techniques for building wealth that we describe in this book are based on compounding. The way to build wealth is to make money on your money, not simply to put money away. Yes, you need to put money away first, but compounding over time is what really builds wealth. In essence, compound interest makes your money work for you, instead of just working for your money.

Four out of five adults falsely believe that that investment growth goes in a straight line. But the reality is that growth is exponential so as your savings compound you earn interest on interest, so you money grows faster and faster.

Compounding serves as the basis of all time value of money considerations. To see how this works, let us look again at our example in which $1,000 is invested at 8 percent for four years. Here is how the amount invested (or principal) would grow using compounding:

At the end of year 1, the $1,000 would have grown to
    $1,080 [$1,000 + ($1,000 × 0.08)].

At the end of year 2, the $1,080 would have grown to
    $1,166.40 [$1,080 + ($1,080 × 0.08)].

At the end of year 3, the $1,166.40 would have grown to
    $1,259.71 [$1,166.40 + ($1,166.40 × 0.08)].

At the end of year 4, the $1,259.71 would have grown to
    $1,360.49 [$1,259.71 + ($1,259.71 × 0.08)].

Due to the effects of compounding, this investor would have earned an additional $40.49 ($360.49 − $320). While this amount might not seem like much, realize that a $1,000 investment for a longer period—say, 40 years—earning 8 percent interest would grow to $21,724.52, providing $20,724.52 in interest over that time period. Simple interest would have resulted in only $3,200 in interest ($1,000 × 0.08 × 40). The benefit of compounding over that time period is an additional $17,524.52 in interest ($20,724.52 − $3,200).

The results are even more dramatic if $1,000 is invested at the end of each year for 40 years. The total at the end of 40 years would be $259,056, with $219,056 representing the interest on the invested funds. This illustration suggests one of the cardinal rules of personal financial planning: Getting rich is not a function of investing a lot of money. It is the result of investing regularly for long periods of time. The greatest investment strategy of all is compounding. Only through compounding will you attain the serious growth of your wealth over time. The sooner you start saving, the less money you have to put away.

1.4b Calculating Future Values

future value

The valuation of an asset projected to the end of a particular time period in the future.

Future value (FV) is the valuation of an asset projected to the end of a particular time period in the future. You can calculate the future value of a lump sum or the future value of a series of deposits.

Future Value of a Lump Sum Equation (1.4) can be used to calculate the future value of a lump sum:

$$FV = (\text{Present value of sum of money}) (1.0 + i)^n \tag{1.4}$$

where i represents the interest rate and n represents the number of time periods. Applying this formula to our earlier example of investing $1,000 at 8 percent for four years, we obtain

$$\$1,360.49 = (\$1,000)(1 + 0.08)^4$$

or

$$\$1,360.49 = (\$1,000)(1.08)(1.08)(1.08)(1.08)$$

Table 1-1   Future Value of $1 After a Given Number of Periods

Periods	1%	2%	3%	4%	5%	6%	7%	8%	9%	10%
1	1.0100	1.0200	1.0300	1.0400	1.0500	1.0600	1.0700	1.0800	1.0900	1.1000
2	1.0201	1.0404	1.0609	1.0816	1.1025	1.1236	1.1449	1.1664	1.1881	1.2100
3	1.0303	1.0612	1.0927	1.1249	1.1576	1.1910	1.2250	1.2597	1.2950	1.3310
4	1.0406	1.0824	1.1255	1.1699	1.2155	1.2625	1.3108	1.3605	1.4116	1.4641
5	1.0510	1.1041	1.1593	1.2167	1.2763	1.3382	1.4026	1.4693	1.5386	1.6105
6	1.0615	1.1262	1.1941	1.2653	1.3401	1.4185	1.5007	1.5869	1.6771	1.7716
7	1.0721	1.1487	1.2299	1.3159	1.4071	1.5036	1.6058	1.7138	1.8280	1.9487
8	1.0829	1.1717	1.2668	1.3686	1.4775	1.5938	1.7182	1.8509	1.9926	2.1436
9	1.0937	1.1951	1.3048	1.4233	1.5513	1.6895	1.8385	1.9990	2.1719	2.3579
10	1.1046	1.2190	1.3439	1.4802	1.6289	1.7908	1.9672	2.1589	2.3674	2.5937

While mathematically correct, these calculations can be cumbersome when using long time periods. Table 1-1 provides a quick and easy way to determine the future dollar value of an investment. For the preceding example, use the table in the following manner: Go across the top row to the 8 percent column. Read down the 8 percent column to the row for four years to locate the factor 1.3605 (at the intersection of the yellow column and row). Multiply that factor by the present value of the cash asset ($1,000) to arrive at the future value ($1,360.50).

Appendix A.1 provides an even more complete table for calculating the future value of lump-sum amounts. Figure 1-5 demonstrates the importance of higher yields and longer time horizons by showing the effects of various compounded returns on a $10,000 investment. The $10,000 will grow to $57,435 in 30 years with an interest rate of 6 percent. Compounding $10,000 at 10 percent yields $174,494 over the same time period; at 14 percent, it yields a whopping $509,502! For practice you might want to confirm these results using Appendix A.1.

DO IT IN CLASS

NUMBERS ON

Understanding Personal Finance

Data from a variety of sources suggest:

- The average score on a national financial literacy test is a lousy 65 out of 100.

- Average household income in the USA is about $59,000.

- A dollar kept under a mattress year ago is worth less now.

- If you want to retire at age 65, you have to save about $4.66 beginning at age 42 to make up for every dollar you did not save at age 22.

- Thirty percent of workers have not yet saved a dime for retirement.

- Investing $50 a month at 8 percent starting at age 45 until you are 65 creates a sum of $27,000, while starting at age 25 provides $155,000.

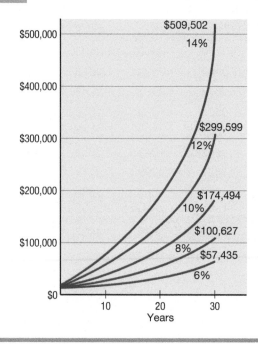

Figure 1-5   **The Importance of Higher Yields and More Time (Future Value of a Single Investment of $10,000)**

Future Value of a Stream of Payments (an Annuity) People often save for long-term goals by putting away a series of payments. Appendix A.3 provides a complete table for calculating the future value of a stream of deposited amounts, referred to as an **annuity**. You can use it to determine the effects of various compounded returns on a $2,000 annual investment made at the end of each year. The $2,000 will grow to $91,524 in 20 years (read across the interest rate row in Appendix A.3 to 8 percent and then down the column to 20 years to obtain the factor of 45.762 to multiply by $2,000) and to $226,566 in 30 years at an 8 percent rate. Compounding $2,000 at 10 percent yields $114,550 in 20 years and $328,988 over 30 years; at 14 percent, it becomes $713,574 after 30 years! As you can see, time builds wealth.

annuity

A stream of payments to be received in the future.

1.4c Finding Present Values Is Called Discounting

Present value (or discounted value) is the current value of an asset (or stream of assets) that will be received in the future. **Discounting** is the process of reducing future values to present values. You can calculate the present value of a lump sum to be received in the future or the present value of a series of payments to be received in the future.

Present Value of a Single Lump Sum The present value of a lump sum is the current worth of an asset to be received in the future. Alternatively, it can be thought of as the amount you would need to set aside today at a given rate of interest for a given time period so as to have some desired amount in the future.

A simple formula for figuring the number of years it takes to double the principal using compound interest is the **Rule of 72**. Simply divide the interest rate that the money will earn into the number 72. The Rule of 72 indicates than an investment earning 9% per year compounded annually will double in 8 years. The rule also means if you want your money to double in 4 years, you need to find an investment that earns 18% per year compounded annually.

MONEY WEBSITES

Informative websites are:
- Bankrate.com
- Bureau of Labor Statistics CNNMoney
- Department of Labor
- Dinkeytown.net
- Federal Reserve Board
- Financial Calculators
- KJE
- Microsoft's MSN MoneyCentral
- Moneychimp
- Intuit's Quicken
- USA Today
- Yahoo Finance

To use the Rule of 72 to determine the approximate length of time it will take for your money to double, simply divide 72 by the annual interest rate. For example, if the interest rate earned is 6%, it will take 12 years (72 divided by 6) for your money to double. If you want your money to double every 8 years, you will need to earn an interest rate of 9% (72 divided by 8).

Here's another way to demonstrate that the Rule of 72 works. Assume you make a single deposit of $1,000 to an account and wish for it to grow to a future value of $2,000 in nine years. What annual interest rate compounded annually will the account have to pay? The Rule of 72 indicates that the rate must be 8% (72 divided by 9 years).

Suppose you want to have $50,000 for the down payment on a new home in ten years. What would you need to set aside today to reach this goal if you could invest your money and receive a 7 percent return? Using Appendix A.2 you could look across the interest rate rows to 7 percent and then down to ten years to obtain the factor of 0.5083. Multiplying $20,000 by this factor reveals that $25,415 set aside today would allow you to reach your goal.

DO IT IN CLASS

Present Value of a Stream of Payments (an Annuity) The present value of an annuity is the current worth of a stream of payments to be received in the future. Alternatively, it can be thought of as the amount you would need to set aside today at a given rate of interest for a given time period so as to receive that stream of payments. Suppose you want to have $30,000 per year for 20 years during your retirement to supplement your expected pension payments. What amount would you need to have invested at retirement to reach this goal if you could invest your money and receive a 7 percent return? Using Appendix A.4 you could look across the interest rate rows to 7 percent and then down to 20 years to obtain the factor of 10.5940. Multiplying $30,000 by this factor reveals that $317,820 (10.5940 × $30,000) set aside at retirement would fund this stream of payments. Note the beauty of compound interest in this result. It takes only $317,820—not $600,000—to fund a $30,000 per year retirement for 20 years if you can earn 7 percent on your financial nest egg.*

CONCEPT CHECK 1.4

1. What are the two common questions about money?
2. Explain the difference between simple interest and compound interest, and describe why that difference is critical.
3. Use Table 1-1 to calculate the future value of (a) $2,000 at 5 percent for four years, (b) $4,500 at 9 percent for eight years, and (c) $10,000 at 6 percent for ten years.

1.5 MAKE SMART MONEY DECISIONS AT WORK

Learning Objective 5

Make smart decisions about your employee benefits.

Making smart decisions about your employee benefits can increase your actual income by 30 percent or more. Such decisions help you recognize the wisdom of young people investing early, regularly, and long-term to extract maximum earnings from their investments.

1.5a Open the New Employee Orientation Package

The rule for you is to open that huge packet on employee benefits you received during new workers orientation. Read it because all employee benefits are noted within and most help you make good personal finance decisions.

*If you are using a financial calculator for time value of money calculations, see "How to Use a Financial Calculator" on the Garman/Forgue companion website, or you can use the present and future value calculators also found on the Garman/Forgue companion website, www.cengagebrain.com.

ADVICE FROM A SEASONED PRO

A Baker's Dozen of Good Financial Behaviors

Good financial behaviors to follow include these:

1. *Develop a plan for your financial future.*
2. *Save regularly and increase savings as income grows.*
3. *Follow a budget or spending plan to control or, if necessary, reduce living expenses.*
4. *Pay credit card bills in full each month.*
5. *Keep all personal debts and installment loans to a minimum.*
6. *If debt becomes unmanageable, get help from a nonprofit credit/budget counselor.*
7. *Set aside an emergency fund sufficient to live on for three to six months.*

8. *Determine how much money is needed for retirement and then begin early to save for it through your employer's plan and/or an individual retirement account.*
9. *Contribute to a flexible spending account if available at your workplace.*
10. *Understand investments and maximize returns through wise asset allocation and fee minimization.*
11. *Comparison shop for major purchases.*
12. *Contemplate how economic events might affect your personal financial decision making and act wisely.*
13. *Consult a fee-only financial planner when faced with challenging financial issues.*

Xiaohui Sophie Li and **Anastasia Theisen,**
Northern Illinois University, DeKalb, Illinois

---

employee benefit

Compensation for employment that does not take the form of wages, salaries, commissions, or other cash payments.

An **employee benefit** is the general term for the indirect benefits one receives at work that are concerned with such things other than compensation for employment that does not take the form of wages, salaries, commissions, or other cash payments. Your benefits package might also include employee benefits like paid vacations and sick days, health insurance, a retirement plan, child care, parental leave, and an education assistance program.

While some benefits are free others will cause you to put out some money. But they also will save you money. What is important is to not procrastinate! Forget your fear of change. Learn about the programs. Then take the effort to sign up at human resources office to slightly reduce your income and spending so you can obtain the values of these benefit programs.

Every time you are faced with a decision to save or spend you need to look at the future consequences of that decision and understand what is important to you now and in the future. There is a tendency to choose smaller rewards in the near term at the expense of a long-term goal. There are costs in all decisions. Be smart.

1.5b Choosing Tax-Free Cafeteria Plan Benefits

cafeteria plan

A type of employee benefit plan where employees are offered a choice between cash (which is taxable) and at least one other nontaxable benefit, which are qualified as nontaxable or tax-sheltered benefits.

A **cafeteria plan** is a type of employee benefit plan where employees are offered a choice between cash (which is taxable) and at least one other nontaxable benefit, which are qualified as nontaxable or tax-sheltered benefits. For example, an employer might offer $4,000 annually to each employee to spend on benefits. The plan might offer health insurance, life insurance, sick leave or disability benefits, medical expense reimbursement, vacation days, dependent care, adoption assistance, and orthodontia treatments. Employees choose the benefits they want and can design their own benefits package.

TURN BAD HABITS INTO GOOD ONES

Do You Do This?

Ignore news about the economy

Buy lots of extra features on products

Focus only on take-home pay

Spend all of your income

Combine all your marital funds into one account

Don't know how much to save for retirement

Rent an expensive apartment

Have not yet started to invest for retirement

Pay out-of-pocket expenses for health care

Skip buying insurance

Get financial advice from friends

Do This Instead!

Watch some business news on cable television

Use marginal costs in buying decisions

Sign up for employer tax-advantaged saving plans

Put money away for a rainy day

Consider having 3 checking accounts: joint, his, and hers

Begin investing as soon as possible

Spend no more than one-third of your budget on housing

Start saving early because your savings will compound

Use employer's cafeteria benefits plan for some expenses

Buy insurance for costly things but not for small risks

Seek advice of fee-only financial planner

1.5c Decisions About Employer's Flexible Spending Accounts

Some employee benefits are tax-sheltered. A **flexible spending account (FSA)**, also called a **flexible spending arrangement,** is a sum of money that the employee sets up at the start of each year that can then be used during the year to pay for health care- and/or dependent-care related items. These are paid with **pretax dollars** (money income that has not been taxed by the government) rather than after-tax income. Under a typical FSA, the employee agrees to have a certain amount deducted from each paycheck that is then deposited into a separate account. There are two types of flexible spending accounts; the *medical and dental expense FSA* and the *dependent care FSA*. FSA contributions are limited to $2,600. Dependent care FSA contributions are limited to $5,000 per year. As eligible expenses are incurred, the employee requests and receives reimbursements from the account.

Funds in a dependent care FSA account may be used to pay for the care of a dependent younger than age 13 or the care of another dependent who is physically or mentally incapable of caring for himself or herself and who resides in the taxpayer's home. Funds in a medical care FSA account may be used to pay for qualified, unreimbursed out-of-pocket expenses for health care, but they may not be used for over-the-counter medicines unless specifically prescribed by a doctor.

Before enrolling in an FSA, you need to estimate your expenses carefully so that the amount in the FSA does not exceed anticipated expenses. According to Internal Revenue Service (IRS) regulations, unused amounts are forfeited and are not returned to the employee—a condition called the "use it or lose it" rule. However, 2/3 of employers offer a 2½-month grace period during which time you can continue to spend up to $500 of the previous year's FSA money.

Some employers offer a *limited purpose FSA* for vision and dental costs. Many employers offer debit cards that withdraw money directly from an employee's FSA. Only about 20 percent of eligible employees participate in flexible spending accounts, even though doing so saves money.

flexible spending account (FSA)
An employer-sponsored account that allows employee-paid expenses for medical or dependent care to be paid with an employee's pretax dollars rather than after-tax income.

pretax dollars
Money income that has not been taxed by the government.

COMMON SENSE
Employees Gain Cash from Flexible Spending Plans

Because many workers pay combined effective marginal income tax rates of about 40 percent, that same percentage can be *saved* by not giving it to the government in taxes. The worker who contributes $5,000, for example, to a flexible spending account (FSA) saves approximately $2,000 ($5,000 × 0.40) in taxes, further reducing his or her overall expenses. That's real cash back into your pocket!

COMMON SENSE
Help With College
Debt

Some employers who want to attract and retain the best workers are offering to help workers with their student loan payments. They are rewarding employees who have been with them for at least 5 years with up to $5,000 in cash to pay toward their student loans in increments of $1,000 each year. Contributions are currently considered taxable income, but Congress might make them tax-free.

health care plans

An employee benefit designed to pay all or part of the employee's medical expenses.

high-deductible health plan (HDHP)

A plan that requires individuals to pay a higher deductible to cover medical expenses before insurance plan payments begin; chosen to save money on premiums.

deductible

An initial portion of any loss that must be paid before collecting insurance benefits.

health savings accounts (HSAs)

Special savings account intended for people who have a high-deductible health care plan (with annual deductibles of at least $1,000 for individuals and $2,000 for families).

1.5d Decisions About Employer-Sponsored Health Care Plans

Many employers offer employees a choice of **health care plans** to assist employees with their health care expenses. The premium for an employee's individual or family plan could be as high as $10,000 or $15,000 annually depending upon the amount of coverage selected. The premiums for employees are often either paid for entirely or partially by the employer. For example, some employers pay the first $3,000 of annual premiums for employee health care coverage and require that employees pay the remainder. Employees usually can make a decision to change health plans once a year as well as when one's family situation changes, such as getting married.

Employers sometimes offer multiple options for health care plans. These may include an expensive traditional health plan, perhaps with a high annual premium that offers comprehensive coverage requiring little out-of-pocket health care spending by the employee. Also frequently available is a **high-deductible health plan (HDHP)**, which has lower premiums than a traditional health plan. In an HDHP the plan member is responsible for paying a deductible that is much greater than in a typical health plan. The **deductible** is the amount paid to cover health care expenses before benefits begin. A policy with perhaps a $3,500 premium might require $6,250 of annual spending on out-of-pocket health care expenses by the employee.

Younger employees, particularly those who are typically healthy, often select high-deductible plans to save on the cost of premiums. For example, if an employer pays only the first $3,000 in health care premiums for employees, an employee selecting the high-cost plan described previously has to pay $6,000 ($9,000 premium − $3,000 employer contribution) annually, or $500 a month in premiums. This contrasts with only a $500 total annual premium for employees who select the high-deductible plan ($3,500 premium − $3,000 employer contribution). The maximum out-of-pocket limit for HDHPs is $6,250 for self-only coverage and $12,500 for self-and-family coverage, after which the policy is supposed to pay for all health expenses. One issue with such plans is that because people are self-insuring such a large amount, they might tend to neglect to get health care when they need it.

Some employers also offer **health savings accounts (HSAs)**. This special savings account is intended for people who have a high-deductible health care plan. Employees make tax-deductible contributions to a savings account to be used for eligible expenses. Employers may also contribute. The employee invests HSA funds, and the money in the account grows tax free. Withdrawals are made to pay for medical expenses. The limits on contributions to an HSA are $3,350 per year for individuals and $6,750 for families. Again, with this plan some participants may be motivated to forgo spending money on health care.

The money in the account remains there even if you do not spend it within a certain time period. After one reaches age 65, money can be withdrawn for non-medical expenses but income taxes must be paid on the withdrawals.

1.5e Decisions About Participating in Employer Insurance Plans

Life, disability, and long-term care insurance coverages are often available through employers. While the premiums charged for the group of employees for life insurance are rarely as low as those available in the general marketplace, some employers pay for part or all of employees' premiums. Coverage is typically one or two times the employee's salary. So, always sign up for free or subsidized life insurance at work. The premiums for disability and long-term care insurance are often less expensive when purchased through one's employer rather than in the general marketplace. Chapters 10, 11, and 12 examine insurances.

1.5f Decisions About Participating in Your Employer's Retirement Plan

When you are young you must start to save something, anything, for retirement because a little saved now will mean having a serious amount of money after compounding for many years. No matter how small the amount—even $5 a week—it is the right amount.

All aspects of retirement are examined in detail in Chapter 17, "Retirement and Estate Planning." When available, sign up at work for the employer's 401(k) retirement plan even if the company does not match your contribution. If that is not available, open a traditional or Roth IRA account. You must become self-reliant and build as much financial security as possible.

About half of all workers are covered by an employer-sponsored, defined-contribution retirement plan, also called a **tax-sheltered retirement plan**. These include 401(k) retirement plans and similar 403(b) and 457 plans. Unfortunately, most workers are either not saving or are under-saving for retirement.

You can secure a financially successful retirement by first realizing that the responsibility of investing funds for retirement and the risk of making poor investments with these funds is totally yours! Then you must choose to carefully read the chapters on investing (Chapters 13, 14, 15, and 16). Finally you need to begin saving and investing for retirement soon after you graduate. To get started, recognize that employer-sponsored retirement plans provide six distinct advantages.

tax-sheltered retirement plan
Employer-sponsored, defined-contribution retirement plans including 401(k) plans and similar 403(b) and 457 plans.

First Advantage: Tax-Deductible Contributions Tax-sheltered retirement plans provide tremendous tax benefits compared with ordinary savings and investment plans. Because pretax contributions to qualified plans reduce taxable income, the current year's tax liability is lowered. The money saved in taxes can then be used to partially fund a larger contribution, which creates even greater returns. The 401(k) plan lets the IRS help employees finance their retirement plans because of the income taxes saved. As illustrated, you can save substantial sums for retirement with only minor effects on your monthly take-home pay. For example, a single man, Yong Liang of Reno, Nevada, with a monthly taxable income of $5,000 pays federal income taxes at the 25 percent marginal tax rate. He forgoes some spending by contributing $500 every month to a tax-sheltered retirement plan. This reduces his monthly take-home pay from $5,000 to $4,500.

The net effect of reduced federal income taxes is that it costs Yong only $375 to put away that $500 per month into his retirement plan. The immediate "return on investment" equals a fantastic 25 percent ($500 − $375 = $125/$500). In essence, the taxpayer puts $375 into his or her retirement plan and the government contributes $125. (Without the plan, the taxpayer would pay the $125 directly to the government in income taxes.)

As shown in Table 1-2, it costs less than the $375 for Yong to save $500 per month for retirement. The net cost for him is only $375.

DO IT IN CLASS

Table 1-2   It Costs Only $375 to Save $500 per Month for Retirement

Monthly Taxable Income	$5,000	Monthly Taxable Income	$5,000
Pretax retirement plan contribution	-0-	Pretax retirement plan contribution	500
Monthly Taxable Income	5,000	Reduced Monthly Taxable Income	4,500
Federal monthly income tax liability*	897	Lower monthly federal income tax liability*	772
Monthly take-home pay	4,103	Reduced monthly take-home pay	3,728
No extra costs	-0-	Cost to put away $500 per month ($4,103 − $3,728)	375

*Single taxpayer; calculations from Chapter 4, Managing Income Taxes, Table 4-2, on page 125.

Patrizia Tilly/Shutterstock.com

Careful planning can result in a much more comfortable life when you retire.

Second Advantage: Employer's Matching Contributions To help retain the best employees as well as to encourage them to save for retirement, many employers also offer employer-paid **matching contributions**. The **match** is in addition to amounts contributed by the employee. Employers may match all or part of their employees' contributions. An employee who saves $250 might receive an additional $125 to $250 a month from his/her employer into the individual's retirement account. That's a 50 to 100 percent return on the employee's $250! Typically, employer's match fifty percent of an employee's contributions up to a certain maximum. It is smart for employees to take the employer's 401(k) match-

match

An employer may voluntarily contribute a certain amount of money to an individual's retirement account according to the amount the employee contributes.

nudge

Policies of employers and/or the government to help get consumers to do what is good for them.

ing contribution by saving whatever amount is required the minute it is offered. It's free money!

Going back to our example of Yong Liang, if he gets a match of 50 percent from his employer, that means the employer puts $250 a month into his retirement account, which adds to his $500 contribution. Thus Jong, who started to save $500 a month, now has $750 ($500 + $250) with his employer's 50 percent matching contribution. That boosts his return even higher! Moreover, why would Jong not save for retirement?

Matching contributions are an example of a **nudge** (to touch or push someone or something gently) offered by employers and/or the federal government to help get consumers to do what is good for them. Many other nudges appear in the IRS tax code. Nudges are part of the economic theory of behavioral economics, which are examined in the behavior "Bias Toward" boxed inserts throughout this book. Nudges help us control our impulses.

DID YOU KNOW

If No Employer's 401(k) Plan?, Open a Roth IRA

You are allowed to open a Roth Individual Retirement Account (Roth IRA) if you earn some income. A **Roth IRA** is a nondeductible, after-tax IRA that offers significant tax and retirement planning advantages. Contributions to Roth IRAs are not tax deductible, but funds in the account grow tax-free. Tax-free withdrawals may be made for qualifying first-time homebuyer costs, medical expenses, or to pay for educational expenses. Roth IRA accounts are discussed in Chapter 17, Retirement and Estate Planning.

Third Advantage: Employer's Contributions Are Not Currently Taxable Income You will pay income taxes on any employer's contributions to your 401(k) retirement plan only when you withdraw from the account. That may not be until you retire and are paying income taxes perhaps at a lower rate than you were in when the contributions were made.

Fourth Advantage: Tax-Deferred Growth Because interest, dividends, and capital gains from qualified plans are taxed only after funds are withdrawn from the plan, investments in tax-sheltered retirement plans grow tax-deferred. The benefits of tax deferral can be substantial.

For example, if a person in the 25 percent tax bracket invests $2,000 at the end of every year for 30 years and the investment earns an 8 percent taxable return (an after-tax return of 6 percent) compounded annually, the fund will grow to $158,116. If the same $2,000 invested annually were instead compounded at 8 percent within a tax-deferred program, it would grow to $226,566! The higher amount results from compounding at the full 8 percent and not paying any income taxes on investment income every year. When the funds are finally taxed upon their withdrawal many years later, the taxpayer may be in a lower marginal tax bracket.

Fifth Advantage: Borrowing Lets You Tap Your Funds Without Income Taxes If you have an immediate need for cash, you might get it quickly by borrowing from your own 401(k) account. Your credit score doesn't matter and interest rates are low. All you need to do is ask your plan administrator for a loan and you do not have to explain why you need the money.

The most you can borrow is 50% of your account balance or $50,000, whichever is less. You have to repay the loan in level amounts over no more than five years (longer if the funds are used to buy a home), but you can pay it off more quickly with no penalty. If you're married, you must obtain your spouse's consent to the loan.

Sixth Advantage: Starting Early Really Pays You One Million Dollars Recall the Rule of 72, which can be used to calculate the number of years it would take for a lump-sum investment to double. An 8 percent rate of return doubles an investment every 8 years. Waiting nine years to begin saving (starting at age 31 instead of 22) results in the loss of one doubling. More emphatically, it is the *last* doubling that is lost, such as from the above $226,566 to $453,132, or $226,566! That's real money.

The financial gains in a 401(k) or other tax-sheltered retirement account will work best for you when you begin to invest early in life. You should not wait until your 40s to begin to save because the compounding boat will have sailed and you will have missed it. The gains are just plain awesome when you consider that when saving for retirement you do not do so just once. Regular, continuing investments really add up and the amounts invested do not have to be large to have a big impact.

For example, Pamela Laborde, an accountant from Gardner, Massachusetts, who starts saving $500 per month (including employer contributions) in a qualified retirement plan starting at age 22 will have almost 1.75 million dollars ($1,745,503) by age 62, assuming an annual rate of return of 8 percent. Waiting until age 32 to start saving results in a retirement fund of *only* about $745,000 by age 62; about $1 million less. The benefit of starting to invest early is about $1,000,000 yet the total extra dollars invested over the first ten years was only about $60,000! This effect occurs because most of the power of compounding appears in the last years of growth. Pamela will have to work an extra ten years to recoup that lost $1 million.

NEVER EVER

Leave Money on the Table!

When the government and/or an employer offers a plan to help you avoid income taxes, take it! Increase your net income by signing up for a flexible benefits program and your employer's 401(k) plan. Reducing your income taxes helps you get as much money back into your net paycheck as possible.

NEVER EVER

Make the Worst Blunders!

1. *Spend more than you earn*
2. *Only think about money matters when you have a financial problem*
3. *Believe and act on financial advice from amateurs rather than trust professional sources*

When you are young you must start to save something, anything, for retirement because a little saved now will mean having a serious amount of money after compounding for many years. No matter how small the amount—even $5 a week—it is the right amount. When available, sign up at work for the employer's 401(k) retirement plan even if the company does not match your contribution. If that is not available, open a Roth IRA account. You must become self-reliant and build as much financial security as possible.

CONCEPT CHECK 1.5

1. What is a *flexible spending account* and what do pretax dollars have to do with it?
2. Summarize the benefits of participating in a high-deductible health care plan at work.
3. Create a math example of why many employees participate in a tax-sheltered employee benefit plan, such as an HSA or 401(k) plan.
4. List two ways you can maximize the benefits from a tax-sheltered retirement program.

1.6 WHERE TO SEEK EXPERT FINANCIAL ADVICE

At various points in their lives, many people rely on the advice of a professional to make financial plans and decisions. Most often financial planning advice is focused on a narrow area of one's finances. Professional advisers, such as lawyers, tax preparers, insurance agents, credit counselors, and stockbrokers, are often relied upon for advice. Much too often, however, these people are salespeople for specific financial services and receive compensation if they make a sale. As a result they typically do not have your best interests at heart.

People often find it helpful to obtain the services of more broadly qualified financial experts. A **financial planner** is an investment professional who evaluates the personal finances of an individual or family and recommends strategies to set and achieve long-term financial goals. The most recognized professional designation for financial planners is the Certified Financial Planner (CFP®).

A good financial planner should be able to analyze a family's total needs in such areas as investments, taxes, insurance, education goals, retirement as well as in managing credit and planned spending, and pull all of the information together into a cohesive plan. The planner may help a client select and prioritize goals and then rearrange assets and liabilities to fit the client's lifestyle, stage in the life cycle, and financial goals. Where appropriate, planners should make referrals to outside advisers, such as attorneys, accountants, trust officers, real estate brokers, stockbrokers, and insurance agents. Effective financial advice helps you make better day-to-day financial decisions so you have more to spend, save, invest, and donate. About half of large employers offer discounted visits to a financial planner.

The shape of the relationship between you and your financial advisor should be clear from the beginning. It should be spelled out in writing, and both you and the advisor should have a copy of the document. When the nature of the advice includes investments you also need an **investment policy statement**. This details your investment philosophy, your financial situation, and the risks you are willing to take, as well as what the advisor will do for you. It provides a road map of how he/she will guide the investing of your money.

1.6a Not Every Financial Advisor Has Your Best Interests in Mind

Despite good intentions, not every financial advisor has your best interests in mind. Most so-called financial advisors are considered **broker-dealers** by the Securities and Exchange Commission. They and most retirement advisors are held to a low **suitability standard** where they are free to sell securities generating the heftiest profits and commissions, as long as they are judged "suitable" for a client based on factors like age or risk tolerance. These people are required to act in the best interest of their employer. Thus they can sell you high-cost stock, bonds, mutual funds, annuities, and other investments that pay them the highest commissions. Steer clear of these advisors. Three-quarters of investors mistakenly think that financial advisers at brokerage firms are required to put clients' interests first. Wrong!

The financial advisor you need is one who adheres to a **fiduciary standard**. This means they are legally obligated to always act in the best interest of the client at all times, even at the cost of their own, when giving advice or recommendations. An investment advisor who is a **registered investment advisor** (RIA) is legally required to act as a fiduciary. Be sure to ask. When you hire a fiduciary financial advisor you will only hear advice that is totally in *your* financial interest. The best way to make sure your advisor is a fiduciary is to have them put it in writing. Only 20 percent of adults have used a financial professional with a fiduciary responsibility.

You can check the background of the planner you are considering. Self-regulatory organizations and government agencies are available to help.

- The Certified Financial Planner Board of Standards (CFP Board) assists those searching for a CFP as well as accepts complaints. Contact www.cfp.net or (800)487-1497.
- The Financial Industry Regulatory Authority (FINRA) regulates U.S. security firms. Contact www.finra.org or (301)590-6500.
- The National Association of Personal Financial Advisors (NAPFA) assists those searching for a fee-only financial planner and sets standards for CFPs who are NAPFA Registered Financial Planners. Contact www.napfa.org or (847)483-5400.
- The Securities and Exchange Commission (SEC) regulates investment advisers and all securities dealers. Contact www.sec.gov or (800)732-0330.

suitability standard
Financial advisors who are held to a standard for advice giving where they are free to sell securities generating the heftiest profits and commissions, as long as they are judged "suitable" for a client based on factors like age or risk tolerance.

fiduciary standard
A financial advisor must always act in the best interest of the client at all times regardless of how it might affect the advisor.

ADVICE FROM A SEASONED PRO

A Baker's Dozen of Bad Financial Behaviors

Poor financial behaviors to avoid include the following:

1. *Purchase things to feel good or important*
2. *Reach the maximum limit on a credit card*
3. *Spend more money than you make*
4. *Make a credit purchase after running out of money*
5. *Obtain a cash advance on a credit card after running out of money or to pay on another credit card*
6. *Ignore an overdue notice from a creditor*
7. *Pay a credit card, utility, telephone, Internet, or any other bill late*

8. *Borrow money from a coworker or employer*
9. *Borrow or lend money from or to friends or family*
10. *Borrow from 401(k) retirement plan at work*
11. *Take your 401(k) money in cash when changing jobs*
12. *Use a debit card (or writing a check) with insufficient funds and incur overdraft fees*
13. *Follow the financial advice of family or friends rather than a financial advisor who is a fiduciary*

Angela W. Taunton
Athens State University, Athens, Georgia

- The National Association of Insurance Commissioners (NAIC) directs inquiries to the appropriate state agency where you can check on planners who also sell insurance products. Contact www.naic.org or (816)842-3600.

1.6b How Financial Planners Are Compensated

One way or another, you will pay to get financial advice—commissions, fees, or lousy financial decisions—so assess the total costs up front as well as the opportunity costs. Financial planners earn their income in one of four ways:

- **Commission-only financial planners and brokers** live solely on the commissions they receive on the financial products (such as investments or insurance) they sell to their clients. In this case, the plan will be "free," but a commission will be paid to the adviser by the source of the financial product, such as an insurance or mutual fund company. Advantage: Save money if you make only a few transactions.
- **Fee-based financial planners** charge an up-front fee for providing services and charge a commission on any securities trades or insurance purchases that they conduct on your behalf. Advantage: Unlimited consultations with broker.

Table 1-3 Financial Planner Professional Certifications

Many financial planners have voluntarily undergone training and satisfied various qualifications for particular professional certifications. Related work experience is often required.

Certification	Description	Contact Information
Accredited Estate Planner	Estate planning	(866) 226-2224 www.naepc.org
Accredited Financial Counselor (AFC®)	Financial counseling and money management	(614) 485-9650 www.afcpe.org
Certified Financial Planner (CFP®)	Best-known financial planning certification	(800) 487-1497 www.cfp.net; www.plannersearch.org
Certified Public Accountant (CPA)	Income tax and estate planning	(888) 777-7077 www.aicpa.org; http://findacpapfs.org
Certified Trust and Financial Advisor (CTFA)	Trusts and taxes	(800) 226-5377 www.aba.com
Chartered Financial Consultant (ChFC®)	Financial planning in insurance and estate planning	(888) 263-7265 www.theamericancollege.edu
Chartered Life Underwriter (CLU®)	Life insurance	(888) 263-7265 www.theamericancollege.edu
Chartered Mutual Fund Counselor (CMF®)	Mutual funds	(800) 237-9990 www.cffpinfo.com/cmfc.html
Investment Advisor	Stockbroker managing less than $100 million	www.nasaa.org; www.finra.org
NAPFA Registered Financial advisor (NRFA)	Source for fee-only financial advisors	(847) 483-5400 www.napfa.org
Personal Financial Specialist (PFS)	Personal finance credential for CPAs	(888) 777-7077 www.aicpa.org
Registered Financial Associate (RIA)	Granted only to recent graduates of approved collegiate programs	Http://www.iarfc.org
Registered Investment Advisor (RIA)	Stockbroker managing more that $100 million	(202) 551-6999 www.sec.gov; www.finra.org

- **Fee-offset financial planners** charge an annual or hourly fee. That fee will be reduced by any commissions earned off the purchase of financial products sold to the client. Advantage: Fee will be reduced as you trade investments.

- **Fee-only financial planners** earn no commissions and work solely on a fee-for-service basis. They charge a specified fee (typically $150 to $300 per hour or 0.75 to 2 percent of the client's assets annually) for the services provided. They usually need five or more one-hour appointments to analyze a client's financial situation and to present a thorough plan that involves all areas of one's personal finances. Also, people pay them a one-time fee to help solve a single unusual financial problem. Advantage: Honesty in recommendations.

Fee-only planners do not sell financial products, such as stocks or insurance. As a result and unlike other financial planners/brokers, they do not recommend products that earn them a commission. Using a fee-only financial planner has one big advantage; unbiased advice. You may want to consider hiring a financial planner once your investment assets reach $50,000.

Remember, it's your money and your financial future. So when you use the services of a financial planner, don't be intimidated. Ask the hardest questions and don't leave the planner's office until you understand the answers.

1.6c Questions to Ask a Financial Planner

Financial planners will influence your life and your future, so be sure to ask them these questions:

1. What experience do you have, such as your work history?
2. What are your qualifications to practice financial planning, such as education, formal training, licenses, and credentials, and who can vouch for your professional reputation including some of your long-term clients?
3. Am I permitted a no-cost, initial consultation, and how much time is allowed?
4. Do you adhere to a fiduciary standard when working with your clients? Why or why not? Will you be the only person working with me or will an associate be involved in evaluating and updating the plan you suggest, and how often are formal reviews held with the client?
5. How do you evaluate my investment performance, and how often?
6. What process do you follow to identify a client's financial goals and may I see representative examples of financial plans, monitoring reports, and portfolios or actual case studies of your clients?
7. How much do you charge, what is your fee structure, how are you personally compensated, and if you earn commissions, how are they earned and from whom?
8. May I have a written agreement that details the points above and the services to be provided?
9. Ask for a copy of the advisor's regulatory disclosure ADV Forms, which outlines any problems with regulators as well as services, fees, and strategies.
10. To whom would I take a complaint, if I had one?
11. Make your check out to an independent custodial institution, typically a brokerage firm.
12. Check up on your advisor by contacting your state securities regulator (www.nasaa.org), FINRA (www.finra.org), and the CFP Board of Standards (www.cfp.net) if he/she claims to be a certified financial planner. Finally, do a Google search on the advisor.

CONCEPT CHECK 1.6

1. How does a professional financial planner differ from a local lawyer or insurance person in your community?
2. What are the four different ways financial planners may be compensated?
3. Describe two professional certification programs for financial planners.
4. List three questions that you think every person should ask a financial planner.

WHAT DO YOU RECOMMEND *NOW?*

Now that you have read the chapter on the importance of personal finance, what do you recommend to Jing Wáng in the case at the beginning of the chapter regarding:

1. Participating in her employer's 401(k) retirement plan?
2. Understanding the effects of her marginal tax rate on her financial decisions?
3. Considering the current state of the economy in her personal financial planning?
4. Using time value of money considerations to project what her IRA might be worth at age 63?
5. Using time value of money considerations to project what her 401(k) plan might be worth at age 63 if she were to participate fully?

qingqing/Shutterstock.com

SUMMARY OF LEARNING OBJECTIVES RECAPPED

LO1 **Recognize the keys to achieving financial success.**

Financial success and happiness come from spending less and saving and investing more. The goal is to achieve a level of living that is very close to your standard level of living. You can do so by spending less so you can save and invest more.

LO2 **Understand how the economy affects your personal financial success.**

Using your knowledge of where we are in the business cycle and tracking a few economic statistics, like the federal funds rate, will guide you to make appropriate adjustments in your financial strategy. Also recognize how inflation and deflation will affect your finances.

LO3 **Think like an economist when making financial decisions.**

Understanding and applying the basic economic principles of opportunity cost, marginal utility and cost, and marginal income tax rate will affect your financial success. The opportunity cost of a decision is the value of the next best alternative that must be forgone. Marginal cost is the additional (marginal) cost of one more incremental unit of some item. When known, this cost can be compared with the marginal utility received. One's marginal tax rate is the tax rate at which your last dollar is taxed.

LO4 **Perform time value of money calculations in personal financial decision making.**

Dollars to be received or paid out in the future are not equivalent to those received or paid out today. A dollar received today is worth more than a dollar received a year from now because today's dollar can be saved or invested. By next year, you expect it to be worth more than a dollar. The time value of money involves two components: future value and present value.

LO5 **Make smart decisions about your employee benefits.**

Smart decisions can increase your actual income by thousands of dollars each year. You need to select wisely among choices within employer-sponsored cafeteria plans; flexible spending accounts; health insurance; life, disability, and long-term care insurance; and retirement. These decisions often require you to calculate the tax-sheltered aspects of the employee benefits.

LO6 **Identify the professional certifications of providers of financial advice.**

When choosing a financial planner, know that many professional designations are meaningful in this field, such as CFP and ChFC. Costs may be charged on a commission-only, fee-based, fee-offset basis, or a fee-only basis. Recognize a list of useful questions to ask a financial planner.

LET'S TALK ABOUT IT

1. **Economic Growth.** What types of federal government efforts to help stimulate economic growth affect consumers?

2. **The Business Cycle.** Where is the United States in the economic cycle now, and where does it seem to be heading? List some indicators that suggest in which direction it may move.

3. **Personal Finance Mistakes.** What are some common mistakes that people make in personal finance? Name two that might be the worst, and why?

4. **Federal Reserve.** Describe some economic circumstances that might persuade the Federal Reserve to lower short-term interest rates.

DO IT IN CLASS
Page 13

5. **Opportunity Costs.** People regularly make decisions in personal finance that have opportunity costs. List three financial decisions you have made recently, and identify the opportunity cost for each.

6. **Inherited Money.** What would you do if you inherited $3,000 from an aunt? Identify three options.

DO THE MATH

1. **Real Income.** Joshua Vermier of Sacramento, California, received a raise after his first year on the job to $45,800 from his initial salary of $44,000. What was Joshua's raise stated as a percentage? If inflation averaged 2.8 percent for the year, what was his real income after the raise? What was his real raise stated as a percentage?

   DO IT IN CLASS
   Page 12

2. **Future Value.** As a graduating senior, Chun Kumora of Manhattan, Kansas, is eager to enter the job market at an anticipated annual salary of $54,000. Assuming an average inflation rate of 3 percent and an equal cost-of-living raise, what will his salary possibly become in ten years? In 20 years? (Hint: Use Appendix A.1.) To make real economic progress, how much of a raise (in dollars) does Chun need to receive next year and the year after?

   DO IT IN CLASS
   Page 19

3. **Present and Future Values.** Megan Berry, a freshman horticulture major at the University of Minnesota, has some financial questions for the next three years of school and beyond. Answers to these questions can be obtained by using Appendix A or the *Garman/Forgue* companion website.

   (a) If Megan's tuition, fees, and expenditures for books this year total $22,000, what will they be during her senior year (three years from now), assuming costs rise 4 percent annually? (Hint: Use Appendix A.1 or the *Garman/Forgue* companion website.)

   (b) Megan is applying for a scholarship currently valued at $5,000. If she is awarded it at the end of next year, how much is the scholarship worth in today's dollars, assuming inflation of 3 percent? (Hint: Use Appendix A.2 or the *Garman/Forgue* companion website.)

   (c) Megan is already looking ahead to graduation and a job, and she wants to buy a new car not long after her graduation. If after graduation she begins an investment program of $2,400 per year in an investment yielding 4 percent, what will be the value of the fund after three years? (Hint: Use Appendix A.3 or the *Garman/Forgue* companion website.)

   (d) Megan's Aunt Karroll told her that she would give Megan $1,000 at the end of each year for the next three years to help with her college expenses. Assuming an annual interest rate of 2 percent, what is the present value of that stream of payments? (Hint: Use Appendix A.4 or the *Garman/Forgue* companion website.)

4. **Future Values.** Using Table 1-1 on page 19, calculate the following:

   (a) The future value of lump-sum investment of $4,000 in four years that earns 5 percent.

   DO IT IN CLASS
   Page 19

   (b) The future value of $1,500 saved each year for three years that earns 6 percent.

   (c) A person who invests $1,200 each year finds one choice that is expected to pay 3 percent per year and another choice that may pay 4 percent. What is the difference in return if the investment is made for four years?

   (d) The amount a person would need to deposit today with a 5 percent interest rate to have $2,000 in three years.

5. Using the present and future value tables in Appendix A, the appropriate calculations on the *Garman/Forgue* companion website, or a financial calculator, calculate the following:

   (a) The amount a person would need to deposit today to be able to withdraw $6,000 each year for ten years from an account earning 6 percent.

(b) A person is offered a gift of $5,000 now or $8,000 five years from now. If such funds could be expected to earn 8 percent over the next five years, which is the better choice?

(c) A person wants to have $3,000 available to spend on an overseas trip four years from now. If such funds could be expected to earn 6 percent, how much should be invested in a lump sum to realize the $3,000 when needed?

(d) A person invests $50,000 in an investment that earns 6 percent. If $6,000 is withdrawn each year, how many years will it take for the fund to run out?

6. **Inflation.** Laureen Mauer's salary a year ago was $52,000. If inflation during the year was 3.5 percent in Tampa where she lives, how much of a decline in her purchasing power occurred? Also, what would be her purchasing power if deflation of 1 percent occurred?

DO IT IN CLASS
Page 12

7. **Employee Benefits Decision.** Ramon Alvarez, of Nome, Alaska, signed up for his employer's flexible spending account plan primarily because he can use the money to pay for unreimbursed medical expenses for himself and his disabled son. Ramon is in the 15 percent marginal tax bracket, pays Social Security payroll taxes of 7.65 percent, and pays a 4 percent state income tax rate. How much will he save in income taxes by participating in the program this year in the amount of $3,000? How much would Ramon save if he was in the 25 percent federal marginal tax bracket?

DO IT IN CLASS
Page 25

8. **Use the Rule of 72.** Using the Rule of 72, calculate how quickly $1,000 will double to $2,000 at interest rates of 2 percent, 4 percent, 6 percent, 8 percent, and 10 percent.

9. **Use the Rule of 72.** Based on the Rule of 72 determine how long it would take to double an investment of $5,000 if you could invest it at 7 percent. How long would it take to triple the investment?

DO IT IN CLASS
Page 21

FINANCIAL PLANNING CASES

CASE 1

Harry and Belinda Johnson Consider Inflation and Children

Throughout this book, we will present a continuing narrative about Harry and Belinda Johnson. Following is a brief description of the lives of this couple.

Harry is 28 years old and graduated five years ago with a bachelor's degree in interior design from a large Midwestern university near his hometown in Indiana. Since graduation Harry has been working in small interior design firm in Kansas City earning a salary of about $50,000.

Belinda is 27, has a degree in business administration from a university on the West Coast, and has been employed in a medium-size manufacturing firm in California for about five years. Harry and Belinda both worked on their schools' student newspapers and met at a conference during their junior year in college.

After all these years they met again socially in January in Kansas City, Missouri where Belinda was visiting relatives and by chance she and Harry were at the same museum. After getting reacquainted they started dating and in only a matter of months Belinda got transferred from California to work in Kansas City and in June they got married. Belinda is now employed as a stockbroker earning about $77,000 annually.

After the wedding they moved into his small apartment. They will face many financial challenges over the next few decades as they buy their first home, decide on life insurance needs, begin a family, change jobs, and invest for retirement.

(a) Harry receives $3,000 in once a year interest income payments from a trust fund set up by his deceased father's estate. The amount will never change until it runs out in 20 years. What will be the buying power of $3,000 in ten years if inflation rises at 3 percent a year? (Hint: Use Appendix A.2.)

(b) Belinda and Harry have discussed starting a family but decided to wait for perhaps five more years in order to get their careers moving along well and getting their personal finances solidly on the road to success. They also know that having children is expensive. The government's figure is that the extra expense of a child would be about $16,000 a year through high school graduation. How much money will they likely cumulatively spend on a child over 18 years assuming a 3 percent inflation rate? (Hint: Use Appendix A.3.)

CASE 2

Victor and Maria Hernandez Look at Future Income

Throughout this book, we will present a continuing narrative about Victor and Maria Hernandez. Following is a brief description of the lives of this couple.

Victor and Maria, both in their late 30s, have two children: Jacob, age 13, and Nicholas, age 15. Victor has had a long sales career with a retail appliance store in Fargo, North Dakota earning $53,000 annually. Maria works as a medical records assistant earning $32,000.

(a) Victor and Maria regularly buy and sell a number of items on eBay, Craig's List, and through the free community newspaper, from which they earn about $4,000 each year. What is the accumulated future value of those amounts over 20 years if the annual earnings were invested regularly and provided a 5 percent return each year? (Hint: Use Appendix A.3.)

(b) What would Victor and Maria's annual income be after 20 years if they both received an average 3 percent raise over their current $85,000 salary ($53,000 + $32,000) every year? (Hint: Use Appendix A.1.)

CASE 3

Julia Price Thinks About the Economy

Throughout this book, we will present a continuing case about Julia Price. Following is a brief description about her. Six years ago, Julia graduated with a degree in aeronautical engineering and went to work as an engineer in Alabama. Last year she moved to Seattle, Washington, to start a job as a mid-level systems engineer on jet aircraft, and some of her design and coordination responsibilities include Department of Defense projects. Julia thinks that the economy is going to get worse in the next two to three years,

perhaps even with prices declining (deflation). Offer your opinions about her thinking.

CASE 4

Reasons to Study Personal Finance

Samantha Beliveau of Ames, Iowa, is a senior in college, majoring in nutrition. She anticipates getting married a year or so after graduation. Samantha has only one elective course remaining and is going to choose between an advanced class in sociology and one in personal finance. As Samantha's friend, you want to persuade her to take personal finance, a course you enjoyed. Give some examples of how Samantha might benefit from the study of personal finance.

CASE 5

A Closer Look at Financial Success

You have been asked to give a brief speech on how to achieve financial success and financial security. Use the five steps in the financial planning process and the building blocks to achieving financial success in your speech. Outline your speech.

BE YOUR OWN PERSONAL FINANCIAL MANAGER

1. **Practice Employment Decisions.** Assume you earn $50,000 annually and your employer offers (a) a flexible spending account to which you can contribute a maximum of $2,000 this year, and (b) a 401(k) retirement account to which you may contribute up to $3,000. Your 401(k) contribution will be matched 50 percent by your employer. Assuming you can only afford to contribute a total of $3,000 to both these benefits, explain what you would do with your $3,000. Write an explanation of your decision and a table similar to Table 1-2 (on page 25) to support your thinking.

2. **Track the Economy.** Complete Worksheet 1: Tracking the Economy from "My Personal Financial Planner" to write up your findings on current data as well as your projections one and two years in the future.

3. **Future Values of a Lump Sum.** Complete Worksheet 2: Calculating the Future Value of a Lump Sum from "My Personal Financial Planner" for the following three questions: (a) $10,000, 2 years, 6%; (b) $22,500, 20 years, 8%; (c) $5,000, 10 years, 7%. Fill out the worksheet including the last two columns.

4. **Future Value of an Annuity.** Complete Worksheet 3: Calculating the Future Value of an Annuity from "My Personal Financial Planner" for the following three questions: (a) $3,000 annually, 5 years, 6%; (b) $1,000 annually, 20 years, 8%; (c) $5,000 annually, 30 years, 7%. Fill out the worksheet including the last two columns.

5. **Present Value of a Lump Sum.** Complete Worksheet 4: Calculating the Present Value of a Lump Sum from "My Personal Financial Planner" for the following three questions: (a) lump sum needed $10,000, 5 years, 6%; (b) lump sum needed $250,000, 30 years, 8%; (c) lump sum needed $30,000, 10 years, 7%. Fill out the worksheet including the last two columns.

6. **Present Value of an Annuity.** Complete Worksheet 5: Calculating the Present Value of an Annuity from "My Personal Financial Planner" for the following three questions: (a) withdraw $12,000 annually for 5 years at 6%; (b) withdraw $2,000 annually for 15 years at 8%; (c) withdraw $3,000 annually for 10 years at 7%. Fill out the worksheet including the last two columns.

ON THE NET

Go to the Web pages indicated to complete these exercises.

1. **Inflation.** Visit the Bureau of Labor Statistics Consumer Price Index homepage at www.bls.gov/cpi/ and link to information for various areas of the country and metropolitan areas of various sizes. Describe how prices have been changing for your area and community during the past year.

2. **Future Direction of the Economy.** Visit the Conference Board website, www.conference-board.org and click on "U.S. Indicators" section for the latest information on the consumer confidence index and the index of leading economic indicators. What do the indexes suggest about the direction of the economy over the next six months to one year?

3. **Economic Trends.** Scan the website of the Economic Policy Institute (www.epi.org/) for insights on the future of the economy.

4. **NAPFA Financial Planners' Code of Ethics.** Visit the website of the National Association of Personal Financial Advisors at http://napfa.org/about/CodeofEthics.asp. Read through the code of ethics for members of the organization. What does the code tell you about the members?

5. **Financial Planning Careers.** Visit the website of the Certified Financial Planner Board of Standards at www.cfp.net and read about "Become a CFP™ Professional." Summarize your findings.

ACTION INVOLVEMENT PROJECTS

1. **Interview a Financial Planner.** Use the Internet and/or Yellow Pages to find a fee-only or fee-based financial planner in your community and telephone that person to ask if he/she would agree to an interview. Take the list of questions in the heading "Questions to Ask a Financial Planner" on page 25, and use it as an outline for your interview. Ask the professional to pick the three questions that he/she considers the most important. Write a summary of your findings.

2. **Smart Money Decisions at Work.** Survey two employed relatives or friends to determine whether or not they take advantage of certain employee benefits at work, such as a cafeteria plan, health care plan, high-deductible health care plan, health savings account, flexible spending account, life insurance, and tax-sheltered retirement plan. Make a written summary of your findings.

3. **Opportunity and Marginal Costs.** Survey two relatives or friends and ask about their decision-making process when they most recently bought a vehicle. Find out if they thought about the opportunity costs when making the purchase. Also ask if they used marginal costs in their thinking. Make a written summary of your findings.

4. **Research Future Direction of the Economy.** Survey three people to determine their opinions on the direction of the economy over the next 12 months. Even though they may not know the meaning of these exact terms, ask about their perceptions on such indicators as the (a) gross domestic product, (b) consumer confidence, (c) inflation and deflation, (d) interest rates, and (e) federal fund rate. Make a table that summarizes your findings.

Visit the Garman/Forgue companion website at www.cengagebrain.com.

2

Career Planning

Decorwithme/Shutterstock.com

Learning Objectives

After reading this chapter, you should be able to:

1 Identify the key steps in successful career planning.

2 Analyze the financial and legal aspects of employment.

3 Practice effective employment search strategies.

WHAT DO YOU RECOMMEND?

Nicole Linkletter, age 21, expects to graduate next spring with a bachelor's degree in business administration. Nicole's grades are mostly As and Bs, and she has worked part-time throughout her college career. Nicole is vice president of the Student Marketing Association on her campus. She would like to work in management or marketing for a medium- to large-size employer. Because she loves the outdoors, Nicole thinks she would prefer a job in the northwest, perhaps in northern California, Oregon, or Washington.

Tyler Olson/Shutterstock.com

What would you recommend to Nicole on the importance of career planning regarding:

1. **Clarifying her values and lifestyle trade-offs?**
2. **Enhancing her career-related experiences before graduation?**
3. **Creating career plans and goals?**
4. **Understanding her work-style personality?**
5. **Identifying job opportunities?**

career

The lifework chosen by a person to use personal talent, education, and training.

career planning

Can help you identify an employment pathway that aligns your interests and abilities with the tasks and responsibilities expected by employers over your lifetime.

You *can* control much of your financial future with effective career planning. A **career** is the lifework chosen by a person using his or her personal talent, education, and training that will lead to a lifestyle a person wants. **Career planning** can help you identify an employment pathway that aligns your interests and abilities with the tasks and responsibilities expected by employers. Career planning is a high-priority, do-it-yourself project, allowing you to take control of where you are going and how you are going to get there. Career planning is absolutely crucial to your happiness and long-term financial success.

Your focus should not be simply a **job**, which is a paid position of regular employment, but a career. The progression of a career will include a number of related jobs. Indeed, the average tenure at a job for U.S. workers is about three years. One in two employees has been at work for less than 5 years. A career is an occupation undertaken for a significant period of a person's life, especially one requiring specialized training, and provides for consecutive progressive achievement. A career gives you a base of income, employee benefits, additional educational experiences, advancement opportunities, and a secure financial future.

Learning Objective 1

Identify the key steps in successful career planning.

career plan

A strategic guide for your career through short-, medium-, longer-, and long-term goals as well as future education and work-related experiences.

breadwinner

The person in a family who earns an income that is primary to a unit of people who are dependent on the person's income.

2.1   DEVELOPING YOUR CAREER PLAN

A **career plan** provides a strategic guide for one's career through short-, medium-, longer-, and long-term goals as well as future education and work-related experiences. You cannot advance very far in planning your financial life without also planning a career that will earn you an adequate income. The **breadwinner** in a family is the person who earns an income that is primary to a unit of people who are dependent on the person's income. A career that suits you well will give you opportunities to display your abilities in jobs you find satisfying while providing balance between work and your personal life.

Sometimes a job opportunity comes your way and the geographic location is not what you wanted. That's okay. Take the job anyway. No matter what job you choose, consider it a chance to do the required tasks effectively and learn more about yourself and your career field. Work hard. You are going to learn a ton in whatever that job is, so don't stress about what it is or where it is. Just take the job, keep your head down, raise your hand for anything anybody asks you to do. Then you can learn how to deal with coworkers and bosses on the job, how to process information, and how to be part of a work team. When it is time the next job will come.

If you are not happy in a job and want to do something else, do not quit. It is easier to get another job when you already have one. It also eliminates the natural interviewer tendency to wonder why you are unemployed.

Every time your life circumstances change, you will likely reconsider your career plan because career planning is a continuous process that lasts forever. Figure 2-1 provides an illustration of the steps in career planning.

2.1a   Clarify Your Values and Interests

Thinking about and discovering what you want out of life gives you guidance for what to do to lead a satisfying life. Understanding yourself enables you to select a career path that best suits you. This requires understanding your values and interests.

Figure 2-1   **Steps in Career Planning**

- Finalize your career plan
- Align yourself with tomorrow's employment trends
- Take advantage of professional and social networking
- Review your abilities, experiences, and education
- Identify one or more desired career fields
- Clarify your values and interests

Values are the principles, standards, or qualities considered worthwhile or desirable. Values provide a basis for decisions about how to live, serving as guides we can use to direct our actions. For something to be a value, it must be prized, publicly affirmed, chosen from alternatives, and acted upon repeatedly and consistently. Values are not right or wrong, or true or false; they are personal preferences. Values are what we believe in. They motivate us and shape our futures.

People may place value on family, friends, helping others, religious commitment, honesty, pleasure, good health, material possessions, financial security, and a satisfying career. The kinds of values employers prefer in employees are personal integrity, adaptability, dedication, dependable, responsible, loyal, passionate, professional, self-confident, self-motivated, and willingness to learn.

Examples of conflicting values are family versus satisfying career, privacy versus social networking, and material possessions versus financial security. When you make important decisions, you might be wise to think carefully to clarify your values before taking action. Consider making a list of your ten most important values.

Your **professional interests** are topics and activities related to employment about which you have feelings of curiosity or concern. Interests engage or arouse your attention. They reflect what you like to do. Interests, including professional interests, are likely to vary over time.

You might consider making a list of your top ten interests. On that list will probably be some things you enjoy but have not done recently. Because of conflicting interests and alternative claims on your time, you cannot pursue all your interests. It is important in career planning to evaluate your interests. If you plan your career with your interests in mind, you will increase the likelihood of career satisfaction.

Interest inventories are measures that assist people in assessing and profiling the interests and activities that give them satisfaction. They compare how your interests are similar or dissimilar to the interests of people successfully employed in various occupations. The theory behind interest inventories is that individuals with similar interests are often attracted to the same kind of work. These inventories can help you identify possible career goals that match your strongest personal interests.

The Strong Interest Inventory assessment is considered by many to be the gold standard of career exploration tools. The opportunity to take one or more interest inventory assessments, usually for free or at a nominal cost, is available at most colleges and state-supported career counseling facilities. These assessments can also be completed online for a fee. (See, for example, www.cpp.com/products/strong/index.aspx.)

values
The principles, standards, or qualities that you consider desirable.

DO IT IN CLASS

professional interests
Long-standing topics and activities that engage your attention.

interest inventories
Scaled surveys that assess career interests and activities.

2.1b Consider Your Current Interests and Possible Career Opportunities

Think about the following questions to help evaluate your interests:

- What courses in college have you enjoyed the most?
- What projects did you enjoy the most?
- Are you a people person or do you prefer to be in the background?
- What are your leisure time activities and hobbies?
- What activities do you that you enjoy the most?

It is good to evaluate yourself by answering these questions because you will gain insights you may not have thought about. Your answers will help you link your current interests to possible career opportunities.

2.1c Identify One or More Desired Career Fields

People a generation or two ago used to take a single job and remain at the same employer until they retired. Now, people may change jobs five to ten times during their working years, staying about 4.6 years per job on

TO-DO SOON

Do the following to begin to achieve financial success:

1. *Prepare your résumé.*
2. *Visit one of your professors to request and attain a mentoring relationship.*
3. *Contact your school's placement office to explore careers in your field.*
4. *Continue your professional education.*
5. *Join a professional association relevant to your career and attend one of their meetings.*

average. Surveys show that 35 percent of employees change jobs at least every 5 years, 18 percent change between 6 and 10 years, and nearly half stay more than 10 years. In contrast, young adults average six jobs before age 26.

Thinking about a career goal helps you focus on what you want to do for a living. A **career goal** can be a specific job (e.g., cost accountant, computer engineer, teacher, human resources manager) or a particular field of work (e.g., health care, communications, green engineering). It helps guide you to do the kind of work you want in life rather than drift from job to job.

career goal

Identifying what you want to do for a living, whether a specific job or field of employment.

You should focus on a series of jobs that form a career ladder. A **career ladder** describes the progression from entry-level positions to higher levels of pay, skill, responsibility, or authority. Formulating a career goal requires thinking about your interests, skills, and experiences and learning about different careers and employment trends. The process of establishing a career goal motivates you to consider career possibilities that you may not have thought of otherwise.

career ladder

Describes the progression from entry-level positions to higher levels of pay, skill, responsibility, or authority.

To create a career goal, explore the jobs, careers, and trends in the employment marketplace that fit your interests and skills. Begin by searching websites such as those for the *Occupational Outlook Handbook* (www.bls.gov/ooh/), the *Occupational Outlook Quarterly* (www.bls.gov/opub/ooq/home.htm), and *The Career Guide to Industries* (www.bls.gov/oco/cg).

These reference books cover more than 8 of 10 jobs in the United States. There are several dozen careers listed in these books, so research the occupation groups that interest you. Take your time to read these pages, study them carefully, and contemplate your future work life. Research the occupational groups that interest you, looking at workstyle, median pay, education, and projected growth. And when you get a chance ask people about their careers.

Benefits and Costs   When making career choices, you must weigh the benefits against the costs. The benefits could include a big salary, likelihood of personal growth and job advancements, and high job satisfaction. For some, the pluses might include the psychic benefit of a prestigious job with a high income. The costs might include living in a less-desirable geographic area and climate, being far from old friends and family, sitting at a desk all day, working long hours, and/or doing too much traveling.

Is a No-Limits Job for You?   Many younger workers are employed in entry-level positions where they are expected to be on-call via a mobile device at all hours of the day and night. These are **no-limits jobs**. They face stressful demands from their companies, such as 300 or 400 daily e-mails and tweets and only a few less on weekends. These communications encourage them to eliminate the boundaries between their life and work. This is affecting the workforce at large. Ask about these things during an interview and factor their answers when deciding about taking the job.

no-limits jobs

Where people, especially younger workers, are employed in entry-level positions where they are expected to be on-call via a mobile device at all hours of the day and night.

Lifestyle Trade-offs   A **lifestyle trade-off** is weighing the demands of particular jobs with your social and cultural preferences. When you consider a career, think about what lifestyle trade-offs are important to you. For example, if access to big-name live entertainment, museums, and artistic activities is important, then working and living in a rural area may not be appropriate. If you like to visit new places, you may choose a career that involves frequent travel or the chance to work overseas.

lifestyle trade-offs

Weighing the demands of particular jobs with your social and cultural preferences.

Consider the following lifestyle options in your decision making:

- Urban/rural setting
- Close/far from work
- Own/rent housing
- City/suburban life
- Warm/cold climate
- Constant/variable climate
- Near/far from relatives

DO IT IN CLASS

The Cost of Career Coaching Privately available career coaching experts are available. For $600 you can buy 5 hours of basic services including identifying career goals, targeting companies, and practicing interviewing skills. For $3,000 you can get customized preparation before each job interview. For $8,000 you get 24/7-access to coaching, mock interviews, and one-on-one advice on salary and benefits.

2.1d Review Your Abilities, Experiences, and Education

A review of your abilities, aptitudes, experiences, and education will help you see how well they match up with your career-related interests. These topics have much to do with **human capital**. This is the skill set, knowledge, and other intangible assets of individuals that can be used to earn income and create economic value for individuals, employers, or communities.

Abilities and Aptitudes Your **professional abilities** are the qualities that allow you to perform job-related tasks physically, mentally, artistically, mechanically, or financially. Most of us think of *ability* as a word describing how well we do something, a proficiency, dexterity, or technique, particularly one requiring use of the mind, hands, or body. Other examples of abilities include being skilled in working with people, being able to easily meet the public, and being good at persuading people.

Employer surveys indicate that the single most important ability needed for career success in the twenty-first century is **digitalization**. This is using digital technologies into everyday life to change a business model. Apple's watch is an example as technology took an everday watch and introduced technology into it with phone capabilities, messaging, and Internet capabilities. They are saying "think digitally." Consider making a list of your top ten professional abilities.

Aptitudes are the natural abilities and talents that people possess. Aptitudes suggest that you have a tendency or inclination to learn and develop certain skills or abilities. Are you good with numbers? Do you find public speaking easy to do? Do you enjoy solving problems? What are your natural talents? Consider making a list of your top ten aptitudes.

Experiences Most college graduates have much more going for them than a degree and a string of part-time job experiences. Reviewing your experiences is a step in career planning. Evaluate what you have been doing in your life, including jobs, participation in student organizations and community and church groups, leadership on school projects, volunteer activities, and internships. Hiring managers say college grads need two internships to be competitive after they graduate. Research shows that students who have completed at least one internship earn $10,000 more in their first job than those who did not intern

Those still in college can enhance their job opportunities by learning as much as possible in school, participating in clubs and other student organizations (including volunteering for committees and campus projects), getting involved in faculty research projects, and attending off-campus professional meetings related to their major. Academic advisers can provide additional suggestions. All these abilities, aptitudes, and experiences can be put on your résumé.

Education and Professional Training The reality is that today's college is yesterday's high school. More than ever before, education determines a worker's earnings over a lifetime.

The college you attend may provide you with all the preparation you need to succeed in the major. But college may not have given you all the skills and abilities to be successfully employed. You may need to seek additional education and professional training. Think about taking extra courses in public speaking, computer software, or business. Perhaps seek an advanced college degree.

2.1e Know Your Preferred Work-Style Personality

Every job requires the worker to function in relation to data, people, and things in differing work environments and corporate cultures. Your

human capital
The skill set, knowledge, and other intangible assets of individuals that can be used to create economic value for the individuals, their employers, or their community.

professional abilities
Job-related activities that you can perform physically, mentally, artistically, mechanically, and financially.

digitalization
This is using digital technologies into everyday life to change a business model.

aptitudes
The natural abilities and talents that individuals possess.

COMMON SENSE
Curiosity Gets You the Job

The one skill set that hiring agents want new employees to possess is curiosity. It is also called "earning agility." Can you grow, learn? Is your mind nimble? Do you read widely and listen to music? Are you interested in life?

DID YOU KNOW ?

Generation Z Will Replace Millennials

Millennials are the demographic cohort born between the early 1980s and the late 1990s. Today they are between 21 to 37 years of age. They are also referred to as "Generation Y" or "Gen Y," the "Echo Boomers," or "Trophy Kids." Millennials were born after the cohorts known in chronological order as Generation X (born 1965–80), Baby Boomers (born 1946–64), and the Greatest/Silent Generation (born 1928–45).

Generation Z (or Gen Z or the iGeneration) were born between 1998 and 2012. It includes the children of the youngest baby boomers. This age group is sometimes called the iGeneration because it was born in the age of the Internet, and the children of this group are growing up using electronics and mobile devices.

This is the generation that is emerging as the next big thing for market researchers, cultural observers, and trend forecasters. They will soon become the dominant youth influencers. They are hard-working, digital natives, technology oriented, conscientious, anxious, pragmatic, multi-taskers, and attentive to the future. Generation Z has come to age in the aftermath of the beginnings of the 9/11 war on terror. They are focused on being mature and in control, and they seek sensible careers.

---

work-style personality

Your own ways of working with and responding to job requirements, surroundings, and associates.

professional networking

Making and using contacts with individuals, groups, and other firms to exchange career information.

social networking

A set of connection of friends, colleagues, and other personal contacts with a common interest who use websites or other technologies to communicate with each other and share information and resources.

work-style personality is a unique set of ways of working with and responding to your job requirements, surroundings, and associates. When making a career selection, you must balance your work-style personality against the demands of the work environment.

You can begin by rating each work value as shown in the Decision-Making Worksheet "What Is Your Work-Style Personality?" Put a check mark in the appropriate column in terms of importance in your career. Armed with this information, you can now more clearly decide on careers that are most suitable for you.

2.1f Take Advantage of Professional and Social Networking

Professional networking is the process of making and using contacts, such as individuals, groups, or institutions, to obtain and exchange information in career planning. Also use **social networking**, which is a set of connection of friends, colleagues, and other personal contacts with a common interest who use websites or other technologies to communicate with each other and share information and resources. Popular social networking sites include Facebook, LinkedIn, Google Plus+, Pinterest, Snapchat, Tumblr, and Twitter.

Spend a few minutes on your favorite sites each day making new connections, and keeping your profile up to date. Always send a personal message with all connection requests. Every person you know or meet is a possible useful contact sometime in the future. And remember that a single crude quote, picture, or selfie on a social-networking site could eliminate you from a job interview. Don't let others tag you at a party as it may come back to haunt you. All recruiters review candidates' social media profiles before making a hiring decision. Therefore, delete any suspicious ones and be professional in all future postings.

Career planning should reflect your lifestyle preferences.

DECISION MAKING WORKSHEET

What Is Your Work-Style Personality?

It would be useful for you to consider a number of work values critical to the process of career selection, particularly in the areas of work conditions, work purposes, and work relationships. Rate how you assess the following work values as either unimportant, somewhat important, or important.

Work-Style Factor	Your Rating of Importance		
	Unimportant	**Somewhat Important**	**Important**
1. Work Conditions			
Independence and autonomy			
Work hours			
Child care costs			
Time flexibility			
Vacation time			
Many e-mails/texts			
Change and variety			
Leave work for child illness			
Stability and security			
Physical challenge			
Mental challenge			
Pressure and time deadlines			
Decision making			
2. Work Purposes			
Material gain			
Truth and knowledge			
Expertise and authority			
Achievement and recognition			
Ethical and moral			
3. Work Relationships			
Working alone			
Public contact			
Close friendships			
Family responsibilities impact advancement			
Influencing others			
Supervising others			

For additional values clarification, go back to the list and *circle the activities* that you want to do more often. The goal is to match your highest work-style values to career choices with similar work-style requirements.

Job referrals are critical in professional networking. A **job referral** is the act of recommending someone to another for possible employment. This helps your résumé get a close look from a hiring manager. When you're referred for a position, and you mention it in your cover letter, you have got a built-in recommendation for the job in the first

job referral
The act recommending someone to another by sending a reference for employment.

Trial hire

Temporary workers that could last a week or two to determine if candidates can do the work and fit in with the corporate culture.

paragraph of your cover letter. It is even better when the person referring you can take a couple of minutes to personally refer you for the job. A referral generally does not include a letter of recommendation.

Companies find one-third of new hires through referrals. Thus you must make a conscious effort to use people you know and meet, especially those met through networking, to maximize your job search process. Networking involves utilizing your social contacts, taking advantage of casual meetings, and asking for personal referrals. Most of your networking contacts will not be able to hire you, but they could refer you to the people who can, or they may be able to give you useful information about a potential employer.

Maintain a continually growing list of people who are family, neighbors, friends, college associates, coworkers, previous supervisors, teachers, professors, alumni, business contacts, and others you know through civic and community organizations such as churches and business and social groups. Take note of where your contacts work and what types of jobs they have. Ask these people for 10 to 20 minutes of their time so you can share a copy of your résumé and seek information and suggestions from them. Perhaps meet at their workplaces (where you might meet other potential networking contacts), and afterward communicate your thanks.

As many as three-quarters of all job openings may never be listed in want ads, so the people in your network become a vital source of information about employment opportunities. For this reason, expanding the number of people in your network is advantageous; some of the people you know will also likely share their networking contacts. Don't forget to keep them informed of your progress and eventual success in obtaining employment.

2.1g Prospective Employers Can Check Your Credit Report

A lousy credit history can suggest a lot about a person's inability to manage important tasks. Federal law requires that individuals (1) be made aware that consumer credit reports can be used for employment purposes and must agree to such use, and (2) are to be notified promptly if information in a consumer report may result in a negative employment decision. About 20 states prohibit employers from using credit reports when hiring.

2.1h Align Yourself with Tomorrow's Employment Trends

What are the trends in employment? The aging U.S. population will create jobs in the service industries of finance, insurance, health care, recreation, and travel. Jobs are gravitating to existing population centers, particularly in warmer climates that have superior transportation systems. Jobs in manufacturing continue to go overseas to Mexico, Asia, Europe, and other countries, with the U.S. job market primarily demanding highly skilled workers in the service industries.

Academic majors leading to jobs with high beginning salaries and substantial demand include computer science, management information systems, software engineering, information technology, economics, civil engineering, statistics, finance, actuarial mathematics, and nursing. In 1950, the Bureau of Labor Statistics tracked 270 careers; now there are over 850.

Your academic choices should, at least in part, be based upon employment trends. If you have the aptitude, you might pursue a degree in a field that pays well. Table 2-1 shows the projected job opportunities in high-growth occupations in the United States.

2.1i Freelancing in the "Gig Economy" and Entrepreneurship

Not too many years ago, the only people who looked for "gigs" were musicians. The rest of us found real, long-term jobs that paid us a fixed full-time

Table 2-1   High-Growth Occupations Projected to 2022

Job Title	Employment in 2022	Median Annual Income
Accountants/auditors	1,442,000	$64,000
Advertising promotions managers	77,000	$95,000
Audiologists	17,000	$70,000
Child and social workers	324,000	$51,000
Compensation benefits managers	70,000	$100,000
Computer system design	2,100,000	$100,000
Green construction	400,000	$75,000
Home health care services	1,900,000	$70,000
Human resource managers	72,000	$122,000
Industrial engineers	205,000	$98,000
Market research analysts and marketing specialists	547,000	$61,000
Marketing managers	228,000	$153,000
Media and communications	46,000	$61,000
Meeting, convention, and event planners	125,000	$46,000
Physical therapists	277,000	$80,000
Public relations specialists	231,000	$66,000
Sales representatives, wholesale and manufacturing	1,600,000	$64,000
Software developers and applications	752,000	$90,000
Social networking	400,000	$85,000
Training and development specialists	261,000	$74,000

Sources: Bureau of Labor Statistics, Table 15, High-growth occupations, by educational attainment cluster and earnings. www.bls.gov/ooh/fastest-growing.htm and www.bls.gov/news.release/ecopro.t05.htm. Projections by authors.

salary every payday. This allowed us to take paid holidays, and gave us the financial basis for planning a stable future

Today, more and more of us choose to make our living working informal gigs rather than taking full-time jobs. The **gig economy** allows these independent contractors (rather than employees) to move from one temporary job to the next without benefits. Gigs allow workers flexibility, autonomy, and the opportunity to seek a better economic future. Gigs are being filled by subcontractors, freelancers, temps, part-timers, on-call workers, and new entrepreneurs.

To the optimists, gigs offer a future of empowered freelancers and entrepreneurs and lots of innovation. To the naysayers, it forsees a dismaying series of part-time jobs hunting for the next piece of self-employment without employee benefits, little social assistance (like workers comp, unemployment, and disability insurance), and nary a cent put away for the last 20 years of life.

Freelancing is where one chooses to be employed with a more flexible work arrangement than full-time on a contract basis, often working at home, for a variety of

gig economy
A workplace economy that allows independent contractors (rather than employees) to move from one temporary job to the next without benefits.

freelancing
One chooses to be employed with a more flexible work arrangement (often part-time) than full-time on a contract basis, often working at home, for a variety of companies, as opposed to working as an employee for a single company.

Coding May Be Your Career Change

Those who can write **modern code**, the language of the digital world, which is writing the source code for a computer program, can immediately earn 6-figure salaries. Lots of people are going to one of the 60-plus coding schools, called boot camps, like Galvanize, Flatiron School, and Hack Reactor, which offer accelerated training in digital skills as a way to rapidly train workers for well-paying jobs.

entrepreneur

One who is starting out a company and is hopeful about their situation because they organize, manage, and assume the risks of a business or enterprise.

modern code

The language of the digital world, which is writing the source code for a computer program.

companies, as opposed to working as an employee for a single company. In a nation of 150 million workers about 30 million people consider themselves freelancers and half of them work at least 15 hours a week. One quarter earn less than $25,000 annually, half make $25,000 to $75,000 and the remaining quarter make more.

An **entrepreneur** is someone who organizes, manages, and assumes the risks of a business or enterprise. Starting a company out of a perceived opportunity occurs when people are hopeful about their situations. They are making a choice between working for someone and working for themselves. Participating in a new business creation is a common activity among U.S. workers over the course of their careers.

Freelancers sometimes move from part-time employment into full-time entrepreneurship. Don't be afraid to take the chance to be part of a start-up company, especially while you are young because if you fail you can always return to the normal working world. If you succeed, well, the world is yours.

2.1j Finalize Your Career Plan

As you near graduation, you should be ready to develop a formal career plan. Figure 2-2 provides an illustrative plan. Your career plan should be realistic and flexible. Your career interests and goals will change over time, especially

Figure 2-2 **Career Plans for Harry Johnson**

Harry Johnson began his working career following graduation from college by obtaining employment with a small commercial interior design firm. He has an undergraduate degree from a university accredited by the American Society of Interior Designers. He is happy that his first professional job is in his major field of interest.

Initial career goal: To become an interior designer. To design, plan, and supervise commercial/contract design projects.

Long-term career goal (20-plus years): Own or become a partner in a medium- to large-size commercial/contract interior design firm.

Short-term plans and goals in career establishment stage (3 to 6 years): Gain work experience in current job; receive employer compliments on quality of work; obtain continuing education credits for professional growth and development; secure higher-level design responsibilities, such as lead professional design team; volunteer for committee responsibilities in local and state professional associations; obtain substantial increases in income; receive promotions; learn operational aspects and marketing of the company.

Medium-term plans and goals in professional growth stage (7 to 12 years): Be promoted to the level of senior designer; consider going to work for another employer as a senior designer and, if necessary, move to another community; volunteer for higher-level service in professional associations; obtain a master of fine arts degree in interior design; become a key assistant to the firm's general manager.

Longer-term plans and goals in advancement stage (13 to 20 years): Become general manager of commercial design firm; seek out potential partners and sufficient financing to either buy out or start up a medium-size design firm.

as you continue your education, gain work experience, and see how your friends fare with their jobs and avocations.

Mary Johnson, of Huntsville, Alabama, teaches music in middle school, but she is starting to realize that the accompanying small income could keep her on a tight financial budget forever. This issue might encourage Mary to consider a total career change—perhaps to sales in the music industry or a related field, where incomes are higher.

Assessing yourself and your career plans every few years is important to achieving success in your working life. What do you find satisfying and not so satisfying? Honest answers will help you, particularly as your interests evolve. Your work experiences should hone your abilities and skills. Learning new skills on the job is common, and if that is not happening in a job, move on and change employers and perhaps careers.

BIAS TOWARD— UNDERESTIMATING INCOMES

People tend to underestimate the fair value of their labor in the future. This suggests that people overvalue the pay of a new job and undervalue the value of future economic benefits. What to do? Consider staying at an employer for a longer time than usual to enjoy the promotions and higher pay later on in life.

CONCEPT CHECK 2.1

1. What is *career planning* and why is it important?
2. How do your values and interests impact your life-style trade-offs in career planning?
3. What can be done to enhance your abilities, experiences and education without working in a job situation?
4. Is the gig economy, freelancing, or entrepreneurship for you? Why or why not?

2.2 FINANCIAL AND LEGAL ASPECTS OF EMPLOYMENT

Learning Objective 2

Analyze the financial and legal aspects of employment.

This section examines financial and legal aspects of employment to consider when analyzing your career plans.

2.2a Is College Worth the Cost?

Concerns about the value of a college degree are nonsense. While a college graduate may not reach the top 10 percent of income earners in life, one does not stand a chance of getting ahead financially without a degree. College graduates earn twice as much as those with a high school diploma, and their unemployment rate is half the high schoolers.

Choosing the right school and major is important, as is how much, if any student debt you take on. If possible, you want to graduate debt free. However, 7 in 10 graduate with college debt.

At College Scoreboard (www.collegescorecard.ed.gov) anyone can browse and compare colleges on metrics such as net price after financial aid, graduation rates and post-college earnings of students who received federal aid. You are able to see how much each school's graduates earn, how much debt they graduate with, and what percentage of a school's students can pay back their loans.

While in school avoid a major with a vague credential, appears low in knowledge and skills, and results in a crippling amount of debt. Besides the **STEM majors** (science, technology, engineering, and mathematics), there are numerous academic majors that teach employable skills and also pay good salaries upon graduation.

Education is more than an investment; it is a treasure. It is priceless. Besides the commercial purpose of learning skills to start a career and earn a living, a college education aims to help you acquire information and learn how to think as well as build an integrated self to live a morally significant life.

College is a place to think, to contemplate, to find out what is valuable, and question the value of what is made. You should be a reasonably

STEM majors
Academic majors in science, technology, engineering, and mathematics.

COMMON SENSE
Incomes and Education

Income varies over the life cycle. Higher incomes typically go to those with more education and/or more specialized education. The U.S. Census Bureau reports that young adults (ages 25–34) with a bachelor's degree earn an average of $47,000. This compares to $17,000 for those who are high school graduates or have a certificate of equivalency, $26,000 for those with some college, and $80,000 for those with advanced degrees.

YOUR GRANDPARENTS SAY

"Never Stop Learning"

"If you have everything all figured out, you the college student are already a loser. Keep learning by staying in school until you finish that degree! You have to listen and learn, especially in college and during your first job."

employee benefits

Forms of remuneration provided by employers to employees that result in the employee not having to pay out-of-pocket money for certain expenses; also known as nonsalary benefits.

literate citizen of the world who had some intelligent understanding of the larger-than-local interests.

Going to college does not require $25,000 or $50,000 in debt. It does not mean you borrow to pay for your rent and food as well as your tuition. If necessary, attend a less expensive school, live at home, work part-time, go to school part-time, and ask parents and other relatives for some financial assistance. Borrow as little money for tuition as possible. And no matter what, do not drop out of school before you graduate.

Nearly 9 out of 10 graduates say their college expenses have been a good investment. The return on investment for a bachelor's degree is about 15 percent a year.

2.2b   Place Dollar Values on Employee Benefits

Employee benefits are tremendously important to employees, especially when comparing those provided by one employer with another. **Employee benefits** (or **nonsalary benefits**) are forms of remuneration provided by employers to employees that result in the employee not having to pay out-of-pocket money for certain expenses. Examples include paid vacations, health care, paid sick leave, child care, tuition reimbursement, and financial planning services.

To put monetary values on employee benefits, you may (1) place a market value on the benefit or (2) calculate the future value of the benefit.

Place a Market Value on the Benefit If instead of enjoying a certain employee benefit, you had to pay out-of-pocket dollars for it, you can easily determine its market value. Private child care might cost $500 a week in your community; thus, when child care is provided free from your employer, that is a whopping $25,000 ($500 × 50 weeks) saved annually. Actually, it is more because after paying federal and state income taxes and Social

DID YOU KNOW ?

Do Not Give Up $160,000 When Changing Employers

When changing jobs, nearly half of workers unwisely cash out all the money in their employer-sponsored retirement plan. Instead they could roll it over to a new employer's 401(k) plan, move it to an IRA rollover account, or leave it with the old employer (if that is allowed). If an individual has $50,000 in a 401(k) account and cashes it out, that person gives up $160,000 in future dollars over the following 20 years earning 6 percent annually.

DO IT IN CLASS

If you cash out $50,000:		If you roll over $50,000:
20% required federal income tax withholding	−$10,000	
5% additional tax (in 25% tax bracket)	−$ 2,500	
10% required early-withdrawal penalty	−$ 5,000	
5% state/local income tax	−$ 2,500	
Total withdrawn	−$20,000	$50,000
Money spent on new vehicle, TV, home repair, vacation, etc.	−$30,000	Money invested in another tax-deferred retirement account that earns 6 percent annually
Total	−$50,000	$50,000
Additional investment actions taken	none	Money grows for 20 years
Investment balance after 20 years	$ 0	$160,000

DID YOU KNOW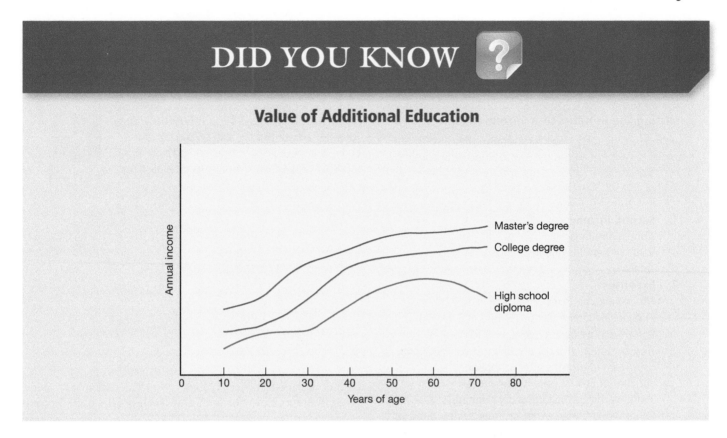

Value of Additional Education

Security and Medicare taxes you would likely have to earn perhaps $40,000 to have $25,000 left over. Another example is an employer-provided paid-for life insurance policy with a face value of $100,000. It might cost $150 to $400 if you had to buy it yourself.

Calculate the Future Value of the Benefit An employer that provides a 401(k) retirement plan offers a valuable benefit. Hopefully, your employer will offer a matching contribution as a nudge to get you to do the right thing in preparing for retirement. Another nudge is to sign up for payroll deduction so you never see the money.

If an employer provides a match of $3,000 a year to your $3,000 in contributions, all the money in the account will grow free of income taxes until the funds are withdrawn. Over 20 years, the annual employee and employer contributions of $6,000 growing at 6 percent annually will be about $240,000 (using Appendix A.3). At 8 percent interest it grows to over $302,000.

If working full-time does not earn you enough to pay all the bills, there is no excuse not to have a side job in the gig economy. The options are virtually unlimited. Remember, too, that this income is not to pad an entertainment budget; it is to fund your retirement plan.

2.2c Know Your Legal Employment Rights

You have legal rights both during the hiring process and after you are hired. When selecting employees, employers may not discriminate based on age, gender, race, color, sex, marital/family status, religion, national origin, birthplace, age, and disability (if the person can perform the essential job tasks). Laws in many states and cities also prohibit discrimination against gays and lesbians in the hiring process. Once hired, you have many rights. Employers must do the following:

- Pay the minimum wage established by federal, state, or local laws
- Provide unemployment insurance
- Provide workers' compensation benefits for job-related injuries or illness
- Pay Social Security taxes to the government, which are then credited to the employee's lifetime earnings account maintained by the Social Security Administration

RUN THE NUMBERS

Assessing the Benefits of a Second Income

A second income might add surprisingly little to your total earnings because of all the costs associated with earning it. In this example, a nonworking spouse is considering a part-time job that pays $30,000 annually. The total net amount of the extra $30,000 income is a mere $8805, thus adding only $734 ($8,805/12 = $734) a month to total earnings.

DO IT IN CLASS

1. Second Income	
Annual earnings	$30,000
Value of benefits (life insurance)	300
Total 1	$30,300
2. Expenses	
Federal income taxes (25% rate × $30,000)	$ 7,500
State/local income taxes (6% rate × $30,000)	1,800
Social Security taxes (7.65% × $30,000)	2,295
Transportation and commuting (50 weeks @ $40)	2,000
Child care (9 months after-school only)	3,600
Lunches out (50 weeks, twice a week at $10)	1,000
Work wardrobe (including dry cleaning)	1,200
Other work-related expenses (magazines, dues, gifts)	300
Take-out food for supper (too tired to cook; $100 per month)	1,200
Guilt complex purchases (to make up for time lost with others)	600
Total 2	$21,495
3. Net Value of Second Income	
Total of 1 from above	$30,300
Subtract total of 2 from above	21,495
Total accurate net amount of second income	$ 8,805 or $734 a month

The law requires that hourly employees be paid overtime for extra work hours put in beyond the standard 40-hour workweek. Salaried employees are not paid overtime, and the vast majority of college graduates have salaried jobs. In addition, a woman cannot be forced to go on maternity leave before she wants to do so if she does choose to take leave. You have the right not to be unfairly discriminated against or harassed and to be employed in a safe workplace.

You have the right to take leave for personal or family medical problems, pregnancy, or adoption. You also have the right to privacy in such personal matters. When you leave an employer, you have the right to continue your health insurance coverage, perhaps for as long as 18 months (using the provisions in the Consolidated Omnibus Budget Reconciliation Act [COBRA] as discussed in Chapter 11), by paying the premiums yourself. If you believe you have been wronged, you may assert your legal rights.

CONCEPT CHECK 2.2

1. Is college worth the cost? Why or why not?

2. How does one put a market value on an employee benefit?

3. Give some examples of legal employment rights.

2.3 PRACTICE EFFECTIVE EMPLOYMENT SEARCH STRATEGIES

Learning Objective 3
Practice effective employment search strategies.

Once you have undertaken some career planning, you will want to start the process of getting a job in your preferred career field. This is an effort that takes much effort. A successful job search might require 25 to 40 hours per week of your time. Effective search strategies follow.

2.3a Assemble an Attention-Getting Résumé

The Internet is a valuable resource for you in all aspects of career planning, including preparing a résumé. A **résumé** is a summary record of your education, training, experience, and other qualifications. It is often submitted with a job application. Your résumé, usually one or two pages in length, should be carefully written and contain zero errors or inconsistencies in message, content, and appearance. A survey of top executives reveals that 75 percent will not even consider an applicant whose résumé has one or more typos. Résumés should be in PDF format so they can be viewed on a variety of mobile devices.

résumé
Summary record of your education, training, experience, and other qualifications.

Its primary function is to provide a basis for screening people out of contention for jobs. When you supply a résumé, you are providing documentation for some kind of subjective evaluation against unknown criteria. Large employers, recruiters, and local and national websites screen résumés using an applicant tracking software system, also known as APS, to screen online résumés.

We live in a world of income inequality based in part on what is known as **skill-based technological change**, and if you do not have the skills you better get some. If you do have the skills, show them off in your résumé. Use nouns and noun phrases, such as "Microsoft Office" or "Excel" so the scanning process picks them up. A good place to find keywords is to review 10 employment ads with similar job titles in your field and see which words are repeatedly mentioned.

A Harvard professor observed that, "The world no longer cares about what you know; the world only cares about what you can do with what you know." Thus, you should focus your résumé on skills and competencies that are most relevant to the position you aspire to hold. When it is necessary to technically fulfill a requirement in the employment process, tailor a special edition of your résumé to fit that special set of circumstances. (See jobsearch.about.com/od/list/fl/list-of-skills-resume.htm.)

Résumés are usually presented in a **chronological format** (information in reverse order with the most recent first), **skills format** (aptitudes and qualities), or **functional format** (career-related experiences). See Figures 2-3, 2-4, and 2-5 for sample resumes. The most common mistake in a résumé is to fill it up with a long list of functions and responsibilities that you had in your previous jobs instead of evidencing the specific accomplishments that made a difference in the companies for which you worked.

chronological format
Résumé that provides your information in reverse order, with the most recent first.

skills format
Résumé that emphasizes your aptitudes and qualities.

functional format
Résumé that emphasizes career-related experiences.

Colleges have career centers with sample résumés and professional staff who can offer personal advice. You can also find examples of résumés on the Internet. Monster.com has more than 1 million online résumés, and it's easy to find résumé templates by searching for them online. However, posting your résumé on an Internet site or sending out résumés is not conducting a significant job search. Know too that if your résumé is posted on the Internet your current employer can view it.

Some high-tech and marketing companies are skipping résumés altogether and hiring based solely on tweets, the online text-based messaging service of up to 140 characters. A tweet or two or five over five days may provide the company with everything they need to know about you and your online personality. But most jobs will still require résumés.

2.3b How to Search for and Target Preferred Employers

A key step in the job search process is to think about both the industries in which you would prefer employment and which employers might be best for you. If, for example, you want to work in the health care industry, you must visit the websites of health trade associations and various health care firms.

DO IT IN CLASS

Figure 2-3 — Sample Chronological Résumé

GORDON CATHEY

SCHOOL ADDRESS:
2824 West Street
Ames, IA 50211
(401) 555-1212
E-mail: cathey@yahoo.com

HOME ADDRESS:
3055 Vallejo Street, Apt.12
Denver, CO 80303
(303) 333-4141

CAREER OBJECTIVE	Entry-level position as a metallurgical engineer.
EDUCATION	Bachelor of Science, Metallurgical Engineering, Iowa State University, Ames, IA, June 2018.
	Associate of Arts, Kishwaukee Community College, Malta, IL, June 2016.
EXPERIENCE	August 2016–May 2018 (academic year, part-time), Iowa State University, Ames, IA, Research Assistant to Professor John Binnion on titanium and plastics, conducted research, performed statistical analyses, wrote reports, led group of interns.
	Summer 2015 and Summer 2016 (full time), Caterpillar's Electro-Motive Diesel, Metallurgical Engineering Department, Chicago, IL, Internship (paid), tested materials, prepared reports, participated in team efforts.
	September 2014–April 2015, Volunteer, Village Nursing Home, Denver, CO, updated some resident activities, organized weekend volunteers.
CAMPUS ACTIVITIES	Associate Editor college newspaper, Iowa State Daily; Vice President, ISU Metallurgical Society; Hispanic Club; Singer, University Chorale; Tutor for College of Engineering computer laboratory; Attended two national conferences of American Society for Metals International.
HONORS	Etta Mae Johnson Scholarship; College of Engineering Academic Scholarship; Most Valuable Member, ISU Metallurgical Society; Julie Lynn Marshall Scholarship.
SKILLS	SAS, Strategic Project Management, Strategic Planning, SAP Material Management, Systems Troubleshooting.
REFERENCES	Available upon request.

DID YOU KNOW ?

Top Skills Employers Want Most

Most employers want a good cultural fit when hiring. Here is what they are looking for:

1. Communication skills inside and outside of company
2. Analytical skills
3. Computer technological literacy
4. Efficiently gather and process information
5. Flexibility
6. Leadership
7. Multicultural awareness
8. Cooperative and empathetic
9. High-energy
10. Confidence
11. Organize, plan, and prioritize properly
12. Solve problems and make decisions
13. Work well as team player
14. Can defend opinions

Figure 2-4   Sample Functional Résumé

Elizabeth Anklin
12144 Southwest 174th Loop
Tupelo, MS 38803
School: (662) 844-5698
Home: (662) 921-1213
Eanklin@hotmail.com

CAREER OBJECTIVE
Public relations or communications department with opportunities to contribute and learn.

EDUCATION
Bachelor of Science, University of Georgia, Financial Planning, Housing and Consumer Economics with a minor in communications, Athens, GA, May 2018; Associate of Arts, Mississippi Valley Community College, Booneville, MS, August 2016.

CAREER-RELATED EXPERIENCES
Organized breakfast meetings, supervised new members, updated membership records, led annual auction, created administrative procedures, Chamber of Commerce, Athens, GA, part-time.
Maintained inventory records, monitored reordering systems, JC Penney Company, Athens, GA, part-time.
Updated merchandising records, redesigned sales floor layout, Johnson's Shoes, Booneville, MS, part-time.
Overseas experience building a school in Botswana, Africa (summer 2014).
Translated Spanish and French to English for Atlanta Translation Services (part-time).

CAMPUS CAREER-RELATED ACTIVITIES
Vice president, Sales and Merchandising Club; Treasurer, Aces Chorale Club; Secretary, National Honor Society; Secretary, Alpha Kappa Alpha Sorority; Co-coordinator Speaker's Committee, Consumer Club; Debate Club; attended Society of Consumer Professionals in Business (SOCAP) meetings in Atlanta; intramural hockey; campus church choir.

COMPUTER SKILLS
Microsoft Office, Corel WordPerfect Office, Corel Paint Shop Pro X, Adobe Acrobat, Dazzle Video Creator, QuickBooks Pro, Computer Assisted Design, Macromedia, FrontPage.

HONORS
Hanna Pallagrosi Academic Scholarship; Modu Samega-Janneh Service Award, College of Family and Consumer Sciences, University of Georgia; Highest Monthly Sales Award, JC Penney; Employee of the Month (twice), JC Penney.

REFERENCES
Furnished upon request.

Figure 2-5   Sample Skills Résumé

Ji-hoon Hyun
2122 South 141th Street West, Apt. 340
San Antonio, TX 78204
School: (210) 207-5454
Home: (210) 419-1445
jhyun@hotmail.com

CAREER OBJECTIVE:
Professional position in human development with administrative responsibilities.

EDUCATION:
Master of Science, 2018, University of Texas at San Antonio, Human Development, San Antonio, TX; Bachelor of Science, 2015, University of Texas at San Antonio, Education and Human Development, San Antonio, TX; Associate of Arts, 2013, San Antonio College, San Antonio, TX.

CAREER-RELATED LEADERSHIP EXPERIENCES
- Organized and coordinated student session at national Family Relations Conference
- Hosted student session at Texas Family Relations Conference
- Led departmental graduate student study committee
- Treasurer of honor society Kappa Omicron Nu
- Organized speaker series for Kappa Omicron Nu
- Chaired Graduate Student Recruitment committee
- Vice President of Study Body, San Antonio College
- Volunteer coordinator for neighborhood Meals-on-Wheels for adults

CAREER-RELATED WORK EXPERIENCE
- Administered intake procedures at Humanas Family Center
- Updated record-keeping systems for Humanas Family Center
- Planned learning activities for Gonzales Child Center
- Supervised parental security for Gonzales Child Center
- Presented research paper at Texas Family Relations Conference
- Attended two state Texas Family Relations Conferences
- Attended University of Utah summer seminar on human development
- Planned curriculum updates for Alamo Elder Center
- Trained and managed interns at campus family counseling center

CAREER-RELATED COMPUTER SKILLS
Word, Excel, Corel Graphics, Adobe Acrobat, SPSS, SAS, Search Engine Marketing.

HONORS
Henry B. Gonzales Public Service Scholarship, Lane Johnson Memorial Scholarship, Outstanding Member of Kappa Omicron Nu.

ADVICE FROM A SEASONED PRO

Career Advancement Tips

The essence of career advancement is to build your job-related knowledge and skills for the future by learning. You do not want to fall behind your coworkers and those who work for other employers, as they may be your future job market competitors. To advance in your career, consider the following:

- **Mentors.** Ask someone a level or two higher than your job rank to serve as your mentor, someone with whom you can regularly discuss your career progress. A **mentor** is an experienced person, often a senior coworker, who offers friendly career-related advice, guidance, and coaching to a less-experienced person.

- **Sponsor.** Getting someone to sponsor you is in some ways even better. A **sponsor** is a powerfully positioned champion who "leans in" with you by advocating on their proteges' behalf and guiding them toward key players and assignments.

- **Traits.** Exhibit passion, self-discipline, confidence, and determination in your everyday responsibilities.

- **Volunteer.** Volunteer for new assignments.

- **Training.** Sign up for employer-sponsored seminars and training and certification opportunities.

- **Advice.** Those who seek advice are perceived as more competent and smarter than those who do not. And

advice seekers stroke the advisor's ego as well as gain valuable insights.

- **Awareness.** An awareness of accounting, finance, and marketing fundamentals.

- **Knowledge.** A knowledge of technology and computer software, such as customer service metrics.

- **Conferences.** Attend meetings and conferences in your field. Become a member of your local professional association and become active in its leadership.

- **College Courses.** Take advanced college courses and complete a graduate degree.

- **Professional Reading.** Stay alert to what is happening in your career field and learning by subscribing to and reading professional and other publications.

- **Current Events.** Be up to date on current events and business and economic news by reviewing websites and reading newspapers, news magazines, and business periodicals.

- **Nonwork Activities.** Be actively involved in something besides work, such as coaching children's athletics, playing softball, singing in a choral group, or teaching reading to illiterate adults.

Dana Wolff
Southeast Technical Institute, Sioux Falls, SD

---

mentor

An experienced person, often a senior coworker, who offers friendly career-related advice, guidance, and coaching to a less-experienced person.

sponsor

A powerfully positioned champion who "leans in" with an employee by advocating on their proteges' behalf and guiding them toward key players and assignments.

Learn as much as you can about the health care industry. How broad is the industry? What types of companies are at the retail level? At the wholesale level? What kinds of firms provide services to the industry? Which companies are the largest? Which have the fastest growth rates? Which employers have employment facilities in geographic areas that are of interest to you? What are the leading companies? Which are the "employers of choice" that are family friendly or offer especially good benefits? What are the employee benefits at different companies?

Knowing the industry and specific employers of interest to you tells you whom to target for employment in your career path. "Liking" a company can mean receiving early notices of job openings and other news.

2.3c Identify Specific Job Opportunities

The next step is to identify specific job opportunities that fit your skill set and provide prospects for early advancement in your career. Record your job search progress below using the Decision-Making Worksheet "Keeping Track of Your Job Search."

Internet, Career Websites, and Job Boards You can use the Internet to obtain career advice, review job opportunities by industry and company, and conduct

DECISION MAKING WORKSHEET

Keeping Track of Your Job Search

Below is a list of task areas in worksheet format that you can use to help keep track of your job search progress. Create more columns to the right so you can input important information, such as dates when you completed each effort.

	Date Done	Deadline to Do More
1. Identify your values.	_____	_____
2. Decide on economic, psychic, and lifestyle trade-offs.	_____	_____
3. Clarify career-related interests.	_____	_____
4. Assess abilities, experiences, and education.	_____	_____
5. Identify employment trends.	_____	_____
6. Create career goals and plans.	_____	_____
7. Target preferred employers.	_____	_____
8. Analyze your work-style personality.	_____	_____
9. Compare salary and living costs in different cities.	_____	_____
10. Calculate values on employee benefits.	_____	_____
11. Create an expanding list of networking contacts.	_____	_____
12. Obtain excellent letters of reference.	_____	_____
13. Compile revealing personal stories.	_____	_____
14. Assemble a résumé.	_____	_____
15. Prepare a cover letter.	_____	_____
16. Identify job opportunities:	_____	_____
a. Career websites	_____	_____
b. Job boards	_____	_____
c. Career fairs	_____	_____
d. Classified advertisements	_____	_____
e. Employment agencies	_____	_____
17. Interviewing:	_____	_____
a. Research the company.	_____	_____
b. Create responses for anticipated interview questions.	_____	_____
c. Create positive responses to list of negative questions.	_____	_____
d. Evaluate your interview performance.	_____	_____
18. Send thank-you notes.	_____	_____
19. Negotiate for salary.	_____	_____
20. Accept the job.	_____	_____

specialized job searches. You also can review résumés, create your résumé, create a cover letter, and post your résumé. The Internet allows you to review salary information, calculate living costs in different communities, and research career fairs. Just about all your search information on the Web can be saved for your future use.

Use **job boards** in your search, too. These are websites devoted to helping employers find suitable new employees by providing job listings, job sites, job search tips, job search engines, and related articles; some allow posting of résumés. Check out targeted industry sites, such as SalesJobs.com, Indeed.com, or Bridgespan.org. Also search Google for "niche job websites" in specific industries.

Career Fairs **Career fairs** are university-, community-, and employer-sponsored opportunities for job seekers to meet with perhaps dozens or even hundreds of potential employers over one or more days. Here you can schedule brief screening interviews with

job boards

A website devoted to helping employers find suitable new employees by providing job listings, job sites, job search tips, job search engines, and related articles; some allow posting of résumés.

career fairs

University-, community-, and employer-sponsored events for job seekers to meet with many employers quickly to screen potential employers.

employment agency

Firm that locates employment for certain types of employees.

cover letter

A letter of introduction sent to a prospective employer to get an interview.

a half-dozen or more employers in a single day. Career fairs are advertised in local newspapers, on television, and on the Internet. Search "career fairs" on the Internet as well as at CareerBuilder.com and NationalCareerFairs. com. There usually are not many jobs at career fairs but participating definitely will help you practice your interviewing skills.

Classified Advertisements Advertisements in newspapers and professional publications usually are not very important in the job search process. However, big newspapers, such as the *Atlanta Journal-Constitution* and *Chicago Tribune*, advertise many jobs in large geographic areas. Others such as *The New York Times* and *The Wall Street Journal* have jobs for the whole country. And the *Financial Times* describe overseas opportunities.

Employment Agencies An **employment agency** is a firm specializing in locating employment positions for certain types of employees, such as secretaries, salespeople, engineers, managers, and computer personnel. Most employment agencies are paid fees by organizations that hire them to find new employees. Others charge the job hunter fees, sometimes very high amounts. Only talk with those firms whose companies pay the fees. Governments also have state or city employment offices that offer free services. Often these are not the best ways to find a good job, although sometimes they are very successful.

2.3d Write an Effective Cover Letter

A **cover letter** is a letter of introduction sent to a prospective employer designed to express your interest in obtaining an interview. An effective cover letter helps introduce and sell you to the prospective employer. The cover letter should be specifically written for each position for which you are applying. See Figure 2-6 for an example. Expand upon a couple of details from your résumé, explaining how your talents and experience

NUMBERS ON

Careers

Data from a variety of sources suggest:

- Four out of 5 jobs created in the USA are in companies with fewer than 100 employees.

- Three-quarters of employers review job applicants' facebook postings and credit reports during background checks to gain insights.

- If your salary does not keep up with inflation (which is what happens with minimum-wage employment), your level of living will decline.

- Sixty percent of firms do telephone interviews.

- Seventy percent of companies conduct face-to-face interviews.

- The length of the interview process typically is 6 days for low-level positions and a month or longer for senior positions.

- Thirty percent of men and women have been at their present jobs for 10 or more years.

- The median job tenure is 15 months for workers aged 20 to 24; it is 3 years for those aged 25 to 34, far short of the 4.6-year average for all workers.

Figure 2-6   **Sample Cover Letter**

June 23, 2018

Ms. Juanita M. Pena, President
Pena Public Relations Agency, Inc.
4235 International Blvd NW
Philadelphia, PA 15101

Dear Ms. Pena:

We met briefly in Atlanta at last January's luncheon meeting of the Society of Consumer Affairs Professionals in Business. My professor at that time, Julia Marlowe, introduced us and stated that your company was "undoubtedly one of the most successful creative agencies" in the Philadelphia community.

My work experience in public relations and sales, academic background in consumer economics and communications, and research about your firm has led me to the conclusion that I am very interested in seeking employment in your organization. Also, a former employee of yours, Brittany Allyson, now with Hewitt Advertising, told me that you were a fine boss and encouraged me to join your fast-growing company.

My abilities to research, organize, communicate, and lead can provide Pena Public Relations with a person with multiple skills who can adapt to fast-changing needs. My strengths include fluency in three languages, serious computer and data analysis skills, technical writing, persuasion, and ease in meeting new people. Attending two colleges and living in three states has broadened my perspectives as has studying public relations from the consumer perspective. See my enclosed résumé for more details.

I look forward to the opportunity to meet with you to better communicate my qualifications and evaluate how they might fit the Pena Public Relations Agency. You may contact me at (662) 921-1213 or Eanklin@hotmail.com. Also, I will telephone you in two weeks.

Sincerely,

Elizabeth Anklin

Elizabeth Anklin
12144 Southwest 174th Loop
Tupelo, MS 38803

Enclosure

---

can benefit the employer. Communicate your enthusiasm for the job. When appropriate, mention a networking contact.

Address your cover letter, written on high-quality paper, to a specific person and request a brief meeting. If the hiring manager's name is not in the job announcement, telephone the employer and speak with a receptionist in the correct department. Be candid about your reason for needing a specific person's name.

Your letter should try to secure a face-to-face meeting to obtain more information and gather impressions. End the letter with a sentence stating that you will be telephoning or e-mailing in about two weeks to reassert your interest in the position. Then, do so! Be sure to use a professional and nondescript e-mail address (like Jsmith@yahoo.com or Jsmith@aol.com) instead of something like cutelady@cutelady.com. Your cover letter should include a signature block that provides a link to your online résumé.

DO IT IN CLASS

2.3e   **Obtain Strong Reference Letters**

College students too often simply ask a couple of professors they like to write them a letter of recommendation. Professors typically give their best judgments in these letters. This may include identifying some student weaknesses as well as strengths. Students who ask for a letter from an instructor who does not know them well also risk receiving a bland, boilerplate, or average kind of reference.

Ask only those professors who know you and your schoolwork well and give them a copy of your résumé. Approach them with a request similar to "Are you willing to give me a strong, *positive* letter of recommendation? I need one that points out my better qualities and performance here at college." If the instructor hesitates too long or gives you some negative feedback, consider asking a different professor for a recommendation. If your recommenders are willing to give you a separate copy of their letters, you will have them in your personal files to photocopy for future use.

ADVICE FROM A SEASONED PRO

Common Job Interview Mistakes

1. *Not arriving on time or on the right date*
2. *Failing to dress appropriately*
3. *Discourteous interactions with the administrative assistant/office staff of interviewer*
4. *Poor eye contact, initial greeting and/or handshake*
4. *Not answering the interview questions asked*
5. *Little knowledge of the business or the industry*
6. *Demonstrating little passion or enthusiasm for the job and/or company*

7. *Inability to discuss your future plans and career goals*
8. *Answering a telephone call or text message during the interview*
9. *Having no questions to ask about the company or the job*
10. *Body language that suggests taking the interview too casually*
11. *Asking for the salary amount in the first interview, before a job offer has been made*

Morgan Bridge and Brian Fraser
Colorado Mesa University, Grand Junction, Colorado

2.3f　Formally Apply for the Job

You cannot get a job without applying for it. Personalize your cover letter and résumé to fit the specific job of interest. Send it to the prospective employer. Many large employers prefer to receive job inquiries via the Internet, often through their website. If so, follow the application instructions perfectly. Other employers prefer a written letter and résumé. It may be smart to do both.

If you have not received a response to a job inquiry within two or three weeks, send a follow-up inquiry by adding a brief new opening sentence to your cover letter and send the revised letter with your résumé. When employers express interest in you as a prospective employee, they may request that you complete their official job application form. Be totally accurate in your responses.

2.3g　Interview for Success

job interview

Formal meeting between employer and potential employee to discuss job qualifications and suitability.

The interview is the single most important part of your search for employment. A **job interview** is a formal meeting to discuss an individual's job qualifications and suitability for an employment position. When you are invited for an interview, that begins an average length of an 6- to 30-day interviewing process from start to finish. Before starting, get *totally* prepared.

NEVER EVER ⚠

Go to a Job Interview Unprepared!

If you are not fully prepared for a scheduled job interview, you should cancel it because you never will get the job. You will waste the interviewer's time and you will be embarrassed about your lack of knowledge. Even if you are a lucky person, success will not happen.

The interview is a sales event in a traditional environment, so be professional. To succeed you should have an up-to-date haircut and wear clothes that are in fashion. Look the interviewer in the eye and lean forward as this suggests you are interested. When talking, focus on the company's needs not yours. Be sure to mention how you have been keeping up with technology and recent changes in your field of work. If you are nervous, do not show it because the interview will doubt your ability. Role play the interview with a friend, mentor, or coach.

When you meet someone for the first time, argues Malcolm Gladwell, author of ***Blink***, "your mind takes about two seconds to jump to a series of conclusions." It is not intuition or a snap judgment; it is rapid rational thinking. A human resources manager can read you the moment you walk into the door from your smile, first few sentences, tone of voice, the way you walk, the clothes you wear, how you stand, the grip of your handshake, and how you sit. You must present yourself—immediately—as a confident and energetic professional. Practice your "blink" before every interview, so you will be ready for a possible meeting on Skype instead of a traditional face-to-face situation. If this happens to you, get ready. If interviewing at home, make the background neat, make sure your face is well lit, eliminate the chance of interruptions, sit still, and practice beforehand with a friend. And give succinct answers to questions by not going on too long with your responses. Professional recruiters estimate that perhaps only 20 percent of college seniors adequately prepare for their interviews.

During an interview be sure to exhibit your "display rules" that are embedded in our culture, employment, and other organizations. These consist of appearing well mannered, kind, friendly, helpful, and generally cheerful. It helps if you are simply positive during the interview.

Rehearse a brief **elevator speech**, too. This is a short (20 to 40 seconds), persuasive summary of your experiences and skills when networking. Make it sound casual, and run through it until you can say it perfectly. Make it memorable and sincere.

elevator speech
This is a short, persuasive summary of your experiences and skills when networking.

Five Points to Raise in an Interview Make five key points during your interview:

(1) "Let me tell you about the time that I solved a similar problem" (and then tell a story),

(2) "I would like to understand that better, please clarify" (demonstrates that you are thorough and want to be accurate),

(3) "I saw that announcement about your company on a website" (shows off your genuine interest in the firm),

(4) "Why did you come to work here?" (shows that you are curious about the company),

(5) "I would love the opportunity to join this company" (implies that you will accept an offer, if made).

Do Lots of Research Before the Interview Before the interview, research the company. Try to know more about it than the interviewer. Learn how the company makes money, its operations and history, profitability, expansion plans, and other recent

DID YOU KNOW ?

How to Interview Over a Meal

More people lose a job interview over lunch than during the official interview because they fail to realize that going to lunch is a continuation of the interview rather than a social situation. Employers want to hire people with some degree of refinement, people who will mix well with clients and executives. It is smart to engage in conversation over a meal, of course, but let the host do most of the talking. Good etiquette tips include the following:

- Order something that is less expensive than what the host has ordered.

- Keep your elbows off the table.

- Break (don't cut) your bread or roll before buttering.

- Use the bread knife (the small knife to the right of your plate) to bring the butter to your bread plate.

- Use the small fork outermost from the plate for the first course.

- Don't salt and pepper your meal before tasting it.

- Cut your meat one bite at a time.

- Don't talk with food in your mouth.

- Don't order beer, wine, or liquor.

- Avoid ordering soup or pastas because both can be too messy.

- Be extremely polite and respectful of the servers.

- Never complain about a meal.

- Leave it to your host to signal the server.

- If confused, be patient and follow the lead of the host.

- Leave your napkin on your chair when excusing yourself.

- When the meal is over, thank the host and state that you remain interested in the job.

NEVER EVER

1. *Neglect to fully research a company before going for an interview.*
2. *Fail to match your interests and preferred work style with the requirements of the career.*
3. *Disregard networking by not getting involved in local, state, and national career-related professional associations.*

developments. Also research the company's competitors and the industry. You cannot spend enough hours on this effort!

Know the major industry trends and news and be able to talk about how they could affect the company. Know what the company is good at and how this relates to your skills. Be familiar with the job description.

Find out what it is like to work at the specific company. When you do a background check on companies, you might seek out candid posts from current or former employees about salaries, company culture, and lousy bosses. However, be wary about unsubstantiated information. See Career-Builder (www.careerbuilder.com), Glassdoor (www.glassdoor.com), Jobster (www. jobster.com), PayScale (www.payscale.com), LinkedIn (www.linkedin .com), and Vault (www.vault.com).

Prepare Responses for Anticipated Interview Questions Your responsibilities during the interview are to remain calm, reveal your personality, be honest, convey your best characteristics, handle questions well, and communicate your enthusiasm about the job. Always answer in a controlled, polite manner. During the interview, be confident that you are the best person for the job so project yourself accordingly.

Job interviewers seem to ask similar questions. You know they are coming so prepare good, personal responses for the following inquiries:

1. Tell me about yourself.
2. How would your instructors, colleagues, and previous employers describe you?
3. What did you like the most about college, and the least?
4. Tell me what you know about our company.
5. Why are you interested in working for this company?
6. What unique abilities and experiences separate you from others?
7. Describe some of your strengths and weaknesses.
8. What motivates you and how do your motivate others?
9. What experiences have you had working with teams and coordinating such efforts?
10. Give an example of an ethical challenge you faced and tell how you handled it.
11. Relate a time when you were faced with a very difficult problem and how you handled it.
12. What are your salary requirements?
13. Are you willing to relocate?
14. Describe the supervisors who motivated you to do your best work.
15. What were some of the best and worst aspects of your last job?
16. What do you do in your leisure time?
17. Describe your career plans for two and five years from now.

DO IT IN CLASS

Create Positive Responses to Negative Questions Be prepared to "turn any negative into a positive" when asked such questions. One popular negative question is, "What are your weaknesses?" Interviewers who ask this type of question want to determine whether the applicant possesses certain qualities such as honesty, self-awareness, humility, sincerity, zest, and skill in managing shortcomings and mistakes. Denying weakness or being evasive means you do not get the job.

Practice your interview skills beforehand. Practice your responses, especially to negative questions. Perhaps make a videotape of a mock interview, and after evaluating your performance, do it again.

Compile Revealing Personal Stories Assemble some personal stories about yourself that reveal some of your better characteristics. For a job at a company you could have five or more interviews in one day, and during the interview process, you are expected to talk about yourself. Therefore, prepare by writing down some concise stories or statements, perhaps about the time you took over caregiver duties for your siblings while your mother was hospitalized, or facilitated resolving some internal conflicts among the officers in your student club, or assisted a high school teacher to coordinate and supervise 20 students on a field trip, or worked 14 straight hours at Walmart during a weather emergency. Show your "grit" in stories, including how you pushed against X until you won. Tell how you struggled and improved.

Preparing as many as a dozen stories will give you many ways to talk about your positive qualities without just saying, "I'm good." Everyone else says that! Communicate that message about yourself in part by telling stories to illustrate your better qualities.

You need not volunteer information in an interview that might hurt you, but respond to questions accurately. Misrepresenting facts, making even small distortions, will cast doubt on everything you said in the interview.

Be certain to ignore phone calls and tweets and do no texting at any time during an interview visit. Even better, turn off your cellphone. Your entire focus should be on the interview experience.

Prepare Questions to Ask the Interviewer A key to success in any interview is to show your enthusiasm and interest in the position and organization. Compliment the interviewer's company based on some facts learned in your pre-interview research. Also, prepare some questions to ask, perhaps about future company plans, company policies, employee benefits, specific duties, and job expectations. You will want to inquire about the corporate culture, too. Write down your questions so you will have your thoughts clear in your mind. Consider the following questions:

- "What qualifications make for an ideal candidate?"
- "What attracted you to this company?"
- "How will the work I'll be doing contribute to the organization's mission?"
- "If you hire me, what can I accomplish in the next six months that will make you glad you did?"
- Toward the end of the interview and after restating your interest in the position, ask, "What is the next step?"

Personality Tests One-third of employers give job candidates personality tests assessing team orientation, strengths important to a job, emotional intelligence, motivation, and true work-style inclinations. This is driven by employers growing belief in **big data**, which is an evolving term preaching the value of collecting as much information as possible about practically everything so it can be mined for lessons and used to make predictions about the future. Personality tests for prospective employees are important in matching people to jobs, fighting turnover, increasing productivity, and raising customer satisfaction.

Popular tests include Gallup's Strengths Finder, Hogan Personality Inventory, MyPlan, Pymetrics, MAPP Assessment, and Cattell's 16 personality factors. When taking such tests do not try to game the employer by telling them what they want to hear—the "right" answer. Being honest confirms what the prospective employer already knows about you.

Be Ready for Telephone Interviews When returning a telephone call or engaging in an interview present yourself in a professional manner. Always have a pen or pencil and paper handy. Be aware of distractions in your surroundings, such as traffic noise. If necessary, arrange to call the interviewer back when you find a quieter place. Speak clearly, and eliminate the "uhs" and "umms." The interviewer will notice if you take a sip of coffee or a bite out of a bagel.

After the Interview, Evaluate It and Send Thank-You Notes After a job interview, take a few minutes to objectively evaluate your performance. Write down any questions you were asked that were different from what you expected and make some notes about ways to improve in your next interview. The more interviews you have, the better you will be able to present yourself. Also, immediately send thank-you notes expressing your appreciation for the opportunity to interview and restate your interest in the position. Four out of five successful job seekers send thank-you notes to *everyone* they meet.

2.3h   How to Compare Salary Offers

DO IT IN CLASS

Comparing salary offers from employers located in different cities can be tricky without sufficient information on the approximate cost of living in each community. Sometimes those costs vary drastically. Information from the Internet reveals, for example, that life in a high-cost city such as Seattle is more expensive than life in a lower-cost city such as Portland, Oregon. The data are reported in index form, with the "average cost" community being given a rating of 100. For details on costs in cities around the world see www.numbeo.com/cost-of-living/.

The following example demonstrates how to compare salary offers in two cities. Assume the Seattle (city 1) index is 138, and Portland's (city 2) is 114. You want to compare the buying power of a salary offer of $52,000 in Portland with a $65,000 offer in Seattle. The costs can be compared using Equations (2.1) and (2.2).

$$\text{Salary in city 1} \times \frac{\text{index city 2}}{\text{index city 1}} = \text{equivalent salary in city 2}$$

$$\text{Seattle salary of } \$65,000 \times \frac{114}{138} = \$53,695 \text{ in buying power in Portland}$$

(2.1)

Thus, the $65,000 Seattle salary offer would buy $53,695 of goods and services in Portland, an amount more than the Portland offer of $52,000. All things being equal (and they are both nice cities), the Seattle offer is slightly better ($53,695 − $52,000 = $1,695), or 3.3 percent more buying power) ($1,695/$52,000).

To compare the buying power of salaries in the other direction, reverse the formula:

$$\text{Salary in city 2} \times \frac{\text{index city 1}}{\text{index city 2}} = \text{equivalent salary in city 1}$$

$$\text{Portland salary of } \$52,000 \times \frac{138}{114} = \$62,947 \text{ in buying power in Seattle}$$

(2.2)

Thus, the $52,000 Portland offer can buy only $62,947 of goods and services in Seattle—an amount less than the $65,000 Seattle salary offer. All things being equal, the Seattle offer is still better. For fairer comparisons, add the value of employee benefits and redo the calculations. Note that nonsalary benefits for college graduates are typically valued at 25 to 30 percent of the salary.

Compare Salary and Cost of Living   You may compare salary figures and the cost of living in different communities at the following websites:

TURN BAD HABITS INTO GOOD ONES

Do You Do This?

Avoid getting to know your professors

Ignore student professional associations

Use an old résumé

Change nothing when writing a cover letter

Plan to move back to your hometown after graduation

Focus primarily on gross pay when deciding on a job opportunity

Do This Instead!

Visit one professor in his/her office on a regular basis

Join and take a leadership role in at least one association

Update your résumé frequently

Write a new cover letter for each job application

Explore employment opportunities in some new cities

Factor take-home pay, employee benefits, and cost of living into your job decisions

- CityRating.com (www.cityrating.com/costofliving.asp).
- Cost of Living (www.coli/org/)
- CNNMoney.com (money.cnn.com/calculator/pf/cost-of-living/)
- Moving.com (www.moving.com/real-estate/compare-cities/index.asp)
- Realtor.com (www.homefair.com/real-estate/cost-of-living.asp)

More Money Does Not Buy Happiness Researchers at Harvard and Princeton found that happiness in the United States peaks at an income of about $75,000. Once you reach $75,000 the beneficial aspects of more money taper off. More stuff does not make you happier either. To be happier, shift your spending from buying stuff, like cars, phones, and other electronics, to experiences, like trips and special evenings out. Focus on what inspires joy. Buying for others increases happiness, too.

Compare Other Community Resources Here are some resources for other important aspects of the decision of whether to relocate:

The cost of housing: www.zillow.com

Moving costs: www.citytocitymoving.us

DO IT IN CLASS

2.3i Ask for the Job

Most interviews conclude when you are told you can expect to hear from the employer within X days or weeks. This is the time to ask for the job! Show your enthusiasm for the job by saying something like, "Based upon my experiences and strong abilities, am I the appropriate fit for this position?" The interviewer's response will be revealing.

2.3j Wait and Be Patient

Be comfortable with silence, and wait for a response. If the offer is less than what you were expecting, explain that point. Be firm but amicable. This will enhance the employer's respect for you. Tell the employer that you are not willing to start at the bottom or middle of the salary ladder. Reiterate your two or three strongest selling points. Be certain to make a short list of these points beforehand. If the employer states that the offer is final, reply that you need a day or two to think it over. Never turn down an offer until you are absolutely positive you must do so. Sixty percent accept the salary they are first offered.

2.3k Negotiate and Accept the Job

Wait until after the job has been firmly offered to discuss salary. Do not be the first to give a definitive dollar amount. Ask for the salary range for the position. Your objective in negotiating is to obtain a salary 20 percent above the highest figure because you are an exceptional candidate and you will perform at the highest level anticipated. Don't sell yourself short.

If the terms are right, accept the job. Give your new employer your acceptance orally as well as in writing. Obtain a letter confirming your acceptance of the job at the agreed-upon salary and benefits. These might include such items as a sign-on bonus, reimbursement for

Seattle has a lot to offer, but it comes at a price.

Rigucci/Shutterstock.com

moving expenses, permission to telecommute one day a week, a staggered work schedule that allows you to start and leave earlier in the day, extra vacation days, assistance in paying for parking, and perhaps a four-day work-week instead of five. It is important to communiate your excitement about the opportunity to begin working for this company.

Four out of five employers expect job candidates to negotiate. Even if the job posting states "salary is not negotiable," do so. Your competitors will. The worst that can happen is that they will say no. Research shows that earning a lower salary in early years is predictive of low salaries during the rest of one's career. So say no to a low salary if you have to. Salary ranges for careers can be found at www.careerjournal.com, www.Indeed.com, www.PayScale.com, www.Salary.com, and www.Glassdoor.com.

Focus on both gross and net pay. A gross income of $60,000 shrinks to about $40,000 after subtracting federal income, Social Security, and Medicare taxes. Additional deductions for contributions for medical care, retirement, and flexible benefits may drop the take-home pay to $37,000, or $3,083 a month. You can then add back the value of employer-paid benefits such as life insurance, child care and the match in their retirement plan.

How to Say "No" When You Have Multiple Job Offers When interviewing at multiple companies, it is important to not accept the first offer too quickly. Assume you are interviewing at companies A, B, and C, and you get an offer from company A. Say "thank you" and add that you are in discussions with companies B and C (but don't say who they really are), and ask company A for time to consider their offers. A week or two should be sufficient, and company A will likely approve of your suggestion. Then contact companies B and C and ask about the timing of their decision.

What to Do if You Have Accepted a Job and a Better One is Offered Ask yourself is the second offer really a great job? Does it meet your financial needs and offer stability? Can you advance in your career? Also seek advice from a mentor (not a friend). Then take the job that is better. Realize, too, that the bulk of earnings growth happens between ages 25 and 35. Thus, do what is best for you!

2.3l How to Move Up at Work

All industries are moving to monthly or even weekly "check-ins" instead of formal once-a-year reviews. Here employees are encouraged to take more initiative to talk with managers about how things are going. Push your boss toward finding out how you are doing and how you can improve.

To move on in your career "ask" others for what you want. Letting someone help you makes you a friend and you gain a strong supporter. Your career and life are not things to be wasted away. Believe in yourself, your ideals and your ideas. Ask your supervisor for suggestions for your professional development. Employers often pay for online education courses. Always be professional by being loyal to and supportive of your boss.

2.3m Getting Paid "Right" in Your Job

Find out what people in your field earn by talking with others, reviewing trade publications, and checking online at sites such as glassdoor.com, vault.com, payscale.com, salary.com, and HotJobs.com. Then get paid what you are worth.

Arrange a meeting with your boss. Beforehand, write down well-defined, achievable, and measurable goals that you can work toward. Document your accomplishments in writing and keep records. Throughout the year, perhaps on a quarterly basis, discuss these with your boss. Do so in sit-down meetings rather than in brief hallway conversations.

ADVICE FROM A SEASONED PRO

What to Do When You Lose Your Job

Be kind to yourself. *Decide to be emotionally, mentally, and physically healthy.*

Reduce your financial stress. *Determine how much money you have and the level of unemployment benefits you might be able to receive, plus calculate how long you can continue to pay your bills in the usual fashion.*

Create a job search plan. *For help with unemployment benefits, resumes, handling stress, and creating a job search plan, see www.CareerOneStop.org/reemployment.*

Think of yourself as being employed. *Your job is to find a new job, so set a daily work schedule for yourself and do it full-time.*

Tap into your social network. *Let people know that you are looking for work, and professionalize your LinkedIn, Facebook, Twitter, Snapchat, and others.*

Consider temping. *Many firms hire temporary workers, and as their business increases they often hire temps full-time.*

Holly Hunts
Montana State University, Bozeman, Montana

If money for a raise does come up in a conversation, suggest a range like $4,000 to $6,000 a year. The range means that you will seem more flexible and cooperative, and this makes it more difficult for a boss to give you a lousy counteroffer. "Seventy-five percent" of people who ask for a raise get one, and 40 percent receive the amount they asked for.

If your company, division, or department is profitable, either get more money today or get a guarantee that you will have another review/salary discussion in six months, not a year. If the boss cannot give you all the money you deserve, ask for a bigger bonus, enhanced health or retirement benefits, a more flexible work schedule, a change in work hours, permission to occasionally telecommute, or more vacation time.

Believe in yourself and get the money you deserve. If necessary, change employers but don't leave a job until you have another one already lined up.

2.3n Periodically Update Your Career Plan

Getting that desired job does not mean that your career planning efforts are over. Indeed, they have only just started. You know that employers formally evaluate their employees on a regular basis and you should do the same for your career plan. Keep a written file at home of tasks you have accomplished quite well because you will need this kind of information for your next job interview.

CONCEPT CHECK 2.3

1. Offer suggestions on correctly assembling a résumé and what style formats are available.
2. Give examples of how to identify specific job opportunities.
3. Give three suggestions on how to succeed in an interview.
4. Explain how to compare salary and living costs in different cities.
5. Give two career advancement tips.

WHAT DO YOU RECOMMEND *NOW*?

Now that you have read the chapter on the importance of career planning, what do you recommend to Nicole Linkletter in the case at the beginning of the chapter regarding:

1. Clarifying her values and lifestyle trade-offs in career planning?
2. Enhancing her career-related experiences before graduation?
3. Creating career plans and goals?
4. Understanding her work-style personality?
5. Identifying job opportunities?

Tyler Olson/Shutterstock.com

SUMMARY OF LEARNING OBJECTIVES RECAPPED

LO1   **Identify the key steps in successful career planning.**

Career planning is identifying an employment pathway that aligns with your interests and abilities and that is expected to provide the lifestyle and work style you find enjoyable and satisfying. It includes clarifying your values and interests; reviewing your abilities, experiences and education; knowing your work-style personality; taking advantage of networking; aligning yourself with tomorrow's employment trends; and finalizing your career plan.

LO2   **Analyze the financial and legal aspects of employment.**

The financial side of career planning includes recognizing the value of a college education, placing

dollar values on employee benefits, and knowing your legal employment rights.

LO3   **Practice effective employment search strategies.**

Smart job search strategies include assembling an attention-getting résumé; targeting your preferred employers; identifying specific job opportunities; writing an effective cover letter; obtaining strong reference letters; formally applying for the job; interviewing for success; dealing with rejection; comparing salary offers; negotiating and accepting the job; and periodically updating your career plans.

LET'S TALK ABOUT IT

1. **Interviewing Tips.** List three interviewing tips for new college graduates looking for employment when in many parts of the country a growing job market exists.

2. **Interview Mistakes.** Thinking about some common mistakes that people make in job interviews, which three are the worst? Make a short list of things people should do to improve success in an interview.

3. **Career Trade-offs.** People regularly make decisions in career planning that have trade-offs. Identify some benefits and costs people are faced with as well as two lifestyle trade-offs.

4. **Keeping Track Topics.** Review the task areas in the Decision-Making Worksheet "Keeping Track of Your Job Search" on page 57, and identify what you think are the three that likely are the most difficult for people to accomplish. For each of the three, offer a suggestion that might help people accomplish the task.

5. **Assessing the Benefits of a Second Income.** Adding a second part-time income to a family either by having another person work or by working two jobs often seems to be a good way to add financial

DO IT IN CLASS
Page 52

resources. But the impact is not always as large as people hope. Review the example given in the "Run the Numbers" box on page 52 and discuss the pros and cons of a second income in that example.

6. **Interviewing Mistakes.** Recall an interview for a job you did not get. What happened to cause it to go wrong? Was there anything you could have done differently/better to prepare?

DO THE MATH

1. **Economic Trade-off of Graduate School.** Jessica Sotomajor, of Bangor, Maine, works for a military contractor and hopes to earn an extra $1,000,000 over her remaining 30-year working career by going back to school to obtain a doctor's degree. If her income projection is correct, that's an average of over $28,000 more income a year. Jessica's employer is willing to pay half, or $45,000, toward the $90,000 cost of the annual Ph.D. program, so she must pay $45,000 of her own money. Jessica wonders if expected extra income would warrant spending the money to get the Ph.D.

DO IT IN CLASS
Page 19

(a) What is the forgone lost future value of her $45,000 over the 30 years at 6 percent? (Hint: See Appendix A.1.)

(b) What would be the forgone lost future value of $90,000 over 30 years if Jessica had to pay all the costs for her doctoral degree? (Hint: See Appendix A.1.)

(c) Advise Jessica as to what she should do.

2. **Comparing Salary Offers.** Using Equations (2.1) or (2.2), if the cost-of-living index was 132 for Chicago and 114 for San Antonio, compare the buying power a $50,000 salary in Chicago with a $47,000 offer in San Antonio.

DO IT IN CLASS
Page 64

3. **Future Value of Employer's Match.** Tyler Winkle's employer in Pittsburgh makes a matching contribution of $2,000 a year to his 401(k) retirement account at work. If the dollar amount of the employer's contribution increases 4 percent annually, how much will the employer contribute to the plan in the twentieth year from now? (Hint: See Appendix A.1.)

4. **Cashing Out 401(k) Plan.** Emily Amarrada of Sioux City, South Dakota has accepted a new job and is thinking about cashing out the $30,000 she has built up in her employer's 401(k) plan to buy a new car. If, instead, she left the funds in the plan and they are projected to earn 6 percent annually for the next 30 years, how much would Emily have in her plan? (Hint: See Appendix A.1.)

DO IT IN CLASS
Page 50

FINANCIAL PLANNING CASES

CASE 1

The Harry and Belinda Johnson Family Might Have a Career Change

Harry has started out fine in his career as his responsibilities have increased since he began working there about five years ago. Belinda recently attended a conference for those in her stock brokerage field and by chance she dropped in at the "career search" room. She saw job opportunities there that fit her skill set that offered salaries of $78,000 to $80,000 in nearby Parkville, Missouri, only about a 30-minute commute away.

(a) If a new employer offered Belinda $80,000 to move and the relative cost index for the new community was 116, how does that compare to her current salary of $77,000 in Kansas City assuming the index in the latter is 122?

(b) Do you think she should take the new job? Give three reasons why or why not?

CASE 2

Victor Hernandez Considers a Career Change

Victor is somewhat satisfied with his sales career and has always wondered about a career as a teacher in a public school. He would have to take a year off work to go back to college to obtain his teaching certificate, and that would mean giving up his $53,000 salary for a year. Victor expects that he could earn about the same income as a teacher.

(a) What would his annual income be after 10 years as a teacher if he received an average 3 percent raise every year? (Hint: Use Appendix A.1.)

(b) Victor also could earn $4,000 each year teaching during the summers. What is the accumulated future value of earning those annual amounts over 10 years assuming a 5 percent raise every year? (Hint: Use Appendix A.3.)

CASE 3

Julia Price's Career Plans Change

Julia has recently undergone a severe career crisis. After nearly ten years as a professional engineer, her position was phased out by her company due to a loss of government contracts, and she has been offered a position in the marketing department. The new job will require that she interact with purchasing agents for various companies that are current and potential customers of her company. The job pays more but will require considerable travel. She will be using her engineering background, but the primary tasks all will relate to presenting herself and her company in the best possible light to these other firms. Julia thinks she should take the new job and make a personal commitment to doing it for one year and, if she does not truly enjoy the work, seek a new engineering job within her company or at another employer. Offer your opinions about her thinking.

CASE 4

Matching Yourself with a Job

After completing his associate of arts degree four months ago from a community college in Oklahoma City, Oklahoma, Juan Ramirez has answered more than three dozen advertisements and interviewed three times in his effort to get a sales job, but he has had no success. Juan has never done sales work before, but he did take some business classes in college, including "Personal Selling." After some of the interviews, Juan telephoned some of those potential employers only to find that even though they liked him, they said they typically hired only those people with previous sales experience or who seemed to possess terrific potential.

(a) If Juan actually were well suited for sales, which work values and work-style factors do you think he would rate as "very important"?

(b) What would you recommend to Juan regarding how to find out about the depth of his interest in a sales career?

(c) Assuming Juan has appropriate personal qualities and academic strengths to be successful in a sales career, what additional strategies should he consider to better market himself?

CASE 5

Career Promotion Opportunity

Nina and Ting Guo of Lima, Ohio, have been together for eight years, having married five years after completing college. Nina has been working as an insurance agent ever since. Ting began working as a family counselor for the state of Ohio last year after completing his master's degree in counseling. Recently Nina's boss commented confidentially that he was going to recommend Nina to be the next person promoted, given a raise of about $15,000, and relocated to the home office in Portland, Oregon. Nina thinks that if offered the opportunity she would like to take it, even if it means that Ting will have to resign from his new job.

(a) What suggestions can you offer Nina when she gets home from work and wants to discuss with her husband her likely career promotion?

(b) What lifestyle factors and benefits and costs issues should Nina and Ting probably discuss?

DO IT IN CLASS
Page 42

BE YOUR OWN PERSONAL FINANCIAL MANAGER

1. **Work-Style Personality.** Do you know your preferred work-style personality? Take the time to complete the worksheet on page 45 or you can use Worksheet 6: What Is My Work Style Personality from "My Personal Financial Planner."

   My Personal Financial Planner

2. **Values Clarification.** Go online and do a Web search or "values clarification assessment" to bring up a long list of possible values clarification exercises. Complete one or more exercises and then compare the results to what you have been thinking in terms of your academic major in college and possible careers.

3. **Career Field Exploration.** Visit the Guide to Industries at www.bls.gov/iag to determine the earnings, benefits, and employment outlook for a position in a career field that interests you. Complete Worksheet 7: Career Field Research from "My Personal Financial Planner" to write up your results including an assessment of how well your work-style personality and values fit the career field that you researched.

4. **Compare Salary Offers.** Use two actual salary offers or two desired offers in two cities of your choosing to compare the salary offers based on the different costs of living in the two cities. See Worksheet 8: Comparing Salary Offers in Two Different Cities from "My Personal Financial Planner," or see the discussion on page 64, as a guide for your analysis.

5. **Assess the Benefits of a Second Part-time Income.** Using real or example data assess the benefits of a second income for a dual-earner household in your salary range. Use the example provided in the text on page 52 or Worksheet 9: Assessing the Benefits of a Second Income from "My Personal Financial Planner" for your assessment.

   My Personal Financial Planner

ON THE NET

Go to the Web pages indicated to complete these exercises.

1. **Research the Occupational Outlook Handbook.** Go to the website for the *Occupational Outlook Handbook* at www.bls.gov/ooh. Select two occupational areas that are of interest to you, and for each, determine the likely starting salary, career path, future salary expectations, and demand for people with the skills appropriate for the occupation.

2. **Research the National Unemployment Rate.** Go to the website for the Bureau of Labor Statistics' assessment of the labor outlook in the United States at www.bls.gov/news.release/pdf/empsit.pdf. Browse through the information provided to determine the current national unemployment rate for the nation as a whole and for a city or area of interest to you. Compare current statistics with those of one year ago and with projections for five and ten years in the future.

3. **Research a Career of Interest.** Check the U.S. Department of Labor Statistics' Occupational Outlook Handbook at www.bls.gov/ooh/occupation-finder.htm to learn about the earnings, benefits, educational requirements, and employment outlook for a career of interest to you. Make a written summary of your findings.

4. **Check Out Income Levels.** Are your current perceptions about the income level typical for various career fields correct? Visit www.payscale.com and research salary data on five career fields.

ACTION INVOLVEMENT PROJECTS

1. **Interview a Human Resource Manager.** Use the Internet and/or Yellow Pages to find a local company that employs people in your prospective career field. Request a brief interview with the human resource manager. Ask about salary levels, employee benefits, and the career ladder. Make a written summary of your findings.

2. **Prepare a Résumé.** Using the Monster.com find a job listing for a position in your career field. Prepare a résumé for the job. Review Figures 2-3, 2-4, and 2-5 on pages 54 and 55 and create or update your résumé accordingly. Take the job listing and documents to your faculty advisor and ask him or her for feedback.
    DO IT IN CLASS
    Page 54

3. **Cover Letter.** Review Figure 2-6 on page 59 and create or update a sample cover letter to accompany your résumé when applying for a job.
    DO IT IN CLASS
    Page 59

4. **Where Do You Want to Live?** It is highly likely that one of the best job opportunities for you at graduation will require that you move away from your hometown and/or where you went to college. While that new location is unknown now, it is not too early to begin thinking of where you might need and/or want to live. Use the list of websites on page 58 to compare housing costs,
    DO IT IN CLASS
    Page 65
    quality of life issues, and moving costs for three cities of interest to you.

5. **Clarify Your Values.** To help you clarify your values, review the section titled "Clarify Your Values and Interests" on pages 40 and 41 and make a list of your 10 most important ones.
    DO IT IN CLASS
    Page 41

6. **Trade-Offs.** To clarify your lifestyle trade-offs, review the section titled "Lifestyle Trade-offs" on pages 42 and 43 and given the list and make a list of your choices for trade-offs.
    DO IT IN CLASS
    Page 42

7. **Anticipated Interview Questions.** Review the questions in the section on "Prepare Responses for Anticipated Interview Questions" on page 62 and write out concise sample responses to each question.
    DO IT IN CLASS
    Page 62

8. **Name Some Possible Mistakes.** Stanford University professors Bill Burnett and Dave Evans bring a fresh perspective to career advice. Their book, *Designing Your Life: How to Build a Well-Lived, Joyful Life,* offers a series of self-evaluation exercises about treating life in a more improvisational way. You can make mistakes. Failure is good. List two mistakes that you might make soon after graduation, and then record what potential solutions might result.

3

Financial Statements, Tools, and Budgets

YOU MUST BE KIDDING, RIGHT?

The world of personal finances is getting more complicated and challenging each year. Which one of the following statements is false?

A. Sixty percent of all adults say they do not budget.

B. Four in ten say they are living beyond their means.

C. Four in ten rate themselves only as "fair" or "poor" in managing money.

D. One-third of Americans say they find it difficult to meet household expenses on time each month.

The answer is "none of the above" because all the statements are true. Clearly, many Americans are having trouble managing their personal finances. You can learn about personal finances so these statements will not apply to you!

Learning Objectives

After reading this chapter, you should be able to:

1. Identify your financial values, goals, and strategies.

2. Use balance sheets and cash-flow statements to measure your financial health and progress.

3. Collect and organize the financial records necessary for managing your personal finances.

4. List a number of money topics to discuss with a partner.

5. Achieve your financial goals through budgeting.

WHAT DO YOU RECOMMEND?

Austin and Emily Patterson, both age 26, have been married for four years and have no children. Austin is a licensed electrician earning $66,000 per year, and Emily earns $46,000 annually as a middle-school teacher. Austin would like to go to half time on his job and return to school on a part-time basis; he is one year short of finishing his bachelor's degree in electrical engineering. His education expenses would be about $25,000 for the year, which could be partially covered by student loans. He has not yet discussed his thoughts with Emily.

Austin and Emily have recently started saving for retirement through their employers and have set aside some savings for emergencies. They have substantial credit card debt and are still paying off student loans. The couple rents a two-bedroom apartment. Austin always thought it smart to save all of their receipts, bank statements, and other financial documents. His system for organizing their records is very simple; each month he puts everything in a manila envelope and then puts the envelopes into a box.

Austin knows that his educational plans will have financial implications for the couple. He wants to factor these financial issues into his discussion with Emily. To this point, they have never developed financial statements or explicit financial goals. He knows that the two of them must be in sync about money issues or they will be going into the future with few goals and no plans for how to achieve them.

Phovoir/Shutterstock.com

What do you recommend to Austin for his talk with Emily on the subject of financial planning regarding:

1. **Setting financial goals?**
2. **Determining what they own and owe?**
3. **Using the information in Austin's newly prepared financial statements to summarize the family's financial situation?**
4. **Evaluating their financial progress?**
5. **Setting up a record-keeping system to better serve their needs?**
6. **Starting a budgeting process to guide saving and spending?**

Sixty percent of all adults say they do not budget. Four in ten say they are living beyond their means. Twenty percent say they regularly spend more money than they earn. Forty percent rate themselves only as "fair" or "poor" in managing money. Three-quarters of adults lose sleep worrying about finances. Forty percent do not have $1,000 in savings. One-third of Americans say they find it difficult to meet household expenses on time each month, and they live paycheck-to-paycheck, and they often turn to credit cards. All these people are poor money matters, and their choices will forever make them the "have nots" in society rather than the "haves."

Smart people sometimes say "The problem is not our income, it is how much we spend, and our spending habits are way too big." Living above your means can lead to financial ruin at a young age. If you regularly live below your means, you will *always* have means. That's the secret! Learn to control your spending, and everything else will fall into place.

To not mess up your financial life you must avoid living paycheck-to-paycheck because this lets your spending dictate your savings. Save first so you can spend later. To truly succeed you need to follow a spending plan that includes savings, take actions to achieve results, and regularly measure your financial progress. One of the easiest ways to save is to have your employer automatically deposit a portion of your paycheck directly into your bank or credit union. What is important is not how much money you have. It is how well you spend your money. Wealth is not measured by how much you earn, rather it is how much you hang onto.

Learning Objective 1

Identify your financial values, goals, and strategies.

values

Fundamental beliefs about what is important, desirable, and worthwhile.

TO-DO SOON

Do the following to begin to achieve financial success:

1. *Develop financial goals and update them annually.*

2. *Set up a spending plan and cash-flow statement for next month and every month.*

3. *Track your net worth and calculate financial ratios each year to assess your financial progress.*

4. *Use an uncomplicated but effective personal financial record-keeping system.*

5. *Honestly communicate about money matters with a key loved one on a regular basis.*

3.1 FINANCIAL VALUES, GOALS, AND STRATEGIES

Identifying your financial values and goals sets the stage for financial success. Values and goals help you keep a balance between spending and saving and make you stay committed to your financial plans. Once goals are set, you can develop the strategies necessary for their achievement.

Financial planning, which is the process of developing and implementing a coordinated series of financial plans, can help you achieve financial success. The first three chapters of this book examine the topic of financial planning so you can do all the appropriate tasks yourself. By planning your personal finances, you seek to manage your income and wealth so that you reach your financial goals throughout your lifetime. If you choose to do little planning, you will not be successful.

Figure 3-1 provides an overview of effective personal financial planning. Table 3-1 illustrates one couple's (Harry and Belinda Johnson) overall financial plan. Such excellent managerial efforts help push them toward achieving financial success. The couple has made plans in 15 specific areas spread across three broad categories: (1) spending, (2) risk management, and (3) capital accumulation.

3.1a Values Define Your Financial Success

Your values provide the underlying support and rationale for your financial and lifestyle goals. Your **values** are your fundamental beliefs about what is important, desirable, and worthwhile. Values are what we believe in. They motivate and shape us. They serve as the basis for your goals.

All of us differ in the ways we value education, security, spiritual life, health, happiness, peace of mind, independence, employment, helping others, credit use, family life, making a difference, and many others. Personal financial goals grow out of these values because we inevitably consider some things more important or desirable than others. We express our values, in part, by the ways we spend, save, invest, and donate our money.

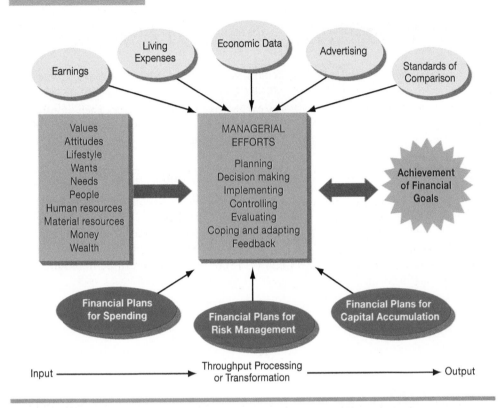

Figure 3-1 **Overview of Effective Financial Planning**

3.1b Saving Is Your Single Most Important Financial Task

One benefit of effective financial planning is learning to wisely use money. People who are smart about their personal finances always value saving some of their income. They adhere to the personal finance philosophy of "Pay myself first!" Think about it: If you earn the money, shouldn't you be paid first?

But Treat Yourself Wise money managers establish a current spending level based on the essentials or the necessities of life, and that probably takes up 50 percent of their income. Then they spend money for their lifestyle, like present and future spending for vehicle purchases, housing, child's education, and vacations. That's another 30 percent. They save the remainder, perhaps 20 percent, for projected future living expenses during retirement. Successful money managers also treat themselves. They use some of their money for travel. They don't buy and accumulate too much stuff. They choose instead to buy things with a purpose.

Commit to Creating an Emergency Savings Fund The biggest worry for most people is how to pay for unexpected emergency expenses. Smart people who are on a limited income—and this includes many new college graduates—who have saved some money in an **emergency fund** are going to do fine financially. This is an account that is used to set aside funds to be used in an emergency, such as the loss of a job, an illness, or one of life's many "what ifs."

Examples of Bad Emergencies You know that financial emergencies are going to happen. Everyone knows. So you should plan for them. When you have an emergency fund built up, then you will not have to pay with plastic for things that are not in your budget.

You ought to eventually save up three to six months of income in an emergency fund. However, as soon as you have $500 to $2,000 in emergency savings, you probably will have enough money to pay for most small crises. However, expensive emergencies will

emergency fund

This is an account that is used to set aside funds to be used in an emergency, such as the loss of a job, an illness, or one of life's many "what ifs."

Table 3-1

Financial Plans, Goals, and Objectives for Harry (Age 28) and Belinda (Age 28) Johnson, Prepared in February 2018

Financial Plan Areas	Long-Term Goals and Objectives	Short-Term Goals and Objectives
FOR SPENDING		
Evaluate and plan major purchases	Purchase a new car in two years.	Begin saving $200 a month for a down-payment for a new car.
Manage debt	Keep installment debt under 10 percent of take-home pay.	Pay off charge cards at the end of each month and do not finance any purchases of appliances or other similar products.
FOR RISK MANAGEMENT		
Medical costs	Avoid large medical costs.	Maintain employer-subsidized medical insurance policy by paying $135 monthly premium.
Property and casualty losses	Always have renter's or homeowner's insurance. Always have maximum automobile insurance coverage.	Make semiannual premium payment of $220 on renter's insurance policy. Make premium payments of $440 on automobile insurance policy.
Liability losses	Eventually buy $1 million liability insurance.	Rely on $100,000 policy purchased from same source as automobile insurance policy.
Premature death	Have adequate life insurance coverage for both as well as lots of financial investments so the survivor would not have any financial worries.	Maintain employer-subsidized life insurance on Belinda and buy some life insurance for Harry. Create advance care documents. Start some investments.
Income loss from disability	Buy sufficient disability insurance.	Rely on sick days and seek disability insurance through private insurers.
FOR CAPITAL ACCUMULATION		
Tax fund	Have enough money for taxes (but not too much) withheld from monthly salaries by both employers to cover eventual tax liabilities.	Confirm that employer withholding of taxes is sufficient. Have extra money withheld to cover additional tax liability because of income on trust from Harry's deceased father.
Revolving savings fund	Always have sufficient cash in local accounts to meet monthly and annual anticipated budget expense needs.	Develop cash-flow calendar to ascertain needs. Put money into revolving savings fund to build it up quickly to the proper balance. Keep all funds in interest-earning accounts.
Emergency fund	Build up monetary assets equivalent to 3 to 6 months' take-home pay.	Put $150 per month into an emergency fund until it totals 3 to 6 month's take-home pay.
Education	Maintain educational skills and credentials to remain competitive. Have employer assist in paying for Belinda to earn a master of business administration (MBA). Have Harry complete a master of fine arts (MFA), possibly a PhD in interior design.	Both take one graduate class per term.
Savings	Always have a nice-size savings balance. Regularly save to achieve goals. Save a portion of any extra income or gifts. Save $26,000 for a down payment on a home to be bought within five years.	Save enough to pay cash for the newest smart phone. Pay off Visa credit card balance of $390 soon. Begin saving $400 per month for a down payment on a new home.
Investment	Own substantial shares of a conservative mutual fund that will pay dividends equivalent to about 10 percent of family income at age 45.	Start investing in a mutual fund before next year.
Retirement and Estate Planning	Own some real estate and common stocks. Retire at age 60 or earlier on income that is the same as the take-home pay earned just before retirement. Provide for a surviving spouse.	Establish individual retirement accounts (IRAs) for Harry and Belinda before next year. Contribute the maximum possible amount to employer-sponsored retirement accounts. Sign so most assets will transfer by contract. Each spouse makes a will.

also occur, and these include things like a trip to the hospital emergency room, surgery that maxes out your insurance, a sick pet, your laptop or smartphone dies, your vehicle breaks down and needs a tow, a plumbing or electrical problem, you get sick and miss work when you have no paid time off, the washer/dryer/fridge/dishwasher/oven/ microwave breaks down, family emergency, a destination wedding for friend/relative, and gifts for baby shower, wedding shower, housewarming. You also may need to pay a handyman to swing by and clean, fix, relocate, or install something.

Note that this list of emergencies does not include auto insurance, holiday gifts, or similar occasional expenses because you know they are coming, so save up and pay them when due. To do so use a revolving savings fund, discussed later in this chapter.

Create Some Margin or Become an Unprepared Borrower Those without an emergency fund who face a financial crisis are stuck with a choice: spend less or acquire more income. Finding, say $1,000 for an emergency, is challenging for many people. If you must borrow to pay for a crisis, you still must come up with a plan to not only pay back what you borrow in a specific period of time but also to quickly and concurrently rebuild your savings.

Those living paycheck-to-paycheck are "unprepared borrowers," and when faced with an emergency expense they are in deep financial trouble. The primary reason why such people never get ahead financially and fail forever and ever is that they cannot create a financial margin of safety by regularly spending less than they earn. This is a skill you must develop!

3.1c Examples of Financial Goals

Some examples of financial goals are finishing a college education, paying off credit card debts, repaying education loans, meeting financial emergencies, taking a vacation, owning a home, accumulating funds to send children through college, owning your own business, and having financial independence at retirement. However, to be achievable each goal must be made more specific.

3.1d Financial Goals Follow Your Values

Successful financial planning evolves from your financial goals. **Financial goals** are the specific long-, intermediate-, and short-term objectives to be attained through financial planning and management efforts. Financial goals should be consistent with your values. Setting goals helps you visualize the gap between your current financial status and where you want to be in the future.

financial goals
Specific objectives addressed by planning and managing finances.

DID YOU KNOW

The Middle Class Shrinks

The Pew Research Center says the middle class is losing ground according to incomes earned. **Middle-income** Americans are adults whose annual household income is two-thirds to double the national median, about $42,000 to $126,000 annually for a 3-person household size. Pew reports that median household income is about $53,000.

Upper-income households have incomes that are greater than double the median. The good news is that over the past 40 years more people moved from the middle class to the upper tier. The not-so-good news is that only 50 percent are now classified as middle class, when it used to be over 70 percent.

Lower-income households have incomes less than two-thirds of the median, and their numbers have grown over those years from 16 to 20 percent. Those Americans without a college degree stand out as having a substantial loss in economic status.

The gap in income between middle- and upper-income households also has widened substantially. In fact, fully half of all income in a recent year went to upper-income households. Upper-income families, which years ago had three times as much wealth as middle-income families now have seven times as much.

To serve as a rational basis for financial actions, a financial goal must be stated explicitly so that a clear result has been defined. Inserting real dollar amounts to each goal is critical. The goal must be measureable so that each task can be defined by how much time and effort it will take to complete. Finally, include the projected time frames by when each goal is to be achieved.

Make Financial Goals Specific Making financial goals specific transforms vague dreams into concrete, achievable goals. Examples: "Finishing my college education within 24 months," "Pay off $3,000 in credit card debt within 3 years," "Repay college loans of $18,000 within 5 years," and "Start savings fund of $300 every month beginning in 3 months to meet annual financial emergencies." It is best if you put the month and year next to each of your specific goals. Making goals specific—with deadlines—empowers the maker to succeed.

Use Pictures, Numbers, and Public Affirmations Here is a thought to help turn a wish into reality. If buying a condo is your goal, tape a photograph of a beautiful one onto your refrigerator. Then tell others about your financial goal. The public affirmations and constant photographic reminders will help you make it into a reality. Also put a list of your financial goals where you can see them every day.

Consider the example of Stephanie Vogel, a dance instructor from Athens, Georgia. Stephanie has just made the last $410 payment on her four-year car loan. She does not like being in debt, so she does not want to take out such a large loan again. Stephanie would like to put the money she has been paying monthly for the loan into a savings account, which would allow her to replace her current vehicle in four or five years. Stephanie figures that it would take about $26,000 to buy another inexpensive high-mileage vehicle in five years. She assumes she could earn a 2 percent return on her savings and, using Appendix A.3, has determined that she would need to save $4,996 per year ($26,000 ÷ 5.2040 for five years at 2 percent interest), or roughly $416 per month ($4,996/12).

Stephanie's thinking offers a good example of how proper financial goal setting works. She recognized the value she put on staying out of debt and proceeded to the general goal of trying to pay cash for her next car. After determining an overall dollar amount needed, she broke that amount down into first annual and then monthly amounts. For only $6 more per month than she has been paying on her loan ($416 − $410), Stephanie will be able to pay cash for her next car. This is the sacrifice she is willing to make to avoid using credit to buy a vehicle in the future.

3.1e Financial Strategies Help Guide Your Financial Success

financial strategies

Pre-established action plans implemented in specific situations.

Financial strategies are pre-established plans of action to be implemented in specific situations. Stephanie Vogel implemented an effective strategy in the preceding example. That is, when a loan has been repaid, start a savings program with the same monthly payment amount. Saving may be easier for Stephanie if she arranges for the amount she would like to save to be automatically deposited from her paycheck into her savings account.

Only 1 in 5 Americans have savings automatically withdrawn from their paychecks. Another useful savings strategy is to arrange for as much as 50 or 75 percent of any raises or bonuses to go into savings before you become accustomed to the additional income. When you get a pay raise that quickly translates into more spending this makes you more dependent upon more income, and that kind of habit can last forever. Instead when you get a pay raise decrease the proportion of your spending by saving and investing more.

3.1f Wealth-Building Principles for Life

Consider adopting the following wealth-building principles for your life:

1. Set clear financial goals both in the short and long term.
2. Save by paying yourself first out of your paycheck.
3. Pay credit card balances in full each month.
4. Spend less than you earn.

5. Participate in the retirement plan at work.
6. Take full advantage of your employer's match on retirement savings.
7. Buy a home for the tax advantages.
8. Pay off your home before retirement.
9. Be patient when investing for the long term.
10. Live every day knowing that your financial future is under control.

CONCEPT CHECK 3.1

1. Summarize the content in Figure 3-1, the overview of effective personal financial planning.
2. What is the biggest financial worry of most individuals, and what can they do about it?
3. Summarize how financial goals follow from one's values.
4. Pick two wealth-building principles for life and explain what they mean to you.

3.2 FINANCIAL STATEMENTS MEASURE YOUR FINANCIAL HEALTH AND PROGRESS

Learning Objective 2
Use balance sheets and cash flow statements to measure your financial health and progress.

Financial statements are compilations of personal financial data that describe an individual's or family's current financial condition. They present a summary of assets and liabilities as well as income and spending of an individual or family. The two most useful statements are the balance sheet and the cash-flow statement.

A **balance sheet** (or **net worth statement**) describes an individual's or family's financial condition on a specified date by showing assets, liabilities, and net worth. It provides a current status report and includes information on what you own, what you owe, and what the net result would be if you paid off all of your debts. It answers the question, "Where are you financially right now?"

Another important financial statement is the **cash-flow statement** (or **income and expense statement**). It lists and summarizes income and expense transactions that have taken place over a specific period of time, such as a month or a year. It tells you where your money came from and where it went. It answers the question, "Where did your money go?"

financial statements
Snapshots that describe an individual's or family's current financial condition.

balance sheet or net worth statement
Snapshot of assets, liabilities, and net worth on a particular date.

cash-flow statement or income and expense statement
Summary of all income and expense transactions over a specific time period.

3.2a The Balance Sheet Is a Snapshot of Your Financial Status Right Now

To benchmark where you are on the wealth-building scale, determine your **net worth**. This is what you are worth after subtracting liabilities from assets. If you are indeed serious about your financial success, then you will sit down soon with pencil and paper or at your computer to see exactly where you stand. You do so by preparing your balance sheet. It should be updated at least once each year and compared to previous ones, so save all your old financial statements. Then you can assess your progress over the years. Net worth grows slowly, but it definitely increases over time.

If you are successful in your career and follow the basic principles outlined in this book, there is no reason why you cannot have a net worth of $1 million, or $2 million or more, later in your life. Net worth typically peaks for people in their 50s or 60s (see Figure 3-2 on page 81).

net worth
What's left when you subtract liabilities from assets.

1. The Three Components of the Balance Sheet A balance sheet consists of three parts: assets, liabilities, and net worth. Your **assets** include everything you own that has monetary value. Your **liabilities** are your debts, the amounts you owe to others. Your **net worth** is the dollar amount left when what is owed is subtracted from the dollar value of what is owned. That is, if all the assets were sold at the listed values and all debts were paid in full. Your net worth is the true measure of your financial wealth.

assets
Everything you own that has monetary value.

liabilities
What you owe.

fair market value
The amount a willing buyer would pay a willing seller for an item.

monetary assets/liquid assets/ cash equivalents
Assets that can be easily converted to cash.

tangible/use/lifestyle assets
Personal property easily converted to maintain your everyday lifestyle.

investment/capital assets
Tangible and intangible items acquired for their monetary benefits.

What Is Owned—Assets Are "The Things You Own." The assets section of the balance sheet lists items valued at their **fair market value**. This is what a willing buyer would pay a willing seller, not the amount originally paid or what it might be worth a year from now. It is useful to classify assets as monetary, tangible, or investment assets.

Monetary assets (also known as **liquid assets** or **cash equivalents**) include cash and low-risk near-cash items that can be readily converted to cash with little or no loss in value such as checking and savings accounts. They are primarily used for maintenance of living expenses, emergencies, savings, and payment of bills.

Tangible (or **use** or **lifestyle**) assets are personal property whose primary purpose is to provide maintenance of one's everyday lifestyle. Tangible assets, such as furniture and vehicles, generally depreciate in value over time.

Investment assets (also known as **capital assets**) include tangible and intangible items that have a relatively long life and high cost and that are acquired for the monetary benefits they provide, such as generating additional income and appreciation (or increasing in value). Examples include stock mutual funds and bonds. Investment assets generally appreciate and are dedicated to the maintenance of one's future level of living.

Following are some examples of each kind of asset.

Monetary Assets

- Cash (including cash on hand, checking accounts, savings accounts, savings bonds, certificates of deposit, and money market accounts)
- Tax refunds due
- Money owed to you by others

Tangible Assets

- Automobiles, motorcycles, boats, bicycles
- House, condominium, mobile home
- Household furnishings and appliances
- Electronic goods
- Personal property (jewelry, furs, tools, clothing)
- Other "big ticket" items

Investment Assets

- Stocks, bonds, mutual funds, gold, partnerships, art, 401(k)s, IRAs
- Life insurance and annuities (cash values only)
- Real property (and anything fixed to it)
- Personal and employer-provided retirement accounts

short-term (current) liability
Obligation paid off within one year.

long-term (noncurrent) liability
Debt that comes due in more than one year.

2. What Is Owed—Liabilities Are "The Money You Owe" The liabilities section of the balance sheet summarizes debts owed, including both personal and business-related debts. The debt could be either a **short-term** (or **current**) **liability**, an obligation to be paid off within one year, or a **long-term** (or **noncurrent**) **liability**, debts that do not have to be paid in full until more than a year from now. To be accurate, record debt obligations at their current payoff amounts (excluding future interest payments). Following are some examples of items to include in the liabilities section of a balance sheet, with some suggested subheadings.

Short-Term (or Current) Liabilities

- Personal loans owed to other people
- Credit card and charge account balances
- Other open-end credit obligations

- Professional services unpaid (doctors, dentists, chiropractors, lawyers)
- Taxes unpaid
- Past-due rent, utility bills, telephone, Internet, and insurance premiums

Long-Term Liabilities

- Automobile loans
- Real estate mortgages
- Student loans
- Home equity and second mortgage loans
- Consumer installment loans and leases
- Margin loans on securities

3. Net Worth—What Is Left Is "A Measure of Your Financial Worth" Net worth is determined by subtracting liabilities from assets, as indicated in (Equation 3.1) the *net worth formula:*

$$\text{Assets} - \text{liabilities} = \text{net worth}$$

or

(3.1)

$$\text{What is owned} - \text{what is owed} = \text{net worth}$$

This formula assumes that if you converted all assets to cash and paid off all liabilities, the remaining cash would be your net worth. For example, Anne Coulty, a college student from Boise, Idaho, had items of value with a fair market value of $8,000 and she owed $4,500 to others, her net worth, or wealth, is $3,500 ($8,000 − $4,500). Figure 3-2 shows median net worth by age. College students typically have more debts than assets. Thus they are technically **insolvent** because they have a negative net worth. Soon after students graduate and take on full-time jobs, typically their balance sheets improve dramatically in only a few years. One in seven households is financially insolvent.

DO IT IN CLASS

insolvent

When a person owes more than he or she owns and the person has a negative net worth.

$\mathcal{Figure}$ **3-2**   **Median Net Worth by Age**

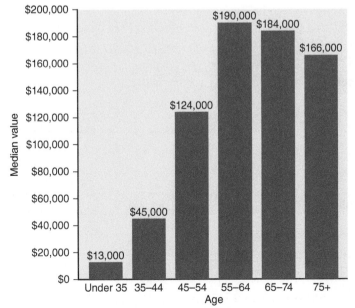

Source: Basic data from *Federal Reserve Bulletin*. Authors' estimates for 2018.

Sample Balance Sheet The total assets on a balance sheet must equal the total liabilities plus the net worth. Both sides must balance, which is the source of the name "balance sheet." You decide how much detail to include to show your financial condition accurately on a given date. The balance sheet shown in Table 3-2 reflects the degree of detail and complexity that might be included for a couple with two children (Victor and Maria Hernandez).

Table 3-2 — Balance Sheet for a Couple with Two Children—Victor and Maria Hernandez, January 1, 2018

ASSETS			
Monetary Assets			
	Cash on hand	1,200	0.3%
	Savings account	4,200	1.1%
	Victor's checking account	2,700	0.7%
	Maria's checking account	3,300	0.8%
	Tax refund due	700	0.2%
	Rent receivable	650	0.2%
	Total Monetary Assets	**$ 12,750**	**3.2%**
Tangible Assets			
	Home	192,000	48.8%
	Personal property	9,000	2.3%
	Automobiles	9,500	2.4%
	Total Tangible Assets	**$210,500**	**53.5%**
Investment Assets			
	Fidelity mutual funds	4,500	1.1%
	Scudder mutual fund	5,000	1.3%
	Ford Motor Company stock	2,800	0.7%
	New York 2038 bonds	4,000	1.0%
	Life insurance cash value	5,400	1.4%
	IRA accounts	34,300	8.7%
	Real estate investment	114,000	29.0%
	Total Investment Assets	**$170,000**	**43.2%**
	Total Assets	**$393,250**	**100.0%**
LIABILITIES			
Short-Term Liabilities			
	Dentist bill due	220	0.1%
	Credit card debt	1,600	0.4%
	Total Short-Term Liabilities	**$ 1,820**	**0.5%**
Long-Term Liabilities			
	Vehicle loan	7,700	2.0%
	Home mortgage loan	92,000	23.4%
	Total Long-Term Liabilities	**$ 99,700**	**25.4%**
	Total Liabilities	**$101,520**	**25.8%**
	Net Worth	**$291,730**	**74.2%**
	Total Liabilities and Net Worth	**$393,250**	**100.0%**

3.2b How to Increase Your Net Worth

You can increase your net worth by increasing assets, decreasing liabilities, or doing both. One way to increase assets and net worth is to cut back on spending. Perhaps consider forgoing the cup of coffee or soda you might buy each day as you head to class. Any decrease in spending leaves money in the bank as an asset. Reducing expenses on high-cost items, such as housing and transportation, will have an even greater effect on assets. A second way to increase net worth is to increase income to build assets or pay down debts. For example, as you earn more money, perhaps consider saving half or more of the difference between your new income and your old income rather than using the added money for more spending. Third, paying off debt, especially high-interest credit card balances, can quickly increase net worth. Fourth think about is taking a part-time job to increase income to acquire assets or pay down debt.

People do not get wealthy by earning an income. Real wealth comes from increases in the value of assets over time such as the growth of investments within a 401(k) retirement program, starting a business, and owning real estate.

BIAS TOWARD— THINKING NEGATIVELY

People tend to compare their success in personal finances to others a lot and care about the results. Sometimes they only feel better when they know others are doing poorly. What to do? Focus on your own goals, and instead of comparing your financial situation to others calculate the numbers on your financial statements to see how well you are doing compared to last year.

3.2c The Cash-Flow Statement Tracks Where Your Money Came From and Went

The **cash-flow (or income and expense) statement** summarizes the total amounts that have been received and spent over a period of time, usually one month or one year. It shows whether you were able to live within your income during that time period, and it reflects the flow of funds in and out.

A cash-flow statement includes three sections: income (total income received); **expenses** (total expenditures made); and **surplus** (or **net gain** or **net income**), when total income exceeds total expenses, or **deficit** (or **net loss**), when expenses exceed income. Such statements are usually prepared on a **cash basis**,* meaning the only transactions recorded are those involving actual cash received or cash that was spent.

Income/Cash Coming In: Where Your Money Comes From You may think of income as simply what is earned from salaries or wages, but there are other types of income that you should include on a cash-flow statement, such as the following:

- Bonuses and commissions
- Child support and alimony
- Public assistance
- Social Security benefits
- Pension and profit-sharing income
- Scholarships and grants
- Interest and dividends received (from savings accounts, investments, bonds, or loans to others)
- Income from the sale of assets
- Other income (gifts, tax refunds, rent, royalties, capital gains)

Expenses/Cash Going Out: Where Your Money Goes All expenditures made during the period covered by the cash-flow statement should be included in the expenses section. The number and type of expenses shown will vary for each individual and family. Many people categorize expenses according to whether they are fixed or variable.

Fixed expenses are usually paid in the same amount during each time period, and they are typically inflexible and often contractual. Examples of such expenses include rent payments and automobile installment loans. It usually takes quite an effort to reduce a fixed expense.

cash-flow statement (or income and expense statement)
Summary of all income and expense transactions over a specific time period.

expenses
Total expenditures made in a specified time such as reported on a cash-flow statement.

surplus (or net gain or net income)
When total income exceeds total expenses such as reported on a cash-flow statement.

deficit
When expenses exceed income on a cash-flow statement.

cash basis
Only transactions involving actual cash received or cash spent are recorded.

DO IT IN CLASS

fixed expenses
Expenses often in the same amount that recur at fixed intervals.

*An alternative method is **accrual-basis budgeting** that recognizes earnings and expenditures when money is earned and expenditures are incurred, regardless of when money is actually received or paid.

variable expenses (or flexible expenses)
Expenses over which you have substantial control.

Variable expenses (or **flexible expenses**) are expenditures over which an individual has considerable control. Food, entertainment, and clothing are variable expenses. Some categories, such as savings, can be listed twice, as both fixed and variable expenses. The following are examples of fixed and variable expenses that you might include in a cash-flow statement:

Fixed Expenses

- Savings and investments
- Retirement contributions to 401(k) plan and IRA account
- Housing (rent, mortgage, loan payment)
- Automobile (installment payment, lease)
- Insurance (health, life, liability, disability, renter's, homeowner's, automobile)
- Installment loan payments (appliances, furniture, electronics)
- Internet service
- Telephone payments
- Taxes (federal income, state income, local income, real estate, Social Security, Medicare, personal property)

Variable Expenses

- Meals (at home and away)
- Utilities (cell phone, electricity, water, gas)
- Transportation (gasoline and maintenance, licenses, registration, public transportation, tolls)
- Medical expenses
- Child care (nursery, baby-sitting)
- Lunches at work
- Dry cleaning
- Clothing and accessories (jewelry, shoes, handbags)
- Snacks (candy, soft drinks, other beverages)
- Education (tuition, fees, books, supplies)
- Household furnishings (furniture, appliances, curtains)
- Cable television
- Personal care (beauty shop, barbershop, cosmetics, dry cleaner)
- Entertainment and recreation (hobbies, socializing, health club, downloads, movie rentals, movies)
- Charitable contributions (gifts, church, school, charities)
- Magazine subscriptions
- Vacations and long weekends
- Credit card payments
- Savings and investments
- Miscellaneous (postage, books, magazines, newspapers, personal allowances, domestic help, membership fees)

When reducing variable expenses, cut back or eliminate overpriced items like café lattes and make bigger budget cuts elsewhere.

There is no rigid list of categories to be used in the expenses section, but you do need to classify all of your expenditures in some way that suits your needs. Rather than just use fixed and variable expenses categories, you might also separate expenditures into savings/investments, debts, insurance, taxes, and household expenses. The more specific your categories, the deeper your understanding of your outlays.

Ridy/Shutterstock.com

Cash Surplus (or Cash Deficit) The surplus (deficit) section shows the amount of cash remaining after you have itemized income and subtracted expenditures from income, as illustrated by the following calculations using Equation (3.2), the **surplus/deficit formula.** A business would call this amount its net profit or net loss.

$$\text{Surplus (deficit)} = \text{total income} - \text{total expenses}$$

or

$$\$1{,}100 \text{ surplus} = \$12{,}500 - \$11{,}400$$
$$(\$800 \text{ deficit}) = \$14{,}900 - \$15{,}700$$

(3.2)

A surplus demonstrates that you are managing your financial resources successfully and do not have to use savings or borrow money to make financial ends meet. When the calculation shows a surplus, that amount is then available (in your checking and savings accounts) to spend, save, invest, or donate. A surplus is not really cash lying around on the kitchen table; it is the cash value reflected in the accounts on your balance sheet. Figure 3-3 shows the typical personal financial situation over the life cycle in present value dollars, from the wealth accumulation years through retirement.

Sample Cash-Flow Statements Table 3-3 shows the cash-flow statement for a couple with two children (Victor and Maria Hernandez). It vividly highlights the additional income needed to rear children and shows the increased variety of expenditures that characterize a family's (rather than an individual's) lifestyle. As a person earns more income, the cash-flow statement usually becomes more involved and detailed.

DID YOU KNOW

Money Websites

Informative websites are:

- Buxfer
- CNNMoney
- HelloWallet
- LearnVest
- Manilla
- Mint
- Mvelopes
- Pageonce

DO IT IN CLASS

surplus
When total income exceeds total expenses on a cash-flow statement.

Figure 3-3   **Personal Finance over the Life Cycle**

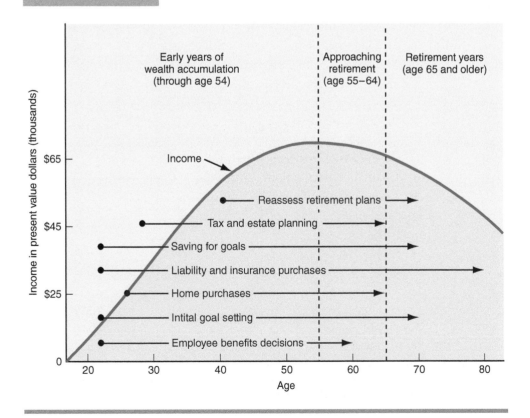

Table 3-3	**Cash Flow Statement for a Couple with Two Children—Victor and Maria Hernandez, January 1–December 31, 2018**

	Dollars	**Percent**
INCOME		
Victor's gross salary	53,000	55.4%
Maria's gross salary	32,000	33.4%
Interest and dividends	1,800	1.9%
Bonus	1,000	1.0%
Tax refunds	200	0.2%
Net rental income	7,720	8.1%
Total Income	**95,720**	**100.0%**
EXPENDITURES		
Fixed Expenses		
Mortgage loan payments	14,400	15.0%
Real estate taxes	4,800	5.0%
Homeowner's insurance	1,200	1.3%
Automobile loan payments	6,000	6.3%
Automobile insurance and registration	2,100	2.2%
Life insurance premiums	1,200	1.3%
Medical insurance (employee portion)	2,800	2.9%
Emergency fund savings	2,400	2.5%
Revolving savings fund	1,800	1.9%
Federal income taxes	10,000	10.4%
State income taxes	2,600	2.7%
City income taxes	600	0.6%
Social Security taxes	6,500	6.8%
Personal property taxes	1,020	1.1%
Retirement IRAs	6,000	6.3%
Total Fixed Expenses	**$63,420**	**66.3%**
Variable Expenses		
Food	7,000	7.3%
Utilities	3,600	3.8%
Gasoline and maintenance	4,200	4.4%
Medical expenses	3,400	3.6%
Medicines	1,750	1.8%
Clothing and upkeep	1,950	2.0%
Church	2,400	2.5%
Gifts	1,400	1.5%
Personal allowances	3,000	3.1%
Children's allowances	3,200	3.3%
Miscellaneous	400	0.4%
Total Variable Expenses	**$32,300**	**33.7%**
Total Expenses	**$95,720**	**100.0%**
SURPLUS (DEFICIT)	**$ 0**	**0.0%**

DID YOU KNOW

Ratios for Evaluating One's Financial Progress

Financial ratios are numerical calculations designed to simplify the process of evaluating your financial strength and the progress of your financial condition. Ratios serve as tools or yardsticks to develop saving, spending, and credit-use patterns consistent with your goals. They are illustrated below using data from the Hernandez family shown in Table 3-2 and Table 3-3. Calculators for These ratios can be found on the **Garman/Forgue** companion website.

DO IT IN CLASS

Ratio	Question It Answers	Calculation	Example	Explanation
Liquidity Ratio	Do I have enough liquidity to pay for emergencies?	Monetary assets divided by monthly expenses	$12,750/$7,977 = 1.58 ratio or about 1 1/2 months	The number of months in which living expenses can be paid should an emergency arise; 3 to 6 months is preferred.
Asset-to-Debt Ratio	Do I have enough assets to meet my debt obligations?	Total assets/total debt	$393,250/$101,520 = 3.873 or a 3.9 to 1 ratio	Provides a broad measure of one's financial liquidity; a high ratio is desirable.
Debt-to-Income Ratio	Is my total debt burden too high?	Annual debt repayments/gross income ×100	$20,400/$95,720 = 21.31%	Compares amount spent on debt repayments to gross income; should be 36 or less and it should decline as one grows older.
Debt Payments-to-Disposable Income Ratio	Is my non-mortgage debt too stressful?	Monthly non-mortgage debt payments/monthly disposable (not gross) income	$500/$6,102 = 0.082 or 8.2%	Estimates funds available for debt repayment; 14 percent or less is desirable and 15 percent or more is problematic.
Investment Assets-to-Total Assets Ratio	Am I saving/investing enough?	Investment assets/total assets	$170,000/$393,250 = 0.432 or 43.2%	How well is one advancing toward their financial goals; ratio of 10 for people in their 20s, 11 to 30 for those in their 30s, and 31 or higher for older adults.

CONCEPT CHECK 3.2

1. Define the balance sheet and give two examples of how to increase one's net worth
2. Define the *cash-flow statement* and explain what it does.
3. How should assets and liabilities be valued for the balance sheet, and why?
4. Distinguish between fixed and variable expenses, and give two examples of each.
5. Which two financial ratios for evaluating financial progress do you like, and why?

financial ratios

Calculations designed to simplify evaluation of financial strength and progress.

3.3 COLLECT AND ORGANIZE YOUR FINANCIAL RECORDS TO SAVE TIME AND MONEY

Learning Objective 3

Collect and organize the financial records necessary for managing your personal finances.

Financial records are documents that evidence financial transactions, such as bills, receipts, credit card receipts and statements, bank records, tax returns, brokerage statements, and paycheck stubs. Your financial records will help determine where you are, where you have been, and where you are going financially. They also help you save

financial records

Documents that evidence financial transactions.

money as well as make money. Good records enable you to review the results of financial transactions as well as permit other family members to find them in an emergency. Organized records help you take advantage of all available tax deductions when filing income taxes and provide you with more dollars to spend, save, invest, or donate.

Table 3-4 shows categories of financial records and the contents that might be included in each. Many people keep duplicates of important records in an envelope at their workplace or with relatives because the likelihood of records at both locations being stolen or destroyed simultaneously is very small. You can purge or shred some of your records when you no longer need them, such as non-tax-related checks and credit card receipts more than a year old, out-of-date warranties, expired insurance policies for which there will be no claims, and records from automobiles you no longer own.

Some records may be safely stored at home in a fire-resistant file cabinet or a safe. Other records should be kept in a **safe-deposit box.** Safe-deposit boxes are secured lock boxes available for rent ($25 to $250 per year) in banks. Two keys are used to open such a box. The customer keeps one key, and the bank holds the other.

Table 3-4   Financial Records: What to Keep and Where

Category	Contents	
	In Home Files and Fireproof Home Safe	**In Safe-Deposit Box**
Financial plans/ budgeting	Financial plans Balance sheets and cash-flow statements Current budget List of safe-deposit box contents Names and contact information for financial advisers	Names and contact information for financial advisers Copy of written financial plans, goals, and budgets
Career and employment	Current resume College transcripts Letters of recommendation Employee benefits descriptions Written career plans	Employer retirement plan correspondence
Banking and financial services	Checkbook, unused checks, and canceled checks List of locations and account numbers for all bank accounts Checking and savings account statements Locations and access numbers for safe-deposit boxes Account transaction receipts	List of financial institutions and account numbers for all financial services accounts Certificates of deposit
Taxes	Copies of all income tax returns, both state and federal, for the past three years, including all supporting documentation Receipts for all donations of cash or property Log of volunteer expenses Receipts for property taxes paid	Copies of all income tax filings, both state and federal, for the past three years Records of securities purchased and sold
Credit	Utility and telephone bills Monthly credit card statements Receipts of credit payments List of credit accounts and telephone numbers to report lost/stolen cards Unused credit cards Credit reports and scores	List of credit accounts and telephone numbers to report lost/stolen cards Loan discharge notice when it is paid off Credit card bills for seven years if they support tax deductions

Table 3-4 **Financial Records: What to Keep and Where (*Continued*)**

Category	Contents	
	In Home Files and Fireproof Home Safe	**In Safe-Deposit Box**
Housing, vehicles, and consumer purchases	Copies of legal documents (leases, mortgage, deeds, titles) Property appraisals and inspection reports Home repair/home improvement receipts Warranties Owner's manuals for purchases Auto registration records Vehicle service and repair receipts Receipts for important purchases	Original legal documents (leases, mortgage, deeds, titles) Copies of property appraisals Vehicle purchase contracts (until vehicle is sold) Photographs or videos of valuable possessions
Insurance	Original insurance policies List of insurance policies with premium amounts and due dates Premium payment receipts Calculation of life insurance needs Insurance claims forms and reports Medical records for family, including immunization records and list of prescription drugs	List of all insurance policies with company and agent names and addresses and policy numbers Listing with photographs or videotape of personal property
Investments	Records of stock, bond, and mutual fund transactions and certificate numbers Mutual fund statements Statements from brokers Reports from financial planner Company annual reports Retirement plan quarterly and annual reports Documents on business interests Written investment philosophy Written investment strategies	Contact information for all investment needs Stock and bond certificates Rare coins, stamps, and other collectibles
Retirement and Estate Planning	Pension and retirement plan information Retirement statements Copies of all retirement plan transactions Copy of Social Security card Trust agreements Information on Social Security Copies of advance directives (wills, living wills, medical powers of attorney, durable powers of attorney with originals kept with physician/attorney) Copies of trust documents (originals with executor, trustees/attorney)	Extra copies of all retirement plan transactions and statements Social Security statements (newest one) Copy of will (original of all estate planning documents should be kept in attorney's office)
Personal information	Copy of birth certificate and marriage license Religious documents Copy of divorce decree, property settlement, and custody agreement Receipts for alimony and child support payments Custodial information for your children, relatives, and/or elderly parent	Passports while not being used Military and adoption papers Originals of birth, marriage, death certificates Originals of Social Security cards Originals of divorce decrees, property settlements, and custody agreements Master list of all important documents and their location Flash drive or CD containing soft copies of many financial records (update once a year)

CONCEPT CHECK 3.3

1. List some advantages of keeping good financial records.
2. Name three financial records that might be best kept in a safe-deposit box or in an envelope at a safe place like at work.

3.4 MONEY TOPICS TO DISCUSS WITH A PARTNER

When you find the right partner, agree to be fully transparent on all financial matters (such as income, assets, debts), and then consider doing the following:

- **Live on one salary and bank all or most of the other.** It is wrong to assume that you will always have the earning of two people. Job loss, career change, family matters, and additional schooling are income interruptions. (See Chapter 1.)

- **Live beneath your rising means.** Leave your spending as it is by budgeting, paying down student debt and credit cards and boosting your savings. Living in a home too big for your needs or driving a vehicle more luxurious than you require will set you back financially. You can still enjoy a gradually improving lifestyle as long as you keep the pace just a tad below your rising income. (See Chapters 2 and 3.)

- **Talk with your partner regularly about financial matters.** Marriage counselors say you will fail in your relationship unless you talk about financial goals, issues, and concerns with your significant other. So mark some dates on your calendar and get talking! Discuss personal finances now while they are still "money talks" and not "money fights." Suggestions on how are in Chapter 5.

- **Tell your money secrets.** One in five Americans have a secret debt their partner does not know about, or has a secret savings stash or checking account. This is the time to talk about such topics.

- **Create a budget and commit to creating an emergency fund.** Understanding how much money comes in and goes out is critical before you begin to spend your money. Getting an emergency fund started quickly takes care of those situations.

- **Max out your retirement savings separately.** Contribute the maximum amount to your retirement plan at work, of more than the match amount. Save no less than 10 percent of your income for each individual. (See Chapters 1 and 17.)

- **Coordinate employee benefits.** Couples often have two incomes so each has a menu of employee benefits from which to choose. One may drop a benefit that is being received via the other's plan. (See Chapters 1 and 2.)

- **Update life insurance coverage.** Focus on term life insurance for the bulk of each of your needs. (See Chapter 12.)

- **Review auto and homeowner's/renter's insurance coverages.** Double check coverage on your vehicles and your personal property. (See Chapter 10.)

- **Update names with government agencies.** If one or both partners' names are changed as a result of your new status, you need to notify the Social Security Administration and driver's licensing office of any change. You will need to show your marriage certificate as proof of the change. (See Chapter 17.)

- **Close redundant bank accounts.** Reducing the number of accounts that each partner brings into the marriage can save money on account fees. Decide which accounts are "yours, mine, or ours." (See Chapters 5 and 6 for more on titling accounts correctly.)

- **Check each individual's credit history.** Find out each person's credit score. Order credit reports for each person. If one has a spotty credit record, do not put that person on as the other's "authorized user" because the previous poor history will appear in the report and the credit score will be dinged. (See Chapter 6.)

- **Focus on being debt free.** Find out how much each one owes and his/her plans for paying the debts off. Find funds soon to pay off credit cards, student loans, and other borrowing, which saves interest from being paid out. (See Chapters 6 and 7.)

- **Avoid debts and similar financial commitments.** People often have a high cost of living because they have gone into debt and signed contracts for telephone, Internet, cable, gym memberships, leases, and service contracts. These contracts mess up your financial decision-making. Such people don't need to earn more to save more; they just need to avoid debt commitments. (See Chapters 6 and 7.)

- **Decide on how to manage money.** Decide on who pays what bills and who makes investment decisions as well as whether or not each person will have individual control over certain money. Who pays for the debt that precedes the relationship. Who pays for gift giving. What money tasks will you do together, such as establishing annual financial goals, making purchases with debt, cost of a wedding, and agreeing on establishing a "slush fund" account with an agreed upon amount, like $200 or less, that can be spent with no questions asked by the other person. (See Chapter 5.)

- **Update estate transfer plans.** With a new "number one" in your life, you should change (or set up) your will and all transfers by contracts (life insurance, mutual funds, and retirement accounts) or property owner designation, and payable-on-death designations, trusts, and advance directives. (See Chapters 11 and 17.)

- **Change beneficiaries.** Life insurance policies, mutual fund accounts, and retirement accounts all have beneficiaries (the people who will receive the funds at your death) named when you set them up. (See Chapters 11 and 17.)

- **Invest in yourselves.** Without furthering your education, there will be nothing to distinguish you from others and no reason for you to be promoted or paid more. (See Chapters 1 and 2.)

- **Keep up to date on money matters.** Stay current on what you need to know to be successful in personal finance. Realize that without good management, your knowledge will not grow into what you would like it to be. (See Chapters 1–17.)

CONCEPT CHECK 3.4

1. Identify two money topics you think might be valuable to discuss with a partner.
2. Identify two money topics that you think might present some challenges when discussing them with a partner.

3.5 REACHING YOUR GOALS THROUGH BUDGETING: YOUR SPENDING/ SAVINGS ACTION PLAN

Learning Objective 5
Achieve your financial goals through budgeting.

Figure 3-4 illustrates how to think about financial statements and budgeting in terms of the past, present, and future. The past is reflected in the cash-flow statement as it focuses on *where you have been* financially. The present is shown in the balance sheet as it shows *where you are* financially at the current time. The future is reflected in the budget as it indicates *where you want to go*.

Your financial success is largely a matter of choice, not a matter of chance. Your budget is where you make and implement those choices. A **budget** is a paper or electronic document used to record both planned and actual income and expenditures over a period of time. Your budget represents the major mechanism through which your financial plans are carried out and goals are achieved.

budget
Paper or electronic document used to record both planned and actual income and expenditures over a period of time.

Your budget is your plan for spending and saving. Budgeting forces you to consider what is important in your life, what things you want to own, how you want to live, what it will take to do that, and, more generally, what you want to achieve in life. The budgeting process gives you control over your finances, and it empowers you to achieve your financial goals while simultaneously (and successfully) confronting any unforeseen events. Budgeting also reduces stress because making and following a budget helps you get more of what you want.

Budgeting today requires little effort. When you have online budgeting apps and can log into your bank statement at any time, it is easier than ever to track your spending. There is no excuse for not budgeting.

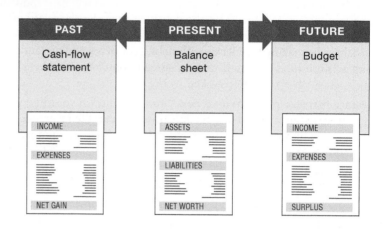

Figure 3-4 **About Financial Statements and Budgets**

PAST	PRESENT	FUTURE
Cash-flow statement	Balance sheet	Budget
INCOME	ASSETS	INCOME
EXPENSES	LIABILITIES	EXPENSES
NET GAIN	NET WORTH	SURPLUS

NEVER EVER

Get Stressed About Money!

Never ever get stressed about money matters. However, money is the number one source of stress among Americans. People worry more about money than about work, family, or health. Three-quarters are worried about money some of the time and another quarter are stressed about finances all the time. Manage your money well and you will not be stressed about your personal finances.

long-term goals

Financial targets to achieve more than five years in the future.

intermediate-term goals

Financial targets that can be achieved within one to five years.

short-term goals

Financial targets or ends that can be achieved in less than a year.

Some people do all their budgeting mentally—and do so successfully. Good for them! Many of us, however, need to see the actual numbers on paper or on a computer screen. Creating and following a budget has three stages: before, during, and after.

3.5a Action Before: Set Financial Goals

Before establishing your budget, take action to set financial goals. **Long-term goals** are financial targets or ends that an individual or family wants to achieve perhaps more than five years in the future. Such goals provide direction for overall financial planning as well as shorter-term budgeting. An example of a long-term goal is to create a $1 million retirement fund by age 60. Goals must be specific. They should contain dollar-amount targets and specific dates for achievement.

Establishing unrealistic short-term goals sets up a high likelihood of failure. Instead, set financial targets that are almost too easy to meet. For example, Michael Philpot, of Huntsville, Alabama, wants to save $500 per month to use as a down payment on a home in five years. Michael might start perhaps rather painlessly by saving $100 per month for a few months. Then put away $150 for two months, $200 for two months, then $250, then $300, and finally $500 so that by the end of the first year he is almost on target.

Intermediate-term goals are financial targets that can be achieved between one year and perhaps three to five years. Examples of intermediate-term goals are creating an emergency fund amounting to three to six months of income within four years, saving $30,000 within three years for a down payment on a home, taking a $5,000 vacation to Asia in two years, paying off $4,000 in credit card debt in one-and-a-half years, and paying off a $12,000 college loan in five years.

Short-term goals are financial targets or ends that can be achieved in less than a year, such as finishing college, paying off an auto loan, increasing savings, purchasing assets (i.e., vehicle, furniture, television, iPhone, stereo, clothes), reducing high-interest debt, taking an annual vacation, attending a wedding, and buying life insurance.

You need to be as clear as possible about what your financial goals are. The goals worksheet in Figure 3-5 provides examples of how much to save to reach long-, intermediate-, and short-term goals. People can view such savings as a fixed expenditure (such as automatically withholding from a paycheck to contribute to an employer's retirement

Figure 3-5   Goals Worksheet for Harry and Belinda Johnson

Date worksheet prepared January 1, 2018					
1	2	3	4	5	6
LONG-TERM GOALS	AMOUNT NEEDED	MONTH/YEAR NEEDED*	MONTHS TO SAVE	DATE TO START SAVING	MONTHLY AMOUNT TO SAVE (2/4)
Home down payment	$30,000	Aug. 2023	60	Aug. '18	$500

Date worksheet prepared January 1, 2018					
1	2	3	4	5	6
INTERMEDIATE-TERM GOALS	AMOUNT NEEDED	MONTH/YEAR NEEDED*	MONTHS TO SAVE	DATE TO START SAVING	MONTHLY AMOUNT TO SAVE (2/4)
European vacation	$6,000	Jul. 2020	30	Jan. '18	$200
New vehicle down payment	5,000	Oct. 2021	45	Jan. '18	111

Date worksheet prepared January 1, 2018					
1	2	3	4	5	6
SHORT-TERM GOALS	AMOUNT NEEDED	MONTH/YEAR NEEDED*	MONTHS TO SAVE	DATE TO START SAVING	MONTHLY AMOUNT TO SAVE (2/4)
House fund	$6,000	Dec. 2018	6	Jun. '18	$500
European vacation fund	2,400	Dec. 2018	12	Jan. '18	200
Summer vacation fund	1,200	Jul. 2018	6	Jan. '18	200
Anniversary dinner party	500	Dec. 2018	12	Jan. '18	42
Emergency fund	2,400	Dec. 2018	12	Jan. '18	200

*Goals requiring five years or more to achieve require consideration of investment return and after-tax yield, which will be discussed in Chapter 4.

plan or to transfer to a savings account). Additional savings, such as saving what is left over after all expenditures are made, will be a variable expense.

Prioritizing your goals makes sense. But what are your most important goals? One certain priority should be to pay off high-interest credit cards as soon as possible because paying 18 percent interest is foolish. Another is to contribute as much as you can afford to a retirement plan at least up until you receive the employer's full matching contribution.

Many college graduates buy a new car soon after getting their first job to celebrate having "made it." Before you're lured into the same fate, give careful consideration to your priorities and remember that every action carries not only the dollar cost of the action taken but also the opportunity cost of the alternatives forgone. To achieve your long-term goals, you may have to sacrifice by deferring some of your short-term desires. Thus, you might consider buying a used car or a low-cost new one.

THERE IS AN APP FOR THAT!

Some of the best apps are:

- Level Money
- Mint
- ReadyforZero
- Splitwise
- You Need a Budget

3.5b Action Before: Make and Reconcile Budget Estimates

In the process of making and reconciling budget estimates of income and expenditures, before the month begins you need to identify how you are spending money now. Then you can resolve conflicting needs and wants by revising estimates as necessary. You cannot have everything in life—especially this month—even though you might want it.

budget estimates

Projected dollar amounts to receive or spend in a budgeting period.

take-home pay/disposable income

Pay received after employer withholdings for such things as taxes, insurance, and union dues.

discretionary or controllable expenses

Money left over after necessities such as housing and food are paid for.

Budget Estimates Gets You from Gross Income to What's Available for Variable Expenses Budget estimates are the projected dollar amounts in a budget that one plans to receive or spend during the period covered by the budget. Begin by estimating total gross income from all sources. For example, Boston's Trevor Noah's annual gross income is $60,000. Typical withholdings from his paycheck and noted as percentages of gross income are: federal income taxes (12%), Social Security taxes (8%), state income taxes (6%), and health insurance premiums (5%). This totals 31% leaving Trevor with 69% in **take-home pay** (also called **disposable income**). This is the pay received after employer withholdings for such things as taxes and insurance. Trevor also contributes 6 percent to his employer's retirement plan and another 5 percent to a Roth IRA, and this reduces his true net income another 11 percent resulting in a total of 42 percent going out. That leaves his with 58 percent, and it is available for budgeting for spending, saving, investing, and donating.

Next Trevor subtracts money for fixed expenses, such as rent (20%) and emergency savings (5%). This totals (25%) for **discretionary** or **controllable expenses**, which make up the bulk of money available to pay for one's various expenses. After paying his fixed expenses Trevor has 33% of his pay left to spend (100% − 42% − 25%) for such variable items as food, electricity, Internet, telephone, cable television, gasoline and maintenance, church and charity, entertainment, and miscellaneous.

Table 3-5 presents budget estimates for a college student, a single working person, a young married couple, a married couple with two young children, and a married couple with two college-age children. The college student's budget requires monthly withdrawals of previously deposited savings to make ends meet. The single working person's budget allows for a vehicle loan, but not much else. The young married couple's budget permits one vehicle loan, an investment program, contributions to retirement accounts, and significant spending on food and entertainment. The budget of the married couple with two young children allows for only an inexpensive vehicle loan payment even though one spouse has a part-time job to help with the finances. The budget of the married couple with two college-age children permits a home mortgage payment, ownership of two paid-for vehicles, savings and investment programs, and a substantial contribution for future college expenses.

It is essential to make reasonable budget estimates. If you have seven holiday gifts to buy and expect to spend $50 for each, it is easy to make an estimate of $350. If you want to go out to dinner once each week with a friend at $60 per meal, estimate an expense of $240 per month. Avoid using unrealistically low figures by simply being fair and honest in your estimates. Then add up your totals.

Revise Budget Estimates to Create a "Balanced Budget" When trying to make your spending conform to your budget goals, sometimes you will find the math is alarming! And you will want to quit. But you must continue.

When initial expense estimates exceed income estimates, three choices are available: (1) earn more income, (2) cut back on expenses, or (3) try a combination of more income and fewer expenses. The process of reconciling needs and wants is a healthy exercise. It helps identify your priorities by telling you what is important in your life at the current time, and it identifies areas of sacrifice that you might make. Revision of your short-term financial goals may also be required.

YOUR GRANDPARENTS SAY

"Cut the Dollars AND the Pennies"

"If you are spending $5 per day on fancy coffee, you will spend $1,250 per year ($5 per day = $25 per week × 50 weeks = 200 workdays). When reducing variable expenses, cut back or eliminate things like café lattes, overpriced vitamin water, and frequent treats, and make bigger budget cuts elsewhere, like in housing, vehicles, insurance, food, preschool, and health care."

Table 3-5 Sample Monthly Budgets for Various Family Units

Classifications	College Student	Single Working Person	Young Married Couple	Married Couple with Two Young Children	Married Couple with Two College-Age Children
INCOME					
Salary 1	$1,000	$4,400	$4,000	$4,000	$8,000
Salary 2	0	0	4,800	4,400	1,600
Interest and dividends	2	20	30	30	80
Student loan withdrawals	300	0	0	0	0
Savings withdrawals	570	0	0	0	0
Total Income	**$1,872**	**$4,420**	**$8,830**	**$8,430**	**$9,680**
EXPENSES					
Fixed Expenses					
401(k) retirement savings	$ 0	$ 70	$ 250	$ 380	$ 500
IRA and Roth IRA contributions	0	20	360	0	200
Savings automatically withheld	0	20	60	0	400
Housing	700	1,100	1,300	1,200	900
Health insurance	0	220	200	500	280
State income taxes	0	40	80	60	80
Life and disability insurance	0	0	60	90	40
Homeowner/renter insurance	0	20	120	140	100
Automobile insurance	0	80	110	180	170
Vehicle loan payments	0	310	390	400	300
Emergency savings	0	50	125	200	200
Student loan payments	0	300	500	300	200
Loans	0	80	220	120	200
Credit card payment	0	40	130	0	200
Federal income taxes	0	670	1080	850	1,000
Social Security taxes	60	340	670	640	730
Real estate taxes	0	0	300	390	330
Investments	0	0	135	100	400
Total fixed expenses	**$ 760**	**$3,360**	**$6,090**	**$5,550**	**$6,230**
Variable expenses					
Other savings	0	20	130	20	200
Food	180	330	500	600	580
Utilities	40	160	230	240	290
Automobile gas, oil, maintenance	0	90	360	300	320
Medical expenses	10	30	80	110	150
Child care	0	0	0	600	0
Clothing	20	50	100	90	150
Gifts and charitable contributions	10	20	80	80	120
Personal allowances	80	150	400	350	500
Education expenses	600	0	0	0	0
Furnishings and appliances	10	10	130	50	70
Personal care	10	70	80	30	120
Entertainment	120	110	300	300	500
Vacations	17	0	150	60	250
Miscellaneous	15	20	200	50	200
Total variable expenses	**$1,112**	**$1,060**	**$2,740**	**$2,880**	**$3,450**
Total Expenses	**$1,872**	**$4,420**	**$8,830**	**$8,430**	**$9,680**

You must reconcile conflicting wants to revise your budget until total expenses do not exceed income. Perhaps you can change some "must have" items to "maybe next year" purchases. Perhaps you can keep some quality items but reduce their quantity. For example, instead of $240 for four meals for you and a friend at restaurants each month, consider dining out twice each month at $70 per evening out. You'll save $100 a month and still have two really nice meals. Your actions on money matters override your words, so act accordingly. Eventually you will finalize your "balanced budget" by making sure planned income equals or exceeds projected expenses.

Unfinished Budget Estimates for Harry and Belinda　Table 3-6 presents the projected annual budget for Harry and Belinda Johnson and reflects their efforts to reconcile their budget estimates. Wisely Harry and Belinda are "paying themselves first." They plan to save about $200 a month in an emergency fund, put away $500 per month to save to buy their own home, save for holiday and summer vacations as well as their planned anniversary party. They also contribute to both their retirement plans at work. However, the Johnsons have failed to complete their budget because their total planned expenses show negative balances especially in the latter months of the year. The Johnsons have a little ways to go to fully reconcile their annual budget estimates.

3.5c　Action Before Budgeting Period: Plan Cash Flows

Before the month begins, you plan your cash flows or where the money will go. Income usually remains somewhat constant month after month, but expenses do rise and fall, sometimes sharply. As a result, people occasionally complain that they are "broke, out of money, and sick of budgeting." This challenge can be anticipated by using a cash-flow calendar and eliminated by using a revolving savings fund.

cash-flow calendar

Budget estimates for monthly income and expenses.

Cash Flow Calendar for Harry and Belinda Johnson　The budget estimates for monthly income and expenses in Table 3-6 have been recast in summary form in Table 3-7, providing a **cash-flow calendar** for the Johnsons. Annual estimated income and expenses are recorded in this calendar for each budgeting time period in an effort to identify surplus or deficit situations. In the Johnsons' case, planned annual expenses exceeds income but they are short in November and December. The couple's year has 10 months of income better than expenses, and then they face planned monthly deficits. The budget still needs work.

Effective management of cash flow can involve curtailing expenses during months with financial deficits, increasing income, using savings, or borrowing. If you borrow money and pay finance charges, the credit costs will further increase your monthly expenses.

revolving savings fund

Variable budgeting tool that places funds in savings to cover emergency or higher-than-usual expenses.

Revolving Savings Fund for Irregular Expenses for Harry and Belinda Johnson　For this reason alone, it is smart to "borrow from yourself" by using a **revolving savings fund**. This is a variable expense classification budgeting tool into which funds are allocated in an effort to create savings that can be used to pay certain expenses that balances the budget so as to avoid running out of money. Establishing such a fund involves planning ahead—much like a college student does when saving money all summer (creating a revolving savings fund) to draw down during the school months.

You establish a revolving savings fund for two purposes: (1) to accumulate funds for large nonmonthly irregular expenses, such as automobile insurance premiums and holiday gifts; and (2) to meet occasional deficits due to income fluctuations.

Examples of Irregular Expenses　Having a revolving saving fund eliminates the most common complaint people offer about their personal finances: They cannot pay irregular bills when they come in. These are not the occasional emergency vehicle repair bill; use your emergency savings fund for that expense. Examples of irregular expenses include twice-a-year auto insurance bill, vacations, travel, tuition and fees, vehicle tag

Table 3-6   2018 Unfinished Annual Budget Estimates for Harry and Belinda Johnson

	Jan.	Feb.	Mar.	Apr.	May	June	July	Aug.	Sept.	Oct.	Nov.	Dec.	Yearly Total	Monthly Averages
INCOME														
Harry's salary	4,080	4,080	4,080	4,080	4,080	4,080	4,080	4,080	4,080	4,080	4,080	4,080	48,960	4,080.00
Belinda's salary	6,400	6,400	6,400	6,400	6,400	6,400	6,400	6,400	6,400	6,400	6,400	6,400	76,800	6,400.00
Interest	30	30	30	30	30	30	30	30	30	30	30	30	360	30.00
Income from trust	0	0	0	0	0	0	0	3,000	0	0	0	0	3,000	250.00
TOTAL INCOME	10,510	10,510	10,510	10,510	10,510	10,510	10,510	13,510	10,510	10,510	10,510	10,510	129,120	10,760.00
EXPENSES														
Fixed Expenses														
Rent	1,600	1,600	1,600	1,600	1,600	1,600	1,700	1,700	1,700	1,700	1,700	1,700	19,800	1,650.00
Health insurance	300	300	300	300	300	300	350	350	350	350	350	350	3,900	325.00
Life insurance	20	20	20	20	20	20	20	20	20	20	20	20	240	20.00
Home purchase fund	0	0	0	0	0	0	0	500	500	500	500	500	2,500	208.33
Renter's insurance	0	0	0	0	0	0	0	220	0	0	0	0	220	18.33
Automobile insurance	0	0	0	0	0	600	0	0	0	0	0	600	1,200	100.00
Auto loan payments	490	490	490	490	490	490	490	490	490	490	490	490	5,880	490.00
Student loan payments	300	300	300	300	300	300	300	300	300	300	300	300	3,600	300.00
Savings/emergencies	100	100	100	100	100	100	100	100	100	100	100	100	1,200	100.00
Harry's retirement plan	195	195	195	195	195	195	195	195	195	195	195	195	2,340	195.00
Belinda's retirement plan	400	400	400	400	400	400	400	400	400	400	400	400	4,800	400.00
Cable TV and Internet	160	160	160	160	160	160	160	160	160	160	160	160	1,920	160.00
Federal income taxes	1,700	1,700	1,700	1,700	1,700	1,700	1,700	1,700	1,700	1,700	1,700	1,700	20,400	1,700.00
State income taxes	500	500	500	500	500	500	500	500	500	500	500	500	6,000	500.00
Social security taxes	800	800	800	800	800	800	800	800	800	800	800	800	9,600	800.00
Automobile registration	0	0	0	0	0	0	0	0	0	0	300	0	300	25.00
Total fixed expenses	6,565	6,565	6,565	6,565	6,565	7,165	6,715	7,435	7,215	7,215	7,515	7,815	83,900	6,991.67
Variable Expenses														
Savings money market	0	0	0	0	0	0	400	3,000	0	0	0	0	3,400	283.33
Revolving savings fund	250	250	210	250	190	0	240	0	200	190	0	0	1,780	148.33
Food (home)	550	550	550	550	550	550	550	550	550	550	550	550	6,600	550.00
Food (out)	300	300	300	300	300	300	300	300	300	300	300	300	3,600	300.00
Utilities	220	220	220	220	220	220	220	220	220	220	220	220	2,640	220.00
Cell phones	110	110	110	110	110	110	110	110	110	110	110	110	1,320	110.00
Auto gas repairs	220	220	220	220	220	220	220	220	220	220	220	220	2,640	220.00
Doctor/dentist/ out-of-pocket	100	100	100	100	100	100	100	100	100	100	100	100	1,200	100.00
Medicines	60	60	60	60	60	60	60	60	60	60	60	60	720	60.00
Clothing and upkeep	170	170	170	170	170	170	170	170	170	170	170	170	2,040	170.00
Church and charity	100	100	100	100	100	60	100	100	100	100	100	100	1,160	96.67
Gifts	80	80	110	75	140	0	120	60	60	50	400	300	1,475	122.92
Public transportation	160	160	160	160	160	160	160	160	160	160	160	160	1,920	160.00
Personal allowances	500	500	500	500	500	500	500	500	500	500	500	500	6,000	500.00
Entertainment	150	150	150	150	150	150	150	150	150	150	150	150	1,800	150.00
European vacation	400	400	400	400	400	400	200	200	200	200	200	200	3,600	300.00
Summer vacation	200	200	200	200	200	200	0	0	0	0	0	0	1,200	100.00
Anniversary dinner party	42	42	42	42	42	42	42	42	42	42	40	40	500	41.67
Miscellaneous	100	100	100	100	100	100	100	100	100	100	100	100	1,200	100.00
Total variable expenses	3,712	3,712	3,702	3,707	3,712	3,342	3,742	6,042	3,242	3,222	3,380	3,280	44,795	3,732.92
TOTAL EXPENSES	10,277	10,277	10,267	10,272	10,277	10,507	10,457	13,477	10,457	10,437	10,895	11,095	128,695	10,724.58
Difference (available for spending, saving, investing, and donating	233	233	243	238	233	3	53	33	53	73	-385	-585	425	
Revolving savings withdrawals	0	0	0	0	0	0	0	0	0	0	385	585	0	

Table 3-7 Cash-Flow Calendar for Harry and Belinda Johnson

Month	1 Estimated Income	2 Estimated Expenses	3 Surplus/ Deficit (1–2)	4 Cumulative Surplus/Deficit
January	$ 10,510	$ 10,277	$233	$ 233
February	10,510	$ 10,277	233	$ 466
March	10,510	10,267	243	$ 709
April	10,510	10,272	238	$ 947
May	10,510	10,277	233	$1,180
June	10,510	10,507	3	$1,183
July	10,510	10,457	53	$1,236
August	13,510	13,477	33	$1,269
September	10,510	10,457	53	$1,322
October	10,510	10,437	73	$1,395
November	10,510	10,895	−385	$1,010
December	10,510	11,095	−585	$ 425
Total	**$129,120**	**$128,695**	**$425**	

renewal fees, property taxes, back-to-school supplies, vet grooming and checkups, dental cleanings, magazine subscriptions, special haircuts, one-time tickets for whatever, birthdays, and Christmas (travel, decorations, gifts). Table 3-8 shows the Johnsons' revolving savings fund. When preparing their budget, the Johnsons realized that they were going to have significant deficits.

Table 3-8 Revolving Savings Fund for Harry and Belinda Johnson

Month	Large Expenses	Amount Needed	Deposit Into Fund	Withdrawal From Fund	Fund Balance
January		$ 0	$ 250	$ 0	$ 250
February		0	250	0	$ 500
March		0	210	0	$ 710
April		0	250	0	$ 960
May		0	190	0	$1,150
June		0	0	0	$1,150
July	Summer vacation	1,200	240	0	$1,390
August		0	0	0	$1,390
September		0	200	0	$1,590
October		0	190	0	$1,780
November	Gifts/Other	385	0	460	$1,320
December	Dinner Party/Other	585	0	220	$1,100
Total		**$2,170**	**$1,780**	**$680**	**−$390**

Harry and Belinda Discuss Budgeting Alternatives The couple has a number of alternatives: (1) Begin putting into savings all of the planned surpluses of January through June to cover the deficits of November and December; (2) use some of Harry's trust fund income to cover the deficit, (3) dip into their emergency savings in November, and December, and/or (4) utilize credit cards to get through the end-of-year expenses. Ideally, the Johnsons want to have sufficient funds by the end of the year to establish their revolving savings fund for the following 12 months.

The Johnsons disagree about their budget priorities. Belinda wants to spend less on food out and to open a credit card account to pay for the deficits later in the year, while Harry wants to spend less on clothing and entertainment and skip their planned anniversary dinner party. They both wonder how they can earn so much money and still have such challenging budgeting problems. The Johnsons might benefit by considering the suggestions in Chapter 5 (see pages 169–173) on how to talk with a significant other about financial matters. The Johnsons need to discuss their spending priorities and make decisions so they can reconcile their budget estimates for the year. Their

ADVICE FROM A SEASONED PRO

Get-Tough Ways to Cut Spending

If you always run out of money before the month is over, you may need to take some drastic steps to get your finances under control. Consider the following:

1. *Stop paying bank fees by maintaining minimum balances and eliminating overdrafts.*

2. *Stop making ATM withdrawals that assess fees.*

3. *Stop getting cash back from debit or credit card purchases to use for pocket money.*

4. *Spend only cash or money that you have, and leave debit and credit cards at home.*

5. *Stop using credit cards.*

6. *Refinance credit card debt at a credit union.*

7. *Do not eat out.*

8. *Cut back on telephone use if it costs money.*

9. *Avoid paying for entertainment; rather do activities that are free.*

10. *Reduce or stop spending on luxuries such as clothing, movies, entertainment, memberships, hobbies, CDs, DVDs, iTunes, phones, and expanded cable channels.*

11. *Drop landline telephone service and use only a cell phone.*

12. *Find cheaper auto insurance.*

13. *Telephone to ask for a price reduction because cable, telephone, Internet and most other companies will reduce monthly charges when asked.*

14. *Plug your TV and cable box into a power strip and save $10 a month by turning it on only in the evenings.*

15. *Install a programmable thermostat (about $90) to shave as much as 15 percent off your cooling and heating bills.*

16. *Sell or give away all that old stuff you crammed into a storage unit.*

17. *Change income tax withholding to increase take-home pay.*

18. *Take a list when shopping, and stick to it.*

19. *Avoid shopping malls and discount stores.*

20. *Sell an asset, especially one that requires additional expenses, such as a boat or second car.*

21. *Build up an emergency fund of savings even if it means temporarily decreasing retirement-plan contributions.*

22. *Only buy used items.*

23. *Consider making Christmas a "nonspend" holiday.*

24. *Move to lower-cost housing.*

25. *Increase income by working overtime or finding a second job.*

Alena C. Johnson
Utah State University, Logan, Utah

budget is not too far from being perfectly balanced and they only need to discuss and agree upon their priorities and make a few changes.

3.5d Action During the Budgeting Period: Control Spending

budget controls

Techniques of planned spending to maintain control over personal spending so that planned amounts are not exceeded.

Budget controls are techniques of planned spending to maintain control over personal spending so that planned amounts are not exceeded. They give feedback on whether spending is on target and provide information on overspending, errors, emergencies, and exceptions or omissions. Following are several examples of budget controls:

Track What You Spend If you spend too much money every month, you need to track what you really spend. For 30 days record in a tablet every penny of what you spend. Start paying cash because cash makes you think more about spending. And take two days to think about any expense over $100. The result: Buying less stuff will make you happier.

Budget for Shopping Trips Set a budget for every shopping trip, and don't spend a cent more.

Record the Purpose of Expenditures Checks contain a space to record the purpose of expenditures. The check stub or register also provides a place to record explanations of expenditures. If you use automatic teller machines (ATMs) to withdraw cash or use debit cards to pay for day-to-day expenditures, record these withdrawals in the check register *immediately*. Retain the paperwork, and write the purpose of each expense on the back of each. Deposit all checks received to your checking account without receiving a portion in cash; if you need cash, write a check or make an ATM withdrawal. If you get cash back when using a credit card, be sure to record why on the receipt.

Track Any Credit Transactions People often do not record their credit transactions until they receive a statement. Thus it is easy to continue buying on credit without recognizing the amount of indebtedness until the statement arrives. Instead you should record each credit transaction when it occurs. If you spend $40 on clothing using a credit card, record the expenditure as clothing expenditure and reduce the amount you have remaining to spend for the month in that category.

Monitor Unexpended Balances to Control Overspending the Number Another method to control overspending is to monitor unexpended balances in each of your budget classifications. You can accomplish this task by using a budget design that keeps a declining balance, as illustrated by parts (a) and (b) of Figure 3-6. Other budget designs, such as those shown in parts (c) and (d) of Figure 3-6, need to be monitored differently. As illustrated in parts (c) and (d) of the figure, simply calculate subtotals every week or so, as needed, during a monthly budgeting period. You can also track your spending using Quicken software or another online program.

budget exceptions

When budget estimates differ from actual expenditures.

Justify Exceptions to Avoid Lying to Yourself Budget exceptions occur when budget estimates in various classifications differ from actual expenditures. Exceptions usually take the form of overexpenditures but can also occur in the over- or under-receipt of earnings. Simply spending extra income instead of recording it is not being honest with yourself. Recording the truth—by writing a few words to explain the exception—gives you the information to control your finances. If the exception is an expenditure, then immediately determine how to make up for the overexpenditure by trying to reduce other expenses in your spending plan.

subordinate budget

Detailed listing of planned expenses within a single budgeting classification.

Use a Subordinate Budget A subordinate budget is a detailed listing of planned expenses within a single budgeting classification. For example, an estimate of $1,200 for a vacation could be supported by a subordinate budget as follows: motels, $700; restaurants, $300; and entertainment, $200.

Figure 3-6 **Record-Keeping Formats**

(a)

Food Budget: $400			
DATE	ACTIVITY	AMOUNT	BALANCE
2-6	Groceries	$80	$320
2-9	Dinner out	45	275
2-14	Groceries	60	

(b)

DATE	ACTIVITY	AMOUNT BUDGETED	EXPENDITURES	BALANCE
2-1	Food Budget	$400		$400
2-6	Groceries		$80	320
2-9	Dinner out		45	230
2-14	Groceries		60	170
2-20	Groceries		50	120
2-28	February Totals	$400	$800	$400

(c)

DATE	ACTIVITY	EXPENDITURES							REMARKS
		Food Budget: $400	Clothing Budget: $30	Auto Budget: $200	Rent Budget: $800	Savings Budget: $90	Utilities Budget: $60	TOTAL Budget: $1,580	
2-1	Gasoline			40				40	
2-6	Groceries	80						80	Had friends over
2-8	Gasoline			37				37	Good price
2-9	Dinner out	45						45	
2-14	Groceries	60						60	Pepsi on sale
2-15	Subtotals	185/400		77/200				262/1580	

(d)

			INCOME			EXPENDITURES							REMARKS
			Salary	Other	TOTAL	Food	Clothing	Auto	Rent	Savings	Utilities	TOTAL	
	Estimates		800	40	840	400	30	200	800	90	60	1580	
	Balance forwarded from January					6		14			2	22	
	Sum		800	40	840	406	30	214	800	90	62	1602	
DATE	ACTIVITY	CASH IN											
2-1	Paycheck	800	800									800	
2-1	Texaco-gasoline							40				40	
2-6	Safeway-groceries					80						80	Had friends over
2-8	7/11-gasoline							37				37	Good price
2-9	Dinner out					45						45	
2-14	Giant-groceries					60						60	Pepsi on sale
2-15	Paycheck	800	800										
2-28	Totals	1600	1600		800	400	30	195	800	90	65	1580	Good month

ADVICE FROM A SEASONED PRO

Secrets of Super Savers

How do some people enjoy the good comfortable life and still find ways to save 20 to 30 percent of their incomes? Like most people, such super savers have home mortgages, pay tuition bills, and take vacations. Also, they tend to have peace of mind about their finances because they have built up a sizable cushion of savings and investments. Some of the secrets of Super Savers include:

- Be goal-oriented about savings and investments to achieve results.

- Shop purposefully (by asking "Do I *really* need it?") so you can ignore impulse buys, which make up 40 percent of purchases.

- Choose to postpone buying anything expensive for two months to see if the "need" is still strong. Avoid debt (installment loans for computers, vehicles, TVs, cell phones,

electronics, and furniture) and using credit cards so you will not spend money you do not have.

- Cut back on spending on expensive items such as homes (not the largest in the neighborhood) and vehicles (drive older ones), and enjoy creative vacations that are not too pricey.

- Choose to spend wisely on everyday expenses by comparison shopping, clipping and using coupons, buying cheaper discounted goods and services, and being careful and mindful about entertainment expenses.

- Make savings automatic by diverting the maximum contribution to your employer's 401(k) retirement plan, and sign up for automatic transfers from a checking to a savings account, a 529 plan, a Roth IRA, and/or a high-yield savings account. Save more as income rises.

Dorothy B. Durband
Kansas State University, Manhattan, Kansas

DID YOU KNOW

You Must "Think Single" in Money Matters

You need to decide that no one is going to take care of you financially and accept the fact that that responsibility falls solely on your shoulders. This goes for both men and women! This thinking is required since at some point in their lives most adults will be managing their money on their own because they are unmarried, divorced, or widowed.

Single is defined as adults who have never been married, are divorced or are widowed. There are 110 million people in the United States who are single, and that means over 40 percent of adults are single. Fifty-three percent are women and 47 percent are men. For every 100 single women, there are 88 single men. A growing number of single Americans are living alone, and they make up one-quarter of all households.

Of the singles, 60 percent of them have never said "I do." Twenty-five percent of singles are divorced. About half of first marriages end in divorce, and 40 percent of those end within 10 years.

Half of all couples have a spouse die, and this often occurs before one is 62 years of age. Seventeen percent of singles are widowed, and 18 percent of singles are 65 years or older.

To cope with these life events, all men and women must start in their twenties—by themselves—to take actions to create a successful financial future. Smart people should always think single!

To help keep to a budget, write checks as often as possible instead of using cash. Also record the purpose of the expenditure on the lower left of the check.

Use the Envelope System for the Strongest Control The **envelope system** of budgeting entails placing exact amounts of money into envelopes for purposes of strict budgetary control. Here you place money equal to the budget estimate for the various expenditure classifications in envelopes at the start of a budgeting period and write the classification name and the budget amount on the outside of each envelope. As expenditures are made, record them on the appropriate envelope and remove the proper amounts of cash. When an envelope is empty, funds are exhausted for that classification. Of course, you must safeguard your cash.

envelope system
Placing exact amounts into envelopes for each budgetary purpose.

DO IT IN CLASS

Download a Financial App Research shows that spending falls after people downloaded and used an app.

3.5e Action After: Evaluate Budgeting Progress to Make Needed Changes

Evaluation occurs at the end of each budgeting cycle. The purpose is to determine whether the earlier steps in your budgeting efforts have worked, and it gives you feedback to use for the next budget cycle. You review by comparing actual amounts with budgeted amounts, evaluating whether your objectives were met, and assessing the success of the overall process as well as your progress toward your short- and long-term goals. The evaluation process helps you to make any needed changes.

In some budget expenditure classifications, the budget estimates rarely agree with the actual expenditures—particularly in variable expenses. A **budget variance** is the difference between the amount budgeted and the actual amount spent or received. The remarks column, as illustrated in parts (c) and (d) of Figure 3-6, can help clarify why variances occurred. Overages on a few expenditures may cause little concern. If large variances have prevented you from achieving your objectives or making the budget balance, then take some action. Serious budget controls might have to be instituted or current controls tightened.

Whatever your goals, it feels good when you make progress toward them, and it is thrilling to achieve them. If you did not achieve some of your objectives, you can

budget variance
Difference between amount budgeted and actual amount spent or received.

NUMBERS ON

Financial Statements, Tools, and Budgets

Data from a variety of sources suggest:

- Four in ten adults say they are living beyond their means.

- One-fourth of people have 6 months or more of saving for a rainy day; one-quarter have savings of 3 to 6 months; one-quarter have less than 3 months; and another one-quarter have zero.

- Average retirement savings balance for people in their 20s is $16,000, and it is $45,000 for people in their 30s.

- Twenty percent of workers receive an annual holiday bonus of $1,000 or more.

- Only one-fifth of adults prepare financial statements.

- Forty percent of adults prepare a monthly budget.

determine why and then adjust your budget and objectives accordingly. It is okay to revise your plans. Suppose at the end of the month Robert Chen, from Tucson, Arizona, finds that he is unable to set aside a planned amount of $250 in monthly savings. By evaluating his budget, perhaps Robert will find that unexpected emergency car repairs led him to spend more than budgeted for the month. Because Robert understands why the objective was not achieved, he can set his sights on reaching the goal during the next budgeting time period.

Bookkeeping The process of recording the sources and amounts of dollars earned and spent is bookkeeping. Recording the estimated and actual amounts for both income and expenditures helps you monitor your money flow. Keeping track of income and expenses is the only way to collect sufficient information to evaluate how close you are to achieving your financial objectives. For those who keep records on paper, Figure 3-6 shows four samples of self-prepared bookkeeping formats that vary in complexity. Most people record earnings and expenditures when they occur. When writing in the "activity" and "remarks" columns in your record, be descriptive because you may need the information later.

Adding Up Actual Income and Expenditures After the budgeting period has ended—usually at the beginning of a new month—you need to add up the actual income received and expenditures made during that period. You can perform this calculation on a form for each budget classification, as shown in parts (a) and (b) of Figure 3-6 or on a form with all income and expenditure classifications, as in parts (c) and (d) of Figure 3-6. Such calculations indicate where you may have overspent within your budget categories. If you are new at budgeting, do not be too concerned about overspending.

It occurs in some classifications almost always, only to be balanced by underspending in other categories. Use such information to refine your budget estimates in the future. In three or four months, you will be able to estimate your expenses much more accurately. The *Garman/Forgue* companion website provides budgeting software as well as numerous other templates, calculators, and worksheets that you can use in your own personal financial planning.

What to Do with Budgeted Money Left Over at the End of the Month At the end of the budgeting time period, some budget classifications may still have a positive balance. For example, perhaps you estimated

NEVER EVER

1. *Fail to plan for non-monthly irregular expenditures.*

2. *Underestimate how much you plan to spend each month.*

3. *Use credit card purchases to "balance" your budget.*

TURN BAD HABITS INTO GOOD ONES

Do You Do This?	Do This Instead!
Spend all your income	Save 10 percent or more
Overspend	Utilize budget controls to reduce spending
Can't find financial records	Create a record-keeping system
Do not know how much you owe	Make a balance sheet
Can't pay for auto insurance premium or vacation	Save for large irregular expenses
Run out of money every few months	Create a cash-flow calendar

the electric bill at $100, but it was only $80. You may then ask, "What do I do with the $20 surplus?" You also may ask, "What happens to budget classifications that were overspent?"

People handle the **net surplus** (the amount remaining after all budget classification deficits are subtracted from those with surpluses) in any of the following ways:

net surplus
Amount remaining after all budget classification deficits are subtracted from those with surpluses.

- Put the money into savings (and this allows the budget to total out to zero)
- Carry the surpluses forward to the following month
- Pay toward credit card debt
- Put surpluses toward a mortgage or other loan
- Put the money into a retirement account
- Spend surpluses like "mad money" on anything you want

The budgeting form in part (d) of Figure 3-6 (page 103) allows for carrying balances forward to the next period. Some people carry forward deficits, with the hope that having less available in a budgeted classification the following month will motivate them to keep expenditures low. Because variable expense estimates are usually averages, it is best not to change the estimate based on a variation that occurs over just one or two months. If estimates are too high or low for a longer period, you will want to make adjustments.

Using financial software for budgeting, like Quicken or Mint, takes some of the drudgery out of making and using a spending plan. And it gets to be pretty easy after a few months. Plus you gain a lot more control over your money.

DID YOU KNOW ?

Hit These Financial Marks While You Are in Your Thirties

- Have about 3 to 6 months of emergency savings available
- Put 15 percent of your income (includes both you and your employer's contributions) into retirement savings

- Buy a home
- Start an investment portfolio for non-retirement goals
- Pay off student loans and credit card debt

CONCEPT CHECK 3.5

1. Explain why setting financial goals is an important step in budgeting.
2. What are *budget estimates*? Offer some suggestions on how to go about making budget estimates for various types of expenses.
3. How might one go about revising budget estimates to create a balanced budget?
4. Explain what a cash-flow calendar accomplishes. Name three techniques to control spending.
5. Name different ways to handle budget variances.

WHAT DO YOU RECOMMEND *NOW*?

Now that you have read the chapter on financial planning, what do you recommend to Austin Patterson for his talk with Emily on the subject of financial planning regarding:

1. Setting financial goals?
2. Determining what they own and owe?
3. Using the information in Austin's newly prepared financial statements to summarize the family's financial situation?
4. Evaluating their financial progress?
5. Setting up a record-keeping system to better serve their needs?
6. Starting a budgeting process to guide saving and spending?

Phovoir/Shutterstock.com

SUMMARY OF LEARNING OBJECTIVES RECAPPED

LO1   Identify your financial values, goals, and strategies.

By identifying your financial values, goals, and strategies, you can always keep a balance between spending and saving and stay committed to your financial success. Financial goals should be specific with target dates. You may create financial plans in three broad areas: plans for spending, plans for risk management, and plans for capital accumulation.

LO2   Use balance sheets and cash-flow statements to measure your financial health and progress.

Financial statements are compilations of personal financial data that describe an individual's or family's current financial condition. The balance sheet provides information on what you own, what you owe, and what the net result would be if you paid off all your debts. The cash-flow statement lists income and expenditures over a specific period of time, such as the previous month or year.

LO3   Collect and organize the financial records necessary for managing your personal finances.

Your financial records will help determine where you are, where you have been, and where you are going financially. They also help you save money as well as make money.

LO4   List a number of money topics to discuss with a partner.

Talking with your partner about money matters on a regular basis likely avoids professional marriage counselors' largest concern about couples who divorce.

LO5   Achieve your financial goals through budgeting.

Budgeting is all about logical thinking about your finances. Budgeting forces you to consider what is important in your life, what things you want to own, how you want to live, what it will take to do that, and, more generally, what you want to achieve in life. A budget is a process used to record both projected and actual income and expenditures over a period of time.

LET'S TALK ABOUT IT

1. **Families.** During slow economic times, the federal government's budgeting priority often is to borrow so it can spend more money than it takes in. What happens to families that try that, and why?

2. **Your Values.** What are two of your most important personal values? Give an example of how each of those values might influence your financial plans.

3. **Cash Flow.** College students often have little income and many expenses. Does this reduce or increase the importance of completing a cash-flow statement on a monthly basis? Why or why not?

4. **Financial Ratios.** Of the financial ratios described in this chapter, which two might be most revealing for the typical college student?

5. **Why Budget.** Do you have a budget or spending plan? Why or why not? What do you think are the two major reasons why people do not make formal written budgets?

6. **Control Spending.** What can a person try to do to genuinely control spending to better achieve financial success?

7. **Financial Mistakes.** Evaluate the biggest three financial mistakes you made over the past 5 years. Are there any patterns in the mistakes?

8. **Budgeting Mistake.** What is the biggest budget-related mistake that you have made? What would you do differently now?

9. **Personal Finances Over the Life Cycle.** Areas of financial decision making change over one's life-cycle. Based on the information provided in Figure 3-3 on page 85 contrast your own areas of concern with those of your parents.   DO IT IN CLASS Page 85

DO THE MATH

1. **Ratio Analyses for Victor and Maria.** Review the financial statements of Victor and Maria Hernandez (Table 3-2 and Table 3-3) and the financial ratios on page 87 and respond to the following questions:

    (a) How would you interpret their investment assets to total assets ratio? The Hernandez family appears to have too few monetary assets compared with tangible and investment assets. How would you suggest that they remedy that situation over the next few years?

    (b) What are your thoughts on the Hernandez's liquidity ratio? How might they address any issues you see?

    (c) Comment on the couple's diversification of their investment assets.

    (d) The Hernandezes seem to receive most of their income from employment rather than investments. What actions would you recommend for them to remedy that imbalance over the next few years?

    (e) The Hernandezes want to take a two-week vacation next summer, and they have only eight months to save the necessary $3,400. What reasonable changes in expenses might they consider to increase net surplus and make the needed $425 per month ($3,400/8)?

2. **Calculating Net Worth and Net Surplus.** Jennifer Pontesso, from Lincoln, Nebraska, wants to better understand her financial situation. Use the following balance sheet and cash flow statement information to determine her net worth and her net surplus for a recent month. Liquid assets: $10,000; home value: $210,000; monthly mortgage payment: $1,300 on $170,000 mortgage; investment assets: $90,000; personal property: $20,000; total assets: $330,000; short-term debt: $5,500 ($250 a month); total debt: $175,500; monthly gross income: $9,000; monthly disposable income: $6,800; monthly expenses: $6,000.   DO IT IN CLASS Pages 81 and 83

3. **Ratio Analyses.** Now that Jennifer better understands her situation she wants to do some analysis of what she has found. Given her balance sheet and cash-flow statements calculate the following ratios:

    (a) Liquidity ratio

    (b) Asset-to-debt ratio

    (c) Debt-to-income ratio

    (d) Debt payments-to-disposable income ratio   DO IT IN CLASS Page 87

    (e) Investment assets-to-total assets ratio

4. **Cash Flow Surplus/Deficit.** Cody Sebastian, of Lubbock, Texas, earns $60,000 a year. He pays 30 percent of his gross income in federal, state, and local taxes. He has fixed expenses in addition to taxes of $1,800 per month and variable expenses that average $1,400 per month. What is his net cash flow (surplus or deficit) for the year?

5. **Construct Financial Statements.** Thomas Green, of Laramie, Wyoming, has been a retail salesclerk for six

years. At age 35, he is divorced with one child, Amanda, age 7. Thomas's salary is $46,000 per year. He regularly receives $400 per month for child support from Amanda's mother. Thomas invests $100 each month ($50 in his mutual fund and $50 in U.S. savings bonds). Using the following information, construct a balance sheet and a cash-flow statement for Thomas.

DO IT IN CLASS
Pages 81 and 83

ASSETS	Amount
Vested retirement benefits (no employee contribution)	$6,000
Money market account (includes $150 of interest earned last year)	5,000
Mutual fund (includes $200 of reinvested dividend income from last year)	5,000
Checking account	1,000
Personal property	5,000
Automobile	12,000
U.S. savings bonds	3,000

LIABILITIES	Outstanding Balance
Dental bill (pays $25 per month and is included in uninsured medical/dental)	$ 450
Visa (pays $100 per month)	3,500
Student loan (pays $100 per month)	7,500

ANNUAL FIXED EXPENSES	Amount
Auto insurance	$ 780
Rent	12,000
Utilities	2,400
iPhone	980
Cable	1400
Internet	800
Food	3,v000
Uninsured medical/dental	1,000

ANNUAL VARIABLE EXPENSES	Amount
Dry cleaning	$ 480
Personal care	420
Gas, maintenance, license	2,120
Clothes	500
Entertainment	2,700
Vacations/visitation/travel	3,300
Child care	5,000
Gifts	400
Miscellaneous	300
Federal income tax	5,600
Social Security taxes	3,500
Health insurance	2,440

6. **Budgeting and Income Projections.** Leyia and Larry Hartley of Columbus, Ohio have decided to start a family next year, so they are looking over their budget (illustrated in Table 3-5 as the "young married couple"). Leyia thinks that she can go on half-salary ($2,400 instead of $4,800 per month) in her job as a college textbook sales representative for about 18 months after the baby's birth; she will then return to full-time work.

   (a) Looking at the Hartley's current monthly budget, identify categories and amounts in their budget where they realistically might cut back $2,400. (Hint: Federal and state taxes should drop about $600 a month ($7,200 annually) as their income drops.)

   (b) Assume that Leyia and Larry could be persuaded not to begin a family for another five years. What specific budgeting recommendations would you give them for handling (i) their fixed expenses and (ii) their variable expenses to prepare financially for an anticipated $2,400 loss of income for 18 months as well as the expenses for the new baby?

   (c) If the Hartley's gross income of $8,830 rises 3 percent per year in the future, what will their income be after five years? (Hint: See Appendix A.1 or the *Garman/Forgue* companion website.)

FINANCIAL PLANNING CASES

CASE 1

The Financial Statements of Harry and Belinda Johnson Suggest Budgeting Problems

Harry has worked at a medium-size interior design firm for five years and earns a salary of $4,080 per month. He also receives $3,000 in interest income once a year from a trust fund set up by his deceased father's estate. Belinda earns a salary of $6,400 per month, and she has many job-related benefits including flexible benefits program, life insurance, health insurance, a 401(k) retirement program, workplace financial education, and a credit union. The Johnsons live in an old apartment located approximately halfway between their places of employment. However, their rent will increase by $100 a month in July. Harry drives about ten minutes to his job, and Belinda travels about 15 minutes via public transportation to reach her downtown job. Harry and Belinda's apartment is very nice, but small, and it is furnished primarily with furniture given to them by some of his friends. Soon after getting married, Harry and Belinda decided to begin their financial planning. Fortunately each had taken a college course in personal finance. After initial discussion, they worked together for three evenings to develop the financial statements presented below. Note that the cash flow statement covered the first six months of their marriage.

(a) Briefly describe how Harry and Belinda probably determined the fair market prices for each of their tangible and investment assets.

(b) Using the data from the cash-flow statement developed by Harry and Belinda, calculate a liquidity ratio, asset-to-debt ratio, debt-to-income ratio, debt payments-to-disposable income ratio, and investment assets-to-total assets ratio. What do these ratios tell you about the Johnsons' financial situation? Should Harry and Belinda incur more debt, such as credit cards or a new vehicle loan?

(c) The Johnsons enjoy a high income because both work at well-paying jobs. They have spent parts of three evenings over the past several days discussing their financial values and goals together. As shown in the upper portion of Figure 3-5, they have established three long-term goals: $6,000 for a European vacation to be taken in 2020, $5,000 needed in October 2021 for a down payment on a new automobile, and $30,000 for a down payment on a home to be purchased in December 2023. As shown in the lower portion of the figure, the Johnsons did some calculations to determine how much they had to save for each goal—over the near term—to stay on schedule to reach their long-term goals as well as pay for two vacations and an anniversary party. After developing their balance sheet and cash-flow statement (shown below), the Johnsons made a budget for the year (shown in Table 3-6 on page 97). They then reconciled various conflicting needs and wants until they found that total annual income was close to the total of planned expenses. Next, they created a revolving savings fund (Table 3-8 on page 99) in which they were careful to include enough money each month to meet all of their short-term goals. When developing their cash-flow calendar for the year (Table 3-7 on page 98), they noticed a problem: substantial cash deficits in November and December. Make specific recommendations to the Johnsons on how they could make reductions in their budget estimates. Do not offer suggestions that would alter their new lifestyle drastically, as the couple would reject such ideas.

Balance Sheet for Harry and Belinda Johnson

January 1, 2018

ASSETS

Monetary Assets

Cash on hand	$ 1,100	3.8%
Savings (First Credit Union)	1,200	4.1%
Savings (Far West Savings Bank)	4,000	13.7%
Savings (Homestead Credit Union)	2,260	7.7%
Checking (First Credit Union)	2,100	7.2%
Total Monetary Assets	**$10,660**	**36.5%**

Tangible Assets

Automobile (3-year old Toyota)	$11,000	37.6%
Personal property	2,300	7.9%
Furniture	1,700	5.8%
Total Tangible Assets	**$15,000**	**51.3%**

Investment Assets

Harry's retirement account	$ 1,170	4.0%
Belinda's retirement account	2,400	8.2%
Total Investment Assets	**$ 3,570**	**12.2%**
Total Assets	**$29,230**	**100.0%**

LIABILITIES

Short-Term Liabilities

Visa credit card	$ 390	1.3%
Target credit card	45	0.2%
Dental bill	400	1.4%
Total Short-Term Liabilities	**$ 835**	**2.9%**

Long-Term Liabilities

Vehicle loan (First Credit Union)	$13,800	47.2%
Student loan (Belinda)	8,200	28.1%
Total Long-Term Liabilities	**$22,000**	**75.3%**
Total Liabilities	**$22,835**	**78.1%**
Net Worth	**$ 6,395**	**21.9%**
Total Liabilities and Net Worth	**$29,230**	**100.0%**

Cash-Flow Statement for Harry and Belinda Johnson July 1–December 31, 2017 (First Six Months of Marriage)

Cash Flow	Dollars	Percent
INCOME		
Harry's gross income	$24,000	37.6%
Belinda's gross income	36,600	57.4%
Interest	180	0.3%
Harry's trust fund	3,000	4.7%
Total Income	**$63,780**	**100.0%**
EXPENDITURES		
Fixed Expenses		
Rent	$ 9,600	15.1%
Health Insurance	1,800	2.8%
Life insurance	120	0.2%
Renter's insurance	220	0.3%
Automobile insurance	600	6.3%
Auto loan payments	2,940	4.6%
Student loan payments	1,800	2.8%
Cable TV and Internet	960	1.5%
Savings/emergencies	960	1.5%
Harry's retirement plan	1,170	1.8%
Belinda's retirement plan	2,400	3.8%
Federal income taxes	10,200	16.0%
State income taxes	3,000	4.7%
Social Security taxes	4,640	7.3%
Automobile registration	300	0.5%
Total Fixed Expenses	**$40,710**	**63.8%**
Variable Expenses		
Savings money market fund	$ 3,000	4.7%
Food (home)	3,800	6.0%
Food (out)	1,860	2.9%

Utilities	1,320	2.1%
Cell phones	660	1.0%
Auto gas/maintenance/repairs	1,150	1.8%
Doctor's and dentist's bills	1,140	1.8%
Medicines	350	0.5%
Clothing and upkeep	1,200	1.9%
Church and charity	550	0.9%
Gifts	1,070	1.7%
Public transportation	940	1.5%
Personal allowances	2,400	3.8%
Entertainment	960	1.5%
Family holiday trip	780	1.2%
Summer vacation	1,200	1.9%
Miscellaneous	560	0.9%
Total Variable Expenses	**$22,940**	**36.0%**
Total Expenses	**$63,650**	**99.8%**
SURPLUS (DEFICIT)	**$130**	**0.2%**

CASE 2

Victor and Maria Hernandez

Victor and Maria, both in their late 30s, have two children: John, age 13, and Joseph, age 15. Victor has had a long sales career with a retail appliance store. Maria works part-time as a medical records assistant. The Hernandezes own two vehicles and their home, on which they have a mortgage. They will face many financial challenges over the next 20 years, as their children drive, go to college, and leave home and go out in the world on their own. Victor and Maria also recognize the need to further prepare for their retirement and the challenges of aging.

Victor and Maria spent some time making up their first balance sheet, which is shown in Table 3-2. Victor and Maria are a bit confused about how various financial activities can affect their net worth.

(a) Assume that their home is now appraised at $200,000 and the value of their automobile has dropped to $8,500. Calculate and characterize the effects of these changes on their net worth and on their asset-to-debt ratio.

(b) If Victor and Maria take out a bank loan for $1,600 and pay off their credit card debts totaling $1,600, what effects would these changes have on their net worth?

(c) If Victor and Maria sell their New York 2038 bond and put the cash into the savings account, what effects would this have on their net worth and liquidity ratio?

CASE 3

Julia Price Thinks About Financial Statements, Tools, and Budgets

Julia graduated over six years ago in aeronautical engineering and changed job once. Her income is more than sufficient for her needs. Julia contributes the maximum into her employer's retirement account and additionally saves about $400 a month. She has only about $1,000 in credit card debt and makes a monthly car payment of $520. With such a strong financial position, she thinks it would be a waste of time to prepare financial statements and create a budget. Offer your opinions about her thinking.

CASE 4

Budget Control for a Recent Graduate

Stephen Bailey, a political scientist from McPherson, Kansas, graduated from college eight months ago and is having a terrible time with his budget. Stephen has a regular monthly income from his job and no really large bills, but she likes to spend. He exceeds his budget every month, and his credit card balances are increasing. Choose three budget control methods that you could recommend to Stephen, and explain how each one could help him gain control of his finances.

DO IT IN CLASS
Page 103

CASE 5

A Couple Creates an Educational Savings Plan

Stanley Marsh and Wendy Testaburger of South Park, Colorado, have two young children. They both work and earn a substantial income, over $100,000 annually. Their monthly budget is illustrated in Table 3-5 on page 96 as the "married couple with two young children." Every month they save quite a bit of money for retirement, and they are paying off their student loans ahead of schedule. They live well but Wendy and Stanley are nervous about not having started an educational savings plan for their children. They have decided that they want to save $200 per month for the children's education.

(a) Review the family's budget and make suggestions about how to modify various budget estimates so that they could save $200 per month for the education fund.

(b) Briefly describe the effect of your recommended changes on the Marsh-Testaburgers' lifestyle.

BE YOUR OWN PERSONAL FINANCIAL MANAGER

1. **Financial Plan.** Use Table 3-1 on page 76 as a guide to making your financial plans, goals, and objectives for spending, risk management, and capital accumulation. Write up your findings.

2. **Balance Sheet.** Use Table 3-2 on page 82 as a guide to create a balance sheet or complete Worksheet 10: My Balance Sheet from "My Personal Financial Planner" to create your own detailed annual balance sheet. Write up your findings.

3. **Cash-Flow Statement.** Use Table 3-3 on page 86 as a guide to create a cash-flow statement or complete Worksheet 11: My Cash-Flow Statement from "My Personal Financial Planner" to create your own cash-flow statement. Write up your findings.

4. **Evaluate Your Financial Ratios.** Use the financial ratios on pages 87 to help evaluate your personal financial condition or complete Worksheet 12: My Financial Ratios from "My Personal Financial Planner" to record your financial ratios.

5. **Categorize Your Financial Records.** Review Table 3-4 "Financial Records: What to Keep and Where" on page 88 to develop a system for your own records or complete Worksheet 13: My Financial Records from "My Personal Financial Planner" to record what records will be placed in your home file, safe-deposit box, or another place.

6. **Monthly Saving to Reach Your Goals.** Use Figure 3-5 "Goals Worksheet for Harry and Belinda Johnson" on page 95 as a guide to develop your own personal savings goals or complete Worksheet 14: Monthly Savings to Reach My Financial Goals from "My Personal Financial Planner" to record the dollar amount, time, and interim short-term goals.

7. **Nonmonthly Expenses.** Complete Worksheet 15: Determining Monthly Budget Amounts for My Nonmonthly Expenses from "My Personal Financial Planner" to carefully plan for your nonmonthly expenses over the year.

8. **Revolving Savings Fund.** Review Table 3-8 "Revolving Savings Fund for Harry and Belinda Johnson" on page 99 to develop a plan for yourself or complete Worksheet 16: My Revolving Savings Fund from "My Personal Financial Planner" to record how you can save to pay for irregular expenses throughout the year.

9. **Create Your Budget.** Use Table 3-6 on page 97 as a guide to create a 12-month budget or complete Worksheet 17: My Budget from "My Personal Financial Planner" to do so.

10. **Control Spending with Budget Worksheets.** Complete Worksheet 18: My Budget Category Ledger Worksheets from "My Personal Financial Planner" to create a system to monitor and control spending.

11. **Organize Your Financial Records.** Use Table 3-4 on page 89 as a guide to helping you get your financial records in order. Write down some notes about your thinking on what documents you will need and where to keep them.

ON THE NET

Go to the Web pages indicated to complete these exercises.

1. **Online Calculators.** Visit MoneyChimp's website (www.moneychimp.com). There you will find an assortment of calculators that can be used in various present and future value calculations. Select three that you believe would be particularly useful in the aspects of personal financial planning that were discussed in this chapter.

2. **More Online Calculators.** Visit CNNMoney's website (money.cnn.com/tools). Select three calculators to try out that you think would be useful in personal finance.

3. **Download 10 Budgets.** Budgets for lots of topics, including travel, college, Christmas gifts at www.makeuseof.com/tag/10-helpful-spreadsheet-templates-help-manage-finances.

4. **Student Budget.** Visit Dinkytown.net at dinkytown.net/java/StudentBudget.html. Use this calculator to help analyze your budget, which is designed to help students understand their expenses and income while college.

5. **Input Your Budget and Compare to Your Projected Expenditures.** Visit the website www.kiplinger.com/tool/spending/T007-S001-budgeting-worksheet-a-household-budget-for-today-a and use the budgeting worksheet and input your projected monthly living costs in various categories. It will compare your projections to what you actually spent.

6. **Can You Make It Through the Month?** "Spent" is an online game that simulates the struggles of homelessness. Accept the challenge and take 10 minutes to play Spent (playspent.org).

ACTION INVOLVEMENT PROJECTS

1. **Money Discussion Topics.** Use "Topics to Discuss with a Partner" as a guide to interview two married couples. Ask them which of the topics they discussed with their partners within the first year of marriage. Make a table that summarizes your findings.

2. **Financial Mistakes.** Survey two people to learn about their financial mistakes in life. Ask each person to cite two financial mistakes he/she has made. Make a table that summarizes your findings.

3. **Short-Term Financial Goals.** Survey two people to ascertain their financial goals. Ask each person, "What are your top two short-term financial goals?" Make a table that summarizes your findings.

4. **Long-Term Financial Goals.** Survey two people to ascertain their financial goals. Ask each person, "What are your top three long-term financial goals?" Make a table that summarizes your findings.

Visit the Garman/Forgue companion website at www.cengagebrain.com.

PART 2

Lucky Business/Shutterstock.com

4 Managing Income Taxes

YOU MUST BE KIDDING, RIGHT?

Bharat Persaud's employer gave him a $2,000 bonus last year, and when Bharat was filling out his federal income tax form, he discovered that $1,000 of it moved him from the 15 percent marginal tax rate to 25 percent. How much additional income tax will Bharat pay on the $2,000?

A. $150   **B.** $180

C. $250   **D.** $400

The answer is C. The federal marginal tax rate is applied to your last dollar of earnings. The first $1,000 of Bharat's bonus is taxed at the marginal tax rate of 15 percent ($150), but the second $1,000 is taxed at 25 percent ($250). Be aware of your marginal tax rate!

Learning Objectives

After reading this chapter, you should be able to:

1 Explain the nature of progressive income taxes and the marginal tax rate.

2 Differentiate among the eight steps involved in calculating your federal income taxes.

3 Use appropriate strategies to avoid overpayment of income taxes.

WHAT DO YOU RECOMMEND?

Ace Steven and Florence Szpanka have known each other for a few years and plan to get married the year after next. Ace earns $74,000 annually as a manager in a copper mining plant. He also earns about $20,000 per year selling jewelry that he designs at craft shows held just about every month in various nearby cities. Soon after they marry, Ace plans to take a year off to go back to college full time to finish the last year of his undergraduate degree. Florence earns $68,000 annually working as an institutional sales representative for an insurance company. Both Ace and Florence each contribute $100 per month to their employer-sponsored 401(k) retirement accounts. Ace has little additional savings, but Florence has accumulated $18,000 that she wants to use for a down payment on a home. Florence also owns 300 shares of stock in an oil company that she inherited six years ago when the price was $90 per share; now the stock is worth $130 per share. Ace and Florence live in a state where the state income tax is 6 percent.

Zero Creatives/Cultura/Jupiter Images

What would you recommend to Ace and Florence on the subject of managing income taxes regarding:

1. Using tax credits to help pay for Ace's college expenses?
2. Determining how much money Florence will realize if she sells the stocks, assuming she pays federal income taxes at the 25 percent rate?
3. Buying a home?
4. Increasing contributions to their employer-sponsored retirement plans?
5. Establishing a sideline business for tax purposes for Ace's jewelry operation?

TO-DO SOON

Do the following to begin to achieve financial success:

1. *Sign up for tax-advantaged employee benefits at your workplace.*
2. *Project your taxable income and total withholding for this year.*
3. *Contribute to your employer-sponsored 401(k) retirement plan at least up to the amount of the employer's matching contribution.*
4. *Buy a home to reduce income taxes.*
5. *Revise the IRS W-4 Form at your human resources office to withhold more or less money for income taxes.*

Managing your personal finances correctly includes not paying unnecessary sums to the federal government in income taxes. Learning about tax-saving techniques will provide you with more money to do with what you want. "The avoidance of taxes is the only intellectual pursuit that carries any reward," wrote economist John Maynard Keynes. You should pay your income tax liabilities in full, but that's all. There is no need to pay a dime extra. Although you should pay your fair share of federal taxes.

To achieve this goal, you need to adopt a **tax planning** perspective designed to eliminate, reduce, or defer some income taxes. To get started, you should recognize that you pay personal income taxes only on your **taxable income**. This amount is determined by subtracting various exclusions, adjustments, exemptions, and deductions from total income, with the result being the income upon which the income tax is actually figured.

Details for these terms and calculations are provided later. For now, simply remember that the main idea in managing income taxes is to reduce your taxable income as much as possible while maintaining a high level of total income. Tax terms can be confusing but are important to master. The better you understand tax terms and how they apply to you, the savvier tax decisions you can make. The result will lower your actual tax liability. Then you will have more money available every year to manage, spend, save, invest, and donate—activities that are the focus of this whole book.

Learning Objective 1

Explain the nature of progressive income taxes and the marginal tax rate.

4.1 PROGRESSIVE INCOME TAXES AND THE MARGINAL TAX RATE

Taxes are compulsory charges imposed by a government on its citizens and their property. The U.S. Internal Revenue Service (IRS) is the agency charged with the responsibility for collecting federal income taxes based on the legal provisions in the *Internal Revenue Code*.

4.1a The Progressive Nature of the Federal Income Tax

Taxes can be classified as progressive or regressive. The federal personal income tax is a **progressive tax** because the tax rate progressively increases as a taxpayer's taxable income increases. A higher income implies a greater ability to pay. As Table 4-1 shows, the higher portions of a taxpayer's taxable income are taxed at increasingly higher rates under the federal income tax.

A **regressive tax** operates in the opposite way. It is a tax imposed in such a manner that the tax rate stays the same for all income with the result that lower-income people pay proportionately more in taxes. An example is the state sales tax, since a rate

tax planning
Seeking legal ways to reduce, eliminate, or defer income taxes.

taxable income
This amount is determined by subtracting various exclusions, adjustments, exemptions, and deductions from total income, with the result being the income upon which the income tax is actually figured.

taxes
Compulsory government-imposed charges levied on citizens and their property.

progressive tax
A tax that progressively increases as a taxpayer's taxable income increases.

Table 4-1   The Progressive Nature of the Federal Income Tax

Single Individuals If taxable income is:	Marginal Tax Rate
Up to $9,275	10%
Over $9,276 but not over $37,650	15%
Over $37,651 but not over $91,150	25%
Over $91,151 but not over $190,150	28%
Over $190,151 but not over $413,350	33%
Over $413,351 but not over $415,050	35%
Over $415,051	39.6%

of perhaps 7 percent might have to be paid by everyone regardless of income. One who earns $30,000 and spends $6,000 on food pays 1.5 percent on food purchases (7% × $6,000 = $420/$30,000 = 1.4%). This compares to another person who earns $100,000 and spends $12,000 on food, thus paying less than 1 percent on sales tax on food purchases (7% × $12,000 − $840/$100,000 = 0.84%).

4.1b   The Marginal Tax Rate Is Applied to the Last Dollar Earned

Note that the marginal tax brackets are progressive. The first portion of someone's income is taxed at the rate in the lowest bracket; the next portion is taxed at the next lowest rate; and the final portion of income is taxed an even higher rate. Because our tax system has graduated tax rates, you do not pay the same tax rate on every dollar subject to tax.

The **marginal tax bracket (MTB)** (or **marginal tax rate**) is the rate at which your last dollar of income is taxed. It refers to the highest tax bracket that your taxable income puts you in. It is illustrated with the seven income-range segments that are taxed at increasing rates as income goes up, as shown in Table 4-1. The tax rates apply only to the income within each tax bracket range.

Depending on their income, taxpayers fit into one of the brackets and, accordingly, pay at one of those marginal tax rates: 10 percent, 15 percent, 25 percent, 28 percent, 33 percent, 35 percent, or 39.6 percent.* In addition, each year the dollar amounts for the taxable income brackets are adjusted for inflation to reduce the effects of inflation in a process called **indexing**. This keeps taxpayers from being forced to pay more taxes as they earn higher incomes.

Your marginal tax rate is perhaps the single most important concept in personal finance. It tells you the portion of any extra taxable earnings—from a raise, investment income, or money from a second job—you must pay in income taxes. It also measures the tax reduction benefits of a tax-deductible expense that allows you to reduce your taxable income.

Consider this example of how the marginal tax rate might apply. Victoria Bassett is from Eau Claire, Wisconsin (see Figure 4-1). Because of the progressive provisions in the tax laws, part of her $60,000 income ($10,350 [$6,300 + $4,050]) is not taxed, the next $9,275 is taxed at 10 percent, the next $28,375 is taxed at 15 percent, and the remaining $12,000 of Victoria's $60,000 income is taxed at 25 percent. Thus, Victoria is in the 25 percent marginal tax bracket because the *last* dollar that she earned is taxed at that level. Her federal income tax liability is $8,183.75 based on her $60,000 in income.

marginal tax bracket (MTB)/ marginal tax rate
One of seven income-range segments at which income is taxed at increasing rates. Also known as marginal tax rate.

indexing
Yearly adjustments to tax brackets that reduce inflation's effects on tax brackets.

DO IT IN CLASS

Figure 4-1   **How Your Income Is Really Taxed (Example: Victoria Bassett with a $60,000 gross income, and she is in the 25% marginal tax bracket)**

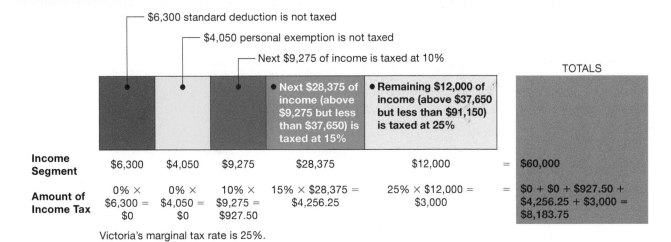

*The history of the latest year when the highest federal marginal tax rates in the United States was applied to taxable income is as follows: 1953 (92%); 1980 (70%); 1986 (50%); 2000 (39.6%).

How to Determine Your Federal Marginal Tax Rate

You can determine your marginal tax rate by following this example.

1. *Start with a single person who has a taxable income of $30,000, and looking at the illustrated tax table (Table 4-3 on page 129), she finds his tax on that amount of income ($4,040).*
2. *Add $100 to the income for a total of $30,100, and find the tax on that amount ($4,055).*
3. *Subtract the difference between the two tax amounts ($4,055 − $4,040). The extra $15 in taxes from a $100 increase in income reflects a federal marginal tax rate of 15 percent.*

effective marginal tax rate

A person's total marginal tax rate on income after adding federal, state, and local income taxes as well as Social Security and Medicare taxes.

The mathematics shown in Figure 4-1 is based either on the **IRS tax table** (used for tax returns with incomes up to $100,000) or the **tax-rate schedules** (used for tax returns with incomes above $100,000). All information cited in this chapter are the most recent available for income tax returns.

4.1c Use Your Marginal Tax Rate to Help Make Financial Decisions

The marginal tax rate can affect many financial decisions that you make. Consider, for example, what happens if you are in the 25 percent marginal tax bracket and you make a $100 tax-deductible contribution to your 401(k) retirement plan at work. Your retirement plan receives the $100, and you deduct the $100 from your taxable income. This deduction results in a $25 reduction in your federal income tax ($100 × 0.25). In effect, you give only $75 (not $100) because the government, in effect, "gives" $25 to your retirement plan.

4.1d Your Effective Marginal Tax Rate Is Higher

The effective marginal tax rate describes a person's total marginal tax rate on income after adding federal, state, and local income taxes as well as Social Security and Medicare taxes. (The last two are called the Federal Insurance Contributions Act [**FICA**] tax that most taxpayers pay.) To determine your effective marginal tax rate on income, add all of these other taxes to your federal marginal tax rate.

To illustrate, a single taxpayer earning a taxable income between $37,651 and $91,150 will pay federal income taxes at a marginal rate of 25 percent and a combined Social Security 6.2%* and Medicare tax rate of 1.45%** that totals 7.65 percent.*** Note that self-employed taxpayers are their own employers and thus pay both portions of the Social Security tax, or 7.65 percent twice, for a total of 15.3 percent. He or she might also pay a state income tax rate of 6 percent;**** and a city income tax rate 2 percent. These taxes result in an effective marginal tax rate of 40 percent for most workers (25 + 7.65 + 6 + 2 = 40.65, or about 40). Thus, most employed taxpayers pay an effective marginal tax rate of about 40 percent.

ADVICE FROM A SEASONED PRO

Your Average Tax Rate Is Low

The **average tax rate** refers to the average amount of one's total taxable income that is paid in taxes. It is always less than your marginal tax rate. It may make one feel good because the tax bite is not as bad as the marginal rate when one does the calculations. For example, a person with a total taxable income of $88,000 pays about $17,777 in federal income taxes because he/she is in a 25 percent marginal tax bracket. His/her average tax rate, however, is only 20.2 percent ($17,800 / $88,000).

Gerard J. Mellnick
Schoolcraft College, Livonia, Michigan

FICA

Social Security and Medicare taxes. Taxes withheld for Social Security and Medicare are known as the Federal Insurance Contributions Act.

*The 6.2 percent Social Security tax is applied to wages up to $118,500.

**The Medicare tax is applied to all wages regardless of amount.

***"Higher-income" taxpayers earning $200,000 (for singles and $250,000 for married), about 4.7 million returns, which is 3.2 percent of all returns, also must pay two additional Medicare taxes: A 3.8 percent surtax on net investment income and a 0.9 percent Medicare contributions tax on self-employment earnings. Those earning $400,000+ also pay a 20 percent rate on all long-term capital gains.

****Check income tax rates in various states at www.bankrate.com/taxes.aspx

CONCEPT CHECK 4.1

1. Distinguish between a progressive and a regressive tax.
2. What is a marginal tax bracket, and how does it impact taxpayers making tax-advantaged contributions to their retirement plans?
3. Explain why some taxpayers have an effective marginal tax rate as high as 40 percent.

average tax rate
*The average amount of one's total **gross** income that is paid in taxes, which is always less than your marginal tax rate.*

4.2 EIGHT STEPS IN CALCULATING YOUR INCOME TAXES

Learning Objective 2

Differentiate among the eight steps involved in calculating your federal income taxes.

There are eight basic steps in calculating federal income taxes:

1. Determine your total income.
2. Determine and report your gross income after subtracting exclusions.
3. Subtract adjustments to income.
4. Subtract either the IRS's standard deduction amount for your tax status or your itemized deductions.
5. Subtract the value of your personal exemptions.
6. Determine your preliminary tax liability.
7. Subtract tax credits for which you qualify.
8. Calculate the balance due the IRS or the amount of your refund.

Figure 4-2 graphically depicts these eight steps in the overall process of federal income tax calculation. The idea is to reduce your income so that you pay the smallest amount possible in income taxes. You do so by reducing total income by removing

Figure 4-2 The Steps in Calculating Your Income Taxes

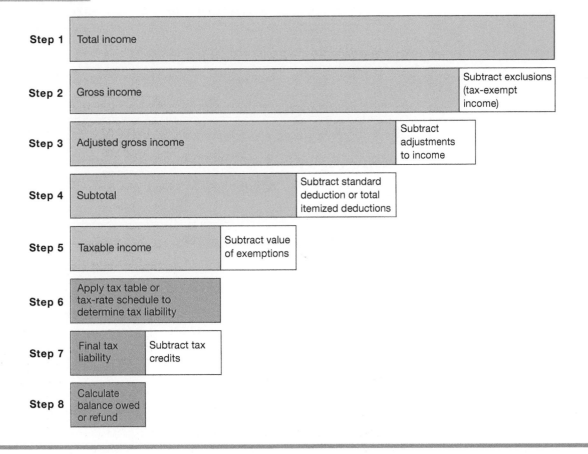

nontaxable income and then subtracting exclusions, deductions, exemptions, and tax credits, as indicated in the unshaded boxes in Figure 4-2.

4.2a Determine Your Total Income

Practically everything you receive in return for your work or services and any profit from the sale of assets is considered income, whether the compensation is paid in cash, property, or services. Listing these earnings will reveal your **total income**—compensation from all sources—and much of it, but not all, will be subject to income taxes.

For most people, **earned income** is income derived from active participation in a trade or business, including wages, salary, tips, commissions, and bonuses. It is reported to them annually on a Form W-2, Wage and Tax Statement. Employers must provide W-2 information (see Figure 4-3) by January 31 of the year following the earned income. If you also receive income from interest or dividends or other sources, you will receive a Form 1099-INT or 1099-DIV, providing appropriate details. The IRS also receives the information on their Form 1099s, which it uses to verify the income you report.

Income to Include The following types of income are included when you report your income to the IRS:

- Wages and salaries
- Commissions
- Bonuses
- Professional fees earned
- Hobby income
- Tips earned
- Severance pay
- Medical insurance rebates because of Patient Protection and Affordable Care Act
- Fair value of anything received in a barter arrangement

total income

Compensation from all sources.

earned income

Compensation for performing personal services.

Figure 4-3 **IRS W-2 Form**

Source: IRS W-2 Form

a Control number				
	22222	OMB No. 1545-0008		
b Employer identification number (EIN) 37-12345678		1 Wages, tips, other compensation 65,000.00	2 Federal income tax withheld 10,400.00	
c Employer's name, address, and ZIP code Financial Knowledge Communications 1245 Oak Street Oak Park, IL 60302		3 Social security wages 65,000.00	4 Social security tax withheld 4,030	
		5 Medicare wages and tips 65,000.00	6 Medicare tax withheld $942.50	
		7 Social security tips	8 Allocated tips	
d Employee's social security number 123-45-6789		9 Advance EIC payment	10 Dependent care benefits	
e Employee's first name and initial Last name Suff. Yasuo Konami		11 Nonqualified plans	12a	
		13 Statutory employee ☐ Retirement plan ☐ Third-party sick pay ☐	12b	
		14 Other	12c	
			12d	
f Employee's address and ZIP code				

15 State Employer's state ID number IL 37-14119877	16 State wages, tips, etc.	17 State income tax $2,801	18 Local wages, tips, etc.	19 Local income tax	20 Locality name

Form **W-2** **Wage and Tax Statement**

Department of the Treasury—Internal Revenue Service

Copy 1—For State, City, or Local Tax Department

- Forgiven or cancelled debt, except for mortgage debt forgiven through foreclosure, short sale, or loan modification
- Alimony received
- Scholarship and fellowship income spent on room, board, and other living expenses
- Grants and the value of tuition reductions that pay for teaching or other services
- Annuity and pension income received
- Withdrawals and disbursements from retirement accounts, such as an individual retirement account (IRA) or 401(k) retirement plan (discussed in Chapter 17, "Retirement and Estate Planning")
- Military retirement income
- Social Security income (a portion is taxed above certain income thresholds)
- Disability payments received if you did not pay the premiums
- Damage payments from personal injury lawsuits (punitive damages only)
- Value of personal use of employer-provided car
- State and local income tax refunds (only if the taxpayer itemized deductions during the previous year)
- Employee productivity awards
- Awards for artistic, scientific, and charitable achievements unless assigned to a charity
- The value of prizes, contest winnings, and rewards
- Gambling and lottery winnings
- All kinds of illegal income
- Fees for serving as a juror or election worker
- Unemployment benefits
- Net rental income
- Royalties
- Investment, business, and farm profits
- Interest income (this includes credit union dividends)
- Dividend income (including mutual fund capital gains distributions even though they are reinvested)

Capital Gains and Losses Are Taxed at Special Low Rates An **asset** is property owned by a taxpayer for personal use or as an investment that has monetary value. Examples of assets include stocks, mutual funds, bonds, land, art, gems, stamps, coins, vehicles, and homes. The net income received from the sale of an asset above the costs incurred to purchase and sell it is a **capital gain**. There is no tax liability on any capital gain until the stock, bond, mutual fund, real estate, or other investment is sold.

capital gain

The net income received from the sale of an asset above the costs incurred to purchase and sell it.

A **capital loss** results when the sale of an asset brings less income than the costs of purchasing and selling the asset. Capital gains and losses on investments must be reported on your tax return. Capital gains from the sale or exchange of property held for personal use, such as on a vehicle or vacation home, must be reported as income, but losses on such property are not deductible.

A **short-term gain** (or **loss**) occurs when you sell an asset that you have owned for one year or less; it is taxed at the same rates as ordinary income, which is all income other than capital gains. A **long-term gain** (or **loss**) occurs when you sell an asset that you have owned for more than one year (at least a year and a day), and it is taxed at special low rates.

long-term gain/loss

A profit or loss on the sale of an asset that has been held for more than a year.

The long-term capital gains rate is zero for taxpayers in the 10 or 15 percent marginal tax brackets. The long-term rate is 15 percent for those in the 25, 28, 33, and 35 percent brackets, and it is 20 percent for those in the 39.6 percent tax bracket. Capital losses may be used first to offset capital gains on your tax return. If there are no capital gains, or if the capital losses are larger than the capital gains, you can deduct

DID YOU KNOW ?

Income Inequality, Incredibly, Gets Worse

Continuing a three-decade trend, in a recent year the wealthiest Americans—the richest 1 percent who have a pre-tax family income above $394,000—earned more than 23 percent of the country's household income. And they earned 95 percent of the increase in income of the last decade. The top 10 percent of earners—those with pre-tax income exceeding $114,000—captured 48 percent of total earnings.

Our economic system is heavily skewed in favor of the wealthiest. Despite rhetoric to the contrary, income and wealth does not trickle down. In fact, both are being sucked upward at a growing rate. When only a few people are winning and millions more are losing, surely something is amiss.

The United States is the top inequality country compared to most developed countries. This is because our taxes, which are low by international standards, and our social welfare programs, which are less generous. Lower taxes means less for government to spend on the needy and middle class.

For example, Social Security typically provides an American retiree with about half of his/her earnings; European countries typically replace two-thirds of retiree income. The USA spends little on early childhood education. Europeans spend less on single-payer national health insurance, and their workers are guaranteed from 20 to 35 days of paid leave annually.

The U.S. is the only developed country in the world that does not guarantee its workers some form of paid family leave, paid sick leave, or paid vacation time. Yet, 4 out of 5 Americans strongly support a law requiring such benefits.

the capital loss against your other income, but only up to a limit of $3,000 in one year. If your net capital loss is more than $3,000, the excess may be carried forward to be deducted on the next tax year's form, again up to an annual $3,000 maximum.

Dividends and Interest Are Treated Differently Owners of stocks in a corporation may receive dividends quarterly. These payments to shareholders are made out of current or accumulated earnings of a corporation and are taxable. Shareholders are annually sent tax forms IRS 1099-DIV that explains what amounts must be reported to the IRS when taxes are filed. Dividends from most domestic corporations and many foreign companies are subject to the same favorable rates as capital gains. Dividends in the form of shares of stock are generally not taxable.

So-called dividends are actually "interest" reported to taxpayers on Form 1099-INT when received from credit unions, cooperative banks, savings and loan associations, building and loan associations, and mutual savings banks. They are subject to ordinary income taxes. Dividends received from a life insurance policy are not taxed because they actually are a refund of your premium.

4.2b   Determine and Report Your Gross Income After Subtracting Exclusions

gross income

All income in the form of money, goods, services, and/or property.

exclusions

Income not subject to federal taxation.

Gross income consists of all income (both earned and unearned) received in the form of money, goods, services, and property before exclusions and deductions that a taxpayer is required to report to the IRS. To determine gross income, you need to determine which kinds of income are not subject to federal taxation and, therefore, need not be reported as part of gross income. These amounts are called **exclusions**.

Income to Exclude The more common exclusions (some are subject to limits) are as follows:

- Gifts
- Inherited money or property
- Income from a carpool
- Income from items sold at a garage sale for a sum less than what you paid

DO IT IN CLASS

- Cash rebates on purchases of new cars and other products
- Tuition reduction, if not received as compensation for teaching or service
- Federal income tax refunds
- State and local income tax refunds for a year in which you claimed the standard deduction
- Scholarship and fellowship income spent on course-required tuition, fees, books, supplies, and equipment (degree candidates only)
- Withdrawals from state-sponsored Section 529 plans (prepaid tuition and savings) used for education
- Prizes and awards made primarily to recognize artistic, civic, charitable, educational, and similar achievements
- Return of money loaned
- Withdrawals from medical savings accounts used for qualified expenses
- Earnings accumulating within annuities, cash-value life insurance policies, Series EE bonds, and qualified retirement accounts
- Interest income received on tax-exempt government bonds issued by states, counties, cities, and districts
- Life insurance benefits received
- Combat zone pay for military personnel
- Welfare, black lung, workers' compensation, and veterans' benefits
- Value of food stamps
- First $500,000 ($250,000 if single) gain on the sale of a principal residence
- Disability insurance benefits if you paid the insurance premiums
- Social Security benefits (except for high-income taxpayers)
- Rental income from a vacation home if not rented for more than 14 days
- First $5,000 of death benefits paid by an employer to a worker's beneficiary
- Travel and mileage expenses reimbursed by an employer (if not previously deducted by the taxpayer)
- Employer-provided per diem allowance covering only meals and incidentals
- Amounts paid by employers for premiums for medical insurance, workers' compensation, and health and long-term care insurance
- Moving expense reimbursements received from an employer (if not previously deducted by the taxpayer)
- Employer-provided payments of $255 per month for transit passes and $255 a month for parking
- Value of premiums for first $50,000 worth of group-term life insurance provided by an employer
- Employer payments (up to $5,000) for dependent care assistance (for children and parents)
- Benefits from employers that are impractical to tax because they are so modest, such as occasional supper money and taxi fares for overtime work, company parties, holiday gifts (not cash), and occasional theater or sporting events
- Employer contributions for employee expenses for education (up to $5,250 annually)
- Employee contributions to flexible spending accounts
- Reimbursements from flexible spending accounts
- Interest received on Series EE and Series I bonds used for college tuition and fees
- Child support payments received
- Property settlement in a divorce
- Compensatory damages in physical injury cases

ADVICE FROM A SEASONED PRO

How to Determine Household Income Under the Affordable Care Act

If you qualify under the Affordable Care Act (see Chapter 11), you must calculate your household income. This means add together your modified adjusted gross income (MAGI) plus the MAGI of your spouse (if you have one) and any tax dependents, and increase it by any excluded foreign income and tax-exempt interest. This number is used to determine eligibility for the premium tax credit and for imposing a penalty on anyone who fails to purchase minimum essential coverage. For most people MAGI is the same as adjusted gross income (AGI).

Stephanie R. Yates
University of Alabama at Birmingham, Birmingham, Alabama

adjustments to income

A special class of a dozen-plus subtractions from gross income that "adjust" or reduce one's income to get the income down to adjusted gross income.

adjusted gross income (AGI)

Gross income less any exclusions and adjustments.

household income

Modified gross income increased by any excluded foreign income and tax-exempt interest. Used under the Affordable Care Act to determine eligibility for the premium tax credit and for imposing a penalty on anyone who fails to purchase minimum essential coverage.

above-the-line deductions

Adjustments subtracted from gross income whether taxpayer itemizes deductions or not.

itemized deductions

Tax-deductible expenses that may be used to directly reduce income and reduce one's tax liability.

DO IT IN CLASS

4.2c Subtract Adjustments to Income

In the effort to reduce your income tax liability, you may take any appropriate **adjustments to income** (or **adjustments**). These are a special class of subtractions from gross income that "adjust" or reduce one's income to get the income down to **adjusted gross income (AGI)**, which is gross income less any exclusions and adjustments.

Subtracting adjustments to income from gross income results in a subtotal. A lower AGI directly cuts your overall tax bill because figuring your AGI is the first step in arriving at one's eventual taxable income amount. The lower your taxable income, the less you will owe the IRS.

The dozen-plus adjustments include the following: moving expenses to a new job location (including college graduates who move to take their first job as long as it is at least 50 miles from their old residence); higher-education expenses (including prepaid charges) for "tuition and fees" (up to $4,000); student loan interest for higher education, including that paid by a parent ($2,500 maximum); military reservists' travel expenses (for more than 100 miles); contributions to qualified personal retirement accounts (IRA and 401(k) accounts) and health savings accounts (up to $3,350 for singles and $6,750 for family coverage); alimony payments; interest penalties for early withdrawal of savings certificates of deposit; $250 for teachers who purchase classroom supplies; and certain expenses of self-employed people (such as health insurance premiums).

To illustrate the value of adjustments to income, consider that Steven Colbert, of Montclair, New Jersey, has a gross income of $85,000. This past year he spent $5,000 moving to New York City, for a new job in broadcasting, and he also paid $2,000 in higher-education expenses working on a graduate degree. The $7,000 in adjustments reduces his gross income from $88,000 to $81,000, and therefore Steven saves $1,750 in income taxes because he is in the 25 percent marginal tax bracket ($7,000 × 0.25).

Adjustments are called **above-the-line deductions** because one subtracts them on the first page of your tax form, just above the last line where you enter your adjusted gross income. Adjustments may be subtracted from gross income regardless of whether or not the taxpayer itemizes deductions or takes the standard deduction amount (discussed next).

4.2d Subtract Either Your Itemized Deductions or the IRS's Standard Deduction for Your Tax Status

Taxpayers may reduce income further by the amount of their **itemized deductions**. These are about 350 possible tax-deductible expenses that can be used to directly reduce income and reduce one's tax liability. Or you can take the government's standard deduction amount, and you want to use the larger of the two figures to further reduce your income.

ADVICE FROM A SEASONED PRO

A Sideline Business Can Reduce Your Income Taxes

A sideline business can open many doors to tax deductions. You should never spend money simply for a tax deduction, after all there is no such thing as a 100 percent marginal tax rate. However, if you're going to spend the money anyway, you should do everything you can to make it tax deductible.

By having your own business, every dollar you spend attempting to make a profit becomes tax deductible in determining one's adjusted gross income (AGI). This is far superior to an employee's business expenses that are only deductible as a miscellaneous itemized deduction to the extent they exceed 2 percent of AGI.

While no deduction is allowed for personal expenses, you can deduct expenses for the business use of your automobile, travel, office (you can get a limited deduction even if the office is in your home as long as you have space exclusively devoted to the business), office equipment (e.g., desk, chair, computer), contributions to self-funded retirement accounts, health insurance premiums, educational expenses, meals and entertainment (50 percent), business gifts (limited to $25 per gift), and more. You can deduct salaries of employees, even if they are your children, other relatives, or friends.

The business does not have to be your primary employment. If you lose money in the business, you can deduct those losses from your other income. The tax law provides that you must do what a "reasonable business person" would do in order to make a profit. If you do not meet that test, the tax law will classify the operation as a hobby, require you to report the income, and disallow all deductions. However, the tax law does provide a presumption that you are engaged in a "for profit" activity as long as your income exceeds your expenses for 3 of the prior 5 years, although this is not a requirement. Even if the activity is deemed a hobby you can deduct expenses up to the amount of revenue derived from such activity.

Howard Davidoff
Brooklyn College, Brooklyn, New York

Table 4-2 Tax Rate Schedules

DO IT IN CLASS

Single Individuals If taxable income is over—	But not over—	The tax is—
$ 0	$ 9,275	10% of the taxable income
$ 9,276	$ 37,650	$927.50 plus 15% of the amount over $9,275
$ 37,651	$ 91,150	$5,183.75 plus 25% of the amount over $37,650
$ 91,151	$190,150	$18,558.75 plus 28% of the amount over $91,150
$190,151	$413,350	$46,278.75 plus 33% of the amount over $190,150
$413,351	$415,050	$119,934.75 plus 35% of the amount over $413,350
Over $415,050	No limit	$120,529.75 plus 39.6% of the amount over $415,050
Married Couples Filing Jointly **If taxable income is over—**	**But not over—**	**The tax is—**
$ 0	$ 18,550	10% of the taxable income
$ 18,551	$ 75,300	$1855 plus 15% of the amount over $18,550
$ 75,301	$151,900	$10,367.50 plus 25% of the amount over $75,300
$151,901	$231,450	$29,517.50 plus 28% of the amount over $151,900
$231,451	$413,350	$51,791.50 plus 33% of the amount over $231,450
$413,351	$466,950	$111,818,50 plus 35% of the amount over $413,350
Over $466,950	No limit	$130,578.50 plus 39.6% of the amount over $466,950

standard deduction

A base amount of income that all taxpayers (except some dependents) who do not itemize deductions regardless of their actual expenses may subtract from their adjusted gross income.

filing status

Defines the type of tax return form an individual will use as it is based on marital status and family situation, and it is a description of one's marital status on the last day of the year.

The **standard deduction** is a base amount of income that all taxpayers (except some dependents) who do not itemize deductions regardless of their actual expenses may subtract from their adjusted gross income. In effect, it consists of the government's permissible estimate of any likely tax-deductible expenses these taxpayers might have. Two out of three taxpayers take the standard deduction.

The standard deduction amount depends on **filing status**, which is an important factor when computing taxable income, as it defines the type of tax return form an individual will use, which is based on marital status and family situation. It is a description of your marital status on the last day of the year. A taxpayer who qualifies for more than one filing status may choose the most advantageous status.

A return can be filed with a status of a single person, a married person (filing separately or jointly), a head of household, or qualifying widow or widower. Certain tax benefits apply to each filing status. For example, the standard deduction amounts are $6,300 for single individuals and twice as much, $12,600, for married people filing jointly.

Additional standard deductions are permitted for those who are blind or over the age of 65. The additional standard deduction for those age 65 or older or who are blind is $1,250 for married individuals and surviving spouses. It is $1,550 for singles age 65 or older or blind filers.

Taxpayers can take the greater of their itemized deductions or the standard deduction but not both. For example, a single person might list all of his or her tax deductions and find that they total $6,900, which is more than the standard deduction amount of $6,300, so he or she takes the $6,900. Someone else with calculated deductions of $4,900 can instead take the standard deduction of $6,300.

The tax form lists the following six classifications of itemized deductions:

1. Medical and Dental Expenses
2. Taxes You Paid
3. Interest You Paid
4. Gifts to Charity
5. Casualty and Theft Losses
6. Job Expenses and Most Other Miscellaneous Deductions

Examples of deductions in each of these categories follow. Note that the deduction amounts allowed are reduced for very high-income taxpayers.

1. Medical and Dental Expenses (Not Paid by Insurance) in Excess of 10 Percent of Adjusted Gross Income*

Charitable contributions—even in cash—are typically tax deductible if you itemize deductions.

- Medicine and drugs
- Insurance premiums for medical, long-term care, and contact lenses
- Medical services (doctors, dentists, nurses, hospitals, long-term health care, acupuncture, chiropractor)
- Mileage traveled to medical appointments
- Sterilizations and prescription contraceptives
- Disability-related home or vehicle modifications
- Addiction treatment, lead paint removal, a guide dog
- Costs of a physician-prescribed course of treatment for obesity

* If you or your spouse is age 65 or older, medical expenses exceeding 7.5 percent of AGI may be claimed.

- Expenses for prescription drugs/programs to quit smoking
- Medical equipment and aids (contact lenses, eyeglasses, hearing devices, orthopedic shoes, false teeth, wheelchair lifts)
- Fees for childbirth preparation classes
- Costs of sending a mentally or physically challenged person to a special school
- Home improvements made for the physically disabled (ramps, railings, widening doors)
- Travel and conference registration fees for a parent to learn about a child's disease
- Long-term care policy premiums and nursing home expenses
- Transportation costs to and from locations where medical services are obtained, using a standard flat mileage allowance

2. Taxes You Paid

- Real estate property taxes (such as on a home or land), including prepaid taxes
- Personal property taxes (such as on an automobile or boat when any part of the tax is based on the value of the asset)
- State, local, and foreign income taxes
- State sales tax (only for residents of states with no or nearly no state income tax, including AK, FL, NV, NH, SD, TN TX, WA, WY); see "sales tax calculator" at www.irs.gov; those who made an expensive purchase, like a vehicle or boat, may claim a even larger deduction.
- Health care penalty tax, which is the greater of a flat dollar amount per individual of $695 or 2.5 percent of MAGI up to a maximum of $2,500; it is indexed to inflation.

3. Interest You Paid

- Interest paid on home mortgage loans
- "Points" treated as a type of prepaid interest on the purchase of a principal residence
- "Points" paid when refinancing a home mortgage (portion deducted over life of the loan)
- Private mortgage insurance (PMI) premiums paid on a home mortgage loan
- Interest paid on home-equity loans
- Interest paid on loans used for investments

DO IT IN CLASS

4. Gifts to Charity

- Cash contributions to qualified organizations such as churches, schools, and charities (keep records of all donations and get receipts for $250 or more)
- Noncash contributions at **fair market value** (what a willing buyer would pay to a willing seller); IRS says that personal property must be in "good used condition or better" to qualify
- Mileage allowance for travel and out-of-pocket expenses for volunteer charitable work
- Charitable contributions made through payroll deduction
- Contributions to charity up to $100,000 from one's individual retirement account (IRA) for those age 70½ or older

5. Casualty and Theft Losses (Not Paid by Insurance) in Excess of 10 Percent of Adjusted Gross Income

- Casualty losses (such as from storms, vandalism, and fires) in excess of $100
- Theft of money or property in excess of $100
- Mislaid or lost property if the loss results from an identifiable event that is unexpected or unusual (such as catching a diamond ring in a car door and losing the stone)

ADVICE FROM A SEASONED PRO

Deduct Work-Related Education as a Business Expense

If you are an employee, you may be able to deduct work-related education or training expenses paid during the year as an itemized deduction. To be deductible, your expenses must be for education that (1) maintains or improves your job skills or (2) that your employer or a law requires to keep your salary, status, or job.

However, even if the education meets either of these tests, the education cannot be part of a program that will qualify you for a new trade or business or that you need to meet the minimal educational requirements of your trade or business. You can deduct the costs of qualifying work-related education as a business expense even if the education could lead to a degree.

Although the education must relate to your present work, education expenses incurred during temporary absence from your job may be deductible. After your temporary absence, you must return to the same kind of work. Usually, absence from work for one year or less is considered temporary.

Expenses that you can deduct include: (1) tuition, books, supplies, lab fees, and similar items; (2) certain related transportation and travel costs; and (3) other educational expenses, such as the cost of research and typing. Travel can be deducted as a business-related or unreimbursed employee expense. Meals (subject to limits) and lodging also may be deductible. Your deduction will be the amount of qualifying work-related education expenses that exceed 2 percent of your adjusted gross income.

If you are self-employed, you may deduct your expenses for qualifying work-related education directly from your self-employment income.

Brianne C. Wilson
Huntingdon College, Montgomery, Alabama

6. Job Expenses and Most Other Miscellaneous Deductions in Excess of 2 Percent of Adjusted Gross Income (Partial Listing)

- Union or professional association dues and membership fees
- Subscriptions to magazines, journals, and newspapers used for business or professional purposes
- Books, software, tools, and supplies used in a business or profession
- Cost of computers and cell phones required as a condition of your job
- Clothing and uniforms not suitable for off-the-job usage as ordinary wearing apparel (protective shoes, hats, safety goggles, gloves, uniforms), laundering and cleaning
- Unreimbursed employee business expenses (but only a portion of the cost of meals and entertainment), including long-distance telephone calls, cleaning and laundry, and car washes of business vehicle
- Investment-related expenses (e.g., computer software, fees for online trading, adviser fees, investment club expenses, IRA fees, safe-deposit box rental, subscriptions to investment magazines and newsletters, tax preparation charges)
- Legal fees that pertain to tax advice in a divorce or alimony payments
- Travel costs between two jobs, using a flat mileage allowance
- Job-related car expenses (but not commuting to a regular job), using a flat mileage allowance or actual expenses
- Commuting costs to a temporary workplace
- Commuting costs that qualify as a business or education expense

- Medical examinations required (but not paid for) by an employer to obtain or keep a job
- Appraisal fees for charitable donations or casualty losses
- Education expenses if required to keep your job or improve your job or professional skills (but not if the training readies you for a new career)
- Job-hunting expenses for typing, printing, resume advice, career counseling, want ads, telephone calls, mailing costs, job placement agency fees, and travel for seeking a job in your current career field
- 50 percent of food and 100 percent of transportation and entertainment costs for job hunting (which does not have to be successful) in your current career
- 100 percent of gambling losses that offset reported gambling income (not subject to 2 percent AGI floor)
- 100 percent of business expenses for workers with disabilities (not subject to 2 percent AGI floor)

exemption (or **personal exemption**)
A legally permitted amount, an allowance to reduce one's taxable income, based on the number of people supported by the taxpayer's income.

dependent
A relative or household member supported by the taxpayer's income for whom an exemption may be claimed.

4.2e Subtract the Value of Your Personal Exemptions

An **exemption** (or **personal exemption**) is a legally permitted amount, an allowance to reduce one's taxable income, based on the number of people supported by the taxpayer's income. A **dependent** is a relative or household member supported by the taxpayer's income for whom an exemption may be claimed. Exemptions may be claimed for the taxpayer and qualifying dependents, such as a spouse (if filing jointly), children, parents, and other dependents earning less than a specific income and for whom the taxpayer provides more than half of their financial support. For example, a husband and wife with two young children would have four exemptions.

A person can serve as an exemption on only one tax return—his or her own or another person's (usually a parent). Each exemption reduces taxable income by $4,050. The value of an exemption is phased out for those with extremely high incomes.

4.2f Determine Your Preliminary Tax Liability

The steps detailed to this point have explained how to determine your taxable income. Taxable income is calculated by taking the taxpayer's gross income, subtracting the adjustments to income, subtracting the amount permitted for the number of exemptions allowed, and subtracting either the standard deduction or total itemized deductions.

The amount of taxable income is then used to determine taxpayers' preliminary tax liability via the tax tables or tax-rate schedules for his or her filing status (such as single or married filing jointly). The following examples illustrate how to determine tax liability. Table 4-3 shows segments of the tax table.

1. A married couple filing jointly has a gross income of $50,500, adjustments of $4,700, two exemptions ($4,050 each), and itemized deductions of $8,285. They take the standard deduction of $12,600 because their itemized deductions do not exceed that amount.

Gross income	$50,500
Less adjustments to income	−4,700
Adjusted gross income	45,800
Less standard deduction for married couple	−12,600
Subtotal	33,200
Less value of two exemptions	−8,100
Taxable income	25,100
Tax liability (from Table 4-3)	$ 2,841

DO IT IN CLASS

Table 4-3

Tax Table*

If Taxable Income Is		Your Tax Is	
At Least	But Less Than	Single	Married Filing Jointly
25,000	25,050	3,290	2,826
25,050	25,100	3,298	2,834
25,100	25,150	3,305	2,841
27,850	27,900	3,718	3,254
27,900	27,950	3,725	3,261
30,000	30,050	4,040	3,576
30,050	30,100	4,048	3,584
30,100	30,150	4,055	3,591
30,150	30,200	4,063	3,599
39,600	39,650	5,678	5,016
39,650	39,700	5,690	5,024
39,700	39,750	5,703	5,031
39,750	39,800	5,715	5,039
40,200	40,250	5,328	5,106
40,250	40,300	5,340	5,114
47,800	47,850	7,228	6,246
47,850	47,900	7,240	6,254
48,550	48,600	7,915	6,359
48,600	48,650	7,928	6,366
48,900	48,950	7,503	6,411
48,950	49,000	8,015	6,419
49,200	49,250	8,078	6,456
49,250	49,300	8,090	6,464
53,050	53,100	9,040	7,034
53,100	53,150	9,063	7,041
56,050	56,100	9,875	7,484
56,100	56,150	9,803	7,491
59,000	59,050	10,528	7,926
59,050	59,100	10,540	7,934
74,100	74,150	14,303	10,191
74,150	74,200	14,315	10,199
90,200	90,250	18,328	14,099
90,250	90,300	18,340	14,111

*These segments of the tax table are derived from the IRS tax-rate schedule illustrated in Table 4-2.

NEVER EVER

Let Someone Else Prepare Your Taxes

You can spend $100 or $200 to have someone else prepare your income taxes, but how are you ever going to learn what exclusions and adjustments to income are available to you and whether or not you can itemize your deductions? Get the software and do your own federal income return. And learn!

tax credit

Allows a reduction in one's tax liability on a dollar-for-dollar basis that is a direct subtraction of your tax liability.

nonrefundable tax credit

A tax credit that can reduce one's tax liability only to zero; however, if the credit is more than the tax liability, the excess is not refunded.

refundable tax credit

A tax credit that can reduce one's income tax liability to below zero with the excess being refunded to the taxpayer.

tax refund

Amount the IRS sends back to a taxpayer if withholding and estimated payments exceed the tax liability.

tax liability

This is the final dollar amount of federal income taxes one will owe the government.

THERE IS AN APP FOR THAT!

Some of the best apps are:

- IRS2GO
- TurboTax
- HRBlock
- Shoebox
- TaxAct
- TaxCaster

2. A single person has a gross income of $66,000, adjustments of $5,000, one exemption, and itemized deductions of $8,400. She subtracts her itemized deductions because the amount exceeds the $6,300 standard deduction value.

Gross income	$66,000
Less adjustments to income	−5,000
Adjusted gross income	61,000
Less itemized deductions	−8,400
Subtotal	52,600
Less value of one exemption	−4,050
Taxable income	48,550
Tax liability (from Table 4-3)	$ 7,915

3. A married couple with a gross income of $137,000 has adjustments of $4,000, two exemptions, and itemized deductions of $9,800. The standard deduction value for a married couple is taken because it exceeds the itemized deductions.

Gross income	$ 137,000
Less adjustments to income	−4,000
Adjusted gross income	133,000
Less standard deduction	−12,600
Subtotal	120,400
Less value of two exemptions	−8,100
Taxable income	112,300
Tax liability (from Table 4-2)*	$19,617.50

4.2g Subtract Tax Credits for Which You Qualify

You may be able to lower your preliminary tax liability through tax credits. A **tax credit** reduces your tax liability on a dollar-for-dollar basis, which is a direct subtraction of your tax liability. A tax deduction or exemption only lowers the amount of your taxable income; they do not benefit you as much as a tax credit. Tax deductions reduce your tax liability by your tax rate for every dollar of the deduction. A $1,000 tax deduction saves $250 in taxes if you are in the 25 percent bracket, but a $1,000 tax credit saves you $1,000.

You may take tax credits regardless of whether you itemize deductions. A **nonrefundable tax credit** may reduce your tax liability to zero (0), but not below. Thus, if the nonrefundable credit amount exceeds the tax you owe, you are not given a refund of the difference. A **refundable tax credit** can reduce your tax liability to below zero (0), and the excess amount will be refunded. To get a refundable tax credit, you must file an income tax return. Credits are often subject to income limits, meaning that high-income taxpayers may not be eligible for a particular credit. A list of tax credits is shown in Table 4-4.

Calculate Your Final Tax Liability Do the math from above to calculate your **tax liability**. This is the final dollar amount of federal income taxes one will owe the government.

4.2h Calculate the Balance Due the IRS or the Amount of Your Refund

After taking all your tax credits, if the amount withheld (shown on your W-2 form) plus any estimated tax payments you made is greater than your final tax liability, then you are entitled to receive a **tax refund**.

*The tax liability is calculated from the tax-rate schedules in Table 4-2 because the taxable income exceeds $100,000. The tax liability is computed on taxable income as follows: $112,300 − $75,300 = $37,000 × 0.25 = $9,250 + $10,367.50 = $19,617.50.

Table 4-4	Tax Credit Programs

Credit Program	Purpose	Details
Health Insurance Premium Tax Credit (HIPTC)	Provides through the Affordable Care Act that individuals and families may take a tax credit to help them afford health insurance coverage.	Insurance premium tax credit is refundable.
American Opportunity Tax Credit (AOTC)	Provides an up to $2,500 per tax credit to help defray college expenses for the first four years of postsecondary education.	Money spent for tuition, fees, books, and course materials paid by the taxpayer during the tax year. Must be enrolled at least half-time.
Hope Scholarship Credit	For those who paid tuition, fees, books, and related expenses for post-secondary education	Up to $2,500 per person in tax credits is partially refundable. One cannot take the Hope, AOTC, and LLC all in the same year.
Lifetime Learning Credit (LLC)	The nonrefundable credit may be claimed every year for tuition and related expenses paid for all years of postsecondary education .	Credit amounts to 20 percent of the first $10,000 paid, for a maximum of $2,000 for all eligible students in a family. One cannot take the LLC, Hope, and AOTC all in the same year.
Earned Income Credit (EIC) (or Earned Income Tax Credit [EITC])	Refundable credit may be claimed not only by low-income workers with a qualifying child but also, in certain cases, by childless workers.	Maximum credit is $506 with no qualifying children, $3,373 with one child, $5,572 with two children, and $6,269 with three or more children.
Child and Dependent Care Credit	For workers who pay employment-related expenses if the care for children under age 13 and/or other dependents gives them the freedom to work.	Part of credit may be refundable.
Child Tax Credits	Taxpayers can claim a **child tax credit (CTC)** of nonrefundable credit of up to $1,000 per child under age 17.	Some parents also may qualify for a refundable **additional child tax credit** if the child portion of the child and dependent care tax credit exceeds their tax liability.
Adoption Credit	Refundable credit.	Up to $13,400 is available for the qualifying costs of an adoption.
Mortgage Interest Credit	Nonrefundable credit of up to $2,000 for mortgage interest paid may be claimed under special state and local government programs that provide a "mortgage credit certificate."	For people who purchase a principal residence or borrow funds for certain home improvements. The home must not cost more than 90 to 110 percent of the average area purchase price.
Retirement Savings Contribution Credit	Nonrefundable credit of up to $1,000 is available.	Credit of 50, 20, or 10 percent of contribution is calculated based on a percentage of your retirement contributions.
Elderly or Disabled Tax Credit	Lower income individuals who are age 65 or older or who are permanently and totally disabled.	Nonrefundable federal tax credit that can be as much as $1,125.

DID YOU KNOW ?

About the Alternative Minimum Tax

The **alternative minimum tax (AMT)** takes back some of the tax breaks allowed for regular tax purposes for very high-income taxpayers who previously were escaping paying income taxes through legitimate means. Some high-income taxpayers (roughly between $200,000 and $500,000) are pushed into paying the higher AMT tax instead of the regular tax when claiming excess itemized deductions, certain tax-exempt interest, and/or a substantial number of exemptions.

When the value of those benefits is added back to one's income, it may result in an AMT calculation that exceeds one's regular tax. About four million taxpayers pay the AMT tax rate at 28 percent, which typically amounts to an additional tax liability of about $4,000.

If the amount is less than your final tax liability, then you have a **tax balance due**. If you owe money, you pay by check, money order, or credit card. The IRS imposes a convenience fee of 2.5 percent of the amount charged on a credit card.

4.2i What Form Do You Use to File?

To file your income tax return, you record all your tax information on the correct tax form and submit it to the Internal Revenue Service by mail or electronically. Use the IRS tax form that is appropriate for your circumstances:

- **Form 1040EZ.** You are single or married, under age 65, and have no dependents; your income consists of less than $100,000 in wages, salary, and tips, and no more than $1,500 in interest; and you do not claim any tax credits or adjustments or itemize deductions.
- **Form 1040A.** Your income is less than $100,000 and you use the standard deduction and/or take adjustments to income or tax credits.
- **Form 1040.** You itemize your deductions. Figure 4-4 shows a completed 1040 Form for a taxpayer.
- **Form 1040X.** You are eligible for a deserved refund or refundable tax credit, or you want to correct any tax filing mistake, or claim an overlooked deductions for any of the past three years.

4.2j You Should File Your Return on Time

You usually should file by April 15 to avoid a penalty. If you owe the IRS and you are broke, you can borrow to pay the taxes or contact the IRS about setting up an installment plan to repay the debt within three years.

Taxpayers hear from the IRS within three weeks if they have failed to sign the return, neglected to attach a copy of the Form W-2, made an error in arithmetic, owe a tax penalty, or figured the tax incorrectly. Once taxpayers file their federal return, they can track the status of their refunds by using the "Where's My Refund?" tool, located on the front page of www.irs.gov.

NUMBERS ON

Income Taxes

Data from a variety of sources suggest that:

- The main sources of federal tax revenue ($3.7 trillion) are individual income taxes (47 percent), payroll taxes (33 percent), and corporate income taxes (10 percent); and 10 percent from excise and other taxes and fees.
- Forty-five percent of Americans do not pay any federal income taxes as half of them do not work (too old, sick, or handicapped) and the other half pay zero because of tax credits targeted at lower- and middle-income taxpayers.

- The top-earning 1 percent of taxpayers paid nearly half of the federal income taxes.
- The top 50 percent of income earners paid 98 percent of the nation's federal income compared to the bottom 50 percent who paid 2 percent.
- The average tax rate for Americans is 13 percent.

4.2k The Best Tax Guides and Other Help

Your Federal Income Tax: For Individuals, Publication 17, is the IRS's detailed 100-plus-page book for preparing your income taxes. A good, readable tax guide is the annual *J. K. Lasser's Your Income Tax* (www. jklasser.com). All federal income tax forms, regulations, guides, and answers to frequently asked questions can be obtained from the IRS at (800) TAX-3676, or at www.irs.gov. The IRS help line is (800) TAX-1040. Most taxpayers can obtain free tax preparation from the Volunteer Income Tax Assistance (VITA) program (www.vita-volunteers.org/index.htm, or call (800) 906-9887).

4.2l File Your Income Taxes Electronically for Free and Get Your Refund Within Days

Ninety percent of taxpayer's returns are filed electronically, either by themselves or they pay someone else to file for them. Seventy percent pay someone to prepare the return. They think it is complicated even though for most people it is not. To file your income taxes online by yourself, visit the website of the Internal Revenue Service (www.irs.gov) and click on "IRS E-file."

Alternatively, you may choose to click on "IRS Free File" because it provides options for free brand-name tax software or online fillable forms plus free electronic filing for most taxpayers. E-filers may request that their refund be deposited directly into their bank account, and it usually will be deposited within ten days of filing. The average refund last year was over $3,200.

4.2m People Pay Their Income Tax Liability in One or Two Ways

The federal income tax is a "pay as you go" tax. Through **payroll withholding**, an employer takes a certain amount from an employee's income as a prepayment of an individual's tax liability for the year and sends those dollars to the IRS, where they are credited to that particular taxpayer's account. People who are self-employed or who receive substantial income from an employer that is not required to practice payroll withholding, such as lawyers, accountants, consultants, investors, authors, and owners of rental property, must pay **estimated taxes**. They are required to estimate their tax liability and pay their estimated taxes in advance in quarterly installments on April 15, June 15, September 15, and the following year's January 15.

MONEY WEBSITES

Informative websites are:

- Bankrate.com's tax estimator
- Bankrate
- Center for American Progress
- Dinkytown's tax estimator
- H&R Block's TaxCut
- Internal Revenue Service
- IRS *Publication* 17
- Lasser's Your Income Tax
- Quicken's TurboTax
- TaxACT
- Volunteer Income Tax Assistance
- Worldwide-Taxes

payroll withholding
The IRS requirement that an employer withhold a certain amount from an employee's income as a prepayment of that individual's tax liability for the year. It is sent to the government where it is credited to the taxpayer's account.

estimated taxes
People who are self-employed or receive substantial income from an employer that is not required to practice payroll withholding (such as lawyers and owners of rental property) are required by the IRS to estimate their tax liability and pay their taxes in advance in quarterly installments.

CONCEPT CHECK 4.2

1. Give five examples of income that must be included in income reported to the Internal Revenue Service.
2. How are long-term and short-term capital gains treated differently for income tax purposes?
3. Give five examples of income that is excluded from IRS reporting.
4. List three examples of adjustments to income.
5. Distinguish between a standard deduction and a personal exemption.
6. What advice on filing a Form 1040X can you offer someone who did not file a federal income tax return last year or in any one of the past three years?
7. List five examples of tax credits.

Figure 4-4   Federal Income Tax Form 1040 (Yasuo Konami)

Form **1040**
Department of the Treasury—Internal Revenue Service   (99)
U.S. Individual Income Tax Return   OMB No. 1545-0074   IRS Use Only—Do not write or staple in this space.

See separate instructions.

Your first name and initial	Last name	Your social security number
Yasuo	Konami	123 45 6789

If a joint return, spouse's first name and initial	Last name	Spouse's social security number

Home address (number and street). If you have a P.O. box, see instructions.   Apt. no.
1245 Oak Street

▲ Make sure the SSN(s) above and on line 6c are correct.

City, town or post office, state, and ZIP code. If you have a foreign address, also complete spaces below (see instructions).
Oak Park, FL 60302

Presidential Election Campaign
Check here if you, or your spouse if filing jointly, want $3 to go to this fund. Checking a box below will not change your tax or refund.   ☐ You ☐ Spouse

Foreign country name	Foreign province/state/county	Foreign postal code

Filing Status

Check only one box.

1 ☒ Single
2 ☐ Married filing jointly (even if only one had income)
3 ☐ Married filing separately. Enter spouse's SSN above and full name here. ▶
4 ☐ Head of household (with qualifying person). (See instructions.) If the qualifying person is a child but not your dependent, enter this child's name here. ▶ _____
5 ☐ Qualifying widow(er) with dependent child

Exemptions

6a ☒ **Yourself.** If someone can claim you as a dependent, **do not** check box 6a . . . . .
b ☐ **Spouse** . . . .

c **Dependents:** (1) First name Last name	(2) Dependent's social security number	(3) Dependent's relationship to you	(4) ✓ if child under age 17 qualifying for child tax credit (see instructions)
			☐
			☐
			☐
			☐

If more than four dependents, see instructions and check here ▶ ☐

d Total number of exemptions claimed . . . .

Boxes checked on 6a and 6b 1
No. of children on 6c who:
• lived with you
• did not live with you due to divorce or separation (see instructions)
Dependents on 6c not entered above
Add numbers on lines above ▶

Income

Attach Form(s) W-2 here. Also attach Forms W-2G and 1099-R if tax was withheld.

If you did not get a W-2, see instructions.

7	Wages, salaries, tips, etc. Attach Form(s) W-2		7	65,000 —
8a	**Taxable** interest. Attach Schedule B if required		8a	200 —
b	**Tax-exempt** interest. **Do not** include on line 8a . .	8b		
9a	Ordinary dividends. Attach Schedule B if required		9a	
b	Qualified dividends	9b		
10	Taxable refunds, credits, or offsets of state and local income taxes		10	
11	Alimony received		11	
12	Business income or (loss). Attach Schedule C or C-EZ		12	
13	Capital gain or (loss). Attach Schedule D if required. If not required, check here ▶ ☐		13	
14	Other gains or (losses). Attach Form 4797		14	
15a	IRA distributions . 15a	b Taxable amount . . .	15b	
16a	Pensions and annuities 16a	b Taxable amount . . .	16b	
17	Rental real estate, royalties, partnerships, S corporations, trusts, etc. Attach Schedule E		17	
18	Farm income or (loss). Attach Schedule F		18	
19	Unemployment compensation		19	
20a	Social security benefits 20a	b Taxable amount . . .	20b	
21	Other income. List type and amount		21	
22	Combine the amounts in the far right column for lines 7 through 21. This is your **total income** ▶		22	65,200 —

Adjusted Gross Income

23	Educator expenses	23		
24	Certain business expenses of reservists, performing artists, and fee-basis government officials. Attach Form 2106 or 2106-EZ	24		
25	Health savings account deduction. Attach Form 8889 .	25		
26	Moving expenses. Attach Form 3903	26		
27	Deductible part of self-employment tax. Attach Schedule SE .	27		
28	Self-employed SEP, SIMPLE, and qualified plans . .	28		
29	Self-employed health insurance deduction . . .	29		
30	Penalty on early withdrawal of savings	30		
31a	Alimony paid b Recipient's SSN ▶	31a		
32	IRA deduction	32	4,000 —	
33	Student loan interest deduction	33	1,100 —	
34	Tuition and fees. Attach Form 8917	34		
35	Domestic production activities deduction. Attach Form 8903	35		
36	Add lines 23 through 35	36		5,100 —
37	Subtract line 36 from line 22. This is your **adjusted gross income** . . . . . . ▶	37		60,100 —

For Disclosure, Privacy Act, and Paperwork Reduction Act Notice, see separate instructions.   Cat. No. 11320B   Form **1040** (2013)

(Continued)

Figure 4-4 Federal Income Tax Form 1040 (Yasuo Konami) (*Continued*)

Form 1040 (2013)   Page **2**

Tax and Credits	38	Amount from line 37 (adjusted gross income)	38	60,100	—
	39a	Check if: ☐ **You** were born before January 2, 1949, ☐ Blind. ☐ **Spouse** was born before January 2, 1949, ☐ Blind. } Total boxes checked ▶ 39a			
Standard Deduction for—	b	If your spouse itemizes on a separate return or you were a dual-status alien, check here ▶ 39b☐			
• People who check any box on line 39a or 39b **or** who can be claimed as a dependent, see instructions.	40	**Itemized deductions** (from Schedule A) **or** your **standard deduction** (see left margin) . .	40	6,950	—
	41	Subtract line 40 from line 38	41	53,150	—
	42	**Exemptions.** If line 38 is $150,000 or less, multiply $3,900 by the number on line 6d. Otherwise, see instructions	42	3,950	—
	43	**Taxable income.** Subtract line 42 from line 41. If line 42 is more than line 41, enter -0- . .	43	49,200	—
• All others:	44	**Tax** (see instructions). Check if any from: **a** ☐ Form(s) 8814 **b** ☐ Form 4972 **c** ☐ _____	44	8,078	—
Single or Married filing separately, $6,200	45	**Alternative minimum tax** (see instructions). Attach Form 6251	45		
Married filing jointly or Qualifying widow(er), $12,400	46	Add lines 44 and 45 . . . . ▶	46		
	47	Foreign tax credit. Attach Form 1116 if required	47		
	48	Credit for child and dependent care expenses. Attach Form 2441	48		
Head of household, $9,100	49	Education credits from Form 8863, line 19	49		
	50	Retirement savings contributions credit. Attach Form 8880	50		
	51	Child tax credit. Attach Schedule 8812, if required . . .	51		
	52	Residential energy credits. Attach Form 5695	52		
	53	Other credits from Form: **a** ☐ 3800 **b** ☐ 8801 **c** ☐ _____	53		
	54	Add lines 47 through 53. These are your **total credits**	54		
	55	Subtract line 54 from line 46. If line 54 is more than line 46, enter -0- . . . . . ▶	55		
Other Taxes	56	Self-employment tax. Attach Schedule SE	56		
	57	Unreported social security and Medicare tax from Form: **a** ☐ 4137 **b** ☐ 8919 . .	57		
	58	Additional tax on IRAs, other qualified retirement plans, etc. Attach Form 5329 if required	58		
	59a	Household employment taxes from Schedule H	59a		
	b	First-time homebuyer credit repayment. Attach Form 5405 if required	59b		
	60	Taxes from: **a** ☐ Form 8959 **b** ☐ Form 8960 **c** ☐ Instructions; enter code(s) _____	60		
	61	Add lines 55 through 60. This is your **total tax** . . . . ▶	61		
Payments	62	Federal income tax withheld from Forms W-2 and 1099 . .	62		
	63	2013 estimated tax payments and amount applied from 2012 return	63		
If you have a qualifying child, attach Schedule EIC.	64a	**Earned income credit (EIC)**	64a		
	b	Nontaxable combat pay election	64b			
	65	Additional child tax credit. Attach Schedule 8812	65		
	66	American opportunity credit from Form 8863, line 8 . . .	66		
	67	Reserved	67		
	68	Amount paid with request for extension to file	68		
	69	Excess social security and tier 1 RRTA tax withheld . . .	69		
	70	Credit for federal tax on fuels. Attach Form 4136	70		
	71	Credits from Form: **a** ☐ 2439 **b** ☐ Reserved **c** ☐ 8885 **d** ☐	71		
	72	Add lines 62, 63, 64a, and 65 through 71. These are your **total payments** . . . . . ▶	72	10,400	—
Refund	73	If line 72 is more than line 61, subtract line 61 from line 72. This is the amount you **overpaid**	73	2,322	—
	74a	Amount of line 73 you want **refunded to you.** If Form 8888 is attached, check here . ▶☐	74a		
Direct deposit? See instructions.	b	Routing number _____ ▶**c** Type: ☐ Checking ☐ Savings			
	d	Account number _____			
	75	Amount of line 73 you want **applied to your estimated tax** ▶	75		
Amount You Owe	76	**Amount you owe.** Subtract line 72 from line 61. For details on how to pay, see instructions ▶	76		
	77	Estimated tax penalty (see instructions)	77		

Third Party Designee	Do you want to allow another person to discuss this return with the IRS (see instructions)? ☐ **Yes.** Complete below. ☐ **No**
	Designee's name ▶ _____ Phone no. ▶ _____ Personal identification number (PIN) ▶ _____

Sign Here

Under penalties of perjury, I declare that I have examined this return and accompanying schedules and statements, and to the best of my knowledge and belief, they are true, correct, and complete. Declaration of preparer (other than taxpayer) is based on all information of which preparer has any knowledge.

Joint return? See instructions. Keep a copy for your records.	Your signature *Yasuo Konami* Date 04-15-18 Your occupation Media Specialist		Daytime phone number 630-555-1234
	Spouse's signature. If a joint return, **both** must sign. Date Spouse's occupation		If the IRS sent you an Identity Protection PIN, enter it here (see inst.)

Paid Preparer Use Only	Print/Type preparer's name	Preparer's signature Date	Check ☐ if self-employed PTIN
	Firm's name ▶		Firm's EIN ▶
	Firm's address ▶		Phone no.

Form **1040**

4.3 STRATEGIES TO REDUCE YOUR INCOME TAXES

While the U.S. tax laws are strict and punitive about compliance (although the IRS audits less than 0.5 percent of all returns), they remain neutral about whether the taxpayer should take advantage of every "tax break" and opportunity possible. The strategies described here will help you to reduce your tax liability.

4.3a Practice Legal Tax Avoidance, Not Tax Evasion

tax evasion

Deliberately and willfully hiding income from the IRS, falsely claiming deductions, or otherwise cheating the government out of taxes owed; it is illegal.

tax avoidance

Reducing tax liability through legal techniques.

Tax evasion involves deliberately and willfully hiding income, falsely claiming deductions, or otherwise cheating the government out of taxes owed. It is illegal. A waiter who does not report tips received and a babysitter who does not report income are both evading taxes, as is a person who deducts $150 in charitable contributions but who does not actually make the donations.

Tax avoidance means reducing tax liability through legal techniques. It involves applying knowledge of the tax code and regulations to personal income tax planning. Tax evasion results in penalties, fines, interest charges, and a possible jail sentence. In contrast, tax avoidance boosts your income because you pay less in taxes. As a result, you will have more money available to spend, save, invest, and donate.

4.3b Strategy: Reduce Taxable Income via Your Employer

It may seem illogical to suggest that to lower your tax liability you should reduce your income. But it is not. The objective is to reduce *taxable* income. Reducing your federal taxable income also will reduce the personal income taxes imposed by state and local governments. Four useful ways of reducing taxable income are premium-only plans, transit spending accounts, dependent care flexible spending accounts, and defined-contribution retirement plans.

Premium-Only Plan Many large employers offer a **premium-only plan (POP)** that allows employees to withhold a portion of their pretax salary to pay their premiums for employer-provided health benefits. Benefits could include health, dental, vision, and disability insurance. Amounts withheld are not reported to the IRS as taxable income. For example, if Nhon Ngo, a restaurant manager in Dallas, has $400 per month ($4,800 annually) withheld through his employer to pay for his share of the employer-sponsored health insurance premium, he saves as much as $1,920 ($4,800 × 0.40 [his effective marginal tax rate]) a year because he does not have to send that amount to the government in taxes.

Transit Spending Account A transportation reimbursement plan is a similar pretax program. This employer plan allows you the opportunity to save money by using payroll deduction with pretax salary dollars to pay for work-related transportation expenses, such as transit passes ($255) and qualified parking ($255). If Nhon contributes $510 in pretax income to his employer's transportation plan, he saves as much as $204 ($255 + $255 = $510 × 0.40).

FSA debit card (also known as flexcard)

A card used to access and spend funds from a flexible spending account.

Flexible Spending Account A benefit for employees who pay for child care or provide care for a parent is a salary reduction plan known as a **flexible spending account (FSA)**, also called a **flexible spending arrangement**. An FSA allows an employee (and an employer) to fund qualified expenses on a pretax basis through salary reduction to pay for out-of-pocket unreimbursed expenses for medical and dental expenses (maximum for employees is $2,600 annually) and dependent care (maximum is $5,000 annually). The expenses are those that are not covered by insurance. Examples are annual deductibles, office co-payments, orthodontia, prescriptions, and over-the-counter drugs for which one has a doctor's prescription. Paper forms or an **FSA debit card**, sometimes known as a **flexcard**, may be used to spend the funds. The salary reductions are not included in the individual's taxable earnings reported on Form W-2, and reimbursements from an FSA account are tax free.

FSAs are subject to a "**use-it-or-lose-it rule**," which means that any unspent dollars in the account at the end of the year are forfeited and not returned to the employee. As a result, you should make conservative estimates of your expenses when you elect your FSA choices. For example, if you had $1,000 withheld for medical expenses but spent only $700 over the year the balance of $300 will go back to your employer, not to you. The IRS does allow a 2½-month additional "grace period" if one's employer permits such an extension.

In summary, suppose Nhon in the preceding example has $4,800 annually withheld through his employer's premium-only plan to be used to pay out-of-pocket medical expenses, another $510 to the transit reimbursement plan, plus another $3,000 to pay out-of-pocket expenses for dependent care of his child. Thus, Nhon saves a whopping $3,324 ($4,800 + $510 + $3,000 × .40) in federal income taxes by contributing to IRS-approved employer provided programs.

Defined-Contribution Retirement Plan Contributing money to a qualified employer-sponsored retirement plan also reduces income taxes. A **defined-contribution retirement plan** (discussed in Chapter 17) is an IRS-approved retirement plan sponsored by an employer to which employees may make pretax contributions that lower their tax liability. The most popular plan is known as a 401(k) retirement plan, although other variations exist as well.

The amount of money that an employee contributes to his or her individual account via salary reduction also does not show up as taxable income on the employee's W-2 form. For example, if you contribute $2,000 to your employer's retirement plan and you are in the 25 percent tax bracket, this immediately saves you at least $500 ($2,000 × 0.25) that you will not have to pay in income taxes this year.

An extra benefit of a defined-contribution retirement plan is that employers often offer full or partial **matching contributions** to employees' accounts up to a certain proportion. For example, if you invest $2,000 into your 401(k) plan and your employer matches half of what you contribute, that is an immediate return of 50 percent ($1,000 / $2,000) on your investment! The employer's "match" is essentially free money.

All of the dollars in a qualified retirement plan are likely to be invested in mutual funds where they will grow free of income taxes. Income taxes must eventually be paid when withdrawals are made, presumably during retirement when the marginal tax rate may be lower than during one's working years.

4.3c Strategy: Prune Taxable Investments

If you have some investments in your portfolio that have lost value, you may want to sell them before the end of the year. Then you can use those capital losses to offset any capital gains earned that year from other investments. If you do not have gains to offset, you can deduct up to $3,000 annually in losses against your regular income. Another strategy is to donate stocks that have appreciated in value to charity. In addition to obtaining the substantial charitable tax deduction, you avoid having to pay taxes on the gain.

4.3d Strategy: Make Tax-Sheltered Investments

Investments are often made with **after-tax dollars**, which means that the individuals earned the money and paid income taxes on it. Then they take their after-tax money and invest it. The returns earned from these investments typically again result in taxable income. Investment alternatives are examined in Chapters 13 through 16.

Tax laws encourage certain types of investments or other taxpayer behaviors by giving them special tax advantages over other activities, and as a result, numerous **tax-sheltered investments** exist. A tax shelter is any financial arrangement (as a certain kind of investment) that results in a reduction or elimination of taxes due. The tax laws allow certain income to be exempt from income taxes in the current year or permit an

---

YOUR GRANDPARENTS SAY

"Don't Pay the IRS First"

The federal government has many programs that allow taxpayers to reduce their income *before* calculating how much they owe in income taxes, so see your employer and sign up to contribute your pre-tax money for retirement, flexible benefits, transit, and children's education.

---

use-it-or-lose-it rule

An IRS regulation requiring that unspent dollars in a flexible spending account at the end of a calendar year be forfeited, unless the employer allows a 2 1/2-month grace period for spending the funds.

defined-contribution retirement plan

IRS-approved retirement plan sponsored by employers that allows employees to make pretax contributions that lower their tax liability.

matching contributions

Employer programs that match employees' 401 (k) contributions up to a particular percentage.

after-tax dollars

Money on which an employee has already paid taxes.

tax-sheltered investments

A financial arrangement that results in a reduction or elimination of taxes due.

DID YOU KNOW ?

Create Future Tax-Free Income with Your Refund

You can instruct the IRS to deposit your tax refund directly into a Roth IRA. This IRA account can be opened online in minutes without making an initial deposit. All the money will grow tax-free, and future withdrawals will be tax-free too.

tax sheltered

Income, dividends, or capital gains that are allowed to grow without taxes until distributions are taken.

Roth IRA

An individual retirement account of investments made with after-tax money; the interest on such accounts is allowed to grow tax-free, and withdrawals are also tax-free.

traditional individual retirement account (IRA)

Investment account that reduces current year income, and the funds in the account accumulate tax-free.

Coverdell education savings account (or education savings account)

An IRS-approved way to pay the future education costs for a child younger than age 18 whereby the earnings accumulate tax-free and withdrawals for qualified expenses are tax-free.

adjustment, reduction, deferral of income tax liability. When making investment decisions, investors should consider tax-sheltered investments.

Invest with Pretax Income Making an investment contribution with **pretax income** means that you do not have to pay taxes this year on the income. In effect, investing with pretax income is an interest-free deferral of income taxes to another year. An example is to make pre-tax contributions to work-related retirement plans.

Make Your Investments Grow Tax Sheltered When income, dividends, or capital gains are tax sheltered, the investor does not pay the current-year tax liability on the income and instead shifts the income and any tax liability to a later year. This benefit is substantial. Investments can grow faster because the money that would have gone to the government in taxes every year can remain in the investment for many years to accumulate. In effect, the government "loans" tax-free money to taxpayers to help fund their investment and retirement plans. The tax-free growth of such investments is called **tax-sheltered compounding**.

Eights Examples of Tax-Sheltered Investments Numerous tax-sheltered investments exist, and some popular ones follow.

Roth IRA Accounts Contributions (up to $5,500 annually) to a Roth IRA accumulate tax-free and withdrawals are tax-free. There is no tax break on Roth IRA contributions, as they are made with after-tax money. This is an excellent investment vehicle for people with a long-term investment horizon who want to save more money for retirement than they can through an employer-sponsored retirement plan. All types of IRA accounts and other retirement plans are examined in Chapter 17.

Individual Retirement Accounts The amount contributed (up to $5,500 annually) to a **traditional individual retirement account (IRA)** is considered an adjustment to income, which reduces your current-year income tax liability. Investments inside the IRA (such as stocks and stock mutual funds) accumulate tax sheltered. Income taxes are owed on the eventual withdrawals, likely during retirement.

Coverdell Education Savings Accounts Contributions of up to $2,000 per year of after-tax money may be made to a **Coverdell education savings account** (also known as an **education savings account** and formerly known as an "Education IRA") to pay future education costs. Earnings accumulate tax-free, and withdrawals for qualified expenses are tax-free. The money can be used to pay for public, private, or religious school expenses, in college or graduate school. It can pay for tuition, fees, room and board, tutoring, uniforms, home computers, Internet access and related technology, transportation, and extended day care.

Qualified Tuition Programs There are two types of **qualified tuition programs**, and these are known as **529 plans**. Under the **prepaid educational service plan**, an individual purchases tuition credits today for use in the future. Also known as a state-sponsored **prepaid tuition plan**, this program allows parents, relatives, and friends to purchase a child's future college education at today's prices by guaranteeing that amounts prepaid will be used for the future tuition at an approved institution of higher education in a particular state. The funds may be used to pay for tuition only—not room, board, or supplies.

The second qualified IRS Section 529 tuition program, called a **college savings plan**, is set up for a designated beneficiary; these are administered mostly by state governments. Withdrawals are tax-free if made for qualified education expenses such as tuition, room, and board. If one child does not go to college, the funds may be transferred to another relative. One may contribute to both a Section 529 plan and a Coverdell education savings account for the same beneficiary in the same year.

Government Savings Bonds Series EE and Series I **government savings bonds** are promissory notes issued by the federal government. The income is exempt from state and local taxes. You may defer the income tax until final maturity (**30 years**) or report

DID YOU KNOW

How to Save for a Child's College Education

Good ways to save for a child's college education while taking advantage of some income tax breaks are as follows:

The **Section 529 College Savings Plan** is named after the related section of the Internal Revenue Service Code, and all states have established at least one **Section 529 college savings plan**. Deposits into a 529 plan are not deductible, but withdrawals (including tax-free growth) for qualified educational expenses are tax-free.

A **Coverdell Education Savings Account** accepts nondeductible contributions up to a maximum of $2,000 per year for a child younger than 18 to pay his or her future education costs. The money and earnings on the account may be withdrawn tax-free to pay for qualified expenses.

Traditional Individual Retirement Accounts (IRAs) are designed primarily for retirement savings but under certain circumstances withdrawals can be used to pay for qualified college expenses for the account holder, child or grandchild. Early withdrawal penalties are waived if the funds are used for education expenses.

A **custodial account** may be opened in the name of a child younger than age 14 under the provisions of the uniform Gifts to Minors Act. College students usually are in the 10 or 15 percent tax bracket and they may be able to sell

assets given to them without paying any capital gains taxes. The **kiddie tax** also applies to income of a minor child earned off the assets (such as interest and dividends). For children younger than age 18, the first $1,050 of unearned income (the income earned from an investment) earned on custodial account assets is tax-free to the child. The next $1,050 is taxed at the child's tax rate. Income in excess of $2,100 is taxed at the parent's (likely higher) rate. When a child is age 18, he or she pays taxes based on his or her own income tax bracket.

Discount bonds (also called **zeroes** or **zero coupon bonds**) are corporate and government bonds that pay no annual interest. Instead, discount bonds are sold to investors at sharp discounts from their face value, which may be redeemed at full value upon maturity. For example, a $10,000 **Series EE savings bond** sold by the federal government can be purchased for $5,000, one-half its face amount. The interest accumulates within the bond itself, and this phantom income earned by a child is generally so small that little, if any, income taxes are due each year as the bond matures. Taxes on the interest earned each year may be deferred until redemption and are tax-free when the proceeds are used to fund a child's college education.

---

the interest annually. Reporting the interest in a child's name is advisable especially when it can be offset totally by the child's standard deduction. You may exclude accumulated interest from bonds from income tax in the year you redeem the bonds to pay qualified educational expenses. (See Chapter 14 for more information.)

Tax-Exempt Municipal Bonds Tax-exempt **municipal bonds** (also called **munis**) are long-term debts issued by local governments and their agencies that are used to finance public improvement projects. Interest is free from federal and state taxes if the bond is purchased in one's state of residence. Taxpayers in higher-income brackets (28 percent or more) often take advantage of these kinds of investments. (See Chapter 14.) Smart investors choose the bonds that pay the better return after payment of income taxes. The formula to decide whether a taxable investment or nontaxable investment is better for you appears in the box "How to Compare Taxable and After-Tax Yields" on page 140.

Capital Gains on Housing A big tax shelter is available to homeowners when they sell their homes. Those with appreciated principal residences are allowed to avoid taxes on capital gains of up to $500,000 if married and filing jointly and on gains up to $250,000 if single. The home must have been owned and used as the taxpayer's private residence for two out of the five years immediately prior to the date of the sale.

Savings Plans for the Disabled The Achieving Better Life Experience (ABLE) savings plans permit after-tax contributions up to $14,000 to care for those adults with a severe disability, such as autism, Down syndrome, or

NEVER EVER

1. *Turn all your income tax planning over to someone else instead of doing it yourself.*

2. *Overwithhold your income taxes to receive a big refund next year causing you to lose interest on the potential earnings.*

3. *Ignore the impact of income taxes in your personal financial planning.*

DID YOU KNOW ?

How to Compare Taxable and After-Tax Yields

Investors may choose to put their money into vehicles that provide taxable income, such as stocks, corporate bonds, and stock mutual funds. Taxpayers also have the opportunity to lower their income tax liabilities by investing in tax-exempt municipal bonds, money market funds that invest in municipal bonds, and other tax-exempt ventures. (These investment alternatives are discussed in Chapter 14.)

Because of their tax-exempt status, these investments offer lower nominal returns than taxable alternatives. But after considering the effects of taxes, the actual return to an investor on a tax-exempt investment may be higher than the after-tax yield on a taxable corporate bond.

To find out whether a taxable investment pays a higher after-tax yield than a tax-exempt alternative, the investor must determine the after-tax yield of each alternative. The **after-tax yield** is the percentage yield on a taxable investment after subtracting the effect of federal income taxes that will need to be paid on the investment. The after-tax yield on a tax-exempt investment is the same as the nominal yield because you do not have to pay income taxes on income from this kind of investment. So the question is, "How does the investor calculate the after-tax yield on a taxable investment?"

When you know the taxable yield, use Equation (4.1) to determine the equivalent after-tax yield on a taxable investment. Only then can you decide which investment is better. For example, suppose Bobby Bigbucks pays income taxes at

DO IT IN CLASS

the 35 percent combined federal and state marginal tax rate and is considering buying either a municipal bond that pays a 3.5 percent yield or a taxable corporate bond that pays a 5.7 percent yield. Equation (4.1) calculates the equivalent after-tax yield on the corporate bond:*

$$
\begin{aligned}
\text{After-tax yield} &= \text{taxable yield} \\
&\quad \times (1 - \text{federal marginal tax rate}) \\
&= 5.7 \times (1.00 - 0.35) \quad \textbf{(4.1)}^\dagger \\
&= 5.7 \times 0.65 \\
&= 3.71
\end{aligned}
$$

The answer is 3.71 percent. Thus, a 5.7 percent taxable yield is equivalent to an after-tax yield of 3.71 percent. Eureka! Bobby now knows that he should buy the corporate bond paying 5.7 percent because its after-tax yield of 3.71 percent is higher than the 3.5 percent paid by the municipal bond. These differences may look small, and they are, but over time they add up. For example, the extra 0.21 percent (3.71 − 3.50) yield on a $20,000 bond investment for 20 years amounts to $840 [$20,000 × 0.0021 × 20 (bond interest is not compounded)]. That's real cash!

The higher your federal tax rate, the more favorable tax-exempt municipal bonds become as an investment compared with taxable bonds. The tax-exempt status of municipal bonds does not apply to capital gains. When you sell an investment for more than what you paid for it, you will owe federal income taxes on the capital gain.

*This and similar equations can be found and used on the *Garman/Forgue* companion website.

†The formula can be reversed to solve for the equivalent taxable yield when one knows the tax-exempt yield. To continue the example, the return for Bobby on a 3.71 percent tax-exempt bond is equivalent to a taxable yield of 5.7 percent [3.71 ÷ (1.00 − 0.35)]. If Bobby finds a tax-exempt bond paying more than 3.71 percent, he should consider buying it.

after-tax yield

The percentage yield on a taxable investment after subtracting the effect of federal income taxes that will need to be paid on the investment.

blindness. The money grows tax-free and can be used for technology, transportation, housing, and job training.

4.3e Strategy: Defer Income

A popular way to reduce income tax liability is to shelter income by deferring it. You will not have to pay taxes on income earned after December 31st until April the following year or 15 months in the future. This goal is achieved by purposefully making arrangements to receive some of this year's income in the next year, when your marginal tax rate might be lower, perhaps only 25 percent rather than 28 percent. A 3 percent tax savings (paying at the 25 percent rate rather than 28 percent) on $3,000 of income is $90 ($3,000 × 0.03), enough to pay for a good meal in a restaurant. Your employer might be willing to give you a bonus or commission check in January rather than in December, and those who are self-employed can ask clients and customers to wait until January to pay their bills.

You might expect to be in a lower tax bracket in the following year because you anticipate fewer sales commissions or know that you will not work full time.

Capital gains are taxable income but up to $500,000 for couples might be exempt on a profitable sale.

For example, if you return to school, have a child, or decide to travel. Retired people may be able to postpone withdrawals of income from retirement plans, and entrepreneurs may delay billing customers for work.

4.3f   Strategy: Accelerate Deductions

This strategy allows you to lower your taxable income sooner rather than later, which is usually a good idea. Many people find that they do not have enough itemized deductions to exceed the standard deduction amount. By shifting the payment dates of some deductible items, you can increase your deductions. For example, if a single person has about $6,000 of deductible expenses this year, she could prepay some items in December to push the total over the $6,300 threshold and benefit by taking the excess deductions now. The next year, perhaps she can take the standard deduction amount instead of itemizing.

This process is known as **accelerating deductions**. Items that may be prepaid include medical expenses, dental bills, real estate taxes, state and local income taxes, the January payment of estimated state income taxes, personal property taxes that have been billed (e.g., on autos and boats), dues in professional associations, and charitable contributions. You may mail the payments or charge them on credit cards by December 31.

4.3g   Strategy: Take All of Your Legal Tax Deductions

Although you should not spend money just to create a tax deduction, you are encouraged to take all of the deductions to which you are entitled. One way to increase itemized deductions, for example, is to purchase a home with a mortgage loan. The large amounts of money homeowners expend for both interest and real estate taxes are deductible. Plus, if your property taxes and interest exceed the standard deduction amount, then you are able to take additional deductions that were ineligible because of the threshold.

Here are some other approaches to increase your deductions and keep more tax dollars in your pocket. Assume you are in the 25 percent marginal tax bracket and itemize deductions. Cash contributions made to people collecting door to door or at a shopping center during holidays are deductible, even though receipts are not given. Fifty dollars in contributions deducted can save you $12.50 in taxes. Instead of throwing out an old television set, donate it, as an $80 charitable contribution for a TV will save you

ADVICE FROM A SEASONED PRO

Buy a Home to Reduce Income Taxes

Hanna Pallagrosi of Rome, New York, took a sales position at a retail chain store two years ago, where she earned a gross income of $66,000. Hanna wisely made a $3,000 contribution to her 401(k) retirement plan. Her itemized deductions came to only $6,000, so she took the standard deduction and personal exemption amounts. The result was a tax liability of $5,425. Hanna was not happy about paying what she thought was a large tax bill that year.

Gross income	$66,000
Less adjustment to income	−3,000
Adjusted gross income	63,000
Less value of one exemption (old figure)	−4,000
Subtotal	59,000
Less standard deduction (old figure)	−6,200
Taxable income	52,800
Tax liability (from old tax table not shown)	$ 9,056

Last year, Hanna did not receive a raise. Nonetheless, Hanna continued to contribute $3,000 into her 401(k). To reduce her federal income taxes, she also became a homeowner after using some inheritance money to make the down payment on a condominium. During the year, she paid out $9,000 in mortgage interest expenses and $2,000 in real estate taxes. After studying various tax publications, Hanna determined that she had $4,000 in other itemized deductions that, when combined with the interest and real estate taxes, then came to a grand total of $15,000. These deductions reduced Hanna's tax liability dramatically.

Gross income	$66,000
Less adjustment to income	−3,000
Adjusted gross income	63,000
Less value of one exemption	$ 4,050
Subtotal	$58,950
Less itemized deductions	−15,000
Taxable income	$43,950
Tax liability (from Table 4-2)	$ 6,759

Hanna correctly concluded that the IRS "paid" $2,297 ($9,056 − $6,759) toward the purchase of her condominium and her living costs because she did not have to forward those dollars to the government. An additional benefit for Hanna is that she now owns a home whose value could appreciate in the future. Buying a home often reduces one's income taxes.

Frances C. Lawrence
Louisiana State University, Baton Rouge, LA

---

unearned income

Investment returns in the form of rents, dividends, capital gains, interest, or royalties.

$20 in taxes. These amounts may sound like "small change," but lots of little tax deductions can quickly add up to more than $100, and that soon becomes real money!

Expenses for business-related trips can be a fruitful area for tax deductions. If you are in the 25 percent tax bracket and take one business trip per year, perhaps incurring $800 in deductible expenses, you will save $200 in taxes, assuming your miscellaneous deductions already exceed 2 percent of your AGI. The IRS also permits tax deductions for the costs expended on occasional job-hunting trips. In other words, depending on your tax bracket, the U.S. government pays the bill for 25 percent of such expenditures.

4.3h Strategy: Shift Income to a Child

A parent who runs his or her own business may pay a child up to $10,350 ($6,300 [value of standard deduction]) + $4,050 [value of exemption]) in "earned income" before any income tax liability occurs for the child. This assumes the child has no other income. Plus, the parent can deduct the payments as business expenses.

However, giving unearned income to children is treated differently by the IRS. **Unearned income** is interest from a savings account, bond interest, alimony, and dividends from stock that comes from investments. This excludes income from wages or self-employment.

TURN BAD HABITS INTO GOOD ONES

Do You Do This?	Do This Instead!
Did not file an income tax return	File a return to obtain amounts over withheld
Pay too much in income taxes	Use the strategies in this chapter to reduce your tax liability
Wish you could itemize instead of using the standard deduction	Buy a home so you can deduct mortgage interest and property taxes as well as take other deductions
Forget to take certain tax credits in the last three years	File 1040X amended returns to get the refunds
Neglect to save for retirement	Save money by contributing to a qualified retirement plan
Let a tax preparer fill out your income tax forms every year	Get smart about how to reduce your income tax liability and use software to prepare your own tax return

The **kiddie tax** is applied to a child's unearned income of more than $2,100, and it impacts children under age 19 (or up to 24 for full-time students). The tax is meant to discourage parents from reducing their own taxes by shifting lots of investment income to their children, who generally have lower tax brackets.

Under the kiddie tax, a parent can shift income-generating investment assets to the name of a child who then may receive $1,050 tax-free. The next $1,050 of such unearned income is taxed at the child's tax rate, perhaps only 10 percent. All of the child's unearned income in excess of $2,100 is taxed at the parents' tax rate, which could be as high as 39.6 percent.

4.3i Strategy: Buy and Manage a Real Estate Investment

Tax losses are paper losses in the sense that they may not represent actual out-of-pocket dollar losses, and they are created when deductions generated from an investment (such as depreciation and net investment losses) exceed the income from an investment.

Taxpayers are allowed to deduct certain real estate losses against ordinary taxable income, such as salary, interest, dividends, and self-employment earnings. Deductions are allowed for real estate investors who (1) have an adjusted gross income of $150,000 or less and (2) actively participate in the management of the property. Here the investor may deduct up to $25,000 of net losses from a "passive investment," such as real estate, against income from "active" sources, such as salary. For example, a residential real estate investment property might generate an annual cash income $1,000 greater than the out-of-pocket operating costs associated with it. However, after depreciation expenses on the building are taken as a tax deduction, the resulting $1,500 tax loss may then be used to offset other income. (For more details, see Chapter 16, "Real Estate and High-Risk Investments.")

COMMON SENSE
The USA Is a Low-Tax Country

Contrary to the hype in the media, surveys show that 60 percent of taxpayers understand the truth: The U.S. tax burden is the lowest among industrialized countries in the world. Compared to other modern countries the United States total tax burden is 33 percent. Seventeen countries have higher rates, including Denmark (48%), Belgium (44%), France (42%), Australia (42%), Hungary (38%), Germany (36%), and United Kingdom (35%). Federal taxes on middle-income Americans are near historic lows.

tax losses
Created when deductions generated from an investment (such as depreciation and net investment losses) exceed the income from an investment.

CONCEPT CHECK 4.3

1. Distinguish between two major types of tax-sheltered investment returns.
2. Explain how to reduce income taxes via your employer, and name three employer-sponsored plans to do so.
3. Summarize the differences between a traditional individual retirement account (IRA) and a Roth IRA.
4. Identify three strategies to avoid overpayment of income taxes, and summarize the essence of each.

WHAT DO YOU RECOMMEND *NOW*?

Now that you have read the chapter on managing income taxes, what advice can you offer Ace and Florence in the case at the beginning of the chapter regarding:

1. Using tax credits to help pay for Ace's college expenses?

2. Determining how much money Florence will realize if she sells the stocks, assuming she pays federal income taxes at the 25 percent rate?

3. Buying a home?

4. Increasing contributions to their employer-sponsored retirement plans?

5. Establishing a sideline business for Ace's jewelry operation?

SUMMARY OF LEARNING OBJECTIVE RECAPPED

LO1 **Explain the nature of progressive income taxes and the marginal tax rate.**

The federal personal income tax is a progressive tax because the tax rate increases as a taxpayer's taxable income increases. The marginal tax rate is applied to your last dollar of earnings. Your effective marginal tax rate is probably 40 percent. Your average tax rate is much lower.

LO2 **Differentiate among the eight steps involved in calculating your federal income taxes.**

There are eight steps in calculating your income taxes. Certain types of income may be excluded. Regulations permit you to subtract exclusions,

adjustments to income, exemptions, deductions, and tax credits before determining your final tax liability.

LO3 **Use appropriate strategies to avoid overpayment of income taxes.**

You can reduce your tax liability by following certain tax avoidance strategies, such as putting your money in tax-sheltered investments, reducing pretax income via your employer, and investing pre-tax money for tax-deferred compounding. Other strategies are to postpone income, accelerate deductions, take all your legal deductions, and buy and manage a real estate investment.

LET'S TALK ABOUT IT

1. **During Slow Economic Times.** Congress often reduces taxes on middle- and low-income taxpayers with the expectation that consumers will spend most of that money and help create more economic growth. Is this idea good or not, and why?

2. **Filing a Tax Return.** Many college students choose not to file a federal income tax return, assuming that the income taxes withheld by employers "probably" will cover their tax liability. Is such an assumption correct? What are the negatives of this practice if the employers withheld too much in income taxes? What are the negatives if the employers did not withhold enough in income taxes? Will any tax credits be lost?

3. **Fairness of Capital Gains.** The long-term capital gains rate is zero for taxpayers in the 10 or 15 percent marginal tax brackets. The long-term rate is 15 percent for those in the 25, 28, 33, and 35 percent brackets, and it is 20 percent for those in the 39.6 percent tax bracket. What is your opinion on the fairness of these lower capital gains tax rates as compared with the marginal rates applied to income earned from employment that range as high as 39.6 percent?

4. **Reporting Cash Income.** Some college students earn money that is paid to them in cash and then do not include this as income when they file their tax returns. What are the pros and cons of this practice?

5. **Sideline Business.** Identify one possible sideline business that you might engage in to reduce your income tax liability.

6. **Tax Credits.** Name three tax credits that a college student might take advantage of while still in school or during the first few years after graduation.

7. **Reduce Tax Liability.** Identify three strategies to reduce income tax liability that you may take advantage of in the future.

8. **Eliminate Tax Credits.** Review the list of tax credits on pages 130 and 131 and select 2 you think ought to be eliminated, and explain your reasoning.

9. **Strategies to Reduce Income Taxes.** Review the list of strategies to reduce your income taxes on pages 136 through 143 and select 2 you think you might use in the future, and explain your reasoning.

DO THE MATH

1. **Calculate Tax Liability.** What would be the tax liability for a single taxpayer who has a gross income of $50,050? (Hint: Use Table 4-3, and don't forget to subtract the value of a standard deduction and one exemption.)

2. **Marginal Tax Rate.** What would be the marginal tax rate for a single person who has a taxable income of (a) $31,560, (b) $58,150, (c) $66,450, and (d) $100,580? (Hint: Use Table 4-2.)

3. **Determine Tax Liability.** Find the tax liabilities based on the taxable income of the following people: (a) married couple, $92,225; (b) married couple, $74,170; (c) single person, $27,880; (d) single person, $56,060. (Hint: Use Table 4-3.)

DO IT IN CLASS
Page 129

4. **Use Tax Rate Schedule.** Jared Goff, of Los Angeles, determined the following tax information: gross salary, $160,000; interest earned, $2,000; IRA contribution, $5,000; personal exemption, $4,050; and itemized deductions, $8,000. Calculate Jared's taxable income and tax liability filing single. (Hint: Use Table 4-2.)

DO IT IN CLASS
Page 125

5. **Use Tax Rate Schedule.** Carson Wentz, of Philadelphia, determined the following tax information: salary, $144,000; interest earned, $2,000; qualified retirement plan contribution, $6,000; personal exemption, $4,050; itemized deductions, $10,000. Filing single, calculate Carson's taxable income and tax liability. (Hint: Use Table 4-2.)

DO IT IN CLASS
Page 125

6. Review Figure 4-1 on page 117 and comment on the logic of how different segments of Victoria Bassett's income is taxed.

DO IT IN CLASS
Page 117

FINANCIAL PLANNING CASES

CASE 1

The Johnsons Calculate Their Income Taxes

Several years have gone by since Harry and Belinda graduated from college and started their working careers. They both earn good salaries. They believe that they are paying too much in federal income taxes. The Johnsons' total income last year included Harry's salary of $73,000 and Belinda's salary of $94,000. She contributed $3,000 to her 401(k) for retirement. They earned $400 in interest on savings and checking and $3,000 interest income from the trust that is taxed in the same way as interest income from checking and savings accounts. Harry contributed $3,000 into a traditional IRA.

(a) What is the Johnsons' reportable gross income on their joint tax return?

(b) What is their adjusted gross income?

(c) What is the total value of their exemptions?

(d) How much is the standard deduction for the Johnsons?

(e) The Johnsons are buying a home that has monthly mortgage payments of $3,000, or $36,000 a year. Of this amount, $32,800 goes for interest and real estate property taxes. The couple has a $14,000 in other itemized deductions. Using these numbers and Table 4-2, calculate their taxable income and tax liability.

(f) Assuming they had a combined $24,000 in federal income taxes withheld, how much of a refund will the Johnsons receive?

(g) What is their marginal tax rate?

(h) List three additional ways that the Johnsons might reduce their tax liability next year.

CASE 2

Victor and Maria Reduce Their Income Tax Liability

The year before last, Victor earned $85,000 from his retail management position, and Maria began working full-time and earned $52,000 as a medical technician. After they took the standard deduction and claimed four exemptions (themselves plus their two children), their federal income tax liability was about $20,000. After being convinced by friends that they were paying too much in taxes, the couple vowed to try to never again pay that much. Therefore, the Hernandezes embarked on a yearlong effort to reduce their income tax liability. This year they tracked all of their possible itemized deductions, and both made contributions to retirement plans at their places of employment.

(a) Calculate the Hernandezes' income tax liability for this year as a joint return (using Table 4-2) given the following information: gross salary income (Victor, $85,000; Maria, $52,000); state income tax refund ($400); interest on checking and savings accounts ($250); holiday bonus from Maria's employer ($1,000); contributions to qualified retirement accounts ($5,500); itemized deductions (real estate taxes, $4,600; mortgage interest, $6,300; charitable contributions, $2,500); and exemptions for themselves and their two children ($4,050 each).

DO IT IN CLASS
Page 125

(b) List five additional strategies that Victor and Maria might consider for next year's tax planning to reduce next year's tax liability.

CASE 3

Julia Price Thinks About Reducing Her Income Taxes

Julia does well financially because she earns a good salary as an engineer, is somewhat frugal, and is making the maximum contribution to her employer-sponsored retirement plan. After reading about ways to decrease her income tax liability, she has some thoughts. Buying a home is an option, but Julia is worried about the changing prices of housing. As an accomplished sculptural artist, she is thinking about creating a sideline business to sell some of her work and convert some everyday expenses into business expenses. She is considering taking a tax-deductible job-hunting trip and then stretching the trip into a vacation. Also on her possibilities list is to start a master's degree program in engineering or a master's in business administration to enhance her skills. Finally, Julia figures she could contribute $300 a month to a Roth IRA account. Offer your opinions about her thinking.

CASE 4

A New Family Calculates Income and Tax Liability

Kate Beckett and her two children, Austin and Alexandra, moved into the home of her new husband, Richard Castle, in New York City. Kate is a novelist, and her husband is a police detective. The family income consists of the following: $60,000 from Kate's book royalties; $90,000 from Richard's salary; $10,000 in life insurance proceeds from a deceased aunt; $140 in interest from savings; $4,380 in alimony from Kate's ex-husband; $14,200 in child support from her ex-husband; $500 cash as a Christmas gift from Richard's parents; and a $1,600 tuition-and-books scholarship Kate received to go to college part time last year.

(a) What is the total of their reportable gross income?

(b) After Richard put $5,600 into qualified retirement plan accounts last year, what is their adjusted gross income?

(c) How many exemptions can the family claim, and how much is the total value allowed the household?

(d) How much is the allowable standard deduction for the household?

(e) Their itemized deductions are $13,100, so should they itemize or take the standard deduction?

(f) What is their taxable income for a joint return?

(g) What is their final federal income tax liability, and what is their marginal tax rate? (Hint: Use Table 4-2.)

(h) If Richard's employer withheld $25,000 for income taxes, does the couple owe money to the government or do they get a refund? How much?

CASE 5

Taxable Versus Tax-Exempt Bonds

Paxton Lynch, radio station manager in Denver, Colorado, is in the 25 percent federal marginal tax bracket and pays an additional 5 percent in income taxes to the state of Colorado. Paxton currently has more than $20,000 invested in corporate bonds bought

DO IT IN CLASS
Page 140

at various times that are earning differing amounts of taxable interest: $10,000 in ABC earning 5.9 percent; $5,000 in DEF earning 5.5 percent; $3,000 in GHI earning 5.8 percent; and $2,000 in JKL earning 5.4 percent. What is the after-tax return of each investment? To calculate your answers, use the after-tax yield formula (or the reversed formula) on page 140, or the *Garmam/Forgue* companion website.

CASE 6

Taxable Versus Nontaxable Income

Identify each of the following items as either part of taxable income or an exclusion, adjustment, or an allowable itemized deduction from taxable income for Brian Collins and Morgan Smithfield, a married couple from San Diego, who have two children plus Brian's child from his first marriage:

DO IT IN CLASS
Page 122

(a) Brian earns $75,000 per year.

(b) Brian receives a $10,000 bonus from his employer.

(c) Morgan receives $70,000 in commissions from her work.

(d) Brian receives $800 in monthly child support from his ex-wife.

(e) Brian receives $600 each month in alimony.

(f) Brian contributes $6,000 to his retirement account.

(g) Morgan inherits a car from her aunt that has a fair market value of $13,000.

(h) Morgan sells the car and donates $1,500 to his aunt's church.

(i) Brian receives a $5,000 gift from his mother.

BE YOUR OWN PERSONAL FINANCIAL MANAGER

1. **Keep Track of Your Sources of Income.** Complete Worksheet 19: My Sources of Taxable Income from "My Personal Financial Planner" to record all of your various income sources throughout the tax year so that you will not forget to report them to the Internal Revenue Service. Record the names of the income sources in the spaces provided. Record the amounts in the appropriate spaces.

   My Personal Financial Planner

2. **Estimate Your Income Tax Liability.** Complete Worksheet 20: Estimate Your Income Tax Liability from "My Personal Financial Planner" to determine an estimate of your income tax liability (for either last year or next year).

   My Personal Financial Planner

3. **Should You File an Income Tax Return to Obtain a Refund?** Complete Worksheet 21: Determining Whether

 I Should File for a Refund from "My Personal Financial Planner." Even if you are not required to file a return perhaps because you did not earn enough money, you should file if you have a refund coming—that is, if you had more taxes withheld from your paychecks than you ultimately owed. Follow the steps to make the determination.

   My Personal Financial Planner

4. **Strategies to Reduce Your Income Tax Liability.** Complete Worksheet 22: Strategic Reduce My Income Tax Liability: "My Personal Financial Planner." There are several ways to reduce your income tax liability. For each strategy that might be of interest, make checkmarks to identify what characteristics you like about each and which strategies you might follow during your tax-paying life.

   My Personal Financial Planner

ON THE NET

Go to the Web pages indicated to complete these exercises.

1. **IRS Publication 17.** Go to the Internal Revenue Service website address www.irs.gov/publications/pl7. There you will find the IRS's entire Publication 17 online. This is the government's detailed explanation of all aspects of federal income taxes where you can look up almost any possible tax question. Summarize your observations about this publication.

2. **Estimate Your Tax Refund.** Visit the website for BankRate.com (www.bankrate.com/calculators/

tax-planning/1040-form-tax-calculator.aspx) to estimate your tax refund. Fill in a few numbers and get an answer.

3. **Estimate Your Income Taxes.** Enter your filing status, income deductions and credits, and the calculator at Dinkytown (www.dinkytown.net/taxes.html), select the current year, and based on your inputs (filing status, income, deductions, and credits) and projected withholdings for the year, it can estimate your tax refund or amount you may owe the IRS next year.

4. **Check Taxes in Your State to Determine Your Effective Tax Rate.** Visit Bankrate.com's website (www.bankrate.com/finance/taxes/check-taxes-in-your-state.aspx). Click on the map to find your state income tax, if applicable. What is your combined federal and state marginal tax rate? Add in another 7.65 percent for Social Security and Medicare taxes to determine your effective marginal tax rate.

ACTION INVOLVEMENT PROJECTS

1. **Telephone the Internal Revenue Service.** Dial 1 (800) TAX-3676 (or 1 (800) 829-3676) to pose a question for an IRS spokesperson. Think of a question before you call. Perhaps it has to deal with whether or not you qualify for a specific tax credit, can deduct expenses for a sideline business, or can make Roth IRA contributions. Be patient. Write a summary of your findings.

2. **Tax Reform Proposals.** Type "tax reform" into your browser and skim read what you find of interest on three websites. Write a summary of your findings and include your views of what reform(s) you might prefer.

3. **Who Pays Income Taxes?** Type "income taxes, who pays" into your browser and skim read what you find of interest on three websites. For starters, you will discover that almost half of Americans do not pay any federal income taxes and that the top 1 percent of earners pay 46 percent of all personal income tax revenues. Write a summary of your findings, and cite your sources.

4. **Tax Bills Lowest Since 1950s.** Read the FactCheck.org article on taxes in the United States at www.factcheck. org/2012/07/tax-facts-lowest-rates-in-30-years. In addition, search the Web for a more recent report on the same topic and write a summary of your findings.

5. **Corporate and Individual Tax Rates Around the World.** Some countries have a value-added tax paid by consumers. Others provide free health care to citizens, while people in some countries have to pay health care premiums. Review the table provided by Congressional Research Service at www.fas.org/sgp/crs/misc/R41743.pdf, and write a brief summary of your impressions.

6. **Corporate Tax Avoidance.** Read the article on the Center for American Progress (https://www.americanprogress.org/issues/tax-reform/report/2012/02/10/11064/why-we-need-a-minimum-tax-on-u-s-corporations-foreign-profits) to discover how many billions the large multinational corporations in the United States do or do not pay in income taxes in this country. Write a summary of your findings.

5

Managing Checking and Savings Accounts

Learning Objectives

After reading this chapter, you should be able to:

1. Identify the goals of monetary asset management and sources of such financial services.

2. Understand and employ the various types of accounts available to meet the goals of monetary asset management.

3. Establish ownership of assets wisely.

4. Describe your legal protections when conducting monetary asset management electronically.

5. Discuss your money and personal finances effectively with loved ones.

Iconic Bestiary/Shutterstock.com

WHAT DO YOU RECOMMEND?

Nathan Rosenberg and Avigail Abramovitz are to be married in two months. Both are employed full time and currently have their own apartments. Once married, they will move into Avigail's apartment because it is larger. They plan to use Nathan's former rent money to begin saving for a down payment on a home to be purchased in four or five years. Nathan has a checking account at a bank near his workplace where he deposits his paychecks. He also has three savings accounts—one at his bank and two small accounts at a savings and loan association near where he went to college. Nathan pays about $30 per month in fees on his various accounts. In addition, he has a $10,000 certificate of deposit (CD) from an inheritance, and it will mature in five months. Avigail has her paycheck directly deposited into her account at the credit union where she works. She has a savings account at the credit union as well as a money market account at a stock brokerage firm that was set up years ago when her father gave her 300 shares of stock. She also has $9,300 in an individual retirement account (IRA) invested through a mutual fund.

iStockphoto.com/Sturti

What would you recommend to Avigail and Nathan on the subject of managing checking and savings accounts regarding:

1. Where they can obtain the services that they need for managing their monetary assets?

2. Their best use of checking and savings accounts as they begin saving for a home?

3. The use of an asset management account for managing their monetary assets?

4. Their use of electronic banking?

5. How they can best discuss the management of their money and finances?

Your financial success will depend in part on how well you manage your **monetary assets**. These assets were defined in Chapter 3 as cash and low-risk, near-cash items that can be readily converted to cash with little or no loss in value, such as checking and savings accounts. If you are a college student, your monetary assets are probably the largest component of your net worth and are the major focus of the activities you consider "personal finance." Monetary assets may represent all your money.

People use monetary assets in one of three ways. First, they use them for day-to-day spending. They buy food, clothing, entertainment, and many products and services. Spending usually requires cash or the use of a check or a debit card to access funds in a checking account. (Using credit is covered in Chapters 6 and 7.) Checking accounts are appropriate places to keep money that you will spend within the next three to six months or so. Not all people save, however. One in three adults does not have any savings at all. And 40 percent say they do not have enough money saved to pay for a $2,000 financial shock, perhaps for car bills, home repairs, or medical emergencies.

The second way that people use monetary assets is to accumulate funds to meet needs that will occur six months to, perhaps, three to five years in the future. You could keep these funds in a checking account, but some types of savings accounts pay more interest. With savings accounts, the focus is on holding money safely until needed in the future for spending or investing. The money in most checking and savings accounts is fully insured by the federal government.

The third way that people use monetary assets is to make investments. Investments are the best places to put money you will not need for 5, 10, or even 20 years in the future. The magic of the world of investments is that over long periods of time, it is quite possible to watch your money triple or quadruple over the original amount invested. Investments are examined in Chapters 1 and 13 through 16.

5.1 WHAT IS MONETARY ASSET MANAGEMENT?

Monetary asset management is the task of maximizing interest earnings and minimizing fees on all of your funds kept readily available for day-to-day living expenses, emergencies, and savings and investment opportunities. Successful monetary asset management allows you to earn interest on your money while maintaining reasonable liquidity and safety. **Liquidity** refers to the speed and ease with which an asset can be converted to cash. **Safety** means that your funds are free from financial risk.

5.1a Who Provides Monetary Asset Management Services?

The **financial services industry** comprises companies that provide checking, savings, and money market accounts and possibly credit, insurance, investment, and financial planning services. These companies include depository institutions such as banks and credit unions, stock brokerage firms, mutual funds, financial services companies, and insurance companies. Table 5-1 matches these various types of firms with the financial products and services that they offer. As you can see, there is considerable overlap. For example, State Farm, which most people recognize as an insurance company, also owns a mutual fund and a bank.

Depository Institutions **Depository institutions** are financial institutions in the United States that are legally allowed to offer checking and savings accounts to individuals and businesses as well as provide loans. They all can offer some form of government account insurance on deposited funds and are government regulated. Examples of depository institutions are commercial banks, savings banks, and credit unions. Although each is a distinct type of institution, people often call them all simply *banks*.

Table 5-1	Providers of Monetary Asset Management Services	
Providers	**What They Sell**	**Examples of Well-Known Company Names**
Depository institutions (banks, mutual savings banks, and credit unions)	Checking, savings, lending, credit cards, investments, and trust advice	Bank of America, Citibank, Chase, Wells Fargo
Mutual funds	Money market funds, tax-exempt funds, bond funds, and stock funds	Fidelity, T. Rowe Price, Vanguard
Stock brokerage firms	Securities investments (stocks and bonds), mutual funds, and real estate investment trusts	Fidelity, Schwab
Financial services companies	Checking, savings, lending, credit cards, securities investments, real estate investments, insurance, accounting and legal advice, and financial planning	American Express, Edward Jones, Raymond James
Insurance companies	Property and liability, health and life insurance, credit services, financial planning services	Allstate, Aetna, State Farm

Commercial banks are a type of bank that accepts deposits in checking and savings accounts and provides transactional services such as accepting deposits, making business loans, and offering basic investment products. They are under federal and state regulations. They offer numerous consumer services, such as checking, savings, loans, safe-deposit boxes, investment services, financial counseling, and automatic payment of bills.

Community banks are a type of commercial bank that focuses on providing traditional banking services in their local communities, where they obtain most of their core deposits locally and make many of their loans to local businesses. Thus, they are considered to be "relationship" bankers as opposed to "transactional" bankers.

Mutual savings banks are a type of thrift institution that also accept deposits and make housing and consumer loans. Originally designed to serve low-income individuals, they historically invested in long-term, fixed-rate assets such as mortgages. Initiated 200 years ago MSBs are located in 17 mid-Atlantic and industrial northeast regions of the United States. They are called "mutual" because the depositors own the institution and share in the earnings.

Savings Institutions (also called **thrift institutions**) accept deposits and provide mortgage and personal loans to individuals. They focus less on commercial loans than banks.

Online banks are regulated just like any other bank, even those they operate entirely over the Internet. Because they avoid the building costs of conventional institutions they often pay higher interest rates than other institutions. Some of the highest rated online banks include Ally Bank, Discover Bank, and Redneck Rewards Checking.

Savings and loan associations (S&Ls) focus primarily on accepting savings and providing mortgage and consumer loans. They offer checking services through interest-earning NOW accounts (discussed later in this chapter). Savings banks generally pay depositors an interest rate about 0.10 to 0.20 percentage points higher than rates at commercial banks.

commercial banks
A type of bank that accepts deposits in checking and savings accounts and provides transactional services such as accepting deposits, making business loans, and offering basic investment products.

community banks
A type of commercial bank that focuses on providing traditional banking services in their local communities, where they obtain most of their core deposits locally and make many of their loans to local businesses.

mutual savings banks
A type of thrift institution that also accept deposits and make housing and consumer loans.

savings institutions (also called **thrift institutions**)
Accept deposits and provide mortgage and personal loans to individuals.

online banks
Banks that are regulated just like any other bank, even those they operate entirely over the Internet, yet because they avoid the "bricks and mortar" costs of conventional institutions they often pay higher interest rates than other institutions.

savings and loan associations (S&Ls)
Thrift institutions that focus primarily on accepting savings and providing mortgage and consumer loans.

bots (or **chatbots**)

Online texting services offered by all financial institutions and other venders who provide information and services, which can conduct human-like conversation formerly reserved for people.

DO IT IN CLASS

credit unions

Not-for-profit institutions that accept deposits and make loans, and the members/owners all share some common bond, such as having the same employer, working for or attending the same school, or living in the same community.

MONEY WEBSITES

Credit unions also accept deposits and make loans, and they operate on a not-for-profit basis. The members/owners of the credit union all share some common bond, such as living in a defined region, have the same employer, attend or work for the same college, or have some other affiliation. People in the family of a member are also eligible to join, and if a parent is a member a child can join. Credit unions generally pay higher interest rates on saving accounts than other institutions, and their rates on loans, such as to finance a vehicle purchase, are often lower than other lenders.

Federal Insurance Protects Your Deposits Deposits in depository institutions are insured against loss of both the amount on deposit and the accrued interest by various insurance funds. Not a single depositor has lost a dime of insured funds since the **Federal Deposit Insurance Corporation (FDIC)** was created. The insurance for your deposits at any one institution works as follows:

1. The maximum insurance on all of your single-ownership (individual) accounts (held in your name only) is $250,000.
2. The maximum insurance on all of your joint accounts (accounts held with other individuals) is $250,000.
3. The maximum insurance on all of your retirement accounts is $250,000.
4. A maximum of $250,000 in insurance per beneficiary is available on payable on death accounts.

Thus individuals might have several increments of insurance for their accounts at any one institution. Funds on deposit at other institutions will also have these same limits. So if a rich uncle Tony Stewart, of Milwaukee, Wisconsin, has $140,000 in individual accounts at each of two different institutions, he would have a total of $280,000 of deposit insurance.

Federally chartered credit unions have their accounts insured through the National Credit Union Share Insurance Fund (NCUSIF), which is administered by the National Credit Union Administration (NCUA). State-chartered credit unions are often insured by NCUSIF, and most others participate in private insurance programs. Credit unions usually pay higher interest rates and charge lower fees than other institutions.

Other Financial Services Providers Are Not Federally Insured Depository institutions are not the only providers of monetary asset management services. Mutual funds, stock brokerage houses, and insurance companies provide some monetary asset management services as well. The services they do not provide are government-insured checking and savings accounts. However, many of these companies also own banks and thus do provide insured deposits through their banking entities.

Mutual funds are investment companies that raise money by selling shares to the public and then invest that money in a diversified portfolio of investments. Most have created cash management accounts to provide a convenient and safe place to keep money while awaiting alternative investment opportunities.

Stock brokerage firms are licensed financial institutions that specialize in selling and buying stocks, bonds, and other investments and providing advice to investors. They earn commissions based on the buy and sell orders that they process. Stock brokerage firms typically offer cash or mutual fund accounts into which clients may place money while waiting to make investments. The noninvestment portion of an account (for example, cash held in the account prior to making an investment) is protected by the Securities Investor Protection Corporation (SIPC), a nongovernment entity.

Insurance companies provide property, liability, health, life, and other insurance products. (These topics are covered in Chapters 10–12.) Many offer monetary asset services, such as money market accounts.

All these other financial service providers are described in later chapters. They are important providers of useful services in personal finance.

5.2 OPEN CHECKING AND MONEY MARKET ACCOUNTS

Learning Objective 2

Understand and employ the various types of accounts available to meet the goals of monetary asset management.

There are two popular monetary asset accounts that are appropriate for most people: A checking account and a money market account. You need to put cash for everyday use into a checking account and open a money market account in which to put money for later purchases and investments.

5.2a Checking Accounts

A **checking account** is a deposit account held at a financial institution that performs transactions that allow for withdrawals and deposits by the account depositor. Checks may be written against amounts on deposit. Money held in a checking account is very liquid, and can be withdrawn using checks, automated cash machines and electronic debits, among other methods. A checking account is sometimes called a **transaction account**.

Whenever you deposit money into, withdraw funds from, or make any payment out of a checking account, you should record the transaction. To do so record the date, amount, and purpose of the transaction in the *check register* provided with your paper

checking account (transaction account)

A deposit account held at a financial institution that performs transactions that allow for withdrawals and deposits.

ADVICE FROM A SEASONED PRO

When "Free Checking" Isn't Free!

Beware! A "free checking" account may not be as free as you think. Some banks charge up to 50 different checking account fees, including charges for using ATMs, seeing a human teller, account maintenance, low balance, bounced checks (insufficient funds), stop-payment orders, check deposit, overdrafts, returned deposit charge, excessive withdrawals, lost debit card, paper statement, foreign transactions, redeeming account points, returned mail, and early account closure. Whew! Be a smart consumer and make sure you understand exactly what your bank requires to get truly "free checking."

Daniel Roccato
Rutgers University, Camden, New Jersey

negotiable order of with-drawal (NOW) account

A interest-earning checking account at a depository institution.

share draft account

The credit-union version of a negotiable order of withdrawal (NOW) account.

tiered interest

The combination of a base interest rate and a higher rate paid on interest-earning accounts.

checks or in an electronic recordkeeping software program and calculate your new account balance.

Checking accounts may or may not pay interest. **Demand-deposit accounts** are checking accounts that typically pay no interest. An interest-bearing checking account is any account upon which you can write check that pays interest. Therefore, select an **interest-earning checking account** (also called a **negotiable order of withdrawal [NOW] account**). A **share draft account** is the credit-union version of a NOW account. NOW accounts and share draft accounts may pay slightly higher interest rates on larger balances (such as amounts above $1,000).

The combination of a base interest rate and a higher rate is called **tiered interest**. For example, an account that pays 0.30 percent on the first $1,000 and perhaps 0.40 percent on any additional funds above the first $1,000 in the account.

ADVICE FROM A SEASONED PRO

Avoiding Overdraft Fees

An **overdraft**, or bounced check, occurs any time one writes a check or uses a debit card when there are insufficient funds in the account. If funds to cover the usage are not available, the bank will charge you a $35 fee or more. The merchant to whom a bad check was written will also charge a similar fee. The costs could total $60 to $80 for one bad check or overdraft!

It is easy to fall victim to these charges if you are not careful. One reason is that banks can choose the order in which they process checks/debits. Let's say you write a large check one day. The next day you use your debit card for three small purchases and the check shows up at your bank for payment. There might be enough money in your account to cover the three small items but not the check. The bank can choose to process the check first. You are overdrawn and the three debit card items are overdrafts, as well, thus you now have four overdrafts. If the bank had cleared the debits first, you would only have had one overdraft.

Your financial institution likely offers three ways to avoid overdraft fees:

1. *Automatic funds transfer agreement.* The amount necessary to cover an overdraft will be transmitted from your savings account to your checking account, as long as you keep sufficient funds in your savings account. This is the least expensive alternative.

2. *Automatic overdraft loan agreement.* The needed funds will be automatically loaned to you by your bank if you have an overdraft line of credit or will be charged as a cash advance to your Visa or MasterCard credit card

account with the same bank. Note that the loan may be advanced in fixed increments of $100. If you need only $10, for example, you will consequently be responsible for paying interest on amounts not needed. A cash advance fee of $20 or more may also be assessed by the credit card company and a high interest rate starts just as soon as you access the funds. This is expensive.

3. *"Opt-in" overdraft/bounce protection.* The bank will honor overdrafts up to a certain limit, such as $1,000, by loaning the money to the account holder. In return, the customer must pay a $25 to $40 fee for each overdraft. Then, the customer must repay the funds usually within a month. With some plans, the money is repaid as soon as any money is deposited back in the account. This is very expensive.

The Dodd-Frank Wall Street Reform and Consumer Protection Act requires that you "opt in" for the opt-in protection. Think twice before you do so. Many new users of checking accounts rack up high levels of fees because they do not understand opting-in. **Opting in** means that the bank will not alert or stop you when you use your debit card or write a check when there are insufficient funds. Use of a debit card for $5.50 for a drink and some chips could trigger a fee ten times as high.

You must keep track of your own account balance and ensure that you have enough in your account each and every time you access your funds. So, check your math to be certain you always know how exactly much money is in your checking account.

Erica Tobe
Michigan State University Extension, East Lansing, Michigan

ADVICE FROM A SEASONED PRO

Do Not Pay for an Idle Bank Account

If you have money untouched in an account for too long of a time period (such as 6 months), the bank may assess you with an "inactivity fee" of perhaps $10 per month. One way to beat the fee is to have another account automatically deposit a small amount into the account each month so it will not be idle.

Katie M. Barrow
Louisiana Tech University, Ruston, Louisiana

A **student checking account** is one offered by credit unions and banks that is better for students than a traditional bank account. It offers excellent benefits to college students, including a low minimum balance, small fees, free online bill pay, free ATM use or ATM rebates, free checks, online statements, mobile deposits or transactions, online transfers, and free debit cards.

Having no monthly fees is a good thing, but you don't want to end up paying for it in other areas, so read all the details to avoid other charges like $35 for **non-sufficient funds (NSF)**. This term is used in the banking industry to signify that there is not enough money in an account in order to honor a check drawn on that account. This is also known as a "bounced check" or "bad check."

A **lifeline banking account** is streamlined checking designed for low-income customers that has low balance requirements, no monthly fees, and is offered by large financial institutions as a way to offer basic banking services to the broad public. **Super NOW accounts** are also available at banks. They pay slightly higher interest rates than a regular checking account but place a limit on the number of checks that can be written each month.

Endorse Your Checks Correctly Endorsement is the process of writing on the back of a check to legally transfer its ownership, usually in return for the cash amount indicated on the face of the check. Choosing the proper type of endorsement can protect you from having the check cashed by someone else against your wishes.

A check with a **blank endorsement** contains only the payee's signature on the back. Such a check immediately becomes a **bearer instrument**, meaning that anyone who attempts to cash it will very likely be allowed to do so, even if the check has been lost or stolen.

A **restrictive endorsement** uses the phrase *For deposit only* written on the back along with the signature and can only be deposited into an account. For further safety, you can include the name of your financial institution and account number as part of the endorsement.

A **special endorsement** can be used to limit who can cash a check. To make this kind of endorsement, you write the phrase *Pay to the order of [person's name]* on the back along with your signature. The person named in such a "two-party check" will likely only be able to deposit it in an account at a financial institution.

Checking Account Balance Requirements Most interest-earning checking accounts have a balance requirement that, if not met, will result in the assessment of a monthly fee and forfeiture of any interest earned for the month.

student checking account
A checking account offered by credit unions and banks that is better for students than another type of bank account, usually because they offer excellent benefits, including a low minimum balance, minimized fees, and free online bill pay.

COMMON SENSE
Pay Bills Online

Paying bills online is a fast and convenient way to stay in control of your finances by paying anyone you would normally pay by check. A service with one password can help you pay your bills, make one-time or recurring payments online in just a few seconds or a minute, and it is quicker and easier than writing and mailing paper checks.

BIAS TOWARD— THE FAMILIAR

People tend toward sticking with the familiar and comfortable. Young adults often bank where their parents do or where they go to college, making it easy for mom to dad to make deposits. They often stay with that institution for years. What to do? Look for the institution that charges the lowest fees and pays the highest interest, which is often a credit union associated with your school or a money market fund.

Balance requirements are structured as either a minimum-balance or average-balance requirement. With a **minimum-balance account**, the customer must keep a certain amount (perhaps $500 or $1,000) in the account throughout a specified time period (usually a month or a quarter) to avoid a flat service charge (usually $10 to $25 a month). A fee is assessed whenever the triggering event occurs, that is when the balance drops below the specified minimum. With an **average-balance account**, a service fee is assessed only if the average daily balance of funds in the account drops below a certain level (perhaps $800 or $1,200) during the specified time period.

What Happens When You Write a Check? When you write a paper check, you either simultaneously make a copy that serves as your record that the check was written or make a note of the transaction in your check register. When the check is paid by your bank, it is said to have *cleared* the bank.

The check itself is treated in one of two ways. In the traditional method, a *canceled check* is sent to your bank so that the funds can be paid to whomever you had written the check. Typically today, the check is scanned by the receiving bank or the business to which you wrote it and an electronic *substitute check* is created and transmitted electronically to your institution. As a result, the check can clear your bank more quickly.

Whether you get your account statements by mail, online, or both, review account statements every month to make sure they are correct and report errors immediately. Also watch for any changes in your minimum balance requirement, fees, or other account terms. Under the Check Clearing for the 21st Century Act, your bank must correct any errors in the processing of paper and substitute checks.

A **stop-payment order** is a notice made by a depositor to his or her bank directing the bank to refuse payment on a specific check drawn by the depositor. To issue such an order, you may telephone your bank and stop payment on the check or you may do it online. You will need the check number, which is in the upper right hand corner, the dollar amount of the check, the date on the check or the date the check was issued, the person the check is payable to and finally the reason for issuing a stop payment.

A stop-payment order works only if the check has not yet cleared. A fee of $30 to $40 will be charged. If the stop payment order is issued in time the person in receipt of the check will not be able to cash it.

Special Purpose Checks There are three special purpose checks that sometimes are useful. A **certified check** is a personal check drawn on your checking account on which your financial institution imprints the word *certified*, signifying that the account has

DID YOU KNOW

ATM Fees Reach Record Highs

There are three types of ATMs The first is owned and operated by your bank or credit union, and the second type is an ATM offered by ATM networks or other financial institutions in partnership with your bank or credit union. Usually neither of these charge any ATM fees. The third type is an ATM that your financial institution does not own and shares no affiliation. This includes most ATMs in convenience stores and ATMs owned by other financial institutions. Most of the time, you are charged two fees for using these ATMs.

The first fee is a transaction fee ranging from $0.50 to $3.50. The second fee is from the unaffiliated ATM company itself, and the charge is usually between $1 and $3 for each withdrawal. For a $20 withdrawal you can easily pay $4.00! That's 20% of the withdrawal! This amounts to $500 a year for twice weekly withdrawals. And these fees keep rising every year. Withdrawing your own cash can be expensive.

NUMBERS ON

Bank Fees

Typical bank fees are: Monthly maintenance fee, $12; early account closure fee, $25; minimum balance unmet, $15; returned deposit, $15; foreign transaction fee, 3 percent; lost debit card, $8; paper statement fee, $2 a month; redeeming awards, $25; returned mail, $9; human teller, $4.

DO IT IN CLASS

DID YOU KNOW

How to Reconcile Your Checking Account

It is good to maintain records of the activities occurring in your various financial accounts. You should record all checks written, debit card transactions, automatic bill payments, electronic payments, and deposits in your check register as they take place. It is also smart to go online every few days to confirm your deposits, withdrawals, and checking transactions.

You should conduct an **account reconciliation** in which you compare your records with your bank's records, checking the accuracy of both sets of records and identifying any errors. The best time to do so is when you receive your monthly statement from your bank.

Reconciling your checking account is a three-step process:

1. Bring your own records up to date.
2. Bring the bank's records up to date.
3. Reconcile the results from Steps 1 and 2.

If the revised balance in your records and the revised balance from the bank statement differ, you will need to find where the error occurred. First, check the additions and subtractions in your records. Next, make sure that all previous entries in your records are properly reported on the account statement.

Trying to find errors when Steps 1 and 2 yield differing results is a necessary but tedious task. Fortunately, it is less likely to be necessary today because of electronic banking. Many people go online almost daily to check their balances and review their account activity for accuracy. In this way,

they can catch errors early and are always confident that their balances are exactly as shown in their own records. Here is a table you can use to guide your reconciling efforts.

STEP 1: Bring Your Own Records Up to Date	Amount
1. Enter balance from your check register.	$
2. Add deposits not yet recorded.	$
3. Subtract checks and other withdrawals not yet recorded.	$
4. Subtract bank fees and charges included in the monthly statement and not yet recorded.	$
5. Add interest earned.	$
ADJUSTED CHECKBOOK REGISTER BALANCE	$

STEP 2: Bring the Account Statement Up-to-Date	
1. Enter ending balance from bank statement.	$
2. Add deposits made since bank statement closing date.	$
3. Subtract outstanding checks written since bank statement closing date.	$
ADJUSTED BANK STATEMENT BALANCE	$

STEP 3: Compare adjusted checkbook register balance and adjusted bank statement balance. If the two balances do not match, identify where the error occurred.

You should reconcile your bank account monthly.

sufficient funds to cover its payment. The financial institution simultaneously places a hold on that amount in the account until the check clears. The fee for a certified check is $10 to $20.

cashier's check

A check drawn on the account of the financial institution itself and, thus, backed by the institution's finances.

Some payees insist on receiving payment in the form of a **cashier's check** drawn on the account of the financial institution itself and, thus, backed by the institution's finances. To obtain such a check, you pay the financial institution the amount of the cashier's check and pay a fee of $10 to $20.

money order

A checking instrument bought for a particular amount with a fee assessed based on the amount of the order.

A **money order** is a checking instrument bought for a particular amount with a fee assessed based on the amount of the order. Many financial institutions, including retailers such as Wal-Mart and the U.S. Postal Service, sell money orders.

TURN BAD HABITS INTO GOOD ONES

Do You Do This?	Do This Instead!
Do not save for the future	Begin by aiming to save $1,000, and increase it later
Use savings for wrong reasons	Keep savings in a separate account so you do not access it
Ignore your account statements	Read each statement for accuracy
Talk about money only when there is a problem	Schedule regular "money talks" with your family
Pay fees every month for checking	Explore no-fee checking accounts at credit unions
Pay some bills late	Pay your bills on time
Don't have money to pay for emergencies	Maintain a proper balance of cash in your emergency fund
Overdraw your checking account	Keep track of your balance online and reconcile monthly
Keep most of your money in your checking account	Earn higher returns in a money market account

ADVICE FROM A SEASONED PRO

Why Interest Rates Change

The reasons why interest rates change from time to time are fourfold:

(1) *Monetary policy changes* in the United States, which are controlled by the independent Board of Governors of the Federal Reserve Board, and it occasionally raises or lowers the Fed rate to stimulate or slow down the economy;

(2) *Federal government borrowing* occasionally changes aggregate demand when it needs to borrow more (or less) than its usual amount;

(3) *Businesses borrowing* likewise changes aggregate demand when it borrows more (during expanding economic times) or less (during poor economic times) than their usual amount; and

(4) *Loan rates rise or fall* depending upon the prevailing rates of interest paid on deposits and the risk on loans.

David A. Evans
Purdue University, West Lafayette, Indiana

5.2b Money Market Accounts

When income begins to exceed expenses on a regular basis, perhaps by $200 or $300 each month, a substantial amount of excess funds can quickly build up. Although this situation is a comfortable one, it is wise from a monetary asset management point of view to move some of the excess funds into an account that pays more interest. At a later time the funds could be put into an investment.

A **money market account (MMA)** is any of a variety of interest-earning accounts that pays slightly higher interest rates (compared with regular savings accounts), and they offer some check-writing privileges. MMAs are offered by depository institutions and others. By legal definition, the investments of money market accounts must mature in less than one year. The funds on deposit are not loaned out to consumers but instead are invested in the "money markets" for short-term loans to businesses. **Money market mutual funds (MMMFs)** are money market accounts opened at mutual fund companies.

Money market accounts can be used much like a checking account. Interest is calculated daily, and an investor can withdraw funds at any time. **Money market funds** are accounts in a mutual fund. They historically pay the highest rate of return that can be earned on a daily basis by small investors.

Money market accounts require a minimum deposit ranging from $500 to $2,500. Dozens of mutual fund companies offer unlimited check writing with no minimums on the amount of each check. Electronic transfers are permitted, but ATMs cannot be used. Although MMAs are not insured by any federal agency, they are considered extremely safe. Some popular MMAs are managed by American Century (www.americancentury.com), Dreyfus (www.dreyfus.com), Fidelity (www.fidelity.com), T. Rowe Price (www.troweprice .com), and Vanguard (www.vanguard.com).

5.2c Savings Accounts

When you are trying to accumulate and hold funds you want to take advantage of the time element to earn more interest than a checking account would pay. Most people start out by opening a **savings account**, sometimes called a **statement savings account**. These are deposit accounts held at a bank or other financial institution that provides principal security and a modest interest rate. Funds on deposit in a savings account are considered **time deposits** (rather than demand deposits). These require

money market account (MMA)
Any of a variety of interest-earning accounts offered by depository institutions that pays slightly high interest rates (compared with regular savings accounts) and offers some check-writing privileges.

money market mutual funds (MMMFs)
Money market accounts offered by a mutual fund investment company (rather than at a depository institution).

money market fund (MMF)
Money market account in a mutual fund rather than at a depository institution.

savings account (statement savings account)
A deposit account held at a bank or other financial institution that provides principal security and a modest interest rate.

time deposits
Funds on deposit in a savings account (rather than demand deposits), and technically these require that account holders give 30 to 60 days notice for withdrawals.

ADVICE FROM A SEASONED PRO

Start Your Emergency Savings Fund Now

To get started on setting aside enough money into an emergency fund, you need to get started. After you receive your paycheck put some money into savings. As soon as you save perhaps $500 or even $2,000, you probably will always have enough money to pay for most emergency vehicle repairs and other unexpected expenses.

An appropriate savings goal for almost anyone going to work after college is to put aside $83 a month for 12 months. You will have $1,000 after one year. That's a good start on an emergency savings fund.

Some people complain that they just cannot save. What if your boss announced that profits are way down and employees like you have a choice. You can "lose your job completely or take a pay cut of 10 percent." Of course, you would take the pay cut and continue working. And you would find the 10 percent. Well, the logic is much the same. Start today to find the 10 percent for your emergency savings fund and save it! Then you will not have to pay with plastic for things that are not in your budget.

Geraldine Ann Chambers
The Villages, Florida

---

money market deposit account (MMDA)

A deposit account that requires a larger initial deposit to open (often $2,500), and it requires a minimum balance to be maintained, checks must be written for a minimum amount, and it only allows a limited number of checking transactions per month.

annual percentage yield (APY)

Return on total interest received on a $100 deposit for 365-day period, given the institution's simple annual interest rate and compounding frequency.

COMMON SENSE
People Don't Save Because They Fear Change

People are afraid to save money, or more money, because they fear change. They associate change with pain. Savings means reducing take-home pay. Savings means cutting back one's spending. Savings means changing one's lifestyle. If you are not willing to make genuine changes in your spending patterns so you can save, you may not really want to save to build an emergency fund, to buy a home, or to save for retirement.

that account holders give 30 to 60 days notice for withdrawals, although this restriction is almost never enforced. Although savings account deposits are extremely safe, the interest rate paid is only slightly higher than on a checking account.

A **money market deposit account (MMDA)** is a deposit account that requires a fairly large initial deposit to open (often $2,500), and it requires a minimum balance to be maintained, checks must be written for a minimum amount, and it only allows a limited number of checking transactions per month. Thus they pay slightly higher interest rates.

The actual dollar amount of interest you will earn depends on four variables:

1. Amount of money on deposit
2. Method of determining this balance
3. Interest rate applied to the balance
4. Frequency of compounding (such as annually, semiannually, quarterly, monthly, or daily)

The Truth in Savings Act requires depository institutions to disclose a uniform, standardized rate of interest so that depositors can easily compare various checking and savings options that pay interest. This rate, called the **annual percentage yield (APY)**, is a percentage based on the total interest that would be received on a $100 deposit for a 365-day period given the institution's annual rate of simple interest and frequency of compounding. The more frequent the compounding, the greater the effective return for the saver.

A **grace period** is the time in days during which deposits or withdrawals can be made and still earn interest from a given day of the interest period. For example, if deposits are made by the tenth day of the month, interest might be earned from the first day of the month. For withdrawals, the grace period generally ranges from three to five days. Thus, if a saver like Dick Morse, of Manhattan, Kansas, withdrew money from an account within three to five days of the end of the interest period, the savings might still earn interest as if the money remained in the account for the entire period.

5.2d Certificates of Deposit

Some time deposits, such as a certificate of deposit, are classified as a **fixed-time deposit**. As such, they have a specific time period that the savings must be left on deposit. Otherwise a penalty is assessed for early withdrawal. A **certificate of deposit (CD)** is an interest-earning savings instrument purchased for a fixed period of time, such as 6 months or 1, 2, or even 5 years. The required deposit amounts range from $100 to $100,000. The interest rate in force when the CD is purchased typically remains fixed for the entire term of the deposit. Depositors collect their principal and interest when the CD matures. Certificates of deposit are insured similarly to checking and savings accounts.

Variable-rate (or **adjustable-rate**) **certificates of deposit** pay an interest rate that is adjusted (up or down) periodically. Typically, savers may pay a fee to be allowed to "lock in," or fix, the rate at any point before their CDs mature.

CDs might appear to be a low-risk place to hold funds. There is a risk, however, if interest rates in general go up while your money is in the CD. The risk is that you have the opportunity cost of not being able to move your money to an account that is paying the newer higher interest rate. The uncertainty about changing rates is referred to as **interest-rate risk**, which is the risk that an investment's value will change due to a change in the absolute level of interest rates.

A **bump-up CD** is a savings certificate entitling the bearer to take advantage of rising interest rates with a one-time option to "bump up" the interest rate received. Thus, if interest rates in general are rising, the holder can elect to increase the interest rate to the soon to rise higher going rate.

Brokered certificates of deposit often pay the highest yields and are available through stockbrokerage firms. Brokered CDs are bought by a brokerage firm in bulk for the purpose of reselling to brokerage customers. They are FDIC insured and usually do not have sales commissions.

Avoid **investment certificates** because they are not CDs. They are an investment product offered by an investment company or brokerage firm designed to offer a competitive yield to an investor. They are not insured and can be recalled by the financial institution and reissued at a lower interest rate prior to their maturity. Sometimes the issuer goes bankrupt and the saver loses 100 percent of his/her money. Ask "Is this a CD or an investment certificate?" Then verify the response.

Money withdrawn from a CD before the end of the specified time period is subject to interest penalties, and these vary by institution. The most common penalty is three months' interest for CDs with maturities of less than one year, and six months' interest for CDs with maturities of one year and longer. If the penalty exceeds the interest amount, you will get back less than you deposited. Before putting money into a CD, make sure that it is appropriate to tie up your funds in this way.

fixed-time deposit
A certificate of deposit that has a specific time period that the savings must be left on deposit; otherwise a penalty is assessed for early withdrawal.

certificate of deposit (CD)
An interest-earning savings instrument purchased for a fixed period of time, such as 6 months or 1, 2, or even 5 years.

variable-rate (adjustable-rate) certificates of deposit
Certificates of deposit that pay an interest rate that is adjusted (up or down) periodically.

interest-rate risk
The risk that an investment's value will change due to a change in the absolute level of interest rates.

YOUR GRANDPARENTS SAY

"Save Automatically"

"The way to save automatically is to treat savings like any other recurring expense, like rent or a vehicle loan. Make that happen by setting up an automatic transfer from your paycheck (or checking account), perhaps in the amount of 5 percent of your net pay, into a savings account to best meet your savings needs."

ADVICE FROM A SEASONED PRO

Never Open an Electronic Communication from a Bank

Never provide account information in response to an e-mail or text message from your financial institution, or any other financial institution. Do not open the message because it is most likely from a scam artist as banks never seek account information from customers via email or text.

Melinda Carlson
Eastern Michigan University, Ypsilanti, Michigan

DID YOU KNOW

Asset Management Accounts

An asset management account (AMA) at a financial institution is one that includes checking services, credit cards, debit cards, margin loans, the automatic sweep of cash balances into a money market fund, as well as brokerage services. Also known as a central asset account, AMAs are offered through depository institutions, stock brokerage firms, financial services companies, and mutual funds. The company sweeps your funds into and out of an account with a depository institution on your behalf. AMAs enable you to conduct all of your financial business with one institution.

Ten thousand dollars is required to open an AMA, and they often assess an annual fee of $100. AMAs usually have other features that are free, such as checks, unlimited check writing, safe deposit box, online banking, and a bill-pay program.

CD laddering

A strategy in which an investor divides the amount of money to be invested into equal amounts to certificates of deposit (CDs) with different maturity dates; it decreases both interest rate and re-investment risks.

CD laddering is a strategy in which an investor divides the amount of money to be invested into equal amounts to certificates of deposit (CDs) with different maturity dates; it decreases both interest rate and re-investment risks. Here's how laddering works. Let's say you have $10,000 you would like to put into a CD. To start, simply go to www.bankrate.com and find the best rate you can get at the time. Then you purchase five CDs: CD #1 for $2,000 for a one-year term, CD #2 for $2,000 for a two-year term, CD #3 for $2,000 for a three-year term, CD #4 for $2,000 for a four-year term, and CD #5 for $2,000 for a five-year term.

As the CDs mature, you renew each of them for five years. After five years, you continue to have one CD mature each year, and you renew at the highest current market rate you can find. You do not have to stay with the same financial institution. As interest rates fluctuate over time, you always have some CDs at lower rates and some at higher rates. As a result, you are always earning an average rate overall, thus avoiding the possibility of having your money earning very low rates. And you always will be able to access at least some of your money within a relatively short time frame.

CONCEPT CHECK 5.2

1. Explain why opening a checking account and a money market account are appropriate actions for most people, and tell how each will be used.
2. Summarize what happens when you write a check.
3. Distinguish between a money market account and a money market mutual fund account.
4. Explain the benefits and drawbacks of certificates of deposit.

Learning Objective 3

Establish ownership of assets wisely.

5.3 ESTABLISH OWNERSHIP OF ASSETS WISELY

When you open a new account, you will be asked to sign a signature card that can be used to verify the signatures of the owners of the account. Accounts can be owned either individually or jointly.

An *individual account* has one owner who is solely responsible for the account and its activity. At the death of the individual owner, the account becomes part of his or her estate and will go to heirs in accordance with the owner's will. If desired, individual accounts can be set up with a **payable on death (POD)**. This is also known as a **Totten trust** designation. A POD is an arrangement between a bank or credit union whereby upon the death of the client the assets are immediately transferred to the designated beneficiaries. A POD does not give the person any rights to the account while the owner is still alive.

A *joint account* has two or more owners, each of whom has legal rights to the funds in the account. The forms of joint ownership discussed here apply to all types of property, including automobiles and homes, as well as checking and savings accounts. Three types of joint ownership exist:

1. **Joint tenancy with right of survivorship** (also called simply **joint tenancy**) is the most common form of joint ownership, especially for husbands and wives. In this case, each person owns the whole of the asset and can dispose of it without the approval of the other(s). With accounts at financial institutions, the financial institution will honor checks or withdrawal slips possessing any of the owners' signatures. An advantage of a joint account is that in case of death of one of the owners, the property continues to be owned by the surviving account holder(s).

2. **Tenancy in common** is a form of joint ownership in which two or more parties own the asset, but each retains control over a separate piece of the property rights. In most states, the ownership shares are presumed to be equal unless otherwise specified. When one owner dies, his or her share in the asset is distributed to his or her heirs according to the terms of a will (or if no will exists, according to state law) instead of going to the other co-owners.

3. **Tenancy by the entirety** is a type of shared ownership of property recognized in most states, available only to married couples. Much like in a joint tenancy, spouses who own property as tenants by the entirety each own an undivided interest in the property, each has full rights to occupy and use it and has a right of survivorship. Tenants by the entirety also cannot transfer their interest in the property without the consent of the other spouse.

Nonworking spouses should get their name on all deeds and investments. In the event of divorce, courts typically award property to the people who legally own it. Dual-earner couples often prefer to own some property together and some property separately. If you own a business and default on a loan, for example, your creditors usually cannot attach your home if it is in your spouse's name.

joint tenancy with right of survivorship (joint tenancy)
The most common form of joint ownership, especially for husbands and wives. In this case, each person owns the whole of the asset and can dispose of it without the approval of the other(s).

DO IT IN CLASS

tenancy in common
A form of joint ownership in which two or more parties own the asset, but each retains control over a separate piece of the property rights.

tenancy by the entirety
A type of shared ownership of property recognized in most states, available only to married couples, where spouses who own property as tenants by the entirety each own an undivided interest in the property, each has full rights to occupy and use it and has a right of survivorship.

CONCEPT CHECK 5.3

1. Explain why correctly owning assets is important to the personal finances of people, especially couples.
2. Differentiate between ownership via joint tenancy with right of survivorship and tenancy in common.

5.4 ELECTRONIC MONEY MANAGEMENT

Learning Objective 4

Describe your legal protections when conducting monetary asset management electronically.

Electronic money management occurs whenever transactions are conducted without using paper documents. Most of these activities involve **electronic funds transfers (EFTs)**, in which funds are shifted electronically (rather than by check or cash) among various accounts and to and from other people and institutions.

5.4a Why Use Electronic Money Management?

People use online banking, cards and other electronic tools for several reasons. Convenience is big as it is easy to monitor virtually all one's financial activities almost instantly. Costs can be very low because brick-and-mortar buildings are not required in every city. Services are growing all the time, including using your smartphone, key fob, or computer for almost all transactions. Safety, too, is a plus with federal legal protections as well as state laws pertaining to electronic money management.

electronic money management
Occurs whenever transactions are conducted without using paper documents.

electronic funds transfers (EFTs)
When funds are shifted electronically (rather than by check or cash) among various accounts and to and from other people and institutions.

5.4b   Cards Used to Access Your Money

The types of cards used to access your money include.

1. **ATM cards.** Most checking accounts come with a free debit card. These allow you to make purchases and withdraw money from **automatic teller machines (ATMs)**, which allow you to check your balance, withdraw and deposit money, and transfer money between your accounts. ATM cards are used to make the transactions along with a **personal identification number (PIN)**. Or you can use your smartphone.

2. **Debit cards.** A debit card (also known as a bank card or check card) is a plastic payment card that provides the cardholder electronic access to his/her bank account(s) at a financial institution. The cards deduct money directly from a consumer's checking account to pay for a purchase. When you buy something, the cost is electronically deducted (debited) from your bank account and deposited into the seller's account. Debit cards also allow you to withdraw money from your checking account through an ATM or through the *cash-back function* that many merchants offer at the point of sale. Debit cards eliminate the need to carry cash or physical checks to make purchases. In addition, debit cards offer the convenience of credit cards and they have many of the same consumer protections when issued by major payment processors like Visa or MasterCard. Debit cards are also called *bank cards, ATM cards, cash cards,* and *check cards.* Debit cards usually have daily purchase limits, meaning it may not be possible to make an especially large purchase with a debit card.

3. **Prepaid cards.** Prepaid cards are easy to use and reloadable, and they may be used almost anywhere to buy online, make bill payments, get cash at ATMs, get direct deposits, and make everyday purchases. No credit check or bank account is needed as they are only as valuable as the money put on the card. With prepaid debit cards the money is on deposit with the card issuer's computers. These have new legal protections from the Consumer Financial Protection Bureau much like debit cards. Bluebird and Visa dominate.

4. **Stored-value cards.** A stored-value card is a payment card with a monetary value stored on the card itself, not in an external account maintained by a financial institution. Debit cards are usually issued in the name of individual account holders, while stored-value cards are usually anonymous. An example of a stored-value card is a gift card. Gift cards often have an activation fee, expiration date (no shorter than five years), and an inactivity fee if there are no transactions within a year. Cards that can only be used at one retailer are worthless if they go bankrupt.

5. **Credit cards.** A credit card is a plastic card with imprinted numbers and a magnetic strip, issued by a bank or business authorizing the holder to use it as payment instead of cash to buy goods or services on credit. The issuer of the card will later collect payment for any purchases. If payment is made after the grace period, interest will be charged on the account usually one month after a purchase is made. Borrowing limits are pre-set according to the individual's credit rating. A credit card is different from a debit card because money is not tied to or immediately removed from a bank account. (Chapter 7 examines credit cards.)

6. **Key fobs and Smartcards.** A type of security token is a **key fob.** It has built-in mechanisms that let people have access to network services and information, including making mobile and contactless payments. There are many similar devices such as rings, bracelets, fitness and smart bands, stickers, wristbands, clothing, and smartcards. MasterCard, Barclays, Apple, Walmart, and other firms' payment technologies permit people to connect to payment terminals sometimes using facial or voice recognition for identification. You can even pay for your tithe at church. Apple Pay and Android Pay will eventually replace credit and debit cards as well as PIN and magnetic strips. They use two factor authentication. All that's necessary is to just place the one device near the merchant's payment card reader, and the two will interact with one another to complete the transaction. Person-to-Person (P2P)

ATM cards

Plastic cards to make purchases and withdraw money from ATMs that require use of a PIN number.

debit cards

A plastic payment card that provides the cardholder electronic access to his/her bank account(s) at a financial institution.

prepaid cards

A plastic payment card that is easy to use and reloadable, and it may be used almost anywhere to buy online, make bill payments, get cash at ATMs, pay bills, get direct deposits, and make everyday purchases.

stored-value cards

A payment card with a monetary value stored on the card itself, not in an external account maintained by a financial institution, that is usually issued in the name of an individual account holder.

gift card

A stored value card that often has an activation fee, expiration date (no shorter than five years), and an inactivity fee if there are no transactions within a year.

credit cards

A credit card is a plastic card with imprinted numbers and a magnetic strip, issued by a bank or business authorizing the holder to use it as payment instead of cash to buy goods or services on credit.

payments let you send money to another person via the app, e-mail, or text.

7. **Electronic Benefit Transfer (EBT) cards.** An electronic system that allows state welfare departments to issue benefits via a magnetically encoded payment debit cards. They are used to access food stamps and cash benefits that can be obtained at EBT participating merchants, ATM machines, and Point of Sale (POS) terminals.

5.4c Liability Limits for Lost or Stolen Debit Cards

Federal and state regulations have been adopted to provide protections for the use of debit cards and other electronic transactions. The Electronic Funds Transfer Act (ETFA) is the governing law, and additional guidelines are provided by the Federal Reserve Board's Regulation E and the Consumer Financial Protection Bureau.

The financial institution must give the customer notice of their liability in case the card is lost or stolen. This includes a phone number for reporting the loss and a description of its error resolution process.

A customer may be liable for unauthorized withdrawals if their card is lost or stolen and they do not follow certain criteria:

- Loss is limited to $50 if institution is notified within two business days
- Loss could be up to $500 if institution is notified between 3 and 59 days
- If loss is not reported within 60 business days customer risks unlimited loss on transfers made after the 60 day period, as he/she could lose all money in the account plus maximum overdraft if any

5.4d EFT Error Resolution Process

Customers should be diligent in reviewing their EFT statements for possible errors and certain steps must be taken:

- Write or call the financial institution immediately, if possible
- Must be no later than 60 days from the date of erroneous statement
- Explain why they believe there is an error, the type, dollar amount and date
- May be required to send details of the error in writing within 10 business days

Under the Electronic Funds Transfer Act, the financial institution must:

- Promptly investigate the error and resolve it within 45 days
- Errors involving new accounts (opened last 30 days), POS transactions, and foreign transactions may take up to 90 days
- If it takes more than 10 business days to complete the investigation, they must re-credit the amount in question
- Notify customer of the results of investigation:
  —If there was error—correct it or make recredit final
  —If no error—explanation in writing, notify customer of deducted recredit
- Customer has the right to ask for copies of any documents relied on in the investigation

The protections offered for fraudulent use of debit cards are not as strong as when your credit card is used fraudulently. It is much safer to use a credit card for certain transactions, especially those made online. States may have laws that provide additional protection for consumers in EFT transactions. MasterCard became the first debit card

THERE IS AN APP FOR THAT!

Some of the best apps include:

- Acorns
- BillGuard
- Digit
- Dyme
- GoodBudget
- Mevelopes
- Mint
- Payfirma
- Pocket Expense
- Square
- Stripe

DO IT IN CLASS

electronic benefit transfer (EBT) cards

An electronic system that allows state welfare departments to issue benefits via a magnetically encoded payment debit cards.

issuer to extend its zero-liability policy in the U.S. to include both PIN purchases and ATM transactions. Thus their debit cards do have liability protections.

5.4e Avoid Automatic Billing, Renewal and Subscription Services

automatic billing (or **auto-renewal billing**)

A feature that allows a vender to automatically charge a customer's credit (or debit) card or bank account on a regular basis through a recurring profile set up on the account.

People often inadvertently spend many dollars a month automatically paying certain bills—some legitimate and some not—that continue to be paid forever. **Automatic billing** (or **auto-renewal billing**) is a feature that allows a vendor to automatically charge a customer's credit (or debit) card or bank account on a regular basis through a recurring profile set up on the account. Examples include gym and athletic clubs, health and beauty suppliers, cable TV services, magazines, pharmacies, music/video downloads (Spotify and Pandora), games, movie rentals, website domains, Sirius, XM Radio, and OnStar.

To stop such charges keep a close eye on your credit statements for any unauthorized reoccurring charges or debits (withdrawals) from your checking account, and report any fraud. Contact the vendor and follow the refund procedures that should have been provided. Request a refund of your money and prohibit such charges in the future. If you believe you have been a victim of fraud, contact your bank. Tell your bank that you did not okay the debit and that you want to prevent further debiting. Your state Attorney General may be able to help get your money back.

Avoid financial laziness by remembering to never give out the numbers to your credit and debit cards or checking account to anyone unless you know the company and understand why the information is necessary. And, never sign up for a "free trial" using a credit card or bank account number. Don't respond to e-mails requesting you to verify your user name and password. Avoid saying "yes" to any question on the telephone (or on a chatbox menu) because the scammer is recording it as confirmation of your agreement. Finally, realize that unsolicited e-mails, text messages or telephone calls only come from crooks.

5.4f Protect Your Privacy

Here are some tips for reducing the risk:

- Study your statements carefully.
- A false $1 charge to a debit or credit card is a sign of a potential larger theft as it means the perpetrator is checking to see if an account number is valid and hoping that you won't notice.
- Avoid banking via a public computer or network.
- Be cautious with private information when using social networking and job search sites.
- Always hit the "log off" button at the top of the page and close the browser window.
- Regularly change your passwords (except for facial and voice systems)
- Keep your financial information away from others.
- Use a shredder.

5.4g Bitcoin Is a "Fad" Virtual Currency

Bitcoin

A peer-to-peer experimental digital cash currency based on an open source cryptographic protocol that can be bought at an exchange and transferred through a computer or smartphone without an intermediate financial institution.

Bitcoin is a peer-to-peer experimental decentralized digital cash currency based on an open source cryptographic protocol. You can buy them at an exchange and you store them in a "mobile wallet" on your computer or smartphone, and they are not registered with any government or financial authority. Bitcoins, of which there are only 21 million, can be transferred through a computer or smartphone without an intermediate financial institution.

The purchasing power is zero thus Bitcoin has no intrinsic value. It is not protected by a central bank and governments probably will never confer the status of legal currency on a private currency. To buy Bitcoins, see Coinbase or Bitstamp, which also store the currency. Transactions are untraceable. Due to internal disputes, Bitcoin is now known as BitcoinXT. Even as Bitcoin, riven by internal divisions, has struggled, a rival virtual currency, known as Ethereum, has entered the market.

Bitcoin is accepted in trade by some merchants and individuals in parts of the world. A large share of its commercial use is believed to be used in money laundering, terrorist financing, ransom and extortion demands, and purchases of illicit goods such as marijuana, cocaine, prescription painkillers, and gambling transactions. Promoters say Bitcoin helps users avoid taxes, regulations, and government seizures of assets. The lack of regulations allows everything to happen, including fraud.

Many have criticized Bitcoin's highly volatile market value as prices jumped in 3 months from $17 to $230. Then in 2 days it plunged to $68 before returning to a price of $77 a week later. Subsequently it went over $1,200, and then dropped to $380 in one day. Talk about stomach-churning volatility! The Internal Revenue Service does not treat Bitcoin as a currency rather it is classified as "property," hence buying and selling transactions are capital gains.

Critics argue that Bitcoin is volatile, inflexible, and minimally used in legitimate commerce. The largest Bitcoin exchange in Tokyo went bankrupt after nearly half a billion dollars of Bitcoins disappeared, mostly from client accounts. The manager claims a hacker took the funds. A hacker generally needs only an owner's password to steal his or her bitcoins.

The innovations in Bitcoin's technology, known as block-chain, are being viewed as a potentially disruptive force that might help traditional institutions be more efficient in transacting and maintaining financial records. In short, safely move money around the world instantly and almost for free. More than $3 trillion in foreign currency changes hands every day, and that means a lot of middlemen.

CONCEPT CHECK 5.4

1. Distinguish among credit cards, debit cards, and stored-value cards.
2. List the steps you should take if you find an error in your monthly statement regarding an electronic transaction.
3. Summarize the rules that apply if you lose your ATM or debit card and it is used without your authorization.
4. Summarize what you know about Bitcoin.

5.5 THE PSYCHOLOGY OF MONEY MANAGEMENT

Learning Objective 5
Discuss your money and personal finances effectively with loved ones.

A common cause of tension in personal relationships is conflict over money. Mutual trust in money matters can be developed—and must be—to have happy relationships and achieve financial success.

5.5a Managing Money and Making Financial Decisions Are Different

Managing money includes such tasks as handling the checkbook, overseeing the budget, doing the household shopping, and making investments. Couples should agree on who will carry out these day-to-day chores and then carry through on their responsibilities. Financial experts recommend that each person in a relationship keep some money of his or her own. This can encourage independence and self-control in a relationship rather than dependency on the other person. This can be accomplished by setting up three checking accounts: a discretionary account for each individual (two accounts) and a third, joint account. Then clearly specify the budget categories for spending related to each account.

NEVER EVER

1. *Keep too much money in a checking account where it earns very little interest.*
2. *Fail to reconcile your accounts on a regular basis.*
3. *Keep money matters and worries to yourself.*

While managing family money is a significant task, decision making is where most disagreements arise. Shared decision making is the best model when defining goals and setting up a budget; when contemplating any major expense, such as buying vehicles and housing; and when conferring on key topics such as investments, insurance, estate planning, and long-term financial plans.

5.5b People Connect Strong Emotions to Money

People often attach a number of emotions to money, including freedom, trust, self-esteem, guilt, indifference, envy, security, comfort, power, and control. They bring with them the patterns, beliefs, and attitudes that were prevalent in their family of origin.

Author Judith Viorst suggests that becoming responsible and adept at managing one's financial matters represents a true passage into adulthood. This evolution involves communicating effectively with others on money matters. Addressing questions openly and calmly helps keep emotions in check. Separately writing down the answers to the following questions and then bringing the answers to the table in a meeting can be an effective way to begin discussing money matters.

1. What is my biggest money worry today?
2. What are we doing well financially?
3. Is there an issue in our finances that I would like to understand better?
4. If we needed to cut back our spending, what three areas are off limits and what three could be changed?
5. What money issues do we avoid and how can we bring them into the open?

5.5c How to Talk About Financial Matters

In the United States, money is not spoken about very often in social settings. People seem to have been raised to be either quiet or apologetic about money matters. Money matters are shrouded in silence or in hushed tones. More than two-thirds of people did not discuss money with their parents while growing up. This is one of our off-limits conversation topics, one of our "unmentionables" like sex. While talking about sex has improved, money matters are still not discussed as often as they should. In fact, disagreements about personal finances are the number one reason why people get divorced. About 15 percent of young people argue about money matters.

Even though money is considered a private matter, such a "no talk" rule can damage your finances. It is smart to talk with friends and family about money matters, read what the experts write, and consult with successful investors.

If you are married, or in a similarly committed relationship, both people need to communicate and show mutual respect for each other. This helps make a successful relationship. Thus each person must talk about money early on in a relationship. One should take the initiative and get "the money talks" started. Seek common goals on creating an emergency fund and paying off debt.

Discussions about money matters are not always easy, and these conversations can be improved. Some people who are entirely rational about other issues are unpredictable or even careless in money matters. Adults need to accept that honest differences may exist among people and accept these differences, and work with them. The following ideas will help you discuss money with more confidence and candor.

Get to Know Yourself and Your Significant Other The first step in learning to talk with others about financial matters is to understand your own approach to money. Consider the emotions described earlier to help you get started. It is constructive to discuss any differences in how you view yourself as compared with how your partner views you. Write these down. Also don't begrudge your significant other for small indulgences. Each of you should have some money to spend with no questions asked or any explanation required.

ADVICE FROM A SEASONED PRO

How to Develop Money Sense in Children

In many families, money matters are a taboo subject. Parents can help children develop money sense by providing them with opportunities to manage their own money while still young. Do the following to increase your children's ease in handling money:

1. **Give them the opportunity to manage an allowance.** Even children as young as 5 years old should have some money of their own. Allowances are a means for teaching money management. The child should learn not to spend all of the allowance each week. Discuss saving for a future purchase or for future needs. A younger child may be interested in a toy which is not yet on the market or may require additional savings to purchase. An older child may be considering long-term needs such as when he/she goes to college or work, or travel.

2. **Encourage them to work.** Once children reach their preteen years, there are many opportunities to earn their own money. When children see the effort it takes to make money, it is easier for them to know the real cost of spending.

3. **Set reasonable limits.** Children should be given age-appropriate limits for spending in various categories and should be required to save a portion of their money.

4. **Teach them to make good choices.** The dollar amounts and areas of discretionary spending should increase as the child matures. A 7-year-old might be allowed to spend a portion of his or her own money on toys, snacks, and gifts to charity. A 14-year-old might be allowed to buy meals, clothing, and games, as well. Ask the child to consider the value of the purchase from both a short-term and long-term perspective to evaluate their options and ultimate choice. Demonstrate and encourage comparison shopping for the best price.

5. **Help them learn patience.** Children should have autonomy over at least some of their own money. But the remainder, perhaps half, should be saved.

6. **Talk about family finances with children.** Children need to see that parents must work at managing the family finances. They should know what it costs to raise a family and to make ends meet.

7. **Practice what you preach, serve as a role model.** Children learn more from what they see than what they are told. Save money yourself, and tell your children that saving means that you can't always have something right away. Teach by example; avoid impulse buying.

Heidi Kilmer
Northeastern University, Boston, Massachusetts

Focus on Commonalities Successful communication about money requires that the effort is aimed toward agreeing on common goals and reaching a consensus of opinion without substantially compromising the views of others. The task is not to avoid arguments; rather it is to work through them. Focusing on the future helps.

Learn to Manage Financial Disagreements Give all family members time to express their views when discussing financial matters. Each also needs to listen to what others are saying and feeling. If talking proves too difficult, have each person separately write down his or her concerns. By swapping notes, ideas and concerns can be shared. Schedule a time and place for financial talks, decide on agenda items, and leave other conflicts outside the door.

Recall from Chapter 3 that Harry and Belinda Johnson had a disagreement when setting up their budget to allow for their anniversary party and spending for holiday gifts at the end of the year. As a result, they ended up with a draft budget that did not balance for the year as planned expenses exceeded anticipated income. They agreed to disagree and postponed decisions that will need to be made on how to cover their shortfalls. They will need to do better in the future.

Each member of the family should be aware of and involved with important financial decisions.

Use Positive "I" Statements Messages focusing on "I" describe the behavior in question, the feelings you experienced because of the behavior, and any tangible effect on you. For example, a spouse might say, "I feel upset when we use credit cards because I do not know where we will find the money to pay the bills at the end of the month." "I" messages say three things: what (the behavior), I feel (feelings), and because (reason).

A goal of using "I" messages is to remove the emotion as much as possible from these discussions. "I" messages help build stronger relationships because they tell the other person "I trust you to decide what change in behavior is necessary."

Beware of "I" statements that begin with "I need you to...." "You" statements are blaming statements, such as "You always ...," "You never ...," and "If you don't, I will...." These statements have a high probability of being condescending to other people, of making them feel guilty, and of implying that their needs and wants are not as important as yours.

Be Honest and Talk Regularly Achieving consensus requires that each person be honest when talking about money matters. It further demands that couples regularly talk about finances. Perhaps begin by deciding to talk about money matters for only ten minutes at a time. Also be prepared to compromise. When you make decisions together, take action on them. Focus attention on current financial activities and issues as well as long-term financial planning. Use these discussions to forge overall long-term strategies for dealing with your family finances.

Once the proper base has been established, other short-term financial issues are more likely to fall into place. When you start to have these kinds of financial conversations, you will have fewer arguments about money issues and more financial happiness.

5.5d Complications Brought by Remarriage

Remarriage merges financial histories, values, and habits as well as households. Some remarried couples—and those choosing to live together following a previous relationship—may have substantial combined incomes bolstered by child-support

ADVICE FROM A SEASONED PRO

Wisely Save Money for Children's Education in a 529 Plan

As soon as your children are born, save for their college in a 529 plan as it is best for most families. Sponsored in almost every state, **529 plans** (also known as a qualified tuition plans) are designed to encourage saving for future college costs. Your investment grows free of income taxes and all earning are tax free when the money is used for qualified college expenses. The minimum investment is $25 a month, and most states also give you tax breaks, perhaps as much as 25 percent on one's state income taxes. To find the best plan, see http://sites.savingforcollege.com/kiplinger/plan_details.php.

Dana Wolff
Southeast Technical Institute, Sioux Falls, South Dakota

payments from a former spouse. In many cases, at least one person may be paying (instead of receiving) alimony and child support.

After Francesco Martignetti, of Newark, New Jersey, discussed the pluses and minuses of a prenuptial agreement (see Chapter 17), they signed one before their wedding. After marriage they decided to set up separate paying funds for "his," "her," and "our" children's expenses because such costs can be quite steep. Special concerns for blended families include determining who assumes financial responsibility for biological offspring and stepchildren; handling resentment over alimony and child-support payments; and managing unequal assets, incomes, responsibilities, and debts. Even gift giving can become challenging. These topics can be mitigated with effective communication.

Many remarried people use "his" and "her" funds and require the legally responsible parent owing financial support to a previous spouse or to children to make such payments out of his or her own money. There is no right or wrong ways to do these things, just the way that makes you both feel comfortable. Professor Jean Lown of Utah State University suggests that, "What is best is what works for your relationship."

5.5e Check Your Overall Financial Health Online

A number of financial websites aim to provide you with a financial health score by asking you a couple dozen questions about such things as your income, savings, expenses, credit, insurance, money management, investments, and estate planning. They give you a score of 1 to 100, tell you how well you stack up against your similarly aged peers, and offer advice on how to strengthen any weak areas. Many employers and banks offer free scores, and you can retake the quiz yearly or as often as you like. See Charles Schwab's "Financial Fitness Quiz" (www.schwabmoneywise.com/public/moneywise/calculators_tools/fitness_quiz).

CONCEPT CHECK 5.5

1. Explain why it is difficult for many people in relationships to talk about money matters.
2. Identify three ways you might more effectively communicate about money matters.

WHAT DO YOU RECOMMEND *NOW?*

Now that you have read the chapter on managing checking and savings accounts, what would you recommend to Nathan Rosenberg and Avigai Abramovitz in the case at the beginning of the chapter regarding:

1. Where they can obtain the monetary asset management services that they need?
2. Their best use of checking accounts and savings accounts as they begin saving for a home?
3. The use of a money market account for their monetary asset management?
4. Their use of electronic banking in the future?
5. How they can best discuss the management of their money and finances?

SUMMARY OF LEARNING OBJECTIVES RECAPPED

LO1 Identify the goals of monetary asset management and sources of such financial services.

Maximizing interest earnings and minimizing fees on savings and checking accounts is the goal of monetary asset management. The primary providers of monetary asset management services are depository institutions, such as insured accounts at banks and credit unions. Deposit insurance protects your deposits.

LO2 Understand and employ the various types of accounts available to meet the goals of monetary asset management.

Put cash into a checking account for everyday use and open a money market account in which to put money for later investments. A student checking account is also often available. Checking accounts usually have balance requirements. Savings accounts, which are time deposits, pay slightly higher interest rates than checking accounts. Certificates of deposit typically pay the same rate over the time of the certificate.

LO3 Establish ownership of assets wisely.

If desired, an individual checking account may be opened with a payable on death arrangement that upon death immediately transfers ownership to a designated beneficiary. Joint accounts especially for husbands and wives usually are opened with a joint tenancy with right of survivorship.

LO4 Describe your legal protections when conducting monetary asset management electronically.

Electronic money management occurs whenever banking transactions are conducted via computers without the customer using paper documents. Electronic banking includes the use of automatic teller machines (ATMs), debit cards, preloaded debit cards, stored-value cards, credit cards, key fobs, and electronic benefit transfer (EBT) cards. The Electronic Funds Transfer Act protects consumers who use electronic money management. There also is an EFT error resolution process required by federal law.

LO5 Discuss your money and personal finances effectively with loved ones.

Recognize the psychological and emotional aspects of money, and identify your own approaches to money. Communicate openly and frequently about money matters by using "I" statements. Recognize there are complications on money issues brought on by remarriage.

LET'S TALK ABOUT IT

1. **Bank Account Fees.** List two examples of checking account transactions that result in assessment of fees that are avoidable?

2. **Avoiding Overdraft Fees.** You know someone who recently had $90 in overdraft fees for two small debit card transactions. Explain to him why such high fees resulted from such small transactions and the relative benefits of having an automatic funds transfer agreement versus an automatic overdraft loan agreement versus overdraft protection.

3. **Forms of Account Ownership.** When would you recommend using an individual account, a joint tenancy with right of survivorship account, and a tenancy by the entirety account for your monetary assets?

4. **Opting in.** Many people desire protection from the possibility of overdrawing their checking account. Banks make it easy by allowing you to opt into overdraft

protection. Explain how this and other overdraft protections work and why the true cost of opting in may exceed the benefits.

5. **Earning Higher Interest on Your Savings.** When might it be appropriate for you to save via a certificate of deposit versus a money market account?

6. **Lost/Stolen Debit Cards.** What should you do if your ATM or debit card is lost or stolen? Why?

7. **Talking About Money.** Have you ever had a disagreement with a friend or family member over a money issue? How might you communicate differently now?

8. **Questions About Money.** If you have trouble talking about money, complete these sentences with the first words that come to your mind: "Sometimes financially I sabotage myself by...." "Financially, I keep feeling I should...." And "Money creates anxiety for me because...."

DO THE MATH

1. **Invest Now or Later? Twins Natalie and Kaitlyn are both age 27. They both live in Warren, Ohio.** Beginning at age 27, Natalie invests $2,000 per year for ten years and then never sets aside another penny. Kaitlyn waits ten years and then invests $2,000 per year for the next 30 years. Assuming they both earn 7 percent, how much will each twin have at age 67? (Hint: Use Appendixes A.1 and A.3 or visit the *Garman/Forgue* companion website.)

2. **The Benefit of a Higher APY.** Isabel Lopez, from Lewiston, Idaho, is age 19, and she recently received an inheritance of $50,000 from her grandmother's estate. She plans to use the money for the down payment on a home in ten years when she finishes her education. Right now the funds are in a savings account paying 1.0 percent APY. How much would Isabel have in ten years if instead she purchased a ten-year CD paying 3.0 percent? (Hint: Use Appendix A.1 or visit the *Garman/Forgue* companion website.)

3. **Reconciling a Checking Account.** Andrew Parker, of San Marcos, Texas, has a checking account at the credit union affiliated with his university. Illustrated below are his monthly statement and check register for the account. Reconcile the checking account and answer the following questions.

   (a) What is the total of the outstanding checks?

   (b) What is the total of the outstanding deposits?

(c) Why is there a difference between the uncorrected balance in the check register and the balance on the statement?

(d) What is the updated and correct balance in the check register on the next page?

Account Name	Andrew Parker	Period of Activity	11/2/18–12/01/18
Account #	123–45678		
Summary of Your Activity This Month			
Date	Activity	Amount	Balance
11/02			$412.66
11/04	Debit Card POS Transaction	$17.46	395.20
11/09	Check #237	33.33	361.87
11/12	Direct Deposit	876.99	1,238.86
11/13	Debit Card POS Transaction	84.56	1,154.30
11/13	EFT	22.00	1,132.30
11/15	Check#238	645.00	487.30
11/23	Debit Card POS Transaction	68.87	418.43
11/27	Debit Card POS Transaction	43.00	375.43
11/28	Deposit	200.00	575.43
11/30	Check#239	125.00	450.43
11/30	Service Charge	4.50	445.93
11/30	ATM Withdrawal	100.00	345.93
12/01	Check #240	46.00	299.93

DO IT IN CLASS
Page 159

Date	Check #	Payee/ Payor	For	Amount	Balance
11/01					412.66
11/03	Debit Card	CVS	Cold Meds	$ 17.46	395.20
11/05	237	Univ. Book-store	Of Mice and Men	33.33	361.87
11/12	Deposit	PNC Bank	Payday-Yeah!	876.99	1,238.86
11/12	238	ABC Property Mgmt.	Rent	645.00	593.86
11/13	Debit Card	Kroger's	Groceries	84.56	509.30
11/13	Electronic Payment	Maysville Water	Water Bill	22.00	487.30
11/23	Debit Card	Kroger's	Groceries	67.88	419.42
11/23	Debit Card	Applebee's	Dinner with Karen	43.00	376.42
11/27	Deposit	Mom	For Utilities	200.00	576.42
11/27	239	Duke Power	Electric/ Heat Bill	125.00	451.42
11/27	240	Conoco	Gas	46.00	405.42
11/30	Debit Card	ATM With-drawal	Carry Around Money	100.00	305.42
12/01	241	Comcast	Cable Bill	53.88	252.54

4. **Saving for College.** You want to create a college fund for a child who is now 3 years old. The fund should grow to $60,000 in 15 years. If an investment available to you will yield 6 percent per year, how much must you invest in a lump sum now to realize the $60,000 when needed? (Hint: Use Appendix A.2 or visit the *Garman/Forgue* companion website.)

5. **Saving for Retirement.** You plan to retire in 40 years. To provide for your retirement, you initiate a savings program of $4,000 per year yielding 7 percent. What will be the value of the retirement fund after 40 years? (Hint: Use Appendix A.3 or visit the *Garman/Forgue* companion website.)

FINANCIAL PLANNING CASES

CASE 1

How Should the Johnsons Manage Their Cash?

In January, Harry and Belinda Johnson had $10,660 in monetary assets (see page 109): $1,100 in cash on hand; $1,200 in a statement savings account at First Credit Union earning 1.0 percent interest; $4,000 in a statement savings account at the Far West Savings Bank earning 1.1 percent interest; $2,260 in Homestead Credit Union earning a dividend of 1.3 percent; and $2,100 in their regular checking account at First Credit Union earning 1 percent.

(a) What specific recommendations would you give the Johnsons for selecting checking and savings accounts that will enable them to effectively use the first and second tools of monetary asset management?

(b) Their annual budget, cash-flow calendar, and revolving savings fund (see Tables 3-6, 3-7, and 3-8 on pages 97, 98 and 99) indicate that the Johnsons will have additional amounts to deposit in the coming year. What are your recommendations for the Johnsons regarding use of a money market account? Why?

(c) What savings instrument would you recommend for their savings, given their objective of saving

enough to purchase a new home? Support your answer.

(d) If the Johnsons could put most of their monetary assets ($10,660) into a money market account earning 1.4 percent, how much would they have in the account after one year?

(e) Recall from Chapter 3 that Harry and Belinda had some disagreements regarding their anniversary dinner and holiday gift spending and ended up not having a balanced budget for the year. Provide some advice for the couple about how to resolve or, better, prevent such disagreements in the future.

CASE 2

Victor and Maria Hernandez Need to Save Money Fast

The Hernandez family is experiencing some financial pressures, even though the couple has a combined income of $85,000. Also, their eldest son, Joseph, will start college in only three years. Maria is contemplating going to work full time to add about $32,000 to the family's annual income.

(a) How will this change in income affect the family's emergency fund needs?

(b) How much should they save annually for the next three years if they want to build up Joseph's college fund to $30,000, assuming a 3 percent rate of return and ignoring taxes on the interest? (Hint: Use Appendix A.1 or visit the *Garman/Forgue* companion website.)

(c) Given their 25 percent marginal tax rate, what is the Hernandezes' after-tax return on their savings and how would that affect the amount they would need to save each year?

(d) What savings options are open to the Hernandezes that could reduce or eliminate the effects of taxes on their savings program?

CASE 3

Julia Price Thinks About Using Checking and Savings Accounts

Julia's six-figure salary has allowed her to build up a considerable cash reserve of over $20,000. She initially had basic checking and savings accounts. She also has a credit card with her bank that she uses to make most of her purchases, thereby earning reward points. She is careful to pay the account balance in full each month. Over time, she purchased several CDs. About three years ago, she also opened a money market deposit account at her bank in which she keeps almost $10,000. Last week she got a call from the bank suggesting that she open a cash management account to coordinate her accounts and maximize her overall earnings. She is hesitant to do so as she feels her current arrangement meets her needs. Offer your opinions about her thinking.

CASE 4

Liability for a Lost ATM Card

Joshua Franz, of Oxford, Mississippi, earned $4,600 during the summer and put $3,000 of the money in a newly opened savings account for use during the school year. It is now November 25th and Joshua went to the bank to withdraw some cash. The teller informed him that there was only $2,100 in the account. When Joshua protested, the teller informed him that there had been three ATM $300 withdrawals from the account on the last day of the month in August, September and October. Joshua typically neglects to open the statements he had received on the third day of each month. When he got home he could not find the ATM card he had received when he opened the account in August and recalled that he had found his car door open in his parking lot in late August but had thought nothing was taken. When he opened the statements he saw the record of each of the withdrawals. He went immediately back to the bank to tell them of

DO IT IN CLASS
Page 167

the loss. How much money will Joshua lose because of these fraudulent transactions?

CASE 5

The Impact of Federal Deposit Insurance

DO IT IN CLASS
Page 154

Alexandra Bronson, of Pueblo, Colorado, age 58, has done a very good job of accumulating savings over the years. She has all of her accounts at the same depository institution and has multiple accounts. Her balances are as follows:

$130,000 in a joint-checking account with her husband; $145,000 in a joint-savings account with her sister from an inheritance they received; $100,000 in a savings account in her own name with her sister as the payable at death party (also from the inheritance); and $75,000 in a savings account in her own name. She also has an individual retirement account (IRA) in her own name with a balance of $459,000. How much federal deposit insurance does Alexandra have in these accounts, and how much of her funds remain uninsured?

CASE 6

How Ownership Affects Who Will Receive Assets After a Death

Bang Liu, of Scranton, Pennsylvania, passed away recently at age 67. Among his assets were the following items: (a) Checking and savings accounts with a total balance of $45,000 with his widow, Fen, held in joint tenancy with right of survivorship. (b) A paid-for $330,000 home with his widow, Fen, held in joint tenancy with right of survivorship. (c) A $144,000 vacation cottage owned equally with his brother held in tenancy in common. (d) A dry cleaning business valued at $280,000 owned equal shares with his business partner, Fai, held in tenancy in common. (e) An automobile valued at $14,000 owned individually. (f) Two savings accounts of $20,000 each with his daughter named as payable at death party on one and his son named as payable at death party on the other. Bang's will names his widow as his sole heir. For each asset, identify who will receive all, or what portions, of the asset.

DO IT IN CLASS
Page 165

CASE 7

Which Is Better: A Minimum-balance Account or an Average-balance Account?

Aaron Searle, a service station owner from Moscow, Idaho, has been paying $20 per month in fees on his checking account for about a year. He is considering changing banks but fears that the fees will be similar no matter where he banks. He has tracked

DO IT IN CLASS
Page 158

his high-, low- and average-balance on his account for the last six months and found the following:

Month	Highest Balance	Lowest Balance	Average Balance
1	$4,800	$1,200	$2,400
2	$4,300	$300	$1,700
3	$3,600	$900	$1,200
4	$5,100	$1,700	$2,700
5	$3,500	$400	$900
6	$4,100	$1,200	$2,100

(a) In your opinion, would Aaron be better off with a minimum-balance account or an average-balance account to minimize his fees?

(b) What other advice would you have for Aaron regarding the avoidance of a monthly fee on his account?

CASE 8

Deciding Among the Tools of Monetary Asset Management

Kwaku Addo, a licensed physical therapist from Topeka, Kansas, earns $4,200 per month take-home pay and has the funds directly deposited in his checking account. He spends only about $3,500 per month, and the excess funds have been building up in his account for about two years.

(a) What other types of accounts are available to Kwaku?

(b) How might he manage his accounts to earn as much interest as possible and keep his money safe?

(c) How might he use electronic money management to accomplish these tasks?

BE YOUR OWN PERSONAL FINANCIAL MANAGER

1. **Checking and Savings Accounts.** Create a table outlining the rates, rules, and fees of your checking and savings accounts. Assess the appropriateness of the accounts

My Personal Financial Planner

for you and shop for more appropriate accounts if necessary using Worksheet 23: Selecting a Checking Account That Meets My Needs from "My Personal Financial Planner" as a guide for your selection process.

2. **Keep Your Accounts Current.** Go online every few days to monitor checking account activity. Use

My Personal Financial Planner

the "Did You Know?" box on page 159 or Worksheet 24: Reconciling My Checking Account from "My Personal Financial Planner" to help reconcile your account monthly.

3. **Protect Your Privacy.** Confirm the existence and amount of each transaction in your checking and savings accounts soon after receiving your account statements. Report any discrepancies immediately.

4. **Talk About Money.** If married or cohabiting, schedule a regular time to discuss finances with your partner. Use the material on pages 169–173 as a guide for the topics and tone of the discussions. To get your conversation started, you might pose the following questions: If we unexpectedly received $10,000 tax free, what would we do with it? If we had to cut our spending by 10 percent, where would we make the reductions? Plan no more than 15 minutes for this initial conversation.

ON THE NET

Go to the Web pages indicated to complete these exercises.

1. **Simple Savings.** Go to the website of BankRate.com at www.bankrate.com/calculators/savings/simple-savings-calculator.aspx. Input the amount of deposit, interest rate and number of years, and record the calculated answer.

2. **Checking Accounts.** Visit the website for the Federal Reserve Board, where you will find articles (www.federalreserve.gov/consumerinfo/fivetips_checking.htm) on checking accounts. Browse the article to find three things you could do that would help you protect your checking account.

3. **Certificates of Deposit.** Visit the Bankrate.com website at www.bankrate.com where you will find information

about rates of return on certificates of deposit. What is the best rate for a one-year CD and a five-year CD in a large city near your home (look in the state, then the city)? How do these rates compare with the average and the highest rates nationally?

4. **Safe Internet Banking.** Visit the website for FDIC at www.fdic.gov. Use the search box to find articles on "internet banking." Read the article titled "Safe Internet Banking." After reading the information, make a list of important positive and negative aspects of Internet banking. Is Internet banking right for you?

ACTION INVOLVEMENT PROJECTS

1. **Checking Accounts Where You Live.** Select three banks, savings banks, or credit unions in your community. Contact each to gather information on the types of checking accounts they offer and the basic rules of the accounts, including overdraft protections, fees, and interest rates. Make a table that summarizes your findings, and identify one institution that best meets your needs.

2. **Account Monitoring.** Survey three of your friends about their patterns of monitoring their checking and savings accounts. Compare what they do to your own pattern.

3. **Debit and ATM Activity.** Survey three of your friends about the patterns and amounts of their typical debit and ATM card usage. Compare their patterns to your own and those recommended in this chapter.

4. **Money Talk.** Survey three couples to ascertain their patterns of money talk. Ask each the following questions: "What are the areas of your finances that are easiest to discuss?" "What are your areas of most difficulty?" "How do you resolve disagreements?" Make a table that summarizes your findings and identify one institution that best meets your needs.

6 Building and Maintaining Good Credit

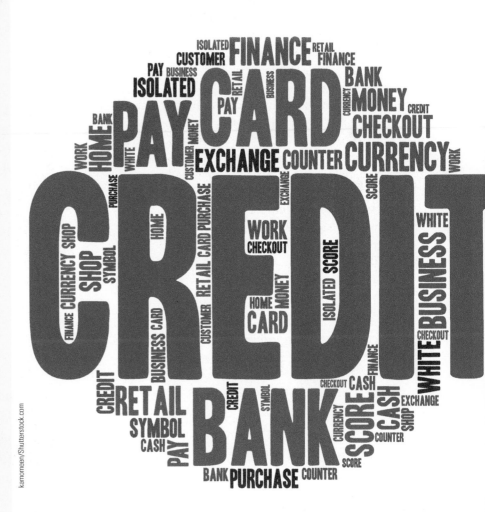

YOU MUST BE KIDDING, RIGHT?

People with no prior credit history or those who show poor repayment patterns in the past often wonder if they will ever be able to get credit, especially during economic times when credit is difficult to obtain. Simply put, will any lender want to trust them? Which of the following is true about the availability of credit for people in such situations?

A. Sadly, they will be doomed to a lifetime of no access to credit.

B. There are a few lenders who will be happy to provide credit to such borrowers.

C. Most of the "big name" banks will grant them credit.

D. Credit will be relatively easy to obtain for such borrowers just about anywhere.

The answer is B. It is difficult for people with poor or no credit to obtain credit from most banks and credit unions. But some lenders do accept such applicants, and they will charge high interest rates. Building and maintaining a good credit history does more than get you access to credit. It will also get you low interest rates!

Learning Objectives

After reading this chapter, you should be able to:

1 List some advantages and disadvantages of using credit.

2 Establish your own debt limit.

3 Obtain credit and build a good credit reputation.

4 Identify signs of overindebtedness, and describe the options that are available for debt relief.

WHAT DO YOU RECOMMEND?

Julia Grace, age 25, is a nurse practitioner with the local health department. She earns $65,000 per year, with about $9,000 of her income coming from overtime pay. Her disposable income is about $3,800 per month. Her employer provides a qualified tax-sheltered retirement plan to which Julia contributes 4 percent of her salary and for which she receives an additional 4 percent matching contribution from her employer. (She could contribute up to 8 percent with an equal employer match.) Julia has $29,000 in outstanding student loans on which she pays $328 per month over the next ten years, and her total credit card debt is $3,000 on which she has been paying $120 per month. Otherwise, she is debt free. Julia would like to purchase a new or late-model used car to replace the car she has been driving since her senior year in high school. She has $2,000 to use as a down payment.

Barry Austin Photography/Getty Images

What would you recommend to Julia on the subject of building and maintaining good credit regarding:

1. How might Julia go about establishing a debt limit?

2. What two or three things can she do help keep her student debt under control?

3. What can Julia do to build a good credit history?

4. Getting a free copy of her credit report?

TO-DO SOON

Do the following to begin to achieve financial success:

1. *Obtain a free copy of your credit report (www.annualcreditreport.com) from one of the three national credit bureaus.*

2. *Confirm the accuracy of the report and, if there are errors or omissions, challenge them.*

3. *Determine your own debt limit rather than relying on a lender before deciding to take on any debt.*

4. *Build a strong credit history and a high FICO score.*

5. *Always repay your debts in a timely manner.*

credit

An arrangement in which goods, services, or money is received in exchange for a promise to repay at a future date.

loan

Consumer credit that is repaid in equal amounts over a set period of time.

credit cards

Cards that allow repeated use of credit as long as the consumer makes regular monthly payments.

interest

The charge for the privilege of borrowing money, typically expressed as an annual percentage rate.

Learning Objective 1

List some advantages and disadvantages of using credit.

finance charge

Total dollar amount paid to use credit.

annual percentage rate (APR)

This is the annual rate that is charged for borrowing expressed as a percentage number that represents the actual yearly cost of funds over the term of a loan.

People have always had a difficult relationship with credit. Credit has long been grouped with the frailties and sins in ancient moral codes. Borrowing is risky, financial decisions are sometimes irrational, and people frequently do not weigh the interests of their present and future.

Your financial success depends heavily on your ability to make the sacrifices necessary to spend less than you earn. This allows you to save money for upcoming uses. Yet, you are likely to use credit to buy housing and vehicles as well as use credit cards and take out student loans. Paying high interest rates and overuse of credit, however, will impede your financial success.

This chapter and the next aim to empower you with the skills to successfully manage your personal finances while in school and beyond, and minimize both dropout and student loan defaults. You will gain the knowledge and skills necessary for making responsible financial decisions.

You should be more likely to set a savings goal, check your FICO credit score, and pay your bills on time. You should be less likely to overspend or spend beyond your means or to default on our student loans and less likely to draw down more money than needed on current student loans.

The term **credit** describes an arrangement in which goods, services, or money is received in exchange for a promise to repay at a future date. Credit represents a form of trust established between a lender and a borrower. If the lender believes that a prospective borrower has both the ability and the willingness to repay money, then credit will be extended. The borrower is expected to live up to that trust by repaying the lender. For the privilege of borrowing, a lender requires that a borrower pay interest and sometimes other charges.

Consumer credit often takes the form of a **loan** that is repaid in equal payments over a set period of time. You also are likely to use **credit cards**, which allow repeated use of credit as long as regular, monthly payments are maintained. Credit cards are an example of open-end credit.

Interest is the charge for the privilege of borrowing money, typically expressed as an annual percentage rate. It represents the "rent" one pays while using someone else's money. When stated in dollars, interest makes up the **finance charge**, which is the total dollar amount paid to use credit (including interest and any other required charges such as a loan application fee).

The Truth in Lending Act requires lenders to state the finance charge both in dollars and as an **annual percentage rate (APR)**. This is the annual rate that is charged for borrowing expressed as a percentage number that represents the actual yearly cost of funds over the term of a loan. This includes any fees or additional costs associated with the transaction. For example, a one-year, single-payment loan for $1,000 with a finance charge of $140 has a 14 percent APR.

6.1 ADVANTAGES AND DISADVANTAGES OF USING CREDIT

6.1a Advantages of Using Credit

There are advantages of using credit: (1) to enjoy the convenience; (2) to enjoy goods and services now; (3) to reduce the need to carry cash; (4) to buy when funds are low; (5) to shop on the Internet and by telephone; (6) to show identification; (7) to enjoy the grace period of 21 days on new credit card purchases; (8) to pay for emergencies; (9) to obtain an education; (10) to make travel reservations; (11) to obtain rebates, such as cash and travel miles; (12) to pay off several purchases with one monthly payment; (13) to easily return merchandise; (14) to protect against seller rip-offs and frauds; (15) to provide recordkeeping for business expenses; (16) to help open a business; and (17) to buy expensive items sooner rather than later, like a home and vehicles.

ADVICE FROM A SEASONED PRO

Debt Crowds Out the Future

Debt is your financial past. Your past is paying for student loans, vehicle purchases, medical bills, and credit cards. These debts prevent you from securing a financial future. People often struggle most of their lives paying debts of the past. The more quickly you eliminate your old past debts, the sooner you can plan and take care of your future.

Jennifer H. Plantier
Hardin-Simmons University, Abilene, Texas

6.1b Disadvantages of Using Credit

There are disadvantages of using credit: (1) it is tempting to spend more money; (2) credit reduces one's future financial flexibility and purchasing power; (3) future income is committed to previous credit contracts; (4) slows progress to achieving financial goals; (5) the risk of overindebtedness is real, (6) interest is costly, perhaps as much as 18 percent or more per month; (7) interest and fees substantially increase the cost of goods and services purchased; (8) increases credit related solicitations via mail, e-mail, text, and telephone calls; (9) reduced privacy when providers sell your personal information to others for solicitation; (10) increases possibility of identity theft; (11) it is much more difficult than you think to pay off old debts later and increase your FICO score; (12) users worry and stress about their debts; (13) may have negative impacts on relationships, (14) may result in property loss via repossession; (15) could result in one declaring personal bankruptcy; (16) can negatively impact one's credit history and credit score; and (17) may result in damaged personal reputation.

6.1c Identity Theft

Identity theft is the fraudulent acquisition and use of a person's private identifying information, usually for financial gain. It is the crime of obtaining the personal or financial information of another person, such as a Social Security or credit card number, for the purpose of assuming that person's name or identity in order to obtain money or credit or to make transactions or purchases. It is rampant especially with the success of **hackers**. The latter are people who secretly get access to computer systems in order to get information, like numbers for credit cards and bank accounts, or to cause damage.

Besides the potential financial loss of identity theft, it can also wreak havoc on one's **credit report**. This is a detailed account of an individual's credit history prepared by a credit bureau and used by a lender to determine a loan applicant's creditworthiness. A consumer who is worried about an identify thief who may open a fraudulent account in the consumer's name may obtain a **credit freeze** (or **credit report freeze**) on his/her credit report. A credit freeze prevents a credit bureau from releasing your credit report to merchants and financial institutions without your consent. You may put a credit freeze in place by contacting one of the credit reporting agencies and requesting that the freeze be put in place, usually for free. You must request the freeze be removed before applying for any new credit. Seventeen percent of the population have been victims of identity theft.

identity theft
The fraudulent acquisition and use of a person's private identifying information, usually for financial gain.

credit report
Information compiled by a credit bureau from merchants, utility companies, banks, court records, and creditors about your payment history.

credit freeze (or **credit report freeze**)
It prevents a credit reporting company from releasing your credit report to merchants and financial institutions without your consent.

YOUR GRANDPARENTS SAY

"Debt Stops Your Financial Progress"

"When young adults take on debt early in life they often neglect to save or invest, and this can compromise one's goal of take actions to become financially successful."

CONCEPT CHECK 6.1

1. Distinguish between the APR (annual percentage rate) and the finance charge on a debt.
2. Which five advantages of credit seem appropriate to you?
3. Which five disadvantages of credit seem appropriate to you?
4. What is identity theft?

Learning Objective 2

Establish your own debt limit.

6.2 THREE WAYS TO SET YOUR OWN DEBT LIMIT

Keep in mind that the only way creditors and lenders make money is to loan it out. They seemingly will give you a great interest rate, a high credit limit, very small payments, really easy repayment schedule, no interest charges for so many months, other special benefits "available for today," and you can take the goods home now but *only* if you borrow or finance with them. And you can do all this even if you are almost broke! If your credit score is a bit low, you will have to pay a little higher interest rate but that's okay. You can handle it. You want to buy and the lender really wants to give you the money. Lenders are saying, "Please borrow!"

Lenders only care about your ability to make debt repayments. They do not want to be bothered about whether or not you are achieving your financial goals. They only profit when you borrow, not when you do not. They want to loan you money because borrowing is what they sell. So you must set your own debt limit and ignore what the creditors and lenders say about whether you can handle the debt.

debt limit

Overall maximum you believe you should owe based on your ability to meet repayment obligations.

A **debt limit** is the overall maximum you believe you should owe based on your ability to meet the repayment obligations. Table 6-1 shows recommended debt limits. It shows some monthly debt-payment limits expressed as a percentage of disposable personal income. You do not want to go over 15 percent as taking on additional debt would be unwise. It would be smart to consider the length of time that high debt payments might last. You could get yourself into financial trouble for many years.

There are three recommended methods for you to determine your own debt limit.

Table 6-1 Debt-Payment Limits as a Percentage of Disposable Personal Income*

Percent	Current Debt Situation	Borrower's Feelings	Take on Additional Debt?
0	No debt at all	Zero stress about personal finances	Taking on some consumer debt is fine
10 or less	Little debt	Borrower feels no stress from debt repayment obligations	More debt could be undertaken cautiously
11 to 14	Safe debt limit but fully extended financially	Borrower is moderately stressed about pressure from debt repayment obligations	Should not acquire more debt, but have reserve capacity for emergencies
15 to 18	Precariously overindebted	Borrower feels seriously stressed about debts and hopes no emergency event arises	Absolutely should not take on more debt and should consider contacting a nonprofit credit counseling agency
19 to 28	Seriously overindebted	Borrower feels overwhelming stress and is desperate about debts	Contact a nonprofit credit counseling company
29+	Excessively overindebted	Borrower feels hopeless and knows his/her debts are so large that financial failure will happen soon	Contact a bankruptcy attorney

*Excluding home mortgage loan repayments and convenience credit card purchases to be repaid in full when the monthly bill arrives.

6.2a   Method 1: Continuous-Debt Method

A useful approach for determining your debt limit is the **continuous-debt method**. If you are unable to get completely out of debt every four years (except for a mortgage loan), you probably lean on debt too heavily. Using debt for more than four years is not short-term consumer debt. You probably are developing a credit lifestyle in which you will never eliminate debt and will continuously pay out substantial amounts for finance charges.

6.2b   Method 2: Debt Payments-to-Disposable Income Method

The **debt payments-to-disposable income method** uses the debt-payments-to-disposable income ratio introduced in Chapter 3 on page 87. Recall that this ratio excludes the first mortgage loan on a home and credit card charges that are paid in full each month. **Disposable income** is the amount of your income remaining after taxes and withholding for such purposes as insurance and flexible benefits programs. Note that the debt payments-to-disposable income method focuses on the amount of monthly debt repayment—not one's total debt.

6.2c   Method 3: Debt-to-Income Method

The **debt-to-income method** also was introduced in Chapter 3 on page 87. Using the debt-to-income method your monthly debt repayments (including your prospective mortgage and any other loan or alimony payments you must make) are divided by your gross monthly income (your income before taxes) and multiplied by 100. A ratio of 36 percent or less is desirable.

Try out examining the impact of credit on your spending plan by looking at the "Run the Numbers" box on the next page. Look at the impact of credit on your spending plan. After deductions for taxes and the like, disposable personal income amounts to $3,656 per month and budgeted expenses consume the entire $3,656. Life with no debt is good as this person has enough money for everything including saving for retirement. Think carefully. Where would you make reductions in the spending plan to pay for increasing levels of debt?

6.2d   Keep Student Loan Debt Under Control

To succeed in keeping your student loan debt under control in the first place, you should not borrow at all to pay for college or borrow as little as possible. To begin your schooling, consider a community college or other less expensive institution. Also, do not borrow to pay for your living expenses. This includes meals at restaurants, clothing, vehicle payments, vacations, alcohol, drugs, and monthly bills, such as mobile phones. Instead work and save, perhaps move in with your parents or another relative. Then work part-time during college to lower the amount you borrow.

Seven out of 10 students do borrow for college and their average debt is $38,000. Forty-three million people have repayment terms for education debt that typically extend to 10 years, and one in six are at least nine months behind on payments. Because of student loan debt, 1 in 4 borrowers put off marriage and delay starting a family.

Upon graduation avoid fees and extra interest costs, keep your payments affordable, and repay on time. Follow these suggestions to keep student debt under control.

1.   **Know Your Loans.** Keep track of the lender, balance, and repayment status for each of your student loans to determine your options for loan repayment and forgiveness.
2.   **Limit Student Debt.** Do not borrow more than 50 percent of your first-year salary, 100 percent at the most. Rather than borrow, get a part-time job to cover living expenses. Choose a school that costs less than the big-name college or university.

DID YOU KNOW ?

Are You Worried About Your Debts?

If you are worried about your debts, then you should be. Your own gut feeling is often the best indicator of carrying too much debt.

continuous-debt method
If you are unable to get completely out of debt every four years (except for a mortgage loan), you probably lean on debt too heavily.

DO IT IN CLASS

debt-to-income method
Your monthly debt repayments (including your prospective mortgage, and any other loan or alimony payments you must make) are divided by your gross monthly income and multiplied by 100.

debt payments-to-disposable income method
Percentage of disposable personal income available for regular debt repayments aside from set obligations.

disposable income
Amount of income remaining after taxes and withholding for such purposes as insurance and union dues.

RUN THE NUMBERS

Make Spending Reductions to Pay for Increasing Credit Usage

Where would you make reductions in the spending plan to pay for increasing levels of debt, such as 10 and

15 percent perhaps for a vehicle lease and/or credit card repayments?

DO IT IN CLASS

Gross Income	$54,000	Your Spending Reductions of 10%	Your Spending Reductions of 15%
Deductions for federal income taxes	$ 6,030	$ 6,030	$ 6,030
Deductions for Social Security/Medicare taxes	$ 4,100	$ 4,100	$ 4,100
Annual disposable personal income	$43,870	$43,870	$43,870
Monthly disposable income	$ 3,656	$ 3,656	$ 3,656
Amount as a Percent of Gross Income	**No Debt**	**10% Debt**	**15% Debt**
Monthly spending plan categories/amounts:			
Monthly debt repayment	**$-0-**	**$366**	**$548**
Rent	1200		
401(k) saving/investing at work	210		
Money market savings account	60		
Student loans	-0-		
Health premiums and out-of-pocket costs	131		
Food at home	250		
Restaurant meals	150		
Utilities (tele; elec; heat; water; Internet)	275		
Insurance (automobile, renter's, and life)	160		
Transportation (gas, repairs, maint.)	250		
Charitable contributions	110		
Entertainment	150		
Clothing	50		
Vacations and long weekends	170		
Medical/dental expenses	60		
Subscriptions	40		
Cable TV	120		
Personal care	30		
Gifts and holidays	110		
Health club	60		
Miscellaneous	70		
Total	$ 3,656	$ 3,656	$ 3,656

3. **Open Every Piece of Lender Mail.** Open and read every piece of mail, paper and electronic, you receive about your student loans.
4. **Keep Lender(s) Up-To-Date on Your Address.** Whenever you move or change your phone number or e-mail address, tell your lender right away. Otherwise you might miss the next payment.

5. **Prepay the Loan If You Can.** If you can afford to pay more than your required monthly payment toward the "loan balance," you can lower the amount of interest you have to pay over the life of the loan.

6. **Pay Off the Most Expensive Loan First.** If you're considering paying off one of your loans ahead of schedule, experts say to start with the one that has the highest interest rate. Others say to first pay off the one with the smallest balance because you will do so more quickly, providing the gratification and momentum to pay off all your debts.

7. **Pick the Right Repayment Option.** When your federal loans come due, your loan payments will automatically be based on a standard 10-year repayment plan. If there are other options, you can change plans down the line if you want or need to.

8. **Know Your Student Loan Grace Period.** A student loan grace period is the period of time a lender gives you to make your repayments without having to pay interest or late fees.

9. **Forgiveness May Be Available.** For those employed in government, nonprofit, and other public service jobs relief may be possible. The lender may offer some type of forbearance, often for a fee, or you may be able to make interest-only payments for some period of time. You also may get deferments, forbearance, and/or an income-based repayment schedule.

10. **Do Not Extend the Loan(s).** Extending your repayment period beyond 10 years can lower your monthly payments, but you'll end up paying more interest.

11. **To Consolidate or Not.** A **consolidation loan** is the combining of several unsecured debts into a single, new loan that is more favorable. It may result in a lower interest rate or a lower monthly payment, or both.

BIAS TOWARD—OVERCONFIDENCE

People tend to being overconfident in credit matters. For example, some people take on large student loan debt and then want to purchase an expensive new vehicle. What to do? Calculate your current debt ratios before taking on any new debt and then calculate what they will be with the new debt. If appropriate, either adjust the borrowed amount down or do not borrow at all.

consolidation loan
The combining of several unsecured debts into a single, new loan that is more favorable, and it may result in a lower interest rate, lower monthly payment or both.

CONCEPT CHECK 6.2

1. Distinguish among the continuous debt method, debt-to-income, debt payments-to-disposable income, and debt-to-income methods for setting your debt limit.
2. What are the borrower's feelings when he/she has a limit of debt of 11 to 14 percent of disposable personal income compared to a debt limit of 15 to 18 percent? (Hint: See Table 6-1.)
3. Summarize the effects of increasing debt payments from 10 percent to 15 percent on a budget. (Hint: See the Run the Numbers worksheet on page 186.)
4. What is the best thought on the list of keeping student loan debt under control?

6.3 OBTAINING CREDIT AND BUILDING A GOOD CREDIT REPUTATION

Credit is widely and readily available to most of us today. It is not unusual for a customer to walk into a retail store, such as Target or Home Depot, and be offered a credit card that can be used immediately. Your success in obtaining credit at a low interest rate depends on an understanding of the credit application, credit report, and your credit reputation.

6.3a The Credit Application and Credit Report

A **credit application** is a request for an extension of credit, either orally or in written form. It demands information that sheds light on your ability and willingness to repay debts, such as your income, assets, and debts. The lender will investigate your credit

credit application
A form and/or an interview that requests information that sheds light on your ability and willingness to repay debts, such as your income, assets, and debts.

NUMBERS ON

Average Debt

Data from a variety of sources suggest the following:

- Seventy percent of households owe consumer debt.

- Vehicle loans/leases: Average debt is $32,000; half of new vehicles are financed for longer than 6 years; half of all vehicle loans are to subprime borrowers.

- Medical debt: Average out of pocket is $3,900; half have trouble paying medical bills.

- Mortgage debt: Average debt is $150,000.

- Student loans: Average debt is $38,000.

- Credit cards: Average debt is $17,000; half of cardholders pay off the bill in full every month and half make monthly payments.

- Delinquencies: Auto loans, 3.5%; student loans, 11.1%; credit cards, 4.8%.

---

credit bureau

Firm that collects and keeps records of many borrowers' credit histories.

prescreened

Refers to a credit card offer that a bank aims at certain consumers based on their borrowing histories, and card approval is likely although not necessarily for the interest rate and credit line outlined in the offer.

invitation-to-apply

Refers to a credit card offer sent without any prior screening, thus one must fill out the application and see if it is approved.

preapproved

Refers to a credit offer based on a pre-qualification of the individual's credit from a credit bureau report, and upon acceptance the issuer obtains more detailed credit information and sets an interest rate.

credit history

Continuing record of a person's credit usage and repayment of debts.

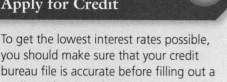

COMMON SENSE
What to Do Before You Apply for Credit

To get the lowest interest rates possible, you should make sure that your credit bureau file is accurate before filling out a credit application. If possible, you should do this at least three months in advance to allow time for you to correct any errors or omissions in your file.

---

history, usually instantly via the Internet and the lender decides whether to extend credit and on what terms.

Applications for consumer loans are usually more involved than for credit cards because institutions want to extend credit to the best risks. Thus, they ask for more details than those applying for credit cards, and they may choose to interview the applicants.

To conduct its credit investigation, the lender obtains a credit report from a **credit bureau** that keeps records of the credit histories of millions of borrowers. Credit bureaus compile information from merchants, utility companies, banks, court records, and creditors. There are three major national credit-reporting bureaus: Experian, TransUnion, and Equifax.

6.3b Prescreened, Invitation-to-Apply, or Preapproved

When you see the term **prescreened** on a credit offer, it is referring to a credit card offer that a bank aims at certain consumers based on their borrowing histories. The bank has done a background check that involved looking at any available personal information, such as your credit score and borrowing history. Since the offers are so well-tailored to the market, eventual card approval is almost guaranteed. However, the offers will not necessarily be for the interest rate and credit line advertised. The average interest rate in the USA on credit cards is 15 percent.

An alternative to prescreened is an **invitation-to-apply**, which is a credit card offer sent without any prior screening. You must fill out the application and wait to see if it is approved.

When a card is **preapproved** it is a conditional offer of credit from a credit card issuer based on a pre-qualification of the individual's credit from a credit bureau report. Upon acceptance, the issuer obtains more detailed credit report information plus data on educational and professional background, telephone service history and ownership of other assets. Then it assigns an APR based on the latest information.

6.3c The Lender Decides on the Application

One-third of people who apply for credit are denied. Half of the unsuccessful applicants have no established **credit history** (a continuing record of a person's credit usage and repayment of debts) or their credit history contains negative information. The other half have low credit scores or are attempting to take on too much debt.

The rejection or approval of credit is based on the lender's judgment of the willingness and ability of the applicant to repay the debt. If the application is accepted, a contract is created that outlines the rules governing the account including the interest rate. For credit cards, this contract is called a **credit agreement**. For loans, the contract is called a **promissory note**.

6.3d Lenders Decides on the Interest Rate

Credit scoring allows lenders to categorize credit users according to the perceived level of risk. Using the concept of **tiered pricing**, lenders may offer the lowest interest rates to applicants with the highest credit scores while charging steeper rates to more risky applicants.

The difference in rates is not much except for those with scores below 620. These people are **subprime borrowers** as their poor credit histories will require that they pay lenders more than others for credit. People with such low credit scores can usually find a lender that will say "yes." However, the interest rates will be much higher than normal. The elevated interest rate reflects the lender's heightened concern that the borrower might not repay his/her financial obligations. The lender (not a credit bureau) always makes the decision about whether to grant credit.

6.3e How to Build Your Foundation for a Good Credit History

Some people who are new to the world of credit wonder whether they will ever get credit when they need it. They will if they establish a good credit history. The following can help you build one.

1. **Establish both a checking account and a savings account.** Lenders see people who can handle these accounts as being more likely to manage credit usage properly.
2. **Have your smartphone and utilities billed in your name.** The fact that you can maintain a good payment pattern on your telephone and utility bills indicates that you can manage your money wisely and will do the same with your credit repayments.
3. **Request, acquire, and use credit cards from retail sellers and businesses.** These cards are relatively easy to obtain. Use the credit sparingly, and pay the entire balance in full and on time each month.
4. **Apply for a bank credit card.** Your own bank is the best place to start your search for a credit card. If not successful there, you usually can find some bank that will issue you a card (search at www.bankrate.com). The credit limit may be low (perhaps $1,000) and the APR high (perhaps 24 percent), but at least the opportunity exists to establish a credit history. Later you can request an increase in the credit limit and a lower APR.
5. **Stay current on your student loans.** Making payments on time and paying off student loans quickly will show prospective lenders that you are a responsible borrower.

6.3f Improving Your Credit History Improves Your Credit Score

A **credit score** is an indication of a person's credit worthiness or how likely the individual will be able to repay any credit extended in a timely manner. The two most widely known credit scoring systems are the **FICO score** developed by Fair Isaac Corporation (www.fico.com) and Vantage (www.vantagescore.com). FICO scores are used by 90-plus percent of companies when making lending decisions because lenders want to know the risk they are taking when lending money.

One's FICO score affects how much money a lender will lend and at what interest rate. FICO scores range from 300 to 850, and higher is better. A high FICO score can often help one qualify for better terms from lenders. FICO does not include insurance,

credit agreement
Contract that stipulates repayment terms for credit cards.

promissory note (note)
Contract that stipulates repayment terms for a loan.

tiered pricing
Lenders that offer the lowest interest rates to applicants with the highest credit scores while charging steeper rates to more risky applicants.

subprime borrowers
People with poor credit histories who are required to pay lenders more than others for credit.

credit score
An indication of a person's credit worthiness or how likely the individual will be able to repay any credit extended in a timely manner.

FICO score
The most widely known credit scoring system developed by Fair Isaac Corporation and used by 90-plus percent of companies when making lending decisions.

ADVICE FROM A SEASONED PRO

Freedom from Discrimination Is the Law

The Equal Credit Opportuntiy Act (ECOA) prohibits credit discrimination on the basis of race, color, religion, national origin, sex, marital status, age, or because one receives public assistance. Creditors may ask for most of this information in certain situations, but they may not use it when deciding whether to give you credit or when setting the terms of the credit extended.

Creditors may not ask if you're widowed or divorced. They may use only the terms: married, unmarried, or separated. Creditors may not ask about your plans for having or raising children, but they can ask questions about expenses related to your dependents. Creditors may not ask if you

receive alimony, child support, or separate maintenance payments, unless you are relying on those payments for income as a basis for obtaining credit.

The ECOA requires lenders to notify an applicant within 30 days about the lender's acceptance or rejection of a credit application. The ECOA also requires the creditor to provide the applicant with a written statement, if requested, detailing the reasons for refusing credit. Rejecting a credit application due to poor credit history is legal. Always request that a lender who turns you down for credit provide you with the credit score it used in the decision and the name of the credit bureau that provided the score.

Linda Meltzer
Queensborough Community College, Bayside, New York

Internet, or cellphone bills in their scoring. FICO recently decided to no longer include in their calculations any unpaid medical bills in collection and other debts in collection that have been settled.

Under the Fair and Accurate Credit Transactions Act, credit bureaus must provide consumers with their credit scores upon request. A fee of no more than $12 is charged for a credit score report. However, if you are **denied credit** altogether or at less than favorable rates you must be told why, and if the reason was your credit score you may request a credit score report at no charge.

denied credit

People who are turned down in their request for credit, and the law requires they must be told why, and if the reason was one's credit score he/she may request a credit score report at no charge.

6.3g   A Free Credit Report is Yours Every Four Months

To obtain a free credit report, simply contact www.annualcreditreport.com. This is the only website that links you directly to the mechanism for obtaining a free report. The law allows you to check your credit for free every four months. How? By staggering your requests once every 4 months to one of the three credit bureaus.

6.3h   FICO Credit Scores

Credit scores are produced via complex statistical models that correlate certain borrower characteristics with the likelihood of repayment. The exact methodologies employed in the models are secret. There are 19 FICO score versions used in mortgage, auto, and credit card lending.

The factors used in the FICO score are shared openly by FICO on their website:

1. *Payment history.* Are you late with your payments? How late? How often? On how many of your accounts? The largest contributor to you getting a high FICO score is to consistently pay your bills and debts on time.

2. *Amounts owed.* What is the balance on each of your credit obligations? (Even if you pay in full each month, there might be a balance on a given date.) How do the amounts owed vary on various types of accounts, such as credit cards versus loans? How many accounts have balances? Are you maxed out or nearly so on your cards, regardless of the dollar amount of your balances? (Credit scores are negatively affected if you have a balance on any card in excess of **30** percent of the credit limit on that card.) On loans, how much of the original loan is still owed?

3. *Length of credit history.* How long have you had each account? How long has it been since you used the accounts?

4. *Taking on more debt.* How many new accounts do you have? How long has it been since you opened a new account? How many recent inquiries have been made by lenders to which you have made application? If you had a period of poor credit usage in the past, for how long have you been in good standing?

5. *Types of credit used.* Do you have a good mix of credit usage, with reliance on multiple types depending on the purpose of the credit (for example, not using a credit card to buy a boat)? How many accounts in total do you have?

The average FICO score is 673. About one-fourth of consumers have a FICO score below 620, making it nearly impossible for them to get a loan from all but the most expensive types of lenders. They are often shut out of most financing because of a negative credit event, such as foreclosure or bankruptcy.

To improve your FICO score consider your **credit utilization ratio**, which is the amount of credit you use as compared to your credit card limits. Keep it below 30 percent on both individual cards as well as all your cards. Carrying a high balance on your cards at any point during the month can damage your credit score. If, for example, you are maxed out on two cards and have low balances on others, you might shift some of the large balances to other cards. Credit utilization ("amounts owed" in Figure 6-1) contributes almost one-third of the weight of your credit score.

Figure 6-1 indicates the relative importance of each of the five factors in the development of FICO scores. Additional tips for improving your FICO credit score are on their website (www.myfico.com/CreditEducation/ImproveYourScore.aspx). FICO scores now are included for free on the credit statements of several issuers. And you can set up "alerts" on your credit cards to let you know when you are nearing your cap.

6.3i   Credit Monitoring is a Waste of Money

Signing up for a **credit-monitoring service** is a waste of money. These services allow one to access his/her credit report as often as daily and obtain a personal FICO credit score.

These types of plans operate on the concept of a **negative option**. This is a business practice in which a customer agrees to have goods or services to be provided automatically, and the customer must either pay for the service or specifically decline it in advance of billing. Thus you will be automatically signed up for a plan costing as much as $100 or more per year every year and your membership will renew automatically unless you cancel. FICO sells this plan, too. This is a waste of money, especially when you can obtain the information in your files for free.

6.3j   How to Fix Errors in Your Credit Report

Because the credit bureaus all gather information from essentially the same sources, you can have some confidence that what appears on one file will be present in the others. If you find an error, contact all three to make the correction.

When you obtain your report, you should thoroughly inspect it for accuracy. If you find an error, the **Fair Credit Reporting Act (FCRA)** allows you to challenge the error as the law requires that reports contain accurate information.

If you find an error or omission in a credit report, you should take steps to correct the information. Notify the credit bureau and the original lender of the error and ask the original lender for confirmation of the debt. You should ask the bureau to confirm the item or delete it.

The credit bureau and lender must reinvestigate the information within 45 days or it must delete the information from your credit file. If the information was erroneous, it must be corrected and a corrected report must be sent to any creditor who sought the report over the past 6 months.

If the credit bureau refuses to make a correction (perhaps because the information was "technically correct"), you may wish to provide your version of the disputed information (in 100 words or less) by adding a **consumer statement** to your credit bureau file. This statement will be included with any future credit reports by that bureau.

Figure 6-1

The Relative Importance of Five Factors in a FICO Score

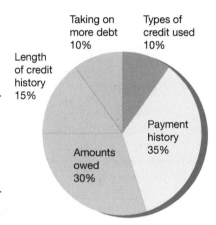

credit utilization ratio
The percentage of a consumer's available credit that he or she has used, which is a key component of one's credit score; a high credit utilization ratio can lower your score.

credit-monitoring service
These companies allow one to access his/her credit report as often as daily and obtain a personal FICO credit score.

negative option
This is a business practice in which a customer agrees to have goods or services to be provided automatically, and the customer must either pay for the service or specifically decline it in advance of billing.

Fair Credit Reporting Act (FCRA)
One part of the law requires that credit reports contain only accurate relevant information and allows consumers to challenge errors or omissions of information in their reports.

consumer statement
Your version of disputed information in your credit report when the credit bureau refuses to remove the disputed item.

THERE IS AN APP FOR THAT!

Some of the best apps are:

- BillGuard
- Credit Karma
- Credit Sesame
- Credit.com
- MintBills.com
- MyFICO

6.3k   Time Limits on Adverse Information in Credit Reports

The FCRA requires deletion of obsolete adverse information. Most of the information in your credit report must be removed after 7 years. However, bankruptcy information is retained for 10 years.

6.3l   Another Person's Credit History

Anyone contemplating marriage or a similar serious commitment must find out the other person's credit history and financial habits. Obtain a copy of the other person's FICO credit report. Look for, ask about, and be aware of job loss, medical expenses, poor/excessive use of credit, divorce/separation, and unexpected expenses due to theft or casualty, home foreclosure, and overspending. It may seem unromantic but it is important because most people do not change much over time.

If one is fully aware of the other person's financial drawbacks and still believes they ultimately can be overcome, good. But the person with a good credit history should keep his or her financial life separate by not adding his/her name to the other's credit accounts as it will reduce one's FICO score. This conversation also could result in keeping your assets separate and maintaining individual checking accounts. It might mean agreeing to a **prenuptial agreement**, which sets forth what will happen to you and your spouse's assets and income in the unfortunate event of separation, divorce, or death.

6.3m   Effects of Divorce on Your Credit

The breakup of a marriage affects the creditworthiness of both partners. Here are suggestions for those who divorce.

Pay careful attention to credit accounts held jointly, including mortgages, second mortgages, and credit cards. The behavior of one divorcing spouse will continue to affect the other individual as long as the accounts are held in both names. One party could make credit card charges, for example, and refuse to pay the debt, leaving the financial burden on the other party. Ask creditors to close joint accounts. Then, if possible, reopen them as individual accounts. Always insist on written confirmation of the effective date of any account closures.

When debts were accumulated in both names, a divorce decree has no legal effect on who technically owes the debt. Creditors can legally collect from *either* of the parties when the accounts were held jointly. If the person absolved of responsibility for the debt under the divorce decree is forced by a creditor to pay off the account, he or she must then go to court to seek enforcement of the divorce decree and collect reimbursement from the former spouse.

Both before and after a divorce, get copies of your credit report from all three credit bureaus. Check them for accuracy and challenge any problem areas, such as accounts, that continue to be shown in both names.

overindebted

When one's excessive personal debts make repayment difficult and cause financial distress.

CONCEPT CHECK 6.3

1. Distinguish among the credit terms: prescreened, invitation-to-apply, and preapproved.
2. What is a credit history, and what role do credit bureaus play in the development of it?
3. Name three steps to help establish a good credit history.
4. List two things to improve someone's lousy FICO credit score.
5. Summarize how to fix errors in your credit report, and explain why some people add a consumer statement to their report.

Learning Objective 4

Identify signs of overindebtedness, and describe the options that are available for debt relief.

6.4   DEALING WITH OVERINDEBTEDNESS

People become **overindebted** when their excessive debts make repayment difficult and cause them financial distress. One should know the signs overindebtedness and steps to take to get out from under excessive debt.

6.4a 11 Signs of Overindebtedness

1. **Not knowing how much you owe.** Have you lost track of how much you owe? Do you avoid reality by not adding up the total? Are you afraid to add up how much debt you have?

2. **Running out of money.** Are you using credit cards on occasions when you previously used cash? Are you borrowing to pay insurance premiums, taxes, or other predictable bills? Are you borrowing to pay for regular expenses such as food and gasoline? Do you try to borrow from friends and relatives to carry you through the month?

3. **Paying only the minimum amount due.** Do you normally pay the minimum payment—or just a little more than the minimum—on your credit cards instead of making large payments to more quickly reduce the balance owed?

4. **Exceeding debt limits and credit limits.** Are you spending 15 percent or more of your take-home pay on nonmortgage credit repayments? Do you sometimes reach or go over the maximum approved credit limits on your credit cards?

5. **Requesting new credit cards and increases in credit limits.** Have you applied for additional credit cards to increase your borrowing capacity? Have you asked for increases in credit limits on your current credit cards?

6. **Using cash advances to pay other credit cards.** Have you obtained a cash advance on one credit card to make a payment due on another card? Have you used a cash advance to pay other bills?

7. **Paying late or skipping credit payments.** Are you late once or more a year in paying your mortgage, rent, vehicle loan or lease, or utility bills? Do you sometimes pay late charges? Are you juggling bills to pay the telephone, utilities, rent, or mortgage? Are creditors sending overdue notices?

8. **Refinancing.** **Refinancing** or taking add-on loans occurs when you refinance or rewrite a loan for an even larger amount before it has been completely repaid. Suppose that a loan of $1,000 has been repaid down to $400. You decide to refinance the debt balance of $400 by borrowing $2,000 and using the additional $1,600 ($2,000 − $400) for other purposes.

9. **Using debt-consolidation loans.** Are you borrowing, perhaps from a new source, to pay off old debts? Such action may temporarily reduce pressure on your budget, but it also indicates that you are overly indebted. A **debt-consolidation loan** is a loan taken out to pay off several smaller debts.

10. **Experiencing garnishment.** **Garnishment** is a court order directing that money or property of a third party (usually wages paid by an employer) be seized to satisfy a debt owed by a debtor to a plaintiff creditor. Wages and salary income, including that of military personnel, can be garnished. The law prohibits more than two garnishments of one person's paycheck and the total amount garnished cannot represent more than 25 percent of a person's disposable income for the pay period or more than the amount by which the weekly disposable income exceeds 30 times the federal minimum wage (whichever is less). The law also prohibits garnishment from being used as grounds for employment discharge.

11. **Experiencing repossession or foreclosure.** **Repossession** is when a financial institution takes back an object that was either used as collateral or rented or leased for nonpayment of a loan. **Foreclosure** is similar. However the law is always involved in repossession since it is the legal process of taking possession of a mortgaged property as a result of the mortgagor's failure to keep up mortgage payments. A **deficiency balance** occurs when the sum of money raised by the sale of the repossessed or foreclosed collateral fails to cover the amount owed on the debt plus any repossession expenses (collection, attorney, and court costs) paid by the creditor.

NEVER EVER

Reaffirm a Debt

Credit collection agencies often contact people years later and demand repayment of an old debt that was written off by a lender. If you repay a single dollar of the old debt, it means you reaffirm the whole debt and you owe everything all over again. Paying a dollar, or any amount, means you have agreed that you again are personally liable for the original debt plus collection expenses. This also occurs if you say "I promise to repay the bill." That means telling the agency that you reaffirm the debt and you owe it again.

refinancing
This occurs when you refinance or rewrite a loan for an even larger amount before it has been completely repaid.

debt-consolidation loan
A loan taken out to pay off several smaller debts.

garnishment
A court order directing that money or property of a third party (usually wages paid by an employer) be seized to satisfy a debt owed by a debtor to a plaintiff creditor.

repossession
When a financial institution takes back an object that was either used as collateral or rented or leased for nonpayment of a loan

foreclosure
The legal process of taking possession of a mortgaged property as a result of the mortgagor's failure to keep up mortgage payments.

deficiency balance
This occurs when the sum of money raised by the sale of the repossessed or foreclosed collateral fails to cover the amount owed on the debt plus any repossession expenses (collection, attorney, and court costs) paid by the creditor.

Fair Debt Collection Practices Act (FDCPA)

Prohibits third-party debt collection agencies from using abusive, deceptive, or unfair practices to collect past-due debts.

6.4b Federal Law Regulates Debt Collection Practices

The **Fair Debt Collection Practices Act (FDCPA)** prohibits debt collectors from using abusive, unfair, or deceptive practices to collect from debtors in the legitimate effort to collect past-due debts. More than one-third of Americans have been reported to collection agencies for unpaid bills.

Under the FDCPA, a **debt collector** is someone who regularly collects debts owed to others. This includes collection agencies, lawyers who collect debts on a regular basis, and companies that buy delinquent debts and then try to collect them.

In some cases, they assist the original lender and charge about 40 percent of what they collect for a fee. In other cases, they take over (purchase) the debt and become a new creditor, and they keep 100 percent of what they collect.

When a debtor offers to make payment for several debts, the FDCPA requires that the amount paid must be applied to whichever debts the debtor desires. Banks, dentists, lawyers, and others who conduct their own collections (second-party collectors) are exempt from the provisions of the FDCPA. Nevertheless, many states have enacted similar laws that govern second-party collectors.

Collection agencies are prohibited from telephoning the debtor at unusual hours, making numerous repeated telephone calls, not applying payments to amounts under dispute, using deceptive practices (such as falsely claiming that their representatives are attorneys or government officials), making threats, and using abusive language. They also are prohibited from contacting a debtor's employer.

If a collection effort is not successful, the creditor may take the debtor to court to seek a legal judgment against the debtor. This judgment may be collected by repossessing some of the debtor's property and/or garnishing wages.

6.4c Ways to Get Out from Under Excessive Debt

Even the most well-meaning credit user can become overextended. The basics of debt reduction are simple: Cut down on your spending and put the extra money toward your debt payments. Suggestions follow:

1. **Determine your account balances and the payments required.** Find out exactly what it would take to pay off all your balances today. This amount is not the same as the total of your remaining payments and this likely includes additional fees, penalties and late charges if you have been late in any of your payments.
2. **If you have a partner, stop fighting with each other.** Debt is a "we" problem not an "I" problem no matter who ran up the bills. Plus married people are always jointly responsible for credit card debt.
3. **Reduce your spending budget by 10 percent.** Do not think you cannot cut your budget this much because you can. Drop cable. Sell a vehicle. Get a cheap non-smart phone at Walmart. Move to a cheaper home. Stop buying stuff.
4. **Take on no new credit.** Return your credit cards to the issuer or lock them up so that you cannot use them. Disciplined action to reduce debt should show results in only a few months. If progress does not occur, seek professional help.
5. **Focus your budget on debt reduction.** Calculate the percentage of your budget necessary to make the payments on your debts, and then add 5 percent. Use this extra money to help pay your creditors by applying the extra money to the debt with the highest APR. Behavioral research shows that people who pay off their smallest credit card balances first (because it feels good!) are more likely to succeed in overall debt reduction.
6. **Contact your creditors.** Try to work out a new repayment plan with your creditors. Many lenders, including those that finance vehicles, may let you skip a payment. They want to see you solve your financial problems so you can avoid bankruptcy.
7. **Increase your income.** Consider whether there is any way to increase your take-home pay. If you get a big tax refund every year, that means you are having

DO IT IN CLASS

TURN BAD HABITS INTO GOOD ONES

Do You Do This?	Do This Instead!
Assume your credit bureau files are correct and up to date	Check your file for free with one of the three credit bureaus alternating every four months
Borrow from your own bank when you need new credit	Shop at various lenders for the best credit terms and lowest APR
Assume you are doing fine if you can make your monthly debt payments	At least once a year, calculate your debt limit using appropriate ratios
Ignore the list of transactions in your credit card account statements	Inspect your statements for errors and signs of identity theft
After paying off a debt, put the old amount back into your regular spending	Put the money you were using to pay off a loan toward your savings goals

too much withheld from your paycheck. If that's the case, you can reduce your withholding by changing your W-4 form at work. Perhaps consider part-time employment.

8. **Debt-consolidation loan.** Some may get a **debt-consolidation loan** through which the debtor exchanges several smaller debts, especially on high-interest credit cards, with varying due dates and interest rates for a single large loan with a lower interest rate. Avoid the temptation to use this strategy simply to lower your total monthly payments.

9. **Avoid debt settlement companies** Debt settlement is the process of offering a large, one-time payment toward an existing credit balance in return for the forgiveness of the remaining larger debt. For example, someone who owes $10,000 on a single credit card may approach their credit card company and offer a one-time payment of $6,000. In return for this one-time payment, the credit card company agrees to forgive or erase the remaining $4,000. You are supposed to stop making payments to your creditors and instead every month set aside a specific amount of money into an escrow-like account so it will accumulate enough savings to pay off any settlement that is reached. Of course, the creditor reports late payments to the credit bureaus. And the IRS may assess you for income taxes due on the value of the debts cancelled.

10. **Free budget and credit advice.** You may be able to obtain free budget and credit advice from your employer, church, bank, or credit union.

11. **Consumer credit counseling agency**. The objective of most onprofit **consumer credit counseling agencies** is to help the creditor avoid bankruptcy, to provide basic education on financial management, and to negotiate with unsecured creditors on behalf of the borrower to reduce interest rates and late fees. Most agencies utilize a **debt management plan (DMP)**, which is an arrangement whereby the consumer provides one monthly payment (usually somewhat smaller than the total of previous credit payments) that is distributed to all creditors. Creditor concessions, such as reduced interest rates, may also allow debtors to repay what they owe more quickly than would otherwise be possible. In effect, the creditor (not the consumer) pays the cost of operating a DMP. Credit counseling services are provided for free or at a nominal cost on a face-to-face basis, online, or via the telephone.

debt-consolidation loan
A loan taken out to pay off several smaller debts.

debt settlement
The process of offering a large, one-time payment toward an existing credit balance in return for the forgiveness of the remaining larger debt.

Consumer credit counseling agencies
The objectives of these nonprofit agencies are to help the creditor avoid bankruptcy, to provide basic education on financial managemen, and to negotiate with unsecured creditors on behalf of the borrower to reduce interest rates and late fees.

NEVER EVER

1. *Fail to regularly check the accuracy of your credit bureau files.*
2. *Let a lender's willingness to grant credit be an indicator that you can afford to repay the debt.*
3. *Pay more than 14 percent of your disposable income toward nonmortgage debt payments.*

6.4d Bankruptcy as a Last Resort

bankruptcy
A constitutionally guaranteed right that permits people (and businesses) to ask a court to find them officially unable to meet their debts.

When debts are so overbearing that life seems really bleak—a situation that may be aggravated by recent unemployment, illness, hospital bills, disability, death in the family, divorce, or small-business failure—many people consider filing a petition in federal court to declare bankruptcy. **Bankruptcy** is a constitutionally guaranteed right that permits people (and businesses) to ask a court to find them officially unable to meet their debts.

A bankruptcy **discharge** releases the debtor from personal liability for certain specified types of debts. In other words, the debtor is no longer legally required to pay any debts that are discharged. Some debts are never excused through bankruptcy. These include education loans that have come due within the previous seven years, fines, alimony, child support, income taxes for the most recent three years, and debts for causing injury while driving under the influence of alcohol or drugs.

Bankruptcy is not a do-it-yourself project. Use a lawyer who specializes in consumer bankruptcies.

What you should not do before declaring bankruptcy is to take money out of your retirement plan at work to "help" pay down your bills when faced with mounting debt. See a bankruptcy attorney who will remind you that bankruptcy law fully protects the assets in your retirement plan. Avoid selling your retirement security in an effort to pay creditors.

Before you can file for bankruptcy, you must complete credit counseling with an agency approved by the United States Bankruptcy Trustee's office. The purpose of this counseling is to give you an idea of whether you really need to file for bankruptcy or whether an informal repayment plan could get you back on your feet financially. You also will have to attend another counseling session to learn more about the fundamentals of personal financial management. Only after you submit proof to the court that you have fulfilled these requirements can your attorney request a bankruptcy discharge wiping out most if not all of your debts.

Bankruptcy Wage Earner Plan, Chapter 13 A **wage earner plan**, subsequently known as Chapter 13, is a bankruptcy protection scheme that allows income earners to satisfy outstanding debts in whole or in part within a specific time frame. It is also called a **regular income plan**.

wage earner plan
Known as Chapter 13 this is a bankruptcy protection scheme that allows income earners to satisfy outstanding debts in whole or in part within a specific time frame.

It is designed for individuals with regular incomes who might be able to pay off some or all of their debts given certain protections of the court. Under this plan, the debtor submits a debt repayment plan to the court that is designed to repay as much of the debt as possible, typically in three to five years.

After the debtor files a petition for bankruptcy, the court issues an **automatic stay**, a court order that temporarily prevents all creditors from recovering claims arising from before the start of the bankruptcy proceeding. This action protects the debtor from collection efforts by creditors, including garnishments. Typically, no assets may be sold by a debtor or repossessed by a lender after a stay is granted.

After the court notifies all creditors of the petition for bankruptcy, a hearing is scheduled. With the help of a **bankruptcy trustee** (an agent of the bankruptcy court), who verifies the accuracy of a bankruptcy petition at a hearing, the proposed repayment plan is reviewed (and modified, if necessary) and finally approved by the court. Then the trustee distributes the assets according to a court-approved plan,

The debtor must then follow a strict budget while repaying the obligations. During this time, the bankrupt person cannot obtain any new credit without the permission of the trustee. If the debtor makes all scheduled payments, he or she is discharged of any remaining amounts due that could not be repaid within the repayment period.

straight bankruptcy
Known as Chapter 7, it provides that a debtor's assets are sold, creditors receive payment, and the debtor is freed from his/her debts.

Bankruptcy Immediate Liquidation Plan, Chapter 7 **Straight bankruptcy**, also called an **immediate liquidations plan**, or **Chapter** 7, provides that a debtor's assets are sold, creditors receive payment, and the debtor is freed from most if not all of his/her debts. This option is permitted by the court when it would be highly unlikely that substantial repayment could ever be made.

Petitioners seeking to file Chapter 7 must pass a **means test** to determine whether an individual debtor's Chapter 7 filing can be presumed to be an abuse of the Bankruptcy laws requiring dismissal or conversion of the case. It is based on the individual's income, amount of debt, and bad faith on the part of the debtor. Those who fail this test because their income is too high must file Chapter 13 instead.

When Chapter 7 is allowed, most of the bankrupt person's assets are given over to the bankruptcy trustee. Any assets that serve as collateral for loans are turned over to the appropriate secured creditors. Most of the remaining assets are sold, and the proceeds of the sales are distributed to the unsecured creditors of the bankrupt person.

If the debtor decides to **reaffirm a debt**, he or she must do so before the bankruptcy discharge is entered. The debtor must sign a written reaffirmation agreement and file it with the court. This is sometimes done with vehicles as the debtor often needs reliable transportation to get to work.

State and federal laws govern what assets the debtor can keep. In general, bankrupt people are allowed to keep a small amount of equity in their homes, an inexpensive vehicle, and limited personal property. Discharged debtors usually emerge with little, if any, debt and a much improved net worth and, of course, a lower credit score.

Bankruptcy should be used as a last resort rather than as a quick fix or cure-all for overuse of credit. Bankruptcy remains on one's credit record for ten years. People who have declared bankruptcy typically face years of trouble when renting housing, obtaining home loans, buying insurance, and obtaining employment. They also cannot use Chapter 7 bankruptcy again for at least six years. Therefore, some creditors will lend to such individuals, but at much higher interest rates than usual.

means test

In bankruptcy a court determines whether an individual debtor's Chapter 7 filing can be presumed to be an abuse of the bankruptcy laws requiring dismissal or conversion of the case.

reaffirm a debt

*If you repay a single dollar of the old debt, and it means you **reaffirm** the debt. Thus you have agreed that you are personally liable for the whole debt again.*

CONCEPT CHECK 6.4

1. Identify four signs of overindebtedness.
2. List the major provisions of the Fair Debt Collection Practices Act.
3. What services are provided by a credit counseling agency, and how might a debt management plan work to provide relief for someone who is having debt problems?
4. Distinguish between Chapter 7 and Chapter 13 bankruptcy, and explain who might be forced to use Chapter 13 rather than Chapter 7.

WHAT DO YOU RECOMMEND *NOW*?

Now that you have read this chapter on building and maintaining good credit, what would you recommend to Julia Grace regarding:

1. How might Julia go about establishing a debt limit?
2. What two or three things can she do help keep her student debt under control?
3. What can Julia do to build a good credit history?
4. Getting a free copy of her credit report?

SUMMARY OF LEARNING OBJECTIVES RECAPPED

LO1   **List some advantages and disadvantages of using credit.**

People borrow for a variety of reasons—for example, to deal with financial emergencies, to have goods immediately, and to obtain discounts in the future. Perhaps the greatest disadvantage of using credit is the ensuing loss of financial flexibility in personal money management. A credit freeze is one technique to try and avoid identify theft.

LO2   **Establish your own debt limit.**

There are three approaches to establish your own debt limit. One is the continuous-debt method. Two is the debt-to-income method. Three is the debt payments-to-disposable income method. There are several techniques to keep your student loan debt under control.

LO3   **Obtain credit and build a good credit reputation.**

Obtaining credit begins with the credit application and your credit report. The lender decides on the application and sets the interest rate. There are ways to build your credit reputation. Improving your credit history improves your credit score. FICO credit scores are important. Errors in your credit report can be fixed.

LO4   **Identify signs of overindebtedness, and describe the options that are available for debt relief.**

Among the signals of being overly indebted are exceeding credit-limit guidelines and running out of money too often. People experiencing serious financial difficulties can obtain professional assistance through nonprofit credit counseling agencies or by contacting an attorney about bankruptcy.

LET'S TALK ABOUT IT

1. **Your Creditworthiness.** What aspects of your financial life make you creditworthy? What aspects might make it difficult for you to obtain credit?

2. **Assessing Your Debt Load.** How might students judge whether they are taking on too high a level of student loan debt?

3. **Managing Student Loan Debt.** Use the information on pages 185, 186 and 187 to discuss how best to deal with student loan debt.

4. **Behind in Repayment.** If you have ever missed a repayment deadline, what was the result? What could you have done differently/better?

5. **Your Privacy.** Are you concerned that the major national credit bureaus may have files containing information about you? What do you think about the process required to correct errors in those files?

6. **Easy Credit.** Is it too easy for college students to get credit cards? Who do you know who has gotten into financial difficulty because of overuse of credit cards, and what happened?

7. **Feelings About Student Loan Bankruptcy.** How do you feel about student loans not being subject to the bankruptcy law? Do you think the law should be changed? Why or why not?

DO THE MATH

1. **Taking Out a Motorcycle Loan.** Kevin Jones, of Elon, North Carolina, is single and recently graduated from law school. He is employed and earns $9,000 per month, an awesome salary for someone only 26 years old. He also has $1,800 withheld for federal income tax, $500 for state income taxes, $700 for Medicare and Social Security taxes, and $230 for health insurance every month. Kevin has outstanding student loans of almost $80,000 on which he pays about $900 per month and a 0% loan on an auto loan payment of $300 on a Ford Fusion Hybrid he purchased new during law school. He is considering taking out a loan to buy a Kawasaki motorcycle.

    DO IT IN CLASS
    page 185

    (a) What is Kevin's debt payments-to-disposable income ratio?

    (b) Based on your answer to (a), how would you advise Kevin about his plan?

2. **Buying a Vacation Home.** Barrie and Inga Adlington, of Birmingham, England, have just finished putting their three daughters through college. As empty-nesters, they are considering purchasing a vacation home in the United States on a lake because prices have dropped in recent years. The house might also serve as a retirement home once they retire in 6 years. The Adlingtons' net worth is $383,000 including their home worth about $265,000 on which they currently owe $43,000 for their first mortgage, with a $778 per month payment. Their outstanding debts in addition to their mortgage include $12,500 on one car loan ($256 monthly payment), $13,700

    DO IT IN CLASS
    Page 185

on a second car loan ($287 monthly payment), and a $25,000 second mortgage on their home taken out to help pay for their daughters' college expenses ($187 monthly payment). Their income is $100,000.

(a) Calculate the Adlingtons' debt-to-income ratio.

(b) Advise them as to the wisdom of borrowing to buy a vacation home at this time.

3. **A Recent Graduate's Debt Status.** Chelsea Menken, of Providence, Rhode Island, recently graduated with a degree in food science and now works for a major consumer foods company earning $70,000 per year with about $58,000 in take-home pay. She rents an apartment for

DO IT IN CLASS
Page 185

$1,100 per month. While in school, she accumulated about $38,000 in student loan debt on which she pays $385 per month. During her last fall semester in school, she had an internship in a city about 100 miles from her campus. She used her credit card for her extra expenses and has a current debt on the account of $8,000. She has been making the minimum payment on the account of about $240 a month. She has assets of $14,000.

(a) Calculate Chelsea's debt payment-to-disposable income ratio.

(b) Calculate Chelsea's debt-to-income ratio.

(c) Comment on Chelsea's debt situation and her use of student loans and credit cards while in college.

FINANCIAL PLANNING CASES

CASE 1

The Johnsons Attempt to Resolve Their Credit and Cash-Flow Problems

Harry and Belinda have a substantial annual joint income—more than $125,000, in fact. Nevertheless, they expect to experience some cash-flow deficits during the months of November and December of the upcoming year (see Tables 3-6 and 3-7 on pages 97–98).

To resolve this difficulty, the couple is considering opening a credit card account and using it exclusively for those expenditures that will cause the deficits they face. They could also open a line of credit that would allow them to borrow money by simply going online and having money placed in their checking account.

(a) What are the advantages and disadvantages of the Johnsons opening these accounts?

(b) What financial calculations should Harry and Belinda undertake to see whether they could afford to borrow more money at this time?

(c) What might Harry and Belinda do before applying for credit to ensure that they will pay the lowest interest rate possible?

(d) Should they use credit to resolve their budget imbalances? Why or why not?

CASE 2

Victor and Maria Advise Their Niece

Victor and Maria have always enjoyed a close relationship with Maria's niece Teresa, who graduated from college with a pharmacy degree. Teresa recently asked Maria for some assistance with her finances now that her education debts are coming due. She owes $29,000 in student loans and has $64,000 in disposable income

annually. Teresa would like to take on additional debt to furnish her apartment and buy a better car.

(a) What advice might Maria give Teresa about managing her student loan debt?

(b) If next year Teresa were to consolidate her education debt into one loan at 6 percent interest, for five years with a monthly payment of $566.

CASE 3

Julia Price Thinks About a Loan to Buy an Inboard Ski/Wakeboard Boat

Julia has been thinking about the purchase of a boat. As a teenager, she was an avid water skier at her parents' summer home. Now that she has moved away, she wants to renew her hobby at a lake nearby. Julia recently received a raise of $200 per month and plans to visit a dealership near the lake to see what kind of boat she can buy with that level of payment. Offer your opinions about her thinking.

CASE 4

Reducing Expenses to Buy a New Car

Courtney Bennett recently graduated from college and accepted a position in Bangor, Maine, as an assistant librarian at the university library. Courtney has no debts, and her budget is shown in the second column (Single Working Person) in Table 3-5 on page 96. She now faces the question of whether to trade in her old car for a new one requiring a monthly payment of $400. Taking the role of a good friend of Courtney, suggest how Courtney might cut back on her expenses so that she can afford the vehicle.

(a) What areas might be cut back?

(b) How much in each area might be cut back?

(c) After finishing your analysis, what advice (and possibly alternatives) would you offer Courtney about buying the new car?

DO IT IN CLASS
Page 186

following list of three topics that Jacob has prepared, provide him with some suggested comments.

(a) What is consumer credit?

(b) Why might graduates use credit?

(c) How can graduates use credit wisely?

CASE 5

Cousins Discuss Their Debt Situations

Melinda Dennis from Sewell, New Jersey, just graduated from college and is concerned about her student loan debts. While at her graduation party she got to talking with three of her cousins, Kyle, Mariah, and Hadrian, who have been out of school for several years and found they each have had somewhat different pattern with using credit and carrying debt. Kyle, who had taken a personal finance class, said he felt good about his credit management and mentioned he has a debt payments-to-disposable income ratio of 7 percent. None of the other three cousins even knew what such ratio was. Kyle offered to do the calculations for the other three cousins. After doing so, he found ratios of 20 percent for Melinda due to her student loan debt, 12 percent for Mariah due primarily to a car loan, and 16 percent for Hadrian due to both a car loan and credit card debt. The cousins are planning to get together next week and discuss what Kyle has found. What assessment and advice should Kyle give to his cousins?

DO IT IN CLASS
Page 185

CASE 6

Preparation of a Credit-Related Speech

Jacob Marchese of Vancouver, Washington, is the credit manager for a regional chain of department stores. He has been asked to join a panel of community members and make a ten-minute speech to graduating high-school seniors on the topic "Using Credit Wisely." In the

CASE 7

Debt Consolidation as a Debt Reduction Strategy

Justin Granovsky, an assistant manager at a small retail shop in Morgantown, West Virginia, has an unusual amount of debt. He owes $5,400 to one bank, $1,800 to a clothing store, $2,700 to his credit union, and several hundred dollars to other stores and individuals. Justin is paying more than $460 per month on the three major obligations to pay them off when due in two years. He realized that his take-home pay of slightly more than $3,100 per month did not leave him with much excess cash. Justin discussed a different way of handling his major payments with his bank's loan officer. The officer suggested that Justin pool all of his debts and take out an $11,000 debt-consolidation loan for seven years at 14 percent interest. As a result, he would pay only $250 per month for all his debts. Justin seemed ecstatic over the idea.

(a) Is Justin's enthusiasm over the idea of a debt-consolidation loan justified? Why or why not?

(b) Why can the bank offer such a "good deal" to Justin?

(c) What compromise would Justin make to remit payments of only $250 as compared with $460?

(d) How much total interest would Justin pay over the seven years, and what would be a justification for this added cost?

DO IT IN CLASS
Page 194

BE YOUR OWN PERSONAL FINANCIAL MANAGER

1. **Your Credit Report.** Visit the website for obtaining a free credit report at www.annualcreditreport.com to order a copy of your credit report. Check the accuracy of the report and follow the directions provided to correct any errors. If no report is available on you, it should be because you have never used credit. If you have used credit and there is no report, you should notify the credit bureaus of this error and ask them to create a file on you.

2. **Set Your Debt Limit.** Based on your personal balance sheet and cash-flow statement, calculate your debt payments-to-disposable income and debt-to-income ratios. Do you feel that you are overly indebted by these

measures? Also consider the continuous-debt method

My Personal
Financial
Planner

in your considerations. Use Worksheet 25: The Effect of Taking on Additional Debt on My Financial Ratios from "My Personal Financial Planner" to determine if you could take on any debt at this time.

3. **List Your Outstanding Installment Loans.** Make an inventory of your installment loans including each

My Personal
Financial
Planner

loan's purpose, to whom the debt was owed, payoff date, monthly payment, and monthly due date using Worksheet 26: My Installment Loan Inventory from "My Personal Financial Planner."

4. **Protect Your Privacy.** A lost or stolen debit or credit card can cost you money and time. Using your credit report and other information from various billing statements, compile a list of all your debit and credit accounts including the telephone number and address of where to send notification if the card is lost or stolen.

5. **List Your Student Loans.** Make an inventory of your student loans including source, amounts currently

My Personal
Financial
Planner

owed, current APR, when payments must begin, approximate monthly payment, and the maximum number of years you will have to repay the loan using Worksheet 27: My Student Loan Inventory from "My Personal Financial Planner."

ON THE NET

Go to the Web pages indicated to complete these exercises.

1. **Credit Cards.** Visit CreditCards.com to see www.creditcards .com/credit-card-news/5-key-laws-protect-credit-cardholders-1377.php. List two protections you were not aware of before.

2. **FICO.** Visit the website for Fair Isaac Corporation at www.myfico.com/crediteducation/creditreports .aspx. Read up on how credit scoring works. Identify two actions you could take to improve your credit score.

3. **Credit Counseling.** Visit the National Foundation for Credit Counseling at www.nfcc.org/our-services/ credit-debt-counseling to read about their services. Click on some of the "frequently asked questions." What did you learn?

4. **Credit Products.** Visit the website for the Center for Responsible Lending at www.responsiblelending.org. Read about the various ways that certain lenders offer credit products and efforts to reign in those products. What do you think of such credit products?

5. **Bankruptcy.** Visit Money Management International at www.bankruptcy.org to learn about bankruptcy. What did you think?

6. **Student Loans.** Visit the National Foundation for Consumer Credit at nfcc.org/our-services/ student-loan-debt-counseling to read about advice on student loans. What did you learn?

ACTION INVOLVEMENT PROJECTS

1. **Understanding Credit Applications.** Visit a local bank or credit union and ask for an application for a credit card. Read through the items of information that are requested. Why do you think that the lender asks for the information requested? Do you think the lender would view the information that you might provide in a positive manner?

2. **Good Uses of Credit.** Survey three of your friends about their perceptions of when it is appropriate to use credit. Compare their views to your own and present your findings in a table.

3. **The Downside of Credit.** Survey three of your friends about their most negative experiences in using credit. Compare their experiences aspects to your own and present your findings in a table.

4. **Perceptions of Bankruptcy.** Survey three of your friends about their feelings about and understanding of bankruptcy. Do their feelings conflict with yours? Is their understanding of bankruptcy accurate?

Visit the Garman/Forgue companion website at www.cengagebrain.com.

7 Credit Cards and Consumer Loans

YOU MUST BE KIDDING, RIGHT?

College students have an average credit card debt of about $4,300 at graduation. If they maintain that level of debt for ten years, how much total interest will they pay over that decade?

A. $4,300   **C.** $7,740

B. $6,450   **D.** $8,400

The answer is C. A credit card with an 18 percent APR translates to a 1.5 percent rate per month (18 ÷ 12). The $4,300 debt multiplied by this rate equals $64.50 ($4,300 × 0.015) per month in interest. And $64.50 multiplied by 120 months equals $7,740. You must pay more than the required minimum monthly amount plus any new charges in order to reduce a credit card debt. Otherwise you will pay many thousands of dollars in interest and be in debt for years and years!

Learning Objectives

After reading this chapter, you should be able to:

1. Distinguish among credit cards and other types of open-emd credit.

2. Manage your credit card accounts wisely.

3. Distinguish among the sources of consumer installment loans.

4. Be familiar with the different types of installment loans.

5. Calculate the interest and annual percentage rate on consumer loans.

WHAT DO YOU RECOMMEND?

iStockphoto.com/serts

Zachary Cochrane, a 31-year-old food scientist made $62,000 last year. Zachary avoided using credit and credit cards until he was 28 years old, when he missed three months of work due to a water-skiing accident. He made ends meet by obtaining two bank credit cards that, because of his lack of a credit history, carry 19.6 and 24 percent annual percentage rates (APRs). Zachary now has 11 credit card accounts: five bank cards and six retail cards. He uses them regularly. He owes $13,000 on the 24 percent APR card and $4,400 on the 19.6 percent APR card. His other three bank cards carry APRs of 11 percent, 12 percent, and 15 percent, and he owes $500 to $700 on each one. For the past year, Zachary has been making only the minimum payments on his bank cards. His cards all carry APRs in excess of 21 percent. Although he has managed to keep from running a balance on those cards during most months, occasionally these accounts have balances as well.

What would you recommend to Zachary on the subject of credit cards and consumer loans regarding:

1. His approach to using credit cards, including the number of cards he has?
2. Estimating the credit card interest charges he is paying each month?
3. How he might lower his interest expenses each month?
4. Consolidating his debts into one installment loan?

Learning Objective 1

Distinguish among credit cards and other types of open-end credit.

open-end credit (revolving credit)

An account under which you are allowed to make repeated purchases or obtain loans and you may pay the balance in full or you may pay in installments.

credit limit

The maximum amount your credit issuer established for you to borrow on a credit card or line of credit.

finance charge

The cost of credit or the cost of borrowing; it is interest accrued on, and fees charged for some forms of credit.

grace period

This is the period of time a creditor, such as a credit card company, gives you to pay your new charges without having to pay interest on the new balance.

You cannot borrow your way to financial success, although advertising suggests otherwise. Realistically, using credit requires deliberate thinking and planning so you do not become overextended. Unfortunately, those who do become overextended often take quite a few years to repay their debts and get back their normal lives.

Before borrowing you need to first consider whether the reason you are borrowing is a good one, and then decide in advance how you will repay the debt. This is especially true for credit cards. Credit card usage can be managed so that you pay no interest at all. This occurs when you pay your card balance in full every month, and about half of cardholders do it.

Planning how to repay an installment loan is also important because here you are committed to make a series of monthly payments for a number of years. Wise borrowers understand the mathematics behind the calculation of the finance charges on installment loans. They focus on the **annual percentage rate (APR)** when comparing sources of credit. The APR is the cost of credit on a yearly basis stated as a percentage rate.

7.1 CREDIT CARDS AND OTHER TYPES OF OPEN-END CREDIT

Consumer credit is debt that someone incurs for the purpose of purchasing a good or service. This includes purchases made on open-end credit, including lines of credit and credit cards, and some loans like those for vehicles and televisions.

7.1a Open-End Credit

Open-end credit is a form of credit extended in advance of any transactions. A retailer or bank agrees to allow the consumer to make purchases and/or borrow up to a specified amount. Issuers like open-end credit because they research demonstrates that consumers tend to spend more using plastic than they would with real cash. When you are not forking over genuine dollar bills there is less sensation of a loss. Upon receiving a credit statement on an open-end account, the borrower may repay the balance in full or in installments.

Access to credit on an open-end account continues unless the borrower exceeds the **credit limit**. This is the maximum outstanding debt allowed on the account. Credit limits vary with the perceived creditworthiness of the borrower. The credit limit amount will be set out in the agreement between the lender and the borrower, although one can request an increase in his/her credit limit.

The account is not considered past due or in default as long as one makes payments according to the terms to which one agreed, such as within the **grace period**. This is the period of time a creditor gives you to pay your new charges without having to make a payment on the new balance. It usually runs from the end of a billing cycle to the next payment due date.

A **finance charge** is the dollar cost of credit or the cost of borrowing. It is interest accrued as well as other charges, such as financial transaction fees. The finance charge may be computed on the unpaid balance of an account when the borrower and a business agree to such terms. The finance charge pays the business, in part, for its expenses in keeping track of your account and processing payments.

Service credit is a form of open-end credit and is granted to consumers by public utilities, physicians, dentists, and other service providers that do not require full payment when services are rendered. For example, your electric company allows you to use electricity all month and then sends you a bill that may not be due for 10 to 20 days. Service credit usually carries no interest, although penalty charges and interest may apply if payments are made late. Service may be cut off for continued slow payment or nonpayment of the debt.

Travel and entertainment (T&E) cards are open-end credit issued by non-banks indicating that the holder has been granted a line of credit. It enables the holder, often a businessperson, to make purchases, like food and lodging when traveling. The full amount of the debt incurred has to be settled at the end of a specified period. Since T&E cards do not offer extended credit, they are not really "credit cards." The holder is usually charged a fee of $90+ annually. T&E cards are not accepted at as many outlets as the more popular bank credit cards. Applicants must have higher-than-average incomes to qualify. Examples are American Express, Diner's Club and Carte Blanche, and these are also known as **corporate cards**.

service credit
A form of open-end credit granted to consumers by public utilities, physicians, dentists, and other service providers that do not require full payment when services are rendered.

travel and entertainment (T&E) cards (corporate cards)
Cards issued by non-banks that are often used by businesspeople for food and lodging expenses while traveling.

7.1b Two Types of Organizations Issue Open-End Credit

One of the two types of organizations that issue open-end credit is **retail sellers and businesses**. These include department stores, clothing stores, oil companies, and car rental agencies that issue plastic cards that only may be used as open-end credit at one of their locations. Often, the balance on the account must be paid in full when the statement is received, and it cannot be rolled over from one billing cycle to the next. Or, the account is open-end credit as described above. The second type of organization that issues open-end credit is **financial institutions** such as banks.

retail sellers and businesses
These include department stores, clothing stores, oil companies, and car rental agencies that issue plastic cards that only may be used as open-end credit at one of their locations.

1. **Retail Sellers and Businesses.** These companies offer credit cards to enhance loyalty among customers. They are known as **retail credit cards** or **proprietary credit cards**, like JCPenney, Macy's, Lowe's, and ExxonMobil. People who have these cards in their wallets do so because they often shop at those stores.

2. **Bank Credit Cards.** These credit accounts are issued by commercial banks and other financial institutions. Bank credit cards usually carry the brand of the major payment processors, Visa or MasterCard although the actual lender is the bank that issues the card. **Bank credit cards** are used for electronic commerce through the Internet and for banking transactions through automatic teller machines (ATMs). The balance on the account may be paid in full when the statement is received or by making a partial payment and whatever balance is left may be rolled over from one billing cycle to the next. Within broad limits, banks can establish their own policies regarding interest rates, grace periods, fees, rewards programs, and other benefits, so there are some dramatic differences among issuers. To make comparisons, see www.bankrate.com.

bank credit cards
Credit cards that are issued by banks or large financial institutions, such as VISA, MasterCard, and Discover.

Bank credit cards not only allow purchase transactions but it may also be possible to withdraw funds up to an approved credit limit. Such **cash advances** are obtained by credit card customers from an ATM or over the counter at a bank or other financial agency. They are activated by using one's bank credit card or by writing a **convenience check** supplied by the lender to make cash advances easier. Cash advances often incur a fee of 3 to 5 percent of the amount being borrowed. When made on a credit card, the interest on a cash advance is often higher than assessed on credit card transactions. The interest compounds daily starting from the day cash is borrowed. Bank credit cards should not be confused with debit cards which give access to your deposited funds rather than allow you to borrow money.

cash advances
Obtained by credit card customers from an ATM or over the counter at a bank or other financial agency, up to a certain limit.

For purchase transactions using retail and bank credit cards, interest charges usually begin one month after a purchase is made. Credit cards have higher interest rates (around 18% per year) than most consumer loans or lines of credit. Bank credit cards may be used for transactions for almost anything anywhere in the world.

Some bank credit cards are promoted as **prestige cards**, often with a precious metal in the brand name such as "gold," "silver," or "platinum." These accounts

prestige cards
Credit cards often with a precious metal in the brand name such as "gold," "silver," or "platinum" that require that the user possess superior credit qualifications and offer enhancements such as higher credit limits.

DID YOU KNOW

Card Blocking Exists

Card blocking is the reserving of a portion of a credit or debit card balance for the cost of services not yet rendered. Credit card blocking is most common in the hospitality and rental car industries. Hotels use credit card blocking to ensure that the individual reserving the room will have sufficient credit available to pay the room fee at check out. The hotel may block all or a portion of the room cost before a stay begins. Rental car companies may place a hold on a credit card that exceeds the cost of renting the vehicle to cover incidental expenses or damages. Even worse, the block can remain for a week or more after the account is settled. Credit card blocking can have a significant impact on cardholders with low credit limits or who have a small amount of credit remaining because the block uses up a substantial amount of credit.

affinity cards

Standard bank cards but with the logo of a sponsoring organization imprinted on the face of the card, meaning that the issuing financial institution donates a small percentage of the amounts charged to the sponsoring organization.

default

This is the failure of a borrower to make a scheduled interest or principal payment, and it is something all borrowers want to avoid.

line of credit

An open-end credit account between a financial institution, usually a bank, and a customer that establishes a maximum loan limit that the bank will permit the person to borrow.

require that the user possess superior credit qualifications and they offer enhancements such as higher credit limits and special services. Prestige cards usually carry annual membership fees. Other bank credit cards are co-branded and known as **affinity cards**. They are standard bank cards but with the logo of a sponsoring organization imprinted on the face of the card. The issuing financial institution donates a small percentage of the amounts charged to the sponsoring organization.

Credit cards are the most convenient type of credit, and it is also the most abused. A wise rule to follow is to keep your credit card transactions limited to what you can pay off in full when the bill arrives. Otherwise you may find that your credit accounts are a revolving door with no exit. All borrowers want to avoid **default**. This is the failure of a borrower to make a scheduled interest or principal payment.

7.1c Revolving Lines of Credit

When using open-end credit, the borrower has a **revolving line of credit**. This is an arrangement between a financial institution and a customer that establishes a maximum credit limit that the lender will permit the person to borrow. You may draw down (borrow against) the **line of credit** at any time, as long as you do not exceed the maximum set in the agreement.

The borrower is under no obligation to actually take out a loan at any particular time, but may take part or all of the funds over a period of years. One may pay back the loan at one's own pace provided he/she pays at least the minimum due each month.

There are three popular types of this non–credit-card debt: unsecured personal loans, home equity credit line, and overdraft protection.

Unsecured Personal Loans. An **unsecured personal loan** is a line of credit available on an as-needed basis. This low-interest cash advance system is accessed by writing special checks. This process avoids having to apply for a new loan every time one needs extra money for a particular purpose. Repayment is in installments usually over 2 to 5 years.

Home Equity Credit Line. A **home equity credit line** is a type of loan in which the borrower uses the equity of his or her home as **collateral**. The amount that may be borrowed is based on the difference between the

DID YOU KNOW

Paying Cash Instead of Using a Credit Card Might Save You Money

The Federal Reserve Board regulations say that merchants are allowed to give discounts for those who pay cash or use a debit card rather than use a credit card. Ask the merchant and you may find that you might save 2 or 3 percent on a purchase, such as for gasoline or for airline tickets.

ADVICE FROM A SEASONED PRO

Smart Cards Do Just About Everything

A **smart card** is any plastic card about the size of a credit card with an embedded microprocessor chip, electronic memory, and a battery. When inserted into a reader (contact smart card) or held within a few inches of the reader (contactless smart card), the card may be used for information storage and management and authentication. It also can be used as a key. A smart card is more secure than cards with a magnetic stripe because the card generates a unique one-time code for each transaction that is impossible to replicate with counterfeit cards.

Smart cards can provide personal identification, authentication, data storage, and application processing. A smart card (some are made from paper or cloth) can be loaded with data and used for phone calls, highway tolls, electronic cash payments, and other applications, and then periodically refreshed for additional use.

Rather than wearables, or technologies embedded in clothing or accessories, today's smart cards may soon be replaced with internables—technologies embedded within the human body. In addtion, smart cards will use biometrics as a form of identification.

Oscar Solis
Virginia Tech, Blacksburg, Virginia

---

current market value of your home and the amount you still owe on the home mortgage loan. Home equity loans are often used to finance major expenses such as home repairs, medical bills, or a college education. These low interest loans are secured with a second mortgage on one's home. Typically, loans may be made only up to 80 percent of the value of the equity. If you cannot repay the loan, you lose your home.

Overdraft Protection. Banks offer an **overdraft protection** line of credit to their customers to cover their check writing overdrafts. Overdraft protection kicks in when a customer writes a check for more than the amount in their account. While it allows customers to escape paying overdraft fees, overdraft protection does charge interest on the amount loaned. Many banks allow their customers to link their bank accounts to a credit card in order to avoid overdraft charges.

collateral
This is something pledged as security for repayment of a loan, to be forfeited in the event of a default.

home equity credit line
A loan in which the lender agrees to lend a maximum amount within a term where the collateral is the borrower's equity in his/her home.

collateral
This is something pledged as security for repayment of a loan, to be forfeited in the event of a default.

CONCEPT CHECK 7.1

1. What is open-end credit and give three examples.
2. Explain the basic features of bank credit cards..
3. Distinguish between an unsecured line of credit and a home equity credit line.

7.2 MANAGING CREDIT CARDS WISELY

Learning Objective **2**
Manage your credit cards wisely.

Credit cards can be a positive tool in personal financial management but only when used appropriately. Your goal should be to use the credit card in a manner that avoids all fees, including finance charges. This means paying your balance in full every month. Otherwise, credit card debt likely will be your most expensive form of debt. As one expert observed, "You want to earn a 21 percent risk-free return on your money? Pay off your credit cards."

credit statement (billing statement)
A periodic report that credit card companies issue to credit card holders showing their recent transactions, balance due and other key information.

billing cycle
The time period between when credit statements are sent to borrowers, which is usually about one month.

7.2a Credit Statements

A **credit statement** (or **billing statement**) is a periodic report that credit card companies issue to credit card holders showing their recent transactions, balance due, and other key information. Billing statements are issued at the end of each **billing cycle**, which is usually about one month long. Figure 7-1 shows an illustrative statement for a credit card.

Figure 7-1 — Statement for a Bank Credit Card Account

XXX Bank Credit Card Account Statement
Account Number XXXX XXXX XXXX XXXX
February 21, 2018 to March 22, 2018
Statement Date 03/22/18

Summary of Account Activity

Previous Balance	$535.07
Payments	–$450.00
Other Credit	–$0.00
Purchases	+$529.57
Balance Transfers	+$785.00
Cash Advances	+$318.00
Past Due Amount	$0.00
Fees Charged	**+$69.45**
Interest Charged	**+$11.05**
New Balance	$1,798.14
Credit limit	$2,000.00
Available credit	$201.86
Statement closing date	3/22/2018
Days in billing cycle	30

Questions?

Call Customer Service	1-XXX-XXX-XXXX
Lost or Stolen Credit Card	1-XXX-XXX-XXXX

Payment Information

New Balance	$1,798.14
Minimum Payment Due	$53.00
Payment Due Date	4/20/18

Late Payment Warning: If we do not receive your minimum Payment by the date listed above, you may have to pay a $25 late fee and your APRs may be increased up to the Penalty APR of 28.99%

Minimum Payment Warning: If you make only the minimum payment each period, you will pay more in interest and it will take you longer to pay off your balance. For example:

If you make no additional charges using this card and each month you pay...	You will pay off the balance shown on this statement in about...	And you will end up paying as estimated total of...
Only the minimum payment	10 years	$3,284
$62	3 years	$2,232 (Savings = $1,052)

If you would like information about credit counseling services, call 1-800-XXX-XXXX

Please send billing inquiries and correspondence to:
PO Box XXXX, Anytown, Anystate XXXXX

Transactions

Reference Number	Trans Date	Post Date	Description of Transaction or Credit	Amount
5884186PS0388W6YM	2/22	2/23	Store #1	$146.19
854338203FS8OO0Z5	2/25	2/25	Pymt Thank You	–
564891561545KOSHD	2/25	2/26	Store #2	$247.36
1542202074TWWZV48	2/26	2/26	Cash Advance	$318.00
4545754784KOHUIOS	2/27	3/1	Balance Transfer	$785.00
2564561023184102315	2/28	3/1	Store #3	$ 34.32
045148714518979874	3/4	3/5	Store #4	$ 29.45
0547810544898718AF	3/15	3/17	Store #5	$ 72.25

Fees				
9525156489SFD4545Q	2/23	2/23	Late Fee	$25.00
84151564SADS874H	2/27	2/27	Balance Transfer Fee	$23.55
256489156189451516L	2/28	2/28	Cash Advance Fee	$20.90
			TOTAL FEES FOR THIS PERIOD	**$69.45**

Interest Charged		
Interest Charge on Purchases		$ 6.40
Interest Charge on Cash Advances		$ 4.65
TOTAL INTEREST FOR THIS PERIOD		**$11.05**

2018 Totals Year-to-Date

Total fees charged in 2018	$90.14
Total interest charged in 2018	$18.27

Interest Charge Calculation

Your Annual Percentage rate (APR) is the stated interest rate on your account.

Type of Balance	Annual Percentage Rate (APR)	Balances Subject to Interest Rate	Interest Charge
Purchases	14.99% (V)	$512.14	$6.40
Cash Advances	21.99% (V)	$253.50	$4.65
Balance Transfers	0.00%	$637.50	$0.00
Penalty APR	28.99%	$ 0.00	$0.00

(V) = Variable Rate

Statement Date The statement date (sometimes called the billing date or closing date) is the last day of the month for which any transactions are reported on the statement. Any transactions or payments made after this date will be recorded on the following month's credit statement. A credit statement is mailed to a cardholder a day or so after the statement date. In Figure 7-1, the statement date is March 22.

Payment Due Date The payment due date is the specific day by which the credit card company should receive payment from you. Federal law states that card issuers have to give card account holders "a reasonable amount of time" to pay on monthly bills. That means payments are due at least 21 days after they are mailed from the issuer. Your payment due date must be the same each month, and if it falls on a weekend or holiday, you have until the following business day to pay. The payment due date is April 20.

Transaction and Posting Dates The date on which a credit cardholder makes a purchase or receives a credit is known as the transaction date ("Trans Date" in Figure 7-1). The posting date is the month, day, and year when a credit card issuer processes a credit card transaction and adds it to the cardholder's account balance. The posting date is sometimes identical to the transaction date, but it is often one to three days later. Any interest is usually charged from the posting date ("Post Date" in Figure 7-1).

Previous Unpaid Balance In Figure 7-1, the cardholder has a previous unpaid balance, $535.07, and was charged interest on the unpaid balance as well as on the new charges made within the billing cycle, starting from the date they were posted to the account. Thus, this example lacks a grace period because of the unpaid balance on the card.

Minimum Payment Due To meet their credit obligations, borrowers must make a minimum payment due monthly that is no smaller than the amount required by the creditor. In Figure 7-1, the cardholder has two options: pay the total amount due, known as the "new balance," of $1,798.14 or make at least the minimum payment of $53. If the borrower pays the total amount due, finance charges on new purchases in the next billing cycle generally can be avoided. If a partial payment, such as $53 is made, additional finance charges will be assessed and will be payable the following month.

Ten Years to Pay Off the Balance Credit card issuers must disclose to cardholders the consequences of making only minimum payments each month, namely how long it would take to pay off the entire balance if users only made the minimum monthly payment. Issuers must also provide information on how much users must pay each month if they want to pay off their balances in 36 months, including the amount of interest. In Figure 7-1, it would take "about 10 years" to pay off the balance making only the minimum payments, resulting in estimated total payments of $3,284. And that is on a balance of only $1,798.14!

Transaction Fees Credit card companies usually charge transaction fees whenever the card is used for a balance transfer or cash advance. Figure 7-1 reveals a late fee of $25, a balance transfer fee of $23.65, and a cash advance fee of $20.90.

Credit for Merchandise Returns and Errors If you return merchandise bought on credit, the merchant will issue you a credit receipt. This is written evidence of the items returned that notes the specific amount of the transaction. The amount of the merchandise credit is charged back to the credit card company and eventually to the merchant. A credit may also be granted by the card issuer when a billing error has been made and when an unauthorized transaction appears. Credits obtained in the current month should appear on the next monthly statement as a reduction of the total amount owed.

Penalty Rates on Credit Cards The penalty rate, also called the default rate, is the very high interest rate charged by the credit card issuer when a borrower violates the card's terms and conditions. It could be 25

COMMON SENSE
Avoid Credit Card Offers by Opting Out

Federal law states that consumers have the right to opt out of receiving unsolicited credit card offers. To put a stop to such mailings, call (888) 5-OPT-OUT or visit www.optoutprescreen.com.

statement date (billing date or closing date)
The last day of the month for which any transactions are reported on a credit card statement.

payment due date
The specific day by which the credit card company should receive payment from the cardholder.

transaction date
The date on which a credit cardholder makes a purchase or receives a credit.

posting date
The month, day, and year when a credit card issuer processes a credit card transaction and adds it to the cardholder's account balance.

minimum payment
The amount due monthly on a credit card statement that is no smaller than the amount required by the creditor.

transaction fees
Whenever a credit card is used for a balance transfer or cash advance such fees are charged to the account.

YOUR GRANDPARENTS SAY

"Don't Use Credit Cards"

"College students often find that credit card charges can quickly spiral out of control. Instead use prepaid cards, debit cards, gift cards, and an interest-bearing checking account."

ADVICE FROM A SEASONED PRO

Which Rewards Credit Card Is Best

You can get "paid" by credit card issuers for things you already do, including shopping, eating, going to theaters and concerts, watching television, staying at hotels, paying bills, renting vehicles, giving to charity, and investing.

Some **rewards credit cards** will pay you 1 to 6 percent cash back on a variety of purchases. The card issuer will send you a check or gift card, give you a statement credit, or deposit funds into a linked account. Others will pay you some "airline miles" to be used on future flights. Still others award "points" for purchases, which can be redeemed for cash, gift cards, merchandise, travel, Amazon orders, and hotel stays. Which type of rewards card is better?

Before you make this decision, you need to examine your own lifestyle and spending patterns. For most people,

especially for those who do not plan to travel much in the future, a cash-back rewards card is more practical.

Avoid any kind of rewards card if you carry a balance because card issuers have to charge high interest rates to pay for rewards. Avoid any rewards card that comes with an annual fee because you have to spend $10,000 on the card each year to pay $100 fee if you earn 1 percent back. Points and miles programs are often complicated and make it challenging to get your money's worth in redemptions. Travelers who spend less than $8000 a year on trips should get a cash-back card. Your points are worthless if they expire, so keep track of your rewards programs. See AwardWallet, NerdWallet, Points.com, and TripIt Pro's Point Tracker.

Ann House
The University of Utah, Salt Lake City, Utah

---

rewards credit card
One that pays the cardholder cash back or airlines miles for future use.

credit receipt
Written evidence of any items returned that notes on a credit card statement the specific amount of the transaction, which will be charged back to the credit card company and eventually to the merchant.

penalty rate (default rate)
The very high interest rate charged by the credit card issuer when a borrower violates the card's terms and conditions.

DO IT IN CLASS

average daily balance
This is the sum of the outstanding balances owed on a credit card each day during the billing period divided by the number of days in the period.

or 35 percent or more. The penalty rate is triggered most often when cardholders are late making monthly payments. This penalty rate can be lowered—or "cured"—if the account holder makes six consecutive on-time payments immediately following the late payment. Then the rate will drop back to a more standard rate, such as 18 percent. In Figure 7-1 the penalty rate is 28.99 percent. The first late fee maxes out at $27, and it can rise to $37.

7.2b   Computation of Finance Charges

Companies that issue credit cards must tell consumers the APR applied as well as the method used to compute the finance charges. Mathematically the APR translates into a **periodic rate**, which is the APR for a charge account divided by the number of billing cycles per year (usually 12). For example, a periodic rate of 1½ percent per month would result from an APR of approximately 18 percent (actually a bit higher because of compounding). Both figures must be disclosed.

The finance charge is typically calculated by first computing the **average daily balance**. This is the sum of the outstanding balances owed each day during the billing period divided by the number of days in the period. The periodic rate is then applied against that balance. For example, a card with an 18 percent APR, a 1½ percent periodic rate, and an average daily balance of $1,000 would have a finance charge for the month of $15 ($1,000 × 0.015). As shown at the bottom on the statement in Figure 7-1, differing APRs were applied for purchases, balance transfers, and cash advances.

7.2c   Liability for Lost or Stolen Cards

The Truth in Lending Act limits a cardholder's **credit card liability** for lost or stolen credit cards. Under the law, if you notify the card issuer within two days of a loss or theft, you are not legally responsible for any fraudulent usage of the card. After two days, your maximum liability for fraudulent usage of the card is $50.

ADVICE FROM A SEASONED PRO

Teaser Rates on Credit Cards

A **teaser rate** (or **introductory rate**) is the annual percentage rate charged by the credit card issuer during an initial period. Federal law requires that teaser rates must stay in effect for six months after the account is opened. These are offered to entice borrowers to apply for an account with their financial organization.

There are three reasons credit card issuers make such an offer: (1) to get their card into your wallet so you will use it plus they earn fees from the merchants you buy from both now and after the introductory period; (2) to encourage you to move any credit card balances you might have to their company via a credit card balance transfer so they receive interest and fees from your activity; and (3) to charge a higher annual percentage rate after the introductory period.

The initial teaser rate can be from 0 to 2.9 percent, but will be higher after the introductory period. You must read the credit card and balance transfer conditions closely to be sure they are in your favor.

Steve Holcombe, Feliccia Smith, and Richard Gianni
North Greenville University, Tigerville, South Carolina

Although your financial liability is low, many companies nevertheless sell credit card insurance to cover the first $50 of unauthorized use of an insured person's lost or stolen credit cards. Such insurance is profitable for the sellers but a wasteful expense for you. If you are insistent, the issuer will waive the $50 fee for unauthorized use as a gesture of goodwill to keep you as a good credit card customer. You also should know that most homeowner's and renter's insurance policies will pay the $50 fee you might be charged for unauthorized use of a lost or stolen credit card, so if needed just file a claim.

Chip and pin technology (or **EMV**) has reduced identity theft for lost and stolen credit cards because each transaction generates a unique code used in approval making them harder to counterfeit. This provides more security than the older magnetic stripe system. **EMV** stands for Europay, MasterCard, and Visa, the three companies that originally created the chip standard. The safer chip technology also is used in debit cards.

DO IT IN CLASS

ADVICE FROM A SEASONED PRO

Card Registration Services Are Unnecessary

Some companies sell a **card registration service** that will notify all companies with which you have debit and credit cards in the event of card loss. In addition, most services will request a replacement card and some advertise that they will reimburse you for fraudulent charges made. Depending upon the company, card registration services can range in price from $50 to $240 a year.

However, you can always notify debit and credit card companies yourself at no cost. Also, thanks to the Fair Credit Billing Act (FCBA), you are only liable for up a maximum of $50 in fraudulent credit card charges per card, and most credit card companies offer 100 percent reimbursement for all unauthorized charges. Thus, making card registration services an unnecessary expense.

Frances C. Lawrence
Louisiana State University, Baton Rouge, Louisiana

ADVICE FROM A SEASONED PRO

Credit Card Insurance Is Overpriced

Many lenders encourage borrowers to sign up for **credit insurance**. This is a policy purchased by a borrower that pays off one or more existing debts in the event of a death, disability, or in rare cases, unemployment. Credit insurance (whether life, disability or unemployment) is usually optional which means you are not required to purchase it. Credit insurance is grossly overpriced and should be avoided.

Linda A. Bradley
California State University, Northridge, California

---

card registration service
Firm that will notify all companies with which you have debit and credit cards if your cards are lost or stolen.

chargeback
The law provides that customers may dispute charges to their credit card when goods or services are not delivered within the specified time frame, goods received are damaged, or the purchase was not authorized by the credit card holder.

Note that chips are not used in telephone and online purchases, where crooks can make unauthorized purchases, so continue to guard your card information.

7.2d Correcting Errors on Your Credit Card Statement

Provisions of the Fair Credit Billing Act (FCBA) provide permit a **chargeback** whereby customers may dispute charges to their credit card when goods or services are not delivered within the specified time frame, goods received are damaged, or the purchase was not authorized by the credit card holder. A customer may dispute a transaction by following the procedures explained on the credit statement or company website. They usually require the customer to provide the rationale for the dispute and, if appropriate, any good-faith efforts they tried to correct the problem. This action temporarily reverses the transaction until the dispute is settled.

For goods and services disputes, the FCBA applies only to charges of more than $50 made in your home state or within 100 miles of your current mailing address. Most lenders apply the spirit of the FCBA to any goods and services disputes, regardless of the geographic distances involved.

Your Time Limits You must make your billing error complaint within 60 days after the date on which the first bill containing the error was mailed to you. The lender then has 30 days to acknowledge your notification and, within 90 days, must either correct the error permanently, return any overpayment (if requested), or provide evidence of why it believes the bill to be correct (such as a copy of a charge slip you supposedly signed).

Lender Responsibilities While the dispute is being investigated, creditors cannot assess interest on or apply penalties for nonpayment of the disputed amount, send **dunning letters** (notices that make insistent demands for repayment), or send negative information about your account to a credit bureau without stating that "some items are in dispute." A lender that does not follow the procedures correctly cannot collect the first $50 of the questioned amount, even if the bill was correct. Back interest and penalties may be charged if the disputed item is shown to be legitimately owed.

Your Action Steps Take these actions when disputing an error on a billing statement:

1. **Notify the merchant** involved of the error. Disputes about the quality of goods and services are not "billing errors," so the dispute procedure does not apply. However, it is often a merchant that caused an

THERE IS AN APP FOR THAT!

Some of the best apps are:

- Bankrate Auto App
- Virtual Wallet by PNC
- SimpleLoanCalculator
- LoanCalculator
- iLoan
- LeanBuddy
- DebtsMonitorFree

error and the merchant is in the best position to clear up most errors.

2. **Write to the creditor** at the address given for "billing inquiries" (not the address for sending your payments), and include your name, address, account number, and a description of the billing error. Provide photocopies of any necessary documentation. Keep the originals to challenge any finding by the company that no error occurred. Alternatively write online using the card issuer's website.

3. **Send your letter** so that it reaches the creditor within 60 days after the first bill with the error was mailed to you. It is a good idea to send your letter by certified mail, and ask for a return receipt so you have proof of what was mailed to the creditor. Include copies (not originals) of sales slips or other documents that support your position. Keep a copy of your dispute letter.

Shoppers frequently rely on purchase loans when buying big ticket items such as furniture and TVs.

4. **Withhold payment for disputed items.** You may withhold payment on the disputed amount (and related charges) during the investigation. You must pay any part of the bill not in question, including finance charges on the undisputed amount.

The creditor must acknowledge your complaint, in writing, within 30 days after receiving it, unless the problem has been resolved. The creditor must resolve the dispute within two billing cycles (but not more than 90 days) after getting your letter. Review your credit bureau file after the dispute has been settled to ensure that it does not include information regarding your refusal to repay the disputed amount.

If the creditor's investigation determines the bill is correct, you must be told promptly and in writing how much you owe and why. You may ask for copies of relevant documents. At this point, you will still owe the disputed amount plus any finance charges that accumulated while the amount was in dispute. You also may have to pay the minimum amount you missed paying because of the dispute.

If you disagree with the results of the investigation, you may write to the creditor, but you must act within 10 days after receiving the explanation, and you may indicate that you refuse to pay the disputed amount. The creditor may begin collection procedures. However, if the creditor reports you to a credit reporting company as delinquent, the report also must state that you do not think you owe the money. The creditor must tell you who gets these reports. The creditor also must promptly report any subsequent resolution of the reported delinquency, to everyone who got a report.

NEVER EVER

Forget to give your change of address to your credit card companies when you move because the 3 months of unpaid bills will find you eventually and then scar your credit history for several years.

CONCEPT CHECK 7.2

1. Distinguish between a statement date and a payment due date on a credit statement.
2. Distinguish between transaction and posting dates on a credit statement.
3. How does a penalty rate work on a credit card?
4. What is the liability for a lost or stolen credit card?
5. What are your action steps to dispute an error on a billing statement?

	Table 7-1	**Traditional Sources of Consumer Loans**

Source	Types of Loans	Interest Rates
Banks	Vehicles, homes, home improvement, home equity, personal, education, credit and cards, personal loans	Low to medium
Savings and loans	Vehicles, homes, home improvement, home equity, personal loans	Low to medium
Credit union	Vehicles, homes, home improvement, credit and debit cards, personal loans	Low to medium
Sales finance companies	Vehicles, consumer products	Low to high
Consumer finance companies (small loans)	Vehicles, consumer products, personal loans	High

Learning Objective 3

Distinguish among the sources of consumer installment loans.

sales finance company

A finance company that buys at a discount the installment sales contracts of merchants or that directly finances retail sales.

7.3 SOURCES OF CONSUMER LOANS

When you need a loan for a specific purpose you will want to shop around for the best deal, and getting the lowest annual percentage rate (APR) on a loan is most important.

Much of what we borrow is for purchases financed through a **sales finance company**. This is a company that finances the installment sales of retail merchants, which is often affiliated with a manufacturer, like Ford or General Electric. The buyer completes the paperwork at the seller's place of operation.

If you want to finance a vehicle, for example, you want an institution to give you a 3- or 4-year loan so you can pay it off before you get too many miles on it. A sales finance company or credit union probably could best meet those terms and at a very low interest rate. Alternatively, if you own stocks you may borrow from the brokerage firm on the value of those stocks (see Chapter 14). You may borrow from your life insurance company if you own a permanent life insurance policy (see Chapter 12). Finally, you may borrow from your retirement plan at work (see Chapter 17). Table 7-1 shows the traditional sources of consumer loans.

CONCEPT CHECK 7.3

1. What is a sales finance company and how does it work?
2. Where would to go to obtain an installment loan to finance a vehicle if you had a good credit rating and wanted to pay a low interest rate?

Learning Objective 4

Be familiar with the different types of installment loans.

installment loan

A system of credit that is repaid by the borrower in regular installments, such as equal monthly payments that include interest and a portion of principal.

7.4 INSTALLMENT LOANS

In contrast to open-end loans, such as credit cards, a **closed-end credit** arrangement is where the full amount owed must be paid back by the borrower by a set point in time. Most real estate and vehicle loans are closed-end credit. The repayment amounts include all the interest and finance charges agreed to at the signing of the credit agreement.

Consumer loans can be either single-payment loans or installment loans. A **single-payment loan** is one that is paid back in a lump sum at a later date. Here a borrower might take out a loan of $2,000 at 12 percent interest for one year. He/she would owe a single payment of $2,240 ($2,000 × $240 interest; $2,000 × 0.12) at the end of one year.

An **installment loan** refers to a system of credit that is repaid by the borrower in regular installments, such as equal monthly payments that include interest and a portion of principal. An example of an installment loan is where an $18,000 loan might require monthly payments of $356 for 60 months at 7 percent interest. Installment loans are used to buy vehicles, appliances, televisions, and other major purchases. Consumers are able to take possession of property today and pay for it within a set amount of time. They benefit by financing expensive items at interest rates that are typically far lower than credit card interest rates.

7.4a The Loan Contract

The **loan contract** (or **loan agreement**) is a document that evidences a loan. It often includes rules, type and and value of collateral pledged, interest rate and fees, and how the loan is to be repaid and over what time period. Also in most states the borrower will sign a formal **promissory note**. This is a financial instrument in which the borrower promises in writing to pay a determinate sum of money to the lender, either at a fixed or determinable future time or on demand of the payee, under specific terms.

7.4b Unsecured and Secured Loans

Credit can either be unsecured or secured.

Unsecured Loans An **unsecured loan** is issued and supported only by the borrower's creditworthiness, rather than by a type of collateral, because it is obtained without the use of property as collateral for the loan. Borrowers generally must have high credit ratings to be approved for an unsecured loan. An example is a **signature loan**. This is an unsecured personal loan because it is not secured by the equity in one's home (as in a home equity loan) or by some other personal property or asset (such as a vehicle loan). Because unsecured loans carry a higher risk than secured debts, the interest rate charged on them is substantially higher. Nearly all purchases on credit cards fall into this category.

Since unsecured loans are risky for lenders they not only have higher interest rates but also stricter conditions. If you do not repay an unsecured debt, the lender can sue and obtain a legal judgment against you. Depending upon your state's rules, the lender may then be able to force you to sell other assets to pay the judgment or, if you are employed by another, to garnish a portion of your wages.

A **student loan** is a form of unsecured credit that is designed to help students pay for college tuition and books, and sometimes living expenses. It differs from other types of loans in that the interest rate may be substantially lower and the repayment schedule may be deferred while the student is still in school. Student loans may be obtained from the federal government or a private lender.

A downside of student loans is that most people incur it at a young age, before they may fully understand the numerous implications of their decision. Student debt also differs from other types of debt in that it cannot be discharged in bankruptcy except in an extremely rare case of undue hardship. Total student debt exceeds aggregate credit card debt. The numbers are massive: more than $1.3 trillion in outstanding student loan debt, 44 million borrowers, and an average balance of $35,000.

Because the federal government gives student loans to all borrowers, this lack of prudence on the front end masks the fact that it becomes a heartless lender when the bills come due. If you don't repay your government student loan, the authorities will use the Internal Revenue Service and private debt collectors and follow you as long as you live.

Secured Loans If the item being purchased is to be used as collateral for a loan (such as a vehicle or television), the loan contract will include a **security agreement**. This identifies whether the lender or borrower retains control over the item being purchased. When the lender maintains a secure interest in a specified asset, the collateral in the event a borrower defaults can be seized and sold by the lender. These are also known as **secured loans** because the borrower has pledged some asset as collateral to guarantee the loan.

The lender typically records a lien in the county courthouse to make the security interest known to the public. When the loan is repaid, the lien is removed. A **lien** is a legal right to keep possession of property belonging to another person until a debt owed by that person is discharged. The lienholder may also dispose of the property (usually they sell) to obtain payment of a claim.

MONEY WEBSITES

Informative websites are:
- AARP
- Bankrate.com Center for Responsible Lending
- Consumer Financial Protection Bureau
- Credit
- Federal Reserve Board
- Federal Trade Commission
- HSH
- Karma MyFICO
- MyMoney
- NOLO

unsecured loan
A loan issued and supported only by the borrower's creditworthiness, rather than by a type of collateral, because it is obtained without the use of property as collateral for the loan.

student loan
A form of unsecured credit that is designed to help students pay for university tuition and books, and sometimes their living expenses.

secured loans
A loan where the borrower has pledged some asset as collateral to guarantee the loan.

lien
A legal right to keep possession of property belonging to another person until a debt owed by that person is discharged; usually recorded in a county courthouse.

ADVICE FROM A SEASONED PRO

Credit Cards Cause Stress

Credit cards and the use of credit can have positive benefits, but credit cards if not managed properly can also have negative consequences. For many, credit card debt is often quite destructive on a personal level. People who overspend on credit cards are kept from achieving their financial goals, such as purchasing a new home or saving for retirement. Couples who are spending more on credit may find that their relationship is falling apart. Marriage counselors say that financial problems are the number one cause of divorce.

Getting wacked every month with a 20 percent interest charge on one's outstanding credit card balance month is stressful. The anxiety is there every day and it smacks you every time the bill arrives. A credit card account with an average balance of $3,000 may wind up costing the cardholder $600 or more annually in interest charges. Additionally, if you make your payment late the credit card company will assess late fees and penalties, which will add to the amount that you must repay over the course of the year. That is all wasted money.

Byron Lynn Morgan
Texas State University, San Marcos, Texas

---

cosigner

When a person (the cosigner) accepts the legal obligation to make payment on another person's debt should that person default.

acceleration clause

Clause in a credit contract that that allow a lender to require a borrower to repay all of an outstanding loan if certain requirements are not met, such as missing one or more repayments.

COMMON SENSE
Good and Bad Debt

Bad debt is money borrowed that is not used to finance an asset, like for a pizza, suppers out, clothing, vehicle, or vacation. Good debt is money borrowed to finance an asset, like a home or an education. But good debt can go bad if you borrow too much using the rationalization that in the end you will be better off financially by borrowing more. Examples are decade-long burdensome student loans and the negative consequences of a mortgage you cannot afford.

Cosigner A special form of collateral happens when a loan has a **cosigner**. This occurs when a person (the cosigner) accepts the legal obligation to make payment on another person's debt should that person default. Having a cosigner is way for individuals with a low income or a poor/limited credit history to obtain financing. A cosigner has the same legal obligations for repayment as the original borrower. The cosigner is on the hook, not just for the loan, but for any late charges or collection fees that may have accrued from the defaulting borrower.

If asked to cosign and you can't afford to pay off the loan, and it is usually for a good friend or a loved one, then no matter how much you love them, how great their need, or how much you want to believe they will pay—you must "just say no."

Ninety percent of private student loans have a parent or grandparent as a cosigner, and they are responsible for repayment even in the event the student borrower dies. Forty percent of cosigners have to make payments. More than one in four student loan borrowers are delinquent or in default.

Acceleration Clause Credit contracts contain an **acceleration clause** that allow a lender to require a borrower to repay all of an outstanding loan if certain requirements are not met, such as missing one or more repayments. Then the loan is considered in default and all remaining installments are due and payable upon demand of the creditor.

Deficiency Payments Clause A **deficiency payments clause** is a loan requirement stating that if one defaults on a secured loan, not only can the lender repossess whatever is secured, but if the sale of that asset does not cover what is owed, the borrower can also be billed for the difference. Thus a repossessed vehicle on which Jamie Johansen, of Bellingham, Washington, owed $11,000 might be sold by the lender for $10,000, and after the lender incurs $400 in attorney and collection fees Jamie will be billed for $1,400 ($11,000 − $10,000 = $1,000 + $400).

Recourse Clause A **recourse clause** in a loan contract defines what actions a lender can take to get money from a borrower in the case of default. A common such action would allow the lender to attach one's wages to pay off a debt.

NUMBERS ON

Credit

Data from a variety of sources suggest:

- Students who regularly pay off credit card balance every month: 20 percent.

- Students who carry an unpaid credit card balance each month: 80 percent

- Average credit card balance of college graduates: $4,300.

- Percentage of college graduates whose card balance is over $7,000: 20 percent.

- Adults who carry credit balances month to month: 50 percent.

- Adult average debt per card that carries a balance: $8,200.

- Average debt per card that does not carry a balance: $1,100.

- Average number of cards held by cardholders: 4.0.

- Average APR on card: 14 percent.

- Card issuer charge-off rate on credit cards: 4 percent.

- Percentage of applicants rejected for a new card or given lower credit limit than requested: 33 percent.

- Average number of adults without a credit card: 25 percent.

7.4c Variable-Rate or Fixed-Rate Loans

A **variable-rate loan** occurs when an interest rate on a loan fluctuates over time because it is tied to an underlying benchmark interest rate that changes periodically. The **prime rate** is sometimes the benchmark as it is the interest rate banks charge their most credit-worthy customers. The advantage of a variable interest rate is that if the underlying interest rate or index declines the borrower's interest payments also fall. Some variable-rate loans are adjusted annually, some monthly. They usually have **interest rate caps** that limit how much the rate can increase over the life of the loan.

A **fixed-rate loan** occurs when the contract calls for the interest rate on a loan to remain fixed either for the entire term of the loan. A fixed interest rate may be attractive to a borrower who feels that the interest rate might rise over the term of the loan, which would increase his/her interest expense.

7.4d Alternative Lenders Offer High-Priced Loans

High-priced credit can come from alternative lenders such as payday lenders, rent-to-own stores, pawnshops, and secured credit cards.

Payday lenders (which are illegal in some states) are businesses that grant credit when they honor a personal check but agree not to deposit the check for a week or longer. The fees for check cashing are often **20** percent or more of the amount of the check, pushing the annual percentage rate from **20** to **300** to **700** percent. Three-quarters of payday borrowers either roll over their loans or take out larger loans further escalating the cost of borrowing.

A **rent-to-own program** offered through a rent-to-own store provides a mechanism for buying an item with little or no down payment by renting it for a period of time, after which it is owned. Items include furniture, appliances, and electronic entertainment.

These programs have some drawbacks. The renter does not own the item until the final payment is made. Paying late or stopping payments will results in the products being repossessed with no allowance made for the previous "rental" payments. And the actual cost for renting items is exorbitantly high. For example, a TV worth $500 might be rented for $39 per week for one year, producing a total charge of $1,028 (52 × $39).

variable-rate loan
A loan where an interest rate on a loan fluctuates over time because it is tied to an underlying benchmark interest rate that changes periodically.

prime rate
The interest rate banks charge their most credit-worthy customers, and it is sometimes used as a benchmark for other variable-rate loans.

interest rate caps
Limits in credit contracts that prohibit how much the interest rate can increase over the life of the loan.

fixed-rate loan
A loan where the contract calls for the interest rate on a loan to remain fixed either for the entire term of the loan.

A **pawnshop** is a business that offers secured loans to people with items of personal property used as collateral that the borrower turns over to the pawnshop. The lender offers single-payment loans, often ranging from $100 to $500, for short time periods (typically two to six months). The dollar amount loaned is typically equal to one-third or less of the value of the item pawned. To get the cash a borrower need merely turn over the item, present identification, and sign on the dotted line.

The pawnshop owner can legally sell the item if the borrower fails to redeem the property by paying the amount due, plus interest, within the time period specified. The pawnshop commonly charges an interest rate of 5 percent per month plus a 2 percent monthly storage fee; thus, the annual combined "interest" amounts to 84 percent [(5 + 2) × 12].

A **secured credit card** (or **collateralized credit card**) is a type of credit card that requires a fee to open, and it is backed by a savings account used as collateral on the credit available with the card. Money is deposited and held in the account backing the card. The limit, often $500 to $1,000, will be based on one's credit history and the amount deposited in the account. Most people do not need to open a secured credit card, but sometimes those who have bad credit ratings or regularly bounce checks are forced to use secured credit cards. Those who have no alternative should consider obtaining one from a reputable institution, such as the Secured MasterCard from Capital One.

CONCEPT CHECK 7.4

1. Distinguish between a single-payment and an installment loan.
2. What is the difference between a secured and an unsecured loan?
3. What reasons do some people offer for not having a relative co sign a student loan?
4. What is an acceleration clause?
5. Which alternative lender probably charges the highest interest rate?

DO IT IN CLASS

7.5 CALCULATING INTEREST ON CONSUMER LOANS

The federal **Truth in Lending Act (TIL)** requires lenders to disclose to credit applicants both the interest rate expressed as an APR and the finance charge.

7.5a Calculating an Installment Loan Payment

Installment credit typically comes with a fixed interest rate or a variable-rate. To help you figure out the required monthly payment for different loan amounts, Table 7-2 shows various monthly installment payments used to repay a $1,000 loan at commonly seen APR interest rates and time periods. For loans of other dollar amounts, divide the borrowed amount by 1,000 and multiply the result by the appropriate figure from the table. For example, an automobile loan for $12,000, financed at 10 percent interest, might be repaid in 36 equal monthly payments of $387.24 ($32.27 × 12). A loan for $3,550 at 16 percent for 24 months will require monthly payments of $173.81 ($48.96 × 3.550).

The finance charge must include all mandatory charges to be paid by the borrower. In addition to interest, lenders may charge fees for a credit investigation; a loan application; or credit life, credit disability, or credit unemployment insurance. When fees are required, the lender must include them in the finance charge in dollars and as part of the APR calculations. When the borrower elects these options voluntarily, the fees are not included in the finance charge and APR calculations, even though they raise the actual cost of borrowing.

It is easy to calculate the finance charge on a consumer loan. First, multiply the monthly payment by the number of months and subtract the original amount borrowed. In the 36-month automobile loan example given earlier, the finance charge would be $1,940.64 [($387.24 × 36) − $12,000]. Second, add any other mandatory charges.

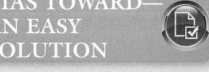

Table 7-2 — Monthly Installment Payments for a Loan (Principal and Interest Required to Repay $1,000*)

	Number of Monthly Payments						
APR[†]	12	24	36	48	60	72	84
5	$85.61	$43.87	$29.97	$23.03	$18.87	$16.10	$14.13
6	86.07	44.32	30.42	23.49	19.33	16.57	14.61
7	86.53	44.77	30.88	23.95	19.80	17.05	15.09
8	86.99	45.23	31.34	24.41	20.28	17.53	15.59
9	87.45	45.68	31.80	24.88	20.76	18.03	16.09
10	87.92	46.14	32.27	25.36	21.25	18.53	16.60
11	88.38	46.61	32.74	25.85	21.74	19.03	17.12
12	88.85	47.07	33.21	26.33	22.24	19.55	17.65
13	89.32	47.54	33.69	26.83	22.75	20.07	18.19
14	89.79	48.01	34.18	27.33	23.27	20.61	18.74
15	90.26	48.49	34.67	27.83	23.79	21.14	19.27
16	90.73	48.96	35.16	28.34	24.32	21.69	19.86
17	91.20	49.44	35.65	28.85	24.85	22.25	20.44
18	91.68	49.92	36.15	29.37	25.39	22.81	21.02
19	92.16	50.41	36.66	29.90	25.94	23.38	21.61
20	92.63	50.90	37.16	30.43	26.49	23.95	22.21

*To illustrate, assume an automobile loan of $14,000 at 8 percent for five years. To repay $1,000, the monthly payment is $20.28; therefore, multiply $20.28 (8% row and 60-month column) by 14 to give a monthly payment of $283.92. For amounts other than exact $1,000 increments, simply use decimals. For example, for a loan of $14,500, the multiplier would be 14.5.

[†]For fractional interest rates of 5.5, 6.5, 7.5, and so on, simply take a monthly payment halfway between the whole-number APR payments. For example, the payment for 48 months at 9.5 percent is $25.12 ($25.36 − $24.88 = $0.48; $0.48/2 = $0.24; $0.24 + $24.88 = $25.12).

minimum payment warning box

The box on credit card statements must show how long it would take to pay off the card's balance by making only the minimum payments, and how much you'd need to pay each month to clear the balance in 36 months.

ADVICE FROM A SEASONED PRO

Avoid the 30-Year Minimum Payment Trap

Do you currently have balances outstanding on your credit cards? If so, how long have you carried those balances? If you open an account in college and already have an unpaid balance of $2,500 upon your graduation, you may find that the balance owed will not drop below $2,500 for many years. This situation occurs when you continue to make purchases with the card but continue to pay only the amounts charged each month.

The CARD Act requires issuers to include a **minimum payment warning box** on credit card statements. That box must show how long it would take to pay off the card's balance by making only the minimum payments, and how much you'd need to pay each month to clear the balance in 36 months. The industry standard is now to calculate the minimum in one of two ways: (1) either 3 percent to 5 percent of the total balance due, or (2) all fees and interest due that month plus 1 percent of the principal amount owed. To avoid paying credit card charges for 6, 10 or even 30 years, which is near perpetual debt, you must make larger monthly repayments that go toward retiring your credit card balances much more quickly.

Jonathan J. Fox
Iowa State University, Ames, Iowa

7.5b Calculation of the Finance Charges and APR for Installment Loans

Interest accounts for the greatest portion of the finance charge. Three methods are used to calculate interest on installment and noninstallment credit: the declining-balance (sometimes called the simple-interest) method, the add-on interest method, and the discount method. The declining-balance method is widely used by credit unions to calculate interest on all loans, and it is always used for credit cards and home mortgages. The add-on method predominates on installment loans at banks, savings banks, and consumer finance companies when financing automobiles, furniture, electronics, and other credit requiring collateral. The following illustrates the calculation of the APR for installment loans using each of the three methods.

1. The Declining-Balance Method Is Fair to Both Lender and Borrower

declining-balance method

A method of calculating the annual percentage rate for installment loans where the interest assessed during each payment period (usually each month) is based on the current outstanding balance of the installment loan.

With the **declining-balance method,** the interest assessed during each payment period (usually each month) is based on the current outstanding balance of the installment loan. The lender initially calculates a schedule (such as that given in Table 7-3) to have the balance repaid in full after a certain number of months. The borrower may vary the rate of repayment by making payments larger than those scheduled or may repay the loan in full at any time.

As shown in Table 7-3, at the end of the first month, a **periodic interest rate** (the monthly rate applied to the outstanding balance of a loan) of 1½ percent (18 percent annually divided by 12 months) is applied to the beginning balance of $1,000, giving an interest charge of $15. Of the first monthly installment of $91.68, $15 goes toward the payment of interest and $76.68 ($91.68 − $15.00) goes toward payment of the principal.

For the second month, the outstanding balance is reduced to $923.32 ($1,000 − $76.68). Since the balance is $78.68 lower, the interest portion of the payment drops to $13.85 (0.015 × $923.32). Because the declining-balance method applies the periodic interest rate to the outstanding loan balance, the APR and the simple interest rate will differ only if fees (such as an application fee) boost the finance charge. (This method of paying off a loan, called "amortization," is also discussed in Chapter 9 when we examine home mortgage loans.) Note that declining-balance loans carry no prepayment penalties.

DO IT IN CLASS

Table 7-3

Declining Balance Method: Sample Repayment Schedule for $1,000 Principal Plus Interest (1½ Percent per Month)

Month	Outstanding Balance	Payment	Interest	Principal	Balance
1	$1,000.00	$91.68	$15.00	$76.68	$923.32
2	923.32	91.68	13.85	77.83	845.49
3	845.49	91.68	12.68	79.00	766.49
4	766.49	91.68	11.50	80.18	686.31
5	686.31	91.68	10.29	81.39	604.92
6	604.92	91.68	9.07	82.61	522.31
7	522.31	91.68	7.83	83.85	438.46
8	438.46	91.68	6.58	85.10	353.36
9	353.36	91.68	5.30	86.38	266.98
10	266.98	91.68	4.00	87.68	179.30
11	179.30	91.68	2.69	88.99	90.31
12	90.31	91.66	1.35	90.31	0

2. The Add-On Method Favors the Lender The add-on method is also widely used for computing interest on installment loans. With this method, the interest is calculated and added to the amount borrowed to determine the total amount to be repaid. Equation (7.1) is used to calculate the dollar amount of interest. Note that the interest rate used in this equation for the add-on method is an add-on rate and should not be confused with the APR.

With the **add-on interest method**, interest is calculated by applying an interest rate to the amount borrowed times the number of years. The add-on interest formula given in Equation (7.1) is used as follows:

$$I = PRT \qquad (7.1)*$$

where

I = Interest or finance charges
P = Principal amount borrowed
R = Rate of interest (simple, add-on, or discount rate)
T = Time of loan in years

For example, assume that Matthew Ferguson of Walnut, California borrows $2,000 for two years at 9 percent add-on interest to be repaid in monthly installments. Using Equation (7.1), his finance charge in dollars is $360 ($2,000 × 0.09 × 2). Adding the finance charge ($360) to the amount borrowed ($2,000) gives a total amount of $2,360 to be repaid. When this amount is divided by the total number of scheduled payments (24), we find that Matthew must make 24 monthly payments of $98.33.

Calculating the APR When the Add-On Method Is Used Add-on rates and APRs are not equivalent. This is because the add-on calculation assumes the original debt is owed for the entire period of the loan. But of course the debt does go down as the debt is repaid. In the example just given, Matthew does not have use of the total amount borrowed for the full two years. Equation (7.2) shows the *n*-ratio method of estimating the APR on her add-on loan.

$$
\begin{aligned}
\text{APR} &= \frac{Y(95P + 9)F}{12P(P + 1)(4D + F)} \qquad (7.2)* \\
&= \frac{(12)(95 \times 24 + 9)(360)}{12(24)(24 + 1)[(4 \times 2,000) + 360]} \\
&= \frac{(12)(2,289)(360)}{(288)(25)(8,360)} \\
&= \frac{9,888,480}{60,192,000} \\
&= 16.4\%
\end{aligned}
$$

Where

APR = Annual percentage rate
Y = Number of payments in one year
F = Finance charge in dollars (dollar cost of credit)
D = Debt (amount borrowed or proceeds)
P = Total number of scheduled payments

Using Equation (7.2), the APR is 16.4 percent. Note that the APR is approximately double the add-on rate because, on average, Matthew has use of only half of the borrowed money during the entire loan period.

The Rule of 78s Determines the Prepayment Penalty When an Add-On Loan Is Repaid Early Most installment loan contracts that use the add-on method include a **prepayment penalty**. This is an additional fee imposed by many loan agreements where a borrower pays off a loan early, before its scheduled pay-off date.

*Calculations involving Equation (7.1) and (7.2) can be found on the Garman/Forgue companion website.

---

add-on interest method
A method of calculating the annual percentage rate for installment loans where interest is calculated by applying an interest rate to the amount borrowed times the number of years.

DO IT IN CLASS

n-ratio method
A method of estimating the annual percentage rate for installment loans where it is an add-on loan.

prepayment penalty
An additional fee imposed by many loan agreements where a borrower pays off a loan early, before its scheduled pay-off date.

TURN BAD HABITS INTO GOOD ONES

Do You Do This?

Skim read your credit card billing statements

Pay with whatever card you pull out first from your wallet or purse

Make only the minimum payment on your credit card

Ignore the potential to earn rewards on your credit cards

Focus on the size of the monthly payment when you take out loans

Do This Instead!

Read each statement for completeness and accuracy

Avoid making purchases that you plan to pay off with a credit card on which you carry a balance

Set a date for paying off that card balance in full and make the payments required to meet your goal

Open an account that provides rewards and make day-to-day purchases paying balances in full when billed

Focus on the annual percentage rate and length of loan

NEVER EVER

1. *Fail to shop for the lowest APR on credit cards and consumer loans.*
2. *Regularly carry balances on credit card accounts.*
3. *Use a credit card rather than lower interest rate installment loans to make expensive purchases.*

rule of 78s (sum of the digits)
The most widely used method of calculating a prepayment penalty where the lender allocates the interest charge on a loan across its payment periods using the numerical values to the sum of all the digits of the periods.

DO IT IN CLASS

Prepayment penalties take into consideration the reality that borrowers should pay more in interest early in the loan period when they have the use of more money and increasingly less interest as the debt shrinks over time.

With an add-on method loan, discussed above, the interest is spread evenly across all payments rather than declining as the loan balance falls. If an add-on method loan is paid off early, the lender will use some penalty method to compensate for the lower interest component applied in the early months.

The **rule of 78s** (also called the **sum of the digits**) method is the most widely used method of calculating a prepayment penalty It is a technique of allocating the interest charge on a loan across its payment periods. Under the rule of 78s, periods are weighted by comparing their numerical values to the sum of all the digits of the periods. The weights are applied in reverse, applying large weights to early periods. Its name derives from the fact that, for a one-year loan, the numbers between 1 and 12 for each month add up to 78 ($12 + 11 + 10 + 9 + 8 + 7 + 6 + 5 + 4 + 3 + 2 + 1$). For a two-year loan, the numbers between 1 and 24 would be added, and so on for loans with longer time periods.

To illustrate the use of the rule of 78s method, consider the case of Devin Grigsby from Lincoln, Nebraska. He borrowed $500 for 12 months plus an additional $80 finance charge and is scheduled to pay equal monthly installments of $48.33 ($580 ÷ 12). Assume Devin wants to pay the loan off after only six months. He might assume—incorrectly—that he would owe only $250 more because after six months he had paid $250 (one-half) of the $500 borrowed and $40 (one-half) of the finance charge, for a total of $290 in payments ($48.33 × 6). Actually, Devin still owes $268.46, including a prepayment penalty of $18.46. To calculate this amount using the rule of 78s method, the lender adds together all of the numbers between 12 and 7 (12 for the first month, 11 for the second, and so on for six months): $12 + 11 + 10 + 9 + 8 + 7 = 57$. The lender assumes that during the first six months $58.46 [(57 ÷ 78) × $80]—not $40—of the finance charges was received from the $290 in payments Devin had made on the loan.* Consequently, only $231.54 ($290.00 − $58.46) was paid on the $500 borrowed, leaving $268.46 ($500.00 − $231.54) still owed, for a prepayment penalty of $18.46 ($268.46 − $250.00).

3. With the Discount Method, Interest Is Paid Up Front The **discount method** is used by creditors whereby the interest amount for an entire loan period (plus other charges, if any) is deducted from the principal at the time a loan is disbursed. The

---

*If the loan was paid off after one month, the amount of interest paid is assumed to be 12/78 of the $80 finance charge, or $12.31. For a loan paid in full after two months, the amount of interest paid is assumed to be 23/78 of the total (12/78 for month 1 plus 11/78 for month 2), or $23.59.

interest is then subtracted from the amount of the loan, and only the difference is given to the borrower. Thus, the interest is paid up front. The borrower then pays off the loan (the full principal amount) as arranged.

When this method is applied to our earlier example involving Matthew Ferguson, he would receive only $1,640 [$2,000 − ($2,000 × 2 × 9%)] at the beginning of the loan period. His monthly payment would be $83.33 ($2,000 ÷ 24). Using Equation (7.2), the APR would be 19.8 percent (the APR rises because only $1,640 is obtained while $2,000 is repaid).

CONCEPT CHECK 7.5

1. Explain how the interest is calculated on a consumer loan that uses the declining-balance method.
2. Summarize how interest is calculated on a consumer loan that uses the add-on method.
3. What is the effect of the rule of 78s when a borrower repays an add-on method loan early?
4. Explain how the interest is calculated on a consumer loan that uses the discount method.

WHAT DO YOU RECOMMEND *NOW*?

iStockphoto.com/serts

Now that you have read this chapter on credit cards and consumer loans, what would you recommend to Zachary Cochrane regarding:

1. His approach to using credit cards, including the number of cards he has?
2. Estimating the credit card interest charges he is paying each month?
3. How he might lower his interest expense each month?
4. Consolidating his credit card debts into one installment loan?

SUMMARY OF LEARNING OBJECTIVES RECAPPED

LO1 **Distinguish among credit cards and other types of open-end credit.**

Open-end credit is form of credit extended in advance of any transactions. A retailer or bank agrees to allow the consumer to make purchases and/or borrow up to a specified amount. Upon receiving a credit statement, the borrower may repay the balance in full or in installments. Bank credit cards are popular examples. They are issued by commercial banks and other financial institutions, such as MasterCard and Visa.

LO2 **Manage your credit cards wisely.**

Credit cards can be a positive tool in personal financial management but only when used appropriately. Understanding your credit statements is critical, especially the years to pay off the balance if you pay only the minimum payment due. Computing the finance charge is fairly simple. There is a limit on the liability for lost or stolen credit cards. Errors on statements may be corrected too.

LO3 **Distinguish among the sources of consumer installment loans.**

When you need a loan for a specific purpose you will want to shop around for the best deal and getting the lowest annual percentage rate (APR) on a loan is most important. Much of what we borrow for is financed through sales finance companies.

LO4 **Be familiar with the different types of installment loans.**

A closed-end credit arrangement is where the full amount owed must be paid back by the borrower by a set point in time. It could be a single-payment or installment loan. Loans can be secured or unsecured.

Loan clauses to be aware of are the deficiency payments clause and the recourse clause. Alternative lenders offer high-priced loans.

LO5 **Calculate the interest and annual percentage rate on consumer loans.**

Both the declining-balance and add-on methods are used to calculate the interest on installment loans, although the annual percentage rate (APR) formula gives the correct rate in all cases. With declining-balance loans, the dollar amount of interest incorporated in each monthly payment declines as the loan balance declines.

LET'S TALK ABOUT IT

1. **Learning More About Credit.** Most young adults form their opinions about credit and debt from what they see in their parents' experiences. How has your perception of carrying credit card debt, student loans, and other borrowing changed as a result of reading Chapters 6 and 7?

2. **What Type of Borrowing Might Be Best?** If you wanted to borrow money to study abroad for a semester and could pay it back within two years after returning, would you prefer a single-payment loan, an installment loan, or a cash advance on a credit card? Why?

3. **Are Rewards Cards a Good Idea?** Some credit cards offer rewards points or a cash back reward for all purchases

made on the card. Which rewards card would you prefer and why?

4. **The Declining-Balance Method.** If you were the borrower, how would you feel about the fact that interest costs are higher in the early months of a declining-balance loan than they are in the later months?

5. **The Rule of 78s.** Are prepayment penalties such as that applied with the rule of 78s justified? Why or why not?

6. **Mistakes in Credit Cards.** Given your experiences in using credit cards, what mistakes or errors have your made? Choose one and concisely share the story.

DO THE MATH

1. **Monthly Payments and Finance Charges or an Add-on Rate Loan.** Zachary Porter of Abilene, Texas, is contemplating borrowing $10,000 from his bank. The bank could use add-on rates of 6.5 percent for 3 years, 7 percent for 4 years, and 8 percent for 5 years. Use Equation 7.1 to calculate the finance charge and monthly payment for these three options.
DO IT IN CLASS
Page 221

2. **Monthly Payments and Finance Charges.** Kimberly Jensen of Storm Lake, Iowa, wants to buy some living room furniture for her new apartment. A local store offered credit at an APR of 16 percent, with a maximum term of four years. The furniture she wishes to purchase costs $4,800, with no down payment required. Using Table 7-2 or the *Garman/Forgue* companion website, make the following calculations:
DO IT IN CLASS
Page 220

   (a) What is the amount of the monthly payment if she borrowed for four years?

   (b) What are the total finance charges over that four year period?

   (c) How would the payment change if Kimberly reduced the loan term to three years?

   (d) What are the total finance charges over that three year period?

   (e) How would the payment change if she could afford a down payment of $500 with four years of financing?

   (f) What are the total finance charges over that four-year period given the $500 down payment?

3. **Average Daily Balance and Finance Charges.** Kayla Sampson, an antiques dealer from Mankato, Minnesota, received her monthly billing statement for April for her MasterCard account. The statement indicated that she had a beginning balance of $600, on day 5 she charged $150, on day 12 she charged $300, and on day 15 she made a $200 payment. Out of curiosity, Kayla wanted to confirm that the finance charge for the billing cycle was correct.
DO IT IN CLASS
Page 210

(a) What was Kayla's average daily balance for April without new purchases?

(b) What was her finance charge on the balance in part (a) if her APR is 19.2 percent?

(c) What was her average daily balance for April with new purchases?

(d) What was her finance charge on the balance in part (c) if her APR is 19.2 percent?

4. **Average Daily Balance.** Alexis Monroe, a biologist from Dyersburg, Tennessee, is curious about the accuracy of the interest charges shown on her most recent credit card billing statement, which appears as Figure 7-1 on page 208. Use the average daily balances provided to recalculate the interest charges, and compare the result with the amount shown on the statement.

5. **Comparing APRs.** James Sprater of Grand Junction, Colorado, has been shopping for a loan to buy a used car. He wants to borrow $18,000 for four or five years. James's credit union offers a declining-balance loan at 9.1 percent for 48 months, resulting in a monthly payment of $448.78. The credit union does not offer five-year auto loans for amounts less than $20,000, however. If James borrowed $18,000, this payment would strain his budget. A local bank offered current depositors a five-year loan at a 9.34 percent APR, with a monthly payment of $376.62. This credit would not be a declining-balance loan. Because James is not a depositor in the bank, he would also be charged a $25 credit check fee and a $45 application fee. James likes the lower payment but knows that the APR is the true cost of credit, so he decided to confirm the APRs for both loans before making his decision.

(a) What is the APR for the credit union loan?

(b) Use the n-ratio formula to confirm the APR on the bank loan as quoted for depositors.

(c) What is the add-on interest rate for the bank loan?

(d) What would be the true APR on the bank loan if James did not open an account to avoid the credit check and application fees?

6. **Rule of 78s.** Miguel Perez of Pamona, California, obtained a two-year installment loan for $1,500 to buy a television set eight months ago. The loan had a 12.6 percent APR and a finance charge of $204.72. His monthly payment is $71.03. Miguel has made eight monthly payments and now wants to pay off the remainder of the loan. The lender will use the rule of 78s method to calculate a prepayment penalty.

(a) How much will Miguel need to give the lender to pay off the loan?

(b) What is the dollar amount of the prepayment penalty on this loan?

DO IT IN CLASS
Page 222

FINANCIAL PLANNING CASES

CASE 1

The Johnsons' Credit Questions

They are considering trading their car in for a newer used vehicle so that Harry can have dependable transportation for commuting to work. The couple still owes $5,130 to the credit union for their current car, or $285 per month for the remaining 18 months of the 48-month loan. The trade-in value of this car plus $1,000 that Harry earned from a freelance interior design job should allow the couple to pay off the auto loan and leave $1,250 for a down payment on the newer car. The Johnsons have agreed on a sales price for the newer car of $21,000.

(a) Make recommendations to Harry and Belinda regarding where to seek financing and what APR to expect.

(b) Using the *Garman/Forgue* companion website or the information in Table 7-2, calculate the monthly payment for a loan period of three, four, five, and six years at 6 percent APR. Describe the relationship between the loan period and the payment amount.

(c) Harry and Belinda have a cash-flow deficit projected for several months this year (see Table 3-6 and Table 3-7 on pages 97–98). Suggest how, when, and where they might finance the shortages by borrowing.

CASE 2

Victor and Maria Have a Billing Dispute

Maria Hernandez was reviewing her recent bank credit card account statement when she found two charges that she and Victor could not have made. The charges were for rental of a hotel room and purchase of a meal on the same day in a distant city. These charges totaled $219.49 out of the couple's $367.89 balance for the month.

(a) What payment should Maria make on the account?

(b) How should she notify her credit card issuer about the unauthorized use?

(c) Once the matter is resolved, what should Maria do to ensure that her credit history is not negatively affected by this error?

CASE 3

Julia Price Thinks About Her Use of Credit Cards

Julia has been thinking about how she uses credit cards. She has two bank cards and three store cards. The APRs on the cards range from 10.5 to 24.9 percent, with the store cards being among the highest. She uses the cards often and picks whatever card she comes to first in her wallet. Most months she pays the balance off in full. However, sometimes she is unable to pay the balance on one or more of the cards, and so she only pays the minimum balance. Julia feels she is doing her best on managing her cards but wants to do better. She is thinking about using just one of her bank cards for any purchases that she thinks she will be unable to pay at the end of the month. Offer your opinions about her thinking.

CASE 4

A Delayed Report of a Stolen Credit Card

Jia Li Sun, of Shreveport, Louisiana, took her sister-in-law Ah-Iam Johnson out for an expensive lunch. When it came for the time to pay the bill, Jia Li noticed that her Visa credit card was missing, so she paid the bill with her MasterCard. While driving home, Jia Li remembered that she had last used the Visa card about a week earlier. She became concerned that a sales clerk or someone else could have taken it and might be fraudulently charging purchases on her card.

(a) Summarize Jia Li's legal rights in this situation.

(b) Discuss the likelihood that Jia Li must pay Visa for any illegal charges to the account.

DO IT IN CLASS
Page 211

CASE 5

Clauses in a Car Purchase Contract

Lauren Rowland is a dentist in Hebron, Kentucky, who recently entered into a contract to buy a new automobile. After signing to finance $38,000, she hurriedly left the office of the sales finance company with her copy of the contract. Later that evening, Lauren read the contract and noticed several clauses—an acceleration, a deficiency payments, a recourse, and a rule of 78s. When she signed the contract, Lauren was told these standard clauses should not concern her.

(a) Should Lauren be concerned about these clauses? Why or why not?

(b) Considering the rule of 78s clause, what will happen if Lauren pays off the loan before the regular due date?

(c) If Lauren had financed the $38,000 for four years at 6 percent APR, what would her monthly payment be, using the information in Table 7-2 or on the *Garman/Forgue* companion website?

BE YOUR OWN PERSONAL FINANCIAL MANAGER

1. **List Your Credit Card Accounts.** Complete Worksheet 28: My Credit Card Inventory from "My Personal Financial Planner," which asks you to make an inventory of your credit cards including the name of the card (Visa, Discover, etc.); issuer; account number; the current APRs for purchases, balance transfers, and cash advances; outstanding balance, if any; usual due dates; and phone numbers to use if the card is lost/stolen or there is a billing error.

   My Personal Financial Planner

2. **Shop for a New Credit Card.** Complete Worksheet 29: Comparing My Credit Card Offers from "My Personal Financial Planner," which asks you to shop for a new credit card from two different sources. If you already have a credit card, include the information on that card in the third column in the worksheet.

   My Personal Financial Planner

   Determine whether your current card is the best of the three, or if you have no current card, choose among the two you have researched.

3. **Monitor Your Credit Card Statements.** Review your most recent credit card statements for accuracy. List the steps you would take if you found an error in the statement

4. **Compare Hypothetical Vehicle Loans.** Assume you have decided to buy a cheap used car by borrowing $6,000 and you have offers for loans at 6, 8, and 10 percent and each can be for 3, 4, or 5 years. Complete Worksheet 30: Monthly Installment Loan Payment Calculator from "My Personal Financial Planner" to determine the monthly payment for each of the six loan arrangements. Which loan is most attractive to you and why?

   My Personal Financial Planner

ON THE NET

Go to the Web pages indicated to complete these exercises.

1. **Review Current Market Interest Rates.** Visit the website for Bankrate.com at www.bankrate.com/credit-cards/low-interest-cards.aspx, where you will find information on bank credit card interest rates around the United States. View the information for the lenders. How does the information compare with the interest rates charged on your own credit card account(s)?

2. **Explore the Impact of Varying Interest Rates and Time Periods on a Loan Payment Amount.** Visit the website for Interest.com at www.interest.com/auto/calculators/auto-loan-calculator. There you will find an auto loan calculator that determines the monthly payment for any declining-balance loan given a specified time period, interest rate, and loan amount. Assume you wish to borrow $32,000 to buy a car. Vary the time period and interest rate of the loan to see how these variations affect your monthly payment.

3. **How Long Will It Take to Pay Off Your Credit Card?** Visit the Bankrate.com website at www.bankrate.com and under "credit cards" click on "Calculators" to find a calculator that will tell you how long it will take to pay off your balances given various monthly payment amounts.

4. **Personal Loans.** Visit LendingTree.org at www.lendingtree.com to compare lending rates for various loans. Compare the rates of personal loans with credit cards.

5. **Debt Free.** Go to CNNMoney at money.cnn.com/calculator/pf/debt-free to input data that will help you determine when you will be debt free. If appropriate, add more debt and try different numbers.

ACTION INVOLVEMENT PROJECTS

1. **Comparing Credit Card Offers.** Select two local retailers, a local bank, and a local credit card and request credit card applications from all four. Compare the applications for the types of information they require. Compare the APRs offered among the cards and others that you may already hold. Make a table that summarizes your findings and write some brief reactions to what you found.

2. **Credit Card Repayment Patterns.** Survey three of your friends about their patterns of using their credit card accounts including, if any, their choice to make the minimum payment rather than pay off the balance in full each month. Compare what they do to your own pattern, and write a summary of your findings.

3. **Credit Card Billing Errors.** Survey three of your friends about experiences they have had concerning a billing error on their credit cards. Compare the steps they took to resolve the error(s) with those recommended in this chapter. Write a summary of your findings.

4. **Installment Loan Interest Methods.** Visit a bank and a credit union in your community. Tell them that you are considering taking out a loan to purchase a vehicle. Inquire whether they offer declining-balance or add-on method loans and which approach they would recommend. Compare the responses to the information provided in this chapter, and write a summary of your findings.

8 Vehicle and Other Major Purchases

YOU MUST BE KIDDING, RIGHT?

When Dora Marquez graduated from college three years ago, she really wanted a fully equipped Honda Accord. Her monthly payment would be about $350 per month, about $70 more than she could afford. To help Dora meet her budget, the dealer suggested that she lease the vehicle and offered a 42-month lease option at $270 per month with a driving maximum of 12,000 miles per year. The contract had a $0.30 per mile fee at the end of the lease for any excess mileage. Now, with six more months left on her lease, Dora is already 1,500 miles over the 42,000 (3.5 × 12,000) mileage limit in her contract. What is Dora's best option at this point?

A. Turn back the vehicle now and pay the $450 (1,500 × $0.30) for excess mileage.

B. Try to cut back on her driving to minimize her excess mileage fee, which could be higher than $2,500 if she keeps driving at the same rate as she has been.

C. Stop driving the car and pay $450 for excess mileage when she turns it back at the end of the lease.

D. Continue driving the vehicle and buy it at the end of the lease by paying the residual value agreed upon when she entered into the contract.

The answer is D. None of the other options is financially practical. Dora learned a hard lesson. Leases may have a lower monthly payment but have hidden costs that often are not known until the very end of the contract!

Learning Objectives

After reading this chapter, you should be able to:

1 Explain the first three steps in the planned buying process that occur prior to interacting with sellers.

2 Describe the process of comparison shopping.

3 Negotiate successfully when making major purchases.

4 Use effective complaint procedures—when appropriate.

FotoYakov/Shutterstock.com

WHAT DO YOU RECOMMEND?

David and Lisa Cosgrove are in their mid-40s and have one child. Their daughter, Alyssa, drives a three-year-old Toyota Camry to community college every day. Last week as Alyssa was pulling into the driveway at home her foot slipped off the brake and she crashed into the rear of her mother's pickup truck, which suffered very little damage perhaps because it has a very high rear bumper. Alyssa's car was a mess. The Cosgroves received an insurance settlement of $14,000 on Alyssa's car, although the loan payoff amount was $16,800. The couple wants to obtain a replacement vehicle that is similar to the one destroyed.

Barry Austin Photography/Getty Images

What do you recommend to David and Lisa on automobiles and other major purchases regarding:

1. How to search for a vehicle to replace Alyssa's?

2. Whether to replace Alyssa's vehicle with a new or used vehicle?

3. Whether to lease or buy a vehicle?

4. How to decide between a rebate and a special low APR financing opportunity if they decide to purchase a new vehicle for Alyssa?

5. How to negotiate with the sellers of the vehicles?

TO-DO SOON

Do the following to begin to achieve financial success:

1. *When shopping for major purchases obtain price information from three sources and negotiate prices and financing terms.*

2. *Fit credit repayments for big-ticket items into your budget before making any purchase decisions.*

3. *When planning to buy a vehicle check repair ratings history in the most recent April issue of Consumer Reports magazine.*

4. *Consider purchasing a late-model used vehicle rather than a new one.*

5. *Seek redress when dissatisfied with purchases or services.*

big-ticket items

Products that have a high selling price that are sometimes called durable goods, which last a relatively long time and provide utility to the user.

Learning Objective 1

Explain the first three steps in the planned buying process that occur prior to interacting with sellers.

need

Item thought to be necessary.

want

Item not necessary but desired.

Planned buying entails thinking about the details of a purchase from the initial desire to buy to your satisfaction after the purchase. You should use planned buying principles any time, but they are especially important when you are buying a vehicle or making other major purchases. You can save thousands of dollars when buying a car and hundreds of dollars when purchasing furniture or a television. You just need to learn how to do it.

Buying a vehicle is probably the first large expenditure that most people make in their lives. You can do it wrong and mess up your personal finances for many years. Or you can do it right and be very satisfied with your purchase.

Only 3 in 4 people age 20 to 24 have a driver's license. So, the remaining one-quarter of young adults likely will not be buying a new vehicle.

You have lots to compare when shopping for a new vehicle. Research shows that good consumer decision making—on large as well as small purchases—results in lower overall spending and more success in long-term financial planning. Your goal when shopping for a vehicle is to avoid making a poor purchasing decision.

Recall that the only way you can achieve long-term financial success is to not spend all of your income. Some money must be saved and invested. Overspending and too much debt are the primary causes of financial failure. These problems can be avoided or minimized when you buy **big-ticket items** using the planned buying process. These are products that have a high selling price that are sometimes called durable goods. They last a relatively long time and provide utility to the user.

The seven distinct steps that lead you through the planned buying process are illustrated in Figure 8-1. Steps 1, 2, and 3 occur before you interact with sellers: prioritizing wants, preshopping research, and fitting a purchase into your budget. Comparison shopping and other interactions with sellers comprise the 4th step in the buying process. Steps 5 and 6—negotiating and making the decision—follow. The 7th and final step—evaluation of the decision—is taken after making the purchase. After reading this chapter, you will understand enough about the planned buying process to save money when buying expensive goods while still meeting your needs and many of your wants.

8.1 BEFORE YOU BUY DO YOUR HOMEWORK

Let's look now at the first three steps in planned buying, all of which should occur before you actually interact with sellers. They are, in a sense, the homework you do when preparing to buy.

8.1a Prioritize Your Wants

A **need** is something thought to be a necessity. A **want** is unnecessary but desired. In truth, very few needs exist. Yet in everyday language, people talk too often of "needing" certain things. Calling something a need makes it no longer open to careful consideration. Instead, consider all purchase options to be wants.

Of course, some wants are more important than others. That is why you must prioritize your wants and consider the benefits and costs of each want. Costs should include opportunity costs as measured by some other want or goal that will become less attainable if a given want is satisfied. For example, buying a car with a retractable sunroof might mean that you cannot afford to purchase one with a remote start feature.

Setting priorities becomes difficult when a decision is complex such as when buying a car or home. Consider the case of Haley Wilson, a physical therapist from Baton Rouge, Louisiana. Haley has been late to work a few times in the past three months because her

Figure 8-1 The Steps in Planned Buying

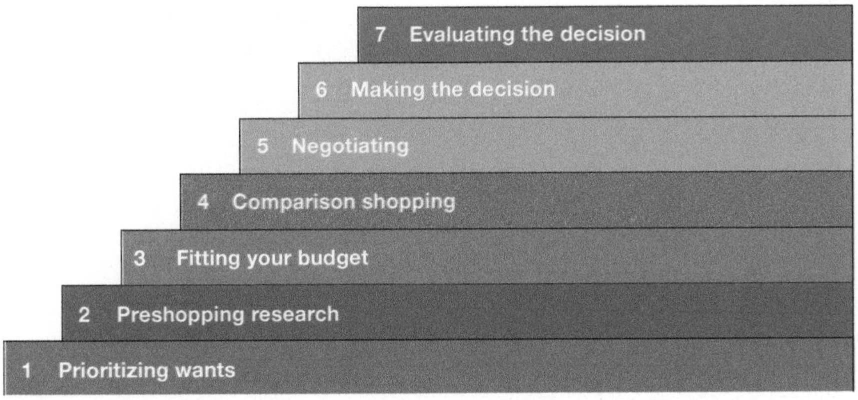

7 Evaluating the decision
6 Making the decision
5 Negotiating
4 Comparison shopping
3 Fitting your budget
2 Preshopping research
1 Prioritizing wants

12-year-old car has been having too many mechanical problems. Haley wants to avoid being late. But how? Should she buy a new car or a used car, lease a new car, repair her current car, or take the bus to work? After considering these options, Haley decided to buy a new car. Now she must determine which features are of high or low priority. To do so, Haley developed the worksheet shown in Figure 8-2. Such a worksheet makes it easier to formalize her wants.

8.1b Conduct Preshopping Research

Smart shoppers learn as much as they can about a product or service before buying. This process starts with **preshopping research**—gathering information before actually beginning to interact with sellers. Manufacturers, sellers, and service providers are all important sources of information about products and services during preshopping research. Two other sources are friends and consumer information in print and on the Internet.

preshopping research
Gathering information before actually beginning to interact with sellers.

When buying vehicles you should research vehicle reviews in *Consumer Reports,* which is the only magazine that objectively tests and reports on numerous product categories. Monthly issues of *Consumer Reports* generally provide a two- to five-page narrative analyzing the products and summarizing the information in chart form. *Consumer Reports Buying Guide,* which is published every December, lists facts and figures for autos and other kinds of products. Each year, the April issue of *Consumer Reports* is devoted entirely to the purchase of automobiles. All this and more can be found at www.ConsumerReports.org.

Know the Price You Should Expect to Pay Advertising is often a key source of information about prices. You can also obtain price information through catalogs, on the telephone, and over the Internet. This situation differs for big-ticket items. While the prices of furniture, appliances, and vehicles may be advertised, that price is almost never the lowest price you can expect to pay. This is because sellers of big-ticket items typically have the authority to negotiate an even lower price, if necessary, to make a sale. You should have a clear understanding what price to expect to pay before going out to shop. Otherwise, you risk buying at a price higher than necessary.

Break the Dealer's Code on New Vehicle Prices You will see two prices when you walk into a vehicle dealer's showroom: (1) manufacturer's suggested retail price, and (2) dealer invoice price. Both are artificial numbers. Thus your negotiation effort should not be to get close to the dealer invoice price but to a lower *real price* you may decide to pay.

Figure 8-2   **Priority Worksheet (for Haley Wilson)**

VEHICLE FEATURE	PRIORITY LEVEL		
	Low	Medium	High
Adaptive front lighting		✔	
Adaptive cruise control		✔	
Air conditioning	✔		
Aluminum wheels		✔	
Automatic transmission	✔		
Backing-up cross-path monitoring		✔	
Blind-spot monitoring			✔
Self-drive autobrake	✔		
Forward-collision warning system		✔	
4-wheel ABS		✔	
4-wheel drive		✔	
Lane departure warning			✔
Leather seats	✔		
Infotainment system		✔	
Pedestrian detection			✔
Pass-through rear seat		✔	
Satellite radio	✔		
Seat belt tightening when braking		✔	
Android Auto/Car Play			✔

manufacturer's suggested retail price (MSRP)

The retail price set by the manufacturer and posted on the federally required side window sticker.

dealer invoice price (base invoice price)

The amount the automaker charges the dealership for new vehicles at the time the dealer buys them; it does not reflect some discounts that the dealer gets.

The **manufacturer's suggested retail price (MSRP)** is the retail price set by the manufacturer and posted on the federally required side window sticker. The dealership wants you to pay full MSRP plus any miscellaneous charges.

The **dealer invoice price** (or **base invoice price**) is the amount the automaker charges the dealership for new vehicles at the time the dealer buys them, and it does not reflect some discounts that the dealer gets. The invoice price typically has some additional charges tacked on by the dealer, which are attempts to generate additional revenue.

Web Sources Are Best for Price Information on Vehicles   The average price for new cars and trucks is over $35,000. Smart buyers can research the average retail and wholesale prices on new and used vehicles by visiting the websites for Edmunds (www.edmunds.com), Kelley Blue Book (www.kbb.com), or the National Automobile Dealers Association (www.nadaguides.com).

Know the Value of Your Trade-in Vehicle   When buying vehicles, it is common but not always advantageous, to trade in an older vehicle when buying a new one. Auto buyers should know the true value of any vehicle they will trade in. Using the websites mentioned earlier, you may find the likely trade-in value of your vehicle (the wholesale price) as well as the amount you could sell it for yourself (the retail price). Armed with this information, you can more effectively negotiate a good trade-in allowance on your existing vehicle with a dealer. If you don't get a good offer on your vehicle from the dealer, shop at another dealer or consider selling it yourself.

Assess Environmental Impact Many products such as vehicles, electronic equipment, and household appliances have an impact on the environment. This factor is part of many people's purchase decisions and relevant information is often available. For example, window stickers on new vehicles include both estimated annual fuel costs and the vehicle's overall environmental impact. The labels also compare vehicles across classes so potential buyers can make more informed decisions. See the app carboncounter.com that compares 125 vehicles to help you save emissions when buying a car.

8.1c Fit Your Budget to the Purchase

When considering a big-ticket item everyone wonders, "Can I afford it?" An unaffordable cash purchase can wreck your budget for one or two months. However, the negative effects of an ill-advised credit or lease contract may last for many years.

Know What You Can Afford Many big-ticket items require the use of credit resulting in an immediate impact on one's budget for months or years into the future. To gauge this impact, consider how Haley Wilson (see Table 8-1) might fit a new car into her budget. She estimates that the dealer invoice price of the car she wants will be about $28,000. This price does not include her highest-priority wants. These options will likely add about $3,300 more to the dealer invoice price: self-drive control, $700; backing-up autobraking, $300; forward-collision braking system, $300; capless fuel filler, $300; power windows, $600; top-level sound system, $800; and satellite ratio, $300. Buying a car with these features will run the cost up to $31,300 ($28,000 + $3,300 for the options). She expects to use $3,500 from her savings account as a down payment, receive $2,000 for trading in her old car, and borrow the remaining amount.

The actual price she will pay for the car will depend on her ability to negotiate the final price down from the dealer invoice price. From her preshopping research, Haley knows that the final agreed upon price should be about 12 percent less than the dealer invoice price. Haley figures she should be able to negotiate the price of the purchase down by at least 10 percent from $31,300 to $28,170 ($31,300 − $3,130 [$31,300 × 0.10]).

The final cost Haley will pay depends on (1) the price she actually pays for the car, (2) the amount of the down payment, (3) the time period for payback of the loan, (4) the amount she receives in trade for her old car, and (5) the interest rate on the vehicle loan. Assuming a car price of $28,170 and another $830 for sales tax and title fees to register the vehicle, Haley will need to finance about $29,000 ($28,170 + $830). The monthly payment over 48 months for a 5 percent loan could be about $668 a month (from Table 7-1 on page 214 [$23.03 × 29]).

DO IT IN CLASS

Fit the Payment into a Monthly Budget The next challenge is to determine if a possible vehicle payment is truly affordable. Haley tried to fit the $668 car payment into her budget as shown in Table 8-1.

Table 8-1 shows Haley's monthly budget. She started with the fact that her take-home pay of $2,440 is totally committed, including $200 in monthly savings. So she juggled the numbers to see if she could finance a new car and found she could only find $330. That's far short of the $668 needed for a monthly payment. By taking out a longer, 60-month 5 percent loan, she could reduce her payments to about $547 per month (29 × $18.87 from Table 7-2 on page 219). Haley's choices are to make more cutbacks in her budget, work overtime, get a part-time job, or buy a less expensive vehicle.

ConsumerReports' | Subscribe to Consumer Reports

Get instant access to thousands of expert Reviews and Ratings.

New Subscribers

- $30.00
  ConsumerReports.org yearly

- $6.95
  ConsumerReports.org monthly

I accept the terms of the User Agreement and would like to subscribe with the convenience of automatic renewal.

Next

Current Subscribers

Active Consumer Reports Magazine subscribers click here for magazine subscriber rate.

Source: Consumer Reports

Time invested in preshopping research pays off in better purchase decisions.

Table 8-1	Fitting a Vehicle Payment into a Monthly Budget (Haley Wilson's $3,440 Disposable Income)		

	Prior Budget	Possible Cutbacks	New Budget
Food	$ 350	$–30	$ 320
Clothing/laundry	120	–50	70
Vehicle maintenance/repairs/tires	80	–30	50
Auto insurance	80		80
Gasoline	160	–20	140
Housing	1,100		1,100
Utilities	150		150
Telephone	70		70
Student loans	400		400
Entertainment	150	–50	100
Gifts	50	–10	40
Church and charity	160		60
Personal care	170	–20	150
Savings	300	–100	200
Miscellaneous	100	–20	80
TOTAL	**$3,440**	**$ 330**	**$3,110**
Car payment			668
TOTAL WITH CAR PAYMENT			**$3,778**

Alternatively, Haley could finance the car over more months. One quarter of new vehicles sold today are financed for more than six years. The average new car loan is $31,000 with a monthly payment of $530. Although paying over more months lowers

ADVICE FROM A SEASONED PRO

Insurance and Maintenance Costs on Vehicles

Maintenance costs for a new vehicle will be lower than for a comparable model 5- or 10-year-old car. This is because repairs on older vehicles can be very expensive as components wear out with age and usage. New cars often have good warranty coverage. In addition, operating costs, such as fuel, will typically be lower on a new vehicle than on a comparable model but older car that gets worse mileage. All of this favors driving a newer car.

However, insurance expenses will typically be lower for the older car. While today's cars are safer and more efficient, collision repair costs are typically higher. Repairing new technology that is damaged in an accident can be very expensive. On an older car, used and/or non-original-manufacturer parts are often used, further reducing repair costs. New cars are designed to crush in an accident to protect the driver, so more extensive repairs are often needed.

Gerson M. Goldberg
Northeastern University, Boston, Massachusetts

ADVICE FROM A SEASONED PRO

How Many Hours of Work Will This Cost?

When buying a new vehicle, smartphone, computer, television, or any big-ticket item, divide the cost of the item by your hourly take- home pay. For example, if you divide the cost of a $360 television by $15 take- home pay ($22 hourly minus taxes), that tells you that you must work 24 hours to pay for it.

Lori Lothringer
Metropolitan Community College, La Vista, Nebraska

the monthly payment, it extends the loan for a long time (perhaps longer than you want to drive the vehicle), and it costs a lot more in total interest. Perhaps she might qualify for a lower interest rate, maybe 3½ percent, at the new car dealer. Then again, Haley could forget the new car entirely and look for a used vehicle that is affordable.

CONCEPT CHECK 8.1

1. What is planned buying?
2. Distinguish between *needs* and *wants*, and explain why it may be better to act as if no needs exist.
3. When shopping for a vehicle what are three things you need to know about when conducting preshopping research?
4. Summarize the process to determine whether you can afford a particular purchase.

8.2 COMPARISON SHOP TO FIND THE BEST BUY

Comparison shopping is the process of comparing products or services to find the best buy. A **best buy** is a product or service that, in the buyer's opinion, represents acceptable quality at a fair or low price for that level of quality. Purchasing the product with the lowest price does not necessarily ensure a best buy because quality and features count, too.

comparison shopping
Process of comparing products or services to find the best buy.

best buy
Product or service that, in the buyer's opinion, represents acceptable quality at a fair or low price for that quality level.

8.2a Comparison Shop for a Vehicle and Think Carefully

Buyers today have more choices than ever before. Electric? Gas? Hybrid? Diesel? Sedan? Coupe? SUV? Pickup? The Internet is a superlative source of information. Begin by checking out ConsumerReports.com, Kiplinger.com, and Edmunds.com. Then go to the vehicle companies themselves, such as Toyota.com, Ford.com, and Honda.com.

Comparison Shop Surveys show that vehicle mileage, reliability, maintenance costs, and safety are all quite important. So read about the items that are of most significance to you. Also think about the options you might want. Consider your likes and dislikes, and their costs. Basically you want to match up your needs and wants with the possibilities. The vehicle must suit your needs and your budget.

Buying a used vehicle is also a possibility. Besides autos there are many products that are worthwhile purchasing used, such as fitness and sporting equipment, electronics, tools, furniture, baby gear, and jewelry. If appropriate, check out eBay, Craig's List,

Amazon, Goodwill, Salvation Army, consignment shops, newspaper ads, pawnshops, and garage sales.

There is no need to hurry the decision. You want to avoid making an **impulse purchase**, an unplanned decision to *buy* a product or service made just before a purchase. You need to carefully identify the best alternatives before making the final decision.

Thinking is important Every buying decision involves a trade-off between spending now versus saving for the future. Buying a vehicle on credit also means that there is the additional cost of interest to pay for as well as making the monthly payments over the coming years.

Specifically, spending on something expensive, like a vehicle, means not spending on something else, like saving to purchase a home or investing for retirement. You must be confident that the vehicle purchase and its accompanying debt payments are not going to make it difficult to achieve your overall financial goals.

The question to ask is "Does the purchase fit within your total financial plans?" If not, then you need to reevaluate whether or not to include the purchase in your financial goals. Experts say that the best way to buy vehicles with the lowest overall cost is to buy late-model used vehicles and drive them for ten or more years or for 200,000 or more miles.

The average vehicle on the road today is 12 years old (16 years for trucks) but you can buy one that is nearly new, just 2 or 3 years old. That choice can save you 40 to 50 percent off the price of a new vehicle.

Seventy percent of new car buyers pay less than $30,000; 42 percent pay less than $20,000. After thinking about the alternatives available and the costs many college graduates choose to purchase a "nearly new" used vehicle rather than a new one. Such a purchase decision, when it is consistent with one's financial plans, can save thousands of dollars and free up money to allocate for other purposes.

ADVICE FROM A SEASONED PRO

Make a List for Every Important Decision

When making important decisions, you want to be level-headed and make the "right" decision. However, what is the right decision? Important decisions such as financing a vehicle or a home can either lead to investment savings to be proud of or daunting buyer's remorse.

Begin by making a list of what you are looking for and explore your options. Be specific. Realize that emotions and persuasive people play a key role in your decision-making. You would do well to try to remove some of those heightened feelings, and stay with the facts.

Also, take your original list and weigh the "pros" and "cons." Make sure to keep a keen eye to both sides

and how you will be affected in both the short and long term.

For instance, while an existing 15-year mortgage can save tens of thousands compared to the traditional 30-year; this choice might cause sleepless nights when higher monthly payments are combined with unforeseen events such as a job loss or death in the family.

Don't complicate the process. Understand your own comfort zone, and make a balanced decision. Then compare what you find with exactly what you want in a vehicle, an apartment or a significant other. Try this process. Stick to it and take pride. A sound plan will work for you.

Bryan Grullón
Polk State College, Lakeland, Florida

8.2b   Comparison Shop for a Safe Vehicle

Here is a list of criteria to use when comparison shopping on how to pick the safest vehicle:

Vehicle size and weight. Smaller, lighter vehicles offer less protection than larger, heavier ones. People in lighter vehicles experience higher crash forces when struck by heavier vehicles.

Forward-collision warning (FCW). Alert you if you get too close to a car in front, and autobrake systems brake if you do not respond in time.

Automatic Emergency Braking (AEB). Sense a potential collision and brakes if you do not.

V2Vcrash-avoidance system. Since 4 out of 5 five accidents are due to driver mistakes, the industry invented V2V, which is short for vehicle-to-vehicle system, which allows automobiles to "talk" to each other and avoid accidents.

Extra airbags. Look for as many airbags as possible. Most new vehicles have six airbags (two front, two front side, and two head-curtain airbags). Knee airbags and back-seat side airbags are becoming popular.

Stability control. These systems use data such as steering-wheel position and yaw and roll rates to detect a skid and then use anti-lock braking and traction-control systems for prevention and recovery.

Adaptive cruise control (ACC). Automatically adjusts vehicle speed to maintain a safe distance from the vehicle in front on you.

Blind-spot warning. Detects and warns of vehicles you cannot see in blind spots to the left and right.

Backup visibility. Backup cameras provide a substantial field of vision.

Automatic high beams. Headlights shift direction as you steer to help improve visibility at night as conditions warrant.

Lane departure warning (LDW). Lets the driver know if the vehicle goes over the line; sometimes the vehicle automatically corrects,

Pothole-Detection Technology. The vehicle's computer detects potholes and immediately adjusts the shock absorbers to keep the tire from dropping too far into the depression.

Parking-assist system. Alerts the driver to how close bumpers, poles, curbs, walls, and shrubbery are when parking.

Self-driving cars. The National Highway Traffic Safety Administration is seeking unified national regulations for states to regulate all self-driving vehicles.

Safety Tests. The National Highway Traffic Safety Administration (NHTSA) and the Insurance Institute for Highway Safety (IIHS) conduct frontal, side, and rollover tests. NHTSA's safest models are those with five-star ratings. At IIHS, the safest models are listed in its yearly "Top Safety Picks."

Recalls on used vehicles. When buying a used vehicle, visit SaferCar.gov to see whether the vehicle has been recalled. If so, confirm that the repairs have been made to the car you are considering. Dealers are required to fix for free vehicles recalled for safety reasons.

8.2c   Comparison Shop by Window Shopping

When you are ready go **window shopping** at vehicle dealers. This is the activity of looking at the goods displayed in shop windows, especially without intending to buy anything. Remember that when window shopping leave your credit and debit cards and checkbook at home because you do not want to be talked into buying until you are fully ready. You next need information on financing options, leasing versus financing, and warranties.

NUMBERS ON

Data from a variety of sources suggest:

- The total number of new sold and leased cars and light trucks is normally 20 million annually.
- Top sellers in descending order are Ford F-Series, Chevrolet Silverado, Ram PU, Toyota Camry, Toyota Corolla, and Nissan Altima.
- Fifteen percent of vehicle owners replace their cars before they have 100,000 miles on the odometer; half replace when it has 100,000 to 250,000 miles; and one-quarter wait until it has been driven more than 250,000 miles.
- Over 260 million vehicles are on the road today, and the average age is 12 years.

- Forty million used vehicles change hands every year.
- Number of vehicles sold each year with false odometer readings: 450,000.
- Over the years the number of fatal automobile accidents decreased from more than 53,000 40 years ago to 36,000 today due to government regulations requiring safer highways and vehicles.
- People are 7 times more likely to die in a vehicle accident than on an airplane.
- Likelihood of fatalities in car crashes: 63% drivers versus 18% passsengers.

8.2d Comparison Shop for Financing

You are probably going to need a loan or lease to drive away in a new vehicle. This commits a large portion of your future income over a number of years. And this will have dramatic impact on your personal finances.

The lowest payment does not mean the best credit plan. Better credit terms are frequently available at lenders not associated with sellers, such as your credit union or a bank that can lend money to make purchases for vehicles, household appliances and other big-ticket items. Also check interest rates on websites such as www.bankrate.com or www.interest.com.

Avoid Long-term Borrowing Beware of taking out a longer loan on a vehicle purchase, such as for five, six, or even more years, because the value of your vehicle may be less than the amount you owe. This is known as being **upside down** due to negative equity.

upside down

A situation where the owner of a financed asset owes more than it is worth, thus creating negative equity.

You are stuck with the vehicle until you pay it off, unless you have enough in savings to make up the difference. If you default on the loan, have an accident, or sell the vehicle, you will have to come up with more money. Rolling the negative equity forward into financing of your next vehicle purchase means that the amount will be added to the price of the new car. Nearly one-third of car owners are currently under water as they owe more than their vehicles are worth. If you must finance a vehicle for five or more years, you really cannot afford to buy it. So, shop for a cheaper new model or a used vehicle.

What Is a Fair Interest Rate? A borrower with a high credit score who can get a one percentage point reduction in interest for a $30,000 loan over 48 months can save hundreds of dollars in interest paid over the life of the loan. Buyers should obtain multiple quotes from credit unions and banks. When shopping for a major purchase, ask your credit union or bank for a **loan preapproval** before you visit sellers. This preshopping step will let you know how much you can borrow and at what interest rate.

Avoiding High Interest Rate Auto Payments The car industry invented the concept of the **bump-up scam**. Auto dealers sometimes tell people that their credit score is not the best and, as a result, they have to pay a higher interest rate. Then the

ADVICE FROM A SEASONED PRO

Avoid Balloon Loans

A **balloon automobile loan** is one that requires a larger-than-usual one-time payment at the end of the term. This allows a borrower to repay only part of the principal of the loan over its term, reducing the monthly repayments in exchange for owing the lender a lump sum at the end of the loan term. However, as vehicle prices fall because of depreciation and/or excessive wear and tear, the odds of owner having positive equity in their vehicle also drops, and he/she may not be able to sell it for the price anticipated. Plus, a problem occurs when the balloon mortgage comes due and the borrower simply cannot afford the payment. When the final payment is due, perhaps when one still owes one, two, or even several thousand dollars, the borrower has five options:

1. *Hand over the cash sum stipulated in your agreement and keep the vehicle.*

2. *Return the vehicle to the lender to pay for the balloon payment (assuming its value satisfies the amount due).*

3. *Refinance with the lender or borrow from another source.*

4. *Sell the motor vehicle and pay the balloon payment with the proceeds (assuming the vehicle will sell for an amount that is high enough).*

5. *Trade the vehicle in on a replacement vehicle, and roll over the balloon amount due into another auto loan for the newer vehicle.*

Clearly, some of these options are not good. Thus buyers need to know what they are getting into it when they sign the dotted line for a balloon automobile loan.

Richard Koza and Jenn J. Dorwart
Chadron State College, Chadron, Nebraska

---

dealer bumps up the interest rate they have to pay to finance their car, truck, or SUV. Over the life of the loan, the extra interest paid costs hundreds or even thousands of dollars in added financing costs.

For example, if your credit is good, you may qualify for a loan with a 4 percent interest rate. But the dealership charges you 8 percent. Or maybe 12 percent. Or even more. The dealer gets a hidden kickback, or fee, from the lender based on the amount of interest you pay. The more you pay in interest, the more profit the dealer makes.

Don't put up with sellers telling that "we have to charge you a higher interest rate." Complain and, if necessary, shop elsewhere for better financing terms. You should know that paying too much every month for years and years will crowd out the amounts you could save to accomplish other financial goals.

Choose Between a Low Interest Rate and a Rebate Often a good source of loans for new vehicles is sales financing arranged through the dealer via the manufacturer. The interest rate on this credit is usually low when manufacturers or dealers want to generate additional sales volume.

Many sellers also offer rebates to encourage people to buy. With a **rebate,** the seller refunds a portion of the purchase price of the product either as a direct payment or a credit against the purchase (sometimes through a gift card). Vehicle manufacturers offer rebates of $1,000 to $5,000 to purchasers of new vehicles as a way to generate more sales volume or to help sell slow-selling models.

DID YOU KNOW

Subprime Lending Is Rising

Today **subprime loans** on vehicles make up 20 percent of all vehicle purchases. These are a type of loan approved for people with substandard credit scores or limited credit histories. Often their FICO scores are lower than 640. These loans are characterized by higher interest rates, poor quality collateral, and less favorable terms in order to compensate for higher credit risk.

This means the industry is making lots of loans to people who may have difficulty maintaining the repayment schedule, sometimes reflecting setbacks, such as unemployment, divorce, and medical emergencies. Subprime loans are characterized by much higher interest rates, poor quality collateral, and less favorable terms in order to compensate for higher credit risk.

RUN THE NUMBERS

Dealer Financing or Rebate?

Advertisements for new vehicles often offer low APRs for dealer-arranged loans. A cash rebate of $1,000 to $3,000 (or more) off the price of the car may be offered as an alternative to the low interest rate. If you intend to pay cash, then the cash rebate obviously represents the better deal. But which alternative is better when you can arrange your own financing?

To compare the two APRs accurately, you must add the opportunity cost of the forgone rebate to the finance charge of the dealer financing. The worksheet provides an example of this process. Suppose a dealer offers 2.9 percent financing for three years with a $1,269 finance charge. Alternatively,

you can receive a $3,000 rebate if you arrange your own financing. The price of the car before the rebate is $32,000. Assume you can make a $4,000 down payment and that you can get a 7 percent loan on your own. This worksheet can be found on the *Garman/Forgue* companion website, or you can find similar worksheet at www.bankrate.com/calculators/auto/car-rebates-calculator.aspx.

DO IT IN CLASS

The lower of the values obtained in steps 3 and 4 is the better deal. In this instance, the financing that you arranged on your own is more attractive. In fact, any loan you arrange that carries an APR lower than 12 percent compares favorably with the dealer-arranged financing in this case.

Step		Example	Your Figures
1.	Determine the dollar amount of the rebate.	$3,000	_____
2.	Add the rebate amount to the finance charge for the dealer financing (dollar cost of credit)	+$1,269	_____
3.	Use the formula from Chapter 7 (Equation [7.2] on page 221 and used here as Equation [8.1]) to calculate an adjusted APR for the dealer financing.		

$$APR = \frac{Y(95P + 9)F}{12P(P + 1)(4D + F)} \quad (8.1)$$

Where

APR = Annual percentage rate
Y = Number of payment periods in one **year**
F = **Finance** charge in dollars
D = **Debt** (amount borrowed)
P = total number of scheduled **payments**

$$APR = \frac{(12)[(95 \times 36) + 9]($3,000 + $1,269)}{12 \times 36(36 + 1)[(4 \times $28,000) + ($3,000 + $1,269)]} = 9.45\%$$

4.	Write in the APR that you arranged on your own.	7%	_____

In most cases, the buyer must choose between the rebate and a low APR loan offer also being offered by the manufacturer. Some people choose to borrow the full price elsewhere and receive the rebate in cash. In effect, this option means that they are borrowing more money than the vehicle actually costs. Plus, the buyers also lose out on the opportunity for the low APR offer.

The Run the Numbers worksheet above provides a way to calculate whether a dealer financing or a rebate is the better option. If you do decide to take the rebate on a new vehicle, you should apply the money to the down payment on the vehicle or pay extra on the first monthly payment on the loan. Rebates are common when purchasing products such as vehicles, cell phones, and computers. The most current details on manufacturers' rebates to both consumers and auto dealers can be found at Edmunds.com (www.Edmunds.com). Just type in "rebates" on the Internet for others.

8.2e   Comparison Shop Between Financing and Leasing

Leasing a new vehicle is an increasingly attractive option to people who are in the market for a car. About 30 percent of the new cars "sold" each year are actually leased. A person leasing a vehicle does not actually own the vehicle. With a **lease** on a vehicle or any other product, you are, in effect, renting the product while the ownership title remains with the lease grantor.

lease
Rental of a product while ownership title remains with the lease grantor.

The reason leasing is popular is people cannot afford the purchase of such an expensive product. You can't afford it! Can you pay $850 a month over three years to buy a vehicle or would you lease it for $550? Or, how about stretching out the payments. Can you pay a lease of $650 for four years or $450 for six years? Those who sell leases will offer you "a deal you can afford."

Pitfalls of Leasing to Avoid   There are a number of problems to avoid when leasing:

1. *Avoid paying money up front.* Consumers are usually asked to shell out several thousand dollars at the beginning of the term to get the lowest lease payment, but if the auto is totally wrecked or stolen the insurance company reimburses the leasing company in full not the consumer. So avoid paying any money up front.

2. *Avoid being upside down with gap insurance.* Because a vehicle depreciates quickly as it is driven off the lot—11 percent immediately—being financially upside down on a lease (or purchase) can be a problem. This is especially true when a new vehicle is stolen or totaled in an accident. Here, the insurance company reimburses the leasing company for the current cash value of the vehicle not the current loan balance. To avoid this problem people purchase **gap insurance** that pays off the remainder of the loan if the insurance payment is insufficient to do so. Dealers sell gap insurance for $500 to $1,000 but you can purchase it much less expensively from an insurance company for under $100. To compare companies and rates see www.gapinsurancequotes.org. You can buy gap insurance whenever you lease or finance a vehicle.

3. *Avoid paying maintenance on leases that are too long.* Once the warranty period is up, usually three years or 36,000 miles, the costs of maintenance is the responsibility of the driver. Paying for new tires and brakes for a vehicle you do not own can be avoided with a shorter lease.

4. *Avoid paying for driving extra miles.* Know your driving habits before committing to a lease. If you usually drive 20,000 miles annually do not sign a lease that limits you to 15,000, otherwise you could wind up owing a lot of money for miles when it's time to turn in the car.

5. *Avoid paying "full market price" for repairs.* When your lease is up and you return the vehicle with small dings, nicks, and little dents this might be okay with the leasing company or it might not. You either get the problems fixed yourself or you pay the dealer the full market price for repairs. Before signing a contract ask for a copy of the lease-end-condition guidelines.

Is leasing a better deal than financing? It could be. Note first that the monthly cost of leasing is always lower than a purchase. This is because the payment is primarily based on the depreciation of the vehicle over the lease time period and also because in most states the sales tax is calculated on the monthly lease payment rather than the full purchase price. Still, you cannot answer this question until you understand some rules and risks of leasing.

Regulation M issued by the Federal Reserve Board governs lease contracts. A requirement of this regulation is a mandatory disclosure of pertinent information about the lease that the consumer is considering. The disclosure form must summarize the offer of the **lessor** (leasing agency) to the **lessee** (consumer). The information in this form should be compared with the actual lease contract prior to signing to ensure that the lease signed is actually what was agreed upon verbally.

Leasing Terminology Five terms are important in leasing:

gross capitalized cost (gross cap cost)

Includes vehicle price plus the cost of any extra features such as insurance or maintenance agreements.

adjusted capitalized cost (adjusted cap cost)

Subtracting the capitalized cost reductions from the gross capitalized cost.

residual value

Projected value of a leased asset at the end of the lease time period.

1. The **gross capitalized cost (gross cap cost)** includes the price of the vehicle plus what the lessee paid to finance the purchase plus any other items the lessee agreed to pay for over the life of the lease, including insurance or a maintenance agreement.
2. **Capitalized cost reductions (cap cost reductions)** are monies paid on the lease at its inception, including any down payment, trade-in value, or rebate.
3. The **adjusted capitalized cost (adjusted cap cost)** is determined by subtracting the capitalized cost reductions from the gross capitalized cost.
4. The **residual value** is the projected value of a leased asset at the end of the lease.
5. The **money factor** (or **lease rate** or **lease factor**) measures the rent charge portion of your payment. Although the money factor is sometimes described by dealers as a figure for comparing leases, lease forms must carry the following disclosure about the money factor: "This percentage may not measure the overall cost of financing this lease."

RUN THE NUMBERS

Finance or Lease?

This worksheet can be used to compare leasing and borrowing to buy a vehicle. Remember that the cost of credit is the finance charge—the extra that you pay because you borrowed. Leases also carry costs, but they are hidden within the contract. Indeed, some may remain unknown until the end of the lease period. These lease costs, which are indicated by an asterisk (*), are negotiable and are defined in the text. Ask the dealer for the price of each item, as these fees must be disclosed by dealers. Then complete the worksheet and compare the dollar cost of leasing with the finance charge on a loan for the same time period.

To make the comparison accurately, you must know the underlying price of the car as if you were purchasing it. Often you are not offered this value with a lease arrangement, so you should always negotiate a price for the vehicle before mentioning your interest in leasing.

DO IT IN CLASS

Also, shop for a lease through dealers and independent leasing companies because costs vary widely. This worksheet can be found on the *Garman/Forgue* companion website, or you can find a similar worksheet at www.bankrate.com /calculators/auto/buy-or-lease-calculator.aspx.

Step		Example	Your Figures
1.	Monthly lease payment (36 payments of $375, for example)	$13,500	_____
2.	Plus acquisition fee* (if any)	400	_____
	Plus disposition charge* (if any)	400	_____
	Plus estimate of excess mileage charges* (if any)	0	_____
	Plus projected residual value of the vehicle	6,500	_____
3.	Amount for which you are responsible under the lease	20,800	_____
4.	Less the adjusted capitalized cost (gross capitalized cost* less the capitalized cost reductions*)	18,000	_____
5.	Dollar cost of leasing to be compared with a finance charge if you purchased the vehicle	2,800	_____

What is most important when considering leasing? Always negotiate the purchase price before discussing a lease! Leasing requires an initial outlay of cash to pay for the first month's lease payment and a security deposit. Payments are based on the capitalized cost of the asset minus any capitalized cost reductions and the residual value. This difference represents the cost of using the asset during the lease period; when divided by the number of months in the contract, it serves to establish the base for the monthly lease payment. Some new vehicles are offered with single-payment leases in which the entire difference between the capitalized cost and residual value is paid up front.

With monthly payment leases, the payments are lower than monthly loan payments for equivalent time periods because you are paying for only the reduction in the asset's value—not its entire cost. To compare the costs of leasing versus buying, use the Run the Numbers worksheet, "Finance or Lease?" Also see www.leasecompare.com.

Open-End and Closed-End Leases A lease may be either open end or closed end. In an **open-end lease,** you must pay any difference between the projected residual value of the vehicle and its actual market value at the end of the lease period. When a vehicle depreciates (goes down in value) more rapidly than expected, the holder of an open-end lease has to pay extra money when the lease expires. For example, a vehicle with an \$11,000 residual value but a \$10,250 market value would require an end-of-lease payment of \$750 (\$11,000 − \$10,250). The Consumer Leasing Act limits this end-of-lease payment to a maximum of three times the average monthly payment. New cars lose about 25 percent of their value in the first year and 40 percent or more by the end of the second year.

Most vehicle leases are closed-end leases. In a **closed-end lease** (also called a **walk-away lease**), the holder pays no charge if the end-of-lease market value of the vehicle is lower than the originally projected residual value. However, closed-end leases may carry some type of end-of-lease charge if the vehicle has greater than normal wear or excess mileage. For example, a four-year closed-end lease might require a \$0.30 per mile **excess mileage charge** in excess of 55,000 miles. If you actually drove the vehicle 60,000 miles during the four years, you would be charged an extra \$1,500 [\$0.30 × 5,000 (60,000 − 55,000)].

With either an open- or closed-end lease, you may purchase the vehicle at the end of the lease period. With an open-end lease, you would pay the actual cash value. With a closed-end lease, you would pay the residual value.

Understand Common Leasing Fees Other charges are possible with a lease. An **acquisition fee** is either paid in cash or included in the gross capitalization cost. It pays for a credit report, application fee, and other paperwork. A **disposition fee** is assessed when you turn in the vehicle at the end of the lease and the lessor must prepare it for resale. An **early termination charge** may also be levied if you decide to end the lease prematurely. Be wary of a lease with an early termination charge, even if you do not plan to end the lease early, because termination also occurs when a leased vehicle is traded in or is totally wrecked or stolen.

Make sure you obtain a written disclosure of these charges before you actually make your decision. The early termination charge is the total amount you would need to repay if you end the lease agreement early. It includes both the early termination charge and the unpaid lease balance. In its early years, your lease may be financially upside down, which means that you owe more on the vehicle than it is worth.

NEVER EVER

Lease Just to Drive a Better Vehicle

Leases work best for people who wish to drive a new vehicle every two or three years and, thus, have decided that they will always have a car payment. If you do choose a leasing option, your goal should be to lower your monthly cost rather than to "buy more car." Otherwise, you will find in just a few years that you have spent big bucks for a vehicle you must turn back in or have to pay extra to buy as a used vehicle.

depreciate
New vehicles and low-mileage used cars go down in value very quickly after purchase, often as much as 20 percent after leaving the dealer's lot.

closed-end lease/walkaway lease
Agreement in which the lessee pays no charge if the end-of-lease market value of the vehicle is lower than the originally projected residual value.

excess mileage charge
Fees assessed at the end of a lease if the vehicle was driven more miles than originally specified in the lease contract.

DID YOU KNOW

It's Possible to Get out of a Lease Early

People eager to get out of a lease might consider a lease-swapping website such as leasetrader.com and swapalease.com. These companies try to match people who want to get out of a lease early with those who want to assume a short-term lease. They charge fees to post your vehicle's information, and your original leasing company likely charges a transfer fee.

BIAS TOWARD— OVERCONFIDENCE

People have a bias toward overconfidence. When negotiating the purchase of a major item like a vehicle people will assume they have sufficient information and skills to obtain the best buy. What to do? Arm yourself with tons of information about the price, interest rate, trade-in value, and dealer holdbacks before negotiating. Also remember that salespeople are professionals at selling and you are a relative amateur at buying, so consider hiring a car buying service to get that vehicle at a good price.

warranty

A type of guarantee that a manufacturer or similar party makes regarding the condition of its product.

warranty of fitness for a particular purpose

Here the seller (or provider or manufacturer) knows the buyer's particular use and the buyer relies on the seller's expertise or judgment in choosing the product.

as is

Way for the seller to get around legal requirements for warranties; the buyer takes all risk of nonperformance or other problems despite any salesperson's verbal assurances.

limited warranty

Any warranty that offers less protection than the three conditions for full warranty.

service contract

An agreement between the contract seller and the buyer of a product to provide repair or replacement for covered components of the product for some specified time period.

Be Cautious About Leasing Getting a good deal on a leased vehicle can be very complicated. Therefore, be cautious if you talk about buying the vehicle all through the negotiation process only to be offered a lease at the last minute. The seller might realize that the purchase price is too high for you and can get you into the same vehicle for a lower monthly payment. But you may be tempted to sign a deal that actually costs considerably more. In addition, make sure all oral agreements related to trade-in value, mileage charges, and rebates are included in the lease contract.

8.2f Comparison Shop for Warranties

A **warranty** is an important consideration in comparison shopping. This is a type of guarantee that a manufacturer or similar party makes regarding the condition of its product. It also refers to the terms and situations in which repairs or exchanges will be made in the event that the product does not function as originally described or intended. The longer the warranty is and the more it covers, the better the warranty.

Implied and Express Warranties Under an **implied warranty,** the product sold is warranted to be suitable for sale (a **warranty of merchantability**) and to work effectively whether or not a written warranty exists. Here the seller (or provider or manufacturer) knows the buyer's particular use and the buyer relies on the seller's expertise or judgment in choosing the product. Then an **implied warranty for fitness for a particular purpose** is created. Implied warranties are required by state law. The only way to avoid them is if the seller states in writing that the product is sold **as is**. If you buy any product as is, you have no legal recourse if it fails to perform, even if the salesperson made verbal promises to take care of any problems. Used cars are often sold as is.

Written and oral warranties are called **express warranties.** Companies that offer written express warranties must do so under the provisions of the federal Magnuson-Moss Warranty Act if the product is sold for more than $15. This law provides that any written warranty offered must be classified as either a full warranty or a limited warranty.

Full and Limited Warranties A **full warranty** includes three stringent requirements:

1. A product must be fixed at no cost to the buyer within a reasonable time after the owner has complained.
2. The owner will not have to undertake an unreasonable task to return the product for repair (such as ship back a refrigerator).
3. A defective product will be replaced with a new one or the buyer's money will be returned if the product cannot be fixed after a reasonable number of attempts.

A **limited warranty** offers less protection than a full warranty. For example, it may offer only free parts, not labor. Note that one part of a product could be covered by a full warranty (perhaps the engine on a lawnmower) and the rest of the unit by a limited warranty. Read all warranties carefully, and note that both full and limited warranties are valid for only a specified time period.

Avoid Service Contracts A **service contract** (or **extended warranty**) is an agreement between the contract seller (the dealer, manufacturer, or an independent company) and the buyer of a product to provide repair or replacement for covered components of the product for some specified time period. Service contracts are purchased separately from the product itself, such as a vehicle, appliance, or electronics equipment. The cost is paid either in a lump sum or in monthly payments. Service contracts are not insurance but act similarly. However, unlike a warranty, a service contract always costs extra.

A service contract means that the buyers are simply purchasing insurance against repair bills. The sales pitch goes, "Why not lock in the price of parts and service now, rather than pay more later?" Keep in mind, too, that the manufacturer's warranty pays for most if not all repairs during the first few years.

To illustrate, a 60-inch LCD/LED flat panel high-definition television could have an extended warranty that promises to fix anything that goes wrong during the third and fourth years of ownership; the manufacturer's warranty covers the first two years. This contract might cost $120 for each year, or $10 per month.

Although buying a service contract might provide peace of mind, it is unwise financially because it makes no economic sense to insure against risks that can, if necessary, be paid for out of current income or savings. Plus extended warranties are horribly overpriced. More than 80 percent of all service contracts are never used, and total payouts to consumers to make repairs amount to less than 10 percent of all money spent on the contracts.

Service contracts are riddled with exclusions. If you have not followed the maintenance schedule, the warranty may exclude a claim. It is the same if a covered part is damaged by a non-covered part. Third-party service contract sellers may limit you to certain repair shops or reimburse you after you pay out-of-pocket for the repairs.

More than half the profits of some electronics dealers come from extended warranty sales, not the products themselves. Extended warranties are not a good choice when buying electronics or autos because the products rarely have problems beyond the warranty period. If you really want to buy an extended warranty, you can purchase one any time before the standard factory warranty runs out. This also gives you extra time to shop for the best price.

On a vehicle extended service contract that costs $1,200, the average payout for claims might be less than $250, with the rest going to administrative costs and profit. And $100 goes to the salesperson. Sellers can afford to be more generous on a deal if they know that most of the money will be made back on the service contract. About one-third of people buy an extended warranty on their new vehicles.

Only half of used car purchasers who purchased a service contract for a vehicle 15 years or newer ever actually filed a claim. Thirty percent of them used the extended warranty policy during the first year of ownership, and two-thirds made a claim in years two thorough five. Four out of five who had to use their service contract said that all their claims were honored. Most of the service contract buyers reported they would purchase a warranty again. That said, it is cheaper to set aside money for rainy-day vehicle repairs.

CONCEPT CHECK 8.2

1. What is the goal of comparison shopping?
2. Summarize what is involved in comparison shopping for a safe vehicle.
3. Explain why lease payments for a new vehicle are lower than loan payments for the same vehicle.
4. How do you choose between a low interest rate and a rebate?
5. How do you comparison shop between financing and leasing?
6. What are some pitfalls of leasing?
7. Explain the difference between an implied warranty and an express warranty, and how do they relate to the term *as is*?
8. What is a service contract and what is its disadvantages?

Learning Objective 3

Negotiate successfully when making major purchases.

8.3 NEGOTIATE SUCCESSFULLY

Sellers of big-ticket products sell every day, and they are highly skilled. In contrast, consumers are amateurs when it comes to buying such items. Thus, smart shoppers must learn to successfully negotiate.

8.3a Successful Negotiators Are Armed with Information

MONEY WEBSITES

Informative websites are:

- AutoTrader
- Beepi
- CarGurus
- CarFax
- CarInsurance
- CarsDirect
- Consumer Reports
- Costco
- Edmunds
- Insurance Institute for Highway Safety
- Kelly Blue Book
- Kiplinger's Personal Finance
- MoneyCNN
- National Highway Traffic Safety Administration
- TrustedChoice
- Vroom

negotiating/haggling

Process of discussing actual terms of agreement with a seller, usually on higher-priced items.

dealer holdback/dealer rebate

A percentage of the total MSRP that the manufacturer holds and then gives back to the dealer, often at the end of the year or quarter.

Negotiating (or **haggling**) is the process of discussing the actual terms of an agreement with a seller. With high-priced items—especially vehicles, appliances, furniture, and fine jewelry—there is an opportunity, and often an expectation, that offers and counteroffers will be made before arriving at the final price. When you are actually shopping to buy bring all your print-outs and magazine articles with you to the dealerships because the salespeople then know you are an informed buyer who must have the best price.

Negotiating is challenging for consumers when buying vehicles because many variables must be considered, including the price of the vehicle, the trade-in value (if any), the possibility of a rebate, the prices of options, the interest rate, and possibly a service contract. The dealer can appear to be cooperative on one aspect and make up the difference elsewhere. Important to successful negotiation is to be armed with accurate information on dealer holdbacks, price, interest rate, and trade-in value.

Discover the Dealer Holdback Consumers have caught on to the fiction of new-car prices and instead focus on the dealer invoice price, which reflects the price the dealer has been billed by the manufacturer.

However, this may not be the price the dealer will pay when the vehicle is sold. This happens because manufacturers often offer a **dealer holdback** (or **dealer rebate**) to dealers. This is a percentage of the total MSRP that the manufacturer holds and then gives back to the dealer, often at the end of the year or quarter. Potential buyers sometimes do not know about holdbacks. Here the dealer can hold back a sum of money from (instead of paying to) the manufacturer, thereby providing the dealer with additional profit on the vehicle.

Because of holdback incentives, dealers can sell a vehicle at or below dealer invoice price and still make a good profit. For example, a vehicle might have a sticker price of $37,000, an invoice price of $34,000, and a dealer holdback of 7 percent, or $2,380. A below invoice negotiated price of $33,500 will still net the dealer a nice profit of $1,880 [$2,380 − ($34,000 − $33,500)].

ADVICE FROM A SEASONED PRO

Buy a Used Car and Save for a Home or Retirement

If a new car payment is $500 versus $250 for a used car, the $250 monthly difference ($500 − $250) for six years of not making installments totals $18,000 ($250 X 72 months). Instead of making new car payments, buy the used vehicle and save the difference for a down payment on a home or for your retirement. Investing $18,000 at an 8 percent return for 30 years equals $180,000! Do you want to drive in a fancy vehicle or buy a home or retire with money?

David Windle
Baker College, Jonesville, Michigan

Always obtain a firm price for a vehicle before negotiating financing or a trade-in.

Both the MSRP and dealer invoice price are artificial numbers set by the manufacturer and dealer to allow lots of room to negotiate a profitable price to the seller. For this reason, do not hesitate to negotiate for a price that is below the dealer invoice price. Visit www.edmunds.com/car-incentives for a listing of current dealer incentive offers.

Negotiate Your Price The complexity and uncertainty involved in negotiating the price of a new vehicle have inspired the development of special services to assist buyers. A **new-vehicle buying service** is an organization that arranges discount purchases for buyers of new cars who are referred to nearby participating automobile dealers that have agreed to charge specific discount prices. After you sign up, a local dealer will call you to offer a no-haggle price, which is often within 4 percent of the dealer invoice price. The buying service earns its income by collecting a finder's fee from the dealer. One of the most popular is www.TrueCar.com.

new-vehicle buying service
Organization that arranges discount purchases for new-car buyers who are referred to nearby participating automobile dealers that have agreed to charge specific discount prices.

Professional shoppers in exchange for a fee of perhaps $150 to $450 will find the best available price from a nearby dealer and finalize the sale. Alternatively, for a lower fee, they will obtain price quotes so you can finalize the deal yourself. Two of the most popular buying services are CarBargains.com and Authority Auto (www.authorityauto.com). Also see car buying programs at Costco, Edmunds, and TrueCar. *Consumer Reports* offers a car buying service that advertises they buy vehicles for people at an average of $3,000 off MSRP.

When negotiating a vehicle purchase, the key is to obtain a firm price from a dealer for the desired vehicle and optional equipment before discussing any other aspects of the deal. Rule number one in auto buying: Do not mention financing or a trade-in until you have obtained a price! You will know from your preshopping research and comparison shopping what a good low price would be for the vehicle in question.

Start your bargaining from this low price rather than the asking price or dealer invoice price on the vehicle. Obtain prices from three dealers and then let each know that you have done so and whether or not their price is the lowest. The dealer will then have the chance to reduce the asking price

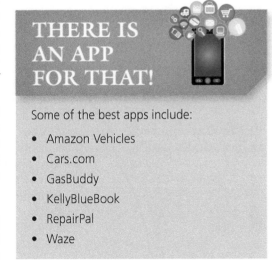

THERE IS AN APP FOR THAT!

Some of the best apps include:

- Amazon Vehicles
- Cars.com
- GasBuddy
- KellyBlueBook
- RepairPal
- Waze

to meet the competition. This smart strategy pressures the dealer to meet your needs rather than the other way around.

Negotiate Your Interest Rate Negotiating the interest rate, or APR, on a vehicle loan is not only possible but also essential to getting a good deal overall. Most vehicle borrowers accept that the dealer-arranged financing is the best they can find since it is usually provided through a sales finance company, although sometimes a credit union is better.

However, buyers may not know that the dealer profits from having the borrower agree to pay a higher interest rate. Here is how the process works. The buyer completes a loan application, which is submitted to one or more lenders with whom the dealer has a pre-existing affiliation. The lenders will assess the application and, if approved, suggest an APR. If the dealer suggests and gets an acceptance for a higher rate by the buyer (perhaps by telling the prospective buyer that his or her credit score is low), the dealer receives a higher fee for arranging the higher APR loan. In this way, the dealer makes money even if the profit off the sale of the vehicle itself is minimal.

You should always arrange your own financing before negotiating and only take the lowest negotiated dealer financing if it beats what you have arranged on your own. It makes sense to save money where you can.

Negotiate Your Trade-in Getting a good deal on a vehicle purchase typically requires one more negotiation: Your trade-in. You can pay a low price for the car you are buying, arrange a low-rate loan, and still not have a good deal if you do not receive what your trade-in is worth.

Success here depends on knowing the value of your vehicle as a trade-in based on your preshopping research. The same online sources you used to get that information also have information on the average price at which similar vehicles are selling.

Trade-ins are another way for a seller to make money on the transaction. In one common sales technique, called **high-balling**, a dealer offers a trade-in allowance that is much higher than the vehicle is worth. This apparent generosity may look very good to a buyer. But beware; the dealer may be making up for this elsewhere, possibly in a higher-than-necessary price for the purchased vehicle. You will not know whether you are being high-balled unless you know the value of your trade-in.

Play "Good Cop-Bad Cop" When Buying a Vehicle Many people are uncomfortable negotiating with sellers. Sellers understand this and are very good at putting people at ease with friendly talk and a supportive tone. But underneath, they are all business. How should you play the game? If you are a good negotiator, bring a friend along to be the friendly good cop while you focus on the deal and ask the hard questions. If you dislike negotiating, you can be the good cop, while your friend can ask the hard questions and focus on getting a good deal.

8.3b Make the Decision at Home Using a Decision-Making Matrix

By waiting until you get home to make the final buying decision, you are free of pressure from a salesperson and free of your own desire to "get it over with." After taking some time to rationally consider all of the consequences of the purchase, you can return to the dealer's showroom and close the sale.

A **decision-making matrix** allows you to visually and mathematically weigh the decision you are about to make. Table 8-2 depicts a matrix for someone deciding among three different smartphones. The first task in developing such a matrix is to determine the various attributes for making the decision. In Table 8-2, these factors include price, durability, screen and input, and styling. Each attribute is assigned a weight that reflects the importance each has in the mind of the purchaser. Each alternative under consideration is then given a score (from 1 to 10 in this case) that indicates how well it performs on that attribute.

high-balling

Sales tactic in which a dealer offers a trade-in allowance that is much higher than the vehicle is worth.

Decision-making matrix

A system that allows one to visually and mathematically weigh the decision you are about to make.

Table 8-2	Decision-Making Matrix (Illustrated for a Smartphone)							
		Alternative A		**Alternative B**		**Alternative C**		
Attribute	**Weight (W)**	**Rating (R)***	**Weighted Rating W × R**	**Rating (R)***	**Weighted Rating W × R**	**Rating (R)***	**Weighted Rating W × R**
Price	30%	9	2.7	7	2.1	5	1.5
Size	20%	6	1.2	8	1.6	8	1.6
Weight	20%	6	1.2	8	1.6	10	2.0
Display Size	10	8	0.8	10	1.0	8	0.8
Warranty	10%	6	0.6	10	1.0	8	0.8
Battery	10%	10	1.0	6	0.6	8	0.8
TOTAL	**100%**		**7.5**		**7.9**		**7.5**

*Using a 10-point scale where 10 is the highest score.

The rating *(R)* is multiplied by the weight *(W)* to obtain a weighted score. The total of the weighted scores for each alternative can then be compared with the totals for the other choices to determine which one "wins." In Table 8-2, Alternative B, which has a total score of 7.9, scores the best.

A matrix of this type helps bring objectivity to your decision-making process and can be of benefit when buying big-ticket items. Also, you may consider other factors in your decision, such as seller reputation.

8.3c Finalizing a Car Deal

After negotiating a good deal and making your final decision, it would be nice if you could simply return to the dealer and sign the necessary papers. But even then there is opportunity for the dealer to push for a little more profit. One technique that is used at this point is called **low-balling.** This involves quoting and getting a verbal agreement from a buyer for an artificially low price. Then the salesperson attempts to raise the already negotiated price when it comes time to finalize the written contract.

To illustrate, after agreeing on the price of a vehicle with a buyer, the salesperson states that, as a formality, the approval of a manager is necessary. While the buyer is dreaming of driving home in the new car, the salesperson and the manager are talking about how much more they can get for the vehicle. When the salesperson returns, he or she indicates that there is a problem. Perhaps the trade-in value is too high, or the dealer invoice price can't be discounted by quite as much as planned, or the price of a certain option has increased. In reality, of course, low-balling is simply a ruse to allow the dealer to get more money. Smart buyers stand firm and insist on the deal that had been negotiated. Otherwise, they walk out the door.

Finally, it is time to sign the papers. Commonly at this point the salesperson turns the buyer over to another member of the sales team whose specific job it is to have all the papers signed to finalize the sale, the loan or lease, and the transfer of the title and registration of the vehicle. Sign only a **buyer's order** that names a specific vehicle and all charges, and do so only after the salesperson and sales manager have signed first. Then verify that all aspects of the deal are as originally agreed, sign your name, and drive away in your new vehicle.

low-balling
A sales tactic where the seller quotes an artificially low price to obtain a verbal agreement from a buyer and then attempts to raise the negotiated price when it comes time to finalize the written contract.

buyer's order
Written offer that names a specific vehicle and all charges; only sign such offers after the salesperson and sales manager have signed first.

DID YOU KNOW ?

The Buyer's Remorse "Legal Right" on Vehicles Is False

Buyer's remorse is a myth pertaining to the buyer's supposed legal right to change his or her mind and return a vehicle after signing a purchase contract. This is a popular misconception. Consumers sometimes falsely believe that they have what is referred to as a three-day "cooling-off period," or three days to decide whether the consumer wants to honor a signed vehicle purchase contract. This simply is not true. As explained elsewhere in this chapter, however, if you buy an item in your home or at a location that is not the seller's permanent place of business, you may have the option to cancel a sale within three days.

8.3d **Evaluate Your Decision**

The planned buying process is complete after you evaluate your decision. The purpose of this step is to think about where things went well and where they went less smoothly. The lessons learned will prove useful when you make a similar purchase in the future.

> **CONCEPT CHECK 8.3**
>
> 1. Why should a shopper negotiate?
> 2. What is dealer holdback and why is it important?
> 3. What three aspects of a vehicle purchase should be negotiated? In what order?
> 4. Why should you make major purchase decisions at home using a decision-making matrix?

Learning Objective 4

Use effective complaint procedures when appropriate.

8.4 COMPLAIN WHEN APPROPRIATE

Despite your efforts to make good consumer buying decisions, not all purchases turn out as well as you want. You may want to try to cancel a contract, use mediation or arbitration, return a vehicle under provisions of a Lemon Law, or file a lawsuit in small claims court.

8.4a **Cancel a Contract Using the Cooling-Off Rule, If It Applies**

If you buy something at a store and later change your mind, you may or may not be able to return the merchandise. However, if you buy an item in your home or at a location that is not the seller's permanent place of business, you may have that option.

cooling-off rule

A Federal Trade Commission rule that gives consumers three days to cancel a contract of $25 or more after signing it for a sale made anywhere other than a seller's normal place of business.

The Federal Trade Commission's (FTC's) **cooling-off rule** gives you three days to cancel a contract of $25 or more after signing it for a sale made anywhere other than a seller's normal place of business. The right to cancel for a full refund extends until midnight of the third business day after the sale. This rule does not apply to vehicle purchases.

The FTC's cooling-off rule applies to sales at the buyer's home, workplace, dormitory, or at facilities rented by the seller on a temporary or short-term basis, such as hotel or motel rooms, convention centers, fairgrounds, and restaurants. The rule applies even when you invite the salesperson to make a presentation in your home. The cooling-off rule does not apply to sales made entirely by mail or telephone, sales that are needed to meet an emergency, or to real estate, insurance, or securities.

Under the FTC rule, the salesperson must tell you about your cancellation rights at the time of sale. In addition, the salesperson also must give you two copies of a cancellation form (one to keep and one to send) and a copy of your contract or receipt. The contract or receipt should be dated, show the name and address of the seller, and explain your right to cancel. The contract or receipt must be in the same language that is used in the sales presentation.

The best way to avoid problems is to read the contract carefully and to fully inspect a new or used product or service before taking ownership. Various states have cooling-off rules that apply even longer cancellation periods to specific types of sales, such as dancing lessons, buying clubs, and timeshares.

8.4b **Mediation and Arbitration**

Vehicle manufacturers utilize mediation and arbitration as part of their warranty procedures. **Mediation** is a procedure in which a neutral third party

---

NEVER EVER ⚠️

1. *Tell a seller what you can afford to pay.*
2. *Rely solely upon the seller for information on price, financing terms, or trade-in value.*
3. *Neglect to complain when products fail to perform as expected.*

TURN BAD HABITS INTO GOOD ONES

Do You Do This?	**Do This Instead!**
Buy on impulse	Create and stick to a shopping list
Buy too much stuff	Write down your needs versus your wants
Get persuaded by ads to "buy now and save"	Realize you are still spending money
Ignore interest rates when financing a purchase	Shop for the best financing terms
Pay too much for vehicle purchases	Learn to comparison shop and get rebates
Can't decide on leasing a vehicle or not	Run the numbers on finance or lease
Buy overpriced extended warranties	Avoid buying such unneeded products

works with the parties involved in the dispute to arrive at a mutually agreeable solution. In **arbitration,** a neutral third party hears (or reads) the claims made and the positions taken by the parties to the dispute and then issues a ruling that may or may not be binding on one or both parties.

DO IT IN CLASS

8.4c   Lemon Laws and Small-Claims Courts

All states have new-vehicle **lemon laws** that provide guidelines used by an arbitrator to order a dealer's buyback of a "lemon." A common definition of a **lemon** in these laws is a vehicle that was in the shop for repairs four times for the same problem in the first year after purchase. (For the specific definition in your state, visit www.carlemon.com.) To enforce a lemon law, the buyer must go through the warranty process specified in the owner's manual. Eventually, if the problem is not resolved, a hearing will be held through which the owner can request a buyback. Some states have also enacted used-vehicle lemon laws.

lemon laws

State laws that provide guidelines for arbitrators to use to order a dealer's buyback of a "lemon" as defined under the law—commonly a car that has been in the shop four or more times to fix the same problem.

8.4d   Small-Claims Court

Sometimes your best efforts at **redress** (to right a wrong) may not prove successful. As a result, you might consider taking legal action in **small-claims court.** In this state court, civil matters are often resolved without the assistance of attorneys. In some states, attorneys are actually prohibited from representing clients. Small-claims courts usually place restrictions on the maximum amount under dispute, typically ranging from $500 to $5,000. To file a small-claims court action, contact your local county courthouse and ask which court hears small claims or check it out on-line.

redress

Process of righting a wrong.

 CONCEPT CHECK 8.4

1. Summarize the FTC's cooling-off rule to cancel a contract.
2. Distinguish between mediation and arbitration.
3. How do lemon laws work?
4. Summarize how a small claims court work.

WHAT DO YOU RECOMMEND *NOW*?

Now that you have read this chapter on vehicle and other major purchases, what do you recommend to David and Lisa Cosgrove regarding:

1. How to search for a vehicle to replace Alyssa's?

2. Whether to replace Alyssa's vehicle with a new or used vehicle?

3. Whether to lease or buy a vehicle?

4. How to decide between a rebate and a special low APR financing opportunity if they decide to purchase a new vehicle for Alyssa?

5. How to negotiate with the sellers of the vehicles?

Barry Austin Photography/Getty Images

SUMMARY OF LEARNING OBJECTIVES RECAPPED

LO1 **Explain the first three steps in the planned buying process that occur prior to interacting with sellers.**

The planned buying process includes three steps that occur prior to interacting with sellers: prioritizing wants, obtaining information during preshopping research, and fitting the planned purchase into the budget. These steps represent the homework needed when preparing to buy.

LO2 **Describe the process of comparison shopping.**

To interact effectively with sellers, you should comparison shop to find the best buy and think carefully. When purchasing vehicles and other big-ticket items, this shopping process includes comparing safe vehicles, window shopping, financing arrangements, interest rates, financing and leasing, warranties, and service contracts.

LO3 **Negotiate successfully when making major purchases.**

Negotiating with sellers involves haggling to obtaining a fair price; discovering the dealer holdback; negotiating the price, interest rate and trade-in; using a decision-making matrix; finalizing a car deal; and evaluating your decision.

LO4 **Use effective complaint procedures when appropriate.**

When the buying process has not gone well, you can use a variety of effective complaint procedures including the FTC's cooling-off rule, mediation, arbitration, lemon laws, or a small-claims court to try to resolve the situation.

LET'S TALK ABOUT IT

1. **Steps in the Planned Buying Process.** Do you think all of the steps in the planned buying process are used when buying simple everyday products (such as a loaf of bread or a half-gallon of milk), or are they used only when buying big-ticket items? Why, or why not?

2. **Positives and Negatives of Leasing.** What benefits do you see in leasing a vehicle? What negatives exist when leasing?

3. **A Bad Purchase Decision.** What is the worst purchase decision you have ever made? What step(s) in the planned buying process could you have done better in that situation?

4. **Do You Complain?** When was the last time you were seriously dissatisfied with a purchase? Did you complain? Why or why not? If you complained, what was the outcome?

5. **A Good Purchase.** Did you ever purchase a big-ticket item and get a good deal? Explain what happened that made it a good purchase.

6. **Credit Card Pain.** Using credit cards is almost like not making a payment. Do you feel less pain when using credit cards? Are your spending decisions made more carefully when you spend cash?

DO THE MATH

1. **Future Value on Cost of Extended Warranty.** Allison Jones of Flagstaff, Arizona, is considering paying $400 a year for an extended warranty on several of her major appliances. If the appliances are expected to last for five years and she can earn 2 percent on her savings, what would be the future value of the amount she will pay for the extended warranty?

2. **Value of Shopping Carefully.** James Canter of Auburn, Alabama, is a good shopper. He always comparison shops and uses coupons every week. James figures he saves at least $40 a month as a result. Assuming an interest rate of 2 percent, what is the future value of this amount over ten years?

3. **Buy Versus Lease.** Amanda Forsythe of Springfield, Missouri, must decide whether to buy or lease a car she has selected. She has negotiated a purchase price (gross capitalized cost) of $35,000 and could borrow the money to buy from her credit union by putting $3,000 down and paying $751.68 per month for 48 months at 6 percent APR. Alternatively, she could lease the car for 48 months at $495 per month by paying a $3,000 capitalized cost reduction and a $350 disposition fee on the car, which is projected to have a residual value of $12,100 at the end of the lease. Use the Run the Numbers worksheet on page 242 to advise Amanda about whether she should finance or lease the car.

DO IT IN CLASS
Page 242

4. **Rebate Versus Low Interest Rate.** Kyle Parker of Concord, New Hampshire, has been shopping for a new car for several weeks. He has negotiated a price of $34,000 on a model that carries a choice of a $2,500 rebate or dealer financing at 2 percent APR. The dealer loan would require a $1,000 down payment and a monthly payment of $578 for 60 months. Kyle has also arranged for a loan from his bank with a 5 percent APR. Use the Run the Numbers worksheet on page 240 to advise Kyle about whether he should use the dealer financing or take the rebate and get financing from the bank.

DO IT IN CLASS
Page 240

FINANCIAL PLANNING CASES

CASE 1

The Johnsons Decide to Buy a Car

After several years of riding a bus to work, Belinda finds that she can no longer do so because her employer moved to a location that is not convenient for public transportation. Thus the Johnsons are in the market for another car. Harry and Belinda estimate that they could afford to spend about $12,000 on a good used car by making a down payment of $2,000 and financing the remainder over 36 months at a 6 percent interest rate for $304 per month.

(a) Make suggestions about how the $304 might be integrated into the Johnsons' budget (Table 3-6 on page 97) by making reductions in certain expense categories.

(b) If they cannot make room in their budget for a $304 monthly car payment, would you recommend they finance a vehicle for 48 or 60 months? Why or why not?

(c) Assume that the Johnsons have narrowed their choices to two cars. The first car is a three-year-old Chevrolet with 44,000 miles; it is being sold for $12,500 by a private individual. The seller has kept records of all maintenance and repairs. The second car is a three-year-old Toyota with 51,000 miles, being sold by a used-car dealership. Harry contacted the previous owner and found that the car was given in trade on another car about three months ago. The previous owner cited no major mechanical problems but simply wanted a bigger car. The dealer is offering a written 30-day warranty on parts only. The asking price is $12,200. Which used car would you advise the Johnsons to buy? Why?

(d) Would you recommend that they purchase or lease a low-priced new vehicle instead of buying a used vehicle? Why or why not?

CASE 2

Victor and Maria Hernandez Buy a Third Car

The Hernandezes' older son, Jacob, has reached the age at which it is time to consider purchasing a car for him. Victor and Maria have decided to give Maria's old car to Jacob and buy a later-model used car for Maria.

(a) What sources can Victor and Maria use to access price and reliability information on various makes and models of used cars?

(b) How might Victor and Maria check out the cars in which they are most interested?

(c) What strategies might Victor and Maria employ when they negotiate the price for the car they select?

CASE 3

Julia Price Wants to Drive a BMW

It has been almost 15 years since Julia graduated with a major in aeronautical engineering, and now she makes "buckets of money" working as a project manager for a large defense contracting company. While she is not very thrifty, she does like a good deal, especially on expensive purchases. Julia recently compared new models of the BMW 320 i, Jaguar XF, and Lexis MDX. She checked out reviews in *Consumer Reports* and other magazines and test drove each vehicle. After deciding on the BMW, Julia shopped online for dealers beyond her community. Julia thinks that she will save about $3,800 if she buys her car from a dealer located 40 miles from her home instead of her hometown seller. She is not sure whether she should take advantage of the dealer's 3 percent financing versus a $4,000 rebate, take the rebate and get a 6 percent loan from a nearby credit union, or lease the vehicle. Offer your opinions about her thinking.

CASE 4

Purchase of a New Refrigerator

Allen Martin, a financial planner from Northridge, California, is remodeling his kitchen. Allen, who lives alone, has decided to replace his refrigerator with a new model that offers more conveniences. He has narrowed his choices to two models. The first is a basic 16-cubic-foot model with a bottom freezer for $1,699. The second is a 25.4-cubic-foot model with side freezer for $2,400. Additional features for this model include icemaker, textured enamel surface, and ice and water dispenser. Allen's credit union will lend him the necessary funds for one year at a 12 percent APR on the installment plan. Following is his budget, which includes $3,345 in monthly take-home pay.

DO IT IN CLASS
Page 233

Food	$400
Entertainment	300
Clothing	100
401(k) retirement plan	400
Gifts	70
Charities	75
Car payment	330
Personal care	120
Automobile expenses	120
Savings	130
Housing	1,200
Miscellaneous	100
Total	**$3,345**

(a) What preshopping research might Allen do to select the best brand of refrigerator?

(b) Using the information in Table 7-1 on page 214 or the *Garman/Forgue* companion website, determine Allen's monthly payment for the two models.

(c) Fit each of the two monthly payments into Allen's budget.

(d) Advise Allen to help him make his decision.

CASE 5

A Dispute over New-Car Repairs

Christopher Hardison, a high school football coach from Buffalo, New York, purchased a new SUV for $38,000. He used the vehicle often. In less than nine months, he put 14,000 miles on it. A 24,000-mile, two-year warranty was still in effect for the power-train equipment, although Christopher had to pay the first $100 of each repair cost. After 16,500 miles and in month 11 of driving, the car experienced some severe problems with the transmission. Christopher took the vehicle to the dealer for repairs. A week later he picked the car up, but some transmission problems remained. When Christopher took the car back, the dealer said that no further problems could be identified. Christopher was sure that the problem was still there, and he was amazed that the dealer would not correct it. The dealer told him he would take no other action.

(a) Was Christopher within his rights to take the car back for repairs? Explain why or why not.

(b) What logical steps might Christopher follow if he continues to be dissatisfied with the dealer's unwillingness or inability to repair the car?

(c) Should Christopher seek any outside help? If so, describe what he could do without spending money on attorney's fees.

DO IT IN CLASS
Page 251

BE YOUR OWN PERSONAL FINANCIAL MANAGER

1. **Can You Afford a Vehicle Payment?** Review Table 8-1, "Fitting a Vehicle Payment into a Monthly Budget," and reflecting upon your own likely financial situation following graduation, write down a few notes explaining how following such an approach might be appropriate for you.

2. **Priority Worksheet.** Review Figure 8-2, "Priority Worksheet (for Haley Wilson)," on page 232 to help you think through the options that you desire in a new vehicle. Tentatively decide on the top five options you would prefer on a new vehicle and write up your findings or complete Worksheet 31: My Top Priority Motor Vehicle Features from "My Personal Financial Planner" to establish your priorities.

3. **Comparing Vehicle Purchase Contracts.** To avoid simply focusing on one or two aspects of buying a vehicle, such as the monthly payment or the trade-in value, com- plete Worksheet 32: Comparing Vehicle Purchase Contracts from "My Personal Financial Planner" to help you focus on effectively comparing what is most important to you.

4. **Lease or Buy a Vehicle?** Review the Run the Numbers worksheet, "Finance or Lease?," on page 242 to help to decide which choice is better for you or complete Worksheet 33: Should I Lease or Buy a Vehicle? from "My Personal Financial Planner."

5. **Rebate or Low-Rate Financing?** Review the Run the Numbers worksheet, "Dealer Finance or Rebate?" on page 240 to help to decide which alternative is better for you when you can arrange your own financing or complete Worksheet 34: Should I Take a New Vehicle Rebate or Low-Rate Financing Offer? from "My Personal Financial Planner."

6. **Major Purchase Decision-Making Matrix.** Review Table 8-2, "Decision-Making Matrix (illustrated for a smart-phone)," on page 249 and think about a purchase you might make. Then complete Work- sheet 35: Decision-Making Worksheet for a Major Product Purchase from "My Personal Financial Planner" and insert the weighted scores you think appropriate.

7. **Sample Complaint Letter.** Draft a letter to seek redress for a deficient product or service you may have had in the past using Worksheet 36: Sample Product or Service Complaint Letter from "My Personal Financial Planner" as a guide.

ON THE NET

Go to the Web pages indicated to complete these exercises.

1. **Keys to Vehicle Leasing.** Visit the website of the Federal Reserve Board at www.federalreserve.gov/pubs/leasing where you will find a link titled "Keys to Vehicle Leasing" that expands on the information in this book. Use this information to generate a list of pros and cons of leasing versus purchasing a vehicle.

2. **Car Buying Advice.** Visit the website of *Consumer Reports* magazine at www.consumerreports.org and click on the "Cars" tab and then see the "Car Buying Advice" section. There you will find lots of information on how to buy cars as well as reliability data. In what ways are the strategies similar and in what ways do they differ from the tips offered in this book for buying a used car?

3. **Consumer Protection Organizations.** Search Google for "consumer protection organizations" that assist consumers with complaints. Create a table showing your findings for three organizations, and include the name, telephone number, Web address, main purpose, and types of problems addressed for each.

4. **Visit Edmunds.com.** Go online to Edmunds.com and search the site carefully. Write a report of your findings.

5. **Shop for a Car.** Visit TrueCar.com at www.truecar.com. Shop for whatever vehicle you might want and see what others paid for the same set of wheels. What do you think of the website?

ACTION INVOLVEMENT PROJECTS

1. **Needs and Wants.** Using Figure 8-2 on page 232 as a guide, make a list of the options in the first column that you would want if you could have any car you wanted. Realizing that getting all the options would be a dream (these are wants), go back to the list, move the priority level on certain items, and move the checkmarks to the second or third priorities. Your needs should now be in the column "high" with wants in the other columns.

2. **Price Available Vehicles.** Telephone two new car dealers to determine if they have a particular make and model of vehicle that is of interest to you, for example, a two-year-old Toyota Prius. Inquire about number of vehicles available of the make and model of interest, colors, options of interest, and asking prices. Make a table of your findings.

3. **Compare Financing Terms.** Telephone two new car dealers to determine some financing details on used vehicles. Inform the dealers that your FICO credit score is above 750 and that you want to finance $28,000 after making a $4,000 down payment. Find out the interest rate, number of years one could finance, and the monthly payments. Make a table of your findings. (Hint: Also see Table 7-2 on page 219.)

9 Obtaining Affordable Housing

YOU MUST BE KIDDING, RIGHT?

Kelvin Lattimore bought a new home and borrowed $230,000 at 5 percent interest for 30 years. His monthly payment for interest and principal will be $1,235. A friend suggested that Kelvin should have been able to find a loan at 4.5 percent with a monthly payment of $1,165. Kelvin dismissed his friend's comments, arguing that the difference in the monthly payments was no big deal. His friend replied, "Kelvin, it's not the monthly payment, it's the interest." Approximately how much more in interest will Kelvin pay over the life of the loan because he took a loan with the higher rate?

A. $1,200

C. $13,000

B. $6,000

D. $25,000

The answer is D. Kelvin will be making a higher payment each and every month for 30 years. While the difference in the monthly payment seems small ($70 [$1,235 − $1,165] per month), even such a little difference in the interest rates on mortgage loans can add up to many thousands of dollars in extra interest over the life of the loan. Paying the lowest interest rate is important when buying a home!

Learning Objectives

After reading this chapter, you should be able to:

1. Decide whether renting or owning your home is better for you.

2. Explain the up-front and monthly costs of buying a home.

3. Describe the steps in the home-buying process.

4. Understand how to finance a mortgage loan and distinguish among ways to purchase a home.

5. Identify some key considerations when selling a home.

WHAT DO YOU RECOMMEND?

Shelby Clark has worked for a major consumer electronics retailer since graduating from college. The company has operations across the country with regional headquarters in Atlanta, Denver, Minneapolis, and Boston. She has been based in the Atlanta area for the past three years, and has begun to think about buying a home rather than renting her townhouse apartment. Then, last month, Shelby was promoted to deputy regional director for the Denver office. The promotion represents a key step for becoming a regional director in four or five years.

Todd Korol/Reuters

What do you recommend to Shelby on the subject of buying a home regarding:

1. Buying or renting housing in the Denver area?

2. Steps she should take prior to actively looking at homes?

3. Finding a home and negotiating the purchase?

4. The closing process in home buying?

5. Selecting a type of mortgage to fit her needs?

6. Things to consider regarding the sale of her new home should she ultimately be promoted to a position in another of the four regions?

TO-DO SOON

Do the following to begin to achieve financial success:

1. *Read your leases and other real estate contracts thoroughly before signing.*

2. *Save the money for a home down payment within a tax-sheltered Roth IRA account.*

3. *Get your finances in order before shopping for a new home by reducing debt, budgeting better, and clearing up anything that keeps you from having a high credit score.*

4. *Buy a home as soon as it fits your budget and lifestyle so you can take advantage of special tax deductions and price appreciation over time.*

5. *Cancel private mortgage insurance as soon as the equity in your home reduces the loan-to-value ratio to 80 percent.*

Learning Objective 1

Decide whether renting or owning your home is better for you.

mortgage loan

Loan to purchase real estate in which the property itself serves as collateral.

rent

The regular payment to a landlord charged for using an apartment or other housing space.

lease

In this context, a contract specifying both tenant and landlord legal responsibilities.

Nine out of ten young adults rent their housing. In contrast, four out of five people aged 55 to 64 are homeowners. Given these statistics, it is likely that one day you will want to buy a home.

At that point, you should be able to mathematically evaluate the financial benefits of renting versus buying and take a hard look at what it really costs to buy a home. If you decide to buy, you will likely obtain a **mortgage loan**—a loan to purchase real estate in which the property itself serves as collateral. There are many types of mortgage loans, and you will need to fully understand your mortgage options before you obligate yourself for 15 to 30 years.

9.1 SHOULD YOU RENT OR BUY YOUR HOME?

One in nine Americans move every year. Whether to rent or buy depends on your preferences and what you can afford. In the short run, renting is usually less expensive than buying. In the long run, the opposite is usually true.

9.1a Renting Housing Is Less Expensive in the Short Term

People may choose to rent their housing for many reasons. Some may simply prefer the easy mobility of renting or want to avoid many of the responsibilities associated with buying. Renting is also good as a temporary move.

Rent is not "money down a rat hole." It frees up cash to keep you living well. In contrast, buying can crimp your income and limit what you can do during some years of your life. Prospective renters need to consider the monthly rental costs, damage and security deposits, the lease agreement and restrictions, and tenant rights.

Rent, Deposit, and Related Expenses **Rent** is the regular payment to a landlord charged for using an apartment or other housing space. It is usually due on a specific day each month, with a late penalty being assessed if the tenant is tardy in making the payment. Other fees could be assessed for features such as use of a clubhouse and pool, tennis courts, exercise facilities, WIFI, cable television, Internet service, and spaces for storage and parking.

A **damage deposit** is a sum of money paid in relation to a rented item to ensure it is returned in good condition. It is common in rented accommodations. It is often charged before the tenant moves in, is often equal to one month's rent, and is refundable if at the end of the lease the tenant leaves the home in good condition. You may also be required to pay a **security deposit** to provide some assurance that you will not move without paying your rent. Again, this amount is often equal to the last month's rent payment. It too is refundable or is applied to the last month's rent. Thus, to rent an apartment might require payment of $1,100 for the first month's rent, a $1,100 security deposit, and a $1,100 damage deposit for a total of $3,300.

Written Lease Contracts Protect All Parties A **lease** is a contract specifying the legal responsibilities of both the tenant and the landlord. It identifies the amount of rent and security deposit, the length of the lease (typically one year), payment responsibility for utilities and repairs, penalties for late payment of rent, eviction procedures for nonpayment of rent, and procedures to follow when the lease ends. Leases often state whether the security deposit accumulates interest, how soon the unit must be inspected for cleanliness after the tenant vacates the premises, and when the security deposit (or the balance) will be forwarded to the tenant. Illustrative leases may be found at Nolo.com. Renting housing without a formal, written lease may seem like an easy and congenial way to do business, but it is fraught with potential for disagreements later.

Two Types of Leases Two types of leases generally govern tenant-landlord relationships. The first provides for **periodic tenancy** (for example, week-to-week or month-to-month residency), where the agreement can be terminated by either of the parties if they give proper notice in advance (for example, one week or one month). Without such notice, the agreement stays in effect. This arrangement also typically applies in situations in which no written lease is established. The second type of lease provides for **tenancy for a specific time**, usually for one year. When this period expires, the agreement terminates unless prior notice is given by both parties that the agreement will be renewed.

Lease Restrictions Lease agreements may contain a variety of restrictions that are legally binding on tenants. For example, pets may or may not be permitted. When they are permitted, landlords often require a larger security deposit. Excessive noise from home entertainment systems or loud parties may be prohibited as well. To protect renters from overcrowding, a clause may limit the number of overnight guests.

An important restriction applies to **subleasing** (wherein an original tenant leases the property to another tenant). Here a tenant who moves before the lease expires may need to obtain the landlord's permission before someone else can take over the rental unit. The new tenant may even have to be approved, and the original tenant often retains some financial liability until the term of the original lease expires.

subleasing
An arrangement in which the original tenant leases the property to another tenant.

9.1b Tenants Have Rights Even in the Absence of a Written Lease

Tenants have a number of legal rights under laws in most states and many local communities. Some important rights are as follows:

- *Retaliatory actions.* Prohibitions against retaliatory actions such as rent increases, eviction, or utility shut-off for reporting building-code violations or otherwise exercising a tenant's legal rights.

- *Habitability.* Assurances of some legally prescribed minimum standard of **habitability** for items such as running water, heat, and a working stove and the safety of access areas such as stairways.

- *Making Repairs.* The right to make minor repairs and deduct the cost from the tenant's next rent payment. This right is subject to certain restrictions, such as giving sufficient prior written notification to the landlord.

COMMON SENSE

Make Sure Your Damage Deposit Is Returned

Use these steps to help ensure that you receive a full refund of your damage deposit:

- Make a list of all damages and defects when you first move into the unit. Have the landlord date and sign this list.

- Maintain the unit and keep it clean.

- Notify the landlord promptly (in writing, if necessary) of any maintenance problems and malfunctions.

- Give proper written notice of your intention to move out at least 30 days in advance of the lease expiration.

- Before moving out but before turning over the keys, make a written list of all damages and defects. Have the landlord date and sign this second list.

- Use certified mail (with a return receipt) to request the return of your security deposit and to inform the landlord of your new address.

- Use small-claims court (see Chapter 8, page 251), if necessary, to obtain a court-ordered refund.

- *Security Deposit Return.* Prompt return of a security deposit, and limits on the kinds of deductions that can be made. Landlords must explain specific reasons for deductions. Some localities require that interest be paid on security deposits.
- *Nonperformance.* The right to file a lawsuit in small-claims court against a landlord for nonperformance.

9.1c   Owned Housing Is Less Expensive in the Long Term

Americans have historically chosen single-family dwellings to satisfy their owned-housing desires. Other alternatives are popular, too, such as condominiums, cooperatives, manufactured housing, and mobile homes.

single-family dwelling
Housing unit that is detached from other units.

condominium (condo)
Form of ownership with the owners holding legal title to their own housing unit among many, with common grounds and facilities owned by the developer or homeowners association.

cooperative (co-op)
Form of ownership in which the owner holds a share of the corporation that owns and manages a group of housing units as well as common grounds and facilities.

Single-Family Dwellings   A **single-family dwelling** is a housing unit that is detached from other units. Buyers have many choices available for both new and existing homes with varying floor plans and home features. Some people prefer the modern kitchens and other features found in newer homes. Others prefer the larger rooms, higher ceilings, and completed landscaping of older homes.

Condominiums and Cooperatives   The terms condominium and cooperative describe forms of ownership rather than types of buildings. These forms of ownership typically cost less than single-family dwellings, offer recreation facilities, and have few if any resident maintenance obligations.

With a **condominium** (or **condo**), the owner holds legal title to a specific housing unit within a multiunit building or project and owns a proportionate share in the common grounds and facilities. The entire development is run by the owners through a **homeowners association**. Besides making monthly mortgage payments, the condominium owner must pay a monthly **homeowners association fee** that is established by the homeowners association. This fee covers expenses related to the management of the common grounds and facilities and insurance on the building.

Some areas of concern for condominium owners include potential increases in homeowner's fees and limited resale appeal of the unit. Condo market prices are much more volatile than for single-family dwellings and condos don't increase as much in value as single-family dwellings. In addition, during a housing downturn, their values decline more than single-family homes.

With a **cooperative** (or **co-op**), the owner holds a share of the corporation that owns and manages a group of housing units. The value of this share is equivalent to the value of the owner's particular unit. The owner also holds a proportional interest in all common areas. A monthly fee for the cooperative covers the same types of items as does a condominium fee and also includes an amount to cover the professional management of the complex as well as payments on the cooperative's mortgage debt. The pro rata share for interest and property taxes is deductible on each shareholder's income tax return.

Manufactured Housing and Mobile Homes Manufactured Housing consists of fully or partially factory-built housing units designed to be transported (often in portions) to the home site. Final assembly and

Be sure to factor homeowners association fees into the monthly income needed to purchase a condominium.

DID YOU KNOW ?

One-Third of Millennials Live with Their Parents

Millennials are the generation born between 1982 and 2004. The millennial generation follows Generation X in order of demographic cohorts. This generation is often associated with technology and social media. They are also known as **Generation Y**.

Thirty-six percent of 18- to 31-year-olds have opted to make home their home again, which is the highest percentage in forty years. That is a record of 22 million boomeranged back to living with mom and dad. Fifty-six percent of adults ages 18 to 24 live at home, and this compares to only 16 percent of 25- to 31-year-olds.

The high cost of living, no down payment money, and increasing student debt are factors that could contribute to the lack of household creation, and it is a drag on the economy. Living at home is a chance for millennials to live with parents, pay down the loan on their vehicle, and save for a wedding and a down payment on a home. It is a time to get ahead in life.

readying of the housing for occupancy occurs at the home site. **Mobile homes**, in contrast, are fully factory-assembled housing units that are designed to be towed on a frame with a trailer hitch. Mobile homes depreciate in value every year just like automobiles.

9.1d So Who Pays More—Renters or Owners?

According to conventional wisdom, homeowners enjoy a financial advantage over renters when total housing costs are calculated over many years. Renters generally pay out less money in terms of annual cash flow, but owners receive annual income tax advantages and they generally can see increases in the value of their homes over time that can improve their financial situation. However, as evidenced by events of recent years, there is no guarantee that housing values will increase in a uniform fashion over time; they might even decline.

Renting, like home ownership, is considered "affordable" if one does not pay more than 30 percent of their disposable income on housing. Zillow reports that the average renter pays 30 percent. In high-cost metro areas, the rental burden rises. Those who spend between 30 and 50 percent are considered "moderately rent-burdened." Those over 50 percent are "severely rent-burdened," and they have difficulty affording necessities such as food, clothing, transportation, and medical care.

An estimated 12 million renter and homeowner households now pay more than 50 percent of their annual incomes for housing. A family with one full-time worker earning the minimum wage cannot afford the local fair-market rent for a two-bedroom apartment anywhere in the United States.

Find out the **price-to-rent ratio** in your community. Either ask your realtor® or look on the Internet. (For current and historical ratios see money.cnn.com/real_estate/storysupplement/price_to_rent/.) This ratio is the median existing home price divided by the average annual rent you would pay for a comparable home in the area.

The national average is 11, although historically it has been 9. The higher the ratio number, especially above 15, is more attractive for renting a home versus buying similar housing. (See Chapter 16, page 495 for more information on price-to-rent ratios.)

Based on Initial Cash Flow, Renters Appear to Win The Run the Numbers worksheet "Should You Buy or Rent?" on page 264 illustrates a comparison between a condominium and an apartment with similar space and amenities. For the apartment, rent would total $1,000 per month. Assume you could buy the condominium for

RUN THE NUMBERS

Should You Buy or Rent?

This worksheet can be used to estimate whether you would be better off renting housing or buying. If you are renting an apartment and planning to buy a house, qualitative differences will enter into your decision. This worksheet will put the financial picture into focus. A similar worksheet can be found at www.finance.yahoo.com/calculator/real-estate/hom06.

DO IT IN CLASS

	Example Amounts		Your Figures	
	Rent	Buy	Rent	Buy
Annual Cash-Flow Considerations				
Annual rent ($1,000/month) or mortgage payments ($863.35/month)*	$12,000	$10,360	_____	_____
Property and liability insurance	360	725	_____	_____
Private mortgage insurance	N/A	0	N/A	_____
Real estate taxes	0	3,000	_____	_____
Maintenance	0	600	_____	_____
Other housing fees	0	1,800	_____	_____
Less interest earned on funds not used for down payment (at 2%)	720	N/A	_____	N/A
Cash-Flow Cost for the Year	**$11,640**	**$16,485**	_____	_____
Tax and Appreciation Considerations				
Less principal† repaid on the mortgage loan	N/A	1,768	N/A	_____
Plus tax on interest earned on funds not used for down payment (25% marginal tax bracket)	180	N/A	_____	N/A
Less tax savings due to deductibility of mortgage interest‡ (25% marginal tax bracket)	N/A	2,148	N/A	_____
Less tax savings due to deductibility of real estate property taxes (25% marginal tax bracket)	N/A	750	N/A	_____
Less appreciation on the dwelling (2.5% annual rate)	N/A	1,800	N/A	_____
Net Cost for the Year	**$11,820**	**$10,019**	_____	_____

*Calculated from Table 9-4 on page 285.
†Calculated according to the method illustrated in Table 9-2 on page 283.
‡Mortgage interest tax savings equal total mortgage payments minus principal repaid multiplied by the marginal tax rate.

$180,000 by using $36,000 in savings as a down payment and borrowing the remaining $144,000 for 30 years at 6.0 percent interest. As the worksheet shows, renting would have a cash-flow cost of $11,640 after a reduction for the interest that could be earned on your savings (after taxes). Buying requires several expenses beyond the monthly mortgage payment, including a monthly $150 homeowner's fee ($1,800 annually) in our example. In this case, the cash-flow cost of buying is $16,485, or $4,845 more than renting.

After Taxes and Appreciation, Owners Usually Win   To make the comparison more accurate, you must also consider the tax and appreciation aspects of the two options. If you rent, you would pay $180 ($720 × 0.25) in income taxes on the interest on the amount in your savings account ($36,000) not used for a down payment. If you buy the condominium, $1,768 of the $10,360 in annual mortgage loan payments during the first year will go toward the principal of the debt, and the remainder—$8,592 ($10,360 − $1,768)—will go toward interest. Both mortgage interest and real estate property taxes qualify as income tax deductions. If you are in the 25 percent marginal tax bracket, your taxes would be reduced by $2,148 ($8,592 × 0.25) as a result of deducting the mortgage interest and by $750 ($3,000 × 0.25) as a result of deducting the real estate tax. In effect, every time you make a payment you will get some of it back from the government.

Condominiums also have a possibility of **appreciation**, or an increase in the home's value. A conservative assumption would be that the condominium will increase in value by 1 percent per year since condo values do not usually rise as fast as single family dwellings. A condominium valued at $180,000 would, therefore, be worth $181,800 ($180,000 × 1.01) after one year, a gain of $1,800. In this case, buying is financially better than renting by approximately $1,801 ($11,820 − $10,019).

The calculations above compare somewhat equivalent housing types. The process is more complicated when you want to compare renting an apartment with buying a house. Further, your costs for renting and buying will continue over time. As a homeowner, you have to pay expenses for maintenance, property taxes, homeowner's insurance, and utilities. While your mortgage payment amount will likely remain the same over time, the other costs typically rise annually. After a few years perhaps a budgeted monthly amount of $1,500 for housing expenses can rise to $2,100. Can you handle a 40 percent increase in expenses for housing?

To make the comparison between renting and buying, *The New York Times* website calculator takes the most important costs associated with buying a house and computes the equivalent monthly rent. See: www.nytimes.com/interactive/2014/upshot/buy-rent-calculator.html?_r=0.

CONCEPT CHECK 9.1

1. Explain the purpose and value of a lease for both the renter and the landlord.
2. Distinguish between periodic tenancy and tenancy for a specific time when renting housing.
3. Identify three ways that home buyers can save on their income taxes.
4. Illustrate how housing buyers can pay less than renters when taxes and appreciation of housing values are considered.

9.2 WHAT DOES IT COST TO BUY A HOME?

Learning Objective 2

Explain the up-front and monthly costs of buying a home.

Buying housing represents the largest outlay of funds over most people's lifetime. Some of these costs occur up front. The big expenditure typically is the down payment. Others, such as the mortgage payment, occur monthly. A few items, such as real estate property taxes, require both an initial outlay and recurring monthly payments. National surveys show that one-third of millennials report they do not own a home because they had not yet saved enough for a down payment.

Table 9-1 illustrates these outlays for the purchase of a $225,000 single-family dwelling with a $25,000 down payment financed by a 30-year mortgage at 4.2 percent interest. (We have used a 4.2 percent rate for illustration purposes. Rates may be lower or higher depending on your credit score and market conditions.) This same example is used repeatedly throughout this chapter to illustrate the costs of home buying as it is near the median price for first-time buyers.

9.2a Pay Up-Front Costs at the Closing

Buyers are faced with substantial initial costs when purchasing a home. These include the down payment and closing costs. **Closing costs** include fees and charges other than the down payment and typically vary from 2 to 7 percent of the mortgage loan amount. The down payment and closing costs must be paid at a meeting called the **closing**, which is the final step in executing a real estate transaction and the ownership of the property is transferred. All the parties to the purchase, sale, and the mortgage loan are represented at the closing. Up-front costs are indicated in Table 9-1.

The Down Payment The **down payment** is an initial payment made in the context of buying expensive items on credit, such as a home or vehicle. The buyer actually writes

closing costs

Include fees and charges other than the down payment and typically vary from 2 to 7 percent of the mortgage loan amount.

down payment

An initial payment made in the context of buying expensive items on credit, such as a vehicle or home.

Table 9-1	Up-Front and Monthly Costs When Buying a Home (Purchase Price of a Home, $225,000 with $25,000 Down; Closing on July 1)	
Home-Buying Costs	**At Closing**	**Monthly**
Payments Required Up-Front		
Down payment	$25,000	
Points (1)	2,000	
Attorney's fee	500	
Title search	200	
Title insurance (to protect lender)	400	
Title insurance (to protect buyer)	400	
Loan origination fee	1,000	
Credit reports	120	
Home inspection	500	
Deed Recording fees	350	
Appraisal fee	350	
Termite and radon inspection fee	130	
Lot survey fee	100	
Home title transfer fee	1,600	
Notary fee	150	
Payments Required Monthly		
Principal and interest (for a $200,000 loan for 30 years at 4.2%)		$978.03
Mortgage insurance		66.66
Warranty insurance		50.00
Payments Required Up-Front and Then Monthly		
Property taxes ($3,180 for the entire year, $1,590 for first half-year, then $265 monthly)	1,590*	265.00
Homeowner's insurance ($1,200 for the entire year; $600 for first half-year, then $100 monthly)	600†	100.00
Subtotal	**$35,005**	**$1,459.69**
Less amount owed by seller	−1,590*	_____
Total	**$33,415**	**$1,459.69**

*Would be received from seller, who legally owes these taxes, and then deposited in escrow account to be available when the tax bill comes due at the end of the year.

†To be deposited in escrow account to be available when the premium for the next year is due.

a check to the seller for the net amount. In this example, we assume that the prospective homeowner has $25,000 saved to use as a down payment on a $225,000 home and will, therefore, need to borrow $200,000.

Points A **point** (or **interest point**) is a fee equal to 1 percent of the total loan amount. Any charges for points must be paid in full when the home is bought, although sometimes they can be added to the amount borrowed. Lenders use points to increase their income return on loans.

For example, a lender might advertise a loan as having an interest rate 0.25 percentage points below prevailing rates but then charge 1 point. Points are, in effect, prepaid interest and compensate the lender for having a lower interest rate. In our example, the lender charged 1 point on the $200,000 loan, resulting in a charge of $2,000. Points are usually used to "buy down" the interest rate, thus the longer you plan to stay in the home the more sense it makes to pay points. By law, interest points must be included when calculating the APR for the loan because they really are interest. Interest points are deductible on federal income tax returns.

Attorney Fees Home buyers should hire an attorney to review documents and advise and represent them prior to and during closing. Attorney fees commonly amount to 0.5 percent of the purchase price of the home, although some attorneys do this work for a flat fee ($500 in our example).

Title Search and Insurance The **title** to real property is the legal right of ownership interest. In real estate transactions, the title is transferred to a new owner through a **deed**, which is a written document used to convey real estate ownership. Although there are several types of deeds, a **warranty deed** is the safest as it guarantees that the title is free of any previous mortgages.

A title search and the purchase of title insurance protect the buyer's title to the property. Your attorney or title company will conduct a **title search** by inspecting court records and prepare a detailed written history of property ownership called an **abstract**. The fees for this process can be paid by the seller or buyer ($200 paid by buyer in our example).

Lenders often require buyers to purchase **title insurance** because it protects the lender's interest if the title is later found faulty. Premiums for title policies vary among title companies. The one-time charge at closing may amount to 0.20 percent of the amount of the loan for each policy ($400 [$200,000 × 0.002] in our example). Homeowners who wish to insure their own interest must purchase a separate title insurance policy (another $400 in our example).

Miscellaneous Fees When a prospective mortgage borrower applies for a loan, the lender may charge a **loan origination fee** at the closing to process the loan ($1,000 or half of a point in our example). In addition, credit reports ($120 in our example) are needed before a home buyer can obtain a loan—and the borrower pays the fee for this report as well. Another important up-front cost is the **home inspection** ($500 in our example) conducted to ensure that the home is physically sound and that all operating systems are in proper order. Title and deed recording fees ($350 in our example) are charged to transfer ownership documents in the county courthouse.

An **appraisal fee** ($350 in our example) may be required to obtain a professionally prepared estimate of the fair market value of the property by an objective party. If you are charged an appraisal fee, you have the right to receive a copy of the appraisal. Occasionally, termite and radon inspections ($130 in our example) are required by local laws, and these are a good idea even when not required. A **survey** ($100 in our example) is sometimes required to certify the specific boundaries of the lot.

Some communities also charge a **home title transfer fee**, which is simply a tax imposed to support community services ($1,600 in our example). Finally, separate **notary fees** ($150 in our example) may be charged for the services of those legally qualified to certify (or notarize) signatures. **Pro-rata interest** may be required if the closing does not occur on the due date of the mortgage payment and interest will accrue before the first payment is due.

point/interest point
Fee equal to 1 percent of the total mortgage loan amount.

title
Legal right of ownership interest to real property.

deed
Written document used to convey real estate ownership.

title insurance
Protects the lender's interest if the title search is later found faulty.

home inspection
Conducted to ensure that the home is physically sound and that all operating systems are in proper order.

appraisal fee
Fee charged for a professionally prepared estimate of the fair market value of the property by an objective party.

9.2b Your Monthly Costs Include Both Principal and Interest

Once a home is purchased, the costs can consume as much as 30 or 40 percent of your monthly disposable income. These outlays include the portion of your monthly payment that goes to **principal** (the amount you owe) and the **interest** on the mortgage loan, which is for the use of money lent. Additional monthly costs can include mortgage insurance, home warranty insurance, property taxes, and homeowner's insurance. Monthly costs are detailed in Table 9-1.

Mortgage Principal and Interest A mortgage loan requires repayment of both principal (P) and interest (I), which are the first two letters of the acronym **PITI**, which real estate agents and lenders often use to indicate a mortgage payment that includes principal, interest, real estate taxes, and homeowner's insurance. In the example in Table 9-1, the mortgage payment for principal and interest on a 30-year mortgage for $200,000 at 4.2 percent is $978.03. (Later in this chapter, you will learn how the P and I components for any mortgage loan are calculated.)

Mortgage Insurance Lenders today expect a 70 to 80 percent **loan-to-value (LTV) ratio** when a home is purchased. The LTV ratio is simply the loan amount divided by the value of the home, which initially is the purchase price. An 80 percent LTV ratio translates into a 20 percent down payment, an amount that is challenging to come by for many first-time buyers. When a buyer makes a lower down payment that results in an LTV higher than that desired by the lender, the lender requires that the borrower purchase mortgage insurance. Two-thirds of home buyers also purchase mortgage insurance, and the cost ranges from 0.375 to 0.05 percent.

Mortgage insurance insures the difference between the amount of down payment required by the lender's desired LTV ratio and the actual, lower down payment. In this way, the lender is assured of payment of the loan balance if the home were later foreclosed for default and sold for less than the amount owed. Mortgage insurance may be obtained from several sources and the homeowner can request that it be canceled when the LTV ratio reaches the desired percent as the loan is paid down. You can obtain mortgage insurance from the following three sources.

- **Private Mortgage Insurance. Private mortgage insurance (PMI)** is obtained from a private company. The largest private mortgage insurer is the Mortgage Guaranty Insurance Corporation (MGIC, pronounced "magic"). The cost of PMI varies from 0.25 to 2.0 percent of the debt, depending on the degree to which the LTV ratio exceeds the lender-desired percentage. In our example, the LTV ratio is 88.8 percent ($200,000 ÷ $225,000), and the lender required 80 percent (20 percent down). As a result, the annual private mortgage insurance premium is 0.4 percent of the mortgage loan (0.004 × $200,000) and is $800, or $66.66 per month ($800 ÷ 12).

- **FHA Mortgage Insurance.** The **Federal Housing Administration (FHA)** of the U.S. Department of Housing and Urban Development (HUD) insures loans that meet its standards. FHA-insured loans can allow one to borrow with as little as 3.5 percent down and a credit score of 580. The insurance is paid for by a combination up-front charge ranging from 1.00 to 2.25 percent of the amount borrowed and a monthly charge of up to 1.15 percent. The maximum amount of the loan varies by geographic region. To obtain such mortgage insurance, the borrower must be creditworthy and the home must meet the FHA's minimum-quality standards. (For information on HUD mortgage programs, visit www.hud.gov/buying /index.cfm.)

- **VA Mortgage Insurance.** The federal **Department of Veterans Affairs (VA)** promotes home ownership among military veterans (active-duty, reserve, and National Guard veterans) by providing the lender with a guarantee against buyer default.

PITI

Elements of a monthly real estate payment consisting of principal, interest, real estate taxes, and homeowner's insurance.

loan-to-value (LTV) ratio

Original or current outstanding loan balance divided by the home value.

mortgage insurance

Insures the difference between the amount of down payment required by an 80 percent LTV ratio and the actual, lower down payment.

private mortgage insurance (PMI)

Mortgage insurance obtained from a private company.

Federal Housing Administration (FHA)

Part of the U.S. Department of Housing and Urban Development (HUD) that insures loans that meet its standards to encourage home ownership.

ADVICE FROM A SEASONED PRO

Cancel Mortgage Insurance as Soon as Possible

Most first-time home buyers cannot make the standard loan-to-value ratio of 80 percent (20 percent down) and must buy mortgage insurance. As the borrower makes mortgage payments over time, the amount of principal remaining to be paid will decline until eventually the 80 percent threshold is reached. At that point, the lender must notify the borrower of the opportunity to drop the insurance. And, by law, the lender must terminate the PMI when the loan-to-value ratio reaches 78 percent based on the market value of the home at the beginning of the mortgage.

But there is no need to wait that long. In this chapter's example mortgage, the borrower starts out owing $200,000 or 88.9 ($200,000/$225,000) percent of the value of the home. It takes about five and one-half years to reach the 80 percent threshold ($225,000 = 0.80 × $180,000)

simply by making loan payments. The good news is that the value of the home may increase faster than the loan principal declines. In the example the 80 percent threshold will be reached in about three years if the value of the home increases at 3 percent per year. When that threshold is attained, the borrower can ask the lender to cancel the mortgage insurance. Lenders usually require an appraisal of the property before doing so, but the cost of the appraisal (perhaps $300) represents money well spent. It is a smart move to make such a request, and it is even smarter to continue making the same monthly payment on the mortgage after the insurance is removed. The extra amount will be applied to the principal of the loan, thereby paying it off even sooner.

Michael Ruff and Sherry Tshibangu
Monroe Community College, Rochester, NY

In effect, the VA (www.benefits.va.gov/homeloans) guarantee operates much like FHA or private mortgage insurance. That is, the lender is guaranteed a portion of the loan's value in the event that the home must be foreclosed and sold below the outstanding balance on the loan.

Fannie Mae or Freddie Mac May Own Your Loan Two quasi-governmental organizations—Fannie Mae and Freddie Mac—underwrite at least half the home mortgages in the country. They purchase home mortgages from lenders, and the money they get from these companies is used to lend money to other borrowers. Thus the company that originated your loan, the one you receive monthly statements from, the one you write a check to each month … isn't necessarily the one who owns your loan. Your lender "services" the loan for the owner by collecting payments, answering questions, handling payoffs, and more.

If Fannie Mae or Freddie Mac owns your loan, you may be eligible for some government programs created to make your mortgage more affordable for you, such as the Home Affordable Refinance Program (HARP) and the Home Affordable Modification Program (HAMP). To find out if Fannie Mae owns your loan see www.fanniemae.com/loanlookup/; see www.freddiemac.com/corporate.

Fannie and Freddie recently started making low-interest mortgage loans directly to consumers with as little as a 3 percent down payment and a 620 credit score. Income limits to qualify typically are no more than 100 percent of the median income in a community.

Home Warranty Coverage All homes for sale carry some type of implied warranty (see page 244 in Chapter 8). Many new-home builders purchase an express warranty good for one year on the new homes they sell. Insurance companies sell **home warranty insurance** on existing homes through real estate agents and builders. It gives assurance to the buyer that all the key home components, such as the air-conditioning, heating, plumbing, and water heater, are in good operating condition. The example in Table 9-1 has a $50-per-month home warranty insurance protection for one year. Typically, the homeowner must pay the first $100 to $500 of any repair. That is not a bad price for some piece of mind.

9.2c Taxes and Insurance Are Paid Both Up Front and Monthly

Some home-buying costs do not fit neatly into an up-front or monthly pattern. This is because they are billed annually, although they often can be paid monthly. Examples are **taxes** *(T)* and **insurance** *(I),* which represent the last two letters of PITI. To ensure that these are paid when due, the lender usually requires that monthly installments be paid into an escrow account. An **escrow account** is a special reserve account at a financial institution in which funds are held until they are paid to a third party. When the insurance and tax bills are due, the institution pays them out of the escrow account.

escrow account

Special reserve account at a financial institution in which funds are held until they are paid to a third party—in this case, for home insurance and for property taxes.

Real Estate Property Taxes **Real estate property taxes** (the *T* in PITI) must be paid to local governments annually and may range from 1 to 4 percent of the value of the home. The total property tax ($3,180 in our example) is due once a year when the government mails out its tax bill. However, if a buyer takes possession during the tax year, the buyer must pay the taxes accrued so far into the escrow account at the closing ($1,590, or 6 × $265 here) to ensure that sufficient funds will be available when the bill comes due at the end of the year. Then the monthly amount ($265 in our example) is paid thereafter into the escrow account. Because it is the seller who really owed the taxes for the six months prior to the sale, the seller will pay the buyer $1,590 on the day of the closing.

Real estate property taxes are based on the value of buildings and land. To calculate these taxes, local government officials first establish a **fair market value,** which is what a willing buyer would probably pay a willing seller for the owner's home and land. Next, the **assessed value** of the property is calculated. This is the dollar value assigned for the purposes of measuring applicable taxes. A home with a fair market value of $200,000, for example, might have an assessed value of $170,000. Some government officials establish the assessed value of a property as the same as the fair market value. You might reduce your property taxes by claiming that the assessed valuation of your home is too high. If successful, your tax bill will be lowered. About one-half of all appeals succeed.

Homeowner's Insurance Lenders always require homeowners to insure the home itself in case of fire or other calamity. Both the home and its contents can be covered in a typical homeowner's insurance policy (the second *I* in PITI). (Chapter 10 covers this information in detail.) The annual premium for such insurance must be paid each year in advance ($1,200 in this example). Lenders require prepayment of the estimated insurance premium each month ($100 here) into the escrow account. In our example illustrated in Table 9-1, the purchaser must be prepared to pay one-half year's premium ($600 here) on the closing day so that there will be sufficient funds in the account to pay the next year's full premium in six months when it is due.

9.2d Make a Decision to Buy (If It Makes Sense) Based on All Costs

The wise financial planner will carefully estimate all initial and monthly costs of housing. Focusing only on the down payment and the monthly payment for principal and interest does not tell the whole story.

In our example, the borrower was able to put less than 20 percent down (11.1% = $25,000 ÷ $225,000). However, with points and other up-front costs, the buyer actually had to come up with $33,415 at the closing. Similarly, the monthly payment for principal and interest was $1,199, but the actual monthly outlay will be $1,680 when taxes and homeowners, mortgage and warranty insurance are added. This is the real dollar amount that this buyer must fit into his or her budget when trying to determine whether he or she can afford to buy a home.

ADVICE FROM A SEASONED PRO

Buy a Home if the Numbers Work Out

Owning a home is the American dream. Growing home equity is a key to long-term economic wealth. Before you buy, however, be certain you plan to stay long enough to recover the upfront costs of moving in and the back-end costs of selling.

Five years is the usual rule for how long you should stay but there are exceptions. Trulia offers a calculator to compare the cost of renting versus buying (www.trulia.com/rentvsbuy).

Lucy Delgadillo
Utah State University, Logan, Utah

CONCEPT CHECK 9.2

1. What is the standard down payment amount on a mortgage loan?
2. If you make a down payment that is lower than standard, identify the extra cost you will be required to pay.
3. Why do lenders use points in home loans, and who is responsible for paying points?
4. Explain why the down payment and mortgage principal and interest understate the actual up-front and monthly costs of home ownership.
5. When should you request that private mortgage insurance be canceled if such insurance was required at the time of purchase of a home?
6. Identify the components of PITI.

9.3 THE STEPS IN HOME BUYING

Do not be in a hurry. Buying a home is the biggest purchase you will likely ever make and **special** attention needs to be paid to the seven steps outlined in Figure 9-1.

> **Learning Objective 3**
> Describe the steps in the home-buying process.

9.3a 1. Get Your Finances in Order

You need to be financially ready to buy a home. So, carefully check your numbers.

Clean Up Your Credit History and Improve Your FICO Score To finance a home purchase you first need a sufficient and steady earnings history. Next your credit history can make or break your chances of buying the home of your dreams. The average FICO credit score for home loan borrowers is above 740. Obtain copies of your credit report and your credit scores from all three major credit reporting agencies (lenders use all three) about six months in advance of starting to buy a home. That way you will have time to clear up any errors and problems before the loan application process begins.

One can easily be disqualified as a potential home buyer with high student loan balance, big vehicle loan, a poor FICO credit score, and/or substantial credit card payments. If you plan on buying a home, you need to be very careful about taking on too much debt while in school and after graduation.

Mortgage lenders charge interest rates based on your credit score. The FICO scores and likely home mortgage rate are as follows: 760–850: 3.7%; 700–759: 3.93; 680–699: 4.1; 660–679: 4.3; 640–659: 4.8; 620–639: 5.3. Loan applicants whose scores are lower than desired are turned down. Current FICO credit scores and mortgage loan interest rates can be found at www.myfico.com/CreditEducation/Calculators/loanrates.aspx.

Figure 9-1 **Steps in the Process of Buying a Home**

You should plan on it taking about 6 months to buy a home from the time you begin your efforts until you actually move in.

6 months before moving in	**1. Get your finances in order.** • Ensure that your credit bureau file is accurate and request any updates or corrections as necessary. • Estimate all your expected monthly housing costs. • Adjust your budget to fit the costs expected.
3 to 5 months before moving in	**2. Prequalify for a mortgage.** • Shop for best rates. • Estimate affordability using front- and back-end ratios. • Consult several lenders and mortgage brokers.
2 to 4 months before moving in	**3. Search for a home online and in person.**
2 months before moving in	**4. Agree to terms with a seller.** • Negotiate a price with the seller and give the seller earnest money. • Have your lawyer go over the purchase contract with you. • Sign the purchase contract. • Have the home inspected by someone you hire.
1 to 2 months before moving in	**5. Obtain a mortgage loan. Decide on the best type of mortgage loan for you.** • Formally apply for a mortgage from the desired lender. • Consider locking-in an interest rate if rates are likely to go up before the closing. • Arrange for a lawyer to help you go over the contract and the good-faith estimate of closing costs.
2 to 4 weeks before moving in	**6. Prepare for the closing.** • Make moving arrangements. • Activate all utilities. • Initiate the change of address process.
Closing day	**7. Attend the closing.** • Correct any errors in the contract or uniform settlement statement. • Sign your name. Write the big checks. • Celebrate!

At that point the borrower may seek a lender in the **subprime market**, which serves higher-risk applicants with low credit scores. Borrowers who are placed in this market are often happy to have obtained a loan. However, such loans carry higher interest rates that may lead to future repayment difficulties. Therefore, it might be better for people with low credit scores to wait and build up their scores before applying for conventional mortgages.

Estimate Your Total Monthly Housing Costs It is vital to have an accurate estimate of what you will have to pay on a monthly basis for your new home. This was amply illustrated in Table 9-1. You should include all likely components of the monthly payment into your budget: the principal and interest, property taxes, homeowner's insurance, mortgage insurance, and perhaps a home warranty fee. You should also consider any additional costs you might pay for utilities. Heating, air-conditioning, electric, and water are all areas for which homeowners generally pay more than renters. Estimating a 50 percent increase from what you are currently spending might be a starting point. Resources are available on the Internet to help estimate housing costs.

1. Choose the type of home you would like to own and the neighborhoods in which you would like to live.
2. Go to the www.realtor.com to search for housing that matches your interests. You will be able to estimate the selling price of similar housing and, by subtracting your available down payment amount, you can estimate the amount you will need to borrow.
3. Go to the www.bankrate.com website to find the current interest rates on mortgage loans.
4. Use the calculator at money.cnn.com/calculator/real_estate /home-afford to estimate the monthly payment for a loan of the amount you need at the prevailing interest rates. Or use Table 9-4 on page 285.
5. Add an additional 30 to 40 percent to the monthly payment on the loan itself for such things as property taxes, homeowner's insurance, warranty insurance, title insurance to protect the buyer, and private mortgage insurance.

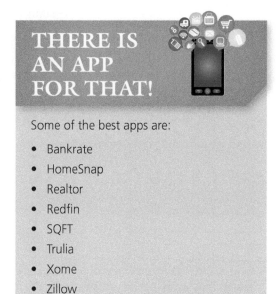

THERE IS AN APP FOR THAT!

Some of the best apps are:

- Bankrate
- HomeSnap
- Realtor
- Redfin
- SQFT
- Trulia
- Xome
- Zillow

Parents Sometimes Help with Down Payment Many young, first-time home buyers look to family members, usually parents, to help them buy a home. Typically they need money to help make the required down payment. If the assistance is a gift to be paid at the closing, the lender will usually require a gift letter with the mortgage application stating that the funds will truly be a gift and from the giver's own funds. Family loans are much more complicated and, if interested, see www.nationalfamilymortgage.com.

Fit the Housing Costs into Your Budget Once you have an estimate of the total monthly costs associated with buying a home, you will need to see how these costs fit into your budget. You can follow a similar process as outlined in Chapter 8 on pages 233 to 235 to fit your payment into your budget. Base the budget on only one person's income. A young couple who buys a home based on their combined incomes is locked into a full-time, dual-income lifestyle to pay the loan. Family obligations or a job loss may later disrupt their ability or willingness to continue that lifestyle. Instead, be smart and base your housing affordability on a single income.

9.3b 2. Get Preapproved for a Mortgage

Before you even start looking at specific homes you should look into whether you will be preapproved for a mortgage loan given the price range of homes that you like and your intended down payment. To be **preapproved** means that a lender believes it is likely that a loan would be granted based on preliminary information provided such as a credit report, amount borrowed and likely down payment. It tells you if you can obtain a loan and the tentative APR.

Make a list of three or four possible lenders at this point including your own bank (see www.bankrate.com). If your budget cannot accommodate the estimate of monthly costs you find in the pre-qualification, you may need to revise your goals by down-sizing the type of home you desire or choose housing in a less expensive neighborhood. Helpful information can be found at the websites for the U.S. Department of Housing and Urban Development (www.portal.hud.gov/hudportal/HUD?src= /topics/buying_a_home) and the Federal National Mortgage Association (www .homepath.com/homebuyers.html). Be aware that being preapproved for a loan carries no guarantee that you will be able to get a loan on a specific property. A purpose of the prequalification is to help you set the price range when you start looking for particular homes.

Shopping for a Mortgage Online Mortgage loans can be found in your hometown as well as online. See SoFi, Lenda and Quicken. Rocket Mortgage from Quicken has streamlined the mortgage application process considerably. Once you give them certain information, they quote you an interest rate quote on the spot. Big players include Bankrate, Freedom Mortgage, HSH, Lending Tree, LightStream, Loan Depot, and Zillow. Local lenders often offer better rates than national lenders Mortgage applicants, however, have to contact banks themselves, going from institution to institution until they have a list of mortgage products and rates for which they qualify.

ADVICE FROM A SEASONED PRO

Singles Can Afford to Buy a Home

Singles often think they cannot afford to buy a home. In reality, most working individuals can qualify for a mortgage and start building equity through homeownership. If you are paying $1,200/month for rent, you could actually afford a mortgage loan of $200,000. However, individuals must make sure their credit score is high enough to receive the best mortgage interest rates.

Many home-buying programs offer down payment assistance options. In addition, there are many programs available for first-time home buyers. Here are some programs to investigate: (1) NeighborWorks America has a variety of local affordable housing programs depending on where you reside (www.neighborworks.org); (2) State Housing Finance Agencies offer a variety of affordable housing options and may even offer down payment saving incentives; (3) USDA

Rural Development offers the single-family direct and guaranteed loan programs based on income; (4) The FHA loan program, insured through the Federal Home Administration, offers a low down payment, low closing costs, and easy credit qualifying; and (5) The VA loan program, which is guaranteed by the U.S. Department of Veterans Affairs, helps you purchase a home with mortgage loan competitive interest rates often without requiring a down payment or private mortgage insurance (for eligible Veterans).

Individuals should not wait to buy a home until they are married. It is important to start building equity and your assets as soon as possible. You could even consider purchasing an investment property such as a duplex; then your tenant could help pay a portion of your mortgage loan payment. Be smart with your money, do the math, and go for it!

Nancy Deringer and Kelsie Smathers
University of Idaho, Moscow, Idaho

TURN BAD HABITS INTO GOOD ONES

Do You Do This?	Do This Instead!
Think a verbal lease for renting is just fine	Get all terms in writing
Move into an apartment without inspecting for defects and damages	Make a written list of all defects and damages at both move-in and move-out and get lists co-signed by landlord
Make your rent payment late from time to time	Make all payments on time; your landlord may report patterns to a credit bureau
Hope, rather than plan, to buy a home	Start saving for a down payment as soon as you get a job after graduation
Want a home just like your parents' home	Recognize that buying a small starter home is just fine

Know that Lenders Use Rules for Home Loans To estimate the maximum affordability of housing expenses for a home loan applicant, lenders carefully apply two rules.

- The **front-end ratio** compares the total annual expenditures for housing (the principal and interest on the mortgage plus the real estate taxes and insurance) with the loan applicant's gross annual income (before taxes). Generally, the total annual expenditures should not exceed 25 to 29 percent of gross annual income. Applying a 28 percent front-end ratio, a young couple with a combined gross annual income of $84,000 could qualify for a mortgage requiring total annual expenditures of less than $23,520 (0.28 × $84,000), or $1,960 per month.

- The **back-end ratio** is also known as the **debt-to-income ratio**. To calculate, divide the total of all monthly debt repayments (for the mortgage, real estate taxes, and insurance, plus auto loans and other debts) by one's gross monthly income (before taxes) and multiply by 100. A ratio of 0.36 or less is desirable. Home loan seekers may not exceed 43 percent to obtain a qualified mortgage, according to the Dobb-Frank law. Applying a back-end ratio of 38 percent, the same couple could qualify for any loan that does not result in total monthly debt repayments exceeding $2,660 (their monthly income of $7,000 [$84,000 ÷ 12] × 0.38). The fastest way to improve (or lower) your back-end ratio is to pay down your debts. See Redfin's home-affordability calculator (www.redfin.com/how-much-house-can-i-afford).

front-end ratio
Compares the total annual PITI expenditures for housing with the loan applicant's gross annual income to assess the borrower's ability to pay the mortgage.

back-end ratio
Compares the total of all monthly PITI expenditures plus auto loans and other debts with gross monthly income.

Use a Realtor® to Help You Look at Properties A **real estate broker (agent)** is a person licensed by a state to provide advice and assistance, for a fee, to buyers or sellers of real estate. Real estate brokers who are members of the National Association of Realtors often use the registered trademark of Realtor® to describe themselves. **Flat-fee brokers**, who charge a flat fee for their services rather than a percentage-based commission, are also available in most real estate markets.

real estate broker (agent)
Person licensed by a state to provide advice and assistance, for a fee, to buyers or sellers of real estate.

Almost any agent can show you housing that is **listed** (under contract with the seller and the broker) by the realty firm. Importantly, buyers should understand that a real estate agent can play various roles.

The Listing Agent Is the Seller's Representative The **listing agent** is the party with whom the seller signs the listing agreement. Listing agents advertise the property, show it to prospective buyers, and assist the seller in negotiations. They receive a commission when the home is sold and owe the seller undivided loyalty. The advantage in working with a listing agent is that because listings may be his or her focus, they have probably figured out how to market properties and how long it takes to get a listing sold.

The Seller's Agent Is the Buyer's Representative A **selling agent** (also **buyers agents**) mostly deal with the homebuyers, usually only listing just a few homes for sale. They also sell the homes that have been placed in the multiple listing service via the listing agents. This person serves as the buyer's representative in the real estate negotiations and transaction. You can find reputable buyer's agents at www.rebac.net/buyers-rep or www.naeba.org.

Brokers typically earn a commission of 6 to 7 percent on the sale price of a home. The seller—not the buyer—usually pays this commission. Commissions are split between the listing agent and the selling agent who represents the buyer. A portion of the agents' commissions then goes to the brokerage firm for whom they work. Two-thirds of brokers admit that they negotiate their commissions at least half the time, and half of brokers say they typically charge a 4 percent commission. Thus commissions are negotiable and available to customers who ask about them.

9.3c 3. Search for a Home Online and in Person

Once you have your finances in order and have received assurances that you can qualify for a mortgage, you can start looking for a home in earnest. Searching for a home requires a commitment of time. You do not want to be impulsive when you will be

DID YOU KNOW ?

How Much Income Do You Need to Qualify for a Mortgage?

The table below gives you a quick idea of how much income you need to buy a home at a certain price using a front-end ratio of 28 percent. The illustration is for a 30-year loan with a 20 percent down payment. For each home price, the top figure in each row shows the monthly payment for principal, interest, real estate taxes, and homeowner's insurance for the interest rates; the bottom figure shows the required gross annual income to qualify

for the loan. For example, a 6 percent loan on a $180,000 home requires a monthly payment of $1,088 plus an income of $46,600 to qualify. Taxes and insurance are assumed to be 1.5 percent of the purchase price (divided by 12 months). Visit the *Garman/Forgue* companion website to perform these calculations for a variety of home prices and interest rates.

DO IT IN CLASS

	Price of Home						
Interest Rate	$120,000	$150,000	$180,000	$210,000	$240,000	$270,000	$300,000
3.0	555	693	832	971	1,109	1,248	1,387
	23,800	29,700	35,700	41,600	47,500	53,500	59,400
3.5	581	726	872	1,017	1,162	1,307	1,453
	24,900	31,100	37,400	43,600	49,800	56,000	62,300
4.0	608	760	912	1,064	1,217	1,368	1,520
	26,100	32,600	39,100	45,600	52,100	58,700	65,200
4.5	636	795	954	1,114	1,272	1,432	1,591
	27,300	34,100	40,900	47,700	54,600	61,400	68,200
5.0	665	832	998	1,164	1,331	1,497	1,663
	28,500	35,700	42,800	49,900	57,000	64,200	71,300
5.5	695	869	1,043	1,216	1,390	1,564	1,737
	29,800	37,200	44,700	52,100	59,600	67,000	74,500
6.0	725	907	1,088	1,269	1,451	1,634	1,814
	31,100	38,900	46,600	54,400	62,200	70,000	77,700
6.5	757	946	1,135	1,324	1,514	1,703	1,892
	32,400	40,600	48,700	56,800	64,900	73,000	81,100
7.0	789	986	1,183	1,380	1,577	1,775	1,971
	33,800	42,300	50,700	59,200	67,600	76,100	84,500
7.5	821	1,027	1,232	1,437	1,642	1,848	2,053
	35,200	44,000	52,800	61,600	70,400	79,200	88,000
8.0	854	1,068	1,282	1,495	1,709	1,922	2,136
	36,600	45,800	54,900	64,100	73,200	82,400	91,500

committing yourself to many thousands of dollars of expense. You can find housing in any number of ways, and the Internet is most helpful.

Never buy without knowing the typical prices for homes in the area in which you wish to buy, not just a particular home of interest. Use Zillow.com or Truvia.com to determine prices for homes that have sold recently in the area. You will be able to see floor plans, photos, descriptions of features and condition, and price-related information.

You can be a more effective house or apartment shopper if you do the following:

- **Make a list** in advance of special features and "must have" items that you are looking for in your new home.

- **Let emotion drive your choices** if a park view trumps a guest bedroom, if a big kitchen is superior to living too close to a thoroughfare, if a particular neighborhood in a charmed setting is perfect even if it means squeezing into a very small apartment, or if a culturally rich environment is more alluring than a spacious apartment.

- **Drive around desirable neighborhoods** before you visit a property. Look at the condition and upkeep of the homes and yards. Are there many homes for sale in the area? Also, get out of the car and listen. Are there industrial noises or excessive highway noises? Any pet noises from neighbors? Look at the availability and quality of parks and schools.

- **Look at only two or three properties** in one day at most. Looking at too many homes at one time can be confusing and exhausting.

- **Bring a notepad and tape measure** with you. Make sketches of the floor plans that you like. Bring along a camera or video equipment. Photos and videos you see on-line are taken from the most advantageous camera angles.

- **Use a checklist** to record, describe, and evaluate features of the home. These can be found on line such as at www.hud.gov/buying/checklist.pdf.

Then contact the seller or the real estate agent handling the properties. Make a list of questions to ask including recent repairs such as to the roof, the cost of utilities over the past year, and any anticipated expenses. A convenient checklist can be found at www.hud.gov/buying/checklist.pdf.

9.3d   4. Agree to Terms with the Seller

If you have found the home you desire, it is time to reach a deal on the price and other details.

Make an Offer to Buy The written offer to purchase real estate is called a **purchase offer** (or an **offer to purchase**). Sellers generally put a price on the property that is 5 to 15 percent higher than the amount that they actually expect to receive. Therefore, you may want to make an offer to buy that is somewhat lower than the asking price. How much

purchase offer/offer to purchase
Written offer to purchase real estate.

NUMBERS ON

Housing

Data from a variety of sources suggest:

- 116 million homes: 70M single family detached; 25M multiunits; 9M mobile homes; 12M other.

- Median price of home on market: $185,000.

- House prices continue an upward trend with annual house price changes settling into a 2- to 3-percent pace.

- 70 percent of homes have a mortgage.

- Purchases of new homes remains sluggish perhaps because of too much student debt.

- Fifty-five percent of parents would allow their boomerang children to come back home, and almost half say it would be rent-free.

- Foreclosure completions continue to decrease as the federal government has modified over 9 million loans.

- Housing affordability remains above historic norms.

- Mortgage delinquency rates past 30 days are low: 2½% for prime borrowers; 25% subprime; 9% FHA loans.

lower is a big question. If you have done your homework and know what homes have been selling for (not *offered* for) in the area, you will be able to make a knowledgeable offer slightly below what you have found. For more on making an offer to buy consult www.homebuyers.mgic.com/buying-your-home/how-to-make-an-offer.html.

earnest money

Funds given to the seller as a deposit to hold the property until a purchase contract can be finalized.

Earnest Money Other aspects of the sale should be included in your offer as well. Examples of contingencies include buyer's ability to secure adequate financing within a specified period of time, seller's ability to deliver marketable title (including certificates of occupancy, work permits, and certificates of completion), successful termite and radon inspections; a home inspection of the plumbing, heating, cooling, and electrical systems; and inclusion of the living room drapes, and appliances in the kitchen and elsewhere. When you make an offer, you need to give the seller some **earnest money** as a deposit. Two or five percent of the purchase price should be sufficient to show your good faith when making an offer to purchase the seller's property. This money is returned if the seller rejects the offer.

Respond to a Counteroffer Most home sellers do not accept the first offer from a prospective buyer. Instead, they usually make a **counteroffer**, which is a legal offer to sell (or buy) a home at a different price and perhaps with different conditions from those outlined in the original offer. You can assume that a seller who is willing to make a counteroffer may also be willing to sell at a slightly lower price. Thus, if you make a counteroffer falling between the two prices, a sale will usually result. It is sometimes common to have other offers outstanding on a home of choice. So, if you push the seller too far, you risk having the seller back out of the negotiations altogether.

purchase contract/sales contract

Formal legal document that outlines the actual agreement that results from the real estate negotiations.

Negotiate a Price and Sign a Purchase Contract A **purchase agreement** (or **purchased contract** or **sales contract**) is the contract outlining the agreed-upon price and terms for the purchase of a home. It includes the final negotiated price and a list of conditions and contingencies that the seller has agreed to accept. When the purchase contract is signed, the seller keeps the earnest money as a deposit. If at this point you simply change your mind about buying, you will forfeit your earnest money and may be sued for damages.

THE TAX CONSEQUENCES OF BUYING A HOME

Home ownership makes you eligible for three big tax breaks.

1. *Mortgage interest and real estate taxes are tax deductible on federal (and most state) income tax returns.* These amounts often exceed the IRS's standard deduction (see Chapter 4). You can then take advantage of even more deduction opportunities that are available to taxpayers who itemize.

2. *You can save the funds to buy a home in a tax-sheltered account.* Individuals can use Roth IRAs (see Chapter 17) to save for retirement. Once the account is five years old, as much as $10,000 may be withdrawn tax free and penalty free by a qualifying, first-time home buyer who uses the funds for home-buying costs.

3. *The profits made by selling a home can be tax free.* If you sell a home for more than you originally paid, you have a **capital gain**. Gains are ordinarily taxable but homeowners can avoid paying taxes on the gain by buying a home that is more expensive, thus rolling the gain into the new home. Also, capital gains of up to $500,000 if married and filing jointly and up to $250,000 if single may be avoided. To qualify, the home must have been owned and used as the principal residence for two of the last five years prior to the date of the sale.

Contingency Clauses to Protect the Buyer A contingency clause is a contract provision that requires a specific event or action to take place in order for the contract to be considered valid. These are very important to a potential buyer because you want to make sure that your earnest money is protected by including one or more clauses in the purchase contract.

One recommended contingency clause would stipulate that the seller must refund the earnest money if the buyer cannot obtain satisfactory financing within a specified time period, usually 30 days. Other important contingency clauses should allow the buyer to opt out of the deal if the appraisal comes in below the agreed upon price or the home fails to pass certain aspects of the home inspection. For example, the inspection uncovers a major structural defect.

9.3e 5. Formally Apply for a Mortgage Loan

Only after you sign a purchase contract do you formally apply for a mortgage loan on the specific home you have selected. Mortgage loan applications are complicated, and providing false information on the form can be considered fraud. Lenders all use the same form found www.fanniemae.com/content/guide_form/1003rev.pdf.

The potential lender usually preapproves or turns down this request within a few days. A **preapproval** is an evaluation of a potential borrower by a lender that determines whether the borrower qualifies for a loan from the lender, or the maximum amount that the lender would be willing to lend. Preapproval letters typically expire between 90 and 120 days, but can be updated with a telephone call to the lender. Half of all consumers who borrow to finance their home purchase unwisely contact but a single lender.

Qualified residential mortgage loan A qualified residential mortgage (QRM) is a descriptor placed on a home loan that meets strict underwriting guidelines and a specified set of product features built into the loan. The QRM was designed to set the standard for residential mortgages and to minimize the risk that borrowers may default. It requires that debt-to-income ratios be limited to 43 percent and loan fees limited to 3 percent, and interest-only loans and negative amortization are not allowed in most cases.

A QRM does not require a special down payment requirement, such as 20 percent. To obtain a QRM, documentation of income must be verified. The lowering of debt-to-income limits on most loans will force some buyers to wait longer and save more to make that first purchase. As a result, these loans will have a lower risk of default compared to a decade ago.

Standardized loan estimate and closing disclosure forms According to provisions of the Dodd-Frank Act, the loan officer assigned to manage your mortgage application gives you two forms to explain mortgage costs and terms. The first form (the **loan estimate**) is designed to provide standardized disclosures that are helpful to consumers in understanding the key features, costs, and risks of the mortgage loan for which they are applying. The loan estimate must be provided to consumers no later than three business days after they submit a loan application. It should reflect a particular loan you discussed with a lender. Check to see that everything matches your expectations.

The second form (the **closing disclosure**) is designed to provide disclosures that will be helpful to consumers in understanding all of the costs of the transaction. The closing disclosure must be provided to consumers three business days before they close on the loan. It discloses categories of information that will vary due to the type of loan, the payment schedule of the loan, the fees charged, the terms of the transaction, and state law provisions. The form helps the borrower double-check that all the details are correct. The format for this document is shown at www.consumerfinance.gov /owning-a-home/closing-disclosure.

The forms were designed by the Consumer Financial Protection Board (CFPB). Consumers can do more research on the "Explore Interest Rates" portion of the

contingency clauses
Specify that certain conditions must be satisfied before a contract is binding.

qualified residential mortgage (QRM)
a descriptor placed on a home loan that meets strict underlying guidelines and a specified set of product features built into the loan.

loan estimate
provides a standardized disclosures that are helpful to consumers in understanding the key features, costs, and risks of the mortgage loan for which they are applying.

closing disclosure
provides disclosures that will be helpful to consumers in understanding all the costs of the home loan transaction.

CFPB's website that is updated daily, See www.consumerfinance.gov/owning-a-home /explore-rate. Another helpful handout from CFPB is the "Your Home Loan Toolkit" that loan officers must give you when you apply for a mortgage loan. See www.files .consumerfinance.gov/f/201503_cfpb_your-home-loan-toolkit-web.pdf.

Table 9-1 provides an example of the basic kinds of information that are in the loan estimate form. Show the loan estimate form to other lenders you have identified to see if they can give you better terms. The format for this document is shown at www.files .consumerfinance.gov/f/201311_cfpb_kbyo_loan-estimate.pdf.

loan commitment
Lender's promise to grant a loan.

Mortgage lock-in agreement The exact interest rate on your mortgage may be the current rate at the time of application or the rate in force at the time of closing. If you expect rates to rise between the time you apply for the loan and the actual closing, you may wish to pay a small fee to obtain a **mortgage lock-in**. This agreement includes a lender's promise to hold a certain interest rate for a specified period of time, such as 30 or 60 days. Make sure you receive a written lock confirmation of the lender's promise. If needed, a lock extension can be obtained for an additional fee. A mortgage lock-in may be part of, but is not the same as, a **loan commitment**, which is a lender's promise to grant a loan.

What if you are turned down for a mortgage loan? A nightmare of many first-time homebuyers is being denied a mortgage. What should you do if you get turned down for a mortgage loan?

1. Find out specifically why you were turned down.
2. Reapply with better information and/or try another lender.
3. Ask for a reappraisal on the under-appraised property.
4. Improve your credit history and FICO score.
5. Save more money.
6. Take steps to improve your front- and back-end ratios.

9.3f   6. Prepare for the Closing

After you have obtained a mortgage, you are not yet finished. Of course, you will want to do all the usual tasks associated with moving: giving notification of your change of address (especially for student loan lenders), hiring a moving company (or not), and getting your utilities shut off at your old residence and turned on in your name at your new one are examples. However, there are two very important additional steps to take that can save you thousands of dollars and many headaches.

Hire a Home Inspector A home inspector is a licensed or certified inspector and he/she should look for termite infestation, wood rot, mold, and radon gas as well as examine the general condition of the home, including heating/cooling, plumbing, and electrical. You should pay the inspector yourself ($250 to $350 is the typical fee). Do not choose one based on the recommendation of the seller's or his/her real estate agent. You want an independent person who is well qualified to look out for your interests. If the inspector finds problems, you can require the seller to fix what needs fixing before you buy the home or you can negotiate with the seller for an adjustment in the purchase price of the home, or use the contingency clause to back out of the deal.

Hire a Qualified Attorney The loan estimate, closing disclosure, and the uniform settlement statement (discussed next) that you receive outlines your entire up-front and monthly home-buying costs. Hiring an attorney to go over these figures and your purchase contract to ensure that everything is in order is money well spent. Many of the closing costs are negotiable, and your attorney can advise on how to keep these costs to a minimum. If you are buying a home that was previously foreclosed, it is absolutely critical that you hire an attorney well experienced in these kinds of special transactions. Some unfortunate buyers of foreclosed properties have later found serious defects in their titles as well as claims against the home.

9.3g 7. Sign Your Name on Closing Day

To complete the sale, the buyer, the seller, and their chosen representatives generally gather in the lender's office for the closing. At the closing, all required documents are signed and payments are made. A key document is the **uniform settlement statement**, which lists all of the costs and fees to be paid at the closing. The final figures are not calculated until right at the end of the deal when all parties know the loan is going to close.

You have the right to see this statement one business day before the closing and again at the closing so that you can avoid surprises and can compare the fees with the good-faith estimate provided earlier. Challenge any discrepancy. You can negotiate every closing cost item.

uniform settlement statement
Lists all of the costs and fees to be paid at the closing.

9.3h 8. Buying a Foreclosed Property

Any slip-up in making mortgage repayments may result in **foreclosure**. This is a specific legal process in which a lender attempts to recover the balance of a loan from a borrower who has stopped making payments by forcing the sale of the asset used as the collateral for the loan.

foreclosure
Process in which the lender sues the borrower to prove default and asks the court to order the sale of the property to pay the debt.

Prior to foreclosure, the homeowner has three options: (1) depart the property and try, for moral reasons, to repay the lender the deficiency, (2) declare bankruptcy, or (3) try to arrange a short sale. Oftentimes the remaining balance owed on the home is more than the property is worth. Unless the lender is willing to modify the terms of the loan, the lender then pursues the homeowner for the deficiency. If interested in buying such a property, you should understand the basic aspects of foreclosed properties:

1. *Preforeclosure.* **Preforeclosure** is the time between when the homeowner has been notified by the lender that he or she is in default and the actual foreclosure has been completed. To purchase such a property, you would negotiate a price directly with the owner The owner may be willing to take a price lower than the market value especially if the offer is above the mortgage balance.

2. *Private Short Sale.* **A private short sale** occurs when a home sale is negotiated with the owner at a price below the actual balance of the debt. The property may or may not be in foreclosure as yet but the seller is trying to get out from under the debt. The lender must approve the short sale.

3. *Lender Short Sale.* In a **lender short sale** the lender accepts less than the full mortgage amount and often forgives whatever debt is left unpaid. The **deficiency amount** is the difference between the amount owed and what the lender collects at the short sale. When a lender agrees to a sale, the homeowner hires an agent to find a buyer. A lender may agree to absorb the loss, although they might demand the homeowner share the loss or make some kind of payment. A short sale may be a buying opportunity for investors, although negotiating with banks is sometimes a cumbersome and lengthy process.

4. *Foreclosure Auction.* Once the foreclosure process has been completed, the lender typically takes ownership of the property. The lender may attempt to sell the property on its own or sell it at a **foreclosure auction**. Most of the people bidding at auction are professional investors. The buyer must come up with the cash immediately.

There are many potential pitfalls when buying a foreclosed residence. The property is likely to need repairs, so insist upon a professional home inspection. Also, taxes and other assessments may be owed. Foreclosure properties can be found on such websites as www.Foreclosure.com, www.Foreclosures.com, and www.RealtyTrac.com, which charge monthly subscription fees for access to their databases. Use a licensed real estate agent and hire a real estate attorney to help when making an offer and for the closing process.

MONEY WEBSITES

Informative websites are:

- **Bankrate**
- **Realtor**
- **Department of Housing and Urban Development**
- **Federal Housing Administration**
- **FSBO**
- **HomeFinder**
- **Kiplinger's Personal Finance**
- **Money MoneyCNN**
- **NOLO**
- **Trulia**
- **Veteran's Administration**
- **Yahoo Finance**
- **Zillow**

Learning Objective 4

Understand how to finance a mortgage loan and distinguish among ways to purchase a home.

9.4 FINANCING A HOME

People often rent housing for five years or more while they save enough to make a down payment to purchase a home. Before buying, you must become knowledgeable about mortgage loans and learn how they are used to purchase a home.

9.4a The Mathematics of Mortgage Loans

Mortgage loans are available from depository institutions (described in Chapters 5 and 7) and **mortgage finance companies** that focus specifically on making mortgage loans. (To find a list of approved lenders in your area go to www.hud.gov/ll/code/llsl-crit.cfm.) In exchange for the loan, the lender (**mortgagee**) has a **lien** on the real estate. Thus, he/she has the legal right to take and hold property or to sell it in the event the borrower (**mortgagor**) defaults on the loan.

mortgage

A loan in which property or real estate is used as collateral.

A mortgage is a loan in which property or real estate is used as collateral. It receives its name from the concept of amortization, which is the process of gradually paying off a loan through a series of periodic payments to a lender. Each payment is allocated in two ways:

1. A portion goes to pay the simple interest on outstanding debt for that month multiplied by the periodic (monthly) interest rate.
2. The remainder goes to repay a portion of the principal, which is the debt remaining from the original amount borrowed.

As the principal is paid down, increasingly smaller portions of the payments will be required to pay interest while the portion of the payments devoted to the principal will grow

Figure 9-2 **Change in Principal and Interest Components of the Monthly Payment on a $200,000 Mortgage Loan at 4.2 Percent Interest Rate for 30 Years**

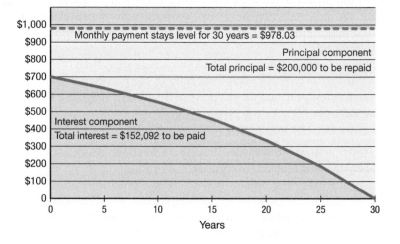

Table 9-2	Amortization Effects of Monthly Payment of $978.03 on a $200,000, 30-Year Mortgage Loan at 4.2 Percent

First Month	$200,000 × 4.2% × 1/12 = $700.00 Interest payment
	$978.03 − 700.00 = $278.03 Principal repayment
	$200,000 − 278.03 = $199,721.97 Balance due
Second Month	$199,800.90 × 4.2% × 1/12 = $699.02 Interest payment
	$978.03 − 699.02 = $279.01 Principal repayment
	$199,721.97 − 279.01 = $199,442.96 Balance due
Third Month	$199,442.96 × 4.2% × 1/12 = $698.05 Interest payment
	$978.03 − 698.05 = $279.98 Principal repayment
	$199,442.96 − 279.98 = $199,162.98 Balance due

larger. These changes in the allocation of each payment are illustrated in Figure 9-2. Note in Figure 9-2 the very slow decline in the amount of each monthly payment going toward interest. It takes 6.5 years before the money going toward interest drops to $600. A high proportion of each monthly payment during the early years of a mortgage loan is allocated to interest.

Table 9-2 shows the interest and principal payment amounts for the first three months of a $200,000, 30-year, 4.2 percent mortgage loan. For the first month, $700 goes for interest costs, and only $278.03 goes toward retirement of the principal of the loan. Table 9-3 provides a partial **amortization schedule** for the same loan. When you take out a mortgage loan, you will receive a full amortization schedule for each month of the loan listing each and every monthly payment, which will show the portions that will go toward interest and principal, and the debt remaining after each payment is made.

It takes many years of monthly payments to significantly reduce the outstanding balance of the loan. At any point, the amount that has been paid off (including the down

DO IT IN CLASS

amortization schedule
List that shows all the monthly payments, the portions that will go toward interest and principal, and the debt remaining after each payment is made throughout the life of the loan.

Table 9-3	Partial Amortization Schedule for a $200,000, 30-Year (360-Payment) Mortgage Loan at 4.2 percent

Payment Number (Month)	Monthly Payment Amount	Portion to Interest	Portion to Principal Repayment	Total of Payments to Date	Outstanding Loan Balance
1	$978.03	$700.00	$278.03	$ 978.03	$199,721.97
2	978.03	699.02	279.01	1,956.06	199,442.96
3	978.03	698.05	279.98	2,934.09	199,162.98
12	978.03	689.10	288.93	14,389.20	196,598.61
24	978.03	676.73	301.30	28,778.40	193,051.57
60	978.03	636.35	341.68	71,946.00	181,472.92
120	978.03	556.66	421.37	143,892.00	158,624.84
180	978.03	458.38	519.65	215,838.00	130,448.00
240	978.03	337.19	640.84	287,784.00	95,699.60
300	978.03	187.73	790.30	359,730.00	52,846.97
360	978.03	3.41	974.62	431,676.00	0.00

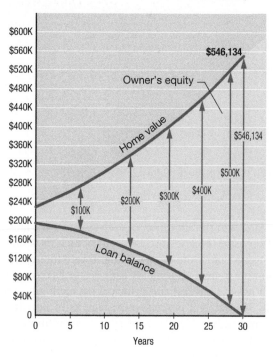

Figure 9-3 Change in Loan Balance and Owner's Equity for a $225,000 Home Purchased with $25,000 Down at a 4.2 Percent Interest Rate for 30 Years (Assumes a 3% Annual Market Price Increase)

homeowner's equity

Dollar value of the home in excess of the amount owed on it.

payment) plus any appreciation in the value of the home represents the **homeowner's equity** (the dollar value of the home in excess of the amount owed on it).

Figure 9-3 illustrates the buildup of equity in a home that results from reductions in the amount owed and the growth in the home's value. Note that the bulk of the increase in equity is a result of increases in the market value of the home. You want to buy a home based on its features and location, not as an investment.

Nonetheless, equity buildup over the long run is a definite plus. If desired, additional payments can be directed toward the principal at any time to reduce the amount owed, increase equity, and reduce the eventual total amount of interest paid on the loan. The equity portion of a mortgage payment is a type of forced savings and helps explain why homeowners typically have a higher net worth than renters.

9.4b Three Factors That Affect the Mortgage Payment

Three factors affect the monthly payment on a mortgage loan: the amount borrowed, the interest rate charged, and the length of maturity of the loan.

1. **Amount Borrowed** The payment schedule illustrated in Table 9-4 on the next page gives the monthly payment required for each $1,000 of a mortgage loan at various interest rates. Using this table, you can calculate the monthly payment for mortgage loans of different amounts. For example, a $200,000 mortgage loan on a $250,000 home at 4.5 percent for 30 years costs $5.0669 per $1,000 per month. Thus, 200 × 5.0669 equals $1,013.38.

    Making a down payment that is larger lowers the borrower's monthly payments. For example, a down payment of 30 percent, or $75,000, would lower the monthly payment on the loan to $886.71 [$5.0669 × ($250,000 − $75,000) ÷ 1,000]. A smaller loan also carries lower total interest costs and may

Table 9-4	Estimating Mortgage Loan Payments for Principal and Interest (Monthly Payment per $1,000 Borrowed)			

	Payment Period (Years)			
Interest Rate (%)	**15**	**20**	**25**	**30**
3.0	$6.9058	$5.5460	$4.7421	$4.2160
3.5	7.1488	5.7996	5.0062	4.4904
4.0	7.3969	6.0598	5.2783	4.7742
4.5	7.6499	6.3265	5.5583	5.0669
5.0	7.9079	6.5996	5.8459	5.3682
5.5	8.1708	6.8789	6.1409	5.6779
6.0	8.4386	7.1643	6.4430	5.9955
6.5	8.7111	7.4557	6.7521	6.3207
7.0	8.9883	7.7530	7.0678	6.6530
7.5	9.2701	8.0559	7.3899	6.9921
8.0	9.5565	8.3644	7.7182	7.3376

Note: To use this table to figure a monthly mortgage payment, divide the amount borrowed by 1,000 and multiply by the appropriate figure in the table for the interest rate and time period of the loan. For example, a $160,000 loan for 30 years at 6.0 percent would require a payment of $959,280 [($160,000 ÷ 1,000) × 5.9955]; over 20 years, it would require a payment of $1,146.29 [($160,000 ÷ 1,000) × 7.1643]. For calculations for different interest rates, visit the *Garman/Forgue* companion website.

qualify for an interest rate that is perhaps 0.5 percentage points lower. In that case, the payment for the same loan would amount to only $835.49 [$4.7742 × ($250,000 − $75,000) ÷ 1,000].

2. **Interest Rate** The higher the interest rate, the higher the monthly payment on a mortgage loan (see Table 9-4). For example, a $1,013.38 monthly payment is required for a $200,000 mortgage loan taken out for 30 years at 4.5 percent. If the interest rate were 5.5 percent, the monthly mortgage payment would be $1,135.58 (200 × $5.6779), an increase of over $120. The effects are even greater when you consider the total of all the monthly payments and the total interest paid over the life of the loan. The 4.5 percent loan will have total payments of $364,816.80 (360 × $1,013.38) with total interest of $164,816.80 ($364,816.80 − $200,000.00). For the 5.5 percent loan, total payments are $408,808.80 (360 × $1,135.58), and total interest is $208,808.80 ($408,808.80 − $200,000.00). Thus, the added cost for the 30-year loan at 5.5 percent is $43,992 ($208,808.80 − $164,816.80) over the life of the loan.

3. **Length of the Loan** Table 9-5 illustrates the relationships among maturity length, monthly payment, and interest cost for a $100,000 loan at various interest rates. A longer term of repayment results in a smaller payment (for loans with the same interest rate). More total interest is paid over the longer repayment time period despite the lower monthly payment. For example, the monthly payment on a 5.5 percent loan is $688 for 20 years but only $568 for 30 years. When the loan is paid back in 20 years, the total interest costs are much lower ($65,100 rather than $104,400, for a savings of $39,300).

Some borrowers choose a mortgage loan with a comparatively short 15-year maturity. Fifteen-year loans usually are one-quarter percentage point lower than 30 year loans. The advantages include a faster buildup of equity, lower total interest, and a quicker payoff of the loan. These advantages can also be gained with a 20- or 30-year mortgage by simply paying additional amounts toward the principal during the time period of the loan. It is wise to take a longer repayment period, such as 30 years, even if you plan to pay off the loan in 15 (or fewer) years. This way the faster payoff is optional rather than mandatory.

DO IT IN CLASS

Table 9-5	Monthly Payment and Total Interest to Repay a $100,000 Loan

Interest Rate	Length of Loan			
	15 years	20 years	25 years	30 years
3.0	$691	$555	$474	$422
	24,400	32,000	42,200	51,900
3.5	715	580	501	449
	28,700	39,200	50,300	61,600
4.0	740	606	528	477
	33,200	45,400	58,400	71,720
4.5	765	633	554	507
	37,700	51,900	66,200	82,500
5.0	791	660	585	537
	42,300	58,400	75,500	93,300
5.5	817	688	614	568
	47,100	65,100	84,200	104,400
6.0	844	716	644	600
	51,900	71,800	93,200	116,000
6.5	871	745	675	632
	56,800	78,800	102,500	127,500
7.0	899	775	707	665
	61,800	86,000	112,100	139,400

Note: Figures are rounded. The top figure in each pair is the monthly payment, and the bottom figure is the total interest paid to the nearest $100.

You can use this table to estimate the monthly payment and total interest on any loan at these same interest rates. Simply divide the amount of the loan by $100,000 and multiply that figure by the amounts shown in the table. For example, the loan of $200,000 at 6.0% for 30 years illustrated in this chapter has a monthly payment of $1,199 (5.9955 × $200) and total interest of $232,000 (2 × $116,000). Note that these figures differ slightly from those earlier due to rounding.

9.4c Conventional Mortgage and Adjustable Mortgage Loans

conventional mortgage
A fixed-rate, fixed-term, fixed-payment mortgage loan.

A **conventional mortgage** is a fixed-rate, fixed-term, fixed-payment mortgage loan. Borrowers like conventional mortgages because they are so predictable. In the example used in this chapter, the $200,000 loan could be granted at a 4.2 percent annual interest rate over a period of 30 years with a fixed monthly payment of $978.03. The payment is the same for month after month and year after year. Ninety percent of borrowers opt for a fixed-rate loan. Most see a conventional fixed-rate loan as the best possible choice because the amount of all future payments are known in advance.

adjustable-rate mortgage (ARM)/variable-rate mortgage
Mortgage in which the borrower's interest rate fluctuates according to some index of interest rates based on the rising or falling cost of credit in the economy—thus transferring interest rate risk to the borrower.

With an **adjustable-rate mortgage (ARM)**—sometimes called a **variable-rate mortgage**—the borrower's interest rate fluctuates according to some index of interest rates based on the rising or falling cost of credit in the economy. With an ARM, the risk of interest rate changes is assumed by the borrower, not the lender. As a consequence, the monthly payment could increase or decrease, usually on an annual basis. If the rate is rising, it does so until it reaches a **cap**. This is a maximum interest rate specified in the contract. Some adjustable-rate loans may have a fixed rate for the first 3 to 10 years after which the rate can vary. Borrowers with ARMs should always determine the "worst case" scenario for interest rate increases under their loan contract and calculate the monthly payment that would result.

ARM rates are usually about 1 percentage point below conventional mortgage rates. Lenders sometimes offer an even lower **teaser rate** to entice people to borrow using an ARM. If you do not feel you can afford even a minimal increase in the rate, you should not take out this type of loan.

ARMs have an **interest-rate cap** limit the amount by which the interest rate can increase to no more than 1 or 2 percent per year and no more than 5 percent over the life of the loan. This may not seem like much, but if the 4.2 percent loan we have been using as an example in this chapter were to go up 5 points after ten years because of rising inflation, the new payment would be almost $1,638, which would be $660, or 67 percent more than the original $978 payment. While such an increase is unlikely, it could happen under the terms of the agreement.

When mortgage rates are low or rising, borrowers are wise to look for a fixed-rate loan. If rates are headed down, consider getting an adjustable mortgage loan.

9.4d Other Housing Financing Arrangements

There are other ways to finance a home purchase.

Growing-Equity Mortgage The **growing-equity mortgage (GEM)** is a fixed rate mortgage on which the monthly payments increase over time. The interest rate on the loan does not change and as the payments increase the additional amounts are applied to the remaining balance and there is never any negative amortization. This shortens the life of the mortgage and increases interest savings.

One form of GEM is the **biweekly mortgage**, which calls for payments to be made every two weeks that represent half of the normal monthly payment. The borrower, therefore, makes 26 payments per year. For example, a $160,000, 6 percent, 30-year loan requires a $959.28 monthly payment for a total of $11,511.36 (12 × $959.28) paid in one year. On a biweekly basis with payments of $479.64 ($959.28 ÷ 2), the total amount paid each year would be $12,470.64 ($479.64 × 26). The difference of $959.28 ($12,470.64 − $11,511.36) is equivalent to one extra monthly payment per year and is applied to the principal of the loan. Under the biweekly repayment plan, a loan will be repaid in approximately 20 years, rather than the 30 years dictated by the monthly payment plan.

All mortgages use the declining-balance method of calculating interest (see Chapter 7 page 220), thus permitting payment of additional amounts toward principal at any time. Thus, you can voluntarily pay additional amounts on the principal without being locked into it as you would with a growing equity mortgage.

Assumable Mortgage With an **assumable mortgage**, the buyer pays the seller a down payment generally equal to the seller's equity in the home and takes responsibility for the mortgage loan payments for the remaining term of the seller's existing mortgage loan. The buyer's goal is to obtain the loan at the original interest rate, which may be below current market rates. This approach will work only if the original mortgage loan agreement does not include a **due-on-sale clause**. Such a clause requires that the mortgage loan be fully paid off if the home is sold. It can impose a burden on the seller because it prohibits a buyer from assuming the mortgage loan.

Seller Financing **Seller financing** occurs whenever the seller of a home agrees to accept all or a portion of the purchase price in installments rather than as a lump sum. Usually seller financing is a short-term arrangement, however, with payments based on

NEVER EVER

Use Found Money to Buy Too Much Home

You receive and inheritance or win a substantial lottery prize and you might be inclined to want to buy a really large home. Stop and think first. Instead, consider paying off your existing home mortgage and enjoy life with a much lower cost of living. That will give you more money for everything else.

teaser rate
Low interest rate that lenders sometimes use to lure buyers; these rates will be low for the first year or so and then will rise to more realistic rates.

biweekly mortgage
A form of growing-equity mortgage (GEM) that calls for payments of half of the normal payment to be made every two weeks; the borrower thus makes 26 payments a year and reduces the principal amount by one full payment each year; this reduces the mortgage term to about 20 years on a 30-year mortgage.

amortization occurring over perhaps 20 years but with a final single **balloon payment** of the total remaining unpaid principal that is due after perhaps five years. Since, the remaining debt is due all at once, the buyer might typically take out a conventional mortgage to finish paying off the purchase.

Reverse Mortgage If you are an older adult, struggling to make ends meet, and have significant equity in your home, you may be eligible for a **home equity conversion mortgage (HECM)** loan, commonly known as a reverse mortgage. These mortgages are insured by HUD or FHA.

reverse mortgage/home-equity conversion loan

Allows a homeowner older than age 61 to continue living in the home and to borrow against the equity in a home that is fully paid for and to receive the proceeds in a series of monthly payments, often for life.

To be eligible someone must be age 62 or older, own your home outright, or have a low mortgage balance that can be paid off at closing with proceeds from the reverse loan, and have the financial resources to pay ongoing property charges including taxes and insurance.

The recipient may receive monthly payments, a line of credit, or a lump sum. The mortgage does not have to be paid back as long as one borrower continues to occupy the property as his/her primary residence and until the last surviving owner sells the house, moves out permanently, or dies. There are some worries in this industry. For example, if only one name is on the mortgage when that person moves out or dies his/her significant other must vacate the premises. For more information on reverse mortgages, go to www.portal.hud.gov/hudportal/HUD?src=/program_offices/housing/sfh/hecm/rmtopten.

NEVER EVER

1. *Take out a mortgage loan with payments that you really cannot afford.*

2. *Neglect to take steps to increase your credit score in the months prior to applying for a mortgage loan.*

3. *Fail to request that private mortgage insurance be canceled when the LTV ratio drops to 80 percent.*

COMMON SENSE
Pay an Extra 10 Percent Toward Your Mortgage

If you can afford it, consider paying an extra 10 percent each month toward your mortgage balance. This would guarantee that your 30-year mortgage will be paid off in about 20 years. That's 10 years of not making mortgage payments that you can now devote to something else, such as funding your retirement or making a real estate investment.

Second Mortgage Loans A **second mortgage** is an additional loan on a residence besides the original mortgage. Because the amount owed on the original mortgage must be paid first the interest rate on a second mortgage is often 2 to 3 percentage points higher than current market rates for first mortgages.

Historically, people have used second mortgages to pay for major remodeling projects, finance college costs for children, pay off medical bills, or start a business. Some people use these funds for everyday living expenses, an unwise practice dubbed "eating one's house."

Two types of second mortgages exist:

- The **home-equity installment loan**, where a specific amount of money is borrowed for a fixed time period with fixed monthly payments.
- The **home-equity line of credit**, where a maximum loan amount is established and the loan operates as open-ended credit, much like a credit card account. These line-of-credit loans often have variable interest rates and flexible repayment schedules.

The credit limit on a second mortgage loan is usually set at 80 to 90 percent of the home's appraised value minus the amount owed on the first mortgage. For example, a person with a home appraised at $200,000 with a balance owed of $100,000 on a first mortgage might be allowed to take out a $60,000 second mortgage [($200,000 × 0.80) − $100,000].

Low- or No-Interest Loans Many states, counties and local governments offer relatively small low- or no-interest mortgage loans that are essentially second mortgages that can be used toward down payment and closing costs. Sometimes they are grants, often for $10,000, that need not be repaid. These are offered to special types of people, such as educators, first-responders, health care workers, and other valued professions to help them afford to live in the community. Search 2,400 communities for eligibility at www.downpaymentresource.com.

RUN THE NUMBERS

When You Should Refinance Your Mortgage

It is sometimes advantageous to refinance an existing mortgage when interest rates decline. In **mortgage refinancing**, a new mortgage is obtained to pay off and replace an existing mortgage. Most often it is undertaken to lower the monthly payment on the home by taking out a new loan with a lower interest rate.

The example here illustrates how to determine whether refinancing your mortgage is a wise choice. The original mortgage for $160,000 was obtained seven years ago at a 5.5 percent interest rate for 30 years. The monthly payment is $908. After seven years, the principal owed has declined to $142,100. If interest rates for new mortgages have declined to 4.5 percent, the owner could take out a new mortgage at the lower rate for a monthly payment of $827. Borrowing $142,100 for 23 years at 4.5 percent saves approximately $81 per month ($908 – $827). However, refinancing may have some up-front costs, including a

DO IT IN CLASS

possible prepayment penalty on the old mortgage and closing costs for the new mortgage. The question then becomes, will these costs exceed the monthly savings gained with a lower payment?

The following worksheet provides a means for estimating whether refinancing offers an advantage. It compares the future value of the reduced monthly payments (line 5) with the future value of the money used to pay the up-front costs (estimated here at 2%) of refinancing (line 8). The homeowner would need to estimate the number of months he or she expects to own the home after refinancing. Given an estimate of four years in this example, the net savings would be $977 (subtracting line 8 from line 5), and refinancing would benefit the owner. In this example, planning to live in the home only three more years would result in it not being financially advantageous to refinance. A similar worksheet can be found at www .bankrate.com/calculators/mortgages/refinance-calculator.aspx.

Decision Factors	Example	Your Figures
1. Current monthly payment	$908	_____
2. New monthly payment	827	_____
3. Monthly savings (line 1 – line 2)	81	_____
4. Additional years you expect to live in the house	4	_____
5. Future value of an account balance after 4 years if the monthly savings were invested at 3% after taxes (using the calculator on the *Garman/Forgue* companion website)	4,175	_____
6. Prepayment penalty on current loan (0%)	0	_____
7. Points and fees for new loan (2%)	2,842	_____
8. Future value of an account balance after 4 years if the prepayment penalty and closing costs ($4,263) had been invested instead at 3% after taxes (using the calculator on the *Garman/Forgue* companion website)	3,198	_____
9. Net saving after 48 months (line 5 – line 8)	$977	_____

It may also be possible to borrow more than the current balance owed on the existing loan, thereby utilizing some of the equity built up in the home. Borrowers refinancing for more than the amount owed should understand that rebuilding the equity to its previous level may take many years. This also is dangerous because if home prices decline the borrower will owe more on the home than it is worth.

CONCEPT CHECK 9.4

1. Explain why the portions of a monthly mortgage payment that are allocated toward interest and toward principal will vary as the loan is repaid.
2. Distinguish between a conventional mortgage loan and an adjustable-rate loan.
3. Identify the two ways that homebuyers build equity in their property.

9.5 SELLING A HOME

defect disclosure form

A state required form that discloses problems that could affect the property's value or desirability, such as a basement that floods in heavy rains.

While most of this chapter deals with buying a home, important considerations also arise when you are selling a home. It is extremely important to do minor painting, cleaning, and repairing before listing your home for sale. When selling your home, you may be obligated to disclose problems that could affect the property's value or desirability using a state required **defect disclosure form**. In most states, it is illegal to fraudulently conceal major physical defects in your property such as a basement that floods in heavy rains. Many states require sellers to make written disclosures about the condition of the property.

9.5a Should You List with a Broker or Try to Sell a Home Yourself?

FSBO

For sale by owner; commonly pronounced "fizbo"; home sold directly by the homeowner to save on sales commission paid to a real estate broker.

Knowing that the sales commission to a broker on a $200,000 home could be $12,000 to $14,000 provides motivation for some homeowners to consider selling their homes themselves. The key to success in a **FSBO** (for sale by owner; commonly pronounced "fizbo") is to know what price to ask for your home. Asking too little could cost you much more than the commission paid to a broker. Setting the price too high keeps potential buyers away.

Many homeowners begin by contacting a few real estate agents to get their opinions on how much the home is worth. Agents are often quite willing to give their opinions because the homeowner might list the home with them if it does not sell quickly. Placing a for-sale sign on your lawn and spending about $500 on advertising the property should keep your telephone ringing with inquiries. If your home does not sell after a few months while other similar properties are selling, you might want to list it with a broker. For more information on selling your own home, visit www.fsbo.com, or www.forsalebyowner.com.

listing agreement

Agreement that brokers require homeowners to sign that permits the broker to list the property exclusively or with a multiple-listing service.

broker's commission

Largest selling cost in selling a home; these commissions often amount to 6 percent of the selling price of the home.

All brokers® require that homeowners sign a **listing agreement** permitting them to list the property exclusively or with a multiple-listing service. A **multiple-listing service** is an information and referral network among real estate brokers allowing properties listed with a particular broker to be shown by all other brokers. Brokers "qualify" prospective buyers—distinguishing between serious buyers and people who are just looking or cannot afford the home. If your broker cannot find a buyer within 60 days, consider signing an agreement with another broker who might prove more aggressive in advertising and selling your property. If a sale occurs (or begins) during the time period of the listing agreement, you must pay a commission to the broker for any sale to a buyer not previously listed as an exception in the listing agreement.

9.5b Selling Carries Its Own Costs

The largest selling cost is the **broker's commission**. These commissions often amount to 6 to 7 percent of the selling price of the home. Sellers are often

FSBOs can save a home seller money but usually take longer to sell.

Stockbyte/Jupiter Images

unaware that brokers may negotiate their commission. Smart sellers also pay for a title search, a professional appraisal, and their own home inspection.

Most mortgage loans are paid off before maturity because people move and sell their homes. Mortgage loan contracts sometimes have a clause that specifies a **prepayment penalty**. A prepayment penalty on a mortgage occurs when buyers sign a contract to pay a penalty stating that if they pay off their mortgage in a set period of time, usually between three and five years, they owe a penalty. They agree because they receive an incentive in the form of a slightly lower initial interest rate, perhaps ¼ of 1 percent, on their original mortgage. Prepayment penalties can range from 2 to 4 percent of the original mortgage loan. On a $160,000 mortgage loan, for example, the charge might vary from $3,200 to $6,400.

Local communities may assess **real estate transfer taxes** that are taxes imposed by states, counties, and municipalities on the transfer of the title of real property within the jurisdiction. These taxes are paid by the seller, and perhaps a mortgage tax to be paid by the homeowner, and they are usually based on the selling price of the home. These tax rates are usually less than 1 percent, but can be as high as 2 percent.

How to Sell a Home in a Hurry What if you want to sell your home in a hurry with lots of other properties on the market? Tell your real estate agent that you are willing to pay a commission of 8 or even 10 percent rather than 6 percent. This will motivate the agent to show your home by bringing lots of people to see it. The agent's broker will also insist that all his or her agents show the property because the broker also will earn more money. The extra you pay in commission (about $4,000 to $6,000 on a $200,000 house) is probably much less than the money you would lose if you are forced to reduce your asking price once, twice, or even more.

prepayment penalty
This occurs when buyers sign a contract to pay a penalty stating that if they pay off their mortgage in a set period of time, usually between three and five years they owe it.

CONCEPT CHECK 9.5

1. List some disadvantages of trying to sell a home yourself.
2. List one advantage and one disadvantage of using a real estate broker to sell a home.
3. Describe two costs associated with selling a home in addition to the real estate commission.

WHAT DO YOU RECOMMEND *NOW*?

Now that you have read the chapter on buying housing, what do you recommend to Shelby Clark regarding:

1. Buying or renting housing in the Denver area?
2. Steps she should take prior to actively looking at homes?
3. Finding a home and negotiating the purchase?
4. The closing process in home buying?
5. Selecting the type of mortgage to fit her needs?
6. Things to consider regarding the sale of her home should she ultimately be promoted to a position in another of the four regions?

SUMMARY OF LEARNING OBJECTIVES RECAPPED

LO1   **Decide whether renting or owning your home is better for you.**

When choosing housing, renters must consider the costs of rent, a security deposit, and renter's insurance. Home buyers can choose among single-family dwellings, condominiums, cooperative housing, manufactured housing, and mobile homes. Renters generally pay out less money in terms of cash flow in the short run, whereas owners enjoy tax advantages and generally see an increase in the market value of their homes, making them better off financially in the long run.

LO2   **Explain the up-front and monthly costs of buying a home.**

Home buyers understand that they will make a down payment and then make monthly principal and interest payments on their mortgage. What some don't understand is that closing costs for interest, points, and other aspects of the purchase can add 2 to 7 percent or more to the amount needed up front at the closing. Similarly, monthly charges for private mortgage insurance, homeowner's insurance, and real estate property taxes can add another 20 percent to their monthly payment. Know all costs before buying.

LO3   **Describe the steps in the home-buying process.**

The home-buying process includes (a) clean up your credit history and improve your FICO score,

(b) estimate your total monthly housing costs, (c) get preapproved for a mortgage, (d) consult multiple lenders, (e) know that lender use rules for home loans, (f) use a realtor® to help you look at properties, (g) search for a home online as in person, (h) agree to terms with the seller, (i) formally apply for a mortgage loan, (j) prepare for the closing, and (k) sign your name on closing day.

LO4   **Understand how to finance a mortgage loan and distinguish among ways to purchase a home.**

Mortgage loans for homes are amortized. Amortization is the process of gradually paying off a mortgage through a series of periodic payments to a lender, with a portion of each payment going toward the principal and another portion going toward the interest owed. The mathematics of buying a home shows how loan payments are calculated and how the portion of each monthly payment that goes toward interest declines, resulting in the portion that goes toward the principal increasing with each subsequent payment. Conventional mortgages and adjustable-rate mortgages are the most common types of housing loans.

LO5   **Identify some key considerations when selling a home.**

When selling a home, it is wise to consider the pros and cons of listing with a real estate broker versus selling the home yourself, the transaction costs of selling, and how to sell a home in a hurry.

LET'S TALK ABOUT IT

1. **Renting Versus Buying.** What do you see as the advantages and the disadvantages for you of renting or buying housing at the current time? How might your feelings change in the future, such as within five years?

2. **Feelings About Long-Term Debt.** In the early years of the standard 30-year mortgage loan, as little as 10 percent of the monthly payment actually goes toward repaying the debt. As a result, it takes many, many years for the loan balance to come down to any significant extent.

Explain how that affects your feelings about taking on such a long-term obligation.

3. **Alternative Mortgages.** Would you prefer a conventional mortgage, an adjustable-rate mortgage, or one of the other financing mechanisms described in this chapter to finance a home purchase? Why?

4. **Negotiating the Purchase of a Home.** Almost all closing costs on a home purchase are negotiable. Would you feel comfortable entering into a discussion of these items? Why or why not?

DO THE MATH

1. **Deciding to Buy.** Dave and Diane Starr of New Orleans, Louisiana, both of whom are in their late 20s, currently are renting an unfurnished two-bedroom apartment for $1,200 per month, plus $230 for utilities and $34 for insurance. They have found a condominium they can buy for $170,000 with a 20 percent down

payment and a 30-year, 6.5 percent mortgage. Principal and interest payments are estimated at $860 per month, with property taxes amounting to $150 per month and a homeowner's insurance premium of $900 per year. Closing costs are estimated at $4,200. The monthly homeowners association fee is $275, and utility costs are estimated at $240 per month. The Starrs have a combined income of $90,000 per year, with take-home pay of $5,800 per month. They are in the 25 percent tax bracket, pay $225 per month on an installment loan (ten payments left), and have $39,000 in savings and investments outside of their retirement accounts.

(a) Can the Starrs afford to buy the condo? Use the results from the *Garman/Forgue* companion website or the information on page 276 to support your answer. Also, consider the effect of the purchase on their savings and monthly budget.

(b) Dave and Diane think that their monthly housing costs would be lower the first year if they bought the condo. Do you agree? Support your answer. Assume that they currently have $10,000 in tax deductible expenses.

(c) If they buy, how much will Dave and Diane have left in savings to pay for moving expenses?

(d) Available financial information suggests that mortgage rates might increase over the next several months. If the Starrs wait until the rates increase ½ of 1 percent, how much more will they spend on their monthly mortgage payment? Use the information in Table 9-4 on page 285 or the *Garman/Forgue* companion website to calculate the payment.

2. **Mortgage Affordability.** Seth and Alexandra Moore of Elk Grove Village, Illinois have an annual income of $110,000 and want to buy a home. Currently, mortgage rates are 5 percent. The Moores want to take out a mortgage for 30 years. Real estate taxes are estimated to be $4,800 per year for homes similar to what they would like to buy, and homeowner's insurance would be about $1,500 per year.

DO IT IN CLASS
Page 276

(a) Using a 28 percent front-end ratio, what are the total annual and monthly expenditures for which they would qualify?

(b) Using a 36 percent back-end ratio, what monthly mortgage payment (including taxes and insurance) could they afford given that they have an automobile loan payment of $470, a student loan payment of $350, and credit card payments of $250? (Hint: Subtract these amounts from the total monthly affordable payments for their income to determine the amount left over to spend on a mortgage.)

(c) Using a 36 percent back-end ratio, if the Moores had zero debt, what monthly mortgage payment (including taxes and insurance) could they afford?

3. **Rent Versus Buy.** Alex Guadet of Nashville, Tennessee, has been renting a two-bedroom house for several years. He pays $900 per month in rent for the home and $300 per year in property and liability insurance. The owner of the house wants to sell it, and Alex is considering making an offer. The owner wants $160,000 for the property, but Alex thinks he could get the house for $150,000 and use his $25,000 in 3 percent certificates of deposit that are ready to mature for the down payment. Alex has talked to his banker and could get a 5 percent mortgage loan for 25 years to finance the remainder of the purchase price. The banker advised Alex that he would reduce his debt principal by $1,700 during the first year of the loan. Property taxes on the house are $1,400 per year. Alex estimates that he would need to upgrade his property and liability insurance to $1,200 per year and would incur about $3,000 in costs the first year for maintenance and improvements. Property values are increasing at about 3 percent per year in the neighborhood. Alex will have to pay $50 a month for private mortgage insurance. He is in the 25 percent marginal tax bracket.

DO IT IN CLASS
Page 264

(a) Use Table 9-4 on page 285 to calculate the monthly mortgage payment for the mortgage loan that Alex would need.

(b) How much interest would Alex pay during the first year of the loan?

(c) Use the Run the Numbers worksheet, "Should You Buy or Rent?" on page 264 to determine whether Alex would be better off buying or renting.

4. **Refinancing a Mortgage.** Kevin Tutumbo of Terre Haute, Indiana, has owned his home for 15 years and expects to live in it for a least five more. He originally borrowed $135,000 at 6 percent interest for 30 years to buy the home. He still owes $96,000 on the loan. Interest rates have since fallen to 4.5 percent, and Kevin is considering refinancing the loan for 15 years. He would have to pay 2 points on the new loan with no prepayment penalty on the current loan.

DO IT IN CLASS
Page 289

(a) What is Kevin's current monthly payment?

(b) Calculate the monthly payment on the new loan.

(c) Advise Kevin on whether he should refinance his mortgage using the Run the Numbers worksheet, "When You Should Refinance Your Mortgage" on page 289.

5. **Illustrating Amortization.** Heather McIntosh of Watertown, South Dakota, recently purchased a home for $190,000. She put $25,000 down and took out a 25-year loan at 5.5 percent interest.

DO IT IN CLASS
Pages 283 and 285

(a) Use Table 9-4 on page 285 to determine her monthly payment.

(b) How much of her first payment will go toward interest and principal and how much will she owe after that first month?

(c) How much will she owe after three months. Hint: Use the logic of Table 9-2 on page 283.

FINANCIAL PLANNING CASES

CASE 1

The Johnsons Decide to Buy a Home

Belinda Johnson's parents and maternal grandmother have combined their finances and presented Harry and Belinda with $50,000 cash gift to use to purchase a home. The Johnsons have shopped and found a house in a new housing development that they like very much. They could either borrow from the developer or obtain a loan from one of three other mortgage lenders. The financial alternatives and data for the home are summarized in the table below.

(a) Which plan has the lowest total up-front costs? The highest?

(b) What would be the full monthly payment for PITI and PMI for each of the options?

(c) If the Johnsons had enough additional cash to make the 20 percent down payment, would you recommend lender 1 or lender 2? Why?

(d) Assuming that the Johnsons will need about $3,000 for moving costs (in addition to closing costs), which financing option would you recommend? Why?

Financing Details on a Home Available to the Johnsons

Price: $290,000. Developer A will finance the purchase with a 10 percent down payment and a 30-year, 5 percent ARM loan with 2 interest points. The initial monthly payment for principal and interest is $1401.10 ($261,000 loan after the down payment is made; 261 × $5.3682). After one year, the rate rises to 5.5 percent, with a principal plus interest payment of $1481.94. At that point, the rate can go up or down as much as 2 percent per year, depending on the cost of an index of mortgage funds. There is an interest-rate cap of 5 percent over the life of the loan. Taxes are estimated to be about $3,800, and the homeowner's insurance premium should be about $1,800 annually. A mortgage insurance premium of $88 per month must be paid monthly on the two 10 percent down options. Figure out the best option for them, and tell why.

Home: Price, $290,000; Taxes, $2,800; Insurance, $1,700

	Developer A	Lender 1	Lender 2	Lender 3
Loan term and type	30-year ARM*	30-year Con[†]	15-year Con	20-year Ren[‡]
Interest rate	5.0%	5.5%	6%	5.5%
Down payment	$29,000	$58,000	$58,000	$29,000
Loan amount	261,000	232,000	232,000	261,000
Points	2	1	0	2
Principal and interest payment	1,401	1,317	1,957	1,795
PMI	88	0	0	88

*Adjustable-rate mortgage.
[†]Conventional.
[‡]Renegotiable every five years.

CASE 2

Victor and Maria Hernandez Learn About Real Estate Agents

Victor and Maria have been thinking about selling their home and buying a house with more yard space so that they can indulge their passion for gardening. Before they make such a decision, they want to explore the market to see what might be available and in what price ranges. They will then list their house with a real estate agent and begin searching in earnest for a new home.

(a) What services could a real estate agent provide for the couple, and what types of agents could represent them as they sell their current home?

(b) A friend has advised them that they really need a buyer's agent for the purchase of the new home. Explain to the Hernandezes the difference between buyer's and seller's agents.

CASE 3

Julia Price Contemplates Buying a Home

Julia has been thinking about buying a home. For several months, she has been watching real estate shows on television and visiting open houses in her community. She thinks it is time to take the plunge and buy a much larger home since she can genuinely afford it. She also thinks that housing prices will rise substantially in the next five years. She has explored the interest rates currently being charged for mortgages and has calculated the amount of money she can afford to pay given her income. She is thinking that her next step would be to call a real estate agent and begin looking in earnest. Offer your opinions about her thinking.

CASE 4

Michael and Maggi Weigh the Benefits and Costs of Buying Versus Renting

Michael Joseph and Maggi Lewis of Saluda, Virginia, are trying to decide whether to rent or purchase housing. Michael favors buying and Maggi leans toward renting, and both seem able to justify their particular choice. Michael thinks that the tax advantages are a very good reason for buying. Maggi, however, believes that cash flow is much better when renting. See whether you can help them make their decision.

DO IT IN CLASS
Page 264

(a) Does the home buyer enjoy tax advantages? Explain.

(b) Discuss Maggi's belief that cash flow is better with renting.

(c) Suggest some reasons why Michael might consider renting rather than purchasing housing.

(d) Suggest some reasons why Maggi might consider buying rather than renting housing.

(e) Is there a clear-cut basis for deciding whether to rent or buy housing? Explain why or why not.

CASE 5

Jeremy Decides to Sell His Home Himself

Jeremy Jorgensen of Lawton, Oklahoma, is concerned about the costs involved in selling his home, so he has decided to sell his home himself rather than pay a broker to do it.

(a) How would you advise Jeremy if he asked you whether he should sell the house himself or list with a broker? Explain your answer.

(b) Would Jeremy really save money by selling his home himself if he considers his time as part of his costs? Why or why not?

(c) Can you suggest any ways that Jeremy might reduce his selling costs without doing the selling himself? Explain.

BE YOUR OWN PERSONAL FINANCIAL MANAGER

1. **Are You Ready to Buy a Home?** Review the material in the Run the Numbers worksheet "Should You Buy or Rent?" on page 264. Then using dollar amounts that fit your situation, complete Worksheet 37: Should I Rent or Buy Housing from "My Personal Financial Planner."

   My Personal Financial Planner

2. **Save to Buy a Home.** Review the material on "Financial Goals Follow From Your Values" on pages 77–78 and then complete Worksheet 14: Monthly Savings Needed to Reach My Goals from "My Personal Financial Planner," which allows you to determine the monthly savings amount you would need to reach a goal of having a down payment on a home.

   My Personal Financial Planner

3. **Can You Afford a Mortgage?** Review the material on "**Did You Know? How Much Income Do You Need to Qualify for a Mortgage?**" on page 276. Then using dollar amounts that fit your situation, complete Worksheet 38: Income Needed to Qualify for a Mortgage

from "My Personal Financial Planner." What price range of home could you afford given the results of your analysis?

   My Personal Financial Planner

4. **Shop for a Mortgage.** If you are ready to buy a home, review the material on "Conventional Mortgage and Adjustable Mortgage Loans" and "Other Housing Financing Arrangements" on pages 286–287. Then using that information complete Worksheet 39: Mortgage Shopping Worksheet from "My Personal Financial Planner" to begin your search for a mortgage.

   My Personal Financial Planner

5. **Should You Refinance Your Mortgage?** Do you have an existing mortgage? Review the material on "When You Should Refinance Your Mortgage" on page 289. Then using dollar amounts that fit your situation, complete Worksheet 42: Should I Refinance My Mortgage? from "My Personal Financial Planner."

   My Personal Financial Planner

ON THE NET

Go to the Web pages indicated to complete these exercises.

1. **Current Interest Rates.** Visit the website for Bankrate .com (www.bankrate.com/mortgage.aspx), where you will find information on mortgage interest rates around the United States. View the information for the lenders in a large city near your home. How does the information compare with the interest rates on your own credit card account(s)? How do the rates in the city you selected compare with other rates found in the United States?

2. **Monthly Home Payment.** Go to AOLReal Estates at realestate.aol.com/blog/zillow-mortgage-calculators and input data to buy, such as price of home, down payment, and type of mortgage and rate. Change financing terms as much as you like What do you think of this website?

3. **Can You Afford to Buy?** Visit the website for Bankrate.com, where you will find a calculator (www.bankrate.com/funnel/mortgages/?ic_id=CR_ SearchMtgProdTypeProduct&prods=1) that helps you determine the amount you can afford for the purchase of a home given your income and funds available for a down payment, points, FICO score, and other home-buying expenses. Enter the data requested for your current situation. What does the calculator tell you about your housing affordability? Change the entered data for some point in the future when you project a better financial situation for yourself. How do the results change?

4. **Searching for a Home to Buy.** Visit the website for the National Association of Realtors (www.realtor.com), where you can search for owned housing in various locales around the United States. Look for housing in your community or in one nearby. Were you able to find housing that meets your price range and other criteria? Also search for similar housing in the San Francisco, CA (high-cost) and Ocala, FL (low-cost) metropolitan areas. Compare these cost results with the housing found in your area.

5. **Search for a Home.** Go to Zillow at www.zillow.com. Insert any address you like and read the output. What do you think of this website?

ACTION INVOLVEMENT PROJECTS

1. **Do Some Home Shopping.** Realtors often open homes for sale to the public on Sunday afternoons. Spend an afternoon looking at housing that is for sale in a neighborhood near you. Gather the information sheets that are provided at the homes and take notes during your visits. Prepare a brief report that summarizes what you have learned about housing costs, features, and locations in the community.

2. **Comparing Leases.** Survey three of your friends who live in rental housing about their feelings about written leases. For those who have written leases, compare some of them for the rights and responsibilities of tenants outlined in the leases. Write a summary of your findings.

3. **Assess the Real Estate Market.** Make an appointment to talk with a real estate agent in your community.

Ask whether home sales are slow or brisk, how long it typically takes for sellers to sell a home, buyers to find a desirable home, whether home values are rising or declining, and tips the agent would give to people in your situation who hope to own their own homes. Write a summary of your findings.

4. **See How Others Go About Buying a Home.** Ask friends and relatives for the names of one or two people who have bought a home in recent years. Contact the home-buyers and ask them for an interview in person or over the phone to discuss how they went about buying a home and their feelings about how the process turned out for them. Compare their procedures and experiences with what you have learned in this chapter.

PART 3

isak55/Shutterstock.com

297

Managing Property and Liability Risk

Chinnapong/Shutterstock.com

YOU MUST BE KIDDING, RIGHT?

Megan Blake recently caused an automobile accident when she had a blowout on the freeway. The cost of repairs to Megan's car will be $13,200. The damage to the other vehicle was $37,900, although miraculously no one was injured in the accident. Megan had purchased an auto insurance policy with a $500 collision deductible and liability limits of $25,000/$50,000/$15,000; the legal minimums in her state. What dollar amount of the losses will Megan have to pay?

A. $500   C. $22,900

B. $13,400   D. $23,400

The answer is D. Megan will be personally responsible for the $23,400. That's the balance remaining after the insurance company payments ($500 + $22,900 [$37,900 − $15,000]). The company will pay her $12,700 after her $500 deductible for the loss of her vehicle. The company will also pay $15,000 for the damage to the other vehicle as that is the limit for property damage liability under her policy. Like most people, Megan did not carry sufficient liability protection. You should!

Learning Objectives

After reading this chapter, you should be able to:

1 Apply the risk-management process to address the risks to your property and income.

2 Explain how insurance works to reduce risk.

3 Design a homeowner's or renter's insurance program to meet your needs.

4 Design an automobile insurance program to meet your needs.

5 Describe other types of property and liability insurance.

6 Summarize how to make an insurance claim.

WHAT DO YOU RECOMMEND?

Nick and Amber Chandler recently had a fire in their garage that destroyed two of their cars and did considerable damage to the garage and to the outside of their home. After receiving their reimbursements from their homeowner's and automobile insurance policies, the Chandlers realized that they were seriously underinsured. One vehicle was not insured for fire, and the insurance on their dwelling amounted to only 60 percent of its current replacement value.

iStockphoto.com/janaiv

What do you recommend to Nick and Amber about managing property and liability risk regarding:

1. **The risk-management steps they should take to update their insurance coverages?**

2. **The relationship between severity and frequency of loss when deciding whether to buy insurance?**

3. **Adequately insuring their home?**

4. **The use of deductibles and policy limits to keep their automobile insurance premiums at a manageable level while still maintaining vital coverage?**

TO-DO SOON

Do the following to begin to achieve financial success:

1. *Identify your exposures to risk and the magnitude of the losses that could occur.*

2. *Assess your automobile insurance coverage and make changes as necessary.*

3. *Buy renter's insurance with limits tied to the actual cash value of your personal property.*

4. *Purchase an umbrella liability insurance policy with a minimum of a $1 million limit.*

5. *Maintain an inventory of all your insured property so that in the event of a loss you can collect what is coming to you.*

Learning Objective 1

Apply the risk-management process to address the risks to your property and income.

risk
Uncertainty about the outcome of a situation or event.

risk management
Process of identifying and evaluating purely risky situations to determine and implement appropriate management.

perils
Any event that can cause a financial loss.

It is important to protect your income, property, and possessions from the possibility of financial loss from accidents, acts of nature, illness or injury, and death. Bad things do happen but, fortunately, not very often. And such losses can be expensive. You can manage the risk of such losses through the use of insurance.

Learning what insurance is, how to buy the right type and amount, how to use it wisely, and how to collect on a loss are examples of smart money management. You can waste hundreds of dollars buying too much or the wrong kind of homeowners, renters, and auto insurance.

More than one-third of insurance buyers simply renew their policies without any reassessment of need or comparison shopping. On average, drivers have not changed insurance companies in a dozen years. If you are single, you probably will spend between $9,000 and $14,000 on auto insurance premiums in the next 10 years. For that amount of money you should make sure you have the right coverage at the right price.

10.1 RISK AND RISK MANAGEMENT

10.1a People Often Misunderstand the Concept of Risk

Risk is uncertainty about the outcome of a situation or event. It arises out of the possibility that the outcome will differ from what is expected. In the area of financial losses, risk consists of uncertainty about both whether the financial loss will occur and how large it might be.

There are two types of risk. **Speculative risk** exists in situations where there is potential for gain as well as for loss. Investments such as those made in the stock market involve speculative risk. **Pure risk** exists when there is no potential for gain, only the possibility of loss. Fires, automobile accidents, illness, and theft are examples of events involving pure risk. Insurance only addresses pure risk.

Many people think of "odds" or games of chance when they hear the word risk. In fact, risk and odds are different concepts. The difference between the two is subtle but very important. An event with a 95 percent chance of occurring is highly likely to occur. Thus, both uncertainty and risk are low. An event with a 0.000001 percent chance of occurring is highly likely *not* to occur. Thus, both uncertainty and risk are low. When an event has a moderate chance of occurring—5 percent, for example—the uncertainty and risk are relatively high because it is difficult to predict the one person in 20 who will experience the event. In such cases, insurance often represents a wise choice for reducing risk.

10.1b Apply the Risk-Management Process

Risk management is the process of identifying and evaluating situations involving pure risk to determine and implement the appropriate means for its management. Risk management involves making the most efficient arrangements *before* a loss occurs. Risk management usually requires the purchase of insurance, although insurance is only one of the ways to handle risk, and it is not always the best choice.

The risk-management process involves five steps:

Step 1: Identify Your Risk Exposures Sources of risk are called **exposures** and these include the items you own and the activities in which you engage that expose you to potential financial loss. Owning and/or driving an automobile are common exposures. To determine your exposures to risk, you should take an inventory of what you own and what you do. You also need to identify the **perils** that you face, which are any events that can cause a financial loss. Fire, wind, theft, vehicle collision, illness, and death are examples of perils.

The items you own and your day-to-day activities expose you to two types of losses: property and liability. **Property insurance** protects you from financial losses resulting from the damage to or destruction of your property or possessions. **Liability insurance** protects you from financial losses suffered by others for which you are held responsible (legally liable). Coverage includes your legal fees if you are sued but does not include coverage for your intentional acts and contractual obligations. The most commonly purchased forms of property and liability insurance are insurance for your home and its contents and insurance for your use and ownership of vehicles.

property insurance

Protection from financial losses resulting from the damage to or destruction of your property or possessions.

liability insurance

Protection from financial losses suffered when you are held liable for others' losses

Step 2: Estimate Your Risk and Potential Losses Next you estimate loss frequency and severity. **Frequency of loss** is the likely number of times that a loss might occur over a period of time. Is the loss highly likely, not very likely to happen, or will it hardly ever happen? **Severity of loss** describes the potential magnitude of a loss. Will the loss be enough to bankrupt you, use up a substantial amount of your resources, or is it an expense you can handle in your budget?

Many people wonder whether they should buy insurance when loss frequency is low, for example, if they are young and healthy or if they live in a safe neighborhood. This is not a good way to think about potential losses because they still could occur, and if loss frequency is low, the cost of insurance would be small. The bottom line is that high severity and low frequency losses should be insured against and low severity and high frequency losses should be prepared for in your budget and savings planning. What is more important is loss severity. "How much might I lose?" is the question to ask. When considering possible property losses, you make an estimate of the value of the property. Liability losses are complicated because the severity of the loss depends on the circumstances of the person you harm. For example, if you caused an accident that permanently disabled a young heart surgeon with three small children, you would be liable for the surgeon's care, lost earnings over his or her lifetime, and future care and education of the children. A loss of several million dollars is not out of the question in such a situation.

Step 3: Choose How to Handle Your Risk of Loss The risk of loss may be handled in multiple ways: risk avoidance, risk retention, loss control, risk transfer, and **risk reduction**. Each strategy may be appropriate for certain circumstances, and the mix that you choose will depend on the source of the risk, the size of the potential loss, your personal feelings about risk, and the financial resources you have available to pay for losses. The five ways to handle risk follow.

risk reduction

Includes mechanisms, such as insurance, that reduce the overall uncertainty about the magnitude of loss.

risk retention

Accepting that some risks simply arise in the course of one's life and consciously retaining that risk.

deductible clause

Requires that the policyholder pays an initial portion of any loss.

loss control

Designing specific mechanisms to reduce loss frequency and loss severity.

- **Risk avoidance.** The simplest way to handle risk is to avoid it. For example, choosing not to own an airplane or not to skydive limits your exposures.

- **Risk retention.** A second way to handle risk is **risk retention**; you either to retain or accept it. For example, you can use a **deductible clause** in an insurance policy to retain an initial portion of the risk. In this way, you pay the first dollars of a loss (perhaps $200 or $500) before the insurance company will reimburse for a loss.

- **Loss control.** **Loss control** is designed to reduce loss frequency and loss severity. For example, installing heavy-duty locks and doors may reduce the *frequency* of theft losses. Installing fire alarms and smoke detectors cannot prevent fires but should reduce the *severity* of losses from them. Insurance companies often require loss-control efforts or give discounts to policyholders who implement them.

- **Risk transfer.** Another way to handle risk is to transfer it to an insurance company.

- **Risk Reduction.** The final way to handle risk is to reduce it to acceptable levels. Insurance is used by policyholders when they arrange for all or a portion of their risk to be covered by an insurance company, thereby reducing their personal level of risk.

BIAS TOWARD—UNDERESTIMATING RISK

People have a bias toward certain behaviors that can be harmful, such as a tendency toward underestimating risk. Many fail to buy insurance for events that are rare and think that a catastrophe will not happen to them. What to do? Recognize that the cost of insurance is very low for rare events and adding to our policy limits is inexpensive.

Renters need insurance too.

large-loss principle

A basic rule of risk management that encourages us to insure the risks that we cannot afford and retain the risks that we can reasonably afford.

Step 4: Implement Your Risk-Management Program

The next step in risk management is to implement the risk-handling methods you have chosen. For most households, this means buying insurance to transfer and reduce risk. This involves selecting types of policies and coverages, dollar amounts of coverage, and sources of insurance protection. Always remember that your goal is to "buy" the insurance you need at a fair price. Do not let yourself be "sold" more or less insurance coverage than you need at unnecessary prices.

People often wonder what types of insurance to buy and how much coverage they should have. You should use the maximum possible loss as a guide for the dollar amount of coverage to purchase.

This way of thinking makes use of the **large-loss principle**, which states: "Insure the risks that you cannot afford and retain the risks that you can reasonably afford." In other words, pay for small losses out of your own pocket and purchase as much insurance as necessary to cover large, catastrophic losses that might ruin you financially. The example earlier of an auto accident that injures a heart surgeon would bring you such financial ruin because a court could hold you responsible for those losses. Consequently, you would want high dollar amounts of liability coverage on your auto insurance.

Step 5: Evaluate and Adjust Your Program The final step in risk management involves periodic review of your risk-management efforts. The risks people face in their lives change continually. Therefore, no risk-management plan should be put in place and then ignored for long periods of time.

An annual review is certainly important but also check your insurance needs when you move, make a major purchase, or if your family situation changes. Many people simply keep old insurance policies that no longer fit their needs (too little or too much coverage) and then find they are inappropriately covered when a loss occurs.

CONCEPT CHECK 10.1

1. Distinguish between pure risk and speculative risk.
2. Explain the distinctions between risk and odds.
3. List, describe, and give an example of each of the five ways to handle risk of loss.
4. When considering likelihood of loss and severity of loss, explain which one of these two concepts is more important when deciding whether to buy insurance and why.

Learning Objective 2
Explain how insurance works to reduce risk.

10.2 UNDERSTANDING HOW INSURANCE WORKS

Insurance is a mechanism for transferring and reducing pure risk through which a large number of individuals share in the financial losses suffered by members of the group as a whole. Insurance protects each individual in the group by replacing an uncertain—and possibly large—financial loss with a certain but comparatively small fee called the **premium**. Insurance premiums are paid for in advance and have four components:

1. The individual's share of the group's losses
2. A share of the company's expenses for administering the insurance plan
3. Insurance company reserves set aside to pay future losses
4. Profit when the plan is administered by a profit-seeking company

The **insurance policy** is the contract between the person buying insurance (the **insured**) and the insurance company (the **insurer**). It contains language that describes the rights and responsibilities of both parties. Most people do not take the time to read and understand their insurance policies. As a result, insurance remains one of the least understood purchases people make. You can do a better job managing your risks if you understand the basic terms and concepts used in the field of insurance, and reading this chapter will improve your knowledge.

10.2a Hazards Make Losses More Likely to Occur

A **hazard** is any condition that increases the probability that a peril will occur. Driving under the influence of alcohol and/or texting represent especially dangerous hazards.

Three types of hazards exist:

- A **physical hazard** is a particular characteristic of the insured person or property that increases the chance of loss. An example of a physical hazard is high blood pressure in a person covered by health insurance.

- A **morale hazard** exists when a person is indifferent to a peril. For example, a morale hazard exists if the insured party, knowing that theft insurance will pay for the loss, becomes careless about locking doors and windows.

- A **moral hazard** relates to the possibility that the insured person will want or even cause a peril to occur in order to collect reimbursement from the insurance company.

Insurance companies often limit or deny coverage if a loss occurs as a result of a morale or moral hazard. An investigation often reveals the truth.

10.2b Only Fortuitous and Financial Losses Are Insurable

Certain minimum requirements must be met for a loss to be considered insurable—in particular, the loss must be fortuitous and financial. **Fortuitous losses** are unexpected in terms of both their timing and their magnitude. A loss caused by a lightning strike and fire to your home is fortuitous; a loss caused by a decline in the market value of your home is not because it is reasonable to expect home values to rise and fall over time. A **financial loss** is any decline in the value of income or assets in the present or future. Financial losses can be measured objectively in dollars and cents.

10.2c The Principle of Indemnity Limits Insurance Payouts

The **principle of indemnity** states that insurance will pay *no more* than the actual financial loss suffered. For example, an automobile insurance policy will pay only the **actual cash value** of a stolen automobile. This is the replacement value less the value of depreciation. This principle prevents a person from gaining financially from a loss (certainly a moral hazard). The principle of indemnity *does not* guarantee that insured losses will be totally reimbursed. Every policy also includes **policy limits** that specify the maximum dollar amounts that will be paid under the policy. As a result, insurance purchasers must carefully select policy limits sufficient to cover their potential losses.

---

insurance

Mechanism for transferring and reducing pure risk through which a large number of individuals share in the financial losses suffered by members of the group as a whole.

premium

The monthly or annual cost paid for insurance.

insurance policy

Contract between the person buying insurance (the insured) and the insurance company (the insurer).

hazard

Any condition that increases the probability that a peril will occur.

principle of indemnity

Insurance will pay no more than the actual financial loss suffered

actual cash value (of personal property)

Represents the purchase price of the property less depreciation.

policy limits

Specify the maximum dollar amounts that will be paid under the policy.

10.2d Ways to Pay Less for Insurance and Still Maintain Sufficient Coverage

Some features of insurance policies can lower your premiums without significantly reducing the protection offered. These features include deductibles, coinsurance, hazard reduction, and loss reduction.

deductible

An initial portion of any loss that must be paid before the insurance company will provide coverage.

1. **Pay the first dollars of a loss yourself. A** deductible is an initial portion of any loss that must be paid before the insurance company will provide coverage. For example, automobile collision insurance often includes a $500 deductible and that means that the first $500 of loss to the car must be paid by the insured. The insurer then pays the remainder of the loss, up to the limits of the policy. The higher the deductible, the more you will save on your premium.

coinsurance

Method by which the insured and the insurer share proportionately in the payment for a loss.

2. **Pay a share of any loss yourself.** Coinsurance is a method by which the insured and the insurer share proportionately in the payment for a loss. For example, a policy may require that the insured pay 20 percent of a loss and the insurer pay the remaining 80 percent. Substantial premium reductions can be realized through coinsurance, but you must be prepared to pay your share of losses. The following **deductible and coinsurance reimbursement formula** can be used to determine the amount of a loss that will be reimbursed when the policy includes both a deductible and a coinsurance clause:

$$R = (1 - CP)(L - D) \quad \textbf{(10.1)}$$

where

R = Reimbursement
CP = Coinsurance percentage required of the insured
L = Loss
D = Deductible

As an example, assume you have an insurance policy with a $100 deductible and a 20 percent coinsurance requirement. If the bill is $10,000, the reimbursement will be $7,920, calculated as follows:

$$R = (1.00 - 0.20)(\$10,000 - \$100)$$
$$= (0.80)(\$9,900)$$
$$= \$7,920$$

3. **Reduce the chances that a loss will occur.** Hazard reduction is action taken by the insured to reduce the probability of a loss occurring. Quitting smoking is an example of hazard reduction related to life and health insurance.
4. **Reduce the dollar amount of a loss. Loss reduction** is action taken by the insured to lessen the severity of loss if a peril occurs. Smoke alarms and fire extinguishers in the home are examples of loss reduction efforts. These items will not prevent fires, but their use may lead to less severe damage.

10.2e Risk Is Reduced for the Insurer through the Law of Large Numbers

Insurance consists of two basic elements: (1) the reduction of risk and (2) the sharing of losses. When you buy insurance, you exchange the uncertainty of a potentially large financial loss for the certainty of a fixed insurance premium, thereby reducing your risk.

As the late baseball player Yogi Berra once said, "It is tough to make predictions, especially about the future." But predictions are much easier for an insurance company than for an individual. This is because risk is reduced for the insurer through the **law of large numbers**. As the number of members in a group increases, predictions about the group's behavior become increasingly more accurate. This greater accuracy decreases uncertainty and, therefore, risk.

law of large numbers

As the number of members in a group increases, predictions about the group's behavior become increasingly accurate.

10.2f Each Insured Benefits Even if One Does Not Suffer a Loss

Individual insurance purchasers benefit regardless of whether they actually suffer a loss because of the reduction of risk. This is the essence of insurance. Reduced risk gives one the freedom to drive a car, own a home, start a business, and plan financially for the future with the knowledge that some unforeseen event will not result in financial disaster.

10.2g How Companies Select among Insurance Applicants

The purchase of insurance begins with an offer by the purchaser in the form of a written or oral policy application. The insurer typically issues a temporary insurance contract, called a **binder,** which is replaced at a later date with a written policy. The application then goes through a process of **underwriting**. This is the insurer's procedure for deciding which insurance applicants to accept. To describe the process of underwriting, it is necessary to first understand how insurance rates are set.

An **insurance rate** is the price charged for each unit of insurance coverage. Rates represent the average cost of providing coverage to various **classes of insureds.** These classes consist of insureds who share similar characteristics. For example, automobile insurance policyholders may be classified by age, gender, marital status, and driving record, as well as by the make and model of vehicle that they drive.

When underwriters receive an application, they assign the applicant to the appropriate class. They then determine whether the rates established for that class are sufficient

DID YOU KNOW

How to Read an Insurance Policy

Insurance policies do not invite casual reading. Consequently, many people neglect to thoroughly examine their policies until a loss occurs, only to find that they had misunderstood the terms of the agreement. You can avoid such problems by systematically reading a policy before you purchase it, focusing on eight points:

1. *Perils covered.* Some policies list only the perils that are covered; others cover all perils except those listed. The definition of certain perils may differ from that used in everyday language.

2. *Property covered.* Like perils, the property covered under a policy may be listed individually, or only the excluded property may be listed. When the property is listed individually, any new acquisitions must be added to the policy.

3. *Types of losses covered.* Three types of property losses can occur: (a) the loss of the property itself, (b) extra expenses that may arise because the property is rendered unusable for a period of time, and (c) loss of income if the property was used in the insured's work.

4. *People covered.* Insurance policies may cover only certain individuals. This information usually appears on

the first page of the policy but may be changed subsequently in later sections.

5. *Locations covered.* Where the loss occurs may have a bearing on whether it will be covered. It is especially important to know which locations are not covered.

6. *Time period of coverage.* Policies are generally written to cover specific time periods. Restrictions may exclude coverage during specific times of the day or certain days of the week or year.

7. *Loss control requirements.* Insurance policies often stipulate that certain loss control efforts must be maintained by the insured. For example, coverage for a vehicle may be denied if the owner knowingly allows it to be driven by an unlicensed person.

8. *Amount of coverage.* All insurance policies specify the maximum amount the insurer will pay for various types of losses.

The information on these eight points may be spread throughout a policy. In fact, coverage that appears to be provided in one location actually may be denied elsewhere. Carefully review the entire policy to determine the protection it provides. If necessary, telephone the salesperson or company to obtain clarification.

to provide coverage for that specific applicant. Underwriters divide insurance applicants into four groups:

1. *Preferred* applicants have lower-than-average loss expectancies and save money because they typically qualify for lower premiums.
2. *Standard* applicants have average loss expectancies for their class and pay the standard rates.
3. *Substandard* applicants have higher-than-average loss expectancies and may be charged higher premiums and have restrictions placed on the types or amounts of coverage they may purchase.
4. *Unacceptable* applicants have loss expectancies that are much too high and are rejected.

You might save money by confirming with your insurance agent that you have been placed in the proper class for premium-determination purposes.

10.2h **Who Sells Insurance?**

insurance agents

Representative of an insurance company authorized to sell, modify, service, and terminate insurance contracts.

Exclusive agents

Companies that market insurance policies through salaried employees, mail-order promotions, newspapers, the Internet, and even vending machines.

Sellers of insurance, called **insurance agents**, represent one or more insurance companies. They have the power to enter into, change, and cancel insurance policies on behalf of these companies. Two types of insurance agents exist: exclusive and independent agents.

Exclusive agents are contracted to sell policies for a single insurance company. They are paid by that one company either with a combination of salary and commissions or with just commissions. They do not shop around at several companies to find a client the best policy for the best price. Most of the insurance companies that are household names, such as MetLife and Aetna, are exclusive agents, sometimes known as **captive agents** or **direct sellers.**

Independent agents can sell the policies of many different companies. They are independent businesspeople who act as third-party links between insurers and insureds. Such agents earn commissions from the companies they represent and will place each insurance customer with the company that they believe best meets that customer's particular needs.

Each type of seller presents both advantages and disadvantages. Independent agents may provide more personalized service and can select among several companies to meet a customer's needs. Exclusive agents can provide personalized service as well but are limited to the policies offered by the one company they represent but their sales commissions tend to be low. For people who know what coverage they need, the lowest-cost insurance premiums can be found with exclusive agents.

CONCEPT CHECK 10.2

1. Define *insurance.*
2. Distinguish among the three types of hazards.
3. Why is the principle of indemnity so important to insurance sellers?
4. Summarize how to use deductibles, coinsurance, hazard reduction, and loss reduction to lower the cost of insurance.
5. Summarize how companies select among insurance applicants.
6. Differentiate between independent agents and exclusive agents.

Learning Objective 3

Design a homeowner's or renter's insurance program to meet your needs.

homeowner's insurance

Combines liability and property insurance coverages that homeowners and renters typically need into single-package policies.

10.3 HOMEOWNER'S INSURANCE

Whether you own or rent housing, you face the possibility of suffering property and liability losses.

10.3a **Coverages**

Homeowner's insurance combines the liability and property insurance coverages needed by homeowners and renters into a single-package policy.

Property Coverage Homeowner's insurance provides protection for various types of property damage losses, including the following:

(1) damage to the dwelling;
(2) damage to other structures on the property, referred to as **appurtenant structures;**
(3) damage to personal property and dwelling contents; and
(4) expenses arising out of a loss of use of the dwelling (for example, food and lodging).

Additional coverages are usually provided for such items as debris removal, trees and shrubs, and fire department service charges. The property protection in a homeowner's policy is written on a named-perils or all-risk basis. **Named-perils policies** cover only those losses caused by perils that are specifically mentioned in the policy. **All-risk (or open-perils) policies** cover losses caused by all perils other than those specifically *excluded* by the policy. All-risk policies provide broader coverage because hundreds of perils can cause property losses, but only a few would be excluded. Common exclusions are flood, earthquake, sewage backup, and mold unless caused by some nonexcluded event such as burst water pipes. Coverage for excluded perils can often be purchased for an additional premium if desired.

named-perils policies
Cover only losses caused by perils that the policy specifically mentions.

all-risk (open-perils) policies
Cover losses caused by all perils other than those that the policy specifically excludes.

Liability Coverage Whenever homeowners are negligent or otherwise fail to exercise due caution in protecting visitors, they may potentially suffer a liability loss. Liability insurers have three major duties: (1) the duty to indemnify, and (2) the duty to settle a reasonable claim, and when appropriate (3) the duty to defend. **Homeowner's general liability protection** applies when you are legally liable for the losses of another person and that includes legal fees and damages assessed up to the limits of the policy.

Homeowners often wish to take responsibility for the losses of another person regardless of the legal liability. Consider, for example, a guest's child who suffers burns from touching a hot barbecue grill. **Homeowner's no-fault medical payments protection** will pay for bodily injury losses suffered by visitors regardless of who was at fault. In the preceding example, such coverage would help pay for the medical treatment of the visitor's burns. **Homeowner's no-fault property damage protection** will pay for property losses suffered by visitors to your home. An example of such a loss might be damage to a friend's leather coat that was chewed by your dog.

homeowner's general liability protection
Applies when you are legally liable for another person's losses, other than those that arise out of use of vehicles or your professional duties.

10.3b Types of Homeowner's Insurance Policies

Six distinct types of homeowner's insurance policies exist: HO-1, HO-2, and HO-3, HO-5, and HO-8, HO-4 and HO-6, as described in Table 10-1. Each is a standardized package of protections designed to cover the perils that commonly affect homeowners and renters. The same terms and identifying numbers are generally used by most insurance companies.

Policies for Owners of Single-Family Dwellings The **basic form (HO-1)** is a named-perils policy that covers 10 property-damage-causing perils and liability-related exposures. The **broad form (HO-2)** is a named-perils policy that covers not 11 but 16 property-damage-causing perils and liability-related exposures. There are special limits on certain classes of personal property, such as loss of jewelry or money. The **special form (HO-3)** is the most common type purchased by homeowners. It provides all-risk protection on the dwelling and 16 listed perils protection on the personal property and protection from liability-related exposures. The **comprehensive form (HO-5)** policy is similar to HO-3 policies except that both the dwelling coverage and personal property coverage are written on an all-risk basis. Again there are special limits on certain classes of personal property, such as loss of jewelry, stamp collections, home office equipment, or money, such as $1,000 or $2,500. If you desire insurance coverage on

YOUR GRANDPARENTS SAY

"Getting a Dog Means Buying Insurance"

"Notify your insurance company if you get a dog, because they might not renew your policy if you make a claim and did not tell them about the animal. One-third of homeowner's insurance liability claims are associated with the 4½ million annual dog bites, and one in five bites requires medical treatment. The average insurance claim is $32,000."

Table 10-1 Summary of Homeowner's Insurance Policies

	HO-1 (Basic Form)	HO-2 (Broad Form)	HO-3 (Special Form)
Perils covered (descriptions are given below)	Perils 1–4, 6, 8–12	Perils 1–16	All perils except those specifically excluded for buildings; perils 1–16 on personal property (does not include glass breakage)
House and any other attached buildings	Amount based on replacement cost, minimum $15,000	Amount based on replacement cost, minimum $15,000	Amount based on replacement cost, minimum $20,000
Detached buildings (appurtenant structures)	10 percent of insurance on the home (minimum)	10 percent of insurance on the home (minimum)	10 percent of insurance on the home (minimum)
Trees, shrubs, plants, etc.	5 percent of insurance on the home, $500 maximum per item	5 percent of insurance on the home, $500 maximum per item	5 percent of insurance on the home, $500 maximum per item
Personal property	50–70 percent of insurance on the home (minimum)	50–70 percent of insurance on the home (minimum)	50–70 percent of insurance on the home (minimum)
Loss of use and/or additional living expense	10 percent of insurance on the home	20 percent of insurance on the home	20 percent of insurance on the home
Credit card, forgery, counterfeit money	$1,000	$1,000	$1,000

Liability coverage/limits (for all policies)		**Special limits of liability**	
Comprehensive personal liability	$300,000	For the following classes of personal property, special limits apply on a per-occurrence basis (e.g., per fire or theft): money, coins, bank notes, precious metals (gold, silver, etc.), $200; computers, $5,000; securities, deeds, stocks, bonds, tickets, stamps, $1,000; watercraft and trailers, including furnishings, equipment, and outboard motors, $1,000; trailers other than for watercraft, $1,000; jewelry, watches, furs, $1,000; silverware, goldware, etc., $2,500; guns, $2,000.	
No-fault medical payments	$1,000		
No-fault property damage	$500		

List of perils covered

1. Theft
2. Fire or Lightning
3. Explosion
4. Smoke
5. Freezing
6. Vehicles
7. Falling Objects
8. Volcanic Eruption
9. Windstorm or Hail

10. Riot or Civil Commotion
11. Damage caused by Aircraft
12. Vandalism or Malicious Mischief
13. Damage due to weight of Ice, Snow, or Sleet
14. Sudden & Accidental Tearing Apart, Cracking, Burning, or Bulging
15. Sudden & Accidental Damage from Artificially Generated Electric Current
16. Accidental Discharge or Overflow of Water from Plumbing, Air conditioning etc.

Table 10-1 Summary of Homeowner's Insurance Policies (*Continued*)

HO-4 (Renter's Contents Broad Form)	HO-6 (For Condominium owners)	HO-8 (For Older Homes)
Perils 1–16	Perils 1–16	Perils 1–4, 6, 8–12
10 percent of personal property insurance on additions and alterations to the apartment	$1,000 on owner's additions and alterations to the unit	Amount based on actual cash value of the home
Not covered	Not covered (unless owned solely by the insured)	10 percent of insurance on the home (minimum)
10 percent of personal property insurance, $500 maximum per item	10 percent of personal property insurance, $500 maximum per item	5 percent of insurance on the home, $500 maximum per item
Chosen by the tenant to reflect the value of the items, minimum $6,000	Chosen by the homeowner to reflect the value of the items, minimum $6,000	50–70 percent of insurance on the home (minimum)
20 percent of personal property insurance	40 percent of personal property insurance	20 percent of insurance on the home
$1,000	$1,000	$1,000

These perils that are typically excluded in all standard homeowners insurance policies and must be purchased as a rider to the policy or separately, if available at all:

1. Earth Movement (earthquake coverage can be endorsed)
2. Ordinance or Law (some coverage may be provided in your policy)
3. Water Damage (Sudden & Accidental Water Damage is automatically included; others can be endorsed onto the policy)
4. Power Failure
5. Neglect
6. War
7. Nuclear Hazard
8. Intentional Loss
9. Government Action
10. Collapse (some coverage may be provided in your policy)
11. Theft to a Dwelling Under Construction
12. Vandalism or Malicious Mischief (only if vacant more than 60 days)
13. Mold, Fungus, or Wet Rot (some coverage may be provided in your policy)
14. Wear & Tear, Deterioration
15. Mechanical Breakdown
16. Smog, Rust & Corrosion
17. Smoke from Agricultural Smudging & Industrial Operations
18. Discharge, Dispersal, Seepage of Pollutants
19. Settling, Shrinking, Bulging, or Expanding
20. Birds, Vermin, Rodents, Insects
21. Animals Owned by Insured

This table describes the standard policies. Specific items differ from company to company and from state to state. When you want a limit that exceeds the standard limit for your company, you usually can increase the limit by paying an additional premium.

such items, you can buy a **rider** for perhaps $10 to $20 per $1,000 in coverage a year. This is a provision of an insurance policy that is purchased separately from the basic policy and that provides additional benefits at additional cost.

The **older home form (HO-8)** is a named-perils policy that provides actual-cash-value protection on the dwelling; not replacement protection. The replacement value of older home may be much higher than its market or actual cash value. Thus, the policy only provides that the dwelling be rebuilt to make it serviceable; not rebuilt to the same standards of style and quality.

Policies for Renters The **renter's contents broad form (HO-4)** is a named-perils policy that protects the insured from losses to the contents of a dwelling rather than the dwelling itself. It covers 17 perils (except for glass breakage) and provides some liability protection. HO-4 also provides for living expenses if the dwelling is rendered uninhabitable by one of the covered perils.

Rider

This is a provision of an insurance policy that is purchased separately from the basic policy and that provides additional benefits at additional cost.

DO IT IN CLASS

renter's contents broad form (HO-4)

Named-perils policy that protects the insured from losses to the contents of a rented dwelling rather than to the dwelling itself.

ADVICE FROM A SEASONED PRO

Applying the Large-Loss Principle to Property and Liability Insurance

You should always select insurance coverage limits for the highest possible loss. Although rare, such losses can destroy your financial future. That thinking underlies the large-loss principle discussed earlier. Here is how to apply the principle to property and liability insurance.

For your personal property insurance, you should select limits that equal the value of the property involved. A $240,000 home should be insured for $240,000. Better yet, you can add **extended-replacement coverage,** which covers the difference if the price to rebuild exceeds your dwelling limit. Select all-risk policies rather than named-peril policies. Yes, the cost may be higher, but the loss of your property could be much worse.

The purchase of an umbrella liability policy is the best way to apply the large-loss principle to liability insurance. Never buy the legal minimums for auto insurance. Causing an accident that destroys one newer-model vehicle

can exceed most state minimum limits. The minimum legally required bodily injury liability coverage is $10,000 to $15,000 in nine states, including California, Florida, and New Jersey. According to the Insurance Information Institute, however, the average bodily injury claim is over $17,000.

You can afford to apply the large-loss principle through the use of higher deductibles. Ask yourself: "What is the largest loss I can afford to cover myself?" Then choose the highest deductible that does not exceed what you can afford to cover. The money saved by selecting a higher deductible can be used to pay for higher policy limits. For example, on a 100/300/50 auto policy with a $100 deductible, you can save as much as $300 per year by simply raising the deductibles to $1,000! Then you can apply some of those savings to buy a $1,000,000 umbrella policy to protect yourself from a catastrophic loss.

Kyoung Tae (KT) Kim
The University of Alabama, Tuscaloosa, Alabama

Policies for Condominium Owners The **condominium form (HO-6)** is a named-perils policy protecting condominium owners from the three principal losses they face: losses to contents and personal property, losses due to the additional living expenses that may arise if one of the covered perils occurs, and liability losses. The building itself is insured by the management of the condominium.

10.3c Buying Homeowner's Insurance

In keeping with the large loss principle you need to select appropriate amounts of coverage on your (1) dwelling, (2) its contents, and (3) liability losses.

1. How Much Coverage Is Needed on Your Dwelling? If you own your home, your first step is to determine the dwelling's replacement value. You could either use the services of a professional liability appraiser and/or consult with your insurance agent to determine replacement value, and as a result the insurance company will not pay the full amount of any losses. Note that over one-half of the homes in the United States are said to be underinsured.

replacement-cost requirement
Stipulates that a home must be insured for 80 percent of its replacement value (some companies require 100 percent) in order for any loss to be fully covered.

Homeowner's insurance policies usually contain a **replacement-cost requirement** that stipulates that a home must be insured for a specified percentage of its replacement value. Historically, the industry standard has been 80 percent, and companies are increasingly requiring 100 percent coverage. Thus, a home with a replacement value of $200,000 would need to be insured for at least $160,000 or perhaps $200,000, and this amount would be the maximum that the insurance company would be obligated to pay for a total loss (after payment of the deductible by the policyholder). If you fail to meet your replacement-cost requirement, you will not be considered fully insured and by default you are coinsuring any losses that may occur. The amount of reimbursement for partial losses will be calculated using the **replacement-cost-requirement formula:**

$$R = (L - D) \times [I \div (RV \times 0.80 \text{ or } 1.00)] \quad \textbf{(10.2)}$$

DO IT IN CLASS

where

   R = Reimbursement payable
   L = Amount of loss
   D = Deductible, if any
    I = Amount of insurance actually carried
 RV = Replacement value of the dwelling

Consider the example of Selena Torres from Henderson, Nevada, who owns a home with a replacement value of $200,000 with a $500 deductible. Some years ago Selena had insured her home for $144,000 and the coverage never increased, even though the policy required coverage of 80 percent of the replacement cost. Last month a fire in her home caused damage amounting to $80,500. Applying Equation (10.2), Selena's calculations are as follows:

$$
\begin{aligned}
R &= (\$80,500 - \$500) \times [\$144,000 \div (\$200,000 \times 0.80)] \\
&= \$80,000 \times (\$144,000 \div \$160,000) \\
&= \$80,000 \times 0.90 = \$72,000
\end{aligned}
$$

As this calculation shows, Selena will be reimbursed for only $72,000 of her loss. Her failure to insure her house for 80 percent of its replacement cost, or $160,000 ($200,000 × 0.80), means she will be covered for only 90 percent ($144,000/$160,000) of its value, and she must pay 10 percent of any partial loss—in this case, $8,000.

Meeting an 80 percent replacement-cost requirement enables you to avoid coinsurance on small losses but might still result in inadequate coverage on large losses that, though rare, exceed the policy limit. Thus, it is wise to insure your dwelling for

ADVICE FROM A SEASONED PRO

Renter's Insurance Is a Must

Have you ever calculated the value of your personal property? Are you financially able to replace all of it in the case of a loss? Your landlord's insurance is only there to cover them and their property, not yours. For a tenant to collect on a loss he/she must prove negligence in court to collect any damages. This is difficult to accomplish, and it may take years.

A renter's insurance policy can cover you in all kinds of real-world situations, such as, theft, vandalism, damage from fire, hail or wind, and personal liability. A standard renter's policy covers $30,000 to replace personal property losses on furniture, carpets, rugs, appliances, clothing, computers, smartphones, and it provides limited coverage on certain other personal items, like jewelry, artwork,

and electronic equipment. If a burglar breaks your car window and steals your laptop, auto insurance may fix the window but renter's insurance will replace the laptop.

Another benefit of renter's insurance is the liability coverage it provides—on and off premises—to pay for medical bills, damages, and legal defense costs from injuries caused by you, members of your family, or a pet. Also it pays for temporary living expenses if your place is damaged and becomes uninhabitable. Renter's insurance is very affordable. The average cost of a rental insurance policy with $30,000 of property coverage and $100,000 of liability coverage is approximately $12 a month but the rates will depend upon the amount and type of coverage you select.

Vicky Swank
Heritage University, Toppenish, Washington

100 percent of its replacement cost. You will also want to sign up for **inflation guard protection** to have your insurance company increase your coverage automatically each year to keep up with inflation.

A standard property insurance policy will replace a damaged property so that it is the same or similar as before. If a house was built a long time ago, building a similar structure as a replacement may not satisfy new building code regulations that will be required in the rebuild. This is especially true in areas that may have experienced natural disasters such as wildfires, windstorms, and flooding. **Law and ordinance protection** is a special insurance endorsement that pays for demolishment and/or repairs to meet modern building standards.

2. How Much Coverage Is Needed on Your Personal Property? Making a **personal property inventory** of, and placing a value on, all the contents of your home are time-consuming but important tasks. Table 10-2 shows the inventory and valuation for the contents of and personal property in a typical living room. You should conduct such an inventory for each room, the basement, garage, shed, and yard possessions. When totaled, these values will enable you to select proper policy coverage limits.

Most homeowner's policies are designed to automatically cover contents and personal property for up to 50 to 70 percent of the coverage on the home. For example, if your home is insured for $200,000, you automatically would have $140,000 in personal property insurance.

Table 10-2 Personal Property Checklist: Living Room

Item	Date Purchased	Purchase Price	Actual Cash Value	Replacement Cost
Furniture				
Sofa	8/15	$ 3,750	$ 2,000	$ 4,000
Chair	11/15	900	400	1,000
Lounger	12/14	1,200	600	1,200
Ottoman	12/14	400	100	400
Bookcase	4/16	400	200	400
End table (two)	7/17	700	350	700
Appliances				
TV	1/17	550	200	600
DVD	6/16	300	100	300
Microwave oven	7/15	100	20	100
Smartphone	7/18	500	300	500
Furnishings				
Rug	6/16	500	100	500
Painting	12/15	350	100	400
Floor lamp	4/15	500	100	500
Art (three items)	10/16	1,200	300	1,200
Table lamp	4/15	300	100	300
Table lamp	5/16	350	100	350
Throw pillows	7/15	90	20	100
TOTAL		**$12,090**	**$5,090**	**$12,550**

Notice that Table 10-2 lists three estimates for the value of the contents of a room: the purchase price, the actual cash value, and the replacement cost. Historically, property insurance policies paid only the **actual cash value** of an item of personal property, which represents the purchase price of the property less depreciation. The **actual-cash-value (ACV) formula** is:

$$ACV = P - [CA \times (P \div LE)] \quad \textbf{(10.3)}$$

where

P = Purchase price of the property
CA = Current age of the property in years
LE = Life expectancy of the property in years

Consider the case of Lindee Holcolm, a college instructor from Kingwood, Texas, whose nine-year-old heating/air-conditioning unit was struck by lightning. The unit cost $2,400 when new and had a total life expectancy of 12 years. Its actual cash value when it was struck by lightning was:

$$ACV = \$2,400 - [9 \times (\$2,400 \div 12)]$$
$$= \$2,400 - (9 \times \$200)$$
$$= \$600$$

Lindee could not replace the unit for $600. A more realistic replacement cost might be $7,000. **Replacement-cost protection** is an option available in homeowner's insurance policies that pays the full replacement cost of any personal property.

replacement-cost protection
Option sometimes available in homeowner's insurance policies (including the renter's form) that pays the full replacement cost of any personal property.

3. How Much Coverage Is Needed for Liability Losses? Newly written standard homeowner's policies provide $300,000 of personal liability coverage, $1,000 of no-fault medical expense coverage, and $500 of no-fault property damage coverage. It is smart to apply the large-loss principle here and increase the policy limits for all three of these coverages (or consider an umbrella liability policy discussed later). The extra cost is small because the odds of such larger losses are low.

ADVICE FROM A SEASONED PRO

What Insurance Covers While at College

The family's homeowner's and auto coverages will only apply to college students if the student (1) lives in a dorm or fraternity/sorority house or (2) lives in off-campus housing in what is clearly a temporary arrangement (that is, the student returns home during semester breaks and over the summer).

Here are some guidelines to remember for those who are on their parent's policies:

1. *Property stored away from home is often only covered for up to 10 percent of the coverage on the home (the rules vary by insurer). If the family home is insured for $200,000, the contents are covered for $140,000 thus $14,000 applies to all college students in the family.*

2. *Expensive items such as jewelry or computers are subject to specific limits in the homeowner's insurance policy.*

3. *Students are covered for liability under the parent's policy but limits are low.*

4. *Auto insurance rates are based on where the vehicle is garaged (or parked) at night. A discount is common for a college student listed on a parent's policy if the student does not have a car at school and the school is at least 100 miles from the parent's home. If used at school, tell your agent because it is better to pay a higher rate than to face possible denial of coverage for a loss because of misinformation.*

Lisa Cole-Martin
Texas Tech University, and Virginia College – Lubbock, Lubbock, Texas

If one makes a claim on his/her homeowner's insurance company, rates will probably rise about 9 or 10 percent next year.

CONCEPT CHECK 10.3

1. List the four types of losses covered under the property insurance portion of a homeowner's policy.
2. Give three examples of liability protection under homeowner's insurance policies.
3. Name the three types of homeowner's insurance policies for most residences: HO-3, HO-4, and HO-6.
4. Identify four types of personal property for which the covered loss is limited to a specific dollar amount under standard homeowner's insurance policies (see Table 10-1).
5. List the three questions you should ask yourself when determining the policy limits for a homeowner's insurance policy.

Learning Objective 4

Design an automobile insurance program to meet your needs.

financial responsibility laws

Those that require vehicle owners to prove they have enough resources to pay for damages resulting from a car accident.

10.4 AUTOMOBILE INSURANCE

Driving a car is the largest single exposure to catastrophic losses for most Americans. A split-second error in driving judgment or bad luck can result in many tens of thousands of dollars of automobile-related property damage and personal injury losses.

Automobile insurance combines the liability and property insurance coverages needed by automobile owners and drivers into a single-package policy. It is illegal to

ADVICE FROM A SEASONED PRO

Financial Responsibility Laws Do Not Work

All states have vehicle insurance requirements. These are called **financial responsibility laws**. These state insurance laws are supposed to protect all drivers on the road. You must carry evidence of financial responsibility in your vehicle at all times and it must be provided when requested by law enforcement, renewing vehicle registration, and when the vehicle is involved in a traffic collision.

While these laws may not specifically require the individual to have *insurance* coverage, they do require the individual to be able to demonstrate the financial capacity to pay damages. Most drivers comply with financial responsibility laws by purchasing auto insurance. State governments try to enforce compulsory auto and motorcycle insurance laws by electronically matching vehicle registration records with insurance policy records.

Two problems, however, exist. First, some drivers refuse to purchase required insurance because either they cannot afford it or they do not want to pay. Auto insurance can be

especially costly for drivers with a history of moving violations and/or accidents. The result is that up to one-quarter of drivers in some states evade the law entirely and drive uninsured. Nationally, one out of every six drivers is uninsured.

The second problem is that even if the other driver is insured, state minimum requirements, where they exist, are so low, that it is possible to not provide enough coverage for the victim. For example, if an uninsured driver totals your new Lexus ES 300h sedan (about $41,000 new), also injuring you, where the state-required minimum coverage is $10,000, that crash leaves you with a substantial financial loss.

Since states are not likely to improve their laws, your only solution is to purchase additional (higher limits) coverage to the uninsured motorist coverage that is part of your own policy, both for bodily injury and for property damage. Otherwise, your losses would be covered as a chargeable accident on your policy, likely to raise your future insurance premiums.

Gerson Goldberg
Northeastern University, Boston, Massachusetts

operate a motor vehicle without assuming financial responsibility for any losses you might cause.

10.4a Losses Covered

Automobile insurance combines four distinct types of coverage: (1) liability insurance, (2) medical payments insurance, (3) protection against uninsured and underinsured motorists, and (4) insurance for physical damage to the insured automobile. Each coverage has its own policy limits, conditions, and exclusions. Table 10-3 summarizes the coverage provided by automobile insurance policies for people not specifically excluded in the policy.

Coverage 1—Liability Insurance Liability insurance covers the insured when he or she is held responsible for losses suffered by others. Two types of liability can arise out of the ownership and operation of an automobile. Bodily injury liability occurs when a driver or car owner is held legally responsible for bodily injury losses suffered by other people, including pedestrians. Property damage liability occurs when a driver or car owner is held legally responsible for damage to the property of others. Such damage can include damage to another vehicle, a building, or roadside signs and utility poles.

Liability Limits. The most common type of automobile insurance policy is the **family auto policy (FAP).** The policy limits for FAPs are quoted as **split liability limits,** usually three numbers such as 100/300/50, with each number representing a multiple of $1,000 (Figure 10-1). The first number gives the maximum that will be paid for liability claims for *one* person's bodily injury losses resulting from an automobile accident ($100,000 in our example). The second number indicates the overall maximum that will be paid

automobile insurance
Combines the liability and property insurance coverages that most car owners and drivers need into a single-package policy.

bodily injury liability
Occurs when a driver or car owner is held legally responsible for bodily injury losses that other people, including pedestrians, suffer.

Table 10-3   Summary of Automobile Insurance Coverages

Section	Type of Coverage	People Covered	Property Covered	Recommended Limits
A	LIABILITY INSURANCE (1) Bodily injury liability	Relatives living in insured's household driving an owned or nonowned automobile	Not applicable	At least legally required minimums or $250,000/$500,000, whichever is greater
	(2) Property damage liability	Relatives living in insured's household driving an owned or nonowned automobile	Automobiles and other property damaged by insured driver while driving	At least legally required minimum or $100,000, whichever is greater
B	MEDICAL PAYMENTS	Passengers in insured automobile or nonowned automobile driven by insured family member	Not applicable	$50,000 or higher
C	UNINSURED AND UNDERINSURED	Anyone driving insured car with permission and insured family members driving nonowned automobiles with permission	Not applicable	$50,000/$100,000 or higher, if available
D	PHYSICAL DAMAGE (1) Collision	Anyone driving insured car with permission	Insured automobile	Actual cash value less deductible
	(2) Comprehensive	Not applicable	Insured automobile and its attached contents	Actual cash value less deductible

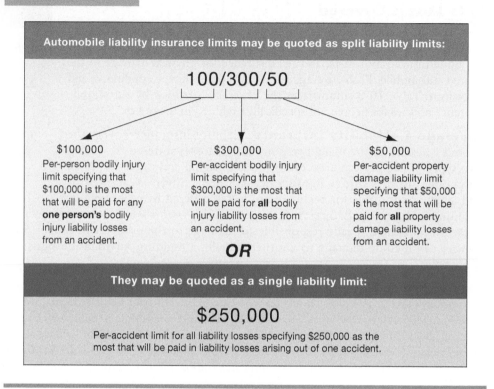

Figure 10-1 **Automobile Liability Insurance Policy Limits**

Automobile liability insurance limits may be quoted as split liability limits:

100/300/50

$100,000	$300,000	$50,000
Per-person bodily injury limit specifying that $100,000 is the most that will be paid for any **one person's** bodily injury liability losses from an accident.	Per-accident bodily injury limit specifying that $300,000 is the most that will be paid for **all** bodily injury liability losses from an accident.	Per-accident property damage liability limit specifying that $50,000 is the most that will be paid for **all** property damage liability losses from an accident.

OR

They may be quoted as a single liability limit:

$250,000

Per-accident limit for all liability losses specifying $250,000 as the most that will be paid in liability losses arising out of one accident.

---

automobile medical payments insurance

Insurance that covers bodily injury losses suffered by the driver of the insured vehicle and any passengers, regardless of who is at fault.

THERE IS AN APP FOR THAT!

Some of the best apps are:

- **Help I Crashed My Car**
- **Car Accident Report**
- **Net Quote**
- **Car Insurance Discounts**
- **iCompare Car Insurance**
- **ESuranceMobile**
- **Car Insurance Quotes Genie**

for bodily injury liability losses to *any number* of people resulting from an automobile accident ($300,000 in our example). The third number specifies the maximum that will be paid for property damage liability losses resulting from an accident ($50,000 in our example).

In some auto insurance policies, the liability limits are stated as a **single liability limit** such as $250,000. Under such policies, all property and bodily injury liability losses resulting from an accident would be paid until the limit is reached. Liability insurance covers only the insured for losses suffered by others. It does not pay for bodily injury losses suffered by the insured or for property damage to the insured's car. Injured passengers of an at-fault driver may collect under the driver's liability coverage, but only after exhausting the coverage provided under medical payments (discussed below) and only after reimbursement is made to people injured in other vehicles or as pedestrians.

Rental Car Liability Driving a rental car exposes you to the same potential liabilities as driving your own vehicle. If you have automobile liability insurance, such liabilities will usually be covered while you drive a rented car. Check with your insurance agent to be certain about your coverage before you rent a car so you can avoid buying overpriced insurance from the rental agency. The odds are with you in not having an accident in a rental car because on average drivers have one accident every 18 years. But you never know.

Coverage 2—Medical Payments Insurance Automobile medical payments insurance can help pay medical expenses no matter who's at fault. It covers you, your passengers, and any family members driving or riding in the insured vehicle at the time of the accident.

Robert Crum/Shutterstock.com

Drivers need to make sure they have sufficient liability coverage in the event of an accident—the person at fault is typically responsible for all damages.

Medical payments coverage is subject to a single policy limit, which is applied per person, per accident. Medical payments also protect insured family members who are injured while passengers in any car or who are injured by a car when on foot or riding a bicycle.

Under medical payments, drivers and their injured passengers collect directly from the driver's insurance. If the driver was not at fault, then the driver's insurer pays the claims and subsequently may choose to exercise subrogation rights against the at-fault party. **Subrogation rights** allow an insurer to take action against a negligent third party (and that party's insurance company) to obtain reimbursement for payments made to an insured.

subrogation rights

Allow an insurer to take action against a negligent third party (and that party's insurance company) to obtain reimbursement for payments made to an insured.

Some states have adopted a version of no-fault automobile insurance where insureds collect first (and possibly *only*) from their own insurance companies for bodily injury losses. In these states, the medical payments coverage is often referred to as **personal injury protection (PIP)** covers the driver and any passengers for bodily injury losses as well as possibly lost wages and rehabilitation expenses. Subrogation rights are limited in no-fault states.

Coverage 3—Uninsured and Underinsured Motorist Insurance

What if you are injured in an accident caused by a driver who has no or insufficient auto liability insurance? You would first be covered by your own medical payments auto insurance but that almost surely will not cover all of the losses.

Uninsured motorist insurance protects you and your passengers from bodily injury losses (and, in a few states, property damage losses) resulting from an automobile accident caused by an uninsured motorist. The cost is about $100 a year.

Underinsured motorist insurance protects the insured and his or her passengers from bodily injury losses (and, in some cases, property damage losses) when the at-fault driver has insurance but that coverage is insufficient to reimburse the losses. This insurance is a smart risk-management choice and carries a very low premium, often less than $1 per month.

uninsured and underinsured motorist insurance

Coverage that an insured can purchase as part of automobile insurance that covers the insured in an accident when an uninsured or underinsured driver is at fault.

Coverage 4—Physical Damage Insurance

Physical damage insurance or (collision and comprehensive coverage) provides protection against losses caused by damage to your vehicle.

NUMBERS ON

Auto Accidents

Data from a variety of sources suggest:

- Every year there are 6 million vehicle accidents and 2.3 million injuries.
- Average likelihood of being in an accident is once every 18 years.
- Seventy percent admit to using a smart phone when driving.

- One-third of drivers admit to reading or writing text messages in past month.
- One-quarter of all accidents involve talking on phone or texting.
- Three in 1,000 accidents involve fatalities.
- Nine people are killed every day when dealing with cellphones, texting, or eating.

collision insurance

Reimburses insureds for losses to their vehicles resulting from a collision with another car or object or from a rollover.

Collision insurance reimburses an insured for losses resulting from a collision with another car or object or from a rollover. The insurer pays the cost of repairing or replacing the insured's car, regardless of who is at fault. When the other driver is at fault, subrogation rights may allow the insurer to obtain reimbursement through that driver's property damage liability protection.

Collision insurance is written with a deductible that usually ranges from $100 to $1,000. If you carry collision insurance coverage on your own car, you are generally covered when you drive someone else's car with that person's permission. Most automobile insurance policies provide for collision coverage on rental cars if such coverage applies to your owned vehicle. Check with your agent before you rent a car. Consider saving up to 40 percent on car insurance by dropping collision coverage when your vehicle reaches 10 years of age or is worth less than perhaps $2,000 or $3,000.

DID YOU KNOW

Auto Premiums Are Based On Your Credit Report

The **premium** for automobile insurance is based on the characteristics of the insured driver, including age, where you live, gender, marital status, coverage you have, type of vehicle, driving record, and amount of deductible. Ratings territories vary according to the number of accidents, claims and costs in each geographic area. Insurers share information through a database called the Comprehensive Loss Underwriting Exchange (CLUE).

When you make an accident claim of $2,000 or more, your insurance premium jumps an average of about 40 percent. A reckless driving ticket boosts rates about 80 percent, which is almost the same increase as adding a new teenage driver to your policy. Speeding 16 to 30 miles per hour too fast will kick premiums up about 25 percent. A DUI probably doubles your rate.

The rating systems are not transparent. They should be based on how you drive not who the companies think you are. Insurers argue that certain factors correlate with increased risk so they should be able to use them in setting rates.

Insurers use about 30 of the almost 130 elements in a credit report to rate drivers. Someone with merely a good credit score could pay as much as $500 more than someone with the best score. Only three states (California, Hawaii, and Massachusetts) prohibit use of credit scores to set prices. Rates for a good driver with excellent credit might be $1,400, $1,700 for good credit, and $3,800 for poor credit. See the data from the study by *Consumer Reports* at www.ConsumerReports.org/FixCarInsurance.

DID YOU KNOW

How Automobile Insurance Would Apply to an Accident

Just how the many provisions in an automobile insurance policy apply to a specific accident mystifies many people. As a result, the claims process may generate considerable dissatisfaction after an accident. The example given here and outlined in the following chart is intended to clarify the application of the multiple coverages and limits

DO IT IN CLASS

In September of last year, Kathy Bonding, a college student from Akron, Ohio, caused a serious accident when she failed to yield to an approaching vehicle while attempting to make a left turn. Kathy suffered a sprained wrist and facial cuts, resulting in medical costs of $11,508. Her passenger, Philip Windsor, was seriously injured with head and neck wounds requiring surgery, a two-week hospital stay, and rehabilitation. Philip's injuries generated medical costs of $137,650. The driver of the other car, Patrick Monk, suffered serious back and internal injuries and facial burns that resulted in some disfigurement. His medical care costs totaled $122,948. His passenger, Annette Monk, suffered cuts and bruises requiring minor medical care at a cost of $2,846.

Both cars were completely destroyed in the accident. Kathy's 10-year-old Buick was valued at $3,150. Patrick's

1-year old Mazda Miata was valued at $19,350. The force of the impact spun Patrick's car around, causing it to destroy a traffic-signal control box (valued at $3,650).

Both Kathy and Patrick were covered by family automobile policies with liability limits of $50,000/$10,000/$25,000 and medical payment limits of $10,000 per person and $100 collision coverage deductibles. In total, Kathy had to pay $155,052 out of her own pocket, as the policy limits were exceeded by her's, Patrick's, and Phillip's medical costs.

An additional point needs to be raised concerning situations in which an accident victim suffers serious, permanent injuries that are not fully reimbursed by the insurance policy protecting the driver at fault. In our example, Patrick suffered very painful injuries resulting in permanent disfigurement. He may wish to sue Kathy for his pain and suffering and for his unpaid medical expenses. If he were to file such a suit, Kathy would be provided with legal assistance by her insurance company. Any judgment that exceeds the policy limits (remember that Kathy's per-person policy limit has already been reached) will be Kathy's responsibility, however. Both Kathy and Patrick were terribly underinsured.

Kathy Bonding's Accident: Who Pays What?

Coverage	Kathy's Policy	Patrick's Policy
Liability (limits)	(50/100/25)	(50/100/25)
Bodily injury:		
Patrick Monk	$50,000	
Annette Monk	2,846	
Philip Windsor	47,154**	
Property damage:		
Patrick Monk's car	19,350	
Traffic-signal control box	3,650	
Medical payments (limits):	($10,000)	($10,000)
Patrick Monk		10,000*
Annette Monk		2,846
Kathy Bonding	10,000	
Philip Windsor	10,000	
Collision coverage (limits):	(ACV, $100 deductible)	(ACV, $100 deductible)
Kathy's car	3,050	
Patrick's car		19,250*
Kathy's out-of-pocket expenses:		
Patrick Monk's bodily injury	72,948	
Phillip Windsor's bodily injury	80,496	
Kathy Bonding's bodily injury	$1,508	
Kathy's collision insurance deductible	100	
TOTAL	**$155,052**	

* Also, included in Kathy's column because Patrick's company filed a claim against Kathy by exercising its subrogation rights.

** Kathy's liability policy paid a total of $52,846 to the passengers in the other car leaving only $47,154 of the $100,000 per accident limit remaining to reimburse Phillip for his medical care that exceeded the medical payments limit of $10,000.

NEVER EVER

Forget to Compare Vehicle Insurance Rates

About three-quarters of insurance customers automatically renew their policies without getting a new quote, even though comparison shoppers save about $180.

comprehensive automobile insurance

Protects against property damage losses to an insured vehicle caused by perils other than collision and rollover.

Comprehensive automobile insurance helps pay for damages that are not caused by a collision or rollover. Covered perils include theft, glass breakage, malicious mischief, theft, hail, and wind, riot, and earthquake, and the policy typically carries a $100 to $1,000 deductible.

When you have a loss that qualifies under collision or comprehensive insurance, an estimate of the repair cost will be made. If this estimate exceeds the value that the insurance company puts on the vehicle, the lower of the two figures is paid, less any deductible. Insurance companies set vehicle values based on the average current selling price of vehicles of the same make, model, and age. Insurance companies will not give you more money because your wrecked vehicle had very low mileage and was in near-perfect condition.

Other Valuable Protections Two other low-or no-cost, but helpful, coverages are available: towing and rental reimbursement. **Towing coverage** pays the cost of having a disabled vehicle transported for repairs. It usually pays only the first $25 or $50 per occurrence but will cover any towing need—not just assistance needed due to an accident. **Rental reimbursement** coverage provides a rental car when

DID YOU KNOW

Steps to Reduce Your Auto and Homeowner's Insurance Costs

There is no point in paying more for insurance than necessary. Here are some suggestions to save money.

Select Appropriate Coverages and Limits. Buy only needed coverages but be certain to select policy limits appropriate for the largest potential losses.

Shop Every Year for Low Cost Coverage. Insurance premiums from one company can be two or three times as another. To save money you can change insurers at any time and get a refund from your old company. Telephone some agents, and do so every year.

Go Online. To obtain comparable quotes go on the Internet and provide some companies your information. Also check out a quote service such as www.insure.com, www.insuremarket.com, or www.insweb.com. If necessary, compare rates at a dozen companies.

Install an Advanced Alarm System. Companies charge lower premiums to policyholders who take steps to reduce the probability or severity of loss. For example, discounts are available if you install dead-bolt door locks, a security system, smoke detectors, or a fire extinguisher in your home or a security system in your vehicle.

Be Nosy. Ask for discounts for which you might qualify. Getting married reduces rates an average of 13 percent.

High Deductible Discounts. Raising your deductibles can save you hundreds of dollars per year.

Bundle Policies Discounts. Most insurance companies offer discounted premiums for policyholders who insure

multiple vehicles or buy multiple policies from them, such as both automobile and renter's insurance.

Driver's Training Discounts. Completing a driver's training program reduces costs. State Farm and Progressive Insurance have helps that monitor your driving habits.

Maintain a Good Grade Point Average. Having a high grade point average in school can reduce rates.

Be Loyal to the Insurer. Some companies give discounts to customers who stay with them for years and years.

Maintain a Safe Driving Record. That means avoiding accidents and traffic violations. One quarter of young drivers got a ticket in the past five years.

Maintain a Good Credit Score. Insurance companies commonly use an applicant's credit rating to provide information in order to help set their auto and homeowner's insurance premiums. In many cases your credit score and whether you use a bank credit card and department store credit card counts more than your driving record. Monitor your credit carefully.

Move to a Rural Community. Homeowners and auto insurance are more expensive in large cities. For example, the same auto insurance coverage in San Francisco, California could cost $1,800 annually compared to $700 in Cleveland, Mississippi.

Pay Annually. Discounts are offered by insurance companies to policyholders who pay annually.

the insured's vehicle is being repaired after an accident or has been stolen. It often has a daily payout limit of $20 to $30 and, therefore, may provide only part of the funds needed to obtain replacement transportation.

CONCEPT CHECK 10.4

1. Identify the four types of automobile insurance coverage.
2. Explain the meaning of the numbers 100/200/75.
3. Identify who is protected by medical payments coverage.
4. Distinguish between collision and comprehensive insurance.
5. Explain why selecting a policy with a high deductible and high liability limits is better than one with a low deductible and low liability limits.

10.5 BUY SPECIALIZED PROTECTION FOR OTHER LOSS EXPOSURES

Learning Objective 5
Describe other types of property and liability insurance.

Some people need protection against property and liability losses that are not covered by or exceed the limits of the standard homeowner's or automobile insurance policies.

10.5a Umbrella Liability Insurance

Umbrella liability insurance is a policy that extends the basic liability coverage provided in different types of policies, including home, auto, boat, and tenant. In short, it protects your assets and future earnings from lawsuits. This type of policy provides broad coverage, meaning that some claims that would not be covered by a standard policy may be covered under the umbrella policy. However, an umbrella policy only pays for losses when the regular coverage amount is exceeded.

Generally, the insured's standard policies must contain minimum levels of liability coverage that are specified by the insurance company in order to add an umbrella policy, and therefore, greater liability coverage. Policy limits are $1 million to $5 million. A $1 million umbrella policy costs $175 to $300 a year. Over three-quarters of umbrella losses are auto-related.

Figure 10-2 shows how a $1 million umbrella policy works. In this example, the insured has an automobile insurance policy with total liability limits of $600,000 (the total liability coverage for one accident is $500,000 per accident plus $100,000 for property damage), a homeowner's insurance policy with liability protection of $200,000, and a $500,000 professional liability insurance policy. If the insured bought an umbrella policy with a $1 million limit and then experienced a $750,000 professional liability loss, the umbrella policy would provide protection of $250,000 after the professional liability policy limits were exceeded. Umbrella policies are relatively low in cost when purchased to supplement basic policies (perhaps $150 to $200 per year for an additional $1 million of protection) and protect against virtually all liability exposures that a person might face.

umbrella (excess) liability insurance
Catastrophic liability policy that covers liability losses in excess of those covered by any underlying homeowner's, automobile, or professional liability policy.

10.5b Flood and Earthquake Insurance

Standard homeowner's insurance policies exclude losses caused by floods, sinkholes, and earthquakes. This is because these types of losses are subject to **adverse selection.** This occurs when people who are most likely to suffer such losses will know that. And those that are least likely to suffer a loss will know that, too. As a result, those people with high probabilities of loss will want to buy the coverage and those will extremely low probabilities will not, thereby violating the law of large numbers. But if you live in a flood-prone area, where sinkholes exist, or in an earthquake zone, your risk of loss should be addressed. The **National Flood Insurance Program** is a federal government program that makes flood insurance available in counties where flood is common (see www.FloodSmart.gov).

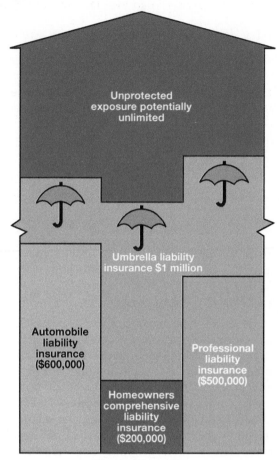

Figure 10-2   **How Umbrella Liability Policies Work**

Unprotected exposure potentially unlimited

Umbrella liability insurance $1 million

Automobile liability insurance ($600,000)

Homeowners comprehensive liability insurance ($200,000)

Professional liability insurance ($500,000)

Types of Exposures

endorsement

An addition to a standard insurance policy designed to expand coverage for a special area of need.

professional liability insurance/ malpractice insurance

Protects individuals and organizations that provide professional services when they are held liable for their clients' losses.

Earthquake insurance can be purchased only from a private insurance company either as a separate policy or as an **endorsement** (an addition to a standard policy) to an existing homeowner's or renter's insurance policy. **Sinkhole insurance** covers damage to your home due to ground collapse. Coverage and availability varies by state but is especially important consideration in Florida, Tennessee, and other states where sinkholes might occur.

10.5c Professional Liability Insurance

Professional liability insurance (sometimes called **malpractice insurance** or **errors and omissions insurance**) protects individuals and organizations that provide professional services (physician, lawyers, psychologists, etc.) when they are held liable for the financial losses suffered by their clients due to professional mistakes or omissions. Policy limits, deductibles, premiums, and other characteristics of such policies vary widely depending on the profession involved. A $1 million professional liability policy written for a family therapist may cost as little as $500 per year; in contrast, some surgeons pay $60,000 or more per year for professional liability insurance. In some states and for certain professions, professional liability insurance may be required by law.

10.5d Floaters

Floaters are additional pieces of insurance coverage designed to cover your valuables with limits above and beyond what your homeowner's policy can deliver. They can provide all-risk protection for accident and theft losses to movable property (such as cameras, sporting equipment, Microsoft's Movies & TV players, and jewelry) regardless of where the loss occurs. Limited floater protection for personal property is part of the standard homeowner's insurance policy. Automobile insurance policies only cover portable personal property that is permanently installed in the vehicle. Property owned for business purposes is excluded from both types of insurance. This means that a mechanic's tools, a lawyer's books, and a karaoke DJ's equipment, for example, would not be covered. A separate floater would be required if you have extensive portable property whether for personal or business use.

floater policies

Provide all-risk protection for accident and theft losses to movable property regardless of where the loss occurs.

CONCEPT CHECK 10.5

1. Explain how purchasing an umbrella liability insurance policy applies the large-loss principle.
2. Who should consider buying flood and earthquake insurance?
3. Are you preparing for a professional career that might expose you to liability losses, and if so how might you protect yourself from such losses?
4. Give two examples of someone who might want to purchase a floater insurance policy.

10.6 HOW TO COLLECT ON YOUR PROPERTY AND LIABILITY LOSSES

Learning Objective 6
Summarize how to make an insurance claim.

The direct benefit of owning insurance becomes evident when a loss occurs and it is time to file a claim. Even when you have a legitimate claim, however, you may want to consider whether you should do so. You might ignore a small claim as it may increase your rate at renewal. One claim increases premiums, on average, 9 or 10 percent. Of course, if you have a large claim, you would want to file for its recovery. Here are the four steps that you should take when you have a loss.

10.6a 1. Contact Your Insurance Agent about Your Loss

If you decide to file a claim, the first step—contacting your agent— should be taken as soon as possible. Follow the agent's instructions regarding who to contact next (including filing a written police report) and what to do to minimize the loss. Then keep the company informed of everything relevant to the loss in a timely manner until the claim is settled. The persistent claimant is more likely to collect fully on a loss.

10.6b 2. Document Your Loss

You carry the burden of proof whenever a property or liability loss occurs. Adequate documentation of the circumstances and the amount of the loss is essential. In the absence of such documentation, the insurance company will generally interpret the situation in the manner most favorable to its interests, not yours.

The best way to document a theft, fire, or other personal property loss is with a visual inventory. Use your phone to photograph or video all valuable property including a written record of the date of purchase, price paid, description, model name and number, and serial number (if any). Keep such records in a safe-deposit box, in a file cabinet at work, or with a relative. If a loss occurs, present a *copy* of your documentation to the agent or insurance company.

You should always file a police report if you become involved in an automobile accident. Make a written record of the accident giving the time and place of the accident,

TURN BAD HABITS INTO GOOD ONES

Do You Do This?

Assume your parents' homeowner's policy covers you at school

Base your potential auto liability losses on your own financial status

Base your insurance decisions on how much coverage will cost

Buy low limits on your liability coverages

Buy policies with the lowest possible deductibles

Do This Instead!

Confirm that you are correct and, if not, buy your own renter's policy

Estimate the maximum loss others could suffer if you caused an accident

Base your decisions on the potential losses you could suffer

Buy higher limits and or an umbrella liability policy

Raise the deductibles on your policies and apply the savings toward higher limits

---

MONEY WEBSITES

Informative websites are:

- 4freequotes
- Insure
- Insurance Institute for Highway Safety
- InstantCarInsurance
- Insweb
- Kiplinger's Personal Finance
- MSN Money
- National Association of Insurance Commissioners
- National Flood Insurance Program
- NerdWallet
- NetQuote
- QuoteWizard
- TheZebra

insurance claim

Formal request to the insurance company for reimbursement for a covered loss.

claims adjuster

Person designated by the insurance company to assess whether the loss is covered and to determine the dollar amount that the company will pay.

release

Insurance document affirming that the dollar amount of the loss settlement is accepted as full and complete reimbursement.

the direction of travel and estimated speed of the cars involved, the road and weather conditions, the behavior of all parties involved and a diagram of the accident scene. Also, obtain the names, driver's license numbers, and contact information for witnesses. Police reports are also advisable (and often required) when filing a theft claim of any type.

10.6c 3. File Your Claim

An **insurance claim** is a formal request to the insurance company for reimbursement for a covered loss. All of the documentation and information will be requested by the insurance agent or a **claims adjuster** (the person designated by the insurance company to assess whether the loss is covered and to determine the dollar amount that the company will pay). Insurance companies require that claims be made in writing, and the adjuster may assist you in completing the necessary forms.

10.6d 4. Sign a Release

Part of the final step in the claims-settlement process is to sign the **release**, which is an insurance document affirming that the dollar amount of the loss settlement is accepted as full and complete reimbursement and that the insured will make no additional claims for the loss against the insurance company. Signing the release absolves the insurance company of any further responsibility for the loss. Resist the temptation to sign a release until you are certain that the full magnitude of the loss has become evident.

 CONCEPT CHECK 10.6

1. What is the best way to establish documentation for potential losses to your personal property?
2. Describe what you should do to file a claim most effectively when involved in an automobile accident.
3. Describe the term *release* and explain why signing a release too soon might work to your disadvantage.

WHAT DO YOU RECOMMEND *NOW*?

Now that you have read the chapter on risk management and property liability insurance, what would you recommend to Nick and Amber in the case at the beginning of the chapter regarding:

1. The risk-management steps they should take to update their insurance coverages?
2. The relationship between severity and frequency of loss when deciding whether to buy insurance?
3. Adequately insuring their home?
4. The use of deductibles and policy limits to keep their automobile insurance premiums at a manageable level while still maintaining vital coverage?

SUMMARY OF LEARNING OBJECTIVES RECAPPED

LO1 Apply the risk-management process to address the risks to your property and income.

Personal financial managers practice risk management to protect their present and future assets and income. Risk management involves identifying the sources of risk, evaluating risk and potential losses, selecting the appropriate risk-handling mechanism, implementing and administering the risk-management plan, and evaluating and adjusting the plan periodically.

LO2 Explain how insurance works to reduce risk.

Hazards make losses more likely to occur. Insurance is a mechanism for reducing pure risk by having a larger number of individuals share in the financial losses suffered by all members of the group. It is used to protect against pure risk but cannot be used to protect against speculative risk, which carries the potential for gain as well as loss. Insurance consists of two elements: the reduction of pure risk through application of the law of large numbers, and the sharing of losses. Only fortuitous and financial losses are insurable. Deductibles and co-insurance are ways to pay less and still maintain sufficient insurance coverage.

LO3 Design a homeowner's or renter's insurance program to meet your needs.

Homeowner's insurance is designed to protect homeowners and renters from property and liability losses. Six types of homeowner's insurance are available, including one geared toward renters. Homeowner's policies can be purchased on a named-perils or an open-perils basis. Buying replacement-cost protection pays more in a loss than actual cash value coverage.

LO4 Design an automobile insurance program to meet your needs.

Automobile insurance is designed to protect the insured against property and liability losses arising from use of a motor vehicle. These policies typically provide liability insurance (both bodily injury and property damage liability), medical payments or personal injury protection insurance, property insurance on your car, and underinsured and uninsured motorist insurance. The most commonly purchased type of automobile insurance is the family automobile policy. The premium for automobile insurance is based on the characteristics of the insured driver, including age, where you live, gender, marital status, coverage you have, type of vehicle, driving record, credit history, and amount of deductible.

LO5 Describe other types of property and liability insurance.

Other important types of property and liability insurance include umbrella liability, flood and earthquake, professional liability, and floater policies.

LO6 **Summarize how to make an insurance claim.**

The insured is responsible for documenting and verifying a loss. Photographs or videotapes of the insured property are ideal for documenting claims made under a homeowner's insurance policy. A police report provides the best documentation for claims made under an automobile insurance policy.

LET'S TALK ABOUT IT

1. **Insurance Underwriting.** How do you feel about being grouped into classes in the insurance underwriting process? Do you feel that insurance companies should treat all such groups of people alike?

2. **Actual Cash Value.** Many people complain that property insurance policies should pay more than what the insurance companies say is the actual cash value of the property, such as for a used motor vehicle with low mileage that is in near-perfect condition. How do you feel about this issue, and what would happen if insurance companies were more generous in their reimbursements?

3. **Auto Liability Limits.** Do you know the liability limits on the automobile insurance policy under which you are covered? Are the limits appropriate?

4. **Personal Property Protection.** Is your personal property, such as furniture and computer, covered under a homeowner's or renter's insurance policy? If so, what are the policy limits? If not, why not?

5. **Auto Insurance Claims.** What experiences have you or a family member had with the automobile insurance claims process? What if anything might have been done differently or better?

6. **Renter's Insurance Claims.** What experiences have you or a family member had with the claims process on a renter's insurance policy? What if anything might have been done differently or better?

DO THE MATH

1. **How Much of Fire Loss Will Be Covered?** Toula and Ian Miller of Gainesville, Florida, recently suffered a fire at their home. The fire, which began in a crawl space at the back of the house, caused $50,000 of damage to the dwelling itself. Their garage, valued at $20,000, was totally destroyed but did not contain a car at the time of the fire. Replacement of the Millers' personal property damaged in the home and garage amounted to $23,000. In addition, $350 in cash and a stamp collection valued at $3,215 were destroyed. While the damage was being repaired, the Millers stayed in a motel for one week and spent $1,350 on food and lodging. The house had a value of $195,000 and was insured for $150,000 under an HO-3 policy with a $250 deductible. Use Table 10-1 on page 309 to answer the following questions. (Hint: You must first determine whether the Millers have adequate dwelling replacement coverage and, if not, what percentage of the necessary 80 percent coverage they do have. The resulting answer will determine the percentage of the loss to the dwelling covered, and consequently the amount to be reimbursed by the insurance company.)

   DO IT IN CLASS Pages 309 and 311

   (a) Assuming that the deductible was applied to the damage to the dwelling, calculate the amount covered by insurance and the amount that the Millers must pay for each loss listed: the dwelling, the garage, the cash and stamp collection, and the extra living expenses.

   (b) How much of the amount of the personal property loss would be covered by the insurance policy? Paid for by the Millers?

   (c) Assuming that they have contents replacement-cost protection on the personal property, what amount and percentage of the total loss must be paid by the Millers?

2. **Sufficient Dwelling Coverage?** Colton Gentry of Lancaster, California, has owned his home for ten years. When he purchased it for $178,000, Colton bought a $160,000 homeowner's insurance policy. He still owns that policy, even though the replacement cost of the home is now $300,000.

   DO IT IN CLASS Page 311

   (a) If Colton suffered a $20,000 fire loss to the home, what percentage and dollar amount of the loss would be covered by his policy?

   (b) How much insurance on the home should Colton carry now to be fully reimbursed for a fire loss?

3. **Coverage on a One-Vehicle Accident.** Bill Converse of Rexburg, Idaho, recently had his truck slide off a gravel road and strike a tree. Bill's vehicle suffered $17,500 in damage. The truck has a book value of $40,000. Bill carried collision insurance with a $500 deductible. How much will Bill be reimbursed by his policy?

4. **How Much of a Major Auto Accident Loss Will Be Covered?** Ashley Diamond of Estes Park, Colorado, drives an eight-year-old Toyota valued at $5,600. She has a $75,000 personal automobile policy with $10,000 per-person medical payments coverage and both collision ($200 deductible) and comprehensive coverage. David Smith of Loveland, Colorado, drives a four-year-old Chevrolet Malibu valued at $9,500. He has a 25/50/15 family automobile policy with $20,000 in medical payments coverage and both collision ($100 deductible) and comprehensive insurance. Late one evening, while he was driving back from Rocky Mountain National Park, David's car crossed the centerline of the road, striking Ashley's car and forcing it into a ditch. David's car also left the road and did extensive damage to the front of a roadside store. The following table indicates the damages and their dollar amounts.

DO IT IN CLASS
Page 319

Item	Amount
Bodily injuries suffered by Ashley	$6,800
Bodily injuries suffered by Fran, a passenger in Ashley's car	28,634
Ashley's car	9,600
Bodily injuries suffered by David	2,700
Bodily injuries suffered by Cecilia, a passenger in David's car	12,845
David's car	9,500
Damage to the roadside store	14,123

Complete the following chart and use the information to answer these questions:

(a) How much will Ashley's policy pay Ashley and Fran?

(b) Will subrogation rights come into play? In what way?

(c) How much will David's bodily injury liability protection pay?

(d) To whom and how much will David's property damage liability protection pay?

(e) To whom and how much will David's medical protection pay?

(f) How much reimbursement will David receive for his car?

(g) How much will David be required to pay out of his own pocket?

David Smith's Accident: Who Pays What?

COVERAGE	David's Policy	Ashley's Policy
Liability (limits)	___	___
Bodily injury		
Ashley	___	___
Fran	___	___
Cecilia	___	___
Medical payments (limits)	___	___
David	___	___
Ashley	___	___
Fran	___	___
Cecilia	___	___
Collision coverage (limits)	___	___
David's car	___	___
Ashley's car	___	___
David's out-of-pocket expenses	___	___
Fran's bodily injury	___	___
Excess property damage losses	___	___
Collision insurance deductible	___	___
TOTAL	___	___

FINANCIAL PLANNING CASES

CASE 1

The Johnsons Decide How to Manage Their Risks

Several years have passed since the Johnsons were married, and their financial affairs have become more complicated. They recently purchased a $200,000 condominium that has added only about $400 per month to their housing expenses. And they have purchased a second used car for $12,000. As a result of these changes, Harry and Belinda realize that they now face greater risks in their financial affairs. They have decided to review their situation with an eye toward managing their risks more effectively. Use the steps in the risk-management process (pp. 300–302), their net worth and income and expense statements in Table 3-6 on page 97 and Table 3-7 on page 98, and other information in this chapter to answer the following questions:

(a) What are Harry and Belinda's major sources of risk from home and automobile ownership, and what is the potential magnitude of loss from each?

(b) Given the choices listed in Step 3 of the risk-management process, how should the Johnsons handle the sources of risk listed in part a?

CASE 2

The Hernandezes Consider Additional Liability Insurance

Victor and Maria's next-door neighbor, Ray Jackson, was recently sued over an automobile accident and eventually was held liable for $437,000 in damages. Ray's automobile policy limits were 100/300/50. Because of the shortfall, he had to sell his house and move into an apartment. Victor and Maria are now concerned that a similar tragedy might potentially befall them. They have a homeowner's policy with $100,000 in comprehensive personal liability coverage and an automobile policy with 50/100/25 limits, and Maria has a small ($100,000) professional liability policy for her work as a medical records assistant.

(a) How might Victor and Maria more fully protect themselves through their homeowner's and automobile insurance policies?

(b) What additional benefits would they receive in buying an umbrella liability policy?

CASE 3

Julia Price Thinks About Managing Her Property and Liability Risk

Julia has always tried to keep her insurance spending under control by purchasing low limits on her policies. Now that her assets and income have grown, she is beginning to reconsider the wisdom of this approach when buying insurance. Julia knows she has a lot more to lose in terms both of property and liability exposures. Last week, she called her insurance agent to discuss raising her policy limits on her homeowner's and automobile insurance policies. The agent suggested she consider an umbrella liability policy. Julia still wants to be frugal and is considering simply raising the limits on the policies she already has rather than obtaining another policy. Offer your opinions about her thinking.

CASE 4

The Princes' Auto Insurance Is Not Renewed

Mark and Kelly Prince of Emmertsburg, Iowa, face a crisis. Their automobile insurance company has notified them that their current coverage expires in 30 days and will not be renewed. Mark and the Prince's younger son each had a minor, at-fault accident during the past year. Their children are otherwise good drivers, as are both parents. The Princes are confused because they know families whose members have much worse driving records but still have insurance.

(a) Explain to Mark and Kelly why their policy might have been canceled.

(b) Use the box on page 319 to give Mark and Kelly some pointers on how to save money when shopping for a new auto insurance policy.

CASE 5

A Student Buys Insurance for a Used Car

Makiko Iwanami, a student from Osaka, Japan, is in one of your classes. She is considering the purchase of a used car and has been told that she must buy automobile insurance to register the car and obtain license plates. Makiko has come to you for advice, and you have decided to focus on three aspects of automobile insurance.

(a) Explain how liability insurance works in the United States. Advise Makiko about which liability insurance limits she should select.

(b) Makiko is especially impressed that automobile insurance includes medical payments coverage because she has no health insurance. Explain why the medical payments coverage does not actually solve her health insurance problem, and describe the type of coverage it provides.

(c) Makiko plans to pay cash for the car and doesn't want to spend more than $5,000. Outline the coverage provided by collision insurance and factors that might make such coverage optional for Makiko.

CASE 6

An Argument About the Value of Insurance

You have been talking at a party to some friends about insurance. One young married couple in the group believes that insurance is almost always a real waste of money. They argue, "The odds of most bad events occurring are so low that you don't need to worry." Furthermore, they say, "Buying insurance is like pouring money down a hole; you rarely have anything to show for it in the end." Based on what you have learned from this chapter, how might you argue against this couple's point of view?

CASE 7

Enlai Contemplates a New Homeowner's Insurance Policy

Enlai Li Zhang of Los Angeles, California recently bought a home for $700,000. The previous owner had a $600,000 HO-1 policy on the property, and Enlai can simply pay the premiums to keep the same coverage in effect. Her insurance agent called her and cautioned that she would be better off to upgrade the policy to an HO-2 or HO-3 policy. Enlai has turned to you for advice. Use the information in Table 10-1 on page 309 to advise her.

 DO IT IN CLASS
Page 309

(a) What additional property protection would Enlai have if she purchased an HO-2 policy?

(b) What additional property protection would Enlai have if she purchased an HO-3 policy?

(c) What property protection would remain largely the same whether Enlai had an HO-1, HO-2, or HO-3 policy?

(d) Advise Enlai on what differences in liability protection, if any, exist among the three policies.

BE YOUR OWN PERSONAL FINANCIAL PLANNER

1. **Property Loss Exposures.** Use Worksheet 43: My Home Inventory from "My Personal Financial Planner" to develop a list of your personal property items, including items you keep at school and those at other locations such as the home of a family member. Use Table 10-1 on page 309 as guides for the types of information to include. Assess the appropriateness of insurance to protect these items from loss.

My Personal Financial Planner

2. **The Risk-Management Process.** Build upon your list of property loss exposures to develop a complete risk-management assessment. Use the risk-management information on pages 300–302 as a guide and use Worksheet 44: My Insurance Inventory from "My Personal Financial Planner" to record the results of your efforts.

My Personal Financial Planner

3. **Evaluate Your Need for Homeowner's or Renter's Insurance.** Determine whether or not you are currently covered by a homeowner's or renter's insurance policy.

If you are, determine whether the policy is adequate for your needs. If you are not, decide what coverage levels you will need.

4. **Evaluate Your Automobile Insurance.** If you drive a vehicle owned by a family member or yourself, you are covered by the insurance policy on that vehicle. Use Table 10-2 on page 312 as a guide to assess the coverage under that policy. Determine whether the policy adequately protects you from loss, and if not, identify what changes you want to make in the policy.

5. **Shop for Automobile Insurance.** Use Worksheet 45: My Comparison of Auto Insurance Providers from "My Personal Financial Planner" to shop for vehicle insurance based on your analysis in item 4 above. Use your current policy for Company A in the worksheet.

My Personal Financial Planner

Then contact two additional companies to obtain quotes on similar coverage to determine whether you are receiving a good value for your current policy or would benefit from switching companies.

ON THE NET

Go to the Web pages indicated to complete these exercises.

1. **Minimum Liability Limits.** Visit the website for the National Association of Insurance Commissioners at www.naic.org/state_web_map.htm, where you will find a map where you can link to the Insurance Commission in your state. Determine the minimum automobile insurance liability limits in your state. How well-insured do you feel someone would be if he or she carried only these minimums?

2. **Insurance Buyer's Guides.** Visit the website for the National Association of Insurance Commissioners, where you will find a map at www.naic.org/state_web_map.htm through which you can link to your state insurance regulator's website. If available in your state, obtain an insurance buyer's guide for automobile and homeowner's insurance that describes policy provisions and compares insurance rates. Use these rate comparisons to select two automobile insurance companies that would be appropriate for your needs. E-mail or telephone the companies to obtain specific premium quotations for the desired insurance protection. Do the same

for single-family dwelling, condominium, or renter's insurance, depending on your circumstances.

3. **Compare Auto Insurance.** Go to CarInsuranceQuotes. com at carinsurancequotesinfo.com. All similar websites require you to input information on you and your vehicle so you might be soon inundated with too much information. Input what you want to see the results. What do you think about the website?

4. **Safe Cars Save Money.** Visit the website for the Insurance Institute for Highway Safety at www. iihs.org/iihs/ratings. For your own vehicle and one or two you would like to own, check how the vehicles stack up against the competition in terms of injury protection.

5. **Compare Renter's/Homeowner's Insurance.** Go to Esurance.com at www.esurance.com/insurance/renters and input data on your housing situation. All similar websites require to you input information on you and your home so you might be soon inundated with too much information. Input what you want to see the results. What do you think about the website?

ACTION INVOLVEMENT PROJECTS

1. **The Benefits of Renter's Insurance.** Identify three of your friends who currently live in rental housing. Ask them if they are covered by a renter's insurance policy. If they are covered, ask them to give their assessment of the costs and benefits of having a policy. If not, ask them why they have not decided to buy such coverage.

2. **Independent Versus Exclusive Insurance Agents.** Interview two insurance agents, one who is an independent agent and one who is an exclusive agent. Ask each to describe the benefits to a customer who buys insurance from that type of agent.

3. **Automobile Insurance Claims.** Interview two or three people who have been involved as an insured party in an automobile accident. Ask them to summarize the claims process as they experienced it and how they now view the process compared to what they expected.

11 Planning for Health Care Expenses

YOU MUST BE KIDDING, RIGHT?

Allison Parker is a 46-year-old unmarried mother with two children, ages 16 and 17. She lives partly on alimony from her former husband and she works part-time out of her home as a medical transcriptionist for a hospital. Last year Allison suffered severe head injuries in a hit-and-run accident when jogging. Her wounds have healed and Allison has regained her ability to speak but is not yet able to walk on her own or use her hands and arms very well. At first she required some mental health counseling. Now she still requires a daily paid caregiver to assist with her personal needs. It may be another six months before she can work again. Which one of the following aspects of her injury was covered by Allison's private health care plan?

A. Hospital stay   **C.** Mental health

B. Rehabilitative care   **D.** All of the above

The answer is "D" or all of the above. Allison had purchased an individual health care policy at HealthCare.gov that covers hospital, surgical, mental health, and rehabilitative care. Therefore, after deductibles and co-pays the Affordable Care Act covered most of her expenses in these areas. Individuals without health insurance can buy a health care policy on a state or federal exchange!

Learning Objectives

After reading this chapter, you should be able to:

1 Explain how the Affordable Care Act works, and how consumers shop and pay for health insurance coverage.

2 Distinguish among the types of health care plans.

3 Describe the typical features and limits of health care plans.

4 Explain the fundamentals of planning for long-term custodial care.

5 Develop a plan to protect your income when you cannot work due to disability.

6 Summarize the benefits of preparing advance medical directive documents.

Sean Locke Photography/Shutterstock.com

WHAT DO YOU RECOMMEND?

Danielle DiMartino is a 32-year-old single mother with one child. Her 8-year-old daughter has a history of ear infections that require doctor's office visits four or five times per year. Danielle's 70-year-old mother lives with the family for financial reasons; she has hereditary high blood pressure and high cholesterol as well as diabetes. Danielle's mother is enrolled in Medicare Parts A and B.

Danielle's employer pays all or a portion of the cost for a health care plan to cover the company's workers, their spouses, and their dependents. Danielle has four options: (1) the basic HMO managed by a local university medical school/hospital with no additional cost for Danielle, but with an additional cost of $290 per month to cover her children, (2) a health insurance plan with a PPO at that same medical center for a total cost of $380 per month, (3) a traditional health insurance plan that provides access to virtually all health care providers in her community for $490 per month, and (4) a health plan with a $5,000 deductible at no additional cost. Danielle's employer offers no disability income or long-term care group plan. She does receive ten sick days per year, which can accumulate if not taken. Danielle has accumulated 30 days.

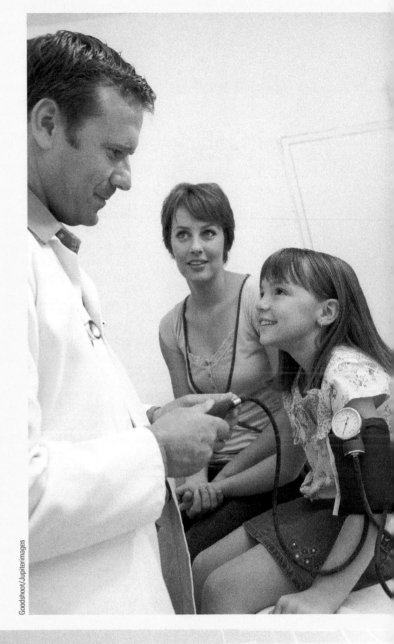

Goodshoot/Jupiterimages

What do you recommend to Danielle DiMartino on the subject of managing health expenses regarding:

1. Choosing among the four alternatives available to her?
2. Danielle's concerns about providing for her mother's health care needs?
3. Danielle's need for disability income insurance?
4. How Danielle can cover her long-term care risk?

Few things in life are more important than your good health. Rare or serious diseases or injuries can wipe out savings and retirement accounts, college education funds, and home equity. This need not happen.

Health insurance is insurance against the risk of incurring medical expenses among individuals. One buys health insurance as part of an effort to plan and control health care expenses, which can be enormous. Insuring against catastrophic events protects one from the economic losses that occur when you become ill, have an accident, or become disabled. The next best thing to enjoying good health is a very good health care insurance policy. This way you can still achieve your lifetime goals.

More than half of Americans have unpaid medical bills, with each owing an average of $1,700. Half of all credit collections are health care related, and 60 percent of all personal bankruptcies are caused by health care bills. Americans now spend 10 percent or more of their income on premiums, deductibles, and related costs for health care. That is up from five percent only a dozen years ago.

You must learn how to protect your health and personal finances. Invest in your own health by eating healthy, staying active, and not smoking. Choose an employer who provides excellent health insurance benefits. When buying the best health insurance policy for yourself, remember to insure the catastrophic losses to keep your premiums low. Alternatively, this also could mean staying on your parents' health care policy until you are age 26. Or, if you qualify you could buy a price-subsidized policy in the private marketplace.

Health care illiteracy is no longer acceptable. You have no choice. You must learn what the insurance vocabulary means as well as all about any exclusions, deductibles, co-pays, and out-of-pocket limits. If you don't, you will lose.

<table>
<tr><td>

Learning Objective 1

Explain how the Affordable Care Act works, and how consumers shop and pay for health insurance coverage.

</td></tr>
</table>

11.1 THE AFFORDABLE CARE ACT AND YOU

11.1a The USA System of Health Care Is the Most Expensive in the World

The current $4.3 trillion U.S. healthcare system costs $11,000 a year for every man, woman, and child. These dollars spent on health care amount to 18 percent of the nation's gross domestic product, which is by far the highest percentage of any country in the world. The industrialized countries of Britain, Canada, Germany, and Norway, as examples, provide health care to all citizens and spend only one-third to one-half as much on health care. Plus their citizens live far longer than those in the United States.

single-payer health system

Where the government, rather than private insurers, pay for all health care costs.

Health care in the USA is not a **single-payer health system**, like in most nations worldwide, where the government, rather than private insurers, pays for all health care costs. People are taxed to pay for it, of course. Instead, we have a highly fragmented system of private and public payers, where all providers make a good profit.

Moreover, the American system is more inefficient and much more costly than others. Our system provides less quality and less value compared to its international counterparts. The USA does not have the best health care system in the world. We are far from it. Our key health statistics are at or near the bottom compared to other industrialized countries.

The United States of America remains the only industrialized country in the world that does not provide universal access to health care to all citizens. This continues despite the fact that every U.S. president in the past 70 years—Democrats and Republicans alike—pushed their Congresses to pass a universal health care law.

11.1b Health Today in the USA

When people who are uninsured suffer any insurable loss, such as a vehicle crash, lost ring, or home fire, they typically bear the full cost of the loss themselves. Health care losses, however, are different. When an uninsured person becomes ill or injured they may obtain care by going to a public hospital for treatment. If they are unable to pay, the costs are primarily shifted first to hospitals because the 1986 Emergency Medical Treatment and Active Labor Act requires hospitals participating in Medicare (and nearly all do) to provide emergency care to anyone who needs it.

That pushes hospitals costs up. Those costs are then shifted to people who do have health insurance in the form of higher costs to insurance companies. The insurers then raise health care insurance premiums (the monthly or annual cost for a health care plan) that partially "cover" those without insurance.

Today about 30 million Americans, about 12 percent of the population, have no health insurance. Every year among all these millions of uninsured men, women, and children 220,000 cancers will be diagnosed and 73,000 will die. Every year another 76,000 will die of heart diseases and 17,000 will die of respiratory diseases. Strokes will kill 16,000. Or they will die from an unexpected diagnosis of a disease like diabetes, nephritis, or influenza. Many lives will be devastated because a loved one dies by a freak accident or an infectious disease.

These illnesses and deaths happen every year to those individuals without insurance. In the eyes of many, including the religious as well as non-believers, their consciences tell them that this history is a moral disgrace to their country.

11.1c The Affordable Care Act

The goal of the 2010 Patient Protection and Affordable Care Act (PPACA), commonly known as the Affordable Care Act (ACA), is to provide affordable health insurance for all U.S. citizens and reduce the growth in health care spending. The ACA has reformed the U.S. health insurance industry and the American health care system as a whole.

Passage of the ACA has made progress in changing the old status quo. The ACA pools risks and shares the costs as broadly as possible so that everyone is protected by affordable health insurance—and often life-saving health care—throughout their lives. The result of the ACA: The number of uninsured Americans has dropped by 21 million.

The ACA covers the uninsured through two channels: (1) Lower-income Americans are covered via a federally funded expansion of Medicaid, and (2) everyone else has access to subsidized policies sold by private insurers, who cannot discriminate based on medical history that are subsidized depending upon one's income. The ACA is an imperfect system, but it is working well.

However, the remaining uninsured population is difficult to reach and is less inclined to become insured. They will likely remain uninsured forever unless the USA goes to a much less expensive government-run single-payer system that covers all persons.

11.1d The ACA Does Not Impact Those Who Already Have Insurance

The 85 percent of Americans who were already covered by a health care plan prior to the ACA's implementation were not impacted by the Affordable Care Act because they already had insurance that meets the law's requirements. They already had a group health care plan offered by an employer, had private insurance, or were enrolled in a government provided insurance plan (e.g., Medicare Part A, Medicaid, CHIP, and TRICARE).

11.1e The ACA Impacts Those Without Health Insurance

The 15 percent without health insurance were required to purchase coverage or pay a penalty tax. Now 15 million of those people bought health insurance, 3 million were added to Medicaid, and 3 million more who were under age 26 were added to their parents' health plan. That is 21 million who now have health insurance for the first time. That reduced the

Patient Protection and Affordable Care Act (ACA)
The law passed by Congress in 2010 to provide affordable health insurance for all US citizens and reduce the growth in health care spending.

TO-DO SOON

Do the following to begin to achieve financial success:

1. *Learn exactly what group health care coverage you actually do have through your job, your school, and/or your family.*

2. *Investigate the possibility of saving on income taxes via a high-deductible health care policy and a health savings account (HSA).*

3. *Consider using a silver-level health plan if you are unable to afford health insurance.*

4. *Think about maintaining coverage for health care expenses when changing employers using the COBRA law.*

5. *Create living will and health care proxy documents.*

uninsured rate in the USA down from 45 million to about 24 million. Hospitals, doctors, and health insurance companies like the ACA because it creates more customers and additional income.

11.1f The ACA Provides Benefits, Rights, and Protections

The ACA offers benefits, rights, and protections to *all* Americans who buy health insurance policies in the individual market. These include a mandate for health insurance companies to cover everyone regardless of pre-existing conditions (which one in two Americans have), stops insurers from charging women more than men, prohibits dropping coverage for any reason except for fraud, eliminates annual and lifetime limits on health care, mandates that insurers cover 10 essential health benefits, wellness visits and preventative services with no out-of-pocket costs, and generally increases the quality of American's health care. The only way health insurance providers can afford all of this is if just about everyone buys insurance.

You Must Have a Health Care Plan If You Are Uninsured No one is guaranteed good health forever. Most people need to see health providers to stay healthy or at least monitor their health. That is why we buy insurance. Just like auto insurance you have to have health insurance as a "what if" something happens. We all wish we could avoid buying any kind of insurance until after the vehicle crashes, or the storm hits, or the home catches on fire, or we get very sick, but that is not how insurance works.

The Affordable Care Act has already reduced the increases in health care costs. It provides affordable health insurance to all Americans and reduces wasteful spending. The ACA focuses on prevention and primary care to help people stay healthy and to manage chronic medical conditions before they become more complex and costly to treat. Provisions of the ACA and answers to many questions may be found at www.irs.gov.aca. Step-by-step help on the law is offered by *Consumer Reports* at HealthLawHelper.org.

quality healthcare plan

An Affordable Care Act provision that requires that all health care policies meet the government's standard for its required "10 essential benefits" of adequate coverage.

individual mandate

An Affordable Care Act provision that require that all Americans and legal residents buy health coverage no matter how sick and regardless of any pre-existing health problems.

individual shared responsibility fee

A tax penalty of the Affordable Care Act that is assessed when one does not buy health insurance.

Quality Health Care Plans Everyone is required to obtain a quality healthcare plan that meets the government's standard for its required "10 essential benefits" of adequate coverage (see next page) either through a private provider, their employer, through a state or federally assisted program, or pay a tax penalty.

Individual Mandate and Shared Responsibility The ACA law requires that all Americans and legal residents buy health coverage no matter how sick and regardless of any pre-existing health problems. That is called the individual mandate. The idea is to encourage all Americans to buy health insurance because whenever anyone receives free urgent medical care the costs are passed on to the rest of society.

If you do not have health insurance, you will be assessed a tax penalty. The IRS calls the tax penalty an individual shared responsibility fee. It goes toward funding the ACA, subsidizing hospitals (which will still have to cover unpaid emergency room visits for those not covered by Medicaid programs in states that do not offer expanded Medicaid [discussed below] and undocumented immigrants), and as a down payment on other uninsured people's almost inevitable use of the health care system. The tax penalty will be assessed when filing your income tax return. It will offset any refund that would otherwise be due or will add to any balance due.

Health insurance coverage gaps of up to three months are allowed and will not violate the individual mandate. But after that, the tax applies to each month within a calendar year that you did not have coverage for yourself or a member of your household. Health insurance plans will provide documentation to prove you had insurance, which is filed with your income tax return.

11.1g Ten Essential Benefits of All New Health Care Plans

Health coverage available in the exchanges is better than the substandard polices that were available to individuals in the health insurance marketplace before because it was dominated by bare-bones, limited-coverage plans. Older policies usually did not cover

DID YOU KNOW ❓

Protections and Benefits of the Affordable Care Act

The Affordable Care Act changed the health insurance industry. While these provisions apply to ACA approved policies, *all* of the insurance industry's other policies now meet the same standards.

- **Ban on Denial for Pre-existing Conditions and Cancellation of Policies.** You cannot be denied coverage because of **pre-existing health conditions** diagnosed prior to signing up for a plan, and this impacts half of all Americans. Nor can an insurer cancel your policy if you get sick or make an honest mistake on your application. Policies can only be canceled for customer fraud.

- **Prohibits Charging Women and Men Different Prices.** The law stops discrimination based on gender, income, and health issues.

- **Prohibits Rationing Health Care.** The law protects consumers from the health care rationing insurance companies have been doing for ages.

- **Lousy Health Policies Are Prohibited.** Prior to passage of the law, the nation saw a race to the bottom as insurers cut benefits to lower premiums. Any policy today offering less than the federal government's "10 Essential Benefits" is prohibited.

- **Required Free Preventive Care and Annual Checkups Without Co-pays.** Plans must eliminate cost-sharing (co-payment, coinsurance, or deductible) for proven preventive measures such as immunizations, mammograms, cancer screenings, well-woman visits, screening for gestational diabetes, colonoscopies, domestic violence screening, breast-feeding supplies, and contraception.

- **Requires Lower Premiums for Prescriptions via Medicare.** The law provides lower prescription drug costs for people on Medicare.

- **Payout Maximums Prohibited.** Major or long-term illness can rack up serious medical bills and health insurance policies may no longer set annual and lifetime limits on how much they would pay for an individual's medical bills.

- **Remain on Parent's Plan Until Age 26.** Young adults may remain as dependents on their parent's policy until they turn 26, regardless of whether they live at home, attend school, or are married, unless they can get coverage at work.

- **Prohibits Overcharging Older Consumers.** Prohibits insurers from charging older people more than three times the amount they charge younger policyholders but premiums are allowed to be higher for tobacco users.

- **Rapid Appeals.** People can appeal insurance company decisions to an independent reviewer and receive a response in 72 hours for urgent medical situations.

- **Required Standard Disclosure Forms.** All plans must use a standardized form to summarize benefits and coverage, including co-payments, deductibles, and out-of-pocket limits, and they must disclose typical out-of-pocket costs for having a baby and treating type 2 diabetes.

- **Requires Justification of Rate Hikes.** The law requires health insurance companies to justify any rate increases above 10 percent to a state agency.

- **Promotes Choice Without a Referral.** Plans must allow people to choose any available participating primary care provider, OB-GYN, or pediatrician in their health plan's network, or emergency care outside of the plan's network, without a referral.

- **Required Premium Rebates if Companies Underspend on Care.** Insurers must spend at least 80 percent (85 percent for insurers covering large employers) of the premiums on medical care, and if insurers spend too much on salaries, bonuses, or administrative costs, instead of health care, they must issue refunds to policyholders.

- **Required Hospital Grading.** Doctors and hospitals are being moved to a system where they are rewarded for providing quality care not quantity. The Medicare Value-Based Purchasing Program means hospitals can lose or gain up to 1 percent of Medicare funding based on a number of quality measures related to treatment of patients with heart attacks, heart failures, pneumonia, certain surgical issues, re-admittance rate, as well as patient satisfaction.

prescription drugs, mental health, maternity, and rehabilitative care. Those lousy policies worked fine for many people as long as they did not discover the limitations of their policies by getting sick, going to the hospital or require some other excluded health care services.

essential health benefits

A list of ten categories of benefits that all health care plans sold on the health insurance exchanges must provide.

The ACA established ten comprehensive **essential health benefits** for adequate coverage that all health care plans now must include:

1. Ambulatory patient services, such as doctor's visits and outpatient services
2. Emergency services
3. Hospitalization
4. Maternity and newborn care
5. Mental health and substance use disorder services, including behavioral health treatment
6. Prescription drugs
7. Rehabilitative services and devices
8. Laboratory services
9. Preventive and wellness services and chronic disease management
10. Pediatric services, including oral and vision care

11.1h   Paying for the Cost of ACA Health Insurance

modified adjusted gross income (MAGI)

The figure the IRS uses to calculate one's health care penalty, and for most people it is the same as adjusted gross income.

One's **modified adjusted gross income (MAGI)** is the figure the IRS uses to calculate one's health care penalty. For most people, MAGI is the same as "adjusted gross income." Technically it is the total of adjusted gross income plus any deductions for IRA contributions, student loan interest or tuition, excluded foreign income, and interest from EE savings bonds used to pay higher education expenses.

If you do not have health insurance you must pay a penalty tax equal to the greater of 2.5 percent or $695 (up to a family maximum of $2,085). You pay whichever is higher. Penalties for children are $347.50, which is half the amount for adults. The tax for future years rises as it is indexed for inflation.

People who are enrolling in ACA approved health care plans are sicker and more heavily subsidized than what the participating insurers had hoped. Many of the healthy uninsured people are instead choosing to pay the penalty tax.

Opting to forego health insurance means that you are rolling the dice on possible costs. You are responsible for paying all of your health care costs, from visits to the doctor's office for vaccinations, health screenings, and check-ups to ambulance rides and emergency room visits for life-threatening situations. You also will not have any protection against enormous medical bills. An emergency room visit can easily cost $10,000. It runs about $30,000 to stay in the hospital for three days or to have a baby, and cancer treatments can cost $100,000 or more. Plus you still have to pay the tax penalty.

healthcare subsidy

A form of cost assistance that lowers the amount you spend on your monthly premium or reduces your out-of-pocket costs.

Subsidies Reduce the Price of Insurance Premiums   The ACA subsidizes low- and middle-income people thus helping them purchase health insurance at a reduced cost so that coverage is more affordable. A **healthcare subsidy** is a form of cost assistance that lowers the amount you spend on your monthly premium or reduces your out-of-pocket costs.

Premiums are determined by supply, demand, geographic location, and competition. Insurance rates are lower in states with vigorous competition in their insurance markets and have robust programs to review rates. Because some insurers were losing money five states now have only one insurer. Thus, the federal government proposes to offer its own health insurance, a so-called "public option" to create competition in some parts of the country to make rates more affordable where there are too fews insurers. Depending upon the state in which you live, the premium could be double that charged in a less expensive state. A subsidized health insurance policy for a young person might cost $800 to $1,600 a year. When insurance premiums increase—and they do every year—the subsidies increase by the same amount.

Nine out of ten people with policies covered under the law receive subsidies. They pay an average of $113 a month. What people pay for subsidized health insurance often is less than their cell phone bill or their cable bill.

health insurance exchange (HIX)

State-by-state mechanisms established by the ACA through which consumers can purchase a health care plan.

Buying Subsidized Health Insurance   Americans may purchase federally regulated and subsidized insurance in their states through **health insurance exchanges (HIX)** (also known as the **health insurance marketplace),** and these are run by the states and/or federal government. This is where the insurance companies compete to sell you their policies. Find your state's shopping portal at www.healthcare.gov.

Affordable health insurance is a policy that costs 8 percent of your income for health care premiums or 9.5 percent of family income if insurance is obtained through an employer. Those who cannot afford health insurance will either qualify for Medicare, Medicaid, or enhanced Medicaid government insurance programs or obtain financial help in the form of tax credits.

11.1j How Subsidy Tax Credits Work Under the ACA

Under the Affordable Care Act there are numerous tax credits and other assistance for low- and moderate-income people. The credit is based on household income and the number of people (adults and children) in the household.

Premium subsidies in the form of federal tax credits are available for people buying their own insurance in the exchanges who have incomes from 100 percent up to 400 percent of the federal poverty level (about $26,000 annually for an individual to about $104,000 annually for a family of four). Middle-income people under age 65, who are not eligible for coverage through their employer or Medicaid, may apply for tax credit subsidies available through state-based exchanges.

While premiums are not cheap, they are a lot lower than they used to be in the private marketplace. Plus they provide much better coverage.

Benchmark Premium The exact amount of the credit is based on a **benchmark premium**, which is the cost of the second-lowest-cost silver plan (described below) in the area where a person lives. The tax credit equals that benchmark premium minus what the individual is expected to pay based on his or her family income. This is calculated on a sliding scale from 2 percent to 9.5 percent of income. The individual can choose to have some, all, or none of the credit applied toward insurance premiums. Any reconciliation may be done on the income tax return when it is filed the following April.

benchmark premium
The amount of the credit provided under the Affordable Care Act that is used to calculate how much an individual will pay for a health care policy.

Estimated Financial Help Calculated Here is an example from the Kaiser Foundation of how the calculation of the credit might work for a 40-year-old individual making $30,000 a year buying a silver plan in Florida:

Estimated financial help:
$67 per month ($810 per year) as a premium tax credit, which covers 24 percent of the monthly cost.

Cost for a silver health care plan:
$208 per month or $2,497 per year in premiums, which equals 8.32 percent of your household income.

The most you have to pay for a silver plan:
8.32 percent of income for the second-lowest cost silver plan

Without financial help, the silver plan would cost:
$276 per month or $3,307 per year

Since prices can go down or rise every year, smart consumers consider switching to another low cost plan, such as going from one silver plan to another silver plan. A calculator from the Kaiser Family Foundation (kff.org/interactive/subsidy-calculator) provides subsidy estimates for families of varying characteristics.

The Kaiser Family Foundation figures that more than half the individuals who buy insurance on their own are eligible for subsidies, which are worth an average of $5,550 per household. This would effectively discount the projected price of insurance premiums by two-thirds, on average.

Who Pays for the Subsidies? The Congressional Budget Office (CBO) calculates that the cost of the ACA subsidies is being paid for by revenues from tax penalties on people who do not sign up for policies and by lowering payments to hospitals. In 2020

NUMBERS ON

Health

Data from a variety of sources suggest:

- The USA, a nation of 330 million, spends at least 50 percent more on health care than any other industrialized country
- USA has the highest rate of death by violence and highest rate of women dying in childbirth
- Medical errors are the number three cause of death in the USA, behind heart disease and strokes
- Smoking causes 480,000 deaths each year
- Smoking contributes to about 90 percent of lung cancer deaths
- Men who smoke are 23 times more likely to develop lung cancer and women are 13 times more likely, compared to having never smoked

- Over 35 million, about 13 percent of people under age 65, remain uninsured and they tend to be low-income families in the South and Southwest
- About 13 percent of adults are disabled
- One in four older adults needs long-term care
- Ninety percent of long-term care is provided by family members
- Forty percent of those receiving long-term care are between age 18 and 64
- Five million suffer from Alzheimer's disease
- The average age when one is admitted to a nursing home is 79 years
- $70,000 to $90,000 is the average annual cost of nursing home care

two new small taxes to pay for ACA are expected to begin: taxing the most expensive health plans and a small tax on the highest-income earners. While premiums for health insurance policies increase almost every year for ACA policies as well as all other health policies, the ACA still costs 25 percent less than projected by nonpartisan congressional experts estimated in 2010.

11.1k Health Care Plans on the Government Exchanges

Today only three factors can affect the cost of your health insurance: (1) age, (2) place of residence, and (3) number of people in your family. Your health history and current illnesses may no longer be used to set premiums.

Individuals, families, and small business owners may shop for health plans in online marketplaces, similar to travel websites. You may choose the provider you want for you, your family, or business based on who offers the most attractive package in terms of affordability and quality of coverage. You choose health plans with high or low premiums using side-by-side benefits and rates. Once you input your information on your state exchange the system will automatically calculate your subsidies.

Plans on the federal and state exchanges are grouped into four categories of "metal" since their quality corresponds to the value of their metal types. They cover 60 to 90 percent of out-of-pocket expenses, which is the most you pay during a policy period (usually a year) before your health insurance or plan begins to pay 100 percent of the allowed amount. The last plan, catastrophic, pays very little (60 percent) and is designed for those under age 30.

The ACA health care plans are:

1. Bronze: Plan pays 60 percent and you pay 40 percent.
2. Silver: Plan pays 70 percent and you pay 30 percent.

3. Gold: Plan pays 80 percent and you pay 20 percent.
4. Platinum: Plan pays 90 percent and you pay 10 percent.

The government also requires that insurers label each plan according to how many doctors are in it. A "standard" label means an average number of doctors for an exchange plan. "Broad" means more doctors while "basic" means less choice in doctors. For certain patients, narrower networks can be appealing because the premiums are perhaps 20 percent lower.

11.1L   Out-of-Pocket Maximum

Your **out-of-pocket maximum** is the largest amount of money you pay toward the cost of your healthcare each year. After you've paid enough in deductibles, copays, and coinsurance to reach your out-of-pocket maximum, your health insurance company pays for all of the rest of your healthcare that year. Keep in mind that you also will pay the premiums, which increases how much you actually pay for health care. It could be $4,000 to $8,000 a year. To keep your costs down, you may comparison shop prices for the price tags of various health care procedures in your area at www.opscost.com. President Donald J. Trump has promised to repeal the Affordable Care Act and replace it with something different.

out-of-pocket maximum

The most you pay during a policy period before your health insurance or plan begins to pay 100 percent of the allowed amount.

CONCEPT CHECK 11.1

1. What does the book say about why the USA has such an expensive health care system?
2. Summarize what the Affordable Care Act is supposed to accomplish.
3. Who does the ACA impact and who does it not?
4. List three of the 10 essential benefits of all new health care plans.
5. Summarize how subsidies reduce the price of insurance premiums under the ACA.
6. If you choose a "silver" health insurance plan, how much of your out-of-pocket medical costs will be paid by the plan?

11.2   TYPES OF HEALTH CARE PLANS

11.2a   Health Care Plans

A **health care plan** is a generic name for any program that pays for or provides reimbursement for health care expenditures. The costs for America's health care bills have been rising through the years, and today health care expenses are extremely high. As a result, both private employers and governments have been making consumers pay more attention to these rising costs. They are encouraging people to seek out less expensive health care and to pay more when they get it.

One key method to reduce health care costs is to require people to use **managed care**. This is a system designed to control the conditions under which health care can be obtained. Examples include preapproval of hospital admissions and restrictions on which hospitals or doctors may be used, and the cost of treatment is monitored by a managing company. Three-quarters of Americans with health insurance are in managed care.

Another way to reduce employer and government costs is to shift more of the expenses to individuals and families. For example, the costs paid by employees for health care averages about $2,900 a year. (Employers pay about $16,000.) Employees also pay out-of-pocket medical costs amounting to $2,200 each year. This is a total payout of $5,100 ($2,900 + $2,200) annually by employees. Families pay more.

health care plan

Generic name for any program that pays or provides reimbursement for health care expenditures.

managed care

A system designed to control the conditions under which health care can be obtained.

There are three health care plans offered by the government: Workers' Compensation, Medicare, and Medicaid, and these are examined later in this chapter. There are several types of health care plans available through employers, including some that utilize managed health. If you are shopping for a health care policy, you need to comparison shop because prices can vary as much as 50 percent for very similar coverage.

11.2b Employer-Provided Group Health Care Plans

If your employer provides you with health insurance, your choices will be limited to what is offered. A **group health plan** refers to the way the policy is sold not to anything specific about the policy. Group policies are to various groups of people, such as employers' employees and members of professional associations. When a group health plan is available as a benefit for active employees, employers today usually pay the cost for each worker (and often subsidizes the costs for other members of the worker's immediate family) for the lowest-cost plan the employer offers. Employees can choose a higher-priced plan or add family members to the coverage by paying an additional charge. These plans are provided by employers to 175 million employees.

Fee-for-Service (Indemnity) Plan A very limited type of health insurance plan is a **fee-for-service** or **indemnity plan.** Under an indemnity plan, you may see whatever doctors or specialists you like, with no referrals required. You pay up front for services and then submit a claim for reimbursement to the insurance company. You must pay an annual deductible before the insurance company begins to pay claims. Then the insurance company will reimburse you directly.

The amount of your claims will be paid at either a fixed amount or as a set percentage of the **usual, customary, and reasonable (UCR) rate** for the service. The latter is the amount paid for a medical service in a geographic area based on what providers in the area usually charge for the same or similar medical service. Alternatively, it might pay a set cash amount of $250 a day for hospital care. The amounts paid to consumers often are woefully inadequate, and not many employers offer this type of health plan.

Traditional Health Insurance Plan A **traditional health insurance** plan provides protection against direct medical expenses resulting from illness and injury based on the concept of payment after an expense occurs. The insurer pays all or most of a portion of the usual, customary, and reasonable fees directly with the insured patient being billed for any remainder. These plans are often referred to as a "fee-for-service" health plan, and the policy actually pays the usual and customary fees. These often are the best health care plans available as they pay almost all health care expenses, and accordingly they are the most expensive.

One well known provider of traditional health insurance for millions of Americans is Blue Cross and Blue Shield. **Blue Cross** provides hospital care benefits while **Blue Shield** provides benefits for surgical and medical services. There are several variations of health care plans offered by employers.

---

fee-for-service or indemnity plan

A health insurance plan where you pay up front for services and then submit a claim for reimbursement to the insurance company.

usual, customary, and reasonable (UCR) rate

The amount paid for a medical service in a geographic area based on what providers in the area usually charge for the same or similar medical service.

Blue Cross

Insurance companies that provide hospital care benefits.

Blue Shield

Insurance company that provides benefits for surgical and medical services.

New employees often must choose from among a menu of health care plans soon after being hired.

Goodluz/Shutterstock.com

1. Managed Care: Health Maintenance Organizations

Health maintenance organizations (HMOs) are pre-paid managed care insurance plans in which individuals or their employers pay a fixed monthly fee for services instead of a separate charge for each visit or service. They offer an array of health care services, including hospital, surgical, preventive health care, and major medical.

A goal of HMOs is to catch any medical problem early, which helps keep overall costs low by reducing the probability of subsequent high-cost medical treatment. Most participants are assigned a primary care physician by the HMO or ask you to choose one from a list of physicians employed by the HMO. The physician must order all approved procedures and approve referrals to specialized health care providers within the HMO.

2. Managed Care: Preferred Provider Organization

A **preferred provider organization (PPO)** is a managed care organization of medical doctors, hospitals, and other health care providers who have agreed with an insurer or a third-party administrator to provide health care at reduced rates to the insurer's clients. Membership allows a substantial discount below the regularly charged rates of the designated professionals partnered with the organization. PPOs have gained popularity because, although they tend to have slightly higher premiums than HMOs and other more restrictive plans, they offer patients more flexibility overall.

A feature of a PPO is that it generally includes a **utilization review**, where representatives of the insurer review the records of treatments provided to verify that they are appropriate for the condition being treated. Also non-emergency hospital admissions and sometimes outpatient surgery must have the prior approval of the insurer.

A PPO is similar to an HMO, but you pay for care when it is received rather than in advance. This discount is then passed along to the policyholders in the form of reductions or elimination of deductibles and coinsurance requirements.

3. Managed Care: Provider-Sponsored Network

A **provider-sponsored network (PSN)** is a managed care organization consisting of a group of doctors, hospitals, and other health care providers (and not insurance companies) who have banded together to offer a health insurance contract. They provide a substantial portion of the health care services for individuals, share some of the financial risk, and own a majority interest in the company. PSN may be either profit or not-for-profit entities, or public or private entities.

Such networks operate primarily in rural areas, where access to HMOs and PPOs may be limited. As a group, the members of the PSN coordinate and deliver health care services and manage the insurance plan financially. They also contract with outside providers for health services that are not available through members of the group.

4. Managed Care: Accountable Care Organization

An **accountable care organization (ACO)** consists of a group of doctors and/or a hospital who have made a deal with a private insurer or Medicare to provide safe and appropriate services, rather than operate as a fee-for-service organization. The goal of coordinated care is to ensure that patients, especially the chronically ill, get the right care at the right time, while avoiding unnecessary duplication of services and preventing medical errors. When an ACO succeeds both in delivering high-quality care and spending health care dollars more wisely, it will share in the savings it achieves for the Medicare program. Keeping people healthy makes them "accountable" for the overall cost and care. Participating in an ACO is purely voluntary for providers, and there is no impact on premiums for policyholders. The distinctions among managed care organizations are becoming blurred.

5. High-Deductible Health Insurance Plan

A **high-deductible health care plan** has a high deductible that you must meet before the insurance will start paying for your office visits, lab tests, and prescriptions. A **deductible** is a clause in health care plan contracts that require you to pay an initial portion of medical expenses annually before receiving reimbursement. In order to qualify as a high-deductible plan the deductible

---

health maintenance organizations (HMOs)

Pre-paid managed care insurance plans in which individuals or their employers pay a fixed monthly fee for services instead of a separate charge for each visit or service.

preferred provider organization (PPO)

A managed care organization of medical doctors, hospitals, and other health care providers who have agreed with an insurer or a third-party administrator to provide health care at reduced rates to the insurer's clients.

utilization review

A feature of managed care health plans where representatives of the insurer review the records of treatments provided to verify that they are appropriate for the condition being treated.

accountable care organization (ACO)

A group of doctors and/or a hospital who have made a deal with a private insurer or Medicare to provide safe and appropriate services, rather than operate as a fee-for-service organization.

deductibles

Clauses in health care plans that require the participant to pay an additional portion of health expenses annually before receiving reimbursement.

DID YOU KNOW ?

Defined Contribution Health Care Plans Replacing Employer-Provided Health Insurance

Many employers are no longer offering fully paid health care as an employee benefit, rather they are subsidizing it. Some companies have dropped offering their health care plan and are instead offering employees a sum of money—perhaps $500 a month in financial assistance—to purchase insurance in the marketplace. Examples are Darden Restaurants, IBM, Trader Joe's, Sears Holdings, and Walgreens.

Within five years some estimates are that more than a quarter of all workers who formerly had an employer-provided group health care plan will get their benefits through employer-provided contributions to defined contribution health plans.

This is a trend away from defined-benefit health coverage offered by employers to defined-contribution coverage. Rather than paying the costs to provide a group health plan benefit (a "defined benefit"), employers reduce their costs by establishing a **defined contribution health plan**. Here a company gives each employee a fixed dollar amount (a "defined contribution") that employees choose how to spend, which includes reimbursing themselves for health insurance costs. Defined contribution health plans are not health insurance plans.

---

must be at least $1,000. The average deductible is $5,000. Often once you have reached the deductible the insurance will kick in with coverage.

Since high-deductible plans cover less they usually have a much lower premium than traditional health plans. Three-quarters of employers offer a high-deductible plan primarily because they are the least expensive. If you are healthy, this may be an option to consider.

health savings account (HSA)

This is a tax-advantaged medical savings account, thus all funds you put in your account are 100 percent tax deductible from gross income as long as they are used for health care expenses.

6. Self-Insured Health Care Plan A key component of the design of a high-deductible health plan is a **health savings account (HSA)**. This is a tax-advantaged medical savings account. All funds you put in your HSA are 100 percent tax deductible from gross income as long as they are used for health care expenses, including certain over-the-counter items. Three quarters of large employers offer them.

An HSA allows one to be partially self-insured. HSA policyholders must have an insurance policy that pays for catastrophic costs that may occur. HSAs can be used for your deductibles, co-payments, prescription drugs, out-of-pocket medical, and dental and vision care, but they cannot be used to pay health insurance premiums. The HSA annual contribution limits are $3,350 for an individual and $6,750 for a family. You can let the money grow for years. Those 55 and older can contribute an extra $1,000. To find an HAS and compare fees, see www.hsasearch.com.

11.2c Government Programs

Three well known programs provide medical coverage for Americans: Workers' Compensation, Medicare, and Medicaid.

Workers' Compensation Plans State **workers' compensation plans** are a form of insurance providing medical benefits and wage replacement to employees injured in the course of employment in exchange for mandatory relinquishment of the employee's right to sue his or her employer for the tort of negligence. Your employer is financially liable for employment-related injuries, no matter who caused it. Employees receive medical costs, rehabilitation expenses, lost wages, and cash benefits for death and dismemberment.

Medicare Over fifty seven million people are enrolled in the federal Medicare program, which is the federal government's single-payer health care program for the elderly. "Single-payer" refers to funding, not delivery. Services are delivered by the private sector. Medicare's primary

NEVER EVER ⚠

Go Without Health Care Insurance

Always buy some kind of health insurance just in case disaster strikes. You can buy a health policy for $150 a month that excludes the first $10,000 in losses but does cover catastrophic losses.

beneficiaries are people age 65 and older who are eligible for Social Security retirement benefits. Medicare is funded by means of the Medicare payroll tax. This tax for most American workers is 1.45 percent of earned income. Both employees and employers pay the 1.45 percent.

It costs only 6 cents on the dollar for the government to run the single-payer Medicare system, which is less than one-third that of privately available health plans. That is an impressive savings for comparing the non-profit federal government program to the private sector where all providers make a profit.

The nation's top 3 percent of unmarried income earners pay an additional 0.09 percent Medicare surtax on incomes over $200,000. Their unearned income (e.g., interest, dividends, capital gains, annuities, rental income) pay a Medicare surtax of 3.8 percent.

Medicare has 4 parts:

- **Hospital Insurance—Medicare Part A** is the hospitalization portion of the program; it requires no premium. Most people do not pay a monthly Part A premium because they or a spouse has 40 or more quarters of Medicare-covered employment.

- **Supplemental Medical Insurance—Medicare Part B** is the supplementary health expense insurance portion for outpatient care, doctor office visits, and certain other services of the Medicare program. It requires payment of a monthly premium of about $130 (but more for higher income older people). Both components require patients to pay a portion of their costs, recently about $170 a year. The federal government pays 75 percent of Part B costs and beneficiaries pay 25 percent.

- **Prescription Drug Coverage—Medicare Part D** provides an optional prescription coverage plan. Participants pay an initial portion of prescription costs, about $30 a month depending on their level of income.

- **Medicare Advantage Plans—Part C.** Some programs compete with Medicare to serve the elderly and their programs are approved by the government. **Medicare Advantage Plans** are health care plans that offer Medicare benefits through private health plans, such as HMOs and PPOs. Medicare pays Medicare Advantage Plans a lump sum annually to provide Plan A and B coverages. The also offer annual

COBRA rights

The Consolidated Omnibus Budget Reconciliation Act of 1985 allows a former employee to remain a member of a group health plan for as long as 18 months if the employee worked for an employer with more than 20 workers.

ADVICE FROM A SEASONED PRO

Maintain Your Health Care Plan Between Jobs

What happens when you no longer work for an employer that offers a group health care plan and you want to continue the coverage? You can assert your **COBRA rights** (Consolidated Omnibus Budget Reconciliation Act of 1985). These rules allow you to remain a member of a group health plan for as long as 18 months if you worked for an employer with more than 20 workers. COBRA applies to you and to any of your dependents who had been covered under the employer's plan. COBRA rights apply to your dependents for 36 months. These rights must be exercised within 60 days after the termination of employment, and you must pay the full premiums (including both the employee's and the employer's portions) plus a 2 percent administrative fee.

You might be tempted to go without coverage for a time because of the high cost of converting your previous plan, you expect to have a job soon that will provide coverage, or simply because you are willing to pay the penalty. This latter reason is shortsighted because young people do get sick and are injured.

So what should you do? Buy a health plan using the government health exchange in your state. Coverage for a premium of perhaps $150 to $250 per month is available. About half of COBRA users are expected to move to the government exchanges.

William Dean
Southern University, Baton Rouge, Louisiana

financial incentives for the better plans. Medicare Advantage plans replace Medicare for one-quarter of the nation's elderly population. Medicare Advantage plans provide broader coverage than Medicare and some also provide prescription drug benefits.

- **Medigap policies.** As the name implies, these policies provide supplemental medical insurance to cover gaps in standard Medicare coverage. There are 10 standardized polices available. Costs usually range from $1,000 to $6,000 annually. Compare costs and benefits at www.healthpocket.com/medicare.

Medicaid

A government health care program for low-income people funded jointly by the federal and state governments.

Medicaid and Expanded Medicaid Medicaid is a joint federal and state funded program that provides health care for over 60 million low-income Americans, mostly children, pregnant women, people with disabilities, and elderly people who need home care or live in nursing homes. Medicaid programs must follow federal guidelines, but they vary somewhat from state to state. Eligibility for Medicaid is based on both household income (less than $16,000) and family size, and it is either free or costs very little.

More than half the states have adopted a voluntary **expanded Medicaid** program, which expands Medicaid eligibility to all individuals (who were not previously eligible) and households with incomes below 138 percent of the Federal Poverty Level.

Expanded Medicaid remains contentious because nearly two dozen states decided not to offer expanded Medicaid to their poorest citizens. This has occurred even though the federal government offered to pay 100 percent of the costs to the states for three years and 90 percent after that. Thus, five million poor families (seven percent of the population) have no affordable health care option at all. These uninsured people will continue to use the last-ditch hospital and emergency services that drive up costs for all taxpayers.

CONCEPT CHECK 11.2

1. Explain how managed care has reduced the cost of health care in America.
2. Summarize how an employer's group health care plan provides coverage to employees.
3. Distinguish between a traditional health insurance plan and a health maintenance organizations (HMO).
4. What is a high-deductible health insurance plan and how does it work with a health savings account (HSA).
5. Distinguish between the government health program called Medicare and Medicaid.

Learning Objective 3

Describe the typical features and limits of health care plans.

certificate of insurance

Document or booklet that outlines group health insurance benefits.

coordination of benefits clause

An insurance clause in all policies that prevents you from collecting more than 100 percent of covered charges by obtaining benefits from more than one policy.

11.3 YOUR HEALTH PLAN BENEFITS AND LIMITS

You can save yourself considerable confusion, delay, and money if you understand your health plan benefits before illness or injury strikes. If you have a group insurance plan, you will receive a **certificate of insurance** that outlines your benefits. HMO participants can obtain a copy of their plan contract. You should become familiar with the details of your health insurance plan. All policies have a **coordination of benefits clause** that prevents you from collecting more than 100 percent of covered charges by obtaining benefits from more than one policy. Below are some questions to ask yourself and background information to understand what you find in these documents.

11.3a What Types of Care Are Covered?

The typical health care plan covers hospital room and board expenses, surgical procedures both as an inpatient and outpatient, prescription drugs, diagnostic tests, visits to the doctor's office, and other aspects of health care. Dental and vision care are now covered as they are part of the required 10 essential benefits.

11.3b Who Is Covered?

A family generally consists of a parent or parents and dependent children. Are the children of a divorced parent who does not have custody covered under that parent's group plan? What about stepchildren? These questions must be answered to ensure that all family members are covered under some plan.

11.3c How Much Is the Premium?

The premium is the amount you pay each month. Paying your premium is sort of like paying into a pool of money with a bunch of other people. Some people will use a lot of care, others will use less. Higher premiums tend to mean lower out-of-pocket costs, specifically lower deductibles, as well as better coinsurance. Health care plans also contain provisions that specify the level of coverage for your expenses and the portion that you must pay yourself.

What Are the Exclusions? All plans also have **exclusions**, or a list of services that are not typically covered in the policy. Ask about the exclusions.

How Much Is Your Deductible? An **annual deductible** is a clause in health care plans that require you to pay an initial portion of medical expenses annually before receiving reimbursement. A deductible of $500 per year, for example, would mean that the patient must pay the first $500 of the medical costs for the year. Family plans generally include a deductible for each family member (again, perhaps $500 per year) with a maximum family deductible (perhaps $1,000 per year). Once the deductible payments for individual family members reach the maximum family deductible ($1,000 in this example), further individual deductibles will be waived. (Under the ACA annual deductibles often range from $3,000 to $7,000.)

How Much Is the Coinsurance Proportion? A **coinsurance clause** requires you to pay a proportion of any loss suffered. The typical share is 80/20, with the insurer paying the larger percentage. Usually, there is a **coinsurance cap** that limits the annual out-of-pocket payments required of the patient when meeting the coinsurance.

How Much Is the Copay? A **copay (or copayment)** requires you to pay a certain dollar amount each time you have a specific covered expense item. A copay is often required for visits to the doctor's office and for prescription drugs. For example, you might have to pay $25 for each prescription, with the insurer paying the remainder. A copay differs from a deductible in that it might require that you pay $35 for each office visit even after the annual deductible is met.

How Much Is the Out-of-Pocket Maximum? This is the most you will pay for covered services in a policy period (usually a year) before your insurer pays 100 percent of covered costs. It can ranges from perhaps less than $50 annually to over $13,000.

The following example illustrates how a deductible of $250 and an 80/20 coinsurance provision with a $1,000 coinsurance cap work together to determine the coverage for an $8,760 health care bill. Because the deductible is the responsibility of the insured party, the patient pays the first $250. The coinsurance ratio is applied to the remaining $8,510 ($8,760 − $250) until the portion paid by the patient reaches the coinsurance cap. Thus, $1,000 is covered by the insured and $4,000 by the insurer. The additional expenses of $3,510 ($8,510 − $1,000 − $4,000) are covered 100 percent by the insurance company.

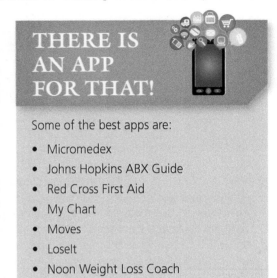

THERE IS AN APP FOR THAT!

Some of the best apps are:

- Micromedex
- Johns Hopkins ABX Guide
- Red Cross First Aid
- My Chart
- Moves
- LoseIt
- Noon Weight Loss Coach
- Healthy Out

Exclusions
A list of services that are not typically covered in a health care policy.

DO IT IN CLASS

coinsurance clause
A clause in a health care plan that requires the participant to pay a proportion of any loss suffered.

copay (or copayment)
A requirement in a health care insurance policy that makes you to pay a certain dollar amount each time you have a specific covered expense item, such as to a doctor's office and for prescription drugs.

DID YOU KNOW ?

Out-of-Pocket Costs Are Killing the Middle Class

Medical costs are crippling the middle class. Workers used to be offered excellent health insurance by employers, which was so good it was known as the "gold standard." Today's employer-provided policies require workers to pay so much out-of-pocket that many are skipping doctor's appointments, postponing medical treatments, and rationing pills. This is pretty much what the uninsured have been doing for years.

The deductibles, copays, coinsurance, and exclusions were intended to help keep costs down by encouraging people to be more cost-conscious if they had more of a financial stake in the game. But a growing number of Americans cannot afford the growing out-of-pocket expenses.

For example, the average cost of a person's typical prescription drugs doubled to more than $11,000 in the past

seven years. Patients sometimes must pay half the cost. These increases are happening in the private sector as well as in the ACA policies, and all health insurances are increasingly requiring larger out-of-pocket payments.

The average deductible on a medical insurance policy is $1,400 a year for individuals, and it is $2,000 for one-fifth of workers. Add to this, copays, co-insurance, and money for procedures not covered, and it is increasingly expensive for average Americans. Five or six thousand in out-of-pocket costs is common. This easily can exceed $10,000 for a family, while median household income is barely over $50,000. Hourly pay in the United States is about $20, almost exactly what it was 50 years ago.

In this example, the insured party will pay $1,250 ($250 deductible + $1,000 coinsurance) and the insurer will pay $7,510 ($4,000 coinsurance + $3,510 remaining charges).

How Good Is the Health Insurance Company? You can compare health care insurance companies by looking at information from the National Committee for Quality Assurance (NCQA). See www.ncqa.org/HEDISQualityMeasurement.aspx. Also more organizations are rating health care providers. Important questions are: Is your current family physician on the provider list? And are services offered nearby?

11.3d   Making Changes in Health Care Plans

open-enrollment period

A time period during which one can make changes in health care insurance coverage or switch among alternative plans.

In almost all health care plans, you must wait until the next **open-enrollment period** to make changes in coverage or switch among alternative plans. Open-enrollment periods are one to two months long. The open-enrollment period for the Affordable Care Act is November 1 through January 31. Plan rules allow changes at other times during the open year if the participant experiences certain family events such as births, adoptions, divorce, and marriage.

CONCEPT CHECK 11.3

1. Distinguish among an exclusion, deductible, coinsurance, and a copay.
2. What is meant by the out-of-pocket maximum?

Learning Objective 4

Explain the fundamentals of planning for long-term custodial care.

11.4   PLANNING FOR LONG-TERM CUSTODIAL CARE

long-term care insurance

Provides reimbursement for costs associated with custodial care in a nursing facility or at home.

Many health care episodes include a period of time when the patient no longer needs skilled medical care but does need assistance to a degree that requires confinement in a nursing home or special help at home. **Long-term care insurance** provides for extended care that consists of help with the activities of daily living such as dressing and bathing, and/or care needed due to severe cognitive impairment, such as caused by Alzheimer's disease. Long-term care insurance is a very long-term contract. You usually buy a policy at age 65 or younger, and you could be making claims in your eighties or nineties. This impacts about 4½ million people. Eleven percent of Americans 85 and older do live in nursing homes.

The need for long-term care is especially prevalent with the extremely elderly and patients with certain conditions such as Alzheimer's disease and related dementias. The cost for such nonmedical assistance is typically not covered by HMOs, health insurance, or Medicare. The elderly who have spent down their assets then may be eligible to receive Medicaid reimbursement for their custodial nursing home care. Middle-income people should realize that insurance costs have risen dramatically in recent years as insurers have recalculated and raised their expense projections. Several factors should be assessed when considering a long-term care policy and these are examined below.

When Benefits Begin Insurance companies use the inability to perform a certain number of **activities of daily living (ADLs)** as a criterion for deciding when the insured becomes eligible for long-term care benefits. A policy typically pays benefits when a person cannot perform two or three ADLs without assistance. The ADLs commonly used in this type of decision making are bathing, bladder control, dressing oneself, eating without assistance, toileting (moving on and off the toilet), and transferring (getting in and out of bed). Because bathing is often one of the first ADLs that is lost, a policy that does not list bathing makes it more difficult to reach the threshold at which benefits become available.

Levels of Care The levels of nursing home care are usually categorized three ways. **Skilled nursing care** is intended for people who need intensive care, meaning 24-hour-a-day supervision and treatment by a registered nurse, under the direction of a doctor. **Intermediate care** is appropriate for people who do not require around-the-clock nursing but who are not able to live alone. **Custodial care** is suitable for many people who do not need skilled nursing care but who nevertheless require supervision (for example, help with eating or personal hygiene).

Person's Age When Purchasing The younger the person is when the policy is purchased, the lower the premium as the odds of needing care increase with age. The trade-off lies between buying young and paying premiums for many years versus waiting to purchase a policy, at which time it may be difficult to afford coverage because of high policy costs.

Benefit Amount Long-term care plans are generally written to provide a specific dollar benefit per day of care. If the cost for nursing homes in your geographic area is $240 a day, you can pay lower premiums by choosing to buy a policy that pays $200 per day, thereby coinsuring for a portion of the expenses.

Benefit Duration The **benefit period** in a long-term care policy is the maximum period of time for which benefits will be paid, typically stated in years. Although it is possible to buy a policy with lifetime benefits, this option can be very expensive. The average nursing home stay is nearly two-and-one-half years. A policy with a three-year limit might cost one-third less than a policy with a lifetime benefit period. Also realize that two-thirds of nursing home patients die within one year of admission.

Waiting Period The **waiting period (elimination period)** in a long-term care policy is the time period between the onset of the need for care and the date that benefits begin. Policies can pay benefits from the first day of nursing home care or they can include a waiting period. Selecting a 30-day or 90-day waiting period can significantly reduce premiums.

Inflation Protection If a policy is purchased prior to age 60, the buyer faces a significant risk in that inflation may render the daily benefit woefully inadequate when care is

activities of daily living (ADLs)
Insurance companies use the inability to perform a certain number of such activities as a criterion for deciding when the insured becomes eligible for long-term care benefits.

custodial care
Suitable for people who do not need skilled nursing care but who nevertheless require supervision (for example, help with eating or personal hygiene).

benefit period
The maximum period of time for which benefits will be paid under a disability income or other insurance policy.

waiting period (elimination period)
The time period between the onset of a disability and the date that disability benefits begin.

NEVER EVER

1. *Pay the tax-penalty assessed under the Affordable Care Act because you fail to enroll in a health care plan.*
2. *Duplicate employer-provided health care protection with your employed spouse.*
3. *Ignore your need for disability income insurance.*

DO IT IN CLASS

ultimately needed. Some policies increase the daily benefit by 2 or 3 percent per year to adjust for inflation, but this protection adds considerably to the premium. The younger your age when a policy is purchased, the more you need inflation protection.

CONCEPT CHECK 11.4

1. What are activities of daily living?
2. Distinguish among the three levels of care in long-term insurance.
3. Distinguish between the benefit period and the waiting period for a long-term care policy.

Learning Objective 5

Develop a plan to protect your income when you cannot work due to disability.

Disability

A self-reported difficulty in one or more of five areas: vision, cognition, mobility, self-care, or independent living.

YOUR GRANDPARENTS SAY

"Discuss Health With Us"

"Health is partially hereditary so talk with your grandparents about health-related decisions. What is the family history of serious and disabling diseases? Have disabilities occurred among relatives? Did anyone require long-term care? Answers can help you make good insurance decisions."

disability income insurance

Insurance that covers a portion of the income lost when you cannot work because of illness or injury.

Social Security Disability Income Insurance

Under this government program, eligible workers can receive some income if their disabilities are total, meaning that they cannot work at any job.

11.5 DISABILITY INCOME INSURANCE

A **disability** is a self-reported difficulty in one or more of five areas: vision, cognition, mobility, self-care, or independent living. This includes driving a vehicle and shopping for groceries. One in five people have a disability.

Accidents or illness can happen to just about anyone at any time. According to the Council for Disability Awareness, one in seven workers can expect to be disabled for five years or more before retirement. The Social Security Administration says three in ten workers entering the labor force today will become disabled. See www.whatsmypdq.org. Today, 8 million people receive Social Security disability benefits. Monthly payments to disabled workers average $1,200, spouses of disabled workers average $320, and children of disabled workers average $350.

Anyone with a job can lose income when he or she becomes sick, injured, or contracts a disease. Many employers voluntarily offer employees sick days and other time off that can be used as necessary, although no federal law requires these policies.

Some employers offer **disability income insurance** that provides regular weekly or monthly cash income to replace a portion of the earnings lost when you cannot work because of illness or injury. These plans come in two forms.

A **short-term disability income insurance plan** replaces a portion of one's income for a short period of time, usually from two weeks up to two years. Short-term plans are sometimes partially paid for by the employer. Employers may also offer a group **long- term disability income insurance plan** for coverage periods of five or more years. The employee is usually required to pay the full premium for such coverage. If your employer does not offer either of these plans, you may buy them on your own.

11.5a Eligible Workers Collect Social Security Disability Income

Workers who are eligible can collect **Social Security Disability Income Insurance** benefits from the federal government. Rules require that the disability is total (meaning they cannot work at any job) and is expected to last one year (or until death if that is anticipated within one year).

The government's Social Security disability income program pays an average of $13,560 annually in tax-free income to the family of an insured disabled worker. See Appendix B at the end of the book or the *Garman/Forgue* companion website for an illustration of how to figure these benefits.

The amount of these benefits is based on the worker's average lifetime earnings subject to Social Security tax. As such, they might not be sufficient to adequately support young workers and their families. Plus seventy percent of Social Security disability applicants are rejected, and this increases the likelihood of one needing to buy disability income insurance.

11.5b Who Needs Disability Insurance?

Long-term disability income loss is often overlooked, though it is vitally important for all workers including young single adults. A male worker has a 21 percent chance of becoming disabled for three months or longer at some point during his working career. Older workers who become disabled may have retirement money available because certain types of pension plans (not 401[k] plans or IRAs) provide benefits to workers who become disabled while still employed. However, such benefit plans often fall far short of fully meeting the needs of most workers.

11.5c What Is Your Level of Need?

The key question to ask when contemplating disability income insurance is, "How much protection do I need?" The dollar limits on disability income policies are written either in increments of $100 per month or as a percentage of monthly income. Policy coverage is limited to 60 to 80 percent of the insured's after-tax earnings.

Determining the amount of additional protection needed is challenging because some sources of help may not actually be available for all disabilities. It is smart to complete the calculations in the Run the Numbers feature, "Determining Disability Income Insurance Needs" on page 352. You can use the figure obtain from the worksheet as a starting point when shopping for disability income insurance protection.

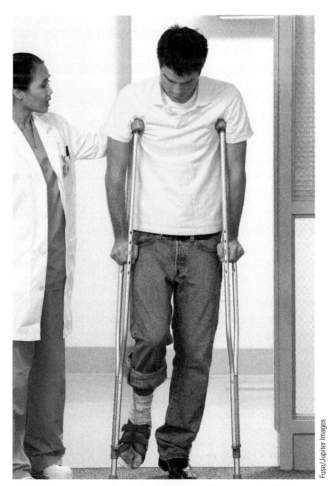

Fuse/Jupiter Images

A young person with no dependents still needs disability income insurance.

MONEY WEBSITES

Informative websites are:
ACA provisions
AARP
Centers for Medicare & Medicaid Services
Department of Health and Human Services
Department of Labor
EHealth
Healthcare portal for states
Kaiser Family Foundation
National Association of Insurance Commissioners
NOLO
Social Security Administration
USA Gov

RUN THE NUMBERS

Determining Disability Income Insurance Needs

The determination of disability insurance needs begins with your current monthly after-tax income. From this figure, subtract the amounts you would receive from Social Security disability and other sources of disability income. The resulting figure will provide an estimate of extra coverage needed.

Decision Factor	Example	Your Figures
1. Current monthly after-tax income	$3,200	_____
2. Minus previous established disability income protections		_____
(a) Monthly Social Security disability benefits	−$1,250	_____
(b) Monthly benefit from employer-provided disability insurance	−$ 600	_____
(c) Monthly benefit from private disability insurance	_____	_____
(d) Monthly benefit from other government disability insurance	_____	_____
Total Subtractions	−$1,850	_____
3. Estimated monthly disability income insurance needs	$1,350	_____

DO IT IN CLASS

11.5d   What Policy Provisions Best Meet Your Needs?

Once you have estimated your level of need, you can begin searching for a disability income insurance policy. These policies are complicated so avoid relying on the verbal assurances of the agent selling the policy. Do your own analysis, and also seek the advice of a financial planner before making a decision. Look first for the major policy provisions discussed in the following five paragraphs.

1. Waiting Period Disability income policies will have a **waiting period** between the onset of the disability and the date that disability benefits begin. Because disability income benefits are paid monthly, the first check will not arrive until 30 days after the end of the waiting period.

2. Benefit Period The **benefit period** in a disability income policy is the maximum period of time for which benefits will be paid. It begins when the elimination period ends. The benefit period is usually stated in years but may instead state a specific age when benefits will cease. Most disability income policies will not pay past age 65.

3. Degree of Disability Policies can be written on an "own-occupation" or "any-occupation" basis. An **own-occupation policy** will provide benefits if you can no longer perform the occupation you had at the time you became disabled. An **any-occupation policy** will provide full benefits only if you cannot perform any occupation. In effect, an any-occupation policy is an income replacement policy, as it makes up a portion of the difference between what you were earning prior to becoming disabled and what you can earn while disabled. Own-occupation policies are more generous and, therefore, cost more.

4. Residual Clause A **residual clause** is a feature of own-occupation policies that allows for some reduced level of disability income benefits when a partial, rather than full, disability occurs. Consider the case of Françoise LaDeux, a criminal lawyer in Columbus, Ohio, who purchased a disability policy offering

BIAS TOWARD— MINIMIZING LOSSES

People have a bias toward minimizing even small, initial losses. An example is demanding a short waiting period on disability and long-term care insurance. Many people fail to understand that having a short waiting period usually means that you are at greater risk of catastrophic losses. This is because the high cost of the short waiting period makes it difficult to afford a long benefit period. What to do? Purchase policies with a six-month or one-year waiting period and apply the premium savings to getting a five-year or longer benefit period.

a benefit of $3,000 per month. Françoise later developed multiple sclerosis and was forced to cut back her workload by 50 percent, thereby taking a 50 percent pay cut. Her disability policy had a residual clause, so she received $1,500 (0.50 × $3,000) per month during her disability.

5. Cost-of-Living Adjustments You are wise to seek out a policy with a **cost-of-living clause** that will increase your benefit amount to keep up with inflation. You might also consider buying a policy that limits benefits to a percentage of income rather than a specific dollar amount per month. With such a policy, your potential monthly benefit would increase automatically as your income increases.

6. Guaranteed Renewability Clause Ask for a policy with guaranteed renewability that also is noncancelable. Then the insurer will not drop you should your health decline.

any-occupation policy
Provides full benefits only if the insured cannot perform any occupation.

residual clause
Feature of own-occupation policies that allows for some reduced level of disability income benefits when a partial—rather than full—disability strikes.

CONCEPT CHECK 11.5

1. Summarize how you determine your level of need for disability income insurance.
2. Explain who needs disability insurance.
3. Identify three policy provisions to consider when purchasing disability income insurance.
4. Distinguish between own-occupation and any-occupation disability income insurance plans.

11.6 ADVANCE DIRECTIVE DOCUMENTS

Advance directives (or **advance medical directives**) are legal documents that explain the type of end-of-life health care you do or do not want when you cannot make your own decisions because of illness or incapacity. You also need to create a document that appoints someone who can speak for you to make sure your wishes are carried out. These documents may be used to retain your dignity and save your loved ones the burden of making some very challenging and difficult decisions. Four out of five adults have no advance directive documents.

There are three types of advance directives: (1) living will, (2) health care proxy, and (3) durable power of attorney. Once you have created advance directive documents, give copies to members of your family and other responsible people in your life, and your wishes in these matters may then be controlled as you desire.

Learning Objective 6

Summarize the benefits of preparing advance medical directive documents.

Advance directives (advance medical directives)
Legal documents that explain the type of end-of-life health care you do or do not want when you cannot make your own decisions because of illness or incapacity.

11.6a A Living Will Specifies End-of-Life Medical Treatments

A **living will** allows you to document in advance your specific wishes concerning medical treatments in an emergency or during end-of-life health care. The document sets forth one's wishes about life-prolonging treatments in case of terminal illness or persistent unconsciousness where the individual is no longer capable of participating in his or her health care decisions. This document only goes into effect if you meet specific medical criteria and are unable to make decisions.

A **Physicians Order for Life Sustaining Treatment (POLST) form** is a similar legal document used for people with advanced illnesses or those in emergency situations. A POLST form is designed to be actionable throughout an entire community, as it is immediately recognizable (as it is brightly colored and on a single page) and can be used by doctors and first responders.

living will
Allows you to document in advance your specific wishes concerning medical treatments in an emergency or during end-of-life health care.

Physicians Order for Life Sustaining Treatment (POLST) form
A legal document similar to a living will used for people with advanced illnesses or those in emergency situations.

11.6b A Health Care Proxy Designates Someone to Make Health Care Decisions

A **health care proxy** is a legal document in which individuals designate another person to make health care decisions on their behalf if they are rendered incapable of making their wishes known. The authorized person executes such decisions or tries to make sure that health care professionals follow the maker's intentions. The person who is

TURN BAD HABITS INTO GOOD ONES

Do You Do This?	Do This Instead!
Simply assume your health care plan provides the coverage you want	Read the plan documents and try to make any changes you desire
Pay all of your medical expenses with after-tax dollars	Sign up for a flexible saving arrangement (Chapter 1) and a health savings account (HSA) to pay for your health insurance premiums.
Ignore the potential for lost income if you became sick or injured	Explore the purchases of disability income insurance through your employer or on your own.
Ignore your employer's open-enrollment period	Use open enrollment to reassess all of your employee benefits including those related to health care
Have no advance medical directive documents	Go online and fill out all necessary forms

authorized is called an attorney-in-fact or proxy. Filling out a health care proxy form does not deprive the creator of the right to make decisions about medical treatment as long as he or she is able to do so.

11.6c   A Durable Power of Attorney Appoints Someone to Handle Legal and Personal Finances

A **durable power of attorney**—gives the designated person virtually absolute power to manage your financial affairs, so choose a trusted individual who knows your wishes. It allows the named individual to make bank transactions, collect Social Security payments, apply for disability, and pay bills while an individual is medically incapacitated. Understand, too, that you may revoke your power of attorney and/or give it to another person as long as you are mentally capable of doing so.

A **limited (or special) power of attorney** is narrower in scope and could be restricted to one specified act or a certain time period, such as signing the maker's name at the closing of the sale of a home or managing the maker's investment accounts. See AARP's printable advanced directives at www.aarp.org/relationships/caregiving/info-03-2012/free-printable-advance-directives.html.

CONCEPT CHECK 11.6

1. Offer some reasons why people should create advance directive documents.
2. What is a living will and what does it try to accomplish?
3. What does a health care proxy achieve?
4. What does a durable power of attorney provide, and can it be changed?

WHAT DO YOU RECOMMEND *NOW*?

Now that you have read the chapter on health care planning, what do you recommend to Danielle DiMartino in the case at the beginning of the chapter regarding:

1. Choosing among the four alternatives available to her?
2. Danielle's concerns about providing for her mother's health care needs?
3. Danielle's need for her own disability income insurance?
4. How Danielle can cover her long-term care risk?

Goodshoot/Jupiterimages

SUMMARY OF LEARNING OBJECTIVES RECAPPED

LO1 **Explain how the Affordable Care Act works and how consumers shop and pay for health insurance coverage.**

The Affordable Care Act was designed to provide affordable health insurance for all American citizens and reduce the growth in health care spending. Americans already covered by a plan prior to 2014 saw little change as a result of the law. The ACA provides a list of benefits, rights and protections for all health insurance buyers. The uninsured have to buy a health care plan or pay an individual shared responsibility fee, a tax penalty. The law provides for health insurance exchanges to allow consumers to find and select a quality health care plan. It also provides subsidies for families whose incomes are up to 400 percent of the poverty level to assist them in buying a health care plan.

LO2 **Distinguish among the types of health care plans.**

Both private employers and governments have been making consumers pay more attention to the rising costs of health care. Managed care has helped keep health care costs in check. The traditional health care policy is the gold standard for insurance as almost all of the policyholder's costs are paid by the policy. There are a number of managed care policies. Major government programs also exist, such as workers' compensation, Medicare, and Medicaid.

LO3 **Describe the typical benefits and limits of health care plans.**

Key in understanding the benefits of health care plans is what types of care are covered and who is covered. Besides asking about the premium addition questions to ask are how much is the deductible, the coinsurance proportion, and the copay.

LO4 **Explain the fundamentals of planning for long-term custodial care.**

Long-term care insurance provides extended care that consists of help with the activities of daily living. Costs have been rising for the three levels of care: skilling nursing care, intermediate care, and custodial care. The person's age when purchasing is important as policies are less expensive when bought at a younger age. The benefit amount impacts premiums, too.

LO5 **Develop a plan to protect your income when you cannot work due to disability.**

Disability income insurance replaces a portion of the income lost when you cannot work as a result of illness, disease, or injury. The amount you need is equal to your monthly after-tax income less any benefits to which you are entitled (for example, Social Security). By selecting among various policy provisions, you can tailor a policy that fills any gaps in your existing disability protection. In deciding on a policy, consider the waiting period, benefit period, and any cost-of-living adjustments.

LO6 **Summarize the benefits of preparing advance medical directive documents.**

Making advance medical directives can save your loved ones the burden of making some difficult and challenging end-of-life decisions in case you become incapacitated. These documents include a living will, health care proxy, and durable power of attorney.

LET'S TALK ABOUT IT

1. **The Affordable Care Act and You.** Are you affected directly by the Affordable Care Act? If so, in what ways.

2. **ACA Protections and Benefits.** Given the list of requirements for the Affordable Care Act, what are your thoughts about yesterday's health policies compared to today's?

3. **Your Health Care Plan.** Are you covered by a health care plan? If so, what do you see as the largest potential for losses if you become ill or injured? How well do you understand the plan?

4. **HMOs Versus Health Insurance.** HMO plans and traditional health insurance plans take different approaches to health care. What are the major differences between the two types of plans? Which plan would you prefer for your own health care protection, and why?

5. **Long-Term Care Insurance.** Are you covered by a long-term care insurance plan? What would happen if you became so incapacitated that such care was necessary? What could you do?

6. **Disability Income Insurance.** Are you covered by disability income insurance? What would happen if you were unable to work for two or three years because of illness or injury?

7. **Disability Social Security.** Are you covered by Social Security disability insurance? What would happen if you were unable to work for a year because of illness or disability?

8. **Advance Directive Documents.** Give some thought to establishing a living will, health care proxy, and a durable power of attorney. What are some provisions that you might put into the documents, and who might you name?

DO THE MATH

1. **Health Care Coverage Amounts.** Michael Howitt of Berkley, Michigan, recently had his gallbladder removed. His total bill for this surgery, which was his only health care expense for the year, came to $13,890. His health insurance plan has a $500 annual deductible and an 80/20 coinsurance provision. The cap on Michael's coinsurance share is $2,000.

   (a) How much of the bill will Michael pay?

   (b) How much of the bill will be paid by Michael's insurance?

   DO IT IN CLASS
   Page 347

2. **Health Care Event Protection.** Christina Haley of Elko, Nevada, age 57, recently suffered a stroke. She was in intensive care for 3 days and was hospitalized for 10 more days. Her total bill for this care was $125,500. After being discharged from the hospital, she spent 25 days in a nursing home at a cost of $270 per day. Christina, who earns $4,500 per month, missed two months of work. Christina had a health insurance plan through her employer. The policy had a $1,000 deductible and an 80/20 coinsurance clause with a $2,000 coinsurance cap. She had also accumulated 21 sick days (equivalent to one month) at work.

   Otherwise she had no long-term care or disability income insurance.

   (a) How much of Christina's direct medical expenses was paid by her insurance policy?

   (b) What did Christina have to pay for her nursing home care?

   DO IT IN CLASS
   Page 347

   (c) How much income did Christina lose?

3. **Social Security Disability Protection.** Sandra Hilton of Sisseton, South Dakota, age 60, recently was in a vehicle accident, was hospitalized, and then suffered a heart attack. She took a leave of absence from her long-time job as a data analyst for an environmental lobbying firm to recuperate. Using Appendix B answer these questions:

   (a) If her earnings averaged $80,000, what would be her monthly Social Security disability benefit?

   (b) If her earnings instead averaged $65,000, what would be the monthly benefit?

FINANCIAL PLANNING CASES

CASE 1

The Johnsons Consider Buying Disability Insurance

Dual-income households often have overlapping health care benefits. For example, both Harry and Belinda Johnson's employers provide partially subsidized family health insurance plans as employee benefits. The Johnsons chose to be covered under Belinda's policy because it provides more protection and is less expensive. Belinda's coverage is fully paid for, and she can add Harry to the plan for only $150 per month. Harry can then drop his health plan through his employer and sign up instead for other benefits such as disability income insurance, flexible benefits coverage, education reimbursement, and/or contribute more to his 401(k) retirement plan. The bad news is that many employers assess an average surcharge of $100 per month when spouses can get health care from their own jobs.

Although Belinda's employer offers a generous employee benefit program, it does not provide disability income protection other than 8 sick days per year, which may accumulate to 20 days. Harry also has no disability income insurance. Although both have worked long enough to qualify for Social Security disability benefits, Based on information they have received from the Social Security Administration, Belinda has figured that Harry would receive about $1,020, and she would receive about $1,330 per month from Social Security. Harry and Belinda realize that they could not maintain their current living standards on only one salary. Thus, the need for disability income insurance has become evident even though they will be challenging to afford such protection at this time. Advise them on the following points:

DO IT IN CLASS
Page 352

(a) Use the Run the Numbers worksheet on page 352 to determine how much disability insurance Harry and Belinda each need. Since it has been more than 10 years since they started working full-time, their incomes have risen about 4 percent annually. Belinda's after-tax income now is $92,000 and Harry's is $58,000.

(b) Use the information on pages 352 and 353 to advise the Johnsons about their selections related to the following major policy provisions:
1. Elimination period
2. Benefit period
3. Residual clause
4. Cost-of-living adjustments

CASE 2

The Hernandezes Face the Possibility of Long-Term Care

Victor Hernandez recently learned that his uncle has Alzheimer's disease. While discussing this tragedy with Maria, he realized that both of his grandparents probably had Alzheimer's or another dementia disease, although no formal diagnoses were ever made. As a result, Victor and Maria have become interested in how they might protect themselves from the financial effects of long-term health care.

DO IT IN CLASS
Page 349

(a) What factors should the Hernandezes consider as they shop for long-term care protection?

(b) Victor is still in his 40s. How does his age affect their decisions related to long-term care protection?

CASE 3

Julia Price Assesses Her Health Care Plan

Julia is about to change jobs. Her new employer offers several different health care plans including a traditional health care plan, an HMO, a PPO, and a high-deductible plan. Her employer will pay the first $300 per month for any plan she chooses. This means that Julia will have to pay the remainder of the premium for the plan plus any out-of-pocket costs. These expenses are higher than they were at her previous employer's, and she is concerned about the added expenses. After talking with the employee benefits office at the new firm, she is considering saving money by opting for the low-cost high-deductible plan and establishing a health savings account. Offer your opinions about her thinking.

DO IT IN CLASS
Page 343

CASE 4

A New Employee Ponders Disability Insurance

Charles Napier of Barstow, California, recently took a new job as a manufacturer's representative for an aluminum castings company. While looking over his employee benefits materials, he discovered that his employer would provide 10 sick days per year, and he can accumulate these to a maximum of 60 sick days if any go unused in a given year. In addition, Charles's employer provides a $3,000-per-month, short-term, one-year total disability policy. When he talked with the human resources office, Charles found that he might qualify for $1,100 per month in Social Security disability benefits if he became unable to work. Charles earns a base salary of $5,000 per month and expects to earn about $40,000 in commissions, for an average after-tax income of $7,000 per month. After considering this information, Charles became understandably concerned that a disability might destroy his financial future.

DO IT IN CLASS
Page 352

(a) What is the level of Charle's short-term, one-year disability insurance needs?

(b) What is the level of Charle's long-term disability insurance needs?

(c) Help Charles select from among the important disability insurance policy provisions to design a disability insurance program tailored to his needs.

CASE 5

A CPA Selects a Health Care Plan

Your friend Taliesha Jackson of Edwardsville, Illinois, recently changed to a new job as a CPA in a moderate-size accounting firm. Knowing that you were taking a personal finance course, she asked your advice about selecting the best health insurance plan. Her employer offered five options. In addition, she could open a flexible spending arrangement to pay some of the premiums:

- **Option A:** A traditional health insurance plan with a $500 annual deductible and an 80 percent/20 percent coinsurance clause with a $2,000 out-of-pocket limit. Taliesha must pay $80 per month toward this plan.

- **Option B:** Same as option A except that a PPO is associated with the plan. If Taliesha agrees to have services provided by the PPO, her annual deductible drops to $200 and the coinsurance clause is waived. As an incentive to get employees to select option B, Taliesha's employer will provide dental expense insurance worth about $40 per month.

- **Option C:** Another PPO health insurance plan with a $200 annual deductible and a 90

percent/10 percent coinsurance clause with a $1,000 out-of-pocket limit. Taliesha must pay $170 per month toward the cost of this plan.

- **Option D:** Membership in an HMO. Taliesha will have to contribute $40 extra each month if she chooses this option.

(a) To help her make a decision, Taliesha has asked you to list two positive points and two negative points about each plan. Prepare such a list.

(b) Why might Taliesha's employer provide an incentive of dental insurance if she chooses option B?

(c) Which plan would you recommend to Taliesha? Why?

BE YOUR OWN PERSONAL FINANCIAL MANAGER

1. **How Do You Pay for Your Health Care?** Make a list of the health care services that you used last year and estimate the cost of each of those services. Then indicate how these costs were paid, whether by yourself as an out-of-pocket expense or by a health care plan. Write a summary of what you have learned about how your health care expenses are paid.

2. **Analyze Your Health Care Plan!** Obtain a copy of your health insurance policy or the explanation of benefits brochure if you are covered by a group plan. Analyze the plan by focusing on the types of care covered, persons covered, its deductibles, coinsurance, and co-pay amounts, and any restrictions on providers of your health care.

3. **What Level of Social Security Disability Benefits Is Available to You?** Visit the website for the Social Security Administration and use its online calculator at www.ssa.gov/planners/retire/AnypiaApplet.html to determine whether you are currently eligible to receive Social Security disability insurance benefits if you become disabled and the projected level of those benefits.

4. **Calculate Your Need for Disability Income Insurance.** Use the Run the Numbers worksheet and material on page 352 or Worksheet 46: Determining My Disability Income Insurance Needs from "My Personal Financial Planner" to estimate the amount you would need to replace should you become disabled.

My Personal Financial Planner

5. **Explore Your Options for Saving on Taxes via Your Health Care Plan.** Are you currently employed and eligible to participate in an employer-sponsored health care plan? Use the material on pages 343–344 to assess the opportunities you have to make use of a high-deductible health care plan and a health savings account to lower your after-tax cost of health care.

6. **Develop Advance Medical Directive Documents.** Complete Worksheet 47: My Advance Directive Documents in "My Personal Financial Planner" by recording which of the three advance medical directives documents the date you prepared and the names of those who know about their location or have a copy.

My Personal Financial Planner

ON THE NET

Go to the Web pages indicated to complete these exercises.

1. **Understanding Health Care Reform.** Visit the website for U.S. Department of Health and Human Services at www.hhs.gov/healthcare/about-the-law/read-the-law/index.html and the Kaiser Family Foundation at www.kff.org for information on the health care reform law aspects of the Affordable Care Act. What provisions in the law might be most beneficial to you in your current life situation? How might the law affect you once you graduate?

2. **Benefiting from Long-term Care Insurance.** Visit the website for U.S. Department of Health and Human

Services at www.longtermcare.gov and read its information on long-term care insurance. How might such protection fit into your risk-management program or that of your family?

3. **Affordable Care Act.** Read about the law at www.hhs.gov/healthcare/. Click on some tabs and learn what you can. What do you think of this website?

4. **ACA Helps Women.** Read about how the Affordable Care Act is helping women at www.hhs.gov/healthcare/facts-and-features/fact-sheets/aca-working-women/index.html. What are your thoughts?

ACTION INVOLVEMENT PROJECTS

1. **Costs and How to Pay for Long-Term Care.** Visit the government's website (longtermcare.gov/the-basics/who-pays-for-long-term-care) to learn the costs and how to pay for long-term care insurance. Write a brief summary of your findings.

2. **Assessment of Your State's Health Insurance Exchange.** Visit your state's health insurance exchange (kff.org/state-health-marketplace-profiles). How easy was it to navigate through the information provided? Why or why not? Would you feel comfortable using the state or the federal health exchange to obtain coverage?

3. **Views Concerning Having Health Care Protection.** Talk to three fellow students who are not taking your personal finance class. Ask them to explain their feelings about their health care plan. Then ask them how they plan to meet their health care needs once they graduate. Make a table that summarizes your findings.

4. **What Is It Like to Choose Among an Employer's Health Care Options?** Survey three individuals or couples who are covered by a group health care plan at work. Ask them how they went about making the choice among the plans the employer offered. Include a discussion of how they approach the same decisions when the open-enrollment period occurs with the plan each year. Write a summary of their responses and how their experiences impacted your thinking about an employer-provided plan.

5. **Applying the Large-Loss Principle to Health Care Planning.** The large-loss principle says that one is better off paying a higher initial portion of any loss and expanding the coverage for the largest and most catastrophic losses. In health care planning, this would mean selecting a health care plan with a high deductible for your health care expenses and a longer waiting period and longer benefit period for your disability income and long-term care insurance plans. Talk to three students in your personal finance class on their views of this approach. Also talk to three people outside of your class who are covered by a health care plan for their views. Write a summary of the responses of these two groups and how their views affect your own thinking about the large-loss principle.

6. **Addressing the Need for Disability Income Insurance.** Talk to a family member who has gone through the process of deciding about disability income insurance. Ask what motivated him or her to decide to buy or not buy such insurance. Also ask about which aspects were the most difficult part of the process. Write a summary of the responses and how your family member's efforts, or lack thereof, affect your thinking about disability income insurance.

7. **Planning for Long-Term Care.** Talk to a family member who has had to decide how to meet the long-term care needs of a loved one. Ask what aspects were the most difficult part of the process. Also ask your family member how going through the process affected his or her thinking about planning for their own long-term care needs. Write a summary of your family member's responses and how his or her efforts, or lack thereof, affect your thinking about long-term care.

12

Life Insurance Planning

Antonio Guillem/Shutterstock

YOU MUST BE KIDDING, RIGHT?

Michelle and Jason Bailey are in their early 30s and expecting their first child next month. Each earns about $60,000 per year. Currently, they have $50,000 life insurance policies on each of their lives with the other named as the beneficiary. They bought these policies a few years ago to pay for death-related expenses if tragedy struck. With the baby coming, they are thinking about buying $300,000 in life insurance coverage on each of their lives so the proceeds could be used to replace the income lost if one of them died. How much will Michelle and Jason each pay for this additional protection?

A. About $25 per month

B. About $50 per month

C. About $100 per month

D. About $200 per month

The answer is A. Term life insurance for people in their 30s can cost about $1 (or less) per $1,000 of coverage per year. Thus, Michelle and Jason could each easily buy this insurance for $300 each or about $25 per month—a small price to pay for the security provided. Always buy inexpensive term life insurance so that you replace the lost income needed by your dependents if you were to pass away!

Learning Objectives

After reading this chapter, you should be able to:

1 Understand why you might need life insurance and calculate the appropriate amount of coverage.

2 Distinguish among types of life insurance.

3 Explain the major provisions of life insurance policies.

4 Apply a step-by-step strategy for implementing a life insurance plan.

WHAT DO YOU RECOMMEND?

Stephanie Bridgeman, age 28, and her husband Will, age 30, recently had their first child. Both have small cash-value life insurance policies ($25,000 and $50,000, respectively) that their parents purchased when they were children. Stephanie is a real estate attorney and earns $90,000 per year. She has continued working after having the baby. Stephanie's employer offers a 401(k) plan into which she can contribute up to 6 percent of her salary each year and qualify for a matching contribution by her employer of one-half of 1 percent for each 1 percent that Stephanie contributes and she can contribute up to another 6 percent that will not be matched. Her employer does not offer employer-paid life insurance. Will is a high-school teacher and track coach and makes $49,000 per year. His employer pays the full cost of his retirement pension plan. An optional supplemental retirement plan is available into which Will can contribute 5 percent of his salary with no employer match, but he has not done so as yet. Will has an employer-provided life insurance policy equal to twice his annual salary. Will and Stephanie have no other life insurance.

Junial/Dreamstime LLC

What do you recommend to Stephanie and Will on the subject of life insurance planning regarding:

1. **Their changing need for life insurance now that they have a child?**
2. **What types of life insurance they should consider?**
3. **Coordinating their retirement savings and other investments with their life insurance program?**
4. **Shopping for life insurance?**

TO-DO SOON

You can start achieving financial success by doing the following:

1. *Use the needs approach to determine your present requirement for life insurance.*

2. *Comparison-shop for term life insurance on the Internet to obtain the lowest possible rates.*

3. *Protect against future premium increases due to health changes by selecting guaranteed renewable term policies and cash-value policies that have a guaranteed insurability option.*

4. *Employ the principle of "buy term life insurance and invest the rest" by purchasing guaranteed renewable term life insurance.*

5. *Partially fund your tax-sheltered retirement plan with the money saved by purchasing term rather than cash-value life insurance.*

life insurance

An insurance contract helps replace lost income if premature death occurs as it promises to pay a dollar benefit to a beneficiary upon the death of the insured person.

Learning Objective 1

Understand why you might need life insurance and calculate the appropriate amount of coverage.

Two financial problems arise because you do not know when you will die. The first problem is the risk of living too long. This raises the possibility that you will outlive your savings during retirement. Life insurance is the wrong way to address the living-too-long problem. For that problem you should invest through tax-sheltered retirement savings plans (discussed in Chapter 17) and over time create a substantial amount of wealth.

The second problem is the risk of dying too soon. This is the possibility that you might die before adequately providing for the financial well-being of loved ones left behind, such as a spouse and children. **Life insurance** helps replace lost income if premature death occurs. As you will see, term life insurance does this best but only 8 in 10 people have purchased a life insurance policy.

People often underestimate how much life insurance coverage they need. Then they buy the wrong type of policy and pay too much for it. Yes, life insurance is confusing. But once you understand the vocabulary and the basic logic of life insurance it becomes a lot less complicated. Then you can make the right purchase at the right price.

The need for life insurance is greatest during the child-rearing years because the income of one or more adults is needed to support a child financially. As children get into their teenage years, they need fewer additional years of financial support. Thus the necessity of life insurance on the income earner begins to decline. And eventually, the children leave home for employment, school, or whatever. Over time, the need for life insurance for the family is eliminated because sufficient funds should be available for survivors through savings and investments that will build up over time.

Life insurance is important. If anyone is dependent upon your income—like a spouse, child, parent, sibling, cousin, or friend—it is wise for the working person to protect them. Otherwise those who cannot take care of themselves financially would be at risk if you were not around. Your children as well as nieces and nephews may need funds to pay for college or to make a down payment on a home.

Ask yourself, "If I die tomorrow will these people have the financial support to take care of themselves?" Even though it may be uncomfortable to deal with the idea of dying, you are smart to protect against the unexpected and take action to deal with it. You are a "financial grown-up" when you make financial decisions to protect someone you love.

12.1 HOW MUCH LIFE INSURANCE DO YOU NEED?

The primary reason for buying life insurance is to allow your family members to continue with their lives free from the financial burdens that your death would bring. Your purchase of life insurance is to benefit your loved ones, not yourself. So if you are young, unmarried, and childless, you need zero life insurance.

Many people do need life insurance, and fortunately costs are quite affordable. For example, a 30-year-old man can buy a $500,000 term policy for $250 a year, or $1 million for $430. Women pay less, perhaps $215 annually for $500,000 and only $360 for a $1 million policy.

12.1a What Financial Needs Must Be Met upon Your Death?

Financial losses that arise from dying too soon are described below.

final expenses

One-time expenses occurring just prior to or after a death.

- **Final-Expense Needs** Final expenses are one-time expenses occurring just prior to or after a death. The largest of these expenses is for the funeral and burial or cremation of the deceased, which could cost as little as $3,000 or as much as

$30,000. In addition, there may be travel, lodging, food, and costs of settling the estate. There are no income or estate taxes due because by law life insurance proceeds are excluded.

- **Income-Replacement Needs** Once someone else becomes financially dependent on you, your income and employee benefits will be the major financial loss resulting from your premature death.

- **Readjustment-Period Needs** Families often need a period of readjustment after the death of a loved one. This period may last for several months to two or three years and may require the surviving spouse to forgo employment for a time and/or obtain further education.

- **Debt-Repayment Needs** A family that has bought sufficient life insurance for the replacement of lost income probably will not need to make specific insurance provisions for the repayment of most debts. It is sometimes helpful, however, to buy an additional amount of life insurance to pay off all nonmortgage debt in order to simplify the finances of the survivors.

- **College-Expense Needs** Death of a parent can impede planning for children's college expenses. A suggested amount of additional life insurance would be the cost of tuition and room and board and expenses for four years at a desired institution.

- **Other Special Needs** Many families have special needs that must be considered in the life insurance-planning process. For example, a family might have a child with special needs who will require medical or custodial care as an adult.

12.1b Three Ways You Can Meet These Financial Needs

There are three ways you can meet your need for protection from losses.

1. Existing Assets Can Help Meet the Need The funds held in savings accounts, certificates of deposit, stocks, bonds, and mutual funds often are specifically earmarked for some special goal, such as retirement, travel, or college for children. These could be used by survivors, even though it might be wiser to retain these funds for their originally intended purposes. Retirement accounts, such as 401(k) plans and IRAs (discussed in Chapter 17), will go to the survivor named as the beneficiary on the account. Younger families should not use these funds earlier in life because such action will jeopardize the surviving spouse's retirement.

2. Government Benefits May Help Meet Some of the Needs Widows, widowers, and their dependents may qualify for various government benefits. **Social Security survivor's benefits** are paid to a surviving spouse with minor children or to the children directly if there is no surviving spouse. Once the youngest child reaches age 18, a surviving spouse enters the Social Security **survivor's blackout period** and is no longer eligible for Social Security survivor benefits. The blackout period ends when the surviving spouse reaches age 60. The surviving spouse may then collect survivor's benefits until age 62, and then may begin collecting Social Security retirement benefits based on his or her own or the deceased spouse's retirement account, whichever provides the higher benefit. The payment could be as high as $2,500 a month although they average less than $1,000.

Social Security survivor's benefits
Government program benefits paid to a surviving spouse and children.

survivor's blackout period
The time frame between when a deceased person with minor children stops receiving Social Security survivor benefits and when he or she begins receiving retirement benefits.

3. Life Insurance Can Close Any Remaining Gap in Needs Life insurance is the simplest form of insurance because it protects against only one peril—death. The benefit the policy will pay in cash is known in advance. This payment to the **beneficiary** (the person named in the policy to receive the funds) will occur within a few days once a death certificate is presented to the insurance company. Some people have existing life insurance that was purchased previously or provided through their employer. These coverages can reduce or eliminate the need for additional life insurance purchases.

beneficiary
Person who receives life insurance proceeds, as per the policy.

12.1c What Dollar Amount of Life Insurance Do You Need?

Half of widows and widowers report that their spouse was inadequately insured. Therefore, correctly determining the magnitude of the losses resulting from a premature

needs-based approach
A superior method of calculating the amount of insurance needed that considers all of the factors that might potentially affect the level of need.

death is extremely important. Do the calculations once and then do them again when a significant life event occurs, such as marriage, birth of a child, and divorce. Two methods are commonly used to determine how much life insurance one needs: a multiple-of-earnings approach and a needs-based approach. The needs-based method is more accurate.

The Multiple-of-Earnings Approach Uses Flawed Logic The **multiple-of-earnings approach** estimates the amount of life insurance needed by multiplying your income by some number, such as 5, 7, or 10. Thus, someone with an annual income of $40,000 would need $200,000 to $400,000 in life insurance. Life insurance agents often suggest this simplistic approach. However, it addresses only one of the factors affecting life insurance needs—income-replacement needs—and does not take into consideration such factors as age, family situation, and other assets that could cover the lost income.

Whatever you do, be certain to insure the breadwinner if others depend upon his/her income. Eight out of 10 American adults have life insurance but they only have $162,000 on average, or three times average annual income.

The Needs-Based Approach Is the Superior Method The **needs-based approach** for estimating life insurance needs considers all of the factors that might potentially affect the level of need. The Run the Numbers worksheet on page 366, "The Needs-Based Approach to Life Insurance," illustrates calculations made via the needs-based approach.

Calculating Life Insurance Needs for a Couple with Small Children Consider the example of Gene Thomas, a 35-year-old chef from Elko, Nevada, who has a spouse, Candice (age 30), and three children (ages 8, 7, and 3 years). Gene earns $56,000 annually and desires to replace his income for 30 years, at which time his spouse would be approaching retirement. The "Example" column of the Run the Numbers worksheet, "The Needs-Based Approach to Life Insurance," expands on the situation faced by Gene.

1. **Final-expense needs.** Gene estimates his final expenses for funeral, burial, and other expenses at $12,000.
2. **Spouse income-replacement needs.** Gene's income of $56,000 is multiplied by 0.75 and the interest factor of 19.6004 (from Appendix A-4). This factor was used because Gene decided that it would be best to replace his lost income for 30 years or until Candice, his wife, reached age 60 and passed through the Social Security blackout period. Gene and Candice are moderate-risk investors and believe that she could conservatively earn a 3 percent after-tax, after-inflation rate of return on life insurance proceeds. Income-replacement needs based on these conditions amount to $823,217.
3. **Readjustment-period needs.** Candice is a reporter for a local newspaper, working half-time and earning an annual income of $38,000. Allocating $19,000 for readjustment-period needs would allow her to take a six-month leave of absence from her job or meet other readjustment needs.
4. **Debt-elimination needs.** Gene and Candice owe $10,000 on various credit cards and an auto loan. They also owe about $128,000 on their home mortgage. Candice would like to pay off all debts except the mortgage debt if Gene dies. The mortgage debt would be affordable if Gene's income were adequately replaced. They also know that the proceeds of one's life insurance are not subject to the claims of creditors.
5. **Dependents' college-expense needs.** Gene estimates that it would currently cost $25,000 for each of his sons to attend the local community college. If he dies, $25,000 of the life insurance proceeds could be invested for each child. The funds should grow at a rate sufficient to keep up with increasing costs of a college education.
6. **Other special needs.** Gene and Candice do not have any unusual needs related to life insurance planning, so they entered zero for this factor.

7. **Subtotal.** The Thomases total items 1 through 6 on the worksheet and determine that the family's financial needs arising out of Gene's death would amount to $939,217. Although this sum seems large to them, they have access to two resources that can reduce this figure, as indicated in items 8 and 9.

8. **Government benefits.** Gene determined from his Social Security Benefits Statement that his family would qualify for monthly Social Security survivor's benefits of $2,725, or $32,700 a year.* These benefits would be paid for 15 years, until his youngest son turns 18. The present value of this stream of benefits is $390,369 (from Appendix A-4), assuming a 3 percent return for 15 years.

DO IT IN CLASS

9. **Current insurance and assets.** Gene has a $50,000 life insurance policy purchased five years ago. His employer also pays for a group policy with a face amount of $50,000. Gene's major assets include his home and his retirement plan. Because he does not want Candice to have to liquidate these assets if he dies, he includes only the $100,000 insurance coverages in item 9.

10. **Life insurance needed.** After subtracting worksheet items 8 and 9 from the subtotal, Gene estimates that he needs an additional $448,848 in life insurance. This amount may be large, but Gene can meet this need through term life insurance for as little as $20 or $30 per month.

Because Candice earns an income that is less than Gene's, her life insurance needs would be lower. To determine the specific amount, the couple must complete a worksheet for her as well. Next, the Thomases will need to decide what type of life insurance is best and from whom to buy the additional life insurance needed. These topics are covered later in this chapter.

Calculating Life Insurance Needs for a Young Professional Baomei Zhao of Lincoln, Nebraska, recently graduated with a degree in tourism management and has accepted a position paying $63,000 per year. Baomei is single and lives with her sister. She owes $24,000 on a car loan and $35,000 in education loans. She has $3,000 in the bank. Among her employee benefits is an employer-paid term insurance policy equal to her annual salary.

Baomei has been approached by a life insurance agent who used the multiple-of-earnings approach to suggest that she needs $315,000 in life insurance, or about five times her income. Does she? If you apply the needs-based approach to Baomei's situation, you will see the following:

- Baomei estimates her final expenses at $12,000, which she entered for item 1.

- Items 2, 3, 5, and 6 in the needs-based approach worksheet on page 366 are zero because Baomei has no dependents.

- Baomei would like to see her $24,000 automobile loan and $25,000 education loans repaid in the event of her death. She feels better knowing that her younger sister could inherit her car free and clear. She entered $59,000 for item 4.

- Baomei's survivors will not qualify for any government benefits, so item 8 will also be zero.

- Baomei has other life insurance and certain assets worth a total of $70,000, so she entered that amount for item 9.

Adequate life insurance can ensure that important goals, such as paying for a child's education, are met should a parent die.

---

* Your personal Social Security benefits can be estimated by requesting a Social Security Statement from the Social Security Administration (www.ssa.gov) or see Appendix B.

RUN THE NUMBERS

The Needs-Based Approach to Life Insurance

This worksheet provides a mechanism for estimating life insurance needs using the needs-based approach. The amounts needed for final expenses, income replacement, readjustment needs, debt repayment, college expenses, and other special needs are calculated and then reduced by funds available from government benefits and any current insurance or assets that could cover the need. This worksheet is also available on the *Garman/Forgue* companion website.

Factors Affecting Need	Example	Your Figures
1. Final-expense needs		
Includes funeral, burial, travel, and other items of expense just prior to and after death	$12,000	$_____
2. Income-replacement needs		
Multiply 75 percent of annual income* by the interest factor from Appendix A-4 that corresponds to the number of years that the income is to be replaced and the assumed after-tax, after-inflation rate of return. ($42,000 × 19.6004 for 30 years at a 3% rate of return)	+823,217	+_____
3. Readjustment-period needs		
To cover employment interruptions and possible education expenses for surviving spouse and dependents	+19,000	+_____
4. Debt-repayment needs		
Provides repayment of short-term and installment debt, including credit cards and personal loans	+10,000	+_____
5. College-expense needs		
To provide a fund to help meet college expenses of dependents	+75,000	+_____
6. Other special needs	+0	+_____
7. Subtotal (combined effects of items 1–6)	+$939,217	+_____
8. Government benefits		
Present value of Social Security survivor's benefits and other benefits. Multiply monthly benefit estimate by 12 and use Appendix A-4 for the number of years that benefits will be received and the same interest rate that was used in item 2. ($2,725 × 12 × 11.9379 for 15 years of benefits and a 3% rate of return)	−390,369	−_____
9. Current insurance assets	−100,000	−_____
10. Life insurance needed	$448,848	$_____

*Seventy-five percent is used because about 25 percent of income is used for personal needs.

The resulting calculations show that Baomei needs no additional life insurance ($12,000 + $49,000 − $70,000 = −$9,000). The agent also suggested that Baomei buy now while she is young and rates are low. This is not a smart idea because you should never buy life insurance simply to lock in low rates. That would be like buying car insurance before you own a vehicle. Besides, life insurance prices have been steadily declining for more than a decade. Unless you have a personal or family-based medical history that might interfere with the purchase of life insurance when needed later, you, like Baomei, should wait until you actually need life insurance before buying a policy.

ADVICE FROM A SEASONED PRO

If I Die Tomorrow, Who Is at Risk?

Life insurance is important. If anyone is dependent upon your income—like a spouse, child, parent, sibling, cousin, niece or nephew, or friend —you would be wise to protect them. If you were not around, those who cannot otherwise properly take care of themselves financially would be at risk. For example, your children may need funds to pay for college or to make a down payment on a home. The financial loss of your death can be easily handled by purchasing an inexpensive term life insurance policy.

If you were to die prematurely, the face value of the policy would be paid to your **beneficiaries**. These are people named in a life insurance policy to receive benefits.

If you buy life insurance, you can dictate how the money will be distributed to those you love, such as a spouse as well as a parent, by naming them as beneficiaries.

If you are a stay-at-home parent with children, protect your partner by buying life insurance on yourself so he/she can hire caregivers to do household tasks and transport children as needed. Likewise, remind your partner that upon his/her death that you do not want to be left high, dry, and broke with kids to support, as child care can easily cost $2,000 a month. And don't forget to update your life insurance beneficiaries when you marry, have a child, or experience any other big changes in your relationships. Life insurance can be of tremendous help in caring for those you love.

Deborah C. Haynes
Montana State University, Bozeman, Montana

Your risk of dying is related to your family history and your health. Thus life insurers ask questions on the application before insuring you. They also may require you to have a free medical exam, including urine and blood tests. Insurers also check to see what information about you is in the clearinghouse file a of the Medical Information Bureau (MIB) at www.mib.com/index.html. This is an association of over 500 U.S. and Canadian insurance companies.

Insurers design rate classification schedules to help them determine an individual's chance of loss. For example, smokers die earlier than others so life insurance premiums for them must be higher than for non-smokers. This is called the process of **underwriting**. They decide whether to insure you and how much to charge.

DO IT IN CLASS

Underwriting
This is the process of insurance companies creating rate classification schedules to help decide whom they will insure and how much to charge.

CONCEPT CHECK 12.1

1. Distinguish between the dying-too-soon problem and the living-too-long problem and the best ways to address each.
2. List five types of needs that can be addressed through life insurance.
3. Explain why the multiple-of-earnings approach is less accurate than a needs-based approach to life insurance planning.
4. Identify periods in a typical person's life when the need for life insurance is low and one when it is high.
5. What two factors in the process of calculating life insurance needs are likely to be the most expensive to replace?

Distinguish among types of life insurance.

term life insurance

"Pure protection" against early death; pays benefits only if the insured dies within the time period (term) that the policy covers.

cash-value life insurance

Pays benefits at death and includes a savings/investment element that can provide a level of benefits to the policyholder prior to the death of the insured person.

face amount

Dollar value of protection as listed in the policy and used to calculate the premium.

guaranteed renewable term insurance

Protects you against the possibility of becoming uninsurable.

12.2 THERE ARE ONLY TWO TYPES OF LIFE INSURANCE

Most people are confused by the wide variety of life insurance plans available. But, in reality, there are only two types of life insurance: term life insurance and cash-value life insurance. **Term life insurance** is often described as "pure protection" because it pays benefits only if the insured person dies within the time period (the "term") covered by the policy. The policy must be renewed if coverage is desired for another time period. In this way, term life insurance acts much like car or homeowner's insurance.

All the other life insurance policies are variations of **cash-value life insurance**. These policies pay benefits at death (like term policies) but also include a savings/investment element that can provide benefits to the policyholder prior to the death of the insured person. This **cash value** factor represents the value of the investment aspect of the life insurance policy. The cash value build up in a policy can either be at a fixed rate or variable rate. Because of the investment aspect of cash-value policies, many people automatically believe cash value life insurance is the better option, but this is a false impression. Cash-value life insurance costs much more than term insurance, often 5 to 8 times more, and there are much better options for investing than through life insurance, as you will learn in upcoming chapters.

12.2a Term Life Insurance Is Pure Protection

Term life insurance contracts are most often written for time periods (or terms) of 1, 5, 10, or even 20 years. If the insured survives the specified time period, the beneficiary receives no monetary benefits. Term insurance can be purchased in contracts with face amounts in multiples of $1,000, usually with a minimum face amount of $50,000. The **face amount** is the dollar value of life insurance protection as listed in the policy and used to calculate the premium.

To renew the policy you must apply for a new contract and sometmes you may be required to undergo a medical examination. The premium will increase slightly with each renewal, reflecting, of course, your increasing age. For example, a $100,000 five-year renewable term policy for a man age 25 might have an annual premium of $100; at age 35, the policy might cost $135; and at age 45, it might cost $220. Term policies are much less expensive than a new cash-value policy at any given age because they do not include a savings/investment element. There are several variations of terms insurance.

Guaranteed Renewable Term Insurance Proving insurability at renewal of a term policy may be difficult if you develop a serious health problem. To avoid this dilemma, term life insurance policies are usually written as **guaranteed renewable term insurance**. The guarantee protects you against the possibility of becoming uninsurable due to health status reasons. The number of renewals you can make without proving insurability may be limited to two or three, and a maximum age may be specified for these renewals (usually 65 or 70 years). Guaranteed renewable term insurance is highly recommended. The additional cost for this guarantee is negligible but the coverage is critically important.

Level-Premium Term Insurance As you grow older, you can avoid term insurance premium increases in part by buying **level-premium term insurance**. This is a term policy with a long time period. Under such a policy, the premiums remain constant throughout the entire life of the policy, perhaps 5, 10, or 20 years. Premiums charged in early years are higher than necessary to balance out the lower-than-necessary premiums in later years covered by the policy. Premiums on policies written for ten or more years usually remain constant for a five-year interval, and then might increase to a new constant rate for another five- or ten-year interval.

Decreasing Term Insurance With **decreasing term insurance,** the face amount of coverage declines every year while the premiums remain constant. The buyer chooses an initial face amount and a contract period, after which the face amount of the policy gradually declines (usually annually) to some minimum in the last year of the contract. For example, a woman age

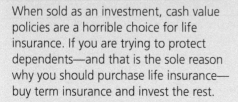

COMMON SENSE
Life Insurance Is
NOT an Investment

When sold as an investment, cash value policies are a horrible choice for life insurance. If you are trying to protect dependents—and that is the sole reason why you should purchase life insurance—buy term insurance and invest the rest.

35 might buy a 30-year $200,000 decreasing term policy that declines by $5,000 each year to a minimum of $50,000.

Convertible Term Insurance Convertible term insurance offers the policyholder the option of exchanging a term policy for a cash-value policy without evidence of insurability. Usually, this conversion is available only during the first five years of the policy. People like this option because they may develop a medical condition and be unable to purchase a new policy, but with a convertible policy you can, although the need is quite rare.

There are two ways to convert a term policy to a cash-value policy. First, you can simply request the conversion and begin paying the higher premiums required for the cash-value policy. Second, you can pay the company the cash value that would have built up had the policy originally been written on a cash-value basis.

The premiums will be based on your health when you originally bought the policy and the age when you convert.

Group Term Life Insurance Group term life insurance is issued to people as members of a group, typically through an employer, rather than as individuals. Group life insurance premiums are average rates based on the characteristics of the group as a whole and, therefore typically, cost *more* than individually purchased plans for healthy individuals. If you are insured under a group plan, however, you do not need to prove your insurability. This is a major benefit for people whose health status makes individual life insurance unaffordable or unattainable. Important to group term life insurance is to determine if the coverage is both renewable and **portable**, meaning you can take the policy with you if you leave the employer.

Credit and Mortgage Term Life Insurance **Credit term life insurance** will pay the remaining balance of a specific loan if the insured dies before repaying the debt. **Mortgage life insurance** specifically pays off a mortgage debt. In essence, both of these types of term insurance are decreasing term insurance with the creditor named as beneficiary. These products are grossly overpriced, and the only people who should consider their purchase are those who are truly uninsurable because of a serious health condition.

12.2b Some Cash-Value Life Insurance Has a Fixed Return

Cash-value life insurance pays benefits upon the death of the insured and also incorporates a savings/investment element. This cash value belongs to the owner of the policy rather than to the beneficiary. While the insured is alive, the owner may obtain the cash value by borrowing some of it from the insurance company or by surrendering and canceling the policy.

convertible term insurance
Offers policyholders the option of exchanging a term policy for a cash-value policy without evidence of insurability.

group term life insurace
A term life insurance policy issued to people as members of a group, typically through an employer rather than as individuals.

ADVICE FROM A SEASONED PRO

Don't Be Fooled by Return-of-Premium Claims

A feature of some term life insurance promoted as a great idea is "return-of-premium (ROP)". Here the salesperson promises the policy will return all the premiums paid if the insured person maintains the policy and lives past a certain number of years— usually 30. These term policies cost much more in order to provide for the return of premiums. Insurance companies promote these policies as a way to avoid "wasting" your money.

In reality, what they are trying to do is to entice you to pay more with the difference becoming analogous to an investment with the profit being the returned premium. Of course, very few policyholders keep their policies for 30 years. And if you die during the policy term you receive nothing on your so-called "investment." Finally, the extra costs may prevent you from buying enough life insurance. This is definitely not a good idea.

Hyungsoo Kim
University of Kentucky, Lexington, Kentucky

Figure 12-1   Comparison of Premium Dollars for Cash-Value and Term Life Insurance

Cash-Value Policy

Premium to pay for insurance protection, and company expenses	Sales commission	Premium to provide for the building of cash value

Term Policy

Premium to pay for insurance protection, and company expenses	Sales commission	Dollars not spent on life insurance and available to invest

NEVER EVER

Pay Premiums Quarterly

If a life insurance premium is $300, be sure to pay it once a year to save money. For example, should you pay quarterly the insurance company will charge you more. A $300 life insurance policy payment divided by 4 quarterly payments is $75 but the insurance company would likely make you pay $81 per quarter (for $324 a year). That extra charge of $24 annually amounts to $240 over 10 years ($24 × 10).

whole life insurance
Form of cash-value life insurance that provides lifetime life insurance protection and expects the insured to pay premiums for life. Also called straight life insurance.

limited-pay whole life insurance
Whole life insurance that allows premium payments to cease before the insured reaches the age of 100.

paid up
Point at which the owner of a whole life policy can stop paying premiums.

Cash-value insurance is referred to as **permanent insurance** because coverage is maintained for the entire life of the insured as long as premiums are paid. The annual premiums for cash-value policies usually remain constant.

The premiums for newly written cash-value policies are always much higher than those for term policies providing the same amount of coverage. This difference arises because only a portion of the premium is used to provide the death benefit; the remainder is used to keep the premium level and to build the cash value. Research shows that half the people who buy cash-value policies drop them within 10 years. They simply stop paying premiums.

Figure 12-1 illustrates the premium differences between cash-value and term life insurance policies. The cash-value policy assesses extremely high sales commissions for the same amount of face value while the term buyer has many dollars not spent on life insurance and available to invest.

Cash-value life insurance actually represents a combination of decreasing term insurance and an investment account that adds up to the face amount of the policy. Figure 12-2 illustrates this concept. Initially, for example, you might have $100,000 of insurance and no savings. About a decade later, you might have built up $2,000 in savings within the policy. In the event of your death, your beneficiary would collect $100,000, of which $2,000 would be your own money. If you lived long enough, the cash value could equal the $100,000 figure. In effect, your beneficiary would then collect your "savings account" rather than an insurance payment. The various types of cash-value policies are discussed below.

Whole Life Insurance   Whole, or **straight life insurance**, is the most popular form of cash-value life insurance, and it provides lifetime life insurance as long as the premiums are paid every year the person is alive. The policy remains in effect and does not need to be renewed.

Limited-Pay Whole Life Insurance   **Limited-pay whole life insurance** is whole life insurance that allows premium payments to cease before you reach the age of 100. Two common examples are **20-pay life policies,** which allow premium payments to cease after 20 years, and **paid-at-65 policies,** which require payment of premiums until the insured turns 65. Although premiums need be paid only for the specified time period in limited-pay policies, the insurance protection lasts for your entire life.

Of course, the annual premiums for limited-pay insurance policies are higher than those for whole life insurance policies because the insurance company has fewer years to collect premiums. Limited-pay policies are said to be **paid up** when the owner can

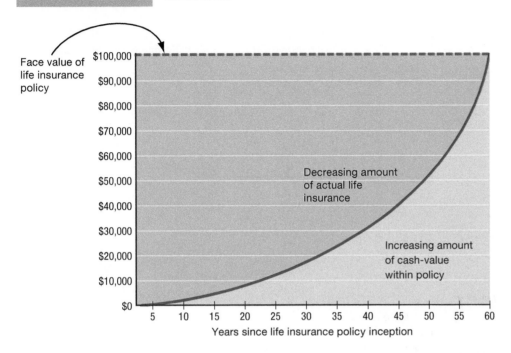

Figure 12-2 **The Fundamental Nature of Cash-Value Life Insurance**

Face value of life insurance policy

Decreasing amount of actual life insurance

Increasing amount of cash-value within policy

Years since life insurance policy inception

stop paying premiums. An extreme version of limited-pay life insurance is **single-premium life insurance,** in which the premium is paid once in the form of a lump sum.

Adjustable Life Insurance **Adjustable life insurance** allows you to modify any one of the three components of life insurance (premium, the face amount of the policy, and the rate of cash-value accumulation) with corresponding changes occurring in the other two. These changes may be made without providing new proof of insurability.

Modified Life Insurance **Modified life insurance** is whole life insurance for which the insurance company charges reduced premiums in the early years and higher premiums thereafter. The premiums are lower in early years because some of the protection during the early years is provided by term insurance. Because modified life insurance uses term insurance in the early years, it accumulates cash value extremely slowly.

12.2c   Some Cash-Value Life Policies Earn a Variable Return

The rate at which the cash value accumulates in a cash-value policy depends on the rate of return paid by the company. All of the cash-value policies described above earn a guaranteed minimum rate of return, often 2 to 4 percent and are known as **fixed-rate policies.** Some cash-value policies, however, may instead pay a higher rate depending on the success of the investments made by the insurance company. Table 12-1 illustrates these rates.

A drawback of policies with a variable return is that they carry high expense loadings and fees. A 2 percent annual fee would change a policy with an annual return of 5 percent on its investments to one with a net 3 percent return. Discussed below are three types of cash-value life insurance policies.

Universal Life Insurance Universal life insurance provides both the pure protection of term insurance and the cash-value buildup of whole life insurance, along with variability in the face amount, rate of cash-value accumulation, premiums, and rate of

BIAS TOWARD— AVOIDING DIFFICULT SUBJECTS

People have a bias to avoid discussing difficult topics. Many people avoid planning for the possibility of death. What to do? Force yourself to do a life insurance needs assessment and purchase the coverage you need to protect who depend upon you financially.

universal life insurance
Provides the pure protection of term insurance and the cash-value buildup of whole life insurance, along with variability in face amount rate of cash-value accumulation, premiums, and rate of return.

Table 12-1	Cash-Value Buildup Illustration—Guaranteed Versus Current Rates*	
Policy Year	**"Guaranteed" Cash-Surrender Value (2.0% rate)**	**"Current Rate" Cash-Surrender Value (3.1% rate)**
1	$0	$0
2	0	96
3	289	354
4	640	730
5	995	1,152
6	1,310	1,475
7	1,730	1,910
8	2,100	2,365
9	2,567	3,420
10	2,910	4,123
15	5,050	6,780
20	7,300	9,355
25	$10,200	$13,630

*Figures are illustrative for a $50,000 universal life policy; the annual premium is $684.

DO IT IN CLASS

return. Initially, the purchaser selects a face amount, and the company quotes an annual premium. The annual premium goes into the cash-value fund, from which the company deducts the cost of providing the insurance protection and charges for company expenses.

As time goes by, the owner of the policy may choose to pay a smaller or larger premium, with corresponding changes occurring in the insurance protection or amount added to cash value. If premiums drop below the amount necessary to cover the insurance protection and expenses, funds are removed from the cash-value account to cover the shortfall. Essentially, universal life insurance combines annual term insurance with a type of investment program.

Variable Life Insurance **Variable life insurance** allows you to choose the investments made with your cash-value accumulations and to share in any gains or losses. The face amount of your policy and the policy's cash value may rise or fall based on changes in the returns earned on the invested funds. The face amount of the policy usually will not drop below the originally agreed-upon amount, however. Instead, the cash value will fluctuate. Variable life insurance policies are complicated and should be read and analyzed very carefully before purchase.

variable-universal life insurance

Form of universal life insurance that gives the policyholder some choice in the investments made with the cash value accumulated by the policy. Also called flexible-premium variable life insurance.

Variable-Universal Life Insurance **Variable-universal life insurance** is a form of universal life insurance that gives the policyholder some choice in the investments made with the cash value accumulated by the policy. Variable-universal life policies usually provide no minimum guaranteed rate of return.

CONCEPT CHECK 12.2

1. Distinguish between term life insurance and cash-value life insurance.
2. Explain why the premiums for term insurance are always so much lower than those of cash-value life insurance.
3. Describe the benefit of buying guaranteed renewable term insurance.
4. Explain why the amount of "insurance" declines over time under a cash-value life insurance policy.
5. Distinguish between cash-value life insurance with a fixed return and with a variable return.

12.3 UNDERSTANDING YOUR LIFE INSURANCE POLICY

A **life insurance policy** is a contract between an insurance policy holder/owner and an insurance company, where the company promises to pay a designated beneficiary a sum of money (the "benefits") upon the death of the insured person. Several parties will be named in the life insurance contract. The **owner**, or **policyholder**, retains all rights and privileges granted by the policy, including the right to amend the policy and the right to designate who receives the proceeds. The **insured** is the person whose life is insured. In addition to the beneficiary who is designated to receive the insurance proceeds, the owner will name a **contingent beneficiary** who will become the beneficiary if the original beneficiary dies before the insured. The same person may be one or more of these parties. Table 12-2 shows illustrative premiums for various types of life insurance policies. These range from annual renewable term to a paid-at-age-65 policy.

12.3a Policy Terms and Provisions Unique to Life Insurance

Life insurance policies define the terminology used in the policy and outline the basic provisions of such insurance. This information serves to clarify the meaning of the policy and the protection afforded the insurer and the policyholder.

The Application The **life insurance application** is the policyholder's offer to purchase a policy. It provides information and becomes part of the life insurance policy. Any errors or omissions in the application may allow the insurance company to deny a request for payment (usually within the first year) of the death benefit and instead any premiums will be refunded.

Lives Covered Most life insurance policies cover the life of a single person—the insured. **First-to-die policies** cover more than one person but pay only when the first insured dies. These policies are less costly than separate policies written on each person, but the survivor then has no coverage after the first person dies. An alternative is the **survivorship joint life policy,** which pays when the last person covered dies.

Incontestability Clause Life insurance policies generally include an **incontestability clause** that places a time limit—usually two years after issuance of the policy—on the right of the insurance company to deny a claim. This clause addresses the problems arising out of erroneous statements that may have been made by the insured on the application.

Suicide Clause Life insurance policies always include a **suicide clause** that allows the life insurance company to deny coverage (although all premiums will be refunded) if the

Learning Objective 3
Explain the major provisions of life insurance policies.

life insurance policy
A contract between an insured (insurance policy holder) and an insurer or assurer, where the insurer promises to pay a designated beneficiary a sum of money (the "benefits") upon the death of the insured person.

owner/policyholder
Retains all rights and privileges granted by the policy, including the right to amend the policy and the right to designate who receives the proceeds.

insured
Individual whose life is insured.

incontestability clause
Places a time limit on the right of the insurance company to deny a claim.

Table 12-2   Annual Premiums for Various Types of Policies—$100,000 Policy*

Policy Type	Policy Year							
	1	2	3	5	10	11	20	Age 65
Annual renewable term (guaranteed renewability to age 70)	$80	$81	$82	$83	$90	$92	$110	$2,400
Decreasing term (over 20 years)	160	160	160	160	160	160	160	0
Convertible term (within 5 years)	170	170	170	170	940	940	940	940
Whole life	870	870	870	870	870	870	870	870
Universal life	590	590	590	590	680	730	760	790
Limited-pay life (paid-at-age 65)	920	920	920	920	920	920	920	0

*Premiums quoted are for a 21-year-old male nonsmoker.

DID YOU KNOW ?

How Insurance Policies Are Organized

All insurance policies have five basic components:

1. **Declarations** provide the basic descriptive information about the insured person or property, the premium to be paid, the time period of the coverage, and the policy limits. Also included may be promises by the insured to take steps to control the losses associated with a specific peril, such as not smoking.

2. **Insuring agreements** are the broadly defined coverages provided under the policy. The insurer makes these promises in return for the premium paid by the insured. For example, in life insurance, the insurer promises to pay the death benefit amount to the beneficiary upon proof of the insured's death.

3. **Exclusions** narrow the focus and eliminate specific coverage broadly stated in the insuring agreements.

The insurer makes no promise to pay for these exceptions and special circumstances. For example, suicide is commonly excluded during the first two years of a life insurance policy. People who do not understand the exclusions in their policies may believe they are covered for a loss when, in fact, they are not.

4. **Conditions** impose obligations on both the insured and the insurer by establishing the ground rules of the agreement. For example, they might include procedures for making a claim after a loss, rules for cancellation of the policy by either party, and procedures for changing the terms of the policy.

5. **Endorsements** (or **riders**) are amendments and additions to the basic insurance policy that can both expand and limit coverage or raise the policy limits to accommodate specific needs.

---

insured commits suicide within the first two years after the policy is issued. If the specified number of years has elapsed, the full death benefit will be paid.

insurance dividends

Surplus earnings of the insurance company when the difference between the total premium charged exceeds the cost to the company of providing insurance.

participating policies

Life insurance policies that pay dividends.

death benefit

Amount that will be paid to the beneficiary when the insured dies.

Cash Dividends Insurance dividends are defined by the Internal Revenue Service as a return of a portion of the premium paid for a life insurance policy. They are not considered taxable income. They represent the surplus earnings of the company when the difference between the total premium charged exceeds the cost to the company of providing insurance. Policies that pay dividends are called **participating policies**, and policies that do not pay dividends are called **nonparticipating policies.** Both term and cash-value policies may pay dividends.

Death Benefit The **death benefit** of a life insurance policy is the amount that will be paid upon the death of the insured person. The amount of the death benefit may be either higher or lower than the face amount. It can be higher due to such items as earned dividends not yet paid or premiums paid in advance. Or it can be lower due to outstanding policy loans or unpaid premiums. Consider a $100,000 participating whole life policy with annual premiums of $1,380. If the insured died halfway through the policy year, with an outstanding cash-value loan of $5,000 and earned but unpaid dividends of $4,000, the death benefit would be $99,690, calculated as follows:

DO IT IN CLASS

$100,000	Face amount
+4,000	Unpaid dividends
+690	Premiums paid in advance (one-half year)
$104,690	Subtotal
−5,000	Outstanding cash-value loan
$99,690	Death benefit

Multiple Indemnity A **multiple indemnity clause** provides for a doubling or tripling of the face amount if death results from certain accidents. It is most often used to double the face amount if death results from an accident. Such a clause is often included automatically as part of the policy at no extra cost.

NUMBERS ON

Life Insurance

Data from a variety of sources suggest the following odds on causes of death in your lifetime:

- Heart disease, 1-in-5
- Cancer, 1-in-7
- Hospital error, such as infection, 1-in-15
- Stroke, 1-in-23
- Base jumping, 1-in-60
- Motorcycle accident, 1-in-50
- Motor vehicle accident, 1-in-100
- Falls, 1-in-120
- Suicide, 1-in-120

- Drug overdose, 1-in-140
- Suicide, 1-in-190
- Firearm, 1-in-300
- Fire, 1-in-1,100
- Drowning, 1-in-9,000
- Airplane crash, 1-in-20,000
- Tornado, 1-in-60,000
- Shark attack, 1-in-61,000
- Lightning, 1-in-84,000
- Sky diving, 1-in-100,000
- Earthquake, 1-in-130,000
- Bicycling, 1-in-140,000
- Terrorist attack, 1-in-230,000

Grace Period Prompt payment of the premium is crucial to the continuation of coverage provided by any insurance policy. A **lapsed policy** is one that has been terminated because of nonpayment of premiums.

To help prevent a lapse, state laws generally require that cash-value and multiyear term policies include a grace period, that is, a period of time (usually 30 days following each premium due date) during which an overdue premium may be paid without a lapse of the policy. During the grace period, all provisions of the policy remain intact if payment is made before the grace period ends.

grace period
Period of time during which an overdue premium may be paid without a lapse of the policy.

Policy Reinstatement If your life insurance policy lapses, it may be possible to reinstate it. To do so, you typically must prove insurability and pay any missed premiums, plus interest, to be reinstated.

12.3b Policy Features Unique to Cash-Value Life Insurance

Cash-value life insurance policies carry special features that all relate to the cash values built up in the policies.

The Policy Illustration Cash-value life insurance policies generally provide a **policy illustration** that charts the projected growth in the cash value. Table 12-1 (on page 372) provides an example of a policy illustration. Policy illustrations can be somewhat helpful, but you should only rely on the guaranteed minimum rate of return. This is the minimum rate that, by contract, the company is legally obligated to pay, and you should understand that the current rate (the rate of return recently paid by the company to policyholders) is merely an estimate of future returns and is quickly outdated. For this reason, it is smart to periodically ask your agent for an **in-force illustration** that shows the cash-value status of the policy and projections for the future given the current rate of return at the time of the illustration (rather than the rate used at the inception of the policy). Reading the middle and right columns in the policy illustration in Table 12-1 reveals that a cash-value policy has very little cash surrender value unless you have held it for ten years or more.

guaranteed minimum rate of return
Minimum rate that, by contract, the insurance company is legally obligated to pay.

current rate
Rate of return the insurance company has recently paid to policyholders.

Asking a few pertinent questions can help cut through some of the misconceptions:

1. Is the "current rate" illustrated actually the rate paid recently? What was the current rate in each of the past five years?
2. What assumptions have been made regarding company expenses, dividend rates, and policy lapse rates?
3. Does all of my cash value earn a return at the current rate? (If not, the current rate is misleading.)
4. Is the illustration based on the "cash surrender value" or the "cash value"? (The cash surrender value is usually the lower value and reflects what will actually be paid if the policy is cashed in.)

nonforfeiture values

Amounts stipulated in a life insurance policy that protect the cash value, if any, in the event that the policyholder chooses not to pay or fails to pay required premiums.

cash surrender value

Represents the cash value of a policy minus any surrender charges.

automatic premium loan

Provision that allows any premium not paid by the end of the grace period to be paid automatically with a policy loan if sufficient cash value or dividends have accumulated.

waiver of premium

A clause in an insurance policy that waives the policyholder's obligation to pay any further premiums should he or she become seriously ill or disabled.

Nonforfeiture Values Nonforfeiture values are important for policyholders. These are amounts stipulated in a life insurance policy that protect the cash value, if any has accumulated, in the event that the policyholder chooses at some point to not pay or fails to pay the premiums.

The policy owner can receive the accumulated cash-value funds in one of three ways. First, the policy owner may continue the policy with the original face amount but for a time period shorter than the original policy. Second, he or she may simply surrender the policy and receive the **cash surrender value**, which represents the cash value minus any surrender charges. Third, the policy may be continued on a paid-up basis, with a new and lower face amount being established based on the amount that can be purchased with the accumulated funds.

Policy Loans The owner of a cash-value policy may borrow all or a portion of the accumulated cash value. Interest rates charged for the loan will range from 2 to 8 percent, depending on the terms of the policy. In addition, the interest rate earned on the remaining cash value typically reverts to the guaranteed minimum rate while the loan remains outstanding. As a result, the cash value ultimately accumulated may be significantly reduced. At a minimum, you must pay the interest on the amount borrowed and any amount owed will be subtracted from the face amount of the policy if you die while the debt remains outstanding.

An **automatic premium loan** provision allows any premium not paid by the end of the grace period to be paid automatically with a policy loan if sufficient cash value or dividends have accumulated. In the first few years of a policy, this provision may not offer much benefit because cash value and dividends accumulate slowly. Eventually these funds may grow enough to pay premiums for a considerable length of time, thereby effectively preventing the lapse of the policy.

MONEY WEBSITES

Informative websites are:

- Accuquote
- CNN Money
- Insweb
- Kiplinger's Personal Finance
- Life Happens
- National Association of Insurance Commissioners
- New York Times
- Master Quote of America
- Quotesmith
- SelectQuote
- Smart Money
- Department of Insurance (name of your state)

Accelerated Death Benefits Some life insurance policies have an **accelerated death benefits clause** (or **living benefit clause**) that allows the payment of a portion of the death benefit prior to death if the insured contracts a terminal illness or requires long-term medical care such as in a nursing home. These early payments are not cash-value loans but do reduce the death benefit ultimately paid.

Viatical companies specialize in buying life insurance policies from terminally ill insureds for a percentage of the death benefit in return for being named owner and beneficiary on the policy. People with AIDS or other serious diseases sometimes allow viatical companies to buy their life insurance policies, and then the viatical company pays the premiums on the policy.

Waiver of Premium A **waiver of premium** is a clause in an insurance policy that waives the policyholder's obligation to pay any further premiums should he or she become seriously ill or disabled. It usually applies when a policyholder becomes totally and permanently disabled, but it may also apply under other conditions, depending on the policy provisions. In effect, the waiver-of-premium option (for an extra cost) protects against the risk of becoming disabled and being unable to pay premiums.

Guaranteed Insurability The **guaranteed insurability** option permits the cash-value policyholder to buy additional stated amounts of cash-value life insurance at stated times in the future without taking a health exam. This option differs from the guaranteed renewability option for term insurance in that it enables the owner to increase the face amount of the policy or to buy an additional policy. The policy might allow the exercise of these options when the insured turns age 30, 35, or 40, or when he or she marries or has children. The added cost of this option is nominal and worthwhile.

12.3c Settlement (or Payout) Options Specify How to Pay the Death Benefit

Settlement options are the five choices that the life insurance policyholder has in determining how the death benefit will be paid:

1. **Lump sum payment.** The death benefit may be received as a lump-sum cash settlement immediately after death. This is often the best approach to take because the beneficiary can invest the proceeds and earn a return higher than the insurance company would pay. The other four methods all require the beneficiary to leave the life insurance proceeds with the insurance company.
2. **Installment payments for a fixed period.** The beneficiary may receive an income from the death benefit for a specific number of years. For example, a widow with small children may choose to receive an income for 18 years. The insurance company would calculate a level of income that would allow for equal proceeds each year, with all funds, including interest, being exhausted at the end of the 18th year.
3. **Income payments of a fixed amount.** The beneficiary may receive a specific amount of income per year from the death benefit. Under this option, payments cease when the death benefit and interest are exhausted. For example, a $100,000 death benefit earning 4 percent interest would provide a $15,000 annual income for approximately eight years.*
4. **Life interest income payments only.** The beneficiary can receive the annual interest earned from the death benefit. For example, the beneficiary would receive $4,000 each year from a $100,000 death benefit earning 4 percent interest. The $100,000 principal would remain intact and would continue to earn interest until the death of the beneficiary, when it becomes part of his or her estate.
5. **Income payments for life.** The beneficiary may elect to receive an income for life. Here the insurance company would use the life expectancy of the beneficiary to calculate the level of income that would allow for equal annual payments so that funds would be exhausted by the expected date of the beneficiary's death. If the beneficiary lives longer than expected, the income payments would continue.

The goal for the lump-sum beneficiary is to invest the life insurance proceeds in a safe, conservative investment, one that totally avoids the occasional downs in market value. It should earn enough income (the interest from a municipal bond, for example) to pay for the beneficiary's expenses. For example, if one invests $1 million life insurance proceeds and earns a 4 percent return (which is discussed in Chapter 14) it will provide the beneficiary $40,000 annually. That amount can be used for expenses, and it assumes the beneficiary does not have to use the principal.

12.3d Delete "Mom" as the Beneficiary on Life Insurance Policies

If you are married, do not let your spouse keep his or her mother's name on their life insurance policy as the beneficiary. People do this a lot when they are single and then forget to change the beneficiary when they marry. Life insurance proceeds are not

NEVER EVER

1. *Let a life insurance agent tell you how much and what type of life insurance to buy.*
2. *Buy expensive cash-value life insurance rather than a cheaper term policy.*
3. *Ignore your changing need for life insurance as you get older.*

guaranteed insurability
Permits the cash-value policyholder to buy additional stated amounts of cash-value life insurance at stated times in the future without evidence of insurability.

settlement options
Choices from which the policyholder can choose in how the death benefit payment will be structured.

* This option and options 4 and 5 are variations of an annuity and are covered further in Chapter 17.

covered by whatever is written in a will. Also make sure your spouse is fully insured. Remind them that upon their death, which is unlikely, you do not want to be left high, dry, and broke with kids to support.

CONCEPT CHECK 12.3

1. Distinguish among the owner, the insured, the beneficiary, and the contingent beneficiary of a life insurance policy.
2. Distinguish between an incontestability clause and a suicide clause in a life insurance contract.
3. What are nonforfeiture values and why are they important?
4. Identify three of the five settlement options for the payment of the proceeds of a life insurance policy to its beneficiary.
5. Distinguish between an automatic premium loan and a waiver-of-premium option in a life insurance policy.
6. Explain how guaranteed renewability for term life insurance and guaranteed insurability for cash-value insurance protect insured people who develop serious health conditions.

Learning Objective 4

Apply a step-by-step strategy for implementing a life insurance plan.

12.4 HOW TO BUY LIFE INSURANCE

Your life insurance needs vary over your life cycle and so should your insurance plan, particularly as it fits into your overall financial planning.

12.4a Integrate Your Life Insurance into Your Financial Plan

Figure 12-3 depicts a life insurance and an investment plan recommended by experts over an individual's life cycle. This plan is built on two foundations: (1) systematic, regular investments, and (2) term insurance.

A base of life insurance can provide for funeral, burial, and other final expenses. A $50,000 to $100,000 guaranteed-renewable term policy is sufficient. The remainder of your life insurance should consist of multiple term insurance policies that you start

As a family ages, life insurance needs typically decrease.

Figure 12-3 **Wisely Using Life Insurance and Investments over the Life Cycle**

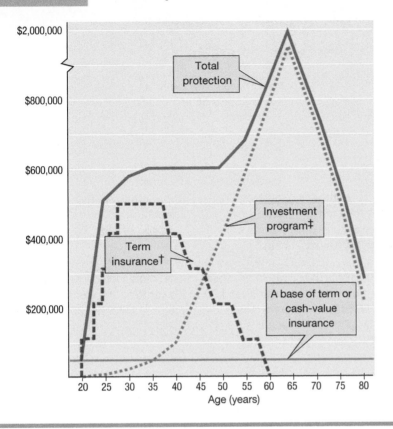

†Layered term insurance policies.
‡Includes vested employer-sponsored retirement (e.g., 401[k]) plans. (See Chapter 17.)

buying when you begin to have dependents. These should be five-or ten-year, level-premium, guaranteed renewable policies in increments of **$100,000**. The policies should be layered so that later on in life you can drop individual policies as your life insurance need declines. By the time you reach retirement, you can drop all your policies as your retirement investment plan hopefully can provide for your survivor's needs.

12.4b Buy Life Insurance from a Financially Strong Company

The most important feature of any life insurance company is its ability to pay its obligations. The company you choose must have the stability and financial strength to survive for the many years your policy will remain in force. Ratings of the financial strengths of insurance companies are available from A.M. Best Company (www.ambest.com), Standard & Poor's (www.standardandpoors.com), Weiss Ratings (www.weissratings.com), Moody's Investor Services (www.moodys.com). Duff and Phelps (www.duffandphelps.com).

12.4c Fair Prices for Term Life Insurance

The price people pay for life insurance depends on their age, health, occupation, and lifestyle. Life insurance companies offer their lowest prices to "preferred" applicants whose health status and lifestyle (for example, nonsmokers) suggest longevity. "Standard" and "impaired" applicants would pay more. Because companies differ in how they assign these labels to applicants, you should comparison-shop for the best treatment. For example, some companies allow an occasional (monthly) cigar smoker to qualify for non-smoker rates.

ADVICE FROM A SEASONED PRO

Buy Term Insurance and Invest the Rest

Americans tend to buy the wrong type of life insurance—cash-value—when term insurance policies cost about 80 percent less. They incorrectly think of life insurance as an investment and not as an expense. And the life insurance industry likes it that way.

Be smart and spend as little money as possible to buy the coverage you need. One way to do this is to use the strategy to "buy term and invest the rest." If you invest the money difference between the cost of premiums for a term life insurance policy and the cost of premiums for a more expensive cash-value policy, you will always come out ahead financially.

To see why, consider the buildup of protection for Seth Cameron, a 30-year-old art gallery administrator from New York City who is considering life insurance policies. Seth could pay an $870 annual premium to buy a $100,000 whole life policy. Alternatively, he could spend $130 for the first-year premium of a $100,000 five-year renewable term policy and invest the $740 difference ($870−$130) in through a tax-sheltered retirement account (assuming a 5 percent after-tax rate of return).

If Seth were to die tomorrow, the policy's beneficiary would receive both the $100,000 in insurance proceeds and the $740 in savings. After five years (age 35), Seth's annual $740 in savings would have grown to $4,293; if he were to die at that time, the total death benefit would be $104,293. If Seth dies years into the future, the estate is even further ahead because of the growing principal in the account. By age 60, Seth's mutual fund investment would have grown to $58,052. If the account earned higher than 5 percent annually, the amount would be much greater. By the time Seth reached age 60, the term insurance premiums would exceed the premiums for the cash-value policy. However, his need for life insurance would presumably be eliminated or greatly reduced at that point. If Seth's children were self-supporting by then, he could probably drop the term insurance policy altogether. Nevertheless, his mutual fund account would remain to provide a financial nest egg of $58,052 or more to his heirs.

With the "buy term and invest the rest" strategy, Seth would have been insured more than 30 years at total premium cost of just $7,350. By contrast, the cash-value policy would have required total premiums of $26,100 ($870 × 30), and the policy's cash value at year 30 would be about $44,000.

For "buy term and invest the rest" to work, however, the difference between the term and cash-value policy premiums *must*, in fact, be invested on a regular basis. Many people say that they will invest this money but then fail to follow through on that promise. You can, like Seth, succeed with a little discipline. The easiest way to ensure that your money is actually invested is to set up an automatic investment program in which a mutual fund company is authorized to withdraw money from your checking account, perhaps monthly, to buy mutual fund shares. When you agree to invest the "difference" automatically, the strategy will work well for you.

Estate Buildup if a Term Life Insurance Buyer Invests the Difference

Age	Premium for Five-Year Renewable Term	Difference (Not Spent on Whole Life)	Total Investment and Earnings* at 5%	Total Estate
30	$130	$740	$740	$100,740
35	150	720	4,293	104,293
40	180	690	9,657	109,657
45	210	660	16,328	116,328
50	240	630	24,668	124,668
60			$58,052	58,052

* This illustration makes the following assumptions: The whole life policy premium for the same $100,000 in coverage is fixed at $870 every year. The buyer pays the five-year renewable term premium at the beginning of each year, and the difference is invested. Those amounts stay in the investments account all year, as does the previous year's ending balance. Investments earn a compounded 5 percent after-tax annual rate of return. Upon the insured's death, the beneficiary would receive the $100,000 face amount of the term life insurance policy plus the amount built up in the investments account earning 5 percent.

Jordan E. Goodman
"America's Money Answers Man" (www.MoneyAnswers.com) and author of *Everyone's Money Book* and *Master Your Money Type*.

Term life insurance premiums are usually quoted in dollars per $1,000 of coverage. Generally, the higher the face amount of the policy, the lower the rate per $1,000. For example, a company might sell term life insurance for $1 per $1,000 per year when purchased in face amounts of $100,000 or more and for $1.25 per $1,000 per year for policies of less than $100,000. Policies with face amounts of $1 million can cost less than $0.50 per $1,000 per year for people younger than age 35.

It is easy to pay too much for term life insurance, especially if you do not comparison-shop. Men pay more than women because they typically die five years earlier. Smokers pay much higher premiums—often triple the price—than nonsmokers because, as a group, smokers die ten years earlier than nonsmokers.

Table 12-3 shows fair prices for term life insurance based on price per $1,000 of coverage. Term insurance prices are by far the lowest, while the cash-value life insurance policies are much more expensive.

12.4d When Buying Life Insurance Get a Great Price Online

Smart personal financial managers take a do-it-yourself approach to life insurance. They calculate their life insurance needs and decide what types of insurance to buy, and then which ones to cancel and when. They use a **premium quote service** that offers computer-generated comparisons from among 20 to 80 different companies. Premium quote services can be found at www.insure.com, www.quotescout.com, and www.accuquote.com. These websites also offer online life insurance needs calculators and a wealth of information on life insurance from an unbiased perspective. In addition, all the major life insurance companies have an online purchase system. Term insurance is easiest to buy this way, but even cash-value insurance can be purchased online.

Don't deal with pushy life insurance sales agents. Instead, get smart about life insurance and shop online. There you are in the power seat, away from persuasive salespersons, and the prices for life insurance are both affordable and competitive.

12.4e Or Contact a Local Insurance Agent

An **insurance agent** is a representative of an insurance company authorized to sell, modify, service, and terminate insurance contracts. In the United States, life insurance is typically sold through **exclusive agents** who represent only one company.

premium quote service
Offers computer-generated comparisons from among 20 to 80 different companies.

insurance agent
Representative of an insurance company who is authorized to sell, modify, service, and terminate insurance contracts.

> **COMMON SENSE**
> **Smokers Pay Much More Than Non-Smokers**
>
> Smokers pay more than twice as much for life insurance than non-smokers. On average they pay 235 percent more. Half of lifetime smokers die before age 70. Don't lie when applying for a policy because the life insurance company will send a nurse to your residence to test your blood for nicotine to be sure you are telling the truth. The only thing, generally, that can void a life insurance policy is fraud on the medical application.

Table 12-3   Fair Prices for Term Life Insurance*

| | Based on Price Per $1,000 of Coverage | | | |
| | Nonsmokers | | Smokers | |
Age	Male	Female	Male	Female
18–30	$0.70	$0.67	$1.00	$0.95
35	$0.83	$0.74	$1.25	$1.15
40	$1.08	$1.00	$1.95	$1.60
45	$1.67	$1.60	$2.80	$2.40
50	$2.30	$2.20	$4.00	$3.25

* Multiply the rate by each $1,000 of coverage and add $60 for estimated administrative fees. For example, a fair annual premium for a $50,000 policy for a 36-year-old male nonsmoker might be $101.50 ($0.83 × 50 = $41.50; $41.50 + $60 = $101.50).

TURN BAD HABITS INTO GOOD ONES

Do You Do This?

Assume that you have life insurance set up by your parents

Put off thinking about life insurance because you are young

Assume a cash-value life insurance policy is the best way to buy life insurance

Rely on a life insurance agent to determine how much and what type of insurance to buy

Do This Instead!

Confirm that you are covered and for how much

Determine the dollar amount of insurance that you need and buy insurance to cover any shortfall

Explore term life insurance as the lowest cost and most appropriate means of protection

Make your own assessments based on your income and family obligations

The life insurance agent must be qualified to design a program tailored to your specific needs and should understand all aspects of life insurance. The agent should have earned the professional designations chartered life underwriter (CLU) and either the certified financial planner (CFP) or chartered financial consultant (ChFC) designation. In addition, you should check your agent's reputation with your state's insurance and securities investment regulatory agencies. See www.naic.org/state_web_map.htm.

YOUR GRANDPARENTS SAY

"Ask About Commissions"

"Knowing that commissions for life insurance agents can be extremely high, ask your agent how much they make on each policy they are discussing with you. You might find out why one policy is being pushed over the others."

DID YOU KNOW

Life Insurance Is Cheap But Half Take a Pass

Most people think that life insurance is expensive but that is false. On the contrary, term life insurance is very affordable, costing as little as $40 per month for a $500,000 policy and $70 per month for a $1 million policy on a person under age 45.

12.4f Sales Commissions Can Amount to 90 Percent of the Annual Premium

Part of the premium you pay for life insurance each year goes toward the sales commissions that are paid to the selling insurance agent. Sales commissions are earned by insurance agents over 10 years, often declining a set percentage every year or two, sometimes much longer. Sales commissions on term insurance policies are very low—often beginning at only 10 percent of the premium, and then it declines.

Cash value policies are different, and that is the major reason why agents try to sell them instead of term policies: They make more money. Sales commissions are as much as 90 to 100 percent of the first-year premium paid for a cash-value life insurance policy. Over the following years, commissions decline annually to 50, 40, 30, 20, and eventually 10 percent. Beginning in the 10th year, the policy builds more cash value.

You can buy cash value life insurance policies with low sales commissions. Such **low-load life insurance** can be bought on the Internet at such sites such as www.llis.com. You can also buy through fee-only financial planners.

12.4g Signs of an Unethical Life Insurance Agent

In an effort to earn maximum commissions and fee revenues, some agents act unethically, and may do any of the following:

1. Five times your salary should do the trick. To assess your insurance needs the agent uses the multiple earnings approach rather than use the needs approach.

2. Cash-value is a great investment. The agent discourages you from buying a term policy and instead pressures you to buy a cash-value policy.

3. I have a better policy for you. The agent encourages you to replace an existing cash-value policy with another (and this is illegal in some states).

4. **The policy pays for itself.** The agent focuses strongly on the poor logic that the net cost of the policy pay for it, rather than how the policy genuinely meets the needs of your family.

5. **Look at how much you will make.** The agent suggests that the high current rate of return is all but guaranteed and unlikely to go down.

6. **I can make you even more money.** The agent says it is a good idea to borrow from a policy to make some other investment such as an annuity.

7. **Act now.** The agent pressures you to sign and pay for a policy without giving you ample time to read it and compare the policy to others.

8. **I will keep your situation to myself.** The agent tells you to misstate your health status or age in order to lower your premium a bit.

9. **I will give you a rebate.** It is illegal for the insurance agent to give you a rebate of premium out of his commission as an inducement for you to buy a policy.

10. **Talk, talk, talk.** The agent does all the talking and uses lots of insurance jargon rather than addresses your issues in understandable language.

THERE IS AN APP FOR THAT!

Some of the best apps are:

- Human Life Value Calculator
- Life Calculate
- Life Happens
- LifePlans.com
- Policy Genius

CONCEPT CHECK 12.4

1. What is meant by integrating your life insurance into your financial plan over the life cycle?
2. Give some examples of fair prices for life insurance and one example of why some people must pay higher premiums than others.
3. List the benefits of buying term and investing the rest.
4. Give three signs of an unethical life insurance agent.

WHAT DO YOU RECOMMEND *NOW*?

Now that you have read the chapter on protecting loved ones through life insurance, what would you recommend to Stephanie and Will Bridgeman in the case at the beginning of the chapter regarding:

1. Their changing need for life insurance now that they have a child?
2. What types of life insurance they should consider.
3. Coordinating their retirement savings and other investments with their life insurance program?
4. Shopping for life insurance?

Junial/Dreamstime LLC

SUMMARY OF LEARNING RECAPPED

LO1 **Understand why you might need life insurance and calculate the appropriate amount of coverage.**

Life insurance is designed to provide financial protection to adequately provide for the financial well-being of loved ones left behind that result from death, such as a spouse and children. The reasons to purchase life insurance evolve over the life cycle. The need for this type of protection is nonexistent children and single adults. Factors affecting life insurance needs include the need to replace income, final-expense needs, readjustment-period needs, debt-repayment needs, college-expense needs, availability of government programs, and ownership of other life insurance and assets. Two methods to calculate life insurance needs are the multiple-of-earnings approach and the needs-based approach.

LO2 **Distinguish among types of life insurance.**

Two types of life insurance exist: term life insurance and cash-value life insurance. Variations on term life insurance include guaranteed renewable term, level-premium term, decreasing term, convertible term, group term, and credit and mortgage term. Variations on cash-value insurance include whole life, limited-pay life, adjustable life, modified life, universal life, variable life insurance, and variable-universal life.

LO3 **Explain the major provisions of life insurance policies.**

A **life insurance policy** is a contract between an insurance policy holder/owner and an insurance company, where the company promises to pay a designated beneficiary a sum of money (the "benefits") upon the death of the insured person when buying life insurance. You should pay attention to the policy's general terms and conditions, the policy features unique to cash-value life insurance, and settlement or payout options.

LO4 **Apply a step-by-step strategy for implementing a life insurance plan.**

Life insurance should be purchased to address the dying-too-soon problem. Your investments should manage the living-too-long problem. Addressing these two problems appropriately requires high amounts of term insurance while you are raising children, and a sound investment program to prepare for your retirement years. You should not purchase life insurance until you have determined the actual dollar amount and type of policy you need and compared premiums using various life insurance cost indices.

LET'S TALK ABOUT IT

1. **Thinking About Life Insurance.** What were your feelings about your need for life insurance before you read this chapter? What are they now?

2. **Are You Insured?** Are you covered by life insurance? If so, how much? Given what you have read, do you feel that you are over- or under-insured?

3. **Term Versus Cash-Value Insurance.** Why do you think people persist in buying cash-value life insurance when,

in most cases, they would be better off buying term insurance and investing the money saved into a retirement account?

4. **Life Insurance for Unmarried Couples.** Many people today choose to cohabitate rather than marry (at least for some time period). How might this affect their thinking about life insurance?

DO THE MATH

1. **Life Insurance Needs for a Young Single.** Matthew Kennedy of Urbana, Ohio, is single and has been working as an admissions counselor at a university for five years. Matthew owns a home valued at $250,000 on which he owes $135,000. He has a two-year-old vehicle valued at $32,000 on which he owes $26,000. He has about $20,000 remaining on his student loans.

DO IT IN CLASS
Page 367

His retirement account has grown to $32,000, and he owns some stock valued at $9,000. Matthew has no life insurance and is considering buying some. How much should he buy?

2. **Life Insurance Needs for a Young Married Couple.** Amy and Mack Holly from Rapid City, South Dakota, have been married for three years. They recently bought a home costing $212,000 using a $190,000 mortgage.

They have no other debts. Mack earns $62,000 per year, and Amy earns $71,000. Each has a retirement plan valued at approximately $20,000. They recently received an offer in the mail from their mortgage lender for a mortgage life insurance policy of $190,000. Their only life insurance currently is a $20,000 cash-value survivorship joint life policy. They each would like to provide the other with support for at least five years if one of them should die.

(a) Assuming $15,000 in final expenses and $20,000 allocated to help make mortgage payments, calculate the amount of life insurance they should purchase using the needs-based approach.

(b) How would their needs change if Amy became pregnant?

3. **Calculating a Death Benefit.** Alexandra Cunningham of Gardner, Massachusetts, has a $100,000 participating cash-value policy written on her life. The policy has accumulated $4,700 in cash value; Alexandra has borrowed $3,000 of this value. The policy also has accumulated unpaid dividends of $1,666. Yesterday Alexandra paid her premium of $1,200 for the coming year. What is the current death benefit from this policy?

DO IT IN CLASS
Page 374

FINANCIAL PLANNING CASES

CASE 1

The Johnsons Change Their Life Insurance Coverage

Harry and Belinda Johnson spend $20 per month on life insurance in the form of a premium on a $10,000, paid-at-65 cash-value policy on Harry that his parents bought for him years ago. Belinda has a group term insurance policy from her employer with a face amount of $200,000. By choosing a group life insurance plan from his menu of employee benefits, Harry now has $100,000 of group term life insurance. Harry and Belinda have decided that, because they have no children, they could reduce their life insurance needs by protecting one another's income for only four years, assuming the survivor would be able to fend for himself or herself after that time. They also realize that their savings fund is so low that it would have no bearing on their life insurance needs. Harry and Belinda are basing their calculations on a projected 4 percent rate of return after taxes and inflation. They also estimate the following expenses: $15,000 for final expenses, $20,000 for readjustment expenses, and $5,000 for repayment of short-term debts.

(a) Should the $3,000 interest earnings from Harry's trust fund be included in his annual income for the purposes of calculating the likely dollar loss if he were to die? (See the discussions about the Johnsons in Chapter 1 beginning on page 34.) Explain your response.

(b) Based on your response to the previous question, how much more life insurance does Harry need? Use the Run the Numbers worksheet on page 366 to arrive at your answer.

(c) Repeat the calculations to arrive at the additional life insurance needed on Belinda's life.

(d) How might the Johnsons most economically meet any additional life insurance needs you have determined they may have?

(e) In addition to their life insurance planning, how might the Johnsons begin to prepare for their retirement years?

CASE 2

Victor and Maria Hernandez Contemplate Switching Life Insurance Policies

Victor and Maria Hernandez have a total of $200,000 in life insurance. Victor has a $50,000 cash-value policy purchased more than 20 years ago soon after when they married and a $100,000 group term policy through his employer. Maria has a $50,000 group term insurance policy through her employer. The couple has been approached by a neighbor who is a life insurance agent. He thinks that they need to change their policy mix because, he says, they are inadequately insured. Specifically, the agent has suggested that Victor cash in his cash-value policy and buy a new variable-universal life insurance policy.

(a) If Victor cashes in his policy, what options would he have when receiving the cash value?

(b) Determine what the $16,000 in cash value in Victor's life insurance policy would be worth in 20 years if that sum were invested somewhere else and earned an 8 percent annual return. (Hint: Use the *Garman/Forgue* companion website.)

(c) Would cashing in the policy be a wise decision? Why or why not?

(d) As the Hernandezes' children are now grown and out on their own, and both Victor and Maria are employed full time, give general reasons why Victor may need more or less insurance.

(e) Explain why it would be a bad idea for Victor to buy a variable-universal life insurance policy.

CASE 3

Julia Starts Thinking About Life Insurance

Julia Price is now in her late 30s and has always wanted children. She has arranged to adopt two siblings from overseas, ages 2 and 4. Julia is happy that she earns enough money to support the children adequately, but the agency sponsoring the adoption also requires that adoptive parents purchase sufficient life insurance. Julia currently has a $20,000 paid-up cash-value life insurance policy purchased by her parents when she was a child. In addition, Julia's employer provides term insurance that matches her salary as an employee benefit. She talked with the agency, and they suggested that she buy a whole life insurance policy in the amount of $450,000 based on her current salary of $150,000. Julia isn't sure this is the way to go. For one thing, the policy would cost about $3,400 per year. Further, she realizes that the amount the agency requires would not maintain the children's lifestyle for long and be insufficient to pay for their college educations. Julia is thinking that guaranteed renewable term insurance would be a better way to go. Offer your opinion about her thinking.

DO IT IN CLASS
Page 379

CASE 4

Life Insurance for a Newly Married Couple

Just-married couples sometimes over-indulge in the type and amount of life insurance that they buy. Hakeem and Leshaniqua Jackson of Barstow, California, took a different approach. Both were working and had a small amount of life insurance provided through their respective employee benefit programs: Hakeem, $60,000, and Leshaniqua, $65,000. During their discussion of life insurance needs and related costs, they decided that if Leshaniqua went back to school full-time and completed her master's degree in industrial psychology, she would have better employment opportunities. Consequently, they decided to use money they had available for additional life insurance to pay for Leshaniqua's education. They both feel, however, that they do not want to have inadequate life insurance.

(a) In what way does Leshaniqua's return to school alter the Jackson's life insurance needs?

(b) Would you agree that the amount of life insurance provided by the Jackson's respective employers is adequate while Leshaniqua is in school? Explain your response.

(c) Summarize how the Jackson's life insurance needs might change over their life cycle.

DO IT IN CLASS
Page 366

CASE 5

Fraternity Members Contemplate Permanent Life Insurance

Biming Chen is a college student from Cleveland, Mississippi. Soon to graduate, Biming was approached recently by a life insurance agent, who set up a group meeting for several members of his fraternity. During the meeting, the agent presented six life insurance plans and was very persuasive about the benefits of a universal life insurance plan that his company calls Affordable Life II. Under the plan, the prospective graduate can buy $100,000 of permanent life insurance for a very low premium during the first five years and then pay a higher premium later when income presumably will have increased. Biming was somewhat confused after the meeting, as were his friends. Armed with your knowledge from this personal finance book, you have been asked to respond to some of their questions.

(a) Do you think universal life insurance is a good deal for these people? Why or why not?

(b) How can the individual fraternity members decide how much life insurance they need?

(c) Life insurance cannot be as confusing as the agent made it seem. What clearer explanation would you give to the fraternity members?

(d) What type of life insurance, if any, would you advise for the fraternity brothers?

(e) How would they know if a life insurance policy is offered at a fair price?

CASE 6

A Married Couple with Children Address Their Life Insurance Needs

Joseph and Marcia Michael of Athens, Georgia, are a married couple in their mid-30s. They have two children, ages 5 and 3, and Marcia is pregnant with their third child. Marcia is a part-time book indexer who earned $30,000 after taxes last year. Because she performs much of her work at home, it is unlikely that she will need to curtail her work after the baby is born. Joseph is a marriage counselor; he earned $75,000 last year after taxes. Because both are self-employed, Marcia and Joseph do not have access to group life insurance. They are each covered by $50,000 universal life policies they purchased three years ago. In addition, Joseph is covered by a $50,000, five-year guaranteed renewable term policy, which will expire next year. The Michaels are currently reassessing their life insurance program. As a preliminary step in their analysis, they have determined that Marcia's three survivors would qualify for Social

Security survivor's benefits of about $1,900 per month, or an annual benefit of $22,800, if she were to die. For Joseph's survivors, the figure would be $2,800 per month, or an annual benefit of $33,600. Both agree that they would like to support each of their children to age 22, but to date, they have been unable to start a college savings fund. The couple estimates that it would cost $300,000 to put all three children through a regional university in their state as measured in today's dollars. They expect that burial expenses for each spouse would total about $12,000, and they would like to have a lump sum of $50,000 to help the surviving spouse make payments on their home mortgage. They also feel that each spouse would want to take a three-month leave from work if the other were to die.

(a) Calculate the amount of life insurance that Marcia needs based on the information given. Use the Run the Numbers worksheet on page 366 or the *Garman/Forgue* companion website. Assume a 3 percent rate of return after taxes and inflation and an income need for 22 years because the unborn child will need financial support for that many years.

(b) Calculate the amount of life insurance that Joseph needs based on the information given. Use the Run the Numbers worksheet on page 366 or the *Garman/Forgue* companion website. Assume a 3 percent rate of return after taxes and inflation and an income need for 22 years because the unborn child will need financial support for that many years.

BE YOUR OWN PERSONAL FINANCIAL MANAGER

1. **Calculating Life Insurance Need.** Review the material in "How Much Life Insurance Do You Need?" on pages 362–367. Then using dollar amounts that fit your personal situation, complete Worksheet 48: Determining My Life Insurance Needs from "My Personal Financial Planner." If you are currently single and childless, for the purposes of this activity, assume that you are 30 years old, have two children under age 5, are married, and earn $60,000 per year and redo the estimate of need. How would having a family change your need for life insurance?

   My Personal Financial Planner

2. **Review Your Life Insurance Program.** Review the material in "There Are Only Two Types of Life Insurance" and "Understanding Your Life Insurance Policy" on pages 368–378. Then examine any life insurance policies on your life. Given what you learn from those policies and your own need for life insurance as determined in item 1 above, decide on the amount and type(s) of additional life insurance you probably need and any appropriate policy features, such as who should own the policy(s) and be named as beneficiaries.

3. **Name Your Beneficiary.** Review the information in "Understanding Your Life Insurance Policy" on pages 373–378. Then revisit the naming of the beneficiary on any policies currently in force on your life and make any changes desired. If you are not currently covered by an insurance policy, assume that you have taken a job after graduation and your employer offers free life insurance as an employee benefit. Who would you name as your beneficiary?

4. **Life Insurance Settlement Options.** Review the material in **"Settlement (or Payout) Options Specify How to Pay the Death Benefit"** on page 377. If you were the beneficiary on another person's life insurance policy in the amount of $100,000, which one of the five ways would you choose to receive the benefits if you were to receive the proceeds of the policy?

5. **Life-Cycle Life Insurance Planning.** Review the information in "Integrate Your Life Insurance into Your Financial Plan," including Figure 12-3 on pages 378–379. Then map out a plan for yourself that integrates life insurance and investments. The plan should protect you from both the dying-too-soon and living-too-long risks that begins on page 362. Make appropriate assumptions for your plans regarding marriage and having children and project your plan out to age 65.

ON THE NET

Go to the Web pages indicated to complete these exercises.

1. **Obtain a Quote on Your Life Insurance.** Visit the website for AccuQuote at www.accuquote.com to obtain a quote for the annual premium on a $200,000 guaranteed renewable, ten-year term policy for you. Then call a life insurance agent in your community to obtain a quote on the same term insurance coverage. How do the term rates quoted by your local agent compare with the rates found over the Internet? Also, ask for the quote on a $100,000 universal life policy with guaranteed insurability and waiver-of-premium options. Ask the agent to explain why the quotes for the two types of policies differ. Report his or her response and write a summary of the agent's observations based on what you learned in this chapter.

2. **Check an Insurance Company's Financial Strength.** Visit the websites for A.M. Best Company at www.ambest .com/ratings/guide.asp and Moody's Investor Services (www.moodys.com) to check the ratings for the insurance company recommended by the agent in Exercise 1 as well as the company with the lowest cost for term insurance that you found on the Web. What do the ratings tell you about the relative strengths of those companies?

3. **How Long Will You Live?** Visit the mortality tables at the Social Security Administration's website (www.ssa.gov/ oact/STATS/table4c6.html) and determine your life expectancy.

4. **Determine Your Need for More Life Insurance.** Visit the Life and Health Insurance Foundation for Education website at www.lifehappens.org. Calculate your current need for life insurance. Then recalculate your need for five years from now given your estimates of your income and family situation.

ACTION INVOLVEMENT PROJECTS

1. **Review Life Insurance Company Websites.** Visit the websites of two large life insurance companies. Focus on how their approaches to educating the public about life insurance are similar to or different from the information provided in this chapter. Write a summary of your findings.

2. **Talk to a Life Insurance Agent.** Visit a life insurance agent and ask for an assessment of your life insurance needs given your current situation. Compare the information you receive with what you have learned in this chapter and write a summary of your findings.

3. **How Others Approach the Need for Life Insurance.** Talk to two friends and/or relatives below age 30 who are married. Ask about their approach to life insurance and how they have gone about setting up a life insurance program. Write a summary of your findings and compare what they have done to what you would do if you were in a similar situation.

4. **Term Versus Cash-Value Life Insurance.** Talk to two of your friends or acquaintances who have never purchased life insurance. Explain to them the differences between term and cash-value life insurance. Then inquire about which type they would prefer to buy. Write a summary of your findings and compare their views with yours.

PART 4

Paul Biryukov/Shutterstock.com

13 Investment Fundamentals

Learning Objectives

After reading this chapter, you should be able to:

1. Explain how to get started as an investor.

2. Identify your investment philosophy and invest accordingly.

3. Describe the major risk factors that affect the rate of return on investments.

4. Accept the realities of the market and avoid investing mistakes that other individuals make.

5. Decide which of the four long-term safe and effective investment strategies you will utilize.

6. Create your own investment plan.

Castlesky/Shutterstock.com

WHAT DO YOU RECOMMEND?

Shanice and Sarena are sisters, both in their early 30s. Shanice drives a leased BMW convertible, and she makes about $50,000, including tips, as a part-time bartender at two different restaurants. Although she has no employee benefits, she enjoys having flexible work hours so that she can go to the beach and the local nightspots. Currently, Shanice has $10,000 in credit card debt. She has $1,500 in a bank savings account, and two years ago she opened an individual retirement account (IRA) with a $1,000 investment in a mutual fund. Her sister Sarena drives a paid-for Honda Civic Coupe, pays her credit card purchases in full each month, and sacrifices some of her salary by putting $200 a month into her employer's 401(k) retirement account. Over the past seven years, the 401(k) account has risen, and Sarena's 401(k) plan is now worth about $30,000. Sarena also has invested about $14,000 in a Roth IRA account that is currently invested in a mutual fund, and she plans to use that money for a down payment on a home purchase. She earns $68,000 as a manager of a restaurant, plus she receives an annual bonus ranging from $2,000 to $5,000 every January that she uses for a spring vacation in the Caribbean. Sarena's employer provides many employee benefits.

What do you recommend to Shanice and Sarena on the subject of investment fundamentals regarding:

1. **Portfolio diversification for Sarena?**
2. **Dollar-cost averaging for Shanice?**
3. **Investment alternatives for Sarena?**

TO-DO LIST

Do the following to begin to achieve financial success:

1. *Start to save a small amount every payday perhaps by signing up to automatically transfer some income to a savings or investment account.*

2. *Start investing early in life by sacrificing some income and putting some cash into an investment for the future.*

3. *Invest regularly through your employer's retirement plan.*

4. *Accept substantial risk when investing for the long term.*

5. *Rebalance your portfolio at least once a year.*

Learning Objective **1**

Explain how to get started as an investor.

At many points in this book, we have encouraged you to set aside funds for the future, especially by accumulating funds through regular savings. Financial guru Andrew Tobias argues that saving more is the smartest, safest investment move you will ever make. Save every nickel you can. Then you will have funds for investing.

The worst financial risk we can take with our money is doing nothing because money sitting in a bank account loses its purchasing power to inflation. When the bank interest rate is less than the rate of inflation, you lose. To win you must invest. Most likely you will invest in stocks, bonds, and mutual funds, all of which pay higher returns than bank accounts. Remember, money wisely invested today increases your future financial security.

Despite the ups and downs of the U.S. and world's stock markets, the best way to make money over the long term—especially for retirement—is to invest. This is true even with occasional serious fluctuations. This chapter explains both why this is true and how to succeed as an investor.

13.1 STARTING YOUR INVESTMENT PROGRAM

To help secure a desirable future lifestyle, you cannot spend every dollar that you earn today. Instead, you must sacrifice by setting aside some of your current income and invest it. When investing you postpone the pleasure of using money for here-and-now consumption so you can have more in the future.

13.1a **Before You Invest**

Before beginning an investment program some things in your financial life should be in order. Ask yourself:

- Are you paying your bills on time?
- Are you paying your credit card bills in full every month?
- Is your budget balanced and are you meeting your basic needs?
- Do you have an adequate emergency fund in cash or liquid saving accounts?
- Do you have access to other sources of credit for an emergency?
- Do you have adequate insurance coverage?
- Are you already contributing the maximum amount needed to earn your employer's match to the 401(k) retirement plan?
- Are you willing to sacrifice some consumption to finance your investments?
- Are you willing to start small by investing just a little on a regular basis?

If you said "yes" to these questions—or soon will be able to say yes—then it is time to learn about investing fundamentals and start investing. If you said "no," you must decide to resolve whatever obstacles remain and begin to invest soon.

To be financially successful, you are wise to start investing early in life, invest regularly, and stay invested. Why? Because, for every five years you delay investing, you will have to double your monthly investment amount to achieve the same goals. Remember: You—and no one else—are responsible for your own financial success.

13.1b **Prioritize Your Investing Goals**

Your investing goals likely include some of the following:

- Take an expensive vacation
- Buy a vehicle or home

- Increase income
- Educate a child
- Accumulate start-up costs for a business
- Build a retirement nest egg.

Once you have your goals you can prioritize them. That helps you know which ones are most important, how much time it will take to reach each goal, and in what order can they be achieved. Then crunch the numbers to determine how much is needed for each. Next think about how much investment risk you can afford to take for each goal. Invest conservatively for short-term goals so you do not lose money. Invest aggressively for long-term goals because you want your money to grow.

13.1c Get the Money to Invest

The most common problem in investing is getting started because most people spend all of their income each month. You must decide to reduce spending on consumption to begin investing. To find money to invest consider the following suggestions:

- Set up a pay-yourself-first plan to accumulate enough savings to make an investment
- Save your net raise after income taxes to use for investments
- Invest any found money (such as tax refunds, bonuses, gifts, inheritances)
- When a debt is repaid continue debt payments to yourself into an investment.
- Go on a budget diet for one month a year to save money to invest
- Take on a second job

13.1d Investing is More than Saving

Savings is the accumulation of excess funds by intentionally spending less than you earn. Investing is more. **Investing** is taking some of the money you are saving and putting it to work so that it makes you even more money. Your goals and the time it will take to reach those goals dictate the investment strategies you follow and the investment alternatives you choose. You start investing when you are organized and have written specific long-term financial goals. The most common ways that people invest are by putting money into assets called **securities**, such as stocks, bonds, and mutual funds (often purchased through their employer-sponsored retirement accounts), and by buying real estate. **Stocks** are shares of ownership in a corporation, and **bonds** represent loans to companies and governments. Essentially, they are IOUs that are bought and sold among investors. All of your investment assets make up your **portfolio**, which is the collection of multiple investments in different assets chosen to meet your investment goals.

13.1e What Long-Term Investment Returns Are Possible?

Figure 13-1 shows the long-term rates of return on some popular investments. Stock market returns have averaged about 9.6 percent over the past 100 years. Since 1927, the *worst* 20-year performance for stocks was a gain of 3 percent annually. Over the past 80 years, the chance of making money during any one year in the stock market has been 66 percent. Over five years, the probability increases to 81 percent; over ten years, it increases to 89 percent.

13.1f Capital Gains Plus Dividends Equals One's Total Return

When people invest their money, they take a **financial risk** (also called **business risk**)—namely, the possibility that the investment will fail to pay any return to the investor. At the extremes, a company could have a very good year earning a considerable profit, or it could go bankrupt, causing investors to lose all of their money.

savings
The accumulation of excess funds by intentionally spending less than you earn.

investing
Putting saved money to work so that it makes you even more money.

securities
Assets suitable for investment, like stocks, bonds, mutual funds, and real estate.

stocks
Shares of ownership in a corporation.

bond
A debt instrument issued by an organization that promises repayment at a specific time and the right to receive regular interest payments during the life of the bond.

portfolio
Collection of investments assembled to meet your investment goals.

DO IT IN CLASS

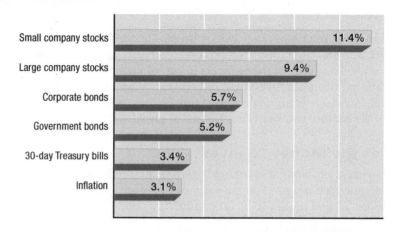

Figure 13-1　**Long-Term Rates of Return on Investments (Annualized returns since 1926)**

Small company stocks — 11.4%
Large company stocks — 9.4%
Corporate bonds — 5.7%
Government bonds — 5.2%
30-day Treasury bills — 3.4%
Inflation — 3.1%

total return

Income an investment generates from current income and capital gains.

current income

Money received while you own an investment; usually received regularly as interest, rent, or dividends.

dividend

A portion of a company's earnings that the firm pays out to its shareholders.

capital gain

Increase in the value of an initial investment (less costs) realized upon the sale of the investment.

Investors expect that their investments will earn them a positive **total return**, which is the income an investment generates from a combination of current income and capital gains. **Current income** is money received while you own an investment. It is usually received on a regular basis as interest, rent, or dividends.

Interest for an investor is the return earned for lending money. **Rent** is payment received in return for allowing someone to use your real estate property, such as land or a building. A **dividend** is a portion of a company's earnings that the firm pays out to its shareholders. For example, Concepcion Rodriguez from Milwaukee, Wisconsin, purchased 100 shares of Apple stock at $125 per share ($12,500) last year. The company paid dividends of $2 per share during the year, so Concepcion received $200 in cash dividends as current income.

A **capital gain** occurs only when you actually sell an investment that has increased in value. It is calculated by subtracting the total amount paid for the investment (including purchase transaction costs) from the higher price at which it is sold (minus any sales transaction costs). For example, if the price of Apple stock rose to $150 during the year, Concepcion could sell it for a capital gain. If she paid a transaction cost of $1 per share at both purchase and time of sale, Concepcion's capital gain would be $2,300 [($15,000 − $100) − ($12,500 + $100)].

ADVICE FROM A SEASONED PRO

Don't Get Scared Out of Buying Stocks and Stock Mutual Funds

Investment expert Peter Lynch says, "The real key to making money in stocks and stock mutual funds is not to get scared out of them." Investing based on the recent past is like driving a car while focused on the rear view mirror: it is stupid and dangerous. Therefore, remain optimistic about stocks and look for moderate gains of 7 to 9 percent annually for the next 10 or 20 years.

Wayne Mackie
Saginaw Valley State University, University Center, Michigan

Capital losses can occur as well. For most investments, a trade-off arises between capital gains and current income. Investments with potential for high capital gains often pay little current income, and investments that pay substantial current income generally have little or no potential for capital gains. Long-term investors are often willing to forgo current income in favor of possibly earning substantial future capital gains.

The **rate of return**, or **yield**, is the total return on an investment expressed as a percentage of its price. It is usually stated on an annualized basis, and it includes dividends and capital gains. For example, if Concepcion sells the Apple stock for $150 per share after one year, she will have a total return of $2,500 ($200 in dividends plus $2,300 in capital gains). Her yield would be 19.8 percent ($2,500 ÷ $12,600).

13.1g   Your Investing Future Looks Promising

One's average investment returns from stocks are likely to be about 6 to 9 percent annually. This is likely to come from a 2 percent dividend yield for stocks and the rest from price increases because of earnings growth. Dividends have roughly accounted for close to one-third of most stocks' total return.

13.1h   Creating Wealth Just Takes Starting Early

What creates wealth? It is not money that creates wealth, it is time. But you must act early to not waste the opportunity. As an example, Barbra starts to save $200 a month at age 25. Debra saves the same amount but waits to begin until she is age 45. Over time both average an 8 percent return. By age 65, Barbra has invested $96,000 ($200 × 12 months × 40 years) while Debra invested $55,000 ($200 × 12 months × 20 years). The investing results: Barbra, $698,000; Debra, $118,000.

Starting early means Barbra's investments will be almost 6 times larger than Debra's. Barbra's $96,000 investment grew to $698,000! The magic of compound interest works wonders over time. The earlier people start to invest, the more time one's money has to get bigger.

capital loss
Decrease in paper value of an initial investment; only realized if sold.

rate of return/yield
Total return on an investment expressed as a percentage of its price.

CONCEPT CHECK 13.1

1. Offer some suggestions on where to get money to invest.
2. How does savings differ from investing?
3. What are the two parts of an investor's total return?
4. What average investment returns from stocks do you anticipate in the future?

13.2   IDENTIFY YOUR INVESTMENT PHILOSOPHY AND INVEST ACCORDINGLY

Achieving financial success requires that you understand your investment philosophy and adhere to it when investing. You also need to know about investment risk and what to do about it.

13.2a   You Must Learn to Handle Investment Risk

Investments are subject to **speculative risk**, which exists in situations that offer potential for gain as well as for loss. **Investment risk** represents the uncertainty that the yield on an investment will deviate from what is expected. For most investments, the greater the risk is, the higher the potential return.

The trust in investments and the stock market among millennials is very low. This is a fear they must get over to become successful investors. Half of them have less than

speculative risk
Involves the potential for either gain or loss; equity investments might do either.

investment risk
The possibility that the yield on an investment will deviate from its expected return.

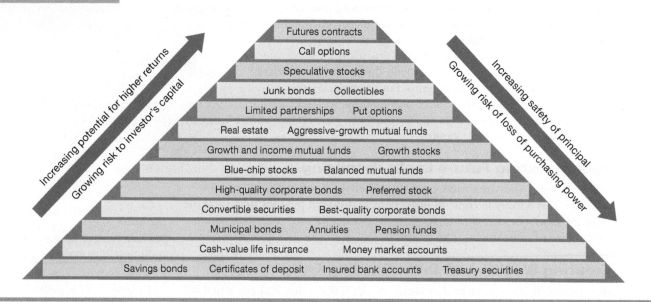

Figure 13-2 **Risk Pyramid Reveals the Trade-Offs Between Risk and Return**

DO IT IN CLASS

$1,000 in investments, and only one-fifth have between $1,000 and $5,000. They must save and invest more for their futures. By accepting exposure to rises in the United States stock market, people can plan for and achieve financially successful lives.

This potential for gain is what motivates people to accept increasingly greater levels of risk, as illustrated in Figure 13-2. Nevertheless, many people remain seriously averse to risk. The figure also gives insights about possible investment choices. Don't be overwhelmed because these investments are explained in the following chapters, and you will never invest in most of them. However, you *will* learn how to make well informed investment decisions for yourself. Why shouldn't you join the rich people who make all their money investing?

13.2b Investors Demand a Risk Premium

T-bill

A government IOU of less than one year.

One popular investment is the short-term Treasury bill, or **T-bill**, which is a government IOU of less than one year. Because T-bills are risk-free investments, they pay too low a return for most people, perhaps only 0.25 or 0.35 percent. Some people invest in T-bills to safeguard their money until it can be invested at a later time.

risk premium (or equity risk premium)

The difference between a riskier investment's expected return and the totally safe return on the T-bill.

Investors need the promise of a high return to warrant placing their money at risk in an investment. When making investments, people demand a **risk premium** (or **equity risk premium**) for their willingness to make investments for which there is no guarantee of future success. This risk premium constitutes the difference between a riskier investment's expected return and the totally safe return on the T-bill.

If the expected return is 8 percent on stocks and 2 percent on ten-year Treasury securities—a risk-free investment similar to T-bills but for a much longer term—the risk premium is 6 percent. Industry experts figure that the amount of the risk premium for most investors is 3 to 6 percent, although the long-term average is 8 percent. Higher-risk investments carry higher-risk premiums.

13.2c What Is Your Investment Philosophy?

risk tolerance

An investor's willingness to weather changes in the value of your investments, that is, to weather investment risk.

Investors have to take risks that are appropriate to reach their financial goals. The task is to find the right balance and make choices accordingly. You must weigh the risks of an investment with the likelihood of not reaching your goal.

Your **risk tolerance** is your willingness to weather changes in the values of your investments. To be successful in investing, your risk tolerance must be factored into your investment philosophy. If you lose sleep over your investments, you know it is time to reduce your risk and adjust your investment philosophy.

Find out how much risk you can comfortably tolerate by taking a risk-tolerance quiz at one of the following websites (1) Bankrate.com: www.bankrate.com/finance/financial-literacy/use-investments-to-reach-your-goals-2.aspx, (2) Kiplinger: www.kiplinger.com/quiz/investing/T031-S001-the-investor-psychology-quiz, and (3) Rutgers Investment Tolerance Quiz: www.njaes.rutgers.edu:8080/money/riskquiz.

An **investment philosophy** is one's general approach to tolerance for risk in investments, whether it is conservative, moderate, or aggressive, given the financial goal(s) to be achieved. The more risk you take, within reason, the more you can expect to earn and accumulate over the long term. However, just because you are comfortable with a risky portfolio does not mean that you actually need one. By the same token, you still need to be aggressive enough to meet your financial goals. Wise investors follow their investment philosophy without wavering unless their basic objectives change.

Are You a Conservative Investor?
If you have a **conservative investment philosophy**, you accept very little risk and are generally rewarded with relatively low rates of return for seeking the twin goals of a moderate amount of current income and preservation of capital. **Preservation of capital** means that you do not want to lose any of the money you have invested. In short, you could be characterized as an investor who is **risk averse**. This is one who tends to dislike risk and is unable to put money into investments that seem risky. About 44 percent of investors describe themselves as conservative investors.

Conservative investors focus on protecting themselves. They do so by carefully avoiding losses and trying to stay with investments that demonstrate gains, often for long time periods (perhaps for five or ten years). Tactically, they rarely sell their investments. Investors who are retired or who are planning to withdraw money from their investments in the near future (less than 5 years) often adhere to a conservative investment philosophy.

Conservative investors typically consider investing in obligations issued by the government. Examples include Treasury bills, notes, and bonds, municipal bonds, high-quality (blue-chip) corporate bonds and stocks, balanced mutual funds (which own both stocks and bonds), certificates of deposit, and annuities. Over the course of a year, a conservative investor with $1,000 could possibly lose $20 and is likely to gain $20 to $30.

Are You a Moderate Investor?
People with a **moderate investment philosophy** seek capital gains through slow and steady growth in the value of their investments along with some current income. They invite only a fair amount of risk of capital loss. Most have no immediate need for the funds but instead focus on laying the investment foundation for later years or building on such a base. Moderate investors are fairly comfortable during rising and falling market conditions. They remain secure in the knowledge that they are investing for the long term. Their tactics might include spreading investment funds among several choices and, if needed, adjusting their portfolio by trading some assets perhaps once or twice a year. About 50 percent of investors describe themselves as moderate investors. People seeking moderate returns consider investing in dividend-paying common stocks, growth and income mutual funds, high-quality corporate bonds, government bonds, and real estate. Over the course of a year, a moderate investor with $1,000 could possibly lose $150 and is likely to gain $60 to $90.

Are You an Aggressive Investor?
If you choose to strive for a very high return by accepting a high level of risk, you have an **aggressive investment philosophy**. As such, you could be characterized as a risk seeker. Aggressive investors primarily seek capital gains. Many such investors take a short-term approach, remaining confident that they can profit substantially during major upswings in market prices. About 6 percent of investors describe themselves as aggressive investors.

DO IT IN CLASS

investment philosophy
Investor's general approach to tolerance for risk in investments, whether it is conservative, moderate, or aggressive, given the investor's financial goals.

conservative investment philosophy (risk aversion)
Investors with this philosophy accept very little risk and are generally rewarded with relatively low rates of return for seeking the twin goals of a moderate amount of current income and preservation of capital.

moderate investment philosophy (risk indifference)
Investors with this philosophy accept some risk as they seek capital gains through slow and steady growth in investment value along with current income.

aggressive investment philosophy (risk seeker)
Investors with this philosophy primarily seek capital gains, often with a short time horizon.

NEVER EVER

Invest Too Conservatively

If you keep your investing money in very conservative choices, such as savings accounts, certificates of deposit, annuities, bonds, and bond mutual funds, you run the risk that your money will not grow enough. Don't be too conservative when investing. Take moderate to aggressive investment risks when you are young because you have time to ride out the downturns and win big on the upturns.

People seeking exceptionally high returns consider investing in common stocks of new or fast-growing companies, high-yielding junk bonds, and aggressive-growth mutual funds. Such investors also may put their money into limited real estate partnerships, undeveloped land, precious metals, gems, commodity futures, stock-index futures, and collectibles. Devotees of this investment philosophy usually do not diversify by spreading their funds among many alternatives. Also, they may adopt short-term tactics to increase capital gains. For example, aggressive investors might place most of their investment funds in a single stock in the hope that it will rise 10 percent over 90 days and then sold, giving a yield of more than 30 percent annually on that one venture. Investment tactics for aggressive investors are discussed in Chapter 16.

Aggressive investors must be emotionally and financially able to weather substantial short-term losses—such as a downward swing in a stock's price of 30 or 40 percent— even though they might expect that an upswing in price will occur in the future. Over the course of a year, an aggressive investor with $1,000 could possibly lose $300 and could gain $100, $200, $300, or even more.

13.2d Should You Take an Active or Passive Investing Approach?

Another aspect of your personal investment philosophy is your level of involvement in investing. That is, do you want to be an active or passive investor?

Active Investing is Hard Work An active investor carefully studies the economy, market trends, and investment alternatives; regularly monitors these factors; and makes decisions to buy and sell, perhaps three or four or more times a year, with or without the advice of a professional. In addition, active investors stay alert because the prices of many investments vary with certain news events, world happenings, and economic and political variables. Knowing what is going on in the larger world helps active investors understand when to buy or to sell investments quickly so as to reap profits and/ or reduce losses. An active investor who selects the right advisor can be rewarded with high returns, net of the high fees and transaction costs of active managers. Such returns can be appealing.

Passive Investing Succeeds over the Long Term A passive investor does not actively engage in trading of securities or spend large amounts of time monitoring his or her investments. They often are **do-it-yourself (DIY) investors**, who do not generally require the advice or services of any financial advisors. Such individuals may make regular investments in securities, such as mutual funds (described in Chapter 15), and his or her assets are rarely sold for short-term profits. Instead, passive investors simply aim to match—not exceed—the diversification, low fees, low trading costs, low risk, and substantial returns of a broad market index. They avoid the higher fees and idiosyncratic risks of managed investments. They ignore "hot" tips and the investment of the day touted in the financial press, and do little trading. They keep their emotions in check, and do not worry because worrying and suffering undue anxiety have no place in investing. The smartest investors are calm and disciplined. As a result, they earn higher returns than active investors over the long term. Most long-term investors utilize a passive approach.

13.2e Identify the Kinds of Investments You Want to Make

The investments you choose should match your interests. Before investing, think about lending versus owning, short term versus long term, and how to select investments that are likely to provide your desired potential total return.

DID YOU KNOW

Calculate the Real Rate of Return (After Taxes and Inflation) on Investments

1. *Identify the rate of return before income taxes.* Perhaps you think that a stock will offer a return of 10 percent in one year, including current income and capital gains.

2. *Subtract the effects of your marginal tax rate on the rate of return to obtain the after-tax return.* If you are in the 25 percent federal income tax bracket, the calculation is $(1 - 0.25) \times 0.10 = 0.075 = 7.5$ percent.

3. *Subtract the effects of inflation from the aftertax return to obtain the real rate of return on the investment after taxes and inflation.* If you estimate an annual inflation of 3 percent, the calculation gives 4.5 percent (7.5 percent − 3.0 percent). Thus, your before-tax rate of return of 10 percent provides a real rate of return of 4.5 percent after taxes and inflation.

Do You Want Lending Investments or Ownership Investments? You can invest money in two ways, by lending or by owning. When you lend your money, you receive some form of IOU and the promise of repayment plus interest. The interest is a form of current income while you hold the investment.

You can lend by depositing money in banks, credit unions, and savings and loan associations (via savings accounts and certificates of deposit) or by lending money to governments (via Treasury notes and bonds as well as state and local bonds), businesses (corporate bonds), mortgage-backed bonds (such as Ginnie Maes), and life insurance companies (annuities).

These lending investments, or **debts**, generally offer both a fixed maturity and a fixed income. With a **fixed maturity**, the borrower agrees to repay the principal to the investor on a specific date. With a **fixed income**, the borrower agrees to pay the investor a specific rate of return for use of the principal. Such investments allow lenders to be fairly confident that they will receive a certain amount of interest income for a specified period of time and that the borrowed funds will eventually be returned. Thus, the return is somewhat assured. No matter how much profit the borrower makes with your funds, the investing lender at best receives only the fixed return promised at the time of the initial investment. Lending investments almost never include capital gains.

An active investor keeps a close watch on the economy and financial markets.

Alternatively, you may invest money through ownership of an asset. Ownership investments are often called **equities** or **ownership equities**. You can buy common or preferred corporate stock (to obtain part ownership in a corporation) in publicly owned companies, purchase shares in a mutual fund company (which invests your funds in corporate stocks and bonds), put money into your own business, purchase real estate, buy commodity futures (pork bellies or oranges), or buy investment-quality collectibles (such as rare antiques or coins). Ownership investments have the potential for providing current income; however, the emphasis is upon achieving substantial capital gains.

Making Short-, Intermediate-, and Long-Term Investments When investing for a short-term goal, such as less than one or even five years, you would want to be very conservative to ensure that a sudden drop in the market would not jeopardize your reaching the goal before the market has time to recover. You want to be confident that you preserve the value of what you have. After all, you don't want to lose money in an investment when you need to use that money for a near-term goal, such as college tuition, or be forced to sell an investment because you need cash in a hurry. People with a short or intermediate time horizon require investments that offer some predictability and stability. As a result, these investors are usually more interested in current income than capital gains. Stick with insured bank certificates of deposit, money market funds and other sure investments. By contrast, if you are investing to achieve long-term goals, you want your money to grow. Long-term investors usually invite more risk by seeking capital gains as well as some current income.

When investing for long-term goals, you can afford to be more aggressive. That is one reason why the stock market is a good place to save for retirement. After you retire, you should still leave a portion of your portfolio in stocks or stock mutual funds since you likely will still have 20 to 25 years before you need the last dollars in your nest egg. Moreover, most people should invest aggressively for the long term and conservatively for the short term.

Long-term investors seek growth in the value of their investments that exceeds the rate of inflation. In other words, they want their investments to provide a positive **real rate of return**. This is the return after subtracting the effects of both inflation and income taxes.

debts
Lending investments that typically offer both a fixed maturity and a fixed income.

fixed maturity
Specific date on which a borrower agrees to repay the principal to the investor.

fixed income
Specific rate of return that a borrower agrees to pay the investor for use of the principal (initial investment).

equities
Ownership equities such as common or preferred stocks, equity mutual funds, real estate, and so on that focus on capital gains more than on income.

real rate of return
Return on an investment after subtracting the effects of inflation and income taxes.

Choose Investments for Their Components of Total Return When investing, you want to build a portfolio of investments that will provide the necessary potential total return through current income and capital gains in the proportions that you desire. One stock might provide an anticipated cash dividend of 1.5 percent and a projected annual price appreciation of 8 percent, for a total anticipated return of 9.5 percent. Another choice offering the same projected total return might be a stock with expected annual cash dividends of 2.5 percent and capital gains of 7 percent.

13.2f   Deal Only with Financial Advisors Who Are Fiduciaries

suitability standard

A requirement followed by financial advisors, consultants, and specialists that requires them to act in the best interest of their employer rather than the best interest of their clients.

Most investors think that financial advisors are required to put clients' interests first. This is false! Most financial advisors are considered **brokers**, and they only adhere to what is known as a **suitability standard**. Thus they are free to sell investments generating the heftiest profits and commissions, as long as they are judged "suitable" for a client based on factors like investment goals, age or risk tolerance. Plus their recommendations usually are not the lowest-cost alternatives. The suitability standard requires that they act in the best interest of their *employer*, not in the best interest of their clients. Those who follow the suitability standard include financial advisors, consultants and specialists.

The financial advisor you need is one who adheres to a **fiduciary standard**. This means they are legally obligated to always act in the best interest of the client at all times, even at the cost of their own, when giving advice or recommendations. To determine which standard your advisor adheres to, just ask; and be wary if the advisor won't answer or says the suitability standard is just fine.

CONCEPT CHECK 13.2

1. Review the risk pyramid in Figure 13-2 to identify three investments that appeal to you and fit your tolerance for risk.
2. Summarize your investment philosophy (conservative, moderate, or aggressive) and say why you hold those views.
3. Indicate whether you view yourself as an active or passive investor, and explain why.
4. Summarize your personal views on lending or owning investments.
5. Comment on how investing differs for both short and long-term investments.

Learning Objective 3
Describe the major factors that affect the rate of return on investments.

13.3   RISKS AND OTHER FACTORS AFFECT THE INVESTOR'S RETURN

To be a successful investor, you must understand the major factors that affect the rate of return on investments. Being informed, you can then take the appropriate risks when making investment decisions.

13.3a   Random Risk Is Reduced by Diversification, Eventually

random/unsystematic risk

Risk associated with owning only one investment of a particular type (such as stock in one company) that, by chance, may do very poorly in the future due to uncontrollable or random factors that do not affect the rest of the market.

diversification

Process of reducing risk by spreading investment money among several different investment opportunities.

Random risk (also called **unsystematic risk**) is the risk associated with owning only one investment of a particular type (such as stock in one company) that, by chance, may do very poorly in the future because of uncontrollable or random factors, such as labor unrest, lawsuits, and product recalls. If you invest in only one stock, its value might rise or fall. If you invest in two or three stocks, the odds are lessened that all of their prices will fall at the same time. Such **diversification**—the process of reducing risk by spreading investment money among several different investment opportunities—provides one effective method of managing random risk as it reduces the ups and downs of a portfolio.

The principle holds that when you own different types of investment assets in a portfolio, some assets should be rising when others are falling. It results in a potential rate of return on all of the investments that is *lower* than the potential return on a single alternative, but the return is more predictable and the risk of loss is lower. Diversification does not mean that you will not lose money. Diversification averages out the high and low returns. While investors might be disappointed with a lower return from a diversified portfolio, they would be even more disappointed by the return in a down market from one that is poorly diversified.

Research suggests that you can cut random risk in half by diversifying into as few as five stocks or bonds; you can eliminate random risk by holding 15 or more stocks or bonds. Rational investors diversify so as to reduce random risk, and over the long term—as little as a decade—it works. You also can diversify by investing in foreign markets.

13.3b Market Risk

Diversification among stocks or bonds cannot eliminate all risks. Some risk would exist even if you owned all of the stocks in a market because stock prices in general move up and down over time. **Market risk** (also known as **systematic** or **nondiversifiable risk**) is the possibility for an investor to experience losses due to unknown factors that affect the overall performance of the financial markets.

What Causes Market Risk? Market risk occurs when the value of an investment drops due to influences and events that affect all similar investments. Examples include a change in economic, social, political, or general market conditions; fluctuations in investor preferences; or other broad market-moving factors, such as a recession, political turmoil, changes in interest rates, and terrorist attacks. Market risk cannot be eliminated but it can be reduced by dividing your portfolio among several different markets.

Market Risk in an Investor's Portfolio Market risk remains after an investor's portfolio has been fully diversified within a particular market. Over the years, market risk for all investments has averaged about 8 percent. As a consequence of this risk, the return on any single securities investment (such as a stock), through no fault of its own, might vary up and down about 8 percent annually. The total risk in an investment consists of the sum of the random risk and the market risk.

13.3c Types of Investment Risks

A number of other investment risks affect investor returns:

- **Business failure risk.** **Business failure risk**, also called **financial risk**, is the possibility that the investment will fail, perhaps go bankrupt, and result in a massive or total loss of one's invested funds.

- **Inflation risk.** Inflation risk may be the most important concern for the long-term investor. **Inflation risk,** also called **purchasing power risk,** is the danger that your money will not grow as fast as inflation and therefore not be worth as much in the future as it is today. Over the long term, inflation in the United States has averaged 3.1 percent annually. Historically, common stocks and real estate have reduced inflation risk, as their values tend to rise with inflation over many years. However, all ownership investments are also subject to **deflation risk.** This is the chance that the value of an investment will decline when overall prices decline.

- **Time horizon risk.** The role of time affects all investments. The sooner your invested money is supposed to be returned to you—the **time horizon** of an investment—the less the likelihood that something could go wrong. The more time

market risk/systematic risk/ undiversifiable risk
The possibility for an investor to experience losses due to unknown factors that affect the overall performance of the financial markets.

business failure risk (financial risk)
Possibility that an investment will fail to pay a return to the investor.

your money is invested, the more it is at risk. For taking longer-term risks, investors expect and normally receive higher returns.

- **Regulatory risk. Regulatory risk** (sometimes called **political risk**) results from changes in the income tax or legal environments imposed by a government. As the government's climate change regulations go into effect, profits for some companies may decrease sharply while others may rise.

- **Business-cycle risk.** As we discussed in Chapter 1, economic growth usually does not occur in a smooth and steady manner and this affects profits as well as investment returns. This is known as business-cycle risk. Periods of expansion lasting three or four years are often followed by contractions in the economy, called **recessions,** that may last a year or longer. The profits of most industries follow the business cycle. Some businesses do not experience business-cycle risk because they continue to earn profits during economic downturns. Examples are gasoline retailers, supermarkets, and utility companies.

- **Market-volatility risk.** All investments are subject to occasional sharp changes in price as a result of events affecting a particular company or the overall market for similar investments, and this is market-volatility risk. For example, the value of a single stock, such as that of a technology company like Apple, might change 5 or even 10 percent in a single day. Also, all technology stocks could decline 2 or perhaps 5 percent if two or three competitors announce poor earnings. In recent years the number of days with a 4 percent swing in the overall stock market prices ranged from 2 to 11.

- **Global investment risk.** The more globally diversified your portfolio, the smoother your total investment returns should be over time. However, it also exposes you to unknowns. It's challenging to invest in overseas markets, and this is particularly relevant when you consider that the outlooks for different regions vary depending on recent economic conditions. Reliable accounting and financial information is often scarce in global investing, as well.

- **Liquidity risk.** Liquidity is the speed and ease with which an asset can be converted to cash. You can sell your stock investments in one day, but rules state that it may take up to four days to have the proceeds available in cash. You will never truly know the value of liquidity until you need it and you do not have it. Liquidity risk is the risk that a given security or asset cannot be traded quickly enough in the market to prevent a loss (or make the required profit). Real estate is **illiquid** because it may take weeks, months, or even years to sell.

- **Marketability risk.** When you have to sell a certain asset quickly, it may not sell at or near the market price. This possibility is referred to as **marketability risk.** Selling real estate in a hurry, for example, may require the seller to substantially reduce the price in order to sell to a willing buyer.

- **Reinvestment risk. Reinvestment risk** is the risk that the return on a future investment will not be the same as the return earned by the original investment.

13.3d **Transaction Costs Reduce Returns**

While you cannot know in advance the return you will earn on an investment, you can calculate in advance the transaction costs. For starters, you can save on commission costs by using less expensive brokers (examined in Chapter 14).

Commissions are usually the largest transaction cost in investments. These are fees or percentages of the units or selling price paid to salespeople, agents, and companies for their services—that is, to buy or sell an investment. The commission charged to buy an investment (one commission) and then later sell it (a second commission) is partially based on the value of the transaction. Commission ranges are as follows: stocks, 1.5 to 2.5 percent (although trades can be made on the Internet for less than $10); bonds, 0 to 2.0 percent; mutual funds, 0 to 8.5 percent; real estate, 4.5 to 7.5 percent; options and futures contracts, 4.0 to 6.0 percent; limited partnerships, 10.0 to 15.0 percent; and collectibles, 15.0 to 30.0 percent.

business-cycle risk
The fact that economic growth usually does not occur in a smooth and steady manner, and this impacts profits as well as investment returns.

market-volatility risk
The fact that all investments are subject to occasional sharp changes in price as a result of events affecting a particular company or the overall market for similar investments.

liquidity
The speed and ease with which an asset can be converted to cash.

liquidity risk
The risk that a given security or asset cannot be traded quickly enough in the market to prevent a loss (or make the required profit).

commissions
Fees or percentages of the selling price paid to salespeople, agents, and companies for their services in buying or selling an investment.

A portfolio of stock mutual funds that charge the cheapest management fees will grow to $1.2 million over 25 years, while a portfolio of those with the most expensive fees will only grow to $850,000. Investing guru Burton Malkiel says "The one thing I know is that the lower the fee, the more money is left for me." Making investments with the lowest possible transaction costs is really important.

13.3e Leverage May or May Not Increase Returns

Another factor that can affect return on investment is leverage. In the leveraging process, borrowed funds are used to make an investment with the goal of earning a rate of return in excess of the after-tax costs of borrowing. You can become financially overextended by using leverage, a factor you should not ignore.

leverage
Using borrowed funds to invest with the goal of earning a rate of return in excess of the after-tax costs of borrowing.

CONCEPT CHECK 13.3

1. What is random risk, and how does it get reduced?
2. Explain market risk, what causes it, and how it fits in one's portfolio.
3. Summarize three other types of investment risks that seem important to you.
4. Explain how transactions costs and leverage may increase or decrease investment returns.

13.4 ACCEPT THE REALITIES OF THE MARKET AND AVOID INVESTING MISTAKES

Learning Objective 4
Accept the realities of the market and avoid investing mistakes that other inviduals make.

Investing is not rocket science! Anyone reading this book and following its recommendations for making long-term investments can become a successful investor, particularly if they are knowledgeable about and avoid the mistakes of other investors.

13.4a Long-Term Investors Understand Bull and Bear Markets and Corrections

Long-term investors understand how the securities markets (places where stocks and bonds are traded) are performing as a whole. That is, are the markets moving up, moving down, or remaining stagnant?

securities markets
Places where stocks and bonds are traded (or in the case of electronic trading, the way in which securities are traded).

Bull Markets Are Profitable for Investors A bull market results when securities prices have risen 20 percent or more over time. Historically, the recent 20 bull markets averaging 55 months in length have seen an average gain of 159 percent.

bull market
Market in which securities prices have risen 20 percent or more over time.

Bear Markets Turn into Bull Markets A securities market in which prices have declined in value by 20 percent or more from previous highs, often over the course of several weeks or months, is called a bear market. Five bear markets have occurred since 1980, and they averaged 17 months in length. Bear markets are what clear the decks for a longer-lasting recovery and drives valuations down to truly low levels from which bigger gains can spring. The last two bear markets were among the worst in American history. On average, investors recoup all their money lost during a bear market in 11 to 44 months.

bear market
Market in which securities prices have declined in value by 20 percent or more from previous highs, often over the course of several weeks or months.

A **bull** in the market is a person who optimistically expects securities prices to go up. A **bear** pessimistically expects the general market to decline. The origin of these terms is unknown, but some suggest that they refer to the ways that the animals attack: Bears thrust their claws downward, and bulls move their horns upward. Historically, bear markets last, on average, about 17 months. The bear market of 2007 to 2009 saw stock prices decline 55 percent. Then the optimistic bull buyers took over thinking that surely the U.S. economy had already reached rock bottom and that stock prices were certain to rise as the economy recovered. Since March 2009 when stock prices stopped falling the U.S. bull market saw a 100+ percent rally in just a few years, a gigantic move, and stocks rose an amazing 300 percent in only 6 years.

THE TAX CONSEQUENCES IN INVESTMENT FUNDAMENTALS

There are some favorable aspects to income taxes to think about when making investments.

1. ***Income versus capital gain.*** *Current investment income, such as dividends and interest, is taxed at one's marginal tax bracket, likely 25 percent. Capital gains are taxed at special lower rates, likely at 10 or 15 percent.*

2. ***Tax-deferred investments.*** *The income and capital gains from investments within employer-sponsored retirement accounts are not subject to income taxes until the funds are withdrawn. Thus such investments rise in value much more quickly than those that are taxed.*

3. ***After-tax return.*** *When comparing similar investments, your objective is to earn the best after-tax return. This return is the net amount earned on an investment after payment of income taxes. (See Equation 4.1 on page 140.)*

4. ***Tax-exempt income.*** *Income earned from municipal bonds is exempt from federal income taxes.*

5. ***Tax-exempt investment account.*** *The income and capital gains from investments within Roth IRA accounts are not subject to income taxes, unless the funds are removed from the account within five years of opening it.*

The lesson after every market crash has been that investors who ride it out or invest more do much better in the long run than people who panic and bail! Stay calm because patience is critically important when investing for the long term. The market will continue its inexorable march upward over the decades on the way to new all-time records.

Market Corrections Also Occur Another type of short-term market trend is called a market correction, which typically occur about every 11 months. A **market correction** is a reverse movement of at least 10 percent in a stock, bond, commodity, or index to adjust for recent, too rapid, price rises. Market corrections interrupt an uptrend in the market or an asset. But the market usually rebounds fairly quickly as opposed to a bear market which requires a longer rebound.

When markets churn and sputter, many investors worry too much because retirement balances shrink some, and then a bit more. Market corrections and bear markets are uncomfortable and painful. Know, however, that as always the stock market will rebound.

13.4b Long-Term Investors Accept Substantial Market Volatility

Market volatility is the price dispersion of a financial instrument based on historical prices over the specified period with the last observation the most recent price. If the prices of a security fluctuate rapidly in a short time span, it is termed to have high volatility. If the prices of a security fluctuate slowly in a longer time span, it is termed to have low volatility. The wider the swings in an investment's price, the harder emotionally it is to not worry. Also realize that price volatility presents opportunities to buy assets cheaply and then sell when they are overpriced. Volatility is also known as how much "excitement" you are willing to live with when investing.

In an average year, the price of a typical stock fluctuates up and down by about 50 percent; thus, the price of a stock selling for $30 per share in January might range from $15 to $45 before the end of the following December. It is not unusual for overall stock market prices to fall (or rise) 3, 4, or 5 percent in a single day. In a recent year the stock market fluctuated 11 times by more than 4 percent in *one day*.

market correction

A short term price decline in the stock markets of at least 10 percent in a stock, bond, commodity or index to adjust for a recent price rises.

market volatility

The likelihood of large price swings in securities due to a company's success (or lack of it) and various market conditions.

Long-term investors—who do not buy and sell very often—must learn to accept—and ignore—market volatility.

13.4c Long-Term Investors Do Not Practice Market Timing

Investors get into trouble when they start to think too much like traders. **Market timers** attempt to predict the short-term movements of various markets (or market segments) and, based on those predictions, move assets from one segment to another in order to capture market gains and avoid market losses. Essentially, market timers try to outguess the trend of stock prices. For example, an investor worried about the future might sell his or her stock investments and move to cash. Another investor who anticipates increasing future stock prices might get 100 percent invested in stocks.

To succeed in timing the market, you need to know just the right time to buy and just the right time to sell, know what signals suggest you take action, and exhibit the discipline to do it. Market timers sometimes sell at the first sign of trouble and then keep their money out of the market until better opportunities are apparent. If you try to time the market, you are just as likely to miss an upswing as you are to avoid a downswing. Note that market timers are competing against graduates from business schools in Chicago, Stanford, and Wharton who learn to do the same job full time for big paychecks.

13.4d Long-Term Investors Avoid Trading Mistakes

Long-term investors avoid making mistakes when making investing decisions, and there are many ways people mess up.

Being Overconfident Investors tend to believe that they know more than they really do. Because they know so much they think they can figure out the future and invest so they can beat the market. A bias toward optimism helps explain why many investors think they can do it.

Setting Unrealistic Goals A common investing mistake is to let unrealistic goals get into your head as wise choices. For example, evaluating success using too short a time frame, perhaps a single year, is inappropriate when perhaps a decade-long perspective would make more sense. Overconfidence can make you take much more risk than you normally would, and it can result in substantial losses.

Trading Too Much One cause of lower returns is trading too much. The more you trade, the more likely you are to make a wealth-destroying mistake. Here investors often fear regret and seek pride. If you sell a losing investment, you are admitting that it was a mistake to buy it in the first place. If you sell a winner, you can be proud. Such investors, who typically are overconfident, often sell winners too soon and keep losers too long. Don't make the mistake of trading when you should be making long-term investments.

Research shows that men make more trading mistakes than women, and it costs them a fortune. Studies of 35,000 households by University of California's professors Barber and Odean demonstrates that women outperform their male counterparts by about 1.0 percentage point each year. The main reason is they trade less often. Trading reduces men's net returns by 2.65 percentage points a year as opposed to women's 1.72 percentage points.

When the return on one's investment portfolio beats another's by about 1 percentage point every year, there are serious long-term results. Investing $4,000 annually for 30 years earning 6 percent shows that the first portfolio will amount to $316,000 and the second earning 5 percent will be $266,000, a $50,000 difference, and that adds up to 18.8 percent more. Proof that trading too much and losing a "little" 1 percent return makes a big difference over time!

BIAS TOWARD—CHASING HOT INVESTMENTS

People have a bias toward pursuing recent performance. They often see investments as good or bad based on the latest performance and chase hot investments expecting to cash in as the investments continue to rise even higher, only to see them drop in price. What to do? Avoid speculation and in the future invest only on fundamentally sound information, not what is hot.

market timers

Investors who attempt to predict the short-term movements of various markets (or market segments) and, based on those predictions, move capital from one segment to another in order to capture market gains and avoid market losses.

THERE IS AN APP FOR THAT!

- Acorns
- Betterment
- FinMason
- Kapitall
- Openfolio
- iQuantifi
- Rebalance IRA
- Robinhood
- SigFig
- Sumday
- Tip'd Off
- Wealthfront

DID YOU KNOW ?

Money Websites for Investment Fundamentals

Informative websites for investment fundamentals, including tips for young adults are:

Fundamentals of Investing (www.financialwisdom.com)

Financial Soundings' auto-rebalance accounts (www.financialsoundings.com)

How To Be Set For Life (www.howtobesetforlife.com/articles/6-investment-fundamentals)

Motley Fool (www.fool.com/how-to-invest/thirteen-steps/index.aspx)

Wikipedia on asset allocation (en.wikipedia.org/wiki/Asset_allocation)

Long-Term Investors Avoid Too Many "Facts."

Buying High and Selling Low Emotion, not logic, too often rules investing decisions. Investors often overreact when buying and selling as their thinking goes through alternating times of panic and euphoria. When plunging portfolio values become too much to accept, investors often just want the pain to end so they sell, which presumably means big losses. This is "buying high and selling low," which is the opposite of what investors should do.

Borrowing to Invest to Recover Losses Sometimes investors will be unwisely tempted to turn to borrowed money to invest. This is almost never smart. Investors often can borrow from their stockbroker.

Taking on Too Much Risk Being realistic is what long-term investing is all about, and it does not include taking on too much risk. Investors who have suffered a substantial loss in a stock position are limited to three options: sell and take a loss, hold and hope, or double down. Selling in such a situation is not fun, so instead an investor may follow the **hold and hope** strategy. It requires waiting for the stock to return to your purchase price, which may take a long time if it ever happens at all.

The **averaging down** (also called **doubling down**) strategy requires that you throw good money after bad in hopes that the stock will perform well, particularly if you are desperate to get even on your investment. Here you buy more shares to reduce your average cost, which includes what you paid for the original shares.

For example if you liked a share of stock when you bought it at $40, you will love it at $20 after the price weakens. Assume you own 100 shares of XYZ stock that cost $40 ($4,000 invested) and it has slowly declined in price to $20. Thus if you sell and take the loss (ignoring transaction expenses), you will be down $2,000 ($4,000 invested versus $2,000 proceeds). When averaging down you would invest $2,000 more (100 shares at $20 each) at the new lower price. Now, you are in for $6,000 (100 shares times today's price of $20 plus $4,000 originally invested). If the price rises to $30 and you sell, you are all square ($30 × 200 total shares = $6,000). If you are confident that only the company's share price had changed, and not its genuine value, then you might average down. In truth, sometimes averaging down works and sometimes it doesn't.

Being Loss Averse Investors who suffer from the **loss aversion effect** are ones who lose money in their investments and later become more reluctant to take risks. Then they strongly prefer avoiding losses in the future. Research shows that losses are twice as powerful, psychologically, as gains. Some such investors sometimes give up on investing permanently; not a prescription for long-term financial success.

13.4e Market Timing Loses Money

Market efficiency (or efficient markets) has to do with the speed at which new information is reflected in investment prices. The theory is that security prices are reflective of their true value at all times because publicly available information has driven market prices to the correct level.

When information is reported in the financial press, it is already too late for most investors to act and make a profit. And they don't always even know what the new information is or if it is even relevant.

As a result, active investors cannot pursue an investment strategy that beats the market because they are just as likely to invest in an overpriced security rather than one that is undervalued. Because of market efficiency, active investors are challenged to buy underpriced securities and sell overpriced securities.

Research shows that individuals are abysmal market timers. Efficient market theory tells you to think twice, and then a third time before you (or your stockbroker) commit to actively investing to beat a market.

Not surprisingly, stock analysts and investment managers believe they can make better choices than the average active investor in part because they can act on information more quickly than others. The reality is, however, that 70 to 80 percent of investment managers, and oftentimes 90 percent in any given year fail to beat the average returns of the stock market.

13.4f Avoid Herd Behavior

When the market prices are rapidly rising, people are fooled into thinking that it is safe to invest more ("I've got to put more money in there"). They lose their sense of caution because it must be safe if everyone else is buying. People with a tendency to join in and follow the crowd tend to push stock prices too far up or down. They look at behavior and assume it is based on knowledge, but often it's not. This is an illustration of **herd behavior**, which arises when investors decide to copy the observed decisions of other investors or movements in the markets rather than follow their own beliefs and information.

herd behavior
When emotion, not logic, rules investing decisions and investors decide to copy the observed decisions of other investors or movements in the markets rather than follow their own beliefs and information.

NUMBERS ON

Investment Fundamentals

- Since 1871, the stock market has spent 40 percent of all years either rising or falling more than 20 percent, thus booms and busts are perfectly normal.

- More than half (52 percent) of Americans are not invested in stocks or mutual funds, or through a retirement account such as a 401(k) or IRA.

- The total market value of publicly traded shares of stock is over $21 trillion.

- Over 40 percent of adults disagree with the statement "My parents provided a good example of how to have a successful financial future."

- When financially successful millennials were asked to describe what money means to them, 42% chose

"security," 22% selected "stress" and 21% chose "comfort."

- Only one-quarter of adults under age 35 own stocks or stock mutual funds.

- Seventy-five percent of adults agree that they could benefit from some advice and answers to financial questions from a professional.

- One-third of adults have made a comprehensive financial plan that goes beyond a simple household budget to cover things like retirement savings and insurance.

- Half of those who have prepared a comprehensive financial plan feel on pace to meet all of their financial goals, such as saving for emergencies and for retirement.

Herd behavior sometimes results in a **stock market bubble** (or **bubble**). It is a surge in equity prices, often more than warranted by the fundamentals and usually in a particular sector, followed by a drastic drop in prices as a massive selloff occurs. Behavioral finance theory attributes stock market bubbles to cognitive biases that lead to groupthink and herd behavior. Valuations sometimes race higher for years before eventually popping. The USA had a dot.com bubble in the late 1990s and a real estate bubble in the mid-2000s. A stock market bubble creates the risk of a significant bear market.

13.4g Ignore 24-Hour Financial News Chatter

Some investors feel compelled to look at prices every day on their smart phones, in the newspapers, or by watching the 24-hour financial news chatter, such as CNBC and CNN. Talking heads spew financial factoids with minute-by-minute updates and sensationalize every blip in the stock markets. Such arcane and sometimes meaningless information creates anxiety or mania that can lead to bad decision making.

Acquiring more "facts" is not the same as gaining knowledge or expertise. You are under no obligation to read or watch financial news. If you do, you are under no obligation to take any of it seriously. The kinds of news and information on cable news and the blogosphere are not designed to appeal to our long-term, rational thought processes. It excites our emotions and fears, and sometimes stokes our prejudices and cynicism. It compels action, not patience. To long-term investors such financial chatter is just noise.

Therefore, don't check your portfolio. Ignore that kind of information. Just go away and live a normal life. Stay focused on your long-term investing strategy and make decisions accordingly. Otherwise, your returns will be less than the averages, like those of most American investors.

CONCEPT CHECK 13.4

1. Distinguish between bull and bear markets.
2. What should long-term investors do about market volatility?
3. Identify three trading mistakes that can be avoided by long-term investors.
4. Summarize how herd behavior sometimes leads to a stock market bubble.

Learning Objective 5

Decide which of the four safe and effective long-term investment strategies you will utilize.

13.5 FOUR SAFE AND EFFECTIVE STRATEGIES FOR LONG-TERM INVESTORS

To succeed financially, you must establish your own long-term investment strategies. And follow them! Don't sabotage your plan by making mistakes, like those described above. There are only four long-term safe and effective investment strategies to follow, and they all hang together.

13.4a Strategy 1: Buy-and-Hold Anticipates Long-Term Economic Growth

The secret to long-term investing success is benign neglect. Long-term investors need to relax with the confidence and knowledge that investing regularly and not trading frequently will create a substantial portfolio over time. Long-term investors do not follow or react emotionally to the day-to-day changes that occur in the market. Ignoring them is the best advice. Because most people are overly sensitive to short-term losses, daily monitoring could motivate one to make shortsighted buying and selling decisions.

Selling high-quality assets in a bear market is a poor strategy because sellers "lock in" their losses. Plus they fail to realize that bear markets are typically short in duration (recently about 17 months). It is smart to buy more shares when prices are lower during market downturns because rising prices in a bull market always follow a bear market.

Most long-term investors use the investment strategy **buy and hold** (also called **buy to hold**). That is, they buy a widely diversified mix of stocks and/or mutual funds, reinvest the dividends by buying more stocks and mutual funds, and hold on to those investments almost indefinitely. With this approach, the investor expects that the values of the assets will increase over the long run in tandem with the growth of the U.S. and world economies. The investments may pay some current income as well. The investor's emphasis is on holding the assets through both good and bad economic times with the confidence that their values will go up over the long term. This is a wise strategy.

Some critics argue that "buy and hold" is a discredited concept. But they are wrong because this remains the best approach for investing over 20 years or longer. Long-term investors must have the patience and fortitude necessary to tolerate bear markets, no matter how severe.

Buy and hold does not mean buy and ignore. Review your whole portfolio once a year to make sure that each remains a good investment. Questions to ask include: "Is the valuation too high?"; "Has the fundamental outlook of the investment changed?"; "Does this asset still fit my investment plan?"; "Would I buy it today?" If absolutely necessary, sell the asset and keep the remainder of your portfolio.

13.4b Strategy 2: Portfolio Diversification Reduces Portfolio Volatility

Owning too much of any one investment creates too great a financial risk. Experts advise that you never keep more than 5 or 10 percent of your assets in one investment, especially including your employer's stock. Many workers who invested too much in their employer's stock have seen their retirement funds disappear or be drastically reduced in value when their employers' stocks plunged in price.

Diversification is the single most important rule in investing. **Portfolio diversification** is the practice of selecting a collection of different asset classes of investments (such as stocks, bonds, mutual funds, real estate, and cash) that are chosen not only for their potential returns but also for their dissimilar risk-return characteristics.

The goal of portfolio diversification is to create a collection of investments that will provide an acceptable level of return and an acceptable exposure to risk. This outcome can be achieved because asset classes typically react differently to economic and marketplace changes. The major benefit of having a diversified portfolio is that when one asset class performs poorly, there is a good chance that another will perform well, and vice versa, thus this strategy helps control your exposure to risk.

As shown in Figure 13-3 diversification reduces portfolio volatility while averaging out an investor's return. If you were totally invested in the investment that rose 13 percent, you would be happy; if you were totally invested in the investment that declined 10 percent, you would be sad. Instead your diversified portfolio over 9 investments averaged 7.1 percent, which is a respectable return. Diversification lowers the odds that you will lose money investing and increases the odds that you will make money.

The lack of diversification can quickly destroy one's investment portfolio. Table 13-1 illustrates the point demonstrating that when stocks crash 50 percent, a $200,000 portfolio that is poorly diversified (too heavy on equities in this case) is devastated, in this case down $85,000.

13.4c Strategy 3: Dollar-Cost Averaging Buys at "Below-Average" Costs

Dollar-cost averaging (or **cost averaging**) is a systematic program of investing equal sums of money at regular intervals regardless of the price of the investment. In this approach, the same fixed dollar amount is invested in the same stock or mutual fund at regular intervals over a long time. Since investments generally increase in price more than they fall, the "averaging" means that you purchase more shares when the price is down and fewer shares when the price is high. Most of the shares are, therefore, purchased at **below-average costs**.

buy and hold/buy to hold
Investment strategy in which investors buy a widely diversified mix of stocks and/or mutual funds, reinvest the dividends by buying more stocks and mutual funds, and hold onto those investments almost indefinitely.

portfolio diversification
Practice of selecting a collection of different asset classes of investments (such as stocks, bonds, mutual funds, real estate, and cash) that are chosen not only for their potential returns but also for their dissimilar risk-return characteristics.

DO IT IN CLASS

dollar-cost averaging/cost averaging
Systematic program of investing equal sums of money at regular intervals, regardless of the price of the investment.

below-average costs
Average costs of an investment if more shares are purchased when the price is down and fewer shares are purchased when the price is high.

Figure 13-3 Diversification Via Asset Allocation Averages an Investor's Return

This chart represents a hypothetical mix of winning and losing various investments after one year. One investment, for instance, increased in value 13 percent; another declined 6 percent. While some investments lost value, over the year those losses were offset with the gains of others, and the overall portfolio earned a 7.1 percent average return.

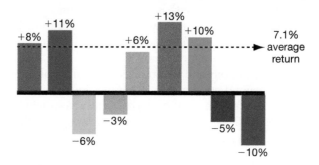

Table 13-1 Market Crashes Destroy Unbalanced Portfolios

Beginning Portfolio Values ($200,000 each)			Ending Portfolio Values	
Portfolio A—Nicely Balanced Between Bonds and Stocks			**Stocks Jump 10%**	**Stocks Crash 50%***
Cash	Bonds	Equities†		
10%	45%	45%		
$20,000	$90,000	$90,000	+$9,000	−$45,000
Portfolio B—Light on Bonds and Heavy on Equities				
Cash	Bonds	Equities†		
5%	10%	85%		
$10,000	$20,000	$170,000	+$17,000	−$85,000

*Decline from previous high in stock market prices during severe economic recession.
†Equity portion of portfolio rises or falls with changes in stock market prices.

This strategy avoids the risks and responsibilities of investment timing because the stock purchases are made regularly (usually every month) regardless of the price. It also ignores all outside events and short-term gyrations of the market, providing the investor with a disciplined long-term buying strategy. Most retirement investors use dollar-cost averaging even if they don't realize it.

Table 13-2 shows the results of dollar-cost averaging for a stock under varying market conditions (commissions are excluded). As an example, assume that you invest $300 into a stock every three months. Notice that dollar-cost averaging is successful in all three scenarios illustrated.

In a Fluctuating Market To illustrate the effects of dollar-cost averaging, assume that you first invested funds during the "fluctuating market" shown in Table 13-2. Because the initial price is $15 per share, you receive 20 shares for your investment of $300. Then the market drops—an extreme but easy-to-follow example—and the price falls

Table 13-2 — Dollar-Cost Averaging for a Stock or Mutual Fund Investment

	Fluctuating Market			Declining Market			Rising Market		
	Regular Investment	Share Price	Shares Acquired	Regular Investment	Share Price	Shares Acquired	Regular Investment	Share Price	Shares Acquired
	$300	$15	20	$300	$15	20	$300	$6	50
	300	10	30	300	10	30	300	10	30
	300	15	20	300	10	30	300	12	25
	300	10	30	300	6	50	300	15	20
	300	15	20	300	5	60	300	20	15
Totals	$1,500	$65	120	$1,500	$46	190	$1,500	$63	140
	Average share price: $13.00 ($65 ÷ 5)* Average share cost: $12.50 ($1,500 ÷ 120)†			Average share price: $9.20 ($46 ÷ 5)* Average share cost: $7.89 ($1,500 ÷ 190)†			Average share price: $12.60 ($63 ÷ 5)* Average share cost: $10.71 ($1,500 ÷ 140)†		

*Sum of share price total ÷ number of investment periods.

† Total amount invested ÷ total shares purchased.

to $10 per share. When you buy $300 worth of the stock now, you receive 30 shares. Three months later, the market price rebounds to $15 and you invest another $300, receiving 20 shares. The price then drops and rises again.

You now own 120 shares, thanks to your total investment of $1,500. The **average share price** is calculated by averaging the amounts paid for the investment: Simply divide the share price total by the number of investment periods. In this example, the average share price is $13 ($65 ÷ 5). The **average share cost**, a more meaningful amount, is the actual cost basis of the investment used for income tax purposes.

It is calculated by dividing the total amount invested by the total shares purchased. In this example, it is $12.50 ($1,500 ÷ 120). Based on the recent price of $15 per share, each of your 120 shares is worth on average $2.50 ($15 − $12.50) more than you paid for it. Thus, your gain is $300 (120 × $2.50; or $15 × 120 = $1,800, $1,800 − $1,500 = $300).

In a Declining Market Markets may also decline over a time period. The "declining market" columns in Table 13-2 (perhaps representing a bear market of 15 months) show purchases of 190 shares for increasingly lower prices that eventually reach $5 per share at the bottom of the business cycle. In a declining market, if you keep investing using dollar-cost averaging, you will purchase a large volume of shares. If you sell when the market is down substantially, you will lose money on your investment.

In this example, you have purchased 190 shares at an average cost of $7.89, and they now have a depressed price of $5. Selling at this point would result in a substantial loss of $550 [$1,500 − (190 × $5)]. Investing in buying more shares during a lousy market can be a benefit because shares are accumulated at low prices.

In a Rising Market During the "rising market" in Table 13-2, you continue to invest but buy fewer shares. The $1,500 investment during the bull market bought only 140 shares for an average cost of $10.71. In this rising market, you profit because your 140 shares have a recent market price of $20 per share, for a total value of $2,800 (140 × $20).

Almost anyone can profit in a rising market. If you use dollar-cost averaging over the long term, you will continue to buy in rising, falling, and fluctuating markets. The overall result will be that you buy more shares when the cost is down, thereby lowering the average share cost to below-average prices.

The totals in Table 13-2, for example, reveal an overall investment of $4,500 ($1,500 + $1,500 + $1,500) used to purchase 450 shares (120 + 190 + 140) for an average cost of

average share price

Calculated by dividing the share price total by the number of investment periods.

average share cost

Actual cost basis of the investment used for income tax purposes, calculated by dividing the total amount invested by the total shares purchased.

ADVICE FROM A SEASONED PRO

Use a Dividend-Reinvestment Plan to Dollar-Cost Average

Many well-known companies allow investors to purchase shares of stock on a dollar-cost basis directly from them without the assistance of a stockbroker and then to continue to invest on a regular basis with low or no brokerage commissions. Such a program is known as a **dividend-reinvestment plan (DRIP).** You simply sign up with the company, agreeing to buy a certain number of shares and to reinvest cash dividends into more shares of stock for little or no transaction fees. Investors' accounts are credited with fractional shares, too.

The Direct Stock Purchase Plan Clearinghouse at www.dripinvestor.com/clearinghouse/home.asp manages the **DRIP** for many companies. Coca-Cola (stock symbol KO) is illustrative. It requires a minimum investment of $500 or minimum monthly investments of $50 each for at least 10 months. The enrollment fee is $10. Coca-Cola will buy back shares for a transaction fee of $15. Other companies offering DRIPs include AT&T, ExxonMobil, Home Depot, McDonald's, Johnson & Johnson, Verizon, and Chevron.

Jon Wentworth
Southern Adventist University, Collegedale, Tennessee

$10 per share ($4,500 ÷ 450). With the recent market price at $20, you will realize a long-term gain of $4,500 ($20 current market price × 450 shares = $9,000; $9,000 − $4,500 invested = $4,500 gain). Note that the dollar-cost averaging method would remain valid if the time interval for investing were monthly, quarterly, semiannually, or annually. The benefits of dollar-cost averaging are derived, in part, from the regularity of investing.

Dollar-Cost Averaging Offers Two Advantages The first advantage is that it reduces the average cost of shares of stock purchased over a relatively long period. Profits occur when prices for an investment fluctuate and eventually go up.

Even when the market if fairly flat and prices are not changing, your money goes further with dollar-cost averaging because you are able to buy more shares at decent prices. This will help you in the future when prices start to rise again. Although this approach does not eliminate the possibility of loss, it does limit losses during times of declining prices. And profits accelerate during rising prices.

The second advantage is that dollar-cost averaging dictates investor discipline. This strategy of investing is not particularly glamorous, but it is the only approach that is almost guaranteed to make a profit for the investor. It takes neither brilliance nor luck, just discipline. People who invest regularly through individual retirement accounts (IRAs), employee stock ownership programs, and 401(k) retirement plans (all discussed in Chapter 17) enjoy the benefits of dollar-cost averaging. Dollar-cost averaging is a systematic strategy that will eventually get your portfolio where you want it to be.

13.4d Strategy 4: Asset Allocation Keeps You in the Right Investment Categories for Your Time Horizon

asset allocation

Form of diversification in which the investor decides on the proportions of an investment portfolio that will be devoted to various categories of assets.

Asset allocation, a form of diversification, is deciding on the proportions of your investment portfolio that will be devoted to various categories of assets. Asset allocation helps preserve capital by selecting assets so as to protect the entire portfolio from negative events while remaining in a position to gain from positive events. This strategy helps control your exposure to risk.

Asset allocation rather than your choice of specific securities is the most important determinant of financial success. Research shows that 93 percent of returns earned by long-term investors result from having one's assets allocated in a diversified portfolio.

Thus you must strive to own the right asset categories at the right time. Of the remaining 7 percent, 2 percent of the return comes from picking the right investments, 2 percent from timing, and 3 percent from luck. The lesson: Use asset allocation and stay diversified.

Your allocation proportions and investment choices need to reflect your age, income, family responsibilities, financial resources, risk tolerance, goals, retirement plans, and investment time horizon. You need not change the proportions of your asset allocation until your broad investment goals change—possibly not for another five or ten years. When your investment objectives change, perhaps because of marriage, birth of a child, child graduating from college, loss of employment, divorce, or death of a spouse, you may need to change your asset allocation as well. Otherwise, stay the course.

Asset Allocation Requires Only Three Types of Investments To achieve an appropriate mix of growth, income, and stability in your portfolio, you need a combination of three investments: (1) stocks and/or stock mutual funds (equities), (2) bonds (debt), and (3) cash (or cash equivalents like Treasury securities). You need a little cash or cash equivalents in your portfolio because this allows you to move more money into stocks when appropriate, like during a down stock market. Asset allocation requires that you keep your equities, debt, and cash at a fixed ratio for long time periods, occasionally rebalancing the allocations, perhaps annually, so as to continue to meet your investment objectives.

Three Asset Allocation Rules of Thumb Consider these three rules of thumb to guide the stock and bond allocation of your portfolio, and a generation ago the first two were followed by most investors:

1. *The 110 Rule.* The percent to invest in equities is 110 minus your age, multiplied by 1.25. For example, if you are 40 years old, calculate as follows: $110 - 40 = 70$; $70 \times 1.25 = 87.5$. Therefore, a 40-year-old investor is advised to maintain a portfolio where 87.5 percent of the assets are in equities and 12.5 percent are in bonds and cash equivalents.
2. *The 120 Rule.* The percent to invest in equities is found by subtracting your age from 120. Put the resulting number in the form of the percentage of your portfolio to invest in stocks. Put the remainder in bonds. So if you are age 30, put 90 percent ($120 - 30$) in stocks and 10 percent in bonds and cash. Every year, subtract your age from 120 again and rebalance your portfolio as needed.
3. *New Portfolio Thinking Rules.* Because people are living longer and interest rates are lower than almost any time in history, investors are adapting. The new rules of thumb follow. They are arranged by age and percentage to invest in stocks and stock mutual funds with the remainder going to bonds and cash: 100 percent for those in their 20s and 30s, 90 to 100 percent for people in their 40s, 75 to 85 percent for investors in their 50s, 70 to 80 percent in your 60s, and 30 to 60 percent in your 70s and later.

Know Your Risk Tolerance and How Much Time You Have to Invest The model portfolios illustrated in Figure 13-4 reflect varying degrees of risk tolerance and time horizons. A 25-year old, risk-tolerant, long-term investor with an aggressive investment philosophy might have a portfolio that is 100 percent in equities because equities offer the highest return over the long term. Younger investors also have ample time to ride out market fluctuations and make up any major losses. A moderate approach with a time horizon of six to ten years might have an equities-bond-cash portfolio of 60/30/10 percent.

Rebalance Your Investment Portfolio at Least Once a Year **Rebalancing** is an account management feature that automatically keeps your 401(k) asset allocation in balance with your most recent asset allocation investment elections. It allows individuals to keep their risk level in check and minimize risk. Rebalancing brings the different asset classes

COMMON SENSE
Consider Be 100 Percent Invested in Stocks

Think long term. If you look at total returns for the S&P 500 across the past 70 holding periods of 20 years starting with 1926–45 and ending last year, not a single 20-year period has posted a loss. In addition, only 8 of those periods posted annual average returns of less than 2% across those years, while 18 posted annual gains of 10 percent or more. The best 20-year period in modern history was up more than 1,200 percent from 1980–99. The likelihood to not lose a dime over the long term along with the chance of a positive increase in stock prices like that makes a long-term investment of 100 percent in stocks a reasonable idea.

Figure 13-4   Asset Allocation and Time Horizons

0–5 Years	6–10 Years	11+ Years	Risk Tolerance/ Investment Philosophy
10% Cash 30% Bonds 60% Equities	20% Bonds 80% Equities	100% Equities	High Risk/Aggressive
20% Cash 40% Bonds 40% Equities	10% Cash 30% Bonds 60% Equities	20% Bonds 80% Equities	Moderate Risk/Moderate
35% Cash 40% Bonds 25% Equities	20% Cash 40% Bonds 40% Equities	10% Cash 30% Bonds 60% Equities	Low Risk/Conservative

DO IT IN CLASS

back into proper relationship following a significant change in one or more of them. You must reset your asset allocation to return your portfolio to the proper mix of stocks, bonds, and cash when they no longer conform to your plan. Here is why.

Assume you have a moderate investment philosophy and started out with a 50/40/10 bond-equities-cash portfolio, as shown in Figure 13-5, and a year later, stock values increased to 49 percent of your portfolio's value while bonds dropped to 42 percent. The result: Your portfolio has drifted too far from your target. It is now too heavy in stocks and too light in bonds. It is too risky compared to your original allocation distribution. As shown in Figure 13-5, this suggests that you sell some of your equities and use the proceeds to buy more bonds, thus rebalancing your portfolio according to your previously determined asset allocations.

Figure 13-5   Rebalance Assets Especially if Assets Increased

Day 1 — Beginning asset allocation of portfolio

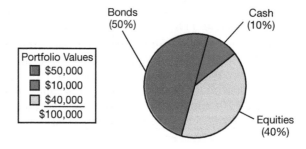

One year later — This allocation needs rebalancing to original percentages

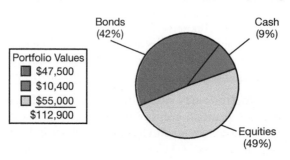

ADVICE FROM A SEASONED PRO

When to Sell an Investment

It is time to consider selling an investment when one of the following conditions has been met:

- **Something changed significantly** about the company's business or its earnings, and things have changed dramatically for the worse since you bought the investment.

- **The investment is doing so well that it is overvalued**, and the share price is much higher than what you believe the company is worth.

- **The investment is performing poorly** and causing you undue anxiety. the great financier Bernard Baruch advised, "Sell down to the level where you are sleeping well."

- **You need cash** for a worthwhile purpose, and this investment appears fully priced.

- **The investment no longer fits** your situation or goals, and you have a more promising place to invest your money.

Diann Moorman
University of Georgia, Athens, Georgia

The beauty of rebalancing is that it forces you to be selling high and buying low—the goal of all investors. It is temperamentally difficult for investors to rebalance. They don't like to sell assets that have increased in value because they hope those values will continue to increase. If you do not rebalance, the lack of change may increase or decrease the risk of your portfolio, and this is not what you decided on in the first place. Regrettably, one-half of employees are unengaged as they do not rebalance their retirement portfolios.

About half of employees who participate in their employer-sponsored retirement plan have access to paid services that automatically rebalance employees' retirement assets. Here a worker can sign up for the services of an **auto-rebalance tool** to do the rebalancing. Once you have signed a contract with a vendor approved by your employer, you decide on your preferred asset allocation. Under supervision by the company you ask them to sell and buy your mutual fund assets, usually quarterly, semi-annually, or annually, on your behalf each time adjusting your portfolio back to your specified level of asset allocation percentages. The contract usually calls for the process to be done automatically.

The service may be paid for entirely or just subsidized by the employer. A study by Financial Engines and Aon Hewitt of 425,000 savers over 5 years found that the median annual returns of those workers who got these services was almost 3 percentage points higher than those who invested on their own. Financial Soundings charges $7 to $14 annually, and both Betterment and SigFig Wealthfront charge 0.25 percent annually. Similar services are offered by Morningstar and Financial Engines.

CONCEPT CHECK 13.5

1. Summarize what the buy-and-hold long-term investment strategy is all about.
2. What is the goal of portfolio diversification, and how is this accomplished?
3. Explain the concept of dollar-cost averaging including why one invests at below-average costs.
4. What is asset allocation, and why does it work?
5. Comment on three popular rules of thumb of asset allocation including being 100 percent invested in stocks.
6. What happens to a worker's 401(k) retirement account if he or she signs up for an auto-rebalance account service?

investment plan
An explanation of your investment philosophy and your logic on investing to reach specific goals.

13.6 CREATING YOUR OWN INVESTMENT PLAN

To create an **investment plan**, which is a reflection of your investment philosophy and your logic on investing to reach specific goals, see the illustrated plan for Christina Garcia in Figure 13-6. Christina's plan includes saving for retirement as well as to buy a vehicle. You can begin creating your own investment plan by identifying your financial goals and explaining your investment philosophy as called for in Steps 1 and 2 in Figure 13-6.

Figure 13-6 **Christina Garcia's Investment Plan**

After some thinking and reading, Christina, age 28, jotted down some investment plan notes.

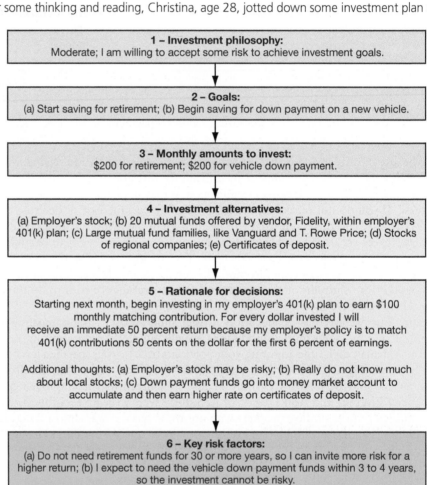

1 – Investment philosophy:
Moderate; I am willing to accept some risk to achieve investment goals.

2 – Goals:
(a) Start saving for retirement; (b) Begin saving for down payment on a new vehicle.

3 – Monthly amounts to invest:
$200 for retirement; $200 for vehicle down payment.

4 – Investment alternatives:
(a) Employer's stock; (b) 20 mutual funds offered by vendor, Fidelity, within employer's 401(k) plan; (c) Large mutual fund families, like Vanguard and T. Rowe Price; (d) Stocks of regional companies; (e) Certificates of deposit.

5 – Rationale for decisions:
Starting next month, begin investing in my employer's 401(k) plan to earn $100 monthly matching contribution. For every dollar invested I will receive an immediate 50 percent return because my employer's policy is to match 401(k) contributions 50 cents on the dollar for the first 6 percent of earnings.

Additional thoughts: (a) Employer's stock may be risky; (b) Really do not know much about local stocks; (c) Down payment funds go into money market account to accumulate and then earn higher rate on certificates of deposit.

6 – Key risk factors:
(a) Do not need retirement funds for 30 or more years, so I can invite more risk for a higher return; (b) I expect to need the vehicle down payment funds within 3 to 4 years, so the investment cannot be risky.

7 – Anticipated return:
(a) Hopefully 6 to 8 percent on the retirement investments; (b) For the down payment funds, hopefully 1 to 1 and 1/2 percent in a money market account, and perhaps 2 to 2 and 1/2 percent in a certificate of deposit.

8 – Actions to take:
(a) Fill out 401(k) forms in Human Resources Department to withhold $200 monthly and invest it in a mutual fund with an investment objective of moderate to high growth; (b) Open an account at large mutual fund company and automatically send $200 monthly from my banking account to a money market account until sufficient funds accumulate to buy a certificate of deposit.

TURN BAD HABITS INTO GOOD ONES

Do You Do This?	Do This Instead!
Make small contribution to employer's retirement plan	Contribute at least the amount to earn the employer's maximum match
Invest conservatively for retirement	Invest aggressively for long-term goals
Try to time investments to market ups and downs	Stay invested for the long term
Ignore transaction costs on investments	Keep transaction costs to the bare minimum
Invest mostly in employer's stock	Reduce holding to no more than 5 or 10 percent

To help in your thinking for Step 3 in Figure 13-6, consider the time horizons of various investments. (Terms new to you are explained in the chapters that follow.) What are the time horizons for each of your investment goals? Are you building up an amount for a down payment on a home, creating a college fund for a child, or putting away money for retirement? Or are all three time horizons relevant? Keep in mind why you are investing and proceed accordingly. Now calculate the numbers. How much money do you need to achieve each goal, and by when? What is the total of your current investment assets? Do the math.

Step 4 in Figure 13-6 asks about investment alternatives. Review Figure 13-1 on page 394 on the long-term rates of return on various investments. Then examine Figure 13-2 on page 396 because it shows the trade-offs between risk and return on investment alternatives. Next take a pencil or pen and delete some investment choices that do not appeal to you or match your investment philosophy. You will be left with alternatives that better fit your investment goals and philosophy.

Now you have started to create an investment plan, so record your responses to Steps 5, 6, and 7. Then create an investment portfolio appropriate for your life now using Figure 13-4 on page 414 as a model. All that remains is to put your plan into action. That means filling out forms to open an investment account, selecting your investments, writing checks for your first investing dollars, and monitoring your investments. These topics are examined in the chapters that follow.

When you take the appropriate retirement planning action steps, including a moderate amount of risk when investing, you will be able to relax with the confidence that you are making wise decisions about your investment assets and the knowledge that your money will grow and will be there to fund your lifestyle during the last quarter of your life.

DID YOU KNOW

Create Your Financial Plan on the Web

To obtain an overall assessment of your financial progress and advice on how to achieve your goals, you may want to consult an online financial advisor to construct a financial plan. Prices vary from $250 to $500 or more. Check out Fidelity.com, Schwab.com, TRowePrice.com, and Vanguard.com.

NEVER EVER

1. *Diversify less than you should.*
2. *Buy and sell more than you should.*
3. *Hold on to a bad investment long after evidence shows it was a bad decision.*

 CONCEPT CHECK 13.6

1. Review Figures 13-1 and 13-2, and record in writing an investment plan to fund your retirement, presumably one of your own long-term goals.

WHAT DO YOU RECOMMEND *NOW?*

Now that you have read the chapter on investment fundamentals, what do you recommend to Shanice and Sarena on the subject regarding:

1. Portfolio diversification for Sarena?
2. Dollar-cost averaging for Shanice?
3. Investment alternatives for Sarena?

SUMMARY OF LEARNING RECAPPED

LO1   **Explain how to get started as an investor.**

To help secure a desirable future lifestyle, you cannot spend every dollar that you earn today. You must decide if you are ready to start your investment program, prioritize your investing goals, and get the money to invest. Before investing, think about how investing is more than savings, the investment returns that are possible, and the long-term rates of return on investment choices. Investors hope that their investments will earn them a positive total return, which is what an investment generates from current income and capital gains.

LO2   **Identify your investment philosophy and invest accordingly.**

Achieving financial success requires that you learn to handle investment risk and understand your investment philosophy; then adhere to it when investing. An investment philosophy is one's willingness to weather changes in the values of your investments. It may be conservative, moderate, or aggressive, given the financial goals to be achieved. Before investing your money, you need to think about taking an active or passive investing approach, wanting to lend or own, making short-term versus long–term investments, and select investments that are likely to provide your desired potential total return.

LO3   **Describe the major risk factors that affect the rate of return on investments.**

Because of the uncertainty that surrounds investments, people often follow a conservative course in an effort to keep their risk low. Being too conservative when investing means that they risk not reaching their financial goals. To be a successful investor, you must understand the major risk factors that affect the rate of return on investments so you can then take the appropriate risks when making investment decisions. Key concepts include random and market risk. Plus there are several other types of investment risks that need to be understood.

LO4   **Accept the realities of the market and avoid investing mistakes that others make.**

Long-term investors understand and accept bull and bear markets as well as corrections. They are willing to accept substantial market volatility. They do not practice market timing and they try to avoid many trading mistakes that others make.

LO5   **Decide which of the four long-term safe and effective investment strategies you will utilize.**

To succeed as an investor, you must establish and follow your own long-term investment strategy. Most long-term investors are passive investors. They wisely ignore the ups and downs of the stock market and the business cycle and simply use any combination of four safe and effective investment strategies of buy and hold, portfolio diversification, dollar-cost averaging, and asset allocation. Rebalancing your portfolio at least once a year is critical to success.

LO6   **Create your own investment plan.**

An investment plan is an explanation of your investment philosophy and your logic on investing to reach specific financial goals. Steps include identifying your goals, contemplating which types of investments might best fit your investment goals, clarifying your investment philosophy, learning about investment alternatives, and narrowing down your choices.

LET'S TALK ABOUT IT

1. **Why Invest.** Why should people invest? Give two reasons each for college students, young college graduates in their 20s, couples with young children, and people in their 50s.

2. **Long-Term Rates of Return.** Review Figure 13-1, "Long-Term Rates of Return on Investments" on page 394, and offer your views on which two investment types would be most suitable for yourself. Explain why.

3. **Market Risk.** What do you think is the likelihood of several consecutive years of poor stock market returns.

4. **What Is Your Tolerance for Risk in Investing?** Is it the same as for other members of your class? Why or why not?

5. **Risk and Return Trade-Offs.** Review Figure 13-2, "The Risk Pyramid Reveals the Trade-Offs Between Risk and Return" on page 396 and give your views on which three investments would be most suitable for you.

6. **Your Investment Philosophy.** Is your investment philosophy conservative, moderate, or aggressive? Give two reasons to support the adoption of your philosophy. How does your view compare with the philosophies of other members of your class?

DO IT IN CLASS
Page 397

7. **Two Worries.** Review the section on "Long-Term Investors Avoid Trading Mistakes" on page 405, and note two that might worry you the most in the world of investing.

8. **Investment Strategy.** Review the "Four Safe and Effective Strategies for Long-Term Investors" that begins on page 408 and select your favorite. Why do you like it so much?

DO IT IN CLASS
Page 409

9. **Invest How Much?** Assume you have graduated from college and have a good-paying job. If you had to commit to investing regularly right now, how much money would you put away every month? Explain why. How does your view compare with the views of other members of your class?

DO THE MATH

1. **Annual Investments.** Sheldon Cooper and Amy Fowler are married and live in Pasadena, California. They have as a new investment goal to create a college fund for their newborn daughter. They estimate that they will need $200,000 in 18 years. Assuming that the Cooper-Fowler family could obtain a return of 5 percent, how much would they need to invest annually to reach their goal? Use Appendix A-3 or the *Garman/Forgue* companion website.

2. **Number of Years.** Mary Cooper, Sheldon's mother, who lives in east Texas, wants to help pay for her grandchild's education. How long will it take Mary to reach her goal of $200,000 if she invests $10,000 per year, earning 6 percent? Use Appendix A-3 or the *Garman/Forgue* companion website.

3. **Future Cost.** If one year of college currently costs $25,000, how much will it cost Grand Rapids, Michigan's resident Michelle Spindle to pay for one year of schooling for newborn daughter, Melissa, 18 years from now, assuming a 5 percent annual rate of inflation? Use Appendix A-1 or the *Garman/Forgue* companion website.

4. **Returns and Actions.** Kunal Nayyar from London, had $50,000 in investments in the USA at the beginning of the year that consisted of a diversified portfolio of stocks (40 percent), bonds (40 percent), and cash equivalents (20 percent). His returns over the past 12 months were 13 percent on stocks, 6 percent on bonds, and 1 percent on cash equivalents.

   (a) What is Kunal's average return for the year?

   (b) If Kunal wanted to rebalance his portfolio to its original position, what specific actions should he take?

DO IT IN CLASS
Page 414

5. **Early Investor Wins.** Jordan and Jeremy, who are twins living in Concord, New Hamphire, took different approaches to investing. Jordan saved $2,000 per year for ten years starting at age 23 and never added any more money to the account. Jeremy saved $2,000 per year for 20 years starting at age 35. Assuming that the brothers earned a 6 percent return, who had accumulated the most by the time they reached age 63? Use Appendix A-1 and Appendix A-3 or the *Garman/Forgue* companion website.

FINANCIAL PLANNING CASES

CASE 1

The Johnsons Embark on a Solid Investment Program

After nearly 14 years of marriage, Harry and Belinda's finances have improved, even though they have incurred debts for an automobile loan and a condominium. Plus they now have a 5-year-old son, Benjamin. They have not yet saved enough for retirement, so they want to catch up. Harry's 401(k) retirement account at work is currently worth only $44,000 and Belinda's at her workplace is $105,000, but they do have $24,000 in investments outside their employers' retirement plans.

Therefore, the Johnsons have decided to seriously forgo some current spending for the next three years to concentrate on getting a solid investment program under way while they still have two incomes available and before they expand their family. In addition to continuing their contributions to their 401(k) programs at work, they are willing to accept a moderate amount of risk and expect to invest $800 per month over the next three years. Respond to the following questions:

(a) In what types of investments (choose only two) might the Johnsons place the first annual installment of $9,600? Review Figures 13-1 on page 394 and 13-2 on page 396 for ideas and available options. Give reasons for your selections.

(b) In what types of investments might they place the second $9,600? Why?

DO IT IN CLASS
Pages 394 and 396

(c) What types of investments should they choose for the third $9,600? Why?

CASE 2

Victor and Maria Hernandez Try to Catch Up on Their Investments

The expenses associated with sending two children through college prevented Victor and Maria Hernandez from adding substantially to their investment program. Now that their younger son, Joseph, has completed school and is working full time, they would like to build up their investments quickly. Victor is 47 years old and wants to retire early, perhaps by age 60. In addition to the retirement program at his place of employment, Victor believes that their investment portfolio, currently valued at $120,000, will need to triple to $360,000 by his planned retirement time, in 13 years. He and Maria realize that they will have to sacrifice a lot of current spending to save and invest for retirement.

(a) What rate of return is needed on the $120,000 portfolio to reach their goal of $360,000 (assuming no additional contributions)? Use Appendix A-1 or visit the *Garman/Forgue* companion website.

(b) Victor and Maria think they will need a total of $600,000 for a retirement financial nest egg to supplement his anticipated small pension from teaching. Therefore, they will need to create an additional sum of about $240,000 through new investments. Assuming an annual return of 8 percent, how much do the Hernandezes need to invest each year to reach their goal of $240,000? Use Appendix A-3 or visit the *Garman/Forgue* companion website.

(c) If they assume a 6 percent annual return, how much do the Hernandezes need to invest each year to reach their goal of $240,000? Use Appendix A-3 or visit the *Garman/Forgue* companion website.

CASE 3

Julia Price's Goal Is to Buy a Luxury Condominium

It has been about 20 years since Julia graduated with a major in aeronautical engineering, and she has been quite successful in her career and her personal finances. Accordingly she wants to sell her home and buy a luxury condominium. She has $40,000 in savings, and she figures that she can continue her savings and investment program for three more years before making a 50 percent down payment on a luxury condominium. The home that she wants to purchase is currently priced at $800,000. Julia thinks she should invest her $40,000 and additional savings during the next three years by using lending investments like certificates of deposit and bonds rather than owning stocks or stock mutual funds. Offer your opinions about her thinking.

CASE 4

A First-Time Investor Gets a Head start

Lucia Gomez, a flight attendant from Kent, Ohio, is thinking about jump-starting her retirement savings plan by investing the $50,000 gift that her elderly uncle gave her. She also wants to invest $3,000 a year for the next 25 years for retirement. Lucia knows little about investments and does not seem to have a big desire to learn.

(a) What can you suggest to Lucia about figuring out her investment philosophy? (Hint: Mention the information in Figure 13-2 on page 396 in your response.)

(b) Would you recommend active or passive investing for her, and why?

(c) Should Lucia be a lender or owner?

(d) Identify three mistakes people make when investing for retirement that Lucia should try to avoid.

(e) Select two of the four recommended investment strategies to recommend to Lucia, and explain why she should follow them.

(f) If Lucia's $50,000 is invested in a standard investment account and her $3,000 yearly is invested in a tax-sheltered account, with each account growing at 8 percent annually for 25 years, how much money will she have accumulated in each account? She is in the 25 percent tax bracket. (Hint: Adjust the lump-sum investment for 25 percent taxes.)

BE YOUR OWN PERSONAL FINANCIAL MANAGER

1. **Your Personal Risk Pyramid.** Review Figure 13-2, "The Risk Pyramid Reveals the Trade-Offs Between Risk and Return," on page 396 and record your opinions on which types of risk you are probably willing to take over the next ten years by listing the names of the investments with which you would be comfortable.

2. **What Is Your Investment Philosophy?** Review the section titled "Identify Your Investment Philosophy and Invest Accordingly" that begins on page 395 and then complete Worksheet 50: My Investment Philosophy from "My Personal Financial Planner" to record various aspects of your approach to investing.

   My Personal Financial Planner

3. **Your Long-Term Investment Strategies.** Complete Worksheet 51: My Preferred Long-Term Investment Strategies from "My Personal Financial Planner" by check marking the strategies you like and that you might follow during your investing life.

   My Personal Financial Planner

4. **Real Return on Investments.** Review the box "Did You Know? Calculate the Real Rate of Return (After Taxes and Inflation) on Investments" on page 398 and complete Worksheet 53: The Real Return on My Investments from "My Personal Financial Planner" by inserting some realistic numbers next to the examples.

   My Personal Financial Planner

ON THE NET

Go to the Web pages indicated to complete these exercises.

1. **Why Invest?** Visit the Bankrate.com website www.bankrate.com/finance/investing/reasons-to-invest-in-the-stock-market-1.aspx and read the article titled "6 Reasons for Investing in the Stock Market" Compare what you read there with what is in this chapter.

2. **Why Invest?** Visit the Motley Food website www.fool.com/investing/beginning/why-should-i-invest.aspx and read the article "Why Invest." Compare what you read there with what is in this chapter.

3. **Risk Tolerance.** Go to the FinMason website www.finmason.com/risk-tolerance/?gclid=CPmTlN-1xMkCFQgUHwodCyQAMg#t7b5BbmXfgOPetia.97 and go through the risk tolerance exercises. Summarize what have you learned.

4. **Investment Philosophy.** Visit the Vanguard website about.vanguard.com/what-sets-vanguard-apart/

principles-for-investing-success and click and read each of the 4 categories. Summarize what you have learned.

5. **Investment Mistakes.** Visit the Investopedia website www.investopedia.com/articles/stocks/07/mistakes.asp?layout=orig and read the article. Compare what you read there with what is in this chapter.

6. **Herd Behavior.** Visit the Investopedia website www.investopedia.com/university/behavioral_finance/behavioral8.asp and read the article on herd behavior. Compare with what you read in this chapter.

7. **Asset Allocation.** Visit the Wikipedia website en.wikipedia.org/wiki/Asset_allocation and read its contents. Compare with what you have read in this chapter.

8. **Investment Plan.** Visit the WikiHow website www.wikihow.com/Create-an-Investment-Plan and read the article. Summarize what you have learned.

ACTION INVOLVEMENT PROJECTS

1. **Your Investment Strategy.** The text discusses four strategies for long-term investors that begins on page 408. Which one appeals to you most and why?

2. **Risk-Tolerance Quiz.** Go to one of the risk-tolerance quiz websites listed in the heading "What is Your Investment Philosophy?" on page 397 and summarize what you have learned.

3. **Current Investment Magazine Article.** Obtain a current issue of *Money* or *Kiplinger's Personal Finance Magazine* and summarize an article that offers suggestions on investing.

4. **Contact a Mutual Fund Company.** Contact a firm like Vanguard or Fidelity and ask what it takes to open an

account as well as what funds they recommend for retirement planning. Summarize their comments.

5. **Telephone a Human Resources Office.** Telephone the human resources office of a large employer and ask them to send you some print information about their company retirement plans. They may have it all on their website. Summarize your findings.

6. **Ask About Retirement Planning.** Contact three people not enrolled in college and ask how well they are prepared for retirement. Ask what sources of retirement income they are counting on in the future. Summarize their responses.

Visit the Garman/Forgue companion website at **www.cengagebrain.com.**

14

Investing in Stocks and Bonds

zimmytws/Shutterstock.com

YOU MUST BE KIDDING, RIGHT?

Brothers Michael and Christopher Morton differ in investment philosophies. Michael is a conservative investor and Christopher holds a moderate investing outlook. Their father left each of them $100,000 when he died ten years ago, and Christopher invested in common stocks while Michael invested in corporate bonds. After ten years, how much more money is Christopher likely to have in his account than Michael?

A. $12,000	**C.** $67,000
B. $21,000	**D.** $148,000

The answer is C, $67,000. One could expect to obtain a long-term average annual return of perhaps 8 percent on U.S. common stocks compared with about 4 percent on corporate bonds. A $100,000 common stock portfolio that returned 8 percent annually would accumulate to over $215,000 in ten years while a bond portfolio earning 4 percent annually over the same time period would grow to $148,000. Christopher's willingness to accept more risk by investing in common stocks may provide him with a balance bigger than his brother's by a whopping $67,000 or 45 percent ($67,000/$148,000). Taking some investment risk is smart!

Learning Objectives

After reading this chapter, you should be able to:

1 Explain how stocks and bonds are used as investments.

2 Describe ways to evaluate stock prices, and calculate a stock's potential rate of return.

3 Use the Internet to evaluate common stocks in which to invest.

4 Summarize how to buy and sell stocks, as well as the techniques of margin buying and selling short.

5 Describe how to invest in bonds.

WHAT DO YOU RECOMMEND?

For the past five years, Ariya Jutanugarn, age 42, has worked as a senior Web designer for Minecraft, a company in Stockholm, Sweden, although she works online from northern California where there are plenty of hills, forests, lakes, and golf courses. She earns $92,000 annually. From her salary, Ariya contributes $460 per month to her 401(k) retirement account, 100 percent matched by her employer for a total of $920 going into her retirement fund, which she totally invests in her employer's company's stock. Ariya is divorced and has custody of her three children, ages 14, 6, and 4. Her ex-husband pays $1,500 per month in child support. Ariya and her former spouse contribute $3,000 each annually to a college fund for their children. Over the past 15 years, Ariya has built a $200,000 portfolio of investments beyond what she has in her 401(k) plan after starting by investing the proceeds of a $100,000 life insurance policy following the death of her first husband. Currently, her portfolio is allocated 40 percent into preferred stocks (paying 4.5 percent); 30 percent into cyclical, blue-chip common stocks (P/E ratio of 14); 10 percent into Treasury bonds (paying 2.99 percent); 10 percent into municipal bonds (paying 1.7 percent); and 10 percent into AA corporate bonds (paying 5.6 percent). Ariya's total return in recent years has been about 7 percent annually. Her investment goals are to have sufficient cash to pay for her children's education and to retire in about 18 years.

Golden Pixels LLC/Shutterstock.com

What do you recommend to Ariya on the subject of stocks and bonds regarding:

1. Investing for retirement in 18 years?

2. Owning blue-chip common stocks and preferred stocks rather than other common stocks given Ariya's investment time horizon?

3. The wisdom of owning municipal bonds rather than corporate bonds?

4. The likely selling price of her corporate bonds, if sold today?

5. Investments that might be appropriate to fund her children's education?

TO-DO SOON

Do the following to begin to achieve financial success:

1. *Don't be afraid of investing in the stock market so include stocks and bonds and/or stock mutual funds in your investment portfolio.*

2. *Use fundamental analysis to determine a company's basic value before investing in any stock, bond, or stock mutual fund.*

3. *Resist putting money into so-called hot investments.*

4. *Invest part of your portfolio in TIPS (Treasury Inflation-Protected Securities) that beat inflation.*

5. *When you have children, consider using zero-coupon bonds (in addition to Roth IRAs) to help save for their education.*

Learning Objective 1

Explain how stocks and bonds are used as investments.

securities

Negotiable instruments of ownership or debt, including common stock, preferred stock, and bonds.

stocks

Shares of ownership in a business corporation's assets and earnings.

common stock

Most basic form of ownership of a corporation.

cash dividends

Cash profits that a firm distributes to stockholders.

market price

The current price of a share of stock that a buyer is willing to pay a willing seller.

To earn a larger return than offered by conservative investments, you must accept more risk. Historically, common stocks, for example, have earned substantially more than corporate bonds, often two or even three times as much. When you invest in stocks, you can increase returns significantly while increasing risk only slightly. These investments belong in everyone's investment portfolio because they provide opportunities for moderate and aggressive investors alike.

The principles of long-term investing remain valid because over time turbulent stock and bond markets calm down and provide investors fairly predictable returns. In fact, a good time to invest is when the share prices of high-quality firms have been beaten down to affordable levels. When the stock markets are down that means that stocks are "on sale," as prices are lower than usual.

You should welcome the fact that economic slumps always spark a powerful market recovery. The typical post-recession rally in prices on the stock market is a 50 percent increase over the following 18 months. History argues that by the time students in college are ready to retire, stock market prices will have tripled or quadrupled.

14.1 THE ROLE OF STOCKS AND BONDS IN INVESTMENTS

Individual investors provide the money corporations use to create sales and earn profits. The stock investor shares when there are profits. A **corporation** is a state-chartered legal entity that can conduct business operations in its own name. A **public corporation** is one that issues stock purchased by the general public and traded on stock markets such as the New York Stock Exchange. In contrast, the stock of a **privately held corporation** is held by a relatively small number of people and is not traded on a public stock exchange.

The ability to sell shares of ownership to investors offers a public corporation the opportunity to develop into a firm of considerable size. It can continue to exist even as ownership of its shares changes hands. For example, the owners of AT&T are the holders of its more than 6.15 million shares of stock.

A corporation's financial needs will vary over time. To begin its operations, a new corporation needs **start-up capital** (funds initially invested in a business enterprise). During its life, a corporation may need additional money to grow. To raise capital and finance its goals, it may issue three types of securities (negotiable instruments of ownership or debt): common stock, preferred stock, and bonds.

14.1a Common Stock

Stocks are shares of ownership in the assets and earnings of a business corporation, and there are 4,300 stocks to choose from in the United States. Each stock investor is a part owner in a corporation. Common stock is the most basic form of ownership of a corporation. For the investor, stocks represent potential income because the investor owns a piece of the future profits of the company.

Investors in common stock usually have two expectations: (1) the corporation will be profitable enough that income will exceed expenses, thereby allowing the firm to pay cash dividends (a share of profits distributed in cash, which is usually between 30 and 70 percent of corporate earnings); and (2) the market price of a share of stock, which is the current price that a buyer is willing to pay a willing seller, will increase over time.

Stocks usually require a low minimum investment. Investors expect to earn annual returns of 8 or 9 percent or higher on average over time from the combination of dividends and capital gains.

Each person who owns a share of stock—called a *shareholder* or *stockholder*—has a proportionate interest in the ownership (an extremely small slice) and, therefore, in the assets and income of the corporation. This **residual claim** means that common stockholders have a right to share in the income and assets of a corporation only after higher-priority claims are satisfied. The higher-priority claims include interest payments to those who own company bonds and dividends to owners of preferred stocks. Stockholders have a **limited liability,** as their responsibility for business losses is limited to the amount invested in the shares of stock owned. These amounts may be small or large, but the most the shareholder can lose is the original amount invested. If the corporation goes bankrupt, the common stockholder's ownership value consists of the amount left per share after the claims of all creditors are satisfied first.

Each *common stockholder* has voting rights, which is the proportionate authority to express an opinion or choice in matters affecting the company. Stockholders vote to elect the company's **board of directors.** This group of individuals sets policy and names the principal officers of the company—**management**—who run the firm's day-to-day operations. The number of votes cast by each shareholder depends on the number of shares he or she owns. Stockholders attend an annual meeting or vote by **proxy**—shareholders' written authorization to someone else to represent them and to vote their shares at a stockholder's meeting.

residual claim

Common stockholders have a right to share in the income and assets of a corporation after higher-priority claims are satisfied.

14.1b   Preferred Stock

Preferred stock is a type of fixed-income ownership security in a corporation. Owners of a preferred stock receive a fixed dividend per share that corporations are required to distribute before any dividends are paid out to common stockholders. They very rarely receive any extra income from the stock other than their fixed dividend, even when the firm is highly profitable. The regular dividend payments appeal to those who desire a reliable stream of income, such as retired investors. While the income stream may be consistent, the market price of preferred stock is sensitive to changes in interest rates. Preferred stockholders rarely have voting privileges.

preferred stock

Type of fixed-income ownership security in a corporation that pays fixed dividends.

Sometimes a corporation decides not to pay dividends to preferred stockholders because it lacks profits or simply because it wants to retain and reinvest all of its earnings. When the board of directors votes to skip **(pass)** making a cash dividend to preferred stockholders, holders of cumulative preferred stock must be paid that dividend before any future dividends are distributed to the common stockholders. For example, assume that a company passes on the first two quarterly dividends of $2.25 each to preferred stockholders, who expect to receive $9 each year ($2.25 × 4 quarters).

If the company prospers and wants to give a cash dividend to its common stockholders in the third quarter, it must first pay the passed $4.50 to the cumulative preferred stockholders. Furthermore, the usual third-quarter cash dividend of $2.25 has to be made to the preferred stockholders before the common stockholders can receive any dividends.

In the case of **noncumulative preferred stock,** the preferred stockholders would have no claim to previously skipped dividends. Convertible preferred stock, a unique security occasionally sold by companies, can be exchanged at the option of the stockholder for a specified number of shares of common stock.

14.1c   Bonds

Individuals who want to invest by loaning their money can do so by buying bonds and becoming a creditor of the business (again a very small one). A **bond** is an interest-bearing negotiable certificate of long-term debt issued by a corporation, the U.S. government, or a municipality (such as a city or state). Bonds are basically IOUs. Corporations and governments often use the proceeds from bonds to finance expensive construction projects and to purchase costly equipment.

NEVER EVER

Fail to Invest

With both regular and retirement investment accounts you can put in a large sum perhaps once a year or choose to invest smaller amounts periodically, perhaps monthly. Don't delay starting to invest. A mere $50 a month—money you will not miss as it is only $12.50 a week— grows at 8 percent to $29,400 in 20 years, $74,000 in 30 years, and $174,000 in 40 years.

Whatever you do, get the habit stated by beginning to invest early in life and do so regularly. If you do not, you give up some of the biggest power of compounding in the value of the asset.

principal
Face amount of a bond.

maturity date
Date upon which the principal is returned to the bondholder.

With bonds, investors lend the issuer a certain amount of money—the **principal**—with two expectations: (1) they will receive regular interest payments at a fixed rate of return for many years, and (2) they will get their principal returned on a specific day in the future, called the **maturity date**. If an investor in bonds wanted to sell before the maturity date, he/she must recognize that the market price of the bonds is sensitive to changes in interest rates.

14.1d An Illustration of Stocks and Bonds: Running Paws Cat Food Company

To better understand how a corporation finances its goals by issuing common and preferred stock while also paying returns for stockholders, consider the example of Running Paws Cat Food Company. When reading through the example, imagine that the numbers have many more zeros to better visualize a company the size of Apple, Alphabet (the parent of Google), or Microsoft.

Running Paws Is Born Running Paws began as a small family business in Pueblo, Colorado, started by Linda Webtek. She developed a wonderful recipe for cat food that contained no corn, corn meal, or corn gluten meal and sold the product through a local grocery store. As sales increased, Linda decided to incorporate the business, expand its operations and share ownership of the company with the public by asking people to invest in the company's future. Running Paws issued 10,000 shares of common stock at $10 per share. Three friends each bought 2,500 shares, and Linda signed over the cat food recipe and equipment to the corporation itself in exchange for the remaining 2,500 shares. At that point, Running Paws had $75,000 in working capital (7,500 shares sold at $10 each), equipment, a great recipe, and a four-person board of directors. Each of the directors worked for the firm, although they paid themselves minimal salaries.

Running Paws Begins to Grow The sales revenues of a corporation like Running Paws are used to pay (1) expenses, (2) interest to bondholders, (3) taxes, (4) cash dividends to preferred stockholders, and (5) cash dividends to common stockholders, in that order. If money is left over after items 1 and 2 are paid, the corporation has earned a **profit**. If funds are available after item 3 is paid, the company has an **after-tax profit**. The average corporation pays out 30 to 70 percent of its after-tax profit in cash dividends to stockholders. The remainder, called **retained earnings**, is left to accumulate and finance the company's goals—often expansion and growth. In its early years, Running Paws retained all of its profits and distributed no dividends.

profit
Money left over after a firm pays all expenses and interest to bondholders.

after-tax profit
Money left over after a firm has paid expenses, bondholder interest, and taxes.

retained earnings
Money left over after a firm has paid expenses, bondholder interest, taxes, preferred stockholder dividends, and common stockholder dividends.

Common stockholders, such as the stockholders of Running Paws Cat Food Company, are not guaranteed dividends. However, most profitable companies do pay common stockholders a small dividend on a quarterly basis until increased earnings justify paying out a higher amount.

Given that Running Paws retained all its earnings, you might wonder why people would invest in such a new company. Two reasons explain the attraction. First, as a company becomes more efficient and profitable, cash dividends to common stockholders may not only begin but also become significant. Second, the market price of the stock may increase sharply as more investors become interested in the future profitability of a growing company. Common stock constitutes a share of ownership; thus as the company grows, the price of its common stock follows suit.

Increasing sales meant more production for Running Paws. Soon more orders were coming in from Chicago than the firm could handle. After three years, the owners of Running Paws decided to expand once again. They wanted to borrow an additional $100,000, but their business was so new and its future so uncertain that lenders demanded an extremely high interest rate. To raise the needed funds, the owners decided to issue 5,000 shares of preferred stock at $20 per share, promising to pay a cash dividend of $1.80 per share annually, providing a 9 percent yield to investors ($1.80/$20). The preferred stock was sold to outside investors, but the original investors retained control of the company through their common stock.

Running Paws Becomes a National Company Following its pattern of expanding into new markets, Running Paws soon developed additional lines of cat food that also sold quite well. With the proceeds from the sale of preferred stock, and after a new plant in Brooklyn, New York, opened, the income of the four-year-old business finally exceeded expenses, and it had a profit of $13,000. The board of directors declared the promised preferred stock dividend of $9,000 (5,000 preferred shares × $1.80) but no dividend for common stockholders. In the following year, net profits after taxes amounted to $28,000. Once again the board paid the $9,000 dividend to preferred stockholders but retained the remainder of the profits to finance continued expansion and improved efficiency. After five years one of the original partners wanted to exit the business and needed to sell her 2,500 shares of stock, for which she had originally paid $25,000. Because Running Paws was beginning to show some profits, two other private investors recommended by a local stockbroker made offers to purchase her shares. The shares were sold at $16 per share, with 1,500 shares going to one investor and 1,000 shares to another investor. Thus, this original investor gained $15,000 in price appreciation ($16 × 2,500 = $40,000; $40,000 − $25,000 = $15,000) when she sold out. (Running Paws did not profit from this transaction.) Now five owners of the common stock, including the two new ones, voted for the board of directors, with each share representing one vote.

During the sixth year, the company's sales again increased and its earnings totaled $39,000. This time the board voted $9,000 for the preferred stockholders and $5,000 ($0.50 per share) for the common stockholders but retained the remaining $25,000. With the $5,000 distribution, the common stockholders finally began to receive cash dividends.

Even with its success, Running Paws faced another decision. To distribute its products nationally would require another $400,000 to $500,000 for expansion costs. After much discussion, the board voted to sell additional shares of stock and issue some bonds. The company planned to sell 10,000 shares of common stock at $25 per share. This would dilute the owners' proportion of ownership by half. Common stockholders, however, have a **pre-emptive right** to purchase additional shares before new shares are offered to the public. Thus, each current stockholder retained the legal right to maintain proportionate ownership by being allowed to purchase more shares.

Bonds were sold, too.* Running Paws issued two hundred $1,000 bonds with a coupon rate of 8 percent. After several months, all of the new stock and bond shares were sold. After brokerage expenses, the company netted more than $190,000 from the bonds to help finance the expansion. On the stock sales, various local stockbrokers took selling commissions totaling $16,000, leaving $234,000 available for the company to use for expansion. These and other investors will follow the progress of Running Paws and buy and sell shares accordingly. The company will not benefit from this trading.

Running Paws and its shareholders expect to benefit from a rising stock price over time because ownership in a growing company becomes increasingly valuable. If Running Paws continues to prosper, its board of directors might work toward having its stock listed on a regional stock exchange to facilitate trading of shares and to further enhance the company's image.

pre-emptive right
Right of common stockholders to purchase additional shares before a firm offers new shares to the public.

CONCEPT CHECK 14.1

1. Distinguish between common stocks and bonds in investments.
2. How do public corporations use stocks and bonds?

---

* Companies that need capital to begin or expand their operations sell new issues of stocks, bonds, or both to the investing public. New issues of stock are referred to as **initial public offerings (IPOs)**. **Investment banking firms** serve as intermediaries between companies issuing new stocks and bonds and the investing public.

14.2 HOW TO EVALUATE COMMON STOCKS

Keep in mind that the risk-return relationship in all types of investments ranges from extremely low risk Treasury bills and bonds to higher paying corporate bonds and preferred stock. (This is illustrated in Figure 13-1 in Chapter 13 on page 394.) More risk and higher returns come from real estate then large corporate stocks followed by small company stocks. The riskiest investments are options, commodities, derivatives, and collectibles and precious metals. When thinking about investing in a stock it is helpful to begin by reviewing Table 14-1, which shows the types of stocks and their characteristics.

income stock

A stock that may not grow too quickly, but year after year pays a cash dividend higher than that offered by most companies.

growth stock

The stock of a company that offers the promise of much higher profits tomorrow and has a consistent record of relatively rapid growth in earnings in all economic conditions.

blue-chip stocks

Stocks that have been around for a long time, have a well-regarded reputation, dominate its industry, and are known for being solid, relatively safe investments.

Countercyclical Stock

The stock of a company whose profits are greatly influenced by changes in the economic business cycle.

value stock

A stock that tends to trade at a low price relative to its company fundamentals (dividends, earnings, sales, and so on) and thus is considered undervalued by a value investor.

Table 14-1 — Characteristics of Stocks

Type of Stock	Characteristics
Income Stock	Company that pays a cash dividend higher than that offered by most companies. Stocks issued by telephone, electric, and gas utility companies; beta often less than 1.0.
Growth Stock	Corporations that are leaders in their fields, that dominate their markets, and that have several consecutive years of above-industry-average earnings; pays some dividends. Investor awareness of such corporations is widespread, and expectations for continued growth are high. The P/E ratio is high; betas of 1.5 or more.
Blue-Chip Stock	A company that has been around for a long time, has a well-regarded reputation, dominates its industry (often with annual revenues of $1 billion or more), and is known for being a solid, relatively safe investment; betas are usually around 1.0.
Countercyclical Stock	A company whose profits are greatly influenced by changes in the economic business cycle in consumer-dependent industries, like automobiles, housing, airlines, retailing, and heavy machinery; betas of about 1.0. A stock with a beta that is less than 1.0 is called a **countercyclical** (or **defensive**) because it exhibits price changes contrary to movements in the business cycle, thus prices remain steady during economic downturns. Examples are cigarette manufacturers, movies, soft drinks, cat and dog food, electric utilities, and groceries.
Value Stock	A company that grows with the economy and tends to trade at a low price relative to its company fundamentals (dividends, earnings, sales, and so on) and thus is considered under-priced by a value investor; beta 1.0 to 2.0.
Large-Cap, Small-Cap, and Mid-Cap stocks	A company's size classification in the stock market is based on market capitalization. **Large caps** are those firms valued at or more than $10 billion. **Mid-caps** are $2 billion to $10 billion. **Small caps** is $300 million to $2 billion.
Tech Stock	A company in the technology sector that offer technology-based products and services, biotechnology, Internet services, network services, wireless communications, and more.
Speculative Stock	A company that has a potential for substantial earnings at some time in the future but those earnings may never be realized; betas above 2.0. Examples: computer graphics firms, Internet applications firms, small oil exploration businesses, genetic engineering firms, and some pharmaceutical manufacturers.

DO IT IN CLASS

14.2a Use Beta to Compare a Stock to Similar Investments

Beta is a number widely used by investors to predict future stock prices. The **beta value** (or **beta coefficient**) is a measure of an investment's volatility compared with a broad market index for similar investments over time. For large-company stocks, the S&P 500 Stock Index often serves as a benchmark. The average for all stocks in the market is a beta of +1.0, thus a stock with a beta of +1.0 typically moves in lockstep with the S&P. A beta greater than 1.0 indicates higher-than-market volatility. Recall from Chapter 13 that market risk is assumed to be 8 percent; thus when the overall stock market increases 8 percent a stock with a 1.0 beta is likely to increase the same amount. A stock with a beta of 1.2 will move 20 percent higher and lower than the index.

Most stocks have positive betas between 0.5 and 2.0. A beta of less than 1.0 (0.0 to 0.9) indicates that the stock price is less sensitive to the market. This is because the price moves in the same direction as the general market but not to the same degree. A beta of more than +1.0 to +2.0 (or higher) indicates that the price of the security is more sensitive to the market because its price moves in the same direction as the market but by a greater percentage. Higher betas mean greater risk relative to the market.

A beta of zero suggests that the price of the stock is independent of the market, much like that of a risk-free U.S. Treasury security. You may look up betas for stocks (just input the stock's symbol) at Calculator Edge (www.calculatoredge.com/finance/betas.htm) or Yahoo! Finance (screener .finance.yahoo.com/stocks.html). Stocks with a negative beta move in the opposite direction of the market.

MONEY WEBSITES

Informative websites are:
- AOL Money Basics
- BloombergBusinessWeek
- CNN Money
- EasyCalculation.com
- Financial Industry Regulatory Authority
- Kiplinger's Personal Finance
- JW Korth Shop-4-Bonds
- MarketWatch
- Morningstar
- Motley Fool
- Municipal Securities Rulemaking Board
- NASDAQ
- Reuters
- Securities Industry and Financial Markets Association
- Value Line Investment Survey
- Yahoo! Finance on bonds Yahoo! Finance on stocks
- Zacks Investment Research

14.2b Most Investors Use Fundamental Analysis to Evaluate Stocks

The theory underlying **fundamental analysis** is that each stock has an intrinsic (or true) value based on its expected stream of future earnings. Most professional stock analysts and investors take this approach to investing as they research corporate and industry financial reports. Fundamental analysis suggests that you can identify some stocks that will outperform others given the state of the economy. The fundamental approach presumes that a stock's basic value is largely determined by its current and future earnings trends, assets and debts, products, competition, and management's expertise to assess its growth potential. The aim is to seek out sound stocks—perhaps even unfashionable ones—that are priced below what they ought to be.

Fundamental analysis suggests that you should consider investing only in companies that will likely be industry leaders—not necessarily the largest firms and fastest-growing industries, but the pacesetters in terms of profitability. You should invest in a stock because you have good reasons related to earnings and profitability. Examples include a new division in a firm that soon is expected to be quite profitable, a firm is starting to outsell its competitors, product research looks promising, or the firm is a leader in an industry that will be a future driver of profits in the economy.

beta value (beta coefficient)
A measure of stock volatility; that is, how much the stock price varies relative to the rest of the market.

fundamental analysis
School of thought in market analysis that assumes each stock has an intrinsic (or true) value based on its expected stream of future earnings.

14.2c Some Investors Use Technical Analysis to Evaluate Stocks

An opposing and minority theory on valuing common stocks is advocated by proponents of **technical analysis**, and often these are authors of investment newsletters. This method of evaluating securities analyzes statistics through the study of past market data, primarily price and volume. Technical analysts do not attempt to measure a security's intrinsic value but instead use charts, graphs, mathematics, and software programs to identify and predict future price movements. Technical analysis has proved to be of little value, although some investors find technical analysts' logic appealing.

14.2d Evaluate Stocks Using Corporate Earnings

Those who use fundamental analysis use several numerical measures to evaluate stock performance. These numbers are readily available to investors on the Internet that will help you assess future stock prices.

corporate earnings

The profits a company makes during a specific time period that indicate to many analysts whether to buy or sell a stock.

Corporate Earnings Corporate earnings are the profits a company makes during a specific time period. Corporate earnings are at the core of fundamental analysis. The investor must study past market data, primarily price and sales volume to learn about an investment's corporate earnings. If a company cannot generate earnings now or in the future, stock market analysts and investors are not going to be impressed. As people reach this conclusion, there quickly will be more sellers than buyers of the company's common stock, and that will depress the stock's market price.

earnings per share (EPS)

A firm's profit divided by the number of outstanding shares.

Earnings Per Share A company's earnings per share (EPS) is annual profit divided by the number of outstanding shares. It indicates the income that a company has available, on a per-share basis, to pay dividends and reinvest as retained earnings. The EPS is a measure of the firm's profitability on a common-stock-per-share basis, and it is helpful because investors can use it to compare financial conditions of many companies. The EPS is reported in the business section of many newspapers as well as online.

In our example, assume that next year, after payment of $9,000 in dividends to preferred stockholders, Running Paws had a net profit of $32,000. With 20,000 shares of stock, the company's EPS would be $1.60 ($32,000 ÷ 20,000).

price/earnings (P/E ratio) (or multiple)

The current market price of a stock divided by earnings per share (EPS) over the past four quarters; used as the primary means of valuing a stock.

Price/Earnings Ratio The price/earnings ratio (P/E ratio) (or multiple) is the current market price of a stock divided by earnings per share (EPS) over the past four quarters. This ratio is the primary means of valuing a stock. It demonstrates how expensive the stock is versus the company's recently reported earnings, by revealing how much you are paying for each $1 of earnings. For example, if the market price of a share of Running Paws stock is currently $25 and the company's EPS is $1.60, the P/E ratio will be 16 ($25 ÷ $1.60 = 15.6, which rounds to 16). This value can also be called a 16-to-1 ratio or multiple, or a P/E ratio of 16. The P/E ratios of many corporations are widely reported on the Internet and in the financial section of newspapers.

To assess a company's financial status, you could compare that firm's P/E ratio with the P/E ratios for other similar stocks. The P/E ratios for corporations typically range from 5 to 25. The historical average P/E ratio for stocks is 15, although it varies for different industries. Financially successful companies with a P/E ratio ranging from 7 to 10 tend

Being invested in the stock market is an excellent way to create wealth.

to have higher dividend yields, less risk, lower prices, and slower earnings growth. Rapidly growing companies would likely have a much higher P/E ratio—13 to 20. Speculative companies might have P/E ratios of 25 or 50 or even higher because they have low earnings now but anticipate much higher earnings in the future.

Inverting a P/E ratio of 12, for example, reveals that stocks have an **earnings yield** of 8.5 percent. In other words, each $100 of stocks is backed by $8.50 in expected earnings. During times of low interest rates, an 8.5 percent yield on stocks looks terrific.

Trailing and Projected Price/Earnings Ratios The standard P/E ratio is, in fact, called a **trailing P/E ratio** measure because it is calculated using recently reported earnings, usually from the previous four quarters. Investors also need to focus on future prospects when analyzing the value of a stock. A **projected P/E** or **forward price/ earnings ratio** divides price by projected earnings over the coming four quarters, an estimate available via online stock quote providers. The **earnings yield,** which is the inverse of the P/E ratio (Running Paws' earnings yield is 6.4 percent [$1.60 ÷ $25]), helps investors think more clearly about expectations for investments.

PEG Ratio Critics of price-earnings ratio argue that those firms with high levels of growth should not be penalized for having high P/E ratios. **PEG ratio**, or **price-earnings growth**, is a way to adjust for this. Divide the P/E ratio by the company's projected growth rate. Going back to Running Paws, divide the firm's P/E ratio of 16 by its projected growth rate of 15 percent (16/15 = 1.07). Investors think a PEG ratio of 1 is fairly priced while a value of 2 or more is too high.

Price/Sales Ratio The **price/sales ratio (P/S ratio)** indicates the number of dollars it takes to buy a dollar's worth of a company's annual revenues. The P/S is obtained by dividing a company's total market capitalization by its sales for the past four quarters. For example, if Running Paws Cat Food Company's common stock currently sells for $25 per share and 20,000 shares of the company's stock are outstanding, its total capitalization is $500,000. If company revenues (sales of dog and cat food) were $750,000 over the past year, the stock's P/S would be 0.67 ($500,000 ÷ $750,000). Stock analysts suggest investors avoid companies with a P/S greater than 1.5 and favor those having a P/S of less than 0.75. Many investors ignore the P/S, but it works better than the highly acclaimed P/E ratio in predicting which companies provide the best return, as explained in James P. O'Shaughnessy's *What Works on Wall Street.*

Cash Dividends Stocks usually pay dividends. Cash dividends are distributions made in cash to holders of stock. They are the current income that you receive while you own shares in the company. The firm's board of directors usually declares a dividend on a quarterly basis (four times per corporate year), typically at the end of March, June, September, and December. Dividends are ordinarily paid out of current earnings, but in the event of unprofitable times (low earnings or none), the money might come from cash reserves held by the company. Occasionally, a company will borrow to pay the dividend so as to maintain its reputation of consistently paying dividends. Later profits can be used to repay any funds borrowed for this purpose.

Dividends per Share The **dividends per share** measure translates the total cash dividends paid out by a company to common stockholders into a per-share figure. For example, Running Paws might elect to declare a total cash dividend of $8,000 for the year to common stockholders. In that case, cash dividends per share would amount to $0.40 ($8,000 ÷ 20,000 shares).

Dividend Payout Ratio The **dividend payout ratio** is the dividends per share divided by EPS. It helps you judge the likelihood of future dividends. For example, imagine that Running Paws Cat Food Company earned $32,000 (after paying preferred stockholders), paid out a cash dividend of $8,000 to company stockholders, and retained the remaining $24,000 to facilitate growth of the company. In this case, the dividend payout ratio

---

earnings yield
The earnings per share of a stock divided by its price; an inversion of the price/earnings ratio; helps investors more clearly see investment expectations.

trailing P/E ratio
Calculated using recently reported earnings, usually from the previous four quarters.

projected P/E ratio (forward price/earnings ratio)
Because investors need to look to the future rather than the past, this measure divides price by projected earnings over the coming four quarters. Also known as forward price/ earnings ratio.

PEG ratio (price-earnings growth)
A way to rationalize buying a stock that has high growth is to calculate by dividing the P/E ratio by the company's projected growth rate.

price/sales ratio (P/S ratio)
Tells the number of dollars it takes to buy a dollar's worth of a company's annual revenues; calculated by dividing company's total market capitalization by its sales for the past four quarters.

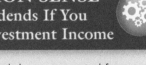

COMMON SENSE
Get Dividends If You
Want Investment Income

Cash dividends have accounted for more than 40 percent of the S&P's total return for 100 years. If you want regular investment income, put some money into dividend-paying stocks and stock mutual funds. You might earn 2 percent in cash dividends plus price appreciation that results in earning 4 or 5 percentage points more than from Treasuries. You may reinvest the income distributions so your returns compound over time. Betas are usually 1.0 or less.

DO IT IN CLASS

book value (shareholder's equity)
Net worth of a company, determined by subtracting total liabilities from assets.

book value per share
Reflects the book value of a company divided by the number of shares of common stock outstanding.

price-to-book ratio (P/B ratio)
Current stock price divided by the per-share net value of a firm's plant, equipment, and other assets (book value).

equals 0.25 ($8,000 ÷ $32,000). For that year, Running Paws paid a dividend equal to 25 percent of earnings.

Newer companies usually retain most, if not all, of their profits to facilitate growth. An investor interested in growth would, therefore, seek a company with a low payout ratio. The lower the payout ratio the greater the likelihood that the company will grow, which results in later capital gains for investors. Examples of companies that historically have a high payout ratio are AT&T (T), Chevron (CVX), Exelon (EXC), Home Depot (HD), Intel (INTC), Merck (MRK), Pfizer (PFE), and Verizon (VZ).

Dividend Yield The dividend yield is the cash dividend paid to an investor expressed as a percentage of the current market price of a security. For example, the $0.40 cash dividend of Running Paws divided by the current $25 market price for its stock reveals a dividend yield of 1.6 percent ($0.40/$25). Growth and speculative companies typically pay little or no cash dividends, so they have limited dividend yields. Such companies may be attractive to investors who are interested in capital gains.

Book Value Book value (also known as shareholder's equity) is the net worth of a company, which is determined by subtracting the company's total liabilities from its assets. It theoretically indicates a company's worth if its assets were sold, its debts were paid off, and the net proceeds were distributed to the investors who own the outstanding shares of common stock.

Book Value per Share The book value per share reflects the book value of a company divided by the number of shares of common stock outstanding. Running Paws has a net worth of $230,000, which, when divided by 20,000 shares, gives a book value per share of $11.50.

Often little relationship exists between the book value of a company and its earnings or the market price of its stock. A stock's price usually exceeds its book value per share. The reason is that stockholders bid up the stock price because they anticipate earnings and dividends in the future and expect the market price to rise even more. When the book value per share exceeds the price per share, the stock may truly be underpriced.

Price-to-Book Ratio The price-to-book ratio (P/B ratio), also called the **market-to-book ratio,** identifies firms that are asset rich, such as many banks, brokerage firms, and insurance companies. The P/B ratio is the current stock price divided by the per-share net value of the company's plant, equipment, and other assets (book value). It tells you the premium that you are paying for the net assets of the company.

In the Running Paws example, the book value per share of $11.50 would be divided into the recent price at which the stock was sold ($25 in this case); thus, the P/B ratio for Running Paws is 2.17. The current P/B ratio for most stocks lies between 2.1 and 1.0. The lower the ratio, the less highly a company's assets have been valued, indicating that the stock may be currently under-priced. If the ratio is less than 1, the assets may be utilized ineffectively. In such cases, an under-performing and undervalued company may become a target of a corporate takeover; where the company may be broken up and sold.

14.2e Calculating a Stock's Potential Rate of Return in Five Steps

There is but a single reason to make an investment: to obtain a positive return. Although you cannot know the exact performance of any investment in advance, you certainly will want to pay no more than the "right price" for the investment given its potential rate of return. Calculating returns on a potential investment involves five steps. Armed with these data, you will be better positioned to make informed decisions:

1. *Use Beta to Estimate the Risk of the Investment* Beta is a useful piece of information when you want to estimate the rate of return you require on an investment in a stock, bond, or mutual fund before putting your money at risk. Betas for individual stocks, mutual funds, and other investments are available online from brokerage firms, advisory services, and investment magazines.

   The following example illustrates how to use beta to estimate the amount of risk in an investment portfolio. Assume you are willing to accept more risk than the general investor and that you buy a stock with a beta of 1.5. If the average price of all stocks rises by 20 percent over time, the price of the stock you chose might rise by 30 percent, which is the beta of 1.5 multiplied by the increase in the market (1.5 × 20%). If the average price of all stocks drops in value by 10 percent, the price of the stock you chose might drop by 15 percent (1.5 × 10%).

DO IT IN CLASS

2. *Estimate the Market Risk* To estimate the required rate of return on an investment, you need to quantify the market risk. **Market risk,** also known as **systematic risk,** which we discussed in Chapter 13, is the possibility for an investor to experience losses due to unknown factors that affect the overall performance of the financial markets. It often causes the market price of a particular stock or bond to change, even though nothing has changed in the fundamental values underlying that security. Historical records indicate that 8 percent represents a realistic estimate of market risk for U.S. stocks. Market risk is high during turbulent times in stock markets, and in the near term, it remains elevated.

3. *Calculate Your Required Rate of Return* The return on short-term Treasury bills (U.S. government securities with maturities of less than one year) has historically exceeded the rate of inflation by a slight degree (but not always as sometimes it is lower). Thus, when T-bills pay 2 percent interest, the inflation rate might hover around 1.7 percent. (The various interest rates in this chapter are chosen to be instructive. Note that the government's real T-bill rate is currently lower than 1 percent.) This circumstance provides almost no gain for the investor because the combination of inflation and income taxes reduce the return to about zero. For this reason, investors often use the yield on Treasury bills as a base number that provides a zero **real rate of return**—that is, a zero return on investment after inflation and income taxes.

Treasury bills (T-bills)
Known as T-bills, U.S. government securities with maturities of less than one year.

To calculate your required rate of return on an investment, multiply the beta value of an investment by the estimated market risk and then add the risk-free T-bill rate, as shown in Equation (14.1). For recent T-bill rates, see www.treasurydirect.gov/indiv/research/indepth/tbills/res_tbill_rates.htm. Use Equation (14.1) to determine an **estimate of the required rate of return on an investment.**

$$\text{Estimate of the required rate of return on an investment} = \text{T-bill rate} + (\text{beta} \times \text{market risk}) \quad \textbf{(14.1)}$$

estimate of the required rate of return on an investment
A calculation that multiplies the beta value of an investment by the estimated market risk and adds the risk-free T-bill rate that suggests to investors the return required to put their money at risk.

For example, assume you are considering investing in Running Paws Cat Food Company, which has a beta of 1.5. If you assume a market risk of 8 percent and the current T-bill rate is 0.5 percent, the total rate of return you will require on this investment is 12.5 percent [0.5 + (1.5 × 8.0)]. Investors need the promise of a return higher than 12.5 percent to put their money at risk in this investment.

4. *Calculate the Stock's Potential Return* The potential return for any investment over a period of years can be determined by adding anticipated income (from dividends, interest, rents, or other sources) to the future value of the investment and then subtracting the investment's original cost. The investor using fundamental analysis can obtain the figures needed to construct the expected stream of future earnings for a company from a variety of sources. For example, you can use estimates for earnings and dividends gathered from large investment data firms such as Value Line, Standard & Poor's, MarketWatch, or Reuters, and then obtain an individual stock analyst's projections or you can create your own numbers.

potential return
Determined by adding anticipated income (from dividends, interest, rents, or other sources) to the future value of investment and then subtracting the investment's original cost.

approximate compound yield (ACY)

A measure of the annualized compound growth of any long-term investment stated as a percentage.

Add Up Projected Income and Price Appreciation Table 14-2 illustrates how to sum up the projected income (dividend income) and price appreciation (earnings). You can convert these figures into a potential rate of return by calculating the **approximate compound yield,** as shown in Equation (14.2). This figure can then be compared with returns on other investments.

$$\text{ACY} = \frac{\text{average annual dividend} + \dfrac{\text{projected price of stock} - \text{current price of stock}}{\text{number of years projected}}}{\dfrac{\text{projected price of stock} + \text{current price of stock}}{2}} \quad (14.2)$$

$$= \frac{\$1.02 + \dfrac{\$60.38 - \$30.00}{5}}{\dfrac{\$60.38 + \$30.00}{2}}$$

$$= \frac{\$1.02 + \$6.08}{\$45.19}$$

$$= 15.7\%$$

Example: Running Paws Cat Food Company Based on a recommendation from his stockbroker, Izzle Stevens, a small business owner who lives in Valdosta, Georgia, is considering Running Paws Cat Food Company as a potential investment. Izzle figures that the company's stock might provide a better return than inflation and income taxes for about five years. He has determined the following information about this stock investment: It is currently priced at $30 per share, its most recent 12-month earnings amounted to $2.40 per share, and the cash dividend for the same period was $0.66 per share.

Izzle began the task of projecting the future value of one share of the stock by using the EPS information. He first calculated the P/E ratio to be 12.5 ($30 ÷ $2.40). Next, as illustrated in Table 14-2, Izzle applied a 15 percent rate of growth estimate (the same rate that occurred in previous years, according to Running Paws' annual report) for the EPS for each year ($2.40 × 1.15 = $2.76; $2.76 × 1.15 = $3.17; and so forth). Using a P/E ratio of 12.5 (the same as the current ratio), Izzle estimated the market price at the end of the fifth year to be $60.38 (12.5 × $4.83). This calculation gives a projected net appreciation in stock price over five years of $30.38 ($60.38 minus the current price of $30).

Table 14-2	Projections of the Earnings and Dividends for Running Paws Cat Food Company

End of Year	Earnings	Dividend Income
1	$2.76	$0.76
2	3.17	0.87
3	3.65	1.00
4	4.20	1.15
5	4.83	1.33
Total dividends		$5.11
Average annual dividend ($5.11 ÷ 5)		$1.02

To project the future income of the investment in Running Paws—the anticipated cash dividends—Table 14-2 shows that Izzle estimated a 15 percent growth rate in the cash dividend ($0.66 × 1.15 = $0.76; $0.76 × 1.15 = $0.87; and so forth). Adding the projected cash dividends over five years gives a total of $5.11. Izzle obtained the potential return for one share of Running Paws over five years by adding anticipated dividend income ($5.11) to the future value of the investment ($60.38) less its original cost ($30.00), for a result of $35.49 ($5.11 + $30.38). Thus, Izzle has projected that $30 invested in one share of Running Paws will earn a potential total return of $35.49 in five years.

The ACY Says What Makes a Good Investment The question now becomes, what is the percentage yield for this dollar return? The **approximate compound yield (ACY)** provides a measure of the annualized compound growth of any long-term investment. In short, it tells you whether or not one stock or another investment is good. You can determine this value by using Equation (14.2). The calculation requires use of an *annual average* dividend rather than the specific projected dividends. In this example, the annual average dividend of $1.02 is computed by dividing the $5.11 in dividend income by five years. Substituting the data from Table 14-2 into Equation (14.2) and using the average annual dividend figure results in an approximate compound yield of 15.7 percent on the potential investment in one share of Running Paws stock for five years. (This formula can be found on the *Garman/Forgue* companion website.)

5. *Compare the Required Rate of Return with the Potential Rate of Return on the Investment* Now the moment of decision making is at hand. You compare the estimated required rate of return on an investment (given its risk) with the investment's potential projected rate of return. In our example involving Running Paws Cat Food Company, the risk suggested a required rate of return of 12.5 percent. The investment's potential rate of return was projected to be 15.7 percent, which suggests that Running Paws is a good buy for Izzle at the current selling price of $30—that is, the stock is under priced. Once armed with projected rate of return information for an investment, you can compare it with other investments.

CONCEPT CHECK 14.2

1. Distinguish between the terms *income stocks* and *growth stocks*.
2. Define *beta* and explain what it means.
3. What is *fundamental analysis* and why is it popular?
4. Choose three measures of corporate earnings that you might use when selecting a stock in which to invest and say why you like them.
5. What are the five steps in figuring a potential rate of return to invest in a stock?

14.3 USE THE INTERNET TO EVALUATE AND SELECT STOCKS

Learning Objective 3

Use the Internet to evaluate common stocks in which to invest.

An overwhelming amount of information is available on stock investments. With about 5,000 U.S. public companies to choose from and another 33,000 stocks in other countries, stock selection takes time. Thousands of investment resources exist, including television and radio shows, books, websites, blogs, and newsletters. What approach should you take? Use the Internet because everything you need is online.

14.3a Begin by Setting Criteria for Your Stock Investments

The process of setting criteria for a stock investment starts with a review of your investment plan, as discussed in Chapter 13 and illustrated in Figure 13-6 on page 416. To make informed selections of the stock investments that match your investment goals, philosophy, and time horizon, begin by making decisions on criteria for your stock investments:

- What classifications of stocks are best suited for your goals?
- What market capitalization size company meets your desires?
- What specific numeric measures do you require on beta, sales, profitability, P/E ratio, dividends, payout ratio, and market price?
- What projected EPS growth do you require?
- Do you want to invest in an industry leader?

14.3b   Investor Education Is Widely Available Online

stock-screening tools

Enable you to quickly sift through vast databases of hundreds of companies to find those that best suit your investment objectives.

Comprehensive investment websites provide updated news headlines; market overviews; market statistics; industry statistics; industry trends; corporate stock symbols; current stock market prices; specific company profiles, history, financials, prices, and outlook for the future; tips on how to build a portfolio; and stock-screening tools with search capabilities. Following are some popular websites on investor education:

- The Investor's Clearinghouse (www.investoreducation.org)
- US Securities and Exchange Commission (investor.gov)
- The Motley Fool (www.fool.com/how-to-invest/index.aspx?source =ifltnvpnv0000001)

14.3c   Why Use Online Stock Calculators?

You can perform almost any kind of mathematical calculation necessary in investing by using one of the online investment websites. For example, by using DailyFinance.com (www.dailyfinance.com/calculators/stocks/), you can get answers to these questions:

- What is the return on my stock if I sell now?
- Should I wait a year to sell my stock?
- Should I sell my stock now and invest the money elsewhere?
- What stock price achieves my target rate of return?
- What is my current yield from dividends?
- How much do fees affect my stock's rate of return?
- Which is better: income or growth stock?
- How do exchange rates affect my foreign stock?
- When will I recover my stock costs?

14.3d   Set Up Your Portfolio Online

You can set up a portfolio through an online brokerage account or by using any of several websites. For example, see WikiHow at www.wikihow.com/Build-a-Stock-Portfolio, and JP Morgan at www.jpmorganfunds.com/cm/Satellite? UserFriendlyURL=buildyourportfolio&pagename=jpmfVanityWrapper. Both let you insert the number of shares you own and at what price. The sites then track stock quotes to update the value of your holdings.

14.3e   Use Stock-Screening Tools

You can research stocks, bonds, and mutual funds by using **stock-screening tools** available on the Internet. Screening enables you to quickly sift through vast databases of numerous companies to find those that best suit your investment objectives. For example, you can use the Kiplinger screening tool to filter thousands of stocks using 27 search criteria, and you can use Kiplinger's or another company's tools to identify dividend-paying stocks,

THERE IS AN APP FOR THAT!

Some of the best apps are:

- Vanguard
- Baton Investing
- Betterment
- Bloomberg
- Chase
- CNBC Real-Time
- EFFdb
- Mint
- Morningstar
- Fidelity
- Forbes
- Motif Investing
- Charles Schwab
- StockTwits
- Wikinvest Portfolio Manager
- Yahoo! Finance

small companies, and growth companies. You simply set the standard for screening, such as high P/E ratios, and the program sorts out the investment choices, including five-year EPS growth projections by professional stock analysts. You may be surprised to find how easy it is to screen stocks. The following websites offer stock-screening tools: Kiplinger, MSN Money, and MarketWatch.

14.3f   Get a Sense of the History of a Stock

You can study the price of stock movements over different time frames, including bull and bear markets, as well as make comparisons to various benchmarks such as the S&P 500 Index. See Market Watch (bigcharts.marketwatch.com/historical). Your task when selecting stocks is to find the right balance between the anticipated return given how much safety and risk are apparent.

14.3g   Go to the Source for Company Information

Corporate filings required by the Securities and Exchange Commission are available on the Internet from the Electronic Data Gathering and Retrieval (EDGAR) project (www.sec.gov/edgar/searchedgar/webusers.htm#.U2p5IaJn34g). Top online sources for stock, bond, and mutual fund information include Morningstar (www.morningstar.com) and Bloomberg (www.bloomberg.com). Each public company has its own website that offers insights from management about the future of the firm, and it is easy to request a company's annual report to obtain management's views.

Every company registered with the Securities and Exchange Commission (SEC) is required to file once each year to ensure public availability of accurate current information about the firm. The company summarizes its financial activities for the year. The **10-Q report** includes the financial results for the quarter, a discussion from management, a list of material events and other risk factors that have occurred (such as legal problems or the loss of a large customer), a forecast of the company's future, and any significant changes or events in the quarter. A similar 10-K report is filed annually. You can obtain both 10-Q and 10-K reports from the SEC online (www.sec.gov). You can find executive compensation details on Form DEF 14A.

10-Q report
A report required by the SEC prepared by the company showing its financial results for the quarter, a discussion from management, a list of material events and other risk factors that have occurred, forecasts of the company's future, and notes of any significant changes or events in the quarter.

There are numerous websites that offer fundamental and technical analysis of stocks. The Motley Fool does so with humor.

annual report

Legally required yearly report about financial performance, activities, and prospects sent to major stockholders and made available to the general public.

prospectus

Highly legalistic information presented by a firm to the SEC and to the public with any new issue of stock.

The company's **annual report** is mostly a numbers-free publication that looks like a slick marketing magazine. While annual reports do contain some summarized financial information, they serve more as promotional corporate brochures.

When a company issues any new security, it files a **prospectus** with the SEC. This disclosure describes the experience of the corporation's management, the company's financial status, any anticipated legal matters that could affect the company, and potential risks of investing in the firm. The language is legalistic and full of technical jargon, but the interested investor may find it useful to sift through the details.

14.3h   Use Stock Analysts' Research Reports

Stock analysts working for independent stock advisory firms or stock brokerages write research reports on companies and industries, as illustrated in Figure 14-1 with a report from Standard & Poor's. Reports based on fundamental analysis are quite informative. The quality of advice is uneven, ranging from brilliant to pedestrian as analysts have a tendency to run with the herd and make similar recommendations. They often recommend buying certain stocks and rarely suggest selling. The prudent investor interprets "hold" recommendations as a signal to sell.

14.3i   Read Research Newsletters

The most popular firms that offer stock advisory research services on a subscription basis to individual investors are Morningstar (www.morningstar.com), Value Line (www.valueline.com), MarketWatch (www.marketwatch.com), and Reuters (www.reuters.com/finance/markets). The cost for some of these services is in the hundreds of dollars per year, and available in large libraries. A Google search for "stock advisory newsletters" will reveal dozens of firms that offer guidance on stock selections, market updates, and investment advice.

You may wish to avoid those that offer suggestions based on a "technical" or "chartist" approach to analyzing stocks; instead select one that uses a mainstream approach emphasizing fundamental research. As the old Wall Street adage says, don't confuse a bull market with genius from a newsletter writer.

securities market index

Measures the average value of a number of securities chosen as a sample to reflect the behavior of a more general market.

14.3j   Be Aware of Economic Trends

To be an effective investor, you need to know the stage of the business cycle (recession or prosperity) and the current rates for interest and inflation. You also need to understand how economic conditions are likely to change over the next 12 to 18 months. (These topics were examined in Chapter 1.) Economic information is available through almost all media:

- *Search engines:* Yahoo!, Google, and Momma
- *Big newspapers: USA Today, Los Angeles Times, The Wall Street Journal*
- *Business news: Business Week, Fortune, Forbes, Financial World*
- *Personal finance: Money magazine and Kiplinger's Personal Finance Magazine*
- *Investment sources: The Wall Street Journal, Barron's, Investor's Business Daily, Market Watch, Reuter's*
- *News magazines: U.S. News & World Report, Time*

YOUR GRANDPARENTS SAY

"Be Prepared to Lose"

"You cannot trade stocks without losing some money. The goal, of course, is for your capital gains on shares to outpace your losses, but when losses do occur they can hit you hard. That's why it's important to trade stocks only with money you're willing to lose: money that was specifically budgeted to stock trading."

14.3k Pay Attention to Securities Market Indexes

Reports on securities market indexes are provided around the clock in almost every media. "The Dow went up 160 points today." "The S&P 500 rose 19 points." When it is reported that "the Dow rose 160 points today in heavy trading," realize that these "points" are changes in the index, not actual dollar changes in the value of the stocks. A **securities market index** is an indicator of market performance. It measures the average value of a number of securities chosen as a sample to reflect the behavior of a more general market. Popular indexes include the following.

Figure 14-1 **Illustrative Stock Analyst's Report**

Stock Report | July 30, 2016 | NNM Symbol: **GOOGL** | **GOOGL** is in the S&P 500

S&P CAPITAL IQ
McGRAW HILL FINANCIAL

Alphabet Inc

S&P Capital IQ Recommendation	**STRONG BUY** ★★★★★	Price	12-Mo. Target Price	Report Currency	Investment Style
		$791.34 (as of Jul 29, 2016 4:00 PM ET)	$900.00	USD	Large-Cap Growth

S&P Capital IQ Equity Analyst S. Kessler

GICS Sector Information Technology
Sub-Industry Internet Software & Services

Summary Alphabet (formerly Google) is the world's largest Internet company, specializing in search and advertising. In October 2015, the company renamed itself, establishing Google as its primary operating unit.

Key Stock Statistics (Source S&P Capital IQ, Vickers, company reports)

52-Wk Range	$810.35–593.09	S&P Oper. EPS 2016**E**	34.09	Market Capitalization(B)	$229.398	Beta	1.09
Trailing 12-Month EPS	$26.19	S&P Oper. EPS 2017**E**	40.24	Yield (%)	Nil	S&P 3-Yr. Proj. EPS CAGR(%)	18
Trailing 12-Month P/E	30.2	P/E on S&P Oper. EPS 2016**E**	23.2	Dividend Rate/Share	Nil	S&P Quality Ranking	A-
$10K Invested 5 Yrs Ago	$39,287	Common Shares Outstg. (M)	685.5	Institutional Ownership (%)	83		

Price Performance

Past performance is not an indication of future performance and should not be relied upon as such.

Analysis prepared by Equity Analyst **S. Kessler** on Jul 29, 2016 10:33 AM, when the stock traded at **$797.21**.

Highlights

➤ We project that revenues will rise 16% in 2016 and 15% in 2017. We see revenue growth being driven by pricing improvements in mobile and increasing traction across display offerings, most notably YouTube. We see a strong U.S. dollar as a negative for top-line growth.

➤ EBTIDA margins narrowed notably in 2012, due to the Motorola purchase, but we have seen improvements thereafter and see this trend continuing through 2018, given a more favorable revenue mix and more disciplined investments. We note continuing spending related to new offerings and government inquiries/investigations, including those involving the European Commission announced in in 2015 and 2016.

➤ In May 2012, GOOGL acquired Motorola Mobility for $12.5 billion. In April 2013, GOOGL sold Motorola's Home unit to Arris in a deal valued at $2.4 billion. In October 2014, GOOGL sold the remainder of Motorola for some $2.9 billion. However, GOOGL retained considerable intellectual property, despite selling related business. GOOGL announced its first stock buyback program, for $5.1 billion, in October 2015.

Investment Rationale/Risk

➤ We see healthy growth, with opportunities related to mobile and video (YouTube, in particular), and note related improving pricing trends. We believe new CFO Ruth Porat, who held the same role at Morgan Stanley, and joined in May 2015, will contribute to greater transparency and more expense discipline. Nonetheless, we see continuing aggressive investments. In August 2015, the company announced it would change its name to Alphabet, and that Google would be its primary operating business.

➤ Risks to our recommendation and target price include the potential for market share losses, excess expenditures associated with expansion and adverse legal and/or regulatory developments.

➤ Our 12-month target price is $900. Global large-cap Internet peers recently had a forward median P/E of 32X and a P/E-to-growth (PEG) ratio of 1.2. Applying these multiples to GOOGL and averaging the outputs results in our target. We have favorable views of the company's balance sheet and capital allocation efforts and potential.

Analyst's Risk Assessment

LOW	**MEDIUM**	HIGH

Our risk assessment reflects significant competition, substantial and increasing investment and related new offerings, considerable ongoing legal and regulatory matters and potential issues related to the pending sale of Motorola Mobility.

Revenue/Earnings Data

Revenue (Million U.S. $)

	1Q	2Q	3Q	4Q	Year
2016	20,257	21,500	--	--	--
2015	17,258	17,727	18,675	21,329	74,989
2014	15,420	15,955	16,523	18,103	66,001
2013	13,969	14,105	14,893	16,858	59,825
2012	10,645	11,807	13,304	14,419	50,175
2011	8,575	9,026	9,720	10,584	37,905

Earnings Per Share (U.S. $)

2016	6.12	7.10	E8.56	E9.61	E34.09
2015	5.20	6.43	5.81	7.16	23.01
2014	5.33	5.09	4.36	5.50	20.27
2013	4.94	3.78	4.36	4.96	18.03
2012	4.38	4.21	3.24	4.34	16.23
2011	2.76	3.84	4.17	4.11	14.88

Fiscal year ended Dec. 31. Next earnings report expected: Late October. EPS Estimates based on S&P Capital IQ Operating Earnings; historical GAAP earnings are as reported in Company reports.

Dividend Data

No cash dividends have been paid.

Past performance is not an indication of future performance and should not be relied upon as such.

Please read the Required Disclosures and Analyst Certification on the last page of this report.

Dow Jones Industrial Average (DJIA)

The most widely reported of all stock market indexes that tracks prices of 30 actively traded blue-chip stocks, including well-known companies such as American Express and AT&T.

The Dow The **Dow Jones Industrial Average (DJIA)** is the most widely reported of all indexes. The most popular DJIA industrial average, also called the "Dow," follows prices of only 30 actively traded blue-chip stocks, including well-known companies such as American Express, Caterpillar, Coca-Cola, Home Depot, Nike, Visa, Walmart, and Walt Disney. The average is calculated by adding the closing prices of the 30 stocks and dividing by a number adjusted for splits, spin-offs, and dividends.* The DJIA also produces a transportation average based on 20 stocks, a utility average based on 15 stocks, and a composite average based on all 65 industrial, transportation, and utility stocks.

Standard & Poor's 500 Index The popular **Standard & Poor's (S&P) 500 Index** reports price movements of 500 stocks of large, established, publicly traded firms. It includes stocks of 400 industrial firms, 40 financial institutions, 40 public utilities, and 20 transportation companies. Companies with the highest market values influence the index the greatest.

NASDAQ Composite Index and Other Indexes The **NASDAQ Composite Index** takes into account virtually all U.S. stocks (about 3,100) traded in the **over-the-counter market** in the automated quotations system operated by the National Association of Securities Dealers. It provides a measure of companies not as popular or as large as those traded on the popular exchanges, including price behavior of many smaller, more speculative companies, although some big companies (such as Cisco Systems, Intel, Microsoft, and Staples) are listed as well. It is often used as a benchmark for the performance of high-tech stocks.

The **Dow Jones Wilshire 5,000 Index** is a market-capitalization-weighted index of the market value of all stocks actively traded in the United States. The total of all the publicly traded stocks in the United States is about 3,700. One point in the index is worth $1 billion; thus when the index is 22,000, that translates to a U.S. stock market valued at over $22 trillion. The **Russell 2,000 Index** is a small-cap stock market index of relatively small capitalized companies and is the most widely quoted measure of the overall performance of the small-cap to midcap company shares. Stock exchanges are located in major cities throughout the world, including London, Sydney, Tokyo, Toronto, Frankfort, Mumbai, Hong Kong, Shenzhen, Shanghai, and Kuala Lumpur. U.S. investors often check the stock exchanges throughout the night to gain a hint of what might happen the next day in the U.S. stock market.

14.3l Securities Exchanges (Stock Markets)

securities exchange (stock market)

Market where agents of buyers and sellers can find each other easily by providing an orderly, open plan to trade securities.

A **securities exchange** (also called a **stock market**) is a market where agents of buyers and sellers can find each other easily by providing an orderly, open plan to trade securities. Each exchange has its own rules, is subject to government regulation, and provides constant supervision and self-regulation.

The transactions were historically performed in an organized physical location, such as the New York Stock Exchange (known officially as NYSE Euronext and listed as NYX), and also known as the **"Big Board"**) as well as the American Stock Exchange (known officially as NYSE MKT LLC and also owned by NYSE Euronext) Both are in New York City.

You may visualize a bustling exchange that ends the trading day with a bell. However, today most stock trading occurs in a fragmented collection of 50 trading platforms, and almost all transactions are performed electronically. The market capitalization of the NYSE Euronext's over 2,800 listed companies is over $22 trillion (which includes 90 percent of the Dow Jones Industrial Average and 80 percent of the S&P 500). As many as 1½ billion shares trade daily on the New York Stock Exchange. There also are regional stock exchanges in many cities that do not meet the stringent requirements for listing on the largest stock markets.

---

* A **stock split** occurs when the shares of a stock owned by existing shareholders are divided into a larger number of shares. This may be an indicator that management expects better profits in the years ahead. Many companies provide a cash dividend to stockholders, and sometimes companies declare a noncash dividend in the form of a **stock dividend.** Here the shareholder receives additional shares of the company's stock.

OTC or Over-the-Counter Trading Over-the-counter (OTC) or off-exchange trading is used to refer to stocks that trade via a dealer network made over a telephone and computer system rather than on the floor of a centralized exchange. This electronic telecommunications network facilitates the buying and selling of securities that usually are not listed on a centralized major exchanges through market makers.

Over-the-counter (OTC) (off-exchange trading)

Refers to stocks that trade via a dealer network made using a telephone and computer system rather than on the floor of a centralized exchange.

14.3m Looking Up a Stock Price

What affects the price of a stock the most is supply and demand. When more people want to buy, the price goes up. When more people want to sell, the price goes down. If you know the company's stock symbol (search Google for "stock symbols"), the current price of any stock may be obtained by inputting the company symbol into Google or any of the other popular investment websites, such as Yahoo! Finance, MSN Money, Reuter's, and MarketWatch.

The millions of daily buying and selling transactions involving stocks, bonds, and mutual funds are summarized in *The Wall Street Journal,* the most widely read financial newspaper in the United States. Many daily newspapers publish abbreviated information, and security prices are quoted and traded to two decimal points. Stock quotations that might appear in *The Wall Street Journal* for Walmart, a retailer, are illustrated in Figure 14-2.

- **Column 1: YTD % Change.** The numbers in this column report the "year to date (YTD) as a percentage" change in the price (+8.6%) of Walmart stock since January 1 of the calendar year.
- **Columns 2 and 3: 52 Weeks, High and Low.** This column shows that Walmart stock traded at a high price of $63.08 and a low price of $41.50 during the previous 52 weeks, not including the previous trading day.
- **Column 4: Stock and Sym.** This column gives the name of the stock (Walmart in this example) and its abbreviated trading symbol (WMT).
- **Column 5: Div.** The dividend amount is based on the last quarterly declaration by the company. For example, Walmart last paid a quarterly dividend that, when converted to an annual basis, amounts to an estimated $0.28 annual dividend.
- **Column 6: Yld %.** The figure in this column represents the yield as a percentage of dividend income, calculated by dividing the current price of the stock into the recent estimated dividend. The yield of the Walmart stock is 0.4 percent.

Figure 14-2 **How Stocks Are Quoted**

1	2	3	4		5	6	7	8	9	10
YTD	52 WEEKS					YLD		VOL		NET
%CHG	HI	LO	STOCK (SYM)		DIV	%	PE	100S	LAST	CNG
+17.2	45.29	28.70	Walgreen	WAG	.14	.4	44	27540	39.45	+0.59
+ 3.7	20.56	14.00	WallaceCS	WCS	.66	3.4	17	714	19.70	+0.06
+ 0.1	34.50	23.00	WaddReed A	WDR	.35	1.1	25	2228	32.24	+0.04
+ 8.6	63.08	41.50	Walmart	WMT	.28	.4	42	104572	62.52	+0.82

Column 7: PE. This figure provides the P/E ratio based on the current price. The earnings figure used to calculate the price is not published in the newspaper but is the latest available. When Walmart's "last" or closing price of $62.52 is divided by earnings, it gives a P/E ratio of 42.

Column 8: Vol 100s. This figure indicates the total volume of trading activity for the stock measured in hundreds of shares. Thus, 10,457,200 shares of Walmart were traded on that day.

Column 9: Last. The price of the last trade of the day before the market closed for Wal-Mart was $62.52.

Column 10: Net Cng. The net change, +0.82%, represents the difference between the closing price (last) on this day and the closing price of the previous trading day. Today's Walmart closing (last) price of $62.52 was up $0.82 from the previous closing price, which must have been $61.70.

14.3n Using Portfolio Tracking to Watch Your Investments

portfolio tracking

Automatically updates the value of your portfolio after you enter the symbols of the stocks you own and the number of shares held.

Watching your investments requires record keeping, particularly for income tax purposes, although when you sell any securities your brokerage firm will provide you with sufficient details. Recordkeeping tasks can be performed easily using the Internet. Portfolio tracking automatically updates the value of your portfolio after you enter the symbols of the stocks you own and the number of shares held. Online portfolio tracking services also alert you to events that may affect your stocks. Tracking helps you stay on top of your holdings so you know which stocks are performing well, which are underperforming, and which might need to be sold. For programs, type in "portfolio tracker" on Google.

NUMBERS ON

Stocks and Bonds

Data from a number of sources suggest:

- CNNMoney reports that the biggest reason why people do not invest is that they don't have the money.

- Only half of American adults (52 percent) say they personally or jointly with a spouse own stock outright or as part of a mutual fund or self-directed retirement account.

- About 40 percent of adults under age 35 own stocks.

- Four in 10 stocks are unprofitable investments.

- Average annual returns in last decade: Stocks, 9.3%; 3-month T-bill, 0.50%; 10-year Treasury Bond, 3.10%.

- Stock market wealth is held by a relatively small number of the most affluent (defined as the 80% of college-educated households who earn more than $75,000) and, as a result, most families have much less than the average amount.

- Surveys say the investments Americans prefer are real estate (27%), cash (23%), stocks (17%), gold (14%), bonds (5%), and others (14%).

- One-third of America's debt is owned by foreigners with the largest holders being China (7.2%) and Japan (7.0%).

- Two-thirds of America's public debt is owned by domestic organizations such as Social Security, 16%; other federal government entities, 13%, and the Federal Reserve, 12%.

CONCEPT CHECK 14.3

1. How does one use a stock screening tool?
2. Name two places where you can go to find information about a company?
3. Distinguish between the Dow Jones Industrial Average and the S&P 500.
4. Where can you go to look up stock symbols and prices?

14.4 BUYING AND SELLING STOCKS

Securities transactions require the use of a licensed broker serving as a middleman between the seller and the buyer and collecting a fee on each purchase or sale of securities. A **stockbroker** (also known as an **account executive**) is licensed to buy and sell securities on behalf of the brokerage firm's clients. You can buy or sell securities through an online or human stockbroker who works for a brokerage firm that has access to the securities markets. Brokerage firms often provide investors with investment advice.

14.4a Opening a Brokerage Account

To trade securities, you will need a brokerage firm to act as your agent. You can open an account at a full-service general brokerage firm or a discount brokerage firm. The firm charges a commission for any trading it conducts on your behalf. You should make clear to the brokerage firm, in writing, your investment objectives and your desired level of risk. A **cash account** is a brokerage account that requires an initial deposit (often as little as $1,000) and specifies that full settlement is due to the brokerage firm within three business days after a buy or sell order has been given. After each transaction, your account is debited or credited, and written confirmation is immediately forwarded.

As a matter of convenience and to facilitate resale, investors prefer to leave securities certificates in the name of their brokerage firm rather than take physical possession themselves. Securities certificates kept in the brokerage firm's name instead of the name of the individual investor are known as the **security's street name**. Brokers have a duty to assess each client's suitability for particular investments. Table 14-3 shows the different types of stock brokerage firms.

Learning Objective 4

Summarize how to buy and sell stocks, as well as the techniques of margin buying and selling short.

stockbroker (account executive)
Professional who is licensed to buy and sell securities on behalf of the brokerage firm's clients.

cash account
A brokerage account that requires an initial deposit (perhaps as little as $1,000) and specifies that full settlement is due to the brokerage firm within three business days after a buy or sell order has been given.

security's street name
Securities certificates kept in the brokerage firm's name instead of the name of the individual investor.

ADVICE FROM A SEASONED PRO

Rules of Thumb on How to Invest

There are certain things that smart people do when investing:

- Trust myself and my intuition
- Get my investment goals straight
- Be knowledgeable before investing
- Be cautious, premeditated, and levelheaded

- Decide where you are on risk tolerance
- Invest little by little
- Start small
- Invest on a regular basis
- Diversify widely
- Learn from any miscalculations

David Leapard
Eastern Michigan University, Ypsilanti, Michigan

general (full-service) brokerage firms

Offer a full range of services to customers, including investment advice and research.

discount brokers

Charge commissions to execute trades that are often 30 to 80 percent less than the fees charged by full-service brokers, but also offer fewer services.

online discount brokers

Such brokers, also called Internet or electronic discount brokers, have reduced the cost of executing a trade to perhaps $20 or even $10 because their primary business is online trading.

Table 14-3	**Types of Brokerage Firms**
General (Full-Service) Brokerage Firm	Offers a full range of services, including investment information and advice; research reports on companies, industries, general economic trends, and world events; an investment newsletter; recommendations to buy, sell, or hold stocks; execution of securities transactions by live brokers and online; and margin loans. Commissions and fees are higher than other firms. See Edward Jones, Raymond James, UBS, Morgan Stanley Smith Barney, and Wells Fargo Advisors.
Discount Brokerage	They charge commissions to execute trades that are often 30 to 80 percent less than the fees charged by full-service brokers. Most offer excellent research and investment tools. See Fidelity, TD Ameritrade, Charles Schwab, USAA Brokerage Services, and Vanguard.
Online Discount Brokerage	**Online discount brokers** (also called Internet or electronic discount brokers) have reduced the cost of executing a trade to perhaps $10 or even $5 because their primary business is online trading. All the discount brokers noted are also online brokers. Additional highly rated online brokers are TD Ameritrade, E*Trade, Fidelity, and Scott Trade.

DID YOU KNOW

Regulations Help Protect Against Investment Fraud

Public trust is vital to the success of the securities industry; without it, consumers will not invest. Regulation occurs at five levels:

1. **Securities and Exchange Commission (SEC).** *The SEC is a federal government agency that focuses on ensuring disclosure of information about securities to the investing public and on approving the rules and regulations employed by the organized securities exchanges. It prohibits manipulative practices, such as using "insider information" for illegal personal gain or causing the price of a security to rise or fall for false reasons. All states require registration of securities sold within their states, and they, too, regulate the securities industry.*

2. **Self-Regulatory Agencies.** *The Financial Industry Regulatory Authority (FINRA) and other self-regulatory organizations, such as the New York Stock Exchange, enforce standards of conduct for their members and*

their member organizations. They dictate rules for listing and for trading securities.

3. **Brokerage Firms.** *Individual brokerage firms have established standards of conduct for brokers that govern how they deal with investors.*

4. **Security Investors Protection Corporation (SIPC).** *The SIPC is a limited insurance program to protect the investing public when an SEC-registered brokerage firm fails. Although investment losses due to fraud, misrepresentation or bad investment decisions are not covered, the SIPC protects each of an investor's accounts at a brokerage firm against financial loss as a result of unreturned securities and cash up to a total of $500,000, but no more than $100,000 in cash.*

5. **Financial Services Oversight Council (FSOC).** *The mission of the FSOC is to eliminate expectations that any American financial firm is "too big to fail" and to respond to emerging threats to U.S. financial stability.*

14.4b Broker Commissions and Fees

Brokerage firms receive a commission on each securities transaction to cover the direct expenses of executing the transaction and other overhead expenses. They have established fee schedules that they use when dealing with any except the largest investors. The fees reflect a commission rate that declines as the total value of the transaction

ADVICE FROM A SEASONED PRO

Day Trading Is Risky

Day trading is speculation in securities, specifically buying and selling financial instruments within the same trading day with the hope that prices will move enough to cover transaction costs and earn some profits. Strictly, day trading is trading only within a day, such that all positions are closed before the market closes for the trading day. Transactions are executed online because they can be done quickly with low commissions. This type of trading often relies on technical analysis, looking at short term price movements, rather than fundamental analysis, looking at underlying value. Day trading is a risky practice.

Studies indicate that most day traders are not profitable. Think of it this way, could the average person compete against a professional athlete? Professional traders and/or sophisticated computer algorithms may be on the other side of your trade.

Jamey Darnell
College of Central Florida, Ocala, Florida

---

increases. For example, in lieu of a minimum commission charge of $25, a brokerage firm might charge 2.8 percent on a transaction amounting to less than $800, 1.8 percent on transactions between $800 and $2,500, 1.6 percent on amounts between $2,500 and $5,000, and 1.2 percent on amounts exceeding $5,000.

Transaction costs are based on sales of **round lots,** which are standard units of trading of 100 shares of stock and $1,000 or $5,000 par value for bonds. An **odd lot** is an amount of a security that is less than the normal unit of trading for that particular security. For stocks, any transaction less than 100 shares is usually considered to be an odd lot. When brokerage firms buy or sell shares in odd lots, they may charge a fee of 12.5 cents (called an **eighth**) per share on the odd-lot portion of the transaction, which is called the **differential.**

The payment of commissions can quickly reduce the return on any investment. A purchase commission of 2 percent is added to a sales commission of another 2 percent, for example, means that the investor has to earn a 4 percent return just to pay the transaction costs. Brokerage commissions typically range from $25 to 3 percent of the value of the transaction. The easiest way to hold down investing costs is to find a brokerage firm that charges low commissions, and that usually means using a discount or online broker, as trades occur with commissions of $10 or less.

One reformed stockbroker admitted what most people already know. When you sell products—such as stocks, bonds, and mutual funds—and get paid on each transaction, your bias is toward selling the ones that pay you the most. And you push more transactions.

14.4c Check the Background of Your Stockbroker or Investment Advisor

See FINRA's BrokerCheck website (www.finra.org/brokercheck) to investigate the background of 440,000 stockbrokers or any of 45,000 brokerage firms. The Financial Industry Regulatory Authority (FINRA) is the nation's largest independent regulatory organization in the securities industry. Also check the disciplinary record of most any financial adviser who manages more than $110 million in assets at the Securities and Exchange Commission at www.adviserinfo.sec.gov. Sometimes the investor receives poor advice.

Seven percent of investment advisors, that's one in every 14, have misconduct records. One year later nearly half of those fired are re-employed in the industry. Don't let one of these people work for you. Don't be ignorant of an advisor's history.

Table 14-4	Instruction Orders Accompanying Stock Transaction

Instruction Order	Process
Market	Buy or sell at current prevailing price
Fill-or-Kill	Immediately buy or sell at current market price or cancel
Matched	Held for minutes, hours or days until executed or cancelled
Negotiated	Buyer "bids" for best price and negotiates until accepted or cancelled
Good-til-Cancelled	Remains valid until executed or cancelled by the investor
Limit	Buy at best possible price "but not above" a specified limit or to sell at a certain price "but not below" a specified price
Stop (or Stop-Loss)	Sell at the market price if it goes below a specified price

14.4d   How to Order Stock Transactions

Hundreds of millions of shares of securities are traded daily on the stock markets in the United States. Every trade brings together a buyer and a seller to complete the transaction at a given price.

Types of Stock Orders Basically, there are only two types of orders—buy and sell. The stockbroker will buy or sell securities according to prescribed instructions in a process called **executing an order**. Those instructions can place constraints on the prices at which those orders are carried out. Table 14-4 shows the instruction orders that accompany stock orders.

14.4f   Margin Buying and Selling Short Are Risky Trading Techniques

For investors interested in taking on additional risk, there are two advanced trading techniques, and both involve using credit: (1) buying stocks on margin and (2) selling short.

Margin Trading Is Buying Stocks on Credit Some investors open a margin account with a brokerage firm in addition to their cash account so they can buy securities using credit provided by the brokerage firm. **Margin buying** requires making a deposit of $2,000 in cash or securities. It is an account offered by brokers that allows investors to borrow money to buy securities. An investor might put down 50 percent of the value of a purchase and borrow the rest. Margin trading allows the investor to apply leverage that magnifies returns or losses.

The **margin rate** is the percentage of the value (or equity) in an investment that is not borrowed. The current requirement for stocks is 50 percent. Thus at least 50 percent of each dollar invested must be the investor's. The remainder may be borrowed from the broker. The securities purchased, as well as other assets in the margin account, are used as collateral.

Buying on margin also can increase returns. Let's say you buy a stock for $50 and the price of the stock rises to $75. If you bought 100 shares of the stock in a cash account and paid for it in full, you'll earn a 50 percent return on your investment ($7,500 − $5,000 = $2,500/$5,000). But if you bought the stock on margin—paying $2,500 in cash and

margin buying

Account at a brokerage firm that requires a substantial deposit of cash or securities and permits the purchase of other securities using credit granted by the brokerage firm.

margin rate

Set by the Fed, percentage of the value (or equity) in an investment that is not borrowed—recently 25 to 50 percent.

THE TAX CONSEQUENCES OF INVESTING IN STOCKS AND BONDS

The government encourages investing through tax policies that favor investors.

Dividends and Interest

Taxes are low on dividend income. Funds put into regular investment accounts represent **after-tax money** where you earn an income on which you pay taxes, and then you invest some of the remaining money. Taxes are due on any interest, dividends, and capital gains in the year in which the income is received. The IRS considers as interest income any increase in the par value on bonds. Interest is taxable at the investor's marginal tax rate. Dividend income is taxed at a maximum rate of 15 percent for most people; a zero percent rate applies to lower-income taxpayers.

Capital Gains and Losses

Capital gains taxes are low. No tax liability is incurred for any capital gains until the stock, bond, mutual fund, real estate, or other investment is sold. When you sell an investment, such as a stock, the gain or loss is calculated by analyzing what you paid for the investment plus broker commissions and fees minus the selling price minus commissions or redemption fees. Short-term gains (for investments held one year or less) are taxed at the same rates as ordinary income. Long-term gains (for investments held at least a year and a day) are taxed at lower rates for most taxpayers. The long-term capital gains rate is zero for taxpayers in the 10 or 15 percent marginal tax brackets; it is 15 percent for those in the 25, 28, 33, and 35 percent brackets; and it is 20 percent for those in the 39.6 percent tax bracket. Capital losses can be used to offset capital gains or even your regular income.

borrowing $2,500 from your broker—you'll earn a 100 percent return on the money you invested ($2,500/$2,500). Of course, you have to repay your broker some interest.

The downside to using margin is that if the stock price decreases, substantial losses can occur. Let's say the stock you bought for $50 falls to $25. If you fully paid for the stock, you'll lose 50 percent of your money. But if you bought on margin, you'll lose 100 percent, and you still must come up with the interest you owe on the loan.

Since the price declined more than 25 percent the **maintenance margin requirement** will be implemented by the broker. This is the minimum amount of equity that must be maintained in a margin account. The typical required minimum level of margin is usually 25 percent of the total market value of the securities in the margin account, although many brokerages have higher maintenance requirements of 30 or 40 percent. When the maintenance margin is not met a representative of the firm will communicate to the investor to immediately either put up more collateral (money or other securities) or face having the investment sold to make up the needed amount in a **margin call** resulting in an even sharper financial loss to the investor.

Selling Short Is Selling Stocks Borrowed from Your Broker Buying a security with the hope that it will go up in value—the goal of most investors— is called **buying long**. You might suspect, however, that the price of a security will drop. You can earn profits when the price of a security declines by **selling short**. In this trading technique, investors sell securities they do not own (borrowing them from a broker) and after so many days or weeks plan to buy back the same number of shares of the security at a lower price (returning them to the broker). Thus, the investor earns a profit on the transaction.

Brokerage firms require an investor to maintain a margin account when selling short because it provides some assurance that the investor can repay the firm for the borrowed stock, if necessary. As a result, some or all of an investor's funds deposited in a margin account are effectively tied up during a short sale. Many brokers hold the proceeds of a short sale, without paying interest, until the customer **covers the position** by buying it back for delivery to the broker.

buying long
Buying a security (especially on margin) with the hope that the stock price will rise.

selling short
Investors selling securities they do not own (borrowing them from a broker) and later buying the same number of shares of the security at a lower price (returning them to the broker).

margin call
Using a margin account to buy securities; allows the investor to apply leverage that magnifies returns—or losses.

NEVER EVER

1. *Invest in stocks that do not match your investment philosophy.*
2. *Fail to use fundamental analysis when making stock investments.*
3. *Buy stocks on margin or sell stocks short.*

Only a small proportion of investors sell stocks short because this approach is so risky. Selling short and buying on margin are techniques to be used only by sophisticated investors.

CONCEPT CHECK 14.4

1. Summarize the differences among discount, online, and full-service brokers.
2. Summarize the differences among types of stock orders: market, limit, and stop order.
3. What is buying on margin and how it can go wrong for an investor?
4. Explain what selling short is and how it can go wrong for an investor.

Learning Objective 5

Describe how to invest in bonds.

investment-grade bonds

Offer investors a reasonable certainty of regularly receiving periodic income (interest) and retrieving the amount originally invested (principal).

zero-coupon bonds (zeros or deep discount bonds)

Municipal, corporate, and Treasury bonds that are issued at a sharp discount from face value and pay no annual interest but are redeemed at full face value upon maturity.

14.5 INVESTING IN BONDS

While bonds usually offer a lower return to investors than stocks, there are good reasons to include bonds in one's portfolio. You should consider investing in bonds if you wish to receive steady income from a portion of your investments. Another is that bonds diversify your investments, which reduces market risk. Others include obtaining a regular source of predictable although low income, the likelihood of profiting from possible future increases in the value of bonds if you own a bond and interest rates decline, and matching some of one's assets to one's investment time horizon. Bonds also can be a safe investment if held to maturity.

A variety of bonds are available to the investor. High quality bonds are called **investment-grade bonds** and they offer investors a reasonable certainty of regularly receiving the periodic income (interest) and retrieving the amount originally invested (principal). Only about 0.001 percent of the 23,000 largest U.S. companies that issue bonds meet the highest investment-grade rating standards for a AAA credit rating. That's a total of 3 companies. Bonds are usually issued at a **par value** (also known as **face value**) of $1,000, and they pay interest semi-annually, which is known as a **coupon rate**.

ADVICE FROM A SEASONED PRO

Zero-Coupon Bonds Pay Phantom Interest

Zero-coupon bonds (also called **zeros** or **deep discount bonds**) are municipal, corporate, and Treasury bonds that pay no annual interest. They are sold to investors at sharp discounts from their face value and may be redeemed at full value upon maturity. For example, a 4 percent, $10,000 zero-coupon bond to be redeemed 15 years from now might sell today for $5,550.

Zeros pay no current income to investors, so investors do not have to be concerned about where to reinvest interest payments. The semiannual interest accumulates within the bond itself, and the return to the investor comes from redeeming the bond at its stated face value at the maturity date. In this manner, zeros operate much like Series EE savings bonds and T-bills. The maturity date for a zero could range from a few months to as long as 30 years. Parents often invest in zero-coupon bonds to help pay for their children's college education, and they wisely establish ownership of the zeros in the child's name. The phantom income "paid" to the child is generally so small that little, if any, income taxes are due.

People planning for retirement often buy zeros because they know exactly how much will be received at maturity. Even though the investor receives no interest money until maturity, the investor still pays income taxes every year on the interest that accumulates within the bond. Investors can avoid income taxes altogether by buying zeros in a qualified tax-sheltered retirement plan account.

Anne Ranczuch
Monroe Community College, Rochester, New York

Speculative-grade bonds pay a high interest rate. These are often derisively called **junk bonds,** and they are long-term, high-risk, high-interest-rate corporate (or municipal) IOUs issued by companies (or municipalities) with weak or no credit ratings. The interest rates paid investors on junk bonds are 3.5 to 8 percentage points more than those of Treasury bonds.

Also more elegantly called **high-yield bonds,** they carry investment ratings that are below traditional investment grade and carry a higher risk of default (not repaying the bond investors). Keep in mind that higher returns require greater risk. A central tenant of investing was violated when a battered company, Third Avenue Focused Credit, blocked investors from redeeming their shares. The SEC approved the delay.

The **default rate** on investment grade AAA-rated bonds is ½ of 1 percent. It is 1.5% on AA bonds; 3% on A bonds; and 10% on BBB bonds. The rate is over 4% for munis. For more information, see Bond Pickers (www.bondpickers.com) or www.defaultrisk .com or search Google using "high-yield bonds."

There are a number of unique characteristics of bonds. They are described in Table 14-5.

speculative-grade bonds
Long-term, high-risk, high-interest-rate corporate (or municipal) IOUs issued by companies (or municipalities) with poor or no credit ratings. Also called junk bonds or high-yield bonds.

default
Not repaying bond investors.

Table 14-5	**Unique Characteristics of Bonds**
Coupon Rate	The bond's **coupon rate** (also known as the **coupon, coupon yield**, or **stated interest rate**) is the interest rate printed on the certificate when the bond is issued. It reflects the total annual fixed rate of interest that will be paid.
Serial or Sinking Fund	Occasionally bonds are retired serially. That is, each bond is numbered consecutively and matures according to a prenumbered schedule at stated intervals. These investments are known as **serial bonds**. Many bonds include a **sinking fund** through which money is set aside with a trustee each year for repayment of the principal portion of the debt.
Secured or Unsecured	A corporation issuing a **secured bond** pledges specific assets as collateral in the **indenture** (written legal agreement between debtor and lenders) the principal and interest guaranteed by another corporation or a government agency. An **unsecured bond** (or **debenture**) does not name collateral as security for the debt and is backed only by the good faith and reputation of the issuing agency.
Registered and Issued	By law, all bonds issued now are **registered bonds**. This provides for the recording of the bondholder's name so that checks or electronic funds transfers for payment of interest and principal can be safely forwarded when due.
Book Entry	All bonds today are issued in **book-entry form**, which means that certificates are not issued. Instead, an account is set up in the name of the issuing organization or the brokerage firm that sold the bond, and interest is paid into this account when due.
Callable	An issuer might desire to exercise a **call option** when interest rates drop substantially. For example, assume a company issues bonds paying a $60 annual dividend (6 percent coupon rate). When interest rates drop perhaps to 4 percent, the 6 percent bonds may represent too high a cost for borrowing to the corporation. If the bonds have a **callable** feature, the issuer can redeem the bonds before the maturity date. The issuer repurchases the bond at par value or by paying a premium, often a partial year's worth of interest. Approximately 80 percent of long-term bonds are classified as callable.

sinking fund
Bond feature through which money is set aside with a trustee each year for repayment of the principal portion of the debt at maturity.

secured bond
Pledges specific assets as collateral in indenture or has the principal and interest guaranteed by another corporation or government agency.

indenture
Written, legal agreement between bondholders and debtor that describes terms of the debt by setting forth the maturity date, interest rate, and other details.

registered bond
Bondholder's name is recorded so that checks or electronic funds transfers for payment of interest and principal can be safely forwarded when due.

call option
Stipulation in some indentures that allows issuer to repurchase the bond at par value or by paying a premium, often one year's worth of interest.

corporate bonds

Interest-bearing certificates of long-term debt issued by a corporation.

14.5a   Corporate Bonds

Corporate bonds are interest-bearing certificates of long-term debt issued by a corporation. They represent a needed source of funds for corporations. The dollar value of newly issued bonds is three times the dollar value of newly issued stocks. Because of tax regulations, corporations often finance major projects by issuing long-term bonds instead of selling stocks. One reason they do so is that payments of dividends to common and preferred stockholders are not tax deductible for corporations, unlike interest paid to bondholders. State laws require corporations to make bond interest payments on time. Therefore, companies in financial difficulty are required to pay bondholders before paying any short-term creditors.

The default risk varies with the issuer. To help you in appraising the risks and potential rewards of bond investments, independent advisory services, such as Moody's Investors Service, Standard & Poor's, and Fitch, grade bonds for credit risk. These firms publish what they describe as unbiased ratings of the financial conditions of corporations and municipalities that issue bonds.

bond rating

An impartial outsider's opinion of the quality—or creditworthiness—of the issuing organization.

default risk (credit risk)

Uncertainty associated with not receiving the promised periodic interest payments and the principal amount when it becomes due at maturity.

A **bond rating** represents the opinion of an outsider on the quality—or creditworthiness—of the issuing organization. It reflects the likelihood that the issuing organization will be able to repay its debt. Ratings for each bond issue are continually re-evaluated, and they often change after the original security has been sold to the public. Investors have access to measures of the **default risk** (or **credit risk**), which is the uncertainty associated with not receiving the promised periodic interest payments as well as the principal amount when it becomes due at maturity.

Table 14-6 shows the bond ratings used by Moody's, Standard & Poor's, and Fitch, all well-known rating services. The higher the rating, the greater the probable safety of the bond and the lower the default risk. The lower the rating of the bond the higher the stated, or effective interest rate. When bonds are reduced in price from their face amount, more risk is involved. Higher ratings denote confidence that the issuer will not default and, if necessary, that the bond can readily be sold before its maturity date.

Investment-grade corporate bonds may provide returns as much as 2.5 percentage points higher than the returns available on comparable U.S. Treasury securities. The interest rate on intermediate term notes and bonds typically deliver about 80 percent of the returns obtained from long-term bonds but at roughly half the risk.

Table 14-6   Summary of Bond Ratings

Ratings			
Moody's	**Standard & Poor's**	**Fitch**	**Creditworthiness**
Aaa	AAA	AAA	*Extremely strong capacity to meet its financial*
Aa1	AA+	AA+	*commitments.*
Aa2	AA	AA	*Strong capacity to meet its financial commitments;*
Aa3	AA−	AA−	*differs only slightly from the highest.*
			Strong capacity to meet its financial commitments.
Baa1	BBB+	BBB+	*Adequate capacity to meet its financial*
Baa2	BBB	BBB	*commitments.*
Baa3	BBB−	BBB−	*Adequate capacity to meet its financial*
			commitments, but vulnerable to changing
			economic conditions.
Caa	CCC	CCC	*Less vulnerable than lower rated bonds but*
Ca	CC	CC	*faces uncertain uncertainties and exposures.*
	C	C	*Currently vulnerable on good economic*
			conditions to meet its obligations.
C	D	D	*Currently in default with little prospect of*
			regaining any investment standing.

14.5b Government Securities

U.S. Treasury securities issued by the federal government are the world's safest investment because it has never intentionally defaulted on its debt. **U.S. Treasury securities** are backed by the "full faith, credit, and taxing power of the U.S. government," and this all but guarantees the timely payment of principal and interest. U.S. debt is denominated in dollars and is the cornerstone of the global financial system.

U.S. government securities are classified into two groups: (1) Treasury bills, notes, and bonds and (2) federal agency issue notes, bonds, and certificates. Treasury bills, notes, and bonds are collectively known as **Treasury securities**, or **Treasuries**. The federal government uses these debt instruments to finance the public national debt. Treasury securities have excellent liquidity and are simple to acquire and sell.

Previously issued marketable Treasury securities are bought and sold in securities markets through banks and brokers. New issues can be purchased online using the Treasury Direct Plan (www.publicdebt.treas.gov), where they are stored electronically. Individuals may buy Treasury securities in amounts as small as $100. Also you may buy Treasury securities via a payroll savings plan through your employer, as it is a safe and effective way to purchase on a regular basis.

The interest rates on federal government securities are lower than those on corporate bonds because they are virtually risk free. The possibility of default is as close to zero as possible. Individuals with a conservative investment philosophy and overseas investors and governments are often attracted to the certainty offered by U.S. government securities. Although interest income is subject to federal income taxes, interest earned on Treasury securities is exempt from state and local income taxes.

Municipal government bonds (also called **munis**) are issued by states, municipalities and local government agencies. Yields on high-quality municipal bonds are normally about 85 percent of those of Treasuries of equal maturity. The investor's interest income on municipal bonds is not subject to federal income taxes. This is because the U.S constitution requires that municipal bond interest be exempt from federal income taxes. To compare the after-tax returns of investments, see page 140.

14.5c Evaluating Bond Prices and Returns

Investors can utilize the standard factors to evaluate bond prices and potential returns: interest rates, premiums and discounts, current yield, and yield to maturity.

Interest Rate Risk Results in Variable Value A bond's price, or its value on any given day, is affected by a host of factors. These include its type, coupon rate, and availability in the marketplace; demand for the bond; prices for similar bonds; the underlying credit quality of the issuer; and the number of years before it matures.

Most important, the price also varies because of fluctuations in current **market interest rates** in the general economy. The state of the economy and the supply and demand for credit affect market interest rates. These are the current long- and short- term interest rates paid on various types of corporate and government debts that carry similar levels of risk.

Long-Term Interest Rates Set by Investors Plus Occasional Fed Interventions Long-term rates largely reflect bond investors' buying and selling decisions, primarily based on their expectations of future inflation. Short-term interest rates are manipulated by the Federal Reserve Board, which is popularly known as the "Fed." When inflation rises, the Fed often raises interest rates to discourage borrowing, which reduces consumer and business spending. When the economy slows, the Fed often lowers the interest rates on short-term Treasury issues in an attempt to stimulate economic activity by making it cheaper for companies and consumers to borrow and expand. Again to stimulate the economy, the Fed sometimes puts more money into the economy by buying long-term mortgage securities and Treasury bonds and notes and related debt for autos and credit cards. Table 14-7 provides details on U.S. government Treasury securities and municipal bonds.

Treasury securities (Treasuries)
Known as Treasuries, securities issued by the U.S. government, including bills, notes, and bonds.

municipal government bonds (munis)
Long-term debts (bonds) issued by local governments (cities, states, and various districts and political subdivisions) and their agencies.

market interest rates
Current long- and short-term interest rates paid on various types of corporate and government debts that carry similar levels of risk.

Table 14-7   **U.S. Government Treasury Securities and Municipal Bonds**

Bond/Security	Details	Description	Purchase	Other
Treasury Bills (or T-bills)	4 to 52 weeks; $1,000 minimum; marketable	Sold at a discount; the difference between the purchase price and face value is interest	Treasury Direct	Interest exempt from state/local income taxes but is subject to federal income taxes
Treasury Notes	2, 3, 5, 7, and 10 years; $100 minimum; marketable	Pay interest every 6 months; returns are higher than the rates for T-bills because the lending period is longer	Treasury Direct, bank or broker	Interest exempt from state/local income taxes but is subject to federal income taxes
Treasury Bonds	30 years; $100; marketable	Pay interest every 6 months; returns are higher than the rates for T-bills and bonds because the lending period is longer	Treasury Direct, bank or broker	Interest exempt from state/local income taxes but is subject to federal income taxes
Treasury Inflation-Protected Securities (TIPS)	5, 10, and 30 years; $100; marketable	Pay interest every 6 months; principal increases/decreases with consumer price index	Treasury Direct, bank or broker	Interest and growth in principal exempt from state/local income taxes but is subject to federal income taxes
Floating Rate Notes (FRNs)	2 years; $100; marketable	Pay interest quarterly	Treasury Direct, bank or broker	Interest exempt from state/local income taxes but is subject to federal income taxes
Series EE/E Savings Bonds	$25 minimum; $10,000 annual maximum; sold at one/half face value; non-marketable	Double in value in 20 years; pay interest for 30 years	Treasury Direct	Fixed rate; redeemed in full at maturity; interest exempt from state/local income taxes; interest excluded from federal taxes if used for education
I-Savings Bonds or I-Bonds	$25 minimum; $10,000 annual maximum; 30 years; non-marketable	Pay variable rate based on inflation and paid only when the bond is cashed in	Treasury Direct	Interest exempt from state/local income taxes but is subject to federal income taxes; interest excluded from federal taxes if used for education
Agency Bonds	Debt instruments issued by a federal agency or an agency affiliated with the federal government; 1 month to 15 years; marketable	Fully guaranteed by the issuing agency but not the full faith and credit of the United States	Credit rating second only to Treasuries; pay 2/10ths to 1 percent higher than comparable Treasury securities	Agencies that can issue these securities include the Federal Home Loan Bank, Farm Credit System, Federal National Mortgage Association, Government National Mortgage Association, and Student Loan Marketing Association
Municipal Government Bonds (or "Munis")	Debt securities issued by a state, municipality or country to finance its capital expenditures; marketable.	$1,000 minimum; pay less than Treasuries but the after-tax returns can be equivalent since they are exempt from state/local income taxes	Known as tax-free or tax-exempt bonds	Municipal bonds are exempt from federal income taxes and from most state and local income taxes, especially if you live in the state in which the bond is issued; 60,000 munis exist

14.5d Pricing a Bond in Today's Market

As we noted in Chapter 13, **interest rate risk** is the risk that interest rates will increase and bond prices will fall, thereby lowering the prices on older bond issues. This decline in value ensures that an older bond and a newly issued bond will offer potential investors approximately the same yield. Bonds generally have a **fixed yield** (the interest income payment remains the same) but a **variable value.**

For example, assume you own a 30-year bond with a face value of $1,000 paying a semiannual coupon interest rate of 6 percent that has 20 years remaining until maturity. If interest rates in the general economy jump to 8 percent after one year, no one will want to buy your 6 percent bond for $1,000 because it pays only $60 per year. If you want to sell it, the price of the bond will have to be lowered, perhaps to $802.08.

The **value of bond** (or **bond selling price**) **formula,** Equation (14.3), shows the calculation involved. If rates on new bonds are now paying 8 percent, then the discount rate is 8 percent (or 4 percent twice a year for 40 payments). The task is to calculate the present value of the interest payments and the repayment lump sum. To do so, use Appendix A.2 and Appendix A.4 and look across the interest rows to 4% and down to 40 "n" periods.

Value of Bond = Present value of interest payments + present value of lump sum

= (Annual interest payment/2 × PVIFA^{i,n}) + (Lump sum × PVIF^{i,n})

Where

i = new annual **interest** rate divided by 2
n = number of years to maturity times 2
= ($60 = 2 × PVIFA$^{4\%,40}$) + ($1,000 × PVIF$^{4\%,40}$)   **(14.3)**
= ($30 × 19.7928) + ($1,000 × 0.2083)
= ($593.78 + $208.30 = $802.08

Conversely, if interest rates on newly issued bonds slip to 4 percent, the price of your 6 percent bond will increase sharply, perhaps to $1,273.55. Thus, investors might be willing to pay a **bond premium** of $273.55 ($1,273.55−$1,000), which is a sum of money paid in excess of the bond's face amount, to buy your $1,000 bond paying 6 percent when other rates are only 4 percent. Remember that bond yields and prices move in opposite directions—as one goes up, the other goes down.

Bond Prices and Interest Rates Have an Inverse Relationship Investors regularly compare the returns on their current investments to what they could get elsewhere in the market. As market interest rates change, a bond's coupon rate—which, remember, is fixed—becomes more or less attractive to investors, who are therefore willing to pay more or less for the bond itself.

Assume the ABC company offers a new issue of 30-year bonds carrying a 7 percent rate. This means it would pay you $70 a year in interest ($35 twice a year). After evaluating your investment alternatives, you decide this is a good deal, so you purchase a bond at its par value, $1,000.

If interest rates in the general economy jump to 8 percent after one year, no one will want to buy your 7 percent bond for $1,000 because it pays only $70 per year. If you want to sell it, the price of the bond will have to be lowered, perhaps to $875 as shown in Figure 14.3. If interest rates dropped to below your original coupon rate of 7 percent, perhaps to 6 percent, your bond would be worth more than $1,166. It would be priced at a premium, since it would be carrying a higher interest rate than what was currently available on the market. Over many years, 90 percent of the returns investors earn from bonds come from interest income with only 10 percent coming from price changes.

Premiums and Discounts When a bond is first issued, it is sold in one of three ways: (1) at its face value (the value of the bond stated on the certificate and the amount the investor will receive when the bond matures), (2) at a discount below its face value, or (3) at a premium above its face value. After a bond is issued, its market price changes

interest rate risk
Risk that interest rates will rise and bond prices will fall, thereby lowering the prices on older bond issues.

DO IT IN CLASS

bond premium
A sum of money paid in addition to a regular price.

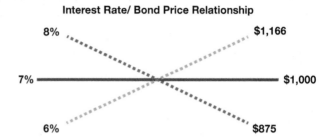

Figure 14-3 Interest Rate/Bond Price Relationship

Interest Rate/ Bond Price Relationship

8% $1,166

7% ━━━━━━━━━━ $1,000

6% $875

in order to provide a competitive effective rate of return for anyone interested in purchasing it from the original bondholder.

As an example, assume that Running Paws Cat Food Company decided to issue 20-year bonds at 8.8 percent. While the bonds were being printed and prepared for sale, the market interest rate on comparable high-risk bonds rose to 9 percent. In this instance, Running Paws would sell the bonds at a slight discount to provide a competitive return. Discounts and premiums on bonds reflect changing interest rates in the economy and the number of years to maturity.

current yield

Equals the bond's fixed annual interest payment divided by its bond price.

Current Yield The current yield equals the bond's fixed annual interest payment divided by its bond price. It is a measure of the current annual income (the total of both semiannual interest payments in dollars) expressed as a percentage when divided by the bond's current market price. When you buy a bond at par, its current yield equals its coupon yield. For example, a bond with a 5.5 percent coupon yield purchased at par for $1,000 has a current yield of 5.5 percent. As bond prices fluctuate because of interest rate changes and other factors, the current yield also changes. For example, if Sarah Jones of Alvin, Texas paid $940 for a $1,000 bond paying $55 per year, the bond's current yield is 5.85 percent, as shown by the **current yield formula,** Equation (14.4).

$$\text{Current yield} = \frac{\text{current annual income}}{\text{current market price}}$$
$$= \frac{\$55}{\$940} \tag{14.4}$$
$$= 5.85\%$$

The current yields for many bonds based on that day's market prices are available online and are published in the financial section of many newspapers.

The total return on a bond investment consists of the same components as the return on any investment: current income and capital gains. In Sarah's case, she will receive $1,000 at the maturity date (20 years from now), even though she paid only $940 for the bond; therefore, her anticipated total return (or effective yield) will be higher than the 5.85 percent current yield. How much higher is accurately revealed by the yield to maturity formula (discussed next).

yield to maturity (YTM)

Total annual effective rate of return earned by a bondholder on a bond if the security is held to maturity—takes into consideration both the price at which the bond sold and the coupon interest rate to arrive at effective rate of return.

Yield to Maturity Yield to maturity (YTM) is the total annual effective rate of return earned by a bondholder on a bond if the security is held to maturity. The YTM is the internal rate of return on cash flows of a fixed-income security. The YTM reflects both the current income and any difference if the bond was purchased at a price other than its face value spread over the life of the bond. The market price of a bond equals the present value of its future interest payments and the present value of its face value when the bond matures.

Three generalizations can be made about the yield to maturity:

1.   If a bond is purchased for exactly its face value, the YTM is the same as the coupon rate printed on the certificate.
2.   If a bond is purchased at a premium, the YTM will be lower than the coupon rate.
3.   If a bond is purchased at a discount, the YTM will be higher than the coupon rate.

For example, because Sarah bought her 20-year bond with a coupon rate of 5.5 percent at a discount for $940, her yield to maturity must be greater than the coupon rate because she will receive $60 more than she paid for the bond when she receives the $1,000 at maturity. Exactly how much greater can be determined by calculating an approximate yield to maturity when contemplating a bond purchase because bonds that seem comparable may have different YTMs.

The **yield to maturity (YTM) formula,** Equation (14.5), which is duplicated on the *Garman/Forgue* companion website, factors in the approximate appreciation when a bond is bought at a discount or at a premium:

$$\text{YTM} = \frac{I + [(FV - CV)/N]}{(FV + CV)/2} \tag{14.5}$$

where

$I = $ **Interest** paid annually in dollars

$FV = $ **Face value**

$CV = $ **current value** (price)

$N = $ **Number** of years until maturity

If Sarah paid $940 for a 20-year bond with a 5.5 percent coupon rate, the YTM is calculated as follows:

$$\text{YTM} = \frac{\$55 + [(\$1,000 - \$940)/20]}{(\$1,000 + \$940)/2}$$

$$= \frac{\$58}{\$970}$$

$$= 5.98\%$$

If you plan to buy and hold a bond until its maturity, you should compare YTMs instead of current yields when considering a purchase because YTMs fairly represent all factors. The current yield on a bond is not an effective measure of the total annual return to the investor. In fact, the fewer years until maturity, the worse an indicator it becomes. As just calculated, Sarah's 20-year bond with a coupon rate of 5.5 percent and a current yield of 5.85 percent has a YTM of 5.98 percent. If the same bond had been purchased with only ten years until maturity, the YTM would be 6.29 percent; with five years until maturity, the YTM would be 6.90 percent; and with two years until maturity, the YTM would be 8.76 percent. Exact YTMs are online and listed in detailed bond tables available online and at brokers' offices.

Four Decisions for Bond Investors Individuals interested in investing in bonds can review resources on the website of the Securities Industry and Financial Markets Association (www.investinginbonds.com). It offers a free, searchable database of the latest corporate, government, municipal, and mortgage-backed bond issues and prices. Bond investors must make four decisions:

1.   **Decide on credit quality.** Consider Treasury/agency, investment-grade corporate and municipal, and below investment-grade corporate and municipal bonds.
2.   **Decide on maturity.** Consider the time schedule of your financial needs: short, intermediate, or long term. Bonds with a short maturity have the lowest current

TURN BAD HABITS INTO GOOD ONES

Do You Do This?	Do This Instead!
Invest only in certificates of deposit	Invest in common stocks, bonds, and mutual funds
Listen to tips and invest in hot stocks	Invest only in stocks with good fundamentals
Invest in speculative stocks	Utilize no more than 5 to 10 percent for speculative stocks
Invest in fewer than five stocks	Invest in more than five stocks or stock mutual funds
Ignore big changes in interest rates	Invest in bonds on interest rate shifts (but not when rates are rising)
Accept broker's advice on stock choices	Use the Internet to research stocks and bonds
Utilize full-service brokers exclusively	Buy and sell online to save on commissions
Deal with a financial advisor who follows the suitability standard	Only use a financial advisor who adheres to a fiduciary standard
Buy on margin and sell short	Never buy on margin and sell short, as it is too risky
Avoid bonds as investments	Buy some TIPS bonds

DID YOU KNOW

If all this stocks and bonds stuff is "way too much," you will enjoy the next chapter. It is so much easier to invest in mutual and exchange traded funds.

yield but excellent price stability. Intermediate maturity bonds pay close to the higher rates earned on long-term bonds and enjoy greater price stability.

3. **Determine the after-tax return.** Assuming equivalent risk, choose the bond that provides the better after-tax return because tax-exempt securities may offer a higher after-tax return than taxable alternatives. To compare the after-tax return of investments, see page 140 in chapter 4.

4. **Select the highest yield to maturity.** Given similar bond securities with comparable risk, maturity, and tax equivalency, investors are wise to choose the one that offers the highest yield to maturity, as calculated by Equation (14.5).

CONCEPT CHECK 14.5

1. Distinguish between investment- and speculative-grade bonds.
2. What are the basic differences between corporate, U.S. government, and municipal bonds?
3. Distinguish among Treasury bills, notes, and bonds.
4. Summarize the differences between I-bonds and TIPS bonds.
5. Summarize why bonds and interest rates have an inverse relationship.
6. Give a math example of how to calculate a bond's yield to maturity that is different than the one in the book.

WHAT DO YOU RECOMMEND *NOW*?

Now that you have read the chapter on stocks and bonds, what do you recommend to Ariya Jutanugarn in the case at the beginning of the chapter regarding:

1. Investing for retirement in 18 years?
2. Owning blue-chip common stocks and preferred stocks rather than other common stocks given Ariya's investment time horizon?
3. The wisdom of owning municipal bonds rather than corporate bonds?
4. The likely selling price of her corporate bonds, if sold today?
5. Investments that might be appropriate to fund her children's education?

Golden Pixels LLC/Shutterstock.com

SUMMARY OF LEARNING OBJECTIVES RECAPPED

LO1 **Explain how stocks and bonds are used as investments.**

Individual investors provide the money corporations use to create sales and earn profits. The investor shares in those profits by investing in corporations' common stock, preferred stock, and bonds.

LO2 **Describe ways to evaluate stock prices, and calculate a stock's potential rate of return.**

Beta value is a measure of an investment's volatility compared with a broad market index over time. Most investors use fundamental analysis to evaluate stocks. To determine a company's basic value, the investor studies certain fundamental factors, such as the company's earnings, price-earnings ratio, and cash dividends. Wise investors also calculate a stock's potential rate of return.

LO3 **Use the Internet to evaluate common stocks in which to invest.**

Individuals begin evaluating stocks by setting criteria for a stock investment. This may involve using online stock calculators, stock-screening software; obtaining security analysts' research reports, annual reports, 10-Q and 10-K reports, and prospectuses; acquiring economic and stock market data; and using portfolio-tracking services.

LO4 **Summarize how to buy and sell stocks, as well as the techniques of margin buying and selling short.**

Securities transactions require the use of a licensed broker serving as a middleman between the seller and the buyer. You can buy or sell securities online or through a live stockbroker who works for a brokerage firm that has access to the securities markets. To reduce transaction costs many individuals use discount and online brokers rather than full-service brokers. Types of stock orders include market, limit, and stop orders. Buying on margin and selling short are risky trading techniques.

LO5 **Describe how to invest in bonds.**

Investment-grade bonds offer a reasonable certainty of regularly receiving the periodic income (interest) and retrieving the amount originally invested (principal). Corporate, U.S. securities (such as Treasury bills, notes, and bonds), and municipal bonds are available. Safe I-bonds and high paying junk bonds are available, too. Corporate bonds usually pay higher returns than government bonds. Long-term interest rates are set by investors. Bonds and interest rates have an inverse relationship. Investors use current yield and yield to maturity formulas to help make buying decisions.

LET'S TALK ABOUT IT

1. **Investing Today.** What counsel can you offer long-term investors who are hesitant to invest in stocks and bonds?

2. **Common or Preferred Stock.** Make a list of the plusses and minuses of investing in either common stock or preferred stock, and give your conclusion as to which is better for you.

3. **Three Good Companies.** Make a list of three products and services that you buy on a weekly or monthly basis and the companies that sell them. Offer your initial views on whether each company would be a good place to invest money.

4. **Two Useful Measures.** The text introduced a variety of ways to measure stock performance. Name two of those measures that you might use in your own decision making. Offer reasons for selecting those measures.

5. **Would You Buy?** You have just heard that Microsoft's stock price dropped $15. If you had the money, would you buy 100 shares? Give three reasons why or why not.

6. **Interesting Stock.** Review the classifications of common stock in Table14-1 on page 428. Based on your personal comfort level for risk, which one type of stock would be of interest to you? Give reasons why.

7. **Sources of Information.** If you had an investment portfolio of stocks worth $20,000, identify three sources for information that you would likely use to keep abreast of current information affecting your investments.

8. **Potential Rate of Return.** Do you think anyone really calculates the potential rate of return on a particular investment? Should they? Why or why not?

9. **Invest Using Credit.** Buying on margin and selling short both involve using credit. Would you invest this way? Give two reasons why or why not.

10. **Interest in Bonds.** Do bonds interest you as an investment? Why or why not?

DO THE MATH

1. **Numerical Measures.** A stock sells at $15 per share.

   (a) What is the EPS for the company if it has a P/E ratio of 20?

   (b) If the company's dividend yield is 3 percent, what is its dividend per share?

   (c) What is the book value of the company if the price-to-book ratio is 1.5 and it has 100,000 shares of stock outstanding?

   DO IT IN CLASS
   Page 432

2. **Bond Selling Price.** What is the market price of a $1,000, 8 percent bond if comparable market interest rates drop to 6 percent and the bond matures in 15 years?

3. **Market Price.** What is the market price of a $1,000, 8 percent bond if comparable market interest rates rise to 10 percent and the bond matures in 14 years?

4. **Equivalent Taxable Yield.** For a municipal bond paying 3.4 percent for a taxpayer in the 25 percent tax bracket, what is the equivalent taxable yield? (Hint: See page 140.)

   DO IT IN CLASS
   Page 140

5. **Equivalent Taxable Yield.** For a municipal bond paying 3.7 percent for a taxpayer in the 33 percent tax bracket, what is the equivalent taxable yield? (Hint: See page 140.)

6. **Yield, Price, and YTM.** A corporate bond maturing in 15 years with a coupon rate of 9.9 percent was purchased for $980 and it now selling for $1,010.

   (a) What is its current yield?

   (b) What will be its selling price in two years if comparable market interest rates drop 1.9 percentage points?

   (c) Calculate the bond's YTM using Equation 14.5 or the *Garman/Forgue* companion website.

7. **Yield, Price, and YTM.** A corporate bond maturing in 22 years with a coupon rate of 8.2 percent was purchased for $1,100 and is now selling for $1,190.

   (a) What is its current yield?

   (b) Calculate the bond's YTM using Equation (14.5) or the *Garman/Forgue* companion website.

   (c) What will the bond's selling price be if comparable market interest rates rise 1.8 percentage points in two years?

   DO IT IN CLASS
   Pages 453 and 455

8. **Beta Calculations.** Michael Margolis is a single parent and motivational training consultant from Palatine, Illinois. He is wondering about potential returns on investments given certain amounts of risk. Michael invested a total of $6,000 in three stocks ($2,000 in each) with different betas: stock A with a beta of 0.8, stock B with a beta of 1.7, and stock C with a beta of 2.5.

   DO IT IN CLASS
   Page 433

(a) If the stock market rises 7 percent over the next year, what will be the likely value of each investment?

(b) If the stock market declines 8 percent over the next year, what will be the likely value of each of Michael's investments?

9. **Investment Calculations.** Xiao and Shiao Jing-jian, newlyweds from Laramie, Wyoming, have decided to begin investing for the future. Xiao is a 7-Eleven store manager, and Shiao is a high-school math teacher. The couple intends to take $3,000 out of their savings for investment purposes and then continue to invest an additional $200 to $400 per month. Both have a moderate investment philosophy and seek some cash dividends as well as price appreciation.

Calculate the five-year return on the investment choices in the table below. Put your calculations in tabular form like that shown in Table 14-2. (Hint: When making your calculations you should assume at the end of the first year. At the end of the first year the EPS for Running Paws will be $2.40 with a dividend of $0.66, and the EPS for Eagle Packaging will be $2.76 with a projected dividend of $0.86.)

(a) Using the appropriate P/E ratios, what are the estimated market prices of the Running Paws and Eagle Packaging stocks after five years?

(b) Show your calculations in determining the projected price appreciations for the two stocks over the five years.

(c) Add the projected price appreciation of each stock to its projected cash dividends, and show the total five-year percentage returns for the two stocks.

(d) Determine the average annual dividend for each stock, and use these figures in calculating the approximate compound yields for each.

(e) Assume that the beta is 2.5 for Running Paws and 2.8 for Eagle Packaging. If the market went up 20 percent during the year, what would be the likely stock prices for Running Paws and Eagle Packaging?

(f) Assume that inflation is approximately 4 percent and the return on high-quality, long-term, corporate bonds is 8 percent. Given the Jing-jians' investment philosophy, explain why you would recommend (1) Running Paws, (2) Eagle Packaging, or (3) a high-quality, long-term corporate bond as a growth investment. Support your answer by calculating the potential rate of return using the information on pages 432–435; or by using the *Garman/Forgue* website. The Jing-jians are in the 25 percent marginal tax bracket.

	Running Paws	Eagle Packaging
Current price	$30.00	$48.00
Current earnings per share (EPS)	$ 2.00	$ 2.30
Current quarterly cash dividend	$ 0.15	$ 0.18
Current P/E ratio	15	21
Projected earnings annual growth rate	20%	20%
Projected cash dividend growth rate	10%	10%

FINANCIAL PLANNING CASES

CASE 1

The Johnsons Want Greater Yields on Investments

The investments of Harry and Belinda have done well through the years. While the cash portion of their portfolio has risen to $16,000, it is earning a minuscule 1 percent in a money market account; thus they are seeking greater yields with bond investments. Examine the following table, which identifies eight investment alternatives, and then respond to the questions that follow. The coupon rates vary because the issue dates range widely, and market prices are above par because older bonds paid higher interest than today's issues.

Name of Issue	Bond Denomination	Coupon Rate Percent	Years Until Maturity	Moody's Rating	Market Price	Current Yield	YTM
Corporate ABC	$1,000	5.4	4	Aa	$1,400		
Corporate DEF	1,000	5.5	20	Aa	1,550		
Corporate GHI	1,000	5.9	12	Baa	1,250		
Corporate JKL	1,000	4.8	5	Aaa	1,500		
Corporate MNO	1,000	4.1	15	B	1,260		
Corporate PQR	1,000	5.3	11	B	1,200		
Treasury note	1,000	2.2	3	—	1,600		
Municipal bond	1,000	2.1	20	Aa	1,200		

(a) What is the current yield of each investment alternative? Use Equation (14.5) or visit the *Garman/Forgue* companion website. (Write your responses in the proper column in the table.)

(b) What is the yield to maturity for each investment alternative? You may calculate the YTMs by using Equation (14.6) or by visiting the *Garman/Forgue* companion website.

(c) Knowing that the Johnsons follow a moderate investment philosophy, which one of the six corporate bonds would you recommend? Why?

(d) Given that the Johnsons are in the 25 percent federal marginal tax rate, what is the equivalent taxable yield for the municipal bond choice? Should they invest in your recommendation in part (c) or in the municipal bond? Why? You may calculate the equivalent taxable yield using the information on page 140.

(e) Which three of the eight alternatives would you recommend as a group so that the Johnsons would have some diversification protection for their $16,000? Why do you suggest that combination?

CASE 2

Victor and Maria Hernandez Wonder About Investing

Victor and Maria have decided to increase their contribution to their investment portfolio since Victor is now age 59 and thinking about retiring in five years. For years, they have followed a moderate-risk investment philosophy and put their money in suitable stocks, bonds, and mutual funds. The value of their portfolio is now $420,000, and this is in addition to their paid-for rental property, which is worth $300,000. They plan to invest about $8,000 every year for the next five years.

DO IT IN CLASS
Pages 428 and 433

(a) Why should Victor and Maria consider buying common stock as an investment with the additional money? Why or why not?

(b) If Victor and Maria bought a stock with a market price of $50 and a beta value of 1.8, what would be the likely price of an $8,000 investment after one year if the general market for stocks rose 6 percent?

(c) What would the same investment be worth if the general market for stocks dropped 8 percent?

(d) Review the types of stocks in Table 14-1 on page 428 and select two that you think Victor and Maria might prefer as investments. Explain why.

(e) Discuss the positives and negatives of preferred stock for Victor and Maria.

CASE 3

Julia Price Seeks Rewards in the Bond Market

Julia's investments survived the last recession and bear stock market declines because she was well diversified and was investing more heavily in bonds in the years preceding the decline. Julia cashed out of some equities and moved most of that money into corporate bonds and Treasuries. As a result, over the past four years, the bond portion of her portfolio rose over 20 percent due to low inflation and declining interest rates, which pushed up the value of her bonds. Now she thinks inflation and bond prices will rise so she is selling all her bonds and investing the proceeds into equities. But the stock market prices seem too high already, so she is hesitating. Offer your opinions about her thinking.

CASE 4

An Aggressive Investor Seeks Rewards in the Bond Market

Jessica Varcoe works as a drug manufacturer's representative based in Irvine, California. She has an aggressive investment philosophy and believes that interest rates on new bonds will drop over the next year or two because of an expected economic slowdown. Jessica, who is in the 25 percent marginal tax rate, wants to profit in the bond market by buying and selling during the next several months. She has asked your advice on how to invest her $15,000.

(a) If Jessica buys corporate or municipal bonds, what rating should her selections have? Why?

(b) Jessica has a choice between two $1,000 bonds: a corporate bond with a coupon rate of 5.1 percent and a municipal bond with a coupon rate of 3.2 percent. Which bond provides the better after-tax return? (Hint: See Equation [4.1] on page 140.)

(c) If Jessica buys fifteen, 30-year, $1,000 corporate bonds with a 5.1 percent coupon rate for $960 each, what is her current yield? (Hint: Use Equation [14.4].)

(d) If market interest rates for comparable corporate bonds drop 1 percent over the next 12 months (from 5.1 percent to 4.1 percent), what will be the approximate selling price of Jessica's corporate bonds in (c)? (Hint: Use Formula 14.3 or the *Garman/Forgue* companion website.)

(e) Assuming market interest rates drop 1 percent in 12 months, how much is Jessica's capital gain on the $15,000 investment if she sells? How much was her current return for the two semiannual interest payments? How much was her total return, both in dollars and as an annual yield? (Ignore transaction costs.) Hint: Use Formula 14.3.

(f) If Jessica is wrong in her projections and interest rates go up 1 percent over the year, what would be the probable selling price of her corporate bonds? (Hint: Use Formula 14.3 or the *Garman/Forgue* companion website.) Explain why you would advise her to sell or not to sell.

CASE 5

Two Brothers' Attitudes Toward Investments

Kyle Broflovski, a high school guidance counselor in South Park, Colorado, has purchased several corporate and government bonds over the years, and his total bond investments now exceeds $40,000. He prefers investments with some inflation protection. His kid brother Ike, a highly paid physician, has more than $150,000 invested in various blue-chip income stocks in a variety of industries.

(a) Justify Kyle's attitude toward bond investments.

(b) Justify Ike's attitude toward stock investments.

Explain why both brothers might be happy investing some of their money in TIPS bonds.

CASE 6

A College Student Ponders Investing in the Stock Market

Ji Wu of Troy, New York, has $5,000 that he wants to invest in the stock market. Ji is in college on a scholarship and does not plan to use the $5,000 or any dividend income for another five years, when he plans to buy a home. He is currently considering a small company stock selling for $25 per share with an EPS of $1.25. Last year, the company earned $900,000, of which $250,000 was paid out in dividends.

(a) Review Table 14-1 on page 428 and explain which classification of common stock would you recommend to Ji? Why?

(b) Calculate the P/E ratio and the dividend payout ratio for this stock. Given this information and your recommendation, would this stock be an appropriate purchase for Ji? Why or why not?

(c) Identify the components of the total return Ji might expect, and estimate how much he might expect annually from each component.

(d) Review the section titled "Evaluate Stocks Using Corporate Earnings" on pages 430–432 and select two that you think Ji would utilize to evaluate when investing in stocks. Explain why.

BE YOUR OWN PERSONAL FINANCIAL MANAGER

1. **Your Stock Preferences.** Complete Worksheet 54: My Preferences Among Stocks from "My Personal Financial Planner" by identifying, for each of the seven types of stock, those that are of interest to you, what you do or do not like about them, and those in which you might invest during your own investing life.

2. **Compare Different Stocks as Investments.** Learn about the stocks of three publically traded companies of interest to you, perhaps General Motors, Ford Motor Company, and Alphabet, by visiting www.kiplinger.com. Then complete Worksheet 55: Comparing Stocks as Investments from "My Personal Financial Planner" by recording for each company each of the several performance variables.

3. **Preference Among Types of Bond.** Complete Work sheet 56: My Preference Among Bonds from "My Personal Financial Planner" by marking for each of the nine types one characteristic you do or do not like about each and which might be of interest to you as an investor.

4. **Taxable Versus Tax-Free Income.** Complete Worksheet 57: Comparing Taxable and Tax-Free Income from "My Personal Financial Planner" by inserting a realistic rate of investment return and tax rate and then performing the appropriate calculations.

5. **Current Yield on a Bond.** Complete Worksheet 58: The Current Yield on My Bond Investment from "My Personal Financial Planner" by inserting realistic different current market prices on two existing bonds (perhaps $980 and $910) and different annual interest payments (perhaps $70 and $80) for two bonds and calculating the current yields.

6. **Current Value of a Bond.** Complete Worksheet 59: The Current Value on My Bond Investment from "My Personal Financial Planner" by going online to find the current market prices of two existing bonds, perhaps individual issues of General Motors and Ford Motor Company, and then inserting the following information in the places provided: annual interest payment and years to maturity. Look online elsewhere

for a current market interest rate on comparable securities, or perhaps use 7 percent, and complete the calculations required.

7. **Yield to Maturity on a Bond.** Complete Worksheet 60: The Yield to Maturity on My Bond from "My Personal

My Personal
Financial
Planner

Financial Planner" by going online to find the following information about two bonds: current market price, face value, number of years until maturity, and annual interest in dollars.

ON THE NET

Go to the Web pages indicated to complete these exercises.

1. **Latest Financial Information.** Go to Kiplinger.com and determine the top three news items that you think are related to personal investing. Note how you can use that information in making a good investment decision.

2. **Stock Quotes.** Visit the website for Kiplinger at www.kiplinger.com, where you can find stock quotes for most publicly traded companies. Type in the symbols for the following companies: Coca-Cola (KO), Google [Alphabet] (GOOGL), Microsoft (MSFT), and Disney (DIS). Evaluate these four firms on the basis of EPS, dividend yield, and P/E ratio. What do these data suggest to you about the relative attractiveness of these companies for investors?

3. **Stock Screener.** Visit the website for Yahoo! Finance, where you can find a stock-screener utility at www.screener.finance.yahoo.com/stocks.html. Search among the S&P 500 stocks for companies with a $50 minimum share price. How many companies meet this criterion? Select again using a P/E ratio from 0 to 20. How many companies meet this new criterion? Why is this list longer? Do you recognize any of the companies on either list?

4. **Bond Calculator.** Go to BondsOnline to input illustrative pricing data on bonds (www.bondsonline.com/Bond_Ratings_Definitions.php). Write what you think of this tool.

5. **Beta Values.** Go to Calculator Edge (www.calculatoredge.com/finance/betas.htm) and input basic information on any stock to calculate its beta. Use 2 percent or a lower figure as the risk-free interest rate.

ACTION INVOLVEMENT PROJECTS

1. **Latest Stock Market Values.** Using a resource like *The Wall Street Journal* or the Internet in general, find the latest values for the following market indexes and indicate how each has performed over the past 12 months: DJIA, S&P 500, NASDAQ Composite, and Dow Jones Wilshire 5000 Index.

2. **Prices of Popular Stocks.** Find the latest values for the following stocks and indicate how each has performed

over the past 12 months: American Express, AT&T, Caterpillar, Coca-Cola, Dell, Merck, Walmart, and Walt Disney.

3. **Characteristics of Bonds.** Review the section "Unique Characteristics of Bonds" on page 449, select 2 that would be critically important to you as a bond investor. Explain why.

15

Mutual and Exchange Traded Funds

YOU MUST BE KIDDING, RIGHT?

Twins Chunhua and Hao Wang invest in mutual funds. Chunhua majored in English in college. For more than 20 years, she invested in managed funds, counting on professional financial advisors to select the winning companies. Hao majored in Finance; he invested in unmanaged index mutual funds that achieve the same return as a particular market index by buying and holding all or a representative selection of securities in the index. After 20 years of investing, what are the odds that Chunhau's investment portfolio balance will be better than Hao's?

A. Zero or less than zero   **C.** 3 to 1

B. 2 to 1   **D.** 4 to 1

The answer is A. Managed mutual funds generally do not earn returns for investors that exceed the overall market indexes. The fact is the average mutual fund manager earns a lower return about 90 percent of the time over 5- and 10-year time periods. Finding a mutual fund investment manager who can consistently beat the market is all but impossible!

Learning Objectives

After reading this chapter, you should be able to:

1   Describe the features, advantages, and unique services of investing through mutual funds.

2   Differentiate mutual funds by investment objectives.

3   Summarize the fees and charges involved in buying and selling mutual funds.

4   Establish strategies to evaluate and select mutual funds that meet your investment goals.

WHAT DO YOU RECOMMEND?

Helen Lamb and David Lilienthal, a couple in their early 30s, have a 2-year-old child and enjoy living in a nice downtown apartment. David, a library director at the Tennessee Valley Authority, earns $80,000 annually. Helen earns $90,000 as a merchandise buyer for a specialty store. They are big savers: Together they have been putting $1,000 to $2,000 per month into CDs, and the couple now has a portfolio worth $240,000 paying about 2 to 3 percent annually. The Lilienthals are conservative investors and want to retire in about 20 years.

wavebreakmedia/Shutterstock.com

What do you recommend to Helen and David on the subject of investing through mutual funds regarding:

1. **Redeeming their CDs and investing their retirement money in mutual funds?**

2. **Investing in growth and income mutual funds instead of income funds?**

3. **Buying no-load rather than load funds?**

4. **Buying mutual funds through their employers' 401(k) retirement accounts rather than saving through a taxable account as they have been doing?**

Most investors prefer to avoid buying individual stocks and bonds because of the high financial risk associated with owning too few investments like two or three stocks or bonds. The average investor usually cannot accumulate a portfolio diversified enough to minimize the risk linked to the failure of a one or two holdings, and there are so many factors to understand when buying a stock or bond. They often also lack both the ability and time required to research individual securities and manage such a portfolio. Moreover, it is not realistic for most people to invest in stocks and bonds.

In an effort to avoid these problems, many people invest *in* the stock and bond markets *through* mutual funds, which usually buy hundreds of different stocks and bonds. Mutual funds make it easy and convenient for investors to select appropriate funds, open an account, and continue investing throughout their lives.

Over the past 30 years investments in mutual funds has grown from $3 trillion dollars to over $20 trillion. Why? Because it is *easy* to find investments in mutual funds that are well matched with your investment objectives. Today more than half of all households invest in mutual funds.

It is a similar story with **exchange traded funds (ETFs)**. These are a cross between a stock and a mutual fund. They hold a basket of securities, such as stocks, bonds, or commodities—exactly like mutual funds—but they trade like stocks. You can trade ETFs all day long while mutual funds are traded only at the end of the market day. Fees on ETFs are extremely low, lower than mutual funds. Today more than half of newly investment money is going into mutual and exchange traded funds.

15.1 WHY INVEST IN MUTUAL FUNDS?

mutual fund

Investment company that pools funds by selling shares to investors and makes diversified investments to achieve financial goals of income or growth, or both.

A **mutual fund** is an investment company that pools funds obtained by selling shares to investors and makes investments to achieve the financial goal of income or growth, or both. Most mutual funds invest in a diversified portfolio of stocks, bonds, short-term money market instruments, and other securities or assets.

The fund might own common stock and bonds in such companies as AT&T, IBM Google (Alphabet), or Running Paws Cat Food Company (our fictional example from Chapter 14). The combined holdings are known as a **portfolio**, as we noted in Chapter 13 and as shown graphically in Figure 15-1. The mutual fund company

Figure 15-1 **How a Mutual Fund Works**

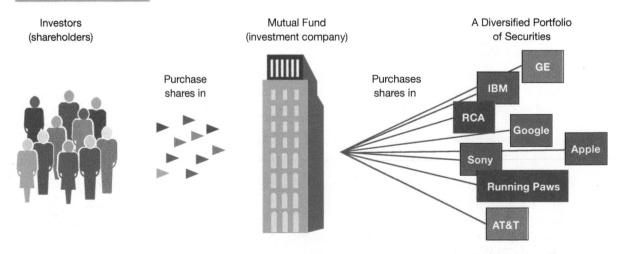

Investors (shareholders) — Purchase shares in — Mutual Fund (investment company) — Purchases shares in — A Diversified Portfolio of Securities: GE, IBM, RCA, Google, Apple, Sony, Running Paws, AT&T

owns the investments it makes and the mutual fund investors own the mutual fund company. Unlike corporate shareholders, holders of mutual funds have no say in running the company, although they have equity interest in the pool of assets and a residual claim on the profits.

Most investors prefer to invest in mutual funds because they provide terrific diversification, are managed by professionals, can achieve remarkable returns, and are easy to select as investments. Mutual funds also can fit just about anyone's investment goals and plans.

15.1a The Net Asset Value Is the Price You Pay for a Mutual Fund Share

One measure of the investor's claim on assets is the net asset value. The **net asset value (NAV)** is the price one pays (excluding any transaction costs) to buy a share of a mutual fund. It is the per-share net worth of the mutual fund. The NAV is calculated by summing the values of all the securities in the fund's portfolio, subtracting liabilities, and then dividing by the total number of shares outstanding.

net asset value (NAV)
Per-share value of a mutual fund.

$$\text{Net asset value} = \frac{\text{market value of assets} \ - \ \text{market value of liabilities}}{\text{number of shares}} \qquad (15.1)$$

For example, a mutual fund has 10 million shares outstanding and a portfolio worth $100 million, and its liabilities are $5 million. The net asset value of a single share is

DO IT IN CLASS

$$\text{Net asset value} = \frac{\$100,000,000 \ - \ \$5,000,000}{10,000,000} = \frac{\$95,000,000}{10,000,000} = \$9.50 \text{ per share}$$

The NAV rises or falls to reflect changes in the market value of the investments held by the mutual fund company. This value is calculated daily after the U.S. stock exchanges close, and a new NAV is posted in the financial media. If the stocks and bonds held in a mutual fund increase in value, the NAV will rise.

For example, if a mutual fund owns IBM and General Electric common stocks and the prices of those stocks increase, the increased value of the underlying securities is reflected in the NAV of fund shares.

This is called **price appreciation**. Some time later when investors sell shares hopefully at a net asset value higher than that paid when they purchased the shares (after transaction costs), they will have a **capital gain.**

The type of mutual fund that is the focus in this chapter is an **open-end mutual fund**. Accounting for more than 90 percent of all funds, open-end mutual funds issue redeemable shares that investors purchase directly from the fund (or through a broker for the fund). They are always ready to sell new shares of ownership and to buy back previously sold shares at the fund's current NAV. Open-end mutual funds number more than 8,100. Table 15-1 lists unique advantages of investing through mutual funds.

price appreciation
The increased value of the underlying securities is reflected in the NAV of fund shares.

open-end mutual fund
Investment that issues redeemable shares that investors purchase directly from the fund (or through a broker for the fund).

15.1b Mutual Fund Dividend Income and Capital Gains Distributions

Mutual fund dividend income is income paid to investors out of profits that the mutual fund has earned from its investments. This **dividend income** represents both ordinary income dividend distributions and capital gains distributions.

Ordinary income dividend distributions occur when the fund pays out dividends from the stock and interest from the bonds it hold in its portfolio. These are passed onto the investor quarterly.

Capital gains distributions represent the net gains (capital gains minus capital losses) that a fund realizes when it sells securities that were held in the fund's portfolio. Mutual funds distribute capital gains once a year, even though the gains occur throughout the year whenever securities are sold at a profit. When a fund pays out these distributions, the NAV drops by the amount paid.

mutual fund dividend
Income paid to investors out of profits earned by the mutual fund from its investments.

ordinary income dividend distributions
Distributions that occur when the fund pays out dividends from the stock and interest from the bonds it hold in its portfolio; these are passed onto the investor quarterly.

capital gains distributions
Distributions representing the net gains (capital gains minus capital losses) that a fund realizes when it sells securities that were held in the fund's portfolio.

redeems
When an investor sells mutual fund shares.

DO IT IN CLASS

exchange privilege
Allowance for mutual fund share-holders to easily swap shares on a dollar-for-dollar basis for shares in another mutual fund within a mutual fund family. Also called switching, conversion, or transfer privilege.

beneficiary designation
Allowance of fund holder to name one or more beneficiaries so that the proceeds bypass probate proceedings if the original shareholder dies.

withdrawal options (systematic withdrawal plans)
Arrangements with a mutual fund company for shareholders who want to receive income on a regular basis from their mutual fund investments.

Table 15-1	**Unique Advantages of Investing Through Mutual Funds**
Diversification	Mutual funds are an easy way to diversify one's investments. When you purchase a mutual fund you are buying a small fraction of an already very diversified portfolio.
Convenience	Funds make it easy to open an account and invest in and sell shares. Fund prices are widely quoted. Services include toll-free telephone numbers, detailed records of transactions, checking and savings alternatives, and the paperwork and record keeping, including accounting for fractional shares.
Liquidity	You can very easily convert mutual fund shares into cash without loss of value because the investor sells (or **redeems**) the shares back to the investment company by using a telephone, wire, fax, mail, or online.
Low Transaction Costs	The costs per trade on most mutual fund investments are much smaller than any other investment, such as stocks and bonds.
Uncomplicated Investment Choices	Selecting a mutual fund is easier than selecting specific stocks or bonds because mutual funds state their investment objectives, allowing investors to select funds that almost perfectly match their own objectives.
Ease of Buying and Selling Shares	Opening an account with a mutual fund company is as simple as opening a checking account. After making your initial investment, you can easily buy more shares. Shares can be bought or sold at any time. Each is redeemed at the closing price—the NAV—at the end of the trading day.
Check Writing and Electronic Transfers	Mutual funds often offer interest-earning, check-writing money market mutual funds in which investors can accumulate cash, accept dividends, or hold their money. Investors can electronically transfer funds to and from mutual funds and banks.
Automatic Reinvestment of Income and Capital Gains	Mutual funds allow investors to choose to receive current income payments or have them automatically reinvested to purchase additional fund shares (often without paying any commissions). This is **automatic reinvestment**, as illustrated in Figure 15-2.
Online and Telephone Exchange Privileges	An **exchange privilege** permits mutual fund shareholders to easily swap shares on a dollar-for-dollar basis for shares in another mutual fund managed by the same mutual fund family, usually at no cost.
Automatic Investment Program (AIP)	Funds often allow investors to make periodic monthly or quarterly payments using money automatically transferred from their bank accounts or paychecks to the mutual fund company. You can invest as little as $25 monthly or quarterly.
Effortless Establishment of Retirement Plans	An employee can fill out a one-page form that directs his or her employer to transfer a specified dollar amount from every paycheck to a mutual fund to buy shares for a 401(k) plan. Similarly, individuals can fill out a one-page form to buy shares for their individual retirement accounts.
Beneficiary Designation	A **beneficiary designation** enables the shareholder to name one or more beneficiaries so that the proceeds go to them without going through probate.
Withdrawal Options	Mutual funds offer **withdrawal options** (also called **systematic withdrawal plans**) to shareholders who want to receive income on a regular basis from their mutual fund investments. The minimum withdrawal amount is $50 at regular intervals. You may make regular withdrawals by (1) taking a set dollar amount each month, (2) cashing in a set number of shares each month, (3) taking the current income as cash, or (4) taking a portion of the asset growth.

Figure 15-2   The Wisdom of Automatic Dividend Reinvestment

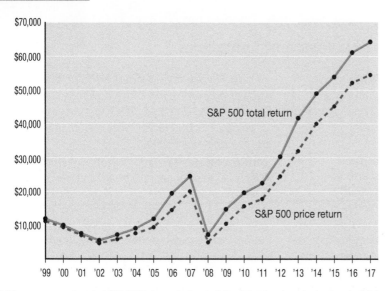

Assume that 20 years ago you invested $10,000 into any index stock fund that benchmarks the Standard & Poor's 500 Index Fund.®* If you agreed to take the dividends every year in cash, your $10,000 would grow to $55,000. If instead you agreed to reinvest the dividends each year, your $10,000 would grow to $65,000.

*Examples of stock index funds that benchmark the S&P 500® are Vanguard 500 Index Fund Investor Shares, Schwab S&P 500 Index Fund, and Fidelity Spartan 500 Index Investor Shares.

When you sell your shares in the mutual fund, you receive the NAV of the share at its current market price. If the price is higher than the price you originally paid, you have a capital gain due to the increase in the NAV.

Reinvesting income greatly compounds share ownership. Figure 15-2 illustrates the positive results obtained by agreeing to automatically reinvest dividends.

15.1c   Mutual Fund Services

A **mutual fund family** is an investment management company that offers a large number of different mutual funds to the investing public, each with its own investment objectives. There are more than 1,300 mutual fund families.

Mutual funds, as shown in Table 15-1, offer a number of advantages that are unique to this type of investment and that are helpful and appealing to investors. More than 40 percent of the total return of the S&P 500 over the past 80 years has come from reinvested dividends. Enrolling in an **automatic reinvestment** program is a smart and easy way of accumulating wealth over time. Most people who invest in mutual funds are very satisfied.

15.1d   Mutual and Exchange Traded Funds Are Similar

An **exchange traded fund (ETF)** is a cross between a stock and a mutual fund. They hold a basket of securities, such as stocks, bonds, currencies, and commodities—just like mutual funds—but they trade like stocks. Their prices are set by market forces since they are listed on securities markets around the world and traded throughout the day (just like stocks) on an "exchange" (hence the name).

ETFs are attractive as investments—particularly for beginning investors who either do not have a lot of investing experience or do not have a lot of cash to put into the market—because of their low costs, tax efficiency, extremely low management fees, and

mutual fund family
Investment management company that offers a number of different funds to the investing public, each with its own investment objectives or philosophies of investing.

automatic reinvestment
Investor's option to choose to automatically reinvest any interest, dividends, and capital gains payments to purchase additional fund shares.

DID YOU KNOW ?

Types of Investment Companies

The federal Investment Company Act distinguishes among investment companies. Open-end mutual funds are by far the most widely owned investment companies. Three other types exist:

1. **Closed-end mutual funds. Closed-end mutual funds** issue a limited and fixed number of shares at inception and do not buy them back. These 80,000 domestic companies operate with a fixed amount of capital. Closed-end shares are bought and sold on a stock exchange or in the over-the-counter market. After the original issue is sold, the price of a share depends primarily on the supply and demand in the market rather than the performance of the investment company assets.

2. **Real estate investment trusts.** A special kind of closed-end investment company is a **real estate investment trust (REIT)**. About 160 REITs invest in a

portfolio of assets as defined in the trust agreement, such as properties, like office buildings and shopping centers (called an equity REIT), or mortgages (a mortgage REIT). Hybrid REITs invest in both. REITs have no predetermined life span.

3. **Unit investment trusts.** A **unit investment trust (UIT)** is a closed-end investment company that makes a one-time public offering of only a specific, fixed number of units. A UIT buys and holds an unmanaged fixed portfolio of fixed-maturity securities, such as municipal bonds, for a period of time. This could be a few months or perhaps 50 years. Each unit represents a proportionate ownership interest in the specific portfolio of perhaps 10 to 50 securities. Sold by brokers for perhaps $250 to $1,000 a unit, there is no trading of these securities, although brokers may repurchase and resell them. There are about 5,400 UITs.

stock-like features. ETFs are passive investments that are best for those who make infrequent transactions and avoid trading fees.

Most of the 1,740 ETFs invest in securities that track an index, such as a stock index or bond index. In effect, ETFs ditch the fund manager and pass the savings on to the investor. It is sort of like an index mutual fund (discussed below), whose investment objective is to achieve the same return as a particular market index by buying and holding all or a representative selection of securities in it. There are ETFs that track the S&P 500, called Spiders; the Dow Jones Industrial Average, called Diamonds; and Qubes based on the NASDAQ 100.

CONCEPT CHECK 15.1

1. Explain how net asset value is calculated and how it is used by mutual funds.
2. List five advantages of investing in mutual funds.
3. Name five services that are unique to mutual funds.

Learning Objective 2

Differentiate mutual funds by investment objectives.

15.2 MUTUAL FUND OBJECTIVES

Most mutual funds are **managed funds,** meaning that professional managers are constantly evaluating and choosing securities using a specific investment approach. On a daily basis, active managers select the stocks and bonds in which to invest and sell them when they deem appropriate. The managers earn a fee often up to 2 percent (or more), for their services, and ultimately their choices are responsible for the performance of the fund.

These also are unmanaged **index mutual funds** (or **index funds**). These are passive investment vehicles that track market averages and minimize transaction costs. Their investment objective is to achieve the same return as a particular market index by buying and holding all or a representative selection of securities in it. Index funds are called **unmanaged funds** because their managers do not evaluate or actively select individual securities that might perform well. Computers do the work. Index mutual funds only buy or sell stocks to match the holdings of the index they seek to track. An S&P 500 index fund would effectively mirror the companies in the index, which are primarily large-cap U.S. stocks. Annual management fees are extremely low, averaging 0.16 percent.

More dollars have flowed to index strategies that track a market benchmark, such as the S&P 500 index, partly because such funds typically have lower costs than active funds and a growing number of investors believe that stock-picking managers cannot regularly beat the financial markets. The overwhelming research evidence says that even professional investors are no more likely to beat the market than monkeys throwing darts at securities listings. Fifteen percent of all money in the stock market is in index funds.

Before investing in any specific mutual fund, you need to decide whether the fund's investment objectives are a good fit for your own investment philosophy and financial goals. The SEC requires funds to disclose their investment objective.

Mutual funds may be classified in one of three categories: (1) income, (2) growth, and (3) growth and income. Each type has different features, risks, and reward characteristics, and the name of a fund gives a clue to its objectives.

15.2a Income Objective

A mutual fund with an **income objective,** such as money market and bond funds, invests in securities that pay regular income in dividends or interest.

Money Market Funds Mutual fund companies and brokerage firms offer **money market funds (MMFs).** They invest in highly liquid, relatively safe securities with very short maturities (always less than one year), such as CDs, Treasury bills, and commercial paper (i.e., short-term obligations issued by corporations). To enhance liquidity, regulations require that MMFs keep 10 percent of their assets in cash or investments that can be converted easily to cash within one day, meaning they are very liquid. You can write checks or use an ATM card to access a money market fund account. Issuers keep the NAV (the price of each share of the fund) at $1.

Money market funds (and there are about 580 of them) pay a higher rate of return than accounts offered through banks and credit unions. They are considered extremely safe. **Tax-exempt money market funds** limit their investments to tax-exempt municipal securities with maturities of less than 60 days, and their earnings are tax free to investors. **Government securities money market funds** appeal to investors' concerns about safety by investing solely in Treasury bills and other short-term securities backed by the U.S. government.

Bond Funds Bond Funds (also called **fixed-income funds**) aim to not incur undue risk while earning current income higher than a money market fund by investing in a portfolio of bonds and other investments, such as preferred stocks and common stocks that pay high dividends. They also earn some capital gains because bond fund prices fluctuate with changing interest rates. Today's nearly 2,000 bond funds are categorized by what they own and the maturities of their portfolio holdings.

- **Short-term corporate bond funds** invest in securities maturing in one to five years.

- **Short-term U.S. government bond funds** invest in Treasury issues maturing in one to five years.

MONEY WEBSITES

Informative websites are:
- Asset Builder
- Betterment
- Buy and Hold
- Business Week Online on funds
- CNNMoney.com on funds
- Financial Guard
- Finish Rich
- Future Advisor
- Jemstep
- Kiplinger's Personal Finance-Kiplinger's model portfolio
- MarketWatch
- Motley Fool
- ShareBuilder
- SigFig
- StrongKids
- Vanguard
- Wealthfront
- Wikipedia
- Yahoo! Finance
- Yahoo! Finance's fund screener

index mutual funds (or index funds)

are those funds whose investment objective is to achieve the same return as a particular market index by buying and holding all or a representative selection of securities in it.

money market funds

are those that invest in highly liquid, relatively safe securities with very short securities, always less than one year.

tax-exempt money market funds

Funds that limit their investments to tax-exempt municipal securities with maturities of 60 days or less.

bond funds (fixed-income funds)

Fixed-income funds that aim to earn current income higher than a money market fund without incurring undue risk by investing in a portfolio of bonds and other low-risk investments that pay high dividends and offer capital appreciation.

- **Intermediate corporate bond funds** invest in investment-grade corporate securities with five- to ten-year maturities.
- **Intermediate government bond funds** invest in Treasuries with five- to ten-year maturities.
- **Long-term corporate bond funds** specialize in investment-grade securities maturing in 10 to 30 years.
- **Long-term U.S. government bond funds** invest in Treasury and zero-coupon bonds with maturities of ten years or longer.
- **Mortgage-backed funds** invest in mortgage-backed securities issued by agencies of the U.S. government, such as Fannie Mae (Federal National Mortgage Association) and Freddie Mac (Federal Home Loan Mortgage Corporation).
- **Junk bond funds** invest in high-yield, high-risk corporate bonds.
- **Municipal bond (tax-exempt) funds** invest in municipal bonds that provide tax-free income. Both investment-grade and high-yield municipal bond funds exist.
- **Single-state municipal bond funds** invest in debt issues of only one state.
- **World bond** funds invest in debt securities offered by foreign corporations and governments.

15.2b Growth Objective

aggressive growth funds (maximum capital gains funds)

Funds that invest in speculative stocks with volatile price swings, seeking the greatest long-term capital appreciation possible. Also known as maximum capital gains funds and capital appreciation funds.

growth funds

Funds that seek long-term capital appreciation by investing in common stocks of companies with higher-than-average revenue and earnings growth, often the larger and well-established firms.

A mutual fund that has a **growth objective** seeks capital appreciation. It invests in the common stock of companies that have above average growth potential, firms that may not pay a regular dividend but have the potential for large capital gains. Growth funds carry a fair amount of risk exposure, and this is reflected in substantial price volatility. Growth funds are categorized by what they own and their investment goals.

Aggressive growth funds (maximum capital gains funds) seek the greatest long-term capital appreciation. Also known as **capital appreciation funds,** they make investments in speculative stocks with volatile price swings. They may employ high-risk investment techniques, such as borrowing money for leverage, short selling, hedging, and options. Lots of buying and selling occurs to enhance returns.

Growth funds seek long-term capital appreciation by investing in the common stocks of companies with higher-than-average revenue and earnings growth, often the larger and well-established firms. Such companies (like Walmart, Microsoft, and Coca-Cola) tend to reinvest most of their earnings to facilitate future growth.

DID YOU KNOW

Bond Funds Drop in Value When Interest Rates Rise

Extremely low interest rates—like those during and following an economic recession—are eventually replaced by rising interest rates because subsequent economic growth eventually results in inflation. When inflation goes up, the value of a bond mutual fund decreases. For every 1 percentage point change in interest rates, the value of the bond fund changes by the amount of the duration of maturity.

For example, if a bond fund has an average duration of seven years and interest rates rise 1 percentage point, the value of the bond fund will drop by 7 percent. Should today's interest rates rise 3 percent over the next few years, the net asset value of a bond mutual fund is likely to decline in value by 21 percent.

Growth and income funds invest in companies that have a high likelihood of both dividend income and price appreciation.

Value funds specialize in stocks that are fundamentally sound and whose prices appear to be low (low P/E ratios), based on the logic that such stocks are currently out of favor and undervalued by the market.

Large-cap funds invest in the stocks of companies with a market capitalization of more than $10 billion.

Midcap funds invest in the stocks of midsize companies with a market capitalization of $2 to $10 billion in size that are expected to grow rapidly.

Small-cap funds (or **small company growth funds**) invest in lesser-known companies with a market capitalization of $300 million to $2 billion in size that offer strong potential for growth.

Microcap funds invest in high-risk companies with a market capitalization of $50 to $300 million.

Sector funds concentrate their investment holdings in one or more industries that make up a targeted part of the economy that is expected to grow, perhaps very rapidly, such as energy, biotechnology, health care, and financial services.

Regional funds invest in securities listed on stock exchanges in a specific region of the world, such as the Pacific Rim, Australia, or Europe.

Precious metals and gold funds invest in securities associated with gold, silver, and other precious metals.

Global funds invest in growth stocks of companies listed on foreign exchanges as well as in the United States, usually multinational firms.

International funds invest only in foreign stocks throughout the world.

Emerging market funds seek out stocks in countries whose economies are small but growing. Fund prices are volatile because these countries tend to be less stable politically.

growth and income funds

Funds that invest in companies that have a high likelihood of both dividend income and price appreciation; less risk-oriented than aggressive growth funds or growth funds.

value funds

Funds specializing in stocks that are fundamentally sound whose prices appear to be low (low P/E ratios) based on the logic that such stocks are currently out of favor and undervalued by the market

---

Figure 15-3   Balancing Risk and Returns on Mutual Funds

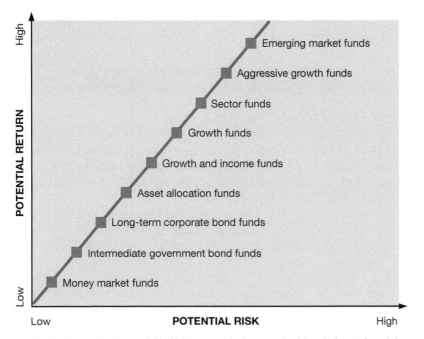

Note that increasing the potential for higher returns also increases the risk to the investor's capital.

15.2c Growth and Income Objective

A mutual fund that has a combined **growth and income objective** seeks a balanced return made up of current income and capital gains. Such funds primarily invest in common stocks. They seek a return not as low as offered by funds with an income objective but not as high as that offered by funds with a growth objective. They invite less risk than growth funds. There are a variety of growth and income funds.

Growth and income funds invest in companies expected to show average or better growth and pay steady or rising dividends.

Equity-income funds invest in well-known companies with a long history of paying high dividends as they emphasize income and capital preservation.

Socially responsible funds invest in companies that meet some predefined standard of moral, ethical, and social behavior. Criteria could be progressive employee relations, strong records of community involvement, an excellent record on environmental issues, respect for human rights, and safe products, as well as no "sinful" products such as tobacco, guns, alcohol, and gambling, as well as utilities that rely upon nuclear power. Faith-based funds also exist. See examples of the 181 socially responsible mutual funds at The Forum for Sustainable and Responsible Investment (www.ussif.org).

Balanced funds (or **hybrid funds**) keep a set mix of stocks and bonds, often 60 percent stocks and 40 percent bonds, in order to earn a well-balanced return of income and long-term capital gains. **Blend funds** invest in a combination of stocks and money market securities, but no fixed-income securities, such as bonds.

Asset allocation funds invest in a mix of assets (usually stocks, bonds, and cash equivalents and sometimes international assets, gold, and real estate), and they buy and sell regularly to reduce risk while trying to outperform the market. The asset mix may be based on risk tolerance (aggressive, moderate, and conservative).

Target-date retirement (life-cycle) funds are asset allocation funds that offer investors premixed portfolios of stocks, bonds, and cash that investors of a certain age and risk tolerance might prefer. They are often named for the year one plans to retire, for example, the "Fidelity Freedom Fund 2050." These are targeted to people in their 30s, 40s, and 50s. Target-date funds shift assets from aggressive to moderate to a more

---

balanced funds

Funds that keep a set mix of stocks and bonds, often 60 percent stocks and 40 percent bonds, in order to earn a well-balanced return of income and long-term capital gains.

asset allocation funds

Investments in a mix of assets (usually stocks, bonds, and cash equivalents and sometimes international assets, gold, and real estate); they buy and sell regularly to reduce risk while trying to outperform the market.

target-date retirement funds (life-cycle funds)

Asset allocation funds that offer investors premixed portfolios of stocks, bonds, and cash that investors of a certain age and risk tolerance might prefer, and they are often named for the year one plans to retire.

ADVICE FROM A SEASONED PRO

Invest Only "Fun Money" Aggressively

Once the investor has his or her financial plan in place and well funded, taking on more risk is acceptable—but *only* within the limits of the individual's definition of **fun money**. This is a sum of investment money that you can afford to lose without doing serious damage to your total portfolio. You might, for example, resolve to trade with a specific sum, such as $5,000, or perhaps no more than 2 or 3 percent of your portfolio. Keep such fun money in a separate account from your long-term investments. Decide mentally that if and when the money is gone, it has been invested in more aggressive stock mutual funds on an

activity that you enjoyed trying, but accept that the money lost is lost forever. Avoid the temptation to "throw good money after bad" by investing more in an effort to try to recover your losses.

The biggest danger of fun-money investing is that you might be successful. Success can give you the confidence—albeit probably false confidence—that you are a great investor. While you might be the next billionaire investor like Warren Buffett, such success is likely to tempt you to aggressively invest even more of the assets in your total portfolio. That approach can result in disaster.

Robert O. Weagley
University of Missouri, Columbia, Missouri

conservative mix of securities as the retirement target date approaches. They seek to first grow and then preserve the portfolio assets. This is a no-hassle, "set-it-and-forget-it" approach to investing for retirement. Regulations require target-date funds provide investors with information that shows the projected allocations over the life of the fund.

Target-risk (lifestyle) funds offer an easy way to diversify one's portfolio based on risk tolerance (such as conservative, moderate or aggressive). These funds maintain their asset allocation over time, unlike target-date retirement funds.

Mutual fund funds earn a return by investing in other mutual funds. This provides extensive diversification, but expenses and fees are higher than average.

Target-risk (lifestyle) funds
Offer an easy way to diversify one's portfolio based on risk tolerance (such as conservative, moderate, or aggressive).

CONCEPT CHECK 15.2

1. Distinguish between a managed mutual fund and an unmanaged mutual fund.
2. Distinguish among mutual funds with an income objective, growth objective, and growth and income objective.
3. Explain why investors like index mutual funds and exchange traded funds.

15.3 MUTUAL FUND INVESTING FEES AND CHARGES

Learning Objective 3
Summarize the fees and charges involved in buying and selling mutual funds.

Individuals who invest through mutual funds pay transaction costs that often are less than those associated with buying individual stocks, bonds, and cash equivalent securities. The expenses one pays when buying a mutual fund are considered as either "ongoing expenses" and/or "sales loads."

15.3a Ongoing Expenses

Ongoing expenses of a mutual fund cover portfolio management, fund administration, daily fund accounting and pricing, and shareholder services (such as call centers and websites). Smart shareholders tend to invest in funds with below-average expense ratios with no distribution charges (known as 12b-1 fees).

These expenses are included in a fund's **expense ratio**, which is the fund's annual expenses that are expressed as a percentage of its assets. The higher the expense ratio, the lower the return. The expense ratio is connected to the **turnover rate**, which is a measure of a mutual fund's trading activity.

To evaluate the fees charged by mutual funds, compare them to the average expense ratio for the fund category. The average management fee for an index equity fund is 11 basis points. This is extremely low and compares well with the average fee for actively managed equity fund which is 86 basis points. A **basis point** is one hundredth of one percent, thus actively managed funds cost more than seven times higher (86/11) than those charged by unmanaged index funds. The average expense ratio for a bond mutual fund 0.57 percent and the average expense rate for a target date mutual fund is 0.55 percent. These terms are discussed later.

expense ratio
Expense per dollar of assets under management.

turnover rate
A measure of a mutual fund's trading activity, and connected to the funds turnover rate.

basis point
One hundredth of one percent.

15.3b Sales Loads

Sales loads are paid at the time of share purchase (front-end loads), when shares are redeemed (back-end loads), and/or over time (level loads).

Load Versus No-Load Funds All mutual funds are classified as either load or no-load funds. This refers to whether or not they assess a sales charge, or load, when shares are purchased. There are also other fees assessed on load and no-load funds that can be avoided through careful research.

Load Funds are "Sold" and Always Charge Transaction Fees Funds that levy a sales charge for purchases are called **load funds**. Load funds are generally sold by stock

load funds
Mutual funds that always charge a "load" or sales charge upon purchase; the load is the commission used to compensate brokers.

front-end load

A sales charge paid when an individual buys an investment, reducing the amount available to purchase fund shares.

stated commission

The sales charge as a percentage of the amount invested.

low-load funds

Funds carrying sales charges of perhaps 1 to 3 percent; sold by brokers, via mail, and sometimes through mutual fund retailers located in shopping centers.

back-end load (contingent deferred sales charge)

A sales commission that is imposed only when shares are sold; often charges are on a sliding scale, with the fee dropping 1 percentage point per year that the investor stays in the fund.

redemption charge (exit fee)

Similar to a deferred load but often much lower; used to reduce excessive trading of fund shares.

no-load funds

Funds that allow investors to purchase shares directly at the net asset value (NAV) without the addition of sales charges.

12b-1 fees (distribution fees)

Annual fees that some "no-load" fund companies deduct from a fund's assets to compensate salespeople and pay other expenses.

trailing commission

Compensation paid to salespeople for months or years in the future.

brokerage firms, banks, and financial planners rather than marketed directly to investors by a mutual fund company. The load is the commission used to compensate sellers for their time and expertise in recommending appropriate funds for investors. This commission, often called a **front-end load**, typically amounts to a level sales charge of 3 to 8.5 percent of the amount invested. This reduces the amount available to purchase fund shares. For example, assume that you and your stockbroker have discussed the investment potential of the Conglomerate Cat and Dog Food Mutual Fund and you decide to invest $10,000. Because this load fund charges a commission of 8.5 percent (the maximum permitted by the SEC), the stockbroker receives $850 ($10,000 $\times$ 0.085). As a result, only $9,150 of your money is actually available to purchase shares.

The sales charge may be shown either as the stated commission or as a percentage of the amount invested. The **stated commission** (8.5 percent in our example) is always somewhat misleading. The "percentage of the amount invested" is a more accurate figure because it is based on the actual money invested and working. A stated commission of 8.5 percent actually amounts to 9.3 percent of the amount invested: $10,000 − $9,150 = $850; $850 ÷ $9,150 = 9.3%. If you want to invest a full $10,000 in this load fund, you will need to pay out $10,930 [$10,930 − ($10,930 $\times$ 8.5%) = $10,000]. Investments of $10,000 or more often receive a discount on the load.

So-called **low-load funds** may carry a front-end sales charge of perhaps 1 to 3 percent. These funds may also be sold by brokers and are sometimes sold via mail and through mutual fund retailers located in shopping centers.

Back-end and Over-time Loads   A **back-end load** (or **contingent deferred sales charge**) is a sales commission that is imposed only when shares are sold. Deferred loads are often on a sliding scale. The fee may decline 1 percentage point for each year the investor owns the fund. For example, a fund might charge a 6 percent fee if an investor redeems the shares within one year of purchase, and then the fee declines on an annual basis, until it reaches zero after six more years. Many no-load funds assess back-end loads and redemption fees.

A **redemption charge** (or **exit fee**) is level to all investors and it is usually 1 percent of the value of the shares redeemed. A fund assesses such a charge to reduce excessive trading of fund shares. The fee disappears after the investment has been held for six months or a year. Long-term investors for retirement do not need to be concerned about paying about back-end loads and exit fees, as these largely disappear over time.

A **no-load fund** sells shares at the net asset value without the addition of sales charges. These mutual fund companies let people purchase shares directly from the mutual fund company without the services of a broker, banker, or financial planner. Interested investors simply seek out advertisements for these funds in financial newspapers, magazines, and the Internet and make contact through toll-free telephone numbers, online, or mail. However, the SEC does allow funds to be called "no-load" even though they assess a service fee of 0.25 percent or less when shares are purchased. No-load funds are usually the best mutual funds in which to invest.

12b-1 Fees are Expensive   A **12b-1 fee** (named for the SEC rule that permits the charge) is an annual charge deducted by the fund company from a fund's assets to compensate underwriters and brokers for fund sales as well as to pay for advertising, marketing, distribution, and promotional costs. A 12b-1 fee is also known as a **distribution fee**. This fee also pays for **trailing commissions**, which is compensation paid to salespeople for months or years in the future. Years ago it was believed that by marketing a mutual fund, its assets would increase and management could lower expenses because of economies of scale. This has yet to be proved. Although the no-load funds do not call 12b-1 fees "loads" because they are not charged up front, they have the same effect as loads—that is, they reduce the investor's return, often quite dramatically. Over 60 percent of funds assess 12b-1 fees, including many no-load funds.

These fees are hidden and they decrease a shareholder's earning power *each year* without being described as a sales commission. A 12b-1 fee is actually a "perpetual sales load" because it is assessed on the initial investment as well as on reinvested dividends, every year, forever. The SEC caps 12b-1 fees at 0.75 percent, although recall that the SEC also permits a 0.25 percent service fee, which brings the total to 1 percent. Some funds stop assessing 12b-1 fees after four to eight years.

15.3c Mutual Fund Share Classes—Designed to Confuse—Are Sold to You

A single mutual fund, with one portfolio and one investment advisor, may offer more than one "class" of its shares to investors. Each class represents a similar interest in the mutual fund's portfolio. The principal difference between the classes is that the mutual fund will charge you different fees and expenses depending upon the class that you choose.

Class A shares typically charge a front-end sales charge and a portion of the dollars you pay is not invested. Class A shares may impose an asset-based sales charge, but it generally is lower than the asset-based sales charge imposed by the other classes.

Class B shares typically do not charge a front-end sales charge, but they do impose asset-based sales charges that may be higher than those that you would incur if you purchased Class A shares. Class B shares also normally impose a contingent deferred sales charge, which you pay when you sell your shares, and they might (if held long enough) allow automatic conversion to share with a lower 12b-1 fee.

Class C shares might have a 12b-1 fee and a redemption charge. Additionally, in most cases your expense ratio would be higher than Class A shares, and even than Class B shares if you hold for a long time.

Moreover, the performance results for each class will differ depending on how long you hold the shares. These shares are sold by brokers and financial planners and can be avoided by investors who choose to invest in no-load funds.

15.3d Use FINRA's Website to Compare Mutual Fund Fees

To compare the costs of various funds and share classes for your expected holding period and estimated returns, see the Financial Industry Regulatory Authority's Mutual Fund Expense Analyzer (apps.finra.org/fundanalyzer/2/fa.aspx). This tool estimates the value of the funds and impact of fees and expenses on your investment and also allows you to look up applicable fees and available discounts for thousands of funds.

The SEC requires that mutual funds provide investors with a summary prospectus—in plain English—of information needed to help make investment decisions, and it appears at the front of a fund's full prospectus. It must include a **standardized expense table** that describes and illustrates in an identical manner the effects of all of its fees and other expenses.

standardized expense table
SEC-required information that describes and illustrates mutual fund charges in an identical manner so that investors can accurately compare the effects of all of a fund's fees and other expenses relative to other funds.

15.3e What's Best: Load or No Load? Low Fee or High Fee?

The best choice is to invest in no-load mutual funds or exchange traded funds (ETFs). Both have extremely low costs. Investors can almost guarantee a poorer return than others if they put their money into a load fund with high management fees. Experts agree that "If you pick your own funds, sales charges and high management fees are a total waste of money."

The SEC says that for a long-term investor a 1 percent fee that increases at 4 percent a year (because the principal increases that much annually) will devour one-third of your eventual total return! And 1 percent is less than the average set of fees.

The sales commissions charged by load funds indisputably reduce total returns. When investment results are adjusted to account for the effects of sales charges, no-load mutual funds always have an initial advantage because the investor has more money at work.

YOUR GRANDPARENTS SAY

"Minimize Expenses"

"Vanguard's Total Stock Index mutual fund charges a mere 0.07% in management expenses. This compares well with the typical actively managed mutual fund charge of 1.4 percent. The results after 30 years of investing $4,000 annually with both accounts earning 5 percent: $258,000 for low management fee and about $209,000 for average management fee. Earning an extra $50,000 for choosing a fund with low fees is worth it!"

12b-1 Fees Kill Long-Term Returns Annual 12b-1 charges are very costly over the long run. If you pay 1 percent per year in 12b-1 fees for a mutual fund in which you invest for ten years, you will be giving up nearly 10 percent of your investment amount in trailing commissions. That fee is charged every year. Yikes!

Avoiding High Fees Is Critical to Investment Success Research has found that over five-year periods, lower-cost funds *always* deliver returns better than those offered by higher-cost funds. It's even harder if you're paying 1.9 percentage points a year for active management. That's like carrying a couple of heavy barbells during a marathon. The equally fast runner without the barbells is going to win over the long run.

The Dark Side of Compounding Fees Will Kill Your Account Balance Assume you and your two siblings each invest $10,000 and earn a 7 percent return every year for 50 years. You each should have a balance of about $295,000. But what about investing expenses? If your asset management fee were only 0.14 percent, you—the smart one in the family—will have $276,000 and have given up only $19,000 in expenses.

Because your first sibling paid an expense ratio of 0.64 percent, he or she ends up with only $218,000 because of $76,000 in expenses. Your truly unlucky second sibling will only have a balance of $168,000 after paying 1.19 percent in fees for $126,000 in expenses. What is wrong with this picture? You have $276,000 versus your sibling's $168,000 after making the exact same return on the investment for 50 years! Those "little" fees made a 64 percent difference in the account balances, or a huge $108,000. Your siblings may want you to take care of them in retirement. To summarize, forget trying to earn the highest return on your investments and instead focus on paying the smallest fees.

15.3f Invest in Index Mutual Funds and ETFs for the Lowest Fees

Twenty percent of money invested in stock funds is invested in index mutual funds. Investors are becoming more aware of their extremely low costs. Their growing popularity makes these funds more competitive than ever with their actively managed peers. Besides, only 4 in 10 of actively managed funds even exist after 10 years.

Instead of looking for a needle in a haystack when investing—finding the best mutual fund—why not buy the whole haystack? The lowest costs in investing can be found among the nation's 373 index funds and 1,400 exchange traded funds (ETFs). ETFs have the same basic advantage that mutual funds do when compared to picking individual stocks: diversification. And that's exactly what every investor needs.

One in four investors has ETFs in their portfolios partly because of the extremely low costs (0.36% annual management fee on average), which are lower than similar index mutual funds (0.76% on average). The lowest annual fee of all ETFs is the largest fund in the world, Vanguard Total Stock Market ETF (VTSAX), with a management fee of only 0.07 percent, which is an unmanaged fund that tracks 3,000 stocks. Schwab's U.S. Broad Market ETF (SCHB) tracks 2,500 stocks with an annual fee of 0.08 percent.

Vanguard's overall fees are the lowest in the industry, averaging 0.16 percent annually compared to 1.16 percent for the industry. That 1 percent difference (1.16 – 0.16) compounded over a lifetime can shrink your retirement nest egg by 40 percent.

The average annual gain of 9.6 percent on stock investments over the long-term is measured by the MSCI USA equity index from 1970 forward. It consists of 3.37 percent from dividends and 6.23 percent in capital gains. Stock pickers who are employed by managed funds have to actively trade and as a result they must obtain a return of 11.6 percent on average to achieve the same result as unmanaged index investment, because their fees and expenses often add up to 2 percent or more.

There is absolutely no scientific evidence that active fund management outperforms index funds and ETFs. Beating an unmanaged index investment may be remotely possible, but in reality it is highly unlikely. Seventy percent of new money coming into mutual and exchange-trade funds has gone into index portfolios.

CONCEPT CHECK 15.3

1. Give three examples of fees or charges associated with load funds.
2. Which is better for most investors, load or no-load funds? Why?
3. Summarize the effects of loads and fees on investment returns.

15.4 HOW TO SELECT THE FUNDS IN WHICH YOU SHOULD INVEST

Learning Objective 4
Establish strategies to evaluate and select mutual funds that meet your investment goals.

Selecting mutual funds in which to invest is a **do-it-yourself (DIY)** effort for no-load investors and it is relatively easy to do. Brokers are not needed because a tremendous amount of objective information is available to help investors evaluate and select funds.

To explain the process of selecting funds, let's follow Catalina Garcia's decision making. She is in her late twenties, lives in San Jose, California, and earns $60,000 annually in her sales management job. Figure 15-4 illustrates the process of selecting mutual fund investments, and Table 15-2 contains performance data for a number of large-cap mutual funds and Table 15.3 illustrates performance data for large exchange traded funds.

Do-it-yourself
Selecting no-load mutual funds in which to invest is relatively easy to do.

Figure 15-4 **Step-By-Step How to Invest in Mutual Funds**

1. Review your investment policy	Conservative Moderate Aggressive
2. Review your investment goals	Goal Time horizon Return Taxes
3. Eliminate funds inappropriate for your investment goals	Income Growth Growth and income Specific fund types
4. Choose low load or no load funds	Low or no-load
5. Determine if investment advice is needed	For immediate investments For later portfolio review
6. Screen and compare funds that meet your investment criteria	Fund-screening tools Fees and charges Performance Services
7. Monitor your mutual fund philosophy	Portfolio monitoring Fund quotations in newspapers

Table 15-2   Mutual Fund Performance

20 Largest Stock Mutual Funds Ranked by Size

Rank/Name	Symbol	Assets in Billions	Total Return 1 year	3 years	5 years	Maximum Sales Charge	Toll-free number (800+)
1. Vanguard Total Stock Market Idx Inv	VTSMX	$300	10%	8%	9%	None	635-1511
2. Vanguard 500 Index Inv	VFINX	180	10	8	9	None	635-1511
3. American Growth Fund of America A	AGTHX	140	10	11	8	5.75%	421-0180
4. American EuroPacific Growth A	AEPGX	120	9	7	11	5.75	421-0180
5. Fidelity Contrafund	FCNTX	130	10	12	13	None	544-9797
6. Vanguard Total Intl Stock Idx Inv	VGTSX	110	9	13	−1	None	635-1511
7. American Capital Income Builder A	CAIBX	90	8	9	8	5.75	421-0180
8. American Inc Fund of America A	AMECX	90	9	8	9	5.75	421-0180
9. Franklin Income A	FKINX	80	9	8	11	4.25	632-2301
10. American Capital World Gro & Inc A	CWGIX	90	9	10	9	5.75	421-0180
11. Vanguard Wellington	VWELX	80	9	8	12	None	635-1511
12. American Balanced A	ABALX	70	10	8	13	5.75	421-0180
13. Fidelity Spartan 500 Index Inv	FUSEX	70	10	8	9	None	544-9797
14. American Washington Mutual A	AWSHX	70	9	8	9	5.75	421-0180
15. American Invstmt Co of America A	AIVSX	70	8	11	7	5.75	421-0180
16. American Fundamental Inv A	ANCFX	60	8	10	8	5.75	421-0180
17. Vanguard Emerging Mkts Stock Idx	VEIEX	60	−2	−1	13	None	635-1511
18. BlackRock Global Allocation A	MDLOX	60	7	6	7	5.25	441-7762
19. American New Perspective A	ANWPX	60	8	10	7	5.75	421-0180
20. Dodge & Cox Stock	DODGX	50	9	10	8	None	621-3979
S&P 500 Stock Index			10%	8%	9%		

Source: Data are authors' estimates calculated supposedly during an upswing in a sustained but slowly growing bull market of 5 years duration, and nothing in this table constitutes investment advice. Returns are illustrative.

Table 15-3   Exchange Traded Funds Performance

10 Largest Exchange Traded Funds Ranked by Size

Name	Symbol	Price (In Dollars)	Annualized Total Return 1 year	3 years	5 years	Recent Yield	Expense Ratio
iShares Core S&P 500	IVV	200	7%	15%	16%	1.1	0.07
iShares Core MSCI EAFE ETS	IEFA	20	5	5	6	1.2	0.11
iShare Core S&P Mid-cap	IJH	140	6	!6	16	1.1	0.14
IShares Core S&P Small –cap	IJR	110	6	18	18	1.3	0.14
Schwab US Large Cap ETF	SCHX	50	6	14	15	1.4	0.06
Vanguard FTSE Developed Markets	VEA	40	−4	11	11	1.2	0.10
Vanguard FTSE Emerging Markets	VWO	40	−3	4	10	1.4	0.17
Vanguard Total International Stock	VXUS	50	−5	9	4	1.3	0.15
Vanguard Small Cap ETF	VB	110	5	7	7	1.2	0.09
Vanguard Total Stock Market	VTI	100	7	10	1	2.0	0.05

*Data are authors' estimates calculated supposedly during an upswing in a sustained but slowly growing bull market of 5 years duration, and nothing in this table constitutes investment advice. Returns are illustrative.

15.4a   1. Review Your Investment Philosophy

Catalina began by reviewing her investment philosophy and financial goals. These topics were examined in Chapter 13. Catalina has a moderate investment philosophy. Thus she seeks capital gains through slow and steady growth in the value of her investments along with some current income. Catalina invites only a fair amount of risk of capital loss. She has no immediate need for the invested money and is focused on laying the investment foundation for later years.

15.4b   2. Review Your Investment Goals

Catalina has a written investment plan (Figure 13-6 on page 416). The investment goal she is interested in investing for now is retirement, and her investment time horizon is the next 30 years or longer. She anticipates an annual return of at least 4 to 5 percent, perhaps more. She does not care about income taxes because these investments will be made within Catalina's tax-deferred 401(k) retirement plan at work, where her earnings will grow tax-free.

Catalina does not have any lump sums available in a savings or money market account to use for investing. To help fund her retirement plan, she decided to have $300 (6 percent of her salary) a month withheld from her paycheck to invest in a mutual fund with a growth investment objective. Catalina's employer's 401(k) plan offers about 20 funds as well as company stock.

15.4c   3. Eliminate Funds Inappropriate for Your Investment Goals

Catalina began by reviewing all fund classifications (pages 470–475) and balancing the risks and returns of various funds as illustrated in Figure 15-3 on page 473. She aims to eliminate mutual funds inappropriate for her retirement investment goal.

Catalina recognizes that increasing the potential for higher returns also increases the risk to the investor's capital. Therefore, she eliminated the following types of funds: sector funds, emerging markets funds, and aggressive growth funds, as well as stock in the company where she works. She also realizes that investing too conservatively invites the risk of failure to achieve her goal of a financially successful retirement. Therefore, Catalina eliminated money market funds.

15.4d   4. Choose Low Load or No Load Funds

Catalina has thought through the choices and is persuaded that no-load funds definitely are the best for her investments. The sales commissions charged by load funds indisputably reduce total returns. Catalina reasoned that since no-load mutual funds have an initial advantage—the investor has more money at work—thus she prefers no-load funds. Because her $300 a month will go into funding her years in retirement, she also thought that 12b-1 fees would be very costly over the long term.

Catalina decided to invest in one or more no-load mutual funds with no 12b-1 fees and very low management expense ratios. Catalina will have to look up some of this information on the Internet since data in Table 15-2 is quite limited. She especially likes the fact that not paying high commissions and wicked fees will guarantee that by the time of retirement she probably will have 30 percent more money.

15.4e   5. Determine if Investment Advice Is Needed

Catalina wants to avoid high management fees that are used to pay for "advice" from professionals. These are the same 70, 80, or 90 percent of professionals who every year lose money, after their commissions and fees, when their performance is compared to

THERE IS AN APP FOR THAT!

Some of the best apps are:

- Bloomberg
- Charles Schwab
- CNNMoney Portfolio
- ETF db
- Fidelity
- Fund Visualizer - Mutual Fund Screener
- Morningstar
- Personal Capital Money and Investing
- SigFig Investment Advisor
- Stock Twits
- Ticker: Stocks Portfolio Manager
- USA Today Stock Portfolio
- Yahoo Finance

NEVER EVER

Keep Too Many Investment Accounts

Having too many investment accounts can be very confusing, especially when you open the mail to read so many reports. It is difficult to comprehend how one is doing financially when each report presents data in different formats. In addition, who wants to pay a $10, $50, or a larger annual custodial fee to maintain each account? Move all your account to the firm with the best investing options and lowest fees.

TURN BAD HABITS INTO GOOD ONES

Do You Do This?

Have only a few investments like stocks and bonds

Find it difficult to reinvest dividends and interest

Buy load funds or those with 12b-1 fees

Seem confused about the right funds in which to invest

Find it difficult to monitor your investments

Do This Instead!

Diversify by investing in mutual funds

Invest in funds that reinvest automatically

Invest in no-load funds or ETFs

Use a free online fund-screening tool

Manage your fund portfolio free online

NUMBERS ON

Mutual Fund Investing

Data from a variety of sources suggest:

- Forty-five percent of individuals own mutual funds, and hold 90 percent of their total mutual fund assets, directly or through 401(k) retirement plans.

- Two-thirds purchased their first mutual fund through an employer-sponsored 401(k) retirement plan.

- Three-quarters of individuals who own mutual funds are married or living with a partner and nearly half are college graduates.

- The average expense ratio for equity mutual funds offered in the United States is 1.33 percent; however 401(k) plan participants pay only 0.54 percent.

- Nine out of 10 dollars invested in through 401(k) accounts are in no-load mutual funds.

- Thirteen percent of mutual funds in 401(k) accounts have a front- or back-end load.

- Seven out of 10 mutual funds underperformed the S&P over the most recent 20-year period.

- Two-thirds of 401(k) plan assets are invested in equity mutual funds, rather in bond, money market, or a mix of stock and bond funds.

- Half of millennials currently seek investment advice online, and four out of 10 have a financial advisor with whom to consult.

- Two-thirds hold more than half of their financial assets in mutual funds.

the stock indexes. And that is her money, not theirs. She reasons that it is crazy to pay too much to brokers.

Instead of simply investing in "this and that" funds, Catalina smartly decided to create a portfolio of mutual funds tailored to her needs. She started her decision-making at www.kiplinger.com/article/investing/T033-C009-S001-kiplinger-25-model-portfolios.html where she found 25 portfolios recommended by *Kiplinger's Personal Finance* editors and writers. Many companies develop and promote lists of good investments, and they are customized for different situations and stages of life. On their websites, she can get updated returns and track the performance of her investments with the benchmark portfolios.

Because Catalina believes she is going to invest in no-load funds or exchange traded funds, she figured she did not need the services of a regular stock broker or financial planner. Instead, she plans to use the tremendous resources that are available via the Vanguard website (www.vanguard.com)—information, education, and professional advice. Vanguard is the largest mutual fund family in the country as it holds over 20 percent of the assets in the industry. Two-thirds of those dollars are in index funds.

Catalina's employer offers investing and retirement planning seminars and workshops provided by Ernst & Young, T. Rowe Price, Vanguard, and other companies. Significant others are welcome to attend. Employer-sponsored financial advice sometimes covers an employee's entire financial situation, including debt reduction, college planning, spousal assets, real estate, and other investments.

Once Catalina's retirement assets build up to a substantial amount, perhaps $50,000 or more, she might consider seeking professional financial advice. However, she has learned that many her working peers who invest through their 401(k) plan want advice now—precisely when they are starting out in their investment program through the workplace. Catalina has learned that her employer is considering hiring a robo-advisor service, and the following is what she found out after going online.

Robo-Advisor Services Available to All Robo-advisors are the way to go, especially if you are a novice investor. A **robo-advisor** is a class of financial advisor that provides portfolio management online with minimal human intervention. These are online wealth management services that provide low-cost automated, algorithm-based portfolio management financial advice without the use of human planners. They offer clear benefits of low cost and ease of use. A robo-advisor service is founded on the belief that traditional Wall Street firms charge way too much.

Robo-advisors offer common sense advice on asset allocation that is at least as good as their competitors—old fashioned human advisors. Their rational advice is offered to middle class people—those long overlooked by the Wall Street financial planning industry—at a good price. Financial advice for average Americans—not just for the wealthy—is finally here.

Robo advisors
Internet based companies that dispense low-cost customized, computer-generated financial advice.

Robo-Advisors for Investments are Mainstream To use a robo-advisor service you answer some online questions about your personal goals, risk tolerance, and time horizon, and a computer program quickly analyzes your responses to generate investment advice using complex algorithms. Robo-advisors apply modern portfolio management theories and calculate thousands of computer simulations about risk-reward scenarios on diversification to help people reach their financial goals. The firm's investment portfolios range from aggressive to conservative. These web-based robo-advisor services give investors with small portfolios access to advice that they would never otherwise receive. They make it push-button easy. And robo-advisors are becoming widely accepted as today's norm.

How Do Robo-Advisor Services Work Robo-advisors keep expenses down by using low-cost exchange traded funds to build portfolios, usually 8 to 12 funds. Fees range from 0.25 to about 1.00 percent per year. Some firms are 100 percent automated while others allow you to talk with a real financial advisor by telephone or online. If specific investment recommendations are made, rather than general asset class advice, the provider must be a registered investment advisor (RIA). This means they are fiduciaries who put the investor's interest ahead of their own or that of their employers.

Most-robo advisors put you into long-term investments that you will own for years, adjusting only for your age or when your goals change. Robo-advisor firms also rebalance your portfolio on a quarterly or annual basis. In short, robo-financial advisors perform virtually all the services one needs as an investor. This assumes you are comfortable using web tools to drive your financial decisions.

The almost-nil fees of Betterment are illustrative of a robo-advisor service: Zero to open an account, no minimum requirement, 400 stock-heavy portfolios aimed at

NEVER EVER

1. *Buy funds with high fees and expenses.*

2. *Withdraw cash dividends rather than reinvesting.*

3. *Chase short-term performance by investing in "hot" funds.*

investors under age 35, annual expenses of 0.14 percent, and a management fee that ranges from 0.15 to 0.35 percent. To learn more, check out Betterment.com, E*Trade.com, SigFig.com, TradeKing.com, Wealthfront .com, and WiseBanyan.com. The big firms, like Fidelity, Schwab, and Vanguard also offer similar services.

Most robo-advisor services offered to the general public also exclude employer-sponsored retirement plan. But a few firms, such as FinancialEngines.com, do specialize in offering such advice to employees through their employers. Ask your employer if they offer access to such a service. This topic is examined in Chapter 17.

15.4f   6. Screen and Compare Funds That Meet Your Investment Criteria

When comparing the track records of mutual funds, there are a number of criteria to consider. These may include expenses; net asset value; minimum initial purchase; size of fund; ratings; past performance (perhaps one, three, five, and ten years); best and worst performance in up and down markets (volatility); fund manager tenure; and services. Catalina is interested in stock funds, international funds and global funds, low management fees, and no 12b-1 fees.

Since today's share prices go up and down quite considerably during any one year, Catalina checked the volatility ratings of funds. **Volatility** characterizes a mutual fund's (or any security's) tendency to rise or fall in price over a period of time. A measure of volatility is the **standard deviation,** which gauges the degree to which a security's historical return rises above or falls below its own long-term average return— and therefore may be likely to do so again in the future. A standard deviation is a probability indicator, not an economic forecast. The bigger an investment's standard deviation, the more volatile its price may be in the future. High volatility suggests greater long-term rewards but a greater-than-normal risk of short-term losses during economic downturns. Other common measures of risk are beta, the Sharpe Ratio, and R-squared. Publications like *Kiplinger's Personal Finance* and *Money* provide volatility ratings for mutual funds.

DID YOU KNOW

The Tax Consequences of Mutual Fund Investing

Ordinary income dividend distributions, capital gains distributions, and realized gains from the sale of mutual funds are generally subject to taxation.

1. In regular investment accounts:

- When you buy and hold mutual fund shares, you owe income taxes on any ordinary income dividends and on the fund's capital gains in the year you receive or reinvest them.

- When you sell shares, you owe taxes on the capital gains earned on the difference between what you paid for the shares and the selling price (less transaction costs).

- Before purchasing a mutual fund toward the end of the year, like in December, determine whether the

fund has already made its end-of-year capital gains distribution. If you buy the fund before the **record date** (the date established by an issuer to determine who is eligible to receive a dividend or distribution), you will receive the income but you also will owe capital gains taxes for the whole year. Buying after the record date avoids that tax because you will not have received the distribution.

2. Interest from a tax-exempt municipal bond fund is
exempt from federal income taxes.

3. In retirement accounts (such as a 401[k] or traditional
IRA account), all taxes are deferred until funds are withdrawn from the account.

Catalina started searching for mutual fund investments at Vanguard (www.kiplinger.com/tool/investing/T052-S001-search-and-compare-stocks-equities/index.php), which is considered one of the best mutual fund screening websites. She began by clicking on the "categories." A **fund screener** or **fund-screening tool** permits an individual to screen all of the mutual funds in the market. Other mutual fund screening tools are available all over the Internet. Just search "stock screener" on Google and try several until you find a favorite. For example, see Yahoo, The Street, Fidelity, and Schwab.

Catalina focused on large-cap funds, including those shown in Table 15-2 on page 480. She researched funds using the Vanguard fund screener. She obtained online a profile prospectus from Vanguard on each of the funds she liked. A **profile prospectus** (or **fund profile**) describes the mutual fund, its investment objectives, and how it tries to achieve its objectives. Written in lay language, it offers a two- to four-page summary presentation of information contained in an SEC-required legal prospectus that answers 11 key investor questions, including risks, fees, and details about the fund's ten-year performance record.

After reading fund details, looking at the numbers, and comparing performance, Catalina decided to split her monthly $300 investment between Vanguard Total Stock Market Index (VTSMX) and Vanguard Emerging Markets Stock Index (VEIEX), partly because of their low to nil expense ratios. (In addition, any minimum initial investment fees are waived for investments via her employer's retirement plan.) Catalina thinks the fund managers will beat the average market returns, such as a S&P 500 index like Vanguard's 500 Index (VFINX). Catalina might be right, or she might be wrong, but she is probably correct.

The next step is for Catalina to contact the human resources department at her employer and sign the documents to withhold $300 a month from her paycheck and invest $150 into each of the two funds. Catalina also knows that for every dollar invested, she gets an immediate 50 percent return because her employer's policy is to match 401(k) contributions 50 cents on the dollar for the first 6 percent of earnings. Catalina's 401(k) balance in 12 months, therefore, will show $3,600 in contributions and $1,800 in employer matching contributions (that's a total of $5,400, which is an immediate 50 percent return on her $3,600!), plus whatever gain occurs (hopefully not a loss) in NAV. Catalina's 401(k) balance this time next year is likely to be more than $5,400. She thinks that is a great start on funding her retirement!

15.4g Monitor Your Mutual Fund Portfolio

Tracking your portfolio is imperative because investors do not want to keep any underperforming mutual funds in their portfolio for very long. If Catalina wants to invest outside of her 401(k) plan in the same or other no-load funds, she can purchase funds directly from mutual fund investment companies, such as family fund companies like Fidelity, T. Rowe Price, or any other mutual fund, like Gabelli, Neuberger, or Calvert.

Use Portfolio Monitoring on the Internet Monitoring a mutual fund portfolio is easy using any of the top-rated mutual fund websites cited earlier. Some services charge nominal fees.

Check Fund Quotations in Newspapers You can check closing prices online any time on the financial websites cited earlier or read quotes in newspapers. See Figure 15-5 for an

COMMON SENSE
How to Ease into
Investing Cautiously

Investors who are fearful of investing in the stock market can try these techniques: (1) Start by buying shares of a diversified stock mutual fund using monthly purchases for 12 months, or (2) Purchase a life cycle or target date mutual fund that contains a premixed allocation of stocks and bonds.

fund screener (fund-screening tool)
Permits investors to screen all of the mutual funds in the market to gauge performance.

profile prospectus (fund profile)
Publication that describes the mutual fund, its investment objectives, and how it tries to achieve its objectives in lay terms rather than the legal language used in a regular prospectus.

It is easy to research mutual funds on the Internet.

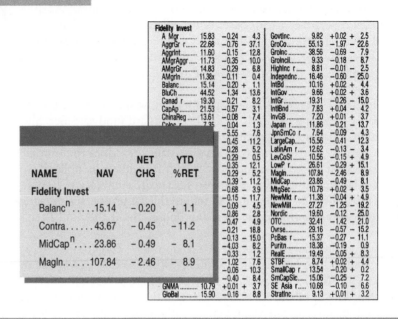

Figure 15-5 How Mutual Funds are Quoted

NAME	NAV	NET CHG	YTD %RET
Fidelity Invest			
Balanc[n]	15.14	– 0.20	+ 1.1
Contra	43.67	– 0.45	– 11.2
MidCap[n]	23.86	– 0.49	– 8.1
MagIn	107.84	– 2.46	– 8.9

illustration. Newspapers' quotations for no-load mutual funds list the name of the fund followed by columns for its net asset value, net change from the previous day, and year-to-date percentage return. For example, within the group listing for Fidelity Investments mutual funds, the Balanced Fund (abbreviated as Balanc) has a net asset value (NAV) of $15.14, a change in the net asset value (NET CHG) of – $0.20 from the closing price of the previous trading day, and a year-to-date percentage return (YTD %RET) of 1.1 percent.

mutual fund bid price

Shareholders receive this amount per share when they redeem their shares, which is the same dollar amount as the NAV.

Mutual Fund Bid Price In mutual funds, the NAV is also known as the **mutual fund bid price**. Shareholders receive this amount per share when they redeem their shares—that is, the company is willing to pay this amount to buy the shares back. Also, the NAV is the amount per share an investor will pay to purchase a fund, assuming it is a no-load fund. A no-load fund is indicated as such by the alphabetic letter *n* at the end of the fund's name.

mutual fund ask (or offer) price

Price at which an investor can purchase a mutual fund's shares; current NAV per share plus sales charges.

Mutual Fund Ask Price The **mutual fund ask price** (or **offer price**) is the price at which a mutual fund's share can be purchased by investors. It equals the current NAV per share plus sales charges, if any. If you wanted to buy or sell shares of Fidelity Balanced Fund, a no-load (note the superscript *n* in Figure 15-5) mutual fund, the price would be $15.14 per share. The funds listed without an *n* are load funds. The SEC requires that appropriate footnotes appear in newspaper listings of mutual funds to indicate other expenses and charges.

CONCEPT CHECK 15.4

1. Explain why it is important to review your investment philosophy and goals when selecting mutual fund investments.
2. Explain how you would eliminate funds inappropriate for your investment goals.
3. How might you go about monitoring your mutual fund investments?

WHAT DO YOU RECOMMEND *NOW?*

Now that you have read the chapter on mutual funds, what do you recommend to Helen and David Lilienthal in the case at the beginning of the chapter regarding:

1. Redeeming their CDs and investing their retirement money in mutual funds?
2. Investing in growth and income mutual funds instead of income funds?
3. Buying no-load rather than load funds?
4. Buying mutual funds through their employers' 401 (k) retirement accounts, rather than saving through a taxable account as they have been doing?

SUMMARY OF LEARNING OBJECTIVES RECAPPED

LO1 **Describe the features, advantages, and unique services of investing through mutual funds.**

A mutual fund is an investment company that pools funds obtained by selling shares to investors and makes investments to achieve the financial goal of income or growth, or both. The net asset value (NAV) is the per-share value of the fund. Advantages of mutual funds include diversification, affordability, and professional management. Unique services include ease of buying and selling, check writing, and easy establishment of retirement plans. A similar investment is an exchange traded funds (ETFs). These are a cross between a stock and a mutual fund. They hold a basket of securities, such as stocks, bonds, or commodities—exactly like mutual funds—but they trade like stocks.

LO2 **Differentiate mutual funds by investment objectives.**

A mutual fund with an income objective invests in securities that pay regular income in dividends or interest. A fund that has a growth objective seeks capital appreciation. A fund that has a combined growth and income objective seeks a somewhat balanced return made up of current income and capital gains. The name of a fund, such as aggressive growth fund, typically gives a clue to its objectives. Index funds and ETFs are popular because they earn almost exactly the same return as a particular market index.

LO3 **Summarize the fees and charges involved in buying and selling mutual funds.**

Individuals who invest through mutual funds pay annual fund operating expenses—management fees—that are deducted from fund assets before earnings are distributed to shareholders. Investors must make decisions on load and no-load funds, 12b-1 fees, deferred load, and redemption fees.

LO4 **Establish strategies to evaluate and select mutual funds that meet your investment goals.**

The process of selecting no-load mutual funds in which to invest is a do-it-yourself effort. The steps are (1) review investment philosophy and investment goals, (2) eliminate funds inappropriate for your investment goals, (3) create a portfolio of funds in which to invest, (4) choose no-load funds with low fees, (5) obtain investment information and advice, (6) screen and compare funds that meet your investment criteria, and (7) monitor your mutual fund investments.

LET'S TALK ABOUT IT

1. **Investing in Tough Economic Times.** Comment on this statement: "A great time to invest is during times of economic turmoil when assets are undervalued."

2. **One Fund of Interest.** Review the three broad objectives of mutual funds. Based on your investment philosophy, which one type of fund would be of most interest to you if you were saving to buy a home several years from now? Give reasons why.

3. **Two Funds.** Assume you graduated from college a few years ago, have a job paying $75,000 annually, and want to invest $300 per month in mutual funds for retirement. Which combination of two or more mutual funds (see pages 471–475) would you think appropriate? Give reasons for each of your selections.

4. **Spread Your Money into Funds.** Assume that your uncle gave you $50,000 to invest solely in mutual funds. Based on your point in the life cycle and your investment philosophy, identify your investment goals and explain how you would spread your money among different funds. (See pages 471–475.)

5. **Good Choices.** Identify the types of mutual funds that would be good choices to meet the following four investment objectives: emergency fund, house down payment, college fund for 2-year-old child, and retirement fund for a 25-year-old. (See pages 471–475.) Give two reasons why each one of your recommendations would be appropriate.

6. **Load or No-Load.** Which is a better choice for you, load or no-load mutual funds? Give some reasons.

7. **Select Two Funds.** Review Table 15-1 on the "Unique Advantages of Investing Through Mutual Funds" on page 468, and select two that would be important to you as an investor. Explain why.

8. **Investing in Mutual Funds.** Have you or anyone in your family invested in mutual funds or exchange traded funds? What positive and/or negative experiences can they report?

DO THE MATH

1. **Net Asset Value.** Last year David McCullough of La Junta, Colorado, bought the XYZ mutual fund, which has total assets of $240 million, liabilities of $10 million, and 15 million shares outstanding.

   DO IT IN CLASS
   Page 467

   (a) What is the net asset value?

   (b) If the current price is $18, is this a good deal?

2. **Back-end Load.** Your neighbor, Kitty Kardashian, of Philadelphia, Pennsylvania, bought $5,000 worth of mutual funds with a back-end load of 5 percent if she sells within the first year. It decreases 1 percent a year afterward.

   (a) If Kitty sells during the third year, how much will be the back-end load?

   (b) Did Kitty make a good decision buying such a mutual fund?

3. **Profits and Taxes.** A year ago, George Jetson, from Orbit City, Texas, invested $1,000 by buying 100 shares of the Can't Lose Mutual Fund, an aggressive growth no-load mutual fund. George reinvested his dividends, so he now has 112 shares. So far, the NAV for George's investment has risen from $10 per share to $13.25.

   (a) What is the percentage increase in the NAV of George's mutual fund?

   (b) If George redeemed the first 100 shares of his mutual fund investment for $13.25 per share, what would be his capital gain over the amount invested?

   (c) Assuming George pays income taxes at the 25 percent rate, how much income tax will he have to pay if he sells those first 100 shares?

4. **Mutual Fund Sales.** Two years ago, Izabella Martinez, from Atlanta, Georgia, invested $1,000 by buying 125 shares ($8 per share NAV) in the Can't Lose Mutual Fund, an aggressive growth no-load mutual fund. Last year, she made two additional investments of $500 each (50 shares at $10 and 40 shares at $12.50). Izabella reinvested all of her dividends. So far, the NAV for her investment has risen from $8 per share to $13.25. Late in the year, she sold 60 shares at $13.25.

   (a) What were the proceeds from Izabella's sale of the 60 shares?

   (b) Investors can use the Internal Revenue Service's "average-cost basis method" to determine the average price paid for one share. Begin by calculating the average price paid for the shares. In this instance, the $2,000 is divided by 215 shares (125 shares + 50 shares + 40 shares). What was the average price paid by Izabella?

   (c) To finally determine the average-cost basis of shares sold, you multiply the average price per share times the number of shares sold—in this case, 60. What is the total cost basis for Izabella's 60 shares?

   (d) Assuming that Izabella has to pay income taxes on the difference between the sales price for the 60 shares and their cost, how much is this difference?

FINANCIAL PLANNING CASES

CASE 1

The Johnsons Decide to Invest Through Mutual Funds

After learning about mutual funds, the Johnsons are confident that they are a great way to invest, especially because of the diversification and professional management that funds offer. The couple has a financial nest egg of $9,500 to invest through mutual funds. They also want to invest another $300 per month on a regular basis.

Although not yet completely firm, Harry and Belinda's goals at this point are as follows:

- They want to continue to build their retirement income to retire in about 26 years.

- They will need about $10,000 in six to eight years to use as supplemental income if Belinda has a baby and does not work for six months.

- They might buy a new automobile requiring a $10,000 down payment if they decide not to have a child.

Knowing that the Johnsons have a moderate investment philosophy, that they live on a reasonable budget, and that they have a well-established cash-management plan, advise them on their mutual fund investments by responding to the following questions:

(a) Some comparable mutual fund performance data on stock funds are shown in Table 15-2 on page 480. Using only that information and assuming that you are recommending some funds for the Johnsons' retirement needs, which two funds would you recommend? Why?

(b) How would you divide the $9,500 between the two stock funds? Why?

(c) How much of the $300 monthly investment amount would you allocate to each of the stock funds? Why?

(d) Assume that both funds increase in value over the next ten years. Another bear market then occurs, causing the NAVs to drop 25 percent from the previous year. Would you recommend that the Johnsons sell their accumulated shares in the funds? Why or why not?

(e) Determine the value of the shares purchased with their $9,500 original investment in ten years, assuming that the two funds' NAVs increase 6 percent annually for the ten years. (Hint: Use Appendix A.1 or the *Garman/Forgue* companion website.)

CASE 2

Victor and Maria Invest for Retirement

Victor and Maria Hernandez plan to retire in less than 15 years. Their current investment portfolio is distributed as follows: 40 percent in growth mutual funds, 40 percent in corporate bonds and bond mutual funds, and 20 percent in cash equivalents. They have decided to increase the amount of risk in their portfolio by taking 10 percent from their cash equivalent investments and investing in some mutual funds with strong growth possibilities.

DO IT IN CLASS
Page 480

(a) Of the stock mutual funds listed in Table 15-2 on page 480, which two would you recommend to meet the Hernandezes' goals? Why?

(b) Would you recommend that the Hernandezes remain invested in those two funds during their retirement years? Why or why not?

CASE 3

Julia Price Is Going to Invest Big in Mutual Funds

It has been over 25 years since Julia graduated with a major in aeronautical engineering, and she has been quite successful in her career as well as in managing her personal finances. She has moved up the career ladder, earns a high salary, has $50,000 in equity in her condo, and has an investment portfolio valued at $400,000 that includes $200,000 in retirement assets through her employer's 401(k) plan. She wants to liquidate her remaining $200,000 investment portfolio now invested in stocks, bonds, and gold and put everything into mutual funds. Julia is optimistic about the future of investing. After serious research, Julia has decided to invest $200,000 into ETFs and index mutual funds rather than actively managed funds. Offer your opinions about her thinking.

CASE 4

Matching Mutual Fund Investments to Economic Projections

Joshua Wickler, an automobile salesperson for the past ten years in Albuquerque, New Mexico, is divorced and contributes to the support of his two children. He is interested in investing in mutual funds. Joshua wants to put $20,000 of accumulated savings into a stock index mutual fund and then continue to invest $200 monthly for the foreseeable future, perhaps using the money for retirement starting in about 25 years. Joshua has limited his choices solely to the index mutual funds listed in Table 15-2 on page 480.

(a) In Table 15-2, note that there are two index funds based on the S&P 500 Index. Suggest a reason why Joshua should invest in one or the other, noting that the returns for the Vanguard 500 Index Fund are about the same as the Fidelity Spartan Index Fund.

(b) Given that Joshua plans to invest $2,400 annually for the next 25 years, which of the other two index funds (Vanguard Total Stock Market Index Fund or Vanguard Emerging Markets Stock Fund) would you recommend, and why?

CASE 5

Selection of a Mutual Fund as Part of a Retirement Plan

Lola Garcia, a single mother of a 6-year-old child, works for a utility company in Baltimore, Maryland, and is willing to invest $3,000 per year in a mutual fund. She wants the investment income to supplement her retirement pension starting in approximately 30 years, and she has a moderate investment philosophy. Lola is concerned about not investing too conservatively because she expects to live a long life, given that her eldest relatives lived well into their 80s and early 90s. Advise Lola by responding to the following questions:

(a) If Lola invests $3,000 annually into two growth mutual funds, which two types would you recommend and why? See the list on page 472.

(b) Alternatively, if Lola invests $3,000 annually into two growth and income funds, which two would you recommend and why? See the list on pages 474–475.

(c) Summarize why these two types of mutual funds might be suitable for Lola.

CASE 6

Selection of an Exchange Traded Fund as Part of a Retirement Plan

Ernesto Melendez, a married father of two adult children, works for a finance company in Las Vegas, Nevada, and is willing to invest $5,000 per year in an exchange traded fund. He wants the asset balance to be available to supplement his retirement pension starting in 20 years. He has a moderate investment philosophy and he is smart enough to know to keep investment costs extremely low. Advise Ernesto by responding to the following questions:

(a) If Ernesto invests $5,000 annually into one ETF, which two would you recommend as finalists to him? See the list on page 480.

(b) Summarize why one or these two ETFs might be most suitable for Ernesto.

DO IT IN CLASS
Page 480

BE YOUR OWN PERSONAL FINANCIAL MANAGER

1. **Your Mutual Fund Preferences.** Review the section "Mutual Fund Objectives" and then complete Worksheet 61: My Mutual Fund Preferences from "My Personal Financial Planner." For each of the types of mutual funds listed, identify which are of interest to you and one characteristic you like about them, and note those in which you might invest during your own investing life.

My Personal Financial Planner

2. **Comparing Mutual Fund Investments.** Learn about three stock mutual funds that might be of interest to you, such as Vanguard Wellington (VWELX), Vanguard Emerging Mkts Stock Idx (VEIEX), and American EuroPacific Growth A (AEPGX), by going online. Then complete Worksheet 62: Comparing Mutual Funds as Investments from "My Personal Financial Planner" by recording the facts requested.

My Personal Financial Planner

3. **Calculating Mutual Fund Returns.** Use the information for the exercises immediately above and complete Worksheet 63: Calculating the Return on Mutual Fund Investments from "My Personal Financial Planner," which will help you deter mine the return from income and capital gains after you make some assumptions, such as a 5-year holding period and the like.

My Personal Financial Planner

4. **Evaluating My Investment Returns.** Complete Worksheet 64: Evaluating the Performance (Gain or Loss) of My Investments from "My Personal Financial Planner" using one example for which you make the assumptions. Perhaps you can use the Fidelity Contrafund (FCNTX) in which you invested $3,000 two years ago for $88 and its present price of $101.

My Personal Financial Planner

ON THE NET

Go to the Web pages indicated to complete these exercises.

1. **Low Cost Mutual Funds.** Visit the Kiplingers website for low-cost mutual funds (www.kiplinger.com/tool /investing/T041-S000-kiplingers-25-favorite-fund /index.php). Summarize why they think these are good investments.

2. **Which ETFs for You?** Visit the website for Vanguard Investments and read its section on exchange traded funds (ETFs) (www.personal.vanguard.com/us/funds /etf). Summarize why you think ETFs might or might not be a good investment for you.

3. **Mutual Fund Information.** Visit the website for CNNMoney. Go to the page titled "What Is a Mutual Fund" at www.money.cnn.com/retirement/guide /investing_mutualfunds.moneymag/index.htm.

Review the dozen or so short articles and compare what you read there with what you read in this chapter. List two things that are new to your understanding.

4. **FINRA on Mutual Funds.** Visit the website for the Financial Industry Regulatory Authority (FINRA) at www.finra.org/Investors/SmartInvesting/Choosing Investments/MutualFunds, where you will find a section titled "Mutual Funds." Review the several paragraphs there and compare what you read with what you read in this chapter. List two things that are new to your understanding.

5. **Mutual Fund Research.** Go to MoneyCentral.com at www.msn.com/en-us/money/investing and type in any fund's name or something similar to it. Read some of the results. What do you think of this website?

ACTION INVOLVEMENT PROTECTS

1. **Review Some Mutual Fund Portfolios.** Go to Kiplinger's article on model portfolios at www.kiplinger.com /article/investing/T033-C009-S001-kiplinger-25 -model-portfolios.html?si=1 and review the three illustrative portfolios that might fit your needs. Summarize your findings.

2. **Using a Fund Screener.** Go to the fund screener of Yahoo! Finance (finance.yahoo.com/funds) and look up three funds of interest to you, perhaps using some of the names of funds you found in the exercise immediately above. Summarize your findings.

3. **Reviewing ETFs.** Go to Fidelity's ETF fund screener website (www.research2.fidelity.com/fidelity/screeners /etf/main.asp) and click on the "Learn More" section of "ETF Portfolio Builder." Compare what you learn there with what is in this book.

4. **Unique Mutual Fund Services.** Review Table 15-1 on "Unique Advantages of Investing Through Mutual Funds" on page 468 and select 2 that would be important to you as a mutual fund investor. Explain why.

DO IT IN CLASS
Page 468

16 Real Estate and High-Risk Investments

YOU MUST BE KIDDING, RIGHT?

Friends David Sanders and Richard Belisle are small town investors. Both have aggressive investment philosophies. Richard invests primarily in residential real estate, and David invests in commodities futures contracts. As longtime investors, they consider themselves experts, but occasionally, they both experience occasional financial losses. What are the odds that an investor, like David, will make money investing in commodities futures contracts?

A. 50%   **C.** 20%

B. 30%   **D.** 10%

The answer is D. Ninety percent of individual investors in futures contracts lose money. Funds used for these investments should be only those that one can afford to lose!

Learning Objectives

After reading this chapter, you should be able to:

1. Demonstrate how you can make money investing in real estate.

2. Recognize how to take advantage of beneficial tax treatments in real estate investing.

3. Calculate the right price to pay for real estate and how to finance your purchase.

4. Assess the disadvantages of investing in real estate.

5. Summarize the risks and challenges of investing in the high-risk investments of collectibles, precious metals, and gems.

6. Explain why options and futures are risky investments.

GongTo/Shutterstock.com

WHAT DO YOU RECOMMEND?

Heide Benser/Corbis/Getty Images

Brittany Day, a 37-year-old managing partner and Realtor® for a large real estate company in an affluent community, earns $110,000 per year. Brittany invests $6,600 annually to her employer's 401(k) retirement plan, and she puts an additional about $800 each month into a mutual fund account, which is worth $320,000.

Ever since her grandfather gave her some stocks as a child, Brittany has loved investing—and she has enjoyed a good track record with her efforts. Brittany is an active investor, often trading every three or four weeks, primarily in the oil, technology, and pharmaceutical prescription drug industries. Every year, she has some losses as well as gains. Brittany has never bought or sold options or futures contracts, but her stockbroker suggested she consider them. Brittany also has a friend who owns several residential rental properties that she bought when prices were low who has asked her to consider investing as her partner in her next real estate venture.

What do you recommend to Brittany on the subject of real estate and high-risk investments regarding:

1. **Investing in real estate?**
2. **Putting some money into collectibles or gold?**
3. **Investing in options and futures contracts?**

TO-DO SOON

Do the following to begin to achieve financial success:

1. *Before deciding to invest in real estate, carefully consider the disadvantages of such investments.*

2. *Invest only in a real estate property that has a positive cash flow.*

3. *Finance real estate investments with conventional mortgages, not mortgages with adjustable interest terms.*

4. *Use the price-to-rent ratio and discounted cash-flow methods to help determine the right price to pay for a real estate investment.*

5. *Do not put any of your long-term investment money into high-risk investments are they are not suitable.*

real estate bubble

Rapid and unsustainable increases in home prices followed by sharp declines in values.

high-risk investments

Assets that present potential for significant fluctuations in return, sometimes over short time periods.

Learning Objective 1

Demonstrate how you can make money investing in real estate.

real estate

Property consisting of land, all structures permanently attached to that land, and accompanying rights and privileges, such as crops and mineral rights.

A home tends to accomplish more than just putting a roof over your head. It is also an investment, because historically housing values have increased about 3 percent annually over the long term. A **real estate bubble** for housing occurred in the United States in the middle of the last decade. The bubble saw rapid increases in home valuations (10-plus percent or more every year) until they were unsustainable.

Then the real estate market crashed as home values plummeted 40 or 50 percent or even more in some communities. The "for sale" signs on millions of foreclosed homes also pulled down the values of nearby homes. Today over 10 percent of all mortgage holders still owe more on their homes than they are worth, thus they are "under water," making it difficult to sell. For too many the American Dream of owning a home was replaced with too much debt, high anxiety, foreclosure, lower credit scores, and homelessness for more than a few. Unemployment and underemployment also makes it challenging for some others to buy homes.

Fortunately, the real estate market has been recovering, so there are some reasonably priced homes available for investment. As a result, suitable investors can once again consider real estate as investment to achieve their long-term goals, such as retirement. Investors with an aggressive investment philosophy who seek high returns and are willing to accept greater risks might consider owning alternative assets such as collectibles, precious metals, gems, options, and futures contracts. All these are referred to as **high-risk** (or **alternative**) **investments** because they have the potential for significant fluctuations in return, sometimes over short time periods.

Many investment advisors today recommend that people put 10 percent of their money into high-risk investments as a way to diversify their money, recommending for example that someone in their twenties have a portfolio of 65% stocks, 15% bonds, 10% high-risk, and 10% cash. They are wrong. High-risk investments are not suitable investments for long-term investing program, such as for your retirement, because they are too uncertain for you to diversify appropriately. Think about it? How many precious metals can you own? How many options and future contacts can you buy?

16.1 HOW TO MAKE MONEY INVESTING IN REAL ESTATE

Sure ways to go wrong in a real estate investment are to pay too much for the property and finance it incorrectly. Real estate investing is not the same as buying a home in which to live, which was the subject of Chapter 9. Investing in real estate might provide you with extra income now and give a boost to your future retirement plans. But you have to do a lot of things right.

Real estate investing is complicated given today's market conditions, thus you must become smart about rental property statistics. You must get data on vacancy days of comparable properties, length of time in tenant turnovers, rental rates in your community, property taxes, insurance, community economics, and general demand. A property might be priced low because rentals are down in that area.

Real estate investments are complex, and they are much riskier than investing in mutual funds and stocks. People often do not possess the mental toughness that it takes because investing in real estate is a "real job." Most people are not cut out to be a do-it-yourself landlord. Dealing with tenants requires a business attitude, not a willingness to view tenants as friends.

Real estate is property consisting of land, all structures permanently attached to that land, and accompanying rights and privileges, such as crops and mineral rights. For example, you can invest directly as an individual or jointly with other investors to buy properties designed for residential living, such as houses, duplexes, apartments, mobile homes, and condominiums. You also could invest in commercial properties designed for business uses, such as office buildings, medical centers, gas stations, and motels.

You might buy raw land or residential lots, although they are extremely risky and often lose money for the investor. For someone considering an investment in real estate, there are some things to do before investing.

16.1a What to Do Before Investing in Real Estate

To protect yourself from making bad decisions when investing in real estate, think about the following:

- Consider investing in properties only in locales where there are thriving businesses located near good schools, supermarkets, and public transportation.
- Line up financing options before searching for properties.
- Hire an inspector to inspect the physical condition of all properties you are seriously considering.
- Hire an accountant experienced in real estate investing.
- Set up a limited liability corporation to own your real estate investments because it protects your personal assets in case someone is injured on your rental property and sues you.
- Consider hiring a licensed contractor for plumbing, electrical, and expensive repair jobs rather than doing them yourself.
- Consider hiring a management company to tend to your property, including maintenance; the cost is usually 8 to 10 percent of monthly rental income.
- Contribute to a reserve fund equal to about 3 to 6 months' expenses for vacancies, repairs, and maintenance.
- Set aside $10,000 as a contingency fund for unanticipated problems with real estate investment property.

16.1b Question 1: Can You Make Current Income While You Own?

The most important consideration for real estate investors in today's real estate market is not whether the price will rise enough in a few years to make a profit. The focus for real estate investors now is whether the rental income will be sufficient to make financial ends meet while waiting for the property to increase in value.

If you invest in a property and you are paying out more than the rental income coming in, the negative cash flow exposes you to two risks: (1) whether you can afford to continue paying out that money month after month and year after year, and (2) whether you can make up for these cash flow losses when the property sells, which you hope will be for more than you paid for it. Get either of these wrong, and you lose your invested money and maybe more.

BIAS TOWARD MINIMIZING INVESTMENT LOSSES

People have a bias toward minimizing their investment losses. People often forget about losses and instead remember more clearly their successes, convinced that they are above-average investors. What to do? When one has investment losses, stop and think, record some notes on what happened and save them in a permanent place, and learn from your mistakes.

Know the Price-to-Rent Ratio To measure the current income in a real estate market, investors can begin by using the **price-to-rent ratio** (PTR). This is a measure of the relative affordability of renting and buying in a given housing market. The lower the ratio the more attractive the decision to buy a home versus renting a similar one.

If the price-to-rent ratio is too high, the prices for homes are likely to be too high. It is calculated as the ratio of home prices to annual rental rates. For example, consider a market where a home worth $200,000 could rent for $1,000 a month. The price-to-rent ratio is 16.67 ($200,000/12 × $1,000).

price-to-rent ratio

The ratio of median residential real estate prices to the median annual rents that can be earned from the real estate.

Therefore, after 16.67 years of paying rent you would have paid the whole price of the home. This is good information for potential renters as well as residential home investors.

The price-to-rent ratio nationally is 13 to 1. For recent information on price-rent ratios see Trulia (www.trulia.com/rent_vs_buy) or SmartAsset (smartasset.com/mortgage/price-to-rent-ratio-in-us-cities).The ratio might range from perhaps 6 in Detroit to 40 in Honolulu depending on local market conditions, meaning how low or high housing prices are.

For investors, the lower the price-to-rent ratio is in a given community and a particular property, the easier it should be to earn back your investment. For example, in San Jose, California, a condominium renting for $2,600 a month might sell for the high price of $890,000 for a price-to-rent ratio of 28.5 (12 × $2,600 = $31,200; $890,000/$31,200).

$$\text{Price-to-rent ratio} = \text{Home price} / \text{annual rent}$$
$$28.5 = (\$890,000/\$31,200 \ [\$2,600 \text{ monthly rent} \times 12]) \qquad (16.1)$$

Alternatively, a home in Pittsburgh, Pennsylvania, might cost $165,000 and rent for $1,200 a month, thus providing a price-to-rent ratio of 11.5 ($165,000/$14,400 [$1,200 × 12]). Investing in rental property with a high ratio will provide a profit only with a future increase in its resale value, which may be difficult to achieve in the near term.

Current Income Results from Positive Cash Flow For an income-producing real estate investment, you pay operating expenses out of rental income. The amount of rental income you have left after paying all operating expenses is called **cash flow**. The amount of cash flow is obtained by subtracting all cash outlays from the cash income. If the property has a mortgage (a common occurrence), payments toward the mortgage principal and interest also must be made out of rental income. Operating expenses such as mortgage payments, real estate property taxes, repairs, and vacancies may eat up half or more of the rental income.

You can expect positive cash flow from an investment property if the monthly rent is at least 1 percent of the purchase price. With a monthly rent of $1,500, you could pay $150,000 for a house and have more income than outflow. If the current owner is asking $140,000, the house might be worth a closer look.

Becoming a landlord is no longer the no-brainer investment it was a few years ago. However, you can count on income for years to come if you choose a property wisely. That means look for a positive cash flow designed to occur every month.

Calculate the Rental Yield Investors also may calculate the **rental yield** on properties, as shown in Equation (16.2). This is a computation of how much income the investor might pocket from rent each year before mortgage payments as a percentage of the purchase price. Most properties yield about 4 percent of income annually, although the rental yield may be as little as 1 or 2 percent or as high as 8 or 9 percent. Less expensive properties often offer higher yields. The formula assumes half of rental income goes for expenses other than debt repayment.

$$\text{Rental yield} = \frac{(\text{rent} \div 2)}{\text{purchase price}} \qquad (16.2)$$

	San Jose	Pittsburgh
Purchase price	$890,000	$165,000
Annual rent	31,200	14,400
Annual rent/2	15,600	7,200
Yield (annual rent/2/purchase price)	1.75%	4.36%

DO IT IN CLASS

cash flow

Amount of rental income you have left after paying all operating expenses.

rental yield

A computation of how much income the investor might pocket from rent each year (before mortgage payments) as a percentage of the purchase price; divide the annual rent by 2 and then divide by the purchase price.

16.1c Question 2: Can You Profit When You Sell the Property?

The **capital gain** earned in a real estate investment comes from price appreciation. It is the amount above ownership costs for which an investment is sold. In real estate, **ownership costs** include the original purchase price as well as expenditures for any capital improvements made to a property prior to sale. **Capital improvements** are costs incurred in making changes in real property—beyond maintenance and repairs—that add to its value. Installing a pool and adding a room represent capital improvements.

Repairs are expenses (usually tax deductible against an investor's annual cash-flow income) necessary to maintain the value of the property. Repainting,

A slowly growing economy can lead to unfinished units and losses for real estate investors.

mending roof leaks, and fixing plumbing are examples of repairs, but in the eyes of the IRS they are not capital improvements. In markets in which real estate is difficult to sell (too many properties on the market and too few buyers), perhaps because of continuing job losses in a sluggish regional economy, residential housing prices might decline 2 or 3 percent annually for a long time. That means continuing deflation in home prices in some markets year after year.

capital improvements
Costs incurred in making value-enhancing changes (beyond maintenance and repair) in real property.

repairs
Usually tax-deductible expenses necessary to maintain property value.

CONCEPT CHECK 16.1

1. Name two things investors should consider doing before investing in real estate.
2. What are the two key questions to consider before investing in real estate?
3. Distinguish between the price-to-rent ratio and the rental yield as measures of current income.
4. Distinguish between capital improvements in real estate investing and repairs.

16.2 TAKE ADVANTAGE OF BENEFICIAL TAX TREATMENTS

The U.S. Congress, through provisions in the Internal Revenue Code, encourages real estate investments by giving investors five special tax treatments.

16.2a 1. Depreciation Is a Tax Deduction

Investors in real estate become successful by understanding the "numbers" of real estate investing. For example, assume that Jisue Han, a lawyer from Dallas, Texas, invested $200,000 in a residential building ($170,000) and land ($30,000). She rents the property to a tenant for $24,000 per year. You might initially think that Jisue has to pay income taxes on the entire $24,000 in rental income. Wrong. IRS regulations allow taxpayers to deduct depreciation from rental income. **Depreciation** represents the decline in value of an asset over time due to normal wear and tear and obsolescence. A proportionate amount of a capital asset representing depreciation may be deducted against income each year over the asset's estimated life. Land cannot be depreciated.

depreciation
Decline in value of an asset over time due to normal wear and tear and obsolescence.

Jisue can deduct from her income taxes on the rental income an equal part of the building's cost over the estimated life of the property. IRS guidelines provide that residential properties may be depreciated over 27.5 years, while nonresidential properties are allowed 39 years. Table 16-1 shows the effects of depreciation rental income after taxes, assuming Jisue pays income taxes at a combined federal and state rate of 36 percent. Jisue calculates the amount she can annually deduct from income to be $6,182 ($170,000 ÷ 27.5). In this example, the depreciation deduction lowers taxable income on the rental income from $24,000 to $17,818 ($24,000 − $6,182). This lowers the tax on the rental income from $8,640 to $6,414. Because depreciation is not an actual out-of-pocket expense for Jisue, her after-tax rental income is $17,586 rather than $15,360.

16.2b　2. Interest Is Also a Tax Deduction

Real estate investors incur many business expenses in attempting to earn a profit: interest on a mortgage, real estate property taxes, insurance, utilities, management bills, homeowner's association fees, capital improvements, repairs, and accounting and legal costs. The largest of these costs often is the interest expense, as properties are often purchased with a mortgage loan.

loan-to-value ratio

Measures the amount of leverage in a real estate investment project by dividing the total amount of debt by the market price of the investment.

The **loan-to-value ratio** measures the amount of leverage in a real estate investment project. It is calculated by dividing the amount of debt by the value of the total original investment. On the property discussed above, Jisue's loan-to-value ratio was 87.5 percent ($175,000/$200,000) because she made a down payment of $25,000, as shown in Figure 16.3 and in Equation 16.3.

Table 16-2 illustrates the effect of interest expenses on income taxes. To purchase her $200,000 investment property, assume Jisue borrowed $175,000 for 15 years at 5 percent with a monthly payment of $1,383 (from Table 9-4 on page 285). After deducting annual depreciation of $6,182 and interest expenses of $7,900 her taxable income is reduced to $9,918. Because her income tax liability is only $3,570, Jisue's after tax return of $12,530 yields 50.12 percent on her leveraged investment. Had Jisue not been able to deduct depreciation, her after-tax yield would have been 41.2 percent.

Tax laws permit investors to deduct interest expenses. The interest deduction gives Jisue a cash flow after paying mortgage interest of $16,100 ($24,000 − $7,900). In essence, the $7,900 in interest is paid with $2,844 ($7,900 × 36 percent combined federal and state income tax rate) of the money that was not sent to the federal and state governments and $5,056 ($7,900 − $2,844) of Jisue's money.

Table 16-1 **Depreciation Reduces Income Taxes and Increases Investor's After Tax Rental Income**

			Without Depreciation	With Depreciation
Total amount invested	$200,000	Gross rental income	$24,000	$24,000
Cost of land	−30,000	Less annual depreciation deduction	0	6,182
Cost of rental building	$170,000	Taxable income	24,000	17,818
Depreciation for 27.5 years	$6,182	Income taxes (36 percent combined federal and state tax rate)	8,640	6,414
		After-tax rental income	$15,360	$17,586

Table 16-2	Interest Paid on Income Taxes Also Increases Investor's Return	
Gross rental income		$24,000
Less annual depreciation deduction		−6,182
Subtotal		$17,818
Less interest expense for the year (5 percent, $175,000 mortgage)		−7,900
Taxable income		$ 9,918
Cash flow after paying interest ($24,000 − $7,900)		16,100
Less income tax liability (0.36 × $9,918)		−3,570
After-tax return ($16,100 − $3,570)		$12,530
After-tax yield [$12,530 ÷ ($200,000 − $175,000)]		50.12%

DO IT IN CLASS

$$\text{Loan-to-Value Ratio} = \frac{\text{Mortgage Amount}}{\text{Appraised Value of the Property}}$$

$$= \frac{\$175,000}{\$200,000} \qquad (16.3)$$

$$= 87.5\%$$

16.2c   3. Capital Gains Are Taxed at Very Low Rates

Capital gains on real estate are realized through price appreciation. For most taxpayers, long-term capital gains are taxed at a rate of 15 percent.

16.2d   4. Exchange of Properties Can Be Tax Free

Another special tax treatment results when a real estate investor trades equity in one property for equity in a similar property. If none of the people involved in the trade receives any other form of property or money, the transaction is considered a **tax-free exchange** (or a **1031 exchange**). If one person receives some money or other property, only that person has to report the extra proceeds as a taxable gain. For example, assume you bought a residential rental property five years ago for $220,000 and today it is worth much more. You trade it with your friend by giving $10,000 in cash for your friend's $280,000 single-family rental home. Your friend needs to report only the $10,000 as income this year. In contrast, you do not need to report your long-term gain, $50,000 ($280,000 – $10,000 – $220,000), until you actually sell the new property.

tax-free exchange (or 1031 exchange)

Arises when a real estate investor trades equity in one property for equity in a similar property and no other forms of property or money change hands.

16.2e   5. Taxes Can Be Lower on Vacation Home Rental Income

If you rent out your vacation property for 14 or fewer days during the year, you can pocket the income tax free because the IRS does not want to hear about this gain. The home is considered a personal residence, so you can deduct mortgage interest and property taxes just as you would for your principal residence. That same tax break is available for those who rent their primary home for 14 days or less, for example, to people attending a major sporting event in your city.

If you rent your property for 15 days or more, you are a landlord and you have turned the endeavor into a business. You may deduct expenses attributable to the rental business, such as mortgage interest, real estate property taxes, depreciation, utilities, repairs, insurance, advertising, homeowner's association fees, and property management fees, as well as auto and other travel expenses.

If you **actively participate** in the management of the property (defined as approving new tenants, deciding on rental terms, or approving repairs and capital improvements), you can deduct rental expenses up to the level of rental income you report prorated for the number of days it was rented out. When your adjusted gross income (AGI) is less than $100,000, a maximum of $25,000 of rental-related losses may be deducted each year to offset income from any source, including your salary. The $25,000 limit is gradually phased out as your AGI moves between $100,000 and $150,000. This ability to shelter income from taxes represents a terrific benefit for people who invest in real estate on a small scale.

CONCEPT CHECK 16.2

1. Summarize how depreciation is used to reduce the taxable income from a real estate investment.
2. Briefly explain how the interest paid on the mortgage of a real estate investment reduces one's income taxes.
3. Summarize the special income tax regulations on renting out vacation homes.

Learning Objective 3

Calculate the right price to pay for real estate and how to finance your purchase.

16.3　PRICING AND FINANCING REAL ESTATE INVESTMENTS

Determining the right price to pay for a real estate investment and how to finance the purchase does not have to be complicated. Certain straightforward calculations can be made to assist you.

16.3a　Pay the Right Price

discounted cash-flow method

Effective way to estimate the value or asking price of a real estate investment based on after-tax cashflow and the return on the invested dollars discounted over time to reflect a discounted yield.

The **discounted cash-flow method** is an effective way to estimate the present value or appropriate price of a real estate investment. It emphasizes after-tax cash flow and the return on the invested dollars discounted over time to reflect a discounted yield. Software programs are available online to calculate the discounted cash flows. (For example, see www.lasvegas4us.com/JwwDCF/discounted_cash_flow_calculator.htm.) You also can use Appendix A-2, as illustrated in Table 16-3.

To see how this method works, assume that you require an after-tax rate of return of 10 percent on a condominium advertised for sale at $210,000. You estimate that rents can be increased about 2 percent each year for five years. After all expenses are paid, you

Table 16-3	Discounted Cash Flow to Estimate Price		
	After-Tax Cash Flow	**Present Value of $1 at 10 Percent***	**Present Value of After-Tax Cash Flow**
1 year	$ 4,000	0.9524	$ 3,809
2 years	4,100	0.9070	3,718
3 years	4,200	0.8638	3,627
4 years	4,300	0.8227	3,537
5 years	4,400	0.7835	3,447
Sale price of property in 5 years	$230,000	0.7835	180,205
Present value of property			$198,343

*From Appendix A-2.

ADVICE FROM A SEASONED PRO

Find Home Prices in Seconds

Someone searching for a new residence can become confused on where to start the process. On-line sites specializing in finding new and used properties are a great place to begin. To find listings and prices for homes anywhere in the country, check out Zillow (www.zillow.com), Trulia (www.trulia.com), or Realtor.com (www.realtor.com). Simply type in an address to obtain an estimate of the price. Or, if you prefer to search by zip code, you can browse listings in the defined area of your search. Be advised, however, that there have been complaints about accurate prices so perhaps check more than one site, or contact the selling agent to verify the listing is accurate.

Mark G. Guild
Southern Adventist University, Collegedale, Tennessee

expect to have after-tax cash flows of $4,000, $4,100, $4,200, $4,300, and $4,400 for the five years. Assuming some price appreciation, you anticipate selling the property for $230,000 after all expenses are incurred. That's a conservative increase in the value of the property of less than 10 percent over 5 years. How much should you pay now to buy the property?

Table 16-3 explains how to answer this question. Multiply the estimated after-tax cash flows and the expected proceeds of $230,000 to be realized on the sale of the property by the present value of a dollar at 10 percent (your required rate of return). Add the present values together to obtain the total present value of the property—in this case, $198,343. The asking price of $210,000 is too high for you to earn an after tax return of 10 percent.

Your choices are to negotiate the price down, accept a return of less than 10 percent, increase rents, hope that the sale price of the property will be higher than $230,000 five years from now, or consider another investment. The discounted cash-flow method provides an effective way to estimate real estate values because it takes into account the selling price of the property, the effect of income taxes, and the time value of money.

DO IT IN CLASS

NEVER EVER

Fail to Take Risks When Investing

Risk does not mean taking a loss. One does not make money in investments without taking some risk because the returns we make on our investments are directly related to the risks we are willing to accept. If you keep your money in a bank, you will actually lose money because inflation typically exceeds any return offered by a financial institution. Thus what seems safe in the short term is quite risky in the long term.

The only way to make sure our dollars will buy what we need when we are older is to create wealth through long-term asset building activities. This means invest in assets that will grow in value.

ADVICE FROM A SEASONED PRO

Timesharing Is a Financial Disaster as an Investment

Timesharing is the joint ownership or lease of vacation property through which 9 million people occupy the property individually for set periods of time. In a typical deal, a buyer pays for a "vacation ownership" or "interval travel" at a resort condominium, maybe one or two weeks a year, and agrees to pay homeowners' association dues covering maintenance and taxes on the property. Some buyers pay upfront, while others finance their purchases often through the company selling the units.

Timesharing is not an investment, although it is promoted as a way to simultaneously invest and obtain vacation housing. It is a lifestyle investment. It is a loser as a financial investment. For an average of $21,000 a unit, buyers, whose average age is 51 (although the average age of recent buyers is 39), can purchase one or more weeks' use of luxury vacation housing furnished right down to the salt-and-pepper shakers. Timeshare owners pay an annual maintenance fee that averages $1,000 for each week of ownership. Maintenance fees increase 2 to 5 percent every year, and occasionally there are special assessment fees.

In the early days of timeshares, owners received deeds specifying their ownership to a fixed-week, fixed-resort timeshare. With **deeded timesharing,** the buyer obtains a legal title or deed to a limited time periods of use of real estate. Purchasers become secured creditors who are guaranteed continued use of the property throughout any bankruptcy proceedings. They really own their week (or two) of the property.

The industry now has moved to a more flexible system where buyers receive a certain number of points they can use for time and amenities, instead of a deed. **Nondeeded timesharing** is a legal right-to-use purchase of a limited, preplanned timesharing period of use of a property. It is a long-term lease, license, or club membership permitting use of a hotel suite, condominium, or other accommodation, and the right to use usually expires in 20 to 25 years. If the true owner of the property—the developer—goes bankrupt, creditors can lock out the timeshare purchasers

(technically they are tenants) from the premises. And it happens.

It is extremely hard to sell a timeshare, almost impossible. Timeshare ownership can become an almost perpetual liability. The average timeshare unit languishes on the market for 4.4 years before being sold. At any point in time, 60 percent of *all* timeshares are up for sale. Timeshare sellers often sell for less than one-half of the initial purchase price, and brokers typically charge a commission of 15 to 40 percent.

Half of the properties that revert to the developer do so by foreclosure. If the seller repossesses a timeshare property because of non-payment, the developer typically pays $1,500 to the homeowner's association and then resells it for $20,000.

If you want to buy a timeshare, you can skip the developer's seductive sales pitch—which includes shills in the audience saying, "Yes, I'll buy!"—and get a juicy discount (one-third to one-half off the retail price) when buying from a current owner. Some timeshares can be purchased for as little as $1. See eBay, RedWeek, Tug2.net, Timeshare Resale Vacations, and www.licensedtiimeshareresalebrokers.org. As one observer said, "If someone tries to sell you a timeshare, run!"

All states have "right of recission" laws that allow timeshare buyers to cancel a purchase contract, usually from 5 to 10 days. Do so in writing and mail it requiring a signed, returned receipt. Transactions in foreign countries are excluded from such laws.

In good economic times or bad, you can find rental lodgings in the same area at a lower price than owning. The one good thing about owning a timeshare is that it forces you to take a yearly vacation, and the vacation will be at the same time and place regardless of where you live in the future. If you want some variety in your vacation time or place, some owners to swap their property for others in distant locations through membership in a worldwide vacation exchange such as My Resort Network at www.myresortnetwork.com/) or www.RCI.com (4,500 affiliated resorts worldwide).

Philip C. Bryant
Ivy Tech Community College, Bloomington, Indiana

16.3b Financing a Real Estate Investment

Borrowing to finance a real estate investment is more expensive than borrowing to buy one's own home. For investment property, the mortgage rate might be 0.5 to 2.0 percentage points above the rate for owner-occupied homes.

There is more risk because the investor does not live at the property. The minimum down payment for investors is often 20 or 25 percent. To make a smaller down payment and perhaps get a lower mortgage rate, some real estate investors buy a home, live in it for a year, and then rent it out as an investment. See the "Did You Know" box on pages 505 and 506 for details on the tax consequences of an income-producing real estate investment.

A popular way to finance a real estate investment is through **seller financing** (or **owner financing**). This occurs when a seller is willing to self-finance a loan by accepting a promissory note from the buyer who makes monthly mortgage payments. No lending agency is involved. Investing buyers pay higher interest rates for seller financing. The seller may accept little or no down payment in exchange for an even higher interest rate, perhaps 1½ to 2½ percent above conventional mortgage rates. Owner-financed deals can be transacted very quickly for investors.

Another way to start in real estate investing is to purchase **sweat equity property**. You buy a fixer-upper at a favorable price and "sweat" by spending many hours cleaning, painting, and repairing it to rent or sell at a profit.

seller financing (owner financing)
When a seller self-finances a buyer's loan by accepting a promissory note from a buyer, who makes monthly mortgage payments.

sweat equity property
Property that needs repairs but that has good underlying value; an investor buys the property at a favorable price and fixes it up to rent or sell at a profit.

CONCEPT CHECK 16.3

1. Summarize how the discounted cash-flow method helps determine the right price to pay for a real estate investment.
2. Comment on the wisdom of buying a timeshare as an investment.
3. List two ways to finance a real estate investment.

16.4 DISADVANTAGES OF REAL ESTATE INVESTING

Learning Objective 4
Assess the disadvantages of investing in real estate.

Real estate investing can be profitable. But it does have some significant disadvantages.

- **Business risk.** It is quite possible to lose money in real estate investments, as lots of investors found out in recent years. A local recession, perhaps because a large employer closed, can depress housing prices. Zoning changes can slash housing values. Rents cannot keep up with costs in communities in which industries and jobs are moving elsewhere or in deteriorating neighborhoods.

- **Foreclosures.** In communities where there are many foreclosures, other sellers have to lower their home prices to compete. This depresses the values of all comparable housing—no matter how wonderful the location or condition—thus making it more difficult for anyone to sell at a reasonable price.

- **Illiquidity.** Besides being expensive, the market for investment property is much smaller than the securities market. As a result, it is common to experience trouble in selling. It may take months or even a year or more to find a buyer, arrange the financing, and close the sale of a real estate investment.

- **Complex Assumptions.** Real estate investments require much more investigation than do most other investments. Numerous assumptions about financial details such as projected rents and the cost of repairs in the future also must be made.

- **Large initial investment.** Direct investment in real estate generally requires many thousands of dollars, often with an initial outlay of $15,000, $30,000, $50,000, or more.

- **Lack of diversification.** So much capital is required in real estate investing that spreading risk is almost impossible.

- **Dealing with rental applicants and tenants.** State laws may make it impossible to evict a deadbeat tenant for several months or a year, or longer. Picking the wrong tenants can quickly turn a real estate property into a big financial loss.

- **Time-consuming management demands.** Managing a real estate investment requires time for conducting regular inspections of the property, dealing with insurance companies, making repairs, and collecting overdue rents.

- **Low current income.** Expenses may reduce the cash-flow return to less than 2 percent or even generate a net loss in a given year.

ADVICE FROM A SEASONED PRO

Screen Rental Applicants and Tenants Yourself

As a rental property owner there are critical decisions that must be made relative to screening applicants. If you do not want to screen rental applicants for their credit histories, criminal records, work references, experience with previous landlords or get calls about clogged toilets in the middle of the night, you can hire a property management company to handle those tasks. Normally, property managers will charge between six (6) to ten (10) percent of the actual rental income plus an additional fee for screening any rental applicants.

Realistically, rental property owners have a better chance of gaining profits if they manage the property themselves. The costs associated with contracting that responsibility out to a third party management company can take a toll on profits. One reliable source for completing criminal background checks is www.mysmartmove.com.

Clarence W. Jones, Jr.
Lane College, Jackson, Tennessee

- **Unpredictable costs.** Estimating costs is problematic. Investors cannot control increasing real estate tax assessments or accurately predict when a central air-conditioning unit might break down.

- **Interest rate risk.** When interest rates rise or unemployment grows, fewer people can afford to buy homes, and this puts downward pressure on prices and rents.

- **Legal fees.** The services of a real estate attorney will be needed to help handle the real estate purchase, sale, building inspections, zoning issues, tenant problems, insurance disputes, accounting, and any liability issues. Title insurance is a critically important expense to investors, particularly when allegations suggest that lenders may or may not have properly inspected the seller's legal documents.

- **High transfer costs.** Substantial transfer costs, often representing 6 to 7 percent of the property's sale price, plus money for fix-up costs, may be incurred when real estate is bought or sold.

ADVICE FROM A SEASONED PRO

Ways to Make $1 Million

Here are some smart strategies on how to surpass $1 million in savings and investments:

1. Limit college debts to federally subsidized loans and avoid over-borrowing
2. Pay yourself first by not overspending
3. Save early and often by contributing to your employer's 401(k) plan
4. Start a business
5. Buy a home with a fixed-rate mortgage
6. When you change jobs rollover your 401(k) to an IRA
7. Buy used vehicles to minimize borrowing on a depreciating asset
8. Fund a Roth IRA with stock mutual funds and ETFs
9. Put 100 percent of any inheritances into investments
10. Buy liability insurance to protect your assets
11. Avoid high-risk investments

Jean Lown
Utah State University, Logan, Utah

THE TAX CONSEQUENCES OF AN INCOME-PRODUCING REAL ESTATE INVESTMENT

When you are considering a real estate investment, you use the investment amount (purchase price or down payment) to begin the process of estimating the likely rate of return. This calculation result may then be compared with other investment alternatives. Because some of the many assumptions in real estate calculations could be incorrect, caution is warranted in real estate analyses.

The following table shows five-year estimates for a hypothetical residential property in Denver, Colorado located close to a well-respected high school with a purchase price of $200,000. The building will be purchased with a $150,000 mortgage loan, so the buyer has to make a $50,000 down payment plus pay $8,000 in closing costs. The gross rental income of $18,000 annually is projected to rise at an annual rate of 5 percent, vacancies and unpaid rent at 10 percent, real estate taxes at 7 percent, insurance at 8 percent, and maintenance at 10 percent. Virtually the entire payment for the 30-year, $150,000, 6½ percent, fixed-rate mortgage loan is assumed to be interest during these early years. For income tax purposes, the land is valued at $20,000, and the building is depreciated over 27.5 years. The amount of annual straight-line depreciation is

calculated to be $6,546 ($200,000 − $20,000 = $180,000; $180,000 ÷ 27.5 = $6,546).

Note (in line D) how challenging it is to earn current income from rental properties. During the first two years, the total cash flow (line D) is projected to be positive ($976 and $652), but for the following three years, the cash flow is expected to be negative (−330, −$10, and −$305). However, because the income tax laws permit depreciation (line E, $6,546) to be recorded each year as a real estate investment expense, even though it is not an out-of-pocket cost, the investor calculates a total taxable loss (line F) for each of the five years of expected ownership (−$5,570 the first year).

These losses can be deducted on the investor's income tax returns. Because the investor pays a 30 percent combined federal and state income tax rate, the loss results in a first-year annual tax savings of $1,671 (line G). Therefore, instead of sending the $1,671 to the government in taxes, the investor can use that amount to help pay the operating expenses of the investment. Consequently, the net cashflow income (line D) of $976 is enhanced by tax savings (line G) of $1,671 to result in a net cash-flow gain after taxes of $2,647 ($1,671 + $976).

Estimates for a Successful Real Estate Investment

		Year			
	1	**2**	**3**	**4**	**5**
A. Gross rental income	$18,000	$18,900	$19,845	$20,837	$21,879
Less vacancies and unpaid rent	1,800	1,890	1,985	2,084	2,188
B. Projected gross income	$16,200	$17,010	$17,860	$18,753	$19,691
C. Less operating expenses					
Principal and interest ($P + I$)	$11,376	$11,376	$11,376	$11,376	$11,376
Real estate taxes (T)	2,600	2,782	2,977	3,185	3,408
Insurance (I)	800	804	933	1,008	1,089
Maintenance	2,400	2,640	2,904	3,194	3,513
Total operating expenses	$17,176	$17,662	$18,190	$18,763	$19,386
D. Total cash flow	$ 976	$ 652	$ (330)	$ (10)	$ (305)
E. Less depreciation expense	(6,546)	(6,546)	(6,546)	(6,546)	(6,546)
F. Taxable income (or loss) ($D − E$)	$(5,570)	$(5,894)	$(6,876)	$(6,556)	$(6,851)
G. Annual tax savings (30 percent marginal rate)	1,671	1,768	2,062	1,966	2,055
H. Net cash-flow gain (or loss) after taxes ($G + D$)	$ 2,647	$ 2,420	$ 1,732	$ 1,956	$ 1,750

Assume that the property appreciates in value at an annual rate of 4 percent and will be worth $243,330 (line K) in five years ($200,000 × 1.04 × 1.04 × 1.04 × 1.04 × 1.04). If it is sold at this price, a 6 percent real estate sales commission of $14,599 ($243,330 × 0.06) would reduce the net proceeds to $228,731 ($243,330 − $14,599).

Now we can calculate the **crude annual rate of return** on the property, as shown in the second table. A crude annual rate of return is a rough measure of the yield on amounts invested that assumes that equal portions of the gain are earned each year. The total return in this example was substantial. The investor made out-of-pocket

(Continued)

cash investments of $50,000 for the down payment and $8,000 in closing costs, and we subtract the accumulated net cash flow (line N) of $10,505 (adding all the numbers across line H because the investor already has received that money) for a total investment (line O) of $47,495. The investor has a capital gain (line M) of $53,461. After dividing to determine the before-tax total return (line R) to obtain 112 percent, the crude annual rate of return (line S) is 22.4 percent annually over the five years (112 percent ÷ 5 years).

Crude Rate of Return on a Successful Real Estate Investment

Taxable cost

I.	Purchase price ($50,000 down payment; $150,000 loan)	$200,000
	Closing costs	8,000
	Subtotal	208,000
J.	Less accumulated depreciation	32,730
	Taxable cost (adjusted basis)	$175,270

Proceeds (after paying off mortgage)

K.	Sale price	$243,330
	Less sales commission	14,599
	Net proceeds	$228,731
L.	Less taxable cost (J)	175,270
M.	Taxable proceeds (capital gain)	$ 53,461

Amount invested

	Down payment	$ 50,000
	Closing costs	8,000
N.	Less accumulated net cash-flow gains	(10,505)
O.	Total invested	$ 47,495

Crude annual rate of return

P.	Total invested	$ 47,495
Q.	Taxable proceeds (capital gain from M)	$ 53,461
R.	Before-tax total return ($53,461/$47,495)	112%
S.	Crude before-tax annual rate of return (112 percent ÷ 5 years)	22.4%

CONCEPT CHECK 16.4

1. Summarize why foreclosures and illiquidity are disadvantages in real estate investing.
2. Briefly comment on why interest rate risk is dangerous to real estate investors.
3. Comment on why real estate investors often have time-consuming management demands.

Learning Objective 5

Summarize the risks and challenges of investing in the high-risk investments of collectibles, precious metals, and gems.

speculator

An investor who buys in the hope that someone else will pay more for an asset in the not-too-distant future.

16.5 INVESTING IN COLLECTIBLES, PRECIOUS METALS, AND GEMS

Investors often think of assets as something they would like to own for the long term. When investing in collectibles, precious metals, and gems, the investor owns illiquid real assets, not intangible items represented by pieces of paper. While an asset may be bought for its long-term investment potential, profits might be earned in the short term.

A **speculator** buys in the hope that someone else will pay more for an asset in the not-too-distant future. Speculators often buy or sell in expectation of profiting from market fluctuations. If you put money into these illiquid assets, limit your speculative investing to no more than 5 to 10 percent of your total investment portfolio, and buy only what you truly adore. Keep in mind that collectibles, precious metals, and gems are not part of your savings plan for retirement. Also, do not invest in anything that you do not know how to sell.

When you sell collectibles, like coins, art, gold, or silver, for a profit the special 0 percent, 15 percent, and 20 percent tax rates on long-term capital gains do not apply. Instead, you will owe tax at your ordinary tax rate, or 28%, whichever is lower. Recall that the typical long-term capital gains rate is 15 percent on investments other than collectibles. As is the case with all assets, short-term capital gains on the sale of collectibles are taxed at ordinary rates.

16.5a Collectibles

Collectibles are cultural artifacts that have value because of their beauty, age, scarcity, or popularity. They include antiques, art, baseball cards, cars, coins, wine, gems, guitars, guns, photographs, paintings, prints, ceramics, comic books, lunchboxes, matchbooks, glassware, posters, rugs, spoons, sports memorabilia, stamps, watches, and fine wines. The collectible markets are fueled by nostalgia, limited availability, and "what is hot to own today." Prices for collectibles often lag the returns of other investments. Collectibles won't beat the return of stocks over the long term, but they are lots of fun to own.

collectibles

Cultural artifacts that have value because of their beauty, age, scarcity, or popularity, such as antiques, stamps, rare coins, art, baseball cards, and so on.

Qualities that Make Collectibles Valuable There are some of the qualities that make collectibles valuable:

- **Rarity.** The law of scarcity says that if there is not a lot of something, it is likely to be worth more, sometimes lots more. Mass-produced "collectibles" like Precious Moments figurines and Hess trucks probably won't be all that valuable later on down the road.

- **Condition.** Invest only in "mint" condition items. The better condition something is in, from an antique chair to a rare coin, the more it will be worth.

- **Authenticity.** An original piece of art is worth more than later prints and copies. If you can prove that a well-known person owned something (think "provenance" as they say on the television production of "Antiques Roadshow"), that's always worth something more as well.

- **Age.** Old age can add value to an item, especially if it is rare, and in reasonably good condition. The older the better in some cases.

Making a Profit on Collectibles Is Not Easy Although buying collectibles can be easy, turning a profit may not. The only return on collectibles occurs through price appreciation, and you must sell to realize a profit. That could be hard for you to do if the collectible gives you pleasure.

Items that are almost certain to lose value include those that are mass produced and marketed as collectibles or limited editions. You often see these kinds of collectibles advertised on television and in newspapers and magazines. Another risk is the wholesale-to-retail price spread, which could be 50 or 100 percent. If you buy from a dealer, you'll probably pay a markup of at least 40 to 50 percent. Investors generally get more for their money buying at an auction, but realize that professional dealers are always bidding there too. Prices on collectibles vary greatly from item to item and year to year. Markets are fickle. If the investor needs to convert the asset to cash, a sale may take days, weeks, or months, and the seller may be forced to accept a lower price.

Buying and Selling Collectibles on the Internet You can buy collectibles on the Internet, using eBay for example, purchasing in minutes what you might never have found even after searching for years in magazines, junk shops, flea markets, and auctions. Buying collectibles on the Internet is efficient and convenient, and it is easy to compare products and prices. It is hard to inspect the collectible before purchase, however. Search Google for "collectibles," but realize that this is a risky way to invest particularly with lots of fakes in existence.

Search for Collectibles Prices at Christie's and Sotheby's online The giant auction houses of Christie's (www.christies.com) and Sotheby's (www.sothebys.com) offer big selections of prints, photographs, watches, wines, furniture, diamond jewelry, and other collectibles. Check out their catalogs and videos on their websites, and consider signing up for text messages and the ability to bid by phone or online.

Sometimes It Is Hard to Sell Losers People have a tendency toward refusing to sell poorly performing investments, including collectibles that have lost value, clinging to the hope that the assets will eventually regain their old values. Instead, regularly monitor your portfolio and make a firm decision to sell investments that are no longer providing the desired return. Then reinvest the money elsewhere.

16.5b Gold and Other Precious Metals

There is an allure to owning gold. You can own and hold it with pride, and it is beautiful to look at. Gold is a uniquely private, personal, and portable way to hold some genuine wealth.

For purposes of investing, however, the reasons for owning it often do not add up. For example, gold does not generate current income while you own it. Its value is determined solely by supply and demand at the time of sale. Thus, investing in gold is speculating. Of all the precious metals available to investors, gold is the most popular.

Fear Pushes Up Gold Prices Fear is what pushes up the price of gold. Some of the world's worried investors purchase gold reasoning that if their national economies crash they will be able to trade gold even if their country's paper currency is devalued. Others who buy gold are concerned about such things as high inflation, rising interest rates, countries seen as printing too much money, economic collapse, possible wars, excessive government borrowing, collapse of the credit system, and international trade wars.

Gold Prices Were Stagnant, Then Soared and Crashed Again Gold sellers make gold sound like an appealing speculative investment, but it is not. Like in never. Consider that if you bought $10,000 in gold in 1980, it would have been worth $10,600 13 years later. If you invested the same $10,000 in 1980 in a mutual fund that tracks the S&P 500, you would have over $200,000 in those 13 years. These are not the kind of data that a gold promoter wants investors to see.

In the last decade gold prices rose from $500 to over $1,200 an ounce. Two months later the price dropped to $1,050. Can the fear and greed of doomsayers, conspiracy theorists, and gold promoters keep gold prices rising, or are today's prices yet another bubble that has happened throughout history? The smart investor proceeds with caution even when speculating.

16.5c You Can Invest in Gold in Several Ways

An initial investment in gold need not be expensive, although buying gold directly can be. There are many ways to invest in gold or other precious metals.

gold bullion

A refined and stamped weight of precious metal.

Gold Bullion Gold bullion is often thought of as the large gold "bricks" that weigh about 28 pounds that people imagine are stored in Fort Knox. Each brick is worth more than $100,000 at today's prices. All the gold in the world weighs 170,000 metric tons, and would create a 68-foot cube and that would fit in a baseball infield.

The term **bullion** simply means a refined and stamped weight of precious metal. Gold bullion is traditionally purchased and traded in 1- and 10-ounce gold bars. Gold as bullion is expensive to own. There are fees for refining, fabricating, and shipping bullion. A sales charge of 5 to 8 percent is common. There are storage costs. When gold is sold, the bank or dealer buying it from an investor may insist on reassaying its quality, yet another cost for the investor. The investor should purchase insurance against fire, theft, and fraud because such transactions are not government regulated.

gold bullion coins

Various world mints issue these coins, which contain 1 troy ounce (31.15 grams) of pure gold.

Gold Bullion Coins Some costs of investing in gold can be avoided by those wanting to take physical possession of gold bullion itself by owning modern **gold bullion coins,** each containing 1 troy ounce (31.15 grams) of pure gold issued by the various world mints. The most popular coins are the South African Krugerrand, Canadian Maple Leaf, and the U.S. Gold Eagle. Other gold bullion coins are available, including the Great Britain Sovereign, Australian Kangaroo Nugget, and Chinese Panda. Minimum orders are ten coins, and commissions are 5 to 6 percent when buying and 1 to 2 percent when selling. These gold bullion coins do not need to be tested for purity, are portable, and have worldwide liquidity. Investors need to store and insure their coins. Visit www.usmint.gov for a list of U.S. Gold Eagle dealers.

Collectible Gold Coins People who buy collectible gold coins buy them in part because of their intrinsic beauty and scarcity. They face high markups, difficulty in grading

Gold and other precious metals are highly volatile investments.

coins (or must pay to hire a grading service), and costs for storage and insurance. Major coin graders include American Numismatic Association Certification Service (www .anacs.com), Numismatic Guaranty Corporation (www.ngccoin.com), and Professional Coin Grading Service (www.pcgs.com). The World Gold Council (www.gold.org) maintains a list of firms that buy and sell gold. Note that the long-term capital gains tax on collectibles, including gold, is 28 percent (or your tax bracket, whichever is lower).

Gold Mining Stocks, Mutual Funds, and ETFs Investors wanting to capitalize on world crises, economic fears, and rising gold prices by investing in smaller amounts may choose to put speculative cash in the stocks of gold mining companies, in mutual funds that own gold companies, and in specialized exchange-traded funds (ETFs). For example, you may have heard of the now defunct Homestake Gold Mine, one of the early enterprises associated with the Gold Rush of 1876 in the northern Black Hills of what was then Dakota Territory. Today, there are a handful of gold mining companies in the United States and dozens around the world.

Popular gold mutual funds include Van Eck International Investors (INIVX), USAA Precious Metals and Minerals (USAGX), Oppenheimer Gold & Special Metals A (OPGSX), and Vanguard Precious Metals and Mining (VGPM). Gold stock prices are much more volatile than the price of gold itself as they can readily swing up or down 50 percent in a matter of months. The largest gold exchange-traded fund (ETF) is SPDR Gold Shares (GLD). Other popular gold ETFs are iShares COMEX Gold Trust (IAU) and Market Vectors Gold Miners ETF (GDX).

16.5d Investing in Other Metals—Silver, Platinum, Palladium, and Rhodium

Some other metals also appeal to certain investors. Silver, platinum, palladium, and rhodium are metals used industrially and occasionally in jewelry. The values of these metals rise and fall with changes in demand. An investor might reason that since palladium is used in auto production that when demand in China and India for vehicles increases substantially, the price of the metal will soar. Prices can drop, too. Illustrative specialized ETFs in these precious metals include iShares Silver Trust (SLV), ETFS Physical Platinum (PPLT), and ETFS Physical Palladium Shares (PALL).

THERE IS AN APP FOR THAT!

Some of the best apps are:

- Betterment
- CBOE Mobile
- KCastGoldAlive
- Property Fixer
- Property Evaluator
- TheLandlordApp
- Zilliow.com/mobile

16.5e Precious Stones and Gems

Precious stones and gems, such as diamonds, sapphires, rubies, and emeralds, are also examples of high-risk investments. Investors purchase investment-grade gems as "loose gems" rather than as pieces of jewelry. Wholesale firms, not jewelers, sell the best-quality precious gems. The gem certification process may be touted as a science, but it is not; rather it is educated guesswork. Obtaining two assessments of a stone's quality, particularly on stones of less than 1 carat, is likely to result in a variation of 10 to 20 percent. There is a lack of price transparency in precious stones and gems and an illiquid trading market. Also, some difficulty exists in establishing uniform standards of quality.

Sales commissions on precious stones are high, and reselling is very difficult. Novice investors often buy at retail and then wind up trying to sell at retail, and then eventually selling at or near wholesale. This approach is the opposite of smart investing, that is, buying low and selling high. Losing 20 to 50 percent of one's investment in precious stones is not uncommon.

16.5f   Speculate by Trading in Currencies

Investors deeply worried about the economic future of their country or world may find it desirable to put some of their assets in the cash of the world's presumed two safest currencies, the U.S. dollar and the Euro. Individuals may speculate on the changing daily values of the dollar, Euro, Yen, Pound, Swiss Franc, and other currencies in the **forex** (foreign exchange trading). A "mini" account can be opened for only $300 at Forex capital Markets (www.FXcM.com) where you try out a practice account and then trade up to 200 times that amount by using margin. Currency trading uses a lot of margin and that is risky!

16.5g   Penny Stocks Are Worth About a Penny

penny stocks
Stocks that trade for less than $5 per share.

The Securities and Exchange Commission (SEC) defines **penny stocks** as those that trade for less than $5 per share. They are unusually vulnerable to fraud because financial information is in short supply, few seasoned professionals follow and analyze the companies, and whatever supposedly unbiased reports are usually written by paid promoters. And they are pushed on the telephone and online by scammers. The risk is so great that the SEC warns penny-stock investors that they "should be prepared for the possibility that they may lose their whole investment." The SEC shuts down hundreds of these companies every year. This is an investment you can totally avoid.

YOUR GRANDPARENTS SAY

"What Makes a Good Investor"

- Self-reliance
- Well informed on investments
- Self-assured but not overconfident
- Cautious risk taker
- Depends on others comfortably

16.5h   Scams Abound in Collectibles, Precious Metals, and Gems

The average investor can't tell a diamond from a cubic zirconium or a Monet from a Manet. The values of collectibles, gold, other precious metals, and precious gems rely in part upon the authority of "experts" who purport to determine their worth. Such blind trust invites risk for potential investors. When an asset does not generate a readily quantifiable return (such as rent, interest, or dividends) its value is determined by supply and demand—as well as lies and rumors. Scams, forgeries, and frauds abound with these investments, as promoters and telemarketers tell tales about skyrocketing prices and high profit potentials to encourage their purchase. Collectibles, precious metals, and gems are not wise choices for the casual investor.

CONCEPT CHECK 16.5

1. Identify one collectible that might be an interesting investment, and explain why it might be difficult to make a profit.
2. Explain why some investors buy gold and other precious metals, and tell why choosing one type of investment might be appealing or unappealing to you.
3. Identify some risks of investing in precious stones and gems.

16.6 INVESTING IN OPTIONS AND COMMODITY FUTURES CONTRACTS

Learning Objective 6
Explain why options and futures are risky investments.

The popular perception of investing in the futures markets is that they are a form of very high risk speculation. This is true. But futures are also widely used as financial tools for reducing risk.

A **derivative** (or **derivative security**) is an instrument used by people to trade or manage more easily the asset upon which these instruments are based. Derivative securities are available for commodities, equities, bonds, interest rates, exchange rates, and indexes (such as a stock market index, consumer price index, and weather conditions). Investors choose derivatives to either reduce future risk by hedging against losses or taking on additional risk by speculating. The investor's returns are derived solely from changes in the underlying asset's price behavior. Two of the most common derivative instruments are options and futures contracts.

16.6a Options Allow You to Buy or Sell an Asset at a Predetermined Price

An **option** is a contract to buy or sell an asset at some point in the future at a specified price. The most common type of option is a **stock option.** This derivative gives the holder (purchaser) the right, but not the obligation, to buy or sell a specific number of shares (normally 100) of a certain stock at a specified price (the **striking price)** before a specified date (the **expiration date,** typically three, six, or nine months). Options are the only investment that tells you in advance (on the expiration date) what day your investment will be worthless.

Two types of option contracts exist: calls and puts. A **call option** gives the option holder (buyer) the right, but not the obligation, to buy the optioned asset from the

NUMBERS ON

Real Estate and High-Risk Investments

Data from various sources suggest:

- Less than 5 percent of invested money is in high-risk alternatives.
- About 10 percent of investors foolishly think gold and precious metals are a good place to invest spare funds.

- If promised returns seem too good to be true, they probably are.
- Most high-risk investors lose money.
- Investing just $25 per week for 40 years grows to more than $250,000; $50 per week accumulates to more than $1 million.

NEVER EVER

1. *Assume that real estate prices will go up and interest rates will not increase.*

2. *Fail to set enough money aside for maintenance, repairs, unanticipated capital improvements, and rising real estate taxes on rental property.*

3. *Invest some retirement money in margin trading, short selling, options, commodity futures, gold, precious metals and gems, currencies, and timeshares.*

covered option

Occurs when an option writer who owns the covered option sells the call.

futures contract

The obligation to make or take delivery of a certain amount of a commodity by a set date.

MONEY WEBSITES

Informative websites are:
- American Numismatic Association Certification Service
- Chicago Board Options Exchange
- Numismatic Guaranty Corporation
- Options Industry Council
- Options Screener
- OptionsXpress
- Realtor.com
- TradeKing
- World Gold Council
- USA Gold
- U.S. Mint
- Yahoo real estate

option writer at the striking price. A **put option** gives the option holder (buyer) the right, but not the obligation, to sell the optioned asset to the option writer at the striking price.

Most option contracts expire without being exercised, and the option seller is the only person to earn a profit. The profit results from the option premium charged when the option was originally sold. Buying and selling options are techniques used by all types of investors.

Conservative Investors Make Money on Options Selling a call option can be a fairly safe way to generate income by conservative option writers who own the underlying asset (the stock). When they sell a call, it is described as a covered option because the writer owns the underlying stock. If the writer does not own the asset, it is a **naked option,** a speculative position. When used effectively by conservative option writers, calls can potentially pick up an extra return of perhaps 1 to 2 percent every three months and minimize risk at the same time. In effect, this conservative investor protects himself financially by hedging his investment against loss due to price fluctuation. You also can conservatively profit by selling a call on stock already owned, giving the buyer the right to purchase your shares at a certain price any time during a relatively short period at a fixed strike price, which is higher than the current price.

Aggressive Investors Profit with Options Aggressive investors in the options market attempt to profit in two ways. First, the investor can hope for an increase in the value of the option. For example, if the price of a stock is rising, the holder of a call option might sell it to another investor for a higher price than that originally paid. Second, the investor can exercise the option at the striking price, take ownership of the underlying securities, and sell them at a profit.

16.6b   Buying and Selling Commodities Futures Contracts

A futures contract is the obligation to make or take delivery of a certain amount of a commodity by a set date. A futures derivative contract requires the holder to buy the asset on the date specified. If the holder does not want to buy the asset, he or she must sell the contract to some other investor or to someone who wants to actually use the asset.

Conservative Economic Needs Creates Futures Markets Farmer Mike Hardesty who planted a 10,000-bushel soybean crop in Chana, Illinois, might want to sell part of it now to ensure the receipt of a certain price when the crop is actually harvested. Similarly, a food-processing company might want to purchase soybeans now to protect against sharp price increases in the future. And an orange juice manufacturer might want to lock in a supply of oranges at a definite price now rather than run the risk that a winter freeze would push up prices. These economic needs create futures markets. You can trade futures on an organized market for lots of commodities, such as coffee, sugar, corn, pigs, plywood, metals, energy, foreign currencies, gold, and other precious metals.

Speculators Trade in Futures Markets The speculative investor who buys or sells a commodity contract is hoping that the market price of the commodity will rise (or fall) before the contract matures, usually 3 to 18 months after it is written. These derivatives offer the potential for extremely high profits because such contracts often are highly leveraged. Depending on the commodity, the volatility of the market, and the brokerage house requirements, an investor can put up as little as 5 to 15 percent of the total value of the contract. Some contracts require a deposit of only $300. Commissions average about $20 for each purchase and sale. You can check the history of advisors at the Commodity Futures Trading Commission's website at SmartCheck.gov.

DID YOU KNOW

About Hedge Funds

Hedge funds are freewheeling risky investment pools for the extremely wealthy that use unconventional investment strategies. They are global companies, beyond most of the regulations of the U.S. government. Hedge funds trade options and commodities, sell short, use leverage, risk arbitrage, buy and sell currencies, and invest in undervalued mature companies, often those in or nearing bankruptcy. Hedge funds can profit in times of market volatility as well as in a falling market. The investors are partners.

Fees charged by the hedge fund manager typically are 2 percent of assets under management and 20 percent of the upside (the "performance fee") of the fund. Most managers assess no full fees until the profits are above 8 percent. None of the 8000 hedge funds can be offered or advertised to the general investing public in the United States. They are limited to "accredited investors and purchasers" who have incomes over $200,000 and a net worth over $1 million and who own more than $5 million in investments. The small investor can buy shares in publicly traded firms, like Blackstone (BX) or Kohlberg Kravis Roberts (KKR), which are parent companies of hedge funds. A number of hedge funds have had catastrophic losses and have gone bankrupt.

Futures Are a Zero-Sum Game In each futures transaction a winner and a loser will emerge. A buyer of a futures contract benefits if the price of the commodity increases, but the seller suffers. When prices decline, the reverse is true. An estimated 90 percent of investors in the futures market lose money. Five percent (mostly the professionals) make profits from the losers and the remaining 5 percent break even.

Trading in futures is a **zero-sum game** in which the wealth of all investors remains the same. The trading simply redistributes the wealth among those traders. Each profit must be offset by an equivalent loss; therefore, the average rate of return for all investors in futures is zero. The return actually becomes negative if transaction costs are included. Most investors do not belong in commodities.

zero-sum game
An investment in which the wealth of all buyers remains the same as the trading simply redistributes the wealth among those traders.

TURN BAD HABITS INTO GOOD ONES

Do You Do This?

Avoid investing in real estate

Buy collectibles, precious metals, and gems

Invest in options and commodity futures for quick profits

Do This Instead!

Do the math to see if it might be profitable

Never put long-term investment money into these assets

Be prepared to lose money

 CONCEPT CHECK 16.6

1. Distinguish between a call and a put for the options investor.
2. Summarize one way a person with a conservative investment philosophy can profit in options.
3. Explain how a speculative options investor can make a lot of money.
4. Offer reasons why futures contracts are not appropriate for the long-term investor.

WHAT DO YOU RECOMMEND *NOW*?

Now that you have read the chapter on real estate and high-risk investments, what do you recommend to Brittany on:

1. Investing in real estate?
2. Putting some money into collectibles or gold?
3. Investing in options and futures contracts?

Heide Benser/Corbis/Getty Images

SUMMARY OF LEARNING OBJECTIVES RECAPPED

LO1 **Demonstrate how you can make money investing in real estate.**

The key questions for real estate investors are: "Can you make current income while you own?" and "Can you profit when you sell the property?" To help find answers, investors calculate the price-to-rent ratio and rental yield.

LO2 **Recognize how to take advantage of beneficial tax treatments in real estate investing.**

The Internal Revenue Service offers the investor five beneficial tax treatments, including depreciation, interest that is deductible, low tax rates on capital gains, tax-free exchanges of real estate, and special tax breaks on renting and vacation homes.

LO3 **Calculate the right price to pay for real estate and how to finance your purchase.**

The discounted cash-flow method is an effective way to estimate the value or asking price of a real estate investment. It takes into account the selling price of the property, the effect of income taxes, and the time value of money. There are various ways to finance a real estate investment.

LO4 **Assess the disadvantages of investing in real estate.**

There are some disadvantages in real estate investing, such as large initial investment, lack of diversification, dealing with rental applicants and tenants, low current income, unpredictable costs, illiquidity, and high transfer costs.

LO5 **Summarize the risks and challenges of investing in the high-risk investments of collectibles, precious metals, and gems.**

When investing in collectibles, precious metals, and gems, the investor owns illiquid real assets, not intangible items represented by pieces of paper. The investor's only return comes from price appreciation, as they do not pay interest or dividends. While prices are set by supply and demand, promoters hype these investments. Changing investor tastes and rumors also influence prices.

LO6 **Explain why options and futures are risky investments.**

Derivatives, such as options and commodity futures, are instruments used by market participants to trade or manage more easily the asset upon which these instruments are based. While all types of investors can profit in options, only speculators with an aggressive investment philosophy should consider trading in futures. Ninety percent of investors in derivatives lose money, and losses can accumulate quickly.

LET'S TALK ABOUT IT

1. **Invest in Real Estate.** Describe what would encourage you to invest in real estate given that in recent years prices in some communities have declined.

2. **The Two Questions of Real Estate Investing.** Which of the two questions in real estate investing is more important? Explain why.

3. **Beneficial Tax Treatments.** Review the five beneficial tax treatments of real estate and explain which one seems most important to you as a real estate investor.

4. **Reasons to Invest.** Assume you have $30,000 in cash. Give reasons why you might want to invest that money in a real estate investment. Offer two reasons

why others might not be willing to invest in real estate.

5. **Manage Rental Applicants and Tenants.** Do you think you could successfully deal with rental applicants, tenants and the management demands required in real estate investing? Why or why not?

6. **Disadvantages of Real Estate.** Review the list of "Disadvantages of Real Estate Investing," and identify one that you think is most important. Explain why.

7. **Timeshares as an Investment.** Explain why timeshares should not be considered an investment. Why do some people buy timeshares?

8. **Put Some Money into High-Risk Investments.** What percentage of your portfolio, if any, do you think should be invested in high-risk investments? Explain.

9. **Invest in Gold?** Would you invest in gold today? Explain why or why not.

10. **Options and Futures.** Both options and futures are risky investments. Identify one that seems like an unwise idea, and explain why it is unappealing.

DO THE MATH

1. **Price-to-Rent Ratios.** Calculate the price-to-rent ratios for the following properties arranged by price of home followed by likely annual rental income: (a) $400,000/$40,000; (b) $300,000/$36,000; (c) $200,000/30,000.

DO IT IN CLASS
Page 496

2. **Real Estate Investment Returns.** Marianne Mooney, benefits manager and her sister, Laureen, a middle-school teacher from Pompano Beach, Florida, are interested in the numbers of real estate investments. They have reviewed the figures in Table 16-2 on page 499 and are impressed with investing together on a 50/50 basis to earn the potential 50.12 percent return after taxes. Assume that they bought the property with each contributed half of the down payment and they financed it with a 7 percent $175,000 30-year mortgage loan with annual interest costs of $11,900. Answer the following questions to help guide their investment decisions:

(a) Substitute the Maureen's 25 percent marginal tax bracket (Florida has no state income tax) in Table 16-2, and calculate her taxable income and return after taxes.

DO IT IN CLASS
Page 499

(b) Substitute Laureen's 15 percent tax rate (no state income tax) in Table 16-2, and calculate her taxable income and return after taxes.

(c) Why does real estate appear to be a favorable investment for Marianne and Laureen?

(d) What one factor might be changed in Table 16-2 to increase their returns?

3. **Review the math in Table 16-3, on page 500.** Discounted Cash Flow to Estimate Price, and give your opinion on which part of the assumptions (rent increase or sales price) is more subject to poor thinking.

DO IT IN CLASS
Page 501

FINANCIAL PLANNING CASES

CASE 1

The Johnsons Consider a Real Estate Investment

Harry and Belinda Johnson are considering purchasing a residential income property as an investment. The Johnsons want to achieve an after-tax total return of 7 percent. They are considering a property with an asking price of $190,000 that should produce $27,000 in gross rental income and $15,000 in net operating income.

(a) Calculate the price-to-rent ratio on the property.

(b) Calculate the present value of after-tax cash flow for the property, assuming that the after-tax cash-flow numbers are $8,000 for the first year, $8,400 for the second year, $8,800 for the third year, $9,200 for the fourth year, and $9,600 for the fifth year, and that the selling price of the property will be

$210,000 in five years. Prepare in a format similar to Table 16-3 on page 500, using Appendix A-2 or the *Garman/Forgue* companion website to discount the future after-tax cash flows to their present values.

(c) Give the Johnsons your advice on whether they should invest in the property at its current price of $190,000.

CASE 2

Victor and Maria Consider Selling Maria's Mother's Home

Victor and Maria Hernandez are thinking about selling her mother's home, which she recently inherited, and use the proceeds to enhance their investments for retirement. Its price increased to about today's value of $300,000. The home is fully paid for.

(a) If the rent is $1,800 a month, what is the rental yield?

(b) If they sold the home, should they invest the proceeds into any high-risk investments, such as gold?

CASE 3

Julia Price Wants to Try High-Risk Investments

Julia continues to be a hard worker and, at age 60, has saved and invested wisely for her planned financially successful retirement. She has an extra $15,000 in a cash management account beyond what she needs for emergency savings. She rejected options and commodity futures as too risky but is considering gold. Julia wonders if the price volatility of gold over the past few years will continue, and she has always thought about investing in antique furniture. Offer your opinions about her thinking.

CASE 4

Real Estate or Stocks?

Keisha Williams, a senior research analyst in San Bernardino, California, has bought and sold high-technology stocks profitably for years. Lately some of her stock investments have done quite poorly, including one company that went bankrupt. Emily, a longtime friend at work, has suggested that the two of them invest in real estate together because property values in some neighborhoods have been rising in anticipation of a large manufacturing company's plans to substantially increase its workforce. Keisha has looked at three small office buildings and some residential duplexes as possible investments.

(a) Contrast the wisdom of investing in commercial office buildings versus the attraction of investing in residential properties.

(b) List three of the advantages associated with real estate investments.

(c) List three things that can go wrong for real estate investors.

CASE 5

From Real Estate to Options and Futures

Jonathan Clark and Cody Adams, longtime dental partners in Basking Ridge, New Jersey, have bought and sold real estate properties for ten years. They have profited on many transactions, although they did have some substantial losses during the last recession. Their portfolio of real estate is worth about $4.7 million, on which they owe $2.9 million. Jonathan has read about investing in options and futures contracts, and last week, he talked with a stockbroker about the possibilities.

(a) Offer some reasons why Jonathan may want to invest $100,000 or more in options and futures contracts.

(b) List some of the risks of options trading for Jonathan and Cody.

(c) From an investor's point of view, contrast trading in futures contracts with buying real estate.

BE YOUR OWN PERSONAL FINANCIAL MANAGER

1. **Before Investing in Real Estate.** Review the information in the heading titled "What to do Before Investing in Real Estate" and identify two suggestions that you definitely would follow if you invested in real estate. Write a summary of your conclusions.

2. **Disadvantages of Real Estate Investing.** Review the list in the "Disadvantages of Real Estate Investing" section and identify two disadvantages that you think might

keep you from personally investing in real estate. Write a summary of your conclusions.

3. **Real Estate ETFs.** Go to the "Real Estate ETF" page for StockEncyclopedia.com (etf.stock-encyclopedia.com) and select three illustrative companies, such as ProShares UltraShort Real Estate Fund. Write a brief report comparing those three ETFs.

ON THE NET

1. **Research Home Prices.** To find prices on homes in your community, go to Zillow (www.zillow.com). Input addresses of homes on three nearby streets and summarize your price information findings.

2. **Research Mortgage Rates.** Find out current mortgage rates for 15-, 20-, and 30-year loans for both residential and investment loans. See LendingTree.com, Quickenloans.com, BankRate.com, or Loan.com. Write a brief report on your findings.

3. **Current Prices of Metals.** Find out the current prices of five popular metals, such as gold, silver, nickel, aluminum, cobalt, copper, lead, palladium, platinum, and silver, at websites like Kitco (www.kitco.com) or USA Gold (www.usagold.com). Write a brief report on your findings.

4. **Gold ETFs.** Go online and search "gold prices per ounce" on Google or Bing. Click on five websites, including Wikipedia's "Gold ETFs," and review what

is written, especially about predictions of future prices. Prepare a report summarizing your findings.

5. **Collectibles Websites.** Search the Internet for two websites featuring one type of collectible that interests you (such as coins, toys, watches, or sports memorabilia). Write a brief report comparing the types of information and features available for buyers of these collectibles.

6. **Research Hedge Funds.** Go online and research two large hedge funds (such as JP Morgan Chase, Bridgewater Associates, and Soros Fund Management) by inserting "hedge fund" after the company name. Write a report comparing what services the two funds perform, participation requirements, and investment returns.

ACTION INVOLVEMENT PROJECTS

1. **Community Real Estate Prices.** Telephone two real estate brokers to determine if the prices of single-family dwellings in your community have been decreasing or increasing over the past four or five years, and ask why. Inquire about homes located near your college as well as those farther away from campus. Prepare a brief report of your findings and include reasons for the change in prices.

2. **Invest in Commercial Real Estate.** Research current commercial properties for sale in your college community by reviewing the real estate section of newspapers and go online. How many listings do you find? How many duplexes? How many small apartment buildings? Select one investment property and prepare a report analyzing it using the price-to-rent ratio and rental yield.

3. **Tax Consequences of Real Estate Investment.** Select a possible commercial real estate investment in your community and make a "first attempt" to prepare an analysis similar in format to that in the Did You Know? box titled "The Tax Consequences of an Income- Producing Real Estate Investment." Make any reasonable assumptions you desire and calculate the numbers. Prepare the table and a brief report of your findings.

17

Retirement and Estate Planning

mstanley/Shutterstock.com

YOU MUST BE KIDDING, RIGHT?

Rachel Jones is 27 years old, and she recently got married and started a new job. Rachel had accumulated $10,000 in her previous employer's 401(k) retirement plan, and she withdrew it to help pay for her honeymoon. How much less money will Rachel have at retirement at age 67 if she could have earned 8 percent on the $10,000?

A. $10,000   **C.** $96,000

B. $46,000   **D.** $217,000

The answer is D. Spending retirement money for discretionary purposes, instead of keeping it in a tax-deferred account where it can compound for many years, is extremely unwise. The lesson is to keep your retirement money where it belongs!

Learning Objectives

After reading this chapter, you should be able to:

1. Estimate your Social Security retirement income benefit.

2. Calculate the amount you must save for retirement in today's dollars.

3. Distinguish among the types of employer-sponsored tax-sheltered retirement plans.

4. Explain the various types of personally established tax-sheltered retirement accounts.

5. Use Monte Carlo advice when investing for retirement.

6. Describe how to avoid penalties and make your retirement money last.

7. Plan for the distribution of your estate.

WHAT DO YOU RECOMMEND?

Chrisanna Pérez Rodríguez and her husband, Fernando, have worked since their early twenties. Chrisanna, age 48, worked for a previous employer for eight years. When she left that job, Chrisanna left her retirement money in that employer's 401(k) retirement plan. The funds are now worth $120,000 and they earn about 4 percent annually. She now works as food services manager for a convention center, earning $110,000 a year. Chrisanna contributes $366 each month (4 percent of her salary) to her employer's 401(k) retirement plan. Her employer's policy is to provide a 100 percent match up to 6 percent of Chrisanna's salary contributions, and allow her to contribute a total of up to 8 percent of her salary on her own. Chrisanna's 401(k) account balance at her new employer is $21,000. They have no other retirement savings. Fernando, age 48, is a computer programmer working independently as a contractor for various companies, and he earns about $90,000 annually. Chrisanna is hoping that she and Fernando can retire when they both are age 65.

What do you recommend to Chrisanna and Fernando on the subject of retirement and estate planning regarding:

1. How much in Social Security benefits can each expect to receive?

2. How much do they each need to save for retirement if they want to spend at a lifestyle of 80 percent of their current living expenses?

3. In which types of retirement plans might Fernando invest for retirement?

4. What withdrawal rate might they use to avoid running out of money during retirement?

5. What two actions might they take to go about transferring their assets by contract to avoid probate?

retirement

The time in life when the major sources of income change from earned income (such as salary or wages) to employer-based retirement benefits, private savings and investments, income from Social Security, and perhaps part-time employment.

Retirement is the time in life when the major sources of income from earned income (such as salary or wages) change to sources like employer-based retirement benefits, private savings and investments, income from Social Security, and perhaps income from part-time employment.

Retirement often is a gradual transition from the workforce rather than sudden cessation. Sixty percent of employees want to spend their retirement in another city or state, typically in a warmer climate. Four out of 10 workers plan to continue having a paid job after retirement, and 3 in 10 people age 65 to 69 are still working.

Yesterday's employers provided pensions for a lifetime that were commonly a reward for 20 or 30 years of working for one company. Today fewer than one in five employers still offer them.

Instead, one-half of employers offer a voluntary retirement plan to which employees may or may not choose to contribute. The other half of the nation's employers do not offer any retirement plan at all, and this number is growing. If your employer does not offer a retirement plan, you can set one up yourself. This chapter provides the details.

The fact today is that you—and only you—are responsible for meeting your retirement income needs. Furthermore, both the responsibility of investing funds saved for retirement and the risk of making poor investments with these funds are also your responsibilities. You are truly in charge of your future, so do not be an amateur investor forever; instead reread chapters 13–16 as well as this chapter.

The biggest mistake people make in thinking about their retirement income is they spend too much on other things today instead of saving for tomorrow's retirement. Thus, they procrastinate on when to begin to save for retirement. The smart assumption is to figure that you are going to live! So save. Hope is not a retirement strategy. Doing nothing is not a strategy. And if it were, it is not the best strategy.

Enjoying financial security during 25 years of retirement takes planning and action. But many adults do not make such efforts early enough in life. Two-thirds of workers age 25 to 34 are not saving at all for retirement through their employers. Some might wake up perhaps at age 53 and say, "I want a great retirement life." With such a delayed start, that future "great retirement" life is definitely not going to happen. For most of the pre-retirees who lack a retirement savings plan, the most common reason cited is procrastination. One-third of adults are not willing to sacrifice quality of life spending to save for retirement.

Such people need to learn how to make a budget, pay off credit cards, save, and invest. They also need to create a financial plan because those who have a plan save three times more than those without a plan. Saving for retirement must be budgeted just like any other item—on a par with creating an emergency fund and paying for vehicles and housing. This means you need to adjust your lifestyle to your savings. You only get one shot at retirement, so plan accordingly. This chapter shows how.

17.1 UNDERSTANDING YOUR SOCIAL SECURITY RETIREMENT INCOME BENEFITS

Social Security is the program that fully one-half of younger workers do not believe will be around for them when they retire. Don't worry because it will be! Older people are voters, too, and they will push Congress to keep our Social Security program. In fact, some politicians are arguing that the retirement benefits should be expanded and increased. Easy fixes that both parties support to save Social Security are: increase the wage cap, increase the payroll tax rate, and change the benefit formula.

The Social Security program is the most successful and popular domestic government program in U.S. history. Forty-two million people currently receive Social Security retirement benefits that average $1,300 a month. Thirty-five percent of workers expect that Social Security will be a major source of income in retirement.

Funding for Social Security benefits comes from a compulsory payroll tax split equally between employees and employers. Social Security taxes withheld from wages are called **FICA taxes** (named for the Federal Insurance Contributions Act). The amounts withheld are put into the Social Security trust fund accounts from which benefits are paid to current program recipients by the Social Security Administration (SSA).

FICA taxes

A 6.2 percent tax paid by both the worker and employer on the worker's employment income up to the maximum taxable yearly earnings.

17.1a Your Taxes Pay Social Security and Medicare Benefits

Wage earners pay both FICA and Medicare taxes to the SSA. The FICA tax is paid on wage income up to the **maximum taxable yearly earnings (MTYE)**, which comprises the maximum amount to which the FICA tax is applied. The MTYE figure—$118,500 for the most recent year—is adjusted annually for inflation. The FICA tax rate is 12.4 percent, consisting of 6.2 percent paid by employees and 6.2 percent paid by employers for their workers for a total of 12.4 percent. Self-employed workers pay a FICA tax rate of 12.4 percent, twice that of wage earners, because they are their own employers.

maximum taxable yearly earnings (MTYE)

The maximum amount to which the FICA tax is applied.

Wage earners and their employers also each pay a 1.45 percent **Medicare tax** on all earnings. The MTYE limit does not apply to the Medicare tax. Thus the 1.45 rate applies to all employment income.

Medicare tax

A 1.45 percent tax paid by both the worker and employer on all the worker's employment income.

Most workers pay 7.65 (6.2 + 1.45) percent of their earnings to the SSA. For example, a person earning $60,000 pays a combined FICA and Medicare tax of $4,590 ($60,000 × 0.0765), and a person earning $100,000 pays $7,650 ($100,000 × 0.0765). A person with annual earnings of $150,000 would pay a combined FICA and Medicare tax of $9,522 [($7,347 = 0.062 × $118,500 [the maximum taxable amount]) + ($2,175 = 0.145 × $150,000)].

17.1b It Takes Ten Years to Qualify for Full Social Security Retirement Benefits

The Social Security program covers nine out of every ten U.S. employees. Employees of some state and local governments are exempt and instead are covered by their state government's retirement plan.

To qualify for Social Security retirement, survivors, or disability insurance benefits for you and your family, you must accumulate sufficient credits for employment in any work subject to the FICA taxes. The periods of employment in which you earn credits need not be consecutive. Military service also provides credits.

You earn **Social Security credits** for a certain amount of work covered under Social Security during a calendar year. For example, workers receive one credit if they earned $1,260 (for the most recent year) during any time during the year. You receive a maximum of four credits if you earned $5,040 (4 × $1,260) during the year. The dollar figure required for each credit earned is raised annually to keep pace with inflation. The number of credits you have earned determines your eligibility for retirement benefits and for disability or survivors benefits if you become disabled or die. The SSA recognizes four statuses of eligibility.

Social Security credits

Accumulated quarterly credits to qualify for Social Security benefits obtained by paying FICA taxes.

1. **Fully Insured** Fully insured status requires 40 credits (10 years of work) and provides the worker and his or her family with eligibility for benefits under the retirement, survivors, and disability programs. Once obtained, this status cannot be lost even if the person never works again. Although it is required to receive retirement benefits, "fully insured" status does not imply that the worker will receive the maximum benefits allowable.

2. **Currently Insured** To achieve **currently insured status**, six credits must be earned in the most recent three years. This status provides for some survivors or disability benefits but no retirement benefits. To remain eligible for these

fully insured Social Security status

Requires 40 credits and provides workers and their families with benefits under the retirement, survivors, and disability programs; once status is earned, it cannot be taken away even if the eligible worker never works again.

benefits, a worker must continue to earn at least six credits every three years or meet a minimum number of covered years of work established by the SSA.

3. **Transitionally Insured** **Transitionally insured** status applies only to retired workers who reach the age of 72 without accumulating 40 credits (ten years). These people are eligible for very limited retirement benefits.

4. **Not Insured** Workers younger than age 72 who have fewer than six credits of work experience are **not insured**.

17.1c Obtain an Estimate of Your Social Security Retirement Benefits

Social Security Estimate

Online Information that the Social Security Administration makes available to all workers, which includes earnings history, Social Security taxes paid, and an estimated benefit amount.

The Social Security Administration makes available your **Social Security Estimate** that includes a record of your earnings history, a record of how much you and your various employers paid in Social Security taxes, and an estimate of the benefits that you and your family might be eligible to receive now and in the future. You can verify that information at www.ssa.gov/myaccount. You also may request an estimate of your expected Social Security benefits at www.ssa.gov/retire/estimator.html.

The actual dollar amount of your eventual Social Security retirement benefits will be based on the average of the highest 35 years of earnings during your working years. In these calculations, your actual earnings are first adjusted, or **indexed**, to account for changes in average wages since the year the earnings were received. The SSA then calculates your average monthly indexed earnings during the 35 years in which you earned the most. The agency applies a formula to these earnings to arrive at your **basic retirement benefit** (or **primary insurance amount**). This is the amount you would receive at your **full-benefit retirement age**—currently 67 for those born in 1960 or later.

basic retirement benefit/ primary insurance amount

Amount of Social Security benefits a worker would receive at his or her full-benefit retirement age.

full-benefit retirement age

Age at which a retiree is entitled to full Social Security benefits; 67 for those born in 1960 or later.

Retirement benefits from Social Security currently average $17,200 per year for men and $13,100 for women. This disparity occurs because women often earn lower incomes, move in and out of the work force to raise children as well as to care for elderly parents, and they live longer than men.

Most people have no idea when, where, or how they will retire. This can turn out badly. So, it is smart to give retirement some thought even when you are young. Perhaps get started by realizing that you have three options about when to begin receiving Social Security retirement benefits. The rule of thumb is the later you claim the better because your check will be bigger.

1. Begin Receiving Benefits at Your Full-Benefit Age Once you have reached your full-benefit retirement age, you are eligible to receive your basic monthly retirement benefit. You can begin collecting these benefits even if you continue working full- or part-time. Your level of employment income will not affect your level of benefits, although it may affect the income taxes that you pay on your Social Security benefits and the amount of your Medicare premiums.

2. Begin Receiving Reduced Benefits at a Younger Age You can choose to start receiving retirement benefits as early as age 62, regardless of your full-benefit retirement age. If you do so, however, your basic retirement benefit will be permanently reduced approximately 6 percent for each year you start early. Thus, if your full-benefit retirement age is 67, your benefits could be permanently reduced by as much as 30 percent (5 years × 6 percent). Should you choose to take the earliest Social Security retirement benefits, you will be ahead financially if you do not survive to about age 80. Sixty percent of retirees elect to take their Social Security benefits early.

People considering early Social Security retirement benefits need to be aware that their checks will be further reduced if they have earned income above the annual limit ($15,720 for the most recent year). The reduction is $1 in benefits for every $2 in earnings. A person entitled to $1,000 per month ($12,000 per year) in early retirement benefits who has an earned income of $20,000, for example, will be penalized

DID YOU KNOW ?

More Than Half Will Be Forced to Retire Early

A study by Transamerica Center for Retirement Studies found that many Americans are putting off saving, and instead plan on working more years. Four out of 5 workers age 60 and older expect to be working past the age of 65. Many plan to keep on working part-time even after they retire. More than half of these people are totally wrong about their future plans!

A study by Voya Financial reveals that 6 in 10 workers had to stop working unexpectedly and were forced to retire ahead of their plans. Life does not always go as planned. Retirement oftentimes does not happen the way people had hoped. They retired earlier than expected, mostly due to circumstances beyond their control, often for health reasons, the need to become a relative's care giver, long-term disability, or loss of employment.

Don't be naive and assume your plans will work out fine. The reality is that the odds say you probably will retire earlier than you want, and it won't be by choice. If you, too, are forced to retire earlier than expected, you will have a smaller amount of money built up in your retirement accounts than originally planned and, therefore, less to live on during your retirement years. The lesson here is to save as much and as soon as you can.

$2,140 in benefits on the income above $15,720 ($20,000 − $15,720 = $4,280/2). It is possible to earn enough to completely eliminate your benefits, so the decision to take Social Security benefits early requires careful analysis.*

3. Begin Receiving Larger Benefits at a Later Age You can delay taking benefits beyond your full-benefit retirement age. In such a case, your benefit would be permanently increased by as much as 8 percent per year. Once you reach age 70 the benefit amount will no longer increase so there is no need to delay receiving benefits beyond that age. You can continue to work even after you begin taking these delayed benefits. Again, your level of employment income will not affect your level of benefits, but it may affect the income taxes that you pay on your Social Security benefits and your Medicare premiums.

Twenty percent of all people in the USA die before age 65. If you are among the 80 percent of people who live to reach age 65, you are expected to live even longer. The Social Security Administration says a man reaching age 65 today can expect to live, on average, until age 83 and a woman to age 87. Half of men and women will live that long and half will not. And a 65-year old couple faces a 1 in 4 chance that one of them will live to age 97.

You can compute your own retirement benefit estimate at www.ssa.gov/OACT/anypia/index.html. To determine which option is best for you, you can do the calculations for an early, on-time, or delayed beginning start date. The logic on the best time is offered at the SSA (www.ssa.gov/pubs/EN-05-10147.pdf), MarketWatch (www.marketwatch.com/story/the-best-time-to-start-taking-social-security-2015-01-15), at The Motley Food (www.fool.com/retirement/general/2014/09/21/why-smart-people-take-social-security-benefits-ear.aspx), and the Consumer Financial Protection Bureau's tool at www.consumerfinance.gov/retirement/before-you-claim.

*In the year you reach your full retirement age, you can earn up to $40,080 between January and your birthday without penalty. Above that amount, your Social Security check will be reduced by about 33 cents for every dollar earned. Also, once you reach full retirement age, your benefits may be recalculated to a higher amount to account for your increased earning record.

Learning Objective 2

Calculate the amount you must save for retirement in today's dollars.

17.2 HOW TO CALCULATE THE AMOUNT YOU MUST SAVE FOR RETIREMENT IN TODAY'S DOLLARS

To plan for a financially successful retirement, you first need to set a "retirement saving goal," which is a dollar amount calculated to earn a certain return so it can pay for your retirement expenses throughout life. Otherwise, as one of the most quoted figures in sports, baseball legend Yogi Berra, once said, "If you don't know where you are going, you will end up somewhere else."

Retirement savings goal (retirement nest egg)

Total amount of accumulated savings and investments needed to support a desired retirement lifestyle.

Your **retirement savings goal**, or **retirement nest egg**, is the total amount of accumulated savings and investments needed to support your desired retirement lifestyle. Financial planners often say that people need 80 to 90 percent of their pre-retirement gross income, including Social Security benefits, to meet their expenses in retirement and maintain their lifestyle. Other experts say 70 to 80 percent is enough. This amount—known as the "replacement ratio"—includes what you pay in income taxes. Aon Hewitt recommends 11 times your salary as rule of thumb on how much to save for retirement.

17.2a What Happens If You Don't Save for Retirement?

If you do not save for retirement or do not save enough, there are consequences. You must begin by accepting the fact that how you are living today is not the way you are going to live in retirement. You will be poorer. Then among your lousy choices will be to:

1. Delay your retirement and continue working full-time in your present job;
2. Consider working later into your 70s to push back drawing down your investments and contributing more to build up a larger nest egg;
3. Work part-time for your present employer or in a retail store;
4. Move to a geographic area that has a lower cost of living, such as a state with no state income taxes;
5. Move into a smaller, cheaper home, perhaps in a rural community;
6. Reduce your level of living in retirement, perhaps by eliminating cable television and vacation travels;
7. Work until you are over 80 years of age, in failing health, or until you die.

Alternatively, you could begin now—early in life—to save for a good retirement by investing enough to live on for those 20 to 25 years. You also could gain an extra $2,000 a month in retirement income by getting totally out of debt and paying off your vehicle and home *before* you retire. Yet one-quarter of retirement-age households still have a home mortgage, and it averages $150,000.

Setting a personally meaningful retirement dollar goal helps motivate people to take the necessary saving and investing actions. Then you can avoid the three pitfalls of saving for retirement: (1) starting too late, (2) investing too little, and (3) investing too conservatively. If you begin to save and invest for retirement early during life, the compounding effect on money over time will make it fairly easy for you to reach your retirement savings goal. If you start late, it will be difficult.

17.2b You Really Can Find Money to Start Saving for Retirement

Some people complain that they cannot save for retirement. Well, here comes a question. What if your boss announced that profits are way down, some are being laid off, and employees like you are given a choice: "You can lose your job completely or take a 10 percent pay cut." Most of us would take the pay cut and continue working. And we would have no choice except to cut back 10 percent in our current spending plan. The logic is much the same for those who do not save for retirement. Make the decision, and then do it! Find the 10 percent in your current spending and save it for retirement!

17.2c How to Find the Money to Save

There are a number of ways to find money to save for retirement:

- Pay yourself first by making it the first expenditure out of every paycheck
- Write a check to yourself when paying your bills and deposit it into an account
- Arrange to have an automatic payroll-deduction savings amount directly withheld from your paycheck and go to an account
- Save half or more of an annual bonus, income tax refund, and any cash gifts received
- After a credit contract is paid off, continue making the same "payments" to your retirement savings account
- Saving one-half of an annual pay raise every year will add $200,000+ to your retirement account balance by age 65.
- Try not spending any money for one month a year and deposit the extra money into savings
- Work overtime or get a part-time job to save the net income
- Smile knowing you are making good progress in your savings program

17.2d Projecting Your Annual Retirement Expenses and Income

"How large a retirement nest egg do I need?" To calculate this amount, you can fill out the Run the Numbers worksheet, "Estimating Your Retirement Savings Goal in Today's Dollars" (page 528). Each spouse in a married couple should prepare a worksheet rather than combine income and savings amounts.

17.2e An Illustration of Retirement Needs

Consider the case of Erik McKartmann, aged 35 and single, who has been the manager of a weight loss and fitness center in South Park, Colorado for 5 years. Erik currently earns $80,000 per year. Last year his employer dropped their defined-benefit retirement plan and put in a defined-contribution 401(k) plan that matches employee contributions up to a maximum of 6 percent of salary at a rate of ½ of 1 percent for every percent Eric contributes. Eric invests $400 per month, or $4,800 annually ($400 × 12 or 6 percent of his salary) plus the addition $200 per month contributed by his employer, into his 401(k) plan, which now has a balance of $7,200. He also has $16,000 in a Roth IRA account he set up some years ago before beginning his current job. Erik hopes to retire at age 62. These numbers are shown on page 528.

1. Erik has chosen not to develop a retirement budget at this time. Instead, he simply multiplied his current salary by 80 percent to arrive at an estimate of the annual income (in current dollars) needed in retirement of $64,000 ($80,000 × 0.80). This amount was

COMMON SENSE
Start Early and Save a Little for Retirement

The old adage is, "Starting behind often means never catching up." Even if you cannot afford to contribute up to the full company match, start saving early perhaps just a small portion of your salary—say, 1 or 2 percent—it's a good start. Just be sure to increase the rate later.

COMMON SENSE
Verify Online the Accuracy of Your Social Security Statement

You have only three years to correct any errors in your Social Security Statement. You should make sure that the SSA's records are up to date and accurate by checking them online. Open an account at the Social Security Administration at www.ssa.gov/myaccount/ and check your statement.

DO IT IN CLASS

entered on line 1 of the worksheet. If Erik wants to increase the amount of dollars to support a higher retirement lifestyle, he can simply increase the percentage in the calculation.

2. Erik checked the Social Security Administration to estimate his benefits in today's dollars. At age 62, he could expect a monthly benefit of $1,600 (in current dollars). Multiplying by 12 gave an expected annual Social Security benefit of $19,200 (in current dollars), which Erik entered on line 2 of the worksheet. (If Erik waited until later to retire, his Social Security benefit would be higher.)

3. Line 3 of the worksheet, which calls for Erik's expected pension benefit, is appropriate for his old defined-benefit retirement plan. After discussing his expected employer pension with the benefits counselor at work, Erik found that his anticipated benefit under the now discontinued retirement plan would amount to approximately $5,800 annually, assuming that he remained with the company until his retirement, so he entered that figure on line 3.

4. Erik adds lines 2 and 3 to determine his total estimated retirement income from Social Security and his employer pension. The amount on line 4 would be $25,000 ($19,200 + $5,800).

5. Subtracting line 4 from line 1 reveals that Erik would need an additional income of $39,000 ($64,000 − $25,000) in today's dollars from savings and investments to meet his annual retirement income needs. All this seems impossible to Erik, but he is willing to continue doing the math.

6. At this point, Erik has considered only his annual needs and benefits. Because he plans to retire at age 62, Erik will need income for 20 years based on his life expectancy. (Of course, Erik could live well into his 80s or 90s, which would mean that he would need to save even more.) Using Appendix A-4 and assuming a return that is 3 percent above the inflation rate, Erik finds the multiplier 14.8775 where 3 percent and 20 years intersect. He then calculates that he needs an additional amount of $580,223 (14.8775 × $39,000) at retirement. That's a big number! And it is in current dollars. The number does not dissuade Erik from saving because he is not nervous. He knows he has plenty of time and the magic of compounding on his side.

DID YOU KNOW ?

Not Saving for Retirement Is Fear Based

Saving for retirement is emotionally difficult for individuals. Many view it as a "loss," and investors fear losses. It is a bit upsetting to give up a dollar you have in hand and save it instead. Spending is reduced because when one is saving the money it hurts. The pain from that loss impacts our perceptions because the long-term benefits of saving for retirement will not be experienced for many, many years.

ADVICE FROM A SEASONED PRO

Buy Your Retirement on the Layaway Plan

The large retirement savings goal dollar amount scares some people. To allay such concerns, the following novel approach to thinking about retirement saving has been suggested. You can look at your retirement as something you "buy." The "retail price" is the retirement nest egg goal itself. From that amount, you can subtract "discounts" for anticipated income from Social Security, employer-sponsored retirement accounts, personal retirement accounts, and any other funds you expect to have accumulated. Then you identify the difference—the shortfall indicated on line 9 of the Run the Numbers worksheet—and buy it on a "layaway plan." The additional amounts you periodically save and invest are, therefore, the "layaway payments" with which you "buy" your retirement. This is smart thinking!

Dennis R. Ackley
Ackley & Associates, Kansas City, Missouri

7. Erik's current savings and investments can be used to offset part of the $580,223 he will need for retirement. Erik has $7,200 invested in his employer's 401(k) account (his $4,800 plus the employer match of $2,400) plus, $16,000 in his Roth IRA account, and $9,000 in aggressive growth stock mutual funds. These amounts are totaled ($32,200) and recorded on line 7E.

8. If left untouched, the $32,200 that Erik has built up will continue to earn interest, dividends, and capital gains until he retires. Because he has 27 more years until retirement, Erik can use Appendix A-1 and, assuming a growth rate of 3 percent over 27 years, find the factor 2.2213 and multiply it by the total amount in line 7. Erik's $32,200 should have a future value of $71,526 at his retirement, so he puts this amount on line 8.

9. Subtracting line 8 from line 6 reveals that Erik's retirement nest egg will need an additional $508,697 ($580,223 − $71,526) at the time of retirement, so he puts this number on line 9.

10. Using Appendix A-3 and a growth rate of 3 percent over 27 years, Erik finds a factor of 40.7096. When divided into $508,697, it reveals that he needs savings and investments of $12,496 per year until retirement, so he puts that number on line 10.

11. Erik records his current 401(k) savings and investments of $7,200 (his $4,800 plus employer's $2,400) per year on line 11.

12. Erik subtracts line 11 from line 10 to determine the additional amount of annual savings that he should set aside in today's dollars to achieve his retirement goal. His shortfall totals $5,296 per year. By saving an extra $441 each month ($5,296 ÷ 12), he can reach his retirement goal established in step 1.

17.2f Suggestions for Funding Erik's Retirement Goal

Erik needs to continue what he is doing—saving and investing—plus save a little more so he can enjoy his lifestyle when his full-time working career ends. Erik should discuss with his benefits counselor how much he can save and invest more via the company's 401(k) program.

Since Eric is allowed to contribute up to a maximum of 8 percent of his salary to the 401(k) plan $6,400 ($80,000 × 0.08), he could bump up his contribution to the workplace program by $1,600 ($6,400 − $4,800). However, this would still leave him short of the additional savings he needs to make. He would need to invest the additional needed savings, or the whole $5,296 shortfall, into a private retirement account, such as an IRA. To create an extra margin of safety Eric could save even more of his salary.

One of the reasons Erik needs to save more is that he plans to retire early at age 62. If he were instead to plan to retire at age 67 (his full-benefit Social Security retirement age), his Social Security benefit would be 30 percent higher ($5,760 more per year) and his retirement nest egg would have 5 more years to grow. He would be wealthy. This is a decision Erik can defer until he gets older. If he is in good health at age 62, he can consider waiting to retire.

Understanding your Social Security and employer-based retirement benefits is a first step in retirement planning.

CONCEPT CHECK 17.2

1. List the steps in the process of estimating your retirement savings goal in today's dollars.

2. In the text example, what can Erik do to save more for his retirement?

RUN THE NUMBERS

Estimating Your Retirement Savings Goal in Today's Dollars

This worksheet will help you calculate the amount you need to set aside each year in today's dollars so that you will have adequate funds for your retirement. The example here assumes that a single person is now 35 years old, hopes to retire at age 62, has a current income of $80,000, currently saves and invests about $4,800 per year to an IRA account, contributes zero to an employer-sponsored retirement plan, anticipates needing a retirement income of $64,000

per year assuming a spending lifestyle at 80 percent of current income ($80,000 × 0.80), and will live an additional 20 years beyond retirement. Investment returns are assumed to be 3 percent after inflation—a reasonable but conservative estimate for a typical portfolio. The financial needs would differ if the growth rate of the investments were less than 3 percent. This approach simplifies the calculations and puts the numbers to estimate retirement needs into today's dollars. The amount saved must be higher if substantial inflation occurs.

		Example	Your Numbers
1.	Annual income needed at retirement in today's dollars (Use carefully estimated numbers or a certain percentage, such as 70% or 80%.)	$ 64,000	_____
2.	Estimated Social Security retirement benefit in today's dollars	$ 19,200	_____
3.	Estimated employer pension benefit in today's dollars (Ask your retirement benefit advisor to make an estimate of your future pension, assuming that you remain in the same job at the same salary, or make your own conservative estimate.)	$ 5,800	_____
4.	Total estimated retirement income from Social Security and employer pension in today's dollars (line 2 þ line 3)	$ 25,000	_____
5.	Additional income needed at retirement in today's dollars (line 1–line 4)	$ 39,000	_____
6.	Amount you must have at retirement in today's dollars to receive additional annual income in retirement (line 5) for 20 years (from Appendix A-4, assuming a 3% return over 20 years, or 14.8775 × $21,000)	$580,223	_____
7.	Amount already available as savings and investments in today's dollars (add lines 7A through 7D, and record the total on line 7E)		
	A. Employer savings plans, such as a 401(k), SEP-IRA, or profit-sharing plan	$ 7,200	_____
	B. IRAs and Keoghs	$ 16,000	
	C. Other investments, such as mutual funds, stocks, bonds, real estate, and other assets available for retirement	$ 9,000	
	D. If you wish to include a portion of the equity in your home as savings, enter its present value minus the cost of another home in retirement	0	
	E. Total retirement savings (add lines A through D)	$ 32,200	
8.	Future value of current savings/investments at time of retirement (using Appendix A-1 and a growth rate of 3% over 27 years, the factor is 2.2213; thus, 2.2213 × $37,000)	$ 71,526	_____
9.	Additional retirement savings and investments needed at time of retirement (line 6–line 8)	$508,697	_____
10.	Annual savings needed (to reach amount in line 9) before retirement (using Appendix A-3 and a growth rate of 3% over 27 years, the factor is 40.7096; thus, $230,239/40.7096)	$ 12,496	_____
11.	Current annual contribution to savings and investment plans	$ 7,200	_____
12.	Additional amount of annual savings that you need to set aside in today's dollars to achieve retirement goal (in line 1) (line 10–line 11)	$ 5,296	_____

17.3 INVEST THROUGH EMPLOYER-SPONSORED RETIREMENT PLANS

Learning Objective 3

Distinguish among the types of employer-sponsored tax-sheltered retirement plans.

Recall that the funds you put into regular investment accounts represent **after-tax money**. Assume, for example, that Pam Knight of Lancaster, California, who is in the 25 percent tax bracket, earns an extra $1,000 and is thinking about investing those funds. She first will pay $250 in income taxes on the extra income, which leaves only $750 in after-tax money available to invest. Furthermore, the yearly earnings from the invested funds are also subject to income taxes each year as they are accrued, also at a tax rate of 25 percent.

Saving for retirement this way is not ideal when saving and investing for retirement. Paying income taxes on your investments annually leaves too little money for growth. To remedy this, years ago the government created policies that help nudge people to save and invest for their retirements in tax-sheltered accounts. Employers sponsor retirement plans are an example. Employers provide voluntary retirement plans as an employee benefit to be competitive with other employers. If two similar employers are both offering you a job and one does not offer a retirement plan, you will not unwisely choose to accept employment there. Why? Because you want to retire one day and having some money then is a good idea.

after-tax money
Funds put into regular investment accounts after paying income taxes.

17.3a How Tax-Sheltered Retirement Accounts Work

You and the various employers who employ you over your lifetime may voluntarily set up tax-sheltered retirement plans. The intention is that the money in these accounts can provide returns for you to use during your years in retirement.

A **tax-sheltered retirement account** is a retirement plan under U.S. law that is generally not taxed, provided certain conditions are met. IRA law allows a tax reduction on a limited amount of contributed saving for retirement.

Therefore, the contributions may be "deductible" from your taxable income in the year they are made. Here you pay zero taxes on the contributed amount of income in the current year. This means that you are investing with **pretax money**, and the salary amount you defer, or contribute, to a tax-sheltered retirement account comes out of your earnings before income taxes are calculated. Thus, you gain an immediate elimination of part of your income tax liability for the current year.

In addition, income earned on funds in tax-sheltered retirement accounts accumulates **tax deferred**. In other words, the individual does not have to pay income taxes on the earnings (interest, dividends, and capital gains) every year as the money accrues as long as the funds are reinvested within the retirement account. Contributors to tax-deferred accounts often assume that they will be in a lower tax bracket when retired and making withdrawals, but this logic is not crucial to investing for the future.

Contributing to a tax-sheltered retirement plan does reduce your tax-home pay. That's the "bad" news. However, it also provides "good" news because the contributions: (1) reduce your income taxes, and (2) the invested dollars grow much faster than money in a pre-tax investment. The result is a much larger balance of invested dollars over time. Another advantage of some tax-sheltered retirement accounts is a **tax-free withdrawal**. Here one may remove assets from an account with no taxes assessed. Zero.

Having a 401(k) plan available the workplace makes a big difference in retirement savings. A Voya study found that people who started saving from the first day on the job with access to a 401(k) were found to have a median savings amount of $200,000 compared to just $50,000 for consistent savers without a plan. The lesson here is to get into a systematic plan to save and invest within a tax-sheltered retirement plan where you just get on the path of investing and the sooner the better.

tax-sheltered retirement accounts
Retirement account for which all earnings from the invested funds are not subject to income taxes.

pretax money
Investing before income taxes are calculated, thus gaining an immediate elimination of part of your income tax liability for the current year.

tax deferred
The individual does not have to pay current income taxes on the earnings (interest, dividends, and capital gains) reinvested in a retirement account.

tax-free withdrawals
Removal of assets from a retirement account with no taxes assessed.

17.3b Employer-Sponsored Retirement Plans Are Government Regulated

An **employer-sponsored retirement plan** is an IRS-approved tax-sheltered retirement plan offered by an employer. These are called **qualified plans**, meaning that they qualify for special tax treatment under regulations of the

employer-sponsored retirement plan
An IRS-approved retirement plan offered by an employer (also called qualified plans).

Employee Retirement Income Security Act (ERISA)

Regulates employer-sponsored plans by calling for proper plan reporting and disclosure to participants in defined-contribution, defined-benefit, and cash-balance plans.

Employer Retirement Income Security Act (ERISA). They are also known as **salary-reduction plans** because the contributed income is not included in an employee's salary. In effect, the contributions to an employer-sponsored retirement plan are an interest-free loan from the government to help you fund your retirement.

ERISA does not require companies to offer retirement plans, but it does regulate those plans that are provided. ERISA calls for proper plan reporting and disclosure to participants. The U.S. Supreme Court held that the ERISA law requires retirement plan sponsors to be legally responsible to continuously monitor investments in their retirement savings plan and, if necessary, remove imprudent investments. Now you may sue if your employer does not offer low-fee mutual funds as an investment choice. Participating in a retirement plan, such as a 401(k), can serve as the cornerstone of your retirement planning.

Beneficiary Designation and Account Trustee When you open a retirement account, you must sign a **beneficiary designation form**. This document contractually determines who will inherit the funds in that retirement account in case you die before the funds are distributed. This designation contractually overrides any provisions in a will.

A special rule applies to 401(k) plans and other qualified retirement plans governed by the ERISA federal law. Your legal spouse is entitled to inherit all the money in the account unless he or she signs a written waiver, consenting to your choice of another beneficiary. It is not enough just to name someone else on the beneficiary form that your employer provides you.

The contributions into an employee's retirement account are deposited with a **trustee** (usually a financial institution, bank, or trust company that has fiduciary responsibility for holding certain assets in the best interest of the client), which according to the employee's instructions invests the money in various securities, including mutual funds, and sometimes the stock of an employer. Each employee's funds are managed in a separate account.

Mistakes to Avoid in Beneficiary Designation Some people make mistakes when choosing the beneficiary on their retirement plan. Singles often list their mothers as the beneficiary, and then fail to change it to their spouse when they marry. Oops! Don't die or the mom may keep all the money. Others keep their first spouse as beneficiary even after they divorce or remarry. Perhaps equally unwise.

Vesting The worker always has a legal right to own the amount of money he or she contributes to his or her account in the employer's plan. The employee determines how the funds are to be invested and withdrawn. Vesting is the process by which employees accrue non-forfeitable rights over their employer's contributions that are made to the employee's qualified retirement plan account. Some employers permit immediate vesting, or ownership, although most employers delay the vesting of their contributions to the employee for three to five years.

vesting

Ensures that a retirement plan participant has the right to take full possession of all employer contributions and earnings.

According to ERISA, the employer can require that the worker must work with the company for three years before vesting begins or he or she will lose any employer contributed money. Employers sometimes permit no vesting for the first two years and then one is fully vested after the third year. This is known as **cliff vesting**. Or it can choose to have the 20 percent of the contributions vest each year over five years, known as graduated vesting.

graduated vesting

Schedule under which employees must be at least 20 percent vested after two years of service and gain an additional 20 percent of vesting for each subsequent year until, at the end of year six, the account is fully vested.

If an employee has not worked long enough for the employer to be vested before leaving his or her job, the employer's contributions are forfeited back to the employer's plan. The employee has no rights to any of those funds until vested.

There are three common types of employer-sponsored retirement plans: (1) defined-contribution, (2) defined-benefit, and (3) cash-balance.

17.3c Type 1: Defined-Contribution Retirement Plans Are Most Common Today

Yesterday's "defined benefit" pensions of baby boomer's parents (discussed in the following section) have been largely replaced by the increasingly popular "defined contribution" retirement plans. The switch over from a pension plan simplified the

COMMON SENSE
Relying on a Voluntary Retirement Program Has Been a Failure

The employer-sponsored voluntary 401(k) retirement program seems to have been designed to fail and it has. Financial experts agree. As a result, we are facing a looming retirement crisis, with tens of millions of Americans facing a sharp decline in living standards at the end of their working lives. Many will choose to work until they cannot continue or until they die. Just as a voluntary Social Security system would have been a disaster, relying on today's do-it-yourself, voluntary 401(k)/IRA retirement savings system has been a failure for the American society.

   This does not have to be you! Start early to save and invest for retirement, invest every payday, and as your income goes up always increase the amount you invest. Then you will retire with plenty of money for your remaining years of living life well.

balance sheets of employers, but requires employees to figure out whether or not to invest, if yes how much to save, where to invest, how to invest, and how to make lump-sum payouts last throughout retirement without running out of money. The responsibilities of today's defined-contribution retirement plans are challenging!

A **defined-contribution retirement plan** voluntarily offered by an employer is designed to provide a retiring employee a lump sum at retirement. This is the most popular retirement plan today. It is distinguished by its "contributions"—that is, the total amount of money put into each participating employee's individual account. The eventual retirement benefit in such a plan consists solely of assets (including investment earnings) that have accumulated in the account.

Contributory and Noncontributory Plans In a **noncontributory plan**, money to fund the retirement plan is contributed only by the employer. In a **contributory plan**, money to fund the plan is provided by both the employer and the participant or solely by the employee. Most plans are contributory.

Get the Employer's Match In a contributory plan the employer may choose to make a **matching contribution** that may fully or partially match (up to a certain limit) the employee's contribution to his or her employer-sponsored retirement account. The matching contribution may be up to a certain dollar amount or a certain percentage of compensation. For example, the match might be $1.00 for every $1.00 the employee contributes up to the first 3 percent of pay. More common is $0.50 per $1.00 up to the first 6 percent of pay. Better employers contribute $1 for every $1 you contribute up to 6 or 8 percent. Workers in their 50s and 60s contribute an average of 8 percent to these plans; those over age 65 contribute 10 percent.

The employer contributions effectively increase your income without increasing your tax liability because you pay no income taxes on matching contributions until they are withdrawn during retirement. Therefore, never turn down free money your employer may put into your retirement plan. Amazingly, 30 percent of employees do not take full advantage of their employer's 401(k) plan match.

When your employer makes a contribution to your account every time you do, you in effect obtain an "instant return" on your retirement savings. Saving $4,000 a year with a $0.50 employer match immediately puts $2,000 more into your retirement account, giving you a **50 percent return** ($2,000/$4,000). This concept is illustrated in Table 17-1, arguing strongly that you should work only for employers whose policy is to offer healthy matching retirement contributions.

defined-contribution retirement plan
A defined-contribution retirement plan is a retirement plan in which a certain amount or percentage of money is set aside each year by a company for the benefit of each of its employees

contributory plan
The most common type of employee-sponsored defined-contribution retirement plan; accepts employee as well as employer contributions.

matching contribution
Employer benefit that offers a full or partial matching contribution to a participating employee's account in proportion to each dollar of contributions made by the participant.

DID YOU KNOW

Save 12 to 15 Percent for Retirement Including Employer Contributions

People who start saving and investing for retirement during their 20s should aim to reserve 12 to 15 percent of their pretax income every year, *including* employer contributions, for this purpose. Those who have delayed planning for retirement until their late 30s or 40s should begin investing 20 to 25 percent annually in an effort to catch up. They have no choice.

Table 17-1 Only Work for Companies Offering a Healthy Match

You should avoid working for an employer that does not offer a 401(k) retirement program with a policy of contributing a healthy match because you will lose big. At retirement the data in the table show which would you rather have after 30 years earning 8 percent? $317,000, $476,000, $634,000, or $952,000. Get a big match!

Salary $70,000	Zero Employee Contribution	100% Match of 2% of Salary	100% Match of 4% of Salary	100% Match of 6% of Salary
Employee contributions	$2,800	$2,800	$2,800	$4,200
Employer contributions	$0	$1,400	$2,800	$4,200
Total annual contributions	$2,800	$4,200	$5,600	$8,400
Account balance after 30 years earning 8%	$317,000	$476,000	$634,000	$952,000

automatic escalation

An employment clause that allows employees to save more for retirement by agreeing to raise their contribution amounts each year.

self-directed

In defined-contribution plans, employees control the assets in their account—how often to make contributions to the account, how much to contribute, how much risk to take, and how to invest.

Employers sometimes reduce or eliminate their matching contributions to retirement plans during times of poor profits. That also is when employees often leave for other employment opportunities. Some employers make their contributions in lump-sum payments to employees' accounts, at the end of the year rather than at the time of each paycheck As a result, their employees miss out on compounding for 12 months and those who leave during the year never receive the funds.

Automatic Enrollment and Automatic Escalation Many employers offer **automatic enrollment**, which is a powerful tool to combat non-participation in retirement plans. Automatic enrollment allows an employer to "enroll" all eligible employees in the employer's plan. Thus workers in these plans automatically begin contributing part of their compensation to their retirement account at the default rate unless they actively choose a different rate (or opt-out completely). The employees' contributions are invested into a fund chosen by the plan sponsor, usually a target-date fund, which is a mutual fund that automatically adjusts toward more conservative investments as the owner approaches retirement age.

Automatic enrollment helps employees deal with nonstop family, health, and life events, and changing financial obligations over the course of one's life. Saving for retirement can easily slip to the bottom of the priority list. If you don't fund your retirement properly, such inaction will seal your fate. Automatic enrollment helps, but smart people need to boost their rate of savings as soon as they can with the goal of getting beyond 10 percent, including employer contributions.

Automatic escalation also can help employees save more for retirement. Such a program automatically increases the employee contribution amounts each year, often by 1 or 2 percent, unless the employee chooses a different amount. This addresses inflation and cost of living increases. It also helps plan participants increase their retirement contributions while not getting distracted by other matters.

Self-Directed Defined-contribution retirement plans are described as **self-directed** because the employee controls where the assets in his or her account are invested. The individual typically selects where to invest, how much risk to take, how much to invest, how often contributions are made to the account, as well as when to buy and sell.

Over time, the balance amassed in such an account consists of the contributions plus any investment income and gains, minus expenses and losses. The contributions devoted to the account are specified ("defined"). The future amount in the account at retirement will not be known until the individual decides to begin making withdrawals. This uncertainty occurs because the sum available to the retiree depends in part on the success of

DID YOU KNOW ?

Save the Match But Even More

Many people save in their employer's retirement plan only up to the amount of the employer's match. Wrong! Financial writer David Bach reminds us that the match is "icing on the cake." You still need to bake the cake by maximizing your contributions because all your money grows, compounded and tax-deferred. So, contribute more than needed for the match, right up to the maximum amount allowed.

the investments made. At retirement, the retiree thus has a lump sum to manage and spend down during the rest of his or her lifetime.

Risks of Investing Through Defined Contribution Retirement Plans

Defined contribution retirement plans are not without risks. In fact, they are considerable because you must decide how much to save, how to invest, and how much to withdraw in retirement so you do not run out of money. And you do not know what the stock markets will do over the next 30 or 40 years. This is an extremely challenging task for novice investors.

The Returns Earned by Typical 401(k) Investors Are Terrible

A Dalbar study reveals that the unmanaged S&P 500 index for two decades earned an average annual return of 9.85 percent. However, the average stock mutual fund investor earned only 5.19 percent, or 4.66 percentage points less than the index.

Viewed in isolation the differences in numbers may seem small. But when they occur year after year the results are devastating. Lousy returns truly translate into life-changing disparities.

Over 40 years a $10,000 investment earning 9.85 percent, with compounding, would grow to over $428,000. This compares to the same $10,000 investment earning 5.19 percent that totals only $75,000 after 40 years. Talk about staggering underperformance!

Why do individual investors do so terribly? Emotions sabotage their efforts. People buy when the stock prices are near the top of the market and sell out at market lows, when they get scared. They also invest in underperforming funds and they trade too much.

When investing for retirement be certain to relentlessly follow your long-term strategy by focusing on the far horizon, and sticking with a simple and cheap investment strategy. Buy to hold in index or target-date mutual funds. And totally avoid any emotional decisions to pull your money in and out of these funds as the market fluctuates over the years.

Names of Defined-Contribution Plans

Several types of employer-sponsored defined-contribution plans exist. These include the 401(k), 403(b), and 457 plans (named after sections of the IRS tax code) and the SIMPLE IRA and SIMPLE 401(k). Each plan is restricted to a specific group of workers. You may contribute to these plans only if your employer offers them.

The **401(k) plan** is the best-known defined-contribution plan. It is designed for employees of private corporations. You can compare the performance and expenses of your employer's 401(k) plan with others at BrightScope (www.brightscope.com). Eligible

BIAS TOWARD INERTIA IN RETIREMENT DECISIONS

People have a bias toward inertia—doing nothing—in retirement planning. Once an employee selects a 401(k) retirement plan contribution rate, such as 3 percent, many never increase it. What to do? You should regularly ratchet up your savings contribution, perhaps when you get a raise each year, and rebalance annually.

401(k) plan
Defined-contribution plan designed for employees of private corporations.

DID YOU KNOW ?

Invest Retirement Money Only in Low-Cost Choices to Earn 42 Percent More

Investing for retirement in low-cost or ultra-low-cost funds, such as an index fund or exchange-traded fund (ETF), is the single most effective strategy to fatten your retirement nest egg. Assume you are 30 years old, earn $60,000, and invest 6 percent of your salary with a $0.50 employer match for every $1.00 you contribute. Your salary increases 3 percent annually, and your investments earn 8 percent a year for 35 years. Ultra-low mutual fund expenses dramatically increase your retirement nest egg: over 42 percent

(0.4257) more in this example ($1,325,300 − $929,600 = $395,700/$929,600).

Cost of Mutual Fund Expenses	Retirement Nest Egg at Age 65
High expenses (2%)	$ 929,600
Moderate expenses (1.0%)	$1,135,800
Low expenses (0.5%)	$1,258,400
Ultra-low expenses (0.25%)	$1,325,300

DID YOU KNOW ?

Predatory Financial Advisors Exist

The government needs to do more to protect investors from predatory advisors. Government has proposed that all retirement plan advisors and salespeople be fiduciaries, which means they always would be required to act in the best interest of employee investors. This would eliminate guiding employee investors to higher-fee products.

Various studies have shown the ill effects of investment costs on portfolio balances. At retirement one's assets become a target for advisors who view it as a pool of money he or she can earn a commission on.

It is disgusting when an ugly thing happens after one exits a job, and rolls over his or her 401(k) balance into an individual retirement account. If an account earning 4¼ percent is compared to one earning 4 percent, the ¼ of 1 percent extra on a $100,000 investment—which is a kickback going to an advisor—results in not having $40,000 to spend during 20 years of one's retirement. That is a balance

of $170,000 accruing at 4 percent compared to $210,000 accruing at 4¼ percent. That portfolio that should be 23 percent larger!

Because of lax long-time government rules about advising retirement investors, these awful returns really matter. Paying an extra 1 percent in annual 401(k) expenses could reduce your nest egg by about one-third come retirement. These things would not happen if advisors who counsel people on whether and how to roll over a 401(k) when leaving a job or retiring were required to be fiduciaries.

Rolling over a large amount of money into an IRA account is one of the most consequential decisions anyone can make and Congress needs to protect investors from those offering self-dealing advice on retirement accounts as well as all investment accounts. You should avoid any financial advisors who do not subscribe to a fiduciary standard.

employees of nonprofit organizations (colleges, hospitals, religious organizations, and some other not-for-profit institutions) may contribute to a **403(b) plan** that has the same contribution limits. Employees of state and local governments and non–church controlled tax-exempt organizations may contribute to **457 plans**; only employees (not employers) make contributions to 457 plans. An employer offering 401(k), 403(b), and 457 plans may also offer Roth versions of these plans calling for after-tax (rather than tax-deferred) contributions but with provisions for tax-free withdrawals during retirement.

When the employing organization has 100 or fewer employees, it may set up a **Savings Incentive Match Plan for Employees IRA (SIMPLE IRA)**. Employers with 25 or fewer employees can offer a **Salary Reduction Simplified Employee Pension Plan (SARSEP)** plan similar to a 401(k) plan. Regulations vary somewhat for each type of plan.

ADVICE FROM A SEASONED PRO

Save for Your Kid's College Education or Your Retirement?

Resist the urge to put your kid's education ahead of saving to finance your retirement years. Half of parents say that rather than have their students take out loans, they prefer to tap their retirement savings. While we want to help our children as much as possible, sometimes it is the wrong thing to do. Your children can borrow to pay for their education, but you cannot borrow to pay for your retirement.

Years ago college was not that expensive and company pensions largely supported former workers. Times have changed on both concerns. Don't be a burden on your children from a financial perspective. Securing your future should be your first priority. That said, if your retirement is secure, an education may be the best gift you ever give your child.

Robert Reagan
Western Dakota Tech, Rapid City, South Dakota

ADVICE FROM A SEASONED PRO

Stable-Value Funds Are Available Only through Employers

Stable-value funds are only available through employer-sponsored retirement plans. They offer attractive returns and liquidity without market risk to defined contribution plan participants (and some "529 tuition-savings plans") because they have contracts with banks and insurance companies designed to permit redemption of shares at book value regardless of market prices. Over the past ten years, stable-value funds returned 3.0 to 5.0 percent annually.

Stable-value funds invest in high-quality, intermediate-term bond funds, including **guaranteed investment contracts (GICs)** offered by insurance companies. A GIC guarantees the owner a fixed or floating interest rate for a predetermined period of time, and the return of principal is guaranteed. The closest thing to a stable value fund in which you can invest privately is a balanced mutual fund.

Dana Wolff
Southeast Technical Institute, Sioux Falls, South Dakota

Limits on Contributions There are limits on the maximum amount of income per year that an employee may contribute to an employer-sponsored plan. The maximum contribution limit to 401(k), 403(b), 457, and Thrift Savings Plan is $18,000. The limit on a SIMPLE IRA is $12,500.

Catch-Up Provision A **catch-up provision** permits workers age 50 or older to contribute an additional $6,000 to most employer-sponsored plans ($2,500 for SIMPLE). Millions of people who are getting a late start on saving can put more money away for retirement.

DID YOU KNOW

Fees Look Like a Nibble But They Sting Like a Bee

So, you think a 1 percent fee on an investment account is nothing, huh? Wrong! It will kill your investment returns. It will take a whopping 30 percent off the total nest egg you were planning on using to live on during retirement. Look below to see the retirement industry's dirty little secret that supports their lifestyles so well. It is scandalous.

A median-income, two-earner household will pay nearly $155,000 over the course of their lifetime in 401(k) fees, according to an analysis by Demos, a public policy organization. Their study, *Retirement Savings Drain: The Hidden and Excessive Costs of 401(k)s,* details how savers are vulnerable to losing about one-third of their investment returns to inefficient stock and bond markets.

Many working employees are not aware that their employer's 401(k) retirement plan charges them fees for recordkeeping, administrative services, and trading and transaction costs. All employers assess fees that are deducted each year from each account before employees see their net returns. According to the Investment Company Institute the average is 0.72 percent for bond mutual funds

and 0.95 percent for stock mutual funds. That amounts to $72 to $95 in fees on every $10,000 of your 401(k) balance every year! Small employers' 401(k) fees average 1.33 percent compared to 0.15 percent for large employers.

High fees can reduce one's ending total 401(k) balance by a minimum of 15 to 20 percent. That cuts $150,000 to $200,000 from an expected balance of $1,000,000, which over the years reduces your account to $800,000 to $850,000. If this fee issue impacts you, contact your employer's human resource department to find out how much in fees you pay each year, what the fees pay for, and what it will take to get them reduced.

All investors are similarly challenged. If you start with $10,000 and invest $500 a month for 30 years into a low-fee index fund charging only 0.2 percent annually and it grows at 8 percent each year, your account will total $818,000. If the fund charges a moderate 1.2 percent, your account total will reach $663,000. That's $155,000 less money because 23 percent of the total went to fees!

portability

Upon termination of employment, employees with portable benefits can keep their savings in tax-sheltered accounts, transferring retirement funds from employer's account directly to another account without penalty.

Portability   An added benefit of employer-sponsored plans is portability. **Portability** means that upon termination of employment, an employee can transfer the retirement funds, when done according to certain rules, from the employer's account to another tax-sheltered account without taxes or penalty.

DOL's Lifetime Income Calculator   The Department of Labor (DOL) is considering proposing a rule that pension benefit statements include the participant's account balance as a single sum as well as an estimated lifetime income stream of level payments using both the participant's current account balance and the projected account balance at retirement. For married participants, the statement must include joint and survivor lifetime income payments. See the DOL's "Lifetime Income Calculator" (www.dol.gov/ebsa/regs/lifetimeincomecalculator.html).

Contribute to a 401(k) Retirement Plan to Create a $2 or $3 Million Portfolio   Here is an example of how to create a million dollars or more portfolio by contributing to an employer's retirement plan. Samantha Smarty participates in her employer's 401(k) retirement plan, and contributes just 7 percent of her gross income. She gets a 50 percent match from her employer. Thus she contributes $6,580 of her $94,000 gross income ($94,000 × 0.07). The match is $3,290, for a total of $9,870 ($6,580 + $3,290) going into her 401(k) retirement plan this year. See Table 17-2 for details.

Since her contributions are tax deductible, this reduces her federal income tax liability by $1,645 ($12,042 − $10,397) and her state tax liability by $263 ($3,280 − $3,017). This reduces her take-home pay only $389 a month ($6,556 − $6,167).

Samantha contributes $548 a month ($6,580/12) but her 401(k) retirement plan grows $822 every month ($6,580 + $3,290 = $9,870/12), so she is already ahead $274 every month ($822 − $548). Thus, Samantha earns a 50 percent return ($274/$548) on her first year's "investment." And that's before her investments earn a dime in return for the year. Whoa! What a great deal!

Note that these figures are based on the assumption that she never gets a raise and never increases her contribution amount. In real life that's not going to happen because raises and increasing contributions are sure to follow for Samantha. Assuming her account earns an 8 percent return, Samantha Smarty's balance after 30 years will reach $1.225 million. If she gets any pay raises in life and/or contributes more, her portfolio could easily reach $2 to $3 million over 30 years.

Table 17-2   **Samantha Pays About $550 a Month to Become a Millionaire (and It Costs Her $389 a Month)**

	Not Participating in 401(k) Plan	Participating in 401(k) Plan
Income	$94,000	$94,000
Contribution to plan	– 0 –	6,580
Taxable income after deductions, personal exemption and plan contribution	82,000	75,420
Matching contribution	– 0 –	3,290
Total available to invest	– 0 –	9,870
Federal income tax*	12,042	10,397
State income tax (4%)	3,280	3,017
Subtotal of taxes	15,322	13,413
Take-home pay	$78,678	$74,007
Monthly tax-home pay	$6,556	$6,167

* From Table 4-2 on page 125.

17.3d Type 2: Defined-Benefit Plans Are Yesterday's Standard

The second type of employer-sponsored retirement plan, a **defined-benefit retirement plan (DB)**, pays lifetime monthly payments to retirees based on a predetermined formula. Defined-benefit plans are commonly called pensions. A **pension** is a sum of money paid regularly as a retirement benefit. The Social Security Administration, various government agencies, and some employers pay pensions to retirees, and sometimes to their survivors.

Defined-benefit plans were the standard retirement plan for previous generations, but today such pensions are offered by only 25 percent of large employers. DB plans were offered by 60 percent of the big Fortune 500 companies as recently as 1998. Eighty percent of state and local government employees are covered by a defined-benefit retirement plan, as are federal government workers. These employers guarantee employer-paid monthly retirement payments for life. Thus the employer—not the employee as in all the defined-contribution retirement plans—accepts the risks of investing.

Pension benefits in defined-benefit plans are based on the years of service at the employer, average pay during the last few working years, and a percentage. For example, an employee might have a defined annual retirement benefit of 2 percent multiplied by the number of years of service and multiplied by the average annual income during the last five years of employment. In this example, a worker with 20 years of service and an average income of $58,000 over the last five years of work would have an annual pension benefit of $23,200 (20 × 0.02 × $58,000), or $1,933 ($23,200/12) per month.

Since the employer contributes all the money, it assumes all the investment risks associated with creating sufficient funds to pay future benefits. Some better employers still

defined-benefit retirement plan (DB)

Employer-sponsored retirement plan that pays lifetime monthly annuity payments to retirees based on a predetermined formula.

COMMON SENSE
Work for an Employer Who Offers a Defined-Benefit Pension

All things being equal, it is much better to work for an employer who offers a defined-benefit pension (DB) plan because the employer contributes to and manages a pool of the money; and, the employer guarantees all of the eventual pension payments (and survivor's benefits) over many years in the future. Thus, the benefits are defined or guaranteed. This guarantee exists no matter if the stock market rises or falls. The risk of market movement is entirely on the provider.

Defined-contribution (DC) plans, such as a 401(k) plans, may or may not include any voluntary matching employer contributions. The contributions from the employee are defined and there are no guarantees about the future performance of the stock market and the value of your retirement account. The risk of market movement is entirely on the employee.

The employee has no choice but to accept full responsibility for the two most important aspects of retirement. First, the employee has to decide (or not) to participate in the plan as well as how much to invest, and second, the employee must accept 100 percent of the risk of poor investment decisions even though odds are that the employee is and will always be an amateur in the world of investing.

While there are no guarantees that once you work for an employer who offers a DB pension plan that they will always keep it; but accrued benefits up to that point are guaranteed by law. In the event of bankruptcy the employer's responsibility is passed to the Pension Benefit Guarantee Corporation (PBGC). Nevertheless, it is a great start for financial stability in retirement.

One in five leading corporations and four out of five governments offer employees DB pension; some offer both DB and DC plans to employees. Most of the people living in retirement communities have DB retirement money coming in. Some have contributed voluntarily to their 401(k) plan or an IRA, so income from those investments supplements their retirement.

ADVICE FROM A SEASONED PRO

PBGC Provides Retirement Plan Insurance

ERISA established the Pension Benefit Guaranty Corporation (PBGC; www.pbgc.gov) to protect the interests of employee benefit plan participants and their beneficiaries. The nation's 24,000 employer-sponsored defined-benefit pension plans pay $3.9 billion in annual insurance premiums to the PBGC, which guarantees a maximum annual benefit of up to about $60,000 a year to 41 million eligible workers should their employers file for bankruptcy protection. The PBGC pays benefits to about 1.5 million people in failed pension plans. PBGC insurance never insures defined-contribution plans, but it does insure some cash-balance plans.

Ashwin Madia

Metropolitan State University, St. Paul, Minnesota, and *North Hennepin Community College,* Brooklyn Park, Minnesota

NEVER EVER

Don't Read Your Retirement Statements!

Jack Bogle, founder of Vanguard Mutual Funds, says "You're gonna get a statement on your retirement account every month, including months when the stock market is going down. Never open it." Checking on how well you are doing financially is counterproductive because it might tempt investors to respond emotionally by selling or buying in response to day-to-day volatility. Retirement is a *long-term* goal so always think long-term, stay invested, and do zero trading inside your retirement accounts, except to rebalance if needed. Of course, you should occasionally check for accuracy since it is important to monitor your investment accounts so you can quickly detect fraud and broker mistakes.

disability benefits
Substantially reduced benefits paid to employees who become disabled prior to retirement.

offer a non-optional defined-benefit retirement plan *and* a voluntary defined-contribution plan to their employees. From a retirement planning perspective, these are the best employers to work for since they offer both plans.

Critics of defined-benefit plans incorrectly claim that recipients of such a retirement plan, such as firefighters, policemen, and teachers, are bankrupting states and localities. In fact it is the politicians who over the years and despite signed agreements have failed to vote to contribute to the plans each and every year. If they had, they would not have any financial shortfalls. Pensions currently take up only 3.8 of state resources annually while states give away over 4 times that amount each year in corporate subsidies.

Should You Take Normal or Early Retirement Under a Defined-Benefit Plan? The earlier you retire, the smaller your monthly retirement pension from a defined-benefit plan will be because you will likely receive income for more years as a retired person. To illustrate, assume you are eligible for a full retirement pension of $28,800 per year at age 65. Your benefit may be reduced 3 percent per year if you retire at age 62. Smaller monthly pension payments are paid to the early retiree in a defined-benefit plan so that he or she will receive, in theory, the same present value amount of pension benefits as the person who retires later.

Disability and Survivors Benefits Disability and survivors benefits also represent important concerns for workers who have spouses or children or are financially responsible for caring for others. A person's full retirement pension forms the basis for any benefits paid to survivors and, when part of a retirement plan, for disability benefits as well.

Disability benefits may or may not be paid to employees who become disabled prior to retirement. It depends upon the employer's pension plan rules. If so, people receiving either disability or survivors benefits from a company pension are entitled to an amount that is substantially less than the full retirement amount. For example, if you were entitled to a retirement pension benefit of $2,000 per month, your disability benefit might be only $1,100 per month.

If a survivor is entitled to benefits, the pension amount must be paid over two people's lives instead of a single person's life. Then the monthly payment is different. A plan might call for a pension of $2,000 a month to the retiree, but a plan with survivor's benefits might pay the retiree only $1,750 a month because of the anticipated costs to pay survivors. Using the benefit described in the preceding example, if your surviving spouse is five years older than you, he or she might be entitled to $1,300 per month. In contrast, if your spouse is five years younger, he or she might be entitled to only $900 per month.

A qualified **joint and survivor benefit** (or **survivor's benefit**) is an annuity whose payments continue to the surviving spouse after the participant's death, often equal to at least 50 percent of the participant's pension benefit. This requirement can be waived if desired, but only after marriage—not in a prenuptial agreement. Federal law dictates that a spouse or ex-spouse who qualifies for benefits under the plan of a spouse or former spouse must agree in writing to a waiver of the spousal benefit.

This **spousal consent requirement** protects the interests of surviving spouses. If the spouse does waive his or her pension survivor benefits, the worker's retirement benefit will increase. Upon the worker's death, the spouse will not receive any survivor benefits. Unless a spouse has his or her own retirement benefits, it is usually wise to keep the spousal pension benefit, if available in a defined-benefit retirement plan.

joint and survivor benefit/ survivor's benefit
Annuity whose payments continue to a surviving spouse after the participant's death; often equals at least 50 percent of participant's benefit.

spousal consent requirement
Federal law that protects the surviving rights of a spouse or ex-spouse to retirement or pension benefits unless the person signs a waiver of those rights.

17.3e Type 3: Cash-Balance Plan Is a Hybrid Employer-Sponsored Retirement Plan

A third type of retirement plan is a hybrid of the defined-contribution and defined-benefit plans. A **cash-balance plan** is a defined-benefit retirement plan that gives each participant an interest-earning account credited with a percentage of pay on a monthly basis. It is distinguished by the "balance of money" in an employee's account at any point in time. The employer contributes 100 percent of the funds, and the employee contributes nothing.

The Pension Protection Act regulates the percentage earned on such accounts. The employer contributes a straight percentage of perhaps 4 percent of the employee's salary every payday to his or her specific cash-balance account. Interest on cash-balance accounts is credited at a rate guaranteed by the employer, and the employer assumes all the investment risk. As a result, the amount in the account grows at a regular rate. Employees can look ahead 5 or 25 years and calculate how much money will be in their account. These plans are less costly for companies but they do offer easy portability to employees who change employers, a common occurrence today.

cash-balance plan
Defined-benefit plan funded solely by an employer that gives each participant an interest-earning account credited with a percentage of pay on a monthly basis.

17.3f Supplemental Employer-Sponsored Retirement Plans

Some employers offer other supplemental savings plans to employees.

Employee Stock-Ownership Plan An **employee stock-ownership plan (ESOP)** is an employer-sponsored benefit plan through which the employer donates company stock into a trust, which is then allocated into accounts for individual employees. When employees leave the company, they get their shares of stock and can sell them. In effect, the supplement retirement fund consists of stock in the company.

Profit-Sharing Plan A **profit-sharing plan** is an employer-sponsored benefit plan that shares some of the profits with employees in the form of end-of-year cash or common stock contributions into employees' 401(k) accounts. The level of contributions made to the plan may reflect each person's performance as well as the level of profits achieved by the employer.

employee stock-ownership plan (ESOP)
Benefit plan in which employers make tax-deductible gifts of company stock into trusts, which are then allocated into employee accounts.

profit-sharing plan
Employer-sponsored plan that allocates some of the employer profits to employees in the form of end-of-year cash or common stock contributions to employees' 401(k) accounts.

CONCEPT CHECK 17.3

1. Distinguish among after-tax money put into investments, pretax money, and vesting.
2. Explain what is meant by tax-sheltered investment growth on money invested through qualified retirement accounts.
3. Summarize the main differences between defined-contribution and defined-benefit pension plans.
4. Explain why defined-contribution retirement plans are called self-directed.
5. Offer your impressions of working for an employer that offers a sizable matching contribution compared with one that does not.

accumulation phase

The years during which you need to save for retirement.

distribution phase

The time period during which you hope that your assets will last throughout retirement.

17.4 MONTE CARLO RETIREMENT ADVICE FOR INVESTORS

Employer-based financial advice for retirement must follow the requirements of the Pension Protection Act. The advice must be based on computer simulations of projected investment performance using **Monte Carlo simulations**. Named for the famous casino site, the advice is used to model the performance of hundreds or even thousands of individual mutual funds and stocks through large numbers of fluctuating securities markets.

17.4a Modern Portfolio Analysis

Monte Carlo simulations are an evolution of the long-term strategy of asset allocation using modern portfolio analysis. The mathematical simulations are based on long-term historical risk and return characteristics for various mixes of stock, bond, and short-term investment asset classes.

The goal is to identify the investor's acceptable level of risk tolerance and time horizon, in order to find an optimal portfolio of assets that may reduce overall portfolio volatility while providing the highest expected returns for that level of risk. This is what occurs in investments made through robo advisors discussed in Chapter 15.

Each simulation estimates how much you need to save—the **accumulation phase**—if your investments performed better or worse than expected, and it gives the odds that your assets will last throughout the retirement time period—the **distribution phase**—after you choose a given set of investments and establish a withdrawal amount.

These calculations are probabilities, not certainties. The simulations allow you to estimate the probability of reaching your financial goals, such as a specific retirement income at a certain point in the future.

By evaluating the trade-offs among various combinations of retirement plan contribution levels, diverse investment mixes, overall portfolio risk, projected retirement age, and retirement income goals, Monte Carlo simulations let you understand how certain changes in these factors will affect the chance that you will have enough money in retirement. Some investors may have to learn to be comfortable with increased risk, while others may have to save more or work longer.

17.4b Online Financial Advice Offered Through Employers

The largest provider in the industry is Financial Engines. They offer assistance in retirement planning to employees through over 600 large employer-sponsored defined contribution retirement plans. They charge a percentage fee, and don't make a commission for selling you anything. They are **fiduciary** advisors and that means they must put your best interests first, not those of their employer or their own. Fiduciaries also must act with the care, skill, prudence, and diligence that a prudent person would exercise.

The Department of Labor (DOL) issued rules requiring stockbrokers, insurance agents, and other financial advisors to meet the high fiduciary standard when selling investments and other products to retirement account owners. Regulations are to go into effect in 2018, however, business groups are lobbying to abolish the law. Sadly, the DOL rules do not affect nonretirement accounts at all, such as investing to buy a home, for your child's education, a car, a wedding, or a vacation. The Securities and Exchange Commission could issue such a rule to cover all types of investing but has not. Realize that not everyone truly has your best interests at heart.

Despite useful employer financial education, investors often learn that they are playing it too safe by investing too conservatively. This may prevent them from investing properly to reach their goals as shown in Figure 17-1.

Financial Engines provides management services and advice so that either they can manage your plan, or you can do it yourself well armed with their information and input. Competitors include The Vanguard Group, FMR,

NEVER EVER

1. *Wait until your thirties, or worse, your forties to start saving for retirement.*

2. *Forget to update forms that contractually award assets upon your death, like life insurance, retirement, and checking accounts.*

3. *Invest in stocks, bond, and stock mutual funds that charge high fees and expenses.*

Figure 17-1 **Monte Carlo Simulations**

You're on track!

The Forecast for your new strategy looks good! Click the **Next** button to receive your Advice Action Kit.

Your decisions	Current	New
Your contribution	$3,400/year	$6,100/year
Employer contribution	$1,300/year	$1,300/year
Your investments	Current	Advice
Your risk level	Mod. conserv.(0.82)	Mod. aggr.(1.25)
Retirement age	65	67
Desired income	$59,000	$59,000
Minimum income	$42,000	$42,000

Your outlook at age 65

	Current strategy	New strategy
Retirement Forecast Chance your investments and benefits will provide $59,000 per year. More...	 FORECAST 8%	 FORECAST 78%
Retirement income Estimated annual income you may have at age 65. More...		
■ Upside - excellent performance*	$63,200	$189,000
■ Median - average performance	$42,600	$82,100
▨ Downside - poor performance*	$31,400	$43,500
Possible 1-year loss Amount you could lose in the next 12 months. More...	9.1% or more	14.1% or more
	Assumptions	Assumptions

*Note: There is a 5% chance you'll have less than the downside amount and a 5% chance you'll have more than the upside amount. Amounts shown are in pre-tax dollars and have been adjusted for inflation.

Your personalized investment advice is based on your decisions. How we created your investment advice.

Investment advice	Current strategy	New strategy
401(k) Account		
Redwood Money Market	5%	0%
Platinum Growth	17%	10%
Cypress Balanced Fund	11%	0%
Maple Bond Market	13%	13%
Sequoia Small Cap	25%	0%
Granite S&P 500 Index	29%	30%
Silver Growth and Income	0%	23%
Chestnut Idx:500 Idx	0%	24%

and Ameriprise Financial. Annual fees at for Monte Carlo advice are usually 0.20 to 0.60 percent, and that will have a significant negative impact on your investment performance over the long-term.

CONCEPT CHECK 17.4

1. Review Figure 17.1, Monte Carlo Simulation, and give your impressions of the "New Strategy" recommendations.
2. What do you think about paying $40 a year for Monte Carlo simulations through your employer from a firm that also offers auto-rebalancing?

Learning Objective 5

Use Monte Carlo Advice when investing for retirement.

17.5 ACHIEVE YOUR RETIREMENT SAVINGS GOAL THROUGH PERSONALLY ESTABLISHED RETIREMENT ACCOUNTS

If you do not have access to an employer's retirement plan, you easily can, and should, set up one or more of your own plans to fund your future retirement. IRS regulations allow you to take advantage of personally established, self-directed tax-sheltered retirement accounts, such as an individual retirement account (IRA). The total maximum annual contribution you may make to any IRA account is $5,500 (or $6,500 for those over age 50). These personally established retirement accounts include Roth IRA accounts, IRAs, and Keogh and SEP-IRA plans.

17.5a Roth IRA Accounts Provide Tax-Free Growth and Tax-Free Withdrawals

Do not pass up the great deal of a Roth IRA. Taxes on your Roth IRA contributions are paid up front, and paying taxes on your contributions in exchange for tax-free withdrawals is appealing to all investors.

Roth IRAs should be considered the "default investment" for retirement planning. This is because despite the head start of a traditional IRA due to the upfront tax break of deductibility, a Roth almost always overcomes that advantage. You take a tax hit upfront but never owe the IRS a penny again

A Roth IRA is not an investment but rather an account in which to hold investments. It can be easily opened account opened at a bank, credit union, or mutual fund company. You may invest once and never do it again or you may contribute regularly for many years, and you may change investments whenever you please.

A **Roth IRA** is a nondeductible after-tax IRA that offers significant tax and retirement planning advantages. Funds in the account grow tax-free. No matter what your income, you do not pay taxes each year on capital gains, dividends, and other distributions from securities held within a Roth IRA account.

Withdrawals from a Roth IRA are tax-free if taken at age 59½ or later (or if you are disabled) from an account held at least five years. If you are under 59½, you may withdraw the exact amount of your Roth IRA contributions with no penalties. Tax-free withdrawals may be made for certain expenses, such as for a first-time home purchase and college expenses. Once you remove money from a Roth IRA, it is a withdrawal (not a loan), and you cannot put it back. There is no mandatory withdrawal schedule for Roth IRAs. You may open a Roth IRA even if you (or your spouse) have a retirement plan at work.

Roth IRAs have no **required minimum distributions (RMDs)**, like other tax-advantaged accounts. RMDs are the amount that most qualified plan participants must

Roth IRA

IRA funded with after-tax money (and thus it is not tax deductible) that grows on a tax-deferred basis; withdrawals are not subject to taxation.

required minimum distributions (RMDs)

The amount that most qualified plan participants must begin distributing from their retirement accounts by April 1 following the year they reach age 70.5.

COMMON SENSE
Everyone Should Invest in a Roth IRA

The bonus of receiving the employer's match on 401(k) retirement contributions at work is appreciated. People also are allowed to invest through a Roth IRA. This is one's best investing friend in life because a Roth IRA is funded with after-tax money.

All the money you put into a Roth IRA and all the growth on that money over the years is tax-free when you remove it. Money coming out of a 401(k) account and a traditional IRA account is taxable, but Roth IRA money is not once your Roth IRA account has been in existence for 5 years.

If you need money in a hurry, you may remove the Roth IRA funds you invested without any tax liability or penalty regardless of your age or how long the money has been growing. Anyone who wants to pay off a home mortgage loan, perhaps just before retirement, may simply withdraw the money in their Roth IRA account and pay it toward the mortgage balance. Everyone earning an income should start a Roth IRA as soon as possible.

begin distributing from their retirement accounts by April 1 following the year they reach age 70.5. With a Roth IRA you can pull out large sums of money to pay for emergencies, such as medical bills, with fear of being pushed into a higher tax bracket.

Equally important is when one is nearing age 50 they should consider shifting their attention toward paying off their home mortgage because retiring mortgage-free is a worthy goal. That may mean contributing less to retirement accounts, and that is okay. If it also means removing money from one's Roth IRA, so be it. You probably want to own your own home free and clear of debt by the time you retire. Pay off your home mortgage ahead of schedule and you will remove one of life's biggest financial worries.

The money in a Roth is all yours. Upon your death the funds in a Roth IRA will transfer to your heirs free of income taxes, which they can withdraw tax-free over their lifetimes.

Just about anyone can open a Roth IRA account. You can contribute up to $5,500 ($6,500 if age 50 or older). Employers have joined in too, as more than half offer Roth IRA and Roth 401(k) accounts.

17.5b   A myRA Is a Starter Savings Opportunity

To help people get started saving for retirement as easily as possible, the **myRA** was invented. Pronounced "my-RAH," it is a no-fee starter savings account for retirement. It is a type of Roth account that accepts after-tax contributions. MyRAs are aimed at low- and middle-income Americans. It is a simple, safe, affordable way to start saving for retirement. It costs nothing to open and has no fees. You contribute whatever amount you choose ($2, $20, or $100), but no more than $5,500 annually. Open a myRA—either through your workplace or by yourself—build up savings, then later on move the funds on to other retirement accounts. Enjoy the advantages of tax-free growth of your funds.

If you change jobs, your myRA account is portable so it goes with you. Plus, after 5 years, you may withdraw the money you put in your account at any time without paying tax and a penalty.

The minimum after-tax investment at a workplace is $25 and payroll deductions may be $5 or more. Funds in the account earn a conservative rate of interest comparable to a federal government securities program, and the principal cannot be lost. Rules for myRA accounts are the same as for Roth IRA accounts.

YOUR GRANDPARENTS SAY

"401(k) Plus a Roth IRA Is the Answer"

"Smart investors contribute the maximum to their employer-sponsored 401(k) retirement plan up to the maximum to enjoy the full employer's match. Then they contribute any other money planned for retirement into a Roth IRA account. This is the answer on how to maximize your retirement savings and benefits."

17.5c Traditional IRAs Result in Tax-Free Growth and Taxable Withdrawals

traditional individual retirement account (IRA)

Personal retirement account to which a person can make contributions that provide tax-deferred growth, and the initial contribution may be tax deductible for the year the IRA was funded.

A **traditional individual retirement account (IRA)** is a personal retirement account into which a person can make one or more annual contributions. An IRA is not an investment but rather an account in which to hold investments. It is much like any other account opened at a bank, credit union, brokerage firm, or mutual fund company. You can invest IRA money almost any way you desire, including collectibles like art, gems, stamps, antiques, rugs, metals, guns, and certain coins.

To fund the account, you may make a new contribution from your checking account or transfer a lump-sum distribution from an employer plan or another IRA account to your IRA account. Taxpayers can even opt on their federal tax return to allocate part or all of their refund for direct deposit into any IRA account. You may not borrow from an IRA.

An IRA offers tax-deferred growth. Your contributions may be tax deductible, which means that you can use all or part of your contributions to reduce your taxable income. You may invest $5,500 ($6,500 if age 50 or older) each year. However, if you (or your spouse) have a retirement plan at work, your contributions to an IRA account may be limited.

17.5d Spousal IRA

spousal IRA

Account set up for spouse who does not work for wages; offers tax-deferred growth and tax deductibility.

Any nonworking spouse can make a deductible IRA contribution to a **spousal IRA** account of up to $5,500 ($6,500 if age 50 or older) as long as the couple files a joint return, and the working spouse has enough earned income to cover the contribution. The IRS requires that withdrawals from traditional IRA accounts begin no later than age 70½.

17.5e Keogh Accounts Are for Self-Employed and Small Business Owners

Keogh

Tax-deferred retirement account designed for high-income self-employed and small-business owners.

A **Keogh** (pronounced "Key-oh") is a tax-deferred retirement account designed for high-income self-employed and small-business owners. Depending on the type of Keogh established (defined contribution or defined-benefit), an individual may save as much as 25 percent of self-employment earned income, with contributions capped at $53,000 per participant. If the income comes from self-employment, contributions can still be made after age 70½.

DID YOU KNOW

States Require Roth IRAs for All Workers

Workers are not saving enough for retirement. Plus half of employers do not offer employees a retirement plan. That means 60 million full- and part-time employees do not have a retirement plan at work.

The danger is that millions of people may live in a state of prolonged poverty during the last years of their lives. As a result, states are passing laws that require private-sector employers to automatically enroll all their workers into a state-run retirement savings plan.

The employees would be obligated to contribute between 3 and 6 percent of their taxable wages. Funds would go into

Roth IRA retirement plans for each worker. Plus, each person would be allowed to opt out.

Participants may put their money into a range of investment options, including low-cost index and target-date funds. All funds are pooled and managed by investment professionals chosen by each state through a bidding process. Thus, fees are both low and transparent. California, Connecticut, Illinois, Oregon, and other states are commencing similar programs.

17.5f Simplified Employee Pension/IRA (SEP/IRA) Is for Self-Employed Workers

A **simplified employee pension/individual retirement account (SEP/IRA)** is a retirement savings account for a person's s self-employment income and those with one or more employees who are looking to save only in profitable years. These often are contract workers. A SEP-IRA is easier to set up and maintain than a Keogh. The total contribution to a SEP-IRA account should not exceed the lesser of 25% of income or $53,000. All employees must receive the same benefits under a SEP plan.

17.5g Solo 401(k) Plan

A **solo 401(k) plan**, also known as an **individual 401(k)** or **uni-k**, works much like a SEP/IRA or traditional employer-provided 401(k) plan. A solo 401(k) is strictly for sole proprietors who have no employees, although one's spouse may contribute if he or she earns income from the business. The solo 401(k) comes in both a traditional and Roth version, just like IRAs. The maximum annual salary deferral is $18,000 or up to 20 to 25 percent of business earnings, up to a total of $53,000, plus $6,000 in catch-up contributions.

17.5h Stay Invested When Changing Employers

When changing employers or retiring, you may have three choices:

1. *Leave it.* You may be able to leave the money invested in your account at your former employer (about half do) until you wish to begin taking withdrawals, but this has some negatives, such as delays in access.
2. *Transfer it.* You may transfer the money to your new employer's plan or to an IRA rollover individual retirement account, but beware of paying higher fees that will reduce your principal, which will shrink your earnings income by 20 to 40 percent during the rest of your life.
3. *Take it.* You can take the money in cash and pay income taxes and penalties.

Options 2 and 3 result in a **lump-sum distribution** because all the money is removed from a retirement account at one time. Such a transfer must be executed correctly according to the IRS's rollover regulations or the taxpayer will be subject to a substantial tax bill and perhaps a need to borrow money to pay the IRS.

A **rollover** is the action of moving assets from one tax-sheltered account to another tax-sheltered account within 60 days of a distribution. This procedure preserves the benefits of having funds in a tax-sheltered account. It is best to never take possession of the money. Instead transfer the funds directly from one financial institution to another.

The IRS has a **one-rollover rule** that says investors can make only one rollover from one IRA to another in any 12-month period. However there is no limit on trustee-to-trustee transfers.

What you don't do when changing employers is to take the cash out of their tax-sheltered retirement plan and spend it. More than 60 percent of workers age 18 to 34 foolishly do that. Taking out $30,000 to pay for a wedding or to buy a car results in about $10,000 in federal and state income taxes and penalties, and this leaves one with net proceeds of $20,000. Worse, they forever have lost over $300,000 to use during retirement (Appendix A-1, 8%, 30 years: 10.0627 × $30,000). Early withdrawals are a gigantic mistake!

one-rollover rule

An IRS rule that says investors can make only one rollover form one IRA to another in any 12-month period.

CONCEPT CHECK 17.5

1. Why should workers choose to save for retirement through a personally established retirement account?
2. Summarize the importance of low-cost investment fees to long-term retirement success.
3. List two differences between a Roth IRA and a traditional IRA.
4. Who would use a Keogh rather than a SEP-IRA to save for retirement?

17.6 AVOID PENALTIES AND DO NOT OUTLIVE YOUR MONEY

Once you have accumulated a substantial retirement nest egg, you can congratulate yourself. For many years, you sacrificed some of your spending and instead wisely saved and invested. However, retirement planning does not end when retirement saving ends.

You will also need to plan your retirement *spending* so you—and perhaps a significant other—can live during retirement without running out of money. To do so, you first must avoid withdrawing your money early in life. You also must carefully manage your retirement assets during the accumulation stage. Then figure out how many years your money will last in retirement, and invest accordingly and plan appropriate account withdrawals. Calculate your life expectancy at www.longevityillustrator.org or www.livingto100com.

17.6a Avoid Withdrawing Retirement Money Early

For many people, the money accumulated in 401(k) or IRA retirement accounts represents most—if not all—of their retirement savings. Withdrawing money early from a retirement account or borrowing some diverts the funds from their intended purpose, and the money is no longer there to grow tax-deferred. When other financial needs present themselves, there is often a desire to tap into the funds for nonretirement purposes. Such uses were not the intent of Congress when it set up the tax-favored status of the accounts. Making early withdrawals means that you either must retire later or retire on schedule at a lower level of living. You want to avoid both.

20 percent withholding rule
The IRS requires plan sponsors to withhold 20 percent of an early withdrawal that is then sent to government to prepay taxes.

early withdrawal penalty
A ten percent penalty over and above the taxes owed when money is withdrawn early from a qualified retirement account.

Beware of the Negative Impacts of Early Withdrawals Early withdrawals typically are defined as a premature distribution before age 59½, and they are taxed as ordinary income. When money is directly withdrawn from a tax-sheltered retirement account before the rules permit—perhaps to buy a car, take a vacation, remodel a home, shell out for tuition, or pay off a credit card debt—four bad things happen:

1. **You must prepay taxes that will be due to the government.** The IRS's **20 percent withholding rule** applies whenever a participant takes direct possession of the funds grown from pretax contributions to a retirement account. This amount is forwarded by the retirement plan account trustee to the IRS to prepay some of the income taxes that will be owed on the withdrawn funds. Thus, if William Wacky withdraws $10,000 he will get a check for only $8,000 ($10,000 less 20% of $10,000). You may avoid the 20 percent withholding rule by transferring the money into a **rollover IRA**, which is an account set up to receive such funds. You must make a **trustee-to-trustee rollover** whereby the funds go directly from the previous account's trustee to the trustee of the new account, avoiding any payment to the employee.

2. **Penalties are assessed.** The IRS assesses a 10 percent **early withdrawal penalty** on such withdrawals. Because William withdrew $10,000, he must also pay a penalty tax of $1,000 ($10,000 × 0.10).

Planning an active retirement can include working part-time at something you enjoy.

Fabio Cardoso/zefa/Corbis

3. **Income taxes must be paid on the withdrawn funds.** Early withdrawals are taxed at one's marginal tax rate. The impact of taxes and the penalty are substantial. Assume William Wacky from above, a 35-year-old with $25,000 in a tax-sheltered retirement account at work, withdrew $10,000 out of the account to take his family on a cruise. William pays federal and state income taxes at a combined 30 percent rate. His $10,000 withdrawal must be included as part of his taxable income. That will cost him a total of $4,000 ($2,000 of which was prepaid). This is due to $3,000 in income taxes ($10,000 × 0.30). Plus, $1,000 due to the early withdrawal penalty ($10,000 × 0.10). These costs will make for a pretty expensive cruise for the Wacky family.

4. **The investment does not grow.** Withdrawing money means that the withdrawn funds no longer grow as part of the invested portfolio. The lost time for compounding will substantially shrink one's retirement nest egg. William forever gave up a future value of a whopping $300,000 to use during retirement (Appendix A-1, 8%, 30 years: 10.0627 × $30,000). Early withdrawals are a big mistake!

Some Penalty-Free Withdrawals Do Exist In spite of the costs associated with early withdrawals, a withdrawal may be needed under certain circumstances. Fortunately, the IRS imposes no penalty for early withdrawals in four situations:

1. **Expenses for medical, college, and home buying.** You can make penalty-free withdrawals from an IRA account (but not an employer-sponsored plan) if you pay for medical expenses in excess of 10 percent of your adjusted gross income, you pay medical insurance premiums after being on unemployment for at least 12 weeks, you are disabled, you pay for qualified higher-education expenses, or the distribution of less than $10,000 is used for qualifying first-time home-buyer expenses.

2. **Account loans.** You may borrow up to half of your accumulated assets in an employer-sponsored account, not to exceed 50 percent of your vested account balance, or $50,000, whichever is less. Here the borrower pays interest on the loan, which is then credited back into the person's account. Loans must be repaid with after-tax money. If the employee changes employers, he or she must repay the unpaid balance of the loan within 30 days. Otherwise, the loan is reclassified as a withdrawal, which will result in additional taxes and penalties. One-quarter of 401(k) investors have loans on their accounts, and half of those borrowers take out additional loans. Some people must think their 401(k) retirement plan is just a piggy bank savings account. Account loans are beneficial only in extreme circumstances and plans should be in place for repayment as soon as the loan is taken.

3. **Hardship withdrawal.** A **hardship withdrawal**, says the IRS, is a distribution from a 401(k) plan made on account of an immediate and heavy financial need of the employee, and the amount must be necessary to satisfy the financial need. Examples are unreimbursed medical expenses, payments to prevent eviction, funeral expenses, payment of college tuition, and purchase of a home. Most 401(k) plans do not allow hardship withdrawals, and those that do report the information to the IRS, which may deem the withdrawal tax-free or may not.

4. **Early retirement.** You may avoid a penalty if you retire early (but not earlier than 59.5 years) or are totally or permanently disabled and you are willing to receive annual distributions according to an IRS-approved method for a time period of no less than five years.

THERE IS AN APP FOR THAT!

Some of the best apps are:

- AARP Retirement Calculator
- ConversationProject
- Eresearchfidelity.com
- ESPlanner
- EverPlans.com
- Fidelity's Income Strategy Evaluator
- iMaximize Social Security
- LifePlanningForYou.com
- LifeReimagined.org
- LivingTo100.com
- Military Retirement
- Personal Capital
- RetirePlan
- Vanguard Nest Egg Retirement Calculator

hardship withdrawal

A distribution from a 401(k) plan to be made on account of an immediate and heavy financial need of the employee, and the amount must be necessary to satisfy the financial need.

17.6b Figure Out How Many Years Your Money Will Last in Retirement

As you near retirement, you will want to ask "How long will my retirement nest egg last?" The answer to this question will depend on three factors: (1) the amount of money you have accumulated, (2) the real (after inflation) rate of return you will earn on the funds, and (3) the amount of money to be withdrawn from the account each year because the higher the rate of your withdrawal, the more likely it is that the assets in your portfolio will not last until you die. Three-quarters of investors overestimate the safe, conservative withdrawal rate of retirement savings.

Appendix A-4 provides factors that can be divided into the money in a retirement fund to determine the amount available for spending each year. Consider the example of Wayne and Melodee Neu, retirees from Sisseton, South Dakota, who want their $500,000 retirement nest egg to last 20 years. They assume that the nest egg will earn a 6 percent annual return in the future and assume an annual inflation rate of 3 percent. The present value factor in the table in the "20 years" column and the "3 percent" row (6 percent investment return minus 3 percent inflation) in Appendix A-4 is 14.8775. Dividing $500,000 by 14.8775 reveals that Wayne and Melodee could withdraw $33,608, or $2,800 per month ($33,608 ÷ 12 months), for 20 years before the fund was depleted.

Because they adjusted their rate of return for inflation, the Neus can safely increase their income by two or three percent each year to safeguard the spending power of their retirement income. But what if they live for 30 more years? The factor for 30 years is 19.6004, and the answer is $25,510, or $2,126 per month; almost $700 less initially.

One of the mistakes that new retirees make is withdrawing money too fast. Table 17-3 shows how long one's retirement money will last using various withdrawal rates.

17.6c Some People Buy an Annuity to "Guarantee" a Portion of Their Retirement Income

The fear of running out of money in retirement looms large for people approaching and during retirement. How can you be sure that declines in the stock market will not cause you to have to significantly decrease your level of living as you age?

First, recognize immediately that the stock market recessions rarely last as long as 1½ or 2 years. The market then comes roaring back to set new record highs in about 2 or 3 years. So, be patient. Consider withdrawing less money for a year or two knowing that stock prices will be sharply higher in the future so do not sell out while the market is down. After it rises you can withdraw more money as needed. Other alternatives

DO IT IN CLASS

| *Table 17-3* | **How Long Will My Retirement Money Last?** |

Here are the rates of withdrawals and the likelihood that a diversified portfolio earning a long-term historical rate of return will last through retirement, assuming 3 percent annual increases for inflation.

Withdrawal Rate Amount	Years in Retirement and Likelihood Money Will Last		
	20	**30**	**40**
3%	99%	99%	93%
4%	99%	86%	68%
5%	93%	61%	41%
6%	74%	35%	18%

to consider include cutting back expenses or getting more income through part-time employment.

On the other hand, rather than continuing to manage your own investments and withdrawals in an effort to make the money last, you could use a portion of your retirement nest egg (such as one-third or one-half) to buy an annuity. Annuities appeal to conservative investors concerned about outliving their income in retirement.

An **annuity** is a contract made with an insurance company that provides for a series of payments to be received at stated intervals (usually monthly) for life or a specified time period. For retirees who buy an annuity, this means that an insurance company will receive a portion of their retirement nest egg and, in return, promise to send monthly payments according to an agreed-upon schedule, usually for the life of the person covered by the annuity (the **annuitant**). As a "risk-pooled mortality product," an annuity contract assumes that a lot of people each pay in, and whoever is alive next year will get a distribution from the pool.

Payments Start Right Away When You Buy an Immediate Annuity People usually buy an **immediate annuity** at or soon after retirement, and the average age is 62. The annuity income payments will then begin at the end of the first month after purchase. You do pay income taxes on the payments received.

Payments Start Years Later With a Deferred Annuity A deferred annuity involves you paying in before retirement but then waiting a certain amount of time to receive any payouts. Once payments begin, they pay you more money than immediate annuities to offset the risk that you might die while paying in before starting to collect.

Fixed and Variable Annuities A **fixed annuity** is a guaranteed payout you receive every year. Two thousand dollars a month might sound good, but how much will

annuity

Contract made with an insurance company that provides for a series of payments to be received at stated intervals (usually monthly) for a fixed or variable time period.

immediate annuity

Annuity, often funded by a lump sum from the death benefit of a life insurance policy or lump sum from a defined-contribution plan, that begins payments one month after purchase.

NUMBERS ON

Retirement and Estate Planning

Data from a variety of sources suggest:

- Ninety percent of young adults are concerned about ensuring that their saving and investing will be enough to live on during retirement.

- More than a third of American adults haven't saved a penny for retirement.

- Only 6 in 10 employees with access to a workplace retirement plan are contributing enough money to take full advantage of the employer match.

- Less than half of working women participate in a retirement plan.

- Average employee savings rate is 8.1 percent, and the average annual contribution is $9,800.

- Roth IRA investors hold 80 percent of their investments in equities.

- Thirty percent of Roth IRA investors are younger than age 40.

- Nine out of 10 households who own mutual funds hold their shares inside employer-sponsored retirement plans, individual retirement accounts (IRAs), and other tax-deferred accounts.

- Three out of five millennials want to retire to some other city or state than where they currently live.

- By 2035, the number of people older than 65 is expected to increase to 20 percent, up from about 12.6 percent in 2018.

- Only 1 in 5 Americans have created a trust as part of their estate plan.

- Average inheritance for the wealthiest 5 percent of households is $1.2 million.

variable annuity

Annuity whose value rises and falls like mutual funds and pays a limited death benefit via an insurance contract.

inflation decrease the buying power of $2,000 over 20 or 25 years? The answer may be over 50 percent. It is hard to buy a $40 restaurant meal when the price 20 years later is $70.

Payments from a **variable annuity** can fluctuate substantially based on how well the premiums are invested by the policyholder/investor. In fact, variable annuities are not guaranteed in any way. Not even the principal. With these types of annuities when you die all payments stop and your heirs receive nothing.

Cash Refund or Life Annuity With a **cash refund or life annuity,** upon your death your heirs will receive a death benefit, either some or all of your remaining payouts. Logically, the monthly payout for the annuitant is less for this kind of policy because it has a death benefit.

Disadvantages of Annuities Annuities are sold aggressively because sellers earn very high sales commissions, often 10 or 15 percent or more, and the insurance company charges substantial annual fees, often 3 percent or more.

Annuities also are illiquid because once your money is invested it is very costly investment decision to reverse. Basically it almost impossible to get your money back. Charges to surrender the investment can be 7 percent. Some companies charge a 25 percent surrender charge for the first 5 or 10 years.

Annuities are extremely complicated contracts, and a lot of that is apparently done on purpose. Thus shopping around is difficult. Annual operating and investment costs are at least 3 to 4 percent, but it is difficult to figure out all the fees and charges as they often are hidden in the contract.

In contrast, equivalent mutual funds and exchange-traded funds assess less than 0.50 in annual costs. Annual returns earned on annuities are 1 to 3 percent, and this contrasts to over 9 percent annually for a stock index fund. Finally, when people purchase an annuity they are buying an illusion of security (years and years of income) at the cost of growth (which is not going to happen due to inflation). People often regret their decision to buy annuity.

Anyone considering the purchase of an annuity might be wise to begin with Vanguard, Fidelity or TIAA-CREF, all of which are low-fee industry leaders. Moreover, if you are thinking about buying an annuity make sure that you fully understand the fees, commissions, and other rules of the contract.

DID YOU KNOW

Hooray! You Are Much Smarter About Personal Finance Now

People often make terrible mistakes in personal finance. They get awful advice, listen to poor advisors, and make abysmal decisions. Then they sometimes give up on their dream of enjoying financial security. That should not be you!

After reading these chapters you now know more than most Americans about what to do right in personal finance and how to avoid the most common pitfalls in investing for retirement. You will likely make a few mistakes in your investing life, but do not let that stop you from continuing

to invest for your financially successful future. You now are already smart enough to spot the bad deals that seem to say "Invest here!" to your money.

Informed personal finance knowledge is your best safeguard against deception, misguidance, and stupid mistakes, so keep learning and continue to get smarter about this subject. And remember that the biggest mistake you can make is to not invest for retirement at all because the only way to create wealth is by investing. We wish the best to you and yours!

CONCEPT CHECK 17.6

1. What are some negative impacts of taking early withdrawals from retirement accounts?
2. Name two types of penalty-free withdrawals from retirement accounts.
3. Summarize how long one's retirement money will last given certain withdrawal rates.
4. Offer some positive and negative observations on the wisdom of buying an annuity with some of your retirement nest egg money when you retire.

17.7 HOW TO PLAN FOR THE DISTRIBUTION OF YOUR ASSETS

Learning Objective 7

Plan for the distribution of your estate.

Estate planning comprises the specific arrangements you make during your lifetime for the administration and distribution of your estate when you die. You need to learn how to transfer assets in such a way that they go to your desired heirs and avoid unnecessary probate court procedures. Most of your assets can be set up to transfer automatically. For the remainder, you need to prepare a will. Estate planning need not be overly complicated but you do need to do it. Upon your death, your surviving family members will not conduct the distribution of your assets. Most of these procedures are set up before your death, as described below. Other procedures are set up through **probate** by which a special **probate court** allows creditors, such as a credit card company, an auto financing company or a mortgage lender, to present claims against an estate and ensures the transfer of a decedent's assets to the rightful beneficiaries. The probate court will make the distributions according to a properly executed and valid will or, when no will exists, to the people or organizations as required by state law.

estate planning
The definite arrangements you make during your lifetime that are consistent with your wishes for the administration and distribution of your estate when you die.

probate
Court-supervised process that allows creditors to present claims against an estate and ensures the transfer of a decedent's assets to the rightful beneficiaries according to a properly executed and valid will or, when no will exists, to the people, agencies, or organizations required by state law.

17.7a Start Right Now by Setting Up Most of Your Assets as Nonprobate Property

Figure 17-2 illustrates the different ways that your property can be distributed after your death. Importantly, nonprobate property is not transferred by the probate court.

TAX CONSEQUENCES IN RETIREMENT AND ESTATE PLANNING

Tax-deferred retirement plans provide these benefits:

- *Your contributions to a tax-sheltered plan are tax deductible and are not subject to federal, state, and local income taxes.*

- *No income taxes are due on any earnings on the invested assets until withdrawn.*

- *Withdrawals are subject to income taxes at your marginal tax rate, which in retirement may be lower than your tax rate today.*

- *Other retirement income, such as from Social Security, pensions, employment, interest, dividends, and capital gains, is subject to income taxes.*

- *To keep income taxes down in retirement when making withdrawals, take money out of taxable accounts first, followed by tax-deferred accounts, and finally Roth IRA accounts.*

- *When you die, any qualified beneficiary may choose to roll your 401(k) and IRA assets into an IRA tax-free.*

- *The likelihood of you paying federal estates taxes is just about zero.*

Figure 17-2 **How Your Estate Is Distributed After Death**

YOUR ENTIRE ESTATE	
Most of your assets are transferred after your death by:	**Your probate property is transferred by the probate court in accordance with:**

1. Contracts you set up before death, including
  ▪ Payable-on-death clauses in bank accounts
  ▪ Assets owned by joint ownership with rights of survivorship
  ▪ Beneficiary designations in life insurance and retirement plans
2. Setting up trusts that designate who will receive the property, including
  ▪ Living trusts established while you are still alive
  ▪ Testamentary trusts designed to take effect at your death
	Your wishes as outlined in your will
	OR
	If you have no will, the intestate succession laws in your state

nonprobate property

Does not go through probate; includes assets transferred to survivors by contract (such as beneficiaries listed on retirement accounts and bank accounts held with another person).

Nonprobate property includes assets transferred to survivors by contract such as by naming a beneficiary for your retirement plan or by owning assets with another person through joint tenancy with right of survivorship. Trusts (discussed below) can also be used to transfer assets outside of probate court.

One of the primary benefits of setting up assets as nonprobate property is time. Nonprobate property transfers immediately upon your death, whereas the legal quagmire of probate can take between 6 months and a year, or longer if there is no will. Avoiding probate court may also save money since your estate pays the cost of the probate process based on the value of the assets it must distribute, and this ranges from hundreds to perhaps thousands of dollars. Avoiding probate additionally maintains your privacy because a public record is maintained of the probate process.

17.7b   Most Assets Are Transferred by Contract

People of average economic means should be able to transfer by contract most or all of their assets outside of probate. Transferring your estate by contract is an easy, do-it-yourself project. You just have to take a few minutes of time to fill out the appropriate forms. There are three ways to transfer assets by contract:

1. Transfers by Beneficiary Designation When you open up investment accounts, you are given a form to complete in order to name your beneficiaries. Changes are made in the same way; you complete a new beneficiary designation form. Examples of accounts like this are IRAs, 401(k) plans, Keogh plans, pension plans, bank and credit union accounts, stock brokerage accounts, mutual funds, and life insurance policies.

beneficiary

A person or organization designated to receive a benefit.

A **beneficiary** is a person or organization designated to receive a benefit. A **beneficiary designation** is a legal form signed by the owner of an asset providing that the property goes to a certain person or organization in the event of the owner's death. The form also contains a place to designate a **contingent (or secondary) beneficiary** in case the first-named **beneficiary**, also known as the primary beneficiary, dies after the form is filled out. If no one has been named as beneficiary for a particular asset or if that person and a named contingent beneficiary has died, the property will go to one's estate and to probate court for distribution. The lesson here: Be certain to name contingent beneficiaries as well as beneficiaries in contracts.

TURN BAD HABITS INTO GOOD ONES

Do You Do This?	**Do This Instead!**
Put off saving for retirement	Save early and often
Avoid risk when saving for retirement	Accept risk knowing that you have time to ride out the highs and lows of the stock market
Rely only on your employer's plan when saving for retirement	Contribute to a Roth IRA to supplement your employer-sponsored plans if necessary to reach your calculated retirement savings goal
Withdraw or borrow money from your retirement accounts when money is desired for other reasons	Keep your hands totally off your retirement money
Put off writing your will	Go online and create a will and revise when needed

2. Transfers by Property Ownership Designation The most common form of joint ownership of assets, especially for husbands and wives is **joint tenancy with right of survivorship**, also called **joint tenancy**. In this case, each person owns the whole of the asset, such as a bank account, vehicle, or home, and can dispose of it without the approval of the other owners. Assets owned in this way often include bank accounts, stocks, bonds, real estate, mutual funds, government bonds, and other assets.

Upon the death of one owner, the surviving owners receive the property by operation of law rather than through the provisions of a will. Simply stated, the surviving owner(s) owned the entire asset before the death and owns all of it after death. The lesson here: If you want an asset to immediately transfer to a particular person upon your death, own it as joint tenants with right of survivorship.

3. Transfers by Payable-on-Death Designation With a **payable-on-death designation** on a bank account the beneficiary has no rights to the funds until you pass on. Until that time, you are free to use the money kept in the bank account, to change the beneficiary, or to close the account. The named beneficiary simply needs to present a copy of your death certificate to the bank and show proper identification, and access to the account will be granted.

17.7c The Rest of Your Estate Can Be Transferred via Your Will

Your **probate property** is simply all assets other than nonprobate property. Your probate property consists of what you owned individually and totally in your name, as well as the value of assets jointly owned through tenancy in common (discussed in Chapter 5). In the latter case, your heirs will receive your share, but not the co-owner's share.

Transfers with a Will Go to Your Desired Heirs A will is the smartest way to transfer your nonprobate assets upon your death. You definitely need a will unless all of your property is nonprobate property and/or will be transferred by contract. It is written after all the other aspects of estate planning are completed.

A **will** is a written document in which a person, the **testator**, tells how his or her remaining assets should be given away after death. In your will, you name an **executor** (or **personal representative**). The executor identifies assets, collects any money due, open up an estate bank account, pays off debts, obtains life insurance proceeds, liquidates assets, files for Social Security burial benefits, prepares final income tax and estate tax returns, and with the court's permission distributes the balance of any remaining money and property to the beneficiaries.

joint tenancy with right of survivorship/joint tenancy
Most common form of joint ownership, especially for husbands and wives, in which each person owns the whole of the asset, such as a bank account or home, and can dispose of it without the approval of the other owner(s).

payable-on-death designation
Status granted to individuals who are not joint tenants and who might need to access accounts without going through probate; the deceased signs the designation before death, and the designee simply presents a death certificate to access the accounts.

DO IT IN CLASS

probate property
All assets other than nonprobate property.

will
Written document in which a person tells how his or her remaining assets should be given away after death; without a will, the property will be distributed according to state probate law.

executor/personal representative
Person responsible for carrying out the provisions of a will and managing the assets until the estate is passed on to heirs.

codicil

Legal instrument with which one can make minor changes to a will.

heir

Person who inherits or is entitled by law or by the terms of a will to inherit some asset.

guardian

Person responsible for caring for and raising any child under the age of 18 and for managing the child's estate.

Relatives and friends are not necessarily the best choice to perform the executor's duties, and many people name an accountant or attorney to play this role since the work is time consuming and challenging for novices and may require the hiring of experts. The person should ideally live in the state where the will is to be probated. A legal background is not necessary, but honesty and maturity are key attributes of a good executor. The executor's basic fee for carrying out these complicated tasks is about 6 percent of the estate (more for smaller estates or less for larger ones) plus a commission of perhaps 5 percent of the value of the estate. Or they can charge an hourly fee.

A simple will that is prepared by an attorney can cost $125 to $400. Minor changes in a will may be made with a **codicil** instead of revoking the existing will and writing a completely new one, as you would when making major changes.

Topics to Include in Your Will

To create a valid will is easy. You actually can do this online instead of paying an attorney to draft one. Before going online write down your responses to these decision topics:

- Decide what property to include.
- Decide who will inherit which assets.
- Identify an executor.
- Choose a guardian for your children.
- Select someone to manage children's inherited assets.
- Input the answers online and print.
- Sign your original will in front of witnesses who also will sign, and make a photocopy.
- Store your original will in a safe deposit box or in another safe place.

See BuildaWill.com, LegacyWriter, LegalZoom, Kiplinger's Quicken Will-maker, RocketLawyer, and WillPower.

A Valid Will Is Not Likely to Be Challenged If you die with a valid will, the probate court will transfer or distribute your property according to your wishes. A person who inherits or is entitled by law or by the terms of a will to inherit some asset is called an **heir**. A will that is properly drafted, signed, and witnessed is unlikely to be successfully challenged by someone who is dissatisfied with the intended distribution of assets, thus reducing the likelihood of family disputes. Leave people in your will $1 if you think he/she might challenge the will, as this avoids them claiming you simply "forgot" to give them something. If you have a complicated estate, you should seek the assistance of an attorney who specializes in estate planning. If you move to another state, update your will since wills are valid under state law, not federal law.

You Need to Appoint a Guardian in Your Will if You Have Minor Children If you have minor children, you should appoint a legal **guardian** for each child in your will. This person is responsible for caring for and raising any child under the age of 18 and for managing the child's estate. The guardian should be someone who shares your values and views on child rearing. You might avoid as potential guardians those who are too old, too ill, or too tired from raising their own children, and those who don't really know the children. Consider naming an alternate candidate in case your first choice cannot take on this responsibility. If you have not taken steps to name a legal guardian, the court will appoint one, perhaps someone you do not know.

Without a Will, State Law Determines the Distribution of Your Property If you don't have a will, and 70 percent of people do not, your state of residence has one for you. If you do not care about what happens to your property, children, vehicle, and favorite pieces of jewelry, the state will make all those decisions. In some states, 50

DID YOU KNOW

Writing a simple will is not that complicated. Here is how Harry Johnson from this book's Harry and Belinda continuing case wrote his.

Last Will and Testament of Harry Johnson

1 Introduction
Being of sound mind and memory, I Harry Johnson, do hereby publish this as my Last Will and Testament. I am married to Belinda Johnson, and my mother is Melinda Johnson.

2 Payment of Debts and Expenses
I hereby direct my Executor to pay my medical and funeral expenses, taxes, debts, and the costs of settling my estate.

3 Distribution of Assets
I give my wife one-half of my possessions and all my personal effects. I give my mother one-quarter of my possessions. I give to Common Cause, a nonprofit organization, one-quarter of my possessions. If my wife, Belinda Johnson, predeceases me, I give her share to my mother, Melinda Johnson.

4 Simultaneous Death of Beneficiary
If any beneficiary of this Will, including any beneficiary of any trust established by this Will, other than my wife, shall die within 60 days of my death or prior to the distribution of my estate, I hereby declare that I shall be deemed to have survived such person.

5 Appointment of Executor and Guardian
I appoint my father-in-law, Martin Anderson, to be the Executor of this will and my estate, and provide if this

executor is unable or unwilling to serve then I appoint the Trust Department of the Bank of America as alternate Executor. My Executor shall be authorized to carry out all provisions of this Will and pay my just debts, obligations, and funeral expenses.

6 Power of the Executor
The executor of this will has the power to receive payments, buy or sell assets, and pay debts and taxes owed on behalf of my estate.

7 Payment of Taxes
I direct my executor to pay all taxes imposed by governments.

8 Execution
In witness therefore, I hereby set my hand to this last Will and Testament, which consists of one page, this 31st day of January 2018.

_____   _____
Signature   Date

9 Witness Clause
The above-named person signed in our presence and in our opinion is mentally competent.

_____	_____	_____
Witness 1	Address	Date
_____	_____	_____
Witness 2	Address	Date

percent of your estate goes to your spouse and 50 percent goes to your children. This could cause some financial and family problems.

When a person dies without a valid will, the deceased is assumed to have died **intestate**. Dying intestate can cost much more in taxes and cause legal, bureaucratic, and emotional struggles for survivors. In such a case, the probate court first ensures that the debts, income taxes, and expenses of the deceased are paid. Remember that if you did not update the beneficiaries on your 401(k), savings account or life insurance policies (what if an ex-spouse is named on everything?), the companies are obligated to send the money to those identified no matter whatever current wishes you may have. After payments are made, the probate court will divide all property and transfer assets to the legal heirs according to state law. If no surviving relatives exist, the estate will go to the state by **right of escheat**. Then your relatives, friends and charities will get nothing.

intestate
When a person dies without a legal will.

17.7d Spouses Have Legal Rights to Each Other's Estates

The **partnership theory of marriage rights** is an assumption in state law that presumes that wedded couples share their fortunes equally. Thus, property acquired during the marriage and titled in the name of only one partner (other than property acquired by gift or inheritance) becomes the property of both spouses.

ADVICE FROM A SEASONED PRO

Three Estate Planning Questions for Mom and Dad

Parents usually do not want their children to know about how they spend every nickel and dime, but there are a few questions that need answering so you all can avoid financial problems in the future:

1. *What types of insurance do you have (e.g., life, health, disability, long-term care), and where are the policies located?*

2. *Are the beneficiaries on life insurance and investment accounts (mutual funds, brokerage, bank, IRAs, 401(k)s, pensions) up to date and as you want them to be?*

3. *Where is a list of your financial accounts, institutions, passwords, safe deposit box (and key), as well as contact information for advisors, brokers, accountants, and lawyers?*

Konnie G. Kustron
Eastern Michigan University, Ypsilanti, Michigan

A decedent who disinherits a surviving spouse or who leaves that person with less than a fair share of the estate is judged to have reneged on the partnership. A surviving spouse disinherited in this manner has some claim in probate court to a portion of the decedent's estate if he or she chooses to elect that option. States give a surviving spouse the right to claim one-fourth to one-half of the other spouse's estate, no matter what a will provides. The remaining portion may pass to other heirs.

In the nine **community property states** where all of the money, assets and debts acquired during a marriage is legally considered the joint property of both spouses, the rights of both husbands and wives are equally protected. Thus, the law assumes that the surviving spouse owns half of everything that both partners earned during the marriage, no matter how much was actually contributed by either partner and even if only one spouse held legal title to the property. In states with community property laws, they provide the same spousal rights for marriages that end in divorce.

These jurisdictions include Arizona, California, Idaho, Louisiana, Nevada, New Mexico, Texas, Washington, and Wisconsin. Alaska is an opt-in community property state that gives both parties the option to make their property community property.

17.7e Who Should Consider Setting Up a Trust?

For most people, a will is the first choice for passing on an estate to heirs. But it is not the only choice. Among other estate planning tools, trusts are gaining in popularity. Trusts may offer before-death and after-death advantages.

People who should consider setting up a trust include those who have complex estates, hold relatively few liquid assets, desire privacy for their heirs, fear a battle over the provisions of a will, or live in a state with high probate costs or cumbersome probate procedures. You can use trusts to transfer assets while avoiding probate court.

Use Trusts to Transfer Assets Trusts may be created to safeguard the inheritances of survivors, fund a child's education, provide the down payment on someone's home, provide financial assistance for minor children, manage property for young children or disabled elders, and provide income for future generations. They also can reduce estate taxes (the subject of the following section). Properly drawn trusts can save you and your family time, trouble, and money. These laudable objectives can be achieved only with the assistance of an experienced attorney who specializes in carefully drafting, planning, and executing strategies and techniques in estate planning.

A **trust** is a legal arrangement between you as the **grantor** or creator of the trust and the **trustee**, the person designated to control and manage any assets in the trust. The agreement requires the trustee to faithfully and wisely manage and administer the assets to the benefit of the grantor and others. Trusts can be established to take effect during the grantor's life as well as upon his or her death.

Living Trusts Are Established while Grantor Is Alive There are two types of trusts: (1) **living trusts** that take effect while the grantor is alive and (2) testamentary trusts (see next section) that go into effect upon death.

Revocable Living Trusts A **revocable living trust** is used to protect and manage a person's assets. The person creating the trust maintains the right to change its terms or cancel the trust at any time, for any reason, during his or her lifetime. Thus, living trusts often establish the grantor as the trustee. A revocable living trust can provide for the orderly management and distribution of assets if the grantor becomes incapacitated or incompetent. A new trustee can easily be named. A revocable living trust operates much like a will and proves difficult to contest. Its assets stay in the estate of the grantor at his or her death.

Use an Irrevocable Charitable Remainder Trust to Boost Your Current Income Effective use of an **irrevocable charitable remainder trust (CRT)** is popular for people who want to leave a portion of their estate to charity because doing so can boost one's income during the grantor's lifetime. You set up the trust and irrevocably give it assets. The trust then pays you income from the assets in the trust for a set period, usually for life, and possibly your spouse's life as well. The charity eventually receives the assets of the CRT when you (and your spouse, if so arranged) die.

For example, Brianna Winston, a widow from Kent, Ohio, increased the after-tax income on her $600,000 investment portfolio from $1,800 to $4,800 per year by creating a CRT, thus giving the assets to the National Wildlife Federation. According to her attorney, Benjamin Pauly, the CRT then reinvested the proceeds, thus earning a higher return for the organization and providing more income to Brianna.

A CRT works well for people who show wealth on paper because of appreciated assets. The projected future value of the gift can be discounted to a present value. This amount can then be written off as a charitable contribution on Brianna's current income tax return, saving her even more money. It is wise to give to a CRT because the donor can avoid capital gains taxes while still realizing the full benefit of the asset's current value.

Irrevocable Living Trusts An **irrevocable living trust** is an arrangement in which the grantor relinquishes ownership *and* control of property. Usually this involves a gift of the property to the trust. It cannot be changed or undone by the grantor during his or her lifetime. The grantor gives up three key rights under an irrevocable living trust: (1) control of the property, (2) change of the beneficiaries, and (3) change of the trustees. Because irrevocable trusts are generally considered separate tax entities, the trust pays any income taxes due. Transfers to a trust made within three years of death may be brought back into the decedent's estate.

Testamentary Trusts Go into Effect Only Upon the Death of the Grantor The other broad category of trusts used in connection with estate planning comprises **testamentary trusts**. A testamentary trust becomes effective upon the death of the grantor according to the terms of the grantor's will or a revocable living trust. Such trusts can be designed to provide money or asset management after the grantor's death, to provide income for a surviving spouse and children, and to give assets to grandchildren or great-grandchildren while providing income from the assets to the surviving spouse and children, among other things.

17.7f Your Letter of Last Instructions Provides Guidance to Those Left Behind

Many people prepare a **letter of last instructions** along with their will that may contain preferences regarding funeral and burial instructions, organ donation wishes, material to

trust
Legal arrangement between you as the creator of the trust and the trustee, the person designated to faithfully and wisely manage any assets in the trust to your benefit and to the benefit of your heirs.

grantor
Creator of a trust—the person who makes a grant of assets to establish a trust. Also called the settler, donor, *or* trustor.

trustee
Person charged with carrying out the trust for the benefit of the grantor(s) and heirs.

living trust
A trust that takes effect while the grantor is still alive.

revocable living trust
Grantor maintains the right to change the trust's terms or cancel it at any time, for any reason, during his or her lifetime.

irrevocable living trust
Arrangement in which the grantor permanently gives up ownership and the right to control of the property, to change the beneficiaries, and to change the trustees.

testamentary trust
Becomes effective upon death of the grantor according to the terms of the grantor's will or a revocable living trust. Such trusts can provide money or asset management after the grantor's death for the heirs' benefit.

letter of last instructions
Nonlegal instrument that may contain preferences regarding funeral and burial, material to be included in the obituary, and other information useful to the survivors, such as the location of important documents.

be included in the obituary, contact information for relatives and friends, and other information useful to the survivors, such as the location of important documents. Family members and others are not legally bound by details in a letter of last instructions, but such a letter relieves them of the stress of making some emotional decisions. A letter of last instructions may specify that certain pieces of jewelry or art not specified in your will that may have more sentimental than monetary value are to go to specific people. If the will contains different instructions on these matters, the will prevails.

Your letter of last instructions and original will should be kept in a safe place, such as a lockable filing cabinet or home safe or at an attorney's office. Copies may be given to certain family members or friends.

17.7g Estate Taxes Impact Only 3,500 People Out of 330 Million

Only about 3,500 of the nation's wealthiest estates each year are required to pay federal estate taxes as owners die, thus nearly 330 million (99.9999 percent) are exempt. Estate taxes only impact the uber-wealthy.

federal estate tax

Assessed against a deceased person's estate before property (real estate, stocks and bonds, business interests, and so on) is transferred to heirs or assigned according to terms of a will or state intestacy laws.

The **federal estate tax** is assessed against the estate of a deceased person before property (real estate, stocks and bonds, business interests, and so on) is transferred to heirs or assigned according to terms of a will or state intestacy laws. It is a tax on the deceased's estate, not on the beneficiary who is to receive the property.

17.7h Exclusion Amount Is $5.45 Million

The **estate and gift tax exemption** is the amount that one can give away during a lifetime or bequest at death without being subject to the federal estate tax. The tax law exempts the first $5,450,000 of an individual's gifts made and estates of decedents dying. This is also called the **exclusion amount.** The tax rate on estates valued above this amount is 40 percent.

The law also offers "portability" of the exemption between married couples as it allows them to add any unused portion of the $5.45 million estate tax exemption of the first spouse to die to carry forward to the surviving spouse's estate tax exemption. Thus married couples may pass $10.9 million on to their heirs free from estate taxes with no planning whatsoever.

17.7i Gift Tax Exclusion Is $14,000 Annually

Giving is a wonderful way to transfer assets before you die, and the recipient of the gift is not taxed. People with extremely high asset values (above $5.45 million) may reduce the taxable total of their estate by donating up to $14,000 annually to a relative or a friend. This is called the **annual exclusion amount.** Only any gifts above $14,000 annually will be included in one's taxable estate.

annual exclusion amount

An annual amount of $14,000 that can be given to a relative or a friend to reduce one's total taxable estate.

When paid directly to an institution such money could pay someone's school tuition and/or medical expenses, including insurance premiums. There are no tax consequences for giving gifts up to $14,000 to as many different people you like. You also could give a recipient up to $28,000 if members of a married couple give individually to the same person.

17.7j State Estate Taxes and Inheritance Taxes

Fourteen states and the District of Columbia have a **state estate tax.** Estate taxes are charged against the estate regardless of who inherits the assets. State estate taxes usually are coupled with the federal estate tax, so when the federal estate tax is zero, those taxes are also zero. States with estate taxes typically exempt much less per estate from their tax and impose a top rate of 12 to 19 percent. Like the federal estate tax, bequests to a spouse are tax-free.

inheritance tax

A tax imposed by eight states that is assessed on the decedent's beneficiaries who receive inherited property.

Once the executor of the estate has divided up the assets and distributed them to the beneficiaries, the inheritance tax comes into play. An **inheritance tax** is levied on the transfer of assets to heirs who *receive* the property. Of the six states with inheritance taxes, Nebraska has the highest top rate at 18 percent; Kentucky and New Jersey are 16 percent. In the case of inheritance taxes, spouses, children, or siblings often have large exemptions. Transfers to spouses, children, parents, and other close relatives may be either totally exempt or be subject to a lower state inheritance tax rate. Relatives would need to have at least several hundred thousand dollars in assets, if not several million, to trigger a tax. The beneficiaries are responsible for paying inheritance taxes.

CONCEPT CHECK 17.7

1. What is probate, and give three examples of how people should transfer assets by contract to avoid probate.
2. Distinguish between probate and nonprobate property.
3. What topics go into a properly drafted will?
4. Distinguish between an irrevocable living trust and testamentary trusts?
5. What is the likelihood of average people paying estate or inheritance taxes?

WHAT DO YOU RECOMMEND *NOW*?

Now that you have read the chapter on estate planning, what do you recommend to Chrisanna and Fernando on the subject of retirement and estate planning regarding:

1. How much in Social Security benefits can each expect to receive?
2. How much do they each need to save for retirement if they want to spend at a lifestyle of 80 percent of their current living expenses?
3. In which types of retirement plans might Fernando invest for retirement?
4. What withdrawal rate might they use to avoid running out of money during retirement?
5. What two actions might they take to go about transferring their assets by contract to avoid probate?

SUMMARY OF LEARNING OBJECTIVES RECAPPED

LO1 Estimate your Social Security retirement income benefit.

You can and, indeed, must save adequately for your retirement. To do so, during your working years you should diversify your investments, keep investment costs low, and live below your means so you can save and invest. The Social Security program, which pays retirement benefits, is funded through FICA taxes on employees and employers, and the amounts withheld are put into trust fund accounts from which benefits are paid to current recipients. You must be fully insured under the Social Security program before retirement benefits can be paid.

LO2 Calculate the amount you must save for retirement in today's dollars.

Your retirement nest egg is the total amount of accumulated savings and investments needed to support your desired retirement. This is calculated by projecting your annual retirement expenses and income and determining the amount of annual savings you need to set aside in today's dollars to achieve your retirement goal.

LO3 Distinguish among the types of employer-sponsored tax-sheltered retirement plans.

The three major types of employer-sponsored retirement plans are defined-contribution, defined-benefit, and cash-balance. Some employers make matching contributions to their employees' accounts. Money invested is tax deductible to the employee and it grows tax deferred. Returns earned by investors are terrible, and this can be avoided. To receive benefits, an employee must be vested in an employer-sponsored retirement plan.

L04 **Explain the various types of personally established tax-sheltered retirement accounts.**

IRS regulations allow you to take advantage of personally established tax-sheltered retirement plans, including the traditional individual retirement account, or IRA, for which contributions are tax deductible and withdrawals are taxed. After-tax contributions may be made to Roth IRAs in which earnings accumulate tax-free and withdrawals can avoid taxation. Keogh plans and SEP-IRA plans are available for the small business owners and self-employed.

L05 **Use Monte Carlo Advice when investing for retirement.**

By using Monte Carlo simulations, investors can get a more realistic view of how much their current investments may yield later on during retirement. Investors may learn that they are playing it too safe by investing too conservatively today, and this may prevent them from reaching their long-term goals. Some investors may have to learn to be comfortable with increased risk, while others may have to save more or work longer. One should stay invested

in a tax-advantaged retirement plan when changing employers.

L06 **Describe how to avoid penalties and make your retirement money last.**

You can save on taxes and make sure your retirement money is maximized by not withdrawing it prior to retirement. Once you have a target nest egg to save for retirement, then figure out how many years your money will last in retirement. Annuities have too many disadvantages but some people still consider them as an option.

L07 **Plan for the distribution of your estate.**

Nonprobate property, which does not go through the court process of probate, includes assets transferred to survivors by contract, such as naming a beneficiary for your retirement plan or with bank accounts owned with another person through joint tenancy with right of survivorship. Assets can be transferred by beneficiary designation, by property ownership, and by payable-on-death designation. By creating one or more trusts, portions of an estate can be transferred in a contractual manner to others in a way that avoids probate. A trust is a legal arrangement between you as the grantor or creator of the trust and the trustee, the person designated to control and manage any assets in the trust. Recognize that relatively few people, about 3,500, pay federal estate taxes and only 8 states have inheritance taxes on recipients.

LET'S TALK ABOUT IT

1. **Why Calculate?** Do you know anyone who has estimated his or her retirement savings goal in today's dollars? Offer two reasons why many people do not perform those calculations. Offer two reasons why it would be smart for people to determine a financial target.

2. **Retirement Investing Today.** What are your thoughts on this comment? "Younger workers today face some serious challenges in deciding where to invest their retirement funds."

3. **Retirement Planning Mistakes.** Of all the mistakes that people make when planning for retirement, which one

might be likely to negatively affect your retirement planning the most? Give reasons why.

4. **Monte Carlo Advice.** What do you think of the Monte Carlo approach to investing? What is good about it?

5. **Wills for College Students.** Do college students really need a will at this point in their lives? Why or why not? What probably would happen to the typical college student's assets if he or she died without a will?

6. **Writing a Letter of Last Instructions.** Identify topics that you would cover in your letter of last instructions.

DO THE MATH

1. **Tax-Sheltered Returns.** Ashley Travis, of Harrisburg, Illinois, is in the 25 percent marginal tax bracket and is considering the tax consequences of investing $2,000 at the end of each year for 30 years in a tax-sheltered retirement account, assuming that the investment earns 8 percent annually.

   (a) How much will Ashley's account total over 30 years if the growth in the investment remains sheltered from taxes?

   (b) How much will the account total if the investments are not sheltered from taxes? (Hint: Use Appendix A-3 or the *Garmim/Forgue* companion website.)

2. **Withdrawal Amount.** Over the years, Ahmed and Aamina El-zayaty, of Berkeley, California, have accumulated $200,000 and $220,000, respectively, in their employer-sponsored retirement plans. If the amounts in their two accounts earn a 6 percent rate of return over Ahmed and Aamina's anticipated 20 years of retirement,

how large an amount could be withdrawn from the two accounts each month? Use the *Garman/Forgue* companion website or Appendix A-4 to make your calculations.

3. **Savings Amount Needed.** Brenda and Dan Domico, of Weatherford, Texas, desire an annual retirement income of $40,000. They expect to live for 30 years past retirement. Assuming that the couple could earn a 3 percent after-tax and after-inflation rate of return on their investments, what amount of accumulated savings and investments would they need? Use Appendix A-4 or the *Garman/Forgue* companion website to solve for the answer.

4. **Annual Earnings.** Jose and Gabriela Perez, of Bridgewater, Virginia, hope to sell their large home for $380,000 and retire to a smaller residence valued at $150,000. After they sell the property, they plan to invest the $200,000 in equity remaining after selling expenses and earn a 4 percent after-tax return. Approximately how much will this nest egg be worth in five years when they retire? Use Appendix A-1 or the *Garman/Forgue* companion website to solve for the answer.

DO IT IN CLASS
Page 19

5. **Twins Invest.** Janet Brooks, of Amarillo, Texas, plans to invest $3,000 each year in a mutual fund for the next 40 years to accumulate savings for retirement. Her twin sister, Rebecca, plans to invest the same amount for the same length of time in the same mutual fund. However, instead of investing with after-tax money, Rebecca will invest through an employer-sponsored tax-sheltered retirement plan. If both mutual fund accounts provide an 8 percent rate of return, how much more will Rebecca have in her retirement account after 40 years than Janet? How much will Rebecca have if she also invests the amount saved in income taxes? Assume both women pay income taxes at a 25 percent rate. Use Appendix A-3 or the *Garman/Forgue* companion website to solve for the answer.

6. **More Aggressive Investing.** Shanice Johnson, of Philadelphia, Pennsylvania, wants to invest $4,000 annually for her retirement 30 years from now. She has a conservative investment philosophy and expects to earn a return of 3 percent in a tax-sheltered account. If she took a more aggressive investment approach and earned a return of 5 percent, how much more would Shanice accumulate? Use Appendix A-3 or the *Garman/Forgue* companion website to solve for the answer.

7. **Disability Before Retirement.** Jackie Facet of Auburn, Alabama, age 60, was planning on retirement and investing well for it because he now has $400,000 in his retirement accounts and would likely to have doubled that by age 67. But, he became permanently disabled after getting into a vehicle accident a few months ago.

   (a) If his average earnings were $65,000, what would be his Social Security disability benefit?

   (b) Social Security Disability benefits end at age 65 and Jackie will switch over to Social Security Retirement benefits. What will his retirement benefit amount be at age 65?

   (c) How much might Jackie earn each year on his $400,000 portfolio if it earns 4 percent?

   (d) How large an amount could be withdrawn from his account each month starting at age 60 over 25 years of retirement? Use Appendix A-4 or the *Garman/Forgue* companion website to solve for the answer.

   (e) Advise Jackie about his options.

FINANCIAL PLANNING CASES

CASE 1

The Johnsons Consider Retirement Planning

Harry Johnson's father, William, was recently forced into early retirement at age 63 because of poor health. In addition to the psychological drawbacks of the unanticipated retirement, William's financial situation is poor because he had not planned adequately for retirement. His situation has inspired Harry and Belinda to take a look at their own retirement planning. Together they now make about $200,000 per year ($110,000 for Belinda and $90,000 for Harry) and would like to have a similar level of living when they retire. Harry and Belinda are both are in their early 40s and they recently received their annual Social Security Benefits Statements indicating that they each could expect about $22,000 per year in today's dollars as retirement benefits in 25 years at age 67. Although their retirement is a long way off, they know that the sooner they put a plan in place, the larger their retirement nest egg will be.

(a) Belinda believes that the couple could maintain their current level of living if their retirement income represented 90 percent of their current annual income after adjusting for inflation. Assuming a 4 percent inflation rate, what would Harry and Belindas's annual income need to be over and above their Social Security benefits when they retire at age 67? (Hint: Use Appendix A-1 or visit the *Garman/Forgue* companion website.)

DO IT IN CLASS
Page 19

(b) Both Harry and Belinda are covered by defined-contribution retirement plans at work. Harry contributes $5,400 to his plan and his employer puts in $2,700. Belinda contributes $6,600 and her employer puts in $3,300. Assuming a 7 percent rate of return, what would their combined retirement nest egg (now valued at $400,000) total 25 years from now if they keep contributing? (Hint: Use Appendix A-3 or visit the *Garman/Forgue* companion website.)

(c) For how many years would the retirement nest egg provide the amount of income indicated in Question (a)? Assume a 4 percent return after taxes and inflation. (Hint: Use Appendix A-4 or visit the *Garman/Forgue* companion website.)

DO IT IN CLASS
Page 548

(d) One of Harry's dreams is to retire in his fifties. What would the answers to Questions (a), (b), and (c) be if he and Belinda were to retire in 12 years?

(e) What would you advise Harry and Belinda to do to meet their income needs for retirement?

CASE 2

Victor and Maria's Retirement Plans

Victor, now age 61, and Maria, age 59, plan to retire at the end of the year. Since his employer changed from a defined-benefit retirement plan to a defined-contribution plan ten years ago, Victor has been contributing the maximum amount of his salary to several different mutual funds offered through the plan, although his employer never matched any of his contributions. Victor's tax-sheltered account, which now has a balance of $300,000, has been growing at a rate of 7 percent through the years. Under the previous defined-benefit plan, today Victor is entitled to a single-life pension of $360 per month ($4,320 annually) or a joint and survivor option paying $240 per month ($2,880 annually). The value of Victor's investment of $20,000 in Pharmacia stock some years ago has now grown to $56,000.

Maria's earlier career as a medical records assistant provided no retirement program, although she did save $10,000 through her credit union, which was later used to purchase zero-coupon bonds now worth $28,000. Maria's second career as a pharmaceutical representative for Pharmacia allowed her to contribute to her retirement account over the past nine years, which is now worth $98,000. Pharmacia matched a portion of her contributions, and that match is now worth $70,000; its growth rate has ranged from 6 to 10 percent each year. When Maria's mother died last year, Maria inherited her home, which is rented for $1,800 per month; the house has a market value of $300,000. The Hernandezes' personal residence is worth $260,000. They pay combined federal and state income taxes at a 30 percent rate.

(a) Sum up the present values of the Hernandezes' assets, excluding their personal residence, and identify which assets derive from tax-sheltered accounts.

(b) Assume that the Hernandezes sold their stocks, bonds, and rental property, realizing a gain of $34,000 after income taxes and commissions. If that sum plus their tax-sheltered accounts earned a 7 percent rate of return over the Hernandezes' anticipated 20 years of retirement, how large an amount could be withdrawn each month? How large an amount could be withdrawn each month if they needed the money over 30 years? How large an amount could be withdrawn each month if the proceeds earned 6 percent for 20 years? For 30 years? Hint: Use Appendix A4.

CASE 3

Julia Price Thinks About Retirement

Julia is now in her early 50s. She has had three jobs in her career so far and participated fully in the defined-contribution retirement plans offered by her employers. When she left her last position, she rolled her retirement account over to the account at her new employer, and it is currently worth about $480,000. Now she is about to change jobs again. But this time, she is taking a job with the Consumer Financial Protection Bureau in Washington, DC. She will also be taking about four months off from working before starting that government job. The federal government retirement program is a defined-benefit plan. That means she cannot transfer her private sector plan to the government plan and therefore must decide whether to leave the funds within her current employer's plan or open a rollover IRA account into which to transfer the funds tax- and penalty-free. Another alternative available to her is to withdraw the $480,000 from her current account, pay income taxes on it this year (probably at a the highest federal marginal tax rate), and invest the proceeds of approximately $300,000 ($480,000 less about $180,000) in a new Roth IRA account. Offer your opinions about her thinking.

CASE 4

Calculation of Annual Savings Needed to Meet a Retirement Goal

Nicci Denny, age 40, single, and from Colorado Springs, Colorado, is trying to estimate the amount she needs to save annually to meet her retirement needs. Nicci currently earns $65,000 per year. She expects to need 80 percent of her current salary to live on at retirement. Nicci anticipates receiving about $1900 per month in Social Security benefits at age 65. Using the Run the Numbers worksheet on page 528, answer the following questions.

(a) What annual income would Nicci need for retirement?

(b) What would her annual expected Social Security benefit be?

(c) Nicci expects to receive $1,500 per month from her defined-benefit pension at work. What is her annual benefit?

(d) How much annual retirement income will she need from her retirement funds?

(e) How much will Nicci need to save by retirement in today's dollars if she plans to retire at age 65 and live to age 90?

(f) Nicci currently has $15,000 in a Roth IRA. Assuming a growth rate of 8 percent, what will be the value of her Roth IRA when she retires? (Hint: Don't take out income taxes.)

(g) How much additional money will she still need to save for retirement?

(h) What is the amount she needs to save each year to reach this goal?

DO IT IN CLASS
Page 526

CASE 5

A Couple Considers the Ramifications of Dying Intestate

Yvonne Moody of Dallas, Texas, is a 34-year-old police detective earning $58,000 per year. She and her husband, Joshua, who is a public school teacher earning $44,000, have two children in elementary school. They own a modestly furnished home and two late-model cars. Morgan also owns a bass fishing boat. Both spouses have 401(k) retirement accounts through their employers, and their employers also provide them with group term life policies that match their salaries. Morgan also has a $100,000 term life policy of her own. The couple has about $5,000 in their joint checking account. Neither has a will.

(a) List four negative things that could happen if either Morgan or Joshua were to die without a will.

(b) What would be the most important negative consequence of not having a will if both Yvonne and Joshua were to die together in a car accident?

(c) Which assets could be jointly owned so that they will automatically transfer to the other spouse if either Yvonne or Joshua dies?

(d) What qualities should Yvonne and Joshua look for when naming the executors of their wills?

(e) Once they have completed and signed their wills, where should the Moody's keep the original documents?

DO IT IN CLASS
Page 553

BE YOUR OWN PERSONAL FINANCIAL MANAGER

1. **Income Needed in Retirement Adjusted for Inflation.** Based on your expected income in your field after you graduate, make an estimate of the dollar amount you would need to make today to live comfortably as a retiree. Then assume that inflation will average 3 per cent per year until you are age 67. Use Appendix A-1 to calculate the dollar amount you would need that year to live at the level of living you estimate as being comfortable today.

2. **Calculate Your Retirement Nest Egg.** Use the Run the Numbers worksheet and material on pages 525–528 or Worksheet 65: My Estimated Retirement Savings Goal in Today's Dollars from "My Personal Financial Planner" to estimate the amount you must save each year to reach your retirement goals.

My Personal Financial Planner

3. **How Long Will Your Retirement Money Last?** If you currently have begun a retirement savings nest egg and/or are currently setting aside funds into an account each year, use Appendix A-1 (for the nest egg) and Appendix A-2 (for the annual deposits) to estimate your full nest egg at an age that you would like to retire. Then use the material on page 548 and Worksheet 66: How Long Will My Retirement Money Last? from "My Personal Financial Planner" to estimate how long that money will last based on the result you obtained for item 1 above.

My Personal Financial Planner

4. **Questions to Ask About an Employer's Retirement Plan.** Are you currently employed and eligible to participate in an employer-sponsored retirement plan? Use Worksheet 67: Questions to Ask About Your Employer's Retirement Plan from "My Personal Financial Planner" to assess the plan and make decisions about your enrollment in the plan.

My Personal Financial Planner

5. **Beneficiary Designations.** Complete Worksheet 68: My Assets to Be Transferred by Beneficiary Designations in "My Personal Financial Planner" by recording your intended beneficiaries for the dozen or more types of assets you either own now or would expect to own in a few years.

My Personal Financial Planner

ON THE NET

Go to the Web pages indicated to complete these exercises.

1. **Calculate Your Benefits.** Visit the website for the Social Security Administration. There you will find a quick benefits calculator at www.socialsecurity.gov/estimator that can be used to estimate your Social Security benefit in today's dollars. Use an income figure that approximates what you expect to earn in the first full year after graduating from college. When the calculator provides your answer, click on "What's the best age?" to see when you would be better off if you had waited until age 67 to begin taking benefits rather than age 62.

2. **How Much Do I Need to Save?** Go to Vanguard.com to use their calculator on how much do I need to save for retirement (personal.vanguard.com/us/insights/retirement/saving/set-retirement-goals). What do you think of the calculator and its assumptions?

3. **How Much Do I Need to Retire?** Go to CNNMoney.com to use their calculator on how much do I need to retire (money.cnn.com/calculator/retirement/retirement-need). Put in your figures and view the results. What do you think of the calculator and its assumptions?

4. **How Much Do I Need to Retire?** Go to Bankrate.com to use their calculator on how much do I need to retire (www.bankrate.com/calculators/retirement/retirement-goal-calculator.aspx). Put in your figures and view the results. What do you think of the calculator and its assumptions?

5. **The Value of Compound Interest.** Go to www.calcxml.com/calculators/interest-calculator?skn put in your figures, including anticipated raises over time, and view the results. How do you like this calculator?

6. **Monthly Sum Needed in Retirement.** Go to CNNMoney (money.cnn.com/tools/annuities) and input some numbers. What do you think of the calculator and its assumptions?

7. **Annuity Calculator.** Go to BankRate.com (www.bankrate.com/calculators/investing/annuity-calculator.aspx) and input some numbers. What do you think of the calculator and its assumptions?

8. **Charitable Remainder Trusts.** View an example of a charitable remainder trust and read the logic behind the donors making such a gift (www.futurefocus.net/crutexample.htm). What are your thoughts about the value to both the donor and the recipient?

9. **Estate Planning.** Go to Nolo (www.nolo.com/legal-encyclopedia/12-simple-steps-estate-plan-29472.html) and review the list of 12 simple steps in estate planning. How does the list compare to what you have read in this chapter?

ACTION INVOLVEMENT PROJECTS

1. **Views Concerning Social Security.** Talk to three fellow students who are not taking your personal finance class. Ask them to explain their feelings about the degree to which Social Security will meet their income needs during retirement. Then ask them how they plan to meet their retirement income needs beyond what Social Security might provide. Make a table that summarizes your findings. Then compare their views and plans with what you have learned from reading this chapter.

2. **What Is It Like to Be Retired?** Survey three individuals or couples who have been retired for more than one year. Ask them how financially well prepared they felt before they retired. Then ask them to assess the financial realities of retirement at the current point in time. Include a discussion of how their investment mix (mutual funds, stocks, bonds, annuities) may or may not have changed since they have retired. Write a summary of their responses and how their experiences may affect your thinking about being retired.

3. **Feelings About Approaching Retirement.** Survey three individuals or couples who are about 10 to 15 years away from retirement. Ask them to explain what steps they have taken to prepare for retirement and how prepared they feel. Also ask them to describe what they will do financially in the next decade to get ready for retirement. Write a summary of their responses and how their experiences impact your own thinking about getting ready for retirement.

4. **Retirement Savings Behavior Early in One's Career.** Survey three individuals or couples who are less than ten years into their professional careers. Ask them if they have started saving for retirement and, if not, why not. Also ask them about the types of investments (mutual funds, stocks, bonds) that they are using or would use to save for retirement. Write a summary of their responses and how their efforts, or lack thereof, impact your thinking about saving for retirement.

5. **Monte Carlo Simulation** Visit the YouTube website www.youtube.com/watch?v=Q5Fw2IRMjPQ and view it. Compare with what you have read in this chapter.

6. **Letter of Last Instructions.** Create a letter of last instructions by giving your personal representative or family member the information needed concerning your personal and financial matters (funeral arrangements, location of will, insurance policies, location of documents, etc.).

7. **Loss of Defined-Benefit Plans.** What do you think of the long-term trend of employers largely moving away from offering employees defined-benefit retirement plans to providing them with defined-contribution plans? Write up you comments.

8. **Low-Cost Fees.** Review the box "Common Sense: Invest Retirement Money Only in Low-Cost Choices to Earn 42 Percent More" on page 533 and offer some comments about the wisdom of its conclusion.

9. **How Long Will Money Last?** Review Table 17-3 on page 548, and offer your comments on what you see.

10. **Transfers.** Make a short list of your assets and determine if upon your death they all will transfer to beneficiaries by contract, property ownership designations, or by payable-on-death designations.

APPENDIXES

S.Dashkevych/Shutterstock.com

Appendix A

PRESENT AND FUTURE VALUE TABLES

Many problems in personal finance involve decisions about money values at varying points in time. These values can be directly and fairly compared only when they are adjusted to a common point in time. Chapter 1 introduced the basic time value concepts. This appendix offers more details about the time value of money. In addition, it provides tables listing the future and present value of $1 with which to make calculations. Four assumptions must be made to eliminate unnecessary complications:

1. Each planning period is one year long.
2. Only annual interest rates are considered.
3. Interest rates are the same during each of the annual periods.
4. Interest is compounded and continues earning a return in subsequent periods.

Tables of present and future values can be constructed to make these adjustments. **Future values** are derived from the principles of compounding the dollar values ahead in time. **Present values** are derived by discounting (which is the inverse of compounding) the dollar values and transferring them to an earlier point in time.

It is usually unnecessary to precisely identify whether the interest is paid/received at the *beginning* of a period or at the end of a period, or to know whether interest compounds daily or quarterly instead of annually. (These calculations require even more tables.) The following present and future value tables assume that money is accumulated, received, paid, compounded, or whatever at the *end* of a period. The tables can be used to compute the mathematics of personal finance with high certainty and to confirm (or reject as inaccurate) what people tell you about financial matters.

The most significant task is to find the correct table. Accordingly, each table is clearly described here, and illustrations of its use appear on the facing page where possible. In addition, the appropriate mathematical equation is shown and can be easily solved using a calculator.

Illustrations Using Appendix A-1: Future Value of a Single Amount ($1)

To use Appendix A-1 on page A-4, locate the future value factor for the time period and the interest rate.

1. You invest $500 at a 15 percent rate of return for 12 years. How much will you have at the end of that 12-year period?

   The future value factor is 5.350; hence, the solution is $500 × 5.350, or $2,675.

2. Property values in your neighborhood are increasing at a rate of 5 percent per year. If your home is presently worth $190,000, what will its worth be in 7 years?

   The future value factor is 1.407; hence, the solution is $190,000 × 1.407, or $267,330.

3. You need to amass $40,000 in the next 10 years to make a balloon payment on your home mortgage. You have $17,000 available to invest. What annual interest rate must be earned to realize the $40,000?

   $40,000 ÷ $17,000 = 2.353. Read down the periods (n) column to 10 years and across to 2.367 (close enough), which is found under the 9 percent column. Hence, the $17,000 invested at 9 percent for 10 years will grow to a future value of slightly more than $40,000.

4. An apartment building is currently valued at $160,000, and it has been appreciating at 8 percent per year. If this rate continues, in how many years will it be worth $300,000?

   $30,000 ÷ $160,000 = 1.875. Read down the 8 percent column until you reach 1.851 (close enough to 1.875). This number corresponds to a period of 8 years. Hence, the $160,000 property appreciating at 8 percent annually will grow to a future value of $300,000 in slightly more than 8 years.

5. You have the choice of receiving a down payment from someone who wants to purchase your rental property as $15,000 today or as a personal note for $25,000 payable in 6 years. If you could expect to earn 8 percent on such funds, which is the better choice?

   The future value factor is 1.587; hence, the future value of $15,000 at 8 percent is $15,000 × 1.587, or $23,805. Thus, it would be better to take the note for $25,000.

6. How much will an automobile now priced at $20,000 cost in 4 years, assuming an annual inflation rate of 5 percent?

   Read down the 5 percent column and across the row for 4 years to locate the future value factor of 1.216. Hence, the solution is $20,000 × 1.216, or $24,320.

7. How large a lump-sum investment do you need now to have $20,000 available in 5 years, assuming a 10 percent annual rate of return?

   The $20,000 future value is divided by 1.611 (10 percent at 5 years), resulting in a current lump-sum investment of $12,415.

8. You have $5,000 now and need $10,000 in 9 years. What rate of return is needed to reach that goal?

   Divide the future value of $10,000 by the present value of the lump sum of $5,000 to obtain a future value factor of 2.0. In the row for 9 years, locate the future value factor of 1.999 (very close to 2.0). Read up the column to find that an 8 percent return on investment is needed.

9. How many years will it take your lump-sum investment of $10,000 to grow to $16,000, given an annual rate of return of 7 percent?

   Divide the future value of $16,000 by the present value of the $10,000 lump sum to compute a future value factor of 1.6; look down the 7 percent column to find 1.606 (close enough). Read across the row to find that an investment period of 7 years is needed.

An alternative approach is to use a calculator to determine the future value, *FV*, of a sum of money invested today, assuming that the amount remains in the investment for a specified number of time periods (usually years) and that it earns a certain rate of return each period. The equation is

$$FV = PV(1.0 + i)^n \tag{A.1}$$

where

$$FV = \textit{Future Value}$$
$$PV = \textit{Present Value} \text{ of the investment}$$
$$i = \textit{Interest} \text{ rate per period}$$
$$n = \textit{Number} \text{ of periods the } PV \text{ is invested}$$

Appendix A-1

Future Value of a Single Amount ($1 at the End of *n* Periods) (Used to Compute the Compounded Future Value of a Known Lump Sum)

n	1%	2%	3%	4%	5%	6%	7%	8%	9%	10%	11%	12%	13%	14%	15%	16%	17%	18%	19%	20%
1	1.0100	1.0200	1.0300	1.0400	1.0500	1.0600	1.0700	1.0800	1.0900	1.1000	1.1100	1.1200	1.1300	1.1400	1.1500	1.1600	1.1700	1.1800	1.1900	1.2000
2	1.0201	1.0404	1.0609	1.0816	1.1025	1.1236	1.1449	1.1664	1.1881	1.2100	1.2321	1.2544	1.2769	1.2996	1.3225	1.3456	1.3689	1.3924	1.4161	1.4400
3	1.0303	1.0612	1.0927	1.1249	1.1576	1.1910	1.2250	1.2597	1.2950	1.3310	1.3676	1.4049	1.4429	1.4815	1.5209	1.5609	1.6016	1.6430	1.6852	1.7280
4	1.0406	1.0824	1.1255	1.1699	1.2155	1.2625	1.3108	1.3605	1.4116	1.4641	1.5181	1.5735	1.6305	1.6890	1.7490	1.8106	1.8739	1.9388	2.0053	2.0736
5	1.0510	1.1041	1.1593	1.2167	1.2763	1.3382	1.4026	1.4693	1.5386	1.6105	1.6851	1.7623	1.8424	1.9254	2.0114	2.1003	2.1924	2.2878	2.3864	2.4883
6	1.0615	1.1262	1.1941	1.2653	1.3401	1.4185	1.5007	1.5869	1.6771	1.7716	1.8704	1.9738	2.0820	2.1950	2.3131	2.4364	2.5652	2.6996	2.8398	2.9860
7	1.0721	1.1487	1.2299	1.3159	1.4071	1.5036	1.6058	1.7138	1.8280	1.9487	2.0762	2.2107	2.3526	2.5023	2.6600	2.8262	3.0012	3.1855	3.3793	3.5832
8	1.0829	1.1717	1.2668	1.3686	1.4775	1.5938	1.7182	1.8509	1.9926	2.1436	2.3045	2.4760	2.6584	2.8526	3.0590	3.2784	3.5115	3.7589	4.0214	4.2998
9	1.0937	1.1951	1.3048	1.4233	1.5513	1.6895	1.8385	1.9990	2.1719	2.3579	2.5580	2.7731	3.0040	3.2519	3.5179	3.8030	4.1084	4.4355	4.7854	5.1598
10	1.1046	1.2190	1.3439	1.4802	1.6289	1.7908	1.9672	2.1589	2.3674	2.5937	2.8394	3.1058	3.3946	3.7072	4.0456	4.4114	4.8068	5.2338	5.6947	6.1917
11	1.1157	1.2434	1.3842	1.5395	1.7103	1.8983	2.1049	2.3316	2.5804	2.8531	3.1518	3.4785	3.8359	4.2262	4.6524	5.1173	5.6240	6.1759	6.7767	7.4301
12	1.1268	1.2682	1.4258	1.6010	1.7959	2.0122	2.2522	2.5182	2.8127	3.1384	3.4985	3.8960	4.3345	4.8179	5.3503	5.9360	6.5801	7.2876	8.0642	8.9161
13	1.1381	1.2936	1.4685	1.6651	1.8856	2.1329	2.4098	2.7196	3.0658	3.4523	3.8833	4.3635	4.8980	5.4924	6.1528	6.8858	7.6987	8.5994	9.5964	10.6993
14	1.1495	1.3195	1.5126	1.7317	1.9799	2.2609	2.5785	2.9372	3.3417	3.7975	4.3104	4.8871	5.5348	6.2613	7.0757	7.9875	9.0075	10.1472	11.4198	12.8392
15	1.1610	1.3459	1.5580	1.8009	2.0789	2.3966	2.7590	3.1722	3.6425	4.1772	4.7846	5.4736	6.2543	7.1379	8.1371	9.2655	10.5387	11.9737	13.5895	15.4070
16	1.1726	1.3728	1.6047	1.8730	2.1829	2.5404	2.9522	3.4259	3.9703	4.5950	5.3109	6.1304	7.0673	8.1372	9.3576	10.7480	12.3303	14.1290	16.1715	18.4884
17	1.1843	1.4002	1.6528	1.9479	2.2920	2.6928	3.1588	3.7000	4.3276	5.0545	5.8951	6.8660	7.9861	9.2765	10.7613	12.4677	14.4265	16.6722	19.2441	22.1861
18	1.1961	1.4282	1.7024	2.0258	2.4066	2.8543	3.3799	3.9960	4.7171	5.5599	6.5436	7.6900	9.0243	10.5752	12.3755	14.4625	16.8790	19.6733	22.9005	26.6233
19	1.2081	1.4568	1.7535	2.1068	2.5270	3.0256	3.6165	4.3157	5.1417	6.1159	7.2633	8.6128	10.1974	12.0557	14.2318	16.7765	19.7484	23.2144	27.2516	31.9480
20	1.2202	1.4859	1.8061	2.1911	2.6533	3.2071	3.8697	4.6610	5.6044	6.7275	8.0623	9.6463	11.5231	13.7435	16.3665	19.4608	23.1056	27.3930	32.4294	38.3376
21	1.2324	1.5157	1.8603	2.2788	2.7860	3.3996	4.1406	5.0338	6.1088	7.4002	8.9492	10.8038	13.0211	15.6676	18.8215	22.5745	27.0336	32.3238	38.5910	46.0051
22	1.2447	1.5460	1.9161	2.3699	2.9253	3.6035	4.4304	5.4365	6.6586	8.1403	9.9336	12.1003	14.7138	17.8610	21.6447	26.1864	31.6293	38.1421	45.9233	55.2061
23	1.2572	1.5769	1.9736	2.4647	3.0715	3.8197	4.7405	5.8715	7.2579	8.9543	11.0263	13.5523	16.6266	20.3616	24.8915	30.3762	37.0062	45.0076	54.6487	66.2474
24	1.2697	1.6084	2.0328	2.5633	3.2251	4.0489	5.0724	6.3412	7.9111	9.8497	12.2392	15.1786	18.7881	23.2122	28.6252	35.2364	43.2973	53.1090	65.0320	79.4968
25	1.2824	1.6406	2.0938	2.6658	3.3864	4.2919	5.4274	6.8485	8.6231	10.8347	13.5855	17.0001	21.2305	26.4619	32.9190	40.8742	50.6578	62.6686	77.3881	95.3962
26	1.2953	1.6734	2.1566	2.7725	3.5557	4.5494	5.8074	7.3964	9.3992	11.9182	15.0799	19.0401	23.9905	30.1666	37.8568	47.4141	59.2697	73.9490	92.0918	114.4755
27	1.3082	1.7069	2.2213	2.8834	3.7335	4.8223	6.2139	7.9881	10.2451	13.1100	16.7386	21.3249	27.1093	34.3899	43.5353	55.0004	69.3455	87.2598	109.5893	137.3706
28	1.3213	1.7410	2.2879	2.9987	3.9201	5.1117	6.6488	8.6271	11.1671	14.4210	18.5799	23.8839	30.6335	39.2045	50.0656	63.8004	81.1342	102.9666	130.4112	164.8447
29	1.3345	1.7758	2.3566	3.1187	4.1161	5.4184	7.1143	9.3173	12.1722	15.8631	20.6237	26.7499	34.6158	44.6931	57.5755	74.0085	94.9271	121.5005	155.1893	197.8136
30	1.3478	1.8114	2.4273	3.2434	4.3219	5.7435	7.6123	10.0627	13.2677	17.4494	22.8923	29.9599	39.1159	50.9502	66.2118	85.8499	111.0647	143.3706	184.6753	237.3763
40	1.4889	2.2080	3.2620	4.8010	7.0400	10.2857	14.9745	21.7245	31.4094	45.2593	65.0009	93.0510	132.7816	188.8835	267.8635	378.7212	533.8687	750.3783	1051.668	1469.772
50	1.6446	2.6916	4.3839	7.1067	11.4674	18.4202	29.4570	46.9016	74.3575	117.3909	184.5648	289.0022	450.7359	700.2330	1083.657	1670.704	2566.215	3927.357	5988.914	9100.438

Illustrations Using Appendix A-2: Present Value of a Single Amount ($1)

To use this table, locate the present value factor for the time period and the interest rate.

1. You want to begin a college fund for your newborn child; you hope to accumulate $30,000 by 18 years from now. If a current investment opportunity yields 7 percent, how much must you invest in a lump sum to realize the $30,000 when needed?

   The present value factor is 0.296; hence, the solution is $30,000 × 0.296, or $8,880.

2. You hope to retire in 25 years and want to deposit a single lump sum that will grow to $250,000 at that time. If you can now invest at 8 percent, how much must you invest to realize the $250,000 when needed?

   The present value factor is 0.146; hence, the solution is $250,000 × 0.146, or $36,500. The present value of $250,000 received 25 years from now is $36,500 if the interest rate is 8 percent.

3. You have the choice of receiving a down payment from someone who wants to purchase your rental property as $15,000 today or as a personal note for $25,000 payable in 6 years. If you could expect to earn 8 percent on such funds, which is the better choice?

   The present value factor is 0.630; hence, the solution is $25,000 × 0.630, or $15,750. Thus, the present value of $25,000 received in 6 years is greater than $15,000 received now, and the personal note is the better choice.

4. You own a $1,000 bond paying 8 percent annually until its maturity in 5 years. You need to sell the bond now, even though the market rate of interest on similar bonds has increased to 10 percent. What discounted market price for the bond will allow the new buyer to earn a yield of 10 percent?

   First, compute the present value of the future interest payments of $80 per year for 5 years at 10 percent (using Appendix A-4): $80 × 3.791, or $303.28. Second, compute the present value of the future principal repayment of $1,000 after 5 years at 10 percent: $1,000 × 0.621, or $621.00. Hence, the market price is the sum of the two present values ($303.28 + $621.00), or $924.28.

An alternative approach is to use a calculator to determine the present value, *PV*, of a single payment received some time in the future. The equation, which is a rearrangement of the future value Equation (A.1), is

$$PV = \frac{FV}{(1.0 + i)^n} \qquad \text{(A.2)}$$

where

$$PV = \textit{Present Value} \text{ of the investment}$$
$$FV = \textit{Future Value}$$
$$i = \textit{Interest} \text{ rate per period}$$
$$n = \textit{Number} \text{ of periods the } PV \text{ is invested}$$

Appendix A-2

Present Value of a Single Amount ($1) (Used to Compute the Discounted Present Value of Some Known Future Single Lump Sum)

n	1%	2%	3%	4%	5%	6%	7%	8%	9%	10%	11%	12%	13%	14%	15%	16%	17%	18%	19%	20%
1	0.9901	0.9804	0.9709	0.9615	0.9524	0.9434	0.9346	0.9259	0.9174	0.9091	0.9009	0.8929	0.8850	0.8772	0.8696	0.8621	0.8547	0.8475	0.8403	0.8333
2	0.9803	0.9612	0.9426	0.9246	0.9070	0.8900	0.8734	0.8573	0.8417	0.8264	0.8116	0.7972	0.7831	0.7695	0.7561	0.7432	0.7305	0.7182	0.7062	0.6944
3	0.9706	0.9423	0.9151	0.8890	0.8638	0.8396	0.8163	0.7938	0.7722	0.7513	0.7312	0.7118	0.6931	0.6750	0.6575	0.6407	0.6244	0.6086	0.5934	0.5787
4	0.9610	0.9238	0.8885	0.8548	0.8227	0.7921	0.7629	0.7350	0.7084	0.6830	0.6587	0.6355	0.6133	0.5921	0.5718	0.5523	0.5337	0.5158	0.4987	0.4823
5	0.9515	0.9057	0.8626	0.8219	0.7835	0.7473	0.7130	0.6806	0.6499	0.6209	0.5935	0.5674	0.5428	0.5194	0.4972	0.4761	0.4561	0.4371	0.4190	0.4019
6	0.9420	0.8880	0.8375	0.7903	0.7462	0.7050	0.6663	0.6302	0.5963	0.5645	0.5346	0.5066	0.4803	0.4556	0.4323	0.4104	0.3898	0.3704	0.3521	0.3349
7	0.9327	0.8706	0.8131	0.7599	0.7107	0.6651	0.6227	0.5835	0.5470	0.5132	0.4817	0.4523	0.4251	0.3996	0.3759	0.3538	0.3332	0.3139	0.2959	0.2791
8	0.9235	0.8535	0.7894	0.7307	0.6768	0.6274	0.5820	0.5403	0.5019	0.4665	0.4339	0.4039	0.3762	0.3506	0.3269	0.3050	0.2848	0.2660	0.2487	0.2326
9	0.9143	0.8368	0.7664	0.7026	0.6446	0.5919	0.5439	0.5002	0.4604	0.4241	0.3909	0.3606	0.3329	0.3075	0.2843	0.2630	0.2434	0.2255	0.2090	0.1938
10	0.9053	0.8203	0.7441	0.6756	0.6139	0.5584	0.5083	0.4632	0.4224	0.3855	0.3522	0.3220	0.2946	0.2697	0.2472	0.2267	0.2080	0.1911	0.1756	0.1615
11	0.8963	0.8043	0.7224	0.6496	0.5847	0.5268	0.4751	0.4289	0.3875	0.3505	0.3173	0.2875	0.2607	0.2366	0.2149	0.1954	0.1778	0.1619	0.1476	0.1346
12	0.8874	0.7885	0.7014	0.6246	0.5568	0.4970	0.4440	0.3971	0.3555	0.3186	0.2858	0.2567	0.2307	0.2076	0.1869	0.1685	0.1520	0.1372	0.1240	0.1122
13	0.8787	0.7730	0.6810	0.6006	0.5303	0.4688	0.4150	0.3677	0.3262	0.2897	0.2575	0.2292	0.2042	0.1821	0.1625	0.1452	0.1299	0.1163	0.1042	0.0935
14	0.8700	0.7579	0.6611	0.5775	0.5051	0.4423	0.3878	0.3405	0.2992	0.2633	0.2320	0.2046	0.1807	0.1597	0.1413	0.1252	0.1110	0.0985	0.0876	0.0779
15	0.8613	0.7430	0.6419	0.5553	0.4810	0.4173	0.3624	0.3152	0.2745	0.2394	0.2090	0.1827	0.1599	0.1401	0.1229	0.1079	0.0949	0.0835	0.0736	0.0649
16	0.8528	0.7284	0.6232	0.5339	0.4581	0.3936	0.3387	0.2919	0.2519	0.2176	0.1883	0.1631	0.1415	0.1229	0.1069	0.0930	0.0811	0.0708	0.0618	0.0541
17	0.8444	0.7142	0.6050	0.5134	0.4363	0.3714	0.3166	0.2703	0.2311	0.1978	0.1696	0.1456	0.1252	0.1078	0.0929	0.0802	0.0693	0.0600	0.0520	0.0451
18	0.8360	0.7002	0.5874	0.4936	0.4155	0.3503	0.2959	0.2502	0.2120	0.1799	0.1528	0.1300	0.1108	0.0946	0.0808	0.0691	0.0592	0.0508	0.0437	0.0376
19	0.8277	0.6864	0.5703	0.4746	0.3957	0.3305	0.2765	0.2317	0.1945	0.1635	0.1377	0.1161	0.0981	0.0829	0.0703	0.0596	0.0506	0.0431	0.0367	0.0313
20	0.8195	0.6730	0.5537	0.4564	0.3769	0.3118	0.2584	0.2145	0.1784	0.1486	0.1240	0.1037	0.0868	0.0728	0.0611	0.0514	0.0433	0.0365	0.0308	0.0261
21	0.8114	0.6598	0.5375	0.4388	0.3589	0.2942	0.2415	0.1987	0.1637	0.1351	0.1117	0.0926	0.0768	0.0638	0.0531	0.0443	0.0370	0.0309	0.0259	0.0217
22	0.8034	0.6468	0.5219	0.4220	0.3418	0.2775	0.2257	0.1839	0.1502	0.1228	0.1007	0.0826	0.0680	0.0560	0.0462	0.0382	0.0316	0.0262	0.0218	0.0181
23	0.7954	0.6342	0.5067	0.4057	0.3256	0.2618	0.2109	0.1703	0.1378	0.1117	0.0907	0.0738	0.0601	0.0491	0.0402	0.0329	0.0270	0.0222	0.0183	0.0151
24	0.7876	0.6217	0.4919	0.3901	0.3101	0.2470	0.1971	0.1577	0.1264	0.1015	0.0817	0.0659	0.0532	0.0431	0.0349	0.0284	0.0231	0.0188	0.0154	0.0126
25	0.7798	0.6095	0.4776	0.3751	0.2953	0.2330	0.1842	0.1460	0.1160	0.0923	0.0736	0.0588	0.0471	0.0378	0.0304	0.0245	0.0197	0.0160	0.0129	0.0105
26	0.7720	0.5976	0.4637	0.3607	0.2812	0.2198	0.1722	0.1352	0.1064	0.0839	0.0663	0.0525	0.0417	0.0331	0.0264	0.0211	0.0169	0.0135	0.0109	0.0087
27	0.7644	0.5859	0.4502	0.3468	0.2678	0.2074	0.1609	0.1252	0.0976	0.0763	0.0597	0.0469	0.0369	0.0291	0.0230	0.0182	0.0144	0.0115	0.0091	0.0073
28	0.7568	0.5744	0.4371	0.3335	0.2551	0.1956	0.1504	0.1159	0.0895	0.0693	0.0538	0.0419	0.0326	0.0255	0.0200	0.0157	0.0123	0.0097	0.0077	0.0061
29	0.7493	0.5631	0.4243	0.3207	0.2429	0.1846	0.1406	0.1073	0.0822	0.0630	0.0485	0.0374	0.0289	0.0224	0.0174	0.0135	0.0105	0.0082	0.0064	0.0051
30	0.7419	0.5521	0.4120	0.3083	0.2314	0.1741	0.1314	0.0994	0.0754	0.0573	0.0437	0.0334	0.0256	0.0196	0.0151	0.0116	0.0090	0.0070	0.0054	0.0042
40	0.6717	0.4529	0.3066	0.2083	0.1420	0.0972	0.0668	0.0460	0.0318	0.0221	0.0154	0.0107	0.0075	0.0053	0.0037	0.0026	0.0019	0.0013	0.0010	0.0007
50	0.6080	0.3715	0.2281	0.1407	0.0872	0.0543	0.0339	0.0213	0.0134	0.0085	0.0054	0.0035	0.0022	0.0014	0.0009	0.0006	0.0004	0.0003	0.0002	0.0001

Illustrations Using Appendix A-3: Future Value of a Series of Equal Amounts (an Annuity of $1 per Period)

To use this table, locate the future value factor for the time period and the interest rate.

1. You plan to retire after 16 years. To provide for that retirement, you initiate a savings program of $7,000 per year in an investment yielding 8 percent. What will the value of the retirement fund be at the beginning of the seventeenth year?

    Your last payment into the fund will occur at the end of the sixteenth year, so scan down the periods (n) column for period 16, and then move across until you reach the column for 8 percent. The future value factor is 30.32. Hence, the solution is $7,000 × 30.32, or $212,240.

2. What will be the value of an investment if you put $2,000 into a retirement plan yielding 7 percent annually for 25 years?

    The future value factor is 63.250. Hence, the solution is $2,000 × 63.250, or $126,500.

3. You are trying to decide between putting $3,000 or $4,000 annually for the next 20 years into an investment yielding 7 percent for retirement purposes. What is the difference in the value of investing the extra $1,000 for 20 years?

    The future value factor is 41.0. Hence, the solution is $1,000 × 41.0, or $41,000.

4. You will receive an annuity payment of $1,200 at the end of each year for 6 years. What will be the total value of this stream of income invested at 7 percent by the time you receive the last payment?

    The appropriate future value factor for 6 years at 7 percent is 7.153. Hence, the solution is $1,200 × 7.153, or $8,584.

5. How many years of investing $1,200 annually at 9 percent will it take to reach a goal of $11,000?

    Divide the future value of $11,000 by the lump sum of $1,200 to find a future value factor of 9.17. Look down the 9 percent column to find 9.200 (close enough). Read across the row to find that an investment period of 7 years is needed.

6. If you plan to invest $1,200 annually for 9 years, what rate of return is needed to reach a goal of $15,000?

    Divide the future value goal of $15,000 by $1,200 to derive the future value factor 12.5. Look across the row for 9 years to locate the future value factor of 12.49 (close enough). Read up the column to find that you need an 8 percent return.

An alternative approach is to use a calculator to determine the total future value, FV, of a stream of equal payments (an annuity). The equation is

$$FV = \frac{[(1.0 + i)^n - 1.0] \times A}{i} \qquad \text{(A.3)}$$

where

$FV = $ *Future Value* of the investment

$i = $ *Interest* rate per period

$n = $ *Number* of periods the PV is invested

$A = $ *Amount* of the annuity

Appendix A-3

Future Value of a Series of Equal Amounts (an Annuity of $1 Paid at the End of Each Period)
(Used to Compute the Compounded Future Value of a Stream of Income Payments)

n	1%	2%	3%	4%	5%	6%	7%	8%	9%	10%	11%	12%	13%	14%	15%	16%	17%	18%	19%	20%
1	1.0000	1.0000	1.0000	1.0000	1.0000	1.0000	1.0000	1.0000	1.0000	1.0000	1.0000	1.0000	1.0000	1.0000	1.0000	1.0000	1.0000	1.0000	1.0000	1.0000
2	2.0100	2.0200	2.0300	2.0400	2.0500	2.0600	2.0700	2.0800	2.0900	2.1000	2.1100	2.1200	2.1300	2.1400	2.1500	2.1600	2.1700	2.1800	2.1900	2.2000
3	3.0301	3.0604	3.0909	3.1216	3.1525	3.1836	3.2149	3.2464	3.2781	3.3100	3.3421	3.3744	3.4069	3.4396	3.4725	3.5056	3.5389	3.5724	3.6061	3.6400
4	4.0604	4.1216	4.1836	4.2465	4.3101	4.3746	4.4399	4.5061	4.5731	4.6410	4.7097	4.7793	4.8498	4.9211	4.9934	5.0665	5.1405	5.2154	5.2913	5.3680
5	5.1010	5.2040	5.3091	5.4163	5.5256	5.6371	5.7507	5.8666	5.9847	6.1051	6.2278	6.3528	6.4803	6.6101	6.7424	6.8771	7.0144	7.1542	7.2966	7.4416
6	6.1520	6.3081	6.4684	6.6330	6.8019	6.9753	7.1533	7.3359	7.5233	7.7156	7.9129	8.1152	8.3227	8.5355	8.7537	8.9775	9.2068	9.4420	9.6830	9.9299
7	7.2135	7.4343	7.6625	7.8983	8.1420	8.3938	8.6540	8.9228	9.2004	9.4872	9.7833	10.0890	10.4047	10.7305	11.0668	11.4139	11.7720	12.1415	12.5227	12.9159
8	8.2857	8.5830	8.8923	9.2142	9.5491	9.8975	10.2598	10.6366	11.0285	11.4359	11.8594	12.2997	12.7573	13.2328	13.7268	14.2401	14.7733	15.3270	15.9020	16.4991
9	9.3685	9.7546	10.1591	10.5828	11.0266	11.4913	11.9780	12.4876	13.0210	13.5795	14.1640	14.7757	15.4157	16.0853	16.7858	17.5185	18.2847	19.0859	19.9234	20.7989
10	10.4622	10.9497	11.4639	12.0061	12.5779	13.1808	13.8164	14.4866	15.1929	15.9374	16.7220	17.5487	18.4197	19.3373	20.3037	21.3215	22.3931	23.5213	24.7089	25.9587
11	11.5668	12.1687	12.8078	13.4864	14.2068	14.9716	15.7836	16.6455	17.5603	18.5312	19.5614	20.6546	21.8143	23.0445	24.3493	25.7329	27.1999	28.7551	30.4035	32.1504
12	12.6825	13.4121	14.1920	15.0258	15.9171	16.8699	17.8885	18.9771	20.1407	21.3843	22.7132	24.1331	25.6502	27.2707	29.0017	30.8502	32.8239	34.9311	37.1802	39.5805
13	13.8093	14.6803	15.6178	16.6268	17.7130	18.8821	20.1406	21.4953	22.9534	24.5227	26.2116	28.0291	29.9847	32.0887	34.3519	36.7862	39.4040	42.2187	45.2445	48.4966
14	14.9474	15.9739	17.0863	18.2919	19.5986	21.0151	22.5505	24.2149	26.0192	27.9750	30.0949	32.3926	34.8827	37.5811	40.5047	43.6720	47.1027	50.8180	54.8409	59.1959
15	16.0969	17.2934	18.5989	20.0236	21.5786	23.2760	25.1290	27.1521	29.3609	31.7725	34.4054	37.2797	40.4175	43.8424	47.5804	51.6595	56.1101	60.9653	66.2607	72.0351
16	17.2579	18.6393	20.1569	21.8245	23.6575	25.6725	27.8881	30.3243	33.0034	35.9497	39.1899	42.7533	46.6717	50.9804	55.7175	60.9250	66.6488	72.9390	79.8502	87.4421
17	18.4304	20.0121	21.7616	23.6975	25.8404	28.2129	30.8402	33.7502	36.9737	40.5447	44.5008	48.8837	53.7391	59.1176	65.0751	71.6730	78.9791	87.0680	96.0217	105.9306
18	19.6147	21.4123	23.4144	25.6454	28.1324	30.9057	33.9990	37.4502	41.3013	45.5992	50.3959	55.7497	61.7251	68.3941	75.8364	84.1407	93.4056	103.7403	115.2659	128.1167
19	20.8109	22.8406	25.1169	27.6712	30.5390	33.7600	37.3790	41.4463	46.0185	51.1591	56.9395	63.4397	70.7494	78.9692	88.2118	98.6032	110.2846	123.4135	138.1664	154.7400
20	22.0190	24.2974	26.8704	29.7781	33.0660	36.7856	40.9955	45.7620	51.1601	57.2750	64.2028	72.0524	80.9468	91.0249	102.4436	115.3797	130.0329	146.6280	165.4180	186.6880
21	23.2392	25.7833	28.6765	31.9692	35.7193	39.9927	44.8652	50.4229	56.7645	64.0025	72.2651	81.6987	92.4699	104.7684	118.8101	134.8405	153.1385	174.0210	197.8474	225.0256
22	24.4716	27.2990	30.5368	34.2480	38.5052	43.3923	49.0057	55.4568	62.8733	71.4027	81.2143	92.5026	105.4910	120.4360	137.6316	157.4150	180.1721	206.3448	236.4384	271.0307
23	25.7163	28.8450	32.4529	36.6179	41.4305	46.9958	53.4361	60.8933	69.5319	79.5430	91.1479	104.6029	120.2048	138.2970	159.2764	183.6014	211.8013	244.4868	282.3618	326.2368
24	26.9735	30.4219	34.4265	39.0826	44.5020	50.8156	58.1767	66.7648	76.7898	88.4973	102.1741	118.1552	136.8315	158.6586	184.1678	213.9776	248.8075	289.4945	337.0105	392.4842
25	28.2432	32.0303	36.4593	41.6459	47.7271	54.8645	63.2490	73.1059	84.7009	98.3471	114.4133	133.3339	155.6196	181.8708	212.7930	249.2140	292.1048	342.6035	402.0424	471.9811
26	29.5256	33.6709	38.5530	44.3117	51.1135	59.1564	68.6765	79.9544	93.3240	109.1818	127.9988	150.3339	176.8501	208.3327	245.7120	290.0883	342.7626	405.2721	479.4305	567.3773
27	30.8209	35.3443	40.7096	47.0842	54.6691	63.7058	74.4838	87.3508	102.7231	121.0999	143.0786	169.3740	200.8406	238.4993	283.5688	337.5024	402.0323	479.2211	571.5223	681.8527
28	32.1291	37.0512	42.9309	49.9676	58.4026	68.5281	80.6977	95.3388	112.9682	134.2099	159.8173	190.6989	227.9499	272.8892	327.1041	392.5027	471.3778	566.4808	681.1116	819.2233
29	33.4504	38.7922	45.2188	52.9663	62.3227	73.6398	87.3465	103.9659	124.1354	148.6309	178.3972	214.5827	258.5834	312.0937	377.1697	456.3032	552.5120	669.4474	811.5228	984.0679
30	34.7849	40.5681	47.5754	56.0849	66.4389	79.0582	94.4608	113.2832	136.3075	164.4940	199.0209	241.3327	293.1992	356.7868	434.7451	530.3117	647.4390	790.9479	966.7121	1181.882
40	48.8864	60.4020	75.4013	95.0255	120.7998	154.7620	199.6351	259.0565	337.8824	442.5925	581.8260	767.0914	1013.704	1342.025	1779.090	2360.757	3134.522	4163.212	5529.829	7343.856
50	64.4632	84.5794	112.7969	152.6671	209.3480	290.3359	406.5289	573.7701	815.0834	1163.908	1668.771	2400.018	3459.507	4994.522	7217.714	10435.65	15089.50	21813.09	31515.33	45497.17

Illustrations Using Appendix A-4: Present Value of Series of Equal Amounts (an Annuity of $1 per Period)

To use this table, locate the present value factor for the time period and the interest rate.

1. You are entering into a contract that will provide you with an income of $1,000 at the end of the year for the next 10 years. If the annual interest rate is 7 percent, what is the present value of that stream of payments?

The present value factor is 7.024; hence, the solution is $1,000 × 7.024, or $7,024.

2. You expect to have $250,000 available in a retirement plan when you retire. If the amount invested yields 8 percent and you hope to live an additional 20 years, how much can you withdraw each year so that the fund will just be liquidated after 20 years?

The present value factor for 20 years at 8 percent is 9.818. Hence, the solution is $250,000 ÷ 9.818, or $25,463.

3. You have received an inheritance of $60,000 that you invested so that it earns 9 percent. If you withdraw $8,000 annually to supplement your income, in how many years will the fund run out?

Solving for *n*, $60,000 ÷ $8,000 = 7.5. Scan down the 9 percent column until you find a present value factor close to 7.5, which is 7.487. The row indicates 13 years; thus, the fund will be depleted in approximately 13 years with $8,000 annual withdrawals.

4. A seller offers to finance the sale of a building to you as an investment. The mortgage loan of $280,000 will be for 20 years and requires an annual mortgage payment of $24,000. Should you finance the purchase through the seller or borrow the funds from a financial institution at a current rate of 10 percent?

$280,000 ÷ $24,000 = 11.667. Scan down the periods (*n*) column to 20 years and then read across to locate the figure closest to 11.667, which is 11.470. The column indicates 6 percent; thus, seller financing offers a lower interest rate.

5. You have the opportunity to purchase an office building for $600,000 with an expected life of 20 years. Looking over the financial details, you see that the before–tax net rental income is $90,000. If you want a return of at least 15 percent, how much should you pay for the building?

The present value factor for 20 years at 15 percent is 6.259, and $90,000 × 6.259 = $563,310. Thus, the price is too high for you to earn a return of 15 percent.

An alternative approach is to use a calculator to determine the present value, *PV*, of a stream of payments. The equation is

$$PV = \frac{[1.0 - (1.0/1.0 + i)^n] \times A}{i} \qquad \text{(A.4)}$$

where

PV = *Present Value* of the investment

i = *Interest* rate per period

n = *Number* of periods the PV is invested

A = *Amount* of the annuity

Appendix A-4

Present Value of a Series of Equal Amounts (an Annuity of $1 Received at the End of Each Period)
(Used to Compute the Discounted Present Value of a Stream of Income Payments)

n	1%	2%	3%	4%	5%	6%	7%	8%	9%	10%	11%	12%	13%	14%	15%	16%	17%	18%	19%	20%
1	0.9901	0.9804	0.9709	0.9615	0.9524	0.9434	0.9346	0.9259	0.9174	0.9091	0.9009	0.8929	0.8850	0.8772	0.8696	0.8621	0.8547	0.8475	0.8403	0.8333
2	1.9704	1.9416	1.9135	1.8861	1.8594	1.8334	1.8080	1.7833	1.7591	1.7355	1.7125	1.6901	1.6681	1.6467	1.6257	1.6052	1.5852	1.5656	1.5465	1.5278
3	2.9410	2.8839	2.8286	2.7751	2.7232	2.6730	2.6243	2.5771	2.5313	2.4869	2.4437	2.4018	2.3612	2.3216	2.2832	2.2459	2.2096	2.1743	2.1399	2.1065
4	3.9020	3.8077	3.7171	3.6299	3.5460	3.4651	3.3872	3.3121	3.2397	3.1699	3.1024	3.0373	2.9745	2.9137	2.8550	2.7982	2.7432	2.6901	2.6386	2.5887
5	4.8534	4.7135	4.5797	4.4518	4.3295	4.2124	4.1002	3.9927	3.8897	3.7908	3.6959	3.6048	3.5172	3.4331	3.3522	3.2743	3.1993	3.1272	3.0576	2.9906
6	5.7955	5.6014	5.4172	5.2421	5.0757	4.9173	4.7665	4.6229	4.4859	4.3553	4.2305	4.1114	3.9975	3.8887	3.7845	3.6847	3.5892	3.4976	3.4098	3.3255
7	6.7282	6.4720	6.2303	6.0021	5.7864	5.5824	5.3893	5.2064	5.0330	4.8684	4.7122	4.5638	4.4226	4.2883	4.1604	4.0386	3.9224	3.8115	3.7057	3.6046
8	7.6517	7.3255	7.0197	6.7327	6.4632	6.2098	5.9713	5.7466	5.5348	5.3349	5.1461	4.9676	4.7988	4.6389	4.4873	4.3436	4.2072	4.0776	3.9544	3.8372
9	8.5660	8.1622	7.7861	7.4353	7.1078	6.8017	6.5152	6.2469	5.9952	5.7590	5.5370	5.3282	5.1317	4.9464	4.7716	4.6065	4.4506	4.3030	4.1633	4.0310
10	9.4713	8.9826	8.5302	8.1109	7.7217	7.3601	7.0236	6.7101	6.4177	6.1446	5.8892	5.6502	5.4262	5.2161	5.0188	4.8332	4.6586	4.4941	4.3389	4.1925
11	10.3676	9.7868	9.2526	8.7605	8.3064	7.8869	7.4987	7.1390	6.8052	6.4951	6.2065	5.9377	5.6869	5.4527	5.2337	5.0286	4.8364	4.6560	4.4865	4.3271
12	11.2551	10.5753	9.9540	9.3851	8.8633	8.3838	7.9427	7.5361	7.1607	6.8137	6.4924	6.1944	5.9176	5.6603	5.4206	5.1971	4.9884	4.7932	4.6105	4.4392
13	12.1337	11.3484	10.6350	9.9856	9.3936	8.8527	8.3577	7.9038	7.4869	7.1034	6.7499	6.4235	6.1218	5.8424	5.5831	5.3423	5.1183	4.9095	4.7147	4.5327
14	13.0037	12.1062	11.2961	10.5631	9.8986	9.2950	8.7455	8.2442	7.7862	7.3667	6.9819	6.6282	6.3025	6.0021	5.7245	5.4675	5.2293	5.0081	4.8023	4.6106
15	13.8651	12.8493	11.9379	11.1184	10.3797	9.7122	9.1079	8.5595	8.0607	7.6061	7.1909	6.8109	6.4624	6.1422	5.8474	5.5755	5.3242	5.0916	4.8759	4.6755
16	14.7179	13.5777	12.5611	11.6523	10.8378	10.1059	9.4466	8.8514	8.3126	7.8237	7.3792	6.9740	6.6039	6.2651	5.9542	5.6685	5.4053	5.1624	4.9377	4.7296
17	15.5623	14.2919	13.1661	12.1657	11.2741	10.4773	9.7632	9.1216	8.5436	8.0216	7.5488	7.1196	6.7291	6.3729	6.0472	5.7487	5.4746	5.2223	4.9897	4.7746
18	16.3983	14.9920	13.7535	12.6593	11.6896	10.8276	10.0591	9.3719	8.7556	8.2014	7.7016	7.2497	6.8399	6.4674	6.1280	5.8178	5.5339	5.2732	5.0333	4.8122
19	17.2260	15.6785	14.3238	13.1339	12.0853	11.1581	10.3356	9.6036	8.9501	8.3649	7.8393	7.3658	6.9380	6.5504	6.1982	5.8775	5.5845	5.3162	5.0700	4.8435
20	18.0456	16.3514	14.8775	13.5903	12.4622	11.4699	10.5940	9.8181	9.1285	8.5136	7.9633	7.4694	7.0248	6.6231	6.2593	5.9288	5.6278	5.3527	5.1009	4.8696
21	18.8570	17.0112	15.4150	14.0292	12.8212	11.7641	10.8355	10.0168	9.2922	8.6487	8.0751	7.5620	7.1016	6.6870	6.3125	5.9731	5.6648	5.3837	5.1268	4.8913
22	19.6604	17.6580	15.9369	14.4511	13.1630	12.0416	11.0612	10.2007	9.4424	8.7715	8.1757	7.6446	7.1695	6.7429	6.3587	6.0113	5.6964	5.4099	5.1486	4.9094
23	20.4558	18.2922	16.4436	14.8568	13.4886	12.3034	11.2722	10.3711	9.5802	8.8832	8.2664	7.7184	7.2297	6.7921	6.3988	6.0442	5.7234	5.4321	5.1668	4.9245
24	21.2434	18.9139	16.9355	15.2470	13.7986	12.5504	11.4693	10.5288	9.7066	8.9847	8.3481	7.7843	7.2829	6.8351	6.4338	6.0726	5.7465	5.4509	5.1822	4.9371
25	22.0232	19.5235	17.4131	15.6221	14.0939	12.7834	11.6536	10.6748	9.8226	9.0770	8.4217	7.8431	7.3300	6.8729	6.4641	6.0971	5.7662	5.4669	5.1951	4.9476
26	22.7952	20.1210	17.8768	15.9828	14.3752	13.0032	11.8258	10.8100	9.9290	9.1609	8.4881	7.8957	7.3717	6.9061	6.4906	6.1182	5.7831	5.4804	5.2060	4.9563
27	23.5596	20.7069	18.3270	16.3296	14.6430	13.2105	11.9867	10.9352	10.0266	9.2372	8.5478	7.9426	7.4086	6.9352	6.5135	6.1364	5.7975	5.4919	5.2151	4.9636
28	24.3164	21.2813	18.7641	16.6631	14.8981	13.4062	12.1371	11.0511	10.1161	9.3066	8.6016	7.9844	7.4412	6.9607	6.5335	6.1520	5.8099	5.5016	5.2228	4.9697
29	25.0658	21.8444	19.1885	16.9837	15.1411	13.5907	12.2777	11.1584	10.1983	9.3696	8.6501	8.0218	7.4701	6.9830	6.5509	6.1656	5.8204	5.5098	5.2292	4.9747
30	25.8077	22.3965	19.6004	17.2920	15.3725	13.7648	12.4090	11.2578	10.2737	9.4269	8.6938	8.0552	7.4957	7.0027	6.5660	6.1772	5.8294	5.5168	5.2347	4.9789
40	32.8347	27.3555	23.1148	19.7928	17.1591	15.0463	13.3317	11.9246	10.7574	9.7791	8.9511	8.2438	7.6344	7.1050	6.6418	6.2335	5.8713	5.5482	5.2582	4.9966
50	39.1961	31.4236	25.7298	21.4822	18.2559	15.7619	13.8007	12.2335	10.9617	9.9148	9.0417	8.3045	7.6752	7.1327	6.6605	6.2463	5.8801	5.5541	5.2623	4.9995

Appendix B

ESTIMATING SOCIAL SECURITY BENEFITS

The Social Security Administration (SSA) provides basic benefits for your retirement, for a period of disability, or for your survivors. To qualify, you must have earned the number of credits required for each benefit program. In 2016, a worker would earn one credit for each $1,260 of income subject to Social Security taxes (this figure is adjusted upward each year for inflation) up to a maximum of 4 credits per year. Once you qualify, the actual dollar level of benefits received is based on your income in years past that was subject to the Federal Insurance Contributions Act (FICA) taxes, commonly known as Social Security taxes. Benefits increase each year based on a cost of living adjustment (COLA) announced by the SSA each October for the following year.

You can obtain a personalized estimate of your benefits from the Social Security Administration at www.ssa.gov/myaccount or www.ssa.gov/planners/benefitcalculators.html. However, if you have not yet earned 40 credits your personalized estimate will underestimate your likely benefits. You can use Appendix B.1 and the income you might expect to make per year at age 30 for a somewhat more accurate estimate. The amounts are for a 30-year-old worker but would not differ significantly for workers up to ten years older.

Social Security Retirement Benefits

To qualify for Social Security retirement benefits, any worker born after 1928 must have earned 40 credits of coverage. Others are eligible to collect benefits based on the covered earnings of the retired worked: dependent children, spouses caring for dependent children, and retired spouses at age 62 (including former spouses if the marriage lasted at least ten years). See www.ssa.gov/retire/index.html.

Social Security Disability Benefits

To qualify for disability benefits, workers need at least 40 credits of coverage, with at least 20 of the credits attained in the previous ten years (depending on year of birth). A worker younger than age 31 must have attained at least six credits or one more than one-half of the total credits possible after age 21, whichever is greater. (For example, a 26-year-old worker would have five years, or 20 credits, possible and would need ten credits of coverage.) Social Security will pay disability benefits to an insured worker, dependent children up to age 18 (or 19, if the child is still in high school), a spouse caring for a dependent child who is younger than age 16 or disabled, and a spouse (even if divorced, but not remarried, provided that the marriage lasted ten years) aged 62 or older. See www.ssa.gov/disabilityssi for more information.

Social Security Survivor's Benefits

For a family to qualify for Social Security Survivor's benefits, the deceased worker must have accrued at least 40 credits of coverage or an average of one credit per year since age 21 to be "fully insured." Other individuals may be considered "currently insured" if they have six credits of coverage in the previous 13 possible calendar credits. The survivors of currently insured workers receive limited types of benefits compared to those available to fully insured workers. Social Security will pay benefits to surviving children younger than age 18 (or 19, if the child is still in high school), to a surviving spouse (even if divorced from the deceased, but not remarried) caring for surviving children who are younger than age 16, and to a surviving spouse (even if divorced, if the marriage lasted at least ten years) aged 60 or older. See www.ssa.gov/survivors for more information.

Appendix B.1   **Estimates of Social Security Benefits for the Three Major Social Security Programs**

	Present Annual Earnings					
	$35,000	**$50,000**	**$65,000**	**$80,000**	**$95,000**	**$120,000**
Monthly Retirement Benefits at Age 67 in Today's Dollars						
Per month	$ 1,480	$ 1,890	$ 2,260	$ 2,450	$ 2,640	$ 2,940
Per year	$17,760	$22,680	$ 27,120	$ 29,400	$ 31,680	$ 35,280
As a percentage of income	51%	45%	42%	37%	33%	29%
Monthly Retirement Benefits at Age 67 in Future Dollars						
Per Month	$ 6,170	$ 7,860	$ 9,550	$ 10,410	$ 11,200	$ 12,440
Per Year	$74,040	$94,320	$114,600	$124,920	$134,400	$149,280
Monthly Disability Benefits if You Became Disabled in 2018						
Individual benefit per month	$ 1,330	$ 1,690	$ 2,040	$ 2,280	$ 2,460	$ 2,720
Individual benefit per year	$15,960	$20,280	$ 24,480	$ 27,360	$ 29,520	$ 32,640
As a percentage of income	46%	41%	38%	34%	31%	29%
Maximum family benefit per month	$ 2,000	$ 2,530	$ 3,060	$ 3,420	$ 3,690	$ 4,080
Maximum family benefit per year	$24,000	$30,360	$ 36,720	$ 41,040	$ 44,280	$ 48,960
As a percentage of income	69%	61%	56%	51%	47%	41%
Monthly Survivor's Benefits if You Died in 2018						
Individual benefit per month	$ 1,040	$ 1,310	$ 1,560	$ 1,750	$ 1,890	$ 2,090
Individual benefit per year	$12,480	$15,720	$ 18,720	$ 21,000	$ 22,680	$ 25,080
As a percentage of income	36%	31%	29%	26%	24%	21%
Maximum family benefit per month	$ 2,380	$ 3,210	$ 3,710	$ 4,090	$ 4,700	$ 4,870
Maximum family benefit per year	$28,560	$38,520	$ 44,520	$ 49,080	$ 52,800	$ 58,440
As a percentage of income	82%	77%	68%	61%	56%	49%

Glossary

10-Q report A report required by the SEC prepared by the company showing its financial results for the quarter, a discussion from management, a list of material events and other risk factors that have occurred, forecasts of the company's future, and notes of any significant changes or events in the quarter.

12b-1 fees (distribution fees) Annual fees that some "no-load" fund companies deduct from a fund's assets to compensate salespeople and pay other expenses.

401(k) plan Defined-contribution plan designed for employees of private corporations.

above-the-line deductions Adjustments subtracted from gross income whether taxpayer itemizes deductions or not.

acceleration clause Clause in a credit contract that that allow a lender to require a borrower to repay all of an outstanding loan if certain requirements are not met, such as missing one or more repayments.

accountable care organization (ACO) A group of doctors and/or a hospital who have made a deal with a private insurer or Medicare to provide safe and appropriate services, rather than operate as a fee-for-service organization.

accumulation phase The years during which you need to save for retirement.

activities of daily living (ADLs) Insurance companies use the inability to perform a certain number of such activities as a criterion for deciding when the insured becomes eligible for long-term care benefits.

actual cash value (of personal property) Represents the purchase price of the property less depreciation.

add-on interest method A method of calculating the annual percentage rate for installment loans where interest is calculated by applying an interest rate to the amount borrowed times the number of years.

adjustable-rate mortgage (ARM)/variable-rate mortgage Mortgage in which the borrower's interest rate fluctuates according to some index of interest rates based on the rising or falling cost of credit in the economy—thus transferring interest rate risk to the borrower.

adjusted capitalized cost (adjusted cap cost) Subtracting the capitalized cost reductions from the gross capitalized cost.

adjusted gross income (AGI) Gross income less any exclusions and adjustments.

adjustments to income A special class of a dozen-plus subtractions from gross income that "adjust" or reduce one's income to get the income down to adjusted gross income.

advance directives Legal documents that explain the type of end-of-life health care you do or do not want when you cannot make your own decisions because of illness or incapacity.

advance medical directives Treatment preferences and the designation of a surrogate decision maker in the event that a person should become unable to make decisions on her or his own behalf.

affinity cards Standard bank cards but with the logo of a sponsoring organization imprinted on the face of the card, meaning that the issuing financial institution donates a small percentage of the amounts charged to the sponsoring organization.

after-tax dollars Money on which an employee has already paid taxes.

after-tax money Funds put into regular investment accounts after paying income taxes.

after-tax profit Money left over after a firm has paid expenses, bondholder interest, and taxes.

after-tax yield The percentage yield on a taxable investment after subtracting the effect of federal income taxes that will need to be paid on the investment.

agency bonds Bonds, notes, and certificates of debt issued by various federal agencies that are government-sponsored enterprises but stockholder owned, such as the Federal National Mortgage Association.

aggressive growth funds (maximum capital gains funds) Funds that invest in speculative stocks with volatile price swings, seeking the greatest long-term capital appreciation possible. Also known as maximum capital gains funds and capital appreciation funds.

aggressive investment philosophy (risk seeker) Investors with this philosophy primarily seek capital gains, often with a short time horizon.

all-risk (open-perils) policies Cover losses caused by all perils other than those that the policy specifically excludes.

amortization schedule List that shows all the monthly payments, the portions that will go toward interest and principal, and the debt remaining after each payment is made throughout the life of the loan.

annual exclusion amount An annual amount of $14,000 that can be given to a relative or a friend to reduce one's total taxable estate.

annual percentage rate (APR) This is the annual rate that is charged for borrowing expressed as a percentage number that represents the actual yearly cost of funds over the term of a loan.

annual percentage yield (APY) Return on total interest received on a $100 deposit for 365-day period, given the institution's simple annual interest rate and compounding frequency.

annual report Legally required yearly report about financial performance, activities, and prospects sent to major stockholders and made available to the general public.

annuity Contract made with an insurance company that provides for a series of payments to be received at stated intervals (usually monthly) for a fixed or variable time period.

any-occupation policy Provides full benefits only if the insured cannot perform any occupation.

appraisal fee Fee charged for a professionally prepared estimate of the fair market value of the property by an objective party.

approximate compound yield (ACY) A measure of the annualized compound growth of any long-term investment stated as a percentage.

aptitudes The natural abilities and talents that individuals possess.

as is Way for the seller to get around legal requirements for warranties; the buyer takes all risk of nonperformance or other problems despite any salesperson's verbal assurances.

asset allocation funds Investments in a mix of assets (usually stocks, bonds, and cash equivalents and sometimes international assets, gold, and real estate); they buy and sell regularly to reduce risk while trying to outperform the market.

asset allocation Form of diversification in which the investor decides on the proportions of an investment portfolio that will be devoted to various categories of assets.

asset management account (AMA, or central asset account) Multiple-purpose, coordinated package that gathers most monetary asset management vehicles into a unified account and reports activity on a single monthly statement to the client.

assets Everything you own that has monetary value.

ATM cards Plastic cards to make purchases and withdraw money from ATMs that require use of a PIN number.

ATM machines Machines that allow you to check your balance, withdraw and deposit money, and transfer money between your accounts.

ATM transaction fee Payments levied each time an automated teller machine (ATM) is used.

automatic billing (or auto-renewal billing) A feature that allows a vender to automatically charge a customer's credit (or debit) card or bank account on a regular basis through a recurring profile set up on the account.

automatic escalation An employment clause that allows employees to save more for retirement by agreeing to raise their contribution amounts each year.

automatic premium loan Provision that allows any premium not paid by the end of the grace period to be paid automatically with a policy loan if sufficient cash value or dividends have accumulated.

automatic reinvestment Investor's option to choose to automatically reinvest any interest, dividends, and capital gains payments to purchase additional fund shares.

automobile insurance Combines the liability and property insurance coverages that most car owners and drivers need into a single-package policy.

automobile medical payments insurance Insurance that covers bodily injury losses suffered by the driver of the insured vehicle and any passengers, regardless of who is at fault.

average daily balance This is the sum of the outstanding balances owed on a credit card each day during the billing period divided by the number of days in the period.

average share cost Actual cost basis of the investment used for income tax purposes, calculated by dividing the total amount invested by the total shares purchased.

average share price Calculated by dividing the share price total by the number of investment periods.

average tax rate The average amount of one's total **gross** income that is paid in taxes, which is always less than your marginal tax rate.

back-end load (contingent deferred sales charge) A sales commission that is imposed only when shares are sold; often charges are on a sliding scale, with the fee dropping 1 percentage point per year that the investor stays in the fund.

back-end ratio Compares the total of all monthly PITI expenditures plus auto loans and other debts with gross monthly income.

balance sheet or net worth statement Snapshot of assets, liabilities, and net worth on a particular date.

balanced funds Funds that keep a set mix of stocks and bonds, often 60 percent stocks and 40 percent bonds, in order to earn a well-balanced return of income and long-term capital gains.

bank credit cards Credit cards that are issued by banks or large financial institutions, such as VISA, MasterCard, and Discover.

bankruptcy A constitutionally guaranteed right that permits people (and businesses) to ask a court to find them officially unable to meet their debts.

basic retirement benefit/primary insurance amount Amount of Social Security benefits a worker would receive at his or her full-benefit retirement age, which is 67 for those born after 1960.

basis point One hundredth of one percent.

bear market Market in which securities prices have declined in value by 20 percent or more from previous highs, often over the course of several weeks or months.

below-average costs Average costs of an investment if more shares are purchased when the price is down and fewer shares are purchased when the price is high.

benchmark premium The amount of the credit provided under the Affordable Care Act that is used to calculate how much an individual will pay for a health care policy.

beneficiary designation Allowance of fund holder to name one or more beneficiaries so that the proceeds bypass probate proceedings if the original shareholder dies.

beneficiary   Person who receives life insurance proceeds, as per the policy.

benefit period   The maximum period of time for which benefits will be paid under a disability income or other insurance policy.

best buy   Product or service that, in the buyer's opinion, represents acceptable quality at a fair or low price for that quality level.

beta value (beta coefficient)   A measure of stock volatility; that is, how much the stock price varies relative to the rest of the market.

big-ticket items   Products that have a high selling price that are sometimes called durable goods, which last a relatively long time and provide utility to the user.

billing cycle   The time period between when credit statements are sent to borrowers, which is usually about one month.

Bitcoin   A peer-to-peer experimental digital cash currency based on an open source cryptographic protocol that can be bought at an exchange and transferred through a computer or smartphone without an intermediate financial institution.

biweekly mortgage   A form of growing-equity mortgage (GEM) that calls for payments of half of the normal payment to be made every two weeks; the borrower thus makes 26 payments a year and reduces the principal amount by one full payment each year; this reduces the mortgage term to about 20 years on a 30-year mortgage.

Blue Cross   Insurance companies that provide hospital care benefits.

Blue Shield   Insurance company that provides benefits for surgical and medical services.

blue-chip stocks   Stocks that have been around for a long time, have a well-regarded reputation, dominate its industry, and are known for being solid, relatively safe investments.

bodily injury liability   Occurs when a driver or car owner is held legally responsible for bodily injury losses that other people, including pedestrians, suffer.

bond funds (fixed-income funds)   Fixed-income funds that aim to earn current income higher than a money market fund without incurring undue risk by investing in a portfolio of bonds and other low-risk investments that pay high dividends and offer capital appreciation.

bond premium   A sum of money paid in addition to a regular price.

bond rating   An impartial outsider's opinion of the quality—or creditworthiness—of the issuing organization.

bond   A debt instrument issued by an organization that promises repayment at a specific time and the right to receive regular interest payments during the life of the bond.

book value (shareholder's equity)   Net worth of a company, determined by subtracting total liabilities from assets.

book value per share   Reflects the book value of a company divided by the number of shares of common stock outstanding.

bots (or chatbots)   Online texting services offered by all financial institutions and other venders who provide information and services, which can conduct human-like conversation formerly reserved for people.

breadwinner   The person in a family who earns an income that is primary to a unit of people who are dependent on the person's income.

broker's commission   Largest selling cost in selling a home; these commissions often amount to 6 percent of the selling price of the home.

budget controls   Techniques of planned spending to maintain control over personal spending so that planned amounts are not exceeded.

budget estimates   Projected dollar amounts to receive or spend in a budgeting period.

budget exceptions   When budget estimates differ from actual expenditures.

budget variance   Difference between amount budgeted and actual amount spent or received.

budget   Paper or electronic document used to record both planned and actual income and expenditures over a period of time.

bull market   Market in which securities prices have risen 20 percent or more over time.

business cycle/economic cycle   Business cycles can be depicted as a wavelike pattern of rising and falling economic activity; the phases of the business cycle include expansion, peak, contraction (which may turn into recession), and trough.

business failure risk (financial risk)   Possibility that an investment will fail to pay a return to the investor.

business-cycle risk   The fact that economic growth usually does not occur in a smooth and steady manner, and this impacts profits as well as investment returns.

buy and hold/buy to hold   Investment strategy in which investors buy a widely diversified mix of stocks and/or mutual funds, reinvest the dividends by buying more stocks and mutual funds, and hold onto those investments almost indefinitely.

buyer's order   Written offer that names a specific vehicle and all charges; only sign such offers after the salesperson and sales manager have signed first.

buying long   Buying a security (especially on margin) with the hope that the stock price will rise.

cafeteria plan   A type of employee benefit plan where employees are offered a choice between cash (which is taxable) and at least one other nontaxable benefit, which are qualified as nontaxable or tax-sheltered benefits.

call option   Stipulation in some indentures that allows issuer to repurchase the bond at par value or by paying a premium, often one year's worth of interest.

capital gain   The net income received from the sale of an asset above the costs incurred to purchase and sell it.

capital gains distributions   Distributions representing the net gains (capital gains minus capital losses) that a fund realizes when it sells securities that were held in the fund's portfolio.

capital improvements Costs incurred in making value-enhancing changes (beyond maintenance and repair) in real property.

capital loss Decrease in paper value of an initial investment; only realized if sold.

capitalism Here a country's economy, its trade and industry, are controlled by private owners who see profit.

card registration service Firm that will notify all companies with which you have debit and credit cards if your cards are lost or stolen.

career fairs University-, community-, and employer-sponsored events for job seekers to meet with many employers quickly to screen potential employers.

career goal Identifying what you want to do for a living, whether a specific job or field of employment.

career ladder Describes the progression from entry-level positions to higher levels of pay, skill, responsibility, or authority.

career plan A strategic guide for your career through short-, medium-, longer-, and long-term goals as well as future education and work-related experiences.

career planning Can help you identify an employment pathway that aligns your interests and abilities with the tasks and responsibilities expected by employers over your lifetime.

career The lifework chosen by a person to use personal talent, education, and training.

cash account A brokerage account that requires an initial deposit (perhaps as little as $1,000) and specifies that full settlement is due to the brokerage firm within three business days after a buy or sell order has been given.

cash advances Obtained by credit card customers from an ATM or over the counter at a bank or other financial agency, up to a certain limit.

cash basis Only transactions involving actual cash received or cash spent are recorded.

cash dividends Cash profits that a firm distributes to stockholders.

cash flow Amount of rental income you have left after paying all operating expenses.

cash surrender value Represents the cash value of a policy minus any surrender charges.

cash-balance plan Defined-benefit plan funded solely by an employer that gives each participant an interest-earning account credited with a percentage of pay on a monthly basis.

cash-flow calendar Budget estimates for monthly income and expenses.

cash-flow statement or income and expense statement Summary of all income and expense transactions over a specific time period.

cashier's check A check drawn on the account of the financial institution itself and, thus, backed by the institution's finances.

cash-value life insurance Pays benefits at death and includes a savings/investment element that can provide a level of benefits to the policyholder prior to the death of the insured person.

CD laddering A strategy in which an investor divides the amount of money to be invested into equal amounts to certificates of deposit (CDs) with different maturity dates; it decreases both interest rate and re-investment risks.

certificate of deposit (CD) An interest-earning savings instrument purchased for a fixed period of time, such as 6 months or 1, 2, or even 5 years.

certificate of insurance Document or booklet that outlines group health insurance benefits.

chargeback The law provides that customers may dispute charges to their credit card when goods or services are not delivered within the specified time frame, goods received are damaged, or the purchase was not authorized by the credit card holder.

checking account (transaction account) A deposit account held at a financial institution that performs transactions that allow for withdrawals and deposits.

chronological format Résumé that provides your information in reverse order, with the most recent first.

claims adjuster Person designated by the insurance company to assess whether the loss is covered and to determine the dollar amount that the company will pay.

closed-end credit An arrangement, such as in secured and unsecured loans, where the full amount owed must be paid back by the borrower by a set point in time.

closed-end lease/walkaway lease Agreement in which the lessee pays no charge if the end-of-lease market value of the vehicle is lower than the originally projected residual value.

closing costs Include fees and charges other than the down payment and typically vary from 2 to 7 percent of the mortgage loan amount.

COBRA rights The Consolidated Omnibus Budget Reconciliation Act of 1985 allows a former employee to remain a member of a group health plan for as long as 18 months if the employee worked for an employer with more than 20 workers.

codicil Legal instrument with which one can make minor changes to a will.

coinsurance clause A clause in a health care plan that requires the participant to pay a proportion of any loss suffered.

coinsurance Method by which the insured and the insurer share proportionately in the payment for a loss.

collectibles Cultural artifacts that have value because of their beauty, age, scarcity, or popularity, such as antiques, stamps, rare coins, art, baseball cards, and so on.

collision insurance Reimburses insureds for losses to their vehicles resulting from a collision with another car or object or from a rollover.

commercial banks A type of bank that accepts deposits in checking and savings accounts and provides transactional services such as accepting deposits, making business loans, and offering basic investment products.

commissions Fees or percentages of the selling price paid to salespeople, agents, and companies for their services in buying or selling an investment.

common stock Most basic form of ownership of a corporation.

community banks A type of commercial bank that focuses on providing traditional banking services in their local communities, where they obtain most of their core deposits locally and make many of their loans to local businesses.

comparison shopping Process of comparing products or services to find the best buy.

compound interest Compound interest is earning of interest on interest and arises when interest is added to the principal so that, from that moment on, the interest that has been added also earns interest.

compounding The addition of interest to principal; the effect of compounding depends on the frequency with which interest is compounded and the periodic interest rate that is applied.

comprehensive automobile insurance Protects against property damage losses to an insured vehicle caused by perils other than collision and rollover.

condominium (condo) Form of ownership with the owners holding legal title to their own housing unit among many, with common grounds and facilities owned by the developer or homeowners association.

conservative investment philosophy (risk aversion) Investors with this philosophy accept very little risk and are generally rewarded with relatively low rates of return for seeking the twin goals of a moderate amount of current income and preservation of capital.

consolidation loan The combining of several unsecured debts into a single, new loan that is more favorable, and it may result in a lower interest rate, lower monthly payment or both.

consumer credit counseling agencies The objectives of these nonprofit agencies are to help the creditor avoid bankruptcy, to provide basic education on financial management, and to negotiate with unsecured creditors on behalf of the borrower to reduce interest rates and late fees.

consumer price index (CPI) A broad measure of changes in the prices of all goods and services purchased for consumption by urban households.

consumer statement Your version of disputed information in your credit report when the credit bureau refuses to remove the disputed item.

contingency clauses Specify that certain conditions must be satisfied before a contract is binding.

contingent (or secondary) beneficiary The beneficiary in case the first-named beneficiary has died; also called the secondary beneficiary.

continuous-debt method If you are unable to get completely out of debt every four years (except for a mortgage loan), you probably lean on debt too heavily.

contributory plan The most common type of employee- sponsored defined-contribution retirement plan; accepts employee as well as employer contributions.

conventional mortgage A fixed-rate, fixed-term, fixed-payment mortgage loan.

convertible term insurance Offers policyholders the option of exchanging a term policy for a cash-value policy without evidence of insurability.

cooling-off rule A Federal Trade Commission rule that gives consumers three days to cancel a contract of $25 or more after signing it for a sale made anywhere other than a seller's normal place of business.

cooperative (co-op) Form of ownership in which the owner holds a share of the corporation that owns and manages a group of housing units as well as common grounds and facilities.

coordination of benefits clause An insurance clause in all policies that prevents you from collecting more than 100 percent of covered charges by obtaining benefits from more than one policy.

copay (copayment) A requirement in a health care insurance policy that makes you to pay a certain dollar amount each time you have a specific covered expense item, such as to a doctor's office and for prescription drugs.

corporate bonds Interest-bearing certificates of long-term debt issued by a corporation.

corporate earnings The profits a company makes during a specific time period that indicate to many analysts whether to buy or sell a stock.

cosigner When a person (the cosigner) accepts the legal obligation to make payment on another person's debt should that person default.

countercyclical stock The stock of a company whose profits are greatly influenced by changes in the economic business cycle.

cover letter A letter of introduction sent to a prospective employer to get an interview.

Coverdell education savings account (or education savings account) An IRS-approved way to pay the future education costs for a child younger than age 18 whereby the earnings accumulate tax-free and withdrawals for qualified expenses are tax-free.

covered option Occurs when an option writer who owns the covered option sells the call.

credit agreement Contract that stipulates repayment terms for credit cards.

credit application A form and/or an interview that requests information that sheds light on your ability and willingness to repay debts, such as your income, assets, and debts.

credit bureau Firm that collects and keeps records of many borrowers' credit histories.

credit card (charge card) A plastic card identifying a credit card holder as a participant in the account plan of a lender, such as a department store.

credit freeze (or credit report freeze) It prevents a credit reporting company from releasing your credit report to merchants and financial institutions without your consent.

credit history Continuing record of a person's credit usage and repayment of debts.

credit limit The maximum amount your credit issuer established for you to borrow on a credit card or line of credit.

credit receipt Written evidence of any items returned that notes on a credit card statement the specific amount of the transaction, which will be charged back to the credit card company and eventually to the merchant.

credit report Information compiled by a credit bureau from merchants, utility companies, banks, court records, and creditors about your payment history.

credit score An indication of a person's credit worthiness or how likely the individual will be able to repay any credit extended in a timely manner.

credit statement (billing statement) A periodic report that credit card companies issue to credit card holders showing their recent transactions, balance due and other key information.

credit unions Not-for-profit institutions that accept deposits and make loans, and the members/owners all share some common bond, such as having the same employer, working for or attending the same school, or living in the same community.

credit utilization ratio The percentage of a consumer's available credit that he or she has used, which is a key component of one's credit score; a high credit utilization ratio can lower your score.

credit An arrangement in which goods, services, or money is received in exchange for a promise to repay at a future date.

credit-monitoring service These companies allow one to access his/her credit report as often as daily and obtain a personal FICO credit score.

cumulative preferred stock Preferred stock for which dividends must be paid, including any skipped dividends, before dividends go to common stockholders.

current income Money received while you own an investment; usually received regularly as interest, rent, or dividends.

current rate Rate of return the insurance company has recently paid to policyholders.

current yield Equals the bond's fixed annual interest payment divided by its bond price.

custodial care Suitable for people who do not need skilled nursing care but who nevertheless require supervision (for example, help with eating or personal hygiene).

dealer holdback/dealer rebate A percentage of the total MSRP that the manufacturer holds and then gives back to the dealer, often at the end of the year or quarter.

dealer invoice price (base invoice price) The amount the automaker charges the dealership for new vehicles at the time the dealer buys them; it does not reflect some discounts that the dealer gets.

death benefit Amount that will be paid to the beneficiary when the insured dies.

debit cards A plastic payment card that provides the cardholder electronic access to his/her bank account(s) at a financial institution.

debt limit Overall maximum you believe you should owe based on your ability to meet repayment obligations.

debt management plan (DMP) Arrangement whereby the consumer provides one monthly payment that is distributed to all creditors.

debt payments-to-disposable income method Percentage of disposable personal income available for regular debt repayments aside from set obligations.

debt settlement The process of offering a large, one-time payment toward an existing credit balance in return for the forgiveness of the remaining larger debt.

debt-consolidation loan A loan taken out to pay off several smaller debts.

debts Lending investments that typically offer both a fixed maturity and a fixed income.

debt-to-income method Your monthly debt repayments (including your prospective mortgage, and any other loan or alimony payments you must make) are divided by your gross monthly income and multiplied by 100.

decision-making matrix A system that allows one to visually and mathematically weigh the decision you are about to make.

declining-balance method A method of calculating the annual percentage rate for installment loans where the interest assessed during each payment period (usually each month) is based on the current outstanding balance of the installment loan.

deductible clause Requires that the policyholder pays an initial portion of any loss.

deductible An initial portion of any loss that must be paid before collecting insurance benefits.

deed Written document used to convey real estate ownership.

default risk (credit risk) Uncertainty associated with not receiving the promised periodic interest payments and the principal amount when it becomes due at maturity.

default This is the failure of a borrower to make a scheduled interest or principal payment, and it is something all borrowers want to avoid.

defect disclosure form A state required form that discloses problems that could affect the property's value or desirability, such as a basement that floods in heavy rains.

deficiency balance This occurs when the sum of money raised by the sale of the repossessed or foreclosed collateral fails to cover the amount owed on the debt plus any repossession expenses (collection, attorney, and court costs) paid by the creditor.

deficit (net loss)   When expenses exceed income on a cash-flow statement.

defined-benefit retirement plan (DB)   Employer-sponsored retirement plan that pays lifetime monthly annuity payments to retirees based on a predetermined formula.

defined-contribution retirement plan   A retirement plan in which a certain amount or percentage of money is set aside each year by a company for the benefit of each of its employees.

deflation   A broad, sustained decline in prices of goods and services that is hard to stop once it takes hold, causing less consumer spending, lower corporate profits, declining home values, rising unemployment, and lower incomes.

deleveraging   A time period when credit use shrinks in an economy instead of expanding as during normal economic times.

denied credit   People who are turned down in their request for credit, and the law requires they must be told why, and if the reason was one's credit score he/she may request a credit score report at no charge.

dependent   A relative or household member supported by the taxpayer's income for whom an exemption may be claimed.

depository institutions   Financial institutions in the United States that are legally allowed to offer checking and savings accounts to individuals and businesses as well as provide loans.

depreciate   New vehicles and low-mileage used cars go down in value very quickly after purchase, often as much as 20 percent after leaving the dealer's lot.

depreciation   Decline in value of an asset over time due to normal wear and tear and obsolescence.

digitalization   This is using digital technologies into everyday life to change a business model.

disability benefits   Substantially reduced benefits paid to employees who become disabled prior to retirement.

disability income insurance   Insurance that covers a portion of the income lost when you cannot work because of illness or injury.

disability   A self-reported difficulty in one or more of five areas: vision, cognition, mobility, self-care, or independent living.

discount brokers   Charge commissions to execute trades that are often 30 to 80 percent less than the fees charged by full-service brokers, but also offer fewer services.

discounted cash-flow method   Effective way to estimate the value or asking price of a real estate investment based on after-tax cashflow and the return on the invested dollars discounted over time to reflect a discounted yield.

discretionary or controllable expenses   Money left over after necessities such as housing and food are paid for.

disposable income   Amount of income remaining after taxes and withholding for such purposes as insurance and union dues.

distribution phase   The time period during which you hope that your assets will last throughout retirement.

diversification   Process of reducing risk by spreading investment money among several different investment opportunities.

do-it-yourself   Selecting no-load mutual funds in which to invest is relatively easy to do.

dollar-cost averaging/cost averaging   Systematic program of investing equal sums of money at regular intervals, regardless of the price of the investment.

Dow Jones Industrial Average (DJIA)   The most widely reported of all stock market indexes that tracks prices of 30 actively traded blue-chip stocks, including well-known companies such as American Express and AT&T.

down payment   An initial payment made in the context of buying expensive items on credit, such as a vehicle or home.

early withdrawal penalty   A ten percent penalty over and above the taxes owed when money is withdrawn early from a qualified retirement account.

earned income   Compensation for performing personal services.

earnest money   Funds given to the seller as a deposit to hold the property until a purchase contract can be finalized.

earnings per share (EPS)   A firm's profit divided by the number of outstanding shares.

earnings yield   The earnings per share of a stock divided by its price; an inversion of the price/earnings ratio; helps investors more clearly see investment expectations.

economic growth   A condition of increasing production (business spending) and consumption (consumer spending) in the economy and hence increasing national income.

economic indicator   Any economic statistic, such as the unemployment rate, GDP, or the inflation rate, that suggests how well the economy is doing now and how well it might be doing in the future.

effective marginal tax rate   A person's total marginal tax rate on income after adding federal, state, and local income taxes as well as Social Security and Medicare taxes.

electronic benefit transfer (EBT) cards   An electronic system that allows state welfare departments to issue benefits via a magnetically encoded payment debit cards.

electronic funds transfers (EFTs)   When funds are shifted electronically (rather than by check or cash) among various accounts and to and from other people and institutions.

electronic money management   Occurs whenever transactions are conducted without using paper documents.

elevator speech   This is a short, persuasive summary of your experiences and skills when networking.

emergency fund   This is an account that is used to set aside funds to be used in an emergency, such as the loss of a job, an illness, or one of life's many "what ifs."

employee benefit Compensation for employment that does not take the form of wages, salaries, commissions, or other cash payments.

employee benefits Forms of remuneration provided by employers to employees that result in the employee not having to pay out-of-pocket money for certain expenses; also known as nonsalary benefits.

Employee Retirement Income Security Act (ERISA) Regulates employer-sponsored plans by calling for proper plan reporting and disclosure to participants in defined-contribution, defined-benefit, and cash-balance plans.

employee stock-ownership plan (ESOP) Benefit plan in which employers make tax-deductible gifts of company stock into trusts, which are then allocated into employee accounts.

employer-sponsored retirement plan An IRS-approved retirement plan offered by an employer (also called qualified plans).

employment agency Firm that locates employment for certain types of employees.

endorsement An addition to a standard insurance policy designed to expand coverage for a special area of need.

entrepreneur One who is starting out a company and is hopeful about their situation because they organize, manage, and assume the risks of a business or enterprise.

envelope system Placing exact amounts into envelopes for each budgetary purpose.

equities Ownership equities such as common or preferred stocks, equity mutual funds, real estate, and so on that focus on capital gains more than on income.

escrow account Special reserve account at a financial institution in which funds are held until they are paid to a third party—in this case, for home insurance and for property taxes.

essential health benefits A list of ten categories of benefits that all health care plans sold on the health insurance exchanges must provide.

estate planning The definite arrangements you make during your lifetime that are consistent with your wishes for the administration and distribution of your estate when you die.

estimate of the required rate of return on an investment A calculation that multiplies the beta value of an investment by the estimated market risk and adds the risk-free T-bill rate that suggests to investors the return required to put their money at risk.

estimated taxes People who are self-employed or receive substantial income from an employer that is not required to practice payroll withholding (such as lawyers and owners of rental property) are required by the IRS to estimate their tax liability and pay their taxes in advance in quarterly installments.

excess mileage charge Fees assessed at the end of a lease if the vehicle was driven more miles than originally specified in the lease contract.

exchange privilege Allowance for mutual fund shareholders to easily swap shares on a dollar-for-dollar basis for shares in another mutual fund within a mutual fund family. Also called switching, conversion, or transfer privilege.

exclusions in health care A list of services that are not typically covered in a health care policy.

exclusions in taxes Income not subject to federal taxation.

exclusive agents Companies that market insurance policies through salaried employees, mail-order promotions, newspapers, the Internet, and even vending machines.

executor/personal representative Person responsible for carrying out the provisions of a will and managing the assets until the estate is passed on to heirs.

exemption (or personal exemption) A legally permitted amount, an allowance to reduce one's taxable income, based on the number of people supported by the taxpayer's income.

expense ratio Expense per dollar of assets under management.

expenses Total expenditures made in a specified time such as reported on a cash-flow statement.

face amount Dollar value of protection as listed in the policy and used to calculate the premium.

Fair Credit Reporting Act (FCRA) One part of the law requires that credit reports contain only accurate relevant information and allows consumers to challenge errors or omissions of information in their reports.

Fair Debt Collection Practices Act (FDCPA) Prohibits third-party debt collection agencies from using abusive, deceptive, or unfair practices to collect past-due debts.

fair market value The amount a willing buyer would pay a willing seller for an item.

fed The Federal Reserve Board, an agency of the federal government.

federal deposit insurance Insures deposits, both principal amounts and accrued interest, up to $250,000 per account for most accounts.

federal estate tax Assessed against a deceased person's estate before property (real estate, stocks and bonds, business interests, and so on) is transferred to heirs or assigned according to terms of a will or state intestacy laws.

federal funds rate The short-term rate at which banks lend funds to other banks overnight so that the borrowing bank has sufficient reserves as mandated by the Fed.

Federal Housing Administration (FHA) Part of the U.S. Department of Housing and Urban Development (HUD) that insures loans that meet its standards to encourage home ownership.

fee-for-service or indemnity plan A health insurance plan where you pay up front for services and then submit a claim for reimbursement to the insurance company.

FICA taxes A 6.2 percent tax paid by both the worker and employer on the worker's employment income up to the maximum taxable yearly earnings.

FICA Social Security and Medicare taxes. Taxes withheld for Social Security and Medicare are known as the Federal Insurance Contributions Act.

FICO score   The most widely known credit scoring system developed by Fair Isaac Corporation and used by 90-plus percent of companies when making lending decisions.

fiduciary standard   A financial advisor must always act in the best interest of the client at all times regardless of how it might affect the advisor.

filing status   Defines the type of tax return form an individual will use as it is based on marital status and family situation, and it is a description of one's marital status on the last day of the year.

final expenses   One-time expenses occurring just prior to or after a death.

finance charge   The cost of credit or the cost of borrowing; it is interest accrued on, and fees charged for some forms of credit.

financial goals   Specific objectives addressed by planning and managing finances.

financial happiness   The experience you have when you are satisfied with your money matters, which is in part a result of practicing good financial behaviors.

financial literacy   Knowledge of facts, concepts, principles, and technological tools that are fundamental to being smart about money.

financial planner   An investment professional who evaluates the personal finances of an individual or family and recommends strategies to set and achieve long-term financial goals.

financial ratios   Calculations designed to simplify evaluation of financial strength and progress.

financial records   Documents that evidence financial transactions.

financial responsibility laws   Those that require vehicle owners to prove they have enough resources to pay for damages resulting from a car accident.

financial security   The comfortable feeling that your financial resources will be adequate to fulfill any needs you have as well as most of your wants.

financial services industry   Companies that provide monetary asset management and other services.

financial statements   Snapshots that describe an individual's or family's current financial condition.

financial strategies   Pre-established action plans implemented in specific situations.

financial success   The achievement of financial aspirations that are desired, planned, or attempted, as defined by the person who seeks it.

financial well-being   A state of being wherein a person can fully meet current and ongoing financial obligations, can feel secure in their financial future, and make choices that allow them to enjoy life.

financially responsible   Means that you are accountable for your future financial well-being and that you strive to make wise personal financial decisions.

fixed expenses   Expenses often in the same amount that recur at fixed intervals.

fixed income   Specific rate of return that a borrower agrees to pay the investor for use of the principal (initial investment).

fixed maturity   Specific date on which a borrower agrees to repay the principal to the investor.

fixed-rate loan   A loan where the contract calls for the interest rate on a loan to remain fixed either for the entire term of the loan.

fixed-time deposit   A certificate of deposit that has a specific time period that the savings must be left on deposit; otherwise a penalty is assessed for early withdrawal.

flexible spending account (FSA)   An employer-sponsored account that allows employee-paid expenses for medical or dependent care to be paid with an employee's pretax dollars rather than after-tax income.

floater policies   Provide all-risk protection for accident and theft losses to movable property regardless of where the loss occurs.

Floating Rate Notes (FRNs)   Two-year note of the federal government that pays interest quarterly.

foreclosure   The legal process of taking possession of a mortgaged property as a result of the mortgagor's failure to keep up mortgage payments.

freelancing   One chooses to be employed with a more flexible work arrangement (often part-time) than full-time on a contract basis, often working at home, for a variety of companies, as opposed to working as an employee for a single company.

front-end load   A sales charge paid when an individual buys an investment, reducing the amount available to purchase fund shares.

front-end ratio   Compares the total annual PITI expenditures for housing with the loan applicant's gross annual income to assess the borrower's ability to pay the mortgage.

FSA debit card (flexcard)   A card used to access and spend funds from a flexible spending account.

FSBO   For sale by owner; commonly pronounced "fizbo"; home sold directly by the homeowner to save on sales commission paid to a real estate broker.

full-benefit retirement age   Age at which a retiree is entitled to full Social Security benefits; 67 for those born in 1960 or later.

fully insured Social Security status   Requires 40 credits and provides workers and their families with benefits under the retirement, survivors, and disability programs; once status is earned, it cannot be taken away even if the eligible worker never works again.

functional format   Résumé that emphasizes career-related experiences.

fund screener (fund-screening tool)   Permits investors to screen all of the mutual funds in the market to gauge performance.

fundamental analysis   School of thought in market analysis that assumes each stock has an intrinsic (or true) value based on its expected stream of future earnings.

future value The valuation of an asset projected to the end of a particular time period in the future.

futures contract The obligation to make or take delivery of a certain amount of a commodity by a set date.

garnishment A court order directing that money or property of a third party (usually wages paid by an employer) be seized to satisfy a debt owed by a debtor to a plaintiff creditor.

general (full-service) brokerage firms Offer a full range of services to customers, including investment advice and research.

gift card A stored value card that often has an activation fee, expiration date (no shorter than five years), and an inactivity fee if there are no transactions within a year.

gig economy A workplace economy that allows independent contractors (rather than employees) to move from one temporary job to the next without benefits.

gold bullion coins Various world mints issue these coins, which contain 1 troy ounce (31.15 grams) of pure gold.

gold bullion A refined and stamped weight of precious metal.

grace period in credit This is the period of time a creditor, such as a credit card company, gives you to pay your new charges without having to pay interest on the new balance.

grace period in insurance Period of time during which an overdue premium may be paid without a lapse of the policy.

graduated vesting Schedule under which employees must be at least 20 percent vested after two years of service and gain an additional 20 percent of vesting for each subsequent year until, at the end of year six, the account is fully vested.

grantor Creator of a trust—the person who makes a grant of assets to establish a trust. Also called the *settler*, *donor*, or *trustor*.

gross capitalized cost (gross cap cost) Includes vehicle price plus the cost of any extra features such as insurance or maintenance agreements.

gross domestic product (GDP) The nation's broadest measure of economic health; it reports how much economic activity (all goods and services) has occurred within the U.S. borders during a given period.

gross income All income in the form of money, goods, services, and/or property.

growth and income funds Funds that invest in companies that have a high likelihood of both dividend income and price appreciation; less risk-oriented than aggressive growth funds or growth funds.

growth funds Funds that seek long-term capital appreciation by investing in common stocks of companies with higher-than-average revenue and earnings growth, often the larger and well-established firms.

growth stock The stock of a company that offers the promise of much higher profits tomorrow and has a consistent record of relatively rapid growth in earnings in all economic conditions.

guaranteed insurability Permits the cash-value policyholder to buy additional stated amounts of cash-value life insurance at stated times in the future without evidence of insurability.

guaranteed minimum rate of return Minimum rate that, by contract, the insurance company is legally obligated to pay.

guaranteed renewable term insurance Protects you against the possibility of becoming uninsurable.

guardian Person responsible for caring for and raising any child under the age of 18 and for managing the child's estate.

hardship withdrawal A distribution from a 401(k) plan to be made on account of an immediate and heavy financial need of the employee, and the amount must be necessary to satisfy the financial need.

hazard Any condition that increases the probability that a peril will occur.

health care plans An employee benefit designed to pay all or part of the employee's medical expenses.

health insurance exchange (HIX) State-by-state mechanisms established by the ACA through which consumers can purchase a health care plan.

health maintenance organizations (HMOs) Pre-paid managed care insurance plans in which individuals or their employers pay a fixed monthly fee for services instead of a separate charge for each visit or service.

health savings account (HSA) A tax-advantaged medical savings account for those who have a high-deductible health care plan whereby all funds put into the account are 100 percent tax deductible from gross income when used for health care expenses.

healthcare subsidy A form of cost assistance that lowers the amount you spend on your monthly premium or reduces your out-of-pocket costs.

hedge funds Freewheeling risky investment pools for the extremely wealthy that use unconventional investment strategies such as trading options and commodities, selling short, using leverage and arbitrage, buying and selling currencies, and investing in undervalued mature companies.

heir Person who inherits or is entitled by law or by the terms of a will to inherit some asset.

herd behavior When emotion, not logic, rules investing decisions and investors decide to copy the observed decisions of other investors or movements in the markets rather than follow their own beliefs and information.

high-balling Sales tactic in which a dealer offers a trade-in allowance that is much higher than the vehicle is worth.

high-deductible health plan (HDHP) A plan that requires individuals to pay a higher deductible to cover medical expenses before insurance plan payments begin; chosen to save money on premiums.

high-risk investments Present potential for significant fluctuations in return, sometimes over short time periods.

home equity credit line A loan in which the lender agrees to lend a maximum amount within a term where the collateral is the borrower's equity in his/her home.

home inspection Conducted to ensure that the home is physically sound and that all operating systems are in proper order.

homeowner's equity Dollar value of the home in excess of the amount owed on it.

homeowner's general liability protection Applies when you are legally liable for another person's losses, other than those that arise out of use of vehicles or your professional duties.

homeowner's insurance Combines liability and property insurance coverages that homeowners and renters typically need into single-package policies.

household income Modified gross income increased by any excluded foreign income and tax-exempt interest. Used under the Affordable Care Act to determine eligibility for the premium tax credit and for imposing a penalty on anyone who fails to purchase minimum essential coverage.

human capital The skill set, knowledge, and other intangible assets of individuals that can be used to create economic value for the individuals, their employers, or their community.

I-bonds Nonmarketable savings bonds backed by the U.S. government that pay an earnings rate that combines two rates: a fixed interest rate set when the investor buys the bond and a semiannual variable interest rate tied to inflation that protects the investor's purchasing power.

identity theft The fraudulent acquisition and use of a person's private identifying information, usually for financial gain.

immediate annuity Annuity, often funded by a lump sum from the death benefit of a life insurance policy or lump sum from a defined-contribution plan, that begins payments one month after purchase.

income stock A stock that may not grow too quickly, but year after year pays a cash dividend higher than that offered by most companies.

incontestability clause Places a time limit on the right of the insurance company to deny a claim.

indenture Written, legal agreement between bondholders and debtor that describes terms of the debt by setting forth the maturity date, interest rate, and other details.

index mutual funds (or index funds) are those funds whose investment objective is to achieve the same return as a particular market index by buying and holding all or a representative selection of securities in it.

index of leading economic indicators (LEI) Four composite index reported monthly by the Conference Board that suggests the future direction of the U.S. economy.

indexing Yearly adjustments to tax brackets that reduce inflation's effects on tax brackets.

individual mandate An Affordable Care Act provision that require that *all* Americans and legal residents buy health coverage no matter how sick and regardless of any pre-existing health problems.

individual shared responsibility fee A tax penalty of the Affordable Care Act that is assessed when one does not buy health insurance.

inflation The process by which the cost of goods and services tends to rise over time.

inheritance tax A tax imposed by eight states that is assessed on the decedent's beneficiaries who receive inherited property.

insolvent When a person owes more than he or she owns and the person has a negative net worth.

installment loan A system of credit that is repaid by the borrower in regular installments, such as equal monthly payments that include interest and a portion of principal.

insurance agents Representative of an insurance company authorized to sell, modify, service, and terminate insurance contracts.

insurance claim Formal request to the insurance company for reimbursement for a covered loss.

insurance dividends Surplus earnings of the insurance company when the difference between the total premium charged exceeds the cost to the company of providing insurance.

insurance policy Contract between the person buying insurance (the insured) and the insurance company (the insurer).

insurance Mechanism for transferring and reducing pure risk through which a large number of individuals share in the financial losses suffered by members of the group as a whole.

insured Individual whose life is insured.

interest inventories Scaled surveys that assess career interests and activities.

interest rate caps Limits in credit contracts that prohibit how much the interest rate can increase over the life of the loan.

interest rate risk Risk that interest rates will rise and bond prices will fall, thereby lowering the prices on older bond issues.

interest The charge for the privilege of borrowing money, typically expressed as an annual percentage rate.

interest-earning checking account Any account on which you can write checks that pays interest.

interest-rate risk The risk that an investment's value will change due to a change in the absolute level of interest rates.

intermediate-term goals Financial targets that can be achieved within one to five years.

intestate When a person dies without a legal will.

investing Putting saved money to work so that it makes you even more money.

investment philosophy Investor's general approach to tolerance for risk in investments, whether it is conservative, moderate, or aggressive, given the investor's financial goals.

investment plan   An explanation of your investment philosophy and your logic on investing to reach specific goals.

investment policy statement   A written document that spells out the relationship between an investor and his or her financial advisor and guides how the advisor will invest the person's money; it should detail the person's investment philosophy, financial situation, and the risks he or she is willing to take, as well as what tasks the advisor will perform.

investment risk   The possibility that the yield on an investment will deviate from its expected return.

investment/capital assets   Tangible and intangible items acquired for their monetary benefits.

investment-grade bonds   Offer investors a reasonable certainty of regularly receiving periodic income (interest) and retrieving the amount originally invested (principal).

investments   Assets purchased with the goal of providing additional future income from the asset itself.

invitation-to-apply   Refers to a credit card offer sent without any prior screening, thus one must fill out the application and see if it is approved.

irrevocable living trust   Arrangement in which the grantor permanently gives up ownership and the right to control of the property, to change the beneficiaries, and to change the trustees.

itemized deductions   Tax-deductible expenses that may be used to directly reduce income and reduce one's tax liability.

job boards   A website devoted to helping employers find suitable new employees by providing job listings, job sites, job search tips, job search engines, and related articles; some allow posting of résumés.

job interview   Formal meeting between employer and potential employee to discuss job qualifications and suitability.

job referral   The act recommending someone to another by sending a reference for employment.

joint and survivor benefit/survivor's benefit   Annuity whose payments continue to a surviving spouse after the participant's death; often equals at least 50 percent of participant's benefit.

joint tenancy with right of survivorship/joint tenancy   Most common form of joint ownership, especially for husbands and wives, in which each person owns the whole of the asset, such as a bank account or home, and can dispose of it without the approval of the other owner(s).

joint-and-survivor annuity   Provides monthly payments for as long as one of the two people—usually a husband and wife—is alive.

Keogh   Tax-deferred retirement account designed for high-income self-employed and small-business owners.

large-cap stocks   Company size classification in the stock market for firms valued at or more than $10 billion.

large-loss principle   A basic rule of risk management that encourages us to insure the risks that we cannot afford and retain the risks that we can reasonably afford.

law of large numbers   As the number of members in a group increases, predictions about the group's behavior become increasingly accurate.

leading economic indicators   Statistics that change before the economy changes, thus helping predict how the economy will do in the future, such as the stock market, the number of new building permits, and the consumer confidence index.

lease   In this context, a contract specifying both tenant and landlord legal responsibilities.

lemon laws   State laws that provide guidelines for arbitrators to use to order a dealer's buyback of a "lemon" as defined under the law—commonly a car that has been in the shop four or more times to fix the same problem.

letter of last instructions   Nonlegal instrument that may contain preferences regarding funeral and burial, material to be included in the obituary, and other information useful to the survivors, such as the location of important documents.

level of living   refers to the level of wealth, comfort, material goods and necessities one is currently living.

liabilities   What you owe.

liability insurance   Protection from financial losses suffered when you are held liable for others' losses.

lien   A legal right to keep possession of property belonging to another person until a debt owed by that person is discharged; usually recorded in a county courthouse.

life insurance policy   A contract between an insured (insurance policy holder) and an insurer or assurer, where the insurer promises to pay a designated beneficiary a sum of money (the "benefits") upon the death of the insured person.

life insurance   An insurance contract helps replace lost income if premature death occurs as it promises to pay a dollar benefit to a beneficiary upon the death of the insured person.

lifestyle trade-offs   Weighing the demands of particular jobs with your social and cultural preferences.

limited warranty   Any warranty that offers less protection than the three conditions for full warranty.

limited-pay whole life insurance   Whole life insurance that allows premium payments to cease before the insured reaches the age of 100.

line of credit   An open-end credit account between a financial institution, usually a bank, and a customer that establishes a maximum loan limit that the bank will permit the person to borrow.

liquidity risk   The risk that a given security or asset cannot be traded quickly enough in the market to prevent a loss (or make the required profit).

liquidity   The speed and ease with which an asset can be converted to cash.

listing agreement   Agreement that brokers require homeowners to sign that permits the broker to list the property exclusively or with a multiple-listing service.

living trust   A trust that takes effect while the grantor is still alive.

living will   Allows you to document in advance your specific wishes concerning medical treatments in an emergency or during end-of-life health care.

load funds   Mutual funds that always charge a "load" or sales charge upon purchase; the load is the commission used to compensate brokers.

loan commitment   Lender's promise to grant a loan.

loan   Consumer credit that is repaid in equal amounts over a set period of time.

loan-to-value ratio   Measures the amount of leverage in a real estate investment project by dividing the total amount of debt by the market price of the investment.

long-term (noncurrent) liability   Debt that comes due in more than one year.

long-term care insurance   Provides reimbursement for costs associated with custodial care in a nursing facility or at home.

long-term gain/loss   A profit or loss on the sale of an asset that has been held for more than a year.

long-term goals   Financial targets to achieve more than five years in the future.

loss control   Designing specific mechanisms to reduce loss frequency and loss severity.

low-balling   A sales tactic where the seller quotes an artificially low price to obtain a verbal agreement from a buyer and then attempts to raise the negotiated price when it comes time to finalize the written contract.

low-load funds   Funds carrying sales charges of perhaps 1 to 3 percent; sold by brokers, via mail, and sometimes through mutual fund retailers located in shopping centers.

managed care   A system designed to control the conditions under which health care can be obtained.

manufacturer's suggested retail price (MSRP)   The retail price set by the manufacturer and posted on the federally required side window sticker.

margin buying   Account at a brokerage firm that requires a substantial deposit of cash or securities and permits the purchase of other securities using credit granted by the brokerage firm.

margin rate   Set by the Fed, percentage of the value (or equity) in an investment that is not borrowed—recently 25 to 50 percent.

marginal cost   The additional (marginal) cost of one more incremental unit of some item.

marginal tax rate   The tax rate at which your last dollar earned is taxed, and it refers to the highest tax bracket that your taxable income puts you in.

marginal utility   The extra satisfaction derived from gaining one more incremental unit of a product or service.

market correction   A short term price decline in the stock markets of at least 10 percent in a stock, bond, commodity, or index to adjust for a recent price rises.

market interest rates   Current long- and short-term interest rates paid on various types of corporate and government debts that carry similar levels of risk.

market price   The current price of a share of stock that a buyer is willing to pay a willing seller.

market risk/systematic risk/undiversifiable risk   The possibility for an investor to experience losses due to unknown factors that affect the overall performance of the financial markets.

market timers   Investors who attempt to predict the short-term movements of various markets (or market segments) and, based on those predictions, move capital from one segment to another in order to capture market gains and avoid market losses.

market volatility   The likelihood of large price swings in securities due to a company's success (or lack of it) and various market conditions.

market-volatility risk   The fact that all investments are subject to occasional sharp changes in price as a result of events affecting a particular company or the overall market for similar investments.

match   An employer may voluntarily contribute a certain amount of money to an individual's retirement account according to the amount the employee contributes.

matching contribution   Employer benefit that offers a full or partial matching contribution to a participating employee's account in proportion to each dollar of contributions made by the participant.

maturity date   Date upon which the principal is returned to the bondholder.

maximum taxable yearly earnings (MTYE)   The maximum amount to which the FICA tax is applied.

means test   In bankruptcy a court determines whether an individual debtor's Chapter 7 filing can be presumed to be an abuse of the bankruptcy laws requiring dismissal or conversion of the case.

Medicaid   A government health care program for low-income people funded jointly by the federal and state governments.

Medicare tax   A 1.45 percent tax paid by both the worker and employer on all the worker's employment income.

mentor   An experienced person, often a senior coworker, who offers friendly career-related advice, guidance, and coaching to a less-experienced person.

mid-cap stocks   Company size classification in the stock market for firms valued between $2 billion and $10 billion.

minimum payment warning box   The box on credit card statements must show how long it would take to pay off the card's balance by making only the minimum payments, and how much you'd need to pay each month to clear the balance in 36 months.

minimum payment   The amount due monthly on a credit card statement that is no smaller than the amount required by the creditor.

moderate investment philosophy (risk indifference) Investors with this philosophy accept some risk as they seek capital gains through slow and steady growth in investment value along with current income.

modern code The language of the digital world, which is writing the source code for a computer program.

modified adjusted gross income (MAGI) The figure the IRS uses to calculate one's health care penalty, and for most people it is the same as adjusted gross income.

monetary asset management The task of maximizing interest earnings and minimizing fees on all of your funds kept readily available for day-to-day living expenses, emergencies, and savings and investment opportunities.

monetary assets/liquid assets/cash equivalents Assets that can be easily converted to cash.

money market account (MMA) Any of a variety of interest-earning accounts offered by depository institutions that pays slightly high interest rates (compared with regular savings accounts) and offers some check-writing privileges.

money market deposit account (MMDA) A deposit account that requires a larger initial deposit to open (often $2,500), and it requires a minimum balance to be maintained, checks must be written for a minimum amount, and it only allows a limited number of checking transactions per month.

money market fund (MMF) Money market account in a mutual fund rather than at a depository institution.

money market mutual funds (MMMFs) Money market accounts offered by a mutual fund investment company (rather than at a depository institution).

money order A checking instrument bought for a particular amount with a fee assessed based on the amount of the order.

monthly statements Monthly reports that show all electronic transfers to and from accounts, fees charged, and opening and closing balances.

mortgage insurance Insures the difference between the amount of down payment required by an 80 percent LTV ratio and the actual, lower down payment.

mortgage loan Loan to purchase real estate in which the property itself serves as collateral.

municipal government bonds (munis) Long-term debts (bonds) issued by local governments (cities, states, and various districts and political subdivisions) and their agencies.

mutual fund ask (or offer) price Price at which an investor can purchase a mutual fund's shares; current NAV per share plus sales charges.

mutual fund bid price Shareholders receive this amount per share when they redeem their shares, which is the same dollar amount as the NAV.

mutual fund dividend Income paid to investors out of profits earned by the mutual fund from its investments.

mutual fund family Investment management company that offers a number of different funds to the investing public, each with its own investment objectives or philosophies of investing.

mutual fund Investment company that pools funds by selling shares to investors and makes diversified investments to achieve financial goals of income or growth, or both.

mutual savings banks A type of thrift institution that also accept deposits and make housing and consumer loans.

named-perils policies Cover only losses caused by perils that the policy specifically mentions.

need Item thought to be necessary.

needs-based approach A superior method of calculating the amount of insurance needed that considers all of the factors that might potentially affect the level of need.

negative option This is a business practice in which a customer agrees to have goods or services to be provided automatically, and the customer must either pay for the service or specifically decline it in advance of billing.

negotiable order of withdrawal (NOW) account An interest-earning checking account at a depository institution.

negotiating/haggling Process of discussing actual terms of agreement with a seller, usually on higher-priced items.

net asset value (NAV) Per-share value of a mutual fund.

net surplus Amount remaining after all budget classification deficits are subtracted from those with surpluses.

net worth What's left when you subtract liabilities from assets.

new-vehicle buying service Organization that arranges discount purchases for new-car buyers who are referred to nearby participating automobile dealers that have agreed to charge specific discount prices.

no-limits jobs Where people, especially younger workers, are employed in entry-level positions where they are expected to be on-call via a mobile device at all hours of the day and night.

no-load funds Funds that allow investors to purchase shares directly at the net asset value (NAV) without the addition of sales charges.

nominal income Also called money income; income that has not been adjusted for inflation and decreasing purchasing power.

nonforfeiture values Amounts stipulated in a life insurance policy that protect the cash value, if any, in the event that the policyholder chooses not to pay or fails to pay required premiums.

nonprobate property Does not go through probate; includes assets transferred to survivors by contract (such as beneficiaries listed on retirement accounts and bank accounts held with another person).

nonrefundable tax credit   A tax credit that can reduce one's tax liability only to zero; however, if the credit is more than the tax liability, the excess is not refunded.

***n*-ratio method**   A method of estimating the annual percentage rate for installment loans where it is an add-on loan.

nudge   Policies of employers and/or the government to help get consumers to do what is good for them.

obsolete knowledge   That which we believe may have been valid at one time, if it ever was true in the first place.

one-rollover rule   An IRS rule that says investors can make only one rollover form one IRA to another in any 12-month period, although there is no limit on trustee-to-trustee transfers.

online banks   Banks that are regulated just like any other bank, even those they operate entirely over the Internet, yet because they avoid the "bricks and mortar" costs of conventional institutions they often pay higher interest rates than other institutions.

online discount brokers   Such brokers, also called Internet or electronic discount brokers, have reduced the cost of executing a trade to perhaps $20 or even $10 because their primary business is online trading.

open-end credit (revolving credit)   An account under which you are allowed to make repeated purchases or obtain loans and you may pay the balance in full or you may pay in installments.

open-end mutual fund   Investment that issues redeemable shares that investors purchase directly from the fund (or through a broker for the fund).

open-enrollment period   A time period during which one can make changes in health care insurance coverage or switch among alternative plans.

opportunity cost   The opportunity cost of any decision is the value of the next best alternative that must be forgone.

ordinary income dividend distributions   Distributions that occur when the fund pays out dividends from the stock and interest from the bonds it hold in its portfolio; these are passed onto the investor quarterly.

out-of-pocket maximum   The most you pay during a policy period before your health insurance or plan begins to pay 100 percent of the allowed amount.

overindebted   When one's excessive personal debts make repayment difficult and cause financial distress.

over-the-counter (OTC) (off-exchange trading)   Refers to stocks that trade via a dealer network made using a telephone and computer system rather than on the floor of a centralized exchange.

owner/policyholder   Retains all rights and privileges granted by the policy, including the right to amend the policy and the right to designate who receives the proceeds.

paid up   Point at which the owner of a whole life policy can stop paying premiums.

participating policies   Life insurance policies that pay dividends.

Patient Protection and Affordable Care Act (ACA)   The law passed by Congress in 2010 to provide affordable health insurance for all US citizens and reduce the growth in health care spending.

pay yourself first   Treating savings as the first expenditure after—or even before getting paid rather than simply the money left over at the end of the month.

Payable On Death (POD) (known as a Totten trust)   An arrangement between a bank or credit union and a client that designates beneficiaries to receive all the client's assets, and the immediate transfer of assets is triggered by the death of the client.

payable-on-death designation   Status granted to individuals who are not joint tenants and who might need to access accounts without going through probate; the deceased signs the designation before death, and the designee simply presents a death certificate to access the accounts.

payment due date   The specific day by which the credit card company should receive payment from the cardholder.

payroll withholding   The IRS requirement that an employer withhold a certain amount from an employee's income as a prepayment of that individual's tax liability for the year. It is sent to the government where it is credited to the taxpayer's account.

PEG ratio (price-earnings growth)   A way to rationalize buying a stock that has high growth is to calculate by dividing the P/E ratio by the company's projected growth rate.

penalty rate (default rate)   The very high interest rate charged by the credit card issuer when a borrower violates the card's terms and conditions.

penny stocks   Stocks that trade for less than $5 per share.

perils   Any event that can cause a financial loss.

personal finance   The study of personal and family resources considered important in achieving financial success; it involves how people spend, save, protect, and invest their financial resources.

Physicians Order for Life Sustaining Treatment (POLST) form   A legal document similar to a living will used for people with advanced illnesses or those in emergency situations.

PITI   Elements of a monthly real estate payment consisting of principal, interest, real estate taxes, and homeowner's insurance.

point/interest point   Fee equal to 1 percent of the total mortgage loan amount.

policy limits   Specify the maximum dollar amounts that will be paid under the policy.

portability   Upon termination of employment, employees with portable benefits can keep their savings in tax-sheltered accounts, transferring retirement funds from employer's account directly to another account without penalty.

portfolio diversification   Practice of selecting a collection of different asset classes of investments (such as stocks, bonds, mutual funds, real estate, and cash) that are chosen not only for their potential returns but also for their dissimilar risk-return characteristics.

portfolio tracking   Automatically updates the value of your portfolio after you enter the symbols of the stocks you own and the number of shares held.

portfolio   Collection of investments assembled to meet your investment goals.

posting date   The month, day, and year when a credit card issuer processes a credit card transaction and adds it to the cardholder's account balance.

potential return   Determined by adding anticipated income (from dividends, interest, rents, or other sources) to the future value of investment and then subtracting the investment's original cost.

preapproved   Refers to a credit offer based on a pre-qualification of the individual's credit from a credit bureau report, and upon acceptance the issuer obtains more detailed credit information and sets an interest rate.

pre-emptive right   Right of common stockholders to purchase additional shares before a firm offers new shares to the public.

preferred provider organization (PPO)   A managed care organization of medical doctors, hospitals, and other health care providers who have agreed with an insurer or a third-party administrator to provide health care at reduced rates to the insurer's clients.

preferred stock   Type of fixed-income ownership security in a corporation that pays fixed dividends.

preloaded debit cards   A plastic payment card that is easy to use and reloadable, and it may be used almost anywhere to buy online, make bill payments, get cash at ATMs, pay bills, get direct deposits, and make everyday purchases.

premium   The monthly or annual cost paid for insurance.

premium quote service   Offers computer-generated comparisons from among 20 to 80 different companies.

prepayment penalty   An additional fee imposed by many loan agreements where a borrower pays off a loan early, before its scheduled pay-off date.

prescreened   Refers to a credit card offer that a bank aims at certain consumers based on their borrowing histories, and card approval is likely although not necessarily for the interest rate and credit line outlined in the offer.

preshopping research   Gathering information before actually beginning to interact with sellers.

prestige cards   Credit cards often with a precious metal in the brand name such as "gold," "silver," or "platinum" that require that the user possess superior credit qualifications and offer enhancements such as higher credit limits.

pretax dollars   Money income that has not been taxed by the government.

pretax money   Investing before income taxes are calculated, thus gaining an immediate elimination of part of your income tax liability for the current year.

price appreciation   The increased value of the underlying securities is reflected in the NAV of fund shares.

price/earnings (P/E ratio) (or multiple)   The current market price of a stock divided by earnings per share (EPS) over the past four quarters; used as the primary means of valuing a stock.

price/sales ratio (P/S ratio)   Tells the number of dollars it takes to buy a dollar's worth of a company's annual revenues; calculated by dividing company's total market capitalization by its sales for the past four quarters.

price-to-book ratio (P/B ratio)   Current stock price divided by the per-share net value of a firm's plant, equipment, and other assets (book value).

price-to-rent ratio   The ratio of median residential real estate prices to the median annual rents that can be earned from the real estate.

prime rate   The interest rate banks charge their most credit-worthy customers, and it is sometimes used as a benchmark for other variable-rate loans.

principal   Face amount of a bond or the original amount invested.

principle of indemnity   Insurance will pay *no more* than the actual financial loss suffered.

private mortgage insurance (PMI)   Mortgage insurance obtained from a private company.

probate property   All assets other than nonprobate property.

probate   Court-supervised process that allows creditors to present claims against an estate and ensures the transfer of a decedent's assets to the rightful beneficiaries according to a properly executed and valid will or, when no will exists, to the people, agencies, or organizations required by state law.

professional abilities   Job-related activities that you can perform physically, mentally, artistically, mechanically, and financially.

professional interests   Long-standing topics and activities that engage your attention.

professional liability insurance/malpractice insurance   Protects individuals and organizations that provide professional services when they are held liable for their clients' losses.

professional networking   Making and using contacts with individuals, groups, and other firms to exchange career information.

profile prospectus (fund profile)   Publication that describes the mutual fund, its investment objectives, and how it tries to achieve its objectives in lay terms rather than the legal language used in a regular prospectus.

profit   Money left over after a firm pays all expenses and interest to bondholders.

profit-sharing plan Employer-sponsored plan that allocates some of the employer profits to employees in the form of end-of-year cash or common stock contributions to employees' 401(k) accounts.

progressive tax A tax that progressively increases as a taxpayer's taxable income increases.

projected P/E ratio (forward price/earnings ratio) Because investors need to look to the future rather than the past, this measure divides price by projected earnings over the coming four quarters. Also known as forward price/earnings ratio.

promissory note (note) Contract that stipulates repayment terms for a loan.

property insurance Protection from financial losses resulting from the damage to or destruction of your property or possessions.

prospectus Highly legalistic information presented by a firm to the SEC and to the public with any new issue of stock.

purchase contract/sales contract Formal legal document that outlines the actual agreement that results from the real estate negotiations.

purchase offer/offer to purchase Written offer to purchase real estate.

purchasing power Measure of the goods and services that one's income will buy.

quality healthcare plan An Affordable Care Act provision that requires that all health care policies meet the government's standard for its required "10 essential benefits" of adequate coverage.

random/unsystematic risk Risk associated with owning only one investment of a particular type (such as stock in one company) that, by chance, may do very poorly in the future due to uncontrollable or random factors that do not affect the rest of the market.

rate of return/yield Total return on an investment expressed as a percentage of its price.

reaffirm a debt If you repay a single dollar of the old debt, and it means you **reaffirm** the debt. Thus you have agreed that you are personally liable for the whole debt again.

real estate broker (agent) Person licensed by a state to provide advice and assistance, for a fee, to buyers or sellers of real estate.

real estate bubble Rapid and unsustainable increases in home prices followed by sharp declines in values.

real estate Property consisting of land, all structures permanently attached to that land, and accompanying rights and privileges, such as crops and mineral rights.

real income Income measured in constant prices relative to some base time period. It reflects the actual buying power of the money you have as measured in constant dollars.

real rate of return Return on an investment after subtracting the effects of inflation and income taxes.

recession A recurring period of decline in total output, income, employment, and trade, usually lasting from six months to a year and marked by widespread contractions in many sectors of the economy.

redeems When an investor sells mutual fund shares.

redemption charge (exit fee) Similar to a deferred load but often much lower; used to reduce excessive trading of fund shares.

redress Process of righting a wrong.

refinancing This occurs when you refinance or rewrite a loan for an even larger amount before it has been completely repaid.

refundable tax credit A tax credit that can reduce one's income tax liability to below zero with the excess being refunded to the taxpayer.

registered bond Bondholder's name is recorded so that checks or electronic funds transfers for payment of interest and principal can be safely forwarded when due.

release Insurance document affirming that the dollar amount of the loss settlement is accepted as full and complete reimbursement.

rent The regular payment to a landlord charged for using an apartment or other housing space.

rental yield A computation of how much income the investor might pocket from rent each year (before mortgage payments) as a percentage of the purchase price; divide the annual rent by 2 and then divide by the purchase price.

renter's contents broad form (HO-4) Named-perils policy that protects the insured from losses to the contents of a rented dwelling rather than to the dwelling itself.

repairs Usually tax-deductible expenses necessary to maintain property value.

replacement-cost protection Option sometimes available in homeowner's insurance policies (including the renter's form) that pays the full replacement cost of any personal property.

replacement-cost requirement Stipulates that a home must be insured for 80 percent of its replacement value (some companies require 100 percent) in order for any loss to be fully covered.

repossession When a financial institution takes back an object that was either used as collateral or rented or leased for nonpayment of a loan.

required minimum distributions (RMDs) The amount that most qualified plan participants must begin distributing from their retirement accounts by April 1 following the year they reach age 70.5.

residual claim Common stockholders have a right to share in the income and assets of a corporation after higher-priority claims are satisfied.

residual clause Feature of own-occupation policies that allows for some reduced level of disability income benefits when a partial—rather than full—disability strikes.

residual value Projected value of a leased asset at the end of the lease time period.

résumé Summary record of your education, training, experience, and other qualifications.

retained earnings Money left over after a firm has paid expenses, bondholder interest, taxes, preferred stockholder dividends, and common stockholder dividends.

retirement savings goal (retirement nest egg) Total amount of accumulated savings and investments needed to support a desired retirement lifestyle.

retirement The time in life when the major sources of income change from earned income (such as salary or wages) to employer-based retirement benefits, private savings and investments, income from Social Security, and perhaps part-time employment.

reverse mortgage/home-equity conversion loan Allows a homeowner older than age 61 to continue living in the home and to borrow against the equity in a home that is fully paid for and to receive the proceeds in a series of monthly payments, often for life.

revocable living trust Grantor maintains the right to change the trust's terms or cancel it at any time, for any reason, during his or her lifetime.

revolving savings fund Variable budgeting tool that places funds in savings to cover emergency or higher-than-usual expenses.

rewards credit card One that pays the cardholder cash back or airlines miles for future use.

rider This is a provision of an insurance policy that is purchased separately from the basic policy and that provides additional benefits at additional cost.

risk management Process of identifying and evaluating purely risky situations to determine and implement appropriate management.

risk premium (or equity risk premium) The difference between a riskier investment's expected return and the totally safe return on the T-bill.

risk reduction Includes mechanisms, such as insurance, that reduce the overall uncertainty about the magnitude of loss.

risk retention Accepting that some risks simply arise in the course of one's life and consciously retaining that risk.

risk tolerance An investor's willingness to weather changes in the value of your investments, that is, to weather investment risk.

risk Uncertainty about the outcome of a situation or event.

robo advisers Internet-based companies that dispense low-cost customized, computer-generated financial advice.

Roth IRA IRA funded with after-tax money (and thus it is not tax deductible) that grows on a tax-deferred basis; withdrawals are not subject to taxation.

rule of 70 A formula to determine how long it will take for the value of a dollar to decline by one-half.

rule of 78s (sum of the digits) This is the most widely used method of calculating a prepayment penalty where the lender allocates the interest charge on a loan across its payment periods using the numerical values to the sum of all the digits of the periods.

safety Your funds are free from financial risk.

sales finance company A finance company that buys at a discount the installment sales contracts of merchants or that directly finances retail sales.

savings account (statement savings account) A deposit account held at a bank or other financial institution that provides principal security and a modest interest rate.

savings and loan associations (S&Ls) Thrift institutions that focus primarily on accepting savings and providing mortgage and consumer loans.

savings institutions (also called thrift institutions) Accept deposits and provide mortgage and personal loans to individuals.

savings Income not spent on current consumption.

secured bond Pledges specific assets as collateral in indenture or has the principal and interest guaranteed by another corporation or government agency.

secured loans A loan where the borrower has pledged some asset as collateral to guarantee the loan.

securities exchange (stock market) Market where agents of buyers and sellers can find each other easily by providing an orderly, open plan to trade securities.

securities market index Measures the average value of a number of securities chosen as a sample to reflect the behavior of a more general market.

securities markets Places where stocks and bonds are traded (or in the case of electronic trading, the way in which securities are traded).

security's street name Securities certificates kept in the brokerage firm's name instead of the name of the individual investor.

self-directed In defined-contribution plans, employees control the assets in their account—how often to make contributions to the account, how much to contribute, how much risk to take, and how to invest.

seller financing (or owner financing) When a seller self-finances a buyer's loan by accepting a promissory note from a buyer, who makes monthly mortgage payments.

selling short Investors selling securities they do not own (borrowing them from a broker) and later buying the same number of shares of the security at a lower price (returning them to the broker).

Series EE/E savings bonds Nonmarketable, interest-bearing bonds issued by the federal government that are issued at a sharp discount from face value and pay no annual interest, and that may be redeemed at full value upon maturity.

service credit A form of open-end credit granted to consumers by public utilities, physicians, dentists, and other service providers that do not require full payment when services are rendered.

settlement options Choices from which the policyholder can choose in how the death benefit payment will be structured.

share draft account The credit-union version of a negotiable order of withdrawal (NOW) account.

sharing economy Refers to person-to-person (P2P) sharing of access to goods and services where owners rent out something they are not using, such as a car, house, or bicycle to a stranger.

short-term (current) liability Obligation paid off within one year.

short-term goals Financial targets or ends that can be achieved in less than a year.

single-family dwelling Housing unit that is detached from other units.

single-payer health system Where the government, rather than private insurers, pay for all health care costs.

sinking fund Bond feature through which money is set aside with a trustee each year for repayment of the principal portion of the debt at maturity.

skills format Résumé that emphasizes your aptitudes and qualities.

small-cap stocks Company size classification in the stock market for firms valued between $300 million and $2 billion.

social networking A set of connection of friends, colleagues, and other personal contacts with a common interest who use a website or other technologies to communicate with each other and share information and resources.

Social Security credits Accumulated quarterly credits to qualify for Social Security benefits obtained by paying FICA taxes.

Social Security Disability Income Insurance Under this government program, eligible workers can receive some income if their disabilities are total, meaning that they cannot work at any job.

Social Security Estimate Online Information that the Social Security Administration makes available to all workers, which includes earnings history, Social Security taxes paid, and an estimated benefit amount.

Social Security survivor's benefits Government program benefits paid to a surviving spouse and children.

speculative risk Involves the potential for either gain or loss; equity investments might do either.

speculative stock A company that has a potential for substantial earnings at some time in the future, but those earnings may never be realized.

speculative-grade bonds Long-term, high-risk, high-interest-rate corporate (or municipal) IOUs issued by companies (or municipalities) with poor or no credit ratings. Also called junk bonds or high-yield bonds.

speculator An investor who buys in the hope that someone else will pay more for an asset in the not-too-distant future.

sponsor A powerfully positioned champion who "leans in" with an employee by advocating on their protégés' behalf and guiding them toward key players and assignments.

spousal consent requirement Federal law that protects the surviving rights of a spouse or ex-spouse to retirement or pension benefits unless the person signs a waiver of those rights.

spousal IRA Account set up for spouse who does not work for wages; offers tax-deferred growth and tax deductibility.

stable-value fund Mutual fund that offers attractive returns and liquidity without market risk to defined contribution plan participants (and some 529 tuition savings plans) because they have contracts with banks and insurance companies designed to permit redemption of shares at book value regardless of market prices.

standard deduction A base amount of income that all taxpayers (except some dependents) who do not itemize deductions regardless of their actual expenses may subtract from their adjusted gross income.

standard of living Material well-being and peace of mind that individuals or groups earnestly desire and seek to attain, to maintain if attained, to preserve if threatened, and to regain if lost.

standardized expense table SEC-required information that describes and illustrates mutual fund charges in an identical manner so that investors can accurately compare the effects of all of a fund's fees and other expenses relative to other funds.

stated commission The sales charge as a percentage of the amount invested.

statement date (billing date or closing date) The last day of the month for which any transactions are reported on a credit card statement.

STEM majors Academic majors in science, technology, engineering, and mathematics.

stockbroker (account executive) Professional who is licensed to buy and sell securities on behalf of the brokerage firm's clients.

stocks Shares of ownership in a business corporation's assets and earnings.

stock-screening tools Enable you to quickly sift through vast databases of hundreds of companies to find those that best suit your investment objectives.

stored-value cards A payment card with a monetary value stored on the card itself, not in an external account maintained by a financial institution, that is usually issued in the name of individual account holders.

straight bankruptcy Known as Chapter 7, it provides that a debtor's assets are sold, creditors receive payment, and the debtor is freed from his/her debts.

student checking account A checking account offered by credit unions and banks that is better for students than another type of bank account, usually because they offer excellent benefits, including a low minimum balance, minimized fees, and free online bill pay.

student loan A form of unsecured credit that is designed to help students pay for university tuition and books, and sometimes their living expenses.

subleasing An arrangement in which the original tenant leases the property to another tenant.

subordinate budget Detailed listing of planned expenses within a single budgeting classification.

subprime borrowers People with poor credit histories who are required to pay lenders more than others for credit.

subrogation rights Allow an insurer to take action against a negligent third party (and that party's insurance company) to obtain reimbursement for payments made to an insured.

suitability standard Financial advisors who are held to a standard for advice giving where they are free to sell securities generating the heftiest profits and commissions, as long as they are judged "suitable" for a client based on factors like age or risk tolerance.

surplus (or net gain or net income) When total income exceeds total expenses such as reported on a cash-flow statement.

survivor's blackout period The time frame between when a deceased person with minor children stops receiving Social Security survivor benefits and when he or she begins receiving retirement benefits.

sweat equity property Property that needs repairs but that has good underlying value; an investor buys the property at a favorable price and fixes it up to rent or sell at a profit.

take-home pay/disposable income Pay received after employer withholdings for such things as taxes, insurance, and union dues.

tangible/use/lifestyle assets Personal property easily converted to maintain your everyday lifestyle.

target-date retirement funds (life-cycle funds) Asset allocation funds that offer investors premixed portfolios of stocks, bonds, and cash that investors of a certain age and risk tolerance might prefer, and they are often named for the year one plans to retire.

tax avoidance Reducing tax liability through legal techniques.

tax credit Allows a reduction in one's tax liability on a dollar-for-dollar basis that is a direct subtraction of your tax liability.

tax deferred The individual does not have to pay current income taxes on the earnings (interest, dividends, and capital gains) reinvested in a retirement account.

tax evasion Deliberately and willfully hiding income from the IRS, falsely claiming deductions, or otherwise cheating the government out of taxes owed; it is illegal.

tax liability This is the final dollar amount of federal income taxes one will owe the government.

tax losses Created when deductions generated from an investment (such as depreciation and net investment losses) exceed the income from an investment.

tax planning Seeking legal ways to reduce, eliminate, or defer income taxes.

tax refund Amount the IRS sends back to a taxpayer if withholding and estimated payments exceed the tax liability.

tax sheltered Income, dividends, or capital gains that are allowed to grow without taxes until distributions are taken.

taxable income This amount is determined by subtracting various exclusions, adjustments, exemptions, and deductions from total income, with the result being the income upon which the income tax is actually figured.

taxes Compulsory government-imposed charges levied on citizens and their property.

tax-exempt income Income from an investment whose earnings are free, or exempt, from taxation.

tax-exempt money market funds Funds that limit their investments to tax-exempt municipal securities with maturities of 60 days or less.

tax-free exchange (or 1031 exchange) Arises when a real estate investor trades equity in one property for equity in a similar property and no other forms of property or money change hands.

tax-free withdrawals Removal of assets from a retirement account with no taxes assessed.

tax-sheltered compounding Tax-free growth of investments and retirement plans.

tax-sheltered income Income that is legitimately exempt from income taxes and may or may not be subject to taxation in a later tax year.

tax-sheltered investments A financial arrangement that results in a reduction or elimination of taxes due.

tax-sheltered retirement accounts Retirement account for which all earnings from the invested funds are not subject to income taxes.

tax-sheltered retirement plan Employer-sponsored, defined contribution retirement plans including 401(k) plans and similar 403(b) and 457 plans.

T-bill A government IOU of less than one year.

teaser rate Low interest rate that lenders sometimes use to lure buyers; these rates will be low for the first year or so and then will rise to more realistic rates.

tech stock A company in the technology sector that offers technology-based products and services, biotechnology, Internet services, network services, wireless communications, and more.

tenancy by the entirety A type of shared ownership of property recognized in most states, available only to married couples, where spouses who own property as tenants by the entirety each own an undivided interest in the property, each has full rights to occupy and use it and has a right of survivorship.

tenancy in common A form of joint ownership in which two or more parties own the asset, but each retains control over a separate piece of the property rights.

term life insurance "Pure protection" against early death; pays benefits only if the insured dies within the time period (term) that the policy covers.

testamentary trust Becomes effective upon death of the grantor according to the terms of the grantor's will or a revocable living trust. Such trusts can provide money or asset management after the grantor's death for the heirs' benefit.

tiered interest The combination of a base interest rate and a higher rate paid on interest-earning accounts.

tiered pricing Lenders that offer the lowest interest rates to applicants with the highest credit scores while charging steeper rates to more risky applicants.

time deposits Funds on deposit in a savings account (rather than demand deposits), and technically these require that account holders give 30 to 60 days notice for withdrawals.

time value of money A method by which one can compare cash flows across time, either as what a future cash flow is worth today (present value) or what an investment made today will be worth in the future (future value). Also, the cost of money that is borrowed or lent; it is commonly referred to as interest and adjusts for the fact that dollars to be received or paid out in the future are not equivalent to those received or paid out today.

title insurance Protects the lender's interest if the title search is later found faulty.

title Legal right of ownership interest to real property.

total income Compensation from all sources.

total return Income an investment generates from current income and capital gains.

trade-off Giving up one thing for another.

traditional (regular) IRA Account that offers tax-deferred growth; the initial contribution may be tax deductible for the year that the IRA was funded.

trailing commission Compensation paid to salespeople for months or years in the future.

trailing P/E ratio Calculated using recently reported earnings, usually from the previous four quarters.

transaction date The date on which a credit cardholder makes a purchase or receives a credit.

transaction fees Whenever a credit card is used for a balance transfer or cash advance such fees are charged to the account.

travel and entertainment (T&E) cards (corporate cards) Charge cards issued by non-banks that are often used by businesspeople for food and lodging expenses while traveling.

Treasury bills Known as T-bills, U.S. government securities with maturities of less than one year.

Treasury Inflation-Protected Securities (TIPS) Marketable Treasury bonds whose value increases with inflation. These inflation-indexed $1,000 bonds are the only investment that guarantees that the investor's return will outpace inflation.

Treasury notes (bonds) Fixed-principal, fixed-interest-rate government security issued for an intermediate term or long term. Notes mature in ten years or less; bonds mature in more than ten years.

Treasury securities (Treasuries) Known as Treasuries, securities issued by the U.S. government, including bills, notes, and bonds.

trial hire Temporary workers that could last a week or two to determine if candidates can do the work and fit in with the corporate culture.

trust Legal arrangement between you as the creator of the trust and the trustee, the person designated to faithfully and wisely manage any assets in the trust to your benefit and to the benefit of your heirs.

trustee Person charged with carrying out the trust for the benefit of the grantor(s) and heirs.

trustee-to-trustee rollover Retirement funds go directly from the previous account's trustee to the trustee of the new account, with no direct payment to the employee occurring, thereby deferring taxation and the early withdrawal penalty.

turnover rate A measure of a mutual fund's trading activity, and connected to the funds turnover rate.

umbrella (excess) liability insurance Catastrophic liability policy that covers liability losses in excess of those covered by any underlying homeowner's, automobile, or professional liability policy.

underwriting This is the process of insurance companies creating rate classification schedules to help decide whom they will insure and how much to charge.

unearned income Investment returns in the form of rents, dividends, capital gains, interest, or royalties.

uniform settlement statement Lists all of the costs and fees to be paid at the closing.

uninsured and underinsured motorist insurance Coverage that an insured can purchase as part of automobile insurance that covers the insured in an accident when an uninsured or underinsured driver is at fault.

universal life insurance   Provides the pure protection of term insurance and the cash-value buildup of whole life insurance, along with face variability in amount, rate of cash-value accumulation, premiums, and rate of return.

unsecured loan   A loan issued and supported only by the borrower's creditworthiness, rather than by a type of collateral, because it is obtained without the use of property as collateral for the loan.

upside down   A situation where the owner of a financed asset owes more than it is worth, thus creating negative equity.

use-it-or-lose-it rule   An IRS regulation requiring that unspent dollars in a flexible spending account at the end of a calendar year be forfeited, unless the employer allows a 2 1/2-month grace period for spending the funds.

usual, customary, and reasonable (UCR) rate   The amount paid for a medical service in a geographic area based on what providers in the area usually charge for the same or similar medical service.

utilization review   A feature of managed care health plans where representatives of the insurer review the records of treatments provided to verify that they are appropriate for the condition being treated.

value funds   Funds specializing in stocks that are fundamentally sound whose prices appear to be low (low P/E ratios) based on the logic that such stocks are currently out of favor and undervalued by the market.

value stock   A stock that tends to trade at a low price relative to its company fundamentals (dividends, earnings, sales, and so on) and thus is considered undervalued by a value investor.

values   Fundamental beliefs about what is important, desirable, and worthwhile.

variable annuity   Annuity whose value rises and falls like mutual funds and pays a limited death benefit via an insurance contract.

variable expenses (or flexible expenses)   Expenses over which you have substantial control.

variable-rate (adjustable-rate) certificates of deposit   Certificates of deposit that pay an interest rate that is adjusted (up or down) periodically.

variable-rate loan   A loan where an interest rate on a loan fluctuates over time because it is tied to an underlying benchmark interest rate that changes periodically.

variable-universal life insurance   Form of universal life insurance that gives the policyholder some choice in the investments

made with the cash value accumulated by the policy. Also called flexible-premium variable life insurance.

vesting   Ensures that a retirement plan participant has the right to take full possession of all employer contributions and earnings.

wage earner plan   Known as Chapter 13 this is a bankruptcy protection scheme that allows income earners to satisfy outstanding debts in whole or in part within a specific time frame.

waiting period (elimination period)   The time period between the onset of a disability and the date that disability benefits begin.

waiver of premium   A clause in an insurance policy that waives the policyholder's obligation to pay any further premiums should he or she become seriously ill or disabled.

want   Item not necessary but desired.

warranty of fitness for a particular purpose   Here the seller (or provider or manufacturer) knows the buyer's particular use and the buyer relies on the seller's expertise or judgment in choosing the product.

warranty   A type of guarantee that a manufacturer or similar party makes regarding the condition of its product.

whole life insurance   Form of cash-value life insurance that provides lifetime life insurance protection and expects the insured to pay premiums for life. Also called straight life insurance.

will   Written document in which a person tells how his or her remaining assets should be given away after death; without a will, the property will be distributed according to state probate law.

withdrawal options (systematic withdrawal plans)   Arrangements with a mutual fund company for shareholders who want to receive income on a regular basis from their mutual fund investments.

work-style personality   Your own ways of working with and responding to job requirements, surroundings, and associates.

yield to maturity (YTM)   Total annual effective rate of return earned by a bondholder on a bond if the security is held to maturity—takes into consideration both the price at which the bond sold and the coupon interest rate to arrive at effective rate of return.

zero-coupon bonds (zeros or deep discount bonds)   Municipal, corporate, and Treasury bonds that are issued at a sharp discount from face value and pay no annual interest but are redeemed at full face value upon maturity.

zero-sum game   An investment in which the wealth of all buyers remains the same as the trading simply redistributes the wealth among those traders.

Index

Note: Boldface type indicates key terms defined in text.